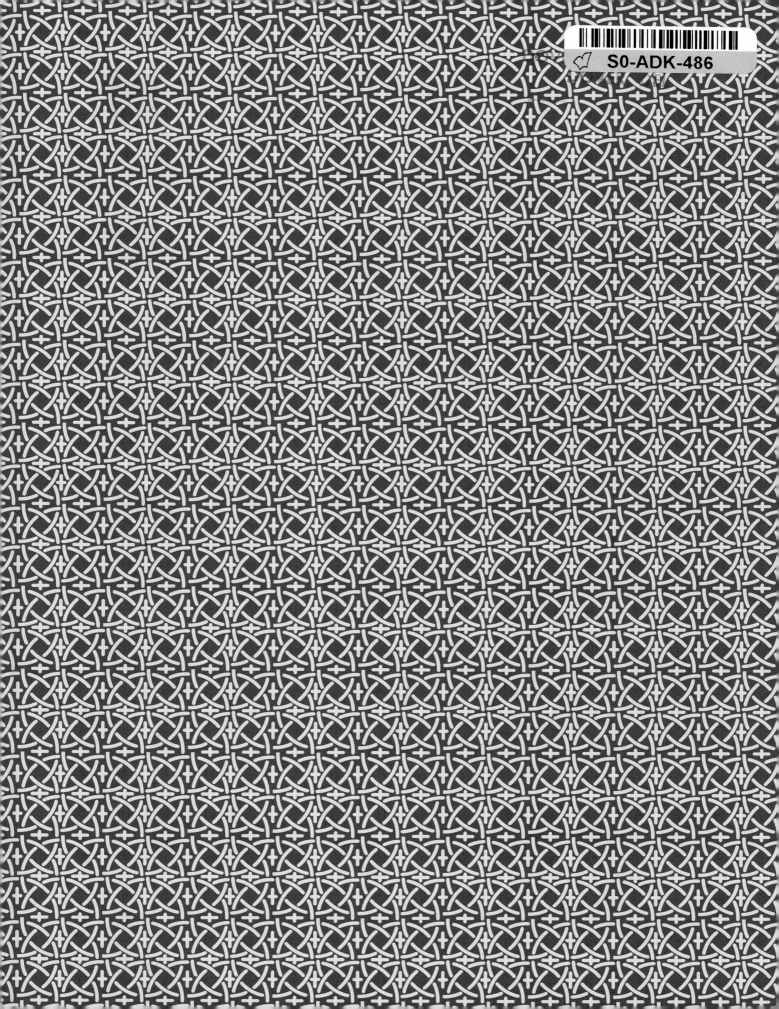

THE OXFORD ENCYCLOPEDIA OF

ARCHAEOLOGY IN THE NEAR EAST

THE OXFORD ENCYCLOPEDIA OF ARCHAEOLOGY IN THE NEAR EAST

PREPARED UNDER THE AUSPICES OF THE

AMERICAN SCHOOLS OF ORIENTAL RESEARCH

Eric M. Meyers

EDITOR IN CHIEF

VOLUME 4

New York Oxford

OXFORD UNIVERSITY PRESS

1997

Oxford University Press

Oxford New York
Athens Auckland Bangkok Bogotá
Bombay Buenos Aires Calcutta Cape Town
Dar es Salaam Delhi Florence Hong Kong Istanbul
Karachi Kuala Lumpur Madras Madrid Melbourne
Mexico City Nairobi Paris Singapore
Taipei Tokyo Toronto

and associated companies in
Berlin Ibadan

Published by Oxford University Press, Inc.,
198 Madison Avenue, New York, New York 10016

Oxford is a registered trademark of Oxford University Press

Library of Congress Cataloging-in-Publication Data
The Oxford encyclopedia of archaeology in the Near East / prepared
under the auspices of the American Schools of Oriental Research;
Eric M. Meyers, editor in chief.
p. cm.
Includes bibliographical references (p.) and index.
1. Middle East—Antiquities—Encyclopedias. 2. Africa, North—Antiquities—
Encyclopedias. I. Meyers, Eric M. II. American Schools of Oriental Research.
DS56.09 1996 96-17152 939′.4—dc20 CIP

ISBN 0-19-506512-3 (set)
ISBN 0-19-511218-0 (vol. 4)

Many photographs and line drawings used herein were supplied by contributors to the work. Others were drawn from the archives of the American Schools of Oriental Research, from commercial photographic archives, and from the holdings of major museums and cultural institutions. The publisher has made every effort to ascertain that necessary permissions to reprint materials have been secured. Sources of all photographs and line drawings are given in the captions to illustrations.

Printing (last digit): 9 8 7 6 5 4 3 2 1

Printed in the United States of America on acid-free paper

ABBREVIATIONS AND SYMBOLS

ACOR	American Center of Oriental Research
AD	*anno Domini,* in the year of the (our) Lord
AH	*anno Hegirae,* in the year of the Hijrah
AIA	Archaeological Institute of America
AIAR	(W. F.) Albright Institute of Archaeological Research
AJA	*American Journal of Archaeology*
Akk.	Akkadian
Am.	*Amos*
ANEP	J. B. Pritchard, ed., *Ancient Near East in Pictures*
ANET	J. B. Pritchard, ed., *Ancient Near Eastern Texts*
AOS	American Oriental Society
APES	American Palestine Exploration Society
Ar.	Arabic
ʿArakh.	*ʿArakhin*
Aram.	Aramaic
ASOR	American Schools of Oriental Research
Assyr.	Assyrian
A.Z.	*ʿAvodah Zarah*
b.	born
B.A.	Bachelor of Arts
Bab.	Babylonian
BASOR	*Bulletin of the American Schools of Oriental Research*
B.B.	*Bava' Batra'*
BC	before Christ
BCE	before the common era
Bekh.	*Bekhorot*
Ber.	*Berakhot*
Bik.	*Bikkurim*
BP	before the present
BSAE	British School of Archaeology in Egypt
BSAI	British School of Archaeology in Iraq
BSAJ	British School of Archaeology in Jerusalem
B.T.	Babylonian Talmud
c.	*circa,* about, approximately
CAARI	Cyprus American Archaeological Research Institute
CAD	computer-aided design/drafting
CAORC	Council of American Overseas Research Centers
CE	of the common era
cf.	*confer,* compare
chap., chaps.	chapter, chapters
1 Chr.	*1 Chronicles*
2 Chr.	*2 Chronicles*
CIG	*Corpus Inscriptionum Graecarum*
CIS	Corpus Inscriptionum Semiticarum
cm	centimeters
CNRS	Centre National de la Recherche Scientifique
col., cols.	column, columns
Col.	*Colossians*
1 Cor.	*1 Corinthians*
2 Cor.	*2 Corinthians*
CTA	A. Herdner, *Corpus des tablettes en cunéiformes alphabétiques*
cu	cubic
d.	died
DAI	Deutsches Archäologisches Institut
diss.	dissertation
Dn.	*Daniel*
DOG	Deutche Orient-Gesellschaft
D.Sc.	Doctor of Science
Dt.	*Deuteronomy*
EB	Early Bronze
Eccl.	*Ecclesiastes*
ed., eds.	editor, editors; edition
ED	Early Dynastic
EEF	Egyptian Exploration Fund
e.g.	*exempli gratia,* for example
Egyp.	Egyptian
Elam.	Elamite
En.	*Enoch*
Eng.	English
enl.	enlarged
esp.	especially
et al.	*et alii,* and others
etc.	*et cetera,* and so forth
Eth.	Ethiopic
et seq.	*et sequens,* and the following
Ex.	*Exodus*
exp.	expanded
Ez.	*Ezekiel*
Ezr.	*Ezra*
fasc.	fascicle
fem.	feminine
ff.	and following
fig.	figure
fl.	*floruit,* flourished
ft.	feet
frag., frags.	fragment, fragments
gal., gals.	gallon, gallons
Geog.	Ptolemy, *Geographica*
Ger.	German
GIS	Geographic Information Systems
Gk.	Greek
Gn.	*Genesis*
ha	hectares
Heb.	Hebrew
Hg.	*Haggai*
Hist.	Herodotus, *History*
Hitt.	Hittite
Hos.	*Hosea*
Hur.	Hurrian
IAA	Israel Antiquities Authority
ibid.	*ibidem,* in the same place (as the one immediately preceding)
IDA(M)	Israel Department of Antiquities (and Museums)
i.e.	*id est,* that is

IEJ	*Israel Exploration Journal*
IES	Israel Exploration Society
IFAPO	Institut Français d'Archéologie du Proche-Orient
Is.	*Isaiah*
IsMEO	Istituto Italiano per il Medio ed Estremo Oriente
Jb.	*Job*
Jer.	*Jeremiah*
Jgs.	*Judges*
Jn.	*John*
Jon.	*Jonah*
Jos.	*Joshua*
JPOS	*Journal of the Palestine Oriental Society*
JRA	*Journal of Roman Archaeology*
J.T.	Jerusalem Talmud
KAI	H. Donner and W. Röllig, *Kanaanäische und aramäische Inschriften*
Kel.	*Kelim*
Ket.	*Ketubbot*
kg	kilogram
1 Kgs.	*1 Kings*
2 Kgs.	*2 Kings*
km	kilometers
KTU	M. Dietrich and O. Lorentz, *Die keilalphabetischen Texte aus Ugarit*
l	liter
l., ll.	line, lines
Lat.	Latin
lb.	pounds
LB	Late Bronze
lit.	literally
Lk.	*Luke*
LM	Late Minoan
Lv.	*Leviticus*
m	meters
M.A.	Master of Arts
masc.	masculine
Mal.	*Malachi*
MB	Middle Bronze
Mc.	*Maccabees*
M.Div.	Master of Divinity
Meg.	*Megillah*
mi.	miles
Mk.	*Mark*
mm	millimeter
mod.	modern
Mt.	Mount
Mt.	*Matthew*
n.	note
NAA	Neutron Activation Analysis
Nat. Hist.	Pliny, *Naturalis Historia* (Natural History)
n.b.	*nota bene*, note well
n.d.	no date
Nm.	*Numbers*
no., nos.	number, numbers
n.p.	no place
n.s.	new series
O.P.	Ordo Praedicatorum, Order of Preachers (Dominicans)
p., pp.	page, pages
para.	paragraph
PEF	Palestine Exploration Fund
Pers.	Persian
Ph.D.	Philosophiae Doctor, Doctor of Philosophy
Phil.	*Philippians*
pl.	plate; plural
PN	Pottery Neolithic
ppm	parts per million
PPN	Pre-Pottery Neolithic
Prv.	*Proverbs*
Ps.	*Psalms*
pt., pts.	part, parts
1 Pt.	*1 Peter*
2 Pt.	*2 Peter*
r.	reigned, ruled
RCEA	*Répertoire chronologique d'epigraphie arabe*
Rev.	*Revelations*
rev.	revised
Ru.	*Ruth*
SBF	Studium Biblicum Franciscanum
SBL	Society of Biblical Literature
SEG	*Supplementum Epigraphicum Graecum*
ser.	series
sg.	singular
Sg.	*Song of Songs*
Shab.	*Shabbath*
S.J.	Societas Jesu, Society of Jesus (Jesuits)
1 Sm.	*1 Samuel*
2 Sm.	*2 Samuel*
sq	square
St., Sts.	Saint, Saints
Sum.	Sumerian
supp.	supplement
Syr.	Syriac
Taʿan.	*Taʿanit*
Th.D.	Theologicae Doctor, Doctor of Theology
Ti.	*Titus*
Tk.	Turkish
1 Tm.	*1 Timothy*
2 Tm.	*2 Timothy*
trans.	translated by
Ugar.	Ugaritic
v.	verse
viz.	*videlicet*, namely
vol., vols.	volume, volumes
vs.	versus
Yad.	*Yadayim*
ZDPV	*Zeitschrift des Deutschen Palästina-Vereins*
Zec.	*Zechariah*
*	hypothetical; in bibliographic citations, English language pages in Hebrew journals
?	uncertain; possibly; perhaps
°	degrees
′	minutes; feet
″	seconds; inches
+	plus
−	minus
±	plus or minus
=	equals; is equivalent to
×	by
1	yields

M

CONTINUED

METALS. [*This entry surveys the history of metal artifacts with reference to the technologies used to create them, the uses to which they were put, and their overall role in the cultures and societies in which they figure. It comprises three articles:*

Typology and Technology
Artifacts of the Neolithic, Bronze, and Iron Ages
Artifacts of the Persian through Roman Periods

The first serves as a general overview, while the remaining articles treat the artifacts of specific periods and regions.]

Typology and Technology

Typological classification, or the ordering of objects into groups and subgroups according to shape, has been the most popular method for studying metal artifacts. Groupings were based on assumed geographical and/or chronological grounds. There are various reasons for this emphasis on typology, not the least of which is that until recently there was hardly any other way to deal with the material. Without the use of modern techniques of scientific analysis, many of which have been applied to the study of archaeological materials only within the last two decades, not much could be said about the materials used or about methods of manufacture. Only the distinction between copper and bronze was emphasized—a difference of real chronological significance as the addition of tin to copper was a relatively late development.

Such basic elemental analyses had been carried out on the metal artifacts excavated at Troy in the late nineteenth century CE as a result of the far-sighted interests of Heinrich Schliemann. [*See the biography of Schliemann.*] Schliemann's conclusion that bronze was used as early as Troy II (EB II) has been confirmed by modern research. That research has also revealed the earlier popularity of an arsenical alloy of copper, beginning at least as early as about 3500 BCE (although not that early at Troy). The use of arsenical copper in the manufacture of metal artifacts in the third millennium BCE had been detected as early as 1906, but it was not until the late 1960s that archaeologists came to appreciate the importance and the extent of the use of arsenical copper. The Early Bronze Age was actually more of an Age of Arsenical Copper (Muhly and Pernicka, 1992).

Another reason for the emphasis on typology in studying metal artifacts was that the vast majority of all surviving pre-Iron Age metal artifacts (in both base and precious metals) came from hoards. Metal, even unalloyed copper, was expensive and metal artifacts were not disposed of. Metal has the property of being endlessly recyclable: broken or worn-out objects were simply melted down and recast. The structure and properties of metal with a long history of reuse are exactly the same as those found in virgin metal just smelted from an ore (and these are the very qualities that have created such problems in using metal analyses to study provenience).

Metal was deliberately taken out of circulation only when metal artifacts were buried with a recently deceased individual as grave goods or when they were buried in the ground as a hoard, a votive deposit, or a foundation deposit (with the last two categories also being designated as hoards). [*See* Grave Goods.] Grave goods can often be dated with some reasonable assurance, especially if a tomb was used for a single burial and also contained datable pottery, but objects from hoards are usually very difficult to date. [*See* Tombs.] Either the pit for the hoard was dug down into earlier strata or else it was dug into sterile soil. An outstanding example of the latter is the Kefar Monash hoard (see below), which was buried in the sand of the Sharon plain in Israel without associated materials either at the findspot or in the immediate area.

In such cases the artifacts from the hoard can only be dated typologically. It is not surprising, therefore, that typology has played such a major role in the study of metal artifacts. As many hoards have been found under less than ideal circumstances, the exact composition of the original hoard is often in dispute, often with serious chronological implications. Again the Kefar Monash hoard provides an instructive example. The consensus of scholars is that the contents of the initial find are most satisfactorily placed in EB I. However, if a crescentic ax found several years later, some 200 m from the original findspot, is considered to be part of the original hoard, it places the entire hoard in EB III (a hoard is dated on the basis of the latest object found in it).

Because so much of the surviving prehistoric metalwork

comes from hoard contexts, the nature of these hoards and the "psychology" of hoarding have been studied intensely by prehistorians, especially by European prehistorians. By studying the metalwork stored in dozens of museums in Europe, the Swedish scholar Gustav Oscar Montelius (1843–1921) was able to work out a comparative typology for the Bronze Age of northern Europe. He worked out a sequence of six periods based on the typological development of bronze tools, implements, weapons, vessels, and ornaments. He later extended it, in both directions, to include four periods of the Neolithic and six periods of the Iron Age. Montelius explained the basis of his typological system in *Die typologische Methode: Die älteren Kulturperioden im Orient und in Europa* (Stockholm, 1903). In a posthumous volume (*La Grèce préclassique,* (Stockholm, 1924), Montelius published drawings of Aegean Bronze Age artifacts that were so good they are reprinted frequently (often without acknowledgment).

Montelius's system was elaborated on by the German prehistorian Paul Reinecke (1872–1958). His four-phase sequential framework for the European Bronze Age, still known as Reinecke A–D (although Reinecke himself never published his system in detail), has long served as the basis for the chronological ordering of the material culture of the European Bronze Age. The sequence was extended into the Iron Age, with Hallstatt A–D, followed by La Tène A–D, which ended with the Roman period. For objects made of base metal, Reinecke's system probably represents the single most successful application of the principles of typological analysis.

One of the main drawbacks of typological analysis is that such work has often resulted in the creation of archaeological cultures having little or nothing to do with historical reality. Present work with metal analyses has created a similar state of affairs, with metal types replaced by metal groups established on the basis of elemental analysis or lead isotope analysis. [*See* Lead Isotope Analysis.]

Scholars not only studied the typology of objects from hoards, they studied the typology of the hoards themselves. European prehistorians came to distinguish between personal hoards (containing the personal property of a single individual), craftsman's hoards (containing the tools used by a particular artisan), merchant's hoards (having freshly made artifacts ready for distribution), and founder's hoards (broken or damaged artifacts destined for the melting pot or crucible).

Although these categories can be extended to the Aegean, they do not seem to work in the Near East. In the first systematic study of hoards from Iraq and Syria dating to before about 2000 BCE, Judith K. Bjorkman concluded that "not a single one can be safely ascribed to a particular occupation" (Bjorkman, 1994, p. 12). The only possible exception would be the Larsa goldsmith's hoard, also the subject of a detailed study by Bjorkman (1993). [*See* Larsa.]

Near Eastern hoards also differ from their European counterparts as regards both size and number. In the hundreds of hoards from the European Bronze Age, many examples have enormous quantities of bronze. In the Cincu-Suseni (Romania) group of seventy hoards, the five largest contained nearly 4,000 kg of bronze. One of the largest of these hoards had 5,812 bronze objects weighing almost 1,100 kg (Sandars, 1983). Nothing like this is known from the Near East, where the largest metal hoard (and also the earliest), from Naḥal Mishmar in Israel's Judean Desert, contained 416 metal artifacts. [*See* Judean Desert Caves.] As to number, Bjorkman, in her catalog of Mesopotamian hoards and deposits, identified only thirty-eight actual hoards from all periods down to about 2000 BCE—most of which are hoards of silver, not bronze.

These figures should be kept in mind in evaluating the role of metals and metallurgy in ancient Mesopotamia. There, metal was never used on anything approaching the scale known from Bronze Age Europe—which must reflect the relative availability of the raw materials, copper and tin, and the accessibility of major ore deposits. The sheer number of artifacts involved is certainly one of the reasons why typological analysis has been carried out with greater success for prehistoric Europe than for ancient Mesopotamia. With more exemplars to work with, it is possible to establish more meaningful categories. The state of preservation of surviving metal artifacts is also a factor: in general, the poor state of preservation of bronze artifacts from the Near East hinders typological classification.

Typology is often used as a means of organizing (and publishing) large bodies of material. This was the case with Jean Deshayes's (1960) two-volume study—the first serious attempt to organize and evaluate a very large number of bronze tools and implements. These volumes were published with boxes containing hundreds of punch cards, eventually either discarded or misplaced by most libraries—an early attempt at the mechanical recovery of data.

The successor to Deshayes's pioneering work is the series of volumes being published under the general title *Prähistorische Bronzefunde,* a monumental research project organized by Hermann Müller-Karpe under the auspices of the Union Internationale des Sciences Préhistoriques et Protohistoriques. Since 1969 a steady stream of volumes has appeared within twenty categories. Eighteen categories are based on type of object: swords, daggers, razors, bracelets, pins, horse trappings—with the nineteenth for specialized bodies of material not otherwise covered; the twentieth is being set aside for general or synthetic studies.

Within each category (or *abteilung*), the material is published geographically. Assembling a complete catalog has meant the inclusion of pieces of questionable context or authenticity, but it does bring together large bodies of material that are otherwise virtually inaccessible. Although the project's main focus has always been prehistoric Europe, there are volumes dealing with material from Greece, Turkey, Cyprus, Israel, Iraq, and Iran, with volumes by Eva A. Braun-Holzinger (1984) on Mesopotamian bronze figurines and statues and by Michael Müller-Karpe (1993) on Mesopotamian bronze vessels.

The fortunes of archaeological discovery play a defining role in any study of ancient Near Eastern metalwork. Certain sites have produced such enormous amounts of metalwork that virtually every category of object includes examples from them. Pride of place must go to the royal cemetery at Ur, including the graves from the Akkadian and Early Dynastic III periods. [*See* Ur; Akkadians.] Much of the Ur material remains unpublished. The final reports of its excavator, C. Leonard Woolley, for all their admirable qualities, often included little more than perfunctory catalogs of metal finds. [*See the biography of Woolley*.] There are also vast numbers of metal artifacts from Nippur, also for the most part unpublished. [*See* Nippur.]

In the case of Nippur the problem is that most of the finds come from the first seasons of excavation, conducted before World War I, and none have any real archaeological context. There is a large body of unpublished Mesopotamian (and Near Eastern) metalwork in the Istanbul Archaeological Museum from the days of the Ottoman Empire (although this material has been studied typologically in an unpublished Turkish dissertation). All excavated Near Eastern sites have produced a fair number of metal finds, but very little of this material has been published in a usable fashion. Such circumstances have discouraged the serious study of ancient Near Eastern, especially Mesopotamian, metalwork.

Conditions are actually somewhat better in the Levant, where a considerable amount of metalwork has been excavated and published. The metal weapons from EB and MB Syria and Palestine have been the subject of a detailed typological study by Graham Philip (1989) that provides the opportunity to examine both the merits and defects of typological analysis. [*See* Weapons and Warfare.]

Within the category of tanged spearheads, Philip gives seventeen separate types. Type number 7, a spearhead with a tang ending in a tightly closed hook, represents a class of objects with very close Anatolian connections. The same holds for type number 15, a spearhead with two parallel slots on either side of the midrib. In these examples the Anatolian connections are so close Philip regards all Levantine examples as Anatolian imports. The objects are also typologically very similar to contemporary metalwork on Cyprus, there representing the beginning of the Cypriot Early Bronze Age, the so-called Philia culture. [*See* Cyprus.] This has been taken to mean that the bronze industry developed on Cyprus, in the third quarter of the third millennium BCE, under a strong Anatolian influence.

Other types of Levantine spearheads appear to have different foreign connections. Type number 3, a spearhead with a leaf-shaped blade, may have strong North Syrian connections, whereas number 9, with a tapering "poker-butt" tang, is a classic Mesopotamian type whose use spread as far as Transcaucasia. The spearhead soon became the characteristic weapon of Mesopotamia, in contrast to Anatolia where the dagger predominated. Spearhead production also marks the beginning of a major metal industry in Mesopotamia, where the earliest example is one excavated by Woolley from an Ubaid period III (c. 5000–4500 BCE) grave at Ur. By the Jemdet Nasr period, Mesopotamia was using the traditional spearhead with a leaf-shaped blade (Frangipane, 1985).

The Mesopotamian connections are even stronger for all Levantine shaft-hole axes. Although Philip recognizes six different types, his total corpus amounts to only thirty-one exemplars, some of which are odd specimens. His type number 6 consists of a group of objects known only from Mari (the palace of Zimrilim). [*See* Mari.] They were published by their excavator, André Parrot, as door hinges (an identification accepted by P. R. S. Moorey, 1994). Type-2 axes, with lobate blades with the cutting edge on their underside, constitute the classic Mesopotamian type of shaft-hole ax. At Ur alone there are at least ninety eight examples, seventy two from Early Dynastic III contexts and twenty-six from the Akkadian period (according to the dating of the Ur burials proposed by Hans Nissen). This type of ax has a distribution along the Euphrates River, from Ur to Habuba Kabira. [*See* Euphrates; Habuba Kabira.] Examples are known as far south as Byblos, but none has ever been found in Israel. [*See* Byblos.] The same holds true for type-3 axes, with horizontally mounted blades. They are known from Syria (Ugarit, Alalakh), but not from ancient Palestine. [*See* Ugarit; Alalakh.]

This evidence certainly indicates that, in the second half of the third millennium BCE, a north–south trade route ran along the Euphrates valley connecting Sumer with the Mediterranean coast of North Syria. Raw materials were conveyed along this route, including copper from Magan (Oman) and tin and lapis lazuli from distant Afghanistan. [*See* Oman.] Armies also marched along this route: inscriptions of Sargon of Akkad and his grandson Naram-Sin record the conquest of Mari, Armanum, and Ebla. [*See* Ebla.]

In the study of ancient Near Eastern metalwork, the fenestrated ax has received a great deal of attention, for it is a type of object thought to have clear chronological significance. Kathleen M. Kenyon even used the presence of such an ax to date temple 4040 at Megiddo to her EB–MB period (also known as EB IV or MB I), although incorrectly. [*See* Megiddo.]

Philip recognizes five types of fenestrated axes, not including the crescentic ax, which he regards as a separate category (with three different types). The crescentic ax has a blade that was attached to the haft by means of one or more tangs; it seems to be a very primitive, almost useless object but one that enjoyed a fair degree of popularity. Examples from ancient Palestine (Jericho, Bab edh-Dhraʿ, Tell el-Ḥesi) all appear to date to EB III, as do the more northern examples known from Byblos and Amarna in Syria. [*See* Jericho; Bab edh-Dhraʿ; Ḥesi, Tell el-.] Byblos produced a mold for casting a crescentic ax, also from the EB III period. The Mesopotamian examples, on the other hand, seem to be somewhat earlier. The examples from the Shara temple at Tell Agrab (in the Diyala region) are Early Dynastic II, while those from the Y cemetery at Kish, found in association with cart burials, could even be late Early Dynastic I. [*See* Diyala; Kish; Carts.]

The classic fenestrated ax is the so-called duckbill ax (Philip, 1989, type 1), which has a narrow, functional blade. An ax of this type is depicted being carried by an Asiatic in an early nineteenth-century BCE painting from Beni Hasan in Lower Egypt, although the ax was foreign to Egypt itself. The date, however, is in keeping with the MB I date suggested for examples from Syrian coastal sites. The best-preserved example of such an ax, which even preserves its distinctive curved wooden handle, comes from the Syrian site of Baghouz and is dated to between 2000 and 1750 BCE (MB I, also known as MB IIA).

Molds for casting duckbill axes are known from Byblos, Ugarit, and Ebla. The Ebla example, from tomb D3712, is made of andesite and is an excellent example of the two-piece, or bivalve, mold. The Ebla mold would have produced a Philip type-2 ax: it has a wider, more D-shaped blade than the narrower type-1 examples. Type-2 axes are known chiefly from the so-called Dépôts des Offrandes at Byblos. These consist of jar deposits containing massive numbers of bronze artifacts, including hundreds of small human figures cut out of thin sheet bronze. Philip convincingly argues that all these hoards are votive deposits, made in association with the Obelisk Temple at Byblos. Similar, though much smaller, deposits at Ugarit are to be associated with the Temple of Baal at Ugarit (Philip, 1988).

The range of metal types in use in Mesopotamia is well indicated by the composition of the Old Babylonian hoard from Tell Sifr. A similar hoard, with hooks, nails, spoons, large rings, needles, tweezers, platters, bowls, mirrors, hoes, sickles, and adzes, is said to have come from Ishchali (Iraq) but was actually purchased in Baghdad in 1930. It is now in the collection of the Museum of the Oriental Institute at the University of Chicago (Moorey, 1994, p. 262).

Vessels were usually made of bronze, but examples in gold, silver, and electrum are also known. A chronological sequence for bronze vessels has been worked out by Müller-Karpe (1993). Statuary in copper and bronze was usually executed on a small scale, as seen in numerous human and animal figurines, usually made of copper (Braun-Holzinger, 1984). The outstanding exception comes in the use of metal for architectural decoration, especially from the Early Dynastic III temple at Tell al-Ubaid, excavated by H. R. Hall and C. Leonard Woolley. [*See* Ubaid.] There, the temple was decorated with large-scale animals—bulls, stags, lions, and leopards—out of hammered thin sheets of copper over a wooden core; the heads (and horns, where present) of the animals were made of cast bronze. This technique of hammering sheet metal over a wooden core was also used in fabricating the lions that guarded the terrace of the Old Babylonian temple of Dagan at Mari.

In the Neo-Assyrian period there was an apparent increase in the use of metal in Mesopotamia, made possible by the tribute in metals paid by vassal states from all parts of the Assyrian empire. The Assyrian kings used some of their newly acquired metal resources to decorate the wooden doors of their temples and palaces with strips of bronze. Such bronze overlays are first mentioned by Adad-Nirari I (1305–1274 BCE) and continued to be used down to the end of the Neo-Assyrian period (late seventh century BCE).

Examples of decorated bronze strips nailed to wooden doors are known from Aššur, Nimrud, Khorsabad, and Tell Hadad (in the Hamrin basin). [*See* Aššur; Khorsabad.] The best-known examples are from the site of Balawat and date to the reign of Shalmaneser III (858–824 BCE). [*See* Balawat.] The bronze bands from Balawat are said to be the earliest examples of true engraving on metal. The cuneiform inscriptions on these bands were cut with steel engraving tools, exactly as they would have been cut into stone. One of the bands shows an Assyrian sculptor cutting cuneiform text on the rock face of a commemorative inscription (Moorey, 1994, pp. 34, 276). The Assyrian king Sennacherib (704–681 BCE) claims that he knew how to melt and cast the metal for making such bronze bands (in his account of the construction of his "Palace without Rival"; cf. Dalley, 1988).

By the tenth century BCE, iron was well on the way to replacing bronze as the basic utilitarian metal. Agricultural tools and implements formerly made of bronze, as documented in cuneiform texts and by the contents of the Tell Sifr hoard (see above), were increasingly made of iron, as documented by the finds from such Palestinian sites as Taʿanach (Stech-Wheeler et al., 1981). [*See* Taʿanach.] The array of iron tools and implements found at Taʿanach nicely parallels the list given in *1 Samuel* 13:19–20. There, in a passage placed in the time of King Saul's wars against the Philistines (c. 1000 BCE), it is stated that "There was no smith to be found in all the land of Israel, for the Philistines had said to themselves, "The Hebrews might make swords or spears!" So all Israel would go down to the Philistines to repair any of their plowshares, mattocks, axes, or sickles." Iron swords were difficult to make and were first found in any quantity on Early Iron Age Cyprus. Spearheads and arrowheads were socketed and, therefore, tended to be made of bronze even in Roman times. It was in the manufacture of objects such as plowshares, axes, adzes, hoes, spades, and shovels, however, that iron soon replaced more expensive bronze.

BIBLIOGRAPHY

Bjorkman, Judith K. "The Larsa Goldsmith's Hoards—New Interpretations." *Journal of Near Eastern Studies* 52 (1993): 1–23.

Bjorkman, Judith K. *Hoards and Deposits in Bronze Age Mesopotamia.* Philadelphia, 1994.

Braun-Holzinger, Eva A. *Figürliche Bronzen aus Mesopotamien.* Prähistorische Bronzefunde 1.4. Munich, 1984.

Dalley, Stephanie. "Neo-Assyrian Textual Evidence for Bronzeworking Centres." In *Bronzeworking Centres of Western Asia c. 1000–539 BC,* edited by John Curtis, pp. 97–110. London, 1988.

Deshayes, Jean. *Les outils de bronze l'Indus au Danube (IVe au IIe millénaire).* Paris, 1960.

Frangipane, Marcella. "Early Developments of Metallurgy in the Near East." In *Studi di Paletnologia in onore di Salvatore M. Puglisi,* edited by Mario Liverani, Alba Palmieri, and Renato Peroni, pp. 215–228. Rome, 1985.

Moorey, P. R. S. *Ancient Mesopotamian Materials and Industries. The Archaeological Evidence.* Oxford, 1994.

Müller-Karpe, Michael. *Metallgefasse im Iraq.* Prähistorische Bronzefunde 2.14. Stuttgart, 1993.

Muhly, J. D., and Ernst Pernicka. "Early Trojan Metallurgy and Metals Trade." In *Heinrich Schliemann. Grundlagen und Ergebnisse moderner Archäologie 100 Jahre nach Schliemanns Tod,* edited by J. Herrmann, pp. 309–318. Berlin, 1992.

Philip, Graham. "Hoards of the Early and Middle Bronze Age in the Levant." *World Archaeology* 20.2 (1988): 190–208.

Philip, Graham. *Metal Weapons of the Early and Middle Bronze Ages in Syria-Palestine.* Oxford, 1989.

Sandars, Nancy. "North and South at the End of the Mycenaean Age: Aspects of an Old Problem." *Oxford Journal of Archaeology* 2 (1983): 43–68.

Stech-Wheeler, Tamara, J. D. Muhly, K. R. Maxwell-Hyslop, and Robert Maddin. "Iron at Taanach and Early Iron Metallurgy in the Eastern Mediterranean." *American Journal of Archaeology* 85 (1981): 245–268.

J. D. MUHLY

Artifacts of the Neolithic, Bronze, and Iron Ages

In the "Three-Age" periodization of human cultural development, first proposed by the Danish scholar Christian J. Thomsen in 1819 (Daniel, 1981, pp. 58–60), the Bronze Age (beginning c. 3000 BCE), marked the change from stone to metal. The metals in question—copper and tin (the latter alloyed with copper to produce bronze)—then dominated the scene until they were replaced by iron (c. 1000 BCE). The Iron Age represented the culmination of the primitive technology characteristic of the ancient world before the emergence of Greco-Roman civilization.

Although world prehistory has largely been rewritten during the last two decades, the three age system is still a useful chronological framework, although it no longer has any technological meaning. Recent advances in what is understood of the beginnings of metallurgy make this very clear: evidence for the first use of metal now goes back to about 8000 BCE. The beginning of the Bronze Age is associated with a series of developments that includes complex political and economic systems requiring stratified societies and systems of writing, international trade, fortified cities, and the use of arsenical copper—not bronze. The alloy of copper and tin, the only copper alloy properly designated bronze, only came into common use during the Middle Bronze Age (c. 2000–1600 BCE). The beginning of the Iron Age has always been put at about 1200 BCE, but only Cyprus and Palestine made any serious use of iron before the first millennium BCE.

Neolithic Period. The first metal used in antiquity was copper, not only because it was a useful metal—being durable, ductile, and easy to work—but also because it exists as a metal in geological context. Nuggets of native copper needed only to be hammered into shape to form the earliest metal artifacts. Small beads, hooks and pins, and reamers/awls of native copper are known from the Aceramic Neolithic site of Çayönü Tepesi in southeastern Anatolia, a site also known for its complex domestic and public architecture (c. 8000 BCE). From a somewhat later period (late eighth millennium) there is a series of copper beads, used in making necklaces, from the site of Aşıklı Höyük in central Anatolia. In about the same time frame, small beads of copper are known from the Iranian site of Ali Kosh and the Mesopotamian site of Tell es-Sawwan. [*See* Ali Kosh.] The earliest substantial copper object is an awl from the northern Mesopotamian site of Tell Magzaliya (see figure 1), dated to the second half of the eighth millennium (Muhly, 1988).

All these early copper finds represent the use of native copper. Quite unexpected is the evidence for the practice of annealing (the heating of copper at low temperatures to prevent cracking during hammering) in the early copper artifacts from Çayönü and Aşıklı. The use of fire (pyrotechnology) was thus employed in working with metal long before it was used with clay, at least in the ancient Near East (in central Europe, animal and human figurines made of fired clay are known from Dolni Veštonice in Czechoslovakia that date to about 24,000 BCE).

The discovery of small pieces of copper smelting slag from level VIA at Çatal Höyük (c. 6000 BCE) suggests the early development of a smelting technology, but there is little other evidence for the use of anything but native copper before about 5000 BCE. [*See* Çatal Höyük.] The lead beads reported from Çatal Höyük VIA are actually made of galena (the lead sulphide ore that would have been smelted to produce metallic lead), and the slags and crucibles from the Anatolian site of Nevalı Çori are from its Early Bronze I levels—not its Aceramic Neolithic ones—which is apparently true for its small copper objects as well. [*See* Nevalı Çori.]

The shaft-hole mace-head from level 2b at Can Hasan (c. 6000 BCE), made of very pure copper, with only 0.05 percent silver as an impurity, must also be made of native copper. The copper beads found in graves at the site of Mehrgarh, in Baluchistan, also date to about 6000 BCE and should also be of native copper. They demonstrate that this simple copper metallurgy had spread to South Asia by the late seventh

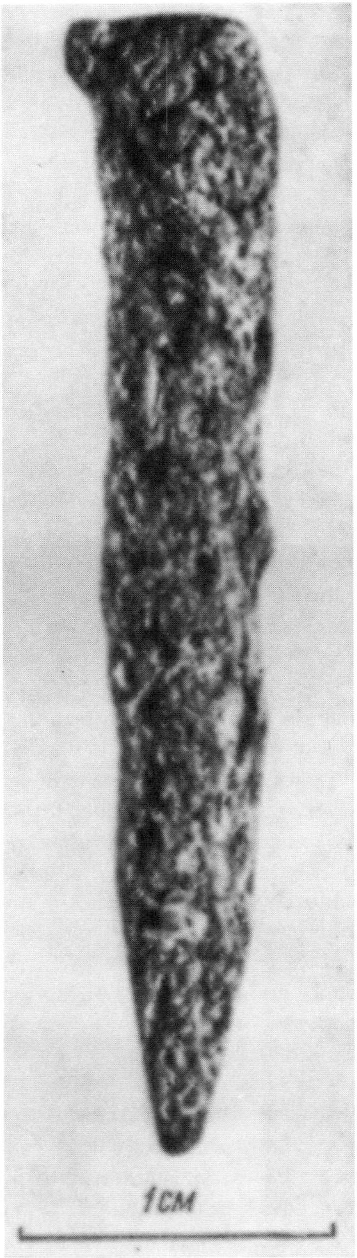

METALS: NEOLITHIC, BRONZE, AND IRON AGES. Figure 1. *Copper awl from the Russian excavations at Tell Magzaliya, Iraq.* (Courtesy Ralf Munchaev; supplied by J. D. Muhly)

millennium. At present, the massive lead bracelet from level XII at the northern Mesopotamian site of Yarim Tepe I (early seventh millennium), stands alone as a Neolithic object made of metal that must have been smelted from an ore.

Metallurgically, the sixth millennium in the ancient Near East seems to have been an uneventful period. The precocious developments of the previous millennium were, for some reason, not carried forth. The sixth seems to have been but a prelude to the great expansion of the following two millennia (c. 5000–3000 BCE)—in many respects the most creative period in prehistoric metallurgy.

From the fifth-millennium Iranian sites of Tell-i-Iblis and Tepe Ghabristan comes the first clear evidence for a copper-smelting technology and the existence of metal workshops. Tall-i-Iblis produced a large number of crucible fragments, while Tepe Ghabristan had an actual workshop, with crucibles, tuyeres, molds, and some 20 kg of copper ore. Contemporary with these finds (c. 4500–4000 BCE, or Sialk III 4–5) are a number of copper artifacts, including fifty-five copper axes from the Susa I (or A) graves representing the mass burials associated with the city's founding (Moorey, 1982). [*See* Susa.]

The second half of the fifth millennium is also when copper metallurgy expanded into the Aegean, the Balkans, and southeastern Europe. Earlier copper objects are known from all these areas, from Early Neolithic (c. 5900–5300 BCE) and Middle Neolithic (c. 5300–4700 BCE) times, but it was in the Late Neolithic (c. 4700–4300 BCE)—also known as the Eneolithic (or Aeneolithic)—that European copper usage exceeded anything known from the Near East. From this period also, the time of the Gumelnitsa, Karanovo VI, Tiszapolgar, Cucuteni, Tripolje, and Sesklo regional cultures, hoards consist of shaft-hole axes as well as flat axes (or celts) and chisels, all made of unalloyed smelted copper. The copper ore came from at least two mining sites that have been securely dated to the second half of the fifth millennium: Rudna Glava, in eastern Serbia, and Ai Bunar in Bulgaria. It was also during the Late Neolithic that gold made its first appearance. A few gold objects are known from sites in northern Greece, but massive quantities were found in the graves of the Varna cemetery on the Black Sea coast of Bulgaria. Nothing comparable is known from the Near East (although claims have been made for Late Neolithic copper smelting in Wadi ʿArabah, at Timnaʿ in Israel (site F2) and at Feinan in Jordan (site Fidan 4). [*See* Timnaʿ (Negev); Feinan.]

Fourth Millennium BCE. Large-scale metallurgy was developed in the ancient Near East in the fourth millennium, replacing the "trinket metallurgy" (cf. Moorey, 1994) of the earlier periods. The best evidence for these developments comes from the Levant—from Israel and Jordan. A great hoard of more than four hundred copper artifacts from Naḥal Mishmar (on the west bank of the Dead Sea) was greeted with incredulity when it was first discovered in 1961. [*See* Judean Desert Caves.] It was thought to be treasure from the Temple in Jerusalem that had been hidden to save it from destruction by the Romans in 70 CE. Now, some thirty objects in the same style are known from excavated Chalcolithic sites that have also produced evidence for copperworking and the casting of the mace heads, standards, and "crowns" still best known from the Naḥal Mishmar hoard (see figure 2). It is still possible that this hoard represents cult paraphernalia, but from the Chalcolithic temple at ʿEin-Gedi, not the Herodian temple in Jerusalem. [*See* Cult; ʿEin-Gedi; Jerusalem.]

Evidence for the Chalcolithic mining of copper is known from Feinan in Jordan (and perhaps also from Timnaʿ in Israel). These mines produced a copper ore consisting of chrysocolla and malachite, but the complex prestige or cult objects were made of a remarkable alloy containing more than 20 percent antimony and more than 8 percent arsenic. The copper for such an alloy could only have come from eastern Anatolia, where it has even been found in an archaeological context at the Chalcolithic site of Noršuntepe. The implications of this evidence are still not understood. It could be argued that the evidence for local metalworking, as known from Tell Abu Maṭar and Shiqmim in Israel, comprising simple bowl furnaces, crucibles, slags, and quantities of copper ore, pertained only to the manufacture of the utilitarian axes and chisels made of unalloyed copper. [*See* Shiqmim.] The ore in question could certainly have come from Feinan, where evidence was also uncovered for Chalcolithic and Early Bronze Age copper smelting, but what then of the cult or prestige objects? The problem is that these objects also seem to be of local manufacture, utilizing an iconography also seen in contemporary objects in clay, stone, and ivory. Apparently, metallic copper, rich in antimony and arsenic, was produced in eastern Anatolia and then shipped to Israel's Negev desert, where it was fashioned into the elaborate objects known from the Naḥal Mishmar hoard.

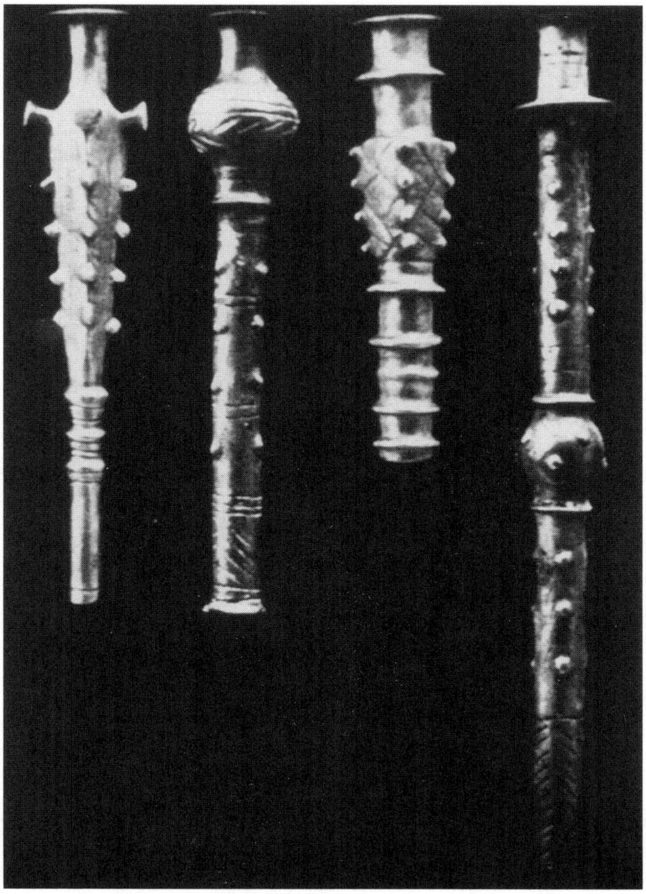

METALS: NEOLITHIC, BRONZE, AND IRON AGES. Figure 2. *Copper Standards from the Naḥal Mishmar hoard.* Israel Museum, Jerusalem. (Courtesy Miriam Tadmor; photograph by Robert Maddin; supplied by J. D. Muhly)

Precious metals are also found for the first time during the Chalcolithic period, in the fourth millennium. A remarkable collection of eight ring-shaped gold objects, with up to 30 percent silver, were found in a cave in Naḥal Qanah, along with prestige objects of alloyed copper. These objects should be described as being made of electrum, as was a remarkable wolf's-head terminal from tomb 114, level X, at Tepe Gawra in northern Mesopotamia (mid-fourth millennium). [*See* Tepe Gawra.] Analysis has shown that many of the objects commonly described in the literature as being of gold are in fact made of electrum, including some of the most famous pieces from the royal cemetery at Ur (see below). [*See* Ur.]

A few pieces of gold jewelry are known from an earlier (level XII) tomb at Tepe Gawra, and more extensive finds, including gold pendants, gold bands, and gold spirals, were found in tombs in levels XI–X. The great age of gold jewelry, however, was the third millennium BCE, a period that, with full justification, could be called the Age of Gold. [*See* Jewelry.]

Electrum normally contains about 60–70 percent gold and 30–40 percent silver. There are examples of high-silver electrum; this so-called aurian silver seems to have been the only type used in ancient Egypt, at least prior to the Middle Kingdom (c. 2000 BCE). In the rest of the ancient Near East, however, silver was extracted from argentiferous galena by a process called cupellation, producing as a by-product a lead oxide known as litharge. The earliest evidence for cupellation comes from the Syrian site of Habuba Kabira (late Uruk period, late fourth millennium). [*See* Habuba Kabira.] The separation of natural electrum into its component parts (gold and silver), a cementation process known as parting, does not seem to have been known before the mid-sixth century BCE.

Silver came into common use in the late fourth millennium. A surprising number of silver objects are known from sites in Anatolia (Beycesultan, level XXXIV; Alişar Höyük, level 14; Arslantepe, level VIA; and from two contemporary rich graves at Koruçutepe), the Levant (especially the rich burials from the Eneolithic cemetery at Byblos), and Egypt (the Predynastic graves at Naqada). [*See* Arslantepe; Grave Goods; Byblos; Naqada.] From the Jemdet Nasr period in

Mesopotamia comes a silver vase and a limestone bull with silver legs (both from Uruk) and, from Proto-Elamite Iran, a magnificent silver kneeling bull holding a vase, an object that, like so many works in precious metal, comes not from a controlled excavation but from the antiquities market. [*See* Jemdet Nasr; Uruk-Warka.] The use of silver inlay in decoration is usually associated with the EB II–III period and is best documented in the inlaid stags from the royal cemetery at Alaca Höyük: the inlaid sword hilts from Arslantepe show, however, that the technique was already in use in the late fourth millennium. Silver is extremely rare from contemporary sites in the Aegean; the only example known to date is a silver pendant from the Alepotrypa cave hoard in Mani, in southern Greece (Muhly, 1985a, p. 112). The lead, produced as a by-product of silver extraction, was also used to make objects, especially a series of vessels from the so-called Jemdet Nasr cemetery at Ur (Moorey, 1994, p. 294).

The prestige objects from Naḥal Mishmar are unusual in their high concentrations of antimony, in addition to the more common arsenic. Arsenical copper was the standard alloy of the fourth millennium, and its use extended into the third as well. The use of arsenical copper is documented in many fourth-millennium copper hoards, including those from Ilipinar, Ikiztepe, Beycesultan, Arslantepe, and Hassek Höyük (in Anatolia), from various sites in Palestine dating to the time of the Naḥal Mishmar hoard, and from late fourth-millennium sites in Mesopotamia, notably Jemdet Nasr and Kish. [*See* Kish.] Arsenical copper was also the dominant alloy in the large hoard of metal objects found at Kefar Monash in Israel that included flat axes, adzes, chisels, large hooked-tang spearheads, and many small, thin copper plates (see figure 3). The hoard also contained some fragments of silver and some carnelian beads and must date to about 3000 BCE (Syro-Palestinian EB I).

METALS: NEOLITHIC, BRONZE, AND IRON AGES. Figure 3. *Copper "scale" from the Kefar Monash hoard.* Israel Museum, Jerusalem. (Courtesy Miriam Tadmor; photograph by Robert Maddin; supplied by J. D. Muhly)

Third Millennium BCE. The use of metal, both precious and base, "exploded" in the entire ancient world during the third millennium BCE, from the Danube to the Indus River. The dominant copper alloy still seems to have been arsenical copper but, as the millennium progressed, the use of bronze steadily increased—in Anatolia, Syria, Mesopotamia, and Iran. The situation in mid-millennium is illuminated by the hoard of metal artifacts found in a large covered and painted clay vessel on the acropolis at Susa in 1907. The entire hoard, consisting of forty-eight (or fifty-seven metal objects, eleven alabaster vessels, six cylinder seals, gold rings and beads, and a tiny frog of lapis lazuli, has come to be known as the *vase à la cachette* ("hidden vase"). It includes objects from the entire first half of the third millennium BCE. Of the forty-two metal artifacts that have been analyzed, only six have at least 2 percent tin, with four of them having more than 7 percent tin. The dominant alloy in use was arsenical copper: thirty-one of the forty-two analyzed objects had at least 1 percent arsenic, including a globular spouted vessel with 6.2 percent; a broad, shallow bowl with 4.7 percent; and a tanged saw with 4 percent arsenic.

The parallel use of bronze and arsenical copper, with the latter predominating, is the technology found across Anatolia, as far as the Troad and the northern Aegean, in the mid-third millennium BCE. Recent analytical work has documented its use at Thermi (Lesbos) and Poliochni (Lemnos). The latter site is of particular interest as the analyses document a gradual but steady increase in the use of bronze, from Poliochni II to V, covering the first half of the third millennium BCE. Arsenical copper was also the predominant alloy in the Cyclades (especially in a hoard thought to be from Kythnos but more likely originating on Naxos) and Crete during the Early Bronze Age. A few bronzes are known from Early Minoan Crete, whose number should increase with the metal finds from the rich cemetery at Ayia Photia. [*See* Crete.]

In Palestine, on Cyprus, and in Egypt, bronze was seldom used before the second millennium BCE. A number of daggers from EB IV tombs in Palestine (Bab edh-Dhraʿ, ʿEinan, Jericho, Motza, Menahemiya) are made of bronze, but the use of this alloy seems restricted to this class of object. [*See* Bab edh-Dhraʿ; ʿEinan; Jericho.] These EB IV bronze daggers have strong Anatolian connections, best seen in the daggers from the hoard found at Soloi-Pompeiopolis. The Anatolian connections could be related to the sources of tin being exploited at the end of the third millennium BCE (see above).

It requires tin to make bronze, and tin deposits are very rare in the lands of the eastern Mediterranean and the ancient Near East. Copper deposits are quite numerous, especially in Anatolia, on Cyprus, and in Iran, but ancient sources of tin have yet to be identified. Some believe that Bronze Age tin, especially EB tin, came from the Taurus Mountains of southeastern Anatolia. [*See* Taurus Mountains.] Others, not impressed by the quantity of cassiterite (or tin oxide, the main source of ancient tin) from the Taurus put their faith in the tin deposits of Afghanistan and Central Asia, where the geological evidence for alluvial cassiterite is far better than anything known from Anatolia. The hypothesis of a Mesopotamian source for tin in Afghanistan is greatly strengthened by the fact that Afghanistan is also known as a major source of lapis lazuli and alluvial gold: these three materials—tin, gold, and lapis lazuli—appear together in the archaeological record in the mid-third millennium BCE. This is best documented in the finds from the royal cemetery at Ur (Early Dynastic IIIA, c. 2600–2500 BCE).

If Afghanistan were indeed a source of tin for the metal industries of EB western Asia, something of a local bronze industry would be expected in Afghanistan itself, the ancient land of Bactria. Indeed, such an industry did exist, but it is known almost entirely from objects purchased on the antiquities market (and from excavated sites such as Mundigak, in the south). "Bactrian bronzes," looted mainly from cemeteries in northern Afghanistan, flooded the antiquities market in the years following the Soviet invasion of Afghanistan in 1979. From the bazaar in Kabul these bronzes made their way to museums and private collections in the West. In addition to a great number of compartmented stamp seals, at first considered to be the work of Nestorian Christians, there were also vessels (including examples in gold, silver, and electrum) and weapons, notably axes. [*See* Weapons and Warfare; Seals.] The axes often are decorated in high relief, there are even examples in silver, ornamented with gold foil. Insofar as it can be determined, these Bactrian bronzes date to the late third and early second millennia BCE (Potts, 1994).

From the mid-third millennium BCE, deposits of gold jewelry, either as hoards or as grave goods, have been uncovered over a vast area, from Greece to southern Mesopotamia. Although chronological uncertainties have long clouded the issue, it now seems that all of these gold treasures, from the Greek mainland (Thyreatis), the northern Aegean (Poliochni), Crete (Mochlos), northwest Anatolia (Troy), central Anatolia (Alaca Höyük, Eskiyapar), and Mesopotamia (Ur) are from roughly the same chronological horizon. Gold, with the exception of Varna (see above) and, to a lesser extent, Tepe Gawra, was rare in archaeological contexts prior to about 2500 BCE. It then appears in (relatively) large quantities and over a vast area. In almost all cases, it appears in conjunction with tin (used in making bronze). Gold jewelry and bronze tools and weapons seem to have something in common. That commonality must reside in the alluvial nature of gold and cassiterite and in the fact that both alluvial materials occur geologically in association with granite rock (not all granites have tin, but there is no tin without granite). In Mesopotamia (Ur) and Syria (Ebla) gold and bronze appear together with lapis lazuli, and all three materials—gold, tin, and lapis lazuli—are found in Afghanistan. [*See* Ebla.] Moreover, lapis lazuli is known only from deposits in northeastern Afghanistan (save for minor deposits in Pakistan).

This conjunction suggests that the great metallurgical expansion of the mid-third millennium BCE was stimulated, in some very significant way, by the establishment of Mesopotamian contact with lands to the east, contacts that tapped into new sources of raw materials, both metals (gold, tin, and perhaps even copper) and semiprecious stones (carnelian and lapis lazuli). This great influx of material wealth stimulated the growth of trade and a commercial expansion that also had a political component. Lapis lazuli was shipped up the Euphrates River and beyond, as far as northern Syria, where blocks of the raw material have been found in the storerooms of palace G at Ebla. [*See* Euphrates; Palace.] It may even have been shipped as far north as Troy, where a ceremonial axe of lapis lazuli was one of four axes that made up Heinrich Schliemann's Treasure L (mid-third millennium BCE). [*See the biography of Schliemann.*] Apart from being at Troy, lapis is unknown at Anatolian Bronze Age sites.

There clearly was a great increase in the amount of precious metal (and tin) in circulation by the middle of the third millennium BCE. The idea that these raw materials came into the land of Sumer from the east is supported by references in Sumerian literary texts to a trade between Sumer and the land of Aratta, described in a Sumerian literary text from Nippur as being "in the midst of the highlands, where the sun rises." [*See* Sumerian; Nippur.] Associated with Aratta is the land of Tukrish, described in the same text as "the mountain land of great food offerings" and as a source of gold and lapis lazuli. Sumer itself was an alluvial floodplain, possessing virtually no natural resources save for clay, reeds, and the Sumerians themselves. All raw materials, including metals, stone, and wood, came, according to Sumerian literary texts, from the eastern highlands.

Silver also played a major role in this trade with lands beyond southern Mesopotamia. An Archaic Sumerian literary text, known from copies found at Ebla and at Abu Salabikh (near Nippur), says of the god Ea that "foreign trade he gave to the traders. [*See* Abu Salabikh.] The lands yielded lapis lazuli and silver, sissoo wood, cedar, cypress, juniper. . . ." The text dates to the very beginning of the Akkadian period (c. 2400–2200 BCE), or just before. In the Akkadian period there was a great increase in the amount of silver in circulation. Mesopotamia went on the "silver standard" and prices for goods were quoted in terms of shekels of silver. It stayed on this standard except for a brief period during Kassite times, when it shifted to gold. [*See*

Kassites.] Neo-Assyrian texts also sometimes quote prices in terms of shekels of copper. [*See* Assyrians.]

A number of silver hoards are known from Akkadian times, including at least four hoards from Tell Brak, two from Tell Taya, and several from Tell Asmar and Khafajeh. [*See* Akkadians; Brak, Tell; Taya, Tell; Khafajeh.] Many contained rings and coils of silver, which are now seen as a premonetary form of currency. The silver coils and rings from the so-called Treasure of Ur, excavated at Mari, indicate that such objects were in use already during the time of the royal cemetery at Ur.

Silver was also much in use in Anatolia during the third quarter of the third millennium BCE; actual ingots of silver are known from Troy and Mahmatlar. Lead-isotope analyses indicate that at least some of the silver used at Troy, and at Mesopotamian sites such as Telloh and Aššur (and even in one of the silver coils from Khafajeh) came from the Taurus Mountains, an area well known as a source of silver until well into Ottoman times. [*See* Aššur.] The great conqueror Sargon of Akkad states that his military campaigns took him "as far as the Cedar Forest and the Silver Mountains." The first is certainly a reference to the cedars of Lebanon; the second must designate the Taurus. There was also a major increase in the use of silver in the Aegean, especially on the islands of the Cyclades, during the third quarter of the third millennium BCE, documented primarily by a group of silver bracelets from Early Cycladic graves. According to lead-isotope analyses, the earlier silver (Early Cycladic I–II) came from the Ayios Sostis mines on Siphnos. Increased demand for silver led to the opening of the Laurion mines, in southern Attica, at the end of Early Cycladic II. The silver known from Early Minoan Crete includes a silver vase from Mochlos.

Although bronze was certainly being produced during the Akkadian period, many of the most famous pieces of Mesopotamian metalwork have proved to be of unalloyed copper. A striking head dated to the time of Sargon of Akkad, but found in a Neo-Assyrian level at Nineveh (where it had been mutilated in the sack of 612 BCE), is made of cast copper, not bronze as usually stated. [*See* Nineveh.] The large-scale statue of a crouching nude male, "discovered" by a bulldozer at the site of Bassetki in northeastern Iraq, is also made of cast copper. It bears an inscription of Naram-Sin, Sargon's grandson, and seems originally to have guarded the gate of a temple. This use of unalloyed copper for sculpture may represent something of a Mesopotamian tradition. There are many Early Dynastic figurines made of cast copper and, from Early Dynastic III, a number of animal heads and relief panels showing animals, probably bulls, are all of cast copper.

According to Sumerian literary and administrative texts, copper came from the land of Magan, now identified as being roughly equivalent to the modern Sultanate of Oman. [*See* Oman.] The copper mines of Oman have been known for many years, but it has only been possible recently to show that these mines were first worked in the late third millennium BCE. The Sumerians sailed to Dilmun, their name for the island of Bahrain, in order to acquire the copper of Magan and, in some periods, sailed directly to Magan. [*See* Dilmun; Bahrain.] In exchange they brought textiles (produced by the extensive textile industry in Sumer) and silver (perhaps from Anatolia). This seaborne trade developed in the second half of the third millennium BCE, replacing the earlier overland trade route that had brought raw materials, including Iranian copper, from the eastern highlands into southern Mesopotamia. The development of this seaborne trade is in some way related to the rise of the Harappan civilization in the Indus Valley, an area known to the Sumerians as the land of Meluḫḫa. In one of his royal inscriptions Sargon of Akkad claims that he "moored the ships of Meluḫḫa, Magan, and Dilmun at the quay of Akkade" (his capital city). [*See* Akkade.] The Sumerian texts refer to gold, and even to tin, from the land of Meluḫḫa, along with stones and exotic woods (Cleuziou, 1986).

As the Mesopotamians had done earlier, the merchants of Meluḫḫa expanded into Central Asia (ancient Bactria) and seem to have been physically present in southern Mesopotamia, where their presence required the services of a translator. The inhabitants of the Indus Valley established some sort of a colony in Afghanistan, at the site of Shortugai. A complex of trade networks came into existence, linking Mesopotamia, Central Asia, and the Indus Valley. The metalwork that resulted from these cultural connections can be seen in such collections of precious materials as the so-called Quetta treasure. The treasure was discovered during the course of digging the foundations for a hotel in modern Quetta and is dated to about 2000 BCE. It includes gold vessels and small objects (especially two bull pendants), as well as copper/bronze implements and alabaster vessels. There is also a hoard of five gold and seven silver vessels said to have been found in 1966 at Khosh Tapa, north of Kabul, also dated to about 2000 BCE. Khosh Tapa is on the other side of the Anjuman Pass, across from the Sar-i-Sang lapis mines. These treasures must reflect the tremendous wealth generated by the international trade of the day (see articles in Ligabue and Salvatori, 1989).

One of the most distinctive objects in the repertoire of late third-millennium BCE jewelry in gold and silver is the quadruple spiral bead. These beads have an extensive geographic distribution, from Anatolia to the Persian Gulf (with later, related examples known from mid-second-millennium sites in Greece). This very distinctive artifact actually provides an excellent object lesson on the dangers inherent in typological dating. While many examples do date from the second half of the third millennium BCE, including specimens from Troy, Alaca Höyük, Tell Selenkahiyeh, Tell Brak, Ur, and Bahrain, others are from the early second millennium BCE (Old Assyrian Kültepe, Aššur tomb 20) and even the late second millennium (twelve examples from a tomb at Mari dated to c. 1400-1200 BCE). Moreover, these beads were still being produced in the Iron Age. Eighteen complete examples in silver were found as part of a hoard excavated at the seventh century BCE site of Tepe Nush-i Jan, in western Iran (Curtis, 1984).

It has been argued that the Nush-i Jan beads represent curated heirlooms and were actually manufactured in the third millennium BCE. This seems most unlikely, given the large number of finds (including a number of fragments), but certainty on such matters will probably forever elude researchers. It certainly is significant that the hoard from Nush-i Jan also included five double spiral pendants in silver, a type known in the Early Uruk period and well documented in graves in the royal cemetery at Ur (Early Dynastic IIIA) and from roughly contemporary examples in Iran (Tepe Hissar IIIB).

The Nush-i Jan hoard also contained thirteen silver bar ingots. Such ingots are known from contexts both a thousand years earlier (Tell Asmar, Larsa) and a thousand years later (from the Late Roman period). [*See* Larsa.] Examples in copper are a distinctive feature of the EB IV period in Palestine. Molds for casting such ingots are known from Tell Brak and Chaghar Bazar (and even from sites as early as Tepe Ghabristan and as late as the Early Iron Age site of Koukos in northern Greece). The distribution of such ingots in Palestine, together with the general lack of EB IV settlements, has suggested the existence of a guild of itinerant metalworkers operating throughout Palestine at the end of the third millennium BCE.

Second Millennium BCE. From a metallurgical perspective the second millennium BCE began with the Old Assyrian trade between Aššur and the *karum* Kaneš, covering the nineteenth century BCE (the time of level II in the *karum*). Hundreds of Old Assyrian letters document a metals trade between northern Mesopotamia and central Anatolia. The Old Assyrian merchants brought tin (and textiles) into Anatolia, there to be exchanged for silver (and gold). The silver was used to purchase more tin, in Aššur, and the process was repeated the following year.

The obvious implication of this trade pattern is that silver was available in Anatolia, whereas tin was not. The texts say nothing about the source(s) of this tin, only that it was brought (from somewhere in the east) to Aššur, where it was purchased by Assyrian merchants, along with textiles from Babylonia. [*See* Babylonians.] Both tin and textiles were then brought by donkey caravan (making use of a special breed of black donkey) to Anatolia. The further implication is that the local Anatolian princes had no access to sources of tin themselves—or, at least, found it more desirable to purchase tin (at somewhat inflated prices) from Assyrian middlemen. The copper used by the Anatolian metalworkers must have been of local origin, and the production and utilization of bronze was also carried out locally. A metal workshop has been excavated in the Ib level in the *karum* Kaneš, the time of Shamshi-Adad I of Assyria.

This pattern of an east–west metals trade, bringing tin from the east (Afghanistan?) to sites west of Mesopotamia, is also documented in the Old Babylonian letters from Mari, covering at least the first half of the eighteenth century BCE. Tin came up the Euphrates to Mari, with Susa serving as a vital link between eastern tin sources and the Euphrates valley. Certain merchants (Akk., *tamkārū*) specialized in this tin trade with Elam, especially one named Isi-Dagan. The good graces of local Elamite officials were essential to maintaining access to this tin and so they were ingratiated with gifts of wine and honey. [*See* Elamites.]

The tin came to Mari in ingot form and was stored there for reshipment. From one text, known as the Mari Tin Inventory, it is known that this tin was shipped to various sites in the west, from Carchemish in the north to Hazor in the south. [*See* Carchemish; Hazor.] From Ugarit the tin was further shipped to the land of Kaptaru, the Akkadian name for the island of Crete. Such long-distance trade was justified by the scarcity (and therefore the cost) of the metal. Metal ratios given in the Mari text reveal that tin was considered to be about one-tenth the price of silver, whereas the price of copper was 150 to 180 times cheaper than silver. Lead, on the other hand, was twelve hundred times cheaper than silver. [*See* Mari Texts.]

There are other references to Kaptaru in the Mari texts, as well as to the exchange of "greeting gifts" between the rulers of the Minoan palaces on Crete and the rulers of Mari. Communication between the merchants of Crete and those of Mari required the services of a translator (Akk., *targamannum,* the Akkadian word eventually borrowed by all European languages as *dragoman*), as had earlier contact between Akkadian merchants and the merchants of Meluḫḫa (see above). The Mari texts also refer to copper from Alashiya, a geographic term usually associated with the island of Cyprus. The Cypriot copper industry was certainly well underway by the eighteenth century BCE. The first evidence for actual copper mining on Cyprus, at the site of Ambelikou *Aletri,* dates to this period. Copper from Alashiya is even mentioned in a text from Babylonia, dated to the fifth year of the reign of Samsuiluna, king of Babylon and the successor of Hammurabi.

This was the international world of the Old Babylonian period, illuminated by many references to metalworking and the metals trade in texts from Mari and Ur. The situation at Mari, however, has been greatly confused by mistranslations in the standard editions of the Mari letters. The translators identified references to a process of ore beneficiation and to a copper-smelting installation. In reality, the texts describe the washing and crushing of ice (Akk., *šurīpum*) and to the storage of that ice in an icehouse *(bīt šurīpim).* A Mari text said to describe the casting of metallic copper actually states that, after the ice freezes, the iceman will send it to Mari for storage in the icehouse. Equally suspect is the interpretation of rooms 216–218 in the palace of Zimrilim as metal workshops. There are, however, many actual references to metalworking in the Mari texts, especially to the manufacture of military equipment and even to the repair of chariots. [*See* Chariots.]

From Ur a group of texts from the time of Rim-Sin, king of Larsa (1822–1763 BCE) deal with the acquisition of copper from Dilmun (the copper actually coming from Oman, ancient Magan). [*See* Larsa.] A trader named Ea-nasir seems to have played a special role in this trade and, according to the surviving texts, may have been a rather unscrupulous individual, trying to pass off ingots of bad copper as good copper. The nature of the objects being produced from this copper can be seen in a hoard of metal artifacts found by W. K. Loftus at the site of Tell Sifr (Iraq) in 1854 (see below). Loftus described the hoard in 1857 as "consisting of large chaldrons, vases, small dishes, and dice-boxes (?); hammers, chisels, adzes, and hatchets; a large assortment of knives and daggers of various sizes and shapes—all unfinished; massive and smaller rings; a pair of prisoners' fetters; three links of a strong chain; a ring weight; several plates resembling horses' shoes, divided at the heel for the insertion of a handle and having two holes in each for pins; other plates of a different shape, which were probably primitive hatchets; an ingot of copper and a great weight of dross from the same smelted metal" (W. K. Loftus, *Travels and Researches in Chaldaea and Susiana,* London, 1857, p. 268).

Although several of the specific identifications Loftus made could be questioned today, it is clear that the Sifr hoard was basically of agricultural tools and that it demonstrates a basic continuity between the agricultural practices of Old Babylonian Mesopotamia and those in use in present-day Iraq. [*See* Agriculture.] Elemental analysis of a number of pieces from the Sifr hoard indicates that tin was used very sparingly, even in the Old Babylonian period. Most of the tools from the Sifr hoard were made of unalloyed copper. The extensive use of unalloyed copper is distinctive of other analyzed groups of second-millennium BCE metalwork as well, including pieces from Tell er-Rimah, Kar-Tukulti-Ninurta, and Bahrain. [*See* Rimah, Tell er-; Kar-Tukulti-Ninurta.]

Old Babylonian work in precious metal is best documented by the contents of the goldsmith's hoard excavated as a jar burial from the site of Larsa. [*See* Burial Techniques.] This deposit included many pieces of scrap metal, both silver and gold, as well as a copper anvil, three copper design blocks, and more than sixty stone weights for use with a pan balance. Such balance weights, often found in complete sets with one or more pan balances, are quite common in the archaeological record, especially in contexts dating to the mid-second millennium BCE (for Larsa hoard see Bjorkman, 1993).

The French excavators of Larsa believe that the room in which this hoard, as well as two others was found, was actually a metal workshop, the atelier of a goldsmith who can even be identified by name. All of this is most unlikely because, while hoards are buried in very improbable places, they are almost never buried in workshops. The goldsmith's hoards from Geometric Eretria (Greece) and the silver hoard from stratum VI (eleventh century BCE) at Megiddo (Israel) certainly did not come from workshop context. [*See* Megiddo.] The same is true of the gold hoard from Late Bronze Age Tell el-ʿAjjul and Beth-Shemesh (Israel; see Tadmor, 1980) and the silver hoards from LB Ugarit and El-Qitar (Syria). [*See* ʿAjjul, Tell el-; Beth-Shemesh; Qitar, El-.] The goldwork of the Middle Bronze Age, like that of the Early Bronze Age, possessed an international character. A gold pendant from Tell ed-Dabʿa (on Egypt's eastern Delta) is very similar to one that is part of a gold hoard said to come from the island of Aegina (Greece). [*See* Dabʿa, Tell ed-; Delta.] Both date to the seventeenth century BCE. However, such goldwork is also found out of context: a gold pendant very similar to one from the Mesopotamian site of Dilbat (seventeenth century BCE) has turned up in a tenth-century BCE burial at the site of Lefkandi on the island of Euboea (Greece).

Nor was metallurgical paraphernalia always stored in a workshop area. Copper/bronze workshops have been identified at Uruk, Ur, Khafajeh, Kish, and Tell Asmar, but none has proved to be very convincing. The only useful example of an Old Babylonian metal workshop is at Tell edh-Dhiba'i, located in what is now a suburb of Baghdad in Iraq (Davey, 1988). Although excavated under conditions that prevented the proper recording of the finds, this workshop contained a rich assemblage of metalworking paraphernalia, including two clay pot bellows, six crucibles, a tuyere, a clay ladle, and a series of molds. The use of the pot bellows to create a forced draft of air to be directed, via the tuyere, into the furnace, is well illustrated in Egyptian tomb paintings, especially those from the tomb of Rekmire. [*See* Tombs; Wall Paintings.] Such bellows are attested at sites in Anatolia, the Levant, the Sinai (Serabit el-Khadem), and Mesopotamia and on Cyprus from throughout the second millennium BCE. They usually are not correctly identified in the relevant excavation reports. Claude F.-A. Schaeffer, for example, thought that the example from Ugarit had been used in making cheese.

The crucibles from Tell edh-Dhiba'i have a distinctive shape; they are best known from Egypt, where in profile the hieroglyphic sign for *metal* (not for *ingot,* as commonly believed) is formed. C. J. Davey (1988) believes that this combination of crucibles, pot bellows, and molds forms the "southern tradition" of metalworking known from Mesopotamia, inland Syria, Palestine, and Egypt. Metalworking in this tradition is depicted in many scenes from Egyptian New Kingdom tombs and is described in many passages in the Amarna letters.

Many passages from the Amarna correspondence describe the greeting gifts exchanged between the pharaoh of Egypt and the rulers of the Hittites, Assyria, Babylonia, and the kingdom of Mitanni. [*See* Hittites; Mitanni.] Egypt was seen as a land rich in gold but, strangely enough, the gifts of gold received from Egypt were considered suspect. Ashur-uballit I, king of Assyria (1353–1318 BCE), says to pharaoh that "gold in your country is dirt; one simply gathers it up" (*EA* 16:6), but the paltry quantity he was sent did not even cover the travel expenses of his messenger. Even worse was the gold sent to Burna-Buriash, king of Kassite Babylonia (1349–1323 BCE). He claims that "the twenty minas of gold that were brought here were not all there. When they put it into the kiln, not five minas of gold appeared" (*EA* 10:4). The Egyptians seem to have held on to their gold for their own use. It is certainly not reasonable to assume that all the gold known from the ancient world in the second half of the second millennium BCE, including the fabulous treasures of the shaft graves of Mycenae and the tholos tombs of Messenia, came from Egypt.

In this period, some of the most interesting work in copper and its alloys come from Susa. The headless statue of Napir-Asu, wife of Untash-Napirisha, king of Anshan and Susa (c. 1250 BCE) is, at 1.29 m, one of the few near life-sized metal sculptures to survive from the second millennium BCE. What makes this work of special interest is the way it was cast: it consists of a copper outer shell cast over a bronze core (not clay as might be expected). This represents a great waste of (expensive) material: the statue, without its head, represents the use of 1,750 kg of metal.

Of equal interest, but for very different reasons, is the bronze object known as the Sit Shamshi, a twelfth-century BCE votive object from the temple of Ninursag on the acropolis at Susa. Inscribed with the name of Shilhak-Inshushinak, son of Shutruk-Nahhunte, the two human figures and the various objects, including jars and altars, which stand on a flat base—some cast as part of the base, others added—must all be connected with a ceremony that was part of the worship of the rising sun. [*See* Altars.] Unfortunately, the lack of comparative material rules out any detailed understanding of this remarkable object.

First Millennium BCE. It has long been argued that, in the confusion created by the various invasions and migrations at the end of the second millennium BCE, the lands of the Aegean and the Levant were cut off from their customary sources of copper and tin. The ensuing bronze shortage forced metalworkers to look for an alternative to bronze: hence, the shift to iron and the birth of the Iron Age. The actual state of affairs was probably much more complex: the degree of disruption at the end of the Bronze Age was not as severe as once believed; metalsmiths in the Aegean and the Levant do not seem to have experienced any bronze shortage as bronze artifacts from the so-called Dark Age (c. 1200–900 BCE) often have a high tin content. Nevertheless, iron did gradually become the dominant utilitarian metal from about 1200 to 800 BCE, with bronze remaining the metal of choice for statues, figurines, and vessels, as well as for weapons and armor.

The shift from bronze to iron probably came about for very practical economic reasons: bronze was always quite expensive, copper was relatively plentiful; but tin was very rare. After a century of speculation scholars are still very uncertain about Bronze Age sources of tin. What the limited textual evidence does make clear is that tin came into the ancient Near East and the eastern Mediterranean from distant lands whose exact location was probably unknown even to the metalworkers at Ur, Tell Brak, Tarsus, and Troy (as it was unknown to Herodotus in the fifth century BCE).

Almost every country of the world, on the other hand, had local deposits of iron ore. To work in iron was to work with local raw materials. The problem was that making use of this ubiquitous resource required a technology quite different from that known for copper, tin, gold, silver, and lead. Those metals could be cast, using molds, for they were all used in the molten state. However, the high melting point of iron (1,534° C) meant that, in the ancient world, iron was always worked in the solid state—except in ancient China. For special reasons, in China a cast-iron industry developed perhaps as early as the eighth century BCE. The Chinese always had cast bronze; they never developed any tradition of hammering sheet metal or of raising a vessel from a sheet of bronze. It seems to have been necessary for them to approach iron in the same way. For lands west of India, however, iron metallurgy was a smithing, not a casting technology. Working with iron was labor intensive, but labor was cheap and the iron ore, to be converted, by smelting and forging, to metallic iron, was readily at hand.

Cheap iron and the alphabet were, for V. Gordon Childe (see below) two of the main factors responsible for the democratization of Iron Age society. In a work first published in 1942, Childe claimed that "cheap iron democratized agriculture and industry and warfare too. Any peasant could afford an iron axe to clear fresh land for himself and iron ploughshares wherewith to break up stony ground. . . . Cheap iron tools abolished or at least reduced the dependence of the small producers on State monopolies and great household stores. With the new metal implements for breaking the ground, clearing it of trees, and digging drainage channels, the small farmer might earn independence by reclaiming for himself a piece of waste . . ." (Childe, *What Happened in History,* rev. ed., New York, 1954, pp. 183, 191).

Childe's observations have strongly influenced subsequent scholarship, especially in biblical studies, in which iron tools have come to be seen as an important factor in making possible the early Israelite settlement of the central hill country. Yet, the concept of cheap iron really does not explain why iron, as a utilitarian metal, only came into general use after 1200 BCE. Objects of metallic iron, often meteoritic iron, were in use in the Early Bronze Age. The best-known example is an iron dagger with a gold-covered hilt from one of the "royal" shaft graves at Alaca Höyük. Numerous iron objects (Sum., AN.BAR; Akk., *parzillu*) are mentioned in Old Babylonian texts from Mari, in mid-second millennium BCE texts from Nuzi, and in Hittite texts from Boğazköy. [*See* Hittite; Boğazköy.] The famous treasure of Tutankhamun contained two ornately decorated ceremonial daggers: one had a gold blade, the other an iron blade. Minoan and Mycenaean tombs have produced a number of iron rings as well as gold rings with an iron bezel. The earliest example of worked iron in the Aegean seems to be the seventeenth-century BCE iron and silver ring from the Anemospilia sanctuary at Arkhanes (Crete).

All this represents the use of iron as an exotic, precious material. To turn iron into a practical metal, possessing properties equal to or better than those found in bronze, it was necessary to develop the techniques of carburization, quenching, and tempering. Simple wrought iron was inferior to bronze, being softer, more subject to oxidation and corrosion, and incapable of taking and holding a decent cutting edge. Quenched, carburized iron (or steel), on the other hand, was superior to the best 10 percent tin-bronze—being harder, more durable, and capable of taking and holding a keen cutting edge. If the steel in question was too hard, and therefore quite brittle from excessive production of martensite, this could be corrected by tempering the metal.

Based on present evidence, the technology of carburization, quenching, and tempering was developed in the eastern Mediterranean, on Cyprus and in Palestine, in the twelfth and eleventh centuries BCE. Various solutions have been proposed, but it is still not clear just why this technology developed where and when it did. Even its localization in the easternmost part of the Mediterranean may reflect nothing more than that region's being where most of the scientific analysis of ancient iron artifacts has so far been carried out. Once perfected, in the eleventh century BCE, the technology spread quickly to other parts of the ancient world. Ideas of a secret technology and of an iron monopoly (exercised by the Hittites and then by the Philistines) are best consigned to the academic dustbin. [*See* Philistines.] Many studies of regional industries have been published recently, including those of Hittite Anatolia, Iron Age eastern Anatolia (kingdom of Urartu), ancient Cyprus, Israel and Assyria.

The emphasis on this new metal and new technology should not be allowed to obscure the fact that bronze continued to be produced in the centuries following 1200 BCE. Indeed, those centuries witnessed the efflorescence of one of the major bronze industries of the ancient world—that covered by the umbrella term *Luristan bronzes*. Although there was an earlier period of bronze production in the Luristan province of the Zagros Mountains, documented by Belgian excavations in western Luristan, the main period covers roughly 1350–750 BCE and is known almost entirely through material illicitly excavated and sold on the antiquities market. The work of the Belgian Luristan Expedition, led by L. Vanden Berghe, has, to some extent, also clarified the chronology of this later period of bronze production in Luristan, as have British excavations at Baba Jan conducted by Clare Goff. The assemblage of bronzes from this period consists of axes, daggers, vessels, and harness trappings for horses, often decorated with contorted animals, principally goats, cast in a fantastic animal style. It is not known how many thousands of bronzes were produced, as Luristan bronzes have found their way into almost every museum and private antiquities collection in the world.

Bronzes inscribed with the names of the later Kassite kings of Babylonia indicate that this period of bronze production began sometime in the fourteenth century BCE. The main period of production seems to have been the Iranian Iron II (c. 1000–800 BCE), contemporary with level IV at Hasanlu. [*See* Hasanlu.] While the nomadic smiths of Luristan worked almost entirely in bronze, a gold bowl also from level IV at Hasanlu helps to date a rich assemblage of gold vessels from Marlik, decorated in high repoussé, to the first two centuries of the first millennium BCE. [*See* Marlik.]

Of the surviving bronzes from the Early Iron Age, the most striking is a series of large bronze cauldrons on iron tripod stands. The rim of each cauldron is decorated with so-called protomes in the shape of griffins, bulls, and sirens (usually four per cauldron). Normally, any one cauldron will have only one class of protome, although the cauldron from tomb 79 at Salamis (late eighth century BCE) has both griffins and sirens—eight of one, four of the other. [*See* Salamis.] Although it was found flattened in the tomb, the Salamis cauldron has been beautifully restored. At 1.25 m in total height, it gives a good idea of the size of such objects that, all too often, are known only from isolated protomes purchased on the antiquities market (Muscarella, 1992).

Once thought to be of Urartian manufacture, such cauldrons are now seen as products of one or more North Syrian workshops, although no examples have yet been found in Syria. [*See* Urartu.] Most surviving examples, in fact, come from sanctuary sites in Greece—from Olympia, Delphi, and Samos. The griffin protomes, of which more than 450 examples are now attested, were either cast or hammered (the cast examples are regarded as being of Greek manufacture). It is possible, however, that all of the cauldrons found in Greece were actually made there. Those who believe otherwise have developed theories of gift exchange, such as is known from the Amarna letters and the world of Homer, with Oriental potentates like Midas, king of Phrygia, sending cauldrons as gifts to Greek sanctuaries (as recorded by Herodotus, 1.14).

BIBLIOGRAPHY

Bjorkman, J. K. "The Larsa Goldsmith's Hoards—New Interpretations." *Journal of Near Eastern Studies* 52 (1993): 1–23.

Braun-Holzinger, Eva A. *Figurliche Bronzen aus Mesopotamien.* Munich, 1984. Well-illustrated, reliable discussion of Mesopotamian bronze sculpture.

Cleuziou, Serge. "Dilmun and Makkan during the Third and Early Second Millennis B.C." In *Bahrain through the Ages: The Archaeology,* edited by Shaikha Haya Ali Al Khalifa and Michael Rice, pp. 143–155. London, 1986.

Curtis, John. *Nush-i Jan III: The Small Finds.* London, 1984. Publication of silver hoard, with excellent discussion of comparative material.

Curtis, John, ed. *Bronze-working Centres of Western Asia, c. 1000–539 B.C.* London, 1988. Valuable collection of articles dealing with Neo-Assyrian, Neo-Babylonian, Iranian, Phoenician, and Phrygian metallurgy.

Daniel, Glyn. *A Short History of Archaeology.* London, 1981.

Davey, Christopher J. "Tell edh-Dhiba'i and the Southern Near Eastern Tradition." In *The Beginning of the Use of Metals and Alloys,* edited by Robert Maddin, pp. 63–68. Cambridge, Mass., 1988. Places the finds from the Tell edh-Dhiba'i workshop in historical context.

De Jesus, Prentiss S. *The Development of Prehistoric Mining and Metallurgy in Anatolia.* 2 vols. British Archaeological Reports, 74. Oxford, 1980. Especially valuable for its presentation of work done by the Turkish Geological Survey (known as MTA).

Gopher, Avi, Tsvika Tsuk, Sariel Shalev, and Ram Gophna. "Earliest Gold Artifacts in the Levant." *Current Anthropology* 31 (1990): 436–443. Analyses of gold and electrum artifacts from Naḥal Qanah.

Hauptmann, Andreas, Gerd Weisgerber and Hans G. Bachmann. "Early Copper Metallurgy in Oman." In *The Beginning of the Use of Metals and Alloys,* edited by Robert Maddin, pp. 34–51. Cambridge, Mass., 1988. Account by the team that has investigated the copper deposits of the Sumerian land of Magan.

Jovanović, Borislav. "Early Metallurgy in Yugoslavia." In *The Beginning of the Use of Metals and Alloys,* edited by Robert Maddin, pp. 69–79. Cambridge, Mass., 1988. Account of early copper mining in the Balkans, by the excavator of Rudna Glava.

Ligabue, Giancarlo, and Sandro Salvatori, eds. *Bactria: An Ancient Oasis Civilisation from the Sands of Afghanistan.* Venice, 1989. Excellent articles, superb illustrations and maps.

Moorey, P. R. S. "Archaeology and Pre-Achaemenid Metalworking in Iran: A Fifteen Year Retrospective." *Iran* 20 (1982): 81–101. Survey of early metallurgical developments.

Moorey, P. R. S. "The Chalcolithic Hoard from Naḥal Mishmar, Israel, in Context." *World Archaeology* 20.2 (1988): 171–189. Good account of the significance of Naḥal Mishmar hoard.

Moorey, P. R. S. *Ancient Mesopotamian Materials and Industries: The Archaeological Evidence.* Oxford, 1994. Definitive work on Mesopotamian metallurgy, as well as on other materials.

Müller-Karpe, Michael. *Metallgefässe im Iraq I: Von den Anfängen bis zur Akkad-Zeit.* Stuttgart, 1993. Typological analysis of all known Mesopotamian metal vessels, down to the late third millennium BCE.

Muhly, J. D. "Beyond Typology: Aegean Metallurgy in Its Historical Context." In *Contributions to Aegean Archaeology: Studies in Honor of William A. McDonald,* edited by Nancy C. Wilkie and William D. E. Coulson, pp. 109–141. Minneapolis, 1985a.

Muhly, J. D. "Sources of Tin and the Beginnings of Bronze Metallurgy." *American Journal of Archaeology* 89 (1985b): 275–291. Development of copper alloys down to about 2000 BCE.

Muhly, J. D. "The Beginnings of Metallurgy in the Old World." In *The Beginning of the Use of Metals and Alloys,* edited by Robert Maddin, pp. 2–20. Cambridge, Mass., 1988. Early use of metal, from Europe to China.

Muhly, J. D. "Early Bronze Age Tin and the Taurus." *American Journal of Archaeology* 97 (1993): 239–253. Critical evaluation of the Taurus Mountains as a source of tin.

Muhly, J. D. "Mining and Metalwork in Ancient Western Asia." In *Civilizations of the Ancient Near East,* edited by Jack M. Sasson, vol. 3, pp. 1501–1521. New York, 1995. General survey to the end of the Iron Age, with references.

Muhly, J. D., Robert Maddin, and Tamara Stech. "The Metal Artifacts." In *Kinneret: Ergebnisse der Ausgrabungen auf dem Tell el-'Orēme am See Gennesaret 1982–1985,* edited by Volkmar Fritz, pp. 159–175. Wiesbaden, 1990. Survey of the development of iron technology, by the team that has done most of the modern analytical work.

Muscarella, Oscar W. "Greek and Oriental Cauldron Attachments: A Review." In *Greece between East and West: 10th–8th Centuries BC,* edited by Gunter Kopcke and Isabelle Tokumaru, pp. 16–45. Mainz, 1992. Survey of scholarship regarding the provenience of caldrons.

Philip, Graham. "Hoards of the Early and Middle Bronze Ages in the Levant." *World Archaeology* 20.2 (1988): 190–208. Argues that metal deposits from Byblos, Ugarit, and elsewhere are hoards.

Potts, Timothy. 1994. *Mesopotamia and the East. An Archaeological and Historical Study of Foreign Relations ca. 3400–2000 BC.* Oxford, 1994. Solid survey, with excellent documentation.

Prag, Kay. "Silver in the Levant in the Fourth Millennium B.C." In *Archaeology in the Levant: Essays for Kathleen Kenyon,* edited by P. R. S. Moorey and Peter J. Parr, pp. 36–45. Warminister, 1978. Archaeological evidence for early silver in Near East.

Tadmor, Miriam. "The Beth Shemesh Hoard of Jewellery." *The Israel Museum News* 16 (1980): 71–79.

Waldbaum, Jane C. "Copper, Iron, Tin, Wood: The Start of the Iron Age in the Eastern Mediterranean." *Archeomaterials* 3 (1983): 111–122. Survey of the evidence for the transition from bronze to iron.

Waldbaum, Jane C. *Metalwork from Sardis: The Finds through 1974.* Cambridge, Mass., 1983. Gives range of metal finds from a single site.

J. D. MUHLY

Artifacts of the Persian through Roman Periods

The metal artifact should be viewed first as a unit of material culture, whereby artifacts themselves—whether a luxury item such as a gold necklace or a utilitarian object such as a corroded iron nail—are seen as equals, in the sense that they illuminate some aspect of daily life in antiquity. Metal objects of the Persian, Hellenistic, and Roman periods served a variety of functions, and the finds themselves number in the thousands. For this reason, this survey relies on a few select examples to suggest the vast corpus of metal artifacts, which are grouped according to cultural function. Gold, silver, electrum, iron, tin, bronze, brass, copper, and lead represent the main metal and alloy types used to manufacture metal objects in the periods under discussion. Major sources of metal ores in the ancient Near East and surrounding regions include the Arabian Peninsula, Asia Minor, Bactria, Cyprus, India, Italy, Lebanon, Nubia, the Sinai Peninsula, Spain, Syria, and Wadi ʿArabah.

Artifacts of Daily Life. Domestic metalwares of the Persian through Roman periods that have come to light in excavations include bowls, plates, cups, goblets, jars, jugs, juglets, pitchers, utensils, lamps, lampstands, pans, strainers, ladles, and trays. Terra-cotta wares were often prototypes for metal vessels. A gold-plated silver bowl with depictions of two elderly Scythian leaders, was discovered with drinking vessels from the Gaymanova Moguila (South Russia). It dates to the second half of the fourth century BCE. (Rolle,

1989). A bronze ladle with a handle decorated with ram heads was recovered from Persian contexts at Gezer (Israel). A sculptured bronze vessel of a seated Nubian boy from Zawiya (Syria) dates to the Early Roman period (Weiss, 1985), and an iron "frying pan" with a folding handle from the Thebes/Luxor region of Egypt is Late Roman (Hayes, 1984).

Chief among the metal artifacts of writing is the inkwell. Although inkwells were commonly made of terra-cotta, several Roman examples in metal have been recovered by archaeologists. A bronze inkwell with a tall, cylindrical body that closely resembles its ceramic counterparts was unearthed at Qumran, Israel (Goranson, 1991). At the monastery site at Deir el-Baḥari (Egypt), a lead (or possibly pewter) inkwell with an iron handle and a rounded body that was raised from a single sheet was found (Hayes, 1984). The artifact dates to the first or second century CE. Lead stationery was also common for the writing of curses and of military diplomas in the Roman period. Examples of such lead sheets with inscribed curses were recently found at Caesarea Maritima (Israel).

Ancient artistic representations of musical instruments and their literary mention abound. [*See* Musical Instruments.] A Late Hellenistic Alexandrian terra-cotta figurine of a seated Syrian musician holding a panpipe connected to a bellow, for example, suggests an organ (Gk., *hydraulis*). Two curved metal trumpets (Heb. *ḥăṣōṣĕrâ*) are depicted on a mosaic floor in the fourth-century CE Samaritan synagogue at el-Khirbe near Sebaste/Samaria (Israel). Ironically, few actual musical instruments have survived from antiquity, chief among them having been the lyre, oboe, lute, pipe, bagpipe, flute, cross flute, panpipe, organ, trumpet, drum, cymbal, rattle, and clappers. Of the various musical instrument types, cymbals, clappers, and rattles are probably the most commonly discovered at archaeological sites. Phoenician cymbals cast in bronze have been recovered at Kerkouane (Tunisia) and date to the third century BCE (Moscati, 1988). They resemble small shallow bowls with raised, domelike centers. A bronze finger cymbal excavated in a military context at the legionary fortress at el-Lejjun (Jordan) is dated to 363–502 CE.

Jewelery represents the most commonly found metal artifact of adornment discovered at ancient Near Eastern sites, primarily finger rings (including signet rings), bracelets, pendants and other necklaces, beads, belts, belt ends and buckles, pins, fibulae, brooches, amulets, and earrings. [*See* Jewelery.] Various decorative techniques—repoussé, cutting, piercing, soldering, and granulation—have been employed by the ancient metalworker in the manufacture of jewelery. A Persian pin with a gold pomegranate-shaped bead and a long silver shank from the Tall-i Takht in Pasargadae (Iran) demonstrates the use of granulation as a decorative technique (Stronach, 1978). A cast, silver signet ring whose oval bezel depicts a woman seated in front of an incense altar was found at Tel Michal (Israel) and dates to the fifth–fourth centuries BCE (Muhly and Muhly, 1989). A gold bangle from Tartus (Syria) represents a superb example of the smithing technique of *opus interrasile,* which, by means of piercing, creates a lacelike decoration. This artifact dates to the late fourth century BCE. A unique pendant from Meroë (Sudan), dating to the second century CE, consists of a single gold nugget on which a cylindrical loop for a chain is attached (Ogden, 1982). The emphasis in this piece on the natural simplicity of the raw metal demonstrates an atypical, virtually modern approach to ancient jewelery design.

Metal artifacts that served a religious, political, or magical function include amulets, altars, censers, crowns, incense shovels, candelabra, lamps, bells, and votive items. A Phoenician faience amulet depicting a cat entwined with gold was recovered at Tharros (Sardinia) and dates to the seventh–fourth centuries BCE (Moscati, 1988). A portable Roman imperial bronze altar (Lat., *arula*) from Lower Egypt consists of a shallow square tray with sloping sides supported by a lathe-turned round drum and a square base (Hayes, 1984). A central shaft fragment with attached branches of a cast-bronze menorah was recovered from a Late Roman context at Sardis (Asia Minor), whose corpus of metal objects is one of the largest and most varied for the Roman and Byzantine Near East (Waldbaum, 1983). Bronze incense shovels from the Faiyum in Egypt date to the first and second centuries CE and consist of a square-to-rectangular central pan with a handle attached to one of the short ends (Hayes, 1984). A Phoenician votive razor (third century BCE) from Carthage (Tunisia) cast in bronze depicts Heracles-Melqart and a male figure slaying an enemy (Moscati, 1985). A votive statuette of a cast-bronze bull from Bludan (Syria), belonging to the corpus of military cult items of the Roman East, was offered to the deity Orion by a soldier, as suggested by a single-line Greek inscription engraved on the base (Weiss, 1985). A collapsible gold crown belonging to a Bactrian nomadic princess was recovered at Tillya-tepe, Afghanistan (Sarianidi, 1985). The crown itself consists of five elaborate palmettes and a fillet-base hand-cut from thin sheet gold.

In healing the sick and the injured, doctors made use of a variety of bronze and iron implements (see figure 1). Roman surgical instruments have widespread distribution across the ancient world. The most common types include bleeding cups, scalpels and dissectors, phlebotomes, retractors, embryo hooks, elevators and chisels, spatulae, spoons (cyathiscomele) and ligulae, probes and needles, tubes, forceps and tweezers, specula, and cylindrical medicine cases. A cranioclast reportedly found at Ephesus (Anatolia) represents the only known example from the Greco-Roman period (Bliquez, 1988; Künzl, 1983). This instrument was used to crush the skull of the fetus in cases of abortion. Representative symbols of the healing gods Hercules (a knotted club pattern), Aesculapius (a snake or head of a snake), and Sminthian Apollo (a mouse) frequently decorate metal surgical instruments. The end of a handle belonging to a sur-

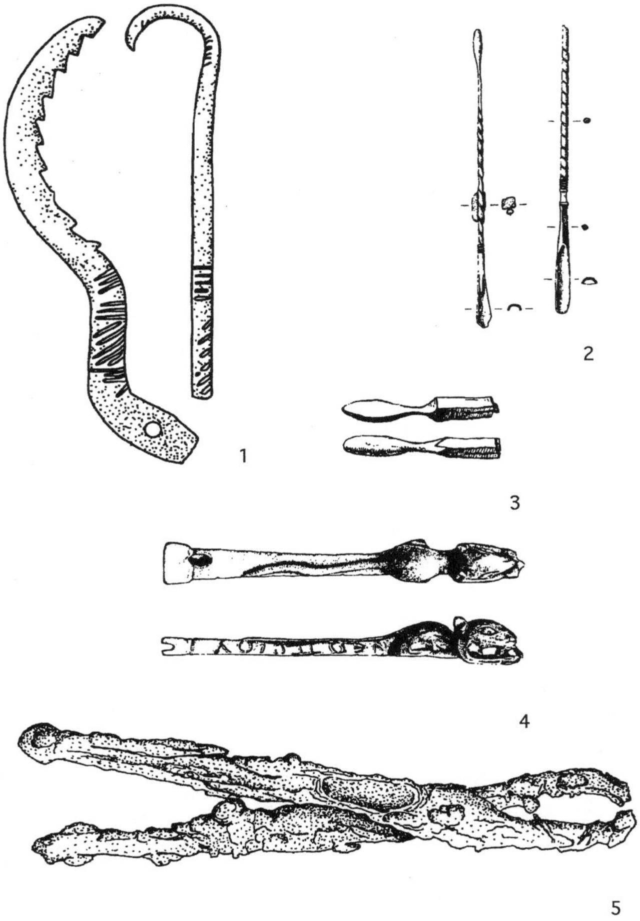

METALS: Persian through Roman Periods. Figure 1. *Near Eastern Roman surgical instruments.* (1) Embryo hooks from Ephesus in Anatolia; (2) spatulae from North Syria; (3) late nineteenth-century illustration of scalpels from Idalion, Cyprus; (4) instrument handle fashioned as a mouse symbolizing the healing god Apollo Smintheus from southwest Asia Minor; (5) dental forceps from a tomb at Gadara, Jordan. (Items 1–4 after Künzl, 1983, figs. 20, 97, 23, and 14 respectively; item 5 after Künzl and Weber, 1991, fig. 4)

gical implement from southwestern Asia Minor is rendered in the shape of a mouse, symbolizing Sminthian Apollo (Künzl, 1983). It was reportedly found with grave goods dating to the first half of the third century CE. A collection of Roman dental instruments (i.e., an iron tooth forceps, tweezers, and shears) was recovered from a grave at the Decapolis city of Gadara/Umm Qeis, Jordan (Künzl and Weber, 1991).

Common metal toilet articles found at sites in the Near East include kohl sticks and tubes, ear spoons, combs, pins, rods, unguent spoons, spatulae, mirrors, tweezers, and razors. A slender cylindrical cosmetic tube, most probably dating to the Roman period, was recovered at Sardis. Although similar to a surgical-probe case, the presence of a black residue inside this artifact of copper alloy suggests that it contained either medicine or cosmetics (Waldbaum, 1983). A collection of bronze kohl tubes and sticks dating to the Persian period was discovered in a tomb at ʿAtlit, Israel (Stern, 1982). The sticks are flat on one side and twisted on the other. A pair of Phoenician cast-bronze tweezers from Kerkouane dates to the fourth century BCE. Bronze tweezers belonging to a military toilet kit were recovered from a Late Roman context at el-Lejjun. In addition to tweezers, the military toilet kit of the Roman period included an ear scoop and nail cleaner. The design and decoration of many cosmetic articles are simple while others are crafted in precious metals with ornate patterns: a gold comb whose handle is fashioned into a dramatic battle scene involving three Scythian warriors was uncovered in a royal tomb of the Solokha kurgan, South Russia (Rolle, 1989). It represents one of the finest pieces of metalwork from the late Persian period (first half of the fourth century BCE).

The range of tools used by the miner, builder, sculptor, artisan, and carpenter in antiquity was not unlike that of today. Metal tools from the archaeological record include planes, hammers, folding rules, plumb bobs, anvils, masons' chisels, compasses, calipers, masons' squares, picks, sledgehammers, punches, and chisels. A Roman iron chisel was recovered by archaeologists from the waste dump of a mine shaft in Wadi Khalid (Jordan). Chemical analyses revealed that its ends are composed of a eutectoid steel with a carbon concentration of about 0.7 percent. Drills used by artisans in antiquity possessed capabilities of the utmost precision, as revealed by microscopic impressions of spiraling grooves left by the head of a very fine iron drill in amber beads from Hajjar ar-Rayḥani (Yemen) dating to the fourth–third centuries BCE (Gwinnett and Gorelick, 1991). Metal spikes, nails, tacks, rivets, wires, staples, and clamps were used in construction, and plows, spades, sickles, pruning hooks, adzes, augers, awls, and axes were commonly used in agriculture. A Late Roman iron pruning hook and sickle were uncovered at Jalame, Israel (Berry, 1988).

The major metal artifacts of trade in antiquity include coins, tesserae, ingots, weights, and weighing instruments, with coins being the most widely circulated. A series of silver coins depicting a dolphin above a murex shell was minted at Phoenician Tyre (Lebanon) in the Persian period. (The Murex shell and its coveted purple dye were closely associated with the international commerce of the city.) Coins also depicted architectural elements of the urban landscape unique to their city of origin. For example, the flight of steps ascending to the Temple of Zeus on Mt. Gerizim is often depicted on coins minted at Neapolis/Nablus (Palestinian Authority), as is the nymphaeum (public fountain) at Pella that appears on coins from this Decapolis city (Jordan). [*See* Coins.]

Cast ingots of gold, silver, iron, or copper further represent a type of metal artifact. They were traded extensively throughout the ancient Near East and provided the metalworker with the core material from which to manufacture objects. A Roman cast-gold bar with Latin stamps originates from Abukir (Egypt).

Persian-period bronze, cube-shaped, as well as zoomorphic weights (e.g., ram, donkey, calf) are known from Ashkelon (Israel). Weights from the Roman East include a rectangular example with beveled edges used with a scalepan balance (Lat., *libra*) and a biconical version used with a steelyard (Lat. *stratera*). Examples of each include the bronze artifacts found at el-Lejjun and Jbail (Syria). In 1985 a unique square lead weight was discovered by archaeologists at Sepphoris (Lower Galilee, Israel). Noteworthy is the mention of Simon, a Jewish *agoranomos,* or "market inspector," in the five-line inscription on the reverse side of the artifact. [*See* Sepphoris.] Weighing instruments, such as a late fourth-century CE bronze steelyard from Jalame or the Roman steelyard from Jbail, are based on the principle of the lever. The Jbail example (and others like it) consists of a central rod with a weight and two hooks—one to support the instrument and the second attached to the end of a chain from which a chosen object is weighed.

Not all metal artifacts served a terrestrial function. Anchors, spikes, nails, staples, hull casings, rams, and sinkers are among the many metal objects associated with ancient seafaring. [*See* Seafaring.] Late Hellenistic hourglass-shaped lead stoves whose broad bases provided considerable stability on rolling seas attest to the ancients' fear of on-board fires (Bass, 1972). With respect to ship construction, copper spikes found at the late fourth-century BCE Kyrenia shipwreck off the northern coast of Cyprus had secured the wooden frames of the ship to its keel. Unlike the Kyrenia wreck, the frames of the Persian shipwreck from Ma'agan Mikha'el (near Haifa, Israel) as well as the Early Roman Kinneret (Sea of Galilee) fishing boat were secured to the hull with iron nails rather than copper spikes. [*See* Ma'agan Mikha'el; Galilee Boat.] Chemical analyses of the Kinneret nails revealed that they are composed of 0.4 percent carbon steel, not unlike present-day steel. A sheathing of lead attached to the Kyrenia vessel's hull by copper tacks—a method commonly used during the Roman period—protected the ship from marine borers. Hundreds of anchor parts made of lead or iron have been recovered in the Mediterranean. [*See* Anchors.] The majority of finds from the Late Persian, Hellenistic, and Early Roman periods suggest that most anchors were made of wood with either lead or stone. After the first century CE, however, anchors were constructed exclusively of iron. One such example of a first-century iron anchor was found in the ancient harbor at Dor (Israel).

Artifacts of War, Oppression, and Death. Important metal weapons and associated equipment recovered from Persian- through Roman-period contexts include swords, daggers, dagger sheaves, penknives, spearheads, arrowheads, javelin heads, bolts, dart points, helmets, breastplates, and chain mail. The arrowhead is perhaps the most commonly found weapon type from archaeological deposits. Specific arrowhead finds include triangular barbed examples from Tell el-Ḥesi, Tel Michal, Gezer, Ḥesban, 'Ein-Boqeq, Masada, and Ḥorvat Eqed (Israel), Pasargadae, Dura-Europos (Syria), and el-Lejjun.

A Late Hellenistic helmet made of two parts, the headpiece and visor, was found at Emesa/Homs (Syria). Both components are cast in iron, but the mask itself is sheathed with solid silver. The thick visor, narrow eye slits, ear guards, and the heavy weight of the helmet attest to its function: protecting its owner in a tournament or battle. A Late Roman bowl-shaped helmet constructed with two iron pieces was recently recovered from the grave of a Roman soldier at el-Haditha (Jordan).

Metal artifacts of oppression include fetters, chains, crucifixion nails, and slave collars. In 1906, a lead collar bearing a single-line Latin inscription was excavated beneath the pavement of the Temple of Apollo area at Bulla Regia (Ḥammam Darradji, Tunisia). The collar was found still attached to the skeleton (neck) of a female who apparently died in midlife. The inscription not only describes the woman as a fugitive, but as a prostitute and as adulterous. The artifact may date to the fourth century CE (Ben Abed Ben Khader and Soren, 1987).

The right heel bone of a crucified male was recovered from a Jewish cemetery at Giv'at ha-Mivatar located north of Jerusalem. It was found in an ossuary engraved with the name of the victim himself, a young man by the name of Yehoḥanan ben Hagkol, who apparently died sometime in the first century CE. An iron nail 11.5 cm long had penetrated the specimen medially. The find is important, for it is the only known archaeological evidence for crucifixion, a widespread form of execution in the ancient Near East (Zias, 1991).

Examples of metal artifacts commonly associated with death and burial include coffins, jewelery, weapons, cosmetic equipment, bells, funerary masks, and metalware. [*See* Grave Goods.] A gold funerary mask from Phoenicia, for example, dates to the fifth–fourth centuries BCE (Moscati, 1988). Lead sarcophagai first begin to appear in the archaeological record in about the first century CE. [*See* Sarcophagus; Burial Sites; Tombs; Burial Techniques.] The base and sides of coffins were often cast in a single mold and their edges further strengthened with lead bars. The lead coffins tend to be long and rectangular and are often decorated with floral and vine patterns. An early Christian coffin of lead has been uncovered at Caesarea Maritima (Israel) and several are known from the Jewish catacombs at Beth-She'arim (Lower Galilee, Israel). [*See* Beth-She'arim.]

Metal objects not only played a role in the customs surrounding death; certain metals even caused it. Lead poisoning was especially widespread in the Roman period. Although miners and metalworkers of lead were most vulnerable, poisoning would also have resulted from nonoccupational exposure to objects either made of lead or containing it. Examples include coins, cosmetics, toys, yarns, drinking vessels, paint pigments, medicines, and water pipes (Nriagu, 1983).

Artifacts of Waste. Slags represent the molten by-product of smelting practices. They are a significant group of metal artifacts because their subsequent chemical and metallographic analyses yield important information about ancient metallurgical techniques (e.g., temperature of the smelting). Depending on the chemical composition of any given slag, the archaeologist can determine the kind of metal smelted at a site. Analysis may even pinpoint the primary source of the ore used in a smelting operation. [*See* DCP Spectrometry; Magnetic Archaeometry.]

Slag heaps often consist of pronounced layering, each stratum of which represents a period of chronologically defined production. By examining layers, the development of technological practices can be traced. On Cyprus alone, seven slag types have been identified and classified (Koucky and Steinberg, 1989). Cypriot slags dating to the Persian through Hellenistic periods include the crucible and blocky shaped varieties. Crucible-shaped iron slags dating to the Late Roman–Early Byzantine periods (see figure 2) were recovered in a barrack at el-Lejjun and suggest a small-scale metalworking operation, substantiating the Roman military author Vegetius's claim that soldiers were skilled in various crafts (Koucky and Lapp, forthcoming). Metal slags also served a secondary use as building blocks in the construction

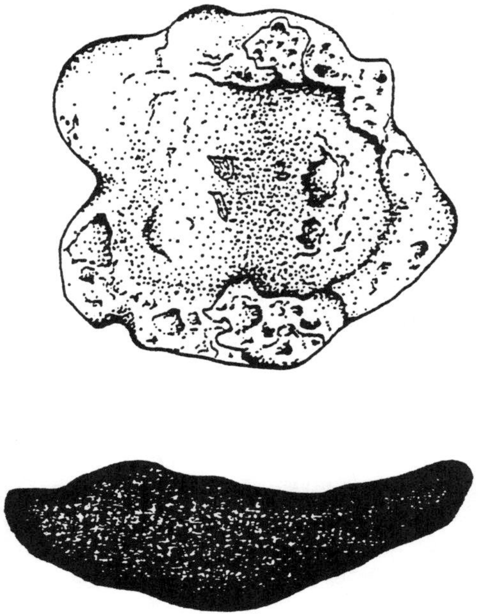

METALS: Persian through Roman Periods. Figure 2. *An iron slag from the legionary fortress of el-Lejjun, Jordan.* (Drawing by Eric C. Lapp)

of walls, as is evidenced at Be'er Ora in Wadi ʿArabah, where Roman stores and workshops were erected with large copper slags (Rothenberg, 1972). In his *Natural History,* which contains important passages regarding the use of metals in antiquity, Pliny notes that both copper and silver slag were considered useful for their medicinal properties, the latter being particularly savvy for closing wounds and remedying sores caused by chafing (33.35.105; 34.24.107).

[*Most of the sites mentioned are the subject of independent entries.*]

BIBLIOGRAPHY

Bass, George F. *A History of Seafaring Based on Underwater Archaeology.* London, 1972. Bass's work represents the most comprehensive to date with respect to the archaeology of ancient as well as historical shipwrecks. It is an important source for the types of metal artifacts found associated with ancient wrecks.

Ben Abed Ben Khader, Aocha, and David Soren, eds. *Carthage: A Mosaic of Ancient Tunisia.* New York, 1987. This well-illustrated work exposes one to the extraordinary material culture of Carthage and other sites in ancient Tunisia.

Berry, Walter. "The Minor Objects." In *Excavations at Jalame: Site of a Glass Factory in Late Roman Palestine,* edited by Gladys Davidson Weinberg, pp. 227–255. Columbia, Mo., 1988. Important primary examples of domesitic, agricultural, and industrial implements and equipment associated with a Late Roman glass factory.

Bliquez, Lawrence J. *Roman Surgical Instruments and Minor Objects in the University of Mississippi.* Göteborg, 1988. Publication of a major collection of ancient surgical instruments.

Goranson, Stephen. "Further Qumran Archaeology Publications in Progress." *Biblical Archaeologist* 54.2 (1991): 110–111. Reinvestigates the ceramic and bronze inkwells from Qumran, themselves important in that they represent some of the very few examples recovered from controlled stratigraphic excavations.

Gwinnett, A. John, and Leonard Gorelick. "Bead Manufacture at Hajar ar-Rayhani, Yemen." *Biblical Archaeologist* 54.4 (1991): 186–197.

Hayes, John W. *Greek, Roman, and Related Metalware in the Royal Ontario Museum: A Catalogue.* Toronto, 1984. Important source of primary metalwares from Greco-Roman Egypt.

Healy, John F. *Mining and Metallurgy in the Greek and Roman World.* London, 1978. Eminently readable, comprehensive, and well-illustrated; draws on a wide range of archaeological evidence and ancient literary sources as they pertain to every technological and administrative mechanism behind Greco-Roman metallurgy.

Koucky, Frank L., and Arthur Steinberg. "Ancient Mining and Mineral Dressing on Cyprus." In *American Expedition to Idalion, Cyprus, 1973–1980,* edited by Lawrence E. Stager and Anita M. Walker, pp. 275–327. Oriental Institute Communications, 24. Chicago, 1989. The most comprehensive treatment of ancient mining, mineral dressing, and slag types found on Cyprus, whose copper industry was one of the most important in antiquity.

Koucky, Frank L., and Eric C. Lapp. "Metallographic Evidence of Ironworking at el-Lejjun: An Archaeometric Study of Roman and Byzantine Iron Slags." In *The Roman Frontier in Central Jordan: Final Report on the Limes Arabicus Project, 1980–1989,* edited by S. Thomas Parker. Washington, D.C., forthcoming. Iron-slag finds at a Roman legionary fortress, attesting to a small-scale metalworking operation in a military context. Chemical and petrological thin-section analyses revealed that their iron content was not unlike that found in slags from sites elsewhere in the Roman world.

Künzl, Ernst. *Medizinische Instrumente aus Sepulkralfunden der römischen Kaiserzeit.* Köln, 1983. Provides a useful comparative catalog of surgical instruments found throughout the ancient world with accompanying discussion and copious illustrations.

Künzl, Ernst, and Thomas Weber. "Das spätantike Grab eines Zahnarztes zu Gadara in der Decapolis." *Damaszener Mitteilungen* 5 (1991): 81–118. Discusses the excavation and burial goods including surgical implements found in this rare grave of an urban Decapolis dentist.

Moorey, P.R.S. *Materials and Manufacture in Ancient Mesopotamia: The Evidence of Archaeology and Art in Metals and Metalwork, Glazed Materials, and Glass.* British Archaeology Reports, International Series, no. 237. Oxford, 1985. Detailed discussion of various techniques employed by artisans; should be consulted in conjunction with other works discussing Early Prehistoric–Persian and middle Hellenistic period metal artifacts of the ancient Near East, particularly from sites in Mesopotamia.

Moscati, Sabatino, ed. *The Phoenicians.* Translated by I. Fenici. Milan, 1988. To date, this landmark work represents the most comprehensive treatment of Phoenician material culture. The numerous metal artifacts included in this impressive, well-illustrated volume provide one with numerous examples of Phoenician metal handicraft.

Munro-Hay, S. C. *Excavations at Aksum: An Account of Research at the Ancient Ethiopian Capital Directed in 1972–4 by the Late Dr. Neville Chittick.* London, 1989. A landmark study of the Ethiopian site of Aksum, whose metalwork finds represent a fascinating mixture of Greco-Roman and African stylistic elements.

Muhly, James D., and Polymnia Muhly. "Metal Artifacts." In *Excavations at Tel Michal, Israel,* edited by Ze'ev Herzog, George Rapp, Jr., and Ora Negbi, pp. 267–295. Publications of the Institute of Archaeology, 8 Minneapolis, 1989. An examination of the important assemblage of metalwork, particularly from the Persian period, recovered by excavations at Tel Michal.

Nriagu, Jerome O. *Lead and Lead Poisoning in Antiquity.* New York, 1983. A comprehensive treatment of lead and its important commercial, medicinal, and often deadly role in ancient society.

Ogden, Jack. *Jewellery of the Ancient World.* London, 1982. Discusses various metals and types of gemstones, glass, enamel, and faience used by ancient smiths to manufacture jewelry; superb illustrations, including several images of metal artifacts taken with the scanning electron microscope to detail smithing techniques.

Rolle, Renate. *The World of the Scythians.* Translated by F. G. Walls. Berkeley, 1989. Discusses metal artifacts in the broader cultural context of the Scythians, including the finds recovered from controlled stratified excavations.

Rothenberg, Benno. *Timna: Valley of the Biblical Copper Mines.* London, 1972. Well-illustrated study addressing six thousand years of metallurgy in the ʿArabah, as evidenced by excavation. The chapter on the Roman copper mines and smelting sites at Be'er Ora provides extraordinary primary archaeological evidence for furnace installations, mining, and smelting.

Sarianidi, V. I. *The Golden Hoard of Bactria.* Translated by Arthur Shkarovsky-Raffé. New York, 1985. An important gold hoard excavated in Afghanistan. Superbly crafted turquoise-inlaid bracelets, ceremonial knives, buckles, and necklaces are presented in detailed color plates.

Stern, Ephraim. *Material Culture of the Land of the Bible in the Persian Period, 538–332 B.C.* Warminster, 1982. Copiously illustrated, comprehensive study of the material culture of Persian Palestine, including chapters on architecture, burial, pottery, metalware, cult objects, seals, weights, and coins.

Stronach, David. *Pasargadae: A Report on the Excavations Conducted by the British Institute of Persian Studies from 1961 to 1963.* Oxford, 1978. The metal artifacts and particularly the jewelry recovered from Persian and Hellenistic contexts at the site demonstrate the sophistication of ancient Iranian metallurgy.

Tylecote, R. F. "Furnaces, Crucibles, and Slags." In *The Coming of the Age of Iron,* edited by Theodore A. Wertime and James D. Muhly, pp. 183–228. New Haven, 1980. Important study with respect to the mechanics behind the manufacture of metal artifacts—furnace types, slags, and crucibles.

Waldbaum, Jane C. *Metalwork from Sardis: The Finds through 1974.* Cambridge, Mass., 1983. Typological and stylistic account of the artifacts and their archaeological context and a thorough commentary on ancient textual sources pertaining to metal artifacts and metallurgy; includes metallographic and chemical analyses of select artifacts.

Weiss, Harvey, ed. *Ebla to Damascus: Art and Archaeology of Ancient Syria.* Washington, D.C., 1985. This exhibition volume of the art and archaeology of ancient Syria is the most comprehensive to date. Its thorough and well-illustrated treatment of the material culture of Syria from the prehistoric through Islamic periods includes significant metal finds.

Zias, Joseph. "Death and Disease in Ancient Israel." *Biblical Archaeologist* 54.3 (1991): 146–159.

ERIC C. LAPP

MICHAL, TEL, site located on the southern part of the Sharon coastal plain, on a *kurkar* (sandstone) cliff overlooking the Mediterranean Sea, about 6.5 km (4 mi.) north of the Yarkon River estuary. The site consists of several areas: a main settlement area, a small high tell (0.3 ha or .75 acre) rising 30 m above sea level; a slightly lower hill to the north that covers about 4 ha (10 acres) and descends toward the north; and three isolated hillocks east of those hills. The site's ancient name is unknown.

The region's sandy soil makes it suitable for cultivating cereals and viticulture. Numerous wine presses were recovered, but wine production alone does not justify occupation of the site or explain the frequent settlement gaps. Rather, the archaeological data show a clear correlation between the periods of occupation and phases of maritime activity; combined with its location, they corroborate the site's *raison d'être* as a coastal trading post. Anchorage for small crafts was possible in a 2-meter-deep and 30–40-meter-wide channel recorded near the mound in an underwater survey conducted in 1978 by Avner Raban of the Center of Maritime Studies, University of Haifa.

In 1958 and 1960 the northeastern hillock was partially exposed by Nahman Avigad, revealing the remains of a ceremonial cult place known as Makmish (Avigad, 1977). The Hebrew name given to the main mound is Tel Michal (or Tel Mikhal). From 1977 to 1980 an expedition from Tel Aviv University, directed by Ze'ev Herzog, conducted a large-scale exploration of the site, in cooperation with the University of Minnesota, the University of Pennsylvania, Brigham Young University, Wisconsin Lutheran Seminary (USA), and Macquarie University (Australia). Several graves were exposed in 1993 at the northern end of the northern hill, during a salvage excavation directed by Herzog and Yossi Levy.

Bronze Age. The first occupation of the site was in the Middle Bronze IIB (stratum XVII, late seventeenth century). To this period, found only on the high tell, belong the remains of an artificial platform that raised and leveled the top of the natural *kurkar* hill. Most of the platform and all the structures built on it are no longer intact, as a result of the collapse of the western seaward side of the site, apparently caused by tectonic shocks. A large amount of Cypriot ware, many "Hyksos"-type scarabs, Egyptian alabasters, and Tell el-Yahudiyeh juglets were collected from the fills on the platform. The construction of this trading station is therefore determined to be connected with the maritime activities of the Hyksos kingdom. [*See* Hyksos.]

The sudden destruction of the settlement, as well as part of the natural hill, forced the planners of the next occupation phase (stratum XVI, Late Bronze Age I) to extend the mound on the east. This was achieved by constructing a tremendous earthen rampart out of alternative layers of debris from the previous settlement, sand, and *hamra* (red sandy soil) in a strip 30 m wide. The scant architectural remains preserved from this period consist of several thick walls found at the northern end of the high tell. These walls were reconstructed in the form of a small rectangular fort. To stratum XVI belongs a group of rare kraters with a single horizontal handle, some decorated in brown and red. In stratum XV (LB IIA) additional earthen fills, supported by solid retaining walls, were laid on the eastern side. In this period the center of the high tell was occupied by domestic structures, and the amount of imported ware decreased. The site was abandoned in the thirteenth century BCE.

There was no occupation at Tel Michal in Iron I (twelfth–eleventh centuries BCE), indicating that Philistine settlements did not cross the Yarkon River valley. After a gap of three hundred years, the site was resettled, in the tenth century BCE (strata XIV–XIII). During this phase, occupation expanded beyond the high tell: all three of the eastern hillocks were occupied for the first time, and the earliest wine presses were constructed. Large domestic units were built on the high tell, some reused in both phases.

The finds on the eastern hillocks for the tenth century were related to ceremonial/cultic uses: an enclosure on the northeastern hillock; and a small chapel with an internal altar and external *favissae* on the eastern hillock, from which large chalices with fenestrated feet and small chalices were recovered. Remains of houses with benches along their walls, which also suggests ceremonial/cultic use, were excavated on the southern hillock.

Two winepresses were found near the eastern hillock, each consisting of two pressing surfaces flanking a storage compartment, a pair of large vats, and a pair of small ones (see figure 1). These plastered installations are a rare example of Iron Age wine presses. The production of wine for the site's ceremonial chapels could have developed into a commercial enterprise. The site was settled as part of the expansion of Phoenician traders along the coast of the eastern Mediterranean, and the cultic chapels may reflect the traders' ceremonial needs. Tel Michal was not settled during the rest of the Iron Age, except for some minor use in the eighth century, indicated by scattered pottery and occupation of the southern hillock (stratum XII).

Persian Period. The most prosperous chapter in the history of Tel Michal began in the late sixth century BCE. In addition to those parts of the site previously occupied, the large northern hill was settled. Six architectural phases (strata XI–VI) were recorded on the high tell covering the period between 525 and 300 BCE (with no cultural break at the beginning of the Hellenistic period). On the high tell a

MICHAL, TEL. Figure 1. *Iron Age wine presses.* (Courtesy Z. Herzog)

large fort or administrative building was constructed with a few residential units to its south. Grain pits dug in the settlement's early phases and a round brick silo from a later stage support the assumption that Tel Michal was one of the stations along the coast that supplied the Persian army on its campaigns against Egypt. Wine production surely played an important role in the economy. A winepress dated to the Persian period was found east of the southern hillock and a smaller one was found on the northern hill. A storeroom with twenty-seven storage jars may have been used as a wine cellar. The jars used in producing and distributing the wine were made locally: similar jars were found in one of the three pottery kilns exposed on the northern hill, which indicates that the kilns had collapsed at the end of the firing process.

The center of the northern hill was densely filled with domestic buildings, a few of which were exposed in excavation. An industrial area was excavated at the edges of the settlement that produced evidence of pottery kilns, wine presses, and metalworking. The northern slope of the northern hill had been used exclusively as a cemetery. In a trench that covers about 10 percent of the area 120 burials of various types were uncovered: cist tombs, pit graves, and infant jar burials. The grave goods included jewelry, bronze bowls and fibulae, and iron tools; bronze and iron nails from wooden coffins also were found. The skeletons had deteriorated from the salty and wet conditions, but from a study of the preserved remains it was concluded that population's lifespan was a low average age of thirty years (Herzog et al., 1989). [*See* Burial Techniques; Grave Goods.]

On the northeastern hillock Avigad exposed a temple in which dozens of clay and stone figurines were found. Trade on an international scale was well attested there by an abundance of luxury goods made of pottery, alabaster, glass, and bronze imported from Cyprus, Egypt, Persia, and Greece. The archaeological data corroborate the political and commercial control of the region by the Phoenicians under Persian hegemony, as recounted in the inscription of Eshmunazar, king of Sidon. [*See* Phoenicians; Eshmunazar Inscription; Sidon.]

Hellenistic, Roman, and Early Arab Periods. The nature of the site changed drastically at the beginning of the third century BCE. Occupation was concentrated again on the high tell, which then housed a large fortress. Three such fortresses were built in consecutive stages in the Hellenistic (strata V–IV) and Hasmonean (stratum III) periods. To the earliest stratum belongs a hoard of forty-seven Ptolemaic silver coins (Kindler, 1978). A large winepress was constructed on the northern hill, cut into the remains of houses of the Persian period. The main vat of the winepress has a capacity of 7,000 l, which demonstrates its role as part of a centralized production system. The northeastern hillock retained its ceremonial function, but the cemetery was not utilized. To the Hasmonaean period are attributed a smaller fort on the high tell and a small winepress, both dated by coins to the days of Alexander Jannaeus.

Following a gap of about fifty years, Tel Michal was reoccupied by a large fortress (37 × 30 m) in the first half of the first century BCE (stratum II). It consisted of rooms arranged around a central courtyard, in the center of which was a massive tower, undoubtedly a lighthouse. This is the only known Roman fortress along the coast of Israel. Its construction may be explained as a measure against Jewish piracy from Jaffa. [*See* Jaffa.] Indeed, the fortress was abandoned when Jaffa was conquered and a Roman camp was built there. After another gap of eight-hundred years, a small watchtower was built on the mound (stratum I), in the ninth–tenth centuries CE.

BIBLIOGRAPHY

Avigad, Nahman. "Makmish, Tell." In *Encyclopedia of Archaeological Excavations in the Holy Land,* vol. 3, pp. 768–770. Englewood Cliffs, N.J., 1976.

Herzog, Ze'ev, et al., eds. *Excavations at Tel Michal, Israel.* Tel Aviv University, Publications of the Institute of Archaeology, 10. Minneapolis, 1989. Full account of the excavations at the site.

Herzog, Ze'ev. "Tel Michal." In *The New Encyclopedia of Archaeological Excavations in the Holy Land,* vol. 3, pp. 1036–1041. Jerusalem and New York, 1993.

Kindler, Arie. "A Ptolemaic Coin Hoard from Tel Michal." *Tel Aviv* 5 (1978): 159–169.

ZE'EV HERZOG

MICROSCOPY. The light microscope, invented in about 1600, became a useful analytical tool in the nineteenth century. Microscopy is a "mature" technique that is invaluable for studying archaeological artifacts. It is usually the first physical technique employed in investigating material culture. A binocular microscope with a magnification of up to 20 × has a depth of focus large enough to provide three-dimensional vision useful for studying surface details or selecting certain mineral grains from a powder.

Higher magnifications require a special sample preparation that depends on the type of material being studied. Transparent materials are usually examined as thin sections of about 0.03 mm thickness in transmitted light, which may be polarized. To prepare a thin section for petrographic analysis, the sample is mounted on a standard-size glass slide (50 × 25 mm) so that a relatively large area can be studied. Mineral grains are identified by their shape (or cleavage pattern), color, and pleochroism (the differential absorption of polarized light in different directions). Rocks are composed of minerals, whose morphologies, relative abundances, and intergrowth may be characteristic of a specific occurrence of a certain rock type. It is therefore possible to relate the raw material of stone artifacts or of rock fragments in coarse-grained pottery to their original source, providing evidence for the transport of raw materials, be it by trade, human migration, or natural events. A classic example is the petrographic study of the bluestones erected at Stonehenge that derive from Pembrokeshire, some 150 miles away. Major applications of this method, often in combination with chemical analyses, have been reported on the provenance of the limestones of Egyptian monuments and on millstones from the eastern Mediterranean. The diorite statues of Manishtushu and of Gudea, the ruler of Lagash, are said to originate in Oman. In pottery, the mineral assemblage can also provide information about firing temperature. [*See* X-ray Diffraction Analysis.]

Organic materials are also regularly studied with this technique. Various sorts of wood differ in their microscopic structure and can therefore be identified from small samples of about 1 mm in diameter. Similarly, textile fibers can be unequivocally identified.

Opaque materials, such as metals, are examined in reflected light. For sample preparation a piece is cut from a metal artifact, embedded in a resin, and polished. The sample can be small (less than 1 cu mm), but larger samples (ideally a thin slice providing a cross-section through the artifact) are easier to work with and yield more information. Often, the polished surface is etched with suitable reagents to enhance the internal structure. Because thermal and/or mechanical treatment like cold-working, annealing, or hot-working results in different microstructures, considerable information on the techniques employed in the fabrication of nonferrous metal artifacts can thus be obtained. Identifying the various phases in iron-carbon alloys sheds light on the processes used in the manufacture of iron and steel artifacts (e.g., carburization, quenching, and tempering) and the progressive evolution of iron metallurgy. Because many ore minerals are also opaque, ores and slags are also often examined using this technique.

As a result of diffraction effects, the limit of resolution of light microscopy is in the order of 1 μm (i.e., 0.001 mm), corresponding to magnifications of about 500 times. Still higher magnifications are obtained in electron microscopes with a resolution of less than one manometer (i.e., 0.000001 mm), which approaches the size of single atoms. For archaeological material, the most useful and widely employed form of electron microscopy is the so-called scanning electron microscope (SEM). A beam of high-energy electrons (up to 100 keV) is focused by a series of magnetic lenses so that the illuminated area of the specimen is about 0.02 μm in diameter—which is also the typical resolution obtainable with this instrument. Additional magnetic coils allow the beam to be deflected so that it scans, in a regular manner, over the surface of the specimen. The primary electron beam stimulates, among other effects, the emission of secondary electrons from the surface of the specimen. These are collected and converted into an electric signal. Because the number of secondary electrons ejected on each spot depends largely on the tilt angle, a grazing beam produces more secondary electrons and, hence, a greater signal than a beam at right angles. The detector is used to modulate the brightness of a display cathode ray (television) tube that has its line scan driven in synchronism with the probe beam in the microscope column. There is a one-to-one correspondence between the brightness of each point on the display tube and the number of secondary electrons emitted from any spot on the surface of the specimen. In this way, a map of a large number of single points (between 50,000 and 100,000) of different brightness is built up that yields a picture of the surface topography of the specimen with a large depth of focus.

The electron beam has to be operated in a vacuum because electrons cannot travel any appreciable distance in air. Therefore, the sample must not contain any substances that are not stable in a vacuum. Otherwise, the requirements for specimen preparation are minimal. Most SEMs have relatively large sample chambers, so that even bulky samples can be accommodated. It is desirable that the specimen be rendered electrically conducting. This is usually achieved by evaporating a thin (10–20 nm) layer of metal or elementary carbon onto the specimen in the vacuum.

Another important feature of the interaction of the electron beam with the sample is the excitation of X-rays characteristic of the chemical composition at the illuminated spot. Hence, it is possible to obtain information on the distribution of certain elements on the sample surface in addition to the topographical picture. However, such analyses can only be considered semiquantitative because of the variable self-absorption of the X-rays in the sample as a result of surface roughness. For quantitative analyses, the electron probe microanalyzer is used. [*See* Analytical Techniques.] The SEM has frequently been used to study the surface microtopography of archaeological materials, especially in investigating ceramic and metal technology and identifying pigments and lime plaster.

BIBLIOGRAPHY

Coghlan, Herbert H. *Notes on Prehistoric and Early Iron in the Old World.* Oxford, 1957. Somewhat dated, but still valuable, account of the use of the microscope for the study of early iron.

Goldstein, Joseph I., et al., eds. *Scanning Electron Microscopy and X-Ray Microanalysis: A Text for Biologists, Materials Scientists, and Geologists.* New York and London, 1981. Comprehensive and very readable text on all aspects of this topic, including practical aspects of sample preparation.

Noll, Walter. *Alte Keramiken und ihre Pigmente: Studien zu Material und Technologie.* Stuttgart, 1991. Comprehensive text on the scientific investigation with the SEM of archaeological pottery and pigments.

Phillips, Victor A. *Modern Metallographic Techniques and Their Applications.* New York, 1971. Standard textbook on metallographic techniques.

Tite, Michael S. "The Impact of Electron Microscopy on Ceramic Studies." In *New Developments in Archaeological Science: A Joint Symposium of the Royal Society and the British Academy, February 1991,* edited by A. M. Pollard, pp. 111–131. Proceedings of the British

Academy, 77. Oxford, 1992. Useful review of scanning electron microscopy in studying ancient ceramic technology.

ERNST PERNICKA

MIDDLE EASTERN CULTURE CENTER IN JAPAN. At the initiative of Prince Takahito Mikasa, and with the close cooperation of the late Sazo Idemitsu, the Middle Eastern Culture Center in Japan was established in October 1979. The first center of its kind in Japan, it provides both researchers and students with a place to conduct intensive studies in various spheres, such as the history and culture of the Near East, and with a forum for exhibiting the results of their work.

A key aim in creating the center was to collect study materials and to design activities that would make the institution inviting to specialists and to the general public. The center is thus furnished with exhibition halls, a library, auditoriums, and research facilities. Among the center's main activities are lectures delivered by foreign scholars and specialists and lectures that supplement special exhibitions of artifacts.

The center sponsors the Biannual Colloquium for Ancient Near Eastern Studies, of which Prince Takahito Mikasa is the honorary president. The center also holds an international Annual Symposium on Anatolian Archaeological Studies.

The center's current overseas projects, both of which were initiated in 1986, are an excavation at Kaman-Kalehöyük in Kirşehir, Turkey, and a general survey of Anatolia. The excavation has unearthed new information regarding the Chalcolithic and Early Bronze periods.

The centers' publications include the *Bulletin of the Middle Eastern Culture Center in Japan* (seven volumes); *Acta Sumerologica* (thirteen volumes); and the *Proceedings of the Anatolian Archaeological Symposium in Japanese* (two volumes). Final reports for the excavation and for the Anatolian survey are published intermittently. The center is a unique institution in Japan because of its area of specialization, the wealth of periodicals in its library, and the opportunity it affords students and researchers to gain first-hand archaeological experience.

SACHIHIRO OMURA

MIDDLE EAST MEDIEVALISTS (MEM) is a professional nonprofit association of scholars interested in the study of the Islamic lands of the Middle East in the medieval period. The organization defines "medieval Middle East" to include northern Africa and Islamic Spain in the period between 500 and 1500 CE. MEM was founded in 1989 and incorporated in the state of Illinois in 1992. Its main goals are to encourage the presentation of panels and papers on subjects relating to the medieval Middle East at scholarly conferences; to support the academic study of the medieval Middle East; and to foster communication among individuals and organizations interested in the medieval Middle East. Membership is open to individuals of all nationalities. In 1995, MEM's membership was about 225 and growing; about 75 percent of its members reside in the United States. The association's first president was Sam I. Gellens (1989–1991). He was succeeded by Fred M. Donner (1992–1994); the current president is R. Stephen Humphreys (1995–1997).

As part of its effort to foster communication among its members, MEM publishes *Al-ʿUsur al-Wusta* (The Bulletin of Middle East Medievalists) semiannually; it contains short articles, reviews of books from the Middle East of interest to MEM's membership, and news of the organization. Exchange programs and summer workshops are planned.

MEM is loosely affiliated with the Middle East Studies Association of North America (MESA) and the American Oriental Society (AOS). It holds its annual business meeting at MESA's annual meeting.

FRED M. DONNER

MIDDLE EAST STUDIES ASSOCIATION. In 1966, a group of American and Canadian scholars founded the Middle East Studies Association (MESA) to promote high standards of scholarship and instruction in the field of Middle East studies, to facilitate communication among scholars through meetings and publications, and to foster cooperation among individuals and organizations concerned with scholarly study of the Middle East. The organization covers the geographic area from the Atlantic to, and more recently including, Central Asia, as well as those lands in Europe once under Islamic political control. The chronological period covered by MESA begins with the rise of Islam. However, most scholarly activities focus on contemporary developments.

MESA publishes both the *International Journal of Middle East Studies* and the *MESA Newsletter* four times a year; the *MESA Bulletin* appears twice a year. Topics of archaeological interest, announcements of conferences, and calls for papers are listed in the Newsletter. The names of those who participate in professional meetings and the titles of the papers presented at those meetings appear in an electronic form. Articles and book reviews related to Islamic archaeology are sometimes included in the *Bulletin.* Tables of contents, notes research and teaching resources, lists of recent conferences, and books in Middle East studies are available on the *MESA Bulletin* gopher site (at gopher.cua.edu) or via World Wide Web connection to URL:gopher://vmsgopher.cua.edu.:70/11gopher_root_mesabul:[000000].

Presentations related to Islamic archaeology are often delivered at the annual MESA meeting. Many of the archaeological sessions at the meeting are sponsored by the North

American Historians of Islamic Art (NAHIA), an organization affiliated with MESA. All of the papers presented at the annual MESA meeting are listed in the *Newsletter*'s fall issue; those papers available for purchase are listed in its winter issue. MESA does not sponsor either archaeological excavations or publications.

JERE L. BACHARACH

MIDIAN. The extreme northwestern corner of the Arabian Peninsula, immediately east of the Gulf of ʿAqaba, was associated by the classical and medieval Arab geographers with the place name Madian or Madiama. It is generally agreed that these preserve the name of Midian, the son of Abraham and Keturah and the ancestor of the Midianites of the Hebrew Bible. It was to Midian that Moses fled after murdering an Egyptian overseer, and it was Zipporah, the daughter of a Midianite shepherd and (possibly) priest, variously named Jethro, Reuel, or Hobab, whom he subsequently married (*Ex.* 2–4, 18; *Nm.* 25, 31). According to one tradition (*Nm.* 10:29–32), Jethro helped guide the Israelites through the desert after their exodus from Egypt. The good relationship initially enjoyed by the two peoples is illustrated by the fact that Moses invited the Midianites to join in the journey to the Promised Land—an offer which was, however, declined. Relations soon deteriorated and, following an incident at Baʿal-Peor in Moab, when an Israelite zealot killed some Midianite princes apparently involved in a fertility rite, the two groups became implacable foes. In *Judges* 6–8 an account is given of an unsuccessful attack by Midianite raiders on the Israelite tribes in northern Canaan led by Gideon, followed by further military action in Transjordan. These events are conventionally dated to the eleventh century BCE. The last mention of the Midianites as a people probably refers to an episode a few decades later, when they are said to have been defeated by the king of Edom (*Gn.* 36:35). After this, the name occurs in the Hebrew Bible only as a geographical expression; it does not appear, either as a gentilic or a locality, in any other ancient texts prior to the classical period.

The Midianites are portrayed in these traditions as nomadic sheep and camel herders, caravaneers, and raiders, ranging over a wide territory to the south and east of Canaan. There is no reason to suppose that this portrayal is not essentially correct, at least in part. However, recent archaeological survey in northwestern Arabia—the heartland of Midian—has indicated that this is not the whole story. There also existed, during the final centuries of the second millennium BCE, sedentary communities that should, in all probability, be included among the Midianites. The evidence lies in the discovery at a number of sites of a distinctive type of painted pottery, stylistically related to certain types of Late Bronze Age pottery of the eastern Mediterranean region. The pottery may ultimately be derived from the Mycenaean pottery of the Aegean, by way of Canaan or Egypt. At the site of Qurayyah a number of kilns used in the manufacture of this pottery have been identified. [*See* Qurayyah.] There is also strong evidence at this site of fortification walls and an irrigated field system contemporary with the pottery. Identical pottery has been excavated at the copper mining and smelting installations at Timnaʿ, in the southern Wadi ʿArabah north of modern Eilat in Israel. That pottery is dated by inscribed Egyptian objects to the nineteenth dynasty (thirteenth–twelfth centuries BCE)—precisely the time to which most authorities ascribe the Hebrew traditions mentioned above. [*See* Timnaʿ (Negev).] There can be no doubt that the Egyptians were engaged, presumably in a controlling capacity, in the ʿArabah mines and that they employed workers from Qurayyah and perhaps from elsewhere in Arabia. There is no evidence for metallurgical activities at Qurayyah itself, however, or at Tayma', where sherds of the same pottery have also been found. [*See* Tayma'.] This suggests that other activities, perhaps the incense trade with Southwest Arabia, played a part in Midian's economy. The field system at Qurayyah indicates that agriculture was also economically important.

It has been suggested that the development of what has been termed oasis urbanism in Midian at this time was largely the result of Egyptian involvement in the economy of the region. This interpretation is controversial, primarily because of the complete lack of evidence in Egyptian texts for such involvement, other than at Timnaʿ. For the Egyptians, the inhabitants of the arid regions of Sinai, the Hijaz, and Transjordan seem to have been subsumed under the term *shasu* and depicted as pastoralists and raiders, much as the Midianites are depicted in the Hebrew Bible. In the present state of research, all further attempts to reconstruct the history of Midian must remain speculative.

BIBLIOGRAPHY

Mendenhall, George E. *The Tenth Generation: The Origins of the Biblical Tradition.* Baltimore, 1973. Chapter 6, "The 'Sea Peoples' in Palestine," contains a stimulating, though very controversial, discussion of the Midianites, suggesting an Anatolian origin.

Parr, Peter J., et al. "Preliminary Survey in North West Arabia, 1968." *Bulletin of the Institute of Archaeology, University of London* 8–9 (1970): 219–241, pls. 21–42. The first account of the archaeological discoveries which began to challenge the conventional view of the history of Midian.

Parr, Peter J. "Pottery of the Late Second Millennium B.C. from North West Arabia and Its Historical Implications." In *Araby the Blest: Studies in Arabian Archaeology,* edited by Daniel T. Potts, pp. 72–89. Copenhagen, 1988. Succinct account and possible interpretation of the recent archaeological discoveries, with full references.

Sawyer, John F. A., and David J. A. Clines, eds. *Midian, Moab, and Edom: The History and Archaeology of Late Bronze and Iron Age Jordan and North-West Arabia.* Sheffield, 1983. Conference papers; see in particular the essays by E. J. Payne ("The Midianite Arc"), E. Axel Knauf ("Midianites and Ishmaelites"), and Beno Rothenberg and Jonathan Glass ("The Midianite Pottery").

PETER J. PARR

MILETUS, the southernmost settlement of Ionia, originally situated on the coast with four harbors but now, as a result of the silting of the Maeander River, in the middle of a plain 3 km (5 mi.) from the sea (37°30′ N, 27°18′ E). A prominent hill several miles to the west of the present theater was, in antiquity, the island of Lade, where the Persian fleet destroyed the Ionian navy in 494 BCE

The site has a long and complex history. Surveys around Miletus conducted under the direction of Volkmar von Graeve have located more than one hundred sites that date from the Neolithic to Byzantine periods. Minoan settlement of the area may date to the sixteenth century BCE, perhaps as part of their maritime expansion throughout the Mediterranean. A city wall and some houses found near the theater date to the Mycenaean period (c. 1400 BCE) and indicate that displacement of the Minoan settlement roughly coincided with the establishment of Mycenaean power on the island of Crete, formerly the center of Minoan power. E. O. Forrer first suggested that Aḫḫijawa in Hittite texts was equated with the Mycenaean Greeks and that Millawanda, also mentioned in the texts, was Miletus. That interpretation has been disputed. James G. Macqueen, for example, argues that Millawanda lay on the shores of the Sea of Marmara in northwest Anatolia (1986, pp. 40–41). The debate continues.

According to literary sources, Miletus (Ionic), or Milatos (Doric), was also known as Pituousa and Anactoria (Herodotos 1.17–20, 141; 6.6; Arrian, *Anabasis* 1.18). In the twelfth century CE, the site was called Balat (from the Greek Palatia) because the inhabitants, then residing upon the completely covered Roman theater, thought they were over a palace.

Scientific excavation of the site (primarily by German archaeologists) began in 1899 under the direction of Theodor Wiegand but were discontinued after the start of World War I. Carl Weickert's excavations, begun in 1938, were halted during World War II. More recently, excavations have been conducted by Gerhard Kleiner, Wolfgang Müller-Wiener, and Volkmar von Graeve. As part of this project, the prehistoric levels are being investigated under the direction of W. D. Niemeier.

Between the ninth and sixth centuries BCE, the city established numerous colonies (ninety, according to literary sources) in lands around the Black Sea (notably Olbia, Sinope, Panticapeion, and Amisos) and around the Mediterranean Sea. At the time, it was the most powerful city in the Ionian world. The Black Sea colonies in particular provided large supplies of needed wheat. Miletus also gave rise to a number of famous philosophers and scientists, including Anaximander, Thales, Anaximenes, Aspasia, and later, Isodoros, the builder of the magnificent Hagia Sophia in Istanbul/Constantinople. [*See* Constantinople.] In addition, according to Greek tradition, Hippodamos, who reconstructed Miletus and other cities after their destruction by the Persians, created a city plan that connected streets at right angles (the Hippodamian plan).

The Milesian alphabet served as the basis for the unification of the Greek states after it was adopted by Athens in the fifth century BCE. Some of the earliest coins were minted at Miletus, including an electrum coin with a lion on one side and three ornamental notches on the other. After the city was demolished by the Persians in 494 BCE, its principal leaders were removed to the mouth of the Tigris River and the rest of the populace enslaved. From that point onward, the city had little influence in the region until the Hellenistic period, when it became an important commercial center. It then had close relationships with the various Hellenistic kings who ruled after the death of Alexander. It became a part of the Roman province of Asia in 129 BCE

The religious center of the town was Delphinion, where Apollo was worshipped. Originally established in the archaic period, the current temenos was enclosed on three of its sides by stoas in the Hellenistic period and further expanded in the Roman period. Other buildings from the Hellenistic period include a gymnasium whose palaestra and propylon have been located. The propylon that leads to the gymnasium is similar to ones encountered at Pergamon and Priene and may have been built as a result of the influence of King Eumenes II of Pergamon. [*See* Pergamon; Priene.] A bouleuterion, also from the Hellenistic period, contains a colonnaded courtyard, an auditorium, and a propylon; it seated approximately fifteen hundred people. An inscription associated with the bouleuterion indicates that it was constructed under the sponsorship of two Milesian brothers, Timarchos and Herakleides, at the behest of Antiochus IV Epiphanes.

An agora in the southern part of the city has been partially excavated and is possibly the largest ever found in the Greek world (about 33,000 sq m). Founded during the Hellenistic period, the stoa on its east had thirty-nine pairs of shops back to back and the one on its south had nineteen. A large stadium was apparently erected during this period, as it is aligned with the bouleuterion and is at right angles to both the south and north agoras. Its gateway is Hellenistic in design.

The Roman theater (built over the earlier Hellenistic one) was one of the largest and most elaborate in Asia, capable of holding upward of fifteen thousand people. [*See* Theaters.] A Jewish presence in the city is confirmed from a second- or third-century CE inscription on a seat in the theater mentioning "the place of the Jews who are also called God fearing." The inscription sheds some light on the current debate over the make-up of the God-fearers (converted Gentiles, pious Jews, etc.) and the degree to which the category is simply a literary creation as Thomas Kraabel has argued. At the least the inscription along with important inscriptions from Panticapaeum and Aphrodisias confirm that such a group existed and was possibly distinct from natural-born Jews (Reynolds and Tannenbaum, 1987, pp. 54–55; see also *Biblical Archaeology Review* 12.5 [1986]: 44–69). The location of the inscription in the fifth row suggests a degree of prestige attributed to the Jews (Paul Trebilco, *Jewish Communities in Asia Minor,* Cambridge, 1991, p. 162). Jews apparently resided in the city beginning in at least the first century CE. Josephus (*Antiq.* 14:244–246) mentions a decree from the Roman proconsul Publius Sevilius Galba who restored the rights of the Jews that had been revoked by the city (e.g., observance of the sabbath, practice of rituals, and collection of tithes). A Roman basilica with an adjacent courtyard was identified by Von Gerkan as a synagogue. [*See* Basilicas; Synagogues.] It was built in the late third or early fourth century but had no Jewish symbols associated with it. The identification, which was based on its architectural similarity to synagogues found in Palestine, is suspect: one column had a decree from Helios Apollo commanding that an altar to Poseidon be built.

A monument with a rounded base near the harbor was apparently set up by the Milesians in honor of an emperor, probably Augustus. Another edifice north of the monument was set up by Grattius, a Roman, and is similar in structure. A large sixteen-harbor gateway with sixteen columns was built in the first half of the first century CE. A processional way flanked by sidewalks went through it. Baths were built by Vergilius Capito, a procurator of Asia Minor under Claudius. A stoa erected by Tiberius Claudius Sophanes lies opposite the north agora and west of the baths. [*See* Baths.] The very well-preserved Faustina baths from the Roman period were sponsored by the wife of Marcus Aurelius (161–180 CE), as was the theater. Other remains of buildings include a temple to Serapis and a *heroon.* The northern gateway of the southern agora has also been reconstructed and is in the Berlin Museum.

A provincial cult, one of three in Asia, was established at Miletus under Caligula. Such a cult indicated that the city was seen as wealthy and of impeccable heritage. It also reveals the political bond that existed between the demos of the city and Rome. The cult lasted only a few years, however. An inscription mentioning it has been found at nearby Didyma, in its Apollo temple, an important cult for Miletus. [*See* Didyma.] The inscription talks about a statue of the emperor Gaius Caesar Germanicus at the time a certain Gaius Vergilius Capito "was high priest of the temple in Miletus of Gaius Caesar for the first time, . . . and (when) Tiberius Julius Menogenes, son of Demetrios the *nomothete* [legislator] was high priest the second time and *neokoros* [cult official] of the temple in Miletus . . ." (Steven J. Friesen, *Twice Neokoros: Ephesus, Asia and the Cult of the Flavian Imperial Family,* Leiden, 1993, p. 22). Capito also had a cult established in his name at Miletus, purportedly the last such cult for a Roman who was not the emperor. When Gaius died, Miletus's provincial cult was discontinued. The cult had been unusual for a provincial cult in not mentioning the senate or Rome or referring to Gaius as divine.

Miletus had close connections with the Temple of Apollo in Didyma, approximately 6 km (10 mi.) to the south. A Sacred Way connecting the two sanctuaries was paved with large limestone slabs sometime during the reign of Trajan—a pattern found in many locations throughout the eastern empire. Fountains, a large gate, and halls with colonnades are associated with the road. Miletus experienced several significant building periods: during the time of Eumenes II, ruler of Pergamon in the second century BCE; and under the emperors Trajan (who also dedicated a monumental nymphaeum to his father) and Marcus Aurelius, primarily through the benefactions of his wife, Faustina (see above).

The site also flourished during the reign of Diocletian, when a good deal of building took place. Shortly afterward, however, buildings fell into disrepair and small, poorly and haphazardly built structures ignored the previous city plan. A modest revival occurred during the reign of Justinian I, in the Byzantine period, when a new cathedral and baths were built and the harbor was dredged. The city also had an archbishop in 536. The exquisite mosque, Ilyas Bey, completed in 1404 is still standing. According to *Acts* 20:15–38, Paul addressed elders from Ephesus here before his return to Jerusalem (cf. 2 *Tm.* 4:20).

BIBLIOGRAPHY

Akurgal, Ekrem. *Ancient Civilizations and Ruins of Turkey.* 7th ed. Istanbul, 1990. Fine summary in English by one of Turkey's most prominent archaeologists.

Forrer, E. O. "Die Griechen in den Boghazköi Texten." *Orientalistische Literaturzeitung* (1924): 113–118.

Forrer, E. O. "Vorhomerische Griechen in den Keilschrifttexten von Boghazköi." *Mitteilungen der deutschen Orientgesellschaft* 63 (1924): 1–22.

Hommel, Hildebrecht. "Juden und Christen im Kaiserzeitlichen Milet: Überlegungen zur Theaterinschrift." *Istanbuler Mitteilungen* 25 (1975): 167–195.

Kleiner, Gerhard. *Die Ruinen von Milet.* Berlin, 1968. Authoritative discussion of the site.

Kleiner, Gerhard. *Das römische Milet.* Weisbaden, 1970. Important discussion of Roman Miletus by one of its principal excavators.

Kleiner, Gerhard. "Miletos." In *The Princeton Encyclopedia of Classical Sites,* pp. 578–582. Princeton, 1976.

Krauss, Friedrich. *Das Theater von Milet.* Milet, vol. 4.1. Berlin, 1973.

Macqueen, James G. *The Hittites and Their Contemporaries in Asia Minor.* London, 1986.

Mayer, M. "Miletos." In *Paulys Real-Encyclopädie der classischen Altertumswissenschaft,* vol. 15, cols. 1622–1655. Stuttgart, 1932.

McRay, John. "Miletus." In *The Anchor Bible Dictionary,* vol. 4, pp. 825–826. New York, 1992.

Milet: Ergebnisse der Ausgrabungen und Untersuchungen seit dem Jahre 1899. Berlin, 1906–1990. Multivolume series published by the Deutsches Archäologisches Institut; the most authoritative presentation of archaeological finds from Miletus, beginning in 1899.

Müller-Wiener, Wolfgang. *Milet 1899–1980, Ergebnisse, Probleme und Perspektiven einer Ausgrabung: Kolloquium Frankfurt am Main 1980*. Istanbuler Mitteilungen, 31. Tübingen, 1986.

Reynolds, Joyce, and Robert Tannenbaum. *Jews and God-Fearers at Aphrodisias: Greek Inscriptions with Commentary*. Proceedings of the Cambridge Philosophical Society, supp. vol. 12. Cambridge, 1987.

Robert, Louis. "Le cult de Caligula à Milet et la province d'Asie." In Robert's *Hellenica*, vol. 7, pp. 206–238. Paris, 1949.

DOUGLAS R. EDWARDS

MINES AND MINING. *See* Metals.

MINḤA, ḤORVAT. *See* Munḥata.

MINOANS. Sir Arthur Evans (1851–1941) gave the modern name Minoan to the Aegean Bronze Age (c. 3000–1100 BCE) inhabitants of the island of Crete. We do not know what they called themselves, or if indeed they were a single ethnic group. They may have been known to their contemporaries in Egypt as *Keftiu* and in Syria as *Kaptarites*.

Systematic excavation of the principal town and palace site at Knossos began in 1900 by Evans under the auspices of the British School at Athens, who used the findings as the basis for his re-creation of Crete's early civilization. In the absence of written history, he devised a tripartite system of relative chronology based on the Egyptian kingdoms but named for the monarch and lawgiver associated with early Crete in later Greek tales, Minos; hence, we speak of the Early, Middle, and Late Minoan periods (EM, MM, and LM, respectively, with divisions of I, II, and III and further subdivisions of A, B, and C). An alternative chronology uses the broad terms *Prepalatial* for EM I to MM IA (c. 3000–1910 BCE), *Protopalatial* for MM IB to MM IIB (c. 1910–1780 BCE), *Neopalatial* for MM III to LM IB (c. 1780–1450 BCE), and *Postpalatial* for LM II and III (c. 1450–1100 BCE). A radiocarbon-based chronology has yet to be widely accepted; the above dates are derived from synchronisms with Egypt and the Near East.

Minoan society before the Postpalatial period is studied on the basis of surviving material culture and the interpretation of complex and detailed iconography in the minor arts, such as on ceramics, seal stones and metal ring bezels, relief carvings on stone vessels, and in wall painting. The absence of obvious political propaganda—for example, there are no representations of named individuals—and an abundance of images, apparently representing ritual behavior, have led to a belief the Minoans were ruled by a priestly class. The frequency of mature women in the iconography has prompted the suggestion that one or more goddesses were the focus of the Cretans' religious beliefs, with a minor emphasis on her youthful male consort.

The earliest inhabitants of Crete seem to have arrived during the Early Neolithic period (c. 6000 BCE). Continuous migration over the next three thousand years must be responsible for the introduction of olives and vines as well as domesticated cattle and sheep and goats. The island's initial attraction may have been its temperate climate and comparative wealth of water and forests. It became densely populated by the Late Bronze Age, with an economy that continued to be based primarily on agriculture but that no doubt took advantage of its median position in the developing east-west Mediterranean trade in metals that preoccupied the Aegean and Near Eastern states in the Middle and Late Bronze Ages. During the palace periods, the Cretans became the producers of luxury goods based on raw materials, both local (ceramic, stone, and textile) and imported (gold, ivory, silver, copper, and semiprecious stones), thereby gaining a reputation abroad as creative artisans.

Settlements seem to have begun as small households in EM I–IIA, for example, at Myrtos-Fournou Korifi and Palaikastro-Roussolakkos. Evidence for substantial structures with possible public functions in EM IIB has been found at Vasiliki, Palaikastro, Knossos, and Phaistos, but later construction has made it difficult to identify the structures clearly. The EM III and MM IA periods are poorly represented, but evidence from Knossos and Mallia—in the form of wall foundations used in the later palaces—may indicate that the planning, at least, for the palaces may have started in EM III or MM IA. Funerary ritual during the Prepalatial period took place in rock shelters and caves throughout the island, and circular stone-built communal monuments, called tholoi, chiefly in south-central Crete, and in rectangular stone-built communal ossuaries, called house tombs, in north-central and eastern Crete. The confusion of bones and grave offerings over long periods may indicate multiple inhumations or the secondary placement of bones following excarnation. Exceptions are rock-cut single inhumations at Aghia Photia in eastern Crete that resemble those at Kouphonisi in the Cyclades.

The palaces at Knossos, Phaistos, and Mallia were built early in the MM IB period. They were erected in prominent positions in their respective towns, which display urban planning, as evidenced by the formal road systems at all three sites; the most impressive example is the Royal Road at Knossos. The palaces themselves incorporated innovations such as facades of quarried and dressed blocks with incised mason's marks, stone pillars and wooden columns, stone-built and ceramic drains and waterpipes, and pattern-painted lime plaster. A formal administration is indicated by the Cretan pictographic, or hieroglyphic, script—as yet undeciphered—that came into use along with a sealing system based on Near Eastern models. An adaptation of the pictographs into the Linear A script, also undeciphered, had taken place by the MM IIA period.

The rectangular complex at Chrysolakkos (Mallia) may represent a new type of civic scale funerary installation near the urban environment, as the tholoi and house tombs of the villages and countryside gradually go out of use during this period, perhaps due to a movement of the population into the emerging palatial centers. Secondary burials in ceramic jars, or pithoi, and ceramic boxes, or larnakes, are found at Ailias near Knossos, and Fourni near Archanes.

The foundation of the palaces coincides with the establishment of remote shrines, including peak sanctuaries and sacred caves, and an elaborately built road system in the countryside, with associated sturdy rectangular structures called watchtowers. It may be that the Early Palace period was a time of emerging competitive states centered on the palaces. Evidence for elaborate protective walls along the north coast at Mallia, Myrtos-Pyrgos, Palaikastro, and in the passes entering the Kato Zakros and Karoumes Bays may confirm this view of formal protection of territorial interests. By the end of the Early Palace period, the preeminent state seems to have been Knossos. The urban defensive works, rural road systems, and towers seem to go out of use, as do most of the remote shrines.

The change from the Old to the New Palace period is not clear. At Knossos, there seems to have been an earthquake in about 1780 BCE that forced the rebuilding of the palace with some architectural innovations—example, the "Minoan Hall" with *polytheron* (multiple doorways); otherwise, the material culture shows little evidence of abrupt change. At Phaistos, the Early Palace shows traces of destruction by fire at roughly the same time, but the palace seems to have been rebuilt in stages and may not have regained its administrative power. A major change may be seen in the appearance of new palaces at Kato Zakros, Archanes-Turkogitonia, Galatas, and most likely Khania, as well as what may be public architecture at numerous coastal sites such as Kommos, Aghia Triadha, Gournia, Mochlos, Palaikastro, and Petras. The countryside during the course of the Neopalatial period filled with rural establishments that may have been centers for localized agricultural and manufacturing concerns responsible, perhaps through taxation, to the palace. The pictographic script was entirely abandoned in favor of Linear A, and the clay roundel became an important administrative device.

The ossuary at Myrtos-Pyrgos and the Temple Tomb at Knossos indicate the continuity of funerary ritual in built civic structures, although these have not been found at other centers. An apparent change in burial practices is indicated by the rock-cut chamber tombs filled with Cretan LM I finds on the island of Kythera. Similar tombs at Poros, the port of Knossos, were reused into the Postpalatial period but certainly were first dedicated in the MM III.

The Neopalatial period fostered the emergence of a lively artistic style that abandoned the codified symbol systems of previous stages and experimented with realism in human and natural representations. The favored group scenes of athletic contests and bull leaping may be related to the social importance of male and female rites of passage and initiation into the social and political elite. By the end of the LM IB period (c.1450 BCE), artists attempted to show depth in their work by sculpting and constructing wall murals in low relief of overlapping subjects with open mouths and exaggerated veins, intended to show the figures' vitality. The close contact of the Mineans with their Near Eastern contemporaries can be seen in the Cretan influences in the representational arts of Syria and perhaps of Egypt during the Hyksos period.

The LM IB ends with clear evidence for burnt destruction throughout Crete and in the Aegean towns that prospered under Cretan influence and control. The subsequent Postpalatial period is marked by the introduction of the Mycenaean Greek language used in an adaptation of Linear A into the Linear B script. Also known as the reoccupation period, many of the oldest settlements were rebuilt, often reusing material from earlier buildings; rarely is there evidence for new quarrying or architectural innovation. Knossos was the main political center, as suggested by the archives there, with secondary centers at Kydonia (modern Khania) and Phaistos. The economy, as understood from the archives, was securely based on the exploitation, in great quantities, of sheep for wool. Early in the period, a new form of burial, primary inhumation with weapons or the warrior grave, appears at Knossos; and large cemeteries of rock-cut chamber tombs appear at a number of locations throughout the island, for example at Armenoi, heralding a major change in funerary ritual. In the arts, a return to flat iconographic representations primarily depicting stationary ritual scenes was witnessed.

A major fire at Knossos in the LM IIIA or Early LM IIIB (c. 1300 BCE) destroyed the majority of the Linear B archives. Tablets found in LM IIIB contexts at Khania and the continued use of the script on transport containers (stirrup jars) may indicate a swing of power to the western town, which now had links with the western Mediterranean. Late in the LM IIIB or early in the LM IIIC there was a gradual move away from the coastal sites to mountaintop areas with access to upland plains—such as Kavousi-Kastro and Karphi-Lasithi—no doubt in response to the general collapse of authority in the Aegean states and the rise of piracy. The material culture of these Postpalatial Cretans was less luxurious than in previous periods, but the iconography of the mature woman as goddess prevailed and continued throughout the subsequent Protogeometric periods, albeit in crude versions.

[*See also* Crete; *and the biography of Evans.*]

BIBLIOGRAPHY

The most useful primary sources for Crete in the Bronze Age are Arthur Evans, *The Palace of Minos*, 4 vols. in 6 (London, 1921–1935), and the *Index* by J. E. Evans (London, 1936). For general surveys the reader may consult Martin S. F. Hood, *The Minoans: Crete in the Bronze Age* (London, 1971), and J. Wilson Myers et al., *The Aerial Atlas of*

Ancient Crete (Berkeley, 1992). The latter contains exceptional aerial views and plans of the most important excavations, as well as recent essays by the excavators and a bibliography. Relative and absolute chronologies are argued in Peter M. Warren and Vronwy Hankey, *Aegean Bronze Age Chronology* (Bristol, 1989), and Philip P. Betancourt, *The History of Minoan Pottery* (Princeton, 1985). Both contain extensive bibliographies. Architecture is discussed in J. Walter Graham, *The Palaces of Crete,* rev. ed. (Princeton, 1987), and J. W. Shaw, *Minoan Architecture: Materials and Techniques* (Rome, 1971). Both works are in need of revision to include theoretical matters. Cretan Hieroglyphic texts may be found in Arthur Evans, *Scripta Minoa,* 2 vols. (Oxford, 1909), and Fernand Chapouthier, *Les écritures minoennes au palais de Mallia* (Paris, 1930), both long out of date and deserving of new corpus. For Linear A, see Louis Godart and Jean P. Olivier, *Recueil des inscriptions en Linéaire A,* 5 vols. (Paris, 1976–1985). Linear B is covered in John Chadwick et al., *Corpus of Mycenaean Inscriptions from Knossos,* vol. 1 (Rome, 1986). Studies on ritual behavior include Geraldine Gesell, *Town, Palace, and House Cult in Minoan Crete* (Göteborg, 1985); Nanno Marinatos, *Minoan Religion* (Columbia, S.C., 1993); and Bogdan Rutkowski, *The Cult Places of the Aegean* (New Haven, 1986). All three are quite speculative. Martin S. F. Hood provides the best treatment of Minoan arts and crafts in *The Arts in Prehistoric Greece* (Harmondsworth, 1978).

J. ALEXANDER MACGILLIVRAY

MIQNE, TEL (Ar., Khirbet el-Muqannaʿ), site located 35 km (22 mi.) southwest of Jerusalem, on the western edge of the inner coastal plain (the frontier zone that separated Philistia and Judah), overlooking the ancient network of highways leading northeast from Ashdod to Gezer (map reference 1356 × 1315). One of the largest Iron Age sites in Israel, Tel Miqne is identified with biblical Ekron, one of the capital cities of the Philistine Pentapolis. The site is composed of a 40-acre lower tell, which in Iron II expanded to 65 acres, and a 10-acre upper tell. William Foxwell Albright (1924) identified Muqannaʿ with biblical Eltekeh, but Joseph Naveh (1958), who subsequently surveyed the site, identified it as Ekron. The current excavations support the latter conclusion.

Written Sources. Ekron is mentioned in the Hebrew Bible in *Joshua* 13:3 as part of "the land that yet remains"; in 15:11 in reference to the northern border of the tribe of Judah running through "*ketef* Ekron northward"; in 15:45–46 in the list of the cities of Judah; and in 19:43 as part of the territory of Dan. In *Judges* 1:18 it is a city conquered by the tribe of Judah; in 1 *Samuel* 5:10 the Philistines take the Ark of the Covenant to Ekron; in 17:52, in the story of David and Goliath, the Philistines are pursued to "the gates of Ekron"; in 2 *Kings* 1:2 King Ahaziah of Israel (ninth century BCE) sent messengers to consult "Baal Zebub, the gods of Ekron"; in *Amos* 1:5 (eighth century BCE) the destruction of Ekron is prophesized, as it is in *Jeremiah* 25:20, *Zephaniah* 2:4, and *Zechariah* 9:5–6 (second half of the seventh century BCE).

In the Assyrian sources the 712 BCE siege of *'amqar(r)una* (Ekron) is depicted on a wall relief in Sargon II's palace in Khorsabad. The 701 BCE conquest of Ekron is described in the royal annals of Sennacherib, and, in first half of the seventh century BCE, in the annals of Esarhaddon, Ikausu, king of Ekron, supplies materials for the construction of the palace in Nineveh, and in 667 BCE, in his annals Ashurbanipal is quoted as ordering the vassal king Ikausu to support his military campaigns against Egypt and Cush. The Babylonian chronicles describe Nebuchadrezzar's campaign against a Philistine city in 603 BCE that may be Ekron.

In the Apocrypha, Ekron appears in 1 *Maccabees* 10:89 and in 14:34 as a toparchy torn from Ashdod. The Roman Jewish historian Josephus (*Antiq.* 13:4:4) reports that in 147 BCE Ekron was given by Alexander Balas to Jonathan the Hasmonean. In the fourth century CE, Eusebius (*Onomasticon,* ed. Klostermann, pp. 22, 11.9–10) mentions "a very large Jewish village called Accaron."

Excavations. The Tel Miqne/Ekron excavation is a joint American-Israeli project directed by Trude Dothan (director, Berman Center for Biblical Archaeology, Hebrew University) and by Seymour Gitin (director, W. F. Albright Institute of Archaeological Research in Jerusalem). Twelve excavation seasons were conducted from 1981 to 1995, exposing 3.5 percent of the site. The primary goal is to examine the process of urbanization of a Philistine city and the geopolitical, economic, cultural, and environmental elements that influenced its development.

A continuous stratigraphic profile of the tell appears only on the acropolis in the upper city (field I), beginning with stratum XI (Middle Bronze Age IIB) and extending through the end of stratum I (Iron IIC). In the lower city (fields III, IV), following stratum XI (sixteenth century BCE), there was a four hundred-year occupational gap until its resettlement in stratum VII at the beginning of Iron I (c. 1200 BCE). Following the Iron I period (end of stratum IV, c. 1000 BCE), there was approximately a 250-year occupational gap in the lower city until it was again resettled at the very end of the eighth century BCE, expanding to its greatest extent in stratum I (seventh century BCE). Both the Iron I and II cities were well designed, with zones of occupation primarily for fortifications, industry, and elite habitation.

Middle Bronze Age. The tell apparently was shaped by the fortifications that encompassed both the upper and lower cities in the Middle Bronze Age. MB II ceramic and fragmentary architectural evidence was found throughout the tell; in addition, three infant burials were found in field IV.

Late Bronze Age. The apparently unfortified LB settlement (strata X–VIII) was confined to the upper city. It contained Cypriot and Mycenaean imports and Anatolian gray-slipped ware, attesting to international maritime trade. The Egyptian impact is evident, inter alia, in a burial containing a nineteenth-dynasty seal and scarab and a fourteenth-century BCE scarab bearing the name of the Egyptian king Amenhotep III and dedicated to the "lady of the sycamore tree," usually associated with the foundations of Egyptian shrines. This scarab was an heirloom found in a later Iron I phase. Stratum VIII, representing the last Canaanite city, was totally destroyed by fire; the destruction was dramatically illustrated by a severely burned storeroom complex with jars containing carbonized grains, lentils, and figs.

Iron Age I. The fortified Iron I settlement (strata VII–IV) encompassed the upper and lower cities. It is characterized by a new material culture introduced by an ethnic group of Aegean origin: the Philistines, one of the Sea Peoples. One of its special features is a megaron-type building with a hearth as its central architectural component. While locally made Mycenaean IIIC:1b pottery (see figure 1) predominates in the earliest phase of occupation (stratum VII), Philistine bichrome pottery with red and black decoration on white slip is predominant in the strata VI–V city. In stratum IV, the material culture reflects the influence of Phoenician culture, with its predominant red-slipped and burnished ceramic vessels.

Upper city (field I). Next to the stratum VII mud-brick city wall was an industrial kiln area and, at the very top of the acropolis, in strata VII–VI, a cluster of large pits. Stratum VI had a large building complex with a cultic room that, in stratum V, became its most prominent feature. It contained votive vessels and incised scapulae, like those from twelfth-and eleventh-century BCE shrines at Enkomi and at Kition on Cyprus. [*See* Enkomi; Kition.] Concentrated in an open activity area to the west were twenty-five circular pebbled hearths—thirteen in stratum VI and twelve in stratum V. Also found in strata VI–V were two infant jar burials.

Stratum IV was attested at the top of the acropolis by the reuse of some stratum V architectural elements and two pebbled hearths. The stratum IV street, with two parallel stone walls, initiated a plan that continued into the Iron II period.

MIQNE, TEL. Figure 1. *Mycenaean IIIC:Ib bowl with antithetic tongue motif.* From the initial Philistine (Sea Peoples) settlement of the early twelfth century BCE. Found in the "elite" zone of occupation. (Courtesy Tel Miqne-Ekron Excavations)

Lower city (field III). Well behind the city wall, stratum VI was represented by a building complex, over which the stratum V monumental building was constructed. Both mud-brick structures had two large units in which were found a mud-brick firebox, a bull-shaped zoomorphic vessel, an incised ivory tube, a conical stamp seal depicting two prancing gazelles, a bronze pin and needle, and two goat skulls. Stratum VI had two examples of the circular pebbled hearths known from fields I and IV. In the stratum V building, a large flagstone pavement formed a monumental entrance with matched wall insets in front of a mushroom stone pillar base. This design is similar to the monumental entrance of the megaron building in field IV. The artifacts, many of which represented a continuation of Aegean traditions, included a rectangular bone plaque painted blue and incised with the back end of a horse, a Mycenaean-type female figurine, a gold spiraled hair ring, an iron knife with an ivory handle, and a pebbled hearth.

Stratum IV consisted of two building complexes and an extended platform that supported a large number of plastered installations. These were in part built over the deep backfill covering stratum V, as in field IV, and in part reused the plan of stratum V. Continuing the Aegean tradition were two pebbled hearths. Immediately behind the fortifications, a large installation of red earth (Ar., *hamra*) and a crucible were found, indicating metal production. Special finds include a gaming piece, copper pins and needles, and an incised scapula similar to those found in field I.

Lower city (field IV). Because of the special nature of its architecture and finds, field IV in the lower city is considered the elite zone. Stratum VII was represented by the earliest appearances of rectangular hearths. In Stratum VI, the western building complex was composed of a temple/palace in the form of a megaron whose central feature was a circular hearth. The origin of the hearth is well attested in megaron buildings of Mycenaean palaces in the Aegean. In stratum VI, the western building complex produced special finds, including a round ivory lid decorated with scenes of animals in battle—gryphons, lions, and bulls—in a distinctly Aegean style.

Stratum V building no. 350 of the western complex, also with a megaron plan, had a main hall with superimposed pebbled hearths, three rooms with benches and *bamot* (altars), one room with twenty clay "lump" loom weights in the Aegean tradition, and a monumental entrance hall with two mushroom-shaped stone pillar bases (see figure 2). This building also produced three miniature bronze wheels from a cultic stand, known from Cyprus and reminiscent of the biblical description of the laver stands (Heb., *mechonot*) in Solomon's Temple in Jerusalem, and a bronze Janus-faced linchpin of a chariot wheel, which can be associated with Cyprus and the Aegean. In addition, it contained an iron knife with a pierced, spool-shaped ivory handle attached by three bronze nails—one of four such handles found at Ekron

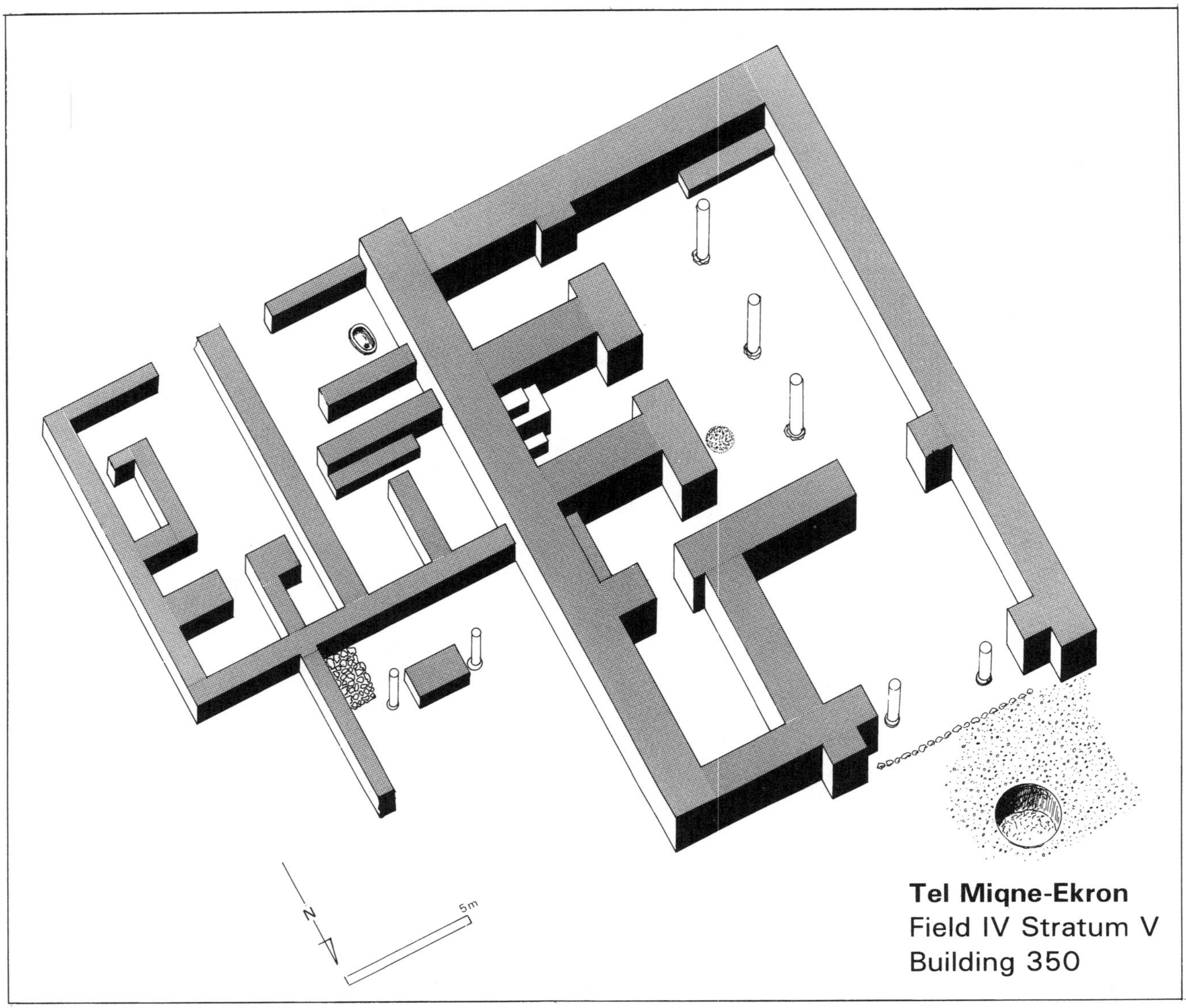

MIQNE, TEL. Figure 2. *Megaron style building 350 in field IV, stratum V.* To the left are adjacent buildings 352, 353, 354. (Courtesy Tel Miqne-Ekron Excavations)

and similar to cultic knife handles known from Tell Qasile, Cyprus, and the Aegean. [*See* Qasile, Tell; Cyprus.]

In strata VI and V, the eastern building complex had extensive living quarters featuring a large stone bath, a monolith, two stone pillar bases, and several hearths, some pebbled. In Stratum IV, the stratum V temple/palace of the western building complex was backfilled, like the stratum V building in field III. Its plan was reused and its cultic functions continued. Its finds include a cache of ivory, faience, and stone objects—decorated earplugs, and a ring depicting the Egyptian goddess Sekhmet. The destruction and abandonment of the lower city of stratum IV marked the end of the early Philistine city and the end of the Iron I period at Ekron.

Iron Age II. In the Iron IIA–B period, strata III–II (c. 1000–700 BCE), Ekron only occupied the 10-acre upper city. Its coastal plain traditions of architecture and pottery evidenced continuity with stratum IV. In stratum IC, the first three-quarters of the seventh century BCE, Ekron became a vassal of the Neo-Assyrian Empire. Its upper and lower cities, which were rebuilt, contained the largest olive oil production center in antiquity. The stratum IB city of the last quarter of the seventh century, which was under Egyptian hegemony, was destroyed in 603 BCE by the Babylonians. Afterward, the site was resettled only sporadically.

Upper city (field I). In strata III–II, Ekron was reduced in size to the area of the acropolis, which was refortified with a new mud-brick city wall and a 7-meter-wide mud-brick tower faced with ashlar masonry. The new Iron II city on the top of the acropolis was built over a series of monumental stone foundations that ran east–west up and across the top of the acropolis, forming part of a huge system of terraces and platforms. Some of these walls contain large ashlar masonry similar to that of the facing of the mud-brick tower.

The central architectural feature of stratum III was a repaved stratum IV street with flanking walls. The monumental architecture of stratum II continued the general plan of stratum III. The two main new elements are a series of rooms, probably shops or market stalls, which opened to the repaved stratum III street, and a stone-lined central drainage system. The ceramic evidence of strata III–II indicates a continuation of the red-slipped and burnished tradition of stratum IV and the introduction of several new forms with red wash and slip. The pottery of stratum II included Judean forms typical of the eighth century BCE, Phoenician-type forms, and local types well known in the eighth-seventh-century BCE coastal ceramic assemblage, best defined in stratum IB. Associated with the end of the eighth century BCE were three *lmlk* stamped jar handles. One, reading *lmlk ḥbrn* ("belonging to the king of Hebron"), is a four-winged type; the others are two-winged, dating from the brief period when Ekron was ruled by Hezekiah, king of Judah. [*See* Judah.]

Lower city (field III). In stratum I, the city was expanded following Sennacherib's conquest in 701 BCE. The Assyrian annals cite Ekron as a vassal city-state of the Neo-Assyrian Empire. The new fortifications of stratum I on the south of the reoccupied lower city included a double system of stone city walls, a line of stables or storehouses, and a three-pier gate protected by a gatehouse, similar to those at Tell Batash, Gezer, Lachish, and Ashdod. [*See* Batash, Tel; Gezer; Lachish; Ashdod.] On the acropolis, the strata III–II mud-brick city wall was rebuilt, and a series of citadel towers was erected.

The most outstanding phenomenon of this new city was the olive-oil industrial zone laid out in a belt along the interior face of the city wall. [*See* Olives.] It was composed of rectangular factory buildings with a tripartite division, including an oil-production room, a room for processing and storage, and an anteroom opening to the street. The oil installation had a large rectangular crushing basin and pressing vats, one on each side of the basin. Other equipment included a stone cylindrical crushing roller and eight 77-kg (170-lb.) stone pressing weights.

Each factory building room produced an average of one hundred restorable ceramic vessels. Special finds include a cache of seven well-preserved large iron agricultural tools and four-horned limestone altars. [*See* Altars.] In all, eighteen altars of this type, usually considered incense altars, were discovered at Ekron. Large numbers of loom weights and installations not associated with the oil-manufacturing process were found throughout the industrial zone, suggesting the presence of a secondary textile industry. [*See* Textiles, *article on* Textiles of the Neolithic through Iron Ages.]

The 115 oil presses thus far found at Ekron have a production capacity of at least 500 tons. To date, Ekron is the largest industrial center for the production of olive oil known from antiquity. This huge industry prospered because of the commercial needs of the expanding Assyrian Empire. [*See* Assyrians.] In the last third of the seventh century (stratum IB), a diminution in olive-oil production is attested by the discarded parts of oil installations. This phenomenon is associated with the end of Assyrian rule (stratum IC) and the establishment of Egyptian hegemony in Philistia in about 630 BCE (stratum IB).

Lower city (field IV). The elite zone had a complex of eight courtyard-type buildings, comprising twenty-one rooms that contained a large percentage of fine and decorated wares (including Assyrian-type and imported East Greek vessels), fourteen inscriptions on storejars, including, among others: *qdš* and *l'šrt,* "dedicated" and "for the goddess Asherah"; *lmkm,* "for the shrine"; the letter *ṭet,* with three horizontal lines below it, probably indicating the allocation of thirty units of produce for tithing; *bt,* designating a storejar capacity of probably 33 l; and inscriptions indicating storejar contents, such as *šmn,* "oil", and *dbl,* "cluster of figs."

These building complexes also produced three caches comprising 157 pieces of silver jewelry, cut pieces of silver—*biṣẓê kesef*—and silver ingots. [*See* Jewelry.] Another cache from the acropolis had thirty one pieces, among which was a silver medallion depicting the goddess Ishtar standing on a lion (see figure 3). A fifth cache was found in field III. Together, these caches represent the richest assemblage of its kind yet found in Israel. The large amount of silver reflects its use as currency, which was an important element in the Assyrian economy and in Phoenician maritime trade.

North of the courtyard building complexes of the elite zone was a monumental Neo-Assyrian-type building. Its front and side entrances each had a single-stone, 4-meter-long threshold. Its special finds include a stela incised with a rosette, a royal Neo-Assyrian emblem, a curated carved elephant tusk with the image of an Egyptian goddess associated with the nineteenth dynasty, a golden cobra, a ureaus, part of the headdress of a statuette of Egyptian royalty or a deity, and a faience amulet of Ptah-patecus, the Egyptian god of craftsmen.

Ekron was destroyed at the end of stratum IB, during Nebuchadrezzar's campaign to Philistia in 603 BCE. Sealed beneath the massive meter-thick layer of destruction debris were thousands of mostly coastal and some inland late seventh-century BCE whole ceramic forms. In stratum IA, apparently only the lower city was occupied. One structure was well preserved, an "Assyrian courtyard" type building that produced typical seventh-/sixth-century BCE coastal ceramic

MIQNE, TEL. Figure 3. *Silver medallion showing a figure praying to the goddess Ishtar, who is standing on a lion.* From a jewelry cache, dated to the end of the seventh century BCE. (Courtesy Tel Miqne-Ekron Excavations)

forms. Thereafter, the city was abandoned until the Roman period. Evidence of Roman, Byzantine, and Islamic settlements was found only at the northern edge of the tell.

Conclusion. The excavations have produced ceramic data indicating that the site was settled almost continuously from the fourth through the third millennia; and stratigraphic, architectural, and artifactual evidence that indicates continuous occupation from the seventeenth through the early sixth centuries BCE. Thereafter, there was sporadic settlement from the Roman through the Islamic periods. The excavations highlight the process of growth, diminution, renewal, and partial abandonment that, during the Iron Age, was the fate of Ekron, a frontier city on the border between Judah and Philistia.

BIBLIOGRAPHY

Albright, William Foxwell. "Researches of the School in Western Judea." *Bulletin of the American Schools of Oriental Research,* no. 15 (1924): 2–11, especially page 8.

Albright, William Foxwell. "The Fall Trip of the School in Jerusalem to Gaza and Back." *Bulletin of the American Schools of Oriental Research,* no. 17 (1925): 5–6.

Clermont-Ganneau, Charles S. *Archaeological Researches in Palestine during the Years 1873–1874.* Vol. 2. London, 1899. See page 195.

Conder, Claude R., and H. H. Kitchener. *The Survey of Western Palestine: Memoirs of the Topography, Orography, Hydrography, and Archaeology,* vol. 2, *Samaria.* London, 1882. See sheet 16, page 425.

Dothan, Trude. *The Philistines and Their Material Culture.* New Haven, 1982. See pages 17–18, 20, 57, 88, 296.

Dothan, Trude. "The Arrival of the Sea Peoples: Cultural Diversity in Early Iron Age Canaan." In *Recent Excavations in Israel: Studies in Iron Age Archaeology,* edited by Seymour Gitin and William G. Dever, pp. 1–14. Annual of the American Schools of Oriental Research, 49. Winona Lake, Ind., 1989.

Dothan, Trude. "Iron Knives in Cult Areas at Ekron" (in Hebrew). *Eretz-Israel* 20 (1989): 154–163.

Dothan, Trude. "Ekron of the Philistines, Part I: Where They Came From, How They Settled Down, and the Place They Worshipped In." *Biblical Archaeology Review* 16.1 (1990): 26–36.

Dothan, Trude. "Bronze Wheels from Tel Miqne–Ekron." *Eretz-Israel* 23 (1992): 148–154.

Dothan, Trude, and Moshe Dothan. *People of the Sea: The Search for the Philistines.* New York, 1992.

Dothan, Trude, and Seymour Gitin. "Ekron." In *The New Encyclopedia of Archaeological Excavations in the Holy Land,* vol. 2, pp. 1051–1059. Jerusalem and New York, 1993.

Dothan, Trude, and Seymour Gitin. "Ekron of the Philistines" (in Hebrew). *Qadmoniot* 105–106 (1994): 2–28.

Dothan, Trude. "Tel Miqne Ekron: The Aegean Affinities of the Sea Peoples' (Philistines') Settlement in Canaan in the Iron Age I." In *Recent Excavations in Israel: A View to the West. Reports on Kabri, Nami, Miqne-Ekron, Dor, and Ashkelon,* edited by Seymour Gitin, pp. 41–59. Archaeological Institute of America Colloquia and Conference Papers, no. 1. Dubuque, Iowa, 1995.

Eitam, David, and A. Shomroni. "Research of the Oil-Industry during the Iron Age at Tel Miqne." In *Olive Oil in Antiquity,* edited by Michael Heltzer and David Eitam, pp. 37–56. Haifa, 1987.

Gitin, Seymour, and Trude Dothan. "The Rise and Fall of Ekron of the Philistines: Recent Excavations at an Urban Border Site." *Biblical Archaeologist* 50 (1987): 197–222.

Gitin, Seymour. "Tel Miqne–Ekron in the Seventh Century BCE: City Plan Development." In *Olive Oil in Antiquity,* edited by Michael Heltzer and David Eitam, pp. 81–97. Haifa, 1987.

Gitin, Seymour. "Incense Altars from Ekron, Israel, and Judah: Context and Typology." *Eretz-Israel* 20 (1989): 52–67.

Gitin, Seymour. "Tel Miqne: A Type-Site for the Inner Coastal Plain in the Iron Age II Period." In *Recent Excavations in Israel: Studies in Iron Age Archaeology,* edited by Seymour Gitin and William G. Dever, pp. 23–58. Annual of the American Schools of Oriental Research, 49. Winona Lake, Ind., 1989.

Gitin, Seymour. "Ekron of the Philistines, Part II: Olive Oil Suppliers to the World." *Biblical Archaeology Review* 16.2 (1990): 32–42, 59.

Gitin, Seymour. "The Impact of Urbanization on a Philistine City: Tel Miqne–Ekron in the Iron Age II Period." In *Proceedings of the Tenth World Congress of Jewish Studies, Jerusalem 1989,* pp. 277–284. Jerusalem, 1990.

Gitin, Seymour. "Last Days of the Philistines." *Archaeology* 45.3 (1992): 26–31.

Gitin, Seymour. "New Incense Altars from Ekron: Context, Typology, and Function." *Eretz-Israel* 23 (1992): 43–49.

Gitin, Seymour. "Scoops: Corpus, Function, and Typology." In *Studies in the Archaeology and History of Ancient Israel: In Honor of Moshe Dothan,* edited by Michael Heltzer et al., pp. 99–126. Haifa, 1993.

Gitin, Seymour. "Seventh Century BCE Cultic Elements at Ekron." In

Biblical Archaeology Today, 1990: Proceedings of the Second International Congress on Biblical Archaeology, Jerusalem, June–July 1990, edited by Avraham Biran and Joseph Aviram, pp. 248–258. Jerusalem, 1993.

Gitin, Seymour. "Tel Miqne–Ekron in the Seventh Century BCE: The Impact of Economic Innovation and Foreign Cultural Influences on a Neo-Assyrian Vassal City-State." In *Recent Excavations in Israel: A View to the West. Reports on Kabri, Nami, Miqne-Ekron, Dor, and Ashkelon,* edited by Seymour Gitin, pp. 61–79. Archaeological Institute of America Colloquia and Conference Papers, no. 1. Dubuque, Iowa, 1995.

Gittlen, Barry M. "The Late Bronze Age 'City' at Tel Miqne/Ekron." *Eretz-Israel* 23 (1992): 50–53.

Gunneweg, Jan, et al. "On the Origin of Pottery from Tel Miqne–Ekron." *Bulletin of the American Schools of Oriental Research,* no. 264 (1986): 3–16.

Hesse, Brian. "Animal Use at Tel Miqne–Ekron in the Bronze Age and Iron Age." *Bulletin of the American Schools of Oriental Research,* no. 264 (1986): 17–27.

Naveh, Joseph. "Khirbet al-Muqannaʿ–Ekron." *Israel Exploration Journal* 8 (1958): 87–100, 165–170.

Porten, Bezalel. "The Identity of King Adon." *Biblical Archaeologist* 44 (1981): 36–52.

Tadmor, Hayim. "Philistia under Assyrian Rule." *Biblical Archaeologist* 29 (1966): 86–102.

TRUDE DOTHAN and SEYMOUR GITIN

MIQVAʿOT. *See* Ritual Baths.

MISHRIFEH, ruin located about 18 km (11 mi.) northeast of Homs and about 35 km (22 mi.) southwest of Salamiyah, on the east side of Wadi Zora, in Syria (34°30′ N, 36°55′ E). The wadi flows from south to north and runs into the al-ʿAsi (Orontes) River. Opposite the southwest corner of the tell is a spring. The houses of the village of Mishrifeh once covered the tell, but in 1980 the inhabitants were removed to a new village along the west side of the tell.

Mishrifeh, a 100-hectare (247 acres) ruin has been identified as Qatna. However, when Robert du Mesnil du Buisson began excavating there, the identification was not yet definite. During his second campaign (1927) many cuneiform tablets were found referring to the site as *alu kat-na, ki, alu kat-na,* and in the Amarna tablets as *alu kat-na, kat-na ki.* In the hieroglyphic texts it was written as *kdn3* by Thutmosis III; *kdn* by Amenhotep II; *kdyn3* by Amenhotep III; *kdn3* by Seti I and Rameses III; and *k3dn3* by Rameses II.

The initial settlement at the site is obscure. In the Paleolithic period it seems to have been a stopping-off place for nomads. Archaeological materials indicate that Qatna played a pivotal role in the trade between Mesopotamia and the Syrian coast at the beginning of the third millennium. A Mesopotamian influence in the period of the third dynasty at Ur appears, particularly in the pottery of tomb IV. [*See* Ur.] Qatna's copperworks demonstrate contact with the Syrian coastal cities. The discovery of Egyptian sculptural fragments and the sphinx of Ita, the daughter of Amenemhat II (1929–1895 BCE) indicate that Qatna had good relations with Egypt in the first two centuries of the second millennium BCE.

Documents from the Mari archive reveal that an Amorite dynasty reigned in Qatna in the first half of the second millennium BCE. [*See* Mari Texts; Amorites.] It also had good relations with Shamshi-Adad of Aššur and his son Ismah-Adad of Mari, as well as with Alalakh, at the time of Alalakh (stratum VII). [*See* Aššur; Alalakh.] However, Qatna's relations with its neighbors were not always good.

At the end of the sixteenth century BCE, the Mitanni spread their control over the kingdom of Aleppo and then in all directions including Qatna in the south, where Hurrian immigrants already lived. [*See* Mitanni; Hurrians.] During the reign of Thutmosis I and Thutmosis III, Qatna was under Egypt's control. To all appearances there was a struggle between Egypt and the Mitanni to pull Qatna into the political sphere of one or the other. The struggle continued between Egypt and the Ḫatti. It is not entirely clear if the Ḫatti or another power destroyed Qatna. Some scholars believe that Šuppiluliuma (1380–1340 BCE) plundered the city. There is, however, evidence that the city was settled by the Arameans in the first half of the first millennium BCE, and that in the Neo-Babylonian period it was an important trading center. [*See* Arameans.]

The Temple of Nin-Egal was identified when cuneiform tablets with an inventory of the temple of the goddess, the lady of Qatna, were discovered. The goddess was worshiped in southern Mesopotamia and the name is Sumerian. [*See* Sumerians.] The plan of the temple is like the court of a palace of the period with a cella in its northeast corner. The palace itself was situated to the east of the temple, opening to the west. It contained a central court; an expanded courtyard; a throne room, whose main entrance is in the south; and two small, square rooms for the toilet. The royal apartment for the habitation of the king's family was situated opposite the north corner of the throne room. It was entered through a door that led to a waiting room. On the west side of the throne room is the royal residence. [*See* Palace.]

The city plan shows Qatna girdled by imposing, approximately square ramparts. Their average height is 15 m and they are constructed of tuff and soil, rather than mud bricks. There are four city gates, one on each side of the wall. The plan of the western and eastern gates, which consists of two pairs of flanking buttresses, resembles those excavated at Gezer in Israel and at Ebla and Tell ʿAṭchana (Alalakh) in Syria. [*See* Gezer; Ebla.]

The so-called inventory of the Temple of Ninegal was found in 1927. It mentions objects, accounts, and administrative arrangements, as well as the names of kings and personal names. The majority of the names are Canaanite and Hurrian, and the syllabary is of a Hurrian type. The archive belongs to the fifteenth century BCE. According to the tablets, Qatna was ruled by Canaanite kings and its population was Canaanite and Hurrite. Besides this inventory, five other tablets were found: a contract, two economic texts, an astrological text, and a fragmentary economic text.

[*See also* Temples, *article on* Syro-Palestinian Temples; *and* Fortifications, *article on* Fortifications of the Bronze and Iron Ages.]

BIBLIOGRAPHY

Bottéro, Jean. "Les inventaires de Qatna." *Revue d'Assyriologie et d'Archéologie Orientale* 43 (1949): 1–41, 137–216.

Bottéro, Jean. "Autres textes de Qatna." *Revue d'Assyriologie et d'Archéologie Orientale* 44 (1950): 105–122.

Du Mesnil du Buisson, Robert. *Le site archéologique de Michrifé-Qatna.* Paris, 1935.

ALI ABOU ASSAF

MITANNI. Probably first attested during the reign of Thutmosis I (1494–1482 BCE), and last mentioned during the reign of Tiglath-Pileser I (1114–1076), Mitanni is the name of a land also known as Hurri, "land of the Hurrians" in Hurrian, Ḫanigalbat (etymology unknown) in Assyrian and in the documents of Nuzi and Arrapḫa, Ḫabigalbat in Babylonian, and Naharina or Nahrima in Egyptian (from the Semitic *nhr,* "river"), the Aram Naharayim of the Bible (*Gn.* 24:10). In about 1450 BCE, the boundaries of Mitanni stretched from the region of modern Kirkuk (Iraq) in the east, to the upper reaches of the Euphrates River in the north, and to the Orontes River and the Mediterranean Sea in the west. Its heartland was the Khabur valley in northern Syria, where its capital, Waššukanni, was located. The exact location of Waššukanni is not known, and its identification with Sikani, modern Tell Fakhariyah is open to question. Mitanni's other important centers were Alalakh (modern Tell Atchana on the Upper Orontes), Nuzi (Gasur) and Arrapḫa in the region of Kirkuk, and Tell Brak in the Khabur, where two tablets recovered in 1984 and 1986 mention the names of two kings of Mitanni.

Mitanni was largely inhabited by Hurrians, an ethnic group attested in cuneiform sources since the third millennium. [*See* Hurrians.] They had migrated from the mountainous areas north and northeast of Mesopotamia into Mesopotamia and Syria, where they were heavily influenced by the local Sumerian and Semitic cultures. They spoke Hurrian, an agglutinative language, which is related to the Urartian language attested during the first millennium BCE. [*See* Hurrian.] Both of these languages are thought to be connected to Caucasian languages. In general, the Hurrians wrote in the Akkadian language, using the cuneiform script, but they also left a few documents written in Hurrian. [*See* Akkadian; Cuneiform.] In about the middle of the second millennium BCE, the Assyrians, a Semitic people who spoke and wrote in Akkadian, were subjects of Mitanni, as were the West Semitic people of the Syrian city-states, such as Aleppo. A group of people speaking an Indo-European dialect also inhabited the land. They had migrated into the area from the east Anatolian mountains at an unknown date, bringing with them Indo-European names of men and gods, as well as Indo-European technical terms related to the breeding and training of horses. The names of the gods whom they worshiped were Mitra, Varuna, Indra, and Nasatya, all known from the Veda. Their onomastica also suggest that they worshiped the *vāyu,* "wind," and *svar,* "heaven." Their term *marijanni-na,* "chariot driver," contains the Old Indian element *márya-*, "young man"; their numbers from one to nine are Vedic. When these speakers of Indo-European ruled Mitanni during the second millennium BCE, they used Hurrian as their official language. A few royal letters written in this language have been found in el-Amarna in Egypt; a few members of the royal family had Hurrian names, such as Gilu-Hepa and Tatu-Hepa, names borne by two princesses. [*See* Assyrians; Indo-European Languages; Amarna, Tell el-.]

The Indo-European speakers ruled over northern Mesopotamia and Syria, playing an important role on the international scene from the seventeenth to the fifteenth centuries BCE. Because the capital and other important Mitanni centers had not yet been discovered, little is known about the beginning of their rise to power. Figure 1 is a list of kings of Mitanni attested by the sources.

The first two kings of Mitanni, Kirta and his son Šuttarna I, are known from a dynastic seal rolled over two documents from Alalakh. Parratarna is known from a tablet from Nuzi and the inscription of Idrimi, king of Ḫalab/Aleppo, accord-

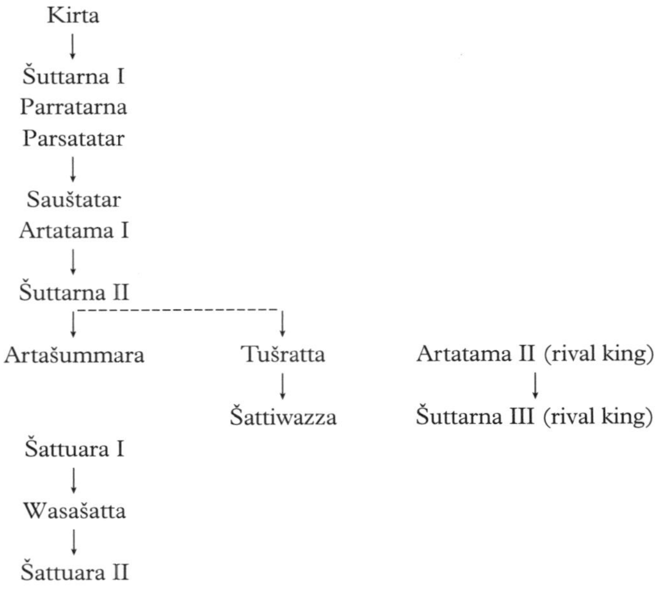

MITANNI. Figure 1. *Kings of Mitanni.* The downward arrows indicate descent from father to son.

ing to which, Parratarna had imposed his hegemony over the king of Ḫalab. Sauštatar and his father Parsatatar are known from a cylinder-seal impression on a letter from Nuzi. The first ruled both Alalakh and Kizzuwatna (later Cilicia), as well as Assyria and Nuzi, thus unifying the kingdom of Mitanni from west to east. According to the treaty between Šuppiluliuma of Ḫatti and Šattiwazza of Mitanni, Sauštatar took away a door of silver and gold from Aššur and installed it in his palace in Waššukanni. Thutmosis III (1478–1424 BCE) and Thutmosis IV (1400–1390 BCE) of Egypt campaigned against Mitanni, aiming at imposing their hegemony over Syria. These campaigns were eventually followed by a peace treaty that was confirmed by diplomatic marriages. Artatama I of Mitanni married his daughter to Thutmosis IV; Šuttarna II married his daughter Gilu-Ḫepa to Amenophis III (1390–1352 BCE); and Tušratta married his daughter Tatu-Ḫepa to the latter, as well as to the latter's successor, Amenophis IV (Akhenaten, (1352–1336 BCE).

Mitanni also faced a new threat to the north, from the Hittites, who later so weakened the land that it was engulfed by its former vassal Assyria. [*See* Hittites.] In a letter from el-Amarna, Tušratta informed his brother-in-law, Amenophis III of Egypt, of a victory over Ḫatti. But after three "Syrian wars," Šuppiluliuma of Ḫatti replaced the Mitanni federation in Syria with a Hittite federation and confined Tušratta and his son Šattiwazza to the Khabur valley in northern Syria. Moreover, he concluded a treaty with a "king of Ḫurri," Artatama II, while Tušratta was still on the throne of Mitanni. The final phase of Mitanni's political survival was marked by Assyrian interference. Ashur-Uballit I (1363–1328) supported Šuttarna III against his enemy Šattiwazza and the latter's Hittite allies and probably annexed Nuzi and Arrapḫa to Assyrian territory. Adad-nirari I (1305–1274) and Shalmaneser I (1273–1244) dealt with the last royal clan of Mitanni: Šattuara I, his son Wasašatta, and his grandson Šattuara II. After the defeat of Šattuara II by Shalmaneser I, very early in the latter's reign, Mitanni was annexed to Assyria and ceased to exist as a political entity.

Mitanni's main cities have not yet been located, and this land's material culture is evidenced only at eastern and western provincial sites, where architecture and sculpture are relatively rare compared with the minor arts (e.g., cylinder-seals, figurines, wares). Mitanni's culture appears essentially to have been eclectic, involving mainly Mesopotamian and Old Syrian traditions. The palaces at Alalakh level IV (from the time of Parratarna and Sauštatar) and at Tell Brak area IV (the time of Tušratta and Artašummara) share such un-Mesopotamian features as a northern location for the major reception rooms and an upper story approached by two stairways. The entrance hall of the palace at Alalakh had a monumental columned portico, a reminder of the *bit-ḫilani,* an architectural style adopted by the Assyrians for their palaces and temples during the Neo-Assyrian period. This architecture was once thought to be of Hurro-Mitannian origin, but recent studies suggest a western, possibly Aegean, influence. The temple at Tell Brak with its broad-room cella and shallow rabbet niche to the north, almost opposite the door, follows an Old Syrian plan known since the third millennium; the inset panels of engaged half columns in the southern and eastern facades reflect the religious architectural tradition of Mesopotamia. The one and only sculpture from Mitanni, a small statue of fine-grained white or gray limestone found at Tell Brak, represents a seated male figure wearing a togalike garment and holding what may be a vase in front of him. The statue shares features with the larger statue of Idrimi of Alalakh, which itself has Egyptian and Old Syrian characteristics. Syro-Mitannian glyptic uses two unequal registers of scenes that depict ritual, hunting, and ceremonial themes. Many other themes found in the glyptic, including winged disks, palmette trees, winged nude females, the storm god, and composite monsters, derive from Mesopotamian, Egyptian, Syrian, Cappadocian, and Aegean repertoires. The heavy use of the drill, a practice known since the third millennium, characterizes Syro-Mitannian seals produced in mass quantities. Nuzi ware, a luxury ware commonly found in temples and palaces, associates Mesopotamian ceramic traditions with western elements of design. It is also attested at Alalakh and Tell Brak, although there local designs were also used. Glass and glazed wares, also luxury products, were produced in large number and widely distributed during the Mitannian period.

[*See also* Alalakh; Brak, Tell; Khabur; Mesopotamia, *article on* Ancient Mesopotamia; *and* Nuzi.]

BIBLIOGRAPHY

Drower, Margaret S. "Syria c. 1550–1400 B.C." In *The Cambridge Ancient History,* vol. 2.1, *History of the Middle East and the Aegean Region c. 1800–1380 B.C.,* edited by I. E. S. Edwards et al., pp. 417–525. 3d ed. Cambridge, 1973. Useful historical survey that should be supplemented by recent studies.

Finkel, Irving. "Inscriptions from Tell Brak, 1984." *Iraq* 47 (1985): 187–201, pls. 34c–d. Includes the only document dated to the reign of Artašummara.

Götze, Albrecht. "The Struggle for the Domination of Syria, 1400–1300 B.C." In *The Cambridge Ancient History,* vol. 2.2, *The Middle East and the Aegean Region c. 1380–1000 B.C.,* edited by I. E. S. Edwards et al., pp. 1–20. 3d ed. Cambridge, 1975. Useful study, although dated by new archaeological and textual discoveries.

Harrak, Amir. *Assyria and Hanigalbat: A Historical Reconstruction of Bilateral Relations from the Middle of the Fourteenth to the End of the Twelfth Centuries B.C.* Hildesheim, 1987. A version of the historical events related to Mitanni's late history; uses archives recently discovered in Syria and Iraq.

Illingworth, N. J. J. "Inscriptions from Tell Brak, 1986." *Iraq* 50 (1988): 87–108.

Moorey, P. R. S. "The Hurrians, the Mittani, and Technological Innovation." In *Archaeologia Iranica et Orientalis: Miscellanea in honorem Louis Vanden Berghe,* edited by Leon De Meyer and E. Haerinck, pp. 273–286. Ghent, 1989. Discusses the role of the Mitannian kingdom in the development of glass and iron technology.

Oates, David. "Excavations at Tell Brak, 1985–86." *Iraq* 49 (1987): 175–191. An exhaustive description of the Mitanni palace uncovered in area HH.

Stein, Diana L. "Art and Architecture." In Gernot Wilhelm's *The Hurrians*, pp. 80–90. Warminster, 1989. Up-to-date archaeological and artistic data related to the Hurrians and the Indo-Aryan kings of Mitanni. Stein has published an illustrated article on the same topic in *Reallexikon der Assyriologie* 8 (1994): 296–299.

Wilhelm, Gernot. *The Hurrians*. Translated by Jennifer Barnes. Warminster, 1989. Comprehensive and authoritative study of the Hurrians, based on available textual and archaeological sources; useful bibliography.

Woolley, C. Leonard. *Alalakh: An Account of the Excavations at Tell Atchana in the Hatay, 1937–1949*. Oxford, 1955. Basic account; must be used with new studies reinterpreting level IV; for a bibliography of the new studies, see Stein above.

AMIR HARRAK

MOAB. Two inscriptions from Luxor, both dating to the reign of Rameses II (c. 1304–1237 BCE), provide the earliest certain epigraphic references to Moab. One of these inscriptions, which apparently commemorates an Egyptian campaign into Moab, is presented with scenes in relief depicting Egyptians attacking fortifications and mentions three towns by name: *b(w)trt, yn(?)d,* and *tbniw*. Both inscriptions render the name *Moab* with the hieroglyphic determinative that indicates a land or a region; other ancient sources verify that Moab was the region immediately east of the Dead Sea. Specifically, the Hebrew Bible refers to the people who lived in that area as Moabites, and two royal inscriptions found there, the Mesha inscription and the Kerak fragment (see below) use the title "king of Moab" for local rulers. The *tbniw* of the Luxor inscription probably is to be identified with Dibon (present-day Dhiban), known otherwise from the Hebrew Bible and the Mesha inscription. The Baluʿ stela also suggests an Egyptian presence in Moab at the end of the Late Bronze Age.

The most important epigraphic source for ancient Moab is the famous Mesha inscription discovered at Dibon/Dhiban in 1868. Written in Canaanite (or Moabite) script on a basalt stela, the thirty-four lines identify Mesha as the king of Moab and report the major deeds of his reign. Those deeds include his successful struggle to "liberate" the region north of Dibon from Israelite control; numerous building projects, such as the temple to Kemosh, where the stela was erected; and the construction of a road across the Arnon River (Wadi el-Mujib). The Hebrew Bible also reports Mesha's successful rebellion against Israel and states that this occurred following King Ahab's death (*2 Ks.* 3:6–27), which would place Mesha's reign in the second half of the ninth century BCE. Parts of only four lines of the Kerak fragment survive, but it is enough to reconstruct the name of one *[K]mšyt,* also identified as king of Moab. It has been suggested that this *[K]mšyt* was Mesha's father, whose name is partially preserved (*Kmš[..]*) in the Mesha inscription. This is what speculative, however, because the theophoric element *Kmš* was typical of royal Moabite names.

Of the few archaeological sites excavated in Moab, most are situated north of the Arnon/Wadi el-Mujib. The following have produced Late Bronze and/or Iron Age remains (listing from north to south): Khirbet el-ʿAl, Ḥesban, Dhiban (Dibon), Lehun, ʿAraʿir, Baluʿ, and Khirbet el-Medeineh (i.e., Medeinet el-Muʿarrajeh, overlooking Wadi el-Lejjun). Especially for the area south of the Arnon/Mujib, therefore, the available archaeological evidence derives largely from surface surveys. It seems clear that the region had a rather sparse sedentary population during the Middle and Late Bronze Ages, but experienced a significant increase in the number of settlements during the Iron Age. This trend probably began near the end of the Late Bronze Age and reached a high point in Iron II. Early in the Iron Age some small but strategically located fortifications already appear—Khirbet ʿAkuzeh, on the southern rim of the Kerak plateau; ed-Deir on its western edge; and the two Khirbet Medeinehs on the eastern side, overlooking Wadi el-Lejjun. These suggest the beginnings of an organized defensive strategy early in the Iron Age, although not necessarily a unified territorial state encompassing the whole area east of the Dead Sea, as the Hebrew Bible seems to presuppose.

Specifically, the Hebrew Bible speaks of a race of giants, the Emim, who occupied the land of Moab before the Moabites (*Gn.* 14:5; *Dt.* 2:10–11). It identifies the Moabites themselves as descendants of Lot's eldest daughter (*Gn.* 19:30–38) and presupposes a unified Moabite kingdom with fixed boundaries already in place when the Israelites passed through Transjordan during their exodus from Egypt (e.g., *Nm.* 21:26; 22:4). The Hebrew Bible is not a firsthand source, however, and the picture it presents of ancient Moab clearly is legendary, as well as influenced by theological and ideal notions regarding early Israel. The various Moabite kings mentioned in the Bible (to the extent that they are in fact historical people), as well as the Shasu king (?) featured in the Baluʿ inscription, may have been tribal chieftains or lords over local city-states. Among the former are Balak, who is said to have engaged the prophet Balaam to curse the Israelites while they were camped in the plains of Moab (*Nm.* 22–24); Eglon, who is reported to have oppressed Israel during the time of the Judges (*Jgs.* 3:12–30); and Mesha, who reportedly paid an annual tribute to Israel of a hundred thousand lambs and the wool of a hundred thousand rams but rebelled after Ahab's death.

The Mesha inscription provides a firsthand look at political circumstances in Moab during the ninth century BCE. The kingdom Mesha inherited from his father seems to have consisted essentially of the city-state of Dibon, for which Wadi el-Mujib and Wadi el-Wale would have provided natural boundaries. From this base he claims to have expanded his domain northward as far as Madaba, fortified ʿAroʿer

(ʿAraʿir), presumably to protect the road he built across the Arnon/Mujib, and conducted at least one military campaign into the region south of the Arnon (depending on the location of Ḥoronaim mentioned in line 31). However, the geographic range of his building activities as reported in the inscription implies that, except for possible military excursions, the Moabite territory south of the Arnon was beyond the limits of his domain. Mesha credited his successes to the Moabite god Kemosh, and the inscription stood in a temple dedicated to Kemosh.

Assyrian texts indicate that Moab, along with the other peoples of Transjordan, became Assyrian vassals following Tiglath-Pileser III's western campaigns in 734–732 BCE. This status involved payments of heavy tribute to Assyria, but also Assyrian protection, which seems to have been needed primarily against the nomadic Qederites, who roamed the desert regions east and southeast of Damascus. Also learned from these Assyrian texts are the names of four additional Moabite kings and other bits of information about Moab's involvement in international affairs. A fragment of a clay tablet discovered at Nimrud lists Salamanu of Moab among the kings who paid tribute to Tiglath-Pileser shortly after 734 BCE. A prism fragment from the reign of Sargon II suggests that Moab was implicated in an anti-Assyrian revolt led by Ashdod in 713 BCE. A Kammusunadbi of Moab is mentioned among local Palestinian kings who sent presents to assure Sennacherib of their loyalty when he marched against Philistia and Judah in 701 BCE. In addition, a King Musuri of Moab appears in a list of kings who transported building materials to Nineveh during the reign of Esarhaddon, as well as in another list of local rulers who sent presents to Ashurbanipal and supported his wars against Egypt. Two more texts from Ashurbanipal's region report Assyrian military action against the Qederites. One of these texts mentions a King Kamashaltu of Moab, who seems to have played a major role in the action. (For documentation of the Assyrian references to Moab, see J. Maxwell Miller, "Moab and the Moabites" in Dearman, ed., 1989, pp. 1–40.)

Josephus (*Antiq.* 10.9.7) states that Nebuchadrezzar made war on the Ammonites and Moabites and brought them under Babylonian control. Presumably, the peoples of Transjordan submitted to Persia as well, but there is no specific evidence of this.

[*See also* ʿAraʿir; Baluʿ; Central Moab; Dibon; Kerak; Lehun; Medeineh, Khirbet el-; *and* Moabite Stone.]

BIBLIOGRAPHY

Bienkowski, Piotr, ed. *Early Edom and Moab: The Beginning of the Iron Age in Southern Jordan.* Sheffield, 1992. Essays focusing on the transition from the Late Bronze to the Iron Age in southern Transjordan and therefore attentive to issues pertaining to the origins of the Moabite and Edomite monarchies. Kenneth A. Kitchen's essay, "The Egyptian Evidence on Ancient Jordan" (pp. 21–30), is especially useful.

Dearman, Andrew, ed. *Studies in the Mesha Inscription and Moab.* Atlanta, 1989. Nine essays that combine to provide a comprehensive overview of recent studies, issues, and views pertaining to ancient Moab. J. Maxwell Miller's essay, "Moab and the Moabites" (pp. 1–40), provides full documentation for references to Moab in biblical and other ancient sources.

Miller, J. Maxwell. "The Israelite Journey through (around) Moab and Moabite Toponymy." *Journal of Biblical Literature* 108 (1989): 577–595. Analysis of key biblical texts relevant for locating Moabite places mentioned in the Hebrew Bible and the Mesha inscription.

Reed, William L., and Fred V. Winnett. "A Fragment of an Early Moabite Inscription from Kerak." *Bulletin of the American Schools of Oriental Research,* no. 172 (1963): 1–9. Initial publication of the fragment that reconstructs the king's name as *[K]mšyt* and identifies him as Mesha's father.

Timm, Stefan. *Moab zwischen den Mächten: Studien zu historischen Denkmälern und Texten.* Wiesbaden, 1989. Comprehensive treatment of epigraphic evidence pertaining to ancient Moab.

Worschech, Udo F. Ch. *Die Beziehungen Moabs zu Israel und Ägypten in der Eisenzeit: Siedlungsarchäologische und siedlungshistorische Untersuchungen im Kernland Moabs (Arḍ el-Kerak).* Wiesbaden, 1990. Based on his own archaeological explorations in the Moabite region, Worschech argues for an early Moabite territorial monarchy already in place by the beginning of Iron I.

J. MAXWELL MILLER

MOABITE STONE. The inscription of Mesha, king of Moab, known both as the Moabite Stone and as the Mesha Stone/Inscription, was the first (1868) of the major epigraphic documents discovered in either Cis- or Transjordan and couched in a language closely related to Hebrew (see figure 1). More than a century later, it is still one of the most important of the Canaanite inscriptions, providing data on the religion, history, geography, language, and thought of the Moabite people.

The discovery did not take place in the course of regular excavations, and attempts by Europeans to obtain the stela from local inhabitants resulted in the inscription being broken into pieces. Many fragments were recovered, but our knowledge of approximately one-third of the text rests on a partial and inexpert copy of the intact stela and on a squeeze hastily taken before the stone was broken. As is often the case with antiquities discovered at the dawn of modern scientific archaeological research, there is no readily identifiable *editio princeps* (on matters of discovery and early publications, see Clermont-Ganneau, 1887, and M. P. Graham in Dearman, 1989, pp. 41–92).

The text deals with the deeds of Mesha, the defeat of his enemies, and the construction projects his new glory permitted (on the questions of text structure and literary genre, see Smelik 1990, 1992). The greatest of these projects was designated by the term *qrḥh,* apparently a quarter of the capital city of Dibon, wherein Mesha erected a *bmt,* a type of sanctuary (cf. Hebrew *bāmâ*), in which the inscription itself was deposited (1.3). He (re)built the walls, the gates, and the towers of the *qrḥh,* as well as a palace within, and installed waterworks (ll. 21–26). For the correlation of archae-

MOABITE STONE. Figure 1. *The Moabite Stone.* (Courtesy ASOR Archives)

ological data from Dibon with the text of the Moabite stone, see A. D. Tushingham (1990). The (re)building activity extended beyond Dibon, to other towns (ll. 26–28).

The enemy was the Israelite Omride dynasty, which had occupied Moab "for many days" (1.5), indeed "forty years" (1.8). Both the Omride occupation and the defeat of the occupiers is described as the work of the deity Kemosh, who had first "been angry with his land" (ll. 5–6) and then "restored it" (ll. 8–9). The interpretation of particular details is uncertain, as is any correlation with data from other sources—for example, the chronology of the Omrides or the geography of both the Israelite occupation and of the Moabite borders with Ammon to the north and Edom to the south (on these matters, see Timm, 1989; Smelik, 1992; and the bibliographies therein).

This text constitutes the primary source for the Moabite language, for most other inscriptions identified as Moabite belong to the category of minor inscriptions, such as seals (Israel, 1987; 1992, pp. 105–110). The primary isoglosses are monophthongization of *-ay-* and *-aw-* diphthongs and *-n* as the plural marker of masculine nouns and adjectives (for details, see Israel, 1984; and K. P. Jackson in Dearman, 1989; pp. 96–130). A fragment of another monumental inscription providing the name of Mesha's father, Kemoshyatti, was published in 1963 (Reed and Winnett, 1963; Swiggers, 1982); more recently, a brief text on papyrus appeared that was identified by its editors as belonging to a dialect of Moabite (Bordreuil and Pardee, 1990).

[*See also* Dibon; *and* Moab.]

BIBLIOGRAPHY

Bordreuil, Pierre, and Dennis Pardee. "Le papyrus du marzeaḥ." *Semitica (Hommages à Maurice Sznycer,* vol. 1) 38 (1990): 49–68. *Editio princeps* of a brief text in what may be a Moabite dialect.

Clermont-Ganneau, Charles S. "La stèle de Mésa." *Journal Asiatique* 9 (1887): 72–112. Early description of the stela and of previous attempts at deciphering the text.

Dearman, Andrew, ed. *Studies in the Mesha Inscription and Moab.* American Schools of Oriental Research, Society of Biblical Literature, Archaeological and Biblical Studies, 2. Atlanta, 1989. Collection of survey articles by various scholars on aspects of Moabite studies. See in particular M. Patrick Graham, "The Discovery and Reconstruction of the Mesha Inscription" (pp. 41–92), and Kent P. Jackson, "The Language of the Mesha Inscription" (pp. 96–130). Contains extensive bibliographical information on previous research; however, data are indicated only in footnotes and with an inconvenient form of cross-reference in subsequent notes.

Israel, Felice. "Geographic Linguistics and Canaanite Dialects." In *Current Progress in Afro-Asiatic Linguistics: Papers of the Third International Hamito-Semitic Congress,* edited by James Bynon, pp. 363–387. Current Issues in Linguistic Theory, vol. 28. Amsterdam, 1984. Linguistic description of Moabite in contrast with neighboring languages.

Israel, Felice. "Studi moabiti I: Rassegna di epigrafia moabita e i sigilli moabiti." In *Atti della 4ª giornata di studi Camito-Semitici e Indeuropei,* edited by Giuliano Bernini and Vermondo Brugnatelli, pp. 101–138. Quaderni della Collana di Linguistica Storica e Descrittiva, 1. Milan, 1987. Overview of Moabite inscriptions, the best attested category being seals.

Israel, Felice. "Note di onomastica semitica 7/2: Rassegna critico-bibliografica ed epigrafica su alcune onomastiche palestinesi; La Transgiordania." *Studi Epigrafici e Linguistici* 9 (1992): 95–114. Moabite onomastics in the Transjordanian context.

Reed, William L., and Fred V. Winnett. "A Fragment of an Early Moabite Inscription from Kerak." *Bulletin of the American Schools of Oriental Research,* no. 172 (1963): 1–9. *Editio princeps* of the Kerak inscription.

Smelik, K. A. D. "The Literary Structure of King Mesha's Inscription." *Journal for the Study of the Old Testament* 46 (1990): 21–30.

Smelik, K. A. D. "King Mesha's Inscription: Between History and Fiction." *Oudtestamentische Studiën* 28 (1992): 59–92. Study of the text as a literary document in praise of Mesha and of its value as a historical document.

Swiggers, Pierre. "The Moabite Inscription of el-Kerak." *Annali: Istituto Universitario Orientale di Napoli* 42 (1982): 521–525. Careful historical and linguistic study of the Kerak inscription.

Timm, Stefan. *Moab zwischen den Mächten: Studien zu historischen Denkmälern und Texten.* Ägypten und Altes Testament, vol. 17. Wiesbaden, 1989. Critical study of all Moabite epigraphic material and of references to Moab in other sources (e.g., Egyptian and biblical).

Tushingham, A. D. "Dhībān Reconsidered: King Mesha and His Works." *Annual of the Department of Antiquities of Jordan* 34 (1990): 183–192. Overview of archaeological work at Tell Dhiban (Dibon), correlated with the Mesha inscription.

DENNIS PARDEE

MOCHA (Ar., al-Mukha), city located in the harbor of a natural lagoon on the Red Sea coast of the Republic of Yemen (13°19′ N, 43°15′ E). The name of the port is synonymous with coffee. Legend attributes the invention of coffee drinking and, hence, the foundation of the town to a local fifteenth-century CE hermit, Shaykh ʿAli ibn ʿUmar Shadhili, who died in 1418 (AH 821). Mocha was the sole port for the shipment of coffee during the Yemeni monopoly on production of the crop (c. 1550–1725 CE). The city was linked by road with Bayt al-Faqih, to the north, which was the emporium for collecting the bales from the mountainous interior where the coffee grew.

Before the arrival of European traders (i.e., before the seventeenth century CE), Mocha served as a small port in the Egypt-India trade. It grew in importance after Ottoman Turkish measures against the Portuguese restricted trading activity at the port of Aden. English and Dutch factories were established first under Ottoman authority in 1618; the height of the coffee trade was reached between about 1660 and 1780. The French did not establish a factory until 1713, but they successfully transplanted coffee bushes to Réunion, breaking the Yemeni monopoly.

There have been no excavations at Mocha. The city's archaeological history is mostly derived from European descriptions, including lithographs. Mocha had no city walls until shortly after 1700. Eighteenth-century descriptions are consistent in their disparaging remarks about the flimsiness of the masonry—too thin to resist canon shot and a suitable deterrent only for cavalry or those without artillery. Aerial photographs taken in the 1970s show the position of the walls and the defensive bastions. The two most significant monuments are the tombs of Shaykh al-Shadhili and Shaykh al-Amudi. The settlement was severely damaged by offshore bombardment during Italian-Turkish engagements before World War I. Worse devastation was inflicted by a flash flood from the mountains that sent a wall of water 1 m deep as far as the sea.

The name of Mocha is inextricably linked with that of Muza, the pre-Islamic port listed in the *Periplus of the Erythraean Sea,* which describes it as a station between Berenice in Egypt and Barygaza in India. The archaeological quest for the location is hampered by the similarity of the names of Muza, Mukha, and Mawzaʿ—the latter located 25 km (15 mi.) inland, which Ptolemy describes as the town associated with the port of Muza. Numerous, mostly informal expeditions have tried to locate Muza, but to no avail. In an analogy with the coastline at Faza, to the north, the harbor of Muza should be sought at least 5 km (3 mi.) south of Mocha and inland: at Faza, early medieval port sites are found stranded to the south and east of present-day lagoons. Prevailing onshore winds and tides have a tendency to create sand bars which form natural anchorages for shallow-drafght boats. In time, the lagoons silt up, and another natural harbor forms farther north.

BIBLIOGRAPHY

Donzel, E. J. van. "Al-Mukhā." In *Encyclopaedia of Islam,* new ed., vol. 7, pp. 513–516. Leiden, 1960–. Covers the Periplus era, as well as the coffee trade.

Hattox, Ralph S. *Coffee and Coffeehouses: The Origins of a Social Beverage in the Medieval Near East* (Seattle, 1985). Provides a more critical analysis of the Shadhili legend than Macro (1960, below).

Huntingford, G. W. B. *The Periplus of the Erythraean Sea.* Hakluyt Society, Second Series, no. 151. London, 1980. Supercedes the much quoted commentary by Wilfred Schoff (New York, 1912).

Macro, Eric. "Notes on Mocha." In *Bibliography on Yemen and Notes on Mocha,* edited by Eric Macro, pp. 31–63. Coral Gables, Fla., 1960.

Macro, Eric. "The Topography of Mocha." *Proceedings of the Seminar for Arabian Studies* 10 (1980): 55–66. This and the above report are supplemented by artist's illustrations published by Macro in *Proceedings of the Seminar for Arabian Studies* (1982, 1984, 1987).

E. J. KEALL

MONASTERIES. The foundation of a monastery was preceded everywhere in the Near East by individual anchorites, whose fame attracted pious individuals to settle near them to benefit from their experience and counsel. It was in this way that communities of monks came into being. Although Eusebius does not mention monasticism in his *Ecclesiastical History,* which was written before 325 CE (suggesting that monasticism was not yet considered a significant trend within Christianity), the first monasteries in Egypt, Syria, and Palestine had already emerged by that time. By the middle of the fourth century the movement had spread, and by the last quarter of that century monasteries were common throughout the Near East. During the fifth and sixth centuries, the movement became strong and wealthy and was a dominant factor in the Christian church and in Byzantine society.

In different parts of the Christian world, depending on local cultural and social and national affinities, there were diverse answers to the question "What is the proper way to conduct monastic life?" The variety of monastic systems gave rise to the emergence of several types of monasteries with particular architectural plans. The design and construction of monasteries were also determined by regional building traditions.

Once the movement had grown and taken shape, two main types of organized monastic life emerged. In each the monks were subordinate to an abbot or priest and their life was regulated by rules, either oral or written. In the cenobium (from the Greek *koinos bios,* "common life"), monks lived within a walled compound; the laura (Gk., "alley") was a community of anchorites in which each monk lived alone in his cell or with one or two fellow monks or disciples. The cells were dispersed around core buildings—a church, kitchen and bakery, storerooms, and other communal buildings. A network of constructed paths communicated between the cells and the core. Cenobitic monks met each other daily, during common meals and prayers. In the laura these encounters occurred only on weekends and at feasts. The framework of the laura can therefore be considered to have been semicenobitic. Cenobia were found everywhere in the Near East, while laurae were restricted mainly to Egypt, Palestine, and Sinai (although they were known in Cappadocia, on Mt. Olympus in Bithynia, and on Mt. Latros [Latmos] in Caria). [*See* Cappadocia.] There were significant differences in the life-styles between the Pachomian cenobia (see below) in Egypt and the Syrian ones, on the one hand, and the Basilian cenobia (see below) of Asia Minor and Palestine on the other hand. There also were differences between the vast anchorite colonies at Nitria, Kellia, and Scetis, where several thousand monks lived in each, and the modest Palestinian laurae or the tiny, remote colonies of Sinai. By the sixth century, a composite institution was also found throughout the Levant: a cenobium with a few anchorites or recluses living within its wall or in immediate proximity to its walls. Almost all of the communal buildings found in a cenobium were also present in the core of a laura, except that the latter had no walls or gates. Typologically, both kinds of monasteries were constructed either on a plain, a moderately hilly area, or steep cliffs.

Egypt. Because, in Egypt, brick was the common building material, the state of preservation of monastery buildings is much poorer than in Syria and Palestine. In the inhabited monasteries, like those in Wadi 'n-Naṭrun, or like St. Antony and St. Paul, medieval and recent reconstruction work masks the original layout.

Two main monastic systems were born in Egypt: one, propagated in Lower Egypt by Antony (251–356 CE) and his disciples, was semicenobitic; the second, founded by Pachomius (c. 290–346 CE) in Upper and Middle Egypt, was a true cenobitic system. The best-known Antonian colonies were those on Mt. Nitria (founded c. 315), in Kellia (established in 338), and in Scetis (established between 330 and 340). The monks in these colonies numbered several thousand. Other communities of this type were the Mustafa Kasif at el-Khargah; Der al-Dik, Der Sombat, and Der Abu Henes in the region of Antinoe (Martin, 1971); and perhaps also the early phases of the excavated Monastery of Apa Apollo at Bawit and Apa Jeremias at Saqqara (Clédat, 1904–1916; Quibel, 1912; Grossmann and Severin, 1982). [*See* Nitria; Saqqara.]

Pachomius founded his first monastery in about 323 in Tabennesi. His second foundation, Phbow (in 329), became his largest and most important. At the time of his death, nine monasteries and two nunneries were united in his community, the Pachomian federation *(koinonia).* They later increased to twenty-four, comprising several thousand monks. A Pachomian monastery was also established in Metanoia, not far from Alexandria. Shenoute, who headed the White Monastery (Deir el-Abiad) near Sohag in the first half of the fifth century, modified the Pachomian system by not advocating extreme asceticism. He permitted a monk to withdraw to the desert after a few years of cenobitic life, without completely cutting ties with the community. Such was the life-style of the cell dwellers associated with the Monastery of Epiphanius near Thebes in Upper Egypt and of the monks who inhabited the cells west of Esna. Egyptian laurae such as these reused the burial caves from the pharaonic and Roman periods that are found along many stretches of the Nile Valley as well as in the Delta (Martin, 1967). [*See* Delta.] Such anchorite settlements had a nearby cenobium serving as its core.

The core buildings at each of the four communities in Scetis included a church; a tower of refuge, or keep (Ar., *qaṣr*); a kitchen, bakery, and dining room; and storehouses for food. The monks' cells were scattered at short distances from each other in unwalled colonies. Unlike Mustafa Kasif and St. Antony, where perimeter walls were built in the fifth and sixth centuries, the core buildings at Scetis were not surrounded by a wall until the ninth century, and in the fourteenth century monks were no longer permitted to dwell outside the walls (Evelyn-White, 1932–1933; Walters, 1974).

The sixth-century laura at Der el-Dik consisted of fifteen rock-cut cells, two churches similarly constructed, and presumably also a *qaṣr.* A large walled structure (146 × 92 m) nearby that might have served as a cenobium was constructed after the cells were abandoned.

Kellia (Gk., "cells") is identified with the sites of Quṣur al-Rubaʿiyyat, Qaṣr Waheida, Quṣur ʿIsa, Quṣur el-ʿIzeila, Quṣur el-ʿAbid, Quṣur Hegeila, and Quṣur ʿEreima. The colony extended for more than 22 km (14 mi.). The collapsed cells, built of mud bricks, created more than fifteen hundred mounds, which are clearly visible on the ground. The mapping of Kellia was done with the aid of aerial photographs, and each mound *(kom)* was given a separate number (Daumas and Guillaumont, 1969; Kasser, 1967, 1972, 1980, 1983, 1984; Bridel, 1986).

The earliest hermitages in Kellia were modest in scale and lacked an encircling wall. However, those built in the late fifth–early sixth centuries were more spacious and elaborate. A typical spacious Kelliot hermitage, dated to the sixth century, is the early phase of *kom* 167, whose rectangular, walled area is about 15 × 27.5 m in size. The *kom* was composed of a spacious dwelling with many rooms; its water-supply installations included a well, a pool, channels, and a toilet; a courtyard area contained a garden. [*See* Pools.] The dwelling (10.30 × 9.70 m) was in two parts, each with several rooms: the larger area included a kitchen and food storerooms and was occupied by the senior monk; the smaller one, attached to it on the south, was used by a disciple or an attendant. Each section had its own chapel (oratory), a spacious room whose walls were ornamented with frescoes. [*See* Wall Paintings.] The ceilings were of brick vaulting.

From the first quarter of the seventh century onward, instead of isolated hermitages dispersed throughout the desert, at Kellia hermitages were grouped into a compound surrounded by a shallow wall. The result was a cenobiumlike construction, a *ma-nshubeh* (Copt., "dwelling"). A *qaṣr* was built later. However, the monks continued to maintain the daily life of hermits, not of cenobites. Such a monastery can be found in the final stage of *kom* 219, excavated by the French expedition (Daumas and Guillaumont, 1969). Within the wall about ten hermitages are each comprised of several rooms. The communal structures included a kitchen, latrines, the courtyard, and cisterns. [*See* Cisterns.] However, isolated hermitages persisted even side by side with these monasteries. There were many churches at Kellia. The main and most ancient church appears to have been the one discovered at Quṣur ʿIṣa (South 1) and excavated by the University of Geneva (Kasser, 1983, 1984). The second ecclesiastical center was at Qaṣr Waheida (= *kom* 34), excavated by the French Institute of Oriental Archaeology at Cairo (Descoeudres, 1988).

The nine cells excavated to the west of Esna, dated to 550–650, are spacious subterranean complexes cut to a depth of about 3.5 m below the surface. The walls and floors were plastered and whitewashed. The simpler type had a single prayer chapel, courtyard, bedroom, and storeroom. The kitchen was equipped with elaborate cooking devices, including a stove and a baking oven with an improved air-circulation system. The second type had two chapels and two courtyards (Sauneron and Jacquet, 1972).

At the Apa Jeremias monastery at Saqqara, the dwellings had three components: a small courtyard, an outer room that served as a living room, and an inner room with a niche in the eastern wall that served as an oratory. It seems that there was also a second story (Quibel, 1912). The structure of the cells at Bawit is similar (Clédat, 1904–1916). At both sites, and near Esna, the rooms also had air shafts.

The Pachomian cenobium, inhabited by several hundred monks, was surrounded by a wall; its plan resembled that of a military camp, although the wall was not a fortification wall. The best-preserved example of a Pachomian cenobium is Deir al-Balaiza near Asyut (Grossman, 1993). It is constructed on a moderate slope that descended eastward; its walls encircle a trapezoidal area (200 × 50–250 sq m). Many of its structures are preserved to two or three stories: three or four churches, a bakery, two refectories, and several dormitories. Its estimated population was about one thousand monks. The wall had a gatehouse on the east, with a guesthouse next to it, on the outside. The entire layout and structure parallel the literary sources (Patrich, 1995, pp. 17–22), according to which a Pachomian monastery included an assembly hall (Gk., *synaxis*) for prayer, a community dining hall, a kitchen, a bakery, a hospital, and storehouses for agricultural produce and other foodstuffs and work tools. There were various workshops and folds for pigs and animals used for plowing and for transport. (Camels and boats were used for transportation.) [*See* Pigs; Camels; Transportation.]

The literary sources report that the monks in each monastery were divided into houses (Gk., *oikoi*) comprised of twenty to forty men. Each three or four houses constituted a tribe. The dwellings created a barracklike structure. Each house was to include an assembly hall for lessons, discourse, and prayer as well. Initially, one monk lived in each cell, but in a later period three monks are known to have lived in a single cell. Such cells were found in the excavations of the sixth-century Monastery of St. Simeon (Anba Hadra) near Aswan. The cells in the monastery's keep opened onto a central corridor (Monneret de Villard, 1927). The cells at Deir Fakhoury near Esna were similarly arranged (Walters, 1974, p. 110). However, at Deir al-Balaiza the monks lived in dormitories (Grossman, 1993).

The refectory at the Apa Jeremias monastery at Saqqara measures about 22 × 10.5 m. Three rows of columns divide the room along its longitudinal axis. Six windows were set in the north wall; traces of stone benches along the eastern wall indicate that the dining tables were long (there are also indications of a round table). Another hall (10 × 20 m) has been identified by inscription as an infirmary (Quibel, 1912; Grossman and Severin, 1982). Niches and cupboards were built in its walls. At Anba Hadra the refectory is also a rectangular hall divided along its axis by a row of four columns. On the stone floor are traces of eight circular brick tables; water tanks were built near the walls. Another refectory with a central row of columns was found in *kom* 34 (Qaṣr Waheida) at Kellia.

Monastic churches are rectangular, oriented to the east, and have straight, outward walls—no apse protrudes. Generally, there were two entrances—on the north and on the south. Where there was a narthex, a third entrance was set in the western wall. The numerous entrances of the White Monastery (Monneret de Villard, 1925–1926) are rare. Churches were basilical in design, with the nave much wider than the aisles. [*See* Basilicas.] Occasionally, galleries are seen. The sanctuary was generally single apsidal or trifoliated, with two sacristies—one on the north and one on the south. On the west there was an endo- and/or an exonarthex. The "southern narthex" in the White and Red Monasteries near Sohag is an unusual feature in its placement. The main building material for churches was brick. Stone was used only for the more important churches, at least in their lower courses. The White Monastery is remarkable because it was built of white limestone, including its floors, doorframes, and decorated architectural members.

The main center of pilgrimage in Egypt was the shrine of St. Menas at the town of Abu Mina (Mareotis; Grossman, 1986).

Sinai. The small monasteries and hermitages in the Sinai desert have been studied extensively in recent years (Finkelstein, 1985; Tsafrir, 1993; Dahari, in press), as has the St. Catherine Monastery (see below). Uzi Dahari (Tsafrir, ed.; 1993) recorded seventy monastic sites in the high mountains of Sinai, seventeen of which appear in the literary sources. He estimates the population of monks in Sinai to have been about six hundred at the apogee of monastic life. A second monastic center, at Rhaithou, was identified by Dahari (Tsafrir, ed., 1993) at modern Sheikh Raia, near the western shore of the peninsula.

The cells discovered in the monastic centers on Jebel Safsafa and Jebel Sirbal in Sinai are generally small, narrow alcoves built under large boulders or in overhangs, with at least one masonry wall. Complex 250 on Jebel Safsafa is unique in that it is more spacious and is composed of a courtyard, vestibule, and a living room; site 2 there, which is a narrow alcove, is the prevalent type of cell (Finkelstein, 1985). The cells at Bir Abu-Sweira, a monastic site near Rhaithou, are also small. Partially rock cut, each cell is a room with several niches in its eastern wall that served as a private chapel. The monks in the high mountains constructed gardens and irrigation systems near their hermitages. Each monk cultivated an average plot of 325 sq m for his livelihood.

The fortified St. Catherine monastery was both a monastic center and a pilgrimage site (Forsyth, 1973; Grossmann, 1988). Most of its structures were two to three stories high and were constructed along the circumference walls (about 75 × 85 m): dwellings, a refectory, a kitchen and a bakery, and storerooms. The magnificent basilical Church of Justinian (20 × 37 m) inside the compound, was built sometime between 548 and 565, next to the "burning bush." Its east–west orientation is askew to the wall lines. A guesthouse and fourth-century tower of refuge are alongside it. The "Well of Moses" is located to the north of the church. The rest of the area inside the walls is free of constructions.

Ancient Palestine. The first monks known by name are Hilarion (291–371) of Tabatha (near Gaza), who started his monastic career about 308, and Chariton, a native of Iconium (Konya) in Asia Minor, the founder of monasticism in the Judean Desert. In the beginning, the laura was the most common type of monastic settlement in the Judean Desert. Chariton established his first monastery, Pharan, there in about 330. At that time anchorites also lived among the reeds of the Jordan River. Chariton later established two other monasteries: Douka, overlooking Jericho, and Souka, not far from Tekoa. [*See* Jericho.] Monasticism spread throughout Palestine during the fourth century, and monasteries—mainly cenobia—were established in Jerusalem, Bethlehem, and in other holy places connected with Jesus' life, as well as in the lowland (Shephelah) and Gaza. [*See* Bethlehem.]

Unlike in Egypt and Syria, Palestinian monasticism was not an indigenous movement; it was mainly a Greek-speaking one, with a cosmopolitan flavor. Influences were introduced both from Egypt and from Asia Minor, from whence most of the Palestinian monastic leaders came. The outcome was something original, however, and in the mid-fifth century Palestine became a monastic center on its own, attracting monks and admirers from the entire Christian world.

The most comprehensive archaeological and historical studies refer to monasticism in the Judean Desert (Hirschfeld, 1992; Patrich, 1995). The ruins of some sixty monasteries and monastic installations were explored in this area, some of which (Khirbet el-Murasas, Khirbet el-Kiliya, Khan el-Ahmar, Khirbet ed-Deir) have been excavated completely (Bottini et al., 1990). All others were surveyed comprehensively. Five monasteries on the fringes of the desert, adjacent to Bethlehem, were excavated by Virgilio Corbo (1955). Information from other regions of the country is more fragmentary.

The sixth-century Monastery of Martyrius (Khirbet el-Murasas) is the best representative among the cenobia. The compound is rectangular (78 × 68 m) and surrounded by a 0.7-meter-thick stone wall preserved to a height of 1–2 m. It originally was about 4 m high. The main entrance was in the eastern wall and had stables next to it. The church, a typical monastery chapel (29.5 × 6.60 m), had a narthex on the west, an elongated diaconicon (15 × 4.6 m) on the south, and a mortuary chapel on the north. The northern wing included the dwelling cave of the founder monk, which later served as a burial ground. [*See* Burial Sites.] The vast refectory (31 × 25 m) was basilical in shape, with galleries on three sides. Adjacent to it was the kitchen, with a cellar and an upper floor. The dwelling areas, with two other chapels, were on the southwest, on the second floor of the structures that surrounded a central courtyard. An exceptional structure, a small bathhouse (9 × 13 m), was located on the west. The monastery was equipped with vast underground cisterns and drainage channels, as well as with storerooms. The floors of all the structures were decorated with colorful mosaics, large portions of which are preserved. [*See* Mosaics.] Open spaces and passages were paved with flagstones. On the exterior, near the northeast corner, was a hostel (28 × 43 m), including a stable and a chapel. Nearby, on the outskirts of the complex, three gardens had been irrigated by stone-cut channels. [*See* Irrigation.]

Generally, monks were interred in the burial chapels and the common cemeteries according to their hierarchy in the monastery: abbots; priests and deacons; and unordained monks. The tomb of the founding father was sometimes marked by a special building, or he was buried in the cave in which he had spent his life. The tomb could become a focal point for veneration by monks and pilgrims. [*See* Martyrion; Tombs.] Monks usually lived alone, but two or three might share a cell or there might have been dormitories, in accordance with the regulations for monks legislated by Emperor Justinian.

The Great Laura of St. Sabas (Mar Saba) is the most elaborate example of a laura (Patrich, 1995). Its remains are distributed along 2 km of the Kidron ravine. There was more than one type of laura hermitage. The simplest cells consisted of a single room and a courtyard; the complex ones consisted of several rooms, including a private chapel or a prayer niche. Most hermitages were intended for a single monk, but there are several dwelling complexes that might have served two, or even three monks. Private chapels were a common feature. Each hermitage had its own water supply provided by drains and cisterns to catch rainwater.

Syria. From the literary sources about eighty monasteries are known to have existed in the sixth century on Syria's limestone massif (the agricultural regions between Antioch and Apamea), with the most important ones being Deir Tell Ade, Qalʿat et-Touffah, Deir Tormanin, and Deir Batabo. [*See* Antioch on Orontes; Apamea.] More than fifty of these monasteries were identified in the surveys of Melchior de Vogüé, Howard C. Butler (1929), Georges Tchalenko (1953–1958), and others. Ten monasteries have been explored in northern Apamene, and still others to the west of Antioch. Ten have been explored in the Hauran and more in the region of Ṭur ʿAbdin. Most monasteries were small, with seven to fifteen monks. Of the fifty-seven cenobia explored by Ignace Peña, P. Castellana, and R. Fernandez (Peña et al., 1983) on Jebel Baricha (northern Syria), thirty-four are small, fifteen medium sized, and only eight are large.

In most regions of Syria monasteries were built of ashlars and, because those communities were deserted by the end of the Byzantine period, the state of preservation of many of them is excellent. Most are known only through an architectural survey; only a few have been excavated. Therefore, information regarding their early stages (fourth–early fifth centuries) is meager, but presumably the earliest structures were humble. The transition from anchoritism to cenobitism passed through the stage of *hîrtâ* (cells arranged irregularly around the cell of the head of the community).

By the first half of the fourth century there were organized monasteries at Osrhoene, Euphrathesia, and Antiochene. Additional centers developed in the second half of the century in the desert of Chalcis, in Cilicia, and in the districts of Apamea, Zeugma, Cyrrhus, and Phoenicia. [*See* Cilicia.] The first known anchorite was Juliana Saba, who lived in the early fourth century in Osrhoene. His disciple, Asterios, had already erected a cenobium. The first anchorite at Antiochene was Ammianos, and his monastery, Teleda (Deir Tell Ade), took the lead in the region. Eusebius, who headed the monastery after 360, promoted monasticism in Antiochene; it was spread from there to Apamene by Agapetus and Symeon, who founded to two monasteries at Nikertai, where the rules of Marcianus, their spiritual father, were implemented.

During the fifth and sixth centuries, the spread of cenobitism was on a large scale: monumental and elaborate communal buildings were arranged efficiently, unlike the unorganized *hîrtâ*. In the larger cenobia, the communal buildings were arranged around a central courtyard and were surrounded by a fence built of unhewn stones. Many cisterns were dug within the enclosure and plots of land were cultivated. Most monasteries were located in the countryside, alongside roads, in agricultural areas, at some distance from villages.

The Antiochene cenobia were comprised of a church; a communal tomb with a burial chapel and underground arcosolia in which the monks were buried according to their monastic rank; a tower used for surveillance or seclusion inside or outside the walls, but nearby; and a monumental communal building of two or three stories that was rectangular, oriented north–south, and surrounded on three or four sides by porticoes of square, plain monolithic pillars supporting an undecorated architrave. There is a debate among scholars about the function of this building (Butler, 1929, Lassus, 1947; Tchalenko, 1953–1958; Peña et al., 1983; Sodini, 1989). It seems that it served as a dormitory for monks and novices, as is recommended by the Justinianic legislation for monks (see above) and by some monastic regulations. Additional use of the ground floor may have included a refectory, house of assembly, infirmary, halls for charitable activities, or workshops. Examples of this type of building, peculiar to monasteries, are preserved at Deir Tell Ade, Deir Turmanin, Deir Simʿan, and Qalʿat Simʿan, as well as at the smaller monasteries of Qaṣr el-Brad and Kimar. The character of the accommodations of the abbot, priest, and other leaders of the community was more private. Those structures may have had more than one story and they lacked porticoes, they were a separate component in the complex.

Early monastic churches in Syria are basilical (e.g., Qaṣr el-Banat, Deir Turmanin, Deir Simʿan [Northwest]), while the late ones are small chapels (Deir Simʿan [Southeast]). The Apamene monastic chapels (e.g., at Dana [South], Btirsa, Shinshara, and el-Breiǧe) are of a transverse type, with a rectilinear sanctuary and a narthex. Those at Ṭur ʿAbdin are of the same type but have an apsidal or triapsidal sanctuary and are roofed with a brick barrel vault rather than with timber (Bell, 1982; Fourdrin, 1985). Monastic churches lack the horseshoe bema, or ambo, located in the central nave in parish churches.

Towers of seclusion and the columns of stylite monks were very common in Antiochea (at Kafr Derian, Kimar, el-Brad), following the habits of the renowned monk Symeon Stylites (d. 459). The monastery built around his column of seclusion between 473 and 491 (Qalʿat Simʿan) became a center of pilgrimage. [*See* Qalʿat Simʿan.] A sacred road led there from Deir Simʿan, and three smaller monasteries and several hostelries for pilgrims were found in that village. The architecture of the Monastery of Symeon Stylites the Younger on Mons Admirabilis, southwest of Antioch, with its cruciform martyrion, is quite similar (Mécérian, 1948, 1965; Lafontaine-Dosogne and Orgels, 1967; Djobadze, 1986). [*See* Martyrion.]

Fifty towers of seclusion were explored on northern Syria's limestone massif (Peña et al., 1975, 1978). The phenomenon of these towers was a late development in Antiochene monasticism (some are dated by inscriptions to the sixth century). The towers are generally spacious hermitages that consist of two, three, and even six stories, each with a single room. The cell on the ground floor was used by the attendant or disciples, while the cell on the upper story served as living quarters for the recluse or as a private chapel. In a two-story hermitage known as the Cell of Gabriel, which was explored in the Abbey of Qartmin near Ṭur ʿAbdin, at the border of the Tigris River, the lower story served as a prayer chapel and the upper one as a living room. A hermit tower of three stories with single rooms is located at a distance of 250 m to the west, outside of the monastery (Palmer, 1990). Each of these towers is generally surrounded by a stone wall enclosing a courtyard and forming a *mandra,* "a fold."

The Apamene monasteries, ten in number, are all located in the northern part of that region; they display a common plan that differs somewhat from those in Antiochea. They appear to have been implemented by a central authority, as a means of disseminating Christianity or Monophysitism. They were isolated from the outside world by a wall and a gate. Except at Frikya, there is no hostel in these monasteries. The collective tomb is located under the church or in a special structure. The absence of traces of cells implies a collective dwelling. In the monasteries of southern Syria, as at ed-Deir, south of Bosra, and in northeast Syria, a symmetrical plan was followed in monasteries. In them, the communal structures were arranged around the atrium of the church, located to its east.

[*See also* Churches.]

BIBLIOGRAPHY

Egypt

Bachatly, Charles. *Le monastère de Phoebamon dans la Thébaïde.* Cairo, 1961–1981.

Bridel, Philippe. *Le site monastique copte des Kellia: Sources historiques et explorations archéologiques.* Actes du Colloque de Genève, 13–15 août 1984. Geneva, 1986.

Chitty, Derwas. *The Desert a City: An Introduction to the Study of Egyptian and Palestinian Monasticism under the Christian Empire.* Oxford, 1966. Includes an extensive bibliography.

Clédat, Jean. *Le monastère et la nécropole de Baouit.* 2 vols. Memoirs de l'Institut Français d'Archéologie Orientale du Caire, vols. 12, 39. Cairo, 1904–1916.

Daumas, François, and Antoine Guillaumont. *Kellia 1, Kôm 219: Fouilles exécutées en 1964 et 1965.* 2 vols. Fouilles de l'Institut Français d'Archéologie Orientale, vol. 28. Cairo, 1969.

Descoeudres, George. "L'architecture des Kellia." *Le Monde Copte* 14/15 (1958): 75–96.

Doresse, Jean. "Monastères coptes aux environs d'Armant en Thébaid." *Analecta Bollandiana* 67 (1949): 327–349, pls. 4–5.

Doresse, Jean. "Nouvelles études sur l'art copte: Les monastères de Saint-Antoine et de Saint-Paul." *Comptes Rendus de l'Académie des Inscriptions et Belles-Lettres* (1951): 268–274.

Doresse, Jean. "Recherches d'archéologie copte: Les monastères de moyenne-Égypte." *Comptes Rendus de l'Académie des Inscriptions et Belles-Lettres* (1952): 390–395.

Evelyn-White, Hugh G. *The Monasteries of the Wâdi 'n Natrûn,* part 2, *The History of the Monasteries of Nitria and Scetis;* part 3, *The Architecture and Archaeology.* New York, 1932–1933.

Fakhry, Ahmed. "The Monastery of Kalamoun." *Annales du Service des Antiquités de l'Égypte* 46 (1947): 63–83.

Godlewski, Włodzimierz. *Le monastère de St. Phoibammon,* translated by Szolt Kiss. Warsaw, 1986.

Grossmann, Peter, and Hans-Georg Severin. "Reinigungsarbeiten im Jeremiaskloster bei Saqqāra: Vierter Vorlaufiger Bericht." *Mitteilungen des Deutschen Archäologischen Instituts, Abteilung Kairo* 38 (1982): 155–193.

Grossmann, Peter. *Abu Mina: A Guide to the Ancient Pilgrimage Center.* Cairo, 1986.

Grossmann, Peter. "Ruinen des klosters Dair al-Balaizā in Oberägypten: Eine Surveyaufnahme." *Jahrbuch für Antike und Christentum* 36 (1993): 171–205.

Husson, Geneviève. "L'habitat monastique en Égypte à la lumière des papyrus grecs, des textes chrétiens et de l'archéologie." In *Hommages à la mémoire de Serge Sauneron,* vol. 2, edited by Jean Vercoutter, pp. 191–207. Cairo, 1979.

Kasser, Rodolphe. *Kellia 1965: Topographie générale.* Recherches Suisses d'Archéologie Copte, vol. 1. Geneva, 1967.

Kasser, Rodolphe. *Kellia: Topographie.* Recherches Suisses d'Archéologie Copte, vol. 2. Geneva, 1972.

Kasser, Rodolphe. "Aux origines du monachisme copte: Fouilles de l'Université de Genève aux Kellia (Basse-Égypte)." *Bulletin de la Société d'Égyptologie, Genève* 3 (1980): 33–38.

Kasser, Rodolphe. *Survey archéologique des Kellia (Basse-Égypte): Rapport de la campagne 1981.* 2 vols. Louvain, 1983.

Kasser, Rodolphe. *Le site monastique des Kellia (Basse-Égypte), Recherches des années 1981–1983.* Louvain, 1984.

Martin, Maurice. "Laures et ermitages du désert d'Égypte." *Mélanges de l'Université Saint-Joseph de Beyrouth* 42 (1966): 181–198.

Martin, Maurice. *La laure de Dêr al Dik à Antinoe.* Cairo, 1971.

Meinardus, Otto F. A. *Monks and Monasteries of the Egyptian Deserts.* Rev. ed. Cairo, 1989.

Monneret de Villard, Ugo. *Les couvents près de Sohâg (Deyr el-Abiad, et Deyr el-Ahmar).* 2 vols. Milan, 1925–1926.

Monneret de Villard, Ugo. *Description générale du monastère de Snt. Siméon à Aswan.* Milan, 1927.

Monneret de Villard, Ugo. *Deyr el-Muharraqah.* Milan, 1928.

Quibell, James R. *The Monastery of Apa Jeremias.* Cairo, 1912.

Sauneron, Serge, and Jean Jacquet. *Les ermitages chrétiens du désert d'Esna.* 4 vols. Cairo, 1972.

Walters, Colin. *Monastic Archaeology in Egypt.* Warminster, 1974.

Winlock, Herbert E., and Walter E. Crum. *The Monastery of Epiphanius at Thebes.* Vol. 1. New York, 1926.

Palestine

Bagatti, Bellarmino. *The Church from the Gentiles in Palestine.* Translated by Eugene Hoade. Jerusalem, 1971. See chapter 11, "The Monasteries."

Bottini, Giovanni Claudio, et al., eds. *Christian Archaeology in the Holy Land, New Discoveries: Essays in Honour of Virgilio C. Corbo.* Jerusalem, 1990. See the essays by Haim Goldfus (pp. 227–244), Yizhar Hirschfeld (pp. 1–90), Yitzhak Magen and Rina Talgam (pp. 91–152), and Joseph Patrich (pp. 205–226).
Corbo, Virgilio. *Gli scavi di Khirbet Siyar el-Ghanam (Campo dei Pastori) e i monasteri dei dintorni.* Jerusalem, 1955.
Corbo, Virgilio. "L'ambiente materiale della vita dei monaci di Palestina nel periodo bizantino." In *Il monachesimo orientale: Atti del convegno di studi orientali, Roma, 9–12 aprile 1958,* pp. 235–257. Orientalia Christiana Analecta, 153. Rome, 1958.
Fitzgerald, Gerald M. *A Sixth-Century Monastery at Beth-Shan (Scythopolis).* Philadelphia, 1939.
Hirschfeld, Yizhar. *The Judean Desert Monasteries in the Byzantine Period.* New Haven, 1992. Includes an extensive bibliography.
Meimaris, Yiannis E. "The Hermitage of St. John the Chozebite, Deir Wady el-Qilt." *Studium Biblicum Franciscanum/Liber Annuus* 28 (1978): 171–192.
Meinardus, Otto F. A. "Notes on the Laurae and Monasteries of the Wilderness of Judaea." *Studium Biblicum Franciscanum/Liber Annuus* 15 (1964–1965): 220–250; 16 (1965–1966): 328–356; 19 (1969): 305–327.
Patrich, Joseph. "The Sabaite Laura of Jeremias in the Judean Desert." *Studium Biblicum Franciscanum/Liber Annuus* 40 (1990): 295–311, pls. 37–40.
Patrich, Joseph. "The Sabaite Monastery of the Cave (Spelaion) in the Judean Desert." *Studium Biblicum Franciscanum/Liber Annuus* 41 (1991): 429–448.
Patrich, Joseph. *Sabas, Leader of Palestinian Monasticism: A Comparative Study in Eastern Monasticism, Fourth to Seventh Centuries.* Dumbarton Oaks Studies, 32. Washington, D.C., 1995. Includes an extensive bibliography.
Piccirillo, Michele. *Mount Nebo.* 2d ed. Jerusalem, 1990.
Saller, Sylvester J. *The Memorial of Moses on Mount Nebo.* 2 vols. Jerusalem, 1941.
Tsafrir, Yoram, ed. *Ancient Churches Revealed.* Jerusalem, 1993. See the essays by Yizhar Hirschfeld (pp. 149–154), Yitzhak Magen (pp. 170–196), and Joseph Patrich (pp. 233–243).

Syria

Bell, Gertrude Lowthian. *The Churches and Monasteries of the Tūr ʿAbdīn.* Edited by Marlia M. Mango. London, 1982.
Butler, Howard Crosby. *Early Churches in Syria, Fourth to Seventh Centuries.* Princeton, 1929. See chapter 4, "The Monasteries."
Canivet, Pierre. "Contributions archéologiques à l'histoire des moines de Syrie, IVe–Ve siècle." *Studia Patristica* 13 (1975): 444–460.
Deichmann, F. W. *Qalb Löze und Qalʿat Semʿan.* Munich, 1982.
Djobadze, Wachtang. *Archeological Investigations in the Region West of Antioch-on-the-Orontes.* Stuttgart, 1986.
Fourdrin, Jean P. "Les églises à nef transversal d'Âpaméne et du Tur Abdin." *Syria* 62 (1985): 319–335.
Lafontaine-Dosogne, Jacqueline, and Bernard Orgels. *Itinéraires archéologiques dans la région d'Antioch: Recherches sur le monastère et sur l'iconographie de S. Syméon Stylite le Jeune.* Brussels, 1967.
Lassus, Jean. *Sanctuaires chrétiens de Syrie.* Paris, 1947. See "La vie monastique et la culte des ascètes."
Mécérian, Jean. "Monastère de Saint-Syméon-Stylite-le-Jeune, exposé des fouilles." *Comptes Rendus de l'Académie des Inscriptions et Belles-Lettres* (1948): 323–328.
Mécérian, Jean. *Expédition archéologique dans l'Antiochène occidentale.* Beirut, 1965.
Palmer, Andrew. *Monk and Mason on the Tigris Frontier: The Early History of Tur Abdin.* Cambridge, 1990. Includes an extensive bibliography.
Peña, Ignace, et al. *Les stylites Syriens.* Jerusalem, 1975.
Peña, Ignace, et al. *Les reclus Syriens.* Jerusalem, 1978.
Peña, Ignace, et al. *Les cenobites Syriens.* Jerusalem, 1983.
Restle, Marcell. "Les monuments chrétiens de la Syrie du Sud." In *Archéologie et histoire de la Syria,* vol. 2, edited by Jean-Marie Dentzer and Winfried Orthmann, p. 381. Saarbrücken, 1989.
Sodini, Jean-Pierre. "Les églises de Syrie du Nord." In *Archéologie et histoire de la Syria,* vol. 2, edited by Jean-Marie Dentzer and Winfried Orthmann, pp. 367–371. Saarbrücken, 1989.
Tchalenko, Georges. *Villages antiques de la Syrie du Nord: Le massif du Bélus à l'époque romaine.* 3 vols. Paris, 1953–1958.
Vööbus, Arthur. *History of Asceticism in the Syrian Orient.* 2 vols. Corpus Scriptorum Christianorum Orientalium, vols. 184, 196. Louvain, 1958–1960.

Sinai

Dahari, Uzi. *Monasteries of Southern Sinai: Archaeological Remnants.* ʿAtiqot, in press.
Finkelstein, Israel. "Byzantine Monastic Remains in the Southern Sinai." *Dumbarton Oaks Papers* 39 (1985): 39–75.
Forsyth, George H., and Kurt Weitzmann. *The Monastery of St. Catherine at Mount Sinai: The Church and Fortress of Justinian.* Ann Arbor, Mich., 1973.
Grossmann, Peter. "Neue baugeschichtliche Untersuchungen im Katharinenkloster im Sinai." *Jahrbuch des Deutschen Archäologischen Instuts. Archäologischer Anzeiger* (1988): 543–558.
Tsafrir, Yoram, ed. *Ancient Churches Revealed.* Jerusalem, 1993. See essays by Uzi Dahari (pp. 341–350), Israel Finkelstein (pp. 334–340), and Yoram Tsafrir (pp. 315–333).

Turkey (Asia Minor)

Gough, Michael. *Alahan: An Early Christian Monastery in Southern Turkey.* Toronto, 1985.
Janin, Raymond. *Les églises et les monastères: Le siege de Constantinople et le patriarcat oecumenique.* 2d ed. Paris, 1969.
Janin, Raymond. *Les églises et les monastères des grands centres byzantins: Bithynie, Hellespont, Latros, Galèsios, Trébizonde, Athenes, Thessalonique.* Paris, 1975.
Rodley, Lyn. *Cave Monasteries of Byzantine Cappadocia.* Cambridge, 1985.
Thiery, Nicole. "Monastères et ermitages en Cappadoce." *Le Monde de la Bible* 70 (1991): 20–26.

JOSEPH PATRICH

MONTET, PIERRE (1885–1966), Egyptologist and archaeologist, born at Villefranche-sur-Saône in 1885. Montet studied Egyptology under Victor Loret at Lyon University. In 1910 he was appointed *pensionnaire* ("fellow") at the French Archaeological Institute in Cairo, where he published, with J. Couyat, *Les inscriptions hiéroglyphiques et hiératiques du Ouâdi Hammâmât.* He was drafted in 1914, and earned medals for distinction during the war. In 1919 he was appointed lecturer and then professor at Strasbourg University. In 1920 Montet excavated Jbail (Phoenician Gebal; Greek Byblos; Crusader Giblet) in Lebanon. He uncovered several royal tombs contemporary with Egypt's Middle Kingdom, along with artifacts that provided evidence for repeated contacts between Byblos and pharaonic Egypt as early as the Old Kingdom. Also found at Byblos was the sarcophagus of Ahiram, which bears the earliest known Phoenician alphabetic inscription. [*See* Ahiram Inscription.]

Montet's work at Byblos between 1920 and 1924 was published in *Byblos et l'Égypte* (1929). He earned his doctorate in 1925 with the thesis "Les scènes de la vie privée dans les tombeaux égyptiens de l'ancien empire." From 1928 onward, he focused on Tanis in Lower Egypt, publishing several monographs. Additional observations on contacts between Egypt and the Levant appear in his 1937 work *Les reliques de l'art syrien dans l'Égypte du nouvel empire.* In 1948 Montet became professor of Egyptology at the Collège de France and in 1953 was appointed a member of the Académie Française des Inscriptions et Belles-Lettres. His two volumes on the *Géographie de l'Égypte ancienne* (1957–1961) serve to summarize his extensive scholarship on ancient Egypt. Pierre Montet bequeathed his Egyptian collection to Strasbourg University, whose Institut d'Égyptologie is named for him.

[*See also* Byblos.]

BIBLIOGRAPHY

Montet, Pierre, and J. Couyat. *Les inscriptions hiéroglyphiques et hiératiques du Ouâdi Hammâmât.* Cairo, 1912.

Montet, Pierre. *Byblos et l'Égypte: Quatre campagnes de fouilles à Gebeil 1921–1924.* Paris, 1929.

Montet, Pierre. *Les nouvelles fouilles de Tanis, 1929–1932.* Paris, 1933.

Montet, Pierre. *Les reliques de l'art syrien dans l'Égypte du nouvel empire.* Paris, 1937.

Montet, Pierre. *Le drame d'Avaris: Essai sur la pénétration des Sémites en Égypte.* Paris, 1941.

Montet, Pierre. *Tanis, douze années de fouilles dans une capitale oubliée du Delta égyptien.* Paris, 1942.

Montet, Pierre. *La Nécropole royale de Tanis.* 3 vols. Paris, 1947–1960.

Montet, Pierre. *Les énigmes de Tanis.* Paris, 1952.

Montet, Pierre. *Géographie de l'Égypte ancienne.* 2 vols. Paris, 1957–1961.

Vandier, Jacques. "Pierre Montet, 1885–1966." *Syria* 43 (1966): 335–338.

HAFEZ K. CHEHAB

MONTGOMERY, JAMES ALAN (1866–1949),

one of the central figures in the early development of the American Schools of Oriental Research (ASOR). Montgomery was the director of the Jerusalem school (1914–1915), chairman of ASOR's board of trustees (1918–1921), and its first president (1921–1934). He was also the first editor of the *Bulletin of the American Schools of Oriental Research (BASOR),* a position he held from 1919 to 1930.

By education and training Montgomery was a biblical scholar and an Orientalist. He held undergraduate (1887) and graduate degrees from the University of Pennsylvania (completing his Ph.D. in 1904). He received his theological training at the Philadelphia Divinity School, graduating in 1890, and subsequently studied at the Universities of Griefswald and Berlin (1890–1892). Montgomery taught Old Testament literature at the Philadelphia Divinity School (1899–1935) and Hebrew and Aramaic at the University of Pennsylvania (1910–1938). During the time he was elected president of the Society of Biblical Literature (in 1918) and the American Oriental Society (1926–1927). He edited each society's journals for extended periods: the *Journal of Biblical Literature* (1909–1913) and the *Journal of the American Oriental Society* (1916–1921, 1924).

Montgomery wrote widely on Semitic philology, Israelite religion, archaeology, Jewish-Christian relations, the history of Israel, Ugaritic, Ethiopic, South Arabian inscriptions, the Hebrew Bible, and the New Testament. He wrote nine full-length books, more than 126 scholarly articles, twenty articles for religious publications, and more than forty-five book reviews. His two contributions to the International Critical Commentary series (on *Daniel* and *Kings*) remain classics, demonstrating his command of Semitic linguistics, textual criticism, and literary genres. Montgomery advanced the study of Biblical and Classical Aramaic significantly. He advocated widespread use of the Aramaic Elephantine texts and various Aramaic inscriptional materials in biblical scholarship. His *Aramaic Incantation Texts from Nippur* (Philadelphia, 1913) is still widely used as the introductory work on these texts. The *Ras Shamra Mythological Texts,* written with Zellig S. Harris (Philadelphia, 1935), represents an early attempt to make use of Ugaritic texts to broaden the understanding of biblical and Canaanite religion.

Montgomery was, however, interested in more than linguistics, literature, and religion. His scholarly breadth allowed him to examine the historical, geographic, and socioeconomic settings of the entire ancient Near East. Two of his works explored these issues. *The Samaritans: The Earliest Jewish Sect* (Philadelphia, 1907) traces the history of Samaritan culture from its origin to the early twentieth century. *Arabia and the Bible* (Philadelphia, 1934), despite some revisions necessitated by recent discoveries (see Van Beek, 1969) remains a sound introduction to the history, geography, and religious and ethic backgrounds of the Arabian Peninsula.

Montgomery became emeritus professor at the University of Pennsylvania and the Philadelphia Divinity School in 1938. His commentary on *Kings,* edited by his student Henry S. Gehman, was published posthumously in 1951.

[*See also* American Oriental Society; American Schools of Oriental Research; Society of Biblical Literature.]

BIBLIOGRAPHY

Gordon, Cyrus H. "A Scholar and Gentlemen: James Alan Montgomery." *Biblical Archaeologist* 46 (1983): 187–189. Brief article providing insight into the personal life of Montgomery as remembered by one of his most prominent students.

King, Philip J. *American Archaeology in the Mideast: A History of the American Schools of Oriental Research.* Philadelphia, 1983. Besides being the standard book on the history of ASOR and its major figures, this work contains valuable information on other related research organizations.

Montgomery, James A. *The Samaritans: The Earliest Jewish Sect.* Philadelphia, 1907.
Montgomery, James A.. *Aramaic Incantation Texts from Nippur.* Philadelphia, 1913.
Montgomery, James A.. *Arabia and the Bible.* Philadelphia, 1934.
Montgomery, James A., and Z. S. Harris. *Ras Shamra Mythological Texts.* Philadelphia, 1935.
Speiser, Ephraim Avigdor. "Bibliography of James Alan Montgomery." *Bulletin of the American Schools of Oriental Research,* no. 117 (1950): 8–13. Complete list of Montgomery's books, articles, and reviews.
Van Beek, Gus W. "Prolegomenon" to reprinted edition of James A. Montgomery, *Arabia and the Bible.* New York, 1969. Critical introduction analyzing and updating Montgomery's book.

CHARLES E. CARTER

MOORTGAT, ANTON (1897–1977), a founder of Near Eastern archaeology as an academic discipline, along with Ernst Herzfeld and Henri Frankfort. The field comprises the investigation of material remains in Asia Minor, Syria, the Arabian Peninsula, Mesopotamia, and Iran from the Neolithic period to the time of Alexander the Great.

Moortgat left his native city of Antwerp, Belgium, for Germany, where he earned his doctorate in classical archaeology at Berlin University in 1923. Following a period of activity at the German Archaeological Institute in Rome, he worked under Walter Andrae in the Near Eastern division of the Berlin museums (1930–1945). As custodian, he held an honorary professorship at the Archaeological Institute of Berlin University in 1941. After World War II, Moortgat accepted the chair of ancient Near Eastern studies at the newly founded Free University of West Berlin (1948), a post he held until his retirement in 1965. Moortgat's chief accomplishment proved to be the working out of a chronologically reliable sequence of styles in the southern Mesopotamian corpus of artistic monuments; at the same time, he investigated artistic activity in this core area's peripheral provinces, with respect to their mutual dependency upon Mesopotamia. It was this schema of cultural groups and his generally reliable system of time periods in the central area that first provided the indispensable prerequisite for further meaningful work in Near Eastern archaeology. Moortgat published his foundational work primarily in *Frühe Bildkunst in Sumer* (Early Imagery in Sumer, 1935); *Vorderasiatische Rollsiegel* (Near Eastern Cylinder Seals, 1940); two articles on Assyrian glyptics (1942, 1944); and *Die Entstehung der sumerischen Hochkultur* (The Development of Sumerian High Culture, 1945).

Because Moortgat based his work on the assumption of ethnically determined artistic regions, he neglected the determining effects of the state on artistic production and ethnological development. Therefore, some of his numerous students rejected aspects of his work and modified and developed his chronological system. Handbooks of art history based on Moortgat's pioneering work are still used as basic texts; examples include Eva Strommenger's *5000 Years of the Art of Mesopotamia* (London, 1964), Barthel Hrouda's *Vorderasien* (Handbuch der Archäologie, vol. 1, Munich, 1971), Winfried Orthmann's *Der alte Orient* (Propyläen Kunstgeschichte, vol. 14, Berlin, 1975), Wolfram Nagel's *Bauern und Stadtkulturen im vordynastischen Vorderasien* (Berlin, 1964), Rainer Boehmer's *Glyptik der Akkad-Zeit* (Berlin, 1965), Peter Calmeyer's *Bronzen aus Luristan* (Berlin, 1969), Ursula Seidl's *Bablyonische Kudurru-Reliefs* (Berlin, 1968), and Jutta Börker-Klähn's *Altvorderasiatische Bildstelen* (Berlin, 1982).

[*See also the biography of Frankfort.*]

BIBLIOGRAPHY

Bittel, Kurt, ed. *Vorderasiatische Archäologie: Studien und Aufsätze Anton Moortgat zum fünfundsechzigsten Geburtstag gewidmet.* Berlin, 1964. Includes a bibliography of Moortgat's work (pp. 12–17).
Moortgat, Anton. *Frühe Bildkunst in Sumer.* Leipzig, 1935.
Moortgat, Anton. *Vorderasiatische Rollsiegel.* Berlin, 1940.
Moortgat, Anton. "Assyrische Glyptik des 13. Jahrhunderts." *Zeitschrift für Assyriologie* 47 (1942): 50–88.
Moortgat, Anton. "Assyrische Glyptik des 12. Jahrhunderts." *Zeitschrift für Assyriologie* 48 (1944): 23–44.
Moortgat, Anton. *Die Entstehung der sumerischen Hochkultur.* Leipzig, 1945.

WOLFRAM NAGEL
Translated from German by Susan I. Schiedel

MOR, TEL (Ar., Tell Mura), a small mound about 1.5 acres in area near the mouth of the Naḥal Lachish, about 2 km (.5 mi.) from the Mediterranean coast in Israel (map reference 1175 × 1368). The site may be ancient Ashdod-Yam, "Ashdod of the Sea." It served as the port of nearby Ashdod in the Bronze and Iron Ages. Tel Mor was excavated in 1959–1960 by Moshe Dothan on behalf of the Israel Department of Antiquities.

Twelve strata were distinguished, extending from the late Middle Bronze Age through the Hellenistic period. The MB remains were scant but included Cypriot and Egyptian imports, as well as local cultic vessels. The Late Bronze Age levels (strata 11–7) indicated a flourishing seaport, especially during the fourteenth century BCE (stratum 9), when a large fortress/storehouse demonstrates that Tel Mor was an important site on the Via Maris. This settlement was destroyed in about 1300 BCE, perhaps during the campaigns of Seti I in Canaan.

The strata 8–7 resettlement, dating mainly to the thirteenth century BCE, saw the construction of another large multiroomed fortress with a courtyard, built on an Egyptian plan. Substantial amounts of Egyptian, Mycenaean, and Cypriot pottery were found in this fortress, which may have been destroyed by fire in the time of Rameses II, or in his son Merneptah's raid in about 1207 BCE. A small tower or fort *(migdal)* in strata 6–5, on the ruins of the fortress, belongs to the late thirteenth–early twelfth centuries BCE. The pottery is transitional LB/Iron I, including local imitations of Cypriot styles. Some Egyptian pottery and scarabs suggest that here, as elsewhere in Canaan, an Egyptian governor was in residence as late as the period of Rameses III.

Strata 4–3 represent the post-Egyptian era, when Philistine material culture dominates, as at other coastal sites. Tel Mor was destroyed again at the end of stratum 3, perhaps in the wars of David against the Philistines. The small resettlement of stratum 2 belongs to the eighth century BCE, with some remains of a casemate-walled fortress. It may have been destroyed by the Neo-Assyrian king Sargon II, who, in the Assyrian annals, is said to have taken Ashdod-Yam and turned the entire territory of Ashdod into an Assyrian province. Following a long abandonment and the transfer of Ashdod's port to a site known later as Hellenistic Azotos (Minet Isdud), only a large public building and a dye-extraction facility were constructed on Tel Mor (stratum 1).

[*See also* Ashdod; Philistines, *article on* Early Philistines.]

BIBLIOGRAPHY

Dothan, Moshe. "Tel Mor (Tell Kheidar)." *Israel Exploration Journal* 9 (1959): 271–272; 10 (1960): 123–125.

Dothan, Moshe. "The Foundation of Tel Mor and Ashdod." *Israel Exploration Journal* 23 (1973): 1–17.

WILLIAM G. DEVER

MOSAICS. In antiquity polychrome mosaic pavements were a conspicuous feature of interior decoration in public and domestic buildings. They survive in great abundance where corresponding wall and ceiling decoration has largely vanished. The earliest floor mosaics were made of small, smooth pebbles, but these were soon replaced by tesserae (small, evenly cut cubes of stone). There are two types of tesserae, each used to achieve different effects: *opus tessellatum* consists of square, or nearly square, stones set in rows and *opus vermiculatum* ("worm-shaped work") are very small tesserae cut in irregular shapes and laid in patterns dictated by a pavement's design. *Opus tessellatum* was used to execute geometric patterns or figures, whereas *opus vermiculatum* was usually reserved for fine details. Tesserae (of local limestone; marble and glass for highlights) were available in a wide range of colors, and several shades of a single color were often used to achieve subtle modeling effects. In Roman mosaic decoration, the average number of colors in the mosaicist's palette was thirty; in Byzantine mosaics the average palette consisted of from ten to twelve colors. Mosaic floors are typically laid on a three-layer foundation consisting of the *rudus* (a bed of packed earth or debris with large stones); the nucleus (several centimeters of mortar made of lime and ash or pottery dust and chips); and the setting bed (a layer of 2–4 cm of limestone plaster into which the tesserae are set).

Although ancient authors (e.g., Vitruvius) mention mosaic pavements, there are no extant texts that describe the making of a mosaic. The process must have involved several specialized craftsmen to prepare the setting bed, to cut the tesserae, and to design and execute the figures. Piles of precut tesserae, sorted according to color, along with the waste stones from which they were cut, have been found at some sites, indicating a degree of industrialization. While even the most complicated geometric patterns could have been executed merely with string and compass, the repetition of nearly identical figural compositions over several centuries and in widely separated geographic areas indicates that some sort of model "books" were used.

Early Pebble Mosaics. The first differentiated floor designs were pebble mosaics. Although some scholars have placed the invention of this technique in the Near East, the most recent studies suggest that pebble mosaics originated in Greece, where they existed as early as the Late Bronze Age. At Gordion, in Asia Minor, three buildings were discovered with multicolored pebble floors that are dated to the eighth century BCE. These Phrygian pavements are composed of scattered geometric motifs with no overall order.

Hellenistic Mosaics. In the Hellenistic period, pebble mosaics were elaborate and representational, often featuring mythological characters (the Scylla mosaic from Nea-Paphos on Cyprus). Floors that incorporate both pebbles and tesserae illustrate the transitional phase in the development of tessellated mosaics (from Alexandria, Egypt: a warrior surrounded by a frieze of griffins; a Hunt with erotes attacking a stag [both now in the Greco-Roman Museum in Alexandria]). As mosaic compositions became more pictorial and dependent on paintings for models, the cutting of the tesserae became more refined. These changes can be charted in the *emblemata,* or portable tray, compositions executed in *opus vermiculatum.* Two very similar mosaics from Thmuis (Tell Timai), with female busts that represent either the city of Alexandria or a Ptolemaic queen (Berenike II?) are striking examples of this technique; their superb execution attests to the virtuosity of the Alexandrian workshops, which some scholars believe specialized in the production of *emblemata.* Close parallels between Alexandrian works and those found in the House of the Faun at Pompeii suggest the influence of Alexandrian artists abroad.

Mesopotamian Mosaics. The art of mosaics was never popular in Mesopotamia. Although the Standard of Ur (in the British Museum) is sometimes described as executed in the mosaic technique, it is not; it is executed with inlay of shell, lapis lazuli, and red limestone. Only four sites with pavements executed in *opus tessellatum* are known from the region, and all date to the third century CE. A personification of the Euphrates River between personifications of Syria and Mesopotamia found at Mas'Udiye has inscriptions in Greek and Syriac that give the name of the artists and the date 539 of the era of the Seleucids (227–228 CE). A well-known mosaic of late Severan date, with the personified provinces, was excavated at Zeugma (Belqis). Better known than either of these are the funerary mosaics at Edessa and the mosaics in the Palace of Shapur I, erected in 260 CE, after his victory over Valerian. In the palace mosaics, geometric panels alternate with figural scenes of dancers, courtesans, musicians, and portraits.

Roman Mosaics. The earliest tessellated mosaics from the Near East follow the compositions of the pebble mosaics of the Hellenistic period (e.g., at Delos and Alexandria)—namely, multiple bands framing a central *emblema* that was usually filled with a geometric design (at Arsamea in ancient Commagene in Turkey). Similar pavements with central designs were found in Israel, on Masada in the Judean Desert and in the Herodian quarter of Jerusalem. They are securely dated to before 70 CE, the year Titus destroyed Jerusalem.

The majority of mosaics from the imperial period are from the private sphere of the Roman house. These are best represented by the extensive series of floors excavated at Antioch in Syria. The taste for illusionistic picture panels arranged within a single composition can be seen in the earliest houses of the first century CE, those constructed before the earthquake of 115 (e.g., the triclinium mosaic in the Atrium House, with its Judgment of Paris, Drinking Contest, and Adonis and Aphrodite). Aside from a rich selection of mythological scenes, apotropaic symbols are introduced at the entrances to rooms and houses (the evil eye or ithyphallic dwarfs). Representations of the months and seasons (House of the Calendar) and personifications of rivers (House of the Porticoes) and provinces (House of Cilicia) also reflect the expansion of the repertoire of mosaic images beyond the narrative models of Greco-Roman painting. Episodes drawn from literary (Greek novels in the House of the Man of Letters, now in the Princeton Museum and the Worcester Art Museum) and theatrical (House of the Red Pavement; House of Iphigenia, now in the Antakya Museum) sources reveal the cultural milieu of Roman cities in the eastern Mediterranean. Sometimes the themes reflect the function of the particular room they decorate—for example, an elaborate table setting replete with foods frames a central medallion with Ganymede serving the Eagle in the apsed triclinium of the House of the Buffet Supper.

This fashion for allegorical and mythological compositions is demonstrated throughout the eastern Mediterranean in the second and third centuries CE. Where entire houses have been excavated, as in the case of the House of Dionysos at Nea-Paphos, there is evidence for reading the selection and placement of certain themes as programmatic. Dionysiac themes (Vintage and Triumph) are typically set into reception rooms or near them (Dionysos's Gift of Wine to Ikarios), while salutatory motifs such as the frontal peacock or Four Seasons are found at or near the house entrance. Often, several themes are incorporated into one grand design, as is the case with the mosaic, reconstructed from numerous fragments, originally found in Gerasa/Jerash (Transjordan): several Dionysiac friezes are stacked vertically and framed by a garland border accented by busts of the Seasons, Muses, and Authors (Homer and Thucydides are extant), each identified by a Greek inscription. The combination of themes in this mosaic, dated on stylistic grounds to the mid-second century CE, may be intentional: they evoke the processions and cult festivals associated with the theatrical guilds of Dionysiac artists. (Most of the mosaic is in the Staatliche Museum in Berlin.)

An equally grand and unusual floor with Dionysiac scenes was produced in the first half of the third century CE for the triclinium of a house in the theater district at Sepphoris in the Galilee. The central composition consists of fifteen panels, each labeled with a Greek inscription, that depict aspects of Dionysiac mythology and ritual. The whole is enclosed by a frame of lush acanthus foliage inhabited by animals and hunters; the bar of the T-shaped mosaic contains a continuous procession of Dionysiac cult followers bearing various gifts and offerings.

Throughout the Near East there was a pronounced taste for mosaic compositions steeped in classical learning. The didactic nature of such displays is emphasized by the popularity of Greek labels. Busts of the Seven Sages (accompanied by their maxims and titles in Greek) and Socrates surround Calliope in a mosaic of Severan date from Baalbek/Suweida in Lebanon. Mythological scenes are also accompanied by inscriptions, and their selection often reflects local lore and interests (the Beauty Contest between Cassiopeia and the Nereids found at Apamea, Palmyra, and Nea-Paphos). The display of philosophical notions of time (*Chronos,* "time"; and *Aion,* "the ages") and the representation of nature by personifications (*Ge,* "earth"; *Georgia,* "agriculture"; and *Tropai,* "turning points of the seasons") are masterfully set out in a mosaic produced in the second half of the third century CE in the city of Shahba/Philippopolis in southern Syria. The discovery of many mythological and allegorical mosaics in Shahba/Philippopolis indicates that a workshop was active there from the second half of the third century through the first half of the fourth.

Late Roman Mosaics. Hellenism continued as a significant force in the cultural life of the Near East through the Late Antique period, as evidenced by the influence of Neoplatonism, especially in Syria. Several of the mosaics found at Apamea, an important Greek city, bear eloquent testimony to the continuation of pagan beliefs and myths. A group of pavements (most are in the Apamea Museum), dated to the reign of Julian the Apostate (360–363 CE), were found in a single building near the Cathedral of Apamea. Among them is a remarkable scene of Socrates seated among the Seven Sages (as well as the Return of Ulysses, with the "Servants" labeled, and the Judgment of the Nereids). The very ambiguity in the scholarly interpretations

MOSAICS. Figure 1. *Mosaic from Shavei-Zion.* (Courtesy Lucille A. Roussin)

of Socrates as a Christlike teacher or a pagan emperor-type implies the degree to which both paganism and Christianity drew inspiration from Platonism. The interpretation of the recondite myths and personifications set out in six elaborate panels in a room from the House of Aion at Nea-Paphos suggests a pagan response to the rise of Christianity. Securely dated to the second quarter of the fourth century, these mosaics include the Childhood and Triumph of Dionysos who, it would appear, is presented as a universal savior. In the adjacent Governor's Palace (House of Theseus), renovations in the fifth century included a grand mosaic with the Birth, First Bath, and Education of Achilles. Scenes from the Life of Achilles are featured on a mosaic from Nablus in Israel, dated to the third/fourth century. The iconography demonstrates the widespread popularity of the myth cycles and the common repertoire of the Near East. Original compositions are rare, but there is an exceptional case from Mariamin (in the Hama Museum in Syria), where the mosaic features a concert with six female musicians, seemingly a record of an actual event.

In the course of the fourth century, figural compositions begin to shift away from pictures in stone to be viewed from a single vantage point to pavements composed of several scenes or single scenes broken up into multiple parts. This change is illustrated by the triclinium pavement in the Constantinian Villa at Antioch (now in the Louvre), where the entire field is divided into a series of irregular panels: sacrifice and hunt scenes fill trapezoidal panels with full-length female Seasons set in the diagonals between them.

Early Christian Mosaics. Although the promulgation of the Edict of Toleration by Constantine in 312/13 CE meant that Christians were free to construct houses of worship, it is not until the third quarter of the fourth century that church building and decoration appear on a large scale in the eastern provinces. The most prolific center for mosaic production was Syria, where the "rainbow style" emerged in the second half of the fourth century. This new style is characterized by complex geometric designs executed in multicolored bands that can be extended in all directions (e.g., the Kaoussié Church in Antioch; the church in Zahrani, Lebanon; and the basilica in Salamis/Constantia, Cyprus). Such designs suited the need for aniconic decoration necessitated by the prohibition against images contained in the Second Commandment.

The increase in mosaic production throughout the Near East in the fifth century is a sign of the region's general prosperity and political stability. Mosaic workshops in Turkey, Syria, and Cyprus continued to flourish, and mosaic production in Lebanon and Palestine increased, especially in the first half of the fifth century. At this time church pavements are decorated with the cross and Christogram (in ancient Palestine at Nahariya, Shavei-Zion (see figure 1), and ʿEvron; on Cyprus there is a mosaic representation of a jeweled cross set into the pavement in the church at Tremithus). The practice continues into the late sixth century, despite the prohibition in the edict of Theodosius II in 427 CE. The crosses and Christograms in these pavements usually mark entrances, altars, and places of special veneration within the churches and may have served an apotropaic function. Specifically religious themes are found in a group of pavements from Cilicia (at Ayas, Karlik, and Korykos) in which the iconography of the Peaceful Kingdom (*Is.* 65:25) is illustrated. This theme continues in popularity in the sixth century in the mosaics from the Madaba region (Baptistery of the Cathedral; Churches of Sts. Lot and Procopius; and the Memorial of Moses on Mt. Nebo). At the same time, the natural world is also brought into the sacred space through the insertion of a great variety of plant and animal motifs into the geometric patterns (in ancient Palestine at the Church of the Nativity, Bethlehem; in Syria at Dibsi Faraj and Khirbet Mouqa; and on Cyprus at Soloi and at the Kourion Baptistery and Basilica).

The most significant development of the latter half of the fifth century is the reintroduction of large-scale animal and

MOSAICS. Figure 2. *Mosaic from Beth-Shean/El-Ḥammam.* (Courtesy Lucille A. Roussin)

hunt carpets. The camel caravan and animal chase mosaic in the portico of the Great Colonnade at Apamea (469 CE) may be the earliest of this type (also at Apamea are mosaics of Amazons hunting and of Atlante and Meleager). The most dramatic and monumental examples of hunt pavements are those discovered at Antioch (the Megalopsychia Hunt from Yakto now in the museum at Antakya, Turkey, and the Worcester Hunt in the Worcester Art Museum). The mosaic of Adam enthroned in Paradise surrounded by wild beasts from the nave of the North Church at Huarte, Syria, is an example of the adaptation of a popular Roman theme—Orpheus charming the beasts—to Christian iconography.

A taste for the personifications of abstract ideas and the elements of nature remain popular from the Late Roman period through the sixth century; for example, *Ananeosis,* or "Renewal," and *Ktisis,* or "Foundation," occur at Antioch (*Ktisis* also appears in the frigidarium of the Baths of Eustolios at Kourion, Cyprus); personifications of the seasons (at Deir es-Sleib, Syria), *Ge* (at Beth Guvrin?), and *Thalassa,* or "Ocean" (at the Church of the Apostles, Madaba). Calendar mosaics expand on the seasons imagery with illustrations of the agricultural labors of each season and month (at Beth-Shean in Israel and el-Ḥammam in the same locale).

In the sixth century, Palestine and Arabia are the most important provincial centers of mosaic productivity. The most popular pattern was the medallion style of the inhabited vine or acanthus scroll rinceaux, which was used for border and field compositions. Within the scrolls of church pavements are miniature versions of hunting themes and pastoral and vintaging scenes (Beth-Shean (see figure 2) and Madaba). Elements of the natural world—flowers (rosettes), animals, birds, baskets of fruit—fill the intervals formed by grid patterns composed of small four-petalled flowers; these petalled trellis designs are widely found—at Antioch, in the House of the Green Carpet; in Lebanon at the church of Khalde; and in Syria at the church at Dibsi Faraj. Classical myths continue to be represented at Madaba with the Dionysiac *thiasos* (revelry) and with Achilles and Patroclus; in Jerusalem, with Orpheus; and at Erez, in Israel, with the Triumph of Dionysos.

Topographical subjects, introduced in the fifth century in the cityscape border of the Megalopsychia Hunt from Antioch and in the Nilotic pavement of the transept of the Church of the Multiplication of Loaves and Fishes at Tabgha, in Israel, are a particularly rich subject for sixth-century mosaicists. The Madaba Map represents the principle cities of Palestine and the Nile Delta, as well as prominent pilgrimage sites. In the borders of the mosaics at Maʿin (719 CE) and Umm er-Rasas (765 CE), in Jordan walled cities and churches represent the principle cities of the patriarchates of Jerusalem, Arabia, Alexandria, and Memphis.

The monumental peristyle (1,900 sq. m) mosaic in the Great Palace in Constantinople provides a rare example of a sixth-century mosaic in an imperial context. Recent excavation has clarified the dating of this monument, which previously ranged from the fourth through the seventh centuries: pottery finds below the mosaic indicate a date in the first half of the sixth century. More than seventy scenes are extant and illustrate heterogeneous episodes drawn from the repertoire of the hunt (outdoors and staged in an amphitheater), rural life, and animal combats, against a neutral white ground.

MOSAICS. Figure 3. *Lion mosaic.* From Byzantine church at Magen in the Negev. (Courtesy ASOR Archives)

Synagogue Mosaics. The majority of synagogue mosaics are found in Israel, where they present iconographic programs distinctly different from those in the Diaspora. The mosaic pavements of the synagogues at Sardis (dated by numismatic evidence to c. 350 CE) and Apamea (dated by inscription to 391/92) are geometric carpets with framed panels of donors' inscriptions interspersed with geometric designs. In contrast, synagogue pavements in Palestine from the fourth through the sixth centuries show a richly developed iconography with representations of the Torah shrine and menorah and other Jewish ritual objects (shofar, lulav, ethrog, incense shovel) used in the liturgy. Signs of the zodiac and personifications of the seasons frame Helios in the mosaics at Hammath Tiberias, Sepphoris, Khirbet Susiya, Naʿaran, Beth-Shean, Beth Alpha, Huṣifah, and Yafia. Biblical scenes are illustrated in the floor mosaics at Gerasa (Noah's family and the animals leaving the Ark), Beth Alpha (the Sacrifice of Isaac), and in Naʿaran and Khirbet Susiya (Daniel in the Lion's Den).

The political unrest produced by the war between the Byzantine and Persian empires and the Arab invasion of 640 brought about a general decline. Mosaic production in Turkey, on Cyprus, and in Phoenicia came to a halt. The discovery of the Church of St. Stephen at Umm er-Rasas, dated to between 756 and 785, indicates that church building in Palestine did not cease. At least some mosaic workshops in Palestine and Arabia flourished long after the Arab conquest.

The Umayyad caliphs employed Byzantine craftsmen to decorate their buildings with mosaics in Syria and Palestine. The most spectacular early Islamic pavement is preserved in the large bath hall at Khirbat al-Mafjar, near Jericho, dated to the second quarter of the eighth century; it consists of thirty-one individual panels filled with geometric designs. A figural mosaic with lions hunting gazelles on either side of a fruit tree is found in the small private room off the hall. Whether this scene can be read as an allegory is debated.

[*See also* Churches; Synagogues. *In addition, many of the sites mentioned are the subject of independent entries (see especially* Madaba).]

BIBLIOGRAPHY

Balty, Janine. *Mosaïques antiques de Syria.* Brussels, 1977.

Campbell, Shelia. "Roman Mosaic Workshops in Turkey." *American Journal of Archaeology* 83 (1979): 287–292.

Daszewski, Wiktor A., and Demetrios Michaelides. *Mosaic Floors in Cyprus.* Ravenna, 1988.

Donceel-Voûte, Pauline. *Les pavements des églises byzantines de Syrie et du Liban.* Louvain-la-Neuve, 1988.

Kitzinger, Ernst. "Stylistic Developments in Pavement Mosaics in the Greek East from the Age of Constantine to the Age of Justinian." In *The Art of Byzantium and the Medieval West,* edited by W. Eugene Kleinbauer, pp. 64–88. Bloomington, 1976.

Lavin, Irving. "The Hunting Mosaics of Antioch and Their Sources." *Dumbarton Oaks Papers* 17 (1963): 181–286.

Levi, Doro. *Antioch Mosaic Pavements.* Princeton, 1947.

Meyers, Eric M., Carol. L. Meyers, and Ehud Netzer. *Sepphoris.* Winona Lake, Ind., 1992.

Michaelides, Demetrios. *Cypriot Mosaics.* Nicosia, 1987.

Ovadiah, Asher, and Ruth Ovadiah. *Hellenistic, Roman, and Early Byzantine Mosaic Pavements in Israel.* Rome, 1987.

Piccirillo, Michele. *Chiese e mosaici di Madaba.* Jerusalem, 1989.

Piccirillo, Michele. *The Mosaics of Jordan* (1986). Amman, 1993.

Trilling, James. "The Soul of the Empire: Style and Meaning in the Mosaic Pavement of the Byzantine Imperial Palace in Constantinople." *Dumbarton Oaks Papers* 43 (1989): 27–72.

CHRISTINE KONDOLEON and LUCILLE A. ROUSSIN

MOSQUE. To the beginning of the eleventh century CE in the Near East, mosque typology is dominated by the plan of the hypostyle (many-columned) courtyard, which in this context is sometimes also referred to as the "Arab" plan. Numerous models from the pre-Islamic period had this layout, but there is little doubt that the Prophet's house in Medina played a key role. This building was not designed to be an exclusive place for prayer. It contained rooms for Muhammad and his wives, and its large open courtyard was used for various social, political, and military functions of the whole Muslim community.

The Prophet led the faithful in prayer on the southern side of the courtyard, facing the shrine at Mecca (that is, the *qiblah*). Here there were two rows of palm tree columns covered with a palm-thatched roof. The collective memory of the significance of this may be thought sufficient for the form's later popularity. Two additional factors may well have contributed to its pervasiveness. The first was its technological simplicity. Trabeated structures (featuring beams or lintels) required little in the way of masonry skills, and reused columns provided a further saving of labor. The second was the flexibility of the hypostyle plan, which permitted expansion in any direction without necessarily altering the overall character of the building.

The expansion of the Prophet's house to become the Great Mosque of Medina shows this process in action. It was one of three major mosques (the others being those of Damascus and Jerusalem) which were built or expanded by Caliph al-Walid (705–715). The Medina mosque was the first to incorporate a *miḥrab* (concave niche), which was situated not at the center of the *qiblab* wall but to one side, corresponding to the axis at which Muhammad led the prayers in the original building. Its first appearance at this site, where it was richly decorated, and its ubiquity in subsequent mosques are strong arguments that it should be seen as a commemoration of the place where the Prophet led the prayers as the first imam. The more frequent explanation, that it indicates the direction of prayer, is less likely for two reasons. First, the *miḥrab* is usually invisible from a substantial portion of the interior of the mosque. Second, the *qiblah* is normally immediately apparent from the direction of the largest roofed area, which is the main prayer hall.

The mosque at Medina was also the first to be provided in al-Walid's rebuilding with tall towers at its corners. These have normally been considered minarets, places from which the call to prayer was given, although recent work by Jonathan Bloom (*Minaret: Symbol of Islam,* Oxford, 1989), has argued that this is a problematic interpretation, and that the minaret did not become a standard feature of mosque architecture until the ʿAbbasid period. Two other features of al-Walid's works at Medina were also widely imitated in other mosques: a finely decorated axial nave and a domed ante-*miḥrab* bay. The rebuilding of the Aqsa mosque in Jerusalem by al-Walid is now thought to have included these two features, although it differs from all early congregational mosques in its lack of a courtyard. This configuration is to be explained by its location within the Ḥaram (the former Temple Mount), where its forecourt could easily have served the same purpose.

Unlike other major early mosques, the Great Mosque of Damascus is essentially basilical in plan rather than hypostyle. The prayer hall has three bays parallel to the *qiblah* wall, interrupted by a transverse nave. It is not certain whether there was originally a dome within this nave; if so, it may have been above the bay in front of the *miḥrab,* rather than the central bay where it is today. The gable that rises above the nave on the courtyard facade is possibly derived from Byzantine palaces. The courtyard is surrounded by one arcade on each side; the combination of basilica and adjacent peristyle courtyard was also common in Roman forums. The Roman temple enclosure, which bounded the mosque, prevented it from being subsequently enlarged. Its already massive size and sumptuous decoration of mosaic landscapes, however, enhanced its prestige and led to frequent copies, the mosques in Khirbet al-Minyeh and the *medina* of Qaṣr al-Ḥair ash-Sharqi being two Umayyad examples.

Smaller Umayyad Mosques. Although it is clear that the prestigious congregational mosques of the Umayyads set the fashion both for later periods and for lesser mosques within their own period, the variety of smaller mosques that has survived has not been fully appreciated. At its simplest the place of prayer could be indicated by a niche in the wall facing Mecca. This *miḥrab* is found, for instance, in the entrance corridor of the caravanserai at Qaṣr al-Ḥayr ash-Sharqi. A passageway also used by animals is an unlikely setting for prayer, but there is a tradition that a mosque is formed wherever one prays, and therefore blocking off this area to other traffic would have been sufficient to form one. The larger enclosure at Qaṣr al-Ḥayr ash-Sharqi has a more substantial courtyard mosque; the mosque of the caravanserai was never designed for many people. In the contemporary caravanserai at Qaṣr al-Ḥayr al-Gharbi the mosque is only slightly more formal, consisting of a wing projecting from the entrance facade. [*See* Qaṣr al-Ḥayr ash-Sharqi; Qaṣr al-Ḥayr al-Gharbi.]

MOSQUE. *Marble mosaic coating of a miḥrab (niche).* Zaynabiyyeh Mosque, Damascus, fourteenth century. (Courtesy K. Toueir)

The mosque at Jabal Says is of the simplest type—a single room—although a central pier awkwardly interrupts the axis between the mihrab and door opposite. Single rooms fronted by a larger courtyard are found at Qastal and Qaṣr Muqatil; the latter is distinguished by a triple entrance to the prayer hall. A possible prototype for these examples or an example that may have occurred concurrently with them is seen at Qaṣr Burquʿ, which consists now only of a low stone wall, but which may well have had a tent erected over it to provide the covered space for prayer. [*See* Qaṣr Burquʿ.]

Three Umayyad mosques, at Khan al-Zabib, Umm al-Walid and Qaṣr al-Ḥallabat, contain the germ of the nine-bay plan, which was to become widespread under the ʿAbbasids. They are square, with an interior whose roof is supported by four piers, although the irregular spacing of the piers and the roofing, either flat or barrel-vaulted and parallel to the *qiblah* distinguish them from the later examples. [*See* Qaṣr al-Ḥallabat.]

ʿAbbasid Congregational Mosques. The major mosques of the ʿAbbasids continued to be courtyard hypostyle buildings, but several features appeared or became standard at this time. The first is the minaret, which usually took the form of a single tower in the middle of the wall opposite the *qiblah* (Siraf, Harran, Samarra). The examples at Samarra are helicoid (spiral shaped), most likely inspired by the then more numerous and better preserved ziggurats of Mesopotamia. The minaret of the mosque of Ibn Tulun in Cairo was probably of the same shape.

The second feature is the *ziyada*, a space that surrounded the mosque on all sides except the *qiblah*. Its purposes are not yet fully understood, especially when to judge from the aerial photographs of the Great and Abu Dulaf Mosques of Samarra, it more than doubled the size of what were already enormous buildings. It is difficult to imagine that these huge buildings (the Great Mosque remains the largest ever built) could ever have been filled for Friday prayers, but recent excavations at Abu Dulaf have shown that double arcades were added to most of the outer walls to accommodate the overflow. The mosque was abandoned before it had been in use for one year. Therefore, these additions must have been a response to a contemporary need. The *ziyada* of Ibn Tulun's mosque is much smaller, but there at least we have some indications of how it was used. The sources mention facilities for ablutions and a small clinic for those attending Friday prayers. The *ziyada* may also have functioned to isolate the prayer area from the noise of the urban surroundings.

The third feature was the use of stucco as a decorative medium. Although this was found on Umayyad palaces, the

ʿAbbasid use of brick rather than stone as the medium of construction must have encouraged its proliferation. The poor state of preservation of the Samarra mosques means that the Ibn Tulun mosque is the place where its effects can be best admired. The soffits (undersides) of the arches each have a different pattern based on abstract vegetal ornament within simple geometric frameworks of intersecting circles and squares, the so-called Samarra B style. The painting which would have adorned these and the friezes that run continuously around the arcades would have made the patterns even more striking.

The state of preservation of the mosque of Ibn Tulun also makes it one of the best places to assess the spatial qualities of the large hypostyle mosque. The repetition of the basic building unit, the arch on piers, allows endless vistas through the arcades to spring up simultaneously in multiple directions. The hypnotic effect that this repetition induces results in the sense of quiet contemplation which pervades the building.

Smaller ʿAbbasid Mosques. The largest corpus of smaller ʿAbbasid mosques is those of the stations of the Darb Zubaydah, the pilgrimage route from Kufah to Mecca which was endowed by Zubaydah, the wife of Harun al-Rashid. More than twenty-five mosques have been recovered in excavations. The simplest plan, as expected, is an undivided room, which occurs both as a single component of a larger building (al-ʿAmya') and in several instances as an isolated rectangular structure, usually with three entrances on the side opposite the *qiblah* (e.g., al-Makhruqa). In other cases courtyards have also been preserved, at least in part, in front of this room (al-Kharaba) and the piers of the wall opposite the *qiblah* show that the three entrances clearly correspond to a division of the interior into three bays (al-Saqiyya).

The most common mosque plan which was added to the *qaṣrs* on the route was a nine-bay type, possibly related to those of Khan al-Zabib, Umm al-Walid, and Qaṣr al-Ḥallabat mentioned above. In five of the *qaṣrs* the nine-bay plan is well-preserved, although in none of them to the extent that the elevation can be deduced. Three of these are roughly square (e.g., Umm aḍ-Ḍamiran), and two are distinctly basilical with engaged piers to either side of the four central ones emphasizing the division into a wider nave and two aisles (al-ʿAqiq).

It is worth noting the resemblance that many of the Darb Zubaydah mosques have to the basilical audience hall of the Dar al-ʿImarah at Kufah, one of the towns on the Darb Zubaydah itself. Rather than necessitating a ceremonial link between these structures, however, it serves to underline the blurring of the meanings of forms which naturally arose from the reuse by Islam of earlier prototypes.

The later ʿAbbasid period sees widespread diffusion of the nine-bay plan. Three Persian examples are known at Balkh, Hazara, and Tirmiz. These were all vaulted; the Hazara example resembles a quincunx (which has central and four corner domes plus four barrel-vaulted bays). That of Balkh is impressive for its stucco decoration. Like the adornment of the mosque of Ibn Tulun, the stucco at Balkh is in Samarra B style, its most easterly diffusion.

Persian Variations. The only well-documented example of a Sasanian four-arched building, that is, a *chahartaq*, being converted into a mosque is that of Yazd-i Khvast. A

MOSQUE. *The al-Aqṣa mosque in Jerusalem.* (Courtesy Pictorial Archive)

similar history has been postulated for several others, raising the question whether dome chambers were later built to stand alone as mosques (i.e., "kiosk" mosques). Most of the discussion has centred around Seljuk monuments, although one ʿAbbasid possibility is the mosque of ʿAli Qundi in Fahraj, a small town that also possesses an ʿAbbasid hypostyle congregational mosque. Whether converted or built anew, it is likely that the presence of these dome chambers stimulated one of the most radical developments in later mosque plans, the incorporation of very large dome chambers in the mihrab area of the hypostyle mosque.

The other radical development of Persian mosques was the incorporation of another pre-Islamic form: the *ayvan.* The Friday Mosque at Nayriz has a large *qiblah ayvan* whose stucco *miḥrab* indicates that it replaced a tenth-century predecessors. It has been suggested that this *ayvan* originally stood alone, although it may be more likely that it was inserted into a hypostyle plan. The real revolution came later, in the eleventh or twelfth century, when the ʿAbbasid plan of the Isfahan Friday Mosque was transformed by the addition of four *ayvans* around its courtyard and became the model for countless others.

At another mosque in Isfahan, the Ḥakim, the remains of an entrance portal decorated in brick and stucco were uncovered in 1955. The style of its inscriptions accords with the textual evidence identifying this as the portal of the Jurjir mosque built by a Buyid vizier about 960–985. Its significance lies in its role as advertising the presence of the mosque through both its elaborate decoration and the multiple reveals of its architecture. This is one of the earliest monumental entrance portals of any Near Eastern mosque.

Fatimid Cairo. The monumental portal soon became widespread. The late tenth-century mosque of al-Ḥakim in Cairo has a projecting axial portal, itself modeled on the earlier mosque in the previous capital of the Fatimids at Maḥdiyya. The early Fatimid mosques in Egypt also borrow some features from other North African prototypes, such as the T-plan and the ante-*miḥrab* dome chamber. However, those features in turn may have been inspired by our first example, the Great Mosque of Medina as restored by al-Walid, where it will be recalled that a shallow dome stood in front of the *miḥrab* and that the arcades were arranged to emphasise the aisle leading to the *miḥrab.*

BIBLIOGRAPHY

Creswell, K. A. C. *Early Muslim Architecture.* 2 vols. Oxford, 1932–1940. Rev. ed. Oxford, 1969. The most detailed treatment of the early mosque.

Creswell, K. A. C., and J. W. Allan. *A Short Account of Early Muslim Architecture.* Aldershot, 1989. Essential revision and expansion of Kreswell's earlier study (above).

Frishman, Martin, and Hasan-Uddin Khan, eds. *The Architecture of the Mosque.* London, 1994. The most comprehensive work on the subject.

Grabar, Oleg. *The Formation of Islamic Art.* Rev. and enl. ed. New Haven, 1987. Chapter 5 deals with the mosque.

Hillenbrand, Robert. "Masdjid." In *Encyclopaedia of Islam,* new ed., vol. 6, pp. 677–684. Leiden, 1960–. The most thoughtful extended summary of mosque architecture yet published.

Hillenbrand, Robert. "Archaeology VI. Islamic Iran." In *Encyclopaedia Iranica,* vol. 2, pp. 317–322. London, 1987–. Includes a thorough bibliography of the archaeological record.

O'Kane, Bernard. "*Čahārṭāq,* Islamic Period." In *Encyclopaedia Iranica,* vol. 4, pp. 639–642. London, 1987–. The most recent discussion of the theory of the "kiosk" mosque.

Pedersen, Johannes. "Masdjid." In *Encyclopaedia of Islam,* new ed., vol. 6, pp. 644–677. Leiden, 1960–. Covers the liturgical and historical background.

BERNARD O'KANE

MOSQUE INSCRIPTIONS. Inscriptions were used in mosques from the earliest times. One of the first congregational mosques, the Umayyad mosque at Damascus built by al-Walid I (r. 705–715 CE), had an extensive epigraphic program in blue and gold mosaic. Although destroyed, the text can be reconstructed from medieval descriptions. It included pious phrases, Qur'anic citations, and the foundation inscription with the caliph's name. Throughout the Islamic world, mosque inscriptions were almost invariably written in Arabic. Although Persian was introduced for commemorative texts and foundation inscriptions in tombs as early as the eleventh century, Arabic remained the primary language for mosque inscriptions, presumably because of the sanctity Arabic was accorded as the language in which the Qur'an was revealed.

The information contained in mosque inscriptions falls into two broad categories, historical and religious. Because each text reads continuously in a single language and script, however, such a division of subject matter is basically a convention of modern scholarship. The standard text begins with the Basmala or invocation to God, followed by Qur'anic citations mixed with the foundation inscription. The basic form was so-and-so ordered the construction of this mosque (Ar. *amara bi-binā' hadhā al-masjid*) at a certain date, but the texts can provide the names of the supervisor and craftsmen and other information about specific parts built or restored. The mosque of Ibn Tulun in Cairo is a good example of the standard text in the early Islamic period: in addition to several Qur'anic citations (among them 9:18, 3:106, 48:29, 2:256, and 24:36–38.) the inscription contains the Basmala, the name of the patron, Ahmad ibn Tulun, and the date AH Ramadan 265 (May 879 CE).

Like inscriptions on other types of buildings and objects, those in mosques became longer and more elaborate over time. Ahmad ibn Tulun is identified by his title *(amir),* his *kunya* or patronymic (Abu'l-ʿAbbas), his *nasab* or genealogy (Ibn Tulun), and his relationship to the ʿAbbasid caliph, client of the commander of the faithful (Ar., *mawlā amīr al-mu'minīn*). Two centuries later when the mosque at Damascus was restored, the inscription records that the work took place during the caliphate of the ʿAbbasid al-Muqtadi, commander of the faithful, the empire of the Seljuq sultan Malik Shah, the governorate of his brother Tutush, and the vizierate of Nizam al-Mulk, all of whom are identified by several names, titles, and epithets. By the fourteenth century under the Mamluks, these titles had doubled in length. Thus, the inscriptions in mosques are useful historical documents to measure political allegiance, for just as the *khutba* or sermon in the congregational mosque was a sign of authority, so the inscription there was a testament to official policy. The inscription served as a legal document of ownership until all work on the building was finished and the endowment deed (Ar., *waqf*) could be drawn up.

The most common Qur'anic text used in mosques is surah 9:18, which says that God's mosques should be reserved for good Muslims who believe in God, pray, pay alms, and worship God alone. One of the few Qur'anic texts to mention mosques (Ar., *masājid*) and the activities associated with them, the text quickly became standard for congregational mosques. Other common Qur'anic citations on mosques include the so-called Throne Verse (2:255) extolling God's majesty, the Light Verse (24:36–38) in which God is eloquently described as the light of the heavens and the earth, and verses from the victory Surah (48) about God's granting a manifest victory. Some Qur'anic verses became associated with parts of mosques because of individual words referring to specific practices: verses 17:78–79 about prayer and vigil, for example, are often found on *miḥrābs* (niches in the wall that indicates the direction of Mecca).

Mosque inscriptions were composed as coherent programs. Those in the earliest mosques seem to illustrate universal or general themes. The Qur'anic inscriptions from the mosque of Damascus, for example, contained eschatological texts about the day of judgment (surahs 79–81). Similarly, the verses carved in stucco on the arcades of the Azhar mosque in Cairo (AH 363/972 CE) described paradise (e.g., 21:101–107). Medieval sources assert that the entire Qur'an was inscribed around the interior of the mosque of Ibn Tulun. Although patently untrue, the report shows that the text was meant to be inclusive. Similarly, the inscriptions around the interior of the mosque of al-Hakim in Cairo, founded in 989 (AH 379), contain the opening verses of various surahs, probably used as synecdoches to suggest the presence of the whole.

With the breakup of the Islamic community in the tenth century, the Qur'anic verses decorating mosques were selected to illustrate specific ideological points. The Fatimids, for example, seem to have chosen verses with key phrases about the Shiʿi *daʿwah* (the call to accept members of the Prophet's family as his rightful successors). A now-lost marble inscription from the exterior of the mosque of al-Hakim, completed in 1010–1011 (AH 401) contains surah 28:4 with the word *a'imma* (leaders), the plural of *īmām,* the title used by the Fatimids. The western minaret of the mosque is inscribed with surah 11:73; it contains the coded phrase *ahl al-bayt* (people of the house), taken by the Fatimids as a direct reference to themselves as descendants of the Prophet's son-in-law ʿAli. Such pointed use of Qur'anic inscriptions only increased with the growing sectarian struggles: the foundation inscription for the mosque of al-Aqmar, dated by inscription to AH 519 (1125–1126 CE) mentions victory over all infidels, referring the Fatimid caliph al-Amir's struggles against either the Crusaders or the recalcitrant Nizaris. The inscription also contains surah 33:33, addressed to the people of the house, a verse which became a code for the Shiʿis who considered it a vindication of their legitimacy.

In addition to Qur'anic citations, *ḥadīth* were also inscribed on mosque furnishings and furniture from the eleventh century. Although a less reverent source of authority than the Qur'an, these prophetic traditions have the advantage of being more diverse and adaptable and could be cited

MOSQUE INSCRIPTIONS. Figure 1. *Isfahan stucco miḥrab.* (Courtesy S. S. Blair)

to support a particular sectarian point of view. The splendid stucco *miḥrāb* added to the congregational mosque at Isfahan in AH Safar 710/July 1310 (see figure 1) just after the Il-Khanid Öljeitü's conversion to Shiism, for example, is inscribed with a tradition of ʿAli ibn Abi Talib that whoever frequents a mosque will receive one of eight benedictions. It was undoubtedly invoked to win over the population in this troublesome sectarian city.

[*See also* Inscriptions, *article on* Inscriptions of the Islamic Period; Mosque.]

BIBLIOGRAPHY

Berchem, Max van, et al. *Matériaux pour un Corpus Inscriptionum Arabicarum.* Cairo, 1894–. The basic survey of Arabic inscriptions on Islamic architecture. The most important volumes are those on Cairo by van Berchem and Gaston Wiet, on Jerusalem by van Berchem, on Aleppo by Ernst Herzfeld, and on Mecca by Hassan el-Hawary and Wiet.

Blair, Sheila S. *The Monumental Inscriptions from Early Islamic Iran and Transoxiana.* Leiden, 1992. Recent corpus.

Bloom, Jonathan M. "The Mosque of al-Hākim in Cairo." *Muqarnas* 1 (1983): 15–36. Discusses the sectarian use of inscriptions in the Fatimid period.

Combe, Étienne, Jean Sauvaget, and Gaston Wiet, eds. *Répertoire chronologique d'épigraphie arabe.* 18 vols. to date. Cairo, 1931–. Corpus of historical inscriptions on Islamic buildings and objects, arranged chronologically. The latest volume covers material up to 1397 CE (AH 800).

Dodd, Erica, and Shereen Khairallah. *The Image of the Word.* 2 vols. Beirut, 1981. Corpus of religious inscriptions on Islamic buildings, arranged by verse number and location.

Finster, Barbara. "Die Mosaiken der Umayyadenmoschee von Damaskus." *Kunst des Orients* 7 (1970–1971): 82–141. Reconstructs the program of inscriptions in one of the earliest mosques.

Sourdel-Thomine, J., et al. "Khāṭṭ (Writing)." In *Encyclopaedia of Islam,* new ed., vol. 4, pp. 1113–1128. Leiden, 1960–.

Sourdel-Thomine, J., et al. "Kitābāt (Inscriptions)." In *Encyclopaedia of Islam,* new ed., vol. 5, pp. 210–233. Leiden, 1960–.

Williams, Caroline. "The Cult of ʿAlid Saints in the Fatimid Monuments of Cairo. Part I: The Mosque of al-Aqmar." *Muqarnas* 1 (1983): 37–52. More on the sectarian use of inscriptions in Fatimid Cairo.

SHEILA S. BLAIR

MOZAN, TELL, site, now positively identified as Urkeš, located in Syria, on the Khabur plains, near the headwaters of Wadi Darʿa, one of the streams feeding the Khabur River, just south of the Mardin pass leading to the Anatolian plateau (37°02′ N, 41°0′ E). The site, with its commanding position, was the major gateway to the copper mines in the north and was a hub in the communication network to the south, along the Khabur, and on the east–west road that flanks the Taurus range. [*See* Taurus Mountains.]

The central High Mound measures 18 ha (45 acres) and stands 25 m above virgin soil. The Outer City extends for 400 m, for a total surface of 135 ha (334 acres). Tell Mozan has been identified as the site of ancient Urkeš, the mythical city of Hurrian mythology and one of the major third-millennium capitals that had so far escaped identification. It is described in later Hurrian myths as the residence of Kumarbi, the major god of the Hurrian pantheon. As such it plays a prominent role in the mythical geography of ancient Syria. The famous bronze lions of King Tish-atal of Urkeš, which had been sold on the antiquities market and are now exhibited in the Louvre and the Metropolitan Museum, are thus to be reinterpreted as having come from Tell Mozan. [*See* Hurrians.]

Tell Mozan was first surveyed and briefly excavated by Max Mallowan in 1934. He dug three trenches (R0, G0, H0) and noted some surface remains, identified as N0. Mallowan first assumed that the site was Roman, which was one reason he chose Chaghar Bazar for his excavations. (The most detailed report is to be found in his wife's autobiography: Agatha Christie, *Come Tell Me How You Live,* New York, 1977, p. 72ff.). [*See the biography of Mallowan.*]

Regular excavations, under the direction of Giorgio Buccellati and Marilyn Kelly-Buccellati, began in 1984; by 1995 eight seasons were completed. The long-term research strategies, favored by the fact that the site has almost no modern occupation, have taken three major directions: extensive surveys (topographic, geophysical, and artifactual) of the entire area; distinct operations on the High Mound, with a view toward obtaining an understanding of different functional units (the city wall in KW; the temple, BA; the royal storehouse, AK; a private house, F1) and different periods (the stepped trench, AS; the deep sounding, S2; the later occupations in BH and C1); and, preliminary soundings in the Outer City, indicating that it was utilized both for burials (OA4, OB1) and domestic structures (OD2, OE1).

The chronological distribution of the occupation of Mozan began in the Halaf period, on the basis of ceramic evidence found on the surface of the Outer City and from the lowest levels of deep sounding S2, just above virgin soil. [*See* Ḥalaf, Tell.] No early third-millennium strata have yet been excavated, but in deep sounding S2 three small pointed-base Ninevite V cups were found in stratum A12 next to a carbon sample for which the calibrated date 2920 ± 170 BCE was obtained. The surface ceramic survey suggested that early-third-millennium sherds were more prevalent on the northern portion of the mound.

The major occupational strata at Mozan and the largest component in the buildup of the high mound can be dated to the second half of the third millennium (a calibrated C-14 date of 2435 BCE ± 60 has been obtained for phase A1 of temple BA). It is remarkable to find structures from this period not only at lower elevations (city wall KW, storehouse AK), but also at middle (private house F1) and topmost elevations (temple BA). This suggests that the city's skyline in the mid-third millennium was already similar in its general outline to the profile of the tell today.

From the initial ceramic survey it appeared that second-millennium BCE occupation was centered on the highest portion of the mound. This was verified in a small sounding (Q1) and in the upper strata of the step trench AS, where traces of a large building have been partially uncovered. The latest levels above temple BA dated to the Khabur period, but no building remains were found. On a lower portion of the high mound, area C1, a single Khabur-period grave was excavated. The latest occupation dates to the Nuzi period and is characterized by private houses (AS, BH) containing very few small finds. Even the ceramics are of the coarser variety, with only portions of two painted goblets found in the excavations.

The earliest phase of temple BA is the best preserved (see figure 1). It had a large interior space (9 × 16.5 m) with a monumental entrance accessed by a long (8 m) stone ramp. The foundations were constructed of large and roughly hewn limestone blocks with mud-brick walls resting immediately on stone foundations. The plan and the exterior dimensions are similar to those of temple G at Ebla and the "Aussenbau" at Chuera (which, however, have an access in antis, as opposed to the Mozan bent-axis approach); at Ebla the walls are twice as thick, which means that the interior space is considerably smaller. [*See* Ebla; Chuera, Tell.] A thick, cementlike pavement covered the entire interior space; it is assumed that, in spite of its large size, this room was roofed and that the roof was pitched.

At the base of a stepped trench on the western side of the tell, portions of a large storehouse have been excavated. Judging from the layout of the excavated portion, this is the southwestern corner of a building that, once excavated, may be three times as large as the present exposure. The plan (see figure 2) consists of an accession suite, a large hall with a closet or vault, and probably a courtyard and an interior storage area behind. The sectors to the east appear to have a plan that is the mirror image of the western half. The lower courses of the walls are stone, up to about 1 m high, with mud brick on top, but they are not plastered. The vault in sector B is a small closet (1.8 × 1.3 m) with thick walls and an anteroom. The notching, or rabbeting, in the doorways is for the most part structural, in that it must have held a door panel—the location of the door coincides in many cases with a strongly marked threshold.

More than six hundred seal impressions, all dated to the early Akkadian period, came from a floor deposit associated with the vault in sector B (stratum B12). More than 150 of these were inscribed: these legends give the name of the king (*endan* in Hurrian) of Urkeš and of the queen, plus other members of the royal court. It appears therefore that this was a royal storehouse, where goods were stored in boxes, baskets, and jars on which the seals were rolled; there were only two door sealings. Since the majority of the seals belonged to the queen, the western wing of AK must have been reserved for goods belonging to her. The iconography and style of the seal impressions are, for the most part, in striking contrast with the more formal early Akkadian glyptic of the south. The seals carved in Urkeš have a unique stylistic vigor that can be traced to the production of different workshops. Distinctive aspects include: the close correlation between the scenes and the individuals mentioned in the legends; the fact that several different seals were used by the same person; various depictions of the royal family with the king, the queen, the crown prince and a smaller child seated on the lap of the queen; the realistic rendering of animal figures, which include a lion crouching under the throne of the king; the extremely fine and naturalistic definition of the figures, resulting in what appears to be portraitlike representations of the queen and the prince.

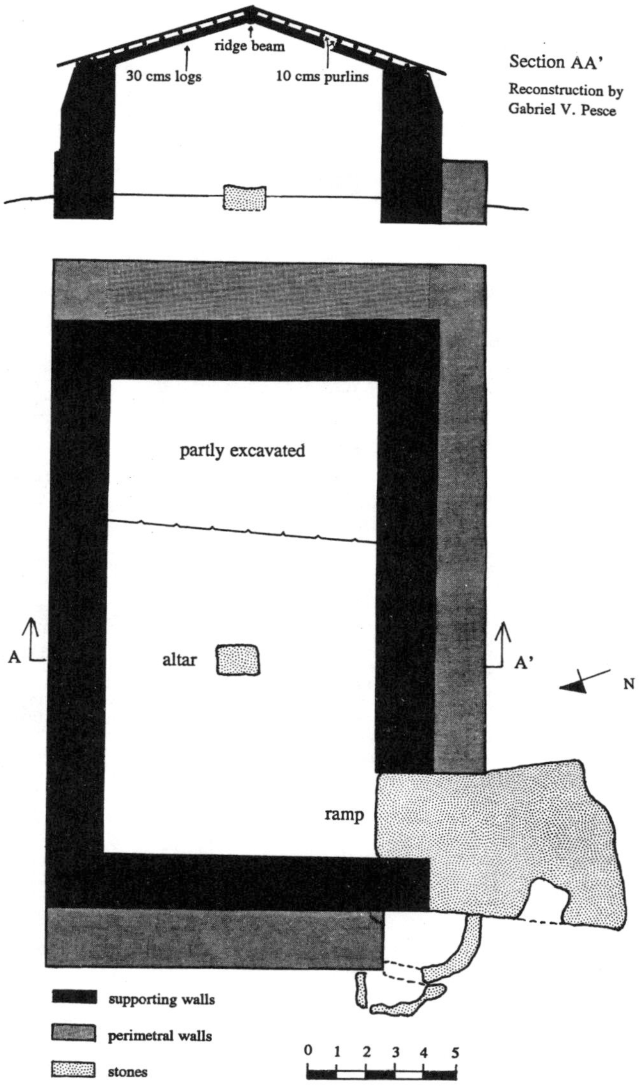

MOZAN, TELL. Figure 1. *Plan of temple BA, phase B1A.* (Courtesy G. Buccellati)

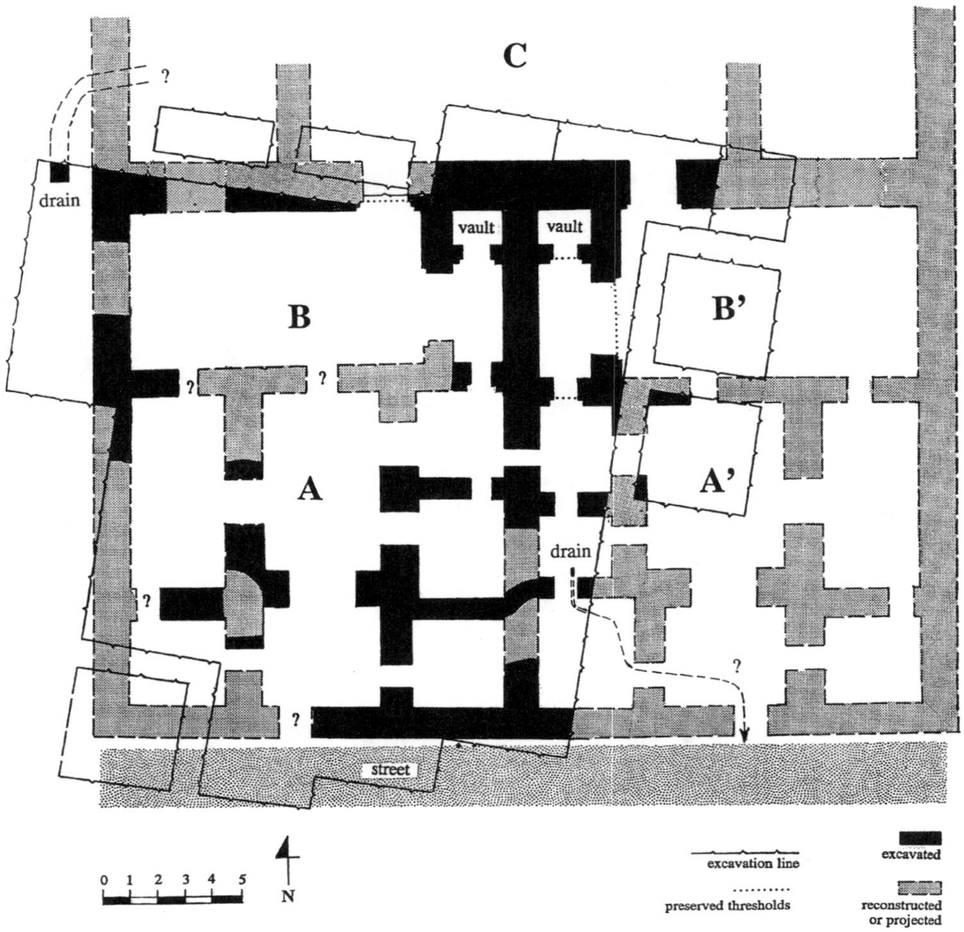

MOZAN, TELL. Figure 2. *Plan of storehouse AK, stratum B12.* (Courtesy G. Buccellati)

Two administrative cuneiform tablets dating to the Late Sargonic period (c. 2250–2000 BCE) were found in F1; they are written in Old Akkadian, but with several Hurrian personal names. A school tablet from AK contains an excerpt of six lines from a list of professions also known from Abu Salabikh and Ebla. [*See* Akkadian; Abu Salabikh.] With it were found one lentoid tablet and fragments of some thirty additional administrative tablets, all from the Early Sargonic period. About eighty seal impressions from AK bore cuneiform legends from the same period. [*See* Seals; Cuneiform.]

More than forty seal impressions were found in KW—mostly door sealings dating to the Early Dynastic III period, some possibly even Early Dynastic II. While some motifs continue into the Early Akkadian period, there are no clearly recognizable Akkadian sealings in the deposit. Prominent among the designs are the nude hero motifs and animal and human combat scenes.

Typical Early Dynastic III ceramics include medium jars with grooved rims, Simple-ware conical cups, and Metallic-ware jars with rounded or ring bases. Akkadian ceramics are characterized by a later variety of metallic ware and a con-

MOZAN, TELL. Figure 3. *Small statue of a lion found in temple BA.* (Courtesy G. Buccellati)

tinuation of the Simple-ware tradition. One tomb with more than fifty vessels excavated in the Outer City (OB1) exhibits the transition between the Late Ninevite 5 tradition and the use of early Metallic ware. During this transition, painted Scarlet-ware stands were utilized at Mozan; they appear to have been manufactured locally because both painted and unpainted examples were found at the site.

From third-millennium contexts a large number of metal objects have been excavated and analyzed—mostly points and pins, but also spears, daggers, and one scraper. A range of metal alloys was used—relatively pure copper, copper alloyed with arsenic, or low-tin bronzes. Some recycling of metals is indicated. The majority of these objects were cast, annealed and finished by cold working.

BIBLIOGRAPHY

Buccellati, Giorgio, and Marilyn Kelly-Buccellati. *Mozan,* vol. 1, *The Soundings of the First Two Seasons.* Bibliotheca Mesopotamica, 20. Malibu, 1988. The first documentary report on the current excavations, with introductory information on the earlier explorations.

Buccellati, Giorgio, and Marilyn Kelly-Buccellati. "Tell Mozan." *Syrian Archaeology Bulletin* 2 (1990): 4–7. Preliminary report on the fifth and sixth seasons.

Buccellati, Giorgio, and Marilyn Kelly-Buccellati. "Tell Mozan." *Les Dossiers d'Archéologie,* no. 155 (1990): 18–23. Introductory overview of the major finds.

Buccellati, Giorgio, and Marilyn Kelly-Buccellati. "Mozan." *American Journal of Archaeology* 95 (1991): 712–714; 98 (1994): 131–133. Preliminary reports on the sixth and seventh seasons of excavation.

Buccellati, Giorgio, and Marilyn Kelly-Buccellati. "Mozan, Tall." In *Reallexikon der Assyriologie und Vorderasiatischen Archäologie,* Berlin, forthcoming. Preliminary report.

Buccellati, Giorgio, and Marilyn Kelly-Buccellati. "The Seventh Season of Excavations at Tell Mozan, 1992." *Annales Archéologiques Arabes Syriennes* (forthcoming). Preliminary report.

Buccellati, Giorgio, and Marilyn Kelly-Buccellati. "The Eighth Season of Excavations at Tell Mozan, 1993." *Annales Archéologiques Arabes Syriennes* (forthcoming).

Kelly-Buccellati, Marilyn. "A New Third Millennium Sculpture from Mozan." In *Essays in Ancient Civilization Presented to Helene J. Kantor,* edited by Albert Leonard, Jr., and Bruce B. Williams, pp. 149–154, pl. 26. Chicago, 1989. Critical analysis of the plowman and herd stelae from temple BA.

Kelly-Buccellati, Marilyn. "Three Seasons of Excavation at Tell Mozan." In *Tall al-Ḥamīdīyā 2,* by Seyarre Eichler et al., pp. 119–132. Orbis Biblicus et Orientalis, Series Archaeologica, 6. Göttingen, 1990. Preliminary report.

Milano, Lucio, et al. *Mozan,* vol. 2, *The Epigraphic Finds of the Sixth Season.* Syro-Mesopotamian Studies, 5.1. Malibu, 1991. Documentary publication of the first find of stratified third-millennium cuneiform texts from Mozan.

GIORGIO BUCCELLATI and MARILYN KELLY-BUCCELLATI

MUNḤATA, site located in the northern Jordan Valley, near the outlet of Naḥal Tabor, 215 m below sea level. Excavations were conducted over a surface area of 2,000 sq m by Jean Perrot (1966) in the 1960s.

The earliest layers (6–3B) are dated to Pre-Pottery Neolithic B (PPNB) period. In layer 6 remains of isolated houses were identified, with foundations built of undressed stones and bricks. In the southern portion of the excavated area, remains of special activities were identified. Five large basalt slabs with wide grooves were uncovered, adjacent to a pavement of large pebbles and a floor with a few fireplaces. In layer 5 the remains of a brick building with a wall more than 20 m long were uncovered. The houses in layer 4 were rectangular, with foundations built of a single course of undressed stones and sun-dried bricks, sometimes containing lime-plaster floors. In layer 3 a large rounded building with pebble flooring was uncovered, as were several rounded, plastered installations, perhaps used for storage.

The lithic industry of the PPNB is characterized by spear points and arrowheads, made mostly from long blades removed from bipolar (naviform) cores and by elongated sickle blades, burins, and retouched blades. The assemblage also includes a large collection of ground-stone tools, including flat bowls, querns, and rubbing stones (Gopher, 1989). Other artifacts recovered include small clay figurines representing both males and females. Among the imports to the site were obsidian from central Anatolia and marine shells. Of the faunal remains, two thirds are of ovicaprids; the rest are pig, cattle, gazelle, and deer. From this evidence, the economic basis seems to have been a mixed strategy of agriculture, herding, and hunting.

Following a short occupational gap (layer 3a), layer 2b belongs to the Pottery Neolithic (PN) period, known as the Yarmukian culture (including both the Shaʿar ha-Golan and Munḥata phases as originally defined by the excavator), tentatively dated to 5500–5000/4800 BCE (uncalibrated). [*See* Shaʿar ha-Golan.]

The Yarmukian habitations are in large pits with numerous underground bell-shaped storage facilities. At least some of these dwellings contain a floor, a fireplace, and a bench-like structure around the walls. The often bell-shaped storage pits are about 1 m deep and 1–1.5 m in diameter at the base.

Recently studied by Yosef Garfinkel (1992), the Yarmukian pottery, the earliest at the site, is characterized by pithoi, holemouth jars, and decorated bowls, as well as handleless jars. Large open bowls are interpreted as food trays, while miniature ones are seen as cosmetic or spice containers. Considered the hallmark of the Yarmukian culture, the incised herringbone pattern, always enclosed by painted lines, is a common decoration. Another pattern is a combination of zigzag and undulating lines. Early assemblages contain pottery decorated with incision and paint.

The objects that most distinguish the Yarmukian culture are the seated female figurines. They are usually represented wearing a conical mask; they have "coffee bean" eyes and their hands are folded under their breasts.

The lithic industry of layer 2b contained denticulate sickle blades, awls and perforators, scrapers and burins, and a few arrowheads and bifacials. The Yarmukian arrowheads are often ʿAmuq and Byblos points, although the smaller type appear in low frequencies. The assemblage resembles that at Shaʿar ha-Golan and may indicate that the sites were occupied by the same people.

Most of layer 2a is related to the Wadi Rabbah phase (4800–4000 BCE), often considered Early Chalcolithic, and reflects Halafian connections. Layer 2a contains the remains of large rectangular structures with mud floors. The lithic industry consists of smaller versions of the same forms as the Yarmukian. Common types of Wadi Rabbah pottery were holemouth jars and pithoi. Slightly less common were bow-rim jars, chalices, and stands.

The stone tools from layer 2 were made using unidirectional cores, a feature that distinguishes them from the PPNB industry, and include sickle blades and scrapers. Layer 1, which was disturbed by agricultural activities, contained remains from the Early Bronze Age.

BIBLIOGRAPHY

Garfinkel, Yosef. *The Pottery Assemblages of the Sha'ar Hagolan and Rabah Stages of Munhata (Israel).* Cahiers du Centre de Recherche Français de Jérusalem, no. 6. Paris, 1992.

Gopher, Avi. *The Flint Assemblages of Munhata: Final Report.* Cahiers du Centre de Recherche Français de Jérusalem, no. 4. Paris, 1989.

Perrot, Jean. "La troisième campagne de fouilles à Munhata (1964)." *Syria* 43 (1966): 49–63.

Ofer Bar-Yosef

MUNSELL CHART. An internationally recognized set of charts that arrange colors on a series of standardized color chips and named for its originator, Albert H. Munsell (1858–1918), is known as the Munsell soil-color charts. In this handbook each chip is identified with a verbal description and a numeric code.

The colors are arranged according to a theoretical three-dimensional cylinder according to three intersecting variables: hue, value, and chroma (or brightness). Hue defines the position of the color in the spectrum arranged around the circumference; the circumference is divided into ten colors that are then subdivided into another ten. Value defines the darkness or lightness of a color along a vertical axis, which is then divided from 0 to 10, with 0 representing black and 10 representing white. Chroma (or brightness) defines the purity or intensity of the color as it radiates from the vertical axis of value (a grayer representation) to its purest state (or brilliance) at the spectrum's outer circumference (usually to 10, but sometimes to an intensity of 16).

Colors represented by these three variables are then given standardized names and numeric codes: for example, yellow 5Y 8/8. The 5Y indicates the hue name—Y for yellow—while the 5 defines the position in the hue range. The 8/ identifies the value of the color on the scale of 0–10 (black–white). The /8 identifies the chroma (or intensity) of the color—hence indicating a fairly pure representation. The numeric code allows a more precise color identification than simply by name; even in the Munsell charts the name *yellow* describes several different color representations—the reason for combining the color name and the code.

The color charts provide more precise color differentiation for both natural and artifactual materials. With soils and sediments, color variations may not only differentiate strata and loci, but may also indicate the presence of organic materials that might prompt further investigation. For artifacts, the most common use of the Munsell charts is in identifying ceramic colors. Their value, however, is not just in color identification (even though the charts provide standards to identify colors beyond such often arbitrary and subjective designations as "burgundy" and "sky blue"): ceramic color, for example, results from a combination of factors, so that assessing color in ceramics can help to identify clay types and technical production procedures.

Although the Munsell charts provide a relative standard of color identification, limitations in their use still exist. Colors ideally should be measured in daylight and preferably at the same time each day, to minimize lighting variations. It is preferable (but usually impossible in the field) to have the colors read by the same person each time because color perceptions vary from person to person.

Despite these limitations, the Munsell soil-color charts are so far the best source of standardization for color identification and are an essential basic tool of modern archaeology.

BIBLIOGRAPHY

Birren, Faber, ed. A Grammar of Color: A Basic *Treatise on the Color System of Albert H. Munsell.* New York, 1969.

Joukowsky, Martha Sharp. *A Complete Manual of Field Archaeology: Tools and Techniques of Field Work for Archaeologists.* Englewood Cliffs, N.J., 1980.

Shackley, Myra L. *Archaeological Sediments: A Survey of Analytical Methods.* New York, 1975.

Shepard, Anna O. *Ceramics for the Archaeologist.* Washington, D.C., 1956.

Dale W. Manor

MURABBAʿAT, a wadi descending from the Judean Desert to the Dead Sea. The wadi's steep slopes contain numerous caves, in four of which were found remains dating from the Chalcolithic period and later. The caves are located about 18 km (11 mi.) south of Qumran and about 25 km (16 mi.) southeast of Jerusalem. Like several of the caves associated with Qumran, those at Murabbaʿat were located by the Taʿamra bedouin searching for written materials they could sell. Because such material began to surface in Jerusalem late in 1951, an archaeological expedition was mounted to explore the wadi and its caves between 21 January and 21 March 1952.

Taking the materials discovered during formal explorations together with what the bedouin had found and sold, the results were considerable: along with various biblical manuscripts, documentary autographs were discovered written in Hebrew, Aramaic, Greek, and Arabic. These materials spanned the period from the first century CE to the tenth century. By far the most important texts dated to the time of the Second Jewish Revolt against Rome, led by Shimʿon Bar Kokhba (132–135 CE). In addition to a number of letters Bar Kokhba sent to his lieutenants (in them his name is revealed to be Simeon b. Kosiba), the Murabbaʿat finds include contracts written during his regime or just prior to it.

At about the same time, bedouin had discovered and were offering for sale additional materials related to this revolt. A proper appraisal of the Murabbaʿat texts requires the use of these related documents. They come from one or more caves in the Wadi Seiyal (Naḥal Ṣeʿelim), and the nearby caves of Wadi Ḥabra (Naḥal Ḥever). After the bedouin pilfering, Israeli archaeologists explored Naḥal Ṣeʿelim between 24 January and 2 February 1960; the documentary finds were fragmentary in the extreme. Archaeologists also investigated Naḥal Ḥever for two weeks in 1960 and a second time in the spring of 1961. It was then that their efforts reaped rich rewards.

One of the Ḥever caves, known as the Cave of Letters, yielded three different collections of documents. The first was a packet of fifteen letters to military leaders in charge of ʿEin-Gedi, an important military supply site during the Second Revolt. Many of these letters were from Bar Kokhba himself, while others had been sent by subordinates. A second group of documents, known as the Archive of the ʿEin-Gedites, consists of six Hebrew and Aramaic contracts leasing state lands. Apparently, like the Roman administration he sought to replace, Bar Kokhba claimed ownership of vast tracts of land, which he leased to tenant farmers. The third collection of documents from the Cave of Letters was the archive of Babatha daughter of Simeon. This group numbered about forty and deals with property and litigation involving Babatha and her family. The texts are inscribed in Aramaic, Nabatean, and Greek; the earliest Babatha text dates to 93/94 CE and the latest to 132 CE.

All of the Murabbaʿat texts have been published in volume 2 of the series Discoveries in the Judaean Desert (Benoît, Milik, and de Vaux, 1961). Texts 42–48 are Bar Kokhba letters; 49–52 may also be Bar Kokhba letters but are too fragmentary to permit certainty even about their genre. The Greek materials in the Babatha archive are also now available (Lewis, Yadin, and Greenfield, 1989). The fifteen letters from Naḥal Ḥever are still unpublished, as are the Semitic portions of the Babatha archive. For these texts there are prepublication descriptions that contain significant excerpts.

Many lacunae exist in the scholarship of the Second Jewish Revolt. The most basic questions—the causes of the outbreak, its geographic extent, and even its dates—cannot be answered with any certainty because of lack of evidence. The Murabbaʿat and related materials do not make it possible to write a history of the revolt, but they do shed important light on limited aspects of it. The materials illumine the course of the war, administration under Bar Kokhba, and the prosopography of those involved in the revolt. They contain precious information on legal and religious practice, the economics of second-century CE Palestine, Jewish literacy, and onomastics. The linguistic information they supply is very considerable and has yet to be fully exploited: the form of both the Hebrew and the Aramaic languages is somewhat different from that known from the Dead Sea Scrolls and later rabbinic literature.

[*See also* Bar Kokhba Revolt; Dead Sea Scrolls; *and* Masada.]

BIBLIOGRAPHY

Benoit, Pierre, J. T. Milik, and Roland de Vaux. *Les grottes de Murabbaʿat.* 2 vols. Discoveries in the Judean Desert, vol. 2. Oxford, 1961. *Editio princeps* of the Murabbaʿat texts, with photographs, transcriptions, French translations, brief notes, and a full discussion of the archaeology.

Fitzmyer, Joseph A. "The Bar Cochba Period." In *The Bible in Current Catholic Thought: Gruenthaner Memorial Volume,* edited by J. L. McKenzie, pp. 133–168. New York, 1962. Good analysis of several texts, with evidence of classical and patristic sources. Deals with most of the big issues but may be overtaken by publication of additional primary source material in the near future.

Isaac, Benjamin, and Aharon Oppenheimer. "The Revolt of Bar Kokhba: Ideology and Modern Scholarship." *Journal of Jewish Studies* 36 (1985): 33–60. Balanced discussion of the major issues and how scholars have evaluated the evidence, including the Murabbaʿat and related texts.

Lewis, Naphtali, Yigael Yadin, and Jonas C. Greenfield. *The Documents from the Bar Kokhba Period in the Cave of Letters: Greek Papyri, Aramaic and Nabatean Signatures and Subscriptions.* Jerusalem, 1989. Excellent analysis of texts and ancillary issues, with photographs, transcriptions, and English translations.

Yadin, Yigael. "Expedition D" and "Expedition D: The Cave of the Letters." *Israel Exploration Journal* 11 (1961): 36–52; 12 (1962): 227–257.

Yadin, Yigael. *Bar-Kokhba.* London, 1971. Along with Yadin's articles (above), this volume provides coverage of the expedition to the Cave of Letters and an analysis of the significance of the texts and related materials, including those from Murabbaʿat. The articles give technical details of the archaeology and many excerpts from texts that remain unpublished; the book contains beautiful color photographs of artifacts and both published and unpublished texts.

MICHAEL O. WISE

MUREYBET, Neolithic site located on the left bank of the Euphrates River, prior to its innundation by the Thawra (Tabqa) dam (36°04′06″ N, 38°05′26″ E). Mureybet is a key site for the Epipaleolithic and Early Neolithic in Syria because its continuous sequence from the Natufian to the Pre-Pottery Neolithic B periods (PPNB) charts the transition from hunting and gathering to agriculture and the passage to a sedentary lifestyle. In-depth studies of the site provide the fullest picture of the Pre-Pottery Neolithic A (PPNA) in the northern Levant.

Salvage excavations were conducted by Maurits N. van Loon in 1965 for the Oriental Institute of the University of Chicago and by Jacques Cauvin from 1971 to 1974 for the Centre National de la Recherche Scientifique. Cauvin found four phases of occupation that incorporate and supercede van Loon's stratigraphy. The earliest is phase I (8500–8200 BCE), in which the semisedentary occupation of a hunting-gathering community was represented in a small excavated area of 35 sq m by a semisubterranean round house, fire pits, and a microlithic tool assemblage, including geometrics. This material culture is considered to be Natufian, thus greatly extending its geographic range beyond the southern Levant. In phase II (8200–8000 BCE), a transitional period that corresponds to van Loon's levels I–VIII, semisedentary occupation continued with monocellular round houses, firepits, and a lithics assemblage with Khiamian arrowheads that, although common, first appeared in phase Ib.

Phase III (8000–7600 BCE; van Loon's levels IX–XVII) represents the Mureybetian, or Middle Euphrates, variant of PPNA culture. At that time innovations in architecture and changes in symbolic representation and an expansion of the settlement to an estimated 2–3 hectares (5–7 acres) took place. Multicellular round houses are internally divided by half-height partition walls that formed storage compartments. Late in phase III, van Loon found multicellular rectilinear structures built with distinctive loaf-shaped cut limestone blocks embedded in a matrix of red clay mortar. The structures were subdivided into compartments thought to be too small for human habitation, and the buildings are believed to have functioned as storehouses. Lithics are characterized by Khiamian and Helwan (notched and tanged) arrowheads. The appearance of rectilinear architecture and Helwan points at Mureybet much earlier than in the southern Levant may indicate their origin on the Middle Euphrates and later diffusion to the southern Levant. Crude female figurines of clay and stone were found. Several ceramic vessels mark an early abortive attempt at pottery manufacture. Subsistence continued to be largely based on hunting and gathering, but there is evidence of some cereal cultivation. Thus, the changes noted above indicate significant transformations in social organization prior to the emergence of a full agricultural system.

In phase IV (7600–6800 BCE) of the PPNB period, the area (28 sq m) excavated included portions of a large rectangular house. Under it were buried several detached skulls, reflecting funerary customs well known in the southern Levant. Lithics are marked by the appearance of Byblos points. Cereals were cultivated and steps were taken toward the practice of animal herding. The occupation of Mureybet from about 8500 to 6800 BCE, during which there were no major cultural breaks, indicates that the trend to sedentism and the emergence of agriculture developed with the same basic population.

[*See also* Euphrates; *and* Euphrates Dams, Survey of.]

BIBLIOGRAPHY

Calley, Sylvie. *Technologie du débitage à Mureybet, Syrie: 9e–8e millénaire.* British Archaeological Reports, International Series, no. 312.1–2. Oxford, 1986.

Cauvin, Jacques. "Les fouilles de Mureybet (1971–1974) et leur signification pour les origins de la sedentarisation au Proche-Orient." *Annual of the American Schools of Oriental Research* 44 (1979): 19–48. Primary publication of Cauvin's excavation.

Cauvin, Marie-Claire, and Danielle Stordeur. "Les outillages lithiques et osseux de Mureybet, Syrie (fouilles van Loon 1965)." *Cahiers de l'Euphrate* 1 (1978): 1–103. See volumes 2–5 for other reports.

Nierlé, M. C. "Mureybet et Cheikh Hassan (Syrie): Outillage de mouture et de broyage (9ème et 8ème millénaires)." *Cahiers de l'Euphrate* 3 (1982): 177–216.

van Loon, Maurits N. "The Oriental Institute Excavations at Mureybiṭ, Syria: Preliminary Report on the 1965 Campaign. Part 1: Architecture and General Finds." *Journal of Near Eastern Studies* 27 (1968): 265–290. Primary report of van Loon's excavation.

Thomas L. McClellan

MURRAY, MARGARET ALICE (1863–1963), first professional woman Egyptologist. Born in Calcutta to English parents who held liberal views concerning female education and non-Christian religions, Margaret Murray earned her doctorate at University College, London, under Flinders Petrie, James H. Walker and Francis Llewellyn Griffith. She was hired 1899 as a junior lecturer and taught elementary Egyptian hieroglyphs, which resulted in a grammar (1905).

Murray's first field experience was with Flinders Petrie at Abydos (1902–1903), when they excavated the mysterious Osireion (thought to be a simulation of the tomb of Osiris or a cenotaph of Seti I). From 1903 to 1904, Murray worked at Saqqara as part of a three-woman team, copying relief scenes in the mastabas. This work resulted in the first and only volume of *Saqqara Mastabas* (1905).

Returning to teaching at University College, Murray organized a comprehensive program in archaeology and continued the language courses. She produced an elementary Coptic grammar in 1911. After Walker's death, she and Flinders Petrie constituted the Department of Egyptology. As he dug in Egypt every winter, starting in November, Murray carried the full burden of teaching but was not appointed an assistant professor until age sixty-one in 1924.

Only summer vacations allowed Murray time for excavations, which she carried out in Europe because of the heat and inundation in Egypt. She spent five seasons investigating megalithic sites on Malta and Minorca. Coincidentally she began studying European folklore and witch cults, publishing *The Witch-Cult in Western Europe* (Oxford, 1921) which won her acclaim among folklorists and the presidency of the Folk Lore Society from 1953 to 1955. Her last field expeditions were at Petra (1937) and at Tell el-ʿAjjul near Gaza with Flinders Petrie and E. J. H. MacKay in 1938.

Murray's bibliography includes more than eighty books and articles. Her best-selling popular book *The Splendour that was Egypt* appeared in 1949. Her last and hundredth year saw the publication of two books, *The Genesis of Religion* and her memoirs, *My First Hundred Years*. Murray's greatest contribution to Egyptology may well have been her dedication to teaching, which resulted in the first integrated program of studies in Egyptology in England, and in training subsequent generations of British archaeologists.

[*See also* Abydos; ʿAjjul, Tell el-; Petra; Saqqara; *and the biography of Petrie.*]

BIBLIOGRAPHY

Dawson, Warren R., and Eric P. Uphill. *Who Was Who in Egyptology*. 2d rev. ed. London, 1972.
Murray, Margaret. *Elementary Egyptian Grammar*. London, 1905.
Murray, Margaret. *Saqqara Mastabas*. Part 1. Publications of the Egyptian Research Account, 10. London, 1905.
Murray, Margaret. *Elementary Coptic (Sahidic) Grammar*. London, 1911.
Murray, Margaret. *The Splendour That Was Egypt*. London, 1949.
Murray, Margaret. *The Genesis of Religion*. London, 1963.
Murray, Margaret. *My First Hundred Years*. London, 1963.

BARBARA SWITALSKI LESKO

MUSEUMS AND MUSEOLOGY. It is often assumed that a fascination with the past is a preoccupation of the modern era, born of a time when the luxury of leisure could permit the retrospective perusal of earlier peoples and cultures. In point of fact many earlier civilizations demonstrated the same curiosity in their ancient antecedents; "museums," in the sense of collections of curios and relics illustrating the past, have existed, in some form, since well before classical times. Nabonidus, the sixth-century BCE ruler of the Neo-Babylonian Empire, is thought to have had a museum, containing ancient inscriptions and other artifacts, at Ur, and possibly another at Babylon. The Greeks also frequently adorned their temples and shrines with statues, paintings, and, in addition to aesthetically interesting artifacts, unusual geological and natural history specimens. Indeed, it was the Greeks who first devised the word *museum,* although the building first named as such, erected by Ptolemy Soter in Alexandria in the third century BCE, was, in reality, more akin to a modern university research institute.

Museums in the currently accepted sense of the term trace their origins to the Renaissance, when an interest in the ancient world was rekindled, and wealthy individuals began to assemble extraordinarily rich and varied collections of art treasures. Nowhere was collecting artifacts and works of art more vigorously pursued than in Italy: in the fifteenth century the Medicis were particularly active in Florence, and in 1471 Pope Sixtus IV established a museum of antiquities on the Capitoline Hill in Rome. More museums were built in the following century. The Belvedere Gardens in Rome became the setting for a fine collection of classical statuary, and the Uffizi Gallery was founded in Florence.

These early museums were essentially private collections, accessible only to their owners; in the seventeenth century, however, it became customary to grant access to learned travelers and educated members of the public, sometimes on receipt of an admission fee. It was out of the tradition of those private collections that the concept of the public museum was born—the creation often inspired by the bequest of the collection to the nation following the death of the owner. Thus it was that the physician Hans Sloane's extensive and diverse collections of antiquities, natural history, and geological specimens, drawings, books, and manuscripts came to form, after his death in 1753, the basis of the first real public museum, the British Museum in London, which first opened its doors to the general public in 1759.

The two hundred years or so following the foundation of this great institution saw the rapid development and proliferation of museums throughout the world; not only museums to serve antiquities and works of art, but museums to document almost every aspect of human experience as well as the natural sciences. As museums have both diversified in terms of their subject matter and specialized with regard to their various points of focus, there has arisen the need for an all-embracing discipline to cope with the numerous aspects and demands of collection curation. The name given to this multifaceted discipline is *museology,* which may be defined as the study of aspects relating to museum collections (in this respect, therefore, the term *museum studies* is to be much preferred because museology might otherwise be taken to indicate a study of museums or even a study of the muses). Clearly, the parameters of this study are variable, depending upon the nature of the collections: the problems facing a museum of philately will not be the same as those confronting a museum of marine transport. In general terms, however, the broad categories of collection care and management are applicable to almost any museum. Restricting the discussion to archaeological museums, the principal subject areas subsumed under the heading of museology or museum studies are display and presentation, conservation and storage, documentation and cataloging, public relations and education, management and policy, and, in the case of some of the larger museums, research.

The issue of display and presentation is perhaps one of the most complex areas of museology, involving, as it often does, a balance between aesthetic values and technical restrictions. The overall design of a particular room or gallery, the arrangement and style of showcases, and the positioning of freestanding exhibits have to be weighed against such factors as access, anticipated number of visitors, and security.

Aesthetically pleasing light levels, both external and in-case, may have to be tempered by consideration of the nature of the objects displayed. Organic materials, textiles, manuscripts, and paintings are light-sensitive, and the level of illumination must consequently be kept low in their display cases. The choice of gallery display materials, again, is a matter to be determined by more than mere physical appearance. In particular, fabrics for case interiors need to be tested rigorously for acidity and sulphide levels, an excess of either being potentially detrimental to the condition of objects placed in close proximity. Control of relative humidity is essential for metal and organic objects, and because the optimum value varies for different materials, it may not be possible to display certain items in the same case. For example, a composite object, such as a bronze daggers with an ivory hilt, would require especially sensitive treatment because the range of relative humidity, acceptable for both materials, may be very narrow indeed. The in-case relative humidity level is normally adjusted by the simple method of inserting a concealed tray of water (to raise the level) or a desiccant such as silica gel (to lower the value). The level is monitored by means of an instrument known as a hygrometer, placed as unobtrusively as possible inside the showcase. Changes in temperature are generally less critical than those in relative humidity. Nevertheless, extremes and large short-term fluctuations must be guarded against if problems such as the stress fracturing of glass and metal artifacts or the softening of materials used in conservation and restoration are to be avoided. It is important, therefore, that the overall design of a gallery incorporate some provision for temperature regulation.

Special attention must also be paid to mounting objects within cases. Mounts to support objects or hold them at particular angles must both protect the item in question, free from stress, and be as unobtrusive as possible. Steel pins, used to mount metal objects on vertical display panels, must be fitted with plastic sleeves to prevent corrosion from the electrochemical reaction contact between the two metals causes.

The layout of a gallery is of prime concern. Archaeologists are notoriously chronologically oriented, an obsession not necessarily shared by the visiting public. While it may seem logical to present archaeological materials chronologically—Chalcolithic, Early Bronze Age, Middle Bronze Age, and so on—thematic presentations may be equally meaningful to the visitor. A gallery could, for example, be organized geographically, or be divided into sections entitled daily life, religion, or weapons and warfare.

The arrangement of objects within cases is largely a matter of taste. Fashions change, and there has been a general tendency in recent years to make displays sparser and more intimate, although there are always instances where greater impact can be gained by presenting objects en masse. Attention should be paid to correct representation: a museum may have a fine collection of, say, unusual Early Bronze Age Syrian terra cottas and jewelry, but to show great numbers of them at the expense of more mundane items would obviously misrepresent the culture. A balance needs to be found between exhibiting objects which are unusual or special and those which are more truly representative.

The provision of labels and information panels constitutes another area of museology for which there are no hard-and-fast rules. Many museums adopt a "house style" to provide a uniformity of in-case labels and information panels throughout their various galleries. Some larger museums, which have their own design department, will be able to produce professional standard panels and labels themselves. Otherwise, this work has to be contracted out, an expensive procedure, especially where graphics or photographs need to be incorporated. Information panels should be exactly that: they should be informative, concise (250 words is the maximum attention limit for most people), and should help to put the exhibited artifacts into context. In-case object labels, similarly, should be clearly and simply worded. Small, unobtrusive numbers, placed next to each item, provide the easiest means of keying the labels to the objects. Labels should, in any event, always include the museum's registration number to assist possible further requests for information. Technical terms should be avoided as much as possible (both on labels and information panels): there is simply no point in specifying the date of an object as "Middle Bronze IIA" (or worse, abbreviated MB IIA) when the vast majority of visitors will barely have grasped the "three ages" system, let alone its idiosyncratic subdivisions. If such terms cannot be avoided, it is essential that a chronological chart with explanatory text be incorporated into the gallery information. Similarly, a map should appear somewhere in the gallery to show the geographic parameters of the exhibits and location of sites.

While display and presentation are arguably the most obvious side of museology (the side seen by the public), there are behind-the-scenes aspects of museum work that are equally important. Storage is often a major problem for museums, especially for those long-established institutions whose space is finite but whose collections continue to grow. Museums that are involved in active fieldwork projects frequently have to resort to outstations in order to cope with processing finds. Their reserve collections, in other words, the items not on permanent exhibition, must be stored following a well-organized system, to keep them accessible to the museum's curators and visiting scholars. Damp, subterranean basements, often the popular image of museum storerooms, are unacceptable. The environmental and climatic control of storage areas is every bit as important as that of the galleries and showcases. This often requires the installation of sophisticated and expensive equipment to handle dust extraction, temperature control, and dehumidification.

Conservation, the preservation of cultural heritage, is an immense subject in itself, covering a wide range of skills and disciplines. At its most basic, "passive conservation" may be seen as the manipulation or control of the environment in order to inhibit the deterioration of an object's condition. A heavily corroded iron dagger placed in appropriately dehumidified storage may not look very attractive, but it will not corrode further. "Active conservation," on the other hand, seeks to arrest and reverse the processes of deterioration by the application of mechanical, chemical, or, in some cases, electrolytic treatments. A bronze bowl, for example, which is found to be deteriorating through the condition known as bronze disease (caused by the presence in the corrosion layer of cuprous chloride) can be mechanically treated using a scalpel. Sites of active bronze disease will be removed, and the overall surface of the bowl will be "cleaned" down to a level within the corrosion layer which is judged to represent the object's original surface. The bowl can then be stabilized using a corrosion inhibitor such as benzotriazole and will then be lacquered to add further protection.

Restoration is the stage beyond conservation, by means of which missing elements of an object are replaced using synthetic materials. A pottery storejar which has been conserved by cleaning and desalinating the individual sherds, and then assembled using an appropriate adhesive, may be found to be missing part of its rim, or to have a broken handle or gaps or holes in the body. Through the process of restoration, these deficiencies can be made good, using a material such as fine dental plaster, which is subsequently painted to provide a near-perfect match.

All three aspects of conservation are relevant to museum collections. The importance of climatic and environmental regulation has already been stressed. In a situation in which this type of control is perfect, the need for active conservation would be minimal beyond the appropriate treatment of new acquisitions. In reality, of course, conditions are never perfect: accidents occur in handling, and many of the materials used in conservation have a finite life-span and may need to be periodically renewed. Small museums may incorporate a laboratory employing one or two conservators who are trained to cope with the full range of materials, or may instead subscribe to a service which provides conservation cover for a number of similar museums in the same region. For large national and international museums, such as the British Museum in London or the Louvre in Paris, both of which have vast and diverse permanent collections, as well as a constant input of archaeological materials from their various field projects, the scale of the operation is much greater. Conservation, in such cases as these, constitutes an established department within the museum, with many laboratories providing facilities for a large number of specialist conservators responsible for individual materials (ceramics, stone, metals, textiles).

A controversial aspect of museology, which draws together display and conservation, lies in the degree to which objects are restored for exhibition. Techniques are so highly refined that it is certainly possible to take, for example, twenty sherds which make up half of the profile of a bowl and produce a complete vessel without even a crack showing. Such a procedure would be seen by most museums as unethical, as would the practice of "completing" an object solely by reference to external evidence. It would not be acceptable, for example, to restore, using a synthetic material, the missing head of a bronze statuette, based on an illustration of a generally similar piece. It would, on the other hand, be perfectly in order to fill in an unsightly gap in the rim of a Greek black-figure vase, or to manufacture the missing second wheel of a terra-cotta chariot model by making a cast of the existing one. While the limits of acceptability vary from museum to museum, most archaeological museums accept a responsibility not to restore beyond what is known or can be established beyond doubt. It is also generally held that the restored elements of an object should be unobtrusive at a distance, but obvious on close examination, leaving no question as to what is original. If an overall trend can be observed in this area, it seems to be one of moving away from restoration. With the viewing public's greater awareness of the processes of archaeology, there is a much greater tolerance and acceptance of artifacts "as found"—pots with gaps and all the breaks showing or animal figurines with missing legs—a recognition of the essential integrity of the objects themselves.

Documentation and cataloging lie at the very heart of any museum's collections. Systems vary, of course, from museum to museum, but whatever method of cataloging is adopted, whether it be on computer, on index file cards, or in bound ledgers, the objective is always the same: to provide for each object in the collection a discrete and specific identification which can be physically applied to the object itself. Catalog entries, whether for Assyrian reliefs or humble potsherds, must be as full and exhaustively documented as possible. This is especially important for archaeological materials where original excavation numbers may have to be removed in favor of the museum's registration number. Clearly, such objects would become utterly meaningless if the catalog entry failed to preserve all details of the context. For any object, the museum's registration entry becomes the primary and fundamental source of information and, as such, should contain the total "profile" of that object. Beyond a physical description (type, material, dimensions, and cultural attributes), each entry should record context details for excavated items and acquisition details for purchased or presented pieces (donor or vendor, source, and price paid). Other relevant information includes publication references, references to any scientific analyses undertaken, details of conservation treatments, references to photographs taken (including appropriate negative numbers), and most importantly of all, an indication of the current location of the object (whether on display or in storage).

Most major museums have adopted computer registration as their normal procedure, opening the way for an international exchange of collections data. Some controls are necessary, however: although it may be extremely convenient and valuable for a curator at the Louvre, for example, to be able to know, at the touch of a button, exactly which bronze items from Beth-Shean stratum VI are held in the collections of the University Museum of the University of Pennsylvania, it may not be appropriate or desirable for, say, the Metropolitan Museum of Art in New York City to know how much the Vienna State Museum paid for a particular Egyptian statuette. Some fields of information may, therefore, need to be restricted, bringing into question ethical issues concerned with freedom of information and access to documentation.

More serious ethical problems have to be addressed with regard to museums' acquisitions policies. Most museums follow ethical codes of practice to ensure that objects illegally exported from their country of origin are not acquired. Regrettably, the guidelines are not followed universally or consistently, and many objects of questionable title find their way into museum collections. It is an unfortunate reality that the trafficking in cultural property involves as much deviousness, misrepresentation, and criminality as the trafficking in drugs. In the case of antiquities, however, the resource is finite; despite claims to the contrary by the so-called legal trade in antiquities, it is undeniably true that any move to purchase items from what is now an international market has a direct, almost proportionate consequence in the looting and destruction of archaeological sites.

In this respect, museums of integrity must adopt the moral high ground. It is becoming increasingly unacceptable for museums to be involved, on any level, with the antiquities trade, either directly through the purchase of objects, or indirectly by offering gallery space to temporary exhibitions of private and often dubiously acquired collections. Such a viewpoint is not incompatible with the desire of museums to add to their collections. National archaeological museums can obviously exploit their own heritage resources through the initiation of home-based field projects.

The international collections of the large multicultural museums, such as the Louvre or the British Museum, need not be static in this respect either. Many countries, in return for the research input, allow a division, or "partage," of excavated finds. Quite apart from the benefits of international cooperation gained through undertaking scientifically controlled research abroad, the objects added to a museum's collections through the process of a legal division will be of immeasurably greater value than the overpriced trinkets of the antiquities market.

The modern archaeological museum has moved a long way from the nineteenth century "cabinet of curiosities." Many of the larger institutions function very much as university faculties, with an overall director or directorate overseeing a number of geographically or chronologically differentiated departments. Each department is staffed by a number of curators responsible for specific and specialized areas; it is their brief not only to superintend the objects within their remit, but more generally to represent their area to the public and to the scholarly community.

Public accountability is of serious concern in state-funded museums, and curators involved in research or field projects must acknowledge an obligation to present the results of their work in exhibitions, public lectures, and publications. These activities may be coordinated through an education department, which not only serves to disseminate the work of the curatorial departments to a wider audience, but also provides guidelines and instructions for teachers and educators.

The modern archaeological museum is, above all, a research institution, often at the very forefront of archaeological and scientific investigation. Many of the larger museums include extensive facilities for scientific analyses, including C-14, neutron-activation, metalography, and petrography—indeed, the full range of analytical techniques designed to complement the work of museum-based excavators and researches and to assist archaeologists from external, often overseas, institutions.

[*See also* Analytical Techniques; Artifact Conservation; Ethics and Archaeology; *and* Restoration and Conservation.]

JONATHAN N. TUBB

MUSICAL INSTRUMENTS. The understanding, sociohistorical interpretation, and research of musical instruments (sound tools) as part of human culture is a *conditio sine que non* of modern scholarship. Modern musicologists define music as a pattern of human behavior in a relevant cultural context, in which sound-producing tools undergo changes based on changes in culture. Musical instruments and their iconographic representations are the only available material evidence from preliterate societies and are the primary source of investigation for societies that have an oral musical tradition. An interdisciplinary approach, combining archaeological, sociohistorical, musicological, and ethnographic-comparative analysis, has turned archaeomusicology (a field established as an independent branch of scholarship only in the late 1970s–early 1980s) into a most effective tool of study of music in ancient cultures.

While archaeological finds of musical instruments may make it possible actually to hear "historical sound," and provide information on the audial ecology of the past, archaeological iconography is more helpful in studying sociocultural matters, performance practices, the social performance environs, and the body language of performers. The central tool of organological research (typological analysis) raises the question of classification (Kartomi, 1990, pp. 12–13). It is assumed that each culture has both its own "culture-emerging," or "natural," musical instrument classification (which scholarship does not necessarily always discover—e.g., Phoenician instruments) and an "observer-imposed," or "artificial," one created for a particular research scheme. Certain Near Eastern cultures (e.g., Sumerian) appear to tend to a natural model guided by the construction material of the musical instrument itself (e.g., determinatives are *giš*, "wood"; *gi*, "cane"; *si*, "horn"; compare Sachs, 1940, p. 164); some (e.g., Hittite) combine this with the method of sound production (*hazzik*, "strike"; *pariparái*, "blow"; Turnbull, 1980, p. 391); others (Israelite/Judean), divide instruments into sacred (horn, trumpet), levitic (lyre), and secular (reed pipes) (Braun, 1994, col. 1512). On the other hand, since the early days of organology, artificial classification systems have been used, although natural systems sometimes contribute more to understanding a certain culture. At present, Erich M. von Hornbostel and Curt Sachs's artificial classification (*Zeitschrift für Ethnologie*, 46 [1914]: 553–590) appears to be the most functional system for ancient cultures. It is based on the source of sound, or the nature of the vibrating body: idiophones, membraphones, aerophones, and chordophones (see below).

The names of the musical instruments are in most cases highly uncertain. Contrary to the conditions in Egypt, where iconographic sources frequently are accompanied by texts bearing the name of the depicted instrument, other Near Eastern archaeological finds lack written comments, and the preserved texts with names of musical instruments include hardly any information on the type of instrument. Only as late as the third century BCE–third century CE do the first known parallels of iconographic and written sources appear (*lilissu*, Akkadian, "kettle drum": Rashid, 1984, p. 140; *zmr*, clarinet-type double pipe with one long pipe and one short one: Braun, 1993, p. 176). Most names of musical instruments have to remain in the realm of suggestions (e.g., *GIS gù-di/dè*, "lute": Anne Kilmer and Dominique Collon, 1980–1983, vol. 6, p. 512), but there are several exceptions (Old Sumerian *balag*, "harp"; Bib. Heb. *ḥăṣōṣĕrâ*, "trumpet"). In certain cases one name is used for different instruments of one type (e.g., *tp*, different drums, most Semitic languages).

The primary importance of ancient Egyptian, Hebrew, Greek, and Roman music cultures has been acknowledged since the beginnings of modern (eighteenth century) music historiography. Carl Engel's study of the music of ancient cultures was the first to focus on archaeological sources (Engel, 1864). The first clear statement on the decisive significance of Near Eastern musical instruments for world music culture was made by the founder of contemporary organology, Curt Sachs (1940). The linguistic approach, which dominated studies of ancient Near Eastern musical instruments, and proved to be insufficient, dominated the period following World War II but was more and more replaced by a combined interdisciplinary approach.

Since World War II, the study of ancient musical instruments has focused on three areas:

1. *Musical instrument types*. Based on a typological approach to musical instruments, the study of instrument types mostly strives for an organological-ergological and historical classification. Its aim is to produce a "history" of the type (see the classical examples of lasting value in Hickmann, 1949–).

2. *Musical instrumentarium of certain cultures or geographic areas*. Socioanthropologically oriented, studies of instrumentarium strive to incorporate archaeomusicological research results into the general framework of historiography. (For Egypt, Mesopotamia, Rome, Greece, Central Asia, and Islam, see the series *Musikgeschichte in Bildern;* for Anatolia see the encyclopedia entries in Max Wegner (1949–) and Harvey Turnbull (1980); for the Sasanian period see Marcelle Duchesne-Guillemin, 1993; and for Israel/Palestine see Joachim Braun (1996).

3. *Artifacts*. Nearly the broadest, in terms of quantity, and developed along with musicologists by archaeologists, historians, and art historians, the study of individual artifacts recovered in excavations stresses the organological-ergological, or socioanthropological, approach.

The few studies designed with a comprehensive Near Eastern approach, continue the approach of Engel and Sachs. However, the discussions of the different Near Eastern areas and cultures are individual and not synthetic. Wegner defends the position that "the ancient Oriental world does not present a unity also in its musical culture" (Wegner, 1950, p. 50), which is especially true, according to the author, of the opposed nature of Near Eastern and Hellenistic musical instruments: the former are changeable and irregular and the latter are stable and invariable. This disputable theory was developed based on Sachs's thesis on the "classical" and quite solemn character of Egyptian Old Middle Kingdom musical instruments, as opposed to the orgiastic, noisy, and savage character of the New Kingdom/Near Eastern sound tools (Sachs, 1940, p. 98). This popular theory was proved wrong by Hickmann (1961b) on the basis of later archaeological discoveries.

The only attempt to discuss Near Eastern musical instruments comprehensively was made by Hickmann (1957, 1961b). His central conclusions are still unchallenged: in certain cases the Egyptian music instrumentarium (e.g., rattles, sistrum, concussion sticks, flute, trumpet) influenced Babylonian cultures; in others primacy belonged to the Sumerians (e.g., lyre, angular harp, cymbals, frame drums); and in still others the development was parallel but independent (e.g., the harp; Hickmann, 1961b, pp. 23, 35). As regards the provenance of the Western instrumentarium, "certain is the Oriental provenance . . . of a number of musical instruments, which are adequate to the common sound-ideal of the Mediterranean countries" (Hickmann, 1957, p. 35). The central Phoenician and Israel/Palestine area of the eastern Mediterranean coast from the Sinai desert to Anatolia was considered to be a transit channel only; its significance as a center with an indigenous culture was ignored, even though a number of musical instruments, and especially new instrumental performance traditions, originated there (see Caubet and Braun in Homo-Lechner, 1994, pp. 129–147).

Idiophones. Self-sounders, or sound produced by vibrations of the substance of the instrument itself (e.g., rattles, cymbals), are known as idiophones.

Natufian strung rattles. Rattles from modern Israel's Carmel range (11,000–9,000 BCE) are the earliest attested sound tools in the Near East (see figure 1). This type of syncretic jewelry/sound cult object, often disregarded by researchers, exists in various forms and has probably always been an artifact of culture.

Concussion sticks. Pictograms from Uruk (Uruk IV period, 3000–2900 BCE) and a carved shell from a burial (no. PG789) at Ur show concussion sticks. A bronze sound tool also was found at Kish from the Jemdet Nasr period (2900–2800 BCE) (Rashid, 1984, ill. 8). Egyptian ivory concussion sticks appear somewhat earlier (first dynasty, 3300–3000 BCE).

Sistrum. In the middle of the third millennium, the sistrum (a type of rattle) appears in both Sumer and Egypt; the Sumerian examples are U-shaped and are open at the top (Rashid, 1984, ills. 8, 42), and the Egyptian examples are rectangular, in the shape of a temple naos, a Hathor image, or a horseshoe (Hickmann, 1961a, p. 160, ills. 26–27). Only two or three centuries later, rectangular metal sistra, ornamented with animal figurines, appeared at the Anatolian sites of Horoztepe, and Alaca Höyük (Turnbull, 1980, p. 388). In all cultures, sistra were cult instruments.

Clay rattles. The most popular Near Eastern idiophones are clay rattles. Among those preserved are egg-shaped examples from the fifth-millennium Lower Egyptian Merimde culture (Hickmann, 1949, p. 70, pl. XLIII); these are the oldest examples and were in use at least until the eighteenth dynasty. Zoomorphic and piecrust shaped clay rattles from the Old Babylonian period (1950–1530 BCE) have been found at nearly every Mesopotamian site (Rimmer, 1969, pl. III), and from the Middle Bronze Age IA–II in ancient Israel/Palestine, some one hundred items in zoomorphic, anthropomorphic, and geometric forms are preserved—the spool shape being the most popular. On Cyprus, the Late

MUSICAL INSTRUMENTS. Figure 1. *Female thigh bone with a fox tooth rattle.* From Hayonim Cave (Mt. Carmel, Israel); early Natufian period. Rockefeller Museum, IAA 79.536. (Courtesy Israel Museum, Jerusalem)

Bronze zoomorphic forms, especially of birds, are found frequently (Cyprus Museum, no. A-990). The quantity, dispersion, and archaeological context of the Near Eastern clay rattles, which preserve an indigenous artistic form in every local culture, confirm their plural function as a cult implement, amulet, sound tool, and game—rather than solely as a child's toy, and substantiates it as a mass produced music, cult, and culture commodity.

Bells. From the early first millennium BCE, bronze bells appear—mostly the sound tool itself (from Nimrud alone there are some one hundred bells that are the property of the British Museum)—that are rarely represented iconographically: the first representations are horse bells on Assyrian bas-reliefs (Rimmer, 1969, pls. XVII, XVIII). Bells are first attested in the tenth century BCE in northern Persia, at Amlash (Rimmer, pl. XIXc–d) and a century later in Assyria, at Nimrud (Rimmer pl. XIXa), and in Israel/Phoenicia, at Megiddo (Oriental Institute, no. M936); two centuries later they are found on Cyprus and in twenty-third-dynasty Egypt at Tell Basta (Hickmann, 1949, pl. XXIIIA). A dispersion from east to west and a Caucasian or Asian provenience are thus plausible. Bells in various sizes (2.5–12 cm) and forms were designed for animals and humans, mostly probably with an apotropaic function (a supposition based on *Ex.* 28:35 and questioned for its uniform interpretation by Peter Calmeyer, (1966, vol. 3, p. 431). Bell-shaped clay rattles and clay bells (Rashid, 1984, ill. 131, Hebrew University, no. 9245; also on Cyprus: Limassol District Museum, no. T474) may indicate a continuity of the social and acoustic function of the two idiophones.

Scrapers. Notched implements, such as scapulae, were scraped with a rigid object to produce sound. Scrapers are known throughout the world from prehistoric times. While they do not appear with any frequency in the Near East, there are examples from Ugarit, thirteenth century BCE (Caubet, 1987, figs. 1, 2) and eleventh century BCE Ekron (Trude Dothan and Seymour Gitin, "Tel Miqne (Ekron) 1982," *Israel Exploration Journal* 33 [1983]: 127–129). A concentration of some ten items was discovered at Kiton, from the twelfth–fifth centuries BCE (Vassos Karageorghis, *Excavations at Kiton,* vol. 5.2, 1985, p. 317); however, the identification of these artifacts as sound tools, based on the presence of trails of erased patina, is doubtful (Karageorghis, 1985 pp. 327–328).

Bronze cymbals. Among the best-attested musical instruments for the entire Near East are bronze cymbals. The earliest representations are on bas-reliefs from southern Babylonia at the end of the third millennium (Rashid, 1984, pp. 70–73). These rather large (some are 20 cm in diameter) cymbals, however, disappeared in Neo-Assyrian times; at Nimrud (ninth century BCE) true cymbals (some 10 cm in diameter) were discovered (Rashid, 1984, p. 110). More than twenty pairs of cymbals (12–8 and 6–4 cm in diameter) dated at least four hundred years earlier have been found at Late Bronze Canaanite/Phoenician sites (Tell Abu Hawam, Hazor, Megiddo). Already mentioned in fourteenth-century BCE sources from Ugarit (Caubet, 1987, p. 734), and frequently encountered in the Hebrew Bible *(mĕṣiltayim),* cymbals disappear from the archaeological finds of Israel/Palestine between the Early Iron Age and the Hellenistic period. Figurines of cymbal players were popular in the Neo-Babylonian kingdom (Rashid, 1964, p. 134), and on Cyprus (Hickmann, 1949, fig. 29; Israel Antiquities Authority, no. P1823); cymbals appear in Anatolia (Bittel, 1968) and Egypt (Marcuse, 1975, p. 10) from the seventh century BCE onward. Cymbals and forked crotala (see below) were widely used at Cybele and Dionysian cult events in Palestine, Anatolia, and Syria, as well as in the Sasanian kingdom.

Forked crotala. Small cymbals attached to a forked handle (forked crotala) and larger cymbals were among the most popular instruments in the Hellenistic–Roman Near East (Farmer, 1966, pp. 18, 23, 27). A frequent combination of instruments seems to be the crotala and the organ (Braun, 1994, p. 142).

Membranophones. Instruments that produce vibrations from a tightly stretched membrane, such as the drum, are known as membranophones. Drums belong to the most ancient and popular category of musical instruments attested in the Near East, where they are the main membranophone. They were made with one or two membranes and in various sizes (20–150 cm) and forms (round and square frame, cylindrical, hourglass, kettle, goblet, and bowl shaped). They were held in several positions (in front of the chest, above the head, under the arm) or placed on the ground. Wall paintings of a hunting shrine at Çatal Höyük in Anatolia (level A.III. 1, seventh millennium) shows men dancing and beating small round-frame drums with a stick (see Doris Stockmann in Lund, 1986, pp. 12–14). This drum (with one or two skins?) appears again at the beginning of the second millennium BCE in a scene of dancing etched on a rock in Israel's Negev desert (Anati, 1963, p. 211) and remains the main membranophone of the Near East. It seems that beginning in the Chalcolithic/EB terra-cotta goblet-, cornet-, chalice- (Ghassulian culture: e.g. IAA, no. 36.66, 36.97) and hour-glass-forms (Gilat, in the Negev: IAA, no. 76.54) were used. In the late third millennium the Mesopotamian giant drum, probably in bronze, or with a bronze frame (Schmidt-Colinet, 1981, ills. 71–75), and in the early second millennium BCE the bronze goblet form, *lilissu* (Schmidt-Colinet, 1981, ills. 76, 77), appeared. A barrel-shaped drum with two skins and a rectangular drum are attested in Middle Kingdom Egypt (Hickmann, 1961a, pp. 28, 106). With rare exceptions, the entire corpus of pre-Iron Age drum iconography shows the instrument in a cultic context.

In the first half of the second millennium BCE in Old Babylonia and later, but especially in the Iron Age, in other Near

Eastern areas, two forms of the female drum player, the most notable indigenous type, appear on deep-relief terracotta plaques. The figures are naked but adorned with a wig or headcover and a disk (drum) is pressed against the chest with both hands (Rashid, 1984, ills. 91–95); and as bell-shaped figures dressed in a long gown, beating the drum, which is in a position perpendicular to the body (Meyers, 1987). Preserved only in Israel/Palestine, there are more than forty items of the first type and some fifteen of the second extant. Mixed types appear on Cyprus and in Syria: pillar figurines with a disk pressed against the chest and figurines on votive stands. It is probably at this time that the drum (*tōph* in the Hebrew Bible) acquired a function in both the cultic and everyday life of the lower strata of the population. The function of this type—homogeneous in its Near Eastern unity and autochthonous—is not yet clear: the range of use is from *dea nutrix* and amulet to apotropaic object and toy; even the identification of the disk type is questioned (drum, solar disk, bread?). The hourglass drum (*darabbuka,* also a popular drum among modern Arabs and Druze), characteristically held under the arm, appears once in the Negev and more frequently in finds from Old Babylonia between the Iron Age and Hellenistic periods. Excavations from the Hellenistic-Roman period confirm the appearance of the Greco-Roman frame drum (mostly on mosaics—e.g., at Sepphoris in Israel; see Meyers, Netzer, and Meyers, 1992, p. 49). In the earliest drum iconography, the membranophone-chordophone in duet is considered to be a typical Near Eastern ensemble (cf. Anati, 1963, p. 211, for Negev rock-etchings; Rashid, 1984, p. 76).

Aerophones. Vibrations of air enclosed in an instrument, produced by wind or breath across its edge (flute), via a reed (clarinet), a double reed (oboe), or the performer's lips (trumpet) distinguish the category of instruments known as aerophones.

Bullroarer. A slab of wood 10–20 cm long, rhomboid in form and frequently carved and ornamented, with a small hole at the end for a cord, is a bullroarer. It is a noisemaker used at ritual and magic events that produces a roaring sound through circular movement. Probably one of the earliest aerophones, it is attested by the finds from the Natufian Kebara cave in Israel's Carmel hills (IAA, no. 13.85) and the Neolithic Nahal Hemar cave (*Treasures of the Holy Land,* Metropolitan Museum of Art, New York, 1986, fig. 17). In Egypt, the bullroarer appears in predynastic times (Hickmann, 1961a, p. 157).

Flute. The first archaeological evidence for flutes is not earlier than the late fourth millennium in Egypt, (Hickmann, 1961a, ills. 1, 4); this flute type, the *nay* (60–90 cm long) is still in use and is usually held at an oblique angle. The flute is also attested in third millennium-Mesopotamia (Rashid, 1984, p. 50). The single flute, however, either was not popular in the ancient Near East, or was not frequently depicted in the Bronze and Iron Ages because of its low status. A corpus of some ten short (7–12 cm) whistles with a single side opening has appeared in areas of Canaan/modern Israel, the earliest dated to the third millennium (Megiddo: IAA, no. 39.680) and the latest to the seventh century BCE. In the first-dynasty royal cemetery at Ur, fragments of silver tubes were discovered that have been interpreted as flutes or other reed instruments.

Double pipe. The most typical aerophone in the ancient Near East was the double pipe (two tubes) with a single or double reed (i.e., a clarinet or an oboe type, not a flute), which produces a rich, harsh, penetrating, and sensual timbre. While the single flute was still in use during the Old Babylonian period (Rashid, 1984, ills. 85, 86), the divergent double pipe with cylindrical tubes, of Cycladian provenience (Aign, 1963, ill. I/5), permeated musical life. The double pipe has been discovered in excavations in contexts from the middle of the second millennium BCE up to Byzantine times; mostly, however, it appears in iconographic material both as a single instrument and in ensembles. The differences in representations are mainly in the degree of divergence of the pipes: length of the longer pipe (possibly a drone), how it is held (horizontally or vertically, together or apart), performance style (position of the hands), and type of reed. Finds from the ninth–seventh centuries BCE (e.g., from Achziv: IAA, no. 44.56; Karatepe: Schmidt-Colinet, 1981, no. 89) show that the double-pipe performer—mostly female—had become a popular Near Eastern terracotta figurine type, along with the drum player (see above.)

The instrument acquired all the signs of the classic aulos; in Greece itself, however, the instrument does not appear prior to 700 BCE. After the seventh century BCE, the *phorbeia* (a leather band passed over the lips and cheeks to secure stability while blowing) appears on Cypriot and Anatolian (see figure 2) figurines (e.g., Schmidt-Colinet, 1981, no. 90; Hermary et al., 1989, no. 578.579), but is absent from Neo-Assyrian examples and in material from Israel/Palestine. The double pipe is frequently part of the Neo-Assyrian orchestra (e.g., the Elamite orchestra, Niniveh, seventh century BCE; see Rashid, 1984, ill. 151), or the membraphone-aerophone-chordophone "Phoenician orchestra" (ninth–seventh centuries BCE: Aign, 1963, figs. 89, 90, 91) that can be traced back to Philistia/Israel ensembles from the eleventh to the tenth centuries BCE (Braun, 1994, p. 143; Ashdod: IAA, no. 68.1182). In Hellenistic-Roman contexts, finds of actual aulos instruments are frequent and seem to indicate microtone scales (e.g., Gezer: IAA, no. 81.1839). In that period, also for the first time, the double pipe with a short melody pipe and long drone (*arghul* type) can be attested with certainty (Safaitic basalt etching: Jordan, J. 1886). Mosaics and other artifacts from the Hellenistic–Roman period show the double pipe both as a musical instrument of lament (e.g., in a wall painting in the Idumean necropolis at Marisa/Mareshah, (in situ) and of orgiastic joy (in a Dionysian context: Braun, 1995).

MUSICAL INSTRUMENTS. Figure 2. *Bell-form figurine with double pipe.* From Achziv, Israel. Dated to the ninth-eighth century BCE. Rockefeller Museum, IAA 44.56. (Courtesy Israel Museum, Jerusalem)

Zamr. A new period in the history of the double pipes, and especially single pipes, began with the use of conoid reed pipes. The *zamr* type of double flute from the seventh century BCE is still dominant in the Near East. Among the first examples to attest this aerophone type is one from Tel Malḥata, in southern Israel: a terra-cotta figurine of a man blowing a divergent conical double pipe (IAA, no. 94.3393); bronze figurines from Anatolia should be associated with this type of aerophone rather than with trumpets (cf. Turnbull, 1980, fig. 8). Single *zamr* instruments appear on numerous artifacts, mostly in pastoral surroundings (Beth-Shean, sixth century, Lady Mary Monastery mosaic, in situ: Farmer, 1966, ill. 5).

Panpipe. The earliest evidence of panpipes *(syrinxes)* in the region is probably from Anatolia (seventh century BCE: Turnbull, 1980, fig. 7). It has been one of the most popular instruments in the Near East since Seleucid times (Rashid, 1984, p. 142) and has kept its autochthonous peculiarities in every area. In the second century CE the panpipe was accepted as a symbol on the city coins of Paneas/Banias in northern Palestine (in the second–third centuries called Caesarea Philippi; see Israel Museum no. 2883). Representations of *zamr* instruments appear on other coins from Paneas, the oldest of which in the Near East is the depiction of a cross flute (Meshorer, 1984–1985, figs. 6a, 27).

Organ. In the third century BCE the organ, based on the panpipe *(hydraulus),* was invented in Alexandria, Egypt. The first iconographic evidence of this instrument are terra cottas from Alexandria (second–first centuries BCE: Perrot, 1971, pl. V), Tarsus (pre-Christian: Perrot, 1971, pl. XVI/1), and Carthage (second century: Perrot, 1971, pl. XII). The most significant example has come to light in a Hamath (Syria) mosaic that depicts a third-century ensemble performance (organ, crotals, lyre, double aulos, bells, sounding bowls). Attention has been drawn to the Samaritan terra-cotta oil lamps, that depict an organ (again with crotala; see Braun in Homo-Lechner, 1994, p. 142); it seems that this instrument was used in both liturgical and secular life.

Animal horns. Comparatively scarcely attested, animal horns may have been used in Anatolian Neolithic cultures (Lund, 1986, p. 20), but they undoubtedly appear in only two finds: in an early second-millennium BCE drawing from Mari (Perrot, 1961, ill. 389) and in a ninth–eighth century BCE stone relief from Carchemish (Schmidt-Colinet, 1981, ill. 75). There is evidence as well of the use of oxhorns in fifteenth-century BCE Egypt during the reign of Amenhotep IV (Marcuse, 1975, p. 747).

Shofar. The ram's horn, or shofar, is the most frequently mentioned music instrument (seventy-two times) in the Hebrew Bible. However, it does not appear in archaeological contexts until the third century (among the earliest appearance is in the Hammath Tiberias synagogue mosaic, in situ): the shofar is always part of a group of synagogue symbols (menorah, shofar, lulav, etrog).

Shell horn. A different type of horn, the shell horn, was used in Israel/Palestine beginning at least in the late second millenium BCE (Tell Qasile: Hebrew University no. 2968:227).

Trumpet. The elite music instrument the trumpet descends from the animal horn and is similar to it. It appears rarely, however. Besides the two famous Tutankhamun trumpets (one silver, 58.2 cm, and the other bronze, 49.4 cm), there are only some fifteen representations of the trumpet from Egypt. Among them, the first certain depiction (sixteenth–fifteenth centuries BCE), shows a clear cultic and military affiliation (Manniche, 1975, pp. 33–35; Hickmann, 1961a, p. 74). Mesopotamian cultures show extremely little evidence for this instrument: there are only two between the Mesalim and Neo-Babylonian periods (Rashid, 1984, ills. 37, 143). The situation is similar in Israel/Palestine, where, contrary to its significance in the Hebrew Bible (e.g., *Nu.* 10:2–10), and in the Dead Sea Scrolls from Qumran (1QM II.15 and VII.9), the only iconographic evidence for the trumpet is on the wall paintings in the Idumean necropolis near Beth-Guvrin (in situ, third–second centuries BCE). There, for the first time in trumpet iconography, the instrument—an early example of the Roman tuba—is part of a hunting scene. The aerophones depicted on the coins minted by Bar Kokhba in 132–135, frequently defined as trumpets, can hardly be considered as such (Sachs, 1940, p. 120), and the two trumpets depicted among the booty from the Jerusalem Temple on the Arch of Titus in Rome may not necessarily be the Temple instruments but, rather, copies of the Roman tuba. There are only isolated instances of trumpet representations from later periods, such as the pair of trumpets on the rock carving at Tak-i-Bostan from the Sasanian period (Behn, 1954, p. 77). In spite of the early appearance and significance of the trumpet in Egypt, and the importance attached to it in Near Eastern written sources, this instrument may actually have been used very little in the Levant.

Chordophones. An instrument in which a stretched string vibrates is known as a chordophone. Its subgroups are the zither, lyre, harp, and lute. The phenomenon of the appearance of sophisticated string instruments at very early stages in the history of music without evidence of earlier rudimentary forms is clearly manifested in the Near East.

Harp. The oldest archaeological document of a chordophone is a stone from Megiddo, strata XIX (figure 3) etched with a female figure with a triangular, fully developed harp. The instrument appears again in Cycladic culture (Aign, 1963, figs. 1–3) but was not witnessed again in the Near East. While other forms of the harp have been attested since the early third millennium in Mesopotamia and the fourth dynasty in Egypt, the harp itself is absent from the central areas along the eastern Mediterranean coast from the Sinai to Anatolia (Caubet and Braun in Homo-Lechner 1994, pp. 132, 141; Turnbull, 1980, p. 388). This strongly questions the popular interpretation of *nēbel* in the Hebrew Bible as the "harp" of ancient Israel.

The early Sumerian harp (Uruk IV and Mesalim periods), a small (50–70 cm), arched instrument, is depicted mainly on seals in a cultic context, frequently being played by animals (Rashid, 1984, pp. 52–59). At the beginning of the second millennium BCE, the arched harp was replaced by the angular harp, which was held vertically or horizontally (Rashid, 1984, figs. 42–49); while the horizontal harp was known only in Mesopotamia, the vertical one was used to the west, especially on Cyprus (Rashid, 1984, fig. 51). Toward the first millennium BCE, the size of the instrument and the number of strings increased. The horizontal harp (eight–twelve strings) was plucked with a plectrum and the vertical harp (eighteen–twenty-two strings) with the hand, which suggests a basso function for the first and a melodic function for the second. The placement of the hands on the strings allows some conclusions about the style of the music being played (Sachs, 1940, p. 82). A new small rectangular vertical harp with upright resonator on the side of the frame appeared during the Seleucid period (Rashid, 1984, p. 150; Behn, 1954, pl. 55; Dor, Exp. no. 61378); in Roman times this type *(sambyke?)* became popular throughout the Near East, Greece, and Rome. The first Egyptian harps, also arched, are dated somewhat later (fourth dynasty; Hickmann, 1961a, pp. 20–27) than the Sumerian but are much larger (150–180 cm); they appear in sophisticated forms, some richly ornamented, with a developed tuning system (up to thirty-six pegs), and others nearly angular (e.g., an example from the tomb of Rameses III: Hickmann, 1961a, pp. 44, 64, 128). There are representations since the eighteenth dynasty of the vertical angular harp, which is considered an import from elsewhere in the Near East (Hickmann, 1961a, pp. 30, 130); smaller harps are depicted as well—the portable "shoulder harp" (Hickmann, 1961a, ill. 95) and the "ladle harp" (Hickmann, 1961a, ills. 93, 94). All of these instruments, mostly built from expensive wood from Lebanon and designed as works of art, seem to have been used only in the highest circles of society. In terms of chronology, the Egyptian harps followed in the footsteps of the Mesopotamian harps but developed greater sophistication in con-

MUSICAL INSTRUMENTS. Figure 3. *Stone etching from Megiddo, showing a figure with a harp.* Dated to the late fourth millennium. Israel Museum, IAA 38.954. (Courtesy Israel Museum, Jerusalem)

struction. In Hellenistic-Roman times, in both the Ptolemaic and Seleucid Empires, the smaller, simply worked, angular harp (Hickmann, 1961a, ill. 109) was played.

Lyre. The primary musical instrument in the Near East was the lyre. From its first appearance on Sumerian seals in the first half of the third millennium, where it is depicted as a perfect chordophone (Rashid, 1984, p. 50), the lyre dominates the musical scene of the region until the Early Byzantine period. The elaborate Sumerian asymmetrical lyres have a resonator in the form of a bull (upright it is some 150 cm high) or are ornamented with a bull's head (portable, 100–120 cm), and have eight–twelve strings. The instruments recovered in excavation and supplemented by iconographic material (Hickmann, 1961a, ills. 11, 28–39) show a royal context for lyre music. The smaller, vertically held, asymmetrical lyre with two unequal side-arms appeared in Akkad and was played also in Carchemish and Babylon (Hickmann, 1961, ill. 43; Aign, 1963, figs. 78, 79). In the late third–early second millennium BCE, when large standing lyres were still in use (in Babylon: Rashid, 1984, ills. 79, 80; in Anatolia: Turnbull, 1980, p. 388), and the first modified forms appeared in the hands of naked dancing women (Negev rock etching, nineteenth century BCE: Anati, 1963, p. 210), dramatic changes took place nearly simultaneously in several places in the Near East. The Sumerian grand royal lyre was replaced by a simply built, small (some 40–50 cm), portable, symmetrical, and sometimes asymmetrical, instrument. For the first time it was held horizontally, in front of the musician; it was played mostly by musicians of low social status, Semitic traveling merchants, and women—the latter often depicted naked (Rashid, 1984, ills. 47, 59, 76, 80; Behn, 1954, pl. 85; Porada, 1956, figs. g–j). The new lyre type entered Egypt from Syria and Canaan. It took root there in its horizontal asymmetrical form and was played only by women. In Late Bronze Age Canaan, a new way to hold the asymmetrical lyre, with the sound box under the arm, can be seen from Megiddo (IAA, no. 38.780). This change significantly increased performance possibilities, and in its new capacity the lyre became the main instrument of priests and musicians in holy places, courts, and elite military orchestras (Rashid, 1984, ills. 120, 142, 145, 148, 150). This new playing technique migrated to Assyria, partly with musicians-prisoners from Judah (Rashid, 1984, ill. 142). The first half of the first millennium BCE is marked by a multitude of lyre forms, demonstrating both the autochthonous creativity of different groups and certain common Near Eastern tendencies. The most common forms follow:

U form. Examples of a U-shaped form with parallel strings can be seen from the eleventh century BCE on Cyprus at Palaipaphos-Xerolimni; in Israel/Palestine at Ashdod; and in Anatolia at Karatepe (Porada, 1956).

Symmetrical square form. Examples of a symmetrical square form with a parallel, or fanlike, arrangement of its strings appeared mainly in Assyria and Israel/Palestine (Rashid, 1984, ill. 150; Braun, 1990–1991, figs. 1, 3; Behn, 1954, fig. 19; Kamid el-Loz excavations, no. 78:504).

Asymmetrical square form. Examples of an asymmetrical square form appear with differently arranged strings throughout the Near East, including Egypt (Hickmann, 1961a, p. 138; Rashid, 1984, pp. 126, 134; Braun, 1990–1991, figs. 4–6).

In Israel/Palestine and Assyria, the preference seems to have been for a parallel string arrangement. In the Hellenistic-Roman period the lyre tended to be the symmetrical Roman type with a rounded or square sound box, animal-horn side arms, and mostly parallel strings; this instrument is often represented in a stylized form (Hickmann, 1961a, ills. 110, 111; Braun, 1994, cols. 1509–10; Rashid, 1984, pp. 152–153; Behn, 1954, pl. 48) and appears in nearly every social context.

Lute. Instruments of the lute type are the most mobile, dynamic, and subject to change among all chordophones. By permitting the performance of a nearly unrestricted number of sounds from one string, they can be adjusted to any kind of tonal system and music style. Their inexpensive and simple construction, as compared to harps and lyres, and their rustic, entertaining, and erotic performance context made them popular among the common people, which may also may explain the comparatively rare depictions of the instrument. The question of the origin of the lute remains unanswered—theories range from the Caucasus and Central Asia (Marcuse, 1975, p. 406), to Syria and Babylon (Turnbull, 1972; Rashid, 1984, p. 92). The first iconographic evidence for the long-necked lute appears on seals from Akkad, probably in a cultic context (Rashid, 1984, ills. 38, 39).

In the Old Babylonian period, the musicians are often naked men and women (Rashid, 1984, pp. 75–76, 81–84); the lute rarely appears then in connection with a cult or temple service, although later it does, in Anatolia (Schmidt-Colinet, 1981, figs. 60, 62). In the middle of the second millennium BCE, probably via Canaan (male terra-cotta figurine, sixteenth century BCE: IAA, no. 33.1567) the lute reached Egypt. While attested in Canaan in two more finds (naked female bronze statuette: IAA, no. M969; dancing minstrel on a terra-cotta plaque: Hebrew Union College, no. 23.095), the lute does not appear in Israel/Palestine again until the Hellenistic period. In Egypt the instrument became very popular and was played by naked females (Hickmann, 1961a, p. 98) and on some occasions by men, possibly in a cultic context (Hickmann, 1961a, ill. 101).

In the earliest depictions, lutes are generally shown with two–three strings marked with decorative tassels at the tuning box. A long, frequently fretted neck emerges from a small, resonator out of wood or tortoise shell and covered with animal hide. Mostly plucked with a plectrum, fastened by a cord to the body of the instrument, the form of the lute has not changed significantly over the centuries. How it was held, however, has changed constantly, and there have been attempts to create a lute chronology according to the playing position: Old-Babylonian period, horizontal; Kassite–Neo-Assyrian period, lute neck at an oblique angle, pointing upward; Seleucid period, lute neck at an oblique angle, pointing downward (Rashid, 1984, p. 146). The short-necked lute with a broad, pear-shaped body, perhaps of Central Asian origins, appeared only rarely in the ancient Near East (it appeared for the first time in the Egyptian nineteenth dynasty: Hickmann, 1961a, ill. 104). In Hellenistic times the instrument is represented on terra cottas from Egypt and Palestine (Hickmann, 1961a, ill. 105; Marisa/Mareshah excavation, no. 1386), and it acquired great popularity in the Sasanian period (Farmer, 1966, ill. 4; Duchesne-Guillemin, 1993), when it developed into one of the most popular traditional instruments of Islamic countries, the *'ud,* predecessor of the European lute.

Zither. The zither type is actually nonexistent in the Near East, and information on this chordophone type, often also called psaltery (*psalteria,* from Gk., *psalmos,* "finger," because in antiquity their strings were plucked with bare fingers) is scarce and confused. The only known example, also interpreted by some scholars as a xylophone (Wegner, 1950, p. 36), is a beautiful carving on an ivory pyxis (BM, no. 118179, ninth–eighth century BCE), where as part of a small Phoenician orchestra two persons are plucking(?) square stringed frames (nine and ten strings) or boxes (Aign, 1963, pp. 158–159)

[*Most of the sites, peoples, and cultures mentioned are the subject of independent entries.*]

BIBLIOGRAPHY

Aign, Bernhard P. *Die Geschichte der Musikinstrumente des Ägäischen Raums bis zum 700 v. Chr.* Frankfurt am Main, 1963. The best discussion of archaeological material from preclassical times, including rich Near Eastern comparative material.

Anati, Emmanuel. *Palestine Before the Hebrews.* New York, 1963, p. 211.

Bayer, Bathja. *The Material Relics of Music in Ancient Palestine and Its Environs: An Archaeological Inventory.* Tel Aviv, 1963. Useful catalog of finds based on a bibliography; does not indicate the artifacts' place of preservation.

Becker, Heinz. *Zur Entwicklungsgeschichte der antiken und mittelalterlichen Rohrblattinstrumente.* Hamburg, 1966. Basic study of ancient reed instruments.

Behn, Friedrich. *Musikleben im Altertum und frühen Mittelalter.* Stuttgart, 1954. Separate chapters on Mesopotamian, Egyptian, Phoenician, Hebrew, Sasanian, and other Near Eastern music cultures, with special stress on organological rather than cultural matters. Includes more than two hundred illustrations.

Bittel, Kurt. "Cymbeln für Kybele." In *Günther Wasmuth zum 80. Geburtstag gewidmet von seinen Freunden, Kollegen und Autoren,* pp. 79–82. Tübingen, 1968.

Braun, Joachim. "Iron Age Seals from Ancient Israel Pertinent to Music." *Orbis Musicae: Essays in Honor of Hanoch Avenary* 10 (1990–1991): 11–26.

Braun, Joachim. "'. . . die Schöne spielt die Pfiefe': Zur nabatäisch-safaitischen Musikpflege." In *Festschrift zum 60. Geburtstag von Wolfgang Suppan,* edited by Bernhard Habla, pp. 167–184. Tutzing, 1993. First attempt to analyze a narrow local musical culture from the Hellenistic period.

Braun, Joachim. "Biblische Musikinstrumente." In *Die Musik in Geschichte und Gegenwart,* vol. 1, pp. 1503–1537. 2d ed. Kassel, 1994.

Braun, Joachim. "Die Musikikonographie des Dionysoskultes im Römischen Palästina." In *Imago musicae,* 8, 109–133. Lucca, 1995.

Braun, Joachim. *Musik in Alt-Israel/Palästina: Studien zu den archäologischen, schriftlichen und vergleichenden Quellen.* Freiburg, 1996.

Calmeyer, Peter. "Glocke." In *Reallexikon der Assyriologie und vorderasiatischen Archäologie,* vol. 3, pp. 427–431. Berlin and New York, 1966.

Caubet, Annie. "La musique à Ougarit." *Comptes Rendus de l'Académie des Inscriptions et Belles-Lettres* (1987): 731–754. The only discussion of Ugaritic musical instruments, stressing the autochthonal character of the musical culture of the eastern Mediterranean coast.

Duchesne-Guillemin, Marcelle. *Les instruments de musique dans l'art Sassanide.* Ghent, 1993.

Ellermeier, Friedrich. "Beiträge zur Frühgeschichte altorientalischer Saiteninstrumenten." In *Archäologie und Altes Testament: Festschrift für Kurt Galling zum 8 January 1980,* edited by Arnulf Kuschke and Ernst Kutsch, pp. 75–90. Tübingen, 1970. Clarifies the interpretation of the Hebrew term *kinor.*

Engel, Carl. *The Music of the Most Ancient Nations.* London, 1864. The first study to emphasize archaeological material, with chapters on the musical cultures of the Assyrians, Egyptians, and Hebrews. Includes more than a hundred illustrations.

Farmer, Henry George. *Musikgeschichte in Bildern,* vol. 3.2, *Islam.* Edited by Heinrich Besseler and Max Schneider. Leipzig, 1966. Along with the other volumes in this series, considered the best study of iconography, both as regards musical instruments and general cultural background. Includes detailed presentations of each artifact, comparative tables, and general musicological discussions.

Fleischhauer, Günter. *Musikgeschichte in Bildern,* vol. 2.5, *Etrurien und Rom.* Edited by Heinrich Besseler and Max Schneider. Leipzig, 1964. See Farmer (1966).

Hass, Gerlinde. *Die Syrinx in der griechischen Bildkunst.* Boelaus, 1985.

Hermary, Antoine, Annie Caubet, and Olivier Masson. *Catalogue des antiquités de Chypre.* Paris, 1989.

Hickmann, Ellen, and David W. Hughes, eds. *The Archaeology of Early Music Culture: Third International Meeting of the ICTM Study Group on Music Archaeology.* Orpheus-Schriftenreihe, vol. 51. Bonn, 1988. Includes an article on harps by O. R. Gurney and B. Lawergren, and Greek and Roman pipes by Annie Bélis.

Hickmann, Hans. *Catalogue général des antiquités égyptiens du Musée du Caire: Instruments de musique.* Cairo, 1949. Classical model of a professional musicological catalog and a monumental independent study of Egyptian musical instruments.

Hickmann, Hans. "Flöteninstrumente," "Glocken," "Harfe," "Horninstrumente," "Klappern," "Klarinette," "Laute," "Leier," "Rassel," and "Trompeteninstrumente I." In *Die Musik in Geschichte und Gegenwart.* Basel, 1949–. Although in need of updating, still valuable entries on the typology of musical instruments.

Hickmann, Hans. "Die Rolle des Vorderen Orients in der Abendländischen Musikgeschichte." *Cahiers d'Histoire Égyptienne* 9.1–2 (1957): 19–37. This and Hickmann (1961b) are the only valuable overall discussions of organological developments in the Near East. Must be read in light of more recent archaeological finds.

Hickmann, Hans. *Musikgeschichte in Bildern,* vol. 2.1, *Ägypten.* Edited by Heinrich Besseler and Max Schneider. Leipzig, 1961a. See Farmer (1966). Additional material may be found in Manniche (1975).

Hickmann, Hans. "Vorderasien und Ägypten im musikalischen Austausch." *Zeitschrift der Deutschen Morganländischen Gesellschaft* 111.1 (1961b): 23–41.

Homo-Lechner, Catherine, ed. *La pluridisciplinarité en archéologie musicale: IVe rencontres internationales d'archéologie musicale d'ICTM, Saint-Germain-en-Laye, octobre 1990.* 2 vols. Paris, 1994. Includes papers on Ugaritic musical instruments by Annie Caubet, the state of archaeomusicological research in Israel by Joachim Braun, Near Eastern string instruments by Bo Lawergren, and the Greek lyre by Annie Bélis.

Karamatov, Fajsulla M., et al., *Musikgeschichte in Bildern,* vol. 2.9, *Mittelasien.* Edited by Werner Bachmann. Leipzig, 1987. See Farmer (1966).

Kartomi, Margaret J. *On Concepts and Classifications of Musical Instruments.* Chicago, 1990. The best contemporary historical, theoretical, and methodological discussion on the classification and research of musical instruments.

Kilmer, Anne, and Dominique Collon. "Laute" and "Leier." In *Reallexikon der Assyriologie und vorderasiatischen Archäologie,* vol. 6, pp. 512–517 and 571–582. Berlin and New York, 1980–1983.

Kilmer, Anne, Richard L. Crocker, and Robert R. Brown. *Sounds from the Silence: Recent Discoveries on Ancient Near Eastern Music.* Berkeley, 1976.

Lund, Cajsa S., ed. *Second Conference of the ICTM Study Group on Music Archaeology, Stockholm, November 19–23, 1984.* Vol. 1. Stockholm, 1986. Includes papers by Doris Stockmann on early Mediterranean drums, Bo Lawergren on the ancient harp of Altai, and Albrecht Schneider on the typology of the ancient reed pipe.

Manniche, Lise. *Ancient Egyptian Musical Instruments.* Munich, 1975. Inefficiently organized catalog; updates Hickmann (1961a).

Marcuse, Sibyl. *A Survey of Musical Instruments.* New York, 1975. Comprehensive contemporary survey organized by instrument type; no references are given for archaeological-iconographic material.

Meshorer, Yaakov. "The Coins of Caesarea Paneas." *Israel Numismatic Journal* 8 (1984–1985): 37–58.

Meyers, Carol L. "A Terracotta in the Harvard Semitic Museum and Disc-Holding Female Figures Reconsidered." *Israel Exploration Journal* 37.2–3 (1987): 116–122. Exemplary discussion of the type.

Meyers, Eric, Ehud Netzer, and Carol L. Meyers. *Sepphoris.* Winona Lake, Ind., 1992.

Nixdorff, Heide. *Zur Typologie und Geschichte der Rahmentrommeln.* Berlin, 1971. The only typological discussion of the ancient drum.

Perrot, Jean. *The Organ from Its Invention in the Hellenistic Period to the End of the Thirteenth Century.* London, 1971. Standard study.

Polin, Claire C. J. *Music in the Ancient Near East.* New York, 1954.

Porada, Edith. "A Lyre Player from Tarsus and His Relations." In *The Aegean and the Near East: Studies Presented to H. Goldmann,* edited by S. Weinberger et al., pp. 185–211. New York, 1956.

Rashid, Subhi Anwar. "Comparative Archaeological Research on the Musical Instruments in Ancient Iraq and Egypt" (in Arabic). *Sumer* 33 (1977): 9–17. Rashid considers Mesopotamia the birthplace of nearly all musical instruments (p. 16). See also Rashid (1984), page 21.

Rashid, Subhi Anwar. *Musikgeschichte in Bildern,* vol. 2, *Mesopotamien.* Edited by Werner Bachmann. Leipzig, 1984. See Farmer (1966).

Rimmer, Joan. *Ancient Musical Instruments of Western Asia in the British Museum.* London, 1969.

Sachs, Curt. *The History of Musical Instruments.* London, 1940. Although somewhat out of date, this volume has not lost its significance as a major classic.

Schmidt-Colinet, Constanze. *Die Musikinstrumente in der Kunst des Alten Orients: Archäologisch-philologische Studien.* Bonn, 1981. Survey of archaeological finds from the Near East, mainly from Mesopotamia, with only casual examples from other areas. Includes some ninety illustrations.

Stauder, Wilhelm. *Die Harfen und Leiern Vorderasiens in babylonischer und assyrischer Zeit.* Frankfurt am Main, 1961.

Turnbull, Harvey. "The Origin of the Long-necked Lute." *Galpin Society Journal* 25 (1972): 58–66.

Turnbull, Harvey. "Anatolia." In *The New Grove Dictionary of Music and Musicians,* vol. 1, pp. 388–393. London, 1980. The only up-to-date and very rich survey of Anatolian musical instruments.

Wegner, Max. "Hethitische Musik." In *Die Musik in Geschichte und Gegenwart,* vol. 6, pp. 330–334. Basel, 1949–.

Wegner, Max. *Die Musikinstrumente des Alten Orients.* Munster, 1950. Includes sections on Egyptian, Mesopotamian, Hittite, Syrian, Israeli, and Greek music.

Wegner, Max. *Musikgeschichte in Bildern,* vol. 2.4, *Griechenland.* Edited by Heinrich Besseler and Max Schneider. Leipzig, 1963. See Farmer (1966).

Wellesz, Egon, ed. *The New Oxford History of Music,* vol. 1. London, 1957, pp. 239–246, 266–274, 294–295. Sections rich with archaeological material are devoted to musical instruments in Mesopotamia and Egypt as opposed to the chapter on music in the Bible, which ignores archaeological sources.

Ziegler, Christiane. *Les instruments de musique égyptiens au Musée du Louvre.* Paris, 1979.

JOACHIM BRAUN

MYRES, JOHN L. (1869–1954), British archaeologist and historian. Myres was a pioneer in applying anthropological techniques to archaeology. His approach was to link history, geography, archaeology, and classical studies. He first visited Greece in 1891 and thereafter traveled widely in Mediterranean lands. In 1893 Myres went to Crete where he recognized the importance of the prehistoric site of Knossos later excavated by Arthur Evans. He established a correlation between the so-called Kamares ware pottery that he had sketched in the Heraklion Museum and the comparable vase fragments found by Flinders Petrie at Kahun in Egypt, dated to the twelfth dynasty. Myres traveled with Evans in Crete and later excavated at Palaikastro and the nearby mountaintop sanctuary at Petsofas. His most profound influence was on Cypriot archaeology. In Cyprus, which he first visited in 1894, he was the first to excavate, particularly at those sites associated with ancient Kition, in a scientific manner in order to reconstruct the island's history. With Max Ohnefalsch-Richter, with whom he conducted an uneasy relationship, he published *A Catalogue of the Cyprus Museum* (1899), which made possible a framework of absolute chronology. In 1914, Myres extended his ideas in the *Handbook of the Cesnola Collection of Antiquities from Cyprus.*

Myres's interest and influence on Cypriot archaeology continued long after he ceased excavating. Instrumental in establishing the Cypriot Department of Antiquities in 1935, he insisted on the proper training of Cypriot archaeologists, most notably Porphyrios Dikaios. In 1910 Myres was elected Wykeham Professor of Ancient History and a fellow of New College, Oxford, a post he held until he retired in 1935. He was knighted in 1943. Although his writings had been mainly in the field of ancient history, Myres again turned his attention to the archaeology of Crete shortly before his death and edited Evans's notes and drawings for *Scripta Minoa* II (1952).

[*See also* Crete; Cyprus; Kition; *and the biographies of Dikaios, Evans, and Ohnefalsch-Richter.*]

BIBLIOGRAPHY

Myres, John L., and Max Ohnefalsch-Richter. *A Catalogue of the Cyprus Museum, with a Chronicle of Excavations Undertaken since the British Occupation and Introductory Notes on Cypriote Archaeology.* Oxford, 1899.

Myres, John L. "Excavations at Palaikastro. II. The Sanctuary-Site at Petsofa." *Annual of the British School at Athens,* no. 9 (1902–1903): 356–387.

Myres, John L. *Excavations in Cyprus, 1913.* London, 1913.

Myres, John L. *Handbook of the Cesnola Collection of Antiquities from Cyprus.* New York, 1914.

Ann C. Brown

N

NABATEAN INSCRIPTIONS. The Nabateans are of Arab descent, as their personal names, certain Arabic words incorporated in their vocabulary, and a recently discovered inscription found in the vicinity of Oboda (Avdat) reveal. The Oboda inscription is written partly in Aramaic and partly in Arabic but rendered entirely in Aramaic letters. The earliest inscriptions written with certainty by Nabateans are in Aramaic, the official language of the Persian Empire. Almost all of the Nabatean-Aramaic inscriptions deal with matters of religion. The earliest inscription, in archaic Aramaic script, dates to 168 BCE and comes from Elusa (Ḥaluṣa) in Israel's central Negev desert. It refers to a shrine in honor of Aretas, king of the Nabateans. The Aslah inscription (c. 90 BCE) found at Petra, in Jordan is also in archaic script and mentions a shrine dedicated to Obodas I, son of Aretas II. It dates to about 67 BCE and was engraved on the base of a statue of King Rabel I.

The bulk of the Nabatean inscriptions come from the vicinity of Petra, the capital of the Nabatean kingdom; Egra (Meda'in Saleh) in northern Arabia; and the Hauran, in southern Syria. Most belong to the reigns of Aretas IV (9 BCE–40 CE), Malichus II (40–70 CE), and Rabel II (70–106 CE). Very few of the texts found at Petra are of any length. The longest is an undated epitaph referring in detail to components of a large funerary monument. Another fairly long and detailed inscription is engraved on what was apparently the base of a statue dedicated to Rabel II. It provides a detailed genealogy of the Nabatean royal house. Most of the inscriptions found in the region of Petra are, however, brief invocations by pilgrims that are engraved along paths leading to open-air high places. In one of these the names Garshu and Raqmu—the Semitic names of Gerasa (Jerash) and Petra—are mentioned.

The northern Arabian group of Nabatean inscriptions comprises some thirty lengthy epitaphs and hundreds of rock inscriptions engraved by pilgrims and soldiers (Cooke, 1903; Jaussen and Savignac, 1909). The detailed funerary inscriptions, written in an elegant cursive script, were engraved on the facades of monuments (there is a direct relationship between the architectural quality of the monument and the length of the inscription). The funerary inscriptions were copies of documents deposited in an office or temple; copies were also distributed among members of the family who had the right of burial. The epitaphs (and the documents) contain the name or names of those who had the monument made, the names of those with the right of burial; a date by regnal years (most monuments were made in the reigns of Aretas IV, Malichus II, and the first five years of Rabel II); a curse on anyone who desecretes the monument; and the amount of the fine to be paid by violators—either to the treasury of a temple or temples or to the treasury of a secular authority (the king or regional governor), and the name or names of the sculptors who made the monument.

The shorter inscriptions were engraved either on the rocks surrounding Petra, where funerary feasts took place, or in the vicinity of Egra, at a place called the Tombs of the Soldiers. Numerous inscriptions were written by soldiers—mostly cavalrymen—in Greek and Latin. The Aramaic-Nabatean inscriptions mention generals in the cavalry and infantry and other military officials.

The inscriptions found in the Hauran were probably engraved by members of the tribe of Obaishat (Gk., Obaisenoi). They consist of dedicatory inscriptions from the temple of Baʿal Shamin at Seeia (built between 33/32 and 2/1 BCE) that mention the building's architectural features, shrines, statues, and other cult objects. One epitaph (c. 270 CE) is for Fero, the teacher of Gadimat, king of Tanuh.

A small group of inscriptions comes from the central Negev, mainly from the religious center at Oboda (Avdat). Some were dedications of the temple and one mentions descendants of Aretas IV. Of special interest is a group of mason's marks engraved by the temple's builders.

The rock inscriptions of southern Sinai (some three thousand graffiti), constitute a discrete group. Most are short invocations containing the word *šlm*, "peace," or a short blessing; the name of the engraver; sometimes also the name of the deceased's brother or brothers, father, and, more rarely, grandfather and ending with another blessing. Only a few are dated (the dates range from 150/51 to 267/68 CE. In a group of inscriptions found at Jebel Moneija, near the oasis of Feiran, the officials of a temple are mentioned (two classes of priests, supervisors of animal victims sacrificed in Nabatean temples, and a scribe).

A few Nabatean inscriptions were found in Wadi Tumilat, in eastern Egypt; a few others were found at various sites within the boundaries of the Roman Empire.

[*See also* Aramaic Language and Literature; Avdat; Ḥaluṣa; Jerash; Nabateans; *and* Petra.]

BIBLIOGRAPHY

Cantineau, Jean. *Le Nabatéen,* vol. 2. Paris, 1932. See pages 11–25.

Cooke, G. A. *A Textbook of North-Semitic Inscriptions.* Oxford, 1903.

Jaussen, Antonin, and Raphael Savignac. *Mission archéologique en Arabia,* vol. 1. Paris, 1909.

Negev, Avraham. *The Inscriptions of Wadi Ḥaqqaq, Sinai.* Qedem, vol. 6. Jerusalem, 1977.

Negev, Avraham. "A Nabatean Sanctuary at Jebel Moneijah, Southern Sinai." *Israel Exploration Journal* 27 (1977): 219–234.

Negev, Avraham. *Personal Names in the Nabatean Realm.* Qedem, vol. 32. Jerusalem, 1991. Contains an extensive bibliography.

AVRAHAM NEGEV

NABATEANS. During the late Hellenistic and Early Roman imperial era, an Arab kingdom centered at Petra in Edomite Transjordan established itself as one of the prominent native independent political powers in the region of the Levant. The territory under its control extended from southern Syria through most of Transjordan, the Negev of Palestine, the Sinai, and the northwestern part of the Hijaz. Strabo, the Roman geographer, and the Jewish historian Josephus offer the fullest discussions of Nabatean history and culture, in the absence of any indigenous Nabatean literary sources. More than four thousand Nabatean Aramaic inscriptions do offer valuable direct testimony from the native population, but the majority are laconic graffiti containing mere stereotyped formulae at best; the few lengthier texts are mostly funerary. Archaeological remains of the material culture suggest that the Nabateans possessed accomplished technical skills. Especially of note is their distinctive hellenized architecture, reflected in rock-cut tombs and temples; peculiar eggshell-thin ceramics of exceptionally high quality; and the hydrological techniques they employed in developing agriculture in the extensive desert landscape they occupied.

Origins. The view that the Nabateans of the classical era are related to the Iron Age people known as the Nabaioth in the Hebrew Bible or the Nabatu of Assyrian texts remains controversial, but linguistic and historical evidence suggest the identification is not without some basis. These indications suggest their homeland was in the region of northeastern Arabia, adjacent to the Persian Gulf. They appear to have migrated westward in the Achaemenid Persian period to settle finally in Petra. [*See* Petra.] The movement was along the North Arabian trade route that connected Babylonia and Egypt and proved to be a vital commercial link even in the Roman era. Of more entrepreneurial importance was their control of the valuable commerce of the frankincense and myrrh of South Arabia transported to the Levant by Minaean and Gerrhean merchants. By 312/11 BCE, the fortune and reputation of the Nabateans were already well established, attracting the interests of Antigonus the One-Eyed, one of the successors of Alexander the Great, who sent his army to Petra in hope of confiscating its wealth. The enterprise failed. According to the Zenon papyri of 259 BCE, the Nabateans also resided in the neighborhood of the Hauran in Syria and were merchants of aromatics with Ptolemaic agents in Moabite Transjordan. By the second century BCE and afterward, they had spread into the Hijaz, the Negev, and Sinai to the borders of Egypt. Their expansion is best perceived as an extensive political alliance of various peoples united under the rule of the Petraean dynasts. [*See* Negev; Sinai.]

Royal Dynasty. During the Hellenistic era, a series of kings is known from literary and epigraphic sources beginning with Aretas I (c. 170 BCE), Rabel I (?), Aretas II (c. 100 BCE), and Obodas I (93–85). Under Aretas III (85–62), Nabatea became a Roman client-state and Malichus I (62–30) was involved with such notable figures as Caesar and Mark Antony. His successor, Obodas II (30–9), was the ally of Augustus, and these relations were continued by the later kings until the reign of the emperor Trajan. Under Aretas IV (9 BCE–40 CE), the Nabatean kingdom flourished and reached its zenith; his reign remains the best known of all the Nabatean dynasts. The reigns of his successors, Malichus II (40–70 CE) and Rabel II (70–106 CE), are more obscure, but the common depiction of this period as one of political and economic decline remains at issue. Because the period between Pompey and Augustus is the best known, the formative character of the monarchy has been seen as a result of Roman rule. However, the Nabatean dynasty reflects all of the aspects of a typical Hellenistic Macedonian monarchy of the Egyptian Ptolemaic type. The kings adopted the traditional titulary slogans of their Hellenistic counterparts on coins and inscriptions: Aretas III was known as *philhellenos;* Aretas IV as "friend of his people," or the equivalent in Greek of *philodemus,* but perhaps better understood as *philopatris;* and Rabel II as "the one who has given life and deliverance to his people," or the *sōtēr,* "savior," of his people. The monarchs also adopted royal consanguineous marriages, typical of the Ptolemaic kingdom of Egypt; intermarriage with the Herodian dynasty is also known. Evidence for a royal dynastic cult is clear from the known apotheosis of Obodas and Malichus; that of the other kings can be inferred from the pseudotheophoric "servant" names combined with the names of the kings and queens and used by many court officials, military personnel, and artisans. After the Roman annexation in 106 CE, the royal family faded from existence and the Nabatean realm was integrated into the new province of Arabia. The Babatha family archive from the Dead Sea documents the transition from the reign of Rabel II to Roman rule. [*See* Dead Sea Scrolls.]

Settlement Pattern. From the royal capital at Petra and the Edomite heartland, Nabatean settlements radiated in all directions. To the south, the port at Leuke Kome on the Red Sea in Midian and inland settlement at Hegra (Meda'in Saleh) in the Hijaz provided bases for transporting South Arabian aromatics on to Petra and elsewhere. [*See* Meda'in Saleh.] From Aila ('Aqaba), routes led northwest to Gaza and north to the Petra. [*See* 'Aqaba.] For the latter, Nabatean road stations and settlements at Khirbet al-Kithara, Khirbet al-Khaldeh, Quweira, Ḥumeima, and Sadaqa sustained traffic to the royal capital. [*See* Khaldeh; Ḥumeima.] The Nabatean temple at Wadi Ram in the Ḥisma was also the center for Nabatean settlers in the desert region. From Petra, another route led west through the Negev via the cities of Oboda/Avdat, Mampsis/Kurnub, Neṣṣana, Sobata/Subeita, and Elusa/Ḥaluṣa; it formed the basis for trade at the ports of Gaza and Rhinocorura on the Mediterranean coast. [*See* Avdat; Kurnub; Subeita; Ḥaluṣa.] Numerous Nabatean inscriptions in the Sinai and the eastern desert of Egypt attest to a substantial Nabatean presence in the area. To the East, a route through the Arabian desert, via the oasis at Dumah al-Jandal (modern Jawf), led to the Persian Gulf and the emporium at Charax Spasinou. To the north through Transjordan, the Nabateans also had a string of settlements in Edom and Moab that extended to Bosra and Damascus, where goods could be transported to the ports along the Phoenician coast. [*See* Edom; Moab; Bosra; Damascus; Phoenicia.] While the Nabatean presence in the hellenized Decapolis region was not substantial, they neither excluded nor avoided the region. [*See* Decapolis.] Both Philadelphia (Amman) and Gerasa/Jerash were the locations of Nabatean communities, and the Hauran of southern Syria has yielded numerous inscriptions and sporadic finds of Nabatean pottery. [*See* Amman; Jerash.] Safaitic inscriptions also attest to Nabatean influence in the region, suggesting that the indigenous population was under the sway of the Nabatean kingdom. [*See* Safaitic-Thamudic Inscriptions.]

Political and Military Organization. The titles of civil and military officials are borrowed from Greek (strategos, chiliarch, and hipparch) and Latin (centurion) and reflect the development of the military system along the lines of a standard professional army of the Hellenistic type. The strategoi were regional district governors and military commanders. Such officials are attested at Sidon in Phoenicia, Dmer and Canatha in southern Syria, Madaba and Umm er-Rasas in Moabite Transjordan, and Hegra (Meda'in Saleh); the Nabatean communities in Edomite Transjordan, the Negev, and perhaps the Sinai, must have been organized in similar fashion, but the evidence is lacking. [*See* Sidon; Madaba; Umm er-Rasas.] There are suggestions that the position was hereditary. For example, the sons of Damasippos at Hegra, Rabîb'el and Ganimu, and his grandson Maliku, were all strategoi at Hegra; another grandson, Damasi, led a revolt later against the ruling dynasty in Petra in the early years of Rabel II's reign. The chiliarchs must have been in charge of infantry units of approximately a thousand men. The hipparchs were commanders of cavalry units of approximately five hundred horsemen. Almost all of the officials with this title are concentrated near Bosra in the far north and Hegra in the far south of the kingdom, but an individual designated the chief of the cavalry *(rb pršy')* is known from Petra. The title may represent the Semitic equivalent of the hipparch or an official of inferior rank in the cavalry unit. Two individuals are designated by the Latin title of centurion, one at Hegra and the other at Leuke Kome, evidently in charge of protecting officials charged with collecting tariffs on trade. In addition, several individuals are designated the chief of the camp *(rb mšryt')* at Petra, Dumah al-Jandal, Luhita, and Abarta', officials perhaps comparable to the *stratopedarch* or *praefectus castrorum* of the Roman army. [*See* Meda'in Saleh.]

In conflicts with Hellenistic armies and the Hasmonean and Herodian dynastic forces, the Nabatean royal army performed fairly efficiently, despite the castigating remarks of Strabo and Josephus about their effectiveness. After the Roman annexation of the kingdom in 106, most of the Nabatean army was transformed into regular Roman military units, comprising at least six regiments of *cohortes Ulpiae Petraeorum* and perhaps several alae regiments of cavalrymen and dromedarii, sometime between 114–116, in connection with Trajan's Parthian campaign. Afterward, these units served in Cappadocia, Syria, and Palestine, and probably their homeland of Arabia as well. [*See* Cappadocia.]

Language and Script. Of the more than four thousand published Nabatean Aramaic inscriptions, the oldest are from the Late Hellenistic era, from Petra (96/5, 70/69), Bostra (51–47) in the Hauran, and Tell el-Shuqafiya (77) in Wadi Tumilat between the modern Suez Canal and Nile River in Egypt, where a recent text is dated to 35/4 BCE, to the reigns of both the Ptolemaic ruler Cleopatra VII Philopater and Malichus I. [*See* Aramaic Language and Literature; Nabatean Inscriptions.] The largest concentration of dated texts is from the tombs at Hegra, which provide important insights as well for the architectural analysis of the tombs at Petra, which have only a single dedicatory inscription. Ironically, the largest concentration of inscriptions is in the forlorn and desolate area of Wadi Mukatteb in the Sinai, where thousands have been recorded. No Nabatean text exists at Petra after its annexation by Rome in 106, although a number of texts dated to the Roman provincial era of Arabia are known from the periphery of the old Nabatean kingdom. The latest dates to 356, from the Hijaz. Although the language of these texts is Aramaic, there are a number of Arabic loanwords utilized for political and religious institutions; the vast majority of personal names in the Nabatean onomasticon are also Arabic, spelled according to the peculiar orthographic practices of Imperial Aramaic of the earlier Persian era. The paleography of the script, with its peculiar ligatures and style, eventually develops into that of the Classical Arabic script. [*See* Arabic.] It is also apparent that some Nabateans used the North Arabian scripts and dialects known as Safaitic and Thamudic (see above). Recent bilingual texts in these pre-Islamic Arabic dialects and Aramaic indicate the Nabatean community was complex, diverse, and basically polylingual, providing a substantial basis for understanding Aramaic as only the formally adopted language of a largely Arabic population.

Economy and Society. Of primary importance for the Nabatean economy was the commerce in aromatics from South Arabia and spices from the Far East. Their activities and fame as traders and merchants extended across the Mediterranean and as far east as Han dynasty China, which knew Petra as Rekem (Chinese, Li-kan). In the fourth century BCE, the Nabateans were already profiting greatly from this exotic commerce, and their activities as merchants in these goods was still recognized by Roman writers in the second century CE. Finds of their typical painted eggshell fineware have been found along the eastern coasts near Bahrain, the ports of Oman and Yemen, and at sites such as Qaryat al-Fau in Saudi Arabia, along the incense route leading north to Petra. [*See* Bahrain; Oman; Yemen; Qaryat al-Fau.] Their Aramaic inscriptions have been found scattered across the Mediterranean at such places as Tenos, Rhodes, Cos, Delos, and Miletus in the Aegean, and Puteoli and Rome in Italy. [*See* Miletus.] The development of agriculture in the Nabatean realm has been viewed as a late development resulting from a decline in commerce when Rome absorbed much of the Red Sea traffic. It is also a product of the social evolutionary anthropological model that characterizes the transition from nomadic pastoralism to sedentary life as a gradual and late development. [*See* Pastoral Nomadism.] In contrast to this cultural scheme, the earliest descriptions of the Nabateans indicate that they possessed advanced technical ability and ingenuity. Their engineering skill is revealed in their developing hydrological systems to support settlements on the desert fringe. [*See* Hydrology.] Such achievements at Ḥumeima in the Ḥisma desert of southern Jordan are particularly impressive and date to the first century BCE, rivaling the later developments in the Negev. In similar fashion, horse breeding must have been a necessity for maintaining the cavalry of the Nabatean army as early as Aretas III—both Petra and Amman seem to have been prime regions for these activities in the Hellenistic era. Furthermore, the art and architecture of the Nabatean realm also reveals creative adaptations of classical styles.

Religion. The principal national god of the Nabateans was Dushares ("belonging to Shara," Edom's mountain range). Other divinities in the pantheon included the goddess Allat, al-Uzza, al-Kutba, Shai al-Qaum, and Baʿal Shamin. Their representations normally were in the betylic form of a rectangular stela (albeit with stylized eyes, nose, and mouth), rather than anthropomorphic form, suggesting to some that there was a cultural inhibition or even prohibition against depicting divinities in human fashion (Patrich, 1990). Other sculptural representations in Hellenic iconographic form suggest the practice was not uniform. Some of the best-preserved sanctuaries are at Petra, Khirbet et-Tannur, and Wadi Ram in Edom; Qaṣr Rabba and Dhat Ras in Moab; and Si in the Hauran. Shrines and cultic centers are abundant throughout the realm, indicating that the Nabateans absorbed the indigenous cults of the Edomites, Moabites, and Syrians into their pantheon. Even the Egyptian cult of Isis flourished at Petra from at least the Augustan era into the later Roman imperial period. Although there is evidence that Petra came increasingly under the sway of Christianity by the fourth century, there are no traces of the new religion in the Nabatean Aramaic inscriptions.

[*See also* Arabian Peninsula, *article on* The Arabian Peninsula before the Time of Islam; Palestine, *article on* Palestine in the Persian through Roman Periods; Syria, *article on* Syria in the Persian through Roman Periods; *and* Transjordan, *article on* Transjordan in the Persian through Roman Periods.]

BIBLIOGRAPHY

Bowersock, Glen W. *Roman Arabia.* Cambridge, Mass., 1983. Superb overview of political developments in the region.

Dentzer, Jean-Marie, ed. *Hauran I: Recherches archéologiques sur la Syrie du Sud à l'époque hellénistique et romaine.* 2 vols. Bibliothèque Archéologique et Historique, vol. 124. Paris, 1985–1986. Basic archaeological investigation of Nabatean southern Syria.

Gatier, Pierre-Louis, and Jean-François Salles. "Aux frontières méridionales du domaine nabatéen." In *L'Arabie et ses mers bordieres,* edited by Jean-François Salles, pp. 173–190. Paris, 1988.

Graf, David F. "The Nabataeans and the Hisma: In the Steps of Glueck and Beyond." In *The Word of the Lord Shall Go Forth: Essays in Honor of David Noel Freedman,* edited by Carol L. Meyers and Michael O'Connor, pp. 647–664. Winona Lake, Ind., 1983.

Graf, David F. "The Origin of the Nabataeans." *ARAM* 2 (1990): 45–75. Synthesis of the recent research on the question of the beginnings of Nabatea.

Graf, David F. "The Nabataean Army and the *Cohortes Ulpiae Petraeorum.*" In *The Roman and Byzantine Army in the East,* edited by Edward Dabrowa, pp. 265–311. Cracow, 1994.

Graf, David F. "The Roman East from the Chinese Perspective." In *Palmyra and the Silk Road.* Damascus, 1995. Discusses the relevant Chinese texts related to Petra and the Near East.

Gruendler, Beatrice. *Development of the Arabic Scripts.* Harvard Semitic Series, 43. Atlanta, 1993. Basic study of the evolution of the Nabatean script into Arabic script.

Hammond, Philip C. *The Nabataeans: Their History, Culture, and Archaeology.* Studies in Mediterranean Archaeology, 37. Gothenburg, 1973.

Healey, John F. *The Nabataean Tomb Inscriptions of Meda'in Salih.* Journal of Semitic Studies, Supplement 1. Oxford, 1993. New edition of older texts, integrating recent linguistic evidence.

Meshorer, Yaʿacov. *Nabataean Coins.* Qedem, vol. 3. Jerusalem, 1975. Basic study now updated by Schmitt-Korte (below).

Negev, Avraham. *Personal Names in the Nabatean Realm*. Qedem, vol. 32. Jerusalem, 1991.

Patrich, Joseph. *The Formation of Nabatean Art*. Leiden, 1990. Provocative study of the iconoclastic tradition in Nabatea.

Schmitt-Korte, Karl, and Mike Cowell. "Nabataean Coinage, Part I: The Silver Content Measured by X-Ray Fluorescence Analysis." *Numismatic Chronicle* 149 (1989): 33–58.

Schmitt-Korte, Karl, and Mike Cowell. "Nabataean Coinage, Part II: New Coin Types and Variants." *Numismatic Chronicle* 150 (1990): 105–133.

Schmitt-Korte, Karl, and Martin Price. "Nabataean Coinage, Part III." *Numismatic Chronicle* 154 (1994): 67–131.

Wenning, Robert. *Die Nabatäer: Denkmäler und Geschichte*. Novum Testamentum et Orbis Antiquus, 3. Göttingen, 1987. Basic bibliographic index of Nabatean archaeology.

Wenning, Robert. "Eine neuerstelle Liste der nabatäischen Dynastie." *Boreas* 16 (1993): 25–38.

Wenning, Robert. "Die Dekapolis und die Nabatäer." *Zeitschrift des Deutschen Palästina-Vereins* 110 (1994): 2–35.

Zayadine, Fawzi, ed. *Petra and the Caravan Cities*. Amman, 1990. Splendid collection of articles on Nabatean religion and culture.

DAVID F. GRAF

NABLUS. *See* Shechem.

NABRATEIN (Ar., "two hills; also known as Kefar Neburaya), site located 4 km (2.5 mi.) north-northeast of Safed in Upper Galilee (33°2′ N, 35°30′ E; map reference 197 × 267). Situated at 650 m above sea level on the summit of a small hill opposite Moshav Dalton, Nabratein lies along a deep ravine on its north side (Naḥal Dalton, or Wadi ʿAmmuqa) that empties eastward into the Hulah Valley at 0.5 km south of Hazor. A perennial spring flows some 250 m southeast of the ruin. Another small site, Khirbet en-Nabrah, which has not been excavated, lies close to the spring and no doubt accounts for the dual form of the name *Nabratein* (Frowald Hüttenmeister and Reeg Gottfried, *Die antiken Synagogen in Israel;* Tübinger Atlas des vorderen Orient, Beiheft B11, vol. 1, Wiesbaden, 1977, pp. 343–347).

Nabratein's ruins were first discovered by the British explorers Claude R. Conder and H. H. Kitchener, who noted the inscription on the synagogue's lintel, which is decorated with a menorah in a wreath. The inscription was deciphered and published by Nahman Avigad in 1960 (see Naveh, 1978, p. 31). It is unique in Hebrew epigraphy because its date, 564 CE, is reckoned from the destruction of the Second Temple in 70 CE: "(According) to the number four hundred and ninety-four years after the destruction, the house was (re)built during the office of Hanina son of Lezer and Luliana son of Yudan." The inscription is incised on a Roman-period architectural fragment. Its decipherment led to a great deal of confusion until recent excavation could demonstrate that a resettlement and rebuilding occurred at the site in the late Byzantine–Early Arab period.

Excavations conducted in 1980 and 1981 were sponsored by the American Schools of Oriental Research and directed by Eric M. Meyers. They focused on the synagogue and its building context, on areas to the northwest presumed to be domestic or agricultural/industrial, and on a smaller area to the southwest in front of the synagogue entryway that did not appear to be a "public" space. Very little debris had accumulated on the site, which is located in a very isolated spot in a reforested area of the Safed mountains. Avigad had

NABRATEIN. Figure 1. *General view of the synagogue.* (Courtesy E. M. Meyers)

removed the incised lintel to the Israel Museum, but its find-spot was known; the central portal of the synagogue on the south side was visible.

Results of the excavation of the synagogue area were surprising and significant. A series of increasingly larger buildings had been built there, which stratigraphic excavation revealed. The oldest and smallest building, synagogue I, dated to the second century CE (c. 135–250), is the oldest post-70 CE, securely dated synagogue in Israel. [*See* Synagogues.] Its dimensions are 11.2 × 9.35 m; its entrance is in the southern wall; and it is a broadhouse building. Benches along its eastern and western walls utilized elements of the older structures below it. It probably had four internal columns, but there is no solid evidence for them in this period. The roof span, however, is sufficiently long to suggest columns. Two stone bemas, or platforms, adorned the southern wall, and the possible imprint of a reader's platform was detected in the plastered floor.

Synagogue II (c. 250–363) was converted to a basilica with six columns (11.2 × 13.85 m), increasing the internal space of the building by 48 percent (see figure 1). The twin bemas were extensively decorated in this phase. The bema at the southwest is adorned with a beautiful Torah shrine whose gabled roof was supported by two rampant lions with a niche for the eternal light carved as a half dome or shell in the key of the pediment. This unique discovery resolved the long-standing question about where in ancient Sacred Jewish architecture the Ark of the Law had been placed (see figure 2). The second bema, in the southeast corner, may have held a menorah or served as the reader's platform.

It is clear that the site was abandoned in about 350–363 as a result of economic hardship and the earthquake of 363. The synagogue was rebuilt in the final phase of occupation, as is demonstrated by the inscription on the lintel (i.e., 564), which lasted into the eighth century, or about 700, when synagogue III was enlarged to an eight-column basilica (11.2 × 16.8 m), 21 percent larger than in the previous phase. A portable wooden Ark of the Law was used in this final phase of the synagogue. This surprising rebuilding, after an abandonment of almost two hundred years, suggests that there was some sort of communal remembrance of the synagogue ruin, which is in keeping with Jewish custom.

The best-preserved Early Roman remains from the site came from the large structure attached to the perimeter wall on the northwest of the synagogue and some 15 m beyond the western areas adjacent to the synagogue. The bedrock installations suggest that the rooms there were basements remodeled and reused in the late second–third centuries. It is not clear whether the area was industrial or domestic. The site's relatively small size (less than a hectare) suggests that the village was not much more than a way station connecting inland Upper Galilee with the nearby Jordan Valley via Wadi Dalton.

The area southwest of the synagogue produced a unique Late Byzantine ceramic piece that depicts the Ark of the Law with the eternal light. The room in which it was found may have served some liturgical function in connection with the synagogue: it may have been where the washing of the feet of the priests took place. The area immediately to the west of the synagogue produced several architectural frag-

NABRATEIN. Figure 2. *Fragment of the Torah Shrine ("Ark").* (Courtesy E. M. Meyers)

ments of interest: part of a lion's body, a lamb's head, and a bird's head, suggesting a loosening of the conservative Jewish attitude toward representational art in the Byzantine period. Numerous impressed sigillata bowls with animals were found in a Late Roman or Byzantine context.

The results of the Nabratein excavations modestly revised views regarding conservatism in Upper Galilee in the Roman through the Byzantine periods, with respect both to art and trade. Because of its location so close to the Jordan Valley, it would not have been oriented to trade with the Phoenician coast. The material culture of the site reflects all of the changes above. Surface sherds, which may have been washed in from the hills above, indicate the presence of an earlier occupation in the area in the Early Bronze Age II–III, Iron II, Persian, and Hellenistic periods. Medieval sherds, from after 700, were found at the second site, some 250 m to the southeast, and dated to the early and late Arab periods.

BIBLIOGRAPHY

Meyers, Carol L., and Eric M. Meyers. "The Ark in Art: A Ceramic Rendering of the Torah Shrine from Nabratein." *Eretz-Israel* 16 (1982): 176–185.

Meyers, Eric M., et al. "The Ark of Nabratein: A First Glance." *Biblical Archaeologist* 44.4 (1981): 237–243.

Meyers, Eric M., et al. "Preliminary Report on the 1980 Excavations at en-Nabratein, Israel." *Bulletin of the American Schools of Oriental Research,* no. 244 (1981): 1–25.

Meyers, Eric M., et al. "Second Preliminary Report on the 1981 Excavations at en-Nabratein, Israel." *Bulletin of the American Schools of Oriental Research,* no. 246 (1982): 35–54.

Naveh, Joseph. *On Stone and Mosaic: The Aramaic and Hebrew Inscriptions from Ancient Synagogues.* Tel Aviv, 1978. See pp. 31–33.

Eric M. Meyers

NAG HAMMADI, city in southern Egypt near discovery site of important Coptic Gnostic texts (26°03′ N, 32°15′ E). The name *Nag Hammadi* has become popular in New Testament studies through its association with the Nag Hammadi Papyri, a collection of Gnostic documents found some miles from Nag Hammadi in Upper Egypt. Being the major urban center in the area, however, Nag Hammadi has been identified as the site of discovery. This small city is located on the west bank of the Nile River, 51 km (32 mi.) northwest of Luxor by a direct route. The discovery was made at the base of Jebel et-Tarif, the high desert cliff face on the north side of the Nile River. Villages in this area between the Nile and the cliff are (from west to east) el-Kasr, el-Busa, Hamra Dom, Sheikh Ali, and Abu Manaa.

In 1945, while digging near Hamra Dom for *sebakh,* a soil mixture used as fertilizer in the Nile Valley, a farmer found a grave containing a skeleton and a jar containing thirteen codices with 1,153 surviving pages, which are now known as the Nag Hammadi papyri (also called the Gnostic papyri). El-Kasr is the ancient site of Chenoboskion, hence the earlier association of the find with this name. Chenoboskion was the site where St. Palamon established one of the first monasteries in Upper Egypt. In the early fourth century CE Pachomius, after a brief association with Palamon, founded his own monastery at Tabennese and later his larger monastery at Pabau (modern Faw Qibli), located about 17.6 km (11 mi.) east of Nag Hammadi on the north side of the Nile. A major phase of the Nag Hammadi excavations focused on this Pachomian monastic complex at Pabau.

Four major seasons of work were conducted from 1975 to 1980. The excavations were organized by James M. Robinson; Torgny Säve-Söderbergh and Bastiaan Van Elderen were the field directors in 1975, and in succeeding seasons Van Elderen served as head. Peter Grossmann of the German Archaeological Institute in Cairo joined the staff in 1976 as chief architect.

The work of the first season was located in the area of Jebel et-Tarif where local people indicated the discovery was made. A major part of this season involved the clearance of six of the more than 150 caves at the middle or top of the cliff face of Jebel et-Tarif. One (T73), a previously published sixth dynasty (c. 2300 BCE) tomb of the provincial governor Tjauti, proved to have lower chambers, previously unknown, with extensive reliefs and hieroglyphs. Some smaller tombs also high up on the cliff face belong to the first centuries CE. A burial cloth found in T117 was dated to the fifth century CE by Carbon-14 testing. Some caves were occupied, presumably by anchorites, during the early Christian centuries. One cave (T8), with the opening lines of the *Book of Psalms* in Coptic inscribed on its walls, was dated to the late sixth or early seventh century by the evidence of coins, epigraphy, and ceramics. In none of these excavations, however, was there clear evidence for the findspot of the codices.

In the second season (1976) the major activity was the excavation of the large monastery-basilica complex of Pachomius in Faw Qibli. The proximity of this complex to the area where the papyri were found suggests that it could throw some possible light on the early Christian movements in this area. Over a wide area on the edge of the village lie the architectural remains, chiefly pillars, of a large building. Seven trenches or squares were sunk in various parts of the site to ascertain the stratigraphy of the area and the dimensions of the major structure.

These probes revealed that the structure was a very large five-aisle basilica. Below these fifth-century ruins two earlier occupation levels were identified: one was a smaller building dated to the fourth century and the other a large late third-century storage room. In addition, in a stratum below this building traces of another building complex, possibly dating from the third century, were found in various parts of the site. The destruction of the basilica, as attributed in literary sources to Khalif el-Hakim in the eleventh century, was confirmed by a destruction level with an ash layer on which architectural members had toppled and building debris had accumulated. This layer was dated by its pottery to the eleventh century.

In the third season (1977–1978) ten new trenches or squares were opened at the site of the basilica of Pachomius. The uncovering of the foundations and lower courses of the north wall, the south wall, and the east wall including the northeast corner provided the dimensions of the basilica—75 m (246 ft.) long and 37 m (121 ft.) wide—which proved to be the largest ancient church in Egypt identified to date.

In the fourth season (1979–1980) eleven new trenches or squares provided additional and new information about the fifth-century basilica and fourth century-building below. Ceramic evidence dated the latter to the fourth century. Correlated with the literary evidence, this building would be the structure built by Pachomius, and the fifth-century basilica would be the structure built by his followers.

In 1980 a team under the direction of H. Keith Beebe as field director conducted a survey of the village of el-Kasr (ancient Chenoboskion) and environs to assess the archaeological remains and the feasibility of further archaeological work. The team identified extensive remains dating from the Roman and Byzantine times.

In addition to a survey of the nearby monastery of St. Palamon, the team also investigated the Wadi Sheikh Ali. In this wadi was located a site with numerous graffiti-like inscriptions. Dozens of Coptic inscriptions were found and additional pharaonic drawings and inscriptions even yielded a cartouche of Menkaure, pharaoh of the fourth dynasty.

The Bodmer papyri were found about the same time as the Nag Hammadi papyri. This collection, named after Martin Bodmer of Geneva, Switzerland, who acquired most of the codices, contains biblical texts, classical texts, early Christian literary texts, and some non-literary texts. Among the biblical texts are some of the earliest sizable copies of New Testament books—*Luke* and *John* (P^{75}), *John* (P^{66})—dating from about 200 CE. The precise provenance of this collection is not known, but local tradition places it near the Pachomian monastic complex, possibly in the Wadi Sheikh Ali.

The findspot of the Nag Hammadi papyri was not verified by the excavations and surveys discussed above. In fact, subsequently in 1988 and 1990 Mohammed Ali suggested another site as the findspot, located approximately one mile northeast from the previous suggestions. This latest suggested site has not been excavated, although its environs are intriguing. Nevertheless, the excavations have set some parameters regarding the findspot and the local Gnostic movement. There is no evidence of a community, settlement, or cemetery in this area. It appears that the grave found in 1945 was a single burial in the low desert. Any suggestion of the size of the Gnostic movement in this area is speculation.

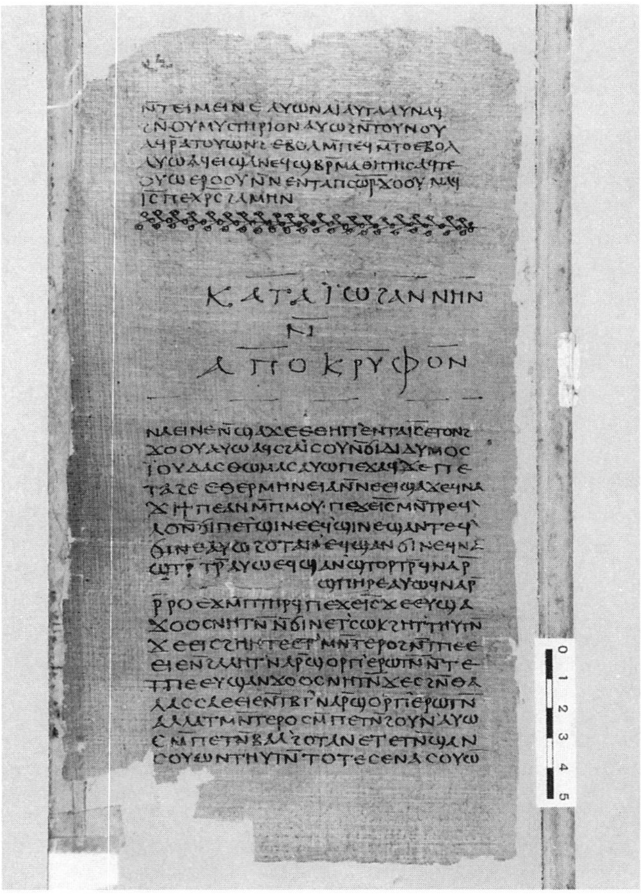

NAG HAMMADI. *The opening page of the Coptic Gospel of Thomas.* (Courtesy ASOR Archives)

Furthermore to claim that the Pachomian monastic compound was Gnostic ignores the close relationship between Pachomius and the Egyptian archbishop Athanasius, who at one time was hiding at the Pachomian complex. Furthermore, the suggestion that the Bodmer papyri were found in this area (possibly in the nearby Wadi Sheikh Ali) implies that there was a strong anti-Gnostic spirit in this vicinity because there are works such as *The Apocryphal Correspondence between the Corinthians and Paul* of this sentiment in the collection of the Bodmer Library. The convergence of the Bodmer Papyri (as early as late second century), the Pachomian monastic complex (fourth century), and the Gnostic papyri in close proximity provides some challenging and interesting problems of integration and historical sequence. Judgment about the Gnostic movement in Upper Egypt must take into account the above data.

The large size of the Pachomian monastic complex confirms the allusions in literary sources to the extent of the monastic movement in Upper Egypt. Along with the contemporaneous extensive rise of monasticism in Lower Egypt (as developed by St. Antony and in the settlements in Wadi 'n-Natrun), this further confirms the major role that monasticism played in Egyptian Christianity.

In view of Athanasius' contacts with the Pachomian monastic movement, the issuance of his canonical list in the Easter letter of 367 may have occasioned the removal of the extracanonical Gnostic papyri and their owners from the Pachomian community. This library may then have been buried with its exiled owners who had settled in the cliff area of Jebel et-Tarif. This hypothesis must await additional surveys and excavation of sites in the vicinity of Nag Hammadi for further confirmation. This area has not been systematically and scientifically surveyed nor additional sites stratigraphically excavated.

BIBLIOGRAPHY

Emmel, Stephen. "Nag Hammadi Library." In *The Coptic Encyclopedia*, edited by Aziz S. Atiya, vol. 6, pp. 1771–1773. New York, 1991.

Facsimile Edition of the Nag Hammadi Codices. 12 vols. Leiden, 1972–1984.

Grossmann, Peter. "The Basilica of St. Pachomius." *Biblical Archaeologist* 42 (1979): 232–236.

Habachi, Labib. "Sixth-Dynasty Discoveries in the Jabal al-Ṭārif." *Biblical Archaeologist* 42 (1979): 237–238.

Kasser, Rodolphe. "Bodmer Papyri." In *The Coptic Encyclopedia*, edited by Aziz S. Atiya, vol. 8, pp. 48–53. New York, 1991.

Lease, Gary. "The Fourth Season of the Nag Hammadi Excavation, 21 December 1979–15 January 1980." *Göttinger Miszellen* 41 (1980): 75–85.

Meyer, Marvin. "Archaeological Survey of the Wadi Sheik Ali, December 1980." *Göttinger Miszellen* 41 (1980): 77–82.

Meyer, Marvin, and H. Keith Beebe. "Literally an Archaeological Survey of al-Qasr." *ARCE Newsletter* 121 (1983): 25–31.

Robinson, James M. "The First Season of the Nag Hammadi Excavation, 27 November–19 December 1975." *Göttinger Miszellen* 22 (1976): 71–79.

Robinson, James M., ed. *The Nag Hammadi Library*. San Francisco, 1990.

Robinson, James M., and Bastiaan Van Elderen, "The Nag Hammadi Excavations." In *Institute for Antiquity and Christianity Report 1972–1980*, edited by Marvin Meyer, pp. 37–44. Claremont, 1981.

Van Elderen, Bastiaan, and James M. Robinson. "The Second Season of the Nag Hammadi Excavation, 22 November–29 December 1976." *Göttinger Miszellen* 24 (1977): 57–73.

Van Elderen, Bastiaan. "The Nag Hammadi Excavation." *Biblical Archaeologist* 42 (1979): 225–231.

BASTIAAN VAN ELDEREN

NAḤAL OREN, prehistoric site located south of the Carmel ridge, close to the outlet of the Oren valley onto the coastal plain. Excavations at the site were begun by Moshe Stekelis in 1942 and were continued from 1954 to 1960 by him and Tamar Yizraeli-Noy, and in 1969–1970 by Noy, Eric Higgs, and Anthony Legge. Because the cave floor is buried under large limestone boulders, the main archaeological operations were conducted on the terrace, over an area of about 400 sq m. Nine layers were uncovered: IX–VII, Kebaran; VI–V, Late Natufian; and IV–I, Pre-Pottery Neolithic A (PPNA) and Pre-Pottery Neolithic B (PPNB).

The Kebaran layer has been radiocarbon dated to 18,250 ±350 to 15,800 ±300 BP. Although a small stone wall was exposed in this layer, most of the remains were animal bones and lithic industries. The Kebaran industry is dominated by microliths, the most common types of which in the lower levels are the obliquely truncated backed bladelets and micropoints. In the uppermost levels, triangles and backed lunates predominate. Among the animal species represented are fallow deer, which indicates that the immediate environment of Mt. Carmel was still covered by oak forest; and gazelle, which were probably hunted in the parkland of the coastal plain. As a result of the lowering of the sea level during the glacial age, the coastal plain was at least 10 km (6 mi.) wide.

Naḥal Oren was unoccupied during the Early Natufian period. The Middle and Late Natufian are represented at the site by flimsy house foundations, well-built terrace walls, small installations, postholes, and a large cemetery. Most of the occupational deposits abut three terrace walls, which were erected in a west–east direction. Deep mortars, also known as "stone pipes," were imbedded in secondary positions in these walls. Small mortars, stone bowls, and numerous pestles, as well as decorated basalt shaft straighteners, were found. The cemetery contained numerous flexed burials with the remains of forty-five humans, ten of which were children. In a central area a large hearth, more than a meter in diameter, was uncovered, surrounded by flat limestone slabs. Three postholes were uncovered nearby around the fireplace.

The Natufian lithic industry is dominated by backed lunates, many of which were made by the microburin technique. Sickle blades, burins, endscrapers, and perforators comprise the rest of the assemblage.

The few art objects recovered include a long bone depicting an ungulate on one end and a human head on the other; a limestone piece interpreted as depicting the heads of a dog and an owl; a gazelle head carved in bone; and a stone figure smeared with red ocher, representing an unidentified animal head but resembling a baboon. Among the objects used as body decorations were bone pendants and numerous dentalium shells.

Layers IV and III contained assemblages associated with the PPNA. The nature of layer IV is unclear but may be related to the Khiamian, the earliest phase within the Neolithic sequence. Layer III contained the remains of twenty domestic structures, often attached, arranged on four terraces. The houses/rooms are 2.5–4.0 m in diameter, with entrances facing south. On the well-preserved floors, rounded hearths surrounded by small stones were uncovered, and next to each was a limestone slab with two to four cup holes. Large, flat, and round grinding stones, as well as rubbing stones, were found, as were two schematic figurines interpreted as representing humans. PPNA burials were rare at Naḥal Oren. Of those burials found, in only one was the skull removed. In this way, the PPNA here differs from contemporary farming communities in the Jordan Valley. [*See* Jericho.]

The layer III lithic industry is comprised of a few arrowheads, ax/adzes, sickle blades, perforators, retouched blades, and a considerable amount of debitage. The Tahunian axes are characterized by a working edge shaped by transverse removals. Among the sickle blades, Beit Ta'amir knives should be noted, as well as el-Khiam arrowheads. Small obsidian blades originated in central Anatolia. It is, however, extremely difficult to determine what part of the microlithic tool assemblage belongs to the PPNA because the leveling of the terraces caused the mixing of Natufian and PPNA artifacts.

Layers II and I contain the remains of small rectangular houses. The remains of six rectangular buildings were exposed, with very few finds. Among the most important objects were querns and rubbing stones. The lithic assemblage includes arrowheads of the Helwan types, Jericho points shaped by pressure flaking, elongated sickle blades with short tangs, and Tahunian axheads, as well as some polished bifacials. The burials are mostly of adults, from which the skulls have been removed. Among the animal remains are ovicaprids, probably domesticated goats, wild boar, gazelle, and some deer.

It seems that Naḥal Oren represents the spreading in the process of acculturation of cultural traits that had originated in the "corridor" of Jericho to the Damascus basin. The small village or hamlet in Naḥal Oren kept its traditional Natufian structure during the PPNA and only modified its architectural forms later, during the PPNB.

BIBLIOGRAPHY

Noy, Tamar, et al. "Recent Excavations at Naḥal Oren, Israel." *Proceedings of the Prehistoric Society* 39 (1973): 75–99.

Stekelis, Moshe, and Tamar Yizraeli. "Excavations at Naḥal Oren: Preliminary Report." *Israel Exploration Journal* 13.1 (1963): 1–12.

OFER BAR-YOSEF

NAJRAN (ancient South Arabian, NGRN; also identified in pre-Islamic literature as Raʿma), also known as al-Ukhdud ("pit," or "trench") in reference to the Qur'anic surah and the Christian martyrdom (see below), a modern oasis located on the fringes of the Arabian shield and on the drainage network of Wadi Najran, which permits large-scale agriculture to the west and south (17°32′ N, 44°12′ E). The wadi disappears eastward into the Rub al-Khali sands. Currently in Saudi Arabia, its ancient historical ties and ecological orientation lie within the framework of ancient South Arabian civilization. Writers from Strabo, Pliny, and Ptolemy (who called it Nagrana) to al-Hamdani, al-Istakhri, and Carsten Niebuhr (1792) have remarked on the area's agricultural and commercial wealth.

Arab travelers referring to the site in 1070 (al-Bakri) and 1230 (Ibn al-Mujawir) suggest the ancient site was abandoned by the early second millennium CE. Niebuhr was the first Westerner to mention the site (1792, p. 61), but it was not visited by a western explorer until Joseph Halévy (1872) in 1870. The next formal investigation of the site was in 1936: St. John Philby described the central walled area, the palatial buildings, the surrounding moats, the cemetery on the south side of the walled area, and the numerous inscriptions in Epigraphic South Arabian (1952, pp. 265–266). His comments on a possible earlier domed structure being a Christian church tied into earlier accounts of the presence of "Omar's mosque" and even the famous Kaʿba of Najran (Shahīd, 1979, pp. 70ff; Zarins et al, 1981, pl. 9). In 1951, Philby revisited the site with the Philby-Ryckmans-Lippens expedition and a more detailed plan of the site was made (Ryckmans, 1981, p. 63). The site was briefly examined in 1967 by Gus Van Beek.

In 1980, the Comprehensive Archaeological Survey of Saudi Arabia, led by Juris Zarins, visited the site to determine the cultural sequence and site layout. A composite section suggested more than 8 m of deposit. In one small sounding, more than 3 m of stratified materials was excavated. Carbon-14 dates from the sounding indicate a range of occupation from 535 BCE to 250 CE for the central citadel area (Zarins et al., 1981, pp. 23–24, pl. 7). Fragmentary Neolithic material was found, but no clear evidence of the Bronze Age (Zarins et al., 1983, p. 36 n. 1). The team revisited the site in 1982 to examine the area in more detail.

Based on the comments and plans of earlier researchers (Philby, 1952; Ryckmans, 1981; Van Beek, n.d.; Zarins et al., 1981; Doe, 1983, pp. 150–152), the site can be divided into several subareas. The citadel area (240–250 m on a side, covering 12.8 acres) is defined by walls of fitted and cut masonry. Its uneven bastions and recesses are typical of South Arabic building (e.g., at Shibam). The straight-axis gate is on the west. The house layout is also typical of South Arabian types (Zarins et al., 1983, pls. 20–21), and their hammered, marginally drafted masonry with inscriptional materials is also well attested (Zarins et al., 1983, pls. 17–20, 34). The moat on at least two sides of the area may be associated with the modern arabic name (al-Ukhdud). The cemetery area noted by others and mapped in 1982 (Zarins et al., 1983, pl. 22) may be the internment area for the Ukhdud settlement (Shahīd, 1979, p. 42), based on the presence of Byzantine period ceramics. Ukhdud (South), a defined area of South Arabic houses, also contained the remains of a seil dam (i.e., for control of flash-flood waters) with accompanying Epigraphic South Arabian inscriptions. The bulk of the site is on the northeast, as the town expanded in the South Arabic, Byzantine, and Islamic periods (Zarins et al., 1983, pp. 22–27, pl. 16).

The excavation area was expanded in 1982 (Zarins et al., 1981, pl. 7; 1983, pl. 23) and a total area surface-collection project begun. The project revealed that the area's South Arabic wares could be divided into at least three subperiods between 500 BCE and 300 CE (Zarins et al., 1981, pp. 28–32), followed by a recognizable Byzantine corpus from between 300 and 700, an Early Islamic (Umayyad/ʿAbbasid) corpus, and, finally, a post-ʿAbbasid corpus of minor importance (Zarins et al., 1981, pp. 32–35; for drawings, cf. Zarins et al., 1981, pls. 22–25; 1983, pls. 24–28). Industrial activities were carried out at the site: copper and iron metallurgy and casting, flint hoe production, steatite working, ceramic production (kilns), and production of huge grinding stones for use in presses and mining (Zarins et al., 1983, 35–36).

Najran was an important commercial center and the northernmost major South Arabian center for transporting incense north along the western Arabian road (Mecca, Yathrib Medina, al-ʿUla/Dedan, Hegra, Tayma', Gaza) and northeast along Jebel Tuwayq (Qaryat al-Fau, Ayun/Layla, al-Yamama, Thaj/Hina). [*See* Mecca; Medina; Dedan, Tayma'; Qaryat al-Fau; Thaj.] Incense burners and inscriptions, particularly the use of the *WD'B* formula praising the deity Wadd at Najran, confirm that Najran was a major handling post for incense, particularly in association with Minaean activities (Doe, 1979; Zarins et al., 1983, pl. 29; Pirenne, 1977). Obsidian was also traded there.

The site became associated with the growth of strong Monophysite Christian belief and their martyrdom, under the Jewish Yemenite king Dhu Nuwas, in 523 CE, is reported in *Martyrium Arethae* (Shahīd, 1971, 1979, 1994; Trimingham, 1979, pp. 287–307; De Blois, 1990). The Qur'anic verse (surah 85.4–7) referring to al-Ukhdud, is taken to refer to these events: the bodies of the victims were thrown into a large trench or pit. Examination of the moats, tumuli, and associated possible Christian-period buildings in the area (Zarins et al., 1983, p. 27), coupled with the strong Byzantine-period ceramic corpus (see above), suggests that future archaeological work may confirm the historical accounts.

BIBLIOGRAPHY

Blois, François de. "The Date of the 'Martyrs of Nagran.'" *Arabian Archaeology and Epigraphy* 1 (1990): 110–128.

Doe, Brian. "The WD'B Formula and the Incense Trade." *Proceedings of the Seminar for Arabian Studies* 9 (1979): 40–44.

Doe, Brian. *Monuments of South Arabia.* New York, 1983.

Halévy, Joseph. "Rapport sur une mission archéologique dans le Yemen." *Journal Asiatique* 19 (1872): 5–98, 129–266, 489–547.

Niebuhr, Carsten. *Travels through Arabia and Other Countries in the East.* 2 vols. Translated by Robert Heron. Edinburgh, 1792.

Philby, H. St. John. *Arabian Highlands.* Washington, D.C., 1952.

Pirenne, Jacqueline. *Corpus des inscriptions et antiquités sud-arabes.* Louvain, 1977.

Ryckmans, Jacques. "Al-Ukhdūd: The Philby-Ryckmans-Lippens Expedition of 1951." *Proceedings of the Seminar for Arabian Studies* 11 (1981): 55–63.

Shahīd, Irfan. *The Martyrs of Najrân: New Documents.* Subsidia Hagiographica, no. 49. Brussels, 1971.

Shahīd, Irfan. "Byzantium in South Arabia." *Dumbarton Oaks Papers* 33 (1979): 25–94.

Shahīd, Irfan. "On the Chronology of the South Arabian Martyrdoms." *Arabian Archaeology and Epigraphy* 5 (1994): 66–69.

Trimingham, J. Spencer. *Christianity among the Arabs in Pre-Islamic Times.* London, 1979.

Van Beek, Gus W. "Preliminary Report on the Nejran Survey, 1967." Unpub. ms., Department of Antiquities, Riyadh, n.d.

Zarins, Juris, et al. "The Second Preliminary Report on the Southwestern Province." *Atlal* 5 (1981): 9–42.

Zarins, Juris, et al. "Preliminary Report on the Najran/Ukhdud Survey and Excavations 1982/1402 AH." *Atlal* 7 (1983): 22–40.

JURIS ZARINS

NAMES AND NAMING. Names are personal (anthroponyms), geographic (toponyms), or divine (DN). They are recorded in various scripts and languages. Most ancient Near Eastern names are Semitic. The remainder are Hamitic (notably Egyptian) and Indo-European (Anatolian and Indo-Iranian) or belong to unclassifiable languages (e.g., Sumerian, Elamite, Hurro-Urartian.).

In antiquity a personal name is not merely a means of identification, but is also considered to be an expression of its bearer's character. Generally, a male is known by his name and patronym. Only rarely is he known by his mother's name. A wife is mentioned in texts together with her husband's name and a slave with his master. Few individuals in Ugarit and early monarchic Israel are known only by their patronyms. Several Israelite personalities, whose names are known, are addressed only by their patronyms—a derogatory usage on the part of their adversaries. In a few cases in the Hebrew Bible, a person is introduced by his full name at the beginning of the narrative and by a short form of his name (a hypocoristicon) in the rest of the story. Many individuals are listed without their genealogy. Extant Mesopotamian and Levantine genealogies generally consist of two generations. The exceptions are Chaldean and Achaemenid Babylonia, where most urbanites are listed with their patronyms and their ancestors' names. Elsewhere, long genealogies are reserved mostly for important personalities. Genealogies are rare in the Old and New Egyptian kingdoms but are common from the Saitic period onward (the longer ones are probably unreliable).

Generally, the newborn is given his name shortly after birth by his mother (Israel and Egypt) or father (Sumer). During his lifetime an individual may acquire an additional name, usually motivated by his extraction, occupation, personality, or physionomy; throne names were current in certain ancient kingdoms. A personal name can be theophoric or "basilophoric" (containing a numen or a royal name, respectively) or profane. From a structural point of view it can be either compound, noncompound (including hypocoristica), or abbreviated. All but atypical names belong to certain languages with various degrees of probability. Almost all the ancient textual corpora contain a small percentage of "atypical" names of various patterns (monosyllabic and reduplicated, anthroponyms including names with identical two final syllables).

Naming (name giving) may be motivated by the circumstances of birth (exclamation names on the one hand, and certain theophoric names invoking a deity with regard to the birth and the newborn on the other), as well as by the unity and succession of the lineage. Naming a child after a grandfather (papponymy) appears in the ancient Near East as early as the first half of the second millennium BCE. The practice became more frequent in the ancient Near East after the second half of the first millennium BCE. It is not documented among preexilic Israelites and, strictly, not among postexilic ones, either, if the highly elaborate genealogies (in all probability invented by the Chronicler or his circle) are ignored. At most, few postexilic Israelites are named after their grandfathers.

Most Mesopotamian individuals are recorded in juridical, administrative, and epistolary documents, whereas the prosopographical Levantine documentation is mainly from seal impressions, bullae, graffiti, ostraca, and votive inscriptions (in Egypt it is mainly from papyri). In order to ascertain ethnolinguistic distributions, not of the number of individual names of a given dialect, but of the number of persons bearing names in that dialect should be calculated. If the name of an individual is indicative of his or her ethnolinguistic affiliation, these statistics are the closest approximations achievable regarding the relative percentage of the ethnolinguistic groups in a given region. However, in most cases it is impossible to draw conclusions on the level of the individual, as relatively few people are listed with their gentilic or place of origin. A prosopographic sampler from a given site does not refer exclusively to residents, but also to visitors and foreigners (especially in capitals and centers of international trade). Except for a very few special cases (such as Puzrish-Dagan—that is, modern Drehem), most individuals were residents of the site in question or its region. The overwhelming majority of the individuals mentioned in a given corpus belonged to the local group, unless there is clear evidence to the contrary. For instance, no more than 10 percent of the more than ten thousand individuals recorded in Babylonia between 580 and 480 BCE were strictly non-Babylonians (actually it was much less than 10 percent, as the Arameans were local). Most individuals in the Hebrew Bible were Israelites.

Like anthroponyms, toponyms (including microtoponyms), or place names, are a rich and enduring source of ethnolinguistic, historical, and folkloristic information. Place names, especially those referring to geomorphologic features like hydronyms and oronyms (e.g., Jordan and Tabor, respectively)—but hardly microtoponyms—are generally more archaic than personal names. They often preserve otherwise unretrievable information concerning early—and often extinct—linguistic strata.

The structure of place names resembles that of personal names, but the distribution of their various patterns is different. Because they have a special function, their topics also generally differ. The following short description is based mainly on the toponymic inventory of Syria-Palestine where the relevant ancient documentation (about one thousand pre-Hellenistic toponyms) is especially abundant and shows a high degree of diversity. Moreover, the later and even modern toponymy of the Syro-Palestinian limestone massif has a sizable hard core of ancient survivals. This is in sharp distinction to the Mesopotamian alluvium, where ecological (the ever-changing arable terrain) and historical factors resulted in much toponymic discontinuity.

Some sentence names are anthroponyms used as unmodified toponyms: *ʿmʿd* and *Yqmʿm* in the Hebrew Bible. Relatively few sentence toponyms describe configurations of the terrain. Most composite toponyms are genitive compounds in which the *nomen regens,* or essential name, is a "ground word" functioning as a geographic definer and followed by a *nomen rectum.* The latter can be an appellative, anthroponym, or divine name. The most frequent ground word is the common Semitic term *byt:* "house;" "temple," "domain." The other ground words (e.g., *ʿyn,* "source" and *bny,* "sons of"—originally a tribal name) are much less common. Noncompound toponyms are, like the corresponding anthroponyms, of various nominal formations. Many noncompound toponyms end in the plural suffixes *-ā/ōt* (even of DN: *ʿntwt, ʿštrwt, Bʿlwt*), and *-īm/n,* as well as in the locative suffix *-aym/n* and *-āʰ*. These suffixes are very rare in genuine anthroponyms. All the toponyms can belong to the following semantic-topical categories:

1. Topographic feature (e.g., *gbʿ(h),* "hill") or position (e.g., *mṣph* "watchtower," "lookout point"; *byt hʿmq,* "house/domain of the valley"), nature of the soil (e.g., ṭwb, *špyr,* "good"), watercourses and sources (e.g., *'bl, 'pq, ḥmt*)
2. Buildings and installations (e.g., *gdr, ḥṣr'dr/'sm*), "fortifications" (e.g., *bṣr, šʿrym*), and worship sites (open or built up, e.g., *bmwt, glgl, qdš, mš'l, 'št'l* [cf. Punic for beg and beseech])
3. Flora (e.g., *bṭnym*)
4. Fauna (e.g., *ḥsr swsym*)
5. Anthroponyms (many second components of ground words).

Moreover, numbers 3–4 may not be primary in many cases but simply an anthroponym deriving from a plant or an animal—as in *(byt) ḥglh* and *ḥṣr (šwʿl).*

A comparison of the percentage of each category in later toponymic documentation groups—namely, those of Hellenistic-Roman (more than 140 new toponyms) and Late Ottoman Palestine—reveals only relatively small differences. These differences are mostly in the realm of human activity as well as in theology. Many fewer place names contain divine names after the Hellenistic period, as a result of the diffusion of monotheism; this is partly remedied by the abundance of saints' toponyms in Byzantine and Islamic Palestine. The toponymy of Palestine the late Ottoman period shows a higher percentage of anthroponyms—an accumulation of ancient layers and a great number of tribal names—as a result of a continuous and massive penetration of seminomads. Thus, the abundant documentation (of about six thousand toponyms) of Palestine in the 1870s can be used as a legitimate comparable corpus for clarifying the functions of ancient Palestinian toponymy.

Theophoric, or divine, elements in names can identify specific deities (Marduk, Sin, Shamash); can be general, using the appellative *ilum*, "god" (pl. *ilū;* or *ilī, ilšu* as a protective deity); can express terms of kinship; or can include other numina (toponyms including temples and sacred objects, for example). In several names the theophoric element is replaced by a personal pronoun (you, he, she, him). Most intelligible personal names in the ancient Near East are theophoric, expressing religiosity and the popularity of the cult of certain deities. It is plausible that bearers of theophoric names were under the protection of the respective deity, but the issue is complicated.

Individual onomastica (corpuses of names) can be described in terms of linguistic affiliation. The discussion that follows is arranged accordingly.

Semitic Onomasticon. The most important Semitic language from the onomastic point of view is Akkadian. The only assured representative of the East Semitic subgroup, its onomasticon has the longest duration—from about 2500 BCE down to the beginning of the Christian era (with later survivals).

The most important type of names in Akkadian are verbal sentence names. The order in early Akkadian (Old Akkadian through Old Babylonian [OB]) is normally verb (imperfect ["preterit"]) as predicate followed by DN as subject. The inverted order occurs only if the verbal form is a ventive. This position (predicate-subject) accords with West Semitic onomastica of the same period (see below). The position changes in post-OB times when there are more Akkadian names with the order subject-predicate (imperfect verb). Again, this tendency is shared by most of the later West Semitic onomastica. Abbreviated names are shortened from compounds. Contrary to male names, most female names in Akkadian and other ancient Semitic onomastica are profane (some based on jewels and related items as a kind of endearment), with a fair percentage of "substitute" names. Several female anthroponyms are genitive compounds, like *Amat/Mārat*-DN ("maid/daughter of [Divine Name]"). Many compound names borne by Semitic females are grammatically masculine; instances of gender congruency are rare. (Note the Septuagent's Elizabeth for *'lyšbʿ* in the Hebrew Bible.) Compound names with two predicates are common in Akkadian but extremely rare in West Semitic.

Eblaite, the second oldest Semitic language, has a considerable number of names, but its classification within Semitic is not yet established. All the texts are from Ebla (Tell Mardikh). Their geographic horizon is roughly between Byblos in the south, Harran in the north, and the Trans-Tigridian regions in the east. Eblaite in this context is necessarily a rather vague designation: the names may belong to several different early and as yet ill-defined Semitic dialects. Names with a verbal form of the prefix conjugation + subject (DN or, conceivably, a divine epithet) are much more common than the inverted order, resembling the situation in early Akkadian and West Semitic. Other Semitic languages belong to the West Semitic subgroup.

Amorite is the earliest West Semitic dialect. It is recorded from about 2100 to about 1180 BCE. Most names are contained in Old and Middle Babylonian texts from Babylonia, the Jezireh, and northeastern Syria. There is not a single Amorite text. The huge Amorite onomasticon (about ten thousand names) is recorded in cuneiform, a writing system that inadequately transmits the inventory of early West Semitic consonantal phonemes. In most cases, cuneiform does not indicate either vowel length or consonant gemination. This is only partly remedied by Egyptian transcriptions (beginning in c. 1800 BCE) of names and words from Canaan.

Early Canaanite can barely be separated from Amorite before the Amarna age because the only criterion—the Canaanite shift of *a* to *o*—was not completed much before 1400 BCE. It is therefore used here only for the sake of convenience. The handful of Late Old Babylonian texts from Palestine contains West Semitic names that cannot be distinguished from Amorite names. The very restricted onomasticon of the Proto-Sinaitic and Proto-Canaanite inscriptions is of the same type. However, the early Canaanite alphabet—and to a great extent Egyptian script—cannot express vowels. Canaanite names in the Amarna correspondence are recorded in Peripheral Middle Akkadian.

Ugaritic was recorded in the fourteenth–thirteenth centuries BCE in the small kingdom of Ugarit on the northwestern coast of Syria. It is written in an invented cuneiform alphabet that transmits the consonantal phonemes adequately, but the vowels only very partially. As far as the abundantly documented local onomasticon is concerned, the alphabetic limitations are in part palliated by the presence of a large corpus of Akkadian texts there. Ugaritic is not a straightforward Canaanite dialect but can be regarded as belonging to the northwestern end of the Amorite dialectal continuum. A small percentage of the names refer to people from Canaan and other Syrian regions. Many of the texts unearthed in the course of controlled excavations belong to archives, which facilitates prosopographic research.

Following a gap in documentation for Syria-Palestine, a negligible number of names are recorded in early Phoenician alphabetic script from the turn of the first millennium BCE. This alphabet was later adopted by both the Arameans in the Jezireh and Syria and by speakers of Canaanite-Hebrew dialects in Palestine and southern Transjordan. Individual scripts do not begin to differentiate until the mid-ninth century BCE. Presumably, script originally expressed the consonantal phonemes of a certain Phoenician dialect, whereas other Northwest Semitic dialects probably had additional consonantal phonemes. These additional phonemes remained unexpressed in script but occasionally occur in transcriptions. All the Canaanite-Hebrew dialects have more or less distinctive onomastica.

Phoenician names are recorded in Phoenician, Akkadian, Greek, and Cypriot transcriptions from about 1000 BCE to the beginning of the Christian era (with some isolated occurrences as late as c. 200 CE). The language later died in the mother country, but Punic, which was spoken by descendants of Phoenician colonists in the western Mediterranean, was still alive as late as the Byzantine period (as Neo-Punic; Phoenician names also appear in Latin transcription). The Phoenician-Punic onomasticon contains hundreds of names referring to thousands of individuals. The poorly documented onomasticon of Philistia is probably very close to Phoenician.

(North-)Israelite and Judahite Hebrew have the largest Canaanite corpus and the richest and most diverse source of data for the Northwest Semitic onomasticon. The first occurrence of the name Israel itself is from 1207 BCE. However, the ensuing documentation is very sparse until the beginning of the eighth century BCE (mostly in the Samaria ostraca). [*See* Samaria Ostraca.] The documentation in Israelite Hebrew ceases after 720 BCE. (The later material from Samaria cannot, strictly speaking, be regarded as an uninterrupted continuation of the North Israelite tradition.) The documentation from Judah is very poor before 720 BCE, but it becomes abundant after the destruction of Samaria. It reaches its peak just before the destruction of Jerusalem in 586 BCE. At least 2,500 individuals, bearing hundreds of different names, are recorded, most of them in late preexilic Judah. The sizable Jewish onomasticon from Achaemenid Egypt and Babylonia is in the same onomastic tradition. The maximum number of Israelite individuals mentioned in the Hebrew Bible is 1,947. Most of them may have lived between 1000 and 300 BCE, and they bore hundreds of different names.

Ammonite, Moabite, and Edomite refer to restricted textual corpora of Canaanite-Hebrew ("fringe Canaanite") from southern Transjordan. Ammonite is written in a variant of Aramaic script, whereas Moabite and Edomite had their own variants of the Phoenician script. There are nearly one hundred Ammonite names (mostly on seals); Moabite has fewer than fifty and Edomite even fewer. The chronological range of these dialects is between about 800 and 500 BCE. Only Edomite survived any later, but merely in the Achaemenid northern Negev and Hellenistic Idumea ("Idumean").

Early Aramaic texts contain a restricted number of anthroponyms. Aramaic texts after 720 BCE and imperial Aramaic documents contain many non-Aramaic names because Aramaic became the language of communication in the vast territories of the Late Assyrian, Neo-Babylonian, and Achaemenid empires. The main sources of the Aramaic onomasticon are the Neo-Assyrian and Neo-Late Babylonian documents and, after the Macedonian conquest, the Greek and then the Latin transcriptions. Altogether there are several thousand names.

Several thousand names are recorded in various ancient Arabian dialects—roughly, from north to south, Safaitic, Thamudic, Taymanite, Lihyanite, Dedanite, Hasean, Minean, Sabean, Qatabanian, Ausanian, and Ḥadhrami, as well as in pre-Islamic classical Arabic. Most of the pre-Islamic Arabian texts consist of graffiti (mainly from the Achaemenid period down to the diffusion of Islam). Earlier Arabian names (no more than one hundred) are recorded in "Proto-Arabian," Assyro-Babylonian, Aramaic, and, later on, Greek and Latin sources. The Ethiopian onomasticon is late (from the Byzantine period onward) and is therefore beyond the scope of this discussion.

West Semitic names are usually transparent as to meaning, for they consist either of a full sentence (e.g., *ntn'l*, "God has given [this child]") or of single-element names, many of which can be identified as abbreviations of sentence names (e.g., *ntn*, "has given"). These single-element names may or may not show a syllable in place of the omitted element, the so-called hypocoristic ending. The sentence names express explicitly various relationships between the deity and the name bearer, while in the single-element names the relationship is not expressed, as in the name *ntn*, historically a verbal form of which any divine name could be the subject. Because any verbal form may in theory be used for the verbal element (though in practice the perfect and the imperfect of the Qal stem are the most common), because any of a great number of nominal patterns may appear, because the order of the elements in sentence names may be reversed or one element may be omitted, and because sentence names may be either declarative or interrogative, the attested number of individual structures is immense (see Zadok, 1988, for an exhaustive listing of the structures attested in Israelite personal names). Finally, though it may be granted that most names were meaningful, one wonders how well names of which the structure is clear but which consist of an archaic element were understood (e.g., Zimri, "my protection [is (in) X-deity]," from an old root ḎMR, meaning "to protect," that was no longer current in biblical Hebrew).

The semantic-topical and theological-ideological evaluation of the ancient Semitic onomastica is necessarily based mainly on the huge, diverse, and fairly well-established Akkadian documentation and much less on the West Semitic (notably Israelite) one. The chronological-historical and social backgrounds of the Akkadian onomasticon are also well known. For many Akkadian names, even the situations and scenarios (concerning mostly the childbirth naming and relationship to deities and relatives) can be reconstructed. The main theological-ideological categories of Akkadian names follow:

Forms of greeting are included in either profane sentence names spoken at the time of birth by a parent (*Balṭu-kašid,* "A healthy one has arrived") or by an older sibling (*Aḫam-arši,* "I have acquired a brother") or theophoric names expressing joy (for the newborn). They are directed to a deity: example, *Sîn-kašid,* "O Sin; he (the newborn) is (here)." In thanksgiving names, such as the latter (generally in the third-person singular), the deity is thought of as having given the child. A name expressing a request (imperative/precative, and generally second-person singular) is *Marduk-iqišanni,* "Give me (a son), O Marduk." The request was uttered by the father before the birth and was eventually fulfilled. A wish (on behalf of the child; imperative) is expressed in *Ilī-uṣuršu,* "O my god, protect him." A complaint and a trust are expressed by *Atanah-Ištar* ("I have become tired, O Ishtar") and *Ana-Sîn-taklaku* ("I trust in Sin"), respectively. The former is motivated by an illness; the latter is placed in the child's mouth. Attribute names refer to characteristics of deities. Praise and endearment names are *Mannum-kīma-*DN ("Who is like DN?") and *Šī-ṭābni,* "She is our (spoken by parents/siblings) joy." "Substitute" names, in which the child is named after a deceased or living relative, are *Ali-ummī,* "Where is my mother?," *Erīb-Sîn,* "Sin has compensated," and *Aḫu-waqar,* "My brother is precious."

Slaves and maids were probably named (in certain cases renamed) by their masters and mistresses, respectively. Many slaves' names contain praises, wishes, and requests for their masters or mistresses, as well as expressions of trust in them. In the same manner, many names of public officials contain praises, wishes, and requests for the king, as well as expressions of trust in him. Priestesses bore more theophoric names than other females. A wide range of occupational terms is attested in anthroponyms, mostly as surnames in Babylonia (especially during the first millennium BCE). Anthroponyms denoting mental characteristics, physical traits, plants, animals, and other realia, as well as gentilics, are well represented in all the Semitic onomastica.

Hamitic Onomasticon. Egyptian, which is written in hieroglyphs and later in derived scripts, has a huge onomastic documentation from about 3000 BCE to the Byzantine period. Very few Libyan and Nubian names are recorded in Egyptian sources. The main Egyptian name types are sentences with finite verbs (in certain tense categories). The second person (singular and plural) is reserved for the imperative. Certain names contain more than one predicate. Nominal sentences contain a substantival, adjectival, or adverbial predicate. There are compound abbreviated names. Short names may or may not bear a hypocoristic suffix.

Indo-European Onomasticon. Hittite, during most of the second millennium BCE, and Luwian for the same period, but continuing into the first half of the first millennium BCE, are written both in cuneiform and hieroglyphs and contain a sizable number of names. Clear compounds are, for example, *piya-,* "give" (preceded or followed by a DN, as in Arma-piya-), the Hittite *asi-,* and the Luwian *wasu-,* "good," "dear" (preceded by DN as in *Laknasu* < *Lak(a)n-asu-*). Both name-types (sequence: subject-predicate) have Indo-European semantic-structural parallels (Greek *Theodoros/Dorotheos* and *Theophilos,* respectively). On the other hand, no such parallels are known for the many names with -ziti-, "man" (Luwian; follows theophoric elements, toponyms, or appellatives); *-muwa-* (signifying "descendance," race; possibly borrowed in Hittite from Luwian), and *-nani,* "brother" (preceded by a DN or an appellative). The fact that Hittite and Luwian stay outside the mainstream of the Indo-European onomastic tradition may be the result of the great antiquity of the Anatolian group and its relative structural isolation within Indo-European. Noncompound names end in various suffixes (either found only in anthroponymy or denoting participles) or are originally appellatives without any modification. Not a few names are originally gentilics in Hittite, Luwian, or Hattic (a non-Indo-European Anatolian language).

Other members of the Indo-European family are Indo-Aryan and Old Iranian. Indo-Aryan has left only remnants in foreign languages—primarily written in cuneiform during most of the second millennium BCE—from Mesopotamia, the Levant, and southeastern Anatolia. The Old Iranian onomasticon (c. 880–330 BCE, and 330 BCE–700 CE, Middle Iranian) is recorded on the Iranian and Armenian plateaus and, during the Achaemenid periods, in other parts of western Asia and Egypt. Indo-Aryan and Old Iranian are an important segment of the rich and well-explored Indo-European onomastic tradition. Two-stem compounds are common in both. The most common type is *bahuvrīhi:* for example, *Miθra-bānu-,* "with Mithra's brilliancy of light." A determinative compound is *Baga-dāta-,* "Created/Given by God," and related names. Compounds with a verbal form are *Dāraya-vahu-,* "He who holds firm the good."

Unclassifiable Onomastica. Sumerian has a very rich onomastic documentation from about 2500 (if not earlier) to the first half of the second millennium BCE. Many genitive compounds start with the initial component *ur,* which looks like the Sumerian appellative for "dog" but is of unknown denotation (perhaps meaning something like "belonging to [DN]"). Other initial components (all like *ur* followed by a theophoric element; the genitive postposition is generally not marked) are, for example, *ir/ir*$_{11}$ "servant," *geme,* "female servant," and *lú,* "man." Genitive constructions without "dependence terms" are ^{d}*En-lil-lá* '("the child belonging") to Enlil' and *Inim-^{d}Utu,* "the word of Utu (is true)." Sentences with a predicate can contain an attribute: *Lugal-ad-da,* "the king is a father" (with a nominal predicate), *Lugal-dingir-mu,* "the king is my god" (with a possessive suffix), *Nanna-lú-du$_{10}$* "Nanna is a good man" (with an adjective as epithet). The predicate can be verbal. Sentence names can express wishes and questions. Hypocoristica are abbreviated from sentence names with omission of the subject, as in *Ma-an-si* < *Dingir-mu-ma-an-si,* or by retention of the participle only (*Du$_{10}$-ga*). Several hypocoristica end in *-mu: A-kal-la-mu,* "my dear Akalla." More than two hundred elements (mostly predicative) are contained in Neo-Sumerian names or serve as such. Flora and fauna are virtually absent in the Neo-Sumerian onomasticon.

Elamite has a sizable number of names from about 2400 BCE to the second century CE. Most compound names consist of two elements and can contain more than one theophoric element. Names with three elements are much less common than those with two. Classification is necessarily tentative. Nominal sentences may consist of substantives, substantive + adjective or vice versa (*^{d}Ri-ša-ap-^{d}la),* substantive + passive participle (*^{d}Sa-ti-šil-ha-ak)* or vice versa (*Šilhak-Inšušinak),* substantive + personal pronoun first person singular (*At-ta-u-ri),* and personal pronoun + passive participle (*Um-mu-ur-da-ik).* A present passive participle follows a substantive (theophoric element as subject) in *At-ta-me-te-en. Hu- ba-nu-du-uk* may consist of a theophoric element plus personal pronoun (*-u-*) plus passive participle (*-k*) of *tu-,* "receive," "take." Verbal sentence names consist of substantive (theophoric element as subject) and verb (mostly ending in *-s,* which marks the personal pronoun third singular: *Hu-pan-mi-ri-iš*). Many names start with *kuk,* "protection," which is followed by a theophoric element. The names look like genitive compounds (if not nominal sentences). Elamite has a sizable number of suffixed hypocoristica, short and atypical names in various patterns.

Kassite and other dialects were spoken in the Iranian plateau and its piedmont before the diffusion of the Old Iranian dialects. Because of the paucity of the material and the lack of any texts in these dialects, no coherent classification of their onomasticon is possible.

Hurrian and Urartian are related to one another. There is a relatively rich Hurrian onomasticon from the Fertile Crescent, the Armenian plateau, parts of Anatolia and the Zagros (predominantly from the second millennium BCE). The Urartian onomasticon has a rather meager documentation and is restricted to the Armenian plateau and adjacent regions during the first half of the first millennium BCE. Most Hurrian names are theophoric compounds. The most common pattern is predicate + theophoric element: *Ehli-, Eni-, Ewri (Ibri), Hišmi-, Taki-, Talmi-, Urhi-Teššup* ("*Tešup* [is] salute/god/lord/brilliant/sure/great/true; *Una-p-Teššup* [with "asservative" -p-], "Teššup [is] surely coming," *Urha-l-enni* [with "superlative" -l-], "the god [is] very steadfast"). Other well-documented elements are *ak (akai,akap),* "to bring," "to guide"; ar- "to give"; *tan-,* "to do"; *tad-,* "to like," "to love"; *hubiti,* "calf"; *keldi,* "peace" (*kili-,* "be in good state," or "peace"); *kiaše,* "sea"; *papa(n),* "mountain"; *pur(u)li,* "house" or "temple"; *šenni,* "brother;" and *wanti,* "just." They form both compounds and single-element names. Hypocoristic suffixes are *-ya* and *-uya.* There are various suffixal formatives.

[See also entries on specific languages and language families.]

BIBLIOGRAPHY

Benz, Frank L. *Personal Names in the Phoenician and Punic Inscriptions.* Rome, 1972.

Gelb, Ignace J., et al. *Nuzi Personal Names.* Chicago, 1943.

Gelb, Ignace J. *Computer-Aided Analysis of Amorite.* Chicago, 1980.

Gröndahl, Frauke. *Die Personennamen der Texte aus Ugarit.* Rome, 1967.

Herr, Larry G. *The Scripts of Ancient Northwest Semitic Seals.* Harvard Semitic Monograph Series, no. 18. Missoula, 1978.

Israel, Felice. "Note di onomastica semitica 7/1-2: Rassegna critico-bibliografica ed epigrafica su alcune onomastiche palestinesi." *Studi Epigrafici e Linguistici* 8 (1991): 119–147; 9 (1992): 95–114.

Jongeling, Karel. "Names in Neo-Punic Inscriptions." Ph.D. diss., Rijksuniversiteit te Groningen, 1984.

Krebernik, Manfred. *Die Personennamen der Ebla-Texte: Eine Zwischenbilanz.* Berlin, 1988.

Laroche, Emmanuel. *Les noms des Hittites.* Paris, 1966.

Limet, Henri. *L'anthroponymie sumérienne dans les documents de la 3e dynastie d'Ur.* Paris, 1968.

Maraqten, Mohammed. *Die semitischen Personnenamen in den alt- und reichsaramäischen Inschriften aus Vorderasien.* Hildesheim, 1988.

Mayrhofer, Manfred. *Onomastica Persepolitana.* Vienna, 1973.

Rainey, Anson F. "Šm, šmwt mqwmwt (Place Names)." In *Encyclopaedia Biblica Instituti Bialik,* vol. 8, cols. 11–29. 1982. Includes an exhaustive bibliography.

Ranke, Hermann. *Die ägyptischen Personennamen.* 2 vols. Glückstadt, 1935–1952.

Rasmussen, Carl G. "A Study of Akkadian Personal Names from Mari." Ph.D. diss., Dropsie University, 1981.

Stamm, J. J. *Die Akkadische Namengebung.* Leipzig, 1939.

Wuthnow, Heinz. *Die semitischen Menschennamen in griechischen Inschriften und Papyri des Vorderen Orients.* Leipzig, 1930.

Zadok, Ran. *The Elamite Onomasticon.* Naples, 1984.

Zadok, Ran. "Zur Struktur der nachbiblischen jüdischen Personennamen semitischen Ursprungs." *Trumah: Jahrbuch der Hochschule für Jüdische Studien Heidelberg* 1 (1987): 243–343. Analyzes not only the postbiblical Jewish names, but also most of the names from Hellenistic–Roman Syria–Palestine and Upper Mesopotamia, including those in Greek and Latin transcription.

Zadok, Ran. *The Pre-Hellenistic Israelite Anthroponymy and Prosopography.* Louvain, 1988.

RAN ZADOK

NAMI, TEL, peninsula situated 15 km (9 mi.) south of Haifa, Israel, and 4 km (2.4 mi.) west of the Carmel ridge (32°39′ N, 34°55′ E). The coastal strip west of the Carmel mountain range is characterized by wavelike parallel series of low sandstone ridges separated by basins filled with clayey alluvium. Tel Nami is part of the westernmost ridge, which is partially submerged. On another ridge, 1 km to the east, a Middle Bronze IIA settlement (c. 2000–1700 BCE) was noted (sites 104–106). Another habitation site, Nami East, was found under the sand dunes 75 m east of the peninsula. Like Tel Nami, it has remains of MB IIA and Late Bronze IIB habitations.

The area's important feature—archaeologically, hydrologically, and geomorphologically—is the course and outlet of Naḥal Meʿarot, which originates in the Carmel ridge, crosses an eastern *kurkar* ("sandstone") ridge, and discharges into the sea in the vicinity of Tel Nami. Ship representations dating to the end of LB II have been observed there. The location of its estuary in antiquity is crucial to understanding the site. Of equal interest is a marshy basin lying between Nami East and another of the *kurkar* ridges. This basin must have been a natural swamp, a shallow or brackish lake, or a lagoon that could have been used in antiquity as a natural anchorage before artificial harbor construction was developed. The site was noted by the Israel Survey in the 1960s and explored in 1975; since 1985 a Land and Sea Project has been carried out by the University of Haifa under the direction of Michal Artzy.

The broadest latitudinal MB IIA exposure thus far was in area D on the tell. There are signs at both Nami East and on the tell that the area was abandoned at the end of MB IIA or the first part of MB IIB. At least two clear architectural phases are apparent, each of which is dictated by the topography, as was a retaining wall that follows the contours of the *kurkar*. At Nami East a possible granary and an unidentified industrial area were excavated. A stone-lined well, already in disuse in MB IIA, has contributed data on sea level for the period. The international character of the anchorage site is demonstrated by imported legumes from the Aegean world, White-Painted ceramics from Cyprus, ʿAmuq/Cilician and Levantine Painted Wares, and a scarab seal weight dated to the milieu of the Egyptian twelfth dynasty. [*See* ʿAmuq; Seals.]

A layer of sand accumulated between MB IIA and the LB II layers. A rampart was constructed at the end of the thirteenth century BCE, probably to combat rising sea levels. On the summit (area G), a cultic precinct was excavated. The finds include kernoi, a seven-spouted lamp, conical cups, pumice, and numerous pieces of metal, including bronze, silver, and gold, which had been prepared for recycling, as well as metalworking tools such as chisels. Part of the floor was paved with sherds of incense burners. Nami East became a necropolis with diverse forms of burials: box and pit, as well as built graves and jar burials. [*See* Tombs; Burial Techniques.] Cypriot, Mycenaean IIIB, and other imported ceramics were noted. The bronze objects recovered include weapons, knives, armor scales, lamps, bowls, strainers, a wine set, incense burners, and scepters. Gold, silver, faience, and ivory objects were also found. For a short time, until its destruction and final abandonment sometime in the first years of the twelfth century BCE, Nami served as an etrepôt for a larger trade network (for incense, among other commodities) that combined maritime and desert routes via the valleys to Transjordan and beyond.

BIBLIOGRAPHY

Artzy, Michal. "Fortress and Settlement: Anchorage System during the Second Millennium Tel Nami?" In *Cities on the Sea, Past and Present,* edited by Avner Raban and Elisha Linder, pp. 14–17. Haifa, 1986.

Artzy, Michal. "Tel Nami, 1985/1988." *Hadashot Arkeologiyot* 9 (1989): 22–24.

Artzy, Michal. "Nami Land and Sea Project, 1985–1988." *Israel Exploration Journal* 40 (1990): 73–76.

Artzy, Michal. "Pomegranate Sceptors and Incense Stand with Pomegranates Found in Priest's Grave." *Biblical Archaeology Review* 16 (1990): 48–51.

Artzy, Michal. "Conical Cups and Pumice: Aegean Cult at Tel Nami, Israel." In *Thalassa, the Prehistoric Aegean, and the Sea: Aegaeum VII,* edited by Robert Laffineur, pp. 203–206. Liège, 1991.

Artzy, Michal, and E. Marcus. "The MBIIA Coastal Settlement at Tel Nami." *Michmanim* 5 (1991): 5*–16*.

Artzy, Michal, and E. Marcus. "Stratified Cypriote Pottery in MBIIA Context at Tel Nami." In *Studies in Honour of Vassos Karageorghis,* edited by G. C. Ioannides, pp. 103–110. Nicosia, 1992.

Artzy, Michal. "Incense, Camels and Collar Rim Jars: Desert Trade Routes and Maritime Outlets in the 2nd Millennium," *Oxford Journal of Archaeology* 13 (1994): 121–147.

Artzy, Michal. "Nami: A Second Millennium International Maritime Trading Center in the Mediterranean," In *Recent Discoveries in Israel: A View to the West,* edited by Seymour Gitin, pp. 17–39. American Institute of Archaeology Series, Colloquia and Conference Papers, 1. 1995.

Artzy, Michal. "Anchorage Systems of the Second Millennium BC at Tel Nami." In *Tropis III: Third International Symposium on Ship Construction in Antiquity,* edited by Harry E. Tzalas, pp. 23–30. Athens, 1995.

Kislev, Mordechai E., et al. "Import of an Aegean Food Plant to a Middle Bronze IIA Coastal Site in Israel." *Levant* 25 (1993): 145–154.

MICHAL ARTZY

NAQADA, important predynastic site in Upper Egypt. The archaeological remains from the Naqada region (Nakada, Negadah; 25°58′ N, 32°44′ E) extend for approximately 8 km (5 mi.) along the desert edge on the western side of the Nile near the modern towns of Naqada and Zawayda and from the Paleolithic to Roman periods. They include scatters of stone tools representing ancient living or working areas, numerous cemeteries, several habitation sites, the ruins of a temple dedicated to the god Seth, and a structure identified by the excavator as a pyramid.

Objects from the area began appearing in museums and private collections in the mid-nineteenth century. The first systematic archaeological investigations were conducted by Flinders Petrie and James E. Quibell in 1894–1895 in the area between Naga Kom Bilal and Zawayda: the archaeological sites of Naqada and Ballas. Two years later, Jacques de Morgan, working on behalf of the Egyptian Antiquities

Service, excavated two cemeteries closer to the village of Naqada. Since that time several surveys and minor excavations have been conducted in the region by various researchers.

The oldest significant remains from the region date to the Predynastic period (c. 3900–3100 BCE). Petrie reported three Predynastic cemeteries near Naqada. He excavated about two thousand graves from the "Great Cemetery." Cemeteries T(umuli) and B(ilal) were significantly smaller. One habitation site of the same period, which Petrie named South Town, and several small predynastic settlements were located nearby. Many pit graves and a number of mastabas of the Early Dynastic period (c. 3100–2700) were also found. The earliest levels of the ancient town of Nubt (classical Ombos), which name probably derives from the ancient Egyptian word for "gold," and the temple of Seth were found to date to the Old Kingdom (2700–2250). Middle and New Kingdom (2050–1050) remains were also recovered from the town and nearby graves. The greatest building phase of the Seth temple dated to the New Kingdom.

To the south of Petrie's excavations, de Morgan found other habitation remains, lithic scatters, and two cemeteries containing predynastic and early dynastic graves. In his southern cemetery, de Morgan uncovered the graves of what he called "indigenous tribes." The northern cemetery contained Early Dynastic burials. The so-called royal mastaba of Naqada is 100 m (328 ft.) north of the northern cemetery. Inscribed objects from this tomb bore the name of the first dynasty ruler Aha and queen Neithhotep. De Morgan thought this was the actual burial place of the ruler, but the current interpretation is that it belonged to an important official.

The predynastic evidence from the Naqada region has been critical to our understanding of developments in Upper Egypt in the fourth millennium. Petrie himself did not initially recognize their significance but thought that the strange objects and burial positions he encountered belonged to invaders, whom he called the New Race and dated to the First Intermediate Period (2250–2050). It was only after the publication of Petrie and Quibell's *Naqada and Ballas* (London, 1896) that de Morgan recognized the true significance of these remains and assigned them to their proper place in history—prior to the beginning of dynastic civilization.

Petrie and Quibell's excavations were the first to bring to light the full complexity of predynastic material culture from mortuary contexts. This inventory included ceramics, stone cosmetic palettes in geometric and animal forms, stone vessels, jewelry of local and imported stones (such as lapis lazuli), and weapons and tools of stone, metal, ivory, and wood. Their work also revealed the increasing sophistication of predynastic tomb architecture, which began with small round or oval holes dug into the ground and developed into large, rectangular pits, some with more than one chamber, lined with wood or mud brick. To deal with the ceramics that he found, Petrie developed a still-used typology of predynastic pottery. He divided the predynastic ceramic corpus into nine classes: B (black topped red), P (polished red), F (fancy), C (white cross-line), N (black incised), W (wavy-handled), D (decorated), R (rough-faced), and L (late).

Petrie and Quibell were the first to note the variation in wealth among the graves at Naqada. Recent anthropological interpretation has posited the development of a stratified social hierarchy, the local elite being buried in Cemetery T. Petrie's theories of ritual cannibalism of the dead and the invasion of a dynastic race have been abandoned by most scholars. It has also been proposed that South Town, with its nearby cemeteries, may have been the center or capital of one of three late predynastic kingdoms or chiefdoms in Upper Egypt.

[*See also the biography of Petrie.*]

BIBLIOGRAPHY

Bard, Kathryn A. *From Farmers to Pharaohs: Mortuary Evidence for the Rise of Complex Society in Egypt.* Oxford, 1994. Recent anthropological study of the funerary remains from Naqada and what they can tell us about predynastic Egyptian society.

Baumgartel, Elise J. *Petrie's Naqada Excavation: A Supplement.* London, 1970. Presents a tabular listing of all known objects recovered by Petrie and Quibell from the cemeteries of Naqada and the southern cemetery at Ballas.

de Morgan, Jacques. *Recherches sur les origines de l'Égypte,* vol. 2, *Ethnographie préhistorique et tombeau royal de Négadah.* Paris, 1897. The primary source for information on these excavations.

Hoffman, Michael A. *Egypt before the Pharaohs.* Rev. and updated ed. Austin, 1991. Excellent review of the state of knowledge on Egyptian prehistory up to 1979, with an addendum updating the work.

Petrie, W. M. Flinders, and James E. Quibell. *Naqada and Ballas* (1896). London, 1974. The best source for information on the sites.

Weeks, Kent R. *An Historical Bibliography of Egyptian Prehistory.* American Research Center in Egypt, Catalog no. 6. Winona Lake, Ind., 1985. Comprehensive bibliography including references to Naqada publications.

PATRICIA V. PODZORSKI

NAQSH-I RUSTAM, a precipitous cliff at the south side of the Husain Kuh, located north of Persepolis, Iran, with rock reliefs ranging from Elamite (second millennium BCE) to Sasanian times (fifth century CE). Surrounding it are other rock installations and some Achaemenid and Sasanian architecture, most of which lies under several meters of debris and has not yet been excavated.

Elamite Periods. The only surviving monument from the pre-Achaemenid period is a relief that was mostly obliterated when the court scene of Bahram II (designated NRm 2) was carved over it. The surface of the original relief curves toward the left and slants back at the right end. The remnants of the scene show an attendant standing behind two seated deities, faced presumably by a standing worshiper, and a head with a mural crown. Only the attendant at the right is preserved in its major features. The bearded face is turned in the direction of the deities, and the hair, projecting in front, is covered with a cloth fastened by ribbons. The view of the body is frontal with the hands clasped at the waist. Only the lower portions of the seated deities are barely discernible. They wear flounced garments and sit on layered thrones representing coiled snakes. To the left of the later carving of Bahram the partially visible feet of a standing figure point toward the deities. The crowned head preserved on the left belongs to a shorter figure whose preserved feet are correspondingly smaller. Another figure stood between this person and the worshipper next to Bahram, as evidenced by the remnants of some curls and a heel. The original height of this figure cannot be reconstructed.

The main part of the relief resembles the central part of the rock sculptures at Kurangun, which can be dated to the late Old Elamite period (c. seventeenth century BCE); however, differences in the shape of the thrones and the slenderness of the figures point to a somewhat later date. The figure with the mural crown at the left may have been added in the early first millennium BCE.

Achaemenid Period. Four tombs of Achaemenid monarchs are cut into the rock of the cliff (Schmidt, 1970). A square tower erected in stone blocks (Kabah-i Zardusht) stands in front of the cliff, and some minor walls of built structures were detected in trenches dug there.

The sepulchral compartments tunneled into the rock differ in plan and in the number of burial cists, but their facades are essentially alike. The oldest (no. I) is dated to Darius I (521–486 BCE) by his inscriptions; the other tombs (nos. II–IV) can be assigned to his successors only through iconography and style (see figure 1).

The facade of tomb I, which faces southeast, lies about 15 m above the surface (see figure 2). Its total height is 22.93 m, but a vertical enlargement toward the bottom may have been intentional as the quarrying slots at the base suggest. The facade is divided into three registers: the bottom register is blank, the middle is sculptured to imitate the front of a palace, and the top shows the monarch at worship on the top of a piece of furniture that is supported by representatives of the nations in his realm.

The middle register, which gives access to the burial chamber, is adorned with a relief representing a building facade. Erich F. Schmidt (1970, p. 81) has shown that the model for it was the facade of the residential palace of Darius at Persepolis (*tačara*: a portico with two rows of four columns *in antis*). In addition to the architectural similarities, Schmidt notes that the principal dimensions are identical (length, height, distances between the centers of the columns, width of the doorway), except for the height of the columns (the lost palace columns are computed from the steps in the antae). This difference arises from a common misunderstanding resulting from the transposition of three-dimensional architecture into two-dimensional relief, however: the capitals, in the shape of addorsed bulls carrying the stepped architrave between their heads, are turned 90 degrees, to be seen in profile; the architrave is consequently shown in cross section and looks instead like small roof beams. If the palace columns are reconstructed with the architrave placed between the bulls' heads of the capitals, they have the same height as the relief columns carved at the tomb. The panels between the columns bear a trilingual cuneiform inscription of Darius I (designated DN b); an Aramaic inscription was added later.

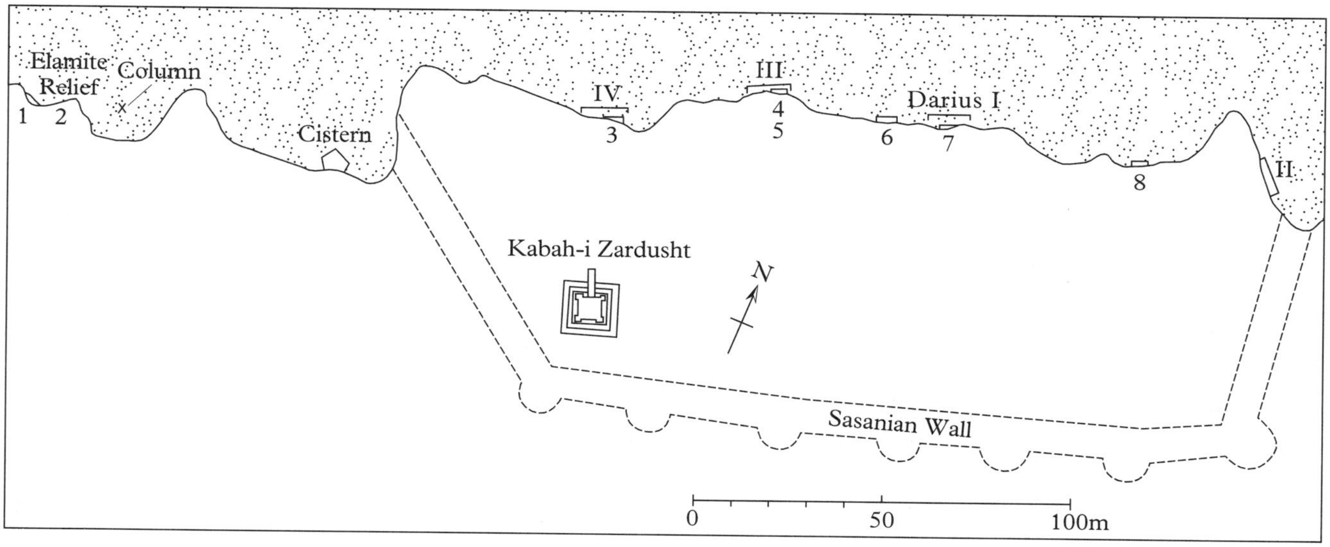

NAQSH-I RUSTAM. Figure 1. *Plan of the site.* Achaemenid tomb facades are numbered in Roman numerals. Sasanian reliefs are numbered 1-8. (Courtesy U. Seidl)

NAQSH-I RUSTAM. Figure 2. *View of Naqsh-i Rustam cliffs.* The entrance to the tomb of Darius I is shown above two Sasanian reliefs. The relief of Shapur I (NRm 6) is at the lower left, and a relief of two jousting scenes (NRm 7) is directly below the tomb entrance. (Courtesy DAI)

The top register is adorned with a framed relief panel showing an imposing estrade (or dais) supported by thirty representatives of the nations of the empire, identified by cuneiform captions. They are arranged in two tiers of fourteen people with raised arms between the legs, and two people on the outside support the feet of the estrade. Unlike the sculptured supporting figures on Assyrian or Urartian furniture, the figures here are actually lifting the dais, and, as they are all facing right, they appear to move it in this direction. On the top, the king, standing on a three-stepped pedestal, faces a fire altar. A figure in a winged disk hovers above, between king and altar, and there is a moon symbol farther to the right. Since the last century, the man in the winged disk has usually been called Ahuramazda, but Shapur Shahbazi (1974) has shown that this interpretation is mainly based on a circular argument. On the tombs and in the Persepolitan palaces, the figure is not only related to the king by his position, he also wears the royal garment and crown; this, along with some written sources, and the Assyrian prototype, points to his being a royal daimon or daimon of kingship. Behind the king is a second inscription of Darius I (DN a). The frame of the relief panel and the projecting side walls are adorned with reliefs. Behind the king stand his spear bearer, the bearer of his battle-ax and bow, and several anonymous spear-bearing Persians. On the opposite strip of frame and wall, several Persians, with their left hands raised to their mouths, face the king.

Three copies of Darius's tomb facade (tombs II–IV) were cut into the same cliff by his successors, but definitive attributions to individual Achaemenid kings have not yet been reached.

The Kabah-i Zardusht is a square tower (12.50 m high

and 7.32 m wide) with reinforced corners that stands on a three-stepped base. It is built of light-colored stone with false windows in dark stone. Most of the tower is solid, but in the upper half a small room with a door facing the cliff can be reached through a stone staircase. An identical monument was built at Pasargadae (Zendan-i Sulaiman). The purpose of these towers is not known, but it has been proposed that it was either a royal tomb, a depository for objects of dynastic or religious importance, or a fire sanctuary. The third can be ruled out because there is no ventilation or outlet for smoke or gases. In the Sasanian period inscriptions of Shapur I and Kerdir the high priest were cut into the tower (see below).

Sasanian Period. Apart from the Aramaic inscription on the tomb of Darius I, presumably cut in the Seleucid period, nothing is known that can be dated to the time between the Achaemenid and the beginning of the Sasanian periods.

Eight rock reliefs were carved on the cliff by Sasanian kings (numbered from west to east NRm 1–8). Although most of the reliefs are difficult to date, they are discussed here in their assumed chronological order.

The oldest relief (NRm 1) was carved at the west end, near the Elamite relief (see above). It shows the investiture of Ardashir I (224–241 CE) by the god Ahuramazda. Both the king and the god are mounted. On the ground under or beside their horses lie their slain enemies, respectively the last Parthian king, Artabanus V, in his royal dress, and Ahriman, the evil genius in the shape of a naked man whose legs end in snakes and whose head is encircled by snakes. The nearby Elamite relief, with its snake throne and perhaps with snake attributes of the gods, was still clearly visible at the time of Ardashir's carving and could have inspired the fashioning of Ahriman.

Ardashir's son and successor, Shapur I (241–272 CE), was the next to carve a relief (NRm 6). He placed his "Victory over the Romans" relief near Darius's tomb (see figure 2). It shows Shapur I on horseback grasping the wrist of a standing Roman (Valerian ?) with his extended right arm. Another Roman emperor (Philip the Arab ?) is kneeling before the Sasamian King. Later, during the reign of Bahram II, the High Priest Kerdir added his picture and a lengthy inscription.

The third relief (NRm 2) shows Bahram II (276–293 CE) with members of his family and court. In carving over an Old Elamite relief (see above) Bahram II made apparent his program to persecute all religions other than Mazdaism. Kerdir, the high priest of Bahram II, writes in his inscriptions, of which two copies are carved on Naqsh-i Rustam monuments (NRm 6 and Kabah-i Zardusht) section 11. "and idols were destroyed and the abode of the demons disrupted. . . ." Was it only the negligence of the sculptor that the portion with the snake thrones remained visible, or was it the intention of a dissident sculptor?

Narseh's (253–302 CE) investiture relief (NRm 8) was never finished. In the main part that is shown, the king receives the ring from the hands of a goddess (Anahita?).

In the fourth century and perhaps also at the beginning of the fifth century reliefs with jousting scenes were carved below the Achaemenid tombs: Hormizd II (302–309) vanquishing his adversary (NRm 5), placed below tomb III; two jousts in two registers below the tomb of Darius I (NRm; see Figure 2), attributed to Bahram IV (388–399) by Hubertus von Gall (1990); the latest joust (NRm 3), dated by von Gall (ibid.) to the fifth century placed below tomb IV; and a relief of a seated king (NRm 4) that is too eroded to be dated. The area of the carvings, excluding the reliefs of Ardashir and Bahram II (NRm 1 and 2), was enclosed by a wall sometime in the Sasanian period. Outside this wall are Sasanian installations that, according to Dietrich Huff (forthcoming), are related to burials: the column on the Husain Kuh, and the so-called fire altars are interpreted as *astodans* (burial urns for the bones of the dead).

[*See also* Elamites; Parthians; Persians; *and* Sasanians.]

BIBLIOGRAPHY

Calmeyer, Peter. "The Subject of the Achaemenid Tomb Reliefs." In *Proceedings of the Third Annual Symposium on Archaeological Research in Iran,* pp. 233–242. Tehran, 1975.

Gall, Hubertus von. *Das Reiterkampfbild in der iranischen und iranisch beeinflußten Kunst parthischer und sasanidischer Zeit.* Teheraner Forschungen, 6 Berlin, 1990. Covers Sasanian reliefs numbers 3, 5, and 7 (pp. 30–36).

Herrmann, Georgina. *Naqsh-i Rustam 5 and 8: Sasanian Reliefs Attributed to Hormuzd II and Narseh.* Iranische Denkmäler, II 8. Berlin, 1977.

Herrmann, Georgina. *The Sasanian Rock Reliefs at Naqsh-i Rustam: Naqsh-i Rustam 6, The Triumph of Shapur I.* Iranische Denkmäler, II 13. Berlin, 1989.

MacKenzie, D. N. "Kerdir's Inscription." In Iranische Denkmäler, II 13, pp. 35–72. Berlin, 1989.

Huff, Dietrich. "Fire Altars and Astodans." In *Proceedings of the International Conference on Parthian and Sasanian Themes in Iranian Art.* London, forthcoming.

Schmidt, Erich F. *Persepolis,* vol. 3, *The Royal Tombs and Other Monuments.* University of Chicago, Oriental Institute Publications, 70. Chicago, 1970. The basic publication for Naqsh-i Rustam.

Seidl, Ursula. *Die elamischen Felsreliefs von Kurangun und Naqsh-i Rustam.* Iranische Denkmäler, II 12. Berlin, 1986. See pages 14–23, pls. 11–15.

Shahbazi, Shapur. "An Achaemenid Symbol I. A Farewell to 'Frahahr' and 'Ahuramazda.'" *Archäologische Mitteilungen aus Iran* N.F. 7 (1974): 135–144.

Vanden Berghe, Louis. *Reliefs rupestres de l'Iran ancien.* Brussels, 1983.

URSULA SEIDL

NAṢBEH, TELL EN-, site located 12 km (8 mi.) north of Jerusalem (31°53′ N, 35°12′ E, map reference 1706 × 1436). The mound is approximately 260 m long by 130 m wide and about 7.7 acres in size. It is usually identified with biblical Mizpah of Benjamin (*Jos.* 18:21–27). The American scholar Edward Robinson traveled past the site but did not connect it with Mizpah, which he located at Nebi Samwil, an identification some still maintain. It was A. Raboisson, in 1897, who first proposed equating Mizpah with Tell en-Naṣbeh. Before the excavation of Tell en-Naṣbeh, those who supported this identification were Gustaf Dalman, Albrecht Alt, Eberhard Baumann, Paul Lohmann, W. Y. Pythian-Adams, and L.-H. Vincent. William Foxwell Albright opposed this view, however, holding to Nebi Samwil instead, and proposing to place Be'erot at Tell en-Naṣbeh; later he contended that Tell en-Naṣbeh was 'Ataroth (Adar) because the Arab village of ʿAṭṭara was located just south of the tell. Alt twice changed his views; he first proposed to locate Gibeon at Tell en-Naṣbeh, with el-Bireh for Mizpah; subsequently, he suggested that Tell en-Naṣbeh was at first called 'Ataroth and after its fortification by Asa was renamed Mizpah. From the time of the excavations to the present, the major supporters of the Tell en-Naṣbeh–Mizpah equation have been F.-M. Abel, William F. Badè, and James Muilenburg.

Tell en-Naṣbeh was excavated in five campaigns between 1926 and 1935 by William F. Badè of the Pacific School of Religion. He uncovered approximately two-thirds of the site, even though the central part was severely eroded, and few occupational deposits, except for rock-cut installations, were recorded. The site's significance today is in the information it provides on town planning in the Iron Age, especially during the little-known Babylonian period. [*See the biography of Badè.*]

The remains uncovered at Tell en-Naṣbeh correlate with what is known of Mizpah. The Mizpah traditions that have the earliest setting revolve around the prophet Samuel, battles with the Philistines, and the election of Saul as king—although not all scholars accept these as early traditions. Mizpah next appears in the reign of Asa of Judah, who fortified the site during his conflict with Baasha of Israel. Its next, and most important, role is as the capital of the Neo-Babylonian province of Judah during the period of the Exile. Inhabitants of Mizpah helped in the restoration of Jerusalem after the Exile. Finally, Judah Maccabee assembled his troops at Mizpah to face the Seleucids.

The earliest remains are from the Late Chalcolithic and Early Bronze I periods: three tombs and two caves on the tell contained ceramics and other material. Early pottery is also found in cavities in the bedrock and scattered in later debris, mainly in the northwest corner of the tell. Other caves used as dwellings and/or tombs were found in the low ridge northwest of the tell.

Tell en-Naṣbeh was uninhabited from the end of EB I to the beginning of the Iron Age. Philistine bichrome pottery and local forms such as collar-rim jars attest to the site's occupation in this latter period. Architectural remains are harder to identify, but many of the rock-cut cisterns and silos were dug then, and many of the houses that were used in Iron II may have been built then as well.

Large parts of the Iron II town were uncovered. Because Tell en-Naṣbeh was not destroyed during that period, many buildings continued in use, with modifications, for more than four hundred years. The Iron II town was protected by a casematelike wall. Later, a wall (4–6 m wide) reinforced by towers and a glacis were built and in places a fosse was erected around the casemate wall, but downslope from the original town. Entrance to the town was through an inner and outer gate complex. (These fortifications are probably the work of Asa.) There were storage bins in the intramural space on the south, and channels to drain off water crossed the northern and western sections. The dwellings usually contain two or three parallel long rooms, with a broad room across the back. The back rooms of the outermost belt of buildings are arranged to form the casemate-like wall and follow the natural oval shape of the mound. These buildings opened onto a ring-road that, with interruptions, circles the site. Facing them across a narrow street is another group. Occasional streets branch off toward the center of the town. Six olive oil presses also belong to this phase. Fragments of contemporary dwellings and agricultural installations were uncovered outside the town wall, in the suburbs of the walled settlement. The Iron Age cemetery was located on the ridge north and west of the tell.

In the Babylonian period, the inner gate and many of the earlier houses went out of use. They were replaced by more spacious houses of the same four-room type, as well as by other, even larger structures whose plans are fragmentary. One may be a palatial building with a large paved central court. The orientation of all of these buildings is completely different from that of the buildings of the previous stratum. It reflects a change in the settlement's purpose from that of a border fortress to a minor provincial capital.

Fragments of walls built over the town wall, isolated walls and rooms scattered across the tell, and two kilns built in front of the outer gate, along with finds of Attic pottery and seal impressions from the Persian period, indicate continued settlement in the Second Temple period. Coins, fragments of Roman pottery, and a possible watchtower attest to at least a minimal late occupation on the tell. The cemetery remained in use until the Byzantine period, and settlement continued in the vicinity, as affected by remains of a church near the western cemetery.

Tell en-Naṣbeh was rich in epigraphic finds. These include private seal impressions and seals; noteworthy is the seal of Jaazaniah, whose title is "the servant of the king." This seal bears one of the earliest representations of a rooster found in Israel. A full range of government seals was uncovered, including *lmlk*, rosette, *mṣh*, and *yhd*. Seven inscribed ostraca were found, as well as an unusual bronze circlet bearing a dedicatory cuneiform inscription.

BIBLIOGRAPHY

Albright, William Foxwell. "Review of McCown and Wampler, *Tell en-Nasbeh I and II.*" *Journal of Near Eastern Studies* 7 (1948): 202–205. Best critical review of the final excavation report.

Avigad, Nahman. "New Light on the MṢH Impressions." *Israel Exploration Journal* 8 (1958): 113–119. Full treatment of this class of seals, most of which come from Tell en-Naṣbeh, including a discussion of their date and function.

Broshi, Magen. "Nasbeh, Tel En-." In *Encyclopedia of Archaeological Excavations in the Holy Land,* vol. 3, pp. 912–918. Englewood Cliffs, N.J., 1975–. Useful summary of the standard interpretations of the Tell en-Naṣbeh material, in the main, accepting the conclusions of the final report.

McClellan, Thomas L. "Town Planning at Tell en-Nasbeh." *Zeitschrift des Deutschen Palästina-Vereins* 100 (1984): 53–69. Best general treatment of the Tell en-Naṣbeh material to appear after the final report and a must for those interested in ancient town planning.

McCown, Chester C. *Tell en-Nasbeh,* vol. 1, *Archaeological and Historical Results.* Berkeley, 1947. Volume 1 of the final report. Includes a concise history of the excavation, a review of Muilenburg's discussion of the site's identification, and a report on the architecture and nonceramic small finds. Not well organized, and a number of conclusions are no longer valid.

Muilenburg, James. "Mizpah of Benjamin." *Studia Theologica* 8 (1954): 25–42. Supplement to the author's chapters in the first volume of the final report; reviews Alt's latest identification of Tell en-Naṣbeh.

Wampler, Joseph C. "Three Cistern Groups from Tell en-Naṣbeh." *Bulletin of the American Schools of Oriental Research,* no. 82 (1941): 25–43. Detailed treatment of the finds, especially the pottery, from three cisterns. This material is only summarized, not analyzed, in the final report.

Wampler, Joseph C. *Tell en-Nasbeh,* vol. 2, *The Pottery.* Berkeley, 1947. Volume 2 of the final report. Includes a general discussion of the types, a list of comparanda as of about 1940, and a catalog of 1,800 types.

Zorn, Jeffrey R. "Tell en Nasbeh: A Re-evaluation of the Architecture and Stratigraphy of the Early Bronze Age, Iron Age and Later Periods." Ph.D. diss., University of California, Berkeley, 1993. A complete detailed restudy of the architectural remains of Tell en-Naṣbeh based on research from the original records.

JEFFREY R. ZORN

NATIONALISM AND ARCHAEOLOGY. Consciously or subconsciously, archaeological interpretation and the public presentation of archaeological monuments are used to support the prestige or power of modern nation-states. Although nationalism is only one of several modern ideologies that have sometimes subtly influenced archaeological interpretation, it is often the most visible, well supported, and socially pervasive. This is the result of the dominating role played by national governmental bodies, such as departments of antiquities, universities, and ministries of tourism and education, in the funding, legal oversight, and logistical support of archaeology. Indeed, national institutions often determine which of a nation's archaeological monuments will be preserved and presented to the public (through special legal decree or inclusion in national park systems) and often approve the contents of widely distributed interpretive information about them (in the form of school textbooks, on-site signage, and promotional tourist brochures). Although scholarly literature is, in most countries, less subject to direct government control, the political context of archaeological work is often unmistakable to academics and to members of the general public. In the Near East—as elsewhere in the world—archaeological finds, interpretations, and hypotheses are often woven into overarching narratives of progress and transformation, used to explain how the particular modern nation's peoples, lifeways, technologies, religions, and even forms of government have roots in a distant past.

Despite bureaucratic apparatus and governmental resources, however, control of archaeology by nation-states has never been either uniform or uncontested. In the Near East, archaeological exploration was long the exclusive province of foreign archaeological expeditions, whose members' direct involvement with particular nationalist ideologies in the region varied from outspoken commitment and political activism to neutrality to open hostility. Because the expansion of archaeological activity in the Near East has long been connected with general religious attachments, resource exploration, and economic development, rather than with specific nationalism, some of the major themes of archaeological interpretation have always highlighted such universal themes as religious evolution, ecological adaptation, and technological innovation, rather than particularist histories. Also working against the power of archaeological nationalism are internal political factors. In recent years, dissident minority and political opposition groups within Near Eastern nations have inspired alternative archaeological interpretations that directly expose or challenge the validity of "official" nationalistic archaeology. Thus, the importance of an examination of the interplay of nationalism and archaeology is not simply one of direct correspondence between a particular political ideology and archaeological interpretation, but rather the illumination of archaeology's relevance to ongoing and often acrimonious philosophical and political discussions about the legitimacy of the modern state and its relationship to the wider world.

In terms of a general definition, nationalism may be described as the philosophical belief in the historical and political legitimacy of territorially circumscribed, often culturally or ethnically homogeneous polities. The conception of the nation-state as the most coherent form of large-scale political organization emerged in Europe in the eighteenth century, when earlier empires based on religious authority or dynastic connections (such as those of the Hapsburgs, the Bourbons, and the Ottomans) had begun to disintegrate. Economic change was also an important factor in the emergence of the modern nation-state in Europe: in place of hereditary aristocracies whose power was largely based on the agricultural surplus of feudal landholdings, there arose urban elites whose power was based on commerce and large-scale production. The new elites became the spokesmen for, and leaders of, territorially and ethnically defined polities of a fairly uniform type. Yet, nationalism cannot be described merely as support of an abstract political formation. Nationalism's potency lies in the concrete manifestations of the patriotism—or chauvinism—of particular nation-states. When taken to extremes in the elevation of the glory of the nation above every other cultural value, nationalism can mobilize citizens to violent action in the pursuit of internal order or external war. Even in its most innocuous manifestations, however, modern nationalism is based on the presumptive antiquity and historical coherence of the boundaries, traditions, customs, and culture of the modern nation. In this respect, archaeology and the other historical disciplines are instrumental in bolstering and legitimizing what might otherwise be considered a thoroughly modern ideology.

Modern nation-states often construct historical narratives that are vividly illustrated by archaeological monuments and bolstered by archaeological interpretations that celebrate the very elements—centralized administration, organized religion, military power—most prized in the modern society (see below). Because these achievements are selectively identified in the archaeological record, the national "spirit" or "character" of the particular modern nation are made to seem timeless, inevitable, or, in some unfortunate and extreme cases, the result of unchanging racial attributes. Although some archaeologists and other scholars have occasionally utilized archaeological data to challenge the basis of modern nationalistic assertions, most scholars have chosen to restrict their interest to narrowly circumscribed research questions, rarely occupying themselves with the possible political implications of their findings. This generally leaves the business of public interpretation and presentation to others—often to officials of the interpretive branches of the national government itself. This sociopolitical phenomenon is strikingly uniform (both in the Near East and throughout the world), despite the antagonism that often arises between competing nations over the interpretation of the same types of artifacts or concerning the same set of historical events.

Archaeological projects, finds, and interpretations serve to legitimate the political power of nation-states in several standard ways. By helping to construct a narrative of the human settlement in the territory of the nation from prehistory to the present, distinguished primarily by the transformation of material culture, archaeology often reinforces the timelessness of modern geographic perceptions and highlights the importance of economic development and technological change. While the sites and archaeological periods of a given nation may be superficially linked to unique historical events or personalities, an equation or correspondence can be made with the historical development of neighboring nation-states or regions using anthropological concepts, Stone/Bronze/Iron Age terminology, or carbon-14 dates. Thus, in providing both a particularistic biography for the nation and in demonstrating that the nation has undergone a development as complex and as lengthy as that of any other nation-state, archaeology provides both a pedigree and a curriculum vitae for the nation's full-fledged participation in the fraternity of modern sovereign states.

While many of the more virulent forms of archaeological nationalism and conflict were abandoned or diluted after the end of the Cold War and its surrogate regional conflicts, the continuing struggle for self-determination by minority ethnic communities throughout the Near East still sometimes finds its symbolic expression in a connection between archaeology and militant nationalism. In this period also, new, more subtle forms of political image making emerged. In a world of transnational economies and worldwide tourism, national identity could sometimes be achieved through the excavation and presentation of archaeological monuments selected for their presumed attraction to foreign visitors rather than for their importance in elaborating a particularistic nationalist ideology.

European Nationalism and Near Eastern Archaeology. The religious and emotional attachment of the various peoples and polities of Western Europe to the antiquities of the Near East can be traced to the early centuries of the Christian era. The discovery and "translation" of relics of saints and biblical figures from the lands of the Bible to European cities established specific geographic and commercial connections. While the Muslim conquests of the early seventh century changed the region's political conditions, the continued European practice of pilgrimage and relic collection served to further the commercial interests of rival European centers under the guise of antiquarian interest or popular piety. The political dimension of the European attachment to Near Eastern relics and ruins was intensified with the establishment of the Crusader kingdoms in the twelfth and thirteenth centuries and the subsequent struggle for power within them by representatives both of church and various European principalities.

Even after the destruction of the Crusader kingdoms, European financial support and religious patronage of Christian shrines and holy places throughout the Near East were sources of political and diplomatic prestige. Yet, the Reformation in Europe in the sixteenth century brought about a significant split in the character of European attachments to Near Eastern antiquities. While the pope and the Catholic powers continued to encourage pilgrimage to the traditional holy sites, the early European Protestant explorers of the region—freed from, and often antagonistic to, the pilgrimage traditions of the Catholic church (and, for that matter, of the Eastern Orthodox churches)—sought to locate what they believed were the "true" locations of the biblical events. Although this antiquarian movement was a manifestation of European theological conflict, it can also be seen as part of an intensifying effort by representatives of trading nations such as England, France, Denmark, and Holland to widen their presence in the region and to contest the long-standing commercial hegemony of Venice and other Italian cities in the Levant.

The political dimension of antiquarian conflict intensified in the seventeenth and eighteenth centuries, as the Ottoman Empire became a tempting target for commercial and ultimately territorial penetration by European powers—notably

England, France, and Prussia, and to a more limited extent Austria, Holland, and Russia. Scholarly pursuits and geographic exploration could not be easily separated from diplomatic, commercial, and religious initiatives at a time when the various nations were attempting to increase their influence in the region. In the field of antiquities and antiquities collection, the acquisition of movable relics began to be seen as an index of national prestige—particularly in Egypt, Asia Minor, and the Aegean—as resident European consuls competed to purchase and remove the most impressive or unusual antiquities.

The first truly national endeavor, however, occurred during the ill-fated Egyptian expedition of Napoleon Bonaparte (1797–1799), when the specially recruited Scientific and Artistic Commission undertook, under French auspices, a comprehensive cartographic and archaeological survey of the Nile River valley and, later, of Palestine. The surrender of one of the commission's prize finds—the Rosetta Stone—to the victorious British forces who supervised the French evacuation from Egypt in 1801 made the political and nationalistic value of the possession of Near Eastern antiquities unmistakable. The Rosetta Stone soon took its place in the British Museum with the Parthenon marbles brought back by Lord Elgin from Greece. In the following decades of the nineteenth century, the competition for antiquities was to become increasingly the activity of national bodies, both scientific and diplomatic, rather than of private individuals. In Egypt, the race for movable inscriptions and statuary intensified between the British and French consuls, and in Syria and Palestine, wide-ranging geographic explorations were undertaken by Ulrich J. Seetzen, on behalf of the Russian government, and Johann Burckhardt, on behalf of the British African Association. In Mesopotamia, in the 1840s, the conflict to excavate and export impressive remains of the Neo-Assyrian palace complexes, waged between the French consul in Mosul, Émile Botta, at Kuyunjik and Khorsabad, and the British consul, Austen Henry Layard, at Nimrud, brought the political competition to a fever pitch. [*See* Nimrud; *and the biographies of Botta and Layard.*]

In fact, the prominent display at the 1851 Crystal Palace exhibition in London of the monumental sculpture recovered by Layard at Nimrud and the conspicuous placement of an Egyptian obelisk in the Place de la Concorde in Paris marked the beginning of an era in which Near Eastern antiquities came to be seen as national trophies, symbols of modern European nations' pretensions to inherit the imperial mantles of the great nations of antiquity. Eventually, permanent national institutions and academic organizations were founded in nearly every European nation to direct and oversee its ongoing exploration of the Near East. Though European scholars of various nations periodically met, debated, and exchanged information, it is significant that the funding and directorship of the early archaeological undertakings in the region were restricted almost entirely to scholars of the same nationality. Thus, for British scholars, the Assyrian Excavation Fund (founded in 1850), the Palestine Exploration Fund (founded in 1865), and the Egyptian Exploration Fund (founded in 1883) became their main practical conduits for Near Eastern archaeological research. For the French, research was done primarily through the Académie des Inscriptions et Belles-Lettres and, in the Holy Land, by the Dominican École Biblique et Archéologique française (founded in 1891); for the Germans, it was through the Deutsche Orient-Gesellschaft (founded in 1898) and, in the Holy Land, by the Deutscher Palästina Verein (founded in 1877); and for the Americans, through the American Palestine Exploration Society (1870–1884) and the American Schools of Oriental Research (founded in 1900). [*See* Palestine Exploration Fund; École Biblique et Archéologique Française; Deutsche Orient-Gesellschaft; Deutscher Palästina Verein; American Palestine Exploration Society; American Schools of Oriental Research.]

European archaeological nationalism was also manifest in the manner in which the monuments were administered and excavation sites were selected. From the 1850s onward in Egypt, French economic and political influence resulted in the customary appointment of a French scholar as director-general of the antiquities service. Regulations enacted at the time of the 1882 British occupation of the country decreed that henceforth a British scholar would serve as deputy director, with extensive powers of his own. While fierce competition for museum-quality antiquities continued (in such cases as the bitter fight between British, French, and Prussian scholars for the famous Moabite Stone in Transjordan in 1868–1870), the claim to rich excavation sites—rather than individual relics—became paramount. [*See* Moabite Stone.] Indeed, with the various European powers preparing to partition the Ottoman Empire toward the end of the nineteenth century, territorial spheres of archaeological influence were established in Asia Minor, Mesopotamia, Palestine, and Egypt. Certain antiquities sites, and indeed entire regions, were regarded as the exclusive provinces of European scholars of particular nationalities. Thus, British predominance in southern Palestine, Sinai, and Lower Egypt; German predominance in central Asia Minor; and French predominance in Lebanon and Syria came to reflect those countries' larger territorial ambitions.

Aside from foreshadowing the direction of future European imperial expansion, nineteenth-century archaeology in the Near East institutionalized a distinctively European approach to the region's past. In former Ottoman provinces, such as Cyprus and Egypt, that came under direct administration by the British, archaeological interpretation began to absorb modern social concepts that far transcended the earlier classicism and historicism of biblical and classical archaeology. Although religious and literary interest continued, the conceptual framework for archaeologically based interpretations of both Near Eastern prehistory and of the later historical periods came increasingly to center on such secular concepts as ethnogenesis, ethnic migrations, state formation, religious evolution, technological development, and military tactics. [*See* Eugenics Movement.] Indeed, the archaeological interest in and elaboration of these concepts occasioned a subtle, yet far-reaching transformation in the modern social implications of the Near Eastern antiquarian enterprise. From passive veneration of religious scriptures, relics, and monuments, European scholars had, by the late nineteenth century, begun to weave a new, material narrative of the rise of the economic, political, and technological institutions of the Western world.

Naturally, the narratives were expressed in terms that were the most congenial to the specific storyteller: the British and American archaeologists in the region, exemplified by William M. Flinders Petrie and George A. Reisner, working under the influence of the generally progressivist model of material culture pioneered by Augustus L.-F. Pitt-Rivers, tended to see the sweep of history as one of increasing technological refinement, characterized by the adoption of ever more efficient and complex military and administrative systems, roughly dated by a regionwide Stone/Bronze/Iron Age scheme. [*See the biographies of Petrie and Reisner.*] In contrast, German and Austrian scholars, such as Friedrich Delitzsch and Hugo Winkler, often preferred to seek origins of cultural and racial characteristics, rather than their outcomes. They attempted to chart the interactions of the world's great cultures: to describe the dynamics of history as the encounter over the millennia of the world's passive peoples with more creative and active ones. This approach became particularly evident in the historical reconstructions of the followers of Delitzsch's *Babel und Bibel* school of the turn of the century, when racial and linguistic theories positing the primacy of the Indo-Aryans finally overcame the apparent Semitocentrism of the Noahide biblical genealogies. Archaeology and indeed Near Eastern historiography as a whole were now resolutely pointed westward. Although Western scholars of varying nationalities might now debate specific chronological and stratigraphic issues, few disputed the mostly unspoken assertion that they—not the local peasants who served them as domestics and excavation laborers—were the true cultural and spiritual heirs of the great empires of the ancient Near East.

A decisive turning point in the political and archaeological history of the region—and in the impact of European-style nationalistic concepts on its peoples—came in the years immediately following World War I. With the final partition of the Ottoman Empire by the victorious allies, the establishment of the Turkish Republic, the granting of at least nominal autonomy to Egypt, and the creation of League of Nations mandates in Palestine, Syria, and Iraq, the future political landscape of the region was envisioned as one of independent nation-states. Under the tutelage of British, French, and Italian administrators, local populations were taught the techniques of self-determination; along with modern finance, education, public works, and public safety departments, archaeological administration in each of the mandated territories was organized as an embryonic national department of antiquities. The Cypriot and Egyptian antiquities services, under direct colonial control, had long been run in this manner, but new archaeological bureaucracies were established in Syria, Palestine, Transjordan, and Iraq. Local participation was, for the most part, restricted to the lower bureaucratic levels of clerks and subregional inspectors. However, for the representatives of the various European powers who served at the higher levels, the period between the two world wars in the Near East was recognized as an archaeological golden age.

Rarely facing effective local political opposition to the expropriation of antiquities sites from the inhabitants of nearby villages, and with the forces of the mandatory regimes cooperating to ensure security and logistical support, massive excavation programs were begun by the various Western institutions in the region. Activities ranged from those of the Oriental Institute of the University of Chicago in Upper Egypt and at Megiddo in Palestine, to the British Museum excavations at Carchemish in Syria, to the French excavations at Ras Shamra/Ugarit, to the continuing German activity in Anatolia and Mesopotamia. The earlier national competition of rival Western archaeological powers continued on an even larger scale. Although some early echoes of local nationalist opposition to foreign expeditions began to be heard in this period, especially in Egypt, the main political context for archaeological activity in the region continued to be primarily that of the scholarly pride and territorial interests of competing European states. Indeed, it was not until after World War II and the end of the colonial era that the peoples of the modern Near East themselves made powerful connections between Near Eastern archaeology and their own emerging national identities.

Archaeological Nationalism and the Rise of Near Eastern Nation-States. Until well into the twentieth century, the empirical archaeological study of Near Eastern antiquities was pursued almost exclusively by visiting or resident European scholars and the few local scholars they had directly educated and trained. For the vast majority of the local population, older traditions of reverence remained potent; remnants of the past such as tombs, ruins, and natural formations ascribed to the activities of legendary or biblical figures were an integral part of a living landscape. They were sites of prayer, pilgrimage, and ritual in which modern peoples drew continuous blessings and inspiration. They were certainly not conceived as discrete research locales. Even the impressive ruins of Egypt and Mesopotamia were woven into Muslim, Jewish, and Christian traditions as the scenes of stereotypical biblical events. Their present ruinous states had clear significance to the larger narrative. The idea of digging up the ruins and removing any interesting artifacts found there clashed directly with time-honored local traditions.

In fact, when European explorers of the late eighteenth and early nineteenth centuries began excavating in the region they were often greeted with horror and outrage by local religious authorities. Excavation was considered to be, at best, a destructive and greedy search for buried treasure, or, at worst, the desecration of sacred sites. For centuries, the interpretation of the past had been the exclusive province of duly ordained religious authorities, guided by traditions and Scripture, be it the Hebrew Bible, New Testament, or Qur'an. The idea that anything meaningful (or previously unknown) could be divined through an examination of fallen stones, broken pottery, or the exhumed bones of the ancients seemed both foolish and heretical. Yet, with the gradual assimilation of the peoples and economies of the Near East into the European world system—and with the concomitant acceptance of European concepts of time, space, and empirical observation—the region's antiquities began to take on a new meaning and a new political significance.

The gradual spread through the region of the modern European-style concepts of nation and national destiny (particularly among Western-educated, urbanized, commercial, or intellectual elites in every region of the former Ottoman Empire) provided the basis for a continuing political struggle for independence. As had already occurred in Europe, images of the past, when loosed from traditional religious moorings, proved to be powerful vessels in the service of modern nationalism. Through the nineteenth century, particularly in Egypt, an entirely new school of nationalist historiography grew up that was not content to dismiss the country's impressive ancient remains as mere biblical relics or ruins of the "time of darkness," the Jahiliyah, the era before the rise of Islam. Instead, they attempted to draw a lesson from the entire narrative of Egypt's history, stretching from the time of the pharaohs to the present. It was almost inevitably concluded that the new awareness of Egypt's great past precluded its continued subjugation by foreign powers. Egypt's ancient past and its modern destiny as an independent culture and an independent polity were therefore seen as essentially parallel.

The rise of political Zionism in the late nineteenth century similarly encouraged a growing number of Jews educated in European universities or otherwise exposed to European political ideologies to see Jewish history as finding fulfillment in the modern world only in the form of a culturally homogeneous, territorially based, modern nation-state. The novelty and potential power of this political conception can be gauged by the initial hostility of both orthodox religious officials and the Ottoman authorities. Yet, the general acceptance of the political program was eventually to be bolstered by assertions about the centrality of Jewish political independence, as suggested by archaeological monuments and finds from the time of Israelite and Judean kings.

The process was similar, if not completely simultaneous, among many of the nationalities and ethnic and religious communities of the region. In Syria, Arab Palestine, Cyprus, Turkey, and Iraq, ancient monuments, landmarks, and decorative motifs began to take on new meanings as symbols of the past greatness of the particular people and sure signs that the greatness could be achieved again. While local Ottoman administrators (or, in the case of Egypt, the only nominally autonomous khedives) had been content to allow Western scholars to excavate and remove antiquities from the country in return for bribes or political favors or in response to diplomatic pressure, the possession and local study of archaeological remains became a matter of national honor in some circles, especially when political independence loomed.

Until the post–World War I era, the notion of archaeological nationalism within the Near East was restricted almost entirely to small circles of intellectuals and often mixed inextricably with uncompromising, often radical, political ideologies. That peripheral status, and the hostility of the authorities, is illustrated by the fact that the members of one of the earliest of the nationalist organizations primarily devoted to archaeology, the Jewish Palestine Exploration Society (founded in 1912), felt it necessary to destroy all of its organization's records at the outbreak of the war. Yet, with the defeat and dismemberment of the Ottoman Empire at the conclusion of the war, and with the declaration of the allies at the San Remo Conference in 1920 that the destiny of all Near Eastern peoples should be one of self-determination, both nationalism and nationalistic archaeology acquired a certain political legitimacy. In Egypt the publicity surrounding the discovery of the tomb of Tutankhamun in 1922 by an English expedition sparked parliamentary protests by the Wafd party. It also led to the enactment of a ban on the export of Egyptian antiquities, a measure designed to end the officially sanctioned plunder of the modern Egyptian people's material patrimony. Although this regulation did not end European hegemony in Egyptological matters, it occasioned a profound shift in the local political context in which it was done.

An even more dramatic change came in Turkey in the 1920s, when the Kemalists began to construct a new, secular history for the republic. They downplayed Turkey's Islamic heritage, stressing instead its historical and ethnic links to the Indo-European Hittites of the second millennium BCE. In Palestine also the continued interest in archaeological remains by the Jewish community began to focus on concrete embodiments of earlier periods of independence and cultural creativity—primarily the tombs, fortifications, and fortresses of the Second Commonwealth and the synagogues of the Byzantine period. Such perceptions would only gradually spread throughout the region. As long as the administration of antiquities remained in the hands of the occupying or colonial powers, ultimately subject to their approval and academic standards, the pursuit of the nationalistic significance of archaeological remains could not always be actively pursued. With the gradual granting of independence to the various countries of the region during World War II, however (in the case of Syria and Lebanon), or in the years that immediately followed (as in the case of Egypt, Israel, and Jordan), the bureaucratic structures of antiquities administration were turned over to newly established governments. Although Western expeditions continued to work in the region, national priorities and nationalist ideologies played increasing roles in determining the pace and progress of Near Eastern archaeology. [*See* Ideology and Archaeology.]

The rise of modern nation-states in the Middle East (as elsewhere) brought about a dramatic shift in the social significance of archaeological work. The region was no longer seen exclusively as the "Fertile Crescent" or the "Cradle of Western Civilization," but was divided into the homelands and autonomous domains of independent peoples. The connection for those people to the land and its archaeological monuments was immediate, not abstract. In each nation, the elaboration of "national" histories was being used as a tool in maintaining the new nation-states' social solidarity. It interpreted archaeological finds as evidence of timeless national character, precocious technological advancement, or as validation of the historicity of prized national myths. In Israel, for example, the emotional connection between the modern Jewish population and the ancient Israelites and Judeans was made explicit through the excavation of biblical sites and their incorporation into a national park system. The much-publicized excavation of the desert palace-fortress of Masada in the 1960s provided the modern nation with a powerful symbol and political metaphor. [*See* Masada.] At the same time, the Hashemite Kingdom of Jordan celebrated images and protected the archaeological remains of the trading Nabateans, the urban populations of the country's Late Roman cities, and the Umayyad caliphs. In Anwar Sadat's Egypt of the 1970s, the power and grandeur of the pharaohs was stressed, while in Iraq in the 1980s, the restoration of Neo-Babylonian monuments was conspicuously associated with the imperial pretensions of Saddam Hussein. Indeed, the establishment of modern nations throughout the region occasioned the adoption of symbolic ancestors and their archaeological monuments. In the Yemen Arab Republic they were the Sabaeans; for the Lebanese Maronites, the Phoenicians; for the Syrians, the Umayyads and, after discoveries in the 1970s, the Early Bronze Age Eblaites.

The list of archaeologically "chosen peoples" and "golden ages" was eventually extended to every country in the Middle East and the eastern Mediterranean basin as traditional religious veneration of the past began to give way to European-style historiography. Despite the distinct images and sites celebrated by each of the nations of the region, the phenomenon was strikingly uniform. It reflected, ironically, the abandonment of time-honored national traditions in preference for the universal celebration of the power of modern archaeology. Thus, throughout the region, national parades and celebrations, postage stamp and banknote symbols, even the rhetoric of newspaper articles and political slogans memorialized and romanticized the symbolic significance of archaeological remains. Archaeological nationalism in the postcolonial period was not, however, restricted only to ideological exploitation of preexisting archaeological images. Ancient ruins, once mute elements of the landscape, became potentially transformable into national shrines and popular tourist attractions. Furthermore, they became the focus of intensifying excavation, following the lead of the earlier European scholars, in the thoroughly empirical study of the material remains of the past.

Departments of antiquities, university archaeology departments, and national museums became the established institutions of historical investigation and instruction, replacing the traditional religious authorities, whose authority became fairly narrowly circumscribed to matters of ritual. The secular institutions were, moreover, entrusted with protecting the nation's sovereignty over its own archaeological heritage. International legal claims began to be expressed for the "repatriation" of antiquities removed during the colonial era: Greek claims for the restoration of the Elgin marbles from England; Egyptian claims for the restoration of the Nefertiti bust from Germany; and Turkish claims for the restoration of the "Treasure of Priam" from the former Soviet Union were merely the most highly publicized.

Here, too, the specific claims should not be permitted to obscure the shared character of a regional phenomenon. Foreign expeditions continued to come to excavate ancient tombs, temples, and cities, but they did so with the express permission and often active cooperation of the local archaeological authorities. Criteria for supervision and control were broadly the same in every country. The conceptual, methodological, and often theoretical frameworks established for archaeology by scholars in the West were closely followed. From a politicosociological perspective, the only elements that differed from nation to nation were the specific sites and cultures selected as the main subjects of research. In this respect, and despite the military and diplomatic enmity between various nations of the region, the symbolic prominence of such archaeological monuments as Masada, the Ishtar Gate, and the Temple of Karnak represented the transformation of Near Eastern regional polities into European-style nation-states. At its core, then, archaeological nationalism in the Near East, as elsewhere, is something of a contradiction in terms. It was only in abandoning traditional national approaches to the past and adopting a more universal conceptual apparatus that the historical inevitability and legitimacy of modern, technologically based nation-states could be historically maintained.

Archaeological Nationalism and "Counterhistories." The establishment of modern nation-states in the Near East and the consequent authority bestowed on national departments of antiquities throughout the region gradually focused scholarly and popular attention on ever-more-tightly bounded areas. Terms such as "the archaeology of Israel" (or of Jordan, Syria, Lebanon, Iraq, or Bahrain) became common, often existing alongside and sometimes even supplanting the archaeological use of such terms as "the Fertile Crescent" and "the Levant." Indeed many important archaeological sites excavated and/or preserved under national auspices became symbolically identified with the modern nation and its ideological interests—by both its most fervent supporters and its external enemies. In this regard, the association of certain Iron Age sites in Israel such as Hazor, Megiddo, and Beersheba with the Early Israelites was both a source of considerable official pride within the country and a source of political criticism by its opponents, who challenged the specific "Israelite" character of the remains (Baramki, 1969). Similarly, the celebration of the grandeur of Persepolis by the shah of Iran (Lewis, 1975) and the attention lavished on pharaonic remains by Sadat in the 1970s (Reid, 1985) were both supported by government resources and condemned and eventually muted by internal Islamic opposition movements. In a more symbolic—if no less direct—manner, archaeological sites in northern Cyprus that had been of considerable ideological importance to the Greek-dominated government of the Republic of Cyprus were subject to plunder and neglect during the years immediately following the Turkish invasion of the island in 1974.

Acts of intellectual, rhetorical, and sometimes physical opposition to "official" national archaeological monuments and narratives are, however, usually underpinned by counternarratives that are no less coherent or politically self-justifying. In none of the cases mentioned above was the critique of a particular nationalist reading put forward in the interest only—or even primarily—of a more scientific or "objective" reading of the past. The critiques are themselves part of an ongoing political struggle for ideological legitimation and political power that frequently cloaks itself in archaeological and historical terms. The source of these counterhistories can be rival governments, opposition political parties, international bodies (whose interests are global rather than national), and—often most powerful and persistent of all—the emerging political elites of ethnic groups or communities struggling for their own statehood or autonomy. These fragmented, subnationalisms have, by their very existence, posed a threat to the coherence of the modern nation and have usually been ignored or moved to the margins of the state's official archaeological history.

In this connection, it is important to note that one of the most pervasive legacies of early European archaeology in the Near East was its chronological imbalance. Because the scholarly representatives of the Western nations saw themselves as the true inheritors of ancient Near Eastern civilization, their interest in the region's material remains extended only to the point where the economic, political, or religious developments they represented were directly relevant to them. Therefore, the eras after the "end of antiquity"—that is, after the seventh-century Muslim conquests, were of relatively less concern that those that preceded them. However, this was ethnocentrism rather than pure nationalism. The nationalistic aspect was emphasized after the end of the colonial period, when new chronological boundaries were determined by every nation-state. As mentioned above, each nation-state saw itself not as a modern political innovation, but as the political resurrection of a long-oppressed people and the fulfillment of that people's history. In that sense, the rise of the modern state was seen to mark the end of the period of cultural subjugation that had followed antiquity, or the people's cherished golden age.

Although the dates and cultural associations for the period of desolation varied with each nation (Islamic, Crusader, Ottoman, or European colonial), the negative associations evoked by the historical period led to a general neglect of its archaeological remains. Except for the interest of art historians and occasional epigraphers, the vast majority of non-monumental, archaeological remains of the medieval and postmedieval periods in the region were consigned to ignorance and oblivion. In practical terms, the otherwise fairly strict archaeological laws of most countries of the region mandated that the material remains of the later periods (with the exception of human remains and impressive standing architecture) were not protected and therefore considered to be removable debris, even by archaeologists undertaking the excavation of important sites.

As a result, a vast discrepancy arose between the scholarly knowledge of the material culture of those periods considered to be truly ancient (Stone, Bronze, and Iron Ages) and those considered to be fairly recent. That differential had a great impact on the nationalistic understanding of history. Because practically no archaeological evidence of material culture change and economic adaptation had been collected from the remains of the periods immediately preceding statehood, the reasons for that political change and resulting modern struggles had to be explained through traditional textual sources. In other instances, those modern developments could be romantically retrojected onto a distant past and be ascribed to inherited traditions or national "character." Whether the neglected archaeological remains came from the time of Ottoman domination (the *Turkokratia* in Greek-speaking countries), the time of Muslim domination in Israel, or the colonial domination of a given region by any and all outsiders, certain material remains were seen as being outside the purview of legitimate archaeology—and thus of little relevance for reconstructing the nation's "real" history.

In other parts of the world, however, such chronological and ideological barriers began to break down during the 1970s and 1980s with the spread of anthropologically oriented historical archaeology. This development would pose an eventual challenge to traditional archaeology in the Near East. Beginning with the theoretical work of James Deetz and Stanley South in the archaeology of colonial North America, it began to be clear that analysis of the material remains of recent or superficially familiar historical periods could provide some striking correctives to conventional understandings. Though the theoretical orientation of historical archaeologists varied from processualist, through structuralist, through neo-Marxist, implicit in the work of all of them was a desire to deepen accepted historical understandings. They wished also to discover some of the underlying causes and contexts for the European commercial and, ultimately, industrial expansion all over the world. In the recognition that material remains permitted analysis of the reality that underlay imperial expansion and the formation of modern nation-states, the historical archaeology of plantations, factories, ghettoes, and workers' housing proved congenial to the antiauthoritarian political reflections of feminism, labor history, social history, the antiapartheid movement in South Africa, and North American African-American history.

Thus, in the early 1980s, when the techniques and theoretical approaches of historical archaeology began to be applied—albeit on a tiny scale—in the Mediterranean basin and the Near East, archaeologists began to recover a material reality that had long been subsumed under the patronizing ethnological rubric of "traditional" everyday life (Ziadeh, 1987; Kardulias, 1994). In the excavations and material culture studies that began to be undertaken at Ottoman-period sites in Israel, Jordan, Syria, Cyprus, Greece, and Turkey, the very act of filling out the archaeological record and demonstrating that every part of the nation's history possessed dynamism, vitality, and complexity helped to undermine the basis of romantic, chronologically imbalanced, nationalistic archaeology.

In the closing decades of the twentieth century, the increasing internationalization of archaeological research in the prehistoric and early historic periods—both in field methodologies and theoretical interpretations—also served to counteract the classical nationalistic archaeology. The adoption of such scientific innovations as radiocarbon dating; chemical provenance studies; geological, botanical, and faunal analysis; and increasingly complex data processing had, by the 1960s, made the ongoing excavations in the Near East among the most technologically sophisticated in the world. The earlier tendency of Near Eastern archaeologists to identify migration and diffusion as the main mechanisms of culture change in the region gradually gave way to a variation of the American "New Archaeology," in which emphasis was placed on the larger systemic concepts of ecological adaptation, resource exploitation, and technological efficiency. [*See* New Archaeology.]

This intellectual development had an unmistakable political context in the post–World War II period, as the Near East underwent unprecedented economic development. In an era when transnational corporations and international development agencies began to devote substantial resources to the study of the environmental, geological, and demographic potential of the various nations of the region, the objectives of Near Eastern archaeology began to reflect a more instrumental, functionalist view of ancient cultures. Particularistic historical questions were being supplemented—and to a certain extent supplanted—by new research questions about agricultural efficiency, economic profits, specialized production, and regional population growth. It was no longer enough merely to describe archaeological remains and link them to historically attested peoples and events. Process and systemic interaction became central. This change in emphasis so neatly parallels the imperatives of modern economic development in the region that it is difficult to ascribe the correspondence to mere coincidence (Miller, 1980; Patterson, 1995). Far more persuasive in its explanatory power is the recognition that the universalist, processualist archaeology was, like the nationalist archaeology it often replaced, a style of historical investigation that had its own implicit ideological subtext: retrojecting into the distant past late-twentieth-century concepts of efficiency, resource extraction, environmental balance, and of the inevitability—or at least imperative—of economic development in all human societies.

In this light, it may be legitimately asked whether archaeological nationalism is a discrete and identifiable—yet ultimately curable—intellectual malady, or whether it is merely one of a limited number of general political assertions that archaeology, throughout its history, has routinely been used to express. The development of new pictures of the past and new technological means of obtaining them have always been tied to economic and cultural change and the emergence of new intellectual and political elites. In the Near East as elsewhere, the acceptance of archaeology has required the abandonment of traditional means of history making—be they legendary, scriptural, or ritual—with all the social and cultural consequences that such an intellectual transformation entails. Whatever the specific nation of the region or the specific subject of archaeological research, politically powerful narratives can make the present seem natural and inevitable. They can also be used to support the power and authority of organized religions, transnational corporations, national liberation movements, and international development agencies—as well as established nation-states.

However, any review of the long history of the interconnections of archaeology and nationalism will demonstrate the particular power and pervasiveness of the nation-state. Although the international legal and scholarly communities have in recent years cooperated to protect and preserve endangered archaeological resources, and to internationalize both the theory and practice of archaeology (Trigger, 1986), conflicts between rival nations in the Near East over control of archaeological remains in disputed territory are seemingly beyond the power of international agencies or individual scholars to discourage or control. As long as control over the practice of archaeology in the Near East remains within the legal purview of national governments, with national departments of antiquities empowered to permit or prevent excavation at certain sites and to provide or withhold funding for public presentation, there is little that international bodies can do to adjudicate conflicting historical claims.

Through the force of archaeological tradition and practice, and through the very structure of modern nation-states in the region, it has become each nation's accepted right to determine the pace and location of excavations within its borders. It has become their right, through national park systems and tourist facilities, to highlight their own chosen peoples and golden ages. Moreover, to interfere with the archaeological agenda of a modern nation—so long as it is conducted along internationally accepted academic standards—is to risk a bitter protest against a violation of sovereignty. Thus, no international scholarly organization has so far been able to formulate and gain acceptance for an enforceable statement of global archaeological rights and obligations that can, when necessary, contest or overrule the narrow pursuit of particularistic national interests. Such an ethical hope may appear quixotic in a world composed of, and ultimately controlled by, nation-states. However, the ethics of the preservation and study of the archaeological remains of the widest possible range of human communities is an essential political and intellectual challenge. It needs to be met if archaeology is ever to be precluded from use primarily as an instrument of nationalism, or ever to serve meaningfully in the resolution—rather than in the promulgation and perpetuation—of national conflicts.

[*See also* Biblical Archaeology; Ethics and Archaeology; Museums and Museology; *and* Tourism and Archaeology.]

BIBLIOGRAPHY

Anderson, Benedict. *Imagined Communities: Reflections on the Origin and Spread of Nationalism.* New York, 1983.

Baramki, Dimitri C. *The Art and Architecture of Ancient Palestine: A Survey of the Archaeology of Palestine from the Earliest Times to the Ottoman Conquest.* Beirut, 1969. Part of a series issued by the Palestine Liberation Organization Research Center; its underlying nationalist orientation is clear.

Broshi, Magen. "Religion, Ideology, and Politics in Palestinian Archaeology." *Israel Museum Journal* 6 (1987): 17–32.

Fagan, Brian M. *The Rape of the Nile: Tomb Robbers, Tourists, and Archaeologists in Egypt.* New York, 1975.

Fagan, Brian M. *Return to Babylon: Travelers, Archaeologists and Monuments in Mesopotamia.* Boston, 1979.

Fowler, Don D. "The Uses of the Past: Archaeology in the Service of the State." *American Antiquity* 52 (1987): 229–248.

Friedman, Jonathan. "The Past in the Future: History and the Politics of Identity." *American Anthropologist* 94 (1992): 837–859. Enlightening essay on the political context for changing national histories.

Gathercole, Peter, and David Lowenthal, eds. *The Politics of the Past.* London, 1990.

Geary, Patrick J. *Furta Sacra: Thefts of Relics in the Central Middle Ages.* Rev. ed. Princeton, 1990. Traces the early religious attachment of certain cities and nations to biblical relics.

Hobsbawm, Eric J. *Nations and Nationalism since 1780.* Cambridge, 1990.

Hunt, E. D. *Holy Land Pilgrimage in the Later Roman Empire, AD 312–460.* Oxford, 1982. Excellent account of the early political significance of relic hunting in the lands of the Bible.

Kardulias, P. Nick. "Towards an Anthropological Historical Archaeology in Greece." *Historical Archaeology* 28.3 (1994): 39–55. Survey of recent developments in constructing histories of neglected archaeological periods.

Kohl, Philip L., and Clare Fawcett, eds. *Nationalism, Politics, and the Practice of Archaeology.* Cambridge, 1995. Wide-ranging collection of essays on the subject from archaeologists working all over the world.

Larsen, Mogens T. "Orientalism and the Ancient Near East." *Culture and History* 2 (1987): 96–115.

Lewis, Bernard. *History Remembered, Recovered, Invented.* Princeton, 1975. Brief survey of manifestations of historical and archaeological nationalism in the Near East.

Lowenthal, David. *The Past Is a Foreign Country.* Cambridge, 1985. Eclectic survey of the modern uses of the past.

Miller, Daniel. "Archaeology and Development." *Current Anthropology* 21 (1980): 709–726.

Patterson, Thomas C. *Toward a Social History of Archaeology in the United States.* Fort Worth, Tex., 1995. Incisive analysis of political power and its effects on the conduct of archaeology.

Reid, Donald M. "Indigenous Egyptology: The Decolonization of a Profession?" *Journal of the American Oriental Society* 105 (1985): 233–246. Survey of the intellectual and political contexts of Egyptology.

Silberman, Neil Asher. *Digging for God and Country: Exploration, Archaeology, and the Secret Struggle for the Holy Land, 1799–1917.* New York, 1982. History of nineteenth-century national and religious conflict over the antiquities of Palestine.

Silberman, Neil Asher. *Between Past and Present: Archaeology, Ideology, and Nationalism in the Modern Middle East.* New York, 1990. Series of essays highlighting the modern social and political context of archaeology in the region.

Silberman, Neil Asher. "The Politics of the Past: Archaeology and Nationalism in the Eastern Mediterranean." *Mediterranean Quarterly* 1 (1990): 99–110.

Silberman, Neil Asher. "Desolation and Restoration: The Impact of a Biblical Concept on Near Eastern Archaeology." *Biblical Archaeologist* 54 (1991): 76–87.

Smith, Anthony D. *The Ethnic Origins of Nations.* Oxford, 1986.

Trigger, Bruce G. "Alternative Archaeologies: Nationalist, Colonialist, Imperialist." *Man* 19 (1984): 355–370.

Trigger, Bruce G. "Prospects for a World Archaeology." *World Archaeology* 18 (1986): 1–20.

Trigger, Bruce G. *A History of Archaeological Thought.* Cambridge, 1989.

Ziadeh, Ghada. "The Present Is Our Key to the Past." *Bir Zeit Research*

Review 4 (1987): 40–65. Theoretical and methodological essay on a new, critical archaeology of Palestine.

NEIL ASHER SILBERMAN

NAUKRATIS (modern Kom Ge'if), site located in the Behera province of the western Nile Delta, about 80 km (50 mi.) southeast of Alexandria, to the west of the Canopic branch of the Nile River. Although Herodotus claimed that it was Pharaoh Amasis (Ahmose, 570–526 BCE) who first allowed Greek merchants to settle and trade at the site, earlier Greek pottery indicates a Hellenic presence in the second half of the seventh century BCE, possibly during the reign of Psamtik (Psammetichus) I (664–610 BCE). Amasis may have simply codified a de facto situation when he made Naukratis the only legal outlet for Greek wares in Egypt. During his reign the city flourished, and nine eastern Greek cities combined their efforts to build the famous Hellenion, described by Herodotus as the "best known . . . most used . . . and . . . largest" of all of the temene, or "sacred precints" at Naukratis.

Naukratis continued to be the foremost commercial city in the Delta for the next few centuries, and when Nectanebo (Nekhtnebef) came to power in 380 BCE, one of his first official acts was to build a temple there. He decreed that 10 percent of the existing levies on "gold, silver, timber, worked wood, and everything coming from the Sea of the Greeks" would be used to provide for its upkeep.

Although the early period of commercial exclusivity ended when Alexander the Great conquered Egypt (332/31 BCE) and founded the Mediterranean port city of Alexandria, the town continued to function as an important transshipment point for goods coming from the Mediterranean to the capital at Memphis, or eastward to Pelusium and beyond. Under the Ptolemies, Naukratis continued (with Alexandria and Ptolemais) to be one of the three major Greek cities in Egypt. The situation becomes less clear during the later Ptolemaic period, as Egypt fell steadily under Roman control.

The events that surrounded the final incorporation of Egypt into the Roman Empire by Octavian (30 BCE) do not seem to have left their mark on Naukratis, but we do know that the old Greek trading center continued to govern itself through the elected members of its own council *(boulē)*. Subsequent documentation for Naukratis, however, is slight, and the date and cause of the city's final demise are unknown. Coptic records sporadically mention bishops from Naukratis through the fourteenth century CE, but by that time the name Naukratis may have been transferred to the neighboring village of Neqrash, where some late artifacts have been recovered.

In 1884, William Flinders Petrie identified the ancient city of Naukratis with the extensive mounds near the village of Qom Ge'if. His excavations (1884–1885) were continued by E. A. Gardner in 1886 and by D. G. Hogarth in 1899 and 1903. Their work uncovered the remains of four Greek sanctuaries (to Apollo, Aphrodite, Hera, and the Dioscuri) that had been founded during the seventh and sixth centuries BCE. In addition, Petrie identified the Hellenion with a large structure (about 260 × 300 m) that he called the Great Temenos, in the southern part of the town. Hogarth, however, found no trace of such a monumental building, he excavated a building in the northern part of the site that he claimed was the Hellenion.

Unfortunately, these early excavators paid little attention to the ancient city's domestic and mercantile character and almost totally ignored the later Ptolemaic and Roman periods. In an attempt to rectify this situation, renewed investigation was conducted from 1978 to 1983 by Albert Leonard, Jr., and W. D. E. Coulson that combined the vertical control of the excavation at Naukratis/Kom Ge'if with a program of regional survey and sounding in an area of 25 sq km around the ancient city. A small mound in the area of Petrie's Great Temenos still survived, and Leonard's excavation produced 6 m of vertical stratigraphy, indicating ten phases of (apparently domestic) occupation, all of which dated to the Ptolemaic period. This argues in favor of Hogarth's identification of the Hellenion. Excavation was also conducted at Qom Hadid, originally part of the Naukratis mounds, where Petrie had recorded Roman structures with painted frescoes. In the reexcavation, however, contiguous architecture was rare, and the artifactual material (almost all of it from secondary deposits) ranged from Ptolemaic times into the Roman period.

Coulson's survey of the area recorded an artifact scatter extending 2 km. to the north and south of the early excavations. The distribution of this material suggests that between the fourth and first centuries CE the city expanded to the north and east, whereas during the Roman period, expansion and growth were to the west. This, too, supports Hogarth's placement of the Hellenion in the northern part of the city.

At present, little survives of the ancient site of Naukratis, and the Delta's high water table persists as a severe obstacle to reaching the early strata of this unique Greco-Egyptian trading center.

[*See also* Delta; *and* Egypt, *article on* Postdynastic Egypt.]

BIBLIOGRAPHY

Coulson, William D. E., and Albert Leonard, Jr., eds. *Cities of the Delta*, vol. 1, *Naukratis*. Malibu, 1981. First volume of the renewed excavation, setting out the project's goals and methodology and providing a good historical summary (by Richard Sullivan).

Coulson, William D. E., and Albert Leonard, Jr. "Investigations at Naukratis and Environs." *American Journal of Archaeology* 86 (1982): 361–380. Good overview and bibliography of past scholarship concerning Naukratis, as well as an exposition of the types of problems and confusion that led to renewed study of the site.

Coulson, William D. E., Albert Leonard, Jr., and Nancy C. Wilkie.

"Three Seasons of Excavations and Survey at Naukratis and Environs." *Journal of the American Research Center in Egypt* 19 (1982): 73–109. Good synthesis of the excavations on the south mound at Naukratis and of soundings at contemporary sites in the survey area.
Venit, Marjorie S. *Greek Painted Pottery from Naukratis in Egyptian Museums*. American Research Center in Egypt Catalogs, vol. 7. Winona Lake, Ind., 1988. The only compilation of this important material in existence. Each sherd is restudied and, when necessary, redated.

ALBERT LEONARD, JR., and WILLIAM D. E. COULSON

NAUTICAL ARCHAEOLOGY. *See* Underwater Archaeology.

NAVILLE, ÉDOUARD (1844–1926), Swiss Egyptologist; specialist in archaeology and philology. Professor of Egyptology at the University of Geneva, his birthplace, Naville was first interested in philology and religious texts. His great four-volume edition of the *Book of the Dead* appeared in 1886, but by then he had begun a long career of excavating on behalf of London's Egypt Exploration Fund (now Society). Hoping to find evidence for the Exodus, Naville first worked in the eastern Delta site of Tell el-Maskhuta. His excavation resulted in *The Store-City of Pithom and the Route of the Exodus* (1885). Further exploration in the Wadi Tumilat, a region in the eastern Delta that includes Tell el-Maskhuta, appeared as *The Shrine of Saft el-Henneh and the Land of Goshen* (1887). Expeditions to Herakleopolis, Mendes, and Tell Muqdam followed, but then Naville turned south to finish the excavation (begun by Auguste Mariette) of Hatshepsut's mortuary temple of Deir el-Baḥari, on the west bank at Thebes. Clearance (1893–1896) was followed by careful epigraphic work, which was published in large folio volumes. In 1903 Naville attacked the mounds to the south of Hatshepsut's temple, discovering tombs and the temple of King Mentuhotep II of the eleventh dynasty.

Unlike Flinders Petrie, Naville found no interest in small antiquities and left this site after the 1907–1908 season, considering it completed, although it would yield still more to the later expedition of New York's Metropolitan Museum of Art in the 1920s. In 1909, Naville was at Abydos, where he cleared the Osireion (presumed to be a cenotaph of Seti I) discovered by Petrie and Murray in 1902. Although Naville had an impressive publication record, his archaeological methodology belongs to the "old school" of Heinrich Schliemann and Mariette, in contrast to Petrie's careful sifting and study of small finds. Undoubtedly much significant material was lost, and Naville's strongly held opinions also tended to color his conclusions.

[*See also* Abydos; Egypt Exploration Society; Maskhuta, Tell el-; *and the biographies of Mariette and Petrie.*]

BIBLIOGRAPHY

Dawson, Warren R., and Eric P. Uphill. *Who Was Who in Egyptology*. 2d rev. ed. London, 1972.
Hall, Henry R. "Édouard Naville." *Journal of Egyptian Archaeology* 13 (1927): 1–6.
Naville, Édouard. *The Temple of Deir el Bahari*. 7 vols. London, 1894–1908.
Naville, Édouard. *The Store-City of Pithom and the Route of the Exodus*. London, 1885.
Naville, Édouard. *The Shrine of Saft el-Henneh and the Land of Goshen*. London, 1887.
Naville, Édouard. *The XIth Dynasty Temple at Deir el-Bahari*. 3 vols. London, 1907–1913.

BARBARA SWITALSKI LESKO

NAZARETH, the town of Jesus' youth, located just west of Mt. Tabor, immediately north of the Jezreel Valley, and 25 km (15 mi.) west of the Sea of Galilee (32°42′ N, 35°18′ E). Nazareth exhibits archaeological remains from the Middle Bronze II, Iron II, and late Hellenistic periods, but its heyday was in the Early Roman period. Judging from the locations of its Early Roman (Herodian) tombs (which must have been located outside the village according to Jewish law), its size then must have been about 900 m from the southwest to the northeast and 200 m southeast–northwest. The total area comes to fewer than 24 ha (60 acres) and reflects a population of some five hundred. It stood in a natural bowl within what is today called the Nazareth Fault, which divides the Jezreel plain from Lower Galilee. Based on its size and locations, Nazareth was surely a dependency of ancient Sepphoris, the capital of Lower Galilee in the Roman period; in the Byzantine period it was the seat of a bishop and an independent city.

Benedict Vlaminck, under auspices of the Custodia Terra Sancta, excavated Nazareth from 1890 to 1910 within the grounds of the Latin churches of St. Joseph and of the Annunciation. In 1889 and then from 1907 to 1910, Prosper Viaud excavated within the same area and published a volume on the two churches. In 1955, Bellarmino Bagatti excavated beneath the Church of the Annunciation, which had been built in 1730, enlarged in 1877, and then demolished to make way for a new church.

Beneath the Church of the Annunciation Bagatti found extensive remains from the Roman–Byzantine village. Cisterns, rooms, chambers, work and storage spaces, tunnels, and other rock-cut areas and installations are evidence that the inhabitants of ancient Nazareth, as of many other Galilean localities, utilized the soft limestone bedrock to increase their living and work spaces.

In two caves beneath the church several layers of plaster were found. Beneath a coat of undecorated white plaster, painted plaster featured a cross in a wreath, some floral designs, and prayers to Jesus in Greek. The prayers are most conservatively dated to the early fourth century CE. These two small caves had been incorporated into the north end of a building whose facade evidently pointed south. The building had a mosaic floor with a large chi-rho cross that pointed north, into the two caves. The excavator interpreted this building as having originally been a Jewish-Christian synagogue because it was oriented south, toward Jerusalem, and because he recovered about seventy architectural fragments nearby that resemble elements of third- or fourth-century Galilean synagogues (e.g., two simple capitals, five column bases, voussoirs of arches). The fragments were found beneath the mosaic floor of a Byzantine (fifth century) monastery.

A Jewish ritual bath, or *miqveh,* from the Roman period was found beneath the mosaic floor with the chi-rho cross. Many plaster fragments had been dumped into the bath when it went out of use and the mosaic floor with its chi-rho cross was installed. Several of the fragments were scratched with graffiti in Greek and Syriac and are Christian in character. They may be remains of a church built over the caves that were seen by the Christian Pilgrim Egeria in the late fourth century CE.

The sequence of occupations at Nazareth follows: (1) Middle Bronze tombs; (2) scattered Iron II remains; (3) Late Hellenistic to Early Roman caves with domestic installations, some used as late as the Byzantine period; (4) a third-century CE, or later, ritual bath; (5) a large public structure, interpreted by the excavator as a Jewish-Christian synagogue; and (6) a fifth-century church with a monastery attached, perhaps the structures seen by the Piacenza Pilgrim in 570 CE.

Nazareth is mentioned in the poem *Mishmaroth* (l. 18; see Michael Avi-Yonah, "A List of Priestly Courses from Caesarea," *Israel Exploration Journal* 12 [1962]: 137–139, pl. 13) as the settlement place of the priestly course of Hapizez, following the destruction of Jerusalem and the Temple in 70 CE. This is repeated in a Byzantine inscription found at Caesarea that contains the priestly courses.

BIBLIOGRAPHY

Bagatti, Bellarmino. *Excavations in Nazareth,* vol. 1, *From the Beginning till the XII Century.* Jerusalem, 1969. Report on the 1955 excavations.

Viaud, Prosper. *Nazareth et ses deux églises de l'Annonciation et de Saint-Joseph.* Paris, 1910. Complete report on the two churches, as of 1910.

JAMES F. STRANGE

NEBI MEND, TELL, site located on the Orontes River in Syria, about 25 km (16 mi.) southwest of the city of Homs (34°33′ N, 36°32′ E). Its identification with Qadesh, the location of the battle between Egyptians and Hittites (early thirteenth century BCE) depicted by Rameses II on the walls of his temples at Karnak and Luxor, was first suggested in 1848 and is universally accepted. The Hittites knew the town as Kinza, and this name appears on an inscribed tablet found in recent excavations at the site. In the late fourth or early third century BCE, the town was refounded, under the Seleucid rulers of Syria, are called Laodiceia-ad-Libanum.

Qadesh is mentioned initially in the textual sources on the occasion of Thutmosis III's battle at Megiddo, when its ruler led the coalition of Canaanite princes attempting to block the Egyptian advance into Syria. It figures in other Egyptian and Hittite texts, including the Amarna letters and the campaign reliefs of Seti I, who captured the city in about 1300 BCE. Its location in the fertile Orontes valley, on one of the few major routes which cross the Levantine coastal mountains to link inland Syria with the Mediterranean, explains its strategic importance. Its siting on the fork of the Orontes and one of its tributaries provides it with natural defensive strength on three sides. Although at about 10 hectares (25 acres) it is not one of the largest of Syria's ancient mounds, it is one of the highest, its summit being 30 m above the surrounding plain. To the south of this mound is an area of comparable extent—with fragmentary remains of walls and column drums—the site of Greco-Roman Laodiceia.

The mound was excavated in 1921–1922 by a French Mandatory government expedition under Maurice Pézard. Large areas on the northeast summit and flanks were investigated and monumental remains uncovered, but the work was entirely devoid of stratigraphic control and was published only in a preliminary manner. Enough was recovered, however, to show that important levels from the Middle and Late Bronze Ages, the Iron Age, and the Greco-Roman period existed. Perhaps the most striking find was part of an Egyptian stela recording Seti I's seizure of the town.

Renewed excavations by an expedition from the University of London, under the direction of Peter J. Parr, commenced in 1975 and is still underway. As a result of the work completed so far, the site's occupational history is postulated as follows.

The earliest settlement took place in the sixth millennium, in the Pottery Neolithic period. The settlers were farmers and lived in houses built of poor mudbrick or *terre pisée,* but with good white plaster floors. After an unknown period of time, and for unknown reasons, this settlement was abandoned (there is no evidence of occupation in the fifth and fourth millennia).

The site was reoccupied in the third millennium, the Early Bronze Age. The substantial and spacious houses uncovered suggest that this settlement was something more than a village, although there is no evidence for urban fortifications. A decline in architectural standards is apparent toward the end of the millennium, however, and the site may have been abandoned again, apart from squatters. A period of vigorous urban growth began in about 2000 BCE, with a new style of architecture and, soon after, massive casemate defensive walls with, in one place at least, a massive, artificial sloping rampart. The site seems to have flourished during this, the

Middle Bronze Age. The settlement came to an end in about 1600 BCE, with the destruction of the fortifications and associated buildings, and there may have been another short period of desertion. The Late Bronze Age (the period of Qadesh's recorded history) is represented archaeologically by remains of large public buildings, none yet sufficiently exposed to provide evidence of their function. Sherds of Cypriot, Mycenaean, and Egyptian pottery show the extent of the city's contacts, as do the few tablets found (letters addressed to its ruler by the prince of Ḫalab [Aleppo]). There is no archaeological record in the areas excavated either of Seti's capture of the city or the battle waged by Rameses II.

Whether, and how, Qadesh was affected by the disturbances which brought the Bronze Age to a close in the Levant is not yet determined. There is significant occupation in the Late Iron Age (eighth–seventh centuries BCE), when an Assyrian garrison was probably stationed at the site. There is nothing to indicate settlement during the Persian period, and the mound may well have been deserted when Laodiceia was founded there. This seems to have been a town of middling importance, judging from surface indications and its virtual absence from the written sources. During the Byzantine period it was the seat of a suffragan bishop, however. The few archaeological finds indicate that the site did not survive beyond the fifth century CE, and that it remained abandoned until the modern village was founded in the early nineteenth century.

BIBLIOGRAPHY

Breasted, James H. *The Battle of Kadesh: A Study in the Earliest Known Military Strategy*. Chicago, 1903. The most thorough English-language account of the battle, with sketches of maps, reproductions of the Egyptian reliefs, and lengthy extracts from texts.

Gardiner, Alan H. *The Kadesh Inscriptions of Ramesses II*. Oxford, 1960. The most scholarly publication of the battle texts in English, correcting some of Breasted's readings.

Parr, Peter J. "The Tell Nebi Mend Project." *Annales Archéologiques Arabes Syriennes* 31 (1983): 99–117. Brief summary of the aims and methods of the current excavations, though now somewhat out of date regarding results. Contains the only accurate published plan of the site.

Parr, Peter J. "The Tell Nebi Mend Project: A Progress Report." *Journal of the Ancient Chronology Forum* 4 (1990–1991): 28–85. Popular account of the most recent excavations.

Pézard, Maurice. *Qadesh: Mission archéologique à Tell Nebi Mend, 1921–1922*. Paris, 1931. Account of the French excavations, useful mainly for the illustrations of the many objects recovered.

PETER J. PARR

NEBO, MOUNT, site rising from the Transjordanian plateau 7 km (4 mi.) west of Madaba, bounded on the east by Wadi ʿAfrit (which extends into Wadi al-Jadidah, Wadi al-Kanisah, and Wadi al-Hary farther south) and on the north by Wadi Abu al-Naml, which extends into Wadi ʿAin Musa. Mt. Nebo's highest crest reaches an altitude of 800 m above sea level. Its other peaks are only slightly lower; of them, the two most important historically are the western peak of Siyagha and the southeastern peak of al-Mukhayyat (map reference 2218 × 1315).

In the Hebrew Bible Mt. Nebo, part of the Abarim Mountain, was located east of the Jordan River, opposite Jericho. It was also known as Pisgah (*Dt.* 34:1; *Nm.* 21:20, 33, 47). As a Christian sanctuary dedicated to Moses, Mt. Nebo was known by scholars and visited by Byzantine pilgrims. Eusebius (*Onomasticon* 136.6) wrote: "Nabau, which in Hebrew is called Nebo, is a mountain beyond the Jordan, in front of Jericho in the land of Moab, where Moses died. Until this day it is indicated at the sixth milestone of the city of Esbus [which lies] to the east." The Roman pilgrim Egeria (381–384) and the bishop of Maiumas of Gaza, Peter the Iberian (fifth century), relate in great detail their visits to the Memorial Church of Moses on Mt. Nebo in Arabia. Egeria, after having crossed the Jordan on her way from Jerusalem, stayed at Livias and then took the road to Esbus. At the sixth Roman mile she took a detour to the Springs of Moses and from there climbed to the summit of Mt. Nebo (*Itinerarium* 10–12). The pilgrim Theodosius (first half of the sixth century) relates that not far from the city of Livias, east of the Jordan River, pilgrims could visit "the water made to flow from the rock, the place of Moses' death and the hot springs of Moses where lepers come to be cured" (Theodosius 19). The pilgrim from Piacenza (second half of the sixth century), adds: "From the Jordan to the place where Moses died, it is eight miles" (*Itinerarium* 10.5).

Moreover, in the Bible, as on the inscription of Mesha, king of Moab, Nebo is a city listed among the Cities of the high plateau of Moab, in the territory of Madaba (*Nm.* 32:3, 38, 33:47; *1 Chr.* 5:8; *Is.* 15:2; *Jer.* 48:1, 22; *1 Mc.* 9:37). The Mesha inscription records that King Mesha conquered the town, killed the inhabitants, and "took from thence the vessels of Yahweh and dragged them before Chemosh" (1. 14–18). [*See* Moabite Stone.] Eusebius (*Onomasticon* 136.9ff.) knew the locality of Nebo as a desert 13 km (8 mi.) from Esbus. The biographer of Peter the Iberian, in the second half of the fifth century, knew Nebo as a village on the mountain inhabited by Christians (*Life* 85). The survival of the name *Nebo* in the region was discovered in 1838 by Edward Robinson and Eli Smith (Robinson and Smith, 1941, vol. 2, p. 307). The local bedouin also know the mountain as Jabal Nabo or Jabal Musa in homonymy to Wadi ʿAin Musa located on the northern slope of the mountain (Saller, 1941, vol. 1, p. 72).

The discovery in Arezzo, Italy, of Egeria's memoirs (edited by Francesco Gamurrini in 1886), and the subsequent discovery of the biography, in Syriac, of Peter the Iberian in 1895 (see above), were decisive in identifying the Memorial of Moses with the ruins at Siyagha on the northwest spur of Mt. Nebo. The ruins were first visited and described in 1864 by the French explorer the Duke de Luynes (1874, vol. 1, pp. 148ff.). In 1933, archaeologists from the Studium Biblicum Franciscanum (SBF) in Jerusalem began exploring Siyagha. Sylvester Saller directed three lengthy excavations, in 1933, 1935, and 1937 that resulted in the discovery of the basilica and of a large monastery that, in the Byzantine period, had grown up around the sanctuary. In 1963, Virgilio Corbo began the restoration of the basilica. Michele Piccirillo has directed the project since 1976. [*See the biographies of Saller and Corbo.*]

The ridge of Mt. Nebo has been inhabited since remote antiquity, as the dolmens, menhirs, flints, tombs, and fortresses from different epochs testify. However, its real fame is derived from the death of Moses described in *Deuteronomy* 34. In the fourth century, the Christians in the region constructed a memorial church in honor of Moses on the Siyagha peak, an obvious effort to perpetuate the memory of the biblical episode. It was a triapsidal church (a *cella trichora*) with a vestibule in front of it, tombs covered by its mosaic floor, and two funeral chapels on each side. An open court in front of the sanctuary's facade was bordered on the north by a covered passageway leading to the diaconicon chapel, including a cruciform baptistery basin (see figure 1). The chapel was lavishly decorated with offerings from the officials of the Byzantine government by a team of three mosaicists: Soelos, Kaiomos, and Elias. The work was completed in August 531, in the time of Bishop Elias of Madaba and of the Roman consuls Lampadius and Orestes.

In the second half of the sixth century the three-nave basilica was built, in the time of Bishop Sergius of Madaba and of Abbott Martyrius. The primitive church Egeria and Peter the Iberian visited became the presbytery of the new sanctuary. The basilica had a long diaconicon on its north side, on a higher level, and a new baptistery chapel (a *fotisterion*) on the south side, with a narthex at the facade. The first stage of the work was completed in 597, as stated in the mosaic inscriptions in the baptistery chapel. The sanctuary was decorated with wall and floor mosaics. At the beginning of the seventh century, in the time of Bishop Leontios and Abbott Theodore, the Chapel of the Theotokos (of the Mother of God) was added on the southern wall, covering two rooms of the monastery. In front of the altar, in the area of the presbytery, a rectangular panel can still be seen of mosaic flowers, gazelles, and two bulls standing before an alter with a ciborium on it. The mosaicist intended to depict the altar in the Temple in Jerusalem.

While the sanctuary was undergoing its various stages of architectural development, the adjacent monastery gradually expanded. Dayr Siyagha reached its maximum size during the sixth century. The monastery, dominated by the Memorial Church of Moses, presents itself as a complex of different, yet interrelated, sectors, composed of several rooms that open into a central courtyard. The sectors seem functionally specialized: community rooms in the atrium of the basilica and living quarters or cells in the southern sector.

NEBO, MOUNT. Figure 1. *The old Diakonikon-Baptistery at Siyagha with mosaic floor.* Dated to 530 CE. (Archive Studium Biblicum Franciscanum; photograph by Michele Piccirillo)

From the archaeological research underway, it appears that the monastery developed from monastic units more or less isolated and situated on the top of or on the slopes of the mountain as the so-called hermitage of Procopius on the west slope (Piccirillo and Alliata, 1990). When the three-naved basilica was completed in 597, the size of the monastery was probably reduced, for unknown reasons, to the area of the atrium in front of the church facade and to the southern sector; the other sectors were abandoned. Archaeological research into the ecclesiastical edifices in the valleys around Mt. Nebo support Saller's conclusion that the superior of the main monastery also had jurisdiction over the monks living in the valleys near the water supply, where the monastery may have had its orchards and vegetable gardens (Saller, 1941). The monastery was completely abandoned in the ninth century.

Khirbet el-Mukhayyat. The fortified place of Khirbet el-Mukhayyat, on the southeast spur of the mountain, with an attested continuity of settlement from the Early Bronze Age to the Roman-Byzantine period, according to its Franciscan excavators, fits well with the locality of Nebo mentioned by ancient sources (Saller and Bagatti, 1949, pp. 207–217). In 1863 the French explorer Félicien de Saulcy listed the name of the tell, but the ruins were not visited until 1881, by Claude R. Conder of the Survey of Eastern Palestine. [*See the biographies of Saulcy and Conder.*] In 1901 Alois Musil visited the site, described it, and was the first to propose its identity. In 1935, the Franciscan Custody of the Holy Land acquired the acropolis. The following year Jerome Mihaic improved the road leading to the ruins and began a program of archaeological research. Saller and Bellarmino Bagatti (1949) published the results. In 1962 Julius Ripamonti of the University of Caracas, Venezuela, undertook a systematic study of the necropolis and at the same time excavated a small monastery and an Iron Age tower (see below). Saller subsequently studied the pottery found in the tombs, which furnished excellent points of reference for establishing a chronological sequence of human habitation at el-Mukhayyat. Bedouin excavated an Early Bronze III tomb on the southwestern slope of the acropolis; Ripamonti excavated several Iron II tombs (Saller, 1966) on the north side of the tell; and Saller (1967) published the tombs of the Hellenistic–Roman period. The Iron Age tower Ripamonti excavated is unpublished.

Three churches and a monastery have been excavated at Khirbet el-Mukhayyat: the Church of Saint George built on top of the acropolis in 536, in the time of Bishop Elias of Madaba and decorated with mosaics by a team of three mosaicists—Nahum, Kiriakos, and Thomas; the Church of Sts. Lot and Procopius built in the time of Bishop John of Madaba (sixth century) on the lower terrace of the acropolis; the Church of Amos and Casiseos on the west slope of Wadi ʿAfrit; and the small monastery on the opposite side of the same valley. [*See* Madaba.]

Recent excavations have proven that the Church of Amos and Casiseos is the oldest in the village (Piccirillo, 1984). It takes its present name from its benefactors, whose names were carved on the chancel posts. The church, poorly paved with stone blocks, may have been built in the second half of the fifth century; it was flanked on the north by a room near a water cistern hewn in the rock of the mountain. In the time of Bishop Phidus of Madaba, under the direction of the priest John and the deacon Silvanus, the area was transformed into a chapel with a mosaic pavement and a square presbytery, preceded by a vestibule also decorated with a mosaic under the deacon Kaiomos. In the time of Bishop John, the chapel was enlarged and rebuilt on higher ground. Based on the style the same team of mosaicists responsible for the mosaic floor in the Church of the Sts. Lot and Procopius executed the mosaic in the new apsed chapel.

The small monastery of al-Kanisah, built following the contours of the terraces of the mountain on the eastern slopes of Wadi ʿAfrit, is composed of a chapel, with a mosaic, on the highest point with respect to the rooms to the south; several rooms are constructed along the slope of the mountain going north. A cave runs underneath the monastery that was used for storage. To the south of the chapel, at a higher point, a wine press was found hewn in the rock, which is typical of agricultural monasteries.

ʿAin Musa Valley. Archaeological exploration of the valley of ʿAin Musa, the toponomic point of reference for the identification of the nearby ruins of Siyagha with the Memorial of Moses, following Egeria's journey, began in 1984. During her visit to Mt. Nebo, the pilgrim Egeria met many monks in the valley near the "springs of Moses" and saw their cells and a tiny church. "Between the church and the cells was a plentiful spring which flowed from the rock, beautifully clear and with an excellent taste," she wrote (*Itinerarium* 11.2).

Before the discovery of Egeria's manuscript, the first account by a modern visitor to the ʿAin Musa was written in 1864 by the Duke de Luynes, who noted the nearby Christian hermitage hewn in the rock (see above). In 1934, Nelson Glueck surveyed the fortress of al-Mashhad near the spring, collecting Iron Age and Nabatean sherds and a number of contemporary clay figurines (see *Annual of the American Schools of Oriental Research* 14 [1933–1934]: 24–27, 15 [1935]: 110). Saller and Bagatti (1949) identified several Byzantine ruins along the path leading to the Roman road on the Mushaqqar ridge, a road with its milestones already known from the survey carried out by J. Jermer-Durand in 1884 ("Voie de Hesban au Jourdain," *Revue Biblique* [1895]: 398–400, [1896]: 613–615). Saller and Bagatti (1949) provided a general sketch of the region with its dolmens, circles, tombs, fortresses, and Byzantine buildings. A more detailed map of the Roman road from Esbus to Livias taken by pilgrims to reach the Memorial of Moses was drawn in 1973 by the members of the Ḥesban (Esbus) expedition, who surveyed and mapped the Roman-Byzantine fortress of al-Mahatta near the sixth Roman milestone.

A rescue excavation by the Studium Biblicum Franciscanum (SBF) under Michele Piccirillo in 1984–1985 in a farmhouse among the vineyards revealed the church of a small monastery, named the Church of Kaianos, with two superimposed mosaic floors: the "upper church," like the "lower" one, had a slightly raised, square presbytery. Iconographically, a unique motif in the mosaic of the upper church is an anonymous Arab camel driver depicted with a loincloth and a mantle over his shoulders. The lower church was built in the time of Bishop Cyrus of Madaba, at the beginning of the sixth century, on top of two tombs. In the area of the presbytery, a bilingual inscription, funerary in character, in Greek and in Christo-Palestinian Aramaic, the language spoken by ordinary people in the region, was recovered (Puech, 1984).

A second church is located along the path connecting the spring with the Roman road. It was part of a small monastery built on the slope of the mountain. It was excavated by the SBF in 1986–1987. It is square and includes a room on the south with a mosaic and a paved courtyard. The church's mosaic floor is nearly intact and is one of the best-preserved works of the local workshops of mosaicists.

In 1994 the SBF excavated a small monastery east of the spring in the Wadi ʿAin al-Kanisah south of the mountain. The chapel was dedicated to the Theotokos as stated in the mosaic inscriptions. It was repaired in 762 at the time of Bishop Job of Madaba (Piccirillo, 1994).

[*See also* Churches; *and* Mosaics.]

BIBLIOGRAPHY

Alliata, Eugenio. "La ceramica dello scavo." *Studium Biblicum Franciscanum (SBF)/Liber Annuus* 34 (1984): 316–317.

Alliata, Eugenio. "La ceramica dello scavo della cappella del Prete Giovanni a Khirbet el-Mukhayyat." *SBF/Liber Annuus* 38 (1988): 317–360.

Alliata, Eugenio. "Nuovo settore del monastero al Monte Nebo–Siyagha." In *Christian Archaeology in the Holy Land, New Discoveries: Essays in Honour of Virgilio C. Corbo,* edited by Giovanni Claudio Bottini et al., pp. 427–466. Studium Biblicum Franciscanum (SBF), Collectio Maior, 36. Jerusalem, 1990.

Bagatti, Bellarmino. "Nuova ceramica del Monte Nebo (Siyagha)." *SBF/Liber Annuus* 35 (1985): 249–278.

Corbo, Virgilio. "Nuovi scavi archeologici nella cappella del battistero della basilica del Nebo (Siyagha)." *SBF/Liber Annuus* 17 (1967): 241–258.

Corbo, Virgilio. "Scavi archeologici sotto i mosaici della basilica del Monte Nebo (Siyagha)." *SBF/Liber Annuus* 20 (1970): 273–298.

Knauf, E. Axel. "Bemerkungen zur frühen Geschichte der arabischen Ortographie." *Orientalia* 53 (1984): 456–458.

Luynes, Duc de. *Voyage d'exploration à la Mer Morte, à Pétra et sur la rive gauche du Jourdain,* vol. 1. Paris, 1874, p. 148ff.

Milani, C. *Itinerarium Antonini Placentini.* Milan, 1977.

Milik, J. T. "Nouvelles inscriptions sémitiques et grecques du pays de Moab." *SBF/Liber Annuus* 9 (1959): 330–358.

Piccirillo, Michele. "Campagna archeologica a Khirbet el Mukhayyet (Città dei Nebo), agosto–settembre 1973." *SBF/Liber Annuus* 23 (1973): 322–358.

Piccirillo, Michele. "Campagna archeologica nella basilica di Mosè Profeta sul Monte Nebo–Siyagha." *SBF/Liber Annuus* 26 (1976): 281–318.

Piccirillo, Michele. "Forty Years of Archaeological Work at Mount Nebo–Siyagha in Late Roman–Byzantine Jordan." In *Studies in the History and Archaeology of Jordan,* vol. 1, edited by Adnan Hadidi, pp. 291–300. Amman, 1982.

Piccirillo, Michele. "Una chiesa nell'wadi ʿAyoun Mousa ai piedi del Monte Nebo." *SBF/Liber Annuus* 34 (1984): 307–318.

Piccirillo, Michele. "The Jerusalem-Esbus Road and Its Sanctuaries in Transjordan." In *Studies in the History and Archaeology of Jordan,* vol. 3, edited by Adnan Hadidi, pp. 165–172. Amman, 1987.

Piccirillo, Michele. "La cappella del Prete Giovanni di Khirbet el-Mukhayyat (Villaggio di Nebo)." *SBF/Liber Annuus* 38 (1988): 297–315.

Piccirillo, Michele, and Eugenio Alliata. "La chiesa del monastero di Kaianos alle ʿAyoun Mousa sul Monte Nebo." In *Quaeritur inventus colitur: Miscellanea in onore di padre Umberto Maria Fasola,* vol. 40, pp. 561–586. Studi di Antichità Cristiana, 40. The Vatican, 1989.

Piccirillo, Michele. *Chiese e mosaici di Madaba.* SBF, Collectio Maior, 34. Jerusalem, 1989. See pages 147–225.

Piccirillo, Michele, and Eugenio Alliata. "L'eremitaggio di Procapis e l'ambiente funerario di Robebos al Monte Nebo–Siyagha." In *Christian Archaeology in the Holy Land, New Discoveries: Essays in Honour of Virgilio C. Corbo,* edited by Giovanni Claudio Bottini et al., pp. 391–426. SBF, Collectio Maior, 36. Jerusalem, 1990.

Piccirillo, Michele. *Mount Nebo.* SBF Guides, 2. 2d ed. Jerusalem, 1990.

Piccirillo, Michele. "Le due inscrizioni della cappella della Theotokos nel Wadi ʿAyn al-Kanisah–Monte Nebo." *Studium Biblicum Franciscanum/Liber Annuus* 44 (1994): 521–538.

Puech, Émile. "L'inscription christo-palestinienne d'ʿAyoun Mousa (Mount Nebo)." *SBF/Liber Annuus* 34 (1984): 319–328.

Robinson, Edward, and Eli Smith. *Biblical Researches in Palestine, Mount Sinai, and Arabia Petraea.* Boston, 1941, vol. 2, p. 307.

Saller, Sylvester J. *The Memorial of Moses on Mount Nebo.* 2 vols. SBF, Collectio Maior, 1. Jerusalem, 1941.

Saller, Sylvester J., and Bellarmino Bagatti. *The Town of Nebo (Khirbet el-Mekhayyat) with a Brief Survey of Other Ancient Christian Monuments in Transjordan.* SBF, Collectio Maior, 7. Jerusalem, 1949.

Saller, Sylvester J. "Iron Age Tombs at Nebo, Jordan." *SBF/Liber Annuus* 16 (1966): 165–298.

Saller, Sylvester J. "Hellenistic to Arabic Remains at Nebo, Jordan." *SBF/Liber Annuus* 17 (1967): 5–64.

Schneider, Hilary. *The Memorial of Moses on Mount Nebo,* vol. 3, *The Pottery.* SBF, Collectio Maior, 1. Jerusalem, 1950.

Stockman, Eugene. "Stone Age Culture in the Nebo Region, Jordan." *SBF/Liber Annuus* 17 (1967): 122–128.

Yonick, Stephen. "The Samaritan Inscription from Siyagha: A Reconstruction and Restudy." *SBF/Liber Annuus* 17 (1967): 162–221.

MICHELE PICCIRILLO

NECROPOLIS. Literally meaning "city of the dead" in Greek, a necropolis is a cemetery of some size exhibiting uniform modes of interment, and usually, though not always, associated with a contemporary settlement. Necropoleis were also used by nonsedentary peoples to bury their dead, as attested, for example, by the Early Bronze Age (EB) IV subterranean charnel houses at Bab edh-Dhraʿ in Jordan. In necropoleis interments took various forms: simple cist graves dug into earth, natural caves or rock-cut chambers, decorative facades hewn into cliff faces, and structures (ranging from simple to grandiose) above or below ground. Necropoleis were normally separated from settlements in order to maintain an acceptable degree of physical and psychical distance between the living and the dead. Intramural interments, as practiced in the Neolithic period, were not, strictly speaking, necropoleis.

Necropoleis first appear in fourth-millennium BCE Egypt (Predynastic Naqada) and Mesopotamia (Ubaid Eridu) during the earliest period of urbanization and state formation. Dolmen fields around the northern Jordan Valley, possibly funerary in character and Chalcolithic in date, may likewise constitute early necropoleis. By the third millennium, the practice of burial in necropoleis was well established, with royal tombs at Ur in Iraq, pyramids and associated elite cemeteries at Giza in Egypt, and typical urban necropoleis as at EB Bab edh-Dhraʿ. With few exceptions (e.g., MB Ebla, LB Ugarit) extramural interment continued throughout the Bronze Age (e.g., MB Jericho, MB/LB Megiddo, LB/Iron Tell es-Saʿidiyeh) and into Iron Age (Tell el-Farʿah [South], Megiddo, Beth-Shean [northern cemetery]).

Necropoleis yield various archaeological data. Undisturbed, they contain quantities of intact objects, mostly pottery vessels, which can be dated using other artifacts such as scarabs found with them or by statistical techniques like seriation, which W. M. F. Petrie applied to Predynastic Egyptian necropoleis. Even necropoleis with no contents, as in Nabatean Petra, can be dated by the styles of decoration on elaborately built or carved burial monuments whose forms offer clues to chronology and cultural associations (McKenzie, 1990). So-called burial customs, the distinctive character of interments within necropoleis, have long been regarded as ethnic indicators. Differences in factors such as tomb size and shape, variety and quality of contents, and disposition of human remains were thought to betoken ethnically distinct peoples, as Kathleen Kenyon assumed for Middle Bronze Jericho (Kenyon, 1979). Alternatively, differences in tomb size, shape, location, and in quantity and quality of contents may reflect the stratification in the society of the living. Old Kingdom Egyptian necropoleis are blatantly stratified: pyramids were the prerogative of pharaohs, nonroyal elites built mastabas, and commoners dug cist graves (Lehner, forthcoming). Burial customs may also reflect kinship structures. Multiple interments accumulated in a single large chamber over a long time span may indicate an extended family resorting generation after generation to an ancestral tomb (Bentley, 1991; Bloch-Smith, 1992). Necropoleis also often contain large numbers of human skeletons that can be analyzed forensically, yielding information about ancient diet, diseases, causes of death, and overall demographic trends.

[*See also* Burial Sites; Catacombs; Pyramids; Skeletal Analysis; *and* Tombs. *In addition, most of the sites mentioned are the subject of independent entries.*]

BIBLIOGRAPHY

There is no general survey of necropoleis for the entire Near East. Published reports on specific necropoleis can be found under entries for the sites of which they are part. The brief list below concerns syntheses of archaeological materials from necropoleis.

Bentley, G. "A Bioarchaeological Reconstruction of the Social and Kinship Systems at Early Bronze Age Bab edh-Dhra', Jordan." In *Between Bands and States,* edited by Susan A. Gregg, pp. 5–34. Southern Illinois University, Center for Archaeological Investigations, Occasional Paper, no. 9. Carbondale, 1991. Reconstruction of Early Bronze society based on results of forensic analyses of human skeletons from a large necropolis in the Jordan valley.

Bloch-Smith, Elizabeth. *Judahite Burial Practices and Beliefs about the Dead.* Journal for the Study of the Old Testament, Supplement 123. Sheffield, 1992. Anthropologically informed investigation of mortuary practice that integrates archaeological data and biblical sources. Includes an annotated catalog of more than 850 Iron Age burials (c. 1200–600 BCE) discovered in modern Israel and Jordan.

Kenyon, Kathleen M. *Archaeology in the Holy Land.* 4th ed. London, 1979.

Lehner, Mark. *The Complete Pyramids.* London, forthcoming. Archaeological and historical survey of the best-known mortuary complex in the Near East, based on recent excavations and surveys of Lehner's Giza Plateau Mapping Project.

McKenzie, Judith. *The Architecture of Petra.* British Academy Monographs in Archaeology, 1. London, 1990. Richly detailed architectural and historical analysis of the funerary facades of Petra, proving that even empty tombs still hold meaning.

Morris, Ian. *Death Ritual and Social Structure in Classical Antiquity.* Cambridge, 1992. Model treatment of the relationship between the living and the dead in classical society, with broad methodological applicability.

JOSEPH A. GREENE

NEDERLANDS HISTORISCH-ARCHEOLOGISCH INSTITUUT TE ISTANBUL.

The Netherlands Historical-Archaeological Institute in Istanbul, Turkey, is an affiliate of the Netherlands Institute for the Near East in Leiden, the Netherlands. Founded in 1953, the Istanbul branch became more fully operational with the opening, in 1958, of an actual institute in the building that had formerly been occupied by the Dutch embassy (Palais de Hollande). While the institutes' financial resources are provided by the Dutch government through Leiden University, individual researchers are often funded independently by the Netherlands Organization for Scientific Research.

The purpose of the institute is to promote research on the archaeology, history, and languages of the countries and cultures of the Near East and to provide logistical support for scholars specializing in Near Eastern studies. In addition, it seeks to foster cultural relations between the Netherlands and various countries in the Near East. The Institute sponsors the publication of the annual *Anatolica* (since 1967), which serves as an international forum for examining the history and archaeology of the Near East in general and of Turkey in particular. Since 1956, the institute has also published a series of monographs in English, German, and French, *Publications de l'Institut Historique-Archéologique Néerlandais de Stamboul.* By 1992, sixty-nine volumes had appeared. In them, individual scholars present the results of their research on various aspects of Near Eastern history and archaeology, from prehistoric to modern times. Since 1979, the institute has participated in the archaeological rescue excavations at Hayaz Höyük and at Kumartepe, both in southern Turkey. In 1985, the institute initiated a major, long-term archaeological project at Ilipinar, in northwestern Anatolia, south of Istanbul.

BIBLIOGRAPHY

Nijland, C. "In Memoriam Arie Abraham Kampman." *Anatolica* 5 (1973–1976): 1–6. Brief account of factors leading to the founding of the institute in Istanbul.

Roodenberg, J., L. Thissen, and H. Buitenhuis. "Preliminary Report on the Archaeological Investigations at Ilipinar in NW Anatolia." *Anatolica* 16 (1989–1990): 61–144. Preliminary but detailed report of the results of the Dutch excavations at Ilipinar, with special emphasis on the prehistoric period.

LEONARD VICTOR RUTGERS

NEGEV. The Negev comprises several different geographic regions, each with climatic, geologic, and topographic peculiarities that influenced the type of settlement it attracted and the course of its history. The regions are the northern Negev, whose most prominent area is the Beersheba basin, which prospered in the Chalcolithic period; the Negev highlands, an area in which settlement flourished in the Early Bronze Age, the Iron Age, and the Nabatean, Roman, and Byzantine periods; and the ʿArabah, the eastern Negev, which flourished principally in the Iron Age and the Nabatean, Roman, and Early Arab periods.

The first periods in the history of the Negev can be characterized as alternating between prosperity and scarcity and abandonment. The region's varied topography, semiarid climate, proximity to Egypt and Sinai as well as the Levant, and its geographic placement at the crossroads between East and West all contributed to the movement of people in and out of the area. It is only since the mid-twentieth century, as a result of numerous archaeological surveys and excavations of the region's major sites—conducted by Nelson Glueck, Yohanan Aharoni, Beno Rothenberg, and Rudolph Cohen—that some of the Negev's ancient history has been recovered. The broadest of the surveys, the Negev Emergency Survey, was carried out by the Israel Department of Antiquities and Museums between 1978 and 1988. [*See the biographies of Glueck and Aharoni.*]

Prehistoric Periods. Surveys in the western Negev sand dunes, the Negev highlands, and the southern Negev have mapped 320 sites, with remains representing all of the prehistoric periods. A connection can be drawn between environmental changes and ongoing geomorphological processes, population growth, and settlement patterns in these periods. The region was extensively populated during the Epipaleolithic (18000–8000 BCE) and, to a certain degree, in the Pre-pottery Neolithic B (Neolithic 2). Avdat, Naḥal Ḥemar, Har-Ḥarif, Naḥal Neṣṣana, Naḥal Issaron, and the ʿUvda Valley are among the important prehistoric sites.

In the Chalcolithic period, a continuous chain of settlement existed from the Beersheba and Arad basins and Naḥal Besor to the interior of the Negev highlands. In the east, sedentarization reached the fringes of the ʿArabah and, in the south, the Timnaʿ region. The focus of settlement, however, was the Beersheba basin. [*See* Timnaʿ (Negev).]

During the course of the Chalcolithic period, groups of pastoralists and possibly hunters, originating in the Beersheba basin and Naḥal Besor, penetrated the Negev highlands. There and in the ʿArabah they established small, unwalled villages and utilized the region's natural caves as dwelling places. In addition, temporary campsites and tent encampments were set up by nomadic or seminomadic tribes who traversed this district, apparently engaged in seasonal animal husbandry and the transport of copper. Major Chalcolithic sites include Beersheba, Gilat, Shiqmim, Naḥal Yattir, Arad, ʿEin-Gedi, and the caves at Naḥal Mishmar. Of special note are the buildings that are probably temples or cultic places, such as those at ʿEin-Gedi and Gilat. [*See* Gilat; Shiqmim; ʿEin-Gedi.]

Early Bronze Age I–III. Widespread sedentarization characterizes the Early Bronze Age in the Negev. The most important Negev site to enjoy significant expansion in this period was the large walled city of Arad. Included among its several public buildings are a sacred area (EB II) with at least one structure its excavator, Ruth Amiran, identified as a temple. Contemporary settlements flourishing in the highlands were unwalled and can be classified as central (upward of 5 acres in area); large (2–4 acres); small (including 2–8 buildings); or temporary. The central and large settlements were located near permanent water sources. Characteristic EB II dwellings are structures with several rooms arrayed around a central courtyard, one-room structures, and round buildings. [*See* Arad, *article on* Early Bronze Age Period.]

The EB II–III population of the Negev highlands included groups of immigrants from the urban culture that had developed to the north. These settlers preserved the pastoral way of life that had flourished in the Chalcolithic period. The Beersheba basin, the previous period's settlement and cultural center, was almost totally abandoned in favor of more southern locations—reaching the southernmost boundaries of the Negev highlands—where the economy was based on agriculture, husbandry, and hunting, as at sites in the Sede Boqer, Ramat Maṭred, and Miṣpe Ramon areas, the ʿUvda Valley, Har-Ḥorsha, and Naḥal Mitnan.

Early Bronze IV. Hundreds of EB IV settlements have been recorded, primarily in the Negev highlands and ʿUvda Valley. None were found in the Beersheba and Arad basins. Excavations at Be'er Resisim, an important EB IV site, were conducted during three seasons by a joint American-Israeli expedition headed by William G. Dever and Cohen. New archaeological techniques focusing on a holistic approach to examining the site were employed. These techniques included climatic, geological, paleozoological, and paleobotanical studies. [*See* Be'er Resisim.]

Arad, which had flourished during EB II, was destroyed and abandoned sometime after the mid-third millennium BCE, as were other larger centers in the Shephelah and southern Transjordan. Most of the population of the Negev highlands and bordering areas, however, was not displaced. In addition, a new ethnic group penetrated the Negev in EB IV. This population established large, dense villages near permanent water sources and lived alongside the settlements of the earlier inhabitants. The social and organizational makeup of the new population differed from that of the earlier Bronze Age people, and its material culture was somewhat more complex.

EB IV settlements fall into three categories: central settlements of 1–5 acres (e.g., ʿEin-Ziq, Mashʿabbe Sadeh, Be'er Resisim, 'Atar Har-Yeruḥam); medium-sized settlements of up to half an acre (Ḥorvat Be'er Ḥayyal, Ramat Boqer, Naḥal Sirpad, Ḥorvat ʿAvnon); and small settlements (Naḥal Revivim, Ḥorvat 'Aḥdir, 'Atar Har-Ramon). Central settlements can be further divided into those characterized by round residences of one to five rooms that share small courtyard; by a coterminous series of rectangular or circular houses whose continuous outer walls served as a parapet for the site; and by residences made up of irregularly shaped rooms built around a large open courtyard.

Far fewer large settlements have been uncovered than small, temporary settlements, perhaps because of the nomadic and seminomadic lifestyle of the region's inhabitants. Most of the small, more distant settlements were occupied periodically, primarily during grazing season, when residents of the larger, more permanent settlements would migrate there with their flocks but return home to the central centers at the end of the season.

Iron Age. The Iron Age was a period of settlement expansion in every area of the Negev. The fortified city of Beersheba was an important site, as was the settlement at Tel Masos and the fortress at Arad. In addition to numerous Hebrew ostraca found in the Arad fortress, the remains of a Judean shrine were uncovered by Aharoni in his excavations there. [*See* Arad Inscriptions.] In the tenth century BCE, following a period of abandonment that lasted almost a millennium, a series of fortified cities came to characterize the Negev highlands, the result of the building programs of David and Solomon. These military installations, surrounded by agricultural settlements, dominated the Negev. The "four-room house," the most prominent dwelling type in the Sede Boqer and Ramat Matred areas, became a distinctive feature of the settlements. [*See* Four-room House.]

Many Iron Age sites have been excavated, most of them fortresses of three main types: oval (the most common, built on axes 15–70 m long), such as those at 'Atar ha-Roʿa and Ḥorvat Ḥaluqim; rectangular (ranging from 78 × 32 to 17 × 15 m), as at Har-Reviv and Naḥal Zenaʿ; and fortresses (from 17 × 11 to 7 × 5 m), such as those at Ḥorvat Ramat Boqer and Be'erotayim. Their common plan was casement rooms around a central courtyard. After these fortresses were destroyed or abandoned—probably in 918 BCE, during Pharaoh Sheshonq's (biblical Shishak) campaign into Judah—the Negev highlands were uninhabited for about four centuries, until the Persian period. [*See* Masos, Tel.]

During the eighth–sixth centuries BCE, the Beersheba basin reached the zenith of its Iron Age occupation, with the establishment and efflorescence of three additional walled cities, at Tel ʿAroʿer, Tel Malḥata, and Tel ʿIra, and the important site of ʿEin-Ḥaṣeva in the ʿArabah. Additionally, many fortresses and forts (e.g., at Arad, Ḥorvat Ṭov, and Qadesh-Barnea) sprang up along the highways of the northeastern Negev. [*See* ʿAroʿer; ʿIra, Tel; Qadesh-Barnea.]

Persian Period. Square fortresses from the Persian period were recently excavated at Meṣudat ha-Roʿa, Ḥorvat Ritma, and Ḥorvat Mesora. Numerous Aramaic ostraca attest to the status of Beersheba as an administrative center and Arad as an important way station. Other centers of note during this period included Tell Jemmeh, Tell el-Farʿah (South), and Gaza. Persian period remains have also been uncovered at Ashkelon by the Leon Levy Expedition headed by Lawrence E. Stager. [*See* Jemmeh, Tell; Farʿah, Tell el- (South); Ashkelon.]

Nabatean, Roman, and Byzantine Periods. Important Nabatean remains lie along the main route traversing the Negev, the "frankincense and myrrh road" leading from Petra to Gaza. These include way stations, forts, towers, and agricultural settlements: Mo'a, Ḥorvat Qaṣra, Meṣad Neqarot, and ʿEin-Saharonim. Significant Nabatean remains were also uncovered during Avraham Negev's excavations at Avdat, Mampsis (Kurnub), and Elusa (Ḥaluṣa). [*See* Avdat; Kurnub; Ḥaluṣa.]

The Roman period is characterized by square fortresses with four projecting corner towers and single square towers erected along roads. ʿEin-Ḥaṣeva, Meṣad Tamar, ʿEin-Boqeq, Yotvata, Meṣad Zohar ʿIllit, and the towers along the Scorpion's Pass are among this period's sites. [*See* ʿEin-Boqeq.]

The Byzantine period represents the Negev's settlement efflorescence. Scores of agricultural settlements have been uncovered, including the cities at Avdat, Mamshit, Reḥovot, Shivtah, and Neṣṣana. Among the most impressive of the remains excavated are several Byzantine churches. These sites apparently constituted the agricultural hinterland of the region's large urban centers and facilitated their economic prosperity. [*See* Reḥovot; Neṣṣana.]

Early Arab Period. While several Byzantine settlements continued to exist after the Arab conquest in the seventh century (at Neṣṣana and Shivtah, to name two), sedentarization in the region declined ending eventually, in the middle of the eighth century CE. A few of the surviving villages and mosques, as well as new settlements, have been excavated (including Sede Boqer, Kefar Shaḥaq, Kibbutz 'Eilot, ʿEin-Yahav, ʿEvrona, and Har-Nafḥa). In the Negev highlands, these new sites follow the distribution of Byzantine-period settlements. This is not the case in the central and southern ʿArabah, however, which witnessed unprecedented settlement in Byzantine times. Both regions experienced an interruption in sedentarization in the fifth–sixth centuries CE.

The sedentary Negev population in this period resided in small villages and on farms, practicing agriculture in the wadis, where seasonal rainwater was collected and utilized for irrigation.

The period's numerous rock inscriptions are mostly graffiti of the type found in abundance in the deserts of northern Arabia, Transjordan, and Sinai and are usually accompanied by engravings of animals. The inscriptions are primarily in Nabatean and Arabic and provide valuable information on the customs and beliefs of the period.

From the inscriptions, as well as from the abundant archaeological remains of settlements, farms, and agricultural installations, it is clear that the semiarid Negev supported a considerable population—partly nomadic and partly sedentary—between the first and seventh–eighth centuries CE.

[*See also* Beersheba.]

BIBLIOGRAPHY

Aharoni, Yohanan. "The Negeb." In *Archaeology and Old Testament Study,* edited by D. Winton Thomas, pp. 385–403. Oxford, 1967.

Aharoni, Yohanan. "The Negeb and the Southern Borders." In *The Age of the Monarchies: Political History,* edited by Abraham Malamat, pp. 290–307. World History of the Jewish People, vol. 4.1. Jerusalem, 1979.

Alon, David, and Thomas E. Levy. "Preliminary Note on the Distribution of Chalcolithic Sites on the Wadi Beer-Sheba–Lower Wadi Besor Drainage System." *Israel Exploration Journal* 30 (1980): 140–147.

Cohen, Rudolph, and William G. Dever. "Preliminary Report of the Pilot Season of the 'Central Negev Highlands Project.'" *Bulletin of the American Schools of Oriental Research,* no. 232 (1978): 29–45.

Cohen, Rudolph. "The Iron Age Fortresses in the Central Negev." *Bulletin of the American Schools of Oriental Research,* no. 236 (1979): 61–79.

Cohen, Rudolph, and William G. Dever. "Preliminary Report of the Second Season of the 'Central Negev Highlands Project.'" *Bulletin of the American Schools of Oriental Research,* no. 236 (1980): 41–60.

Cohen, Rudolph, and William G. Dever. "Preliminary Report of the Third and Final Season of the 'Central Negev Highlands Project.'" *Bulletin of the American Schools of Oriental Research,* no. 243 (1981): 57–77.

Cohen, Rudolph. "New Light on the Date of the Petra-Gaza Road." *Biblical Archaeologist* 45 (1982): 240–247.

Cohen, Rudolph. "The Mysterious MB I People." *Biblical Archaeology Review* 9.4 (1983): 16–29.

Cohen, Rudolph. "The Fortresses King Solomon Built to Protect His Southern Border." *Biblical Archaeology Review* 11.3 (1985): 56–70.

Cohen, Rudolph. "Solomon's Negev Defense Line Contained Three Fewer Fortresses." *Biblical Archaeology Review* 12.4 (1986): 40–45.

Dever, William G. "Village Planning at Be'er Resisim and Socioeconomic Structure in Early Bronze Age IV Palestine." *Eretz-Israel* 18 (1984): 18*–28*.

Glueck, Nelson. *Rivers in the Desert: A History of the Negev.* New York, 1959.

Goring-Morris, A. Nigel. *At the Edge: Terminal Pleistocene Hunter-Gatherers in the Negev and Sinai.* 2 vols. British Archaeological Reports, International Series, no. 361. Oxford, 1987.

Haiman, Mordechai. "Preliminary Report of the Western Negev Highlands Emergency Survey." *Israel Exploration Journal* 39 (1989): 173–191.

Herzog, Ze'ev. "Enclosed Settlements in the Negeb and the Wilderness of Beer-Sheba." *Bulletin of the American Schools of Oriental Research,* no. 250 (1983): 41–49.

Lender, Yeshayahu. *Archaeological Survey of Israel: Map of Har Nafḥa (196) 12–01.* Jerusalem, 1990.

Levy, Thomas E., ed. *Shiqmim,* vol. 1, *Studies Concerning Chalcolithic Societies in the Northern Negev Desert, Israel, 1982–1984.* British Archaeological Reports, International Series, no. 356. Oxford, 1987.

Negev, Avraham. "The Nabataeans and Provincia Arabia." In *Aufstieg und Niedergang der römischen Welt,* vol. II.8, edited by Hildegard Temporini and Wolfgang Haase, pp. 520–686. Berlin and New York, 1977.

Sharon, M. "Arabic Rock Inscriptions from the Negev." In *Archaeological Survey of Israel: Ancient Rock Inscriptions. Supplement to Map of Har Nafḥa (196) 12–01,* edited by Y. Kuris and Lori Lender, pp. 9*–35*. Jerusalem, 1990.

Shiloh, Yigal. "Elements in the Development of Town Planning in the Israelite City." *Israel Exploration Journal* 28 (1978): 36–51.

Stern, Ephraim. *Material Culture of the Land of the Bible in the Persian Period, 538–332 B.C.* Warminster, 1982.

RUDOLPH COHEN

NELSON GLUECK SCHOOL OF BIBLICAL ARCHAEOLOGY.

Located in the Skirball Center for Biblical and Archaeological Research on the campus of Hebrew Union College–Jewish Institute of Religion (HUC-JIR) in Jerusalem, the Nelson Glueck School of Biblical Archaeology is an academic institution with an active field research program focusing on the archaeology of the land of Israel and the world of the Bible. The campus, initially called Hebrew Union College Biblical and Archaeological School, was opened in 1963 by Nelson Glueck, then president of HUC-JIR. The intention of its founders was to provide, among other community services, a base for American scholars and researchers engaged in Near Eastern studies. At the time, some were unable to visit East Jerusalem, where the American School of Oriental Research (now the Albright Institute) is located, then under Jordanian control. At the outset an American scholar was appointed director annually, but in 1968 William G. Dever became its first permanent director; he was followed by Joe D. Seger.

The school began a long-term archaeological project at Gezer in 1964 under the direction of G. Ernest Wright. The enterprise contributed to the school's rapid development into a major archaeological center. In addition to introducing new excavation methods, the Gezer project inaugurated the use of student volunteers in the field. The school also undertook excavations at Jebel Qaʿaqir and Khirbet el-Qom. Final reports of the Gezer excavations appear in the school's Annuals; a *Manual of Field Excavation* was published in 1978.

Following Glueck's death in 1971 and the election of Alfred Gottschalk as president of HUC-JIR, the name of the school was changed to the Nelson Gleuck School of Biblical Archaeology. In 1974 Avraham Biran was appointed director, at which time the school took over the excavation at Tel Dan, which became its major project and is the longest ongoing excavation in Israel. Other excavations were carried out at ʿAroʿer, Yesud ha-Maʿalah, Ras el-Kharrubeh, Deir es-Sid, TelʿIra, Shiqmim, Gilat, and Nahal Tillah.

An integral part of the school is its Skirball Museum, which exhibits material from the school's archaeological projects. The exhibits are based on specific subjects with an emphasis on archaeological objects as works of art and as expressions of the cultural and historical processes that affected the biblical world.

An International Colloqium on Temples and High Places in Biblical Times was held in 1977 and its proceedings published (1981). Congresses, seminars, and lectures complement the school's research activities.

[*See also the biography of Glueck. In addition most sites mentioned are the subject of independent entries; see especially* Dan; *and* Gezer.]

BIBLIOGRAPHY

Biran, Avraham. *Dan: 25 shenot hafirot be-Tel Dan* (Dan: 25 Years of Excavations at Tel Dan). Tel Aviv, 1992.

Biran, Avraham. *Biblical Dan.* Jerusalem, 1994.

Biran, Avraham, ed. *Temples and High Places in Biblical Times: Proceedings of the Colloquium in Honor of the Centennial of Hebrew Union College–Jewish Institute of Religion, Jerusalem, 14–16 March 1977.* Jerusalem, 1981.

Dever, William G., and H. Darrell Lance, eds. *A Manual of Field Excavation: Handbook for Field Archaeologists.* Cincinnati, 1978.

AVRAHAM BIRAN

NEMRUD DAĞI, Late Hellenistic site on the summit of the mountain of the same name, located in southeastern Turkey (36°38′ N, 38°40′ E), in the new (as of 1954) province of Adıyaman, formerly the province of Malatya. Nemrud Dağı is one of the highest mountains of the Anti-Taurus range within the region known in Turkish as the Ankar Dağları. Although some of the neighboring mountains are higher, Nemrud Dağı is unique in that its summit is clearly visible from all directions and the sanctuary on its peak must have been a prominent landmark in antiquity, as it is today. The Turkish Aerial Geodetic Survey in 1954 reported an official height of 2,150 m above sea level for Nemrud Dağı. The elevation was verified in 1986 by the Ministry of Culture and Tourism. More precise data for the coordinates of the peak and the number of the geodetic benchmark on top of the site are not available because Nemrud Dağı lies within a military zone.

The name *Nemrud Dağı* seems to have been first brought to the attention of the West by Charles Sester, a German road engineer and surveyor, when he reported his discovery of the monument to German and Ottoman authorities in 1881. Subsequently, the site was explored briefly and then published by two separate teams. In 1882 and 1883, German teams recorded the major sculptural, epigraphic, and architectural remains, which were published amid descriptions of the team's travels throughout Asia Minor and North Syria (Humann and Puchstein, 1890, pp. 97–406). Also in 1883, O. Hamdy Bey, director of the Imperial Ottoman Museum of Constantinople, and Osgan Effendi, an Armenian technician, made the difficult ascent to Nemrud Dağı and spent five days studying the remains (Hamdy Bey and Osgan Effendi, 1883). Complete investigation of the site's abundant sculptures and inscriptions did not occur until the mid-twentieth century, when an international team, directed by Theresa Goell between 1953 and 1973, carried out thorough excavations, pioneering geophysical explorations, and partial restorations. Other sporadic investigations and reconstructions continued during the late 1980s.

Although Nemrud Dağı is the name used today for the site and the mountain peak, it is uncertain whether this is merely one name among others. For example, William Ainsworth, an English traveler who journeyed through the region in 1839, described the scenery and mentioned an outstanding high conical peak that he called Assur. Later, Humann and Puchstein identified the mountain of Assur as Nemrud Dağı. However, Ainsworth referred also to a more remarkable cone called Ura Baba, which could equally well be the mountain now called Nemrud Dağı.

On top of the mountain peak of Nemrud Dağı is the *hierothesion,* or temple-tomb and common dwelling place of all the gods, of the Late Hellenistic king Antiochus I of Commagene (c. 69–34 BCE). The term *hierothesion* seems to appear only on monuments erected by Antiochus I and at the burial places of his immediate family, at the sites of Nemrud Dağı, Gerger, Karakuş, and Arsameia on the Nymphaios. The numerous inscriptions at Nemrud Dağı do not furnish any precise historical or chronological data regarding the date of the site or the life of its creator. The king's alleged genealogies, carved on the backs of stelae throughout the site, provide a chronological position relative only to two dynastic lines. The site does, however, provide the earliest known extant Greek calendrical horoscope, in the form of a monumental stela depicting a striding lion and a scattering of stars. Representing the constellation Leo and other celestial elements, the particular configuration of astronomical symbols presents a date equivalent to 7 July 62 BCE (for an alternative interpretation of the stela and its date, see Tuman, 1984).

The complete excavation and site clearance led by Theresa Goell finally revealed the true nature of Antiochus's tomb-sanctuary, which his workers had hewed directly from the living rock of Nemrud Dağı. The monuments are made from and rest directly on the peak's limestone; there are no remains of previous occupation. Nevertheless, certain iconographic and architectural similarities between the layout and design of the *hierothesion* and some Hittite and late Hittite monuments in the region hint at the prospect that this prominent summit may once have been a sacred high place. Any remains of such an ancient ritual location are currently buried deep beneath a roughly 50-meter-high conical tumulus that is the focal point and dominant feature of the *hierothesion.*

The whole complex is constructed on a cyclopean scale. Three rock-cut terraces flank the tumulus on its northeast, southwest, and north; each is a terminus for separate sign-posted Processional Ways leading up to Nemrud Dağı from the valleys and towns below. On the East Terrace, the largest and most spacious of the three, the central court is lined on all four sides by a vast array of ritual accessories. Along the west side of the terrace, colossal enthroned statues (originally about 8–9 m high) of Antiochus and his syncretized Greco-Persian tutelary deities rise high above the court on a two-tiered podium cut from the mountain limestone, with the massive tumulus as a backdrop. The seated gods, mostly preserved intact except for their heads, which have fallen to the ground, include a centrally positioned Zeus-Oromasdes, flanked on the north by Apollo-Mithras-Helios-Hermes and Artagnes-Heracles-Ares and on the south by the goddess Commagene and Antiochus himself (see figure 1). The deities are bounded at each end by a pair of guardian figures, an eagle and a lion. Carved on the back of the colossal thrones are monumental Greek inscriptions (*nomos,* or "sacred laws") prescribing the rituals pertaining to the cult of Antiochus and the eternal maintenance of his sanctuary.

Parallel to the colossal statues, but located below, on a lower tier set closer to court level, was a row of four colossal stelae, each depicting Antiochus being greeted by one of his tutelary gods in an act of deification. The lion horoscope stela stood as the northernmost stela in this row; the set was also bounded by guardian animals. These stelae survive only in fragments. A row of contiguous orthostats set into sockets on low plinths define the north and south limits of the East Terrace. The northern stelae depict, on the side facing the court, full-length, overlifesize portraits of the Persian and Commagenian ancestors of Antiochus, beginning with Darius the Great and ending with Antiochus's father. The southern row of stelae portray Antiochus's Macedonian ancestors, from Alexander the Great through Antiochus's mother. On the backs of the ancestor stelae, genealogical inscriptions identify each royal relative on the obverse. Be-

NEMRUD DAĞI. Figure 1. *Antiochus's pantheon.* View across the East Terrace toward the Double Podium, as of the 1954 excavation season. The rubble tumulus rises in the background. (Used with permission of the Nemrud Dag Publication Project)

hind and parallel to each line of ancestors is a shorter, second row of orthostats depicting miscellaneous lesser figures, including Antiochus's children. Only a few stelae survive in large, recognizable pieces.

On the east side of the terrace stands a low, square, stepped platform, now fully restored. The remains lying around the platform suggest that it supported a Persian fire altar and sets of guardian eagles and lions. Other, smaller altars are scattered throughout the terrace: in front of each ancestor stela, by the deification sequence, and at the southwest corner, near a subsidiary collection of carved stelae depicting the investiture of Antiochus.

The West Terrace contains the same set of sculpted features, but they are arranged a bit differently because of the shallow and cramped available floor space. Thus, the West Terrace lacks the stepped platform and high double podium prominent in the East Terrace's grandiose layout. The colossal gods are less well preserved than those on the East Terrace, but the ancestor stelae survive somewhat more completely. The magnificent monumental deification stelae and lion horoscope, which are preserved nearly intact, were recently restored to their original positions. The North Terrace contains only a guardian eagle and a long wall of uncarved orthostats forming one side of the court. A rubble walkway rings the base of the tumulus, connecting all three terraces. If Antiochus's tomb chamber exists within the tumulus, no entrance to it has been detected, despite numerous test trenches and geophysical probes into the mound.

The site's design, use of guardian animals, profuse statuary, and ritual symbols set within a cultic context perpetuate long-established local traits dating from the period of the Hittite Empire. Late Hellenistic architectural vocabulary and contemporary Persian religious iconography were integrated with indigenous features into an elegant and coherent statement of power and piety.

The site is important because (1) it is the most striking and informative monument of the Hellenistic ruler cult; (2) it presents an excellent reflection of the fusion of Anatolian, Persian, and Hellenistic cultural and artistic conventions; (3) it provides telling testimony to the manner in which Mithraism, a new agrarian religion sweeping across borders from east to west, permeated long-established Hellenistic beliefs (the sculpture and inscriptions illustrate remarkably the regional tendency toward religious syncretism in the crucial decades just preceding the Christian era); and (4) the exact date provided by the astronomical data on Antiochus's horoscope stelae furnish a monument firmly placed in the mid-first century BCE, from which to study other Hellenistic monuments that lack fixed dates.

At Antiochus's *hierothesion* the separate elements of architecture, sculpture, inscriptions, and the natural landscape are intertwined in a complex and delicate balance that recalls and reflects the king's immersion in a Greek, Roman, and Parthian military and cultural environment. The total effect of the sanctuary at Nemrud Dağı is unique, as a result not only of Antiochus's syncretistic proclivities, but ultimately of an underlying tenacity of indigenous Anatolian traditions.

[*See also* Hittites.]

BIBLIOGRAPHY

There is currently no complete or fully accurate monograph on Nemrud Dağı, however, a comprehensive excavation report is forthcoming (see Sanders below). The publications by Theresa Goell, director of the site's excavations, are all preliminary, and therefore partial, studies. All other publications about the site are based primarily on the incorrect, fragmentary, and largely inaccessible books by Humann and Puchstein (1890) and Hamdy Bey and Osgan Effendi (1883), or on the early reports by Goell.

Dörner, Friedrich Karl. *Der Thron der Götter auf dem Nemrud Dag: Kommagene, das grosse archäologische Abenteuer in der östlichen Türkei.* 2d ed., rev. Lübbe, 1987. Exhaustive review of Commagenian sites, including Nemrud Dağı, comprising the final compendium of work by a German epigrapher who specialized in Commagenian history. Dörner discovered and excavated Arsameia on the Nymphaios, the *hierothesion* and mountaintop retreat of Mithradates Callinicus, father of Antiochus.

Goell, Theresa. "The Excavation of the 'Hierothesion' of Antiochus I of Commagene on Nemrud Dagh, 1953–1956." *Bulletin of the American Schools of Oriental Research,* no. 147 (October 1957): 4–22. Review of the author's first excavation seasons, including a survey of previous scholarship, the site's regional context, the importance of the site for late Hellenistic scholarship, and problems still to be resolved.

Goell, Theresa. "Throne above the Euphrates." *National Geographic Magazine* 119.3 (1961): 390–405. General essay on the site and brief summary of the basic remains, as well as a colorful description of the region, the author's exploits in the territory, and the conditions under which excavations were carried out. Generously illustrated.

Goell, Theresa. "Geophysical Survey of the Hierothesion and Tomb of Antiochus I of Commagene, Turkey." *National Geographic Society Research Reports: 1963 Projects,* pp. 83–102. Washington, D.C., 1968. Presents the findings of the pioneering geophysical explorations of the mound and terraces, of which the primary objective was to locate the tomb chamber of Antiochus. The seismic refraction and electrical resistivity surveys, equipment and methods used, and the results are presented in somewhat technical language.

Goell, Theresa. "The Nemrud Dagh (Turkey) Geophysical Surveys of 1964." *National Geographic Society Research Reports: 1964 Projects,* pp. 61–81. Washington, D.C., 1969. Summary of the second and last geophysical probing of the mound, using seismic refraction, magnetic, and gravity techniques, with a review of the equipment, methods, and results, and suggestions for further tests.

Hamdy Bey, Osman, and Osgan Effendi. *Le tumulus de Nemroud-Dagh: Voyage, description, inscriptions* (1883). Istanbul, 1987. Remarkable work—given the authors' brief stay at the site and the 4m of snow covering some of the monuments—attributing the site to Antiochus IV, mid-first century CE. The publication was rushed to press to counter preliminary analyses offered in 1882 by Otto Puchstein. Contains numerous illustrations, particularly of the inscriptions.

Humann, Karl, and Otto Puchstein. *Reisen in Kleinasien und Nordsyrien.* 2 vols. Berlin, 1890. The fundamental publication of the site and region, upon which all subsequent interpretations have been based until Goell's excavations dramatically altered our understanding of Nemrud Dağı's design, date, heritage, and art historical significance (see Goell, Sanders). Contains numerous errors in analysis and transcription of the inscriptions, primarily the result of limited excavation time, lack of knowledge regarding the yet to be discovered indigenous Anatolian cultures, and an overwhelming tendency to judge remains against an ideal Greek model. The authors present a date of 17 July 98 BCE for the Lion Horoscope.

Sanders, Donald H., ed. *Nemrud Dağı: The Hierothesion of Antiochus I of Commagene; Results of the American Excavations Directed by Theresa B. Goell.* 2 vols. Winona Lake, Ind., 1995. Final and comprehensive excavation report, including all the work of Goell and her collaborators (most data heretofore unavailable) on the geography of the region, its architecture, sculpture, inscriptions, and small finds, with a synthesis of the geophysical probes. Important as a corrective to the numerous errors and misstatements in previous publications about the site. Lavishly illustrated.

Tuman, V. S. "The Tomb of Antiochus Revisited: Planetary Alignments and the Deification of the King." *Archaeoastronomy* 7.1–4 (1984): 56–69. Suggests an alternative interpretation of the Lion Horoscope stelae, giving a date of 4–5 February 55 BCE on which occurred a significant alignment of planets. The author posits a direct relationship between this event and the selection of Antiochus's pantheon. Although weak on art historical analysis, the reassessment of the site's iconography merits consideration in all future studies.

DONALD H. SANDERS

NEO-HITTITES. The term used to designate the Iron Age states that succeeded the Hittite Empire in southeast Anatolia and North Syria is *Neo-Hittite.* [*See* Hittites.] It reflects the use of the term *Ḫatti* for these peoples by their neighbors, principally the Assyrians. These states no longer used the Hittite language written in cuneiform on clay tablets (like those in the Ḫattuša archives); instead they continued the practice of the Hittite kings in writing monumental inscriptions in the hieroglyphic script and Luwian language. [*See* Luwians.] Evidence suggests that they also wrote their everyday texts on perishable materials that have not survived. The bulk of the population as well as the rulers appear to have been Luwian speaking, which implies a migration of this people from the Anatolian plateau into Syria at the fall of the Hittite Empire.

The Neo-Hittite states seem partly to correspond to old centers and provinces of the Hittite Empire and partly to be new foundations. At the center lay Carchemish, where continuity of occupation from the Hittite Empire is likely. [*See* Carchemish.] Limited excavation of the site by a British expedition (1911–1914) exposed parts of the citadel and fortifications and especially an area of the lower town and recovered a considerable amount of sculpture and inscriptions.

On the east bank of the Euphrates River 20 km (12 mi.) south of Carchemish, Tell Ahmar, ancient Til Barsip, was excavated by a French expedition (1929–1931), revealing a provincial Assyrian palace, under which lay the palace of the earlier rulers (see Thureau-Dangin and Dunand, 1936). [*See* Til Barsip.] Hieroglyphic inscriptions give the history of a Neo-Hittite dynasty of at least four generations. The site, now threatened with flooding by a barrage, is again (1993) under investigation by an expedition from Melbourne University (Bunnens, 1990).

On the west bank of the Upper Euphrates the site of Arslantepe (ancient Melid) was excavated by a French expedition (1932–1933, 1938) that recovered its main Neo-Hittite monument, the Lion Gate, with its sculpture and inscriptions (Delaporte, 1940). [*See* Arslantepe.] A series of royal inscriptions from the valley of the Tohma Su marks the expansion of Melid westward, and a stela from Elbistan records the colonization of that plain by a Melidian king. In 1947, Turkish excavations at the neighboring site of Karahöyük discovered another large stela in situ (Özgüç, 1949). An Italian expedition resumed excavations at Arslantepe in 1961 that are still underway to investigate the mound's levels (for full bibliography, see Frangipane, 1993).

On the Euphrates between Melid and Carchemish lay Kummuh, the Iron Age predecessor of classical Commagene, with its capital at Samsat Höyük on the river. Rescue excavations at sites along the river preceded their flooding by a barrage in 1989, but no very notable Neo-Hittite remains were recovered (see Moore, 1993; Summers et al., 1993). Hieroglyphic inscriptions, the work of a Hittite dynasty, are known from other sites.

West of Kummuh, Marqas (modern Maraş, the capital of the small state of Gurgum), in spite of a complete absence of archaeological investigation, has yielded a series of sculptures and inscriptions. The latter attest the existence of a seven-generation dynasty in the period from 1000–800 BCE; the former are funerary in character, suggesting as provenance the unlocated cemetery.

The Syrian-Hittite Expedition of the University of Chicago (1933–1938) investigated the modern ʿAmuq, the kingdom of Unqi, on the plain of Antioch (Braidwood, 1937; Haines, 1971). [*See* ʿAmuq.] The Iron Age capital at Tell Taʿyinat yielded a typical Neo-Hittite palace-citadel and fortification complex, though the excavated sculpture and inscriptions were badly destroyed, probably in antiquity by the Assyrian conquerors. The Syrian Department of Antiquities has uncovered a massive, early Neo-Hittite temple at ʿAin Daraʿ, another Unqi site (Abou Assaf, 1990). [*See* ʿAin Daraʿ.]

A Danish expedition from the University of Copenhagen (1931–1938) excavated the most southern state with Neo-Hittite remains, Hama, ancient Hamath, which revealed another typical Neo-Hittite citadel of the ninth century BCE, the work of a Hittite dynasty, as its hieroglyphic inscriptions show (Fugmann et al., 1948–1990). [*See* Hama.] By the eighth century BCE, political power had passed to an Aramean dynasty.

In Plain Cilicia another Neo-Hittite kingdom is known, but of its capitals, the site of ancient Adana has not been located, while Tarsus, excavated by an American expedition (1934–1938, 1947–1949) has not yielded substantial remains of the period (Goldmann, 1956–1963). [*See* Cilicia.] Its civilization is thus represented by the small provincial site of Karatepe in the hills north and east of the plain. There, a hilltop fort, excavated by a Turkish expedition since 1947, has two monumental gateways decorated by sculptured orthostats and a large bilingual inscription in hieroglyphic Luwian and alphabetic Phoenician (for bibliography, see Orthmann, 1980). [*See* Karatepe Phoenician Inscriptions.] This bilingual, which has been of great significance in the decipherment of hieroglyphic Hittite, provides the longest inscription of the hieroglyphic corpus and probably also the latest (c. 700 BCE).

The southeast Anatolian plateau is not well known archaeologically in this period, but it is quite rich in monuments. A western group centering on the mountains Karadağ and Kızıldağ probably date to the twelfth century BCE and provide evidence of continuity from the Hittite Empire. The other two groups, a northern one covering the modern provinces of Kayseri and Nevşehir and a southern one covering Niğde, are both late (late eighth century BCE) and attest the works of Anatolian dynasties of the period.

In addition to the evidence of their own hieroglyphic inscriptions, sources for the history of the Neo-Hittite states can be drawn from the inscriptions of the Assyrians, who attacked, harried, and ultimately destroyed them. In the late eighth century BCE, the Assyrians broke up these states one by one, removing their native populations and constituting the resettled territories as Assyrian provinces. This process proved terminal for Hittite civilization, which finally disappeared from history at this date. [*See* Assyrians.]

BIBLIOGRAPHY

Abou Assaf, Ali. *Der Tempel von ʿAin Dārā.* Mainz am Rhein, 1990.

Braidwood, Robert J. *Mounds in the Plain of Antioch.* Oriental Institute Publications, 46. Chicago, 1937.

Bunnens, Guy, ed. *Tell Ahmar, 1988 Season.* Publications of the Melbourne University Expedition to Tel Ahmar, vol. 1. Louvain, 1990. First report on the new series of excavations, with an overview of previous work.

Delaporte, Louis. *Malatya, Arslantepe,* vol. 1, *La Porte des Lions.* Paris, 1940.

Desideri, Paolo, and Anna M. Jasink. *Cilicia: Dall'età di Kizzuwatna alla conquista macedone.* Turin, 1990. The most up-to-date survey of the sources for Cilicia.

Frangipane, Marcella. "Melid. B. Archäologisch." In *Reallexikon der Assyriologie und Vorderasiatischen Archäologie,* vol. 8.1–2, pp. 50–52. Berlin, 1993.

Fugmann, Ejnar, et al. *Hama II: Les premiers habitants et la ville préhellénistique de Hamath,* vol. 1, *L'architecture* (Fugmann); vol. 2, *Les objets de la période dit Syro-Hittite* (P. J. Riis and Marie-Louise Buhl); vol. 3, *Les cimetières à crémation* (Riis). Copenhagen, 1948–1990.

Goldman, Hetty, ed. *Excavations at Gözlü Kule, Tarsus,* vol. 2, *From the Neolithic Period through the Bronze Age;* vol. 3, *The Iron Age.* Princeton, 1956–1963.

Haines, Richard C. *Excavations in the Plain of Antioch,* vol. 2, *The Structural Remains of the Later Phases.* Oriental Institute Publications, 95. Chicago, 1971.

Hawkins, J. D. "The Neo-Hittite States in Syria and Anatolia." In *The Cambridge Ancient History,* vol. 3.1, edited by John Boardman et al., pp. 372–441. 2d ed. Cambridge, 1982. General historical overview, including evidence drawn from detailed interpretations of the hieroglyphic inscriptions.

Hawkins, J. D. "The Syro-Hittite States." In *The Cambridge Ancient History,* plates to vol. 3, pp. 65–92. Cambridge, 1984. Illustrations to citation above, with detailed explanatory text for each picture.

Hawkins, J. D. In *Reallexikon der Assyriologie und Vorderasiatischen Archäologie,* vols. 4–8. Berlin and New York, 1972–1990. See the entries for Halab, Hamath, Hatti, Hattin (Unqi), Hilakku (Cilicia), Irhuleni (Hamath), Jau-bi'di (Hamath), Karatepe, Karkamiš, Kinalua (Unqi), Kummuh, Luhuti (Hamath), Manṣuate (Hamath), Maraş, Marqas, and Melid. General encyclopedia entries with detailed references covering history, excavation, and indigenous sources; includes most of the Neo-Hittite states under one heading or another except Que (Cilicia), Tabal (Anatolian plateau), and Til Barsip (Tell Ahmar).

Hogarth, David G., et al. *Carchemish: Report on the Excavations at Djerabis,* vol. 1, *Introductory* (Hogarth); vol. 2, *The Town Defences* (C. Leonard Woolley); vol. 3, *The Excavations in the Inner Town; The Hittite Inscriptions* (Woolley and R. D. Barnett). London, 1914–1952.

Moore, John. *Tille Höyük 1: The Medieval Period.* British Institute of Archaeology at Ankara, Monograph no. 14. London, 1993.

Orthmann, Winfried. "Karatepe. B. Archäologisch." In *Reallexikon der Assyriologie und Vorderasiatischen Archäologie,* vol. 5.5–6, pp. 411ff. Berlin, 1980.

Özgüç, Tahsin, and Nimet Özgüç. *Ausgrabungen in Karahöyük.* Ankara, 1949.

Summers, G. D., et al. *Tille Höyük 4: The Late Bronze Age and the Iron Age Transition.* British Institute of Archaeology at Ankara, Mongraph no. 15. London, 1993.

Thureau-Dangin, François, and Maurice Dunand. *Tille Barsib.* Paris, 1936.

Wäfler, Markus. "Zu Status und Lage von Tabāl." *Orientalia* 52 (1983): 181–193.

J. D. HAWKINS

NERAB INSCRIPTIONS. Two basalt funerary stelae, inscribed in Aramaic and belonging to two priests of the moon god Śaḥr, were found in 1891 by fellahin digging clay for the walls of their houses on a tell abutting the small village of Nerab (about 7 km, or 4 mi., southeast of Aleppo, Syria). The stelae were associated with an uninscribed sarcophagus hewn from the same material, containing two skeletons. The sarcophagus had been uncovered two years previously in similar circumstances (Clermont-Ganneau, 1897, pp. 183–184). Charles Clermont-Ganneau obtained the stelae for France and had them brought to the Louvre museum, where they remain. He published them in 1897.

Each priest is carved in bas-relief on a stela with a rounded top. In Nerab I (93 × 35 cm), Sin-zer-ibni stands with his right arm raised in a gesture of prayer or adoration. His fringed robe, wrapped around his right shoulder, leaving his left shoulder bare, reaches to his bare feet. He is wearing a round cap and in his left hand he grasps some folded fabric, possibly fringed. The text surrounds his head and then continues across the bottom of his robe from the knee down:

Sin-zer-ibni, priest of Śaḥr in Nerab, deceased. And this is his image and his sarcophagus (?). Whoever you are, should you carry off (?) this image and the sarcophagus (?) from its place, may Śaḥr and Shamash and Nikkal and Nusk tear out your name and your place from life, and may they kill you with a nasty death and destroy your offspring. But if you guard the image and this sarcophagus (?), afterward, may what belongs to you be guarded.

Nerab II (95 × 45 cm) depicts She'gabbar wearing the same cap and robe worn by Sin-zer-ibni on stela I. He sits before a well-stocked offering table, feet resting on a footstool. His left hand holds a drinking cup close to his lips. Facing him from across the table stands an attendant, carved on a smaller scale, either whisking flies from the table or fanning the priest. The text is inscribed on the flat raised surface above this scene:

She'gabbar, priest of Śaḥr in Nerab. This is his image. Because of my righteous conduct before him he gave me a good name and prolonged my days. On the day I died, my mouth was not stopped from speaking; and with my eyes, what was I seeing? Children of the fourth generation wept over me [or: "and with my own eyes I was witnessing the children of the fourth generation. They wept over me . . ."] and became crazed with grief. They did not set any silver or bronze vessel beside me. They set me (here) with my clothes (only) so that, in the future, you would not carry off my sarcophagus (?). Whoever you are—should you commit wrong and carry me off, may Śaḥr and Nikkal and Nusk make his death odious, and may his posterity perish.

The script of the stelae is fairly conservative (Naveh, 1970, pp. 17–18; Gibson, 1975, p. 94). Virtually every form has a precedent in eighth–century BCE Aramaic inscriptions. A number of these forms, however, are at the innovating pole of the comparable forms *(zayin, ḥet, kaph, samekh, ṣade)*. Assuming that the lapidary style was conservative in its own time, the script fits the early seventh century BCE.

Fortunately for dating purposes, She'gabbar of Nerab II has turned up as "Se'gabbari, priest *(šangû)* of Nerab," in a Neo-Assyrian letter addressed to Sargon II (c. 710 BCE) published by Simo Parpola (1985). The same name is attested in two other cuneiform sources from roughly the same temporal and geographic horizon (c. 721–680 BCE; Parpola, 1985, p. 273, n. 2), allowing a date in the first decades of the seventh century BCE for She'gabbar's funerary stela.

The method of writing is *scriptio continua* throughout, without word dividers or spaces between words. The orthography is conservative and conforms to the practice of the Old Aramaic inscriptions of the ninth and eighth centuries BCE. The language is transitional between the Old Aramaic of the ninth and eighth centuries and the Official Aramaic of the Persian period. Certain consonants later lost through merger in the Persian period are still represented as they are in Old Aramaic (cf., e.g., *l't'ḥz* II:4; *'šrh, 'šrk* I:8, 10; *tnṣr, ynṣr* I:12, 13). The form of the negative in the Nerab stelae (II:4, 6, 8) is simply *l-*, as in Old Aramaic generally (and in the Aššur ostracon), in contrast to *l'* in the texts of the Persian period. [*See* Aššur.] On the other hand, the vacillation between assimilated (*ysḥw* I:9) and nonassimilated forms (*tnṣr, ynṣr* I:12, 13) falls between the Old Aramaic inscriptions, which generally (outside of the Tell Fakhariyah inscription) assimilate, and the official and literary documents of the Persian period, which do not assimilate these forms. [*See* Fakhariyah Aramaic Inscription.] The form *yktlwk* (I:11) presupposes the **qṭl* form of the root for "to kill," widely attested from the Persian period, in contrast to the original **qtl* reflected in the Old Aramaic inscriptions (and in cognate languages). Moreover, the language behind the Nerab inscriptions has already developed the quasi-verbal use of the participle (*mḥzh 'nh* II:5) entirely absent in the Old Aramaic inscriptions of the ninth and eighth centuries BCE, but widely attested in the Persian period.

As funerary texts, the Nerab stelae are unique among early epigraphic Aramaic texts. They share a number of structural features with several Phoenician funerary inscriptions, including autobiographical elements and curses pronounced on the would-be violator of the funerary installations. [*See* Phoenician-Punic.] In both inscriptions, but especially in Nerab II, the deceased speaks from beyond the grave. The curses are comparable to similar curses found in other Northwest Semitic funerary, commemorative, and votive inscriptions (Gevirtz, 1961). Hayim Tawil (1974, pp. 57–65) has demonstrated the traditional character of several motifs in Nerab II by adducing parallels in other Northwest Semitic and cuneiform texts. Most impressive, however, is the sequence of motifs (most in the same order) shared with Nerab II by the Harran funerary inscription of Nabonidus's mother Adda-guppi' (Gadd, 1958, pp. 46–51) cited by Tawil (1974, p. 65).

The Nerab stelae exhibit an Assyrian influence in the names of the priests (Kaufman, 1970), in the formulae of the inscription (Tawil, 1974, pp. 57–65), and in the iconography of the bas-reliefs (Gibson, 1975, p. 94). The gods mentioned—Shamash, Nikkal, Nusk, and Sin (in the Aramaic form of Śaḥr)—are Babylonian. Nikkal is the consort of the moon god Sin/Śaḥr, while Nusk (if not also Shamash) is their son. From the letter published by Parpola (1985) it is clear that Nerab (cuneiform evidence points to a vocalization, *Nēreb*) was administratively dependent on Harran, where the same holy family was worshiped. Theophoric names from cuneiform tablets from Nerab of more recent date (c. 560–520 BCE; Dhorme, 1928; Oelsner, 1989, pp. 68–69, 76) indicate the longevity of the cult of this holy family in Nerab.

[*See also* Aramaic Language and Literature; Imperial Aramaic; *and the biography of Clermont-Ganneau.*]

BIBLIOGRAPHY

Clermont-Ganneau, Charles S. "Le stèles araméennes de Neîrab." *Études d'Archéologie Orientale* 2 (1895): 182–223. See with Clermont-Ganneau (1897).

Clermont-Ganneau, Charles S. *Album d'antiquités orientales: Recueil de monuments inédits ou peu connus.* Paris, 1897. With Clermont-Ganneau (1895), the *editio princeps* of the Nerab stelae. Serious study should begin with the photographic plates, which are still the best published, especially for Nerab I. These are more readily available, although reduced and somewhat poorly reproduced, in Driver (1976, pl. 59.1–2) below.

Dhorme, Paul. "Les tablettes babyloniennes de Neirab." *Revue d'Assyriologie* 25.2 (1928): 53–82.

Driver, Godfrey R. *Semitic Writing: From Pictograph to Alphabet.* 3d ed. London, 1976.

Fitzmyer, Joseph A., and Stephen A. Kaufman. *An Aramaic Bibliography,* part 1, *Old, Official, and Biblical Aramaic.* Baltimore and London, 1992. The fullest bibliography on the Nerab inscriptions.

Gadd, C. J. "The Harran Inscriptions of Nabonidus." *Anatolian Studies* 8 (1958): 35–92, pls. 1–16.

Gevirtz, Stanley. "West-Semitic Curses and the Problem of the Origins of Hebrew Law." *Vetus Testamentum* 11 (1961): 137–158.

Gibson, John C. L. *Textbook of Syrian Semitic Inscriptions,* vol. 2, *Aramaic Inscriptions, Including Inscriptions in the Dialect of Zenjirli.* Oxford, 1975. The most up-to-date treatment in English, with useful philological notes, in spite of their brevity (see pp. 93–98). Should be read critically.

Kaufman, Stephen A. "Si'gabbar, Priest of Sahr in Nerab." *Journal of the American Oriental Society* 90 (1970): 270–271.

Naveh, Joseph. "The Development of the Aramaic Script." *Proceedings of the Israel Academy of Sciences and Humanities* 5 (1970): 21–43.

Oelsner, Joachim. "Weitere Bemerkungen zu den Neirab-Urkunden." *Altorientalische Forschungen* 16 (1989): 68–77.

Parpola, Simo. "Si'gabbar of Nerab Resurrected." *Orientalia Lovaniensia Periodica* 16 (1985): 272–275.

Pritchard, James B., ed. *The Ancient Near East in Pictures Relating to the Old Testament.* 2d ed. Princeton, 1969. See plates 280 and 635. Relatively good photographic plates, especially for Nerab II (no. 635); more accessible than Clermont-Ganneau.

Tawil, Hayim. "Some Literary Elements in the Opening Sections of the Hada, Zākir, and the Nērab II Inscriptions in the Light of East and West Semitic Royal Inscriptions." *Orientalia* 43 (1974): 40–65.

DOUGLAS M. GROPP

NEṢṢANA, site located in the western Negev desert, 52 km (32 mi.) southwest of Beersheba (30°53′ N, 34°26′ E). Founded by Nabateans in the Hellenistic period, Neṣṣana was occupied until the Early Arab period. The modern village of Auja al-Hafir is located on the site of the ancient town. It is west of Wadi Ḥafir, below the acropolis where the remains described below are located. The H. Dunscombe Colt expedition excavated the site for two seasons in the 1930s under the auspices of the British School of Archaeology in Jerusalem. Dan Urman (1990–1991) resumed excavations in 1987, on behalf of the Israel Antiquities Authority.

When Neṣṣana was first inhabited is unclear. The earliest remains date to the third century BCE, when Nabateans settled this region of the Negev. Finds from this period include coins from Egypt and Judea (Judah) and imported Hellenistic pottery. The date and function of the earliest building (27 × 25 m) are difficult to determine because in the Byzantine period the North Church was built in the same location. Colt thought the earliest building was a Hellenistic fortress because it had thick walls and towers. Avraham Negev (1993) believes that the walls and towers were Byzantine renovations and suggests that it may have been a Nabatean temple, built between 30 BCE and 60 CE. In the same period, a large staircase was built up to the acropolis.

There is no evidence of new building activity and only a few small finds between 60 and 200 CE. It is possible that the site was abandoned for part of this period. It was occupied after the late third century: a fortress (85 × 35 m) was built adjacent to the south side of the Nabatean temple. It had rooms along the western wall, and, later, rooms were added along the eastern wall. It was probably one of several forts built by Diocletian and Constantine to form a regional defense system in the fourth century. Local troops manned the fort until their unit was disbanded; the building subsequently became part of a monastery.

Not long after the fort was built, a Christian church complex was erected on the foundations of the Nabatean temple. The complex consisted of the church, a courtyard, rooms south of the church, and an atrium to the east of the church. The church is a narrow, three-aisled basilica (19 × 10.7 m). It had a marble floor with opus sectile inlays. West of the nave was a baptistery, and north of it was a chapel. The nave was entered through its south wall, which led into a narrow courtyard. On the south side of the courtyard are several rooms, two of which functioned as a martyrion (a burial chamber with inscriptions to different saints). East of the courtyard and the basilica was an atrium that was connected to the old monumental staircase, the entrance to the complex. Numerous papyri were found in the martyrion, including literary and nonliterary texts. The literary papyri include fragments from classical authors and religious texts. The nonliterary texts are legal documents, such as contracts and receipts or church and military documents. They are written in Greek and Arabic and are dated to between 512 and 689.

In about 601, a second church was built on a hill southwest of the Roman fortress. It, too, was a three-aisled basilica (20.8 × 14.1 m). On the south side of the nave was a smaller chapel (6.22 × 13.2 m), and west of the nave was an atrium. The entire complex was built of well-dressed stone and paved. Neṣṣana flourished after the Islamic conquest until the eighth century. The reasons for its decline are uncertain.

[*See also* Judah; Nabateans; *and* Negev.]

BIBLIOGRAPHY

Casson, Lionel, and Ernest L. Hettich, eds. *Excavations at Nessana,* vol. 2, *Literary Papyri.* Princeton, 1950.

Colt, H. Dunscombe, ed. *Excavations at Nessana.* Vol. 1. Princeton, 1962.

Kraemer, C. J., ed. *Excavations at Nessana,* vol. 3, *Non-Literary Papyri.* Princeton, 1958. This and the volumes above comprise the final report for the 1935–1937 Colt excavations. Volume 1 describes the site's architecture and history and catalogs various finds (glass, coins, lithics, pottery, etc.). The second and third volumes describe the papyri found at Nessana.

Mayerson, Philip. "*P. Ness.* 58 and Two *Vaticinia ex Eventu* in Hebrew." *Zeitschrift für Papyrologie und Epigraphik* 77 (1989): 283–286. Discusses Nessana after the Islamic conquest and how the Umayyad government's policies affected the town.

Negev, Avraham. "Nessana." In *The New Encyclopedia of Archaeological Excavations in the Holy Land,* vol. 3, pp. 1145–1149. Jerusalem and New York, 1993. Excellent summary of excavations at Nessana; overturns some of Colt's theories by using more recent archaeological data and comparing Nessana to other Nabatean sites.

Urman, Dan. "Tel Nessana: A Meeting Place of Cultures during the Byzantine Period." *Bulletin of the Anglo-Israel Archaeological Society* 10 (1990–1991): 103–104. Brief summary of a lecture describing excavations at Nessana (1987–1991); mentions areas excavated by Colt and some new excavations in the lower city.

Adam Lynd-Porter

NEUTRON ACTIVATION ANALYSIS. The chemical composition, or "fingerprint," of an object can be determined by trace- and major-element analysis. The method, neutron activation analysis (NAA), measures the quantities of a large number of constituent elements from only a small sample of an object (typically 50–100 mg). NAA's widest application in archaeology has been in determining the chemical composition of ceramics in order to establish place of origin. NAA has also been applied with great success to obsidian, flint, glass, jade, marble, and basalt. By applying statistical tests to the composition of a collection of samples, it is possible to determine if the samples come from the same or a different source. It is also possible to determine where an artifact originated by matching its chemical composition to that characterizing a particular site.

However, because the methods employed in ceramic production can change the composition of the clay (e.g., if temper is added or clays are mixed) and because the chemical reference compositions characterizing different pottery-production sites may not be available, tracking the sources of ancient pottery is a complicated task. Reference compositions are usually not based on clay analysis but on the chemical analysis of ceramics that can be unequivocally assigned to a specific site or region. The composition of the ceramic reflects the composition of the clay plus whatever else the potter added to the clay. Wasters are ideal for establishing local compositions. Kiln and *tabun* ceramic linings, mud bricks, footbaths, and loom weights can serve as reference materials to establish a local chemical profile. Ceramic chemical compositions that persist over long time periods at a given site and that represent different types of pottery can also serve as reference groups. The use of ceramic rather than clay compositions in NAA is also preferred because the composition of a given clay bed may not be uniform over a wide area and because it usually is not known where ancient potters got their clay. The availability of chemical reference compositions is a technical problem that is gradually being overcome by judicially selected analysis and interlaboratory calibrations. One of the advantages of NAA over other analytical techniques is that NAA laboratories can be intercalibrated very precisely.

A fairly simple way to uncover similarity between chemical compositions, and hence commonality of origin, is to do a regression analysis, in which a constant relationship between two chemical compositions is sought. If a constant factor is found that connects every element of one composition to every element of the other, the two represent the same clay source, diluted to different degrees. Considering dilution is a common but critical factor in chemical analyses of pottery.

In order to determine the place of manufacture of a collection of ceramic objects sampled, the chemical fingerprint of the clay sources or ceramic compositions at various sites across a wide area is needed. Without such reference groups, NAA, coupled with statistical analysis, can only tell whether the objects measured came from one or more sources—although this information is valuable in itself.

NAA provides precision and accuracy for a large number of elements; the method uses instruments (no chemical preparation of the sample is required; hence, I[nstrumental]NAA is often used in tests in place of NAA); many element abundances are measured simultaneously; measurements can be automated; errors of measurement can be precisely determined; and large numbers of samples can be measured in relatively short time round the clock with little human attendance.

[*See also* Analytical Techniques.]

BIBLIOGRAPHY

Perlman, I., and F. Asaro. "Pottery Analysis by Neutron Activation Analysis." *Archaeometry* 11 (1969): 21–52.

Yellin, Joseph, I. Perlman, F. Asaro, H. V. Michel, and D. F. Mosier. "Comparison of Neutron Activation Analysis from the Lawrence Berkeley Laboratory and the Hebrew University." *Archaeometry* 20 (1978): 95–100.

Yellin, Joseph, and A. M. Maier. "Origin of the Picotrial Krater from the 'Mycenaean' Tomb at Tel Dan." *Archaeometry* 34 (1992): 31–36.

Zorn, Jeffrey, Joseph Yellin, and J. Hays. "The M(W)SH Stamp Impressions and the Neo-Babylonian Period." *Journal of the Israel Exploration Society* 44 (1994): 161–183.

Joseph Yellin

NEUVILLE, RENÉ (1899–1952), prehistorian considered, together with Dorothy Garrod and Alfred Rust, to be one of the founders of modern Near Eastern prehistory. Born in Gibraltar, where his father was a diplomat, Neuville was sent to Jerusalem in 1926 as a chancellor of the French general consulate. While in that post (1926–1937), his interest in prehistory emerged under the influence of Father Alexis Mallon when he became involved in Mallon's Chalcolithic excavations for the Pontifical Biblical Institute in Jerusalem at Umm Qaṭafa in the Judean Desert and at Teleilat el-Ghassul.

His own research concentrated on the Paleolithic sites of the Judean Desert and on the Qafzeh cave, near Nazareth. Among the Judean sites at which he worked are Umm Qaṭafa, where Acheulean industries were uncovered; Abu Sif, with a then new kind of Middle Paleolithic assemblage; and ʿErq el-Aḥmar and el-Khiam, with unique stratifications of Upper Paleolithic, Epipaleolithic, and Neolithic layers. Qafzeh cave is well known for the association of modern humans with Middle Paleolithic industries and is of interest because of the presence of the early Upper Paleolithic at the top of the sequence.

As early as 1934, Neuville proposed a first synthesis of the prehistory of Palestine. Using both his results and those from the Carmel caves, he was able to draw a sketch of human occupation in Palestine. [*See* Carmel Caves.] Drawing from the knowledge he had acquired in Europe as a guide, but identifying some of the main specifics of the local tradition, he subdivided the Upper Paleolithic into six phases, avoiding European nomenclature. This work of the 1930s still underlies scholarly interpretations sixty years later.

Neuville left Jerusalem in 1937 and spent several years in Spain and North Africa. Returning to Palestine in 1946, he prepared a monograph (1951) on his work in the Judean Desert. Through their work Neuville, Garrod, and Rust developed the teaching of Jacques de Morgan, according to whom the biblical record was of no value in understanding the prehistory of the Near East. Neuville was a pioneer in considering Near Eastern prehistory in the context of the worldwide study of the oldest developments of human life and in incorporating Near Eastern materials into the general framework of Quaternary research.

[*See also* Judean Desert Caves; Teleilat el-Ghassul; *and the biographies of Garrod and Mallon.*]

BIBLIOGRAPHY

Neuville, René. "Le préhistorique de Palestine." *Revue Biblique* 43 (1934): 237–259.

Neuville, René. *Le Paléolithique et le Mésolithique du désert de Judée.* Archives de l'Institut de Paléontologie Humaine, Mémoire 24. Paris, 1951.

FRANÇOIS R. VALLA

NEVALI ÇORI, prehistoric settlement site below the village of Kantara Köy (now Gülusağı), in the Hilvan district of the province of Şanlı Urfa, Turkey (37°60′ N, 38°70′ E). Since 1992 it has been covered by the Atatürk Reservoir. Settlement was on a 90-meter-long and 40-meter-wide terrace below the Yangıntepe foothills, 490 m above sea level on the right side of the Kantara Çayı, 3 km (2 mi.) from the southeast bank of the Euphrates River in the foothills south of the Taurus.

Nevalı Çori was discovered in 1980 during a systematic survey carried out by Hans Georg Gebel as part of excavations at Lidar Höyük, 9 km (7 mi.) away. It was excavated in 1983, 1985–1987, and 1989–1991 by the University of Heidelberg, under the direction of Harald Hauptmann, in cooperation with the Archaeological Museum of Şanlı Urfa. The aim of the excavations was to investigate the earliest occupation of the settlement, which is dated to the Pre-Pottery Neolithic B (PPNB; 8800–7600 BCE), the beginning of agriculture and the domestication of animals. [*See* Agriculture.]

Stone cist graves in a small cemetery date from the Roman period. The Early Bronze Age IB level (c. 3000–2700 BCE) contained a terraced limestone building. Pits with copper slag and crucibles were evidence of metallurgic activities. Twenty-three stone cist and pithos graves belong to this period as well. [*See* Burial Techniques.] On the basis of the plain simple ware and reserved-slip ware typically found in such burials in North Syria, this settlement is contemporary with Hassek Höyük 0–2, Kurban Höyük VB and VA–B, Noršuntepe XXVI–XXV, and ʿAmuq G. [*See* Grave Goods; ʿAmuq.]

A limestone wall surrounding an open area below the limestone hilltop is to be dated to the Middle Chalcolithic Halaf culture of the second half of the sixth millennium. Along its southern length, it consists of a 13-meter-long double wall with a towerlike round building at each end. A small round structure just northeast of the enclosure contained the skeleton of a seated burial. Good parallels for the monochrome and painted ceramics can be found in the Middle Euphrates area at Kurban Höyük VIII, Cavı Tarlasi, and Tell Damisliya on the Middle Euphrates, and in ʿAmuq D. The site's special significance, however, is in its Early–Middle PPNB settlement, which in the Taurus and its piedmont are represented by Cafer Höyük near Malatya and Çayönü, north of Diyarbakir. [*See* Çayönü.] The core settlement (Nevalı Çori I) contains five building phases, 2 m thick that, for the most part, was investigated (see below). The opposite, west side of the valley was also settled (Nevalı Çori II); however, it consisted of only two building phases.

The basic construction type for the twenty-three limestone and mud-mortar buildings is a freestanding, long rectangle with regular inner divisions and subfloor channels. This building type, characteristic of levels I–V, has a direct correspondence at Çayönü in the Intermediate level.

Level I. In the lowest level (I) at Nevalı Çori, two channels under a house (no. 21 A) floor ran along its long axis. Outside of the house were cooking areas and roasting pits lined with gravel, as at Cafer Höyük and Çayönü. Only wall fragments remain of a "cult building." [*See* Cult.]

Existing carbon-14 dates give a calibrated age of between 8400 and 8100 BCE for this level, making it contemporary with Abu Hureyra 2A, Mureybet IV A, and the older levels at Çayönü in the Early PPNB. [*See* Mureybet.] The stone-implement industry (consisting of flint), in which the bipolar striking technique dominates, supports this dating. The two largest groups of implements found are projectile points, including tanged points of the Byblos type (also known from Bouqras, Jericho, and Ugarit), and harvest implements (i.e., blades with silicate luster). [*See* Bouqras; Jericho; Ugarit.] These indicate an economy based on hunting and the already developed agriculture (see above). Gazelle were especially prized as game animals—along with red deer, fallow deer, and wild boar—while sheep and goats were kept as domestic animals. [*See* Sheep and Goats.] There were plantings of einkorn and emmer (*Triticum boeoticum* and *monococcum* as well as *Triticum dicoccoides* and *dicoccum*); barley (*Hordeum spontaneum [distichon]);* legumes such as lentils (*Lens culinaris);* peas (*Pisum sativum);* and other pulses. The food supply was supplemented by gathering pistachios, almonds, grapes, and wild grasses and bearded wheats (*Aegilops squarosa* or *speltoide*). [*See* Cereals.]

Level II. In level II three buildings were situated next to each other (nos. 12, 21B, 26). The remaining buildings (nos. 16, 22, 25) and a sacred building in the west were set off by a ditch leading from the slope. Along the slope a wall formed the settlement boundary with Yangıntepe. The largest house (no. 26) was 19 m long and 6.5 m wide. The building's 16.10-meter-long main portion (toward the northeast) was a long rectangle with eight rooms arranged in two regular rows. The adjoining main building had its entrance on the side facing the Kantara valley. The outer walls were .50 m thick and the inner walls .40 m thick. The construction, which encompassed five building stages, corresponds to the typical schema at Nevalı Çori: the foundation platform, composed of large stone blocks, consisted of six rectangular strips with spaces (0.25–0.30 m) between them. The spaces were covered with stone slabs to produce subfloor channels. The outer walls and then the rooms were set above this continuous foundation platform, which was made even with stone ballast. The floor was covered with a layer of gravel, and it and the stone walls were plastered with mud. The channels, which run through the platform, are left open on the outside, and so provided ventilation or cooling. The exterior of the house was surrounded by a "bench" consisting of one layer of stone. Posts were set along the long sides to support the roof.

The successor to the oldest cult building was well preserved. Its rectangular outline (13.9–13.5 m to a side) covered a surface of 188 sq m. The surrounding walls, still partially preserved to a height of up to 2.8 m, consisted of layers of undressed stone covered with plaster. Inside, a stone bench was positioned in front of the walls on three sides; eleven monolithic pillars with T-shaped capitals were set into the bench. The entrance, flanked by two pillars, lay in the southwest; in the southeast wall there was a niche for a cult statue. The floor was made from terrazzo. Stone sculptures representing birds and human/animal hybrids belong to this building.

Level III. The settlement showed its most lavish con-

NEVALI ÇORI. *Building 3, view from the northeast.* (Archäologisches Museum Şanliurfa)

struction in level III. In the southeast, four houses (nos. 3, 2, 6, 7) were in parallel alignment. House 2 (16 × 6.8 m) and house 7 (14 × 6.10 m) show the same construction: a foundation platform of rectangular strips (eight and nine of them, respectively) with subfloor channels running through them (seven and eight of them, respectively). An open area separated these houses from those with a different orientation in the west and the latest sacred building erected on the spot of previous ones. The settlement was again closed off with a boundary wall toward the slope. Most of the houses contain up to nine small rooms arranged in three rows and seem to have been storehouses; house 6, however, based on its division into large rooms and its furnishings, can be interpreted as a residence and workshop for the manufacture of stone implements and sculpture.

The cult building was set directly into its underlying predecessor from level II, so that its area was reduced to 155 sq m. On the inside a stone bench covered with monolithic stone slabs was set in front of the walls, except on the entrance side. Ten pillars were inserted between the slabs and an additional two pillars were placed at the entrance. The inside of the room, with two 3-meter-high sculptured pillars, was again outfitted with a terrazzo floor, as in the terrazzo building at Çayönü. A small niche for a cult statue was cut in the rear wall opposite the entrance.

Levels IV–V. Several buildings arranged in parallel rows belong to level IV, among them house 4 (12 × 8 m). A break in the continuity of settlement becomes apparent with the most recent level (V). Only one 10-×-6-meter house (no. 1) survives from level V, and it lacks the previously characteristic channels. The division of space—four equally large rooms with a diagonal area in front of them—corresponds to buildings from the cell building phase at Çayönü.

In addition to skeletons from "contracted-position" burials, deposits of skulls and partial burials were also found in the houses, generally below the floors. They provide evidence for the skull cult, or ancestor worship, practiced in this period. Monumental stone buildings outfitted with life-sized limestone figures provide, for the first time, an idea of Early Neolithic worship. A clean-shaven head with a snake coiling itself like a braid, as well as a human torso, must have belonged to a male figure. In addition, there is a sculpture of a bird in flight and one of a hybrid creature with the body of a standing bird with a stylized human head. A composite figure shows two female figures crouching back to back surmounted by a bird. It and another monumental female head were part of a carved column reminiscent of a totem pole. In the world of ideas, these symbol-laden images anticipate the later wall art at Çatal Höyük; however, in their uniqueness they go far beyond the usual ideas of Neolithic communities in the Near East. [*See* Wall Paintings.]

NEVALI ÇORI. *Limestone bird sculpture.* (Archäologisches Museum Şanliurfa)

In addition to the large statues, a stone bowl with a relief on its exterior of two human figures framing a turtle (representing fertility) and a limestone plate with an engraved hunting scene are especially fine. The small limestone sculptures include naturalistic and stylized human heads and representations of panthers, lions, wild boars, wild horses, bears, and vultures. There are female and male figures in sun-dried and fired clay, as well as polished-stone objects: axes, clubs, arm rings, and beads with single and multiple holes of the older bar form and the later butterfly form. The advanced technical level at the site is documented by a copper bead—evidence of a preliminary stage of early metallurgy (as at Çayönü, Tell Maghzaliyeh, Tell Ramad, and Aşıklı Höyük).

Settlement Differentiation. Nevalı Çori and neighboring settlements provide a differentiated picture of Early Neolithic forms of organization in the southern Taurus piedmont. The settlements had different subsistence economies, which were already highly specialized because of specific environmental conditions. On the Euphrates plain there was agriculture and fishing, and in the fertile alluvial land of the Harran plain (e.g., Gürçütepe) there was gazelle hunting as well. [*See* Fishing; Hunting.] On the limestone hilltops of the steppe, an additional settlement type appeared, as at Göbekli Ziyaret Tepe, in which flint outcroppings were used to produce implements, and the easily worked limestone promoted the manufacture of small figures and large sculptures. In this settlement system, Nevalı Çori may have functioned as a central site, where a central cult was located, tools and objects of religious significance were produced, and provisions stored. Its organization and coherence as a larger settlement strongly suggest such a role.

BIBLIOGRAPHY

Hauptmann, Harald. "Nevalı Çori." *Anatolian Studies* 34 (1984): 228; 37 (1987): 206–207.

Hauptmann, Harald. "Nevalı Çori: Architektur." *Anatolica* 15 (1988): 99–110.

Hauptmann, Harald. "Nevalı Çori: Eine Siedlung des akeramischen Neolithikums am mittleren Euphrat." *Nürnberger Blätter zur Archäologie* 8 (1991–1992): 15–33.
Hauptmann, Harald. "Ein Kultgebäude in Nevalı Çori." In *Between the Rivers and over the Mountains: Archaeologica Anatolica et Mesopotamica, Alba Palmieri Dedicata,* edited by Marcella Frangipane et al., pp. 37–69. Rome, 1993.
Hauptmann, Harald. "Frühneolithische Steingebäude in Südwestasien." In *The Megalithic Phenomenon: Recent Research and Ethno-Archaeological Approaches,* edited by Karl W. Beinhauer et al. Mannheim, 1996.
Mellink, Machteld J. "Nevalı Çori." *American Journal of Archaeology* 88 (1984): 449; 91 (1987): 10; 92 (1988): 104; 93 (1989): 107; 94 (1990): 127; 95 (1991): 126–128; 96 (1992): 123–124; 97 (1993): 108–109.
Schmidt, Klaus. "Nevalı Çori: Zum Typenspektrum der Silexindustrie und der übrigen Kleinfunde." *Anatolica* 15 (1988): 161–201.
Schmidt, Klaus. "The Nevalı Çori Industry: Status of Research." In *Neolithic Chipped Stone Industries of the Fertile Crescent,* edited by Hans G. Gebel and Stefan Kozłowski, pp. 239–252. Studies in Early Near Eastern Production, Subsistence, and Environment, 1. Berlin, 1994.
Schmidt, Klaus. "Nevalı Çori: Chronology and Instrasite Distribution of Lithic Tool Classes. Preliminary Results." In *Neolithic Chipped Stone Industries of the Fertile Crescent, and Contemporary Taxa in Adjacent Regions,* edited by Stefan K. Kozłowski and Hans G. Gebel. Studies in Early Near Eastern Production, Subsistence, and Environment, 3. Berlin, in press.

HARALD HAUPTMANN

Translated from German by Susan I. Schiedel

NEW ARCHAEOLOGY. Originally used by Joseph Caldwell in 1959 to describe the increasing archaeological interest in North America in ecology, settlement patterns, and cultural process (Caldwell, 1959), "New Archaeology" entered the archaeological vernacular in 1962 with the publication of Lewis Binford's "Archaeology as Anthropology" (Binford, 1962). In that landmark article Binford argued that archaeology should be understood as having the same goals as anthropology: the recovery and explanation of patterns of similarity and difference in human cultural behavior. In the 1970s and 1980s, the term became largely synonymous with Processual Archaeology. The interests of the New Archaeology were generally paralleled in England in the work of David Clarke (1968). Many of the same criticisms of the cultural-historical paradigm, and suggestions for a new approach, had been voiced by Walter W. Taylor in his prescient, but neglected 1948 book *A Study of Archaeology* (1948; see generally Trigger, 1989).

The New Archaeology sought to escape historical particularism and address issues of broad comparative and anthropological interest, including subsistence, land use, settlement patterns, demography, and technology. It thus incorporated many of the interests of the cultural ecology approach that had emerged in the 1950s, particularly under the influence of Julian Steward (see especially Steward, 1955). The New Archaeology also incorporated the materialist approach of Leslie White, which saw culture as technological, economic, social, and ideological subsystems determined by the levels of technology and energy capture (White, 1949). These two positions were partially reconciled by the neo-evolutionary cultural anthropologists, such as Elman Service and Morton Fried (Service, 1962; Fried, 1967), whose evolutionary schemes (bands, tribes, chiefdoms, and states) and egalitarian, rank, and stratified societies gave archaeologists fixed typologies with which to theorize and categorize their data. While ahistorical or even antihistorical in practice (Patterson, 1990), New Archaeology therefore had significant interest in social organization and change—which proved especially influential in the emergence of debates over the origins of the state. Discussions over the causes and nature of social evolution, including the origins of the state, had been almost completely ignored by Syro-Palestinian archaeology.

Among the concerns of the New Archaeology were a more rigorous scientific approach to archaeological method, including explicit research design and the use of statistics and computers, sampling strategies, and floral and faunal data. Among the techniques that came into use were flotation of soil samples to recover botanical remains, analysis of animal bones to understand stock raising and utilization patterns, and computers to execute multivariate statistical analyses, especially cluster and regression analyses and tests of significance. An emphasis on explicit research design, which set out the goals and methods of a particular project, was one achievement of the period, though the concept was frequently influenced by a unique epistemological orientation.

The New Archaeology was concerned with more explicit archaeological theory based on scientific reasoning situated broadly within the logical positivist approach. The hypothetical-deductive reasoning espoused by Carl Hempel was most influential. This view held that the only way that scientific explanation could be verified was through the formulation and testing of falsifiable hypotheses (see especially Watson et al., 1971). In this manner archaeologists could generate "covering laws" or "nomothetic paradigms" that would supposedly represent proven patterns of human development and behavior. While possessing an apparent clarity, the hypothetical-deductive approach does not reflect the way "science" is actually done—nor does it account for the inherent limitations, and variability, of archaeological data. The statistical-relevance approach outlined by Wesley and Merrilee Salmon (Salmon, 1982), which accepts a preponderance of affirmative evidence within a contingent context of discovery and analysis as supporting an explanation, more accurately reflects scientific and archaeological reasoning.

Defined as a science, the New Archaeology drew freely from concepts and methods developed in other social sciences, such as economics and political science. The introduction of General Systems Theory, developed originally in evolutionary biology, and systems engineering gave archaeology a highly formalized series of concepts with which to explain social structure and change. Negative and positive feedback had the effects of either maintaining a steady state or bringing about change within a system. Decision-making theories developed originally in management science were also applied to explain how change was formulated and effected in human organization. The New Archaeology generally assumed optimizing and maximizing behavior based on least-effort and least-cost principles, which to an extent rendered past decision makers into protocapitalist businessmen. All these approaches deliberately compartmentalized aspects of the past and negated the role of the individual and of human agency and free will in favor of systems of terms and explanatory frameworks that appeared scientific and potentially quantifiable (see Moore, 1983). The generalizing and rationalizing bases of the New Archaeology attempted to situate archaeology within those sciences relevant to society.

Though originally a marginal or fringe approach centered, to a large extent, around Binford and his students, by the late 1960s and 1970s the New Archaeology had become the conventional mainstream, both in terms of method and theory. By the late 1970s and 1980s, however, the approach per se had been surpassed by other developments, particularly in the areas of theory and epistemology. The emphasis on the material, rather than on the symbolic and ideological, and the social and cultural, rather than the individual, was eventually seen as incomplete and antihumanist. The shortcomings of the hypothetical-deductive approach were also highlighted, though the heightened interest in the philosophy and epistemology of archaeology was a positive outgrowth of the New Archaeology's search for clarity and rigor (Redman, 1991; Watson, 1991; cf. Wylie, 1989). While the theoretical or philosophical underpinnings of the New Archaeology (empiricism and objectivity, scientism, and hypothetical-deductive reasoning) have fallen away, the most significant and enduring legacies have been heightened concern for careful research design, data recovery, and analysis using scientific techniques. In the 1980s and 1990s, American and European archaeologies have to an extent retained rationalist and empiricist practices while hotly debating a variety of theoretical approaches—including some that are explicitly relativistic, antiscientific, and political in orientation (e.g., Shanks and Tilley, 1987a, 1987b; cf. Watson, 1990).

In terms of theory, the New Archaeology, as with previous and subsequent trends in anthropological archaeology, had little impact on Syro-Palestinian archaeology. Outside of the study of prehistory there was little interest in the comparative study of human behavior and societies, and little understanding of how to gain insights through the integration of a variety of archaeological data. In Near Eastern archaeology as a whole, however, the New Archaeology had a significant influence in the 1960s and 1970s on research in Iraq and Iran. Particularly important to the discussion were Robert Braidwood and Robert Adams of the University of Chicago. Braidwood was vehemently opposed to the rhetoric of the New Archaeology, which he viewed as a humorless cult (Braidwood, 1971). His approach was nevertheless congruent with the scientific and problem orientation of the New Archaeology. Adams was heavily influenced by the evolutionary approach of Julian H. Steward and the settlement-pattern techniques that had been used in New World archaeology. He has also been an acute and influential commentator on trends in archaeology and an advocate of bridging the humanities and social sciences (Adams, 1968, 1983). Adams's work on Mesopotamian settlement patterns and social evolution provides some of the best examples of New Archaeology-influenced research in the Near East (e.g., Adams, 1968, 1981). New Archaeology orientation is also reflected in the work of Kent Flannery, Frank Hole, and others on early village life and the origins of food production (Hole et al., 1969) and that of Gregory Johnson on settlement patterns and the rise of the state in southwestern Iran (Johnson, 1973). With the exception of Adams, however, the influence of the New Archaeology has been largely restricted to prehistory and the early historical periods in the Near East.

The positive impact of the New Archaeology on archaeology in the Levant was methodological. A variety of new techniques was eventually incorporated into standard practice, such as animal bone archaeology, paleobotany, geology, and a regional orientation. The most intense internal debates, however, remained parochial and emphasized local issues of philosophy and practice. These included whether archaeology in the southern Levant should be construed as "biblical" or "Syro-Palestinian," whether excavations should emphasize broad horizontal exposures or vertical depth, the relative stratigraphic control involved in these strategies, and the usefulness of section drawings (see Aharoni, 1973; Dever, 1973; 1981). The American Syro-Palestinian archaeology position stressed independence and professionalization over the traditional secondary position of archaeology to biblical and historical studies; it sought to connect with the main stream of anthropological archaeology. Israeli archaeology has tended to absorb methodological innovations and eschew overt theoretical orientations (see generally Bar-Yosef and Mazar, 1982; Glock, 1985; 1986; Broshi, 1987). Jordanian archaeology remains oriented toward cultural resource management issues, and its research agenda is dominated by foreign archaeologists. The development of a local Jordanian school of archaeology continues, with predictable nationalistic and legitimizing orientations. British, French, and German approaches to archaeology in the southern Levant do not appear to have been significantly influenced by the New Archaeology.

Several examples trace the incorporation of new methods into American Syro-Palestinian archaeology (see generally

Dever, 1985; 1988). The excavations at Gezer, in Israel, in the mid- to late 1960s employed a field geologist and also used the then-new flotation method to recover botanical materials. The project also hosted a British team that conducted a site catchment analysis, examining regional pedology and vegetation. The project, however, placed more emphasis on integrating the American orientation toward detailed ceramic typology with the then also new Kenyon-Wheeler, or balk-to-locus, approach to digging (Dever and Lance, 1978). The Gezer final reports emphasize ceramics and stratigraphy rather than an integrated view of the site and its setting through time.

The Gezer project was also the progenitor of a number of projects in the 1970s and 1980s that were executed by former staff members. These include Be'er Resisim, Tell el-Ḥesi, Meiron, Tel Ḥalif, Tel Miqne, and Ashkelon in Israel; Idalion on Cyprus; and the Wadi Tumilat project in Egypt. Each of these projects has also sought explicitly to incorporate new methodologies into its repertoire and has been, to greater and lesser degrees, self-conscious of developments in archaeological theory. These developments have come in part as a response to the institutionalization of the New Archaeology materialist orientation in the United States—and by accompanying changes in the political economy of archaeology. The latter include the need to demonstrate legitimacy through explicit research designs in order to receive funding from agencies such as the National Science Foundation, the Wenner-Gren Foundation for Anthropological Research, and the National Geographic Society (Yellen and Greene, 1985).

The most self-conscious emulation of the New Archaeology appears in the Tell el-Ḥesi project (Worrell, 1989; Rose, 1989). Two of the innovations the project attempted to integrate were an explicit research design, with strong ecological and philosophical components, and a multidisciplinary staff. The staff included a geologist, paleoethnobotanist, and cultural and physical anthropologists. In reality, however, the project had difficulty translating abstract concepts into practical goals for fieldwork. Testing ecological hypotheses became exercises in collecting more and diverse information, rather than specific and constrained investigations. Interest in "lifeways," such as food and craft production, became merely the rationale for careful digging. While admirable in its multidisciplinary orientation, and for its early experimentation with computers, the project was ultimately unable to integrate goals and methods. The project fell prey to lack of direction, and to the formidable challenges of excavating and eventually publishing a large multicomponent tell site. The example demonstrates the difficulty of applying or modifying a methodological program and scientific paradigm originated by and for archaeologists studying small, single-component sites. It further points out inadequacies in the New Archaeology paradigm itself: that of structuring research designs to address highly abstract questions of "evolution" and "process" for the purposes of defining "laws." The Tell el-Ḥesi project has begun to publish its results in a highly traditional fashion, emphasizing stratigraphy, architecture, and material culture.

The most successful examples of the incorporation of methodological advances into archaeological practice are the Bab edh-Dhraʿ and Shiqmim projects, both late prehistoric sites. The Bab edh-Dhraʿ project, for example, examines, with a highly developed multidisciplinary emphasis, an Early Bronze Age site in Jordan, on the southeast plain of the Dead Sea. It includes a physical-anthropological component that has contributed greatly toward understanding the health, nutrition, and demography of the population buried in the site's extensive cemeteries (Ortner, 1979). The geological investigations have led to an understanding of the site and of environmental change, and the ceramic analyses have been strongly emphasized (Beynon et al., 1986; Schaub, 1987). A number of neighboring sites has also been examined, strengthening the project's regional orientation (Coogan, 1984). [*See* Bab edh-Dhraʿ.]

The Shiqmim project examines a Chalcolithic site in Israel's northern Negev desert. The site's actual excavation was preceded by an extensive regional archaeological survey that illuminated Shiqmim's importance and larger context. In the excavation of the site and its associated cemetery particular attention has been paid to questions of subsistence in a semiarid environment, craft production, especially of copper and chipped stone tools, and technological and spatial analyses of the ceramic assemblage. The result has been a number of summary and specialized reports that present and integrate the variety of data (Levy and Menahem, 1987; Levy and Shalev, 1989). While broadly conceived with ecological concerns, the Shiqmim project has concentrated on the practical matters of excavating, and analyzing and publishing data, rather than on self-conscious philosophical discussions. [*See* Shiqmim.]

The most successful example of a project addressing a multicomponent site and its surrounding regions with an explicit theoretical orientation is the Ḥesban project. While the original rationale was to investigate what was hoped would be a biblical site, research was structured around the food-systems concept developed by Øystein LaBianca that broadly addresses changing patterns of food production over time (LaBianca, 1986). This entailed a strong regional orientation, including archaeological and environmental surveys (LaBianca and Lacelle, 1986). The project was also concerned with modern evidence for subsistence and social organization and therefore conducted ethnoarchaeological investigations of surrounding villages and bedouin encampments (LaBianca, 1990). The Madaba Plains Project has continued to creatively combine a variety of approaches within the framework of the food-systems concept (Geraty et al., 1989). [*See* Ḥesban.]

While informed by advances in methodology, Syro-Palestinian archaeology remains firmly rooted in its cultural-historical approach. The discipline stands at a crossroads:

whether to return to a particularist and parochial orientation or to move into the archaeological mainstream, in terms of integrating and contributing to the development of method and theory. The experience of the New Archaeology points out both the advantages and pitfalls of the latter direction.

[*See also* Biblical Archaeology; Environmental Archaeology; Ideology and Archaeology; Settlement Patterns; *and* Statistical Applications. *In addition, many of the sites mentioned are the subject of independent entries.*]

BIBLIOGRAPHY

Adams, Robert McC. "Archaeological Research Strategies: Past and Present." *Science* 160 (1968): 1187–1192.

Adams, Robert McC. *The Evolution of Urban Society: Early Mesopotamia and Prehistoric Mexico.* Chicago, 1971.

Adams, Robert McC. *Heartland of Cities: Surveys of Ancient Settlement and Land Use on the Central Floodplain of the Euphrates.* Chicago, 1981.

Adams, Robert McC. "Natural Science and Social Science Paradigms in Near Eastern Prehistory." In *The Hilly Flanks and Beyond: Essays on the Prehistory of Southwestern Asia Presented to Robert J. Braidwood,* edited by T. Cuyler Young, Jr., et al., pp. 369–374. Studies in Ancient Oriental Civilization, no. 36. Chicago, 1983.

Aharoni, Yohanan. "Remarks on the Israeli Method of Excavation." *Eretz-Israel* 11 (1973): 48*–53*.

Bar-Yosef, Ofer, and Amihai Mazar. "Israeli Archaeology." *World Archaeology* 13 (1982): 310–325.

Beynon, Diane, et al. "Tempering Types and Sources for Early Bronze Age Ceramics from Bab edh-Dhraʿ and Numeira, Jordan." *Journal of Field Archaeology* 13 (1986): 297–305.

Binford, Lewis R. "Archaeology as Anthropology." *American Antiquity* 28 (1962): 217–225.

Braidwood, Robert J. "Distinguished Lecture 1971." *American Anthropological Association Annual Report 1971,* pp. 43–52. Washington, D.C., 1971.

Broshi, Magen. "Religion, Ideology, and Politics and Their Impact on Palestinian Archaeology." *Israel Museum Journal* 6 (1987): 17–32.

Caldwell, Joseph R. "The New American Archaeology." *Science* 129 (1959): 303–307.

Clarke, David L. *Analytical Archaeology.* London, 1968. 2d ed. New York, 1978.

Coogan, Michael David. "Numeira 1981." *Bulletin of the American Schools of Oriental Research,* no. 255 (1984): 75–81.

Dever, William G. "Two Approaches to Archaeological Method: The Architectural and the Stratigraphic." *Eretz-Israel* 11 (1973): 1*–8*.

Dever, William G., and H. Darrell Lance, eds. *A Manual of Field Excavation: Handbook for Field Archaeologists.* Cincinnati, 1978.

Dever, William G. "The Impact of the 'New Archaeology' on Syro-Palestinian Archaeology." *Bulletin of the American Schools of Oriental Research,* no. 242 (1981): 15–29.

Dever, William G. "Syro-Palestinian and Biblical Archaeology." In *The Hebrew Bible and Its Modern Interpreters,* edited by Douglas A. Knight and Gene M. Tucker, pp. 31–74. Chico, Calif., 1985.

Dever, William G. "Impact of the 'New Archaeology.'" In *Benchmarks in Time and Culture: An Introduction to Palestinian Archaeology Dedicated to Joseph A. Callaway,* edited by Joel F. Drinkard et al., pp. 337–352. Atlanta, 1988.

Fried, Morton H. *The Evolution of Political Society: An Essay in Political Anthropology.* New York, 1967.

Geraty, Lawrence T., et al. "An Overview of Goals, Methods, and Findings." In *Madaba Plains Project: The 1984 Season at Tell el-ʿUmeiri and Vicinity and Subsequent Studies,* edited by Lawrence T. Geraty et al., pp. 3–19. Berrien Springs, Mich., 1989.

Glock, Albert E. "Tradition and Change in Two Archaeologies." *American Antiquity* 50 (1985): 464–477.

Glock, Albert E. "Biblical Archaeology: An Emerging Discipline." In *The Archaeology of Jordan and Other Studies Presented to Siegfried H. Horn,* edited by Lawrence T. Geraty and Larry G. Herr, pp. 85–101. Berrien Springs, Mich., 1986.

Hole, Frank A., et al., eds. *Prehistory and Human Ecology on the Deh Luran Plain: An Early Village Sequence from Khuzistan, Iran.* University of Michigan, Memoirs of the Museum of Anthropology, no. 1. Ann Arbor, 1969.

Johnson, Gregory A. *Local Exchange and Early State Development in Southwestern Iran.* University of Michigan, Museum of Anthropology, Anthropological Paper, no. 51. Ann Arbor, 1973.

LaBianca, Øystein S. "The Diachronic Study of Animal Exploitation at Hesban: The Evolution of a Research Project." In *The Archaeology of Jordan and Other Studies Presented to Siegfried H. Horn,* edited by Lawrence T. Geraty and Larry G. Herr, pp. 167–181. Berrien Springs, Mich., 1986.

LaBianca, Øystein S., and Larry Lacelle, eds. *Hesban,* vol. 2, *Environmental Foundations: Studies of Climatical, Geological, Hydrological, and Phytological Conditions in Hesban and Vicinity.* Berrien Springs, Mich., 1986.

LaBianca, Øystein S. *Hesban,* vol. 1, *Sedentarization and Nomadization: Food System Cycles at Hesban and Vicinity in Transjordan.* Berrien Springs, Mich., 1990.

Levy, Thomas E., and N. Menahem. "The Ceramic Industry at Shiqmim: Typological and Spatial Considerations." In *Shiqmim,* vol. 1, *Studies Concerning Chalcolithic Societies in the Northern Negev Desert, Israel, 1982–1984,* edited by Thomas E. Levy, pp. 333–355. British Archaeological Reports, International Series, no. 356. Oxford, 1987.

Levy, Thomas E., and Sariel Shalev. "Prehistoric Metalworking in the Southern Levant: Archaeometallurgical and Social Perspectives." *World Archaeology* 20 (1989): 352–372.

Moore, James A. "The Trouble with Know-It-Alls: Information as a Social and Ecological Resource." In *Archaeological Hammers and Theories,* edited by James A. Moore and Arthur S. Keene, pp. 173–192. New York, 1983.

Ortner, Donald J. "Disease and Mortality in the Early Bronze Age People of Bab edh-Dhraʿ, Jordan." *American Journal of Physical Anthropology* 51 (1979): 589–597.

Patterson, Thomas C. "Some Theoretical Tensions within and between the Processual and Postprocessual Archaeologies." *Journal of Anthropological Archaeology* 9 (1990): 189–200.

Redman, Charles L. "Distinguished Lecture in Archaeology: In Defense of the Seventies—The Adolescence of New Archaeology." *American Anthropologist* 93 (1991): 295–307.

Rose, G. D. "The Methodology of the New Archaeology and Its Influence on the Joint Expedition to Tell el-Hesi." In *Tell el-Hesi: The Site and the Expedition,* edited by Bruce T. Dahlberg and Kevin G. O'Connell, pp. 72–87. Winona Lake, Ind., 1989.

Salmon, Merrilee H. *Philosophy and Archaeology.* New York, 1982.

Service, Elman R. *Primitive Social Organization: An Evolutionary Perspective.* New York, 1962.

Shanks, Michael, and Christopher Tilly. *Re-Constructing Archaeology: Theory and Practice.* Cambridge, 1987a.

Shanks, Michael, and Christopher Tilly. *Social Theory and Archaeology.* Cambridge, 1987b.

Steward, Julian H. *Theory of Culture Change: The Methodology of Multilinear Evolution.* Urbana, Ill., 1955.

Taylor, Walter W. *A Study of Archeology* (1948). Carbondale, Ill., 1983.

Trigger, Bruce G. *A History of Archaeological Thought.* Cambridge, 1989.

Watson, Patty Jo, et al. *Explanation in Archaeology: An Explicitly Scientific Approach.* New York, 1971.

Watson, Richard A. "Ozymandias, King of Kings: Postprocessual Rad-

ical Archaeology as Critique." *American Antiquity* 55 (1990): 673–689.
Watson, Richard A. "What the New Archaeology Has Accomplished." *Current Anthropology* 32 (1991): 275–291.
White, Leslie. *The Science of Culture.* New York, 1949.
Worrell, J. E. "The Evolution of a Holistic Investigation: Phase One of the Joint Expedition to Tell el-Hesi." In *Tell el-Hesi: The Site and the Expedition,* edited by Bruce T. Dahlberg and Kevin G. O'Connell, pp. 68–71. Winona Lake, Ind., 1989.
Wylie, Alison. "The Interpretive Dilemma." In *Critical Traditions in Contemporary Archaeology,* edited by Valerie Pinsky and Alison Wylie, pp. 18–27. Cambridge, 1989.
Yellen, John E., and Mary W. Greene. "Archaeology and the National Science Foundation." *American Antiquity* 50 (1985): 332–341.

ALEXANDER H. JOFFE

NEW TESTAMENT. *See* Biblical Literature, *article on* New Testament.

NEWTON, CHARLES THOMAS (1816–1894), the most influential classical archaeologist in nineteenth-century England. Trained in classics at Oxford University, Newton described himself as a historian rather than an archaeologist. His scholarship was based in the tradition of Johann Joachim Winckelmann, on a thorough knowledge of Latin and Greek texts. The stress Newton placed on the identification of mythological subjects in Greek art prefigured the modern interest in iconography.

Newton entered the British Museum's Department of Antiquities in 1840 and left in 1852 for diplomatic service, mainly in the Aegean area. He was, however, able to devote time to excavations for the British Museum: his work at Kalymnos (1854–1855) produced a large corpus of inscriptions, but his main archaeological achievement was the 1856–1857 expedition to Halikarnassos, Knidos, and Branchidai (Miletus). Newton was supported by a naval vessel and a contingent of Royal Engineers, the latter commanded by Robert Murdoch Smith, who produced plans of the excavations and was the first to locate the actual site of the Mausoleum at Halikarnassos. Newton's excavation methods were primitive, and he did not maintain a daily list of finds, but he was almost the first excavator to employ a photographer.

Newton returned to the British Museum in 1861 as the first keeper of the new Department of Greek and Roman Antiquities. His tenure was marked by spectacular acquisitions, including several major collections and the fruits of excavations conducted by others (e.g., Alfred Biliotti on Rhodes; Robert Murdoch Smith and Edwin Augustus Porcher at Cyrene; Richard Popplewell Pullan at Priene; and John Turtle Wood at Ephesus). The museum's tradition of scholarship was much enhanced by his publications.

Newton also contributed to the advance of classical archaeology in England. He was the first Yates Professor of Art and Archaeology at University College London (1880–1888), and he was active in the founding of the Society for the Promotion of Hellenic Studies (1879), the Egypt Exploration Society (1882), and the British School at Athens (1885).

[*See also* Halikarnassos; Miletus.]

BIBLIOGRAPHY

Works by Newton

Newton, Charles Thomas. *A History of Discoveries at Halicarnassus, Cnidus, and Branchidae.* 2 vols. in 3. London, 1862–1863. Detailed report on Newton's major expedition. Long out of print and rare outside specialized libraries.
Newton, Charles Thomas. *Travels and Discoveries in the Levant.* 2 vols. London, 1865.
Newton, Charles Thomas. *Essays on Art and Archaeology.* London, 1880. Collection of lectures and reprinted articles, illustrating the range of Newton's scholarly interests.
Newton, Charles Thomas, ed. *The Collection of Ancient Greek Inscriptions in the British Museum.* Vols. 1–3. Oxford, 1874–1890.

Works on Newton

Cook, B. F. "Sir Charles Newton, K. C. B." Commemorative lecture on the centenary of Newton's death, given at the Eighteenth British Museum Classical Colloquium, 7–9 December 1994. Sculpture and Sculptors of the Dodecanese and Caria. Publication forthcoming in the Proceedings of the Colloquium, which will also include a detailed bibliography of Newton's works.
Dictionary of National Biography, vol. 22, pp. 1096–1097. London, 1901. Short biography, with references to obituaries. A revised edition of the dictionary is in preparation.
Jebb, R. C. "Sir C. T. Newton." *Journal of Hellenic Studies* 14 (1894): xlix–liv. Contemporary appreciation of Newton.
Jenkins, Ian. *Archaeologists and Aesthetes in the Sculpture Galleries of the British Museum, 1800–1939.* London, 1992. Includes an authoritative modern assessment of Newton's work as excavator and curator, with a bibliography.

B. F. COOK

NICOLAOU, KYRIAKOS (1918–1981), one of the foremost Cypriot archaeologists. Having earned his doctorate from the University of Göteborg (his dissertation was published in 1976), Nicolaou spent most of his working life in the Department of Antiquities of Cyprus. He was archaeological officer between 1957 and 1961, assistant curator of the Cyprus Museum between 1961 and 1964, and curator from 1964 until his retirement in 1978. As curator he was also responsible for the running of all state museums on the island. Nicolaou reorganized the stores and the displays of the Cyprus Museum in Nicosia, and he founded district museums in Famagusta, Larnaca, Limassol, and Paphos, as well as a number of local museums.

Nicolaou surveyed and excavated throughout the island. His main surveys covered a large part of the Kyrenia district and the Yialias River valley. Of his many excavations, the most important were those of the Hellenistic sanctuary of Aphrodite at Morphou, the Late Bronze Age necropoleis of Deneia, Angastina, and Kazaphani, as well as the Geometric-period necropoleis of Marion, which also includes classical sections, and Kythraia. It is, however, for his work in Nea-Paphos that he is most famous. There, apart from a number of important Hellenistic and Roman tombs, he excavated the Greco-Roman odeion and the house of Dionysos with its famous mosaic floors. He also started the excavation of the gymnasium and the Asklepieion, and in general brought Nea-Paphos, the Hellenistic and Roman capital of the island, to the foreground of archaeological research. He published many articles on his discoveries and on Cypriot archaeology in general; and he lectured widely in Europe and the United States. He was a member of many learned societies and was honored by several foreign organizations.

[*See also* Paphos.]

BIBLIOGRAPHY

Nicolaou, I. "Nicolaou, Kyriakos." In *Megale Kypriake Enkyklopaideia* (The Large Cypriot Encyclopaedia), vol. 10, pp. 252–253. Leukosia, Cyprus, 1984–.

Nicolaou, I. "Kyriakos Nicolaou: Biographical Note and List of Publications" (in Greek). *Archaeologia Cypria* 2 (1990): 3–8.

Nicolaou, Kyriakos. "The Topography of Nea Paphos." In *Mélanges offerts à Kazimierz Michałowski,* pp. 561–601. Warsaw, 1966. For many years the only topographical study of the Hellenistic and Roman capital of Cyprus.

Nicolaou, Kyriakos. "Archaeological News from Cyprus." *American Journal of Archaeology* 71 (1967): 399–406; 84 (1980): 63–73. Nicolaou's reports from Cyprus appear more or less annually in the journal from 1966 to 1978.

Nicolaou, Kyriakos. *Nea Paphos: An Archaeological Guide.* Nicosia, 1967. Rev. ed. Nicosia, 1978.

Nicolaou, Kyriakos. *Ancient Monuments of Cyprus.* Nicosia, 1968.

Nicolaou, Kyriakos. *The Historical Topography of Kition.* Göteborg, 1976.

DEMETRIOS MICHAELIDES

NILE. Because ancient Egypt rarely received rainfall, the size and the reliability of the Nile River's annual flooding was the basis for the Egyptians' stable agrarian economy. The inhabitants lived almost exclusively within the river valley and the Delta. They distinguished between these two regions and incorporated them into their world view; the valley was known as Upper Egypt and the Delta as Lower Egypt. The Nile Valley is bounded by the Eastern Desert and the Western or Libyan deserts. These remote regions were beyond the Nile's influence and therefore considered wild uncivilized areas.

Flowing northward from Central Africa's Lake Victoria (White Nile) and the Ethiopian plateau (Blue Nile and Atbara), the Nile entered Egypt at its southernmost point, Elephantine (modern Aswan) at the First Cataract. This 8.5-kilometer-long cataract—five others occur farther upriver in Nubia—consists of a narrowing in the valley made by the granite basement rock that has breached the ground surface. The First Cataract served as a natural barrier preventing unauthorized entrance into Egypt from the south. Farther downriver, the Nile cuts through sandstone until it reaches Gebel el-Silsila where the bedrock changes to softer limestone, allowing a wider floodplain.

The Nile Delta begins north of Memphis (near modern Cairo), formed in part from silt deposited as the river's speed decreases. In antiquity, several branches of the Nile dissected the Delta before emptying into the Mediterranean Sea; only the Rosetta and Damietta waterways survive.

The most important event in the Nile's regime was the annual inundation. Unfailingly each year in late June, the Nile began to rise as large volumes of water from heavy rains in East Africa drained into its system. The initial flood stage coincided with the heliacal rising of the star Sirius, whose reappearance in the sky marked the beginning of the new year. In a matter of weeks, the river overflowed its banks. The waters slowly spread across the floodplain, often to the edge of the low desert margins. The flood reached its apex after two months, although its duration and height varied depending on the site of the flood's measurement. This inundation soaked the soil, leaving behind a layer of rich silt while also replenishing the marshes in which the Egyptians fished and fowled. Gradually the river returned to its banks, and by late October crops could be planted in the sodden basin areas.

Variations in the amount of water entering Egypt determined the flood's height, and significant fluctuations seriously effected the economy. Lower water levels brought diminished crop yields, and an unusually high flood threatened villages, canals, animals, and fields. When the filling of the Aswan Dam began in 1964, this annual inundation ceased.

The river connected the inhabitants of ancient Egypt. They thought of north and south in relation to the river: to travel north (downstream) was written with a hieroglyph of a boat with a steering oar and folded sail, and traveling south (upstream) was identified as a boat in full sail. The valley's topography and the river's cycle impeded overland travel except for short distances, which were covered on paths following irrigation canals.

Given the river's significance to Egyptian life, it is not surprising that Nilotic imagery pervades the culture's mythology. The annual inundation, for example, was seen as a symbol for the creation of the universe. Several deities were associated with the Nile. Hapy symbolized its life-giving properties. The river was also under the protection of Khnum, lord of the First Cataract region, because the inundation was believed to spring from caverns located beneath Elephantine.

[*See also* Delta; Egypt.]

BIBLIOGRAPHY

Abu al-ʿIzz, M. S. *Landforms of Egypt.* Translated by Yusuf A. Fayid. Cairo, 1971. Detailed but quite usable book with a focus on the Nile River and its valley. The bibliography lists only works in English relating to the geology of the Nile Valley within Egypt's modern borders.

Baines, John, and Jaromir Málek. *Atlas of Ancient Egypt.* New York, 1980. Discusses the geology of the river and its valley and its importance to Egyptian culture (see chapter 1).

Butzer, Karl W. *Early Hydraulic Civilization in Egypt: A Study in Cultural Ecology.* Chicago, 1976. Attempts to relate the river and the agricultural cycle to other aspects of ancient Egyptian culture, principally focusing on location of settlements. Remains an interesting if dated work.

James, T. G. H. *Egypt: The Living Past.* London, 1992. Includes a discussion of the adaptation of ancient and modern Egyptian life to the Nile Valley and river's yearly cycle (see pp. 8–74).

Kees, Hermann. *Ancient Egypt: A Cultural Topography.* Translated by Ian F. D. Morrow. London, 1961. Includes a very readable discussion of the importance of the Nile River in ancient Egyptian culture (see chapter 3).

DIANA CRAIG PATCH

NIMRIN, TELL (Tell esh-Shuna; Tell Shuna South), site located in the Jordan Valley, approximately 12 km (7 mi.) north of the Dead Sea and 16 km (10 mi.) east of Jericho (31°54′00″ N, 35°37′30″ E; map reference 2094 × 1451).

F. M. Abel, William Foxwell Albright, Claude R. Conder, Alexis Mallon, and Selah Merrill were among the nineteenth- and early twentieth-century explorers and archaeologists to visit and comment on the site. Nelson Glueck was the first to conduct a systematic archaeological survey there, early in 1943 (Glueck, 1943, pp. 7–26). He described Tell Nimrin as a "natural mound" and noted that he had collected "large numbers of Roman through mediaeval Arabic sherds," but found no evidence of pre-Roman ceramics (Glueck, 1951, pp. 367, 368).

Like other Western explorers before him, Glueck was especially interested in biblical associations. He suggested that the biblical "Waters of Nimrîn" (*Is.* 15:6; *Jer.* 48:34) might refer to the Wadi Nimrin, otherwise known as Wadi Shaʿib. He thought that Tell Nimrin itself undoubtedly, but mistakenly, preserved the ancient biblical name Beth-Nimrah found in *Numbers* 32:36 and *Joshua* 13:27 (Glueck, 1943, p. 11; 1951, pp. 367–368). Lacking evidence for Bronze and Iron Age occupation, Glueck followed Albright and Mallon in identifying nearby Tell Bleibil with biblical Beth-Nimrah, arguing that the name had likely migrated to Tell Nimrin during the Hellenistic period (Glueck, 1951, pp. 368, 371). Glueck was confident that Tell Nimrin was the site referred to as Bethnamaris by Eusebius and Jerome in the fourth century CE (Glueck, 1943, p. 11). The site is also mentioned in the Byzantine synagogue mosaic at Reḥob in the Beth-Shean Valley (Naveh, 1978, p. 81, l. 16).

Glueck's conclusions were generally accepted as authoritative until the site was reexamined in 1976 in a surface survey that recovered pottery dating from the Early Bronze–Middle Bronze, Iron I, Iron II, Umayyad, ʿAbbasid, Ayyubid/Mamluk, and Ottoman periods (Ibrahim et al., 1988, p. 192). In 1980, a sixth-century Byzantine church was excavated on the western slope of the mound by the Jordanian Department of Antiquities (Piccirillo, 1982).

The first full-scale excavation of Tell Nimrin was conducted by James W. Flanagan and David W. McCreery under the auspices of Case Western Reserve University during the summer of 1989. Khair N. Yassine joined the project as a codirector in 1990. The project's two seasons were organized as a salvage operations designed to clarify the occupational sequence and assess the importance of the site before modern development projects created further damage. An intensive surface survey of the mound was followed by the excavation of ten 5-meter squares. With the help of a road cut that exposed a section of the tell from top to base, the squares were strategically placed in order to test each level of the site. Approximately 12 m of stratigraphy, accumulated in a four-thousand-year occupational sequence, were documented.

The results of field readings of pottery from the surface survey and excavation, attested the site's occupational history. First settled near the end of EB IV (c. 2000 BCE), Nimrin was occupied throughout the MB period. Nearly 6 m of MB stratification are preserved, including monumental walls constructed in late MB II. During the Late Bronze and Early Iron I, the site was unoccupied (for approximately five hundred years, c. 1500–1000 BCE). Settlement resumed in Late Iron I/Early Iron II, when tenth-century structures were built immediately above the late MB II stratum. At least part of the site was destroyed by fire in the late tenth century BCE.

The Iron II occupational evidence is preserved in mudbrick walls, living surfaces, and almost 4 m of other stratified material. Late ninth-century and seventh-century destruction levels were encountered, but their extent was not determined in the first season of excavation. The site was continuously occupied from the Persian through the Mamluk periods. Most of the post-Hellenistic material has been bulldozed from the top of the tell, but classical through late Islamic strata are well preserved on the western slope.

Contrary to Glueck's conclusions, excavation has demonstrated that the site is a true tell, rather than a natural mound, and that occupation during the MB and Iron II periods was extensive. In light of this new evidence, there is no reason to prefer Tell Bleibil over Tell Nimrin as the site of biblical Beth-Nimrah. However, Tell Nimrin's long history of occupation and its rich deposits overshadow its relative insignificance as a biblical site. The site has yielded paleoagronomic remains rich enough to indicate that it and the region were fertile and productive zones in the MB period. Other material and textual artifacts suggest, as R. H. Dornemann (1983) hypothesized, that the Jordan Valley and Tell Nimrin enjoyed a simple but rich and independent life in the midst of surrounding centers of power.

BIBLIOGRAPHY

Albright, William Foxwell. "The Jordan Valley in the Bronze Age." *Annual of the American Schools of Oriental Research* 6 (1926): 13–74.

Dornemann, Rudolph Henry. *The Archaeology of the Transjordan.* Milwaukee, 1983.

Flanagan, James W., and David W. McCreery. "First Preliminary Report of the 1989 Tell Nimrin Project." *Annual of the Department of Antiquities of Jordan* 34 (1990): 131–152.

Glueck, Nelson. "Some Ancient Towns in the Plains of Moab." *Bulletin of the American Schools of Oriental Research,* no. 91 (1943): 7–26.

Glueck, Nelson. *Explorations in Eastern Palestine.* Vol. 4. Annual of the American Schools of Oriental Research, 25/28. New Haven, 1951.

Ibrahim, Moʿawiyah, et al. "The East Jordan Valley Survey, 1976." In *Archaeology of Jordan: Essays and Reports,* edited by Khair Yassine, pp. 189–207. Amman, 1988.

Khouri, Rami G. "Tell Nimrin." In his *The Antiquities of the Jordan Rift Valley,* pp. 70–72. Amman, 1988.

Naveh, Joseph. *On Stone and Mosaic: The Aramaic Hebrew Inscriptions from Ancient Synagogues* (in Hebrew). Tel Aviv, 1978.

Piccirillo, Michele. "A Church at Shunat Nimrin." *Annual of the Department of Antiquities of Jordan* 26 (1982): 335–342.

JAMES W. FLANAGAN and DAVID W. MCCREERY

NIMRUD, site located in northern Iraq, on the east bank of the Tigris River, southeast of Mosul (36°06′ N, 43°19′ E). The site covers an area of about 360 hectares (889 acres) and consists of a walled enclosure with a Citadel in the southwest corner, on which there were many public buildings, and an arsenal, known as Fort Shalmaneser, in its southeast corner. There has been little excavation in the outer town. In Assyrian texts the city is known as Kalḫu (the biblical equivalent is Calah), first attested in the thirteenth century BCE. The modern name of Nimrud derives from an association with Nimrod, "the mighty hunter," whose legend is described (rather differently) in both the Bible (*Gn.* 10:8–12) and the Qur'an (21:52–69). The site's first excavator, A. H. Layard, originally thought it was Nineveh. It was not until 1853 that H. C. Rawlinson demonstrated that it was in fact Kalḫu.

Although Nimrud is mainly known as a Neo-Assyrian capital, the site was occupied from prehistoric times, as attested by Ḥalaf- and Ubaid-period sherds found on the surface. Layard found pottery vessels of incised Ninevite V ware, and W. K. Loftus discovered a stone cist grave in the southeast part of the Citadel dating to the mid-second millennium BCE or slightly earlier. M. E. L. Mallowan found evidence of Middle Assyrian occupation in the so-called 1950 Building on the Citadel and in private houses built against the town wall on the east side of the Citadel (TW 53). It was this time that Shalmaneser I (1273–1244 BCE) did some building at Nimrud; however, it was not until the reign of Ashurnasirpal II (883–859 BCE) that it became a royal capital. This king initiated a major construction program continued by some of his successors, including Shalmaneser III (858–824 BCE), Adad-Nirari III (810–783 BCE), and Tiglath-Pileser III (744–727 BCE). During the reign of Sargon (721–705 BCE) the royal capital was moved to Khorsabad, but Kalḫu remained an important provincial capital. Esarhaddon (680–669 BCE) undertook some further building work here. In 614–612 BCE, Nimrud, together with other Assyrian centers, was destroyed by the Medes; extensive traces of this destruction were found in the excavations. There is evidence for limited occupation in the post-Assyrian period, albeit of an impoverished kind. There are also slight traces of habitation in the Achaemenid period, supported by the observations of Xenophon, who passed the site (which he called Larissa) in 401 BCE. Remains of the Hellenistic period are more substantial, particularly in the southeast part of the Citadel, where a succession of settlements was excavated dating from about 240 to 140 BCE. This occupation may have continued into Parthian and Sasanian times. Thereafter, Nimrud remained for all intents and purposes, unoccupied.

The first recorded excavations at Nimrud were undertaken by G. P. Badger in 1844, but it was Layard who realized the site's true potential and whose name is firmly linked with it. He worked there from 1845 to 1847 and 1849 to 1851, supported first by Sir Stratford Canning and then by the trustees of the British Museum. He was helped by a young Chaldean Christian from Mosul, Hormuzd Rassam. The results were spectacular. In the Northwest palace of Ashurnasirpal II he excavated mainly in the state apartments to the south of the main entrance. Lack of funds prevented him from completely excavating many of the rooms; he contented himself with trenching round the walls. Nevertheless, he uncovered many stone relief slabs and a number of colossal stone gateway figures, some of which are now in the British Museum. Elsewhere on the site, Layard excavated in the Ninurta and Ishtar Šarrat-niphi temples, and the Central, South-East and South-West palaces. In front of the so-called Central Building he found the black obelisk of Shalmaneser III that shows the biblical king Jehu submitting to the Assyrian king and tribute being brought from various parts of the Near East. He even worked briefly around the Ziggurat and Fort Shalmaneser. It is difficult to overestimate the enormity of Layard's contribution, not only to what is known about Nimrud, but to Mesopotamian archaeology in general.

A complete plan of the city, which is still useful today, was produced by Captain Felix Jones of the Indian Navy in 1852. In 1854–1855 W. K. Loftus, working on behalf of the Assyrian Excavation Fund, excavated mainly in the Central Palace area, the South-East and South-West palaces, and the Nabu Temple. His most interesting results, however, were obtained in the Burnt Palace, where he found an important collection of ivories. He also discovered a grave dating from the early–mid-second millennium BCE. For the next eighteen years no serious archaeological work was done at Nimrud, but two large collections of sculptures were removed during this time and sent to Zurich and Paris. In 1873

NIMRUD. *Relief from Nimrud depicting a battle scene.* Musée du Louvre, Paris. (Alinari/Art Resource, NY)

the cuneiform scholar George Smith of the British Museum worked briefly at Nimrud, investigating various buildings on the Acropolis, but without achieving any significant results. Then, from 1877 to 1879, Hormuzd Rassam returned to Nimrud, also sent by the trustees of the British Museum. In addition to working in the Nabu Temple and the South-East and Central Palace areas, he discovered the Kidmuri Temple northeast of the North-West Palace.

After Rassam's departure, there was a lull in archaeological work at Nimrud until 1949 when M. E. L. (Sir Max) Mallowan resumed work on behalf of the British School of Archaeology in Iraq. This expedition worked at Nimrud until 1963—after 1958 under the direction of David Oates and in 1963 of Jeffrey Orchard. In the North-West Palace, the British School team excavated the domestic quarters to the south of passage P and cleared part of the Administrative Wing (ZT) on the north side. They also cleared out the wells in rooms AB and NN. Elsewhere on the Acropolis the British School expedition worked mainly in the Ninurta Temple, the 1950 Building, the Governor's Palace, the Nabu Temple, the Burnt Palace, and the South-East Palace. They also investigated houses abutting the town wall (TW53) and cleared a stretch of stone wall on the west side of the Acropolis. From 1958 onward, the building in the southeast corner of the city (Fort Shalmaneser) was the main focus of attention. This vast building's ground plan was established, and many of its chambers were cleared, producing extensive and varied collections of carved ivories.

From 1974 to 1976, a Polish team led by Janusz Meuszyński worked in the central part of the Nimrud Acropolis on what he termed the Central Building, probably a temple built by Ashurnasirpal II, and on the Central Palace of Tiglath-Pileser III. The Poles were followed, from 1987 to 1989, by an Italian team from the Centro Scavi, Turin, led by Paolo Fiorina. They completed a contour plan of the entire city and undertook a surface-sherd survey. Otherwise, their attention was focused on Fort Shalmaneser. They investigated the wall separating the fort compound from the rest of the city and its junction with the main city wall; they also excavated or reexcavated a number of storerooms in the southwest sector, particularly SW36 and SW37. They recovered a number of ivories, but outstanding among the finds from this area was a bronze and iron model of a turreted fortress on wheels. In 1989, a British Museum team, directed by John Curtis and Dominique Collon, returned to Nimrud and also worked in Fort Shalmaneser. They partially excavated room T20, finding a bronze horse harness and glazed bricks of Shalmaneser III with Aramaic signs and pictographic symbols on their unglazed surfaces. They also

NIMRUD. *Assyrian relief from the palace of Ashurnasirpal II.* Detail from Ashurnasirpal's siege of a city showing King Ashurnasirpal in royal progress. Dated to the seventh century BCE. Musée du Louvre, Paris. (Foto Marburg/Art Resource, NY)

found clear evidence of rebuilding activities, probably in the reign of Esarhaddon.

Meanwhile, the Iraq Department of Antiquities had begun restoration work at Nimrud in 1956; they continued the project in 1959–1960. Since 1969 the work has been carried out annually. The emphasis is on reexcavation and restoration, principally in the North-West Palace and the Nabu Temple. In 1975, the clearance of the well in room AJ, directed by Muyasser Sa'id, produced another spectacular collection of ivories. Even more remarkable discoveries were made in a series of four tombs excavated between spring 1988 and November 1990 by Muzahim Mahmud in the southern part of the North-West Palace. These tombs contained vessels in precious metal and an astonishing array of gold jewelry; the tombs seem to have been the graves of the consorts of a number of Assyrian kings.

Nimrud's Citadel was surrounded by its own mud-brick wall, which, on the west side, overlooking the Tigris floodplain, was faced with stone blocks (sometimes called the quay wall). The largest and most important building on the Citadel in the North-West Palace, built by Ashurnasirpal II and partly restored by several later kings. It measures about 200 m north–south, although its southern limit has not been established. In the center were state apartments lavishly decorated with sculptured stone slabs as well as painted plaster and glazed bricks. In several of the more important gateways were colossal stone figures of human-headed lions or bulls. The northern wing of the palace (ZT) held offices and storerooms, while the southern wing held private apartments and what may have been the harem. The more important finds from the palace include the so-called banquet stela of Ashurnasirpal II describing his conquests and building works at Nimrud and ending with a description of the banquet to celebrate the building of the palace. This was found in a recess near gate E. The excavation of room AB recovered a large collection of bronzes, including furniture ornaments and bowls decorated in Syrian and Phoenician style, and several interesting glass vessels, including a vase inscribed with the name of Sargon. Important finds also came from a number of the wells. In the well in room NN a collection of ivories was discovered that includes the two well-known heads of women popularly known as the Mona Lisa and the Ugly Sister and two ivory plaques with traces of gold overlay, each showing a lioness mauling an African. In the well in room AB were ivory and wood writing boards with wax-coated surfaces. More ivories were recovered from the well in room AJ, including pyxides, bowls, small human heads, and carved tusks.

The palace's south wing is notable for the discovery there of a series of rich graves, all apparently of high-ranking women. Beneath the floor of room DD, Mallowan had found a terra-cotta coffin with a female skeleton and the so-called Nimrud jewel, but Mahmud's recent discoveries overshadow this grave. He found four subterranean chambers with barrel-vaulted roofs, three of which held astonishing collections of jewelry. The first tomb, in room MM, contained a pottery sarcophagus and jewelry that included a gold fibula and chain attached to a stamp seal in a gold mount. The second tomb, in room 49, had various inscriptions mentioning Yabâ, Banîti, and Atalia, "queens" or "palace women" of Tiglath-Pileser III, Shalmaneser V (726–722 BCE), and Sargon, respectively. A stone coffin held at least two bodies and a vast array of grave goods, including gold bowls, earrings, and necklaces. A Phoenician-style gold bowl has embossed decoration showing boats in a papyrus thicket. The third tomb, in room 57, was originally the grave of Mulissu-mukannišat-Ninua, a queen of Ashurnasirpal II, but it had been reused. The original stone sarcophagus was empty, but badly preserved bones and an stunning variety of grave goods were found in three bronze coffins in the antechamber. The large number of gold objects included an intricate crown or headdress. The fourth tomb contained large numbers of glazed pottery and alabaster vessels.

NIMRUD. *Head of "Madonna" in ivory from Nimrud.* Dated to 720 BCE. Iraq Museum, Baghdad. (Scala/Art Resource, NY)

At the extreme northwest corner of the Citadel was the Ziggurat, and sandwiched between it and the North-West Palace was the Ninurta Temple, built by Ashurnasirpal II. At one entrance a pair of human-headed lions stood watch, while outside a second entrance a massive, round-topped stela of Ashurnasirpal II showed the king with symbols of the gods. Stone reliefs at these entrances show protective genies; one remarkable example shows a god battling with a monster that is a mixture of an eagle and a lion.

There were two other temples in this area, one dedicated to Ishtar Šarrat-niphi and the other to the Kidmurri. The former had colossal lions flanking the doorway; a magnificent limestone statue of Ashurnasirpal II standing on a red stone base was set up inside.

In the middle of the Citadel, among other important buildings, was the so-called Central Building and the Central Palace of Tiglath-Pileser III. Painted decoration and winged bulls were found here, as well as sculptured slabs, stacked and ready for reuse in the South-West Palace.

To the east of the Central Palace was the Governor's Palace, the residence of the governor of Kalḫu in the eighth century BCE. An important Archive of administrative tablets was found there. South of this building were the Burnt Palace and the Nabu Temple. The Burnt Palace was a ninth-century building that was subsequently rebuilt twice—the second time by Sargon, who may have used it as a royal residence. An important collection of ivories come from this palace (see above).

The Nabu Temple included shrines dedicated to Nabu and his consort Tashmetum and a reception suite. Ashurnasirpal claimed to have founded the building, but much of the construction work was done in the reign of Adad-Nirari III. A number of tablets were found here, including the "vassal treaties" of Esarhaddon. The temple held two pairs of statues of attendant gods, one colossal and one life-sized; inscriptions on the latter mention Adad-Nirari III. There was also a round-topped stela of Shamshi-Adad V (823–811 BCE), showing the king with symbols of gods. A number of incised ivory plaques in Assyrian style were found in this building.

The excavation of the two buildings at the extreme south end of the Citadel is incomplete. The South-West Palace was built by Esarhaddon and was decorated with reliefs of Ashurnasirpal II and Tiglath-Pileser III in secondary use. The so-called South-East Palace was apparently built by Shalmaneser III and later restored.

The building known as Fort Shalmaneser in the southeast corner of the city was a palace for reviewing troops *(ekal māšarti)* built by Shalmaneser III and restored by Esarhaddon. It is within a walled enclosure that covers about 30 hectares (74 acres). Later, stone walls with a postern gate in the south part were built by Esarhaddon. The building includes a block of state apartments (T) as well as storerooms and barracks grouped around courtyards. Outstanding finds include the throne-base of Shalmaneser III from throne room (T1). The sides are carved with scenes of tribute being brought to the king. A panel of painted and glazed bricks set above a doorway in courtyard T, which shows Shalmaneser III standing beneath a winged disk, within a framework of goats and floral motifs. In addition, important collections of smaller items have come from many of the rooms: ivories from rooms SW7, SW12, SW37, NW15, and NW21 and bronze furniture from room NE26. Tablets, including wine-ration lists, were found at various locations.

[*See also the biographies of Layard, Mallowan, and Rawlinson.*]

BIBLIOGRAPHY

In addition to the works listed below, readers may wish to consult various articles related to the topic, too numerous to list here, that appeared in the journal *Iraq* between vol. 12 (1950) and vol. 25 (1963).

Curtis, J. E., Dominique Collon, and A. R. Green. "British Museum Excavations at Nimrud and Balawat in 1989." *Iraq* 55 (1993): 1–37.
Dalley, Stephanie, and J. N. Postgate. *The Tablets from Fort Shalmaneser.* Cuneiform Texts from Nimrud, 3. London, 1984.
Herrmann, Georgina. *Ivories from Room SW37, Fort Shalmaneser.* Ivories from Nimrud, 4. London, 1986.
Herrmann, Georgina. *The Small Collections from Fort Shalmaneser.* Ivories from Nimrud, 5. London, 1992.
Layard, Austen H. *Discoveries in the Ruins of Nineveh and Babylon.* London, 1853.
Layard, Austen H. *Nineveh and Its Remains* (1849). New York, 1970.
Mallowan, M. E. L. *Nimrud and Its Remains.* 3 vols. London, 1966.
Mallowan, M. E. L., and L. G. Davies. *Ivories in Assyrian Style.* Ivories from Nimrud, 2. London, 1970.
Mallowan, M. E. L., and Georgina Herrmann. *Furniture from SW7, Fort Shalmaneser.* Ivories from Nimrud, 3. London, 1974.
Orchard, J. J. *Equestrian Bridle-harness Ornaments.* Ivories from Nimrud, 1.2. London, 1967.
Postgate, J. N., and J. E. Reade. "Kalḫu." In *Reallexikon der Assyriologie,* vol. 5, pp. 303–323. Berline, 1977–1980.
Postgate, J. N., ed. and trans. *The Governor's Palace and Archive.* Cuneiform Texts from Nimrud, 2. London, 1973.
Reade, J. E. "Nimrud." In *Fifty Years of Mesopotamian Discovery,* edited by J. E. Curtis, pp. 99–112. London, 1982.
Wilson, J. V. Kinnier. *The Nimrud Wine Lists.* Cuneiform Texts from Nimrud, 1. London, 1972.

John Curtis

NINA-SIRARA. *See* Girsu and Lagash.

NINEVEH, ancient Ninua, one of the noted sites of antiquity, situated on the east bank of the Tigris River, close to the confluence of the Tigris and the Khosr Rivers (36°24′ N, 44°08′ E). Distinguished by the tall mounds of Kuyunjik and Nebi Yunus and the remains of a roughly rectangular perimeter wall that is about 2 km wide (1 mi.) and 5 km (3 mi.) long, the visible ruins of Nineveh are currently invested on all sides by recent additions to the city of Mosul, in modern Iraq. While the core mound, known today as Kuyunjik, may have been occupied almost continuously from the seventh millennium down to early Islamic times (when the focus of settlement moved to the site of medieval Mosul on the opposite bank of the Tigris), Nineveh's reputation principally rests on its role as the last great capital of the Assyrian Empire. In particular, Nineveh's destruction at the hands of the Medes and Babylonians in 612 BCE still stands as a vivid paradigm for a sudden fall from unrivaled wealth and dominion.

Exploration and Excavation. The first European traveler to take note of the location of ancient Nineveh was Benjamin of Tudela, the Spanish traveler and rabbi, in the twelfth century. Others who commented on the site in succeeding centuries included the Danish scholar Carsten Niebuhr, whose visit took place in 1766. The earliest detailed examination of Nineveh is owed to Claudius James Rich, whose admirable map of the site was completed in 1820. Twenty-two years later, Paul-Émile Botta, the consul of France at Mosul, opened the first trenches on Kuyunjik with little success. Then, following a prior period of concentration on the Assyrian remains at Nimrud, Austen Henry Layard began his own excavations at Nineveh in 1846. [*See* Nimrud.] Before he left Nineveh in 1851 to take up a career in politics, Layard had revealed a good part of the plan of the Southwest Palace, "the palace without a rival" (Luckenbill, 1924, p. 96) of the redoubtable Sennacherib (704–681 BCE). Within this structure he revealed close to 3 km (2 mi.) of carved stone reliefs, including those depicting Sennacherib's spectacular siege and capture of the Judean city of Lachish. [*See* Lachish; *and the biographies of Botta and Layard.*]

Layard's work on behalf of the British Museum was subsequently taken up by Hormuzd Rassam, his resourceful assistant, beginning in 1852. Rassam succeeded in discovering the North Palace of Ashurbanipal, where he not only excavated sculptured slabs depicting memorable lion-hunt sequences, but also a substantial portion of the twenty-four

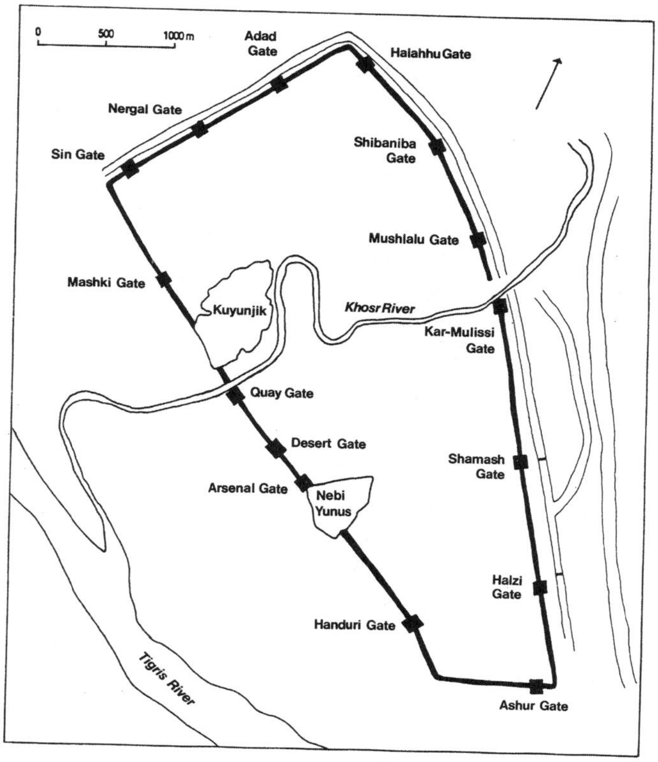

NINEVEH. *Plan of certain main elements of the city in the seventh century BCE.* The terrain outside the city wall was marked by the presence of substantial moats and ditches, especially to the east. (Courtesy D. Stronach)

thousand cuneiform tablets that make up the so-called Library of Ashurbanipal (an invaluable resource on ancient Mesopotamia, variously composed of archival documents, manuals, and cultic literary works). [*See* Cuneiform; Tablet; Libraries and Archives.] The year 1852 also saw the completion of a further exemplary survey of Nineveh (by the trained cartographer Felix Jones). It was, in addition, the approximate moment when it first became possible to affirm the long-suspected identity of the site on the basis of excavated cuneiform records. Among other excavators who worked at Nineveh in the latter part of the nineteenth century, it is impossible to pass over the name of the gifted cuneiform scholar, George Smith. In 1872 Smith electrified Victorian England by discovering the greater part of the Babylonian account of the Flood among the tablets excavated by Layard and Rassam. [*See* Babylonians; *and the biography of Smith.*] Charged with the task of finding the missing portions of the story, he effectively achieved this aim within days of reaching Nineveh in the spring of 1873. Tragically, however, he was to die of dysentery soon after the end of his 1876 season. He was no more than thirty-six years old.

Subsequent British excavators include R. Campbell Thompson, who was at Nineveh in 1904–1905 and from 1927–1932. While Campbell Thompson did much to explore the poorly preserved remains of both the Nabu temple and the adjacent Temple of Ishtar (where he discovered the magnificent copper head that has been variously ascribed to either Sargon of Akkad or Naram-Sin), he also elected to introduce a sounding through the deep prehistoric strata of Kuyunjik in the course of his final season. This last, pioneer endeavor was supervised by his assistant, M. E. L. Mallowan, whose account (Mallowan, 1933) duly provided the first available overview of the early pottery sequence in northern Mesopotamia. [*See the biography of Mallowan.*]

Each of the more recent excavations at Nineveh—beginning with those of the Iraqi Department of Antiquities and Heritage from the second half of the 1960s onward and ending with those of the University of California at Berkeley between 1987 and 1990—have been shaped, at least in part, by the rapid post-1960 growth of the city of Mosul. Expressly, it was the pressure posed by a series of new building projects that persuaded Tariq Madhloom of the Department of Antiquities to devote a good part of his own efforts between 1965 and 1971 to the task of precisely locating, and then restoring, critical portions of the walls and gates of Nineveh's Neo-Assyrian defenses. In a direct complement to Madhloom's work, one of the main concerns of the Berkeley team, led by David Stronach, was to learn more about the nature of Nineveh's extensive lower town, especially within its still largely undisturbed northern sector.

Early Nineveh. While little is yet known in any detail about Kuyunjik's very earliest phases of occupation, the site seems to have been closely related to innovative developments in southern Mesopotamia during the Uruk period (c.

4000–3000 BCE). There are also indications that the subsequent Ninevite-5 settlement (c. 3000–2500 BCE) was at least as large as any that had preceded it. However, the original, enduring fame of Nineveh stemmed from the repute of the city's time-honored diety, Ishtar of Nineveh. In an allusion, for example, to an event that had taken place five hundred years before his own reign, Shamshi-Adad I of Assyria (c. 1813–1781 BCE) boasted in an inscription that he was the first monarch to renovate the Temple of Ishtar "since Manishtushu, son of Sargon, king of Akkad." [*See* Assyrians.]

Later Nineveh. Beginning in the reign of Shalmaneser I (1273–1244 BCE), a number of Middle Assyrian, and then Neo-Assyrian, rulers chose to erect a royal residence on the high summit of Kuyunjik. Elsewhere, the flat ground directly to its north appears to have become the hub of a sizable lower town from at least the beginning of the first millennium BCE. The principal expansion of Nineveh is directly related, however, to a somewhat later sequence of events: to the ignominious death in 705 BCE of the father of Sennacherib, Sargon II, and to Sennacherib's subsequent decision to move the capital from Dur Sharrukin (Khorsabad)—Sargon's newly created and patently inauspicious seat of government—to the long-hallowed "eternal foundation" of Nineveh (Luckenbill, 1924, p. 94). [*See* Khorsabad.]

As can be gauged from Sennacherib's successive building inscriptions, the main axis of his palace eventually came to measure a remarkable 500 m in length. Among this structure's many "objects of astonishment" (to use Sennacherib's own phrase; see Luckenbill, 1924, p. 97) certain of its tall columns were supported by resplendent bronze lions, each cast in a striding but at the same time weight-bearing pose. The city as a whole was expanded to include an area of 750 ha (1,852 acres) and its imposing double walls came to cover a distance of some 12 km (7 mi.). While the massive inner mud-brick wall is likely to have been at least 25 m high, the less lofty outer wall would have presented a gleaming facade of finely dressed limestone masonry, capped by continuous stone crenellations. No fewer than fifteen city gates pierced this circuit. Of these, the Nergal Gate in the north wall was the most sumptuously appointed. Guarded by giant winged colossi, it stood on the course of a paved royal road that led southward to the palace mound of Kuyunjik. [*See* Palace.] At the same time, the northwestern portion of the lower town appears to have included both a crowded industrial quarter not far from the Sin Gate and, just inside the Mashki Gate (at a point closer to Kuyunjik), a more affluent district distinguished by spacious courtyard houses.

With the death of Sennacherib, the pace of construction slowed considerably. Esarhaddon (680–669 BCE) and Ashurbanipal (668–627 BCE) both continued to build on Tell Nebi Yunus, the second mound of Nineveh, where Sennacherib had already founded an imperial arsenal. However, much of this later work was never finished and, when it came to the construction of Ashurbanipal's extensive North Palace, toward the north end of Kuyunjik, it is perhaps telling that no attempt was made to replicate the 40-ton monolithic winged bulls of his grandfather's time. Conversely, the quality of at least a part of Ashurbanipal's relief sculpture, and most especially that depicting the great lion hunt (see above), can be ranked as unsurpassed in the history of Mesopotamian art. An informative relief from about 645 BCE, which shows a royal park watered by a tall aqueduct, also provides one of several indications of the keen delight that Sennacherib and his successors took in providing Nineveh and its environs with parks, gardens, and even nature reserves. It demonstrates as well the singular feats of engineering, including dam and aqueduct construction, that made such choice amenities possible. [*See* Aqueducts; Gardens, *article on* Gardens in Preclassical Times.] As has been recently pointed out, in fact, the true locale of the famed Hanging Gardens may not have been Babylon but, given the nature of the extant evidence, Assyrian Nineveh (Dalley, 1994).

Biblical References. Many of the biblical references made to Nineveh can be seen to reflect either changing historical circumstances, competing religious messages, or descriptive matter that ranges from the legendary to the real. In *Genesis* 10:11–12, Nineveh is listed as one of the major cities of Mesopotamia that owed its foundation to Nimrod,

NINEVEH. *Entrance to the recently excavated Halzi Gate.* Located at the south end of Nineveh's long eastern wall, this gate was narrowed to a width of two meters in anticipation of the final Median and Babylonian assault. The gateway was nonetheless forced and the bed of the roadway (beneath the horizontal scale) was strewn with the heaped remains of those killed in that constricted space. (Courtesy D. Stronach)

the great grandson of Noah. The erstwhile glory of Nineveh is perhaps best reflected, however, in the *Book of Jonah* (where, as an object of god's grace, the city is said to have been spared, not overthrown). In a reference to the exceptional size of Nineveh, it is said to have taken "three days' journey" to cross it (*Jon.* 3:3). This is known to be hyperbole and, on the evidence of the three-day period Jonah is said to have spent in the belly of the great fish, a formulaic use of the number 3 can be assumed. On the other hand, the ingathering of people and livestock that would certainly have occurred at the time of the siege of Nineveh could perhaps have brought the city's suddenly swollen population to the figure of "six score thousand persons" (together with "much cattle") that is specified in *Jonah* 4:11. Apart from the fact that Muslim tradition places the tomb of Jonah on Tell Nebi Yunus ("the mound of the prophet Jonah"), Jonah's connection with Nineveh is also recalled in *Matthew* 12:41 and *Luke* 11:30, 32. These last passages assert that the inhabitants of Nineveh, the "men of Nineveh" to whom Jonah had preached, would arise at the Last Judgment to condemn the generation of Jesus.

Other biblical references to Nineveh are of a more historical nature. These include two that allude to Sennacherib residing at Nineveh (*2 Kgs.* 19:36; *Is.* 37:37) and another that records his assassination by his sons at the same location (*2 Kgs.* 19:37). Of most interest, however, is the "vision of Nahum" in which the overthrow of Nineveh (at the command of, in this case, a vengeful and wrathful god) is "foretold." Despite having been written well after the event, most probably in the Achaemenid period, the *Book of Nahum* carries the impact of an eyewitness account of the city's terrible fall. To begin with, the forceful image of the "myriads of slain" and the "heaps of corpses" that resulted from the sack of "the bloody city" (*Na.* 3:1–3) can be said to have found an all-too-realistic counterpart in the outstretched, tangled skeletons that came to light during the recent excavations at the Halzi Gate (Stronach, 1992). In additions, an insistence on the key role that water was made to play in the events that accompanied Nineveh's destruction (*Na.* 2:6) is not only echoed in other sources (see below), but would seem to stem from a detailed knowledge of the physical nature of the city's devastation.

Other Literary References. The Babylonian Chronicle indicates that Nineveh fell in the high summer of 612 BCE following a siege of three months. The same source also relates that Nabopolassar (625–605 BCE), the victorious king of Babylon, held court in the palace at Nineveh before returning to his homeland with ashes collected from the ruins of the Assyrian capital. [*See* Babylon.] Herodotus is less informative. He refers to the march on Nineveh of Cyaxares, the king of Media (1.104); promises to relate in full the details of the fall of Nineveh (1.106); and, in the end, neglects to do so. According to Diodorus Siculus, writing in the late first century CE, Nineveh fell in the third year of a prolonged siege, when the Euphrates River rose in flood and breached the wall of the city (Diodorus 1.27.1–2). [*See* Euphrates.] In reality, however, neither the Tigris nor the Euphrates (invoked in obvious error) would ever have been in flood at the height of summer. Indeed, in following the details of Nahum's account, which mentions the opening of "the gates of the rivers," the dissolving of "the palace" (an expression best taken to refer to rather less-vaunted structures at the level of the plain), and a degree of flooding that turned Nineveh into "a lake" (*Na.* 2:6, 8), it is preferable to suppose that the various sources for such an inundation consisted of the waters of the Khosr (which could have been effectively undammed upstream and redammed within the limits of the city) and the discharge of a number of Nineveh's still-operative canals. In sum, Nineveh was not only overthrown, it was also afflicted, after its fall, with many of the almost ritual terms of destruction (e.g., flooding and the removal of ashes) that Sennacherib had imposed on Babylon seventy-seven years earlier. Yet, the city of Nineveh did rise again (if never to its previously exalted status), especially during the last few centuries BCE and the first centuries CE, when it is known that a limited Hellenistic occupation was followed by an interval when both the Parthians and the Romans left a definite imprint on the site.

NINEVEH. *Detail of a number of tangled skeletons on the partly cobbled roadway of the Halzi Gate.* Those cut down at this spot recall Nahum's image of Nineveh's "myriads of slain" (*Na.* 3:1–3). (Courtesy D. Stronach)

BIBLIOGRAPHY

Barnett, Richard D. *Sculptures from the North Palace of Ashurbanipal at Nineveh, 668–627 B.C.* London, 1976.

Bleibtreu, Erika, et al. *The Southwest Palace of Sennacherib at Nineveh.* London, 1996.
Dalley, Stephanie. "Nineveh, Babylon, and the Hanging Gardens: Cuneiform and Classical Sources Reconciled." *Iraq* 56 (1994): 45–58.
Eiland, M. L. "Roman Coins Found at Nineveh Provide Evidence of Trade between Rival Empires." *The Celator* 6.10 (1992): 30–32.
Hill, George F. "A Hoard of Coins from Nineveh." *Numismatic Chronicle* 12 (1931): 160–170.
Jacobsen, Thorkild, and Seton Lloyd. *Sennacherib's Aqueduct at Jerwan.* Oriental Institute Publications, 24. Chicago, 1935.
Layard, Austen H. *Nineveh and Its Remains.* 2 vols. London, 1849.
Layard, Austen H. *Discoveries in the Ruins of Nineveh and Babylon.* London, 1853.
Luckenbill, Daniel D. *The Annals of Sennacherib.* Oriental Institute Publications, 2. Chicago, 1924.
Madhloom, Tariq. "Excavations at Nineveh: A Preliminary Report." *Sumer* 23 (1967): 76–79.
Madhloom, Tariq. "Nineveh: The 1967–68 Campaign." *Sumer* 24 (1968): 45–51.
Madhloom, Tariq. "Nineveh: The 1968–69 Campaign." *Sumer* 25 (1969): 43–49.
Mallowan, M. E. L. "The Prehistoric Sondage of Nineveh, 1931–32." *Annals of Archaeology and Anthropology, University of Liverpool* 20 (1933): 127–186.
Rassam, Hormuzd. *Asshur and the Land of Nimrod.* Cincinnati, 1897.
Reade, Julian. "Sources for Sennacherib: The Prisms." *Journal of Cuneiform Studies* 27 (1975): 189–196.
Reade, Julian. "Studies in Assyrian Geography, Part I: Sennacherib and the Waters of Nineveh." *Revue d'Assyriologie et d'Archéologie Orientale* 72 (1978): 47–72, 157–180.
Reade, Julian. *Assyrian Sculpture.* London, 1983.
Russell, John M. *Sennacherib's Palace without Rival at Nineveh.* Chicago, 1991.
Scott, M. Louise, and John Macginnis. "Notes on Nineveh." *Iraq* 52 (1990): 63–73. Includes a full list of Nineveh's excavators.
Scurlock, J. A. "The Euphrates Flood and the Ashes of Nineveh." *Historia* 39 (1990): 382–384.
Stronach, David, and Stephen Lumsden. "U.C. Berkeley's Excavations at Nineveh." *Biblical Archaeologist* 55 (1992): 227–233.
Stronach, David. "Village to Metropolis: Nineveh and the Beginnings of Urbanism in Northern Mesopotamia." In *Nuove Fondazioni nel Vicino Oriente Antico: Realta e ideologia,* edited by Stefania Mazzoni, pp. 85–114. Pisa, 1994.
Stronach, David. "Notes on the Topography of Nineveh." In *Neo-Assyrian Geography,* edited by Mario Liverani. Rome, 1996.
Thompson, R. Campbell, and Richard W. Hutchinson. *A Century of Exploration at Nineveh.* London, 1929.
Turner, Geoffrey. "The State Apartments of Late Assyrian Palaces." *Iraq* 32 (1970): 177–213.
Turner, Geoffrey. "Tell Nebi Yūnus: The *Ekal Māšarti* of Nineveh." *Iraq* 32 (1970): 68–85.
Ussishkin, David. *The Conquest of Lachish by Sennacherib.* Tel Aviv, 1982.

David Stronach and Kim Codella

NIPPUR (modern Niffar or Nuffar), ancient Mesopotamian city and cult center located at the center of the southern Mesopotamian floodplain (32°10′ N, 45°11′ E), just north of Afak, about 180 km (112 mi.) southwest of Baghdad. Nippur stands nearly 20 m above the immediately surrounding plain and measures more than 1.5 km across, northeast–southwest. It is divided into an eastern and a western portion by the dried bed of a canal, the Shatt en-Nil. The southern tip of the eastern mound, known as Tablet Hill or the Scribal Quarter because of the large number of tablets found there, is separated from the northern part by a shallow gully. The northern part of the eastern mound is commonly termed the Religious Quarter because of the ziggurat complex located there. [*See* Ziggurat.] Austen Henry Layard reported that local Arabs referred to the ziggurat area as Bint il-Amir, "daughter of the emir," and had a tradition that a golden boat lay buried in the mound (*Discoveries in the Ruins of Nineveh and Babylon,* New York, 1985, p. 473). Chains of low mounds, the remains of the city's fortification wall, are visible on the far northeast and southwest. [*See the biography of Layard.*]

Hermann V. Hilprecht (*Die Ausgrabungen in Bel-Tempel zu Nippur,* Leipzig, 1903, p. 11) noted that Oppert first identified Nuffar as ancient Nippur. Henry C. Rawlinson had already linked Nuffar with ancient Nippur and biblical Calneh (*Gn.* 10:10) in 1861 (*Cuneiform Inscriptions of Western Asia,* vol. 1, London, 1861, pl. 1) and Hilprecht also noted the link (*Explorations in Bible Lands during the 19th Century,* Philadelphia, 1903, p. 294). The identification of Calneh with Nippur is based on a Talmudic tradition (Seder *Mo'ed* 3 *(Yoma')*. *Genesis* 10:10 reads "And his kingdom began at Babel and Erech and Accad and Calneh *(wkhalneh)* in the land of Shinar." In large part because there was no record of a southern Mesopotamian Calneh, William Foxwell Albright suggested that the Masoretic text was corrupt and should be emended to read *wkhullanah. Genesis* 10:10 would then read "And his kingdom began at Babel and Erech and Accad, and all of them were in the land of Shinar" (Albright, "The End of Calneh in Shinar," *Journal of Near Eastern Studies* 3 [1944]: 254–255). Albright's suggestion obviates any link between Nuffar/Nippur and a city mentioned in the Bible. [*See the biographies of Hilprecht, Rawlinson, and Albright.*]

Settlement History. Nippur was already occupied in the early sixth millennium. Sherds from the second (Hajji Muhammad) phase of the Ubaid period have been found on the surface of the mound and recovered from excavated contexts. The main mound continued to be occupied until 800 CE. Small mounds west of the site date to roughly 900–1200 BCE, however, and recent work has uncovered traces of an occupation dating to the fourteenth century BCE just northeast of the mound. McGuire Gibson has provided a concise summary of the history of settlement at Nippur (Gibson, 1992, pp. 33–54).

Throughout its early history, Nippur occupied a preeminent, if not unique, position among the cities of Mesopotamia. Not only was it equidistant between Sippar in the north and Ur in the south—in effect on the border between Sumer and Akkad—but Nippur was also the site of Ekur, the temple of Enlil, the paramount deity of the pantheon, and the city served as the major religious center of Mesopotamia. [*See* Sippar; Ur; Sumerians; Akkade.] Probably because of its geographically strategic position and religious character, it was early on made a "neutral" city. There exists no trace in Mesopotamian historical tradition of any king or dynasty centered on Nippur holding political dominance, but nearly all of the kings of Sumer and Akkad sought legitimacy for their rule through recognition there. The city was large—by the end of the third millennium, 135–150 ha (334 acres) inside its walls—and prosperous, the object of continuous royal/state investments in the form of construction projects such as its fortification wall and temple buildings (and, concomitantly, pious donations to temples).

In the late eighteenth century BCE, however, Nippur's fortunes began to fluctuate. Perhaps because of a combination of politicoeconomic and environmental factors, including drought and the instability of the branch of the Euphrates River on which it was located, Nippur experienced periodic "abandonments" and, conversely, resurgences as a result of or accompanied by royal/state investments. The archaeological and written evidence suggests, for example, that the city was largely abandoned for three hundred years from the late eighteenth through the end of the fifteenth centuries BCE, but was revitalized under the Kassite kings in the fourteenth and thirteenth centuries. [*See* Kassites.] So, too, Nippur also appears to have been largely abandoned in the first century and a half of the Parthian era—the last 150 years BCE, but was reinvigorated by Vologases II as part of a deliberate strategy to control international trade by curbing the expansionist policies of Characene. [*See* Parthians.]

Excavations. Excavations have been carried out at Nippur since the beginning of archaeological work in Iraq, almost 140 years ago. Layard excavated for roughly two weeks in January and February 1851 and seems to have been disheartened by the results of his work, wondering whether extensive excavations would produce any important results (*Discoveries,* 1985, p. 477). An American expedition affiliated with the University of Pennsylvania carried out work at Nippur in the late nineteenth century. From 1888 to 1900 the expedition undertook four major campaigns at the site. Accounts of their work appeared in popular works by two of the excavators, John Punnett Peters and Hermann V. Hilprecht, but only one volume in the planned series of final reports was ever published.

In 1948 The University Museum of the University of Pennsylvania and the Oriental Institute of the University of Chicago reopened excavations at Nippur. This Joint Expedition, under the direction of Donald E. McCown, focused its work on the ziggurat complex, in particular on the so-called kitchen temple, and began two soundings (TA, TB) on Tablet Hill, to the southeast. The expedition continued to work in those areas in its second (1949–1950) and third (1951–1952) seasons. The results were published in *Nippur I* (McCown and Haines, 1967).

In the course of the third season, with work on the ziggurat complex and TA and TB nearing completion, the Joint Expedition undertook a number of soundings on the east mound designed to locate promising areas for future excavations. One of the soundings (E) was laid out about 325 m to the northwest of the ziggurat. The sequence of Early Dynastic and Akkadian temples—the so-called North Temple—encountered there became the primary focus of the fourth season's (1953–1954) work. The University Museum withdrew from the excavations at the end of the third season and the Baghdad School of the American Schools of Oriental Research joined the Oriental Institute in the fourth season in sponsoring the excavations. A final report was published in *Nippur II* (McCown et al., 1978).

A second of the third season's soundings (B) was on the northwest slope of a low rise just southwest of the ziggurat. There the excavators came down into the Temple of Inanna. Sounding B was expanded in the fourth season, and the Temple of Inanna was the major focus of work in the fifth–seventh seasons, although small-scale excavations were also carried out in the ziggurat complex in the fifth and sixth seasons. In the eighth season (1962–1963) the expedition continued work on the lower levels of the Inanna temple and undertook test soundings on the east mound. Richard C. Haines, who had earlier been the expedition's architect, acted as field director during the work on the temple. Only preliminary reports on the temple excavations have appeared to date.

After a break of two years and the near termination of the program of excavations begun in 1948, the Oriental Institute reopened the Nippur excavations in November 1964. In both the ninth and tenth seasons, the expedition, under James Knudstad's direction, turned its attention to delimiting the large Parthian fortress that overlay the ziggurat complex as a first step to excavating earlier levels of Ekur. However, it was not possible, largely for political reasons, and work at Nippur had to be halted after two seasons. The results of the excavations of the Parthian fortress have been published only in preliminary reports.

The Oriental Institute's expedition resumed work at Nippur in the early 1970s. In the eleventh (1972–1973) and twelfth (1973) seasons, the excavators, led by Gibson, worked in two areas on the west mound: area WA (and a sounding called WA 50c near the main opertion) and area WB. The excavators continued work in those areas in the thirteenth season (1975), but also began a program of excavations at the far southwestern end of the site (area WC). The stated purpose of the work in area WC was to uncover the remains of the city's wall, but a large Kassite building (area WC-1) and a series of private houses dating to the seventh century BCE (area WC-2) were also uncovered. The expedition continued work in area WC in the fourteenth (1976) and fifteenth seasons (1981–1982), undertaking extensive excavations of the city wall (WC-3), in addition to work in WC-1 and WC-2. The final report on the excavations in area WC-1 was published in *Nippur III* (Zettler, 1993).

The sixteenth's season's work at Nippur (1985) was an outgrowth of excavations in area WC-2. The remains from the WC-2 houses were difficult to date, and so a sounding (area TC) was made at the southern end of area TA to provide a well-stratified sequence for the range of time in question and to provide a check on the published stratigraphy of area TA. In addition to work in area TC, two excavation areas (WD, WE) were established at the southern tip of the western mound as alternate excavation sites for those days when work in TC had to be halted because of sandstorms.

In recent years, the excavators undertook a series of operations in various areas, intended, in some cases, to check and expand on the results of earlier work and, in others, to provide a sequence through poorly known periods. In the seventeenth season (1987), for example, in addition to continuing work on the western city wall (area WC-3), the excavators focused their efforts on the eastern city wall (areas EA, EB, EC), previously excavated by the University of Pennsylvania, and on a low Islamic mound to the northeast of site (area M). In the eighteenth season (1989), the excavators located a 10-×-10-meter sounding (area WF) north of WA-50c. The sounding was undertaken there because excavations in area WA-50c in the early 1970s had shown readily accessible mid- to late third-millennium occupation levels. In addition, the excavators worked on the top of the west mound just west of area WA (area WG). Area WG was intended to check the transition from the pre-Islamic to the Islamic periods at the site. In the nineteenth season (1990), in addition to continuing work in Area WF, the excavators resumed work on the WA sequence of temples that had been the focus of excavations in the early 1970s. Successive campaigns of work that began with the eleventh season in 1972 have included environmental and landscape studies. (Brandt, 1990, pp. 67–73).

Excavation Results. The University of Pennsylvania's expeditions worked largely on the ziggurat complex and Tablet Hill, leaving only the far western end of the mound untouched. Aside from the ziggurat, perhaps the best-known architectural remains excavated by the expedition was the Court of Columns uncovered on the western mound in the vicinity of area WA. The Court of Columns features a megaron hall with *prodomos* opening off a columned court. The plan led the excavators to identify the building as a Mycenaean palace, but recent excavations have shown that it could not have been built before the end of the third century BCE (Gibson, 1978, p. 19).

In addition to architecture, the nineteenth-century Nippur expeditions recovered tens of thousands of tablets and fragments, which, along with economic documents, include lexical tablets and exemplars of almost all important Sumerian literary works, most of which probably came from private houses on Tablet Hill (for a bibliography of publications of Nippur tablets, see Bregstein and Schneider, 1992). On Tablet Hill, the area TA sounding (20 × 40 m) was located roughly in the center of the mound. Area TB was located approximately 30 m northeast of area TA at the bottom of a large cut made by the Pennsylvania expedition. The remains uncovered in areas TA and TB span a period of nearly two thousand years, from the time of the dynasty of Akkad through the Achaemenid era. Private houses were uncovered in both areas. The character of the excavated remains in area TB, however, changed over time. The buildings uncovered in the earliest, or lowest, levels (XIII–X) were probably private houses. They were replaced by a large "public" building that was rebuilt four times (levels IX–IV). That public building was, in turn, replaced in the latest area TB levels by private houses. The area TB public building was a private house and "office" of a high state official concerned with the administration of agricultural lands (Zettler, 1991, pp. 251–281).

The Inanna temple represents the longest continuous archaeological sequence available for Mesopotamia: twenty-two building levels spanning the Middle Uruk through Late

NIPPUR. *Bronze statue of King Ur-Nammu.* Dated to 2100 BCE. Iraq Museum, Baghdad. (Scala/Art Resource, NY)

Parthian periods. The Early Dynastic temples (levels IX–VII) have a unique building plan with two sanctuaries. The temples yielded important relief-carved plaques, sculpture in the round, and clay sealings (Hansen, 1963, pp. 145–166; 1971, pp. 47–54). The sequence of buildings and associated artifacts has provided the basis for Donald P. Hansen's redefinition of the phases of the Early Dynastic period. Where the Diyala sequence provided for a threefold division of the period (Early Dynastic I–III), the Inanna temple sequence suggested a twofold division (Hansen, 1965, pp. 201–213; Porada et al., 1992, pp. 103–113). The Parthian temples are particularly interesting in that they demonstrate the continuation of ancient Mesopotamian cults and traditional temple architecture into late periods (Keall, 1970).

While E. J. Keall discusses the Parthian Inanna temple, he focuses largely on the fortress built over the top of the ruined ziggurat. Excavations of the Parthian fortress showed that the fort went through three distinct phases of growth, and none of the plans was completed before being abandoned in favor of more ambitious constructions. In the latest phase (phase III), the north quadrant of the fort had a monumental complex that included a court with four iwans. The three phases of the fortress date to the first and second centuries BCE.

The excavations in area WA yielded a sequence of temples from the end of the Third Dynasty of Ur through the Achaemenid period. Based on inscriptions and figurines recovered from the excavations, Gibson has suggested that the WA temple was dedicated to Gula, a healing goddess and the wife of Ninurta. The WA excavations also provided additional evidence bearing on the so-called Mycenaean palace uncovered by the University of Pennsylvania.

In area WB, the lower levels contained private houses occupied for roughly fifty years from the end of the reign of Rim-Suen (1822–1763 BCE) to the time of Samsuiluna (1749–1712 BCE). A Kassite palace (level II) with a plan similar to the ʿAqar Quf (Dur Kurigalzu) palace was uncovered above the Old Babylonian houses. The palace, which dates to the thirteenth century BCE is probably the building from which the University of Pennsylvania recovered a large number of Kassite tablets and would appear to have been the governor's residence. The latest occupation phases (levels I, G–F) in area WB were poorly preserved. Level IB contained jar burials. One of the jars had a number of unbaked clay tablets packed into the cut into which it had been set. The tablets date to late eighth and early seventh centuries BCE and represent one of the few sources of information for that poorly documented period (Cole, 1990).

At the southwest end of the site, excavations in area WC-1 yielded remains of the city wall and a large Kassite house whose lower level (level III) had been rebuilt three times; the upper level (level II) provided evidence of two main construction phases. Both levels contained a formal court-

NIPPUR. *Statuette of a couple.* Iraq Museum, Baghdad. (Art Resource, NY)

yard and reception room, as well as a domestic suite of rooms. The upper level could be assigned to the thirteenth century BCE, based on a dated tablet. Surface remains in area WC-1 contained fragmentary floors and two chronologically discrete groups of burials. The earlier group of jar burials dated to the early first millennium BCE, while the later group of simple inhumations was probably late Parthian. In area WC-2 the excavations yielded two occupational phases of private houses that could be dated to the seventh century BCE. The earlier phase also contained a small chapel (Armstrong, 1989). Work in area WC-3 focused on disentangling the various phases of the western stretch of the city wall. Aside from the work in area WA, the most important recent excavations at the site have been in areas TC and WF. The sounding carried out in area TC provided incontestable evidence for the abandonment of the site between the Old Babylonian and Late Kassite periods (fourteenth and thirteenth centuries BCE) and made possible a reassessment of the stratigraphy of area TA (Armstrong, 1989). The sequence uncovered in area WF has been discussed in the context of the transition from the Early Dynastic to Akkadian periods at Nippur (McMahon, 1993).

[*See also* Mesopotamia, *article on* Ancient Mesopotamia; *and* Temples, *article on* Mesopotamian Temples.]

BIBLIOGRAPHY

Albright, William Foxwell. "The End of 'Calneh in Shinar.'" *Journal of Near Eastern Studies* 3 (1944): 254–255.

Armstrong, James A. "The Archaeology of Nippur from the Decline of the Kassite Kingdom until the Rise of the Neo-Babylonian Empire." Ph.D. diss., University of Chicago, 1989. The results of excavation of post-Kasite Nippur, including a discussion of the building levels of area TA.

Brandt, Margaret C. "Nippur: Building an Environmental Model." *Journal of Near Eastern Studies* 49 (1990): 67–73.

Bregstein, Linda B., and Tammi J. Schneider. "Nippur Bibliography." In *Nippur at the Centennial,* edited by Maria deJong Ellis, pp. 337–357. Philadelphia, 1992. A comprehensive bibliography of the primary publications of Nippur tablets that includes tablets from the post–World War II seasons of excavations.

Cole, Steven. "Nippur in Late Assyrian Times, 750–612 B.C." Ph.D. diss., University of Chicago, 1990. Discusses the area WB unbaked clay tablets from the jar burials (eighth–seventh centuries BCE).

Crawford, Vaughn E. "Nippur, the Holy City." *Archaeology* 12 (1959): 74–83.

Fisher, Clarence S. *Excavations at Nippur.* Philadelphia, 1905.

Franke, Judith Ann. "Artifact Patterning and Functional Variability in the Urban Dwelling: Old Babylonian Nippur, Iraq." Ph.D. diss., University of Chicago, 1987. Focuses on the area WB private houses.

Gibson, McGuire. *Excavations at Nippur: Eleventh Season.* Chicago, 1975.

Gibson, McGuire. *Excavations at Nippur: Twelfth Season.* Chicago, 1978a.

Gibson, McGuire. "Nippur (1975)." *Sumer* 34 (1978b): 114–121.

Gibson, McGuire, et al. "The Southern Corner of Nippur: Summary of Excavations during the Fourteenth and Fifteenth Seasons." *Sumer* 39 (1983): 170–190.

Gibson, McGuire. "Patterns of Occupation at Nippur." In *Nippur at the Centennial,* edited by Maria deJong Ellis, pp. 33–54. Philadelphia, 1992.

Hansen, Donald P., and George F. Dales. "The Temple of Inanna, Queen of Heaven at Nippur." *Archaeology* 15 (1962): 75–84.

Hansen, Donald P. "New Votive Plaques from Nippur." *Journal of Near Eastern Studies* 22 (1963): 145–166.

Hansen, Donald P. "The Pottery Sequence at Nippur from Middle Uruk to the End of the Old Babylonian Period, 3400–1600 B.C." In *Chronologies in Old World Archaeology,* edited by Robert W. Ehrich, pp. 201–213. Chicago, 1965.

Hansen, Donald P. "Some Early Dynastic I Sealings from Nippur." In *Studies Presented to G. M. A. Hanfmann,* edited by D. G. Mitten et al., pp. 47–54. Cambridge, 1971.

Hilprecht, Hermann V. *Die Ausgrabungen in Bel-Tempel zu Nippur.* Leipzig, 1903a.

Hilprecht, Hermann V. *Explorations in Bible Lands during the Nineteenth Century.* Philadelphia, 1903b. See pages 289–577.

Keall, E. J. "The Significance of Late Parthian Nippur." Ph.D. diss., University of Michigan, 1970.

Knudstad, James E. "Excavations at Nippur." *Sumer* 22 (1966): 111–114; 24 (1968): 95–106.

Layard, Austen H. *Discoveries in the Ruins of Nineveh and Babylon.* London, 1853. Reprint, New York, 1985. See page 562.

McCown, Donald E., and Richard C. Haines. *Nippur I: Temple of Enlil, Scribal Quarter, and Soundings.* Chicago, 1967.

McCown, Donald E., et al. *Nippur II: The North Temple and Sounding E.* Chicago, 1978.

McMahon, Augusta Madeline. "The Early Dynastic to Akkadian Period Transition in Southern Mesopotamia." Ph.D. diss., University of Chicago, 1993.

Peters, John P. *Nippur.* 2 vols. New York, 1897.

Porada, Edith, et al. "The Chronology of Mesopotamia, ca. 7000–1600 B.C." In *Chronologies in Old World Archaeology,* edited by Robert W. Ehrich, vol. 1, pp. 77–121, vol. 2, pp. 90–124. 3d ed. Chicago, 1992.

Rawlinson, Henry Creswicke. *Cuneiform Inscriptions of Western Asia.* Vol. 1 London, 1861.

Stone, Elizabeth C. *Nippur Neighborhoods.* Chicago, 1987. Synthetic study of the buildings, artifacts, and texts from the Isin-Larsa and Old Babylonian levels of areas TA and TB.

Zettler, Richard L. "Nippur under the Third Dynasty of Ur: Area TB." *Aula Orientalis* 9 (1991): 251–281.

Zettler, Richard L. *Ur III Temple of Inanna at Nippur.* Berlin, 1992. A study of the architecture, artifacts, and tablets from the level IV temple.

Zettler, Richard L. *Nippur III: Kassite Buildings in Area WC–1.* Chicago, 1993.

RICHARD L. ZETTLER

NISHAPUR, site located in Khorasan province, northeastern Iran, about 65 km (40 mi.) west of Mashhad. Founded by Shapur II in the Sasanian period, Nishapur was one of the major cities of the region during the Middle Ages. However, during the Sasanian and Early Islamic periods, Nishapur had been a somewhat marginal town, even though one of the most important Sasanian fire temples was located in its vicinity. Nishapur gained prominence when the Tahirids proclaimed their dynasty to be semiautonomous and made the city their capital; the founder of this dynasty was ʿAbd Allah ibn Tahir (AH 213–230/828–845 CE). Nishapur's importance was enhanced under the Samanids (tenth–eleventh centuries), when it began to decline; various factors contributed to this process, such as wars and earthquakes, culminating in its sacking by the Mongols in the thirteenth century. The city was never to regain its former prominence.

Under the Samanids, Nishapur competed with several other courts of semiautonomous princes, such as Merv, Rayy/Tehran and Bukhara, attaining a high level of cultural and intellectual activity. The city became a flourishing commercial center, producing luxury goods such as textiles and remarkable ceramics.

In the city a well-known mosque and the palace of the governor were adjacent to the citadel and another quarter. The city appears to have been planned on the classical pattern, with four gates that must have led to a *cardo* and a *decumanus* (most of the streets in the commercial district ran in parallel north–south and east–west directions, intersecting at right angles).

What is known of Nishapur is largely the result of excavations conducted by a team from the Metropolitan Museum of Art (New York City), primarily from 1935 to 1940, with a final season in 1947. The finds were distributed among several mounds (*tepes*), and were mostly attributed to the ninth–thirteenth centuries. The majority of the material consisted of pottery, both complete vessels and sherds, but kilns were also found, testifying to the local manufacture of these ceramics (Wilkinson, 1973). The ceramics are both unglazed and glazed. The unglazed pieces are plain for the most part, though some are decorated by a variety of methods; molds were used, some of which were recovered and are particularly noteworthy. The various groups of glazed ceramics include a number of distinctive types: buff ware with an underglaze and painted decoration and black-on-white pottery with abundant epigraphic motifs. Glass, an extensive array of metalwork (Allan, 1982), coins, and fragments of frescoes were also among the finds.

[*See also* Ceramics, *article on* Ceramics in the Islamic Period; Metals, *article on* Artifacts of the Byzantine and Islamic Periods; *and* Persia, *article on* Persia in the Islamic Period.]

BIBLIOGRAPHY

Allan, J. W. *Nishapur: Metalwork of the Early Islamic Period.* New York, 1982.

Wilkinson, Charles K. *Nishapur: Pottery of the Early Islamic Period.* New York, 1973.

MYRIAM ROSEN-AYALON

NITRIA, monastic settlements near Alexandria, visited in the fourth and fifth centuries CE by Greek and Latin writers who came to Egypt to see its holy men. The visitors called the settlements Nitria, or more properly, "the mount of Nitria" (Gk., *ho oros tēs Nitrias;* Lat., *mons Nitriae*). In the Latin text of the *Historia Monachorum in Aegypto,* attributed to Rufinus (c. 345–410 CE), who spent eight years in Egypt and was a leading figure in Palestinian monasticism, Nitria was about 65 km (40 mi.) from Alexandria and took its name from a nearby town, a center for the collection of salts *(nitratos).* Its precise location has not been identified; the description in the *Historia Monachorum,* as well as other references to Nitria by Palladius (c. 363–431), author of the *Lausiac History;* Cassian (c. 360–435); and other Christian writers, suggests that the region was settled near the modern village of El-Barnugi, about 14 km (9 mi.) southwest of Damanhur. In antiquity it lay on the edge of cultivation, in an area of marshy, marginal land.

Tradition ascribes the initial settlement to the ascetic Amoun (Ammon), a contemporary of Antony (c. 251–356), father of Egyptian monasticism. Unlike the coenobitic system introduced by Pachomius (c. 290–346) in Upper Egypt, in which formal, written rules regulated every detail of the monks' daily life, the system developed under the spiritual direction of Antony and Amoun allowed freer associations. The monks lived, according to Rufinus, in about fifty individual dwellings (lauras) set close together: in some, many monks lived together, in others only a few, and in still others, there were some true solitaries. The pattern of religious life allowed the monks to determine their own course to salvation, leading a life of prayer and penance in their cells. They met on Saturdays and Sundays for a common celebration of the Eucharist, the church being described by Palladius as being large but not magnificent. It was administered by priests who were subject to the authority of the bishop at Damanhur.

Monks supported themselves by tending small vegetable gardens and by selling mats and baskets plaited from halfa grass or palm fiber in the villages and in Alexandria. They hired themselves out as laborers at harvest time or wove flax. Their daily life, ascetic practices, conduct and behavior to one another, and relations with the secular world are exemplified in an anonymous compilation known as the *Sayings of the Fathers (Apophthegmata Patrum; Verba Seniorum),* dating from at least the middle of the fifth century, with translations into Coptic (the last stage of the native language of Egypt), Syriac, and Latin.

The proximity of Nitria to Alexandria attracted visitors in great numbers. There was a guest house and a bakery near the church. This influx of visitors and the growing number of disciples resulted in the withdrawal of individuals farther inland to an area that is referred to in the literary sources as Kellia ("cells"). The textual evidence for the site of Kellia confirms that it was in an area of some six hundred mounds of varying height, in the sandy country 16–17 km (11 mi.) southwest of El-Barnugi, remote from the settlements near Qusur el-ʿIlzeila and Qusur al-Rubaʿiyyat.

The area's archaeological significance was first noticed in 1925, but it was not until 1964 that it became the focus of a joint scientific mission carried out by Geneva University and the French Archaeological Institute of Cairo. After publishing a preliminary report on their findings, the missions proceeded separately with the work, which has not yet been completed. The report on the site's eroded brick buildings—of differing sizes, some with painted scenes—reflects a conglomerate of hermit dwellings, the larger more elaborate than might be supposed from the literary tradition. When the fieldwork is completed, the finds fully documented and published, and the site's chronological sequences defined, it should be possible to use the archaeological evidence to supplement the literary evidence for the monks' daily life, to clarify the relationship of Kellia with the less remote community of Nitria, and to trace the movement toward more closely knit monastic communities.

The literary evidence, supported by the study and analysis of pottery from Kellia, suggests that the settlements of Nitria and Kellia were in decline at the end of the fifth century and were abandoned in the ninth. In contrast, a third area, even more remote, called Scetis (Shiet) in the ancient texts, has had a continuous but checkered history of occupation. It lies within a depression below sea level, now known as Wadi 'n-Naṭrun, that takes its name from a chain of salt lakes fringed with reed beds. Its origins, in the fourth century, are traditionally associated with Macarius the Great (c. 330–390). There is little detailed information about how anchorite settlements developed into today's imposing monasteries, fortified with walls and keeps, with individual cells and communal refectories, gardens, wells, oil and wine presses, bakeries, storerooms, and churches with wall paintings. Weakened by doctrinal disputes and subject to raids from Berber tribes to the west, the monks experienced periods of decline interspersed with periods of material prosperity. The history of construction at the different monasteries is complex: existing buildings, restored and enlarged, obscure more ancient construction that dates to the eighth century.

Four monasteries are still active, three of which date to the fourth century: Deir Abu-Maqar (Convent of St. Macarius), Deir Anba Bishoi (Convent of St. Pschoi), and Deir el-Baramous (Convent of the Romans—that is, of the two Roman saints Maximus and Domitius, said to be the sons of the emperor Valentinian, 364–375 CE). The fourth monastery is known as Deir as-Suryan (Convent of the Syrians). Originally founded in the sixth century, it was inhabited by Syrian monks from Mesopotamia in the ninth century. It was still active in the seventeenth century, when the great monasteries of Iraq, Syria, and eastern Turkey had already disappeared. Its library, whose fortunes can be traced back almost continuously to the ninth century, contained important Syriac manuscripts.

These communities are the center of Egyptian monasticism and have, since the seventh century, attracted European travelers in search of ancient manuscripts. Notable among travelers who left vivid accounts of their experiences was Robert Curzon. His *Visits to Monasteries in the Levant,* first published in 1849, is a minor classic.

[*See also* Monasteries.]

BIBLIOGRAPHY

General Sources

Badawy, Alexander. *Coptic Art and Archaeology: The Art of the Christian Egyptians from Late Antique to the Middle Ages.* Cambridge, Mass., 1978. General study, particularly good on architecture, including a short account of Kellia.

Chadwick, Owen. *Western Asceticism.* London and Philadelphia, 1958. Selected translations, with introductions and notes, of the *Sayings of the Fathers, Conferences of Cassian,* and the *Rule of Saint Benedict.*

Evelyn-White, Hugh G. *The Monasteries of the Wâdi 'n Natrûn,* part 2, *The History of the Monasteries of Nitria and of Scetis,* edited by Walter Hauser; part 3, *The Architecture and Archaeology.* New York, 1932–1933. Fundamental study arising from the mission of the Egyptian Expedition of the Metropolitan Museum of Art, New York, 1910–1911 and 1920–1921. Part 1, published in 1926, is a catalogue of new Coptic texts from the Monastery of Saint Macarius, with an introduction to the library.

Leroy, Jules. *Les peintures de couvents du Quadi Natroun.* Mémoires de l'Institut Français d'Archéologie Orientale, C1. Cairo, 1982. The only full discussion of the paintings in the monasteries of Wadi 'n-Natrun, with 147 plates.

Meinardus, Otto F. A. *Monks and Monasteries of the Egyptian Deserts.* Rev. ed. Cairo, 1989. Up-to-date general account, with bibliography.

Russell, Norman. *The Lives of the Desert Fathers.* Cistercian Studies Series, no. 34. London, 1980. Translation, with an introduction by Benedicta Ward SLG, of the *Historia Monachorum in Aegypto,* with a bibliography of selected primary and secondary sources.

Walters, Colin. *Monastic Archaeology in Egypt.* Warminster, 1974. General survey of the material culture of the Egyptian monasteries up to the twelfth century.

Excavation Reports

Daumas, François, and Antoine Guillaumont. *Kellia 1, Kôm 219: Fouilles executées en 1964 et 1965.* 2 vols. Fouilles de l'Institut Français d'Archéologie Orientale, vol. 28. Cairo, 1969.

Egloff, Michel. *Kellia: La potterie copte.* 2 vols. Geneva, 1977.

Egloff, Michel. *Survey archéologique des Kellia (Basse Égypte): Rapport de la campagne 1981.* Louvain, 1983.

Kasser, Rodolphe. *Kellia 1965.* 2 vols. Recherches Suisses d'Archéologie Copte, nos. 1–2. Geneva, 1967.

Kasser, Rodolphe. *Kellia: Topographie.* Geneva, 1972.

A. F. SHORE

NORTH AFRICA. Occuping the entire northwestern quarter of the African continent, North Africa, or the Maghreb, embraces modern Tunisia, Algeria, Morocco, and sometimes Libya. North Africa came in contact with the ancient Near East through the Phoenicians, who founded Carthage and other settlements across the region early in the first millennium BCE.

What the Phoenicians called this newly found land is uncertain because, in antiquity, North Africa had many names. To the Greeks it was Libya, by which they denoted everything from the Nile River westward to the Pillars of Hercules (Straits of Gibraltar). [*See* Libya.] The Romans called it Africa, subdividing the region according to political and economic organization or ethnic affiliation. Carthago in northern Tunisia was the city and territory of Phoenician Carthage. [*See* Carthage.] Emporia (Gk., "markets") denoted the eastern coast of central Tunisia. Tripolitania designated three Phoenician city-states along the coast in southeastern Tunisia and western Libya: Labdah (Leptis Magna), Trablus (Oea), and Sabratha. [*See* Leptis Magna.] Numidia in eastern Algeria was the territory of indigenous pastoralists, the Numidians (Gk., *nomades,* "nomads"), and Mauretania in western Algeria and northern Morocco, that of the native Maures. (Roman Mauretania should not be confused with the modern northwest African country of the same name but different location.) Medieval Arab geographers took the name *ifraqiya* ("Africa") from the Byzantines, but also coined their own, more descriptive phrase, *al-djezirat al-maghreb,* "the island of the west." Shortened to *al-maghreb,* "the west," this is today transliterated as Maghreb. No record survives of what the Phoenicians called their adoptive land in their own Semitic tongue; nor is there any trace of how it was named by its native peoples, the Numidians, Maures, Garamantes, and others—later known collectively as Berbers.

By whatever name the Phoenicians knew it, these newcomers to North Africa found a landscape there not unlike the one they had left behind in the east: a narrow coastal plain enclosed by echelons of low hills and high mountains, beyond which stretched hot, dry desert. The terrain of North Africa, however, is far less compact than that of Lebanon or Syria, and, except in Tripolitania, the desert is far removed from the coast. East and south, the Sahara effectively isolates the Maghreb from the Nile Valley and from equatorial Africa. The waters of the Mediterranean Sea and South Atlantic Ocean border it on the north and west, respectively. Within these boundaries the Atlas Mountains, a chain of densely folded limestone ridges, form an interior massif extending 2,000 km (1,240 mi.) from the Atlantic coast of Morocco to the Straits of Sicily east of Carthage. Inland, the topography is sharply dissected by numerous short, seasonal wadis that drain the watersheds of the Atlas into the surrounding seas or into marshy, internal depressions. There are numerous rocky headlands and offshore islands along the lengthy North African coastline but few natural harbors, a circumstance that influenced where on the coast the seafaring Phoenicians made landfall during their journeys westward.

The North African climate is Mediterranean, with hot, dry summers and cool, wet winters. The upper elevations of the Atlas are colder and wetter, and the Saharan desert fringes, hotter and drier than the coastal zones. Since the Neolithic period, typical Mediterranean modes of subsistence have prevailed. Cereal agriculture and sheep/goat pastoralism are long-established livelihoods in North Africa. [*See* Cereals; Sheep and Goats.] Rainfall is usually adequate for dry cultivation and the annual renewal of pastures, but the amount of precipitation can vary considerably from year to year—with potentially disastrous consequences for both farmers and herders. The landscape once supported a natural-climax forest vegetation of cedar, pistachio, holm oak, and pine and the wild progenitors of domesticated olive and grape. It proved hospitable to the domesticated vines and olive trees introduced there by the Phoenicians. [*See* Viticulture; Olives.] Since the time of Phoenician contact, however, the human populations in North Africa have greatly altered its original environment. Millennia of exploitation by agriculturalists and pastoralists have resulted in familiar Mediterranean patterns of woodland destruction and ensuing soil erosion.

Phoenicians and Libyans comprised the two main groups of people inhabiting North Africa in antiquity. The Libyans were aborigines, descended probably from the region's original prehistoric inhabitants. The Phoenician newcomers arrived only in the early first millennium BCE. Classical authors also recognized a mixture of the two groups, so-called Libyphoenicians, that inevitably sprang up wherever the Phoenicians landed in North Africa (Livy, 20.22.3).

Phoenicians in North Africa are often referred to as Punic. This is an English transliteration of the Latin *poeni,* itself a Latin transliteration of the ancient Greek *phoinix,* a common noun for the color purple. In Greek it was also the gentilic name for Semitic speakers of the Syrian coast who specialized in the manufacture of purple dye. These were Canaanites, whose name may come from *kinaḫḫu,* a Semitic word for purple. [*See* Canaanites.]

The modern academic distinction between *Phoenician* and *Punic* is based on chronology, geography, and language. "Phoenician" history and archaeology are divided from "Punic" at about the beginning of the sixth century BCE, the time of the Neo-Babylonian siege and conquest of Tyre (586–573 BCE). [*See* Babylonians; Tyre.] Subsequently, Carthage emerged as the leading Phoenician city in the west. Geographically, the Mediterranean is separated into a Phoenician east and a Punic west. In language, older Phoenician grammatical forms, onomastica, and scripts are differentiated from linguistically and paleographically evolved Punic ones. [*See* Phoenician-Punic.] The distinction is not a rigid one, however, and artifacts, monuments, and settlements in North Africa are sometimes described somewhat ambiguously as Phoenician-Punic.

In this regard, St Augustine of Hippo (354–430 CE), a native North African, made a trenchant comment. Speaking of the indigenous inhabitants *(rustici)* of North Africa, he observed that they still (early fifth century CE) referred to themselves in their own (Punic) language as *Chananaei,* or "Canaanites" (*Letters* 209.2–3). This suggests that in North Africa the Phoenicians may never have ceased being Canaanites.

The Canaanites who "discovered" North Africa discovered that it was already occupied. The foundation legends of Carthage, transmitted through classical sources (cf. Justin 18.5 for the fullest account), mention native inhabitants who contested the newcomers' right to settle their land. Beyond the bare fact of their existence, however, little else is known. There is a dearth of direct archaeological data to support generalizations about the society and economy of the native populations of North Africa in the millennium leading up to their first contact with the Iron Age civilizations of the Near East. The best appraisal of the people encountered by the founders of Carthage is that they were probably ceramic Neolithic farmers and herders clustered in villages or camping in tents and possessing no knowledge of metal or of writing. The Stone Age prehistory of the Maghreb is well understood into the third millennium, but there is no evidence for a native "Bronze Age" in North Africa. The handful of indigenous inscriptions is chronologically very late. Even those that occur bilingually with Punic texts have never been satisfactorily deciphered.

What the natives called themselves in their own tongue is not known. Classical authors lumped them under one rubric, Libyans, though these same writers did record the names and the locations of traditional territories of some native tribes or tribal confederations. These include the Garamantes of the Sahara, the Massylies and Masaesylii of Numidia (central North Africa), and the Mauri of Mauretania (western North Africa). The ancient writers also distinguish between native groups that farmed and those that herded. According to the written sources, agriculture was practiced in the Mediterranean zones of the northern and western Maghreb, while sheep/goat pastoralists ranged south and east along the Saharan fringe. (Camels and camel pastoralism were introduced into the region very late, probably in the Roman period.) [*See* Agriculture; Pastoral Nomadism; Camels.]

Today, native North Africans are collectively called Berbers, a transmutation of an ancient Greek epithet for non-Greek speakers, *barbaroi.* The modern Berber language is written in Arabic script and is laden with loanwords, but it remains identifiable with its remote linguistic ancestors, ancient Semitic and Egyptian.

Carthage. The best-known and most thoroughly explored of the ancient Near Eastern settlements in North Africa is Carthage. According to legend it was established by Phoenicians from Tyre and Cyprus in the late ninth century BCE. The early date, though not yet the specific origin, of Carthage is now supported by archaeological evidence. Utica, a neighboring site to the north, was (also according to legend) an earlier foundation (1101 BCE); archaeologically, however, the site does not date to before the eighth century BCE.

Carthage (Lat., Carthago) transliterates the Phoenician words *qart ḥadasht,* "new town," an approprite name for a colonial foundation. In the Persian and Hellenistic periods, Carthage emerged as a military and economic rival to Rome, ultimately contesting with that city, in a series of three so-called Punic Wars (in 264–241 BCE, 218–200 BCE, 149–146 BCE), for control of the entire western Mediterranean world. In the end, Phoenician Carthage lost that struggle. Afterward, the city reemerged as the capital of Roman Africa, ranking in size and importance with Alexandria in Egypt and Antioch in Syria. [*See* Alexandria; Antioch on Orontes.] After the Vandal interregnum (439–533 CE), Carthage remained under Byzantine rule until the Islamic conquest in 700.

The ruins of ancient Carthage—Phoenician, Roman, Vandal, and Byzantine—now lie in the coastal suburbs of modern Tunis, Tunisia. In antiquity the city spread over the southern tip of the Carthage peninsula, a low ridge of sandstone hills joined to the mainland by a broad, flat, sandy isthmus. The locale is often described as typically Phoenician: an offshore island or remote promontory providing safe haven from the sea and protective isolation from the mainland. Already partly enclosed by the Gulf of Tunis, the twin lagoons north and south of the peninsula offered ancient mariners a choice of sheltered anchorages, depending on the direction of the winds. As late as the Byzantine period (sixth–seventh centuries CE) these lagoons were still navigable, but continual siltation from adjacent rivers since the end of antiquity has almost cut them off from the sea.

Archaeological excavations, ongoing at Carthage since the nineteenth century, have revealed many, though not all, of the principal features of the Phoenician city: features excavated in whole or in part include the citadel (Byrsa), cemeteries of all periods, dwellings, fortifications, industrial installations of Old and New Carthage, the port, and the tophet, where the Carthaginians allegedly practiced (and archaeological evidence now suggests, actually did practice) child sacrifice. Much recent data have resulted from the International Campaign to Save Carthage carried out during the 1970s and 1980s by expeditions from a score of countries under the auspices of UNESCO.

Byrsa. The citadel of Carthage, the Byrsa was so called because its boundaries were legendarily delimited by the city founders with thongs of oxhide (Gk., *bursa*). The Byrsa rises 50 m (164 ft.) above the surrounding landscape and was always the focus of settlement in ancient Carthage. No trace of the earliest occupation survives on the summit, however, because Roman engineers truncated it in order to terrace the hilltop for their later monumental constructions. Flanking the crest of the hill and undisturbed by later occupation are seventh-century BCE extramural tombs built of monolithic sandstone blocks (see figure 1). Above the tombs are the well-preserved remains of the second-century BCE multistory townhouses of wealthy urbanites destroyed in the final Roman assault on the citadel in 146 BCE. These are the townhouses so vividly described by the Latin author Appian (*Libyca* 96), who also left an account of the Carthaginian ports. Ruins of these townhouses were later engulfed by debris pushed downslope from the summit during the massive Roman terrace building. Some of the townhouse walls are preserved to a height of more than 2 m.

Cemeteries. From the seventh century BCE onward, cemeteries spread north and east from the Byrsa in ever-widening, concentric semicircles. Their progressive enlargement and increasing distance from the Byrsa suggest that the town underwent a gradual expansion through the first three centuries of its existence, followed by an episode of rapid growth after 500 BCE. This growth corresponds with what can be gleaned from the meager written sources, which refer to an Old Carthage and a New Carthage—the latter possibly laid out on an orthogonal grid sometime in the fifth century BCE.

Old and New Carthage. Vestiges of both Old Carthage and New Carthage were revealed in German excavations in the 1970s and 1980s under the auspices of the German Archaeological Institute (Rome section), directed by Friedrich Rakob, and the University of Hamburg, directed by Hans-Georg Niemeyer, on the seafront east of the Byrsa and north of the port. Unearthed there were fifth-century BCE dwellings protected by a sandstone seawall that also functioned as part of the city's fortifications. These structures had been erected on backfill containing debris of seventh-century BCE buildings apparently razed to make way for them. In orientation, the new houses conformed to an orthogonal plan set at right angles to the coastline. In the third–second centuries BCE, larger, more sumptuous seaside villas succeeded the fifth-century dwellings but maintained the same alignment. [*See* Villa.] The orientation of the city plan of Roman Carthage corresponds closely to this pre-Roman grid.

To the west, farther from the sea and closer to the foot of the Byrsa, in trenches that reached sterile soil, the German team found several meters of occupational debris laid down in eleven floor levels. The architecture consisted of mud-brick structures built on stone foundations with pillar-and-rubble walls. (Pillar-and-rubble wall construction, already in use at Megiddo in the tenth century BCE, was so widespread in North Africa the Romans dubbed it *opus Africanum*, "African work.") [*See* Megiddo.] Ceramics from these floor and fills, especially imported Greek wares, date this architecture indubitably to the eighth–sixth centuries BCE. Almost a third of the ceramics found in the basal deposits was not imported Phoenician or Greek, but indigenous handmade ware, a vestige of early contact between the incoming Phoenicians and indigenous Libyans. Also in this area were signs of industrial activity of the seventh–sixth centuries BCE: pottery kilns, metalworking installations, and purple-dye works. The picture emerging from these excavations is that of a seaside industrial area between the Byrsa and the tophet taken over for urban housing and public buildings as the Iron Age/Persian-period city developed into a Hellenistic metropolis. Late in this process, Carthage was provided with a new port befitting its status as a major Mediterranean trading city.

Port of Carthage. At the time of the final Punic War, the port of Carthage, according to Appian (*Libyca* 96), consisted of a rectangular harbor for merchantmen and an adjacent circular one for warships in the city's southeast quarter. American (ASOR Punic Project directed by Lawrence E. Stager, Oriental Institute, University of Chicago) and British (British Academy Excavations at Carthage directed by H. Hurst, Institute of Archaeology, Oxford University) excavations in the 1970s confirmed conclusively that the shallow lagoons southeast of the Byrsa (one rectangular, one circular) were indeed the remains of this port. Moreover, both were shown to be relatively late features of the city, built only after about 350 BCE. The location of the pre-Hellenistic harbor remains a mystery.

The commercial harbor was a rectangular artificial basin (Gk., *cothon*) surrounded by a quay wall built of monumental sandstone ashlars more than 2 m on a side and almost 1 m high. Near the quayside the American excavators discovered a large warehouse constructed in the typical Phoenician pillar-and-rubble technique (Stager, 1979). The harbor seems to have been only lightly damaged in the final Punic War, and the Romans soon put it back in service. The thickly plastered surface of the first-century CE Augustan quayside overlay a half meter of Punic destruction debris dumped as leveling fill by the Romans. The refurbished Punic port continued to serve the Roman city well into Late Antiquity.

The military harbor adjoined the commercial one. Investigations in the circular lagoon by British mission in the 1970s demonstrated that it too was part of the port described by Appian. This lagoon also was an artificial basin with an island created in the center. Based on the excavator's estimates, the military harbor (see figure 2) could accommodate 170 to 180 warships in timber-and-stone drydock ramps built on the central island and around the shore of the lagoon (Hurst and Stager, 1978). (Appian put its capacity at 220

NORTH AFRICA. Figure 1. *View of seventh-century* BCE *Punic tombs on the Byrsa hill, Carthage.* Looking northwest toward the summit. Note the triangular roofed tomb. (Photograph by J. A. Greene)

ships.) Such ramps had existed earlier in the eastern Mediterranean, as in the sixth-century BCE *cothon* at Phoenician Kition (Larnaca) on Cyprus. [*See* Kition.] The date of the military harbor is surprisingly late—no earlier than the second century BCE, when Carthage was on the brink of the last Punic War. Less surprisingly, the military harbor was heavily destroyed in the aftermath of that war but was later rebuilt along different lines by the Romans.

Tophet. The tophet, or Precinct of Tanit, was near the port but was founded much earlier. There, the Carthaginians practiced child sacrifice, or so charged Greek and Latin textual accounts. Owing to the fate of the city's library after 146 BCE (the Romans gave it to their Punic-speaking Numidian allies and it was subsequently lost), no Phoenician account of the city's history is preserved. Until archaeological evidence for a tophet at Carthage was discovered accidently in 1921, the classical sources might have been dismissed as mere adverse propaganda.

The tophet at Carthage was a typical open-air Phoenician sanctuary (see figure 3): an area delimited by a temenos wall and filled with urn burials containing cremated remains of humans or animals surmounted by stone markers, usually decorated or inscribed, or sometimes both. [*See* Burial Sites; Burial Techniques.] Other such sanctuaries were later discovered at Phoenician sites in North Africa and on Sicily and Sardinia. [*See* Sardinia.] They are now known at Amathus on Cyprus and in Tyre in Lebanon. [*See* Amathus; Tyre.] Tophets at other North African sites in the region of Byzacium to the south and along the Mediterranean coast of Algeria continued to be used into the Christian era, though by then animal substitution rather than actual human sacrifice was apparently the norm. The term *tophet* (meaning, perhaps, "roaster") is taken from *2 Kings* 23:10, which describes a tophet in the valley of Hinnom outside Jerusalem. The Jerusalem tophet was obliterated in the sixth century BCE, during Josiah's reforms "so that no one would make a son or daughter pass through the fire as a *mulk*-sacrifice" (NRSV, adapted). Excavations have shown that the tophet at Carthage was in continuous use from the founding of the city in about 800 BCE until its destruction by the Romans in 146 BCE.

Excavations at the Carthage tophet began immediately after its discovery, with campaigns of François Icard and Paul Gielly (Tunisian Department of Antiquities, 1922), Francis Kelsey (University of Michigan, 1925), G. G. Lapeyre (Tunisian Department of Antiquities, 1934–1936), and Pierre Cintas (Tunisian Department of Antiquities, 1944–1947). None was ever fully published, though Donald Harden, a junior member of Kelsey's expedition, synthesized the 1925 results in two brief articles that accurately fixed the relative sequence (Tanit I–III) and absolute chronology (eighth–second centuries BCE) of the tophet urn burials (summarized in Harden, 1980, pp. 82–90).

Excavations by the American Schools of Oriental Research Punic Project during the UNESCO Save Carthage Campaign in the 1970s verified the broad outlines as well as

NORTH AFRICA. Figure 2. *Model of the second-century* BCE *ship sheds at the circular harbor, Carthage.* (Courtesy British Academy Carthage Excavations)

NORTH AFRICA. Figure 3. *General view of the Carthage Tophet excavations, looking west.* (Courtesy ASOR Punic Project)

many details of Harden's analysis. The Punic Project uncovered more than four hundred whole or fragmentary burial urns containing the cremated remains of children and young animals. Analysis of the contents and stratigraphic contexts of the urns, together with a reconsideration of the biblical and extrabiblical written sources, demonstrates beyond doubt that child sacrifice was practiced at Carthage.

In the area excavated at least nine phases of burials were dated, from about 750 to 146 BCE. The lowest levels, on bedrock, corresponded to the earliest period of the tophet, about 750–600 BCE (phases 1–4 = Harden's Tanit I). The intermediate levels spanned the fifth–fourth/third centuries BCE (phases 5–8 = Harden's Tanit II). The uppermost stratum, dating to the third–second centuries BCE (phases 9 = Harden's Tanit III), was mostly destroyed by the Romans, leaving little of the final level of the tophet in situ.

A typical burial consisted of an urn placed in a stoned-lined pit capped by a flat cobble. All of the urns contained the charred bones of sacrificial victims, either children (newborns or two–four-year-olds) or animals (lambs, kids, birds). Animal substitutes were interred with the same rites as human victims, including the provision of grave offerings (see figure 4 (glass beads, carved amulets and, more rarely, miniature pottery vessels) and sometimes a burial monument. [*See* Grave Goods.] The monuments, sandstone cippi or limestone stelae, were used frequently (though not invariably) to mark the burials. The earliest markers were undecorated, L-shaped sandstone cippi. By the fourth century BCE, the monuments were often embellished with the symbols of the deities Tanit and Ba'al Hammon; they were sometimes inscribed with the dedicant's name, profession, and genealogy.

Contrary to expectation, animal substitution did not gradually supplant human sacrifice. In the earliest phases (750–600 BCE), one urn in three contained the charred remains of lambs, kids, or birds. In later levels (phases 5–8) only one urn in ten contained the remains of an animal substitute. In all cases the integrity of individual skeletons in the urns in-

NORTH AFRICA. Figure 4. *Tanit I urn amulet group from the Tophet, Carthage.* (Courtesy ASOR Punic Project)

dicated that a deliberate effort had been made by those conducting the sacrifice to collect from the pyre the particular remains of each victim—human or animal—and place them in a separate urn.

The approximate age, but not the sex, of the human victims can be determined. Infant skeletons are composed of a high percentage of cartilage, all of which is destroyed by burning. Only the more completely ossified portions of the skeleton survive. Teeth are the most heat resistant, and the stage of dental development provides important clues for establishing the victim's age at death. While the sex of such young individuals cannot be determined from the skeletal evidence, the textual sources suggest that the rite was not limited to first-born males and that sons or daughters served equally as offerings to Tanit and Baʿal Hammon.

Child sacrifice at Carthage not only had religious dimensions, but also social and economic ones. Viewed in a comparative cultural perspective, ritual infanticide at Carthage may be seen to fulfil many of the same functions as more informal modes of infanticide—exposure, drowning, strangulation, poisoning—practiced in the contemporary Greek and Roman world. Thus, the practice served as a mechanism for regulating population growth. It was less hazardous to the health of the mother than abortion of an unborn fetus and allowed parents to select for the sex and birth order of children. Among the economic elite of Carthage, the religious institution of child sacrifice may have been used by wealthy families to consolidate and maintain their fortunes by allowing them to regulate the number of male heirs among whom inheritance would have to be shared and the number of females who would have to be dowered into marriage. Some scholars reject such a materialist analysis and contend that Phoenician tophets merely represent cemeteries of children who perished of natural causes and whose remains were accorded special treatment.

Cap Bon, Byzacium, and Tripolitania. Outside Carthage, to the south and west, lay other regions of North Africa: Cap Bon, Byzacium, Numidia, Mauretania, and the outer limits of the known world in antiquity beyond the Pillars of Hercules.

Cap Bon. A broad peninsula, Cap Bon's low mountains and hilly plains stretch north and east from Carthage. Its extreme eastern tip lies only 150 km (93 mi.) from Sicily, a propinquity that proved advantageous when the Phoenicians controlled Sicily and Sardinia; it was far less advantageous later, when, from the fifth century CE onward, Carthage faced military threats from Greek Sicily and from Rome. Easier to reach by sea than by land, Cap Bon formed a hinterland and resource base for the city. The sandstone so ubiquitous in public and private architecture of all periods at Carthage was quarried at El Houaria on Cap Bon's northwestern shore (see figure 5). By the late fourth century BCE, if not before, the peninsula was richly planted with olive groves, vineyards, and fruit orchards interspersed with pasture for sheep, cattle, and horses and dotted with luxurious country houses. [*See* Cattle and Oxen.] In 310 BCE the army

NORTH AFRICA. Figure 5. *Roman sandstone quarries at El Houaria, Cap Bon.* Note the quarried blocks of sandstone. These were taken both directly from the surrounding cliffs and from the extensive system of underground caves. (Photograph by J. A. Greene)

of Agathocles, the Syracusan tyrant, marched through this countryside to attack Megalopolis, a town of unknown location somewhere on Cap Bon (Diodorus Siculus 20.8.3–4). Historical sources record that three cities on Cap Bon—Nepheris, Aspis (modern Kelibia), and Neapolis (modern Nabeul)—remained loyal to Carthage until its ultimate defeat by Rome in 146 BCE. For that loyalty they paid with their own destruction (Strabo 17.3.16). The two sites whose locations are known have, however, yielded very little archaeological evidence of that destruction or of any pre-Roman occupation. Archaeological surveys by a joint Tunisian-Italian team at the northern end of Cap Bon have found surface traces of Phoenician occupation at smaller sites. Excavations by this same team at three sites (Djebel el-Fortras, Ras ed-Drek, Aspis/Kelibia) uncovered what have been interpreted as "forts" dating to the fifth century BCE. Also found at Ras ed-Drek was a temple, dated by its excavators to the third–second centuries BCE (Barreca and Fantar, 1983). The earliest and most substantial evidence for Phoenician settlement on the peninsula, however, is from Kerkouane, on the northeast coast of Cap Bon.

Kerkouane. Except for Carthage, Kerhouane is, to date, the best-preserved and most extensively excavated Phoenician town in North Africa. Its ancient name is lost; the surviving written sources mention only the larger Phoenician cities of Cap Bon. Archaeologically, however, ancient Kerkouane is quite well known. It was founded in the sixth century BCE and inhabited until the mid-third century BCE. There were two main periods of occupation, the first from its founding down to the late fourth century BCE, about the time of Agathocles' invasion from Sicily. Rebuilt, its second phase of occupation lasted fifty more years, until the town was abandoned permanently in the course of the First Punic War. Because there was no later occupation, the excavators of the Tunisian Institut National du Patrimonie, directed by M. Fantar, were able to recover substantially complete plans of structures wherever they dug.

A double fortification wall surrounded the town, enclosing an area of 7 or 8 ha (17 or 20 acres). Within the walls a well-planned system of wide streets intersected at regular angles, unpaved but provided with stone-lined drains. Courtyard houses opened onto the streets through narrow vestibules. Each house had a cistern sunk into the courtyard to provide water, as well as its own private bath (see figure 6). [*See* Cisterns; Baths.] Near the town center a large courtyard structure with pillars flanking its entrance and subsidiary rooms was surrounded by benches. Although very likely a temple, nothing found inside this structure offered a clue about the cult celebrated there. [*See* Cult.] At the edge of the town was an industrial zone of pottery and figurine workshops and kilns. Piles of broken Murex shells unearthed nearby suggest the presence a typical Phoenician enterprise, purple-dye works. Tombs dating from the sixth to the third centuries BCE lay, as expected, outside the town walls. Significantly, there is no natural harbor near the site. Kerkouane was an agricultural village, according well with Diodorus's depiction of Cap Bon as an agricultural hinterland.

NORTH AFRICA. Figure 6. *Bath in a fourth-century* BCE *private house, Kerkouane.* (Photograph by J. A. Greene)

Byzacium. South of Cap Bon lay Byzacium (the modern Tunisian Sahel), a flat, fertile, sandy plain known in Greek as Emporia. Along its littoral, from the base of Cap Bon to the border of Tripolitania, stretched a string of Phoenician towns: Hadrumetum (Sousse), Rusapina (Monastir), Lepti (Lemta), Thapsus (Ras Dimass), Mahdia (ancient name unknown), Sullecthum (Salakta), and Acholla (Ras Botria). These are known mainly from textual traditions. There are few ancient traces of Hadrumetum and Rusapina because they are buried beneath modern Sousse and Monastir. The accidental discovery and subsequent excavation at Hadrumetum of burial urns and carved stelae by Pierre Cintas revealed that a tophet was in use there from at least the seventh to the first centuries BCE (Lancel, 1995, pp. 291–292). Cemeteries dating to the fourth century BCE have also been found. By contrast, Rusapina, Thapsus, Mahdia, and Sullecthum are, before the Roman period, virtually blank archaeologically. Their locations on headlands or near offshore islets are, however, suggestive of Phoenician foundations, as are the presence at some of difficult-to-date harbor works, such as a *cothon* at Mahdia and a mole at Thapsus. Lepti, rechristened Leptis Minor by the Romans, to distinguish it from Leptis Magna, its greater neighbor in Tripolitania, similarly lacks any known Phoenician remains; however, the site and its region are now the object of renewed archaeological investigations by a joint Tunisian-American project that may file this lacuna. Pliny the Elder remarked on the cultural and ethnic particularity of Byzacium, identifying its inhabitants as Libyphoenicians (*Nat. Hist.* 5.24). This characterization is reflected archaeologically in cemeteries on the coast at Lepti and inland at Smirat that reveal indigenous (as distinct from Phoenician) funerary practices. Unlike Cap Bon, Byzacium sided with Rome in the final

Punic War and in return was spared destruction. Its reluctance to take a stake in Carthage's quarrel with Rome is perhaps explained by its mixed population, partly Canaanite, mostly Libyan.

Tripolitania. South of Byzacium lay Tripolitania ("three cities"), colonized by Phoenicians in the seventh century BCE. It took its name from its three principle cities: Labdah/Leptis Magna, Trablus/Oea, and Sabratha. Until 146 BCE, Tripolitania formed the eastern province of a western Phoenician realm dominated by Carthage. After Carthage's destruction, Rome ceded Tripolitania to its Numidian allies but later absorbed it as a Roman province.

Numidia, Mauretania, and Beyond the Pillars of Hercules. West of Carthage, the Mediterranean seaboard of North Africa is marked at roughly equal intervals by Phoenician coastal settlements, either known or conjectured, on or near prominent headlands or estuarine embayments. Some are no more than place names cited by ancient authors, with no firm connection to an identified archaeological site. Others are demonstrably ancient foundations firmly dated by excavated artifacts to as early as the sixth century BCE. Archaeologists have noted this uniform spacing—in time about one day's sail, in distance measured coastwise some 30–40 km (19–25 mi.)—and have connected it with the system of cabotage (short-distance coastal sailing and trading) described in documentary sources for the sixteenth-century Mediterranean. The Phoenicians were supposed to have practiced a first-millennium BCE version of cabotage as they expanded into the western Mediterranean. The data, though suggestive, are not in perfect accord with this reconstruction. The spacing of sites is not invariable, and archaeological evidence is often absent or chronologically too late. Some site identifications are based on nothing more than onomastic guesswork supported by the ambiguous testimony of the classical geographers.

At some coastal sites, extant remains are no earlier than the era of the Punic Wars (third–second centuries BCE). Hippo Regius (modern Anaba on the Tunisian-Algerian frontier) has yielded inscribed tophet stelae and evidence of a temple to African Saturn (i.e., Baʿal Hammon), all dated to the third–second centuries BCE. Beyond Hippo, from east to west along the Algerian coast, other late sites include Rusicada (modern Skikda), Chullu (Collo), Iqilgili (Gigel), Salda (Begaya), Iomnium (Tigzirt), Rusucurru (Dellys), and Rusguniae (Tametfoust). Rusazus, Rusippisir, and Cissi are known only by name and have yet to be located. At several of the excavated sites (Iomnium, Rusucurru, Rusguniae), the presence of inscribed tophet stelae dating to as late as the second century CE suggest the continuation of rites connected with child sacrifice (though perhaps not the actual practice itself) long after the Romans suppressed it at Carthage.

Near modern Algiers the data are better. While Icosium (Algiers) can be dated no earlier than the third–second centuries BCE, Tipasa (Zeralda), to the west, had a sizable occupation in the fifth and fourth centuries BCE, with strong Libyan funerary traditions and a tophet in use up to the first century CE. West of Tipasa, Iol (Roman Caesarea, modern Cherchel) was founded by the sixth or fifth century BCE. Literary traditions make it a Numidian royal city by the third century BCE. A second-century BCE Neo-Punic inscription found there mentions a temple dedicated to the Numidian king Micipsa, successor to Massinissa; two second–first-century BCE Neo-Punic texts attest a local cult of Saturn. West of Iol, Gunugu (Gouraya) has produced fifth-century BCE ceramics, Neo-Punic inscriptions, and Neo-Punic stelae from the second–third centuries CE mentioning Saturn.

Phoenician sites in the Gulf of Oran are separated by 160 km (99 mi.) from those near Algiers. The intervening stages are not yet located. The ancient name of Les Andalouses, a site 30 km (19 mi.) west of Oran, is uncertain. It has two cemeteries, a western one dating to the sixth century BCE and an eastern one dating to the late fourth–second centuries BCE. In between is a fourth–second-century BCE settlement of about 3 ha (7 acres). Both the settlement and the eastern cemetery show strong ceramic affinities with Phoenician Iberia. At Mersa Madakh (ancient name unknown) is a necropolis dating to about the sixth century BCE. [*See* Necropolis.] It too has ceramic connections with Phoenician Iberia and with Phoenician sites on the Atlantic coast of Morocco. Siga (Takembrit), founded in the fifth century BCE, became, in the third century BCE, a Numidian royal city occupied by Syphax, king of the Masaesyles. Neo-Punic inscribed stelae from the third–first centuries BCE attributed to Siga (and now in the Oran Museum) and second–third-century CE anepigraphic stelae excavated near Siga witness the continuity of the cult of Saturn at the site for at least five hundred years. Finally, there is Rachgoun, an island near shore on the Gulf of Oran, with a necropolis and dwellings dating to about 650–600 to 500 BCE. It is the earliest site thus far found on the Algerian coast; it too exhibits ceramic parallels with Phoenician Iberia, moreso than with Carthage.

To the west, of the known Phoenician settlements on the Moroccan Mediterranean coast, only Sidi Abdelsalem el Bahar shows any signs of occupation in the fifth century BCE. The others, Rusaddir (Mellila), Emsa, and Tamuda (Tetouan), range from the fourth to second centuries BCE.

There are strong literary traditions that the Phoenicians early (mi 1110 BCE) went beyond the Pillars of Hercules to found settlements at Gadir (Cadiz) on the southwest coast of Spain and, even before that, at Lixus (Larache) on the Atlantic coast of Morocco (Pliny, *Nat. Hist.* 19.63). There is at present, however, no archaeological support for such early foundations. At Tingis (Tangier) there is a necropolis from perhaps the seventh century BCE. The evidence for Phoenician occupation at Lixus is substantial, however: cemeteries and remains of habitations and a temple, but none date to before the seventh century BCE. Mogador, 700 km (434 mi.) south of Tingis, is in a typically Phoenician location, an offshore island close to a small river mouth. Excavations there in the 1950s by A. Jodin have found Attic and Ionian amphora and Phoenician red-slip pottery diagnostic of the seventh century BCE, but the overall nature of the occupation is unclear. In all cases, these sites show the same material cultural connections with Phoenician Iberia demonstrated by those on the western Algerian coast.

If evidence of settlement is lacking, the written sources do suggest extensive Phoenician contacts with the western coast of North Africa. Herodotus (4.196) recorded their custom of silent barter with Libyans on the coast beyond the Pillars, a wordless exchange of Phoenician trade goods for North African gold. The *Periplus of Hanno* (a set of sailing instructions) recounts the voyage of a Carthaginian, Hanno, and his fleet of sixty ships down the west coast of Africa in perhaps the late fifth century BCE "to found cities of Libyphoenicians." The expedition may have gone as far as modern Sierra Leone, or perhaps farther, to Cameroon or Gabon (the coastal features described are consistent for either location) before turning back, their supplies exhausted, without founding any new settlements. By its own account, the text of the *Periplus* was inscribed on a tablet displayed in the Temple of Kronos (Baʿal Hammon) in Carthage.

[*See* also American Institute for Maghreb Studies; *and* American Schools of Oriental Research.]

BIBLIOGRAPHY

North Africa is difficult to grasp bibliographically: books and articles concerned with its history and archaeology and its connections with the ancient eastern Mediterranean are numerous and published in many different languages. What follows serves to introduce essential bibliography by signaling classic works, sound interpretations of the existing evidence across a range of topics, and recent publications of important new data.

Because North African archaeology has long been a preserve of European scholars, mainly French and Italian, much past and present work appears in those languages. Fundamental early studies, all in French, are accessible only in major research libraries. Published proceedings of recent international conferences, despite their titles in French, Italian, and German, frequently contain important contributions in English. The major relevant museum collections are in North Africa and Europe; very few exhibits of this material travel to North America. As a result, exhibition catalogs are usually not in English. A notable exception is *Carthage: A Mosaic of Ancient Tunisia.* Despite this, much is accessible in English, either as original work or in translation.

Scholarly journals in English (e.g., the *Journal of Roman Archaeology, Libyan Studies*) often contain articles on North African archaeology. The French journal *Antiquités Africaines,* which focuses on ancient North Africa, sometimes includes lengthy English-language contributions. The *American Journal of Archaeology* from time to time publishes a "North Africa Newsletter" summarizing recent developments. One of these comprises a comprehensive bibliography for archaeology in Tunisia (exclusive of Carthage) from 1956 to 1980: Abdelmajid Ennabli, "North Africa Newsletter 3: Part 1. Tunisia, 1956–1980," *American Journal of Archaeology* 87 (1983): 197–206. For general bibliographies, see Richard I. Lawless, *Algeria* (Oxford, 1980), and Allan M. Findlay and Richard I. Lawless, *Tunisia* (Oxford, 1982) and *Morocco* (Oxford, 1984), in the World Bibliographical Series (vols. 19, 33, 47).

Early Studies

Babelon, Ernest, et al. *Atlas archéologique de la Tunisie au 1:50.000.* Paris, 1893. Compiled by French army surveyors, this atlas records the locations (but little else) of hundreds of "Roman ruins" (not all are Roman) in northern and western Tunisia. Rare but worth searching for.

Cintas, Pierre. *Manuel d'archéologie punique.* 2 vols. Paris, 1970–1976. Comprehensive survey of the subject by the doyen of Phoenician-Punic archaeology. Volume 2 appeared posthumously at the start of the UNESCO Save Carthage Project; the manual is thus dated but still essential.

Gauckler, Paul. *Nécropoles puniques de Carthage.* Paris, 1915. Reproduces Gauckler's notebooks from his cemetery excavations at Carthage; to be used with Hélène Benichou, *Les tombes puniques de Carthage: Topographie, structures, inscriptions et rites funéraires* (Paris, 1982), which is indispensable for understanding Gauckler's work.

Gsell, Stéphane. *Histoire ancienne de l'Afrique du Nord.* 8 vols. Paris, 1913–1930. First and still fundamental historical study framing the basic questions of North African history.

Tissot, Charles J. *Exploration scientifique de la Tunisie: Géographie comparée de la province romaine d'Afrique.* 2 vols. Paris, 1884–1888. Detailed historical geographical study based on texts and inscriptions; the basis for many site identifications proposed in the *Atlas archéologique* above.

Pre-Phoenician Period

Camps, Gabriel. "Beginnings of Pastoralism and Cultivation in North-West Africa and the Sahara: Origins of the Berbers." In *The Cambridge History of Africa,* vol. 1, edited by J. Desmond Clark, pp. 548–623. Cambridge, 1982. Summarizes the author's lifelong study of pre- and protohistoric North Africa; full bibliography in French.

Carthage and North Africa

Barreca, F., and M. Fantar. *Propezione archeologia al Capo Bono II.* Rome, 1983.

Charles-Picard, Gilbert, and Colette Charles-Picard. *The Life and Death of Carthage.* Translated by Dominique Collon. New York, 1969. Overview of the history, archaeology, and religion of Punic Carthage by two noted scholars of ancient North Africa.

Ennabli, Abdelmajid, ed. *Pour sauver Carthage: Exploration et conservation de la cité punique, romaine et byzantine.* Paris and Tunis, 1992. Comprehensive summary in French of the results of the UNESCO Save Carthage Project; contains a complete bibliography of all UNESCO project publications with valuable full listings of titles in multi-authored volumes. Not widely distributed in North America.

Gras, Michel, et al. *L'univers phénicien.* Paris, 1989. Latest synthesis from leading French Phoenician scholars.

Gras, Michel, et al. "The Phoenicians and Death." Translated by Helga Seeden. *Berytus* 39 (1991): 127–176. Chapter 6 of *L'univers phénicien,* a thorough exposition of the "revisionist" view that the Carthaginians did not practice child sacrifice.

Greene, Joseph A. *Ager and ʿArosot: Rural Settlement and Agrarian History in the Carthaginian Countryside.* Redditch, forthcoming. Results of archaeological survey in the city's hinterland; covers the Phoenician/Punic, Roman, and Byzantine periods.

Harden, Donald B. *The Phoenicians.* 3d ed. Harmondsworth, 1980. Best summary in English of Phoenician archaeology (more concise than Cintas, above), with an extensive discussion of Carthage and annotated topical bibliography current to 1980.

Hurst, H., and Lawrence E. Stager. "A Metropolitan Landscape: The Late Punic Port at Carthage." *World Archaeology* 9 (1978): 334–346.

Lancel, Serge. *Carthage: A History.* Translated by Antonia Nevill. Cambridge, Mass., 1995. The 1992 French edition, much enriched by

Lancel's inclusion of information from previously unpublished nineteenth- and twentieth-century excavations in Tunisia.

Law, R. C. C. "North Africa in the Period of Phoenician and Greek Colonization, c. 800 to 323 B.C." and "North Africa in the Hellenistic and Roman Periods, c. 323 B.C. to A.D. 305." In *The Cambridge History of Africa,* vol. 2, edited by J. D. Fage, pp. 87–147, 148–209. Cambridge, 1978. Up-to-date historical summaries (with bibliographies); geographically broader than Warmington (below).

Niemeyer, Hans-Georg. "The Phoenicians in the Mediterranean: A Non-Greek Model for Expansion and Settlement in Antiquity." In *Greek Colonists and Native Populations: Proceedings of the First Australian Congress of Classical Archaeology, Sidney 1985*, edited by Jean-Paul Descoeudres, pp. 469–489. Canberra, 1990. Argues for a new interpretation of the archaeological evidence for Phoenician settlement at Carthage. An updated version, presenting new data from his excavations in Carthage, is forthcoming in Markoe (below).

Stager, Lawrence E. "Carthage: The Punic Project." *Annual Report of the Oriental Institute, 1978–1979*, pp. 52–59. Chicago, 1979.

Stager, Lawrence E., and Samuel R. Wolff. "Child Sacrifice at Carthage: Religious Rite or Population Control?" *Biblical Archaeology Review* 10.1 (1984): 30–51. Well-illustrated discussion of a much-debated topic in North African archaeology; an updated version will appear in Markoe.

Warmington, Brian H. *Carthage.* 2d ed. London, 1969. Best treatment in English of the history of Phoenician-Punic Carthage, based on written sources.

International Conferences

Acquaro, Enrico, et al., eds. *Atti del II congresso internazionale di studi fenici e punici.* 3 vols. Collezione di Studi Fenici, 30. Rome, 1991.

Bartoloni, Piero, et al., eds. *Atti del I congresso internazionale di studi fenici e punici, Roma, 5–10 novembre 1979.* 3 vols. Collezione di Studi Fenici, 16. Rome, 1983. See Acquaro (above) for the second congress; proceedings of a third congress (Tunis, 1991) are in press. A fourth congress was held in Cadiz, Spain, in 1995.

Devijver, Hubert, and Lipiński, Éduard, eds. *Studia Phoenicia X: Punic Wars.* Orientalia Lovaniensia Analecta, 33. Louvain, 1989. Proceedings of an annual Belgian conference on Phoenician archaeology and history; a new topic is selected yearly (see Lipiński, below, as well).

Lipiński, Éduard, ed. *Studia Phoenicia VI: Carthago.* Orientalia Lovaniensa Analecta, 26. Louvain, 1988.

Markoe, Glenn E., ed. *Carthage Reexplored.* Cambridge, Mass., 1996. Cincinnati conference held in 1990 devoted to final reports on the UNESCO Save Carthage Project. The volume will include new syntheses of Carthaginian child sacrifice (by Stager and Paul Mosca) and early Phoenician settlement at Carthage (by Niemeyer and Greene).

Niemeyer, Hans-Georg, ed. *Phönizier im Westen: Die Beiträge des Internationalen Symposiums über "Die phönizische Expansion im westlichen Mittelmeeraum" in Köln, 24–27 April 1979.* Madrider Beiträge, 8. Mainz am Rhein, 1982. Conference on Phoenician archaeology in the western Mediterranean.

Pedley, John G., ed. *New Light on Ancient Carthage.* Ann Arbor, 1980. Conference held in 1979 on initial results of the UNESCO Save Carthage Project; bibliography of preliminary reports.

Senay, Pierre, ed. *Carthage VI–IX: Actes du congrès.* 4 vols. Cahiers des Études Anciennes, Trois-Rivières, 16–19. Montreal, 1984–1986. Proceedings of a 1984 conference devoted to interim reports on the UNESCO Save Carthage Project.

Exhibition Catalogs

Ben Khader, Aïcha Ben Abed, and Soren, David, eds. *Carthage: A Mosaic of Ancient Tunisia.* New York, 1987. Exhibition organized by the American Museum of Natural History that toured extensively in North America, 1987–1990.

Moscati, Sabatino, ed. *The Phoenicians.* New York, 1988. Based on an exhibition at the Palazzo Grassi, Venice, this lavishly illustrated catalog includes topical essays and an extensive bibliography. Translated from the Italian edition, *I Fenici* (Milan, 1988).

JOSEPH A. GREENE

NORTHERN SAMARIA, SURVEY OF. The area designated in the Bible and Bronze Age sources as Mt. Manasseh or Mt. Shechem is now known as the northern Samarian hills. This broad syncline, extending along a southwest–northeast axis, terminates to the west and north in the ʿAnabta and Umm el-Fahm anticlines and to the east in the Farʿah anticline. Rising out of the center of the region are mountain ranges that are higher than the surrounding anticlines. (The tallest of these, Mt. Ebal, is 940 m above sea level.) Of Eocene origin, the syncline is hatched in a southeast–northwest direction by a lattice of Neogene faults. Six interior valleys formed along these faults, as did Wadi Farʿah and Wadi el-Maliḥ on the syncline's eastern side. Numerous springs can be found from north of Jenin to the foot of Mt. Gerizim in the south. Abundant water sources, as well as the region's arable soil and broad interior valleys, distinguish the northern Samarian hills from the more rugged hill country to the south, the Ephraim and Judean anticlines.

Archaeological investigation of northern Samaria has been ongoing since the early years of the twentieth century, primarily because of its biblical importance as the site of three Israelite capitals. Shechem, the earliest Israelite religious center, was excavated by Ernst Sellin in 1913–1914 and again in 1926–1927. Samaria (Sebaste), the religious and administrative capital of the northern kingdom for most of its independent history, was excavated in 1908–1910 by George A. Reisner and Clarence S. Fisher. The latter's work was continued between 1931 and 1935 by the Palestine Exploration Fund, and resumed by a Drew University–McCormick Theological Seminary expedition between 1956 and 1964. Tell el-Farʿah (North), identified as biblical Tirzah, the capital city of Jeroboam I, first king of the northern kingdom, was excavated by Roland de Vaux between 1946 and 1960. [*See the biographies of Sellin, Reisner, Fisher, and de Vaux.*]

A few sites on Mt. Manasseh were surveyed before the 1960s, but a systematic examination of the region was not undertaken until 1967–1968, when an emergency survey was conducted by Israeli archaeologists Zecharia Kallai, Ram Gophna, and Yosef Porath. Beginning in 1978, Adam Zertal led the first comprehensive survey of the region for Tel Aviv and Haifa Universities and for the Israel Exploration Society. By 1991 three-quarters of the northern Samarian hills, about 1,800 sq km (1,116 sq. mi.), had been surveyed and some 821 ancient sites classified—632 of them new discoveries—with every archaeological era from the Chalcolithic through the Ottoman periods represented. The survey also determined that, in terms of the region's settlement history and morphology, the division between north and south was not between Judea (Judah) and Samaria, as was formerly believed, but between the Ephraim and Judean anticlines and the Shechem syncline.

The history of northern Samaria can be characterized by dense settlements alternating in fairly quick succession with periods of rapid decline. Settlement was affected by political events as well as the region's diverse topography: internal valleys, particularly the Tubas (Thehez) and Zababdeh valleys in the east, the Mikhmetat valley in the south, and the er-Rameh and Dothan valleys in the west and north, where settlement was centered; hard limestone and dolomite hills to the west of these valleys, where forests of Palestinian terebinth and evergreen oak once stood (and where some specimens still stand); and a broad band of desert margin to the east, descending into the Jordan Valley.

Chalcolithic and Bronze Ages. An important survey finding was that most Early Bronze Age settlements were established in EB I (start of the third millennium BCE) rather than, as had been assumed, in EB II–III, when settlement actually declined. EB I settlements, like those of the Chalcolithic, were concentrated along Wadi Farʿah, Naḥal Shechem, and the western slope of the syncline, an area replete with water sources. Of the seventy-eight EB I sites, nineteen were fortified mounds, some indicative of large settlements. Six fortified enclosures, each positioned for defense, also were discovered. Not all of these enclosures housed settlements, but they probably served as a safe haven for the inhabitants of the nearby valleys. After two periods of decline, settlement activity increased significantly in EB IV, when fifty-five settlements were established, several of them likely serving a cultic function. Unlike the earlier EB sites, those from EB IV were situated along the desert margin and in the eastern valleys, where water was scarce and the soil poor. Large and clustered in groups, these settlements were characterized by a central fortified enclosure and an abundance of potsherds and architectural remains.

As well as can be determined from pottery dating to the Middle Bronze period (beginning of the second millennium BCE), settlement activity came to a virtual standstill in MB I but then exploded in MB II—to 161 sites, a number unequaled anywhere else in Palestine. Many new tells were founded at the region's largest sites (among them, Shechem, Tirzah, Dothan, and Jenin), each protected by exterior walls and earthen ramparts; smaller settlements, some with exterior protection, developed simultaneously on the edges of valleys. The contemporary Egyptian Execration texts refer to the region as Mt. Shechem, or the land of Shechem, but no evidence has been uncovered as to the area's political and ethnic makeup in this period.

Although settlement decreased in general during the Late Bronze Age (latter half of the second millennium BCE), extensive historical data from the period indicate that for a certain time the area extended into the Jezreel Valley and was ruled by the family of Lab'ayu of Shechem, the hill country's most powerful prince. The number of sites decreased substantially in LB I (to twenty-three), possibly as a result of a decline in rainfall and the desiccation of springs on the eastern edge of the syncline at the end of the sixteenth century BCE. These environmental changes were no doubt exacerbated by the widespread destruction wrought by the eighteenth-dynasty Egyptian pharaohs during their military incursions into Canaan.

Iron Age. Pottery remains from the thirteenth and twelfth centuries BCE indicate that seminomads did enter northern Samaria at the beginning of the Iron Age (c. 1200 BCE), the period of Israelite settlement. Moving through Naḥal Tirzah (Wadi Farʿah), the trade route that connected the northern Samarian hills with Transjordan, they settled initially in the Jordan Valley, along Wadi Farʿah and Wadi Maliḥ, and in the eastern valleys of Mt. Manasseh, all areas of light Canaanite settlement. The first cultic center of the period probably was Shechem and possibly Mt. Ebal. Ceramic evidence, especially three types of cooking pots, indicates that these settlers moved gradually into the central and northern valleys and later, in search of arable land, into the forested areas and south toward Mt. Ephraim. This interpretation requires further study and is contested by some scholars (e.g., Dever, 1993), but it helps to explain some of the contradictory biblical references regarding the beginnings of Israelite settlement on Mt. Manasseh.

By Iron II northern Samaria was fully inhabited, the number of settlements reaching a high of 238. Israelite administration of the region is illuminated by the Samaria Ostraca, which date to this period. [*See* Samaria Ostraca.] Political upheavals caused by the Assyrian conquest of Samaria in 722 BCE resulted in a sharp decrease in settlements on Mt. Manasseh in Iron IIC (721–530 BCE), during which the fleeing inhabitants built fortified farms along the desert margin, from Wadi Farʿah to Wadi el-Maliḥ. A new pottery group was introduced, probably by Cuthean settlers who were sent into the region from Mesopotamia in the eighth–seventh centuries BCE, when Samaria was a province of the Babylonian Empire.

Persian through Ottoman Periods. Political stability returned to Mt. Manasseh in the Persian period (sixth–fourth centuries BCE). As a result, settlement was heavy, particularly in the Dothan valley. These settlements, and other findings of the survey, support A. Grintz's assertion that Samaria as well as Judea (Judah) was resettled by those returning from captivity in Babylon after 538 BCE. Settlement was cut in half during the Hellenistic period, however, primarily in the wake of the Samaritan Revolt of 332 BCE, when the inhabitants of the region resisted the legions of Alexander the Great. [*See* Samaritans.] Stability returned during the Early Roman period, when settlement surged and new sites were founded in the northwest, in the area linked to the small state of Narbata. Of all the historical periods, the greatest density of settlement on Mt. Manasseh occurred in the Byzantine period—358 sites—but that number was cut in half in both the Early Arab and the medieval periods (seventh–fourteenth centuries CE), again as a result of political upheavals. Evidence of renewed settlement, including fortified settlements, was found for the Mamluk period, but another significant decline—to less than a quarter of the number of Byzantine settlements—occurred in the Ottoman period.

[*See also* Dothan; Far'ah, Tell-el (North); Jordan Valley; Judah; Samaria; Shechem; *and* Southern Samaria, Survey of.]

BIBLIOGRAPHY

Albright, William Foxwell. "The Site of Tirzah and the Topography of Western Manasseh." *Journal of the Palestine Oriental Society* 11 (1931): 241–251.

Dever, William G. "Cultural Continuity: Ethnicity in the Archaeological Record and the Question of Israelite Origins." *Eretz-Israel* 24 (1993): 22–33.

Zertal, Adam. "Har Menashe Survey, 1982." *Excavations and Surveys in Israel* 2 (1983): 43–44.

Zertal, Adam. "The Water Factor during the Israelite Settlement Process in Canaan." In *Society and Economy in the Eastern Mediterranean c. 1500–1000 B.C.*, edited by Michael Heltzer and Éduard Lipiński, pp. 341–352. Orientalia Lovaniensia Analecta, 23. Louvain, 1988.

Zertal, Adam. "The Wedge-Shaped Decorated Bowl and the Origin of the Samaritans." *Bulletin of the American Schools of Oriental Research*, no. 276 (1989): 77–84.

Zertal, Adam. "The Pahwah of Samaria (Northern Israel) during the Persian Period." *Transeuphratène* 3 (1990): 9–30.

Zertal, Adam. "Israel Enters Canaan: Following the Pottery Trail." *Biblical Archaeology Review* 17.5 (1991): 28–47.

ADAM ZERTAL

NORTHWEST SEMITIC SEAL INSCRIPTIONS.

Reflecting a long tradition of seal inscriptions in Egypt and Mesopotamia, cylinder and stamp seals from Ugarit and other second-millennium BCE Syro-Palestinian sites are inscribed in Egyptian hieroglyphics, syllabic cuneiform, or bilingual Akkadian-Hittite. On one tablet, the dynastic cylinder *aban kunukku ša šarri* ("seal of the king") is placed next to a king's personal alphabetical stamp seal (MÍŠMN). In the first millennium BCE, the use of bullae to seal papyri became widespread. Hebrew used two Egyptian words for *seal, ḥôtām* and *ṭabba'at*, to refer to royal Egyptian (*Gn.* 41:22) and Persian (*Est.* 3:10; cf. Aram. *'izqah, Dn.* 6:18) stamp seals, respectively. The seals are most often made of hard, semiprecious stones such as carnelian.

Aramaic cylinder seals were in use from about 800 BCE until the end of the Achaemenid Empire (c. 330 BCE). Descended from Egyptian scarabs and used until about 100 BCE, scaraboid stamp seals were strung on cords or mounted on rings. A typical example might measure 20 × 15 × 8 mm, with a surface area of 3 sq cm. The characters are usually legible on the imprints. The decoration, often engraved first by a skilled craftsman, may relate to the inscription (Pierre Bordreuil, "Sceau en calcèdoine grise en forme de canard" BAALIM III, *Syria* 63 [1986], p. 429), or not (Galling, 1941, no. 97; Bordreuil, 1986, nos. 29, 139). More than 1,200 different seals are attested either by the seal itself or by an impression: 150 Phoenician, nearly 500 Hebrew, including 220 bullae from the end of the preexilic period, (about 2,000 "royal" stamp sealings on which the text is "LMLK + toponym" are not included), more than 350 Aramaic, about 100 Ammonite, about 40 Moabite, and about 10 Edomite.

Corpora. The study of Northwest Semitic seals was inaugurated by James Tassie and Rudolf E. Raspe (1791), Moritz A. Levy (1857), Henry C. Rawlinson (1864), Melchior de Vogüé (1868), and M. A. Levy (1869). In 1883 Charles Clermont-Ganneau listed thirty seals and in volume 2 of the *Corpus Inscriptorum Semiticarum* (*CIS;* Paris, 1889) forty-two seals from different collections were reedited. Hebrew inscriptions stamped on earthenware jars in Palestine were known to scholars by the end of the nineteenth century: the stamps were inscribed YH(W)D ("Judah") or LMLK ("belonging to the king"), followed by a place name and the depiction of a flying scarab. In 1934, David Diringer summarized the one hundred and four known inscribed Hebrew seals, and in 1941, Kurt Galling assembled a catalog of 183 illustrated inscribed seals (Galling, 1941). In 1946, Nahman Avigad began publishing a number of then newly discovered seals (selected bibliography, *Eretz Israel* 18 [1985], Nahman Avigad Volume). In 1951, Sabatino Moscati expanded Diringer's list. Beginning in 1969, Francesco Vattioni assembled lists of known inscribed seals: 452 in Hebrew (1971, 1978), 178 in Aramaic (1971), and 104 in Phoenician (1981). In 1976, Avigad published more than seventy new Aramaic bullae dating from 515 to 445 BCE and a catalog of the inscribed seals in collections in the museums of Israel (Hestrin and Dayagi-Mendels, 1979) gathered 136 documents. The importance of Transjordanian glyptic has in recent years been made apparent (more than 150 inscribed seals in Moabite, Ammonite, and Edomite; cf. Herr, 1978, pp. 55–78). In 1986 Avigad published 255 bullae of high officials dating to the end of the seventh century BCE (e.g., BRKYHW BN NRYHW HSPR, YRḤM'L BN HMLK; cf. *Jer.* 36:4, 26) and a catalog of 139 seals from various museums in Paris. The principle museum collections of inscribed seals are those in the Biblioteque Nationale (106 examples), the Louvre (27), the Israel Museum (124), the British Museum (56), and the Vorderasiatisches Museum, Berlin (11).

Inscriptions. The first Phoenician seals date from the middle of the eighth century BCE. The lapidary script is illustrated by the scaraboid 'ŠTRT'Z (Bordreuil, 1986, no. 17). Systematic excavations have uncovered seals and seal impressions at Khorsabad (*ibid.*, no. 8), ʿAtlit (Galling, 1941, no. 110a), Sarepta (Vattioni, 1981, no. 350), Byblos, Tell Anafa, Tell Kazel, Ras Ibn Hani, Cyprus, various sites in the western Mediterranean basin, and on Delos (a bulla dating to 128/27 BCE; Bordreuil, 1992, col. 143ff.).

Shortly after 800 BCE, the two Hebrew sigillary scripts, Israelite and Judean, diverged, only to be replaced by Aramaic script just before 500 BCE. The writing on the Judean intaglio L'BYW ʿBD ʿZYW (Bordreuil, 1986, no. 40: "minister of ʿUzziyahu" [781–740?]) is typical of the dominant cursive, whereas the writing on the contemporary seal LŠMʿ ʿBD YRBʿM from Megiddo (Galling, 1941, no. 17: "minister of Jeroboam [II]," 787–747?) is quite different. Other examples come from Samaria, Shechem, Jerusalem, Lachish, Arad, Gibeon, Ramat Raḥel, and Wadi ed-Daliyeh.

Because of the prolonged use and geographic extent of the Aramaic language and script on seals, many varieties of the script are attested. By iconographic criteria the cylinder seals can be dated to between about 800 BCE (Bordreuil, 1986, no. 85) and about 600 BCE (Galling, 1941, no. 148). The conoids date from 700 BCE (*ibid.*, no. 113) to 450 BCE (Bordreuil, 1986, no. 132). The writing on the stamp seal of Nurshi' ("servant of ʿAtarshumki"; *ibid.*, no. 86), and on that of Bar Rakib son of Panamou (Vattioni, 1971, no. 129), is still monumental in style; beginning in about 750 BCE, until the end of its use shortly before 300 BCE, Aramaic script (*ibid.*, nos. 63, 64) was influenced by cursive writing. Because Aramaic was an important chancery language in the Achaemenid period, many "Arameo-Persian" cylinder seals have been in use.

The first Transjordanian seals were not discovered in excavation until after 1945. The Ammonite sigillary script was first identified by Avigad on Vattioni's (1969, 1978), no. 98: L'DNPLṬ ʿBD ʿMNDB. The person in question had already been identified as an official of a king of ʿAmmon, just as in the case of L'DNNR ʿBD ʿMNDB (Vattioni, 1969, 1978, no. 164), whose seal was discovered in a tomb. The succession of kings and the evolution of the Ammonite sigillary script in the seventh century BCE were established when the personnages BYD'L ʿBD PD'L (Bordreuil, 1986, no. 69) and MLKM'WR ʿBD BʿLYŠʿ (Bordreuil, 1992, col. 154) were identified. This writing was replaced between 600 and 500 BCE first by Aramaic script and later by the Aramaic language. The iconography is typified by the use of animal figures.

Three Moabite seals have come from excavations: KMŠNTN from Ur, BʿLNTN from Tello, and PLṬY BN M'Š HMZKR from Amman. Qos, the principal diety of the Edomites, appears as the theophoric element in various names attested on Transjordan seals.

Personal Names and Titles. Proper names, official titles, and professional titles are, with a few rare place names, the principal information given by the inscribed glyptics. These are not negligible, for not only do they sometimes expand our knowledge of theophorous names (derived from the names of deities), but they also present, on occasion, new proper names.

Phoenician names. In the Phoenician language, personal names may be of one of five constructions: (1) in a verbal phrase: perfect predicate-subject, ŠT'L ("El has put"; Bordreuil, 1986, no. 20); subject-predicate, BʿLYTN ("Baal has given"; Vattioni, 1981, no. 25); imperfect predicate-subject, YḤZBʿL ("Baal will look"; *ibid.*, no. 87); subject-predicate, BʿLYSP ("Baal will add"; Vattioni, 1969, no. 219), abbreviated, YZBL ("he will exalt"; Vattioni, 1969, 1978, no. 215), or the interrogative, MK'L ("who [is] like El?"; Vattioni, 1981, no. 84); (2) in a nonverbal phrase: nominal predicate-subject, NʿM'L ("El [is] agreeable"; Vattioni, 1969, no. 95); subject-predicate, ʿŠTRTʿZ ("Astart [is] strength"; Bordreuil, 1986, no. 17); or a construct state, GR'ŠMN ("host of Eshmun"; Vattioni, 1981, no. 93); (3) as a single noun, KPR ("lion"; Bordreuil, 1986, no. 24); (4) a hypocoristic verbal, ŠB' ("the divinity has returned"; Vattioni, 1981, no. 71); or (5) a divine name, a place name, such as ṢRPT (Sarepta), or an occupation, such as H'MN ("the artisan"; Vattioni, 1978, no. 256).

Hebrew names. Personal names in the Hebrew language may be of one of four constructions: (1) in a verbal phrase: perfect predicate-subject, 'MRYHW ("Y said"; Vattioni, 1978, no. 211); subject-predicate, 'LḤNN ("El favored"; Vattioni, 1969, no. 5); abbreviated 'ḤZ ("he took"; *ibid.*, no. 141); imperfect predicate-subject, Y'ZNYHW ("Y will hear"; Vattioni, 1969, 1978, no. 69); subject-predicate, YHWYḤY ("Y will make live"; Avigad, *Eretz Israel* 20 [1989], no. 3), abbreviated, Y'R ("he will make light"; Vattioni, 1969, no. 104); the imperative, DMLYHW ("live before Y"; *ibid.*, no. 19); the interrogative, M(Y)KYHW ("who is like Y?"; *ibid.*, no. 30); (2) a nonverbal phrase: nominal predicate-subject, 'BY(H)W ("Y [is] father"; Bordreuil, 1986, no. 40); subject-predicate, YW'B ("Y [is] father"; Vattioni, 1969, no. 9); prepositional, BDYHW ("in the hand of Y"; Vattioni, 1978, no. 393); (3) a construct state relation, 'Ḥ'B ("father's brother"; Vattioni, 1969, no. 57); an abstract noun, MTNYHW ("gift of Y"; Vattioni, 1978, no. 268); and (4) a single noun, 'PRḤ ("chick"; *ibid.*, no. 239); hypocoristic verbal, BRKY ("the divinity has blessed"; Vattioni, 1969, no. 193); nominal 'B' ("the divinity [is] father"; *ibid.*, no. 160); or a construct state: 'ŠN' ("gift [of god]"; *ibid.*, no. 141); place name, D'R (Vattioni, 1978, no. 323; or title of occupation, 'ŠR ʿL HBYT ("majordomo"; *ibid.*, no. 149).

Aramaic names. In Aramaic, personal names may be one of six constructions: (1) in a verbal phrase: perfect predicate-subject, YPʿHD ("Hadad made resplendent"; Vattioni, 1971, no. 72); subject-predicate, 'LYHB ("El has provided"; *ibid.*, no. 70); abbreviated, NTN ("he has given"; *ibid.*, no. 85); imperfect predicate-subject, YʿDR'L ("El will aid"; *ibid.*, no. 19); abbreviated, YG'L ("he will buy back"; Vattioni, 1978, no. 309); verbal adjective, BLḤY ("Bel is living"; Vattioni, 1971, no. 116); (2) a nonverbal phrase:

nominal predicate-subject, GBR⟨H⟩D ("Hadad [is] powerful"; *ibid.*, no. 63); subject-predicate, 'BRM ("the father [is] elevated"; Vattioni, 1969, no. 66); prepositional, HDBʿD ("Hadad [is] behind"; Vattioni, 1971, no. 55); (3) a construct state, NRŠ' ("light of sin"; Bordreuil, 1986, no. 86); (4) using nouns, SʿLY (= ŠʿLY, "little fox"; Vattioni, 1971, no. 7), BRWK (Heb., "blessed"; Vattioni, 1978, no. 308); (5) using a transcription 'N'Ḥ'TN (Vattioni, 1971, no. 124) of the Akkadian *'Anu-aḫa-iddin(a)* ("Anu has given a brother"), of the Egyptian, ḤRḤRBY ("Horus of Kheb"; *ibid.*, no. 91), or of the Persian, 'RTDT/Artadata ("given by justice"; *ibid.*, no. 75); or (6) a hypocoristic verbal, BRKY ("the divinity has blessed"; Bordreuil, 1986, no. 95); an interrogative MYKH ("who [is] like the divinity?"; Vattioni, 1978, no. 313); the nominal 'DY ("the divinity [is] Adad"; Bordreuil, 1986, no. 127); or the title of an occupation PḤW' ("governor"; Vattioni, 1978, no. 306).

Ammonite names. In Ammonite, personal names may be one of five constructions: (1) a verbal phrase: perfect postpositive subject, 'MR'L ("El said"; Battioni, 1978, no. 259); prepositive subject, 'LZKR ("El remembered"; Bordreuil, 1986, no. 82); an abbreviated form, ŠMʿ ("he has heard"; Vattioni, 1978, no. 440); the imperfect postpositive subject YNḤM'L (unpublished; "El will console"); the abbreviated form, YNḤM ("he will console"; Vattioni, 1969, no. 103); and the interrogative, MKM'L ("who [is] like El?"; *ibid.*, no. 445); (2) in a nonverbal phrase: nominal predicate subject, NʿMʿM (Vattioni, 1969, no. 29, new reading: "the paternal uncle [is] agreeable"); subject-predicate, 'BGD ("the father [is] fortune"; *ibid.*, no. 234); prepositional, BDMLKM ("in the hand of Milkom"; Vattioni, 1971, no. 16); (3) in a construct state, MQNMLK ("possession of milk"; Bordreuil, 1986, no. 73); (4) in a noun, ŠʿL ("fox"; Vattioni, 1969, no. 41); (5) in a transcription of the Akkadian, MNG' NRT/Mannu-ki Ninurta ("who [is] like Ninurta?"; Vattioni, 1978, no. 225); in a hypocoristic verbal, TMK' ("the divinity has supported"; *ibid.*, no. 318); in an interrogative, 'Y' ("where [is] the divinity?"; Bordreuil, 1986, no. 72); in a nominal 'L' ("the divinity [is] El"; Vattioni, 1978, no. 262); and in a construct state, 'BD' ("servant of the divinity"; *ibid.*, no. 217) or an occupation, HNSS ("the standard bearer"; *ibid.*, no. 261).

Moabite names. In Moabite, personal names may be one of four constructions: (1) in a verbal phrase: perfect predicate-subject, ʿD'L ("El testified"; Vattioni, 1969, no. 146); subject-predicate, KMŠNTN ("Kamosh has given"; *ibid.*, no. 265); imperfect subject-predicate, KMŠYḤY ("Kamosh will make live"); (2) in a nonverbal phrase: nominal predicate-subject, GDMLK ("milk [is] fortune"; *ibid.*, no. 64); subject-predicate, KMŠ'L ("Kamosh [is] god"; *ibid.*, no. 113); a construct state; ʿBDYRḤ ("servant of Yarih"; Vattioni, 1971, no. 86); (3) in a noun, 'MṢ ("fort"; Vattioni, 1969, no. 74); or (4) in a hypocoristic, YŠʿ' ("the divinity has saved"; *ibid.*, no. 85), a gentilic, MṢRY ("Musrite"; Bordreuil, 1986, no. 65), or an occupation, HSPR ("the scribe"; Vattioni, 1969, no. 74).

Edomite names. In Edomite, personal names may be one of the following constructions: in a nominal phrase, subject-predicate, QWS G [BR] ("Qos [is] strong"; F. Israel, *Rivista Biblica Italiana* 27 [1979], no. 5, p. 172); a prepositional phrase, BʿZR'L ("with the aid of El"; Vattioni, 1969, no. 118); a hypocoristic phrase, QWS' ("Qos [is] god"; Israel, *Rivista Biblica Italiana* 27 [1979], no. 16, p. 176); or an occupation, ʿBD HBʿL ("servant of the master"; Bordreuil, 1992, col. 197).

Titles. Seals belonging to "servants" of kings, such as Shemaʿ and Abyau (see above), of YHWZ⌈R⌉Ḥ . . . ʿBD ḤZ⌈Q⌉YHW (Hestrin and Dayagi-Mendels, 1979, no. 4), of ŠBNYW ʿBD ʿZYW (Bordreuil, 1986, no. 41), of ʿŠN' ʿBD 'ḤZ (Galling, 1941, no. 1a; Hestrin and Dayagi-Mendels, 1979, no. 40), of ʿBD'L . . . ʿBD MTT . . . ("king of Ashkelon"; Vattioni, 1969, no. 73), of BYD'L, 'DNNR, and of MLKM'WR (see above) include an epigraphic and/or iconographic version of their title. The sovereign is occasionally designated anonymously: Y'ZNYHW ʿBD HMLK (Vattioni, 1979, no. 69). A ʿBD HML'K ("servant of the king") may have been in charge of palace provisions. Was the title YHW'ḤZ BN HMLK ("son of Josiah"? [*2 Kgs.* 23:30ff.]; *ibid.*, no. 252) common to the royal family? Did YRḤM'L BN HMLK (Avigad, 1986, no. 8) participate in the arrest of Jeremiah (*Jer.* 36:26)?

'MT ("female servant"; *ibid.*, no.157), as in ŠLMYT 'MT 'LNTN P⌈Ḥ⌉[W'], may have been a woman in charge of the provincial archives, subject to the provincial governor (Avigad, 1976, no. 14). 'ŠT ("wife"), as in 'ḤTMLK 'ŠT YŠʿ (Vattioni, 1969, no. 63), may be ascribed an important status on the basis of the iconography of the seal. A PḤW' was a "governor" in the Achaemenid administration (cf. the bulla in Vattioni, 1978, no. 408 belonging to the PḤT of Samaria Sin-uballit [e.g., *Neh.* 2:10]). HMZKR ("the herald"; Bordreuil, 1992, col. 187) announces (ZKR) royal decisions. HSPR ("the scribe") could receive an order of the king (Vattioni, 1969, no. 41). BRKYHW BN NRYHW HSPR (Avigad, 1986, no. 9) was in all likelihood Jeremiah's secretary (*Jer.* 36:26). HNSS was "the standard bearer" (Vattioni, 1969, no. 261). GDLYHW 'ŠR ʿL HBYT was a "major-domo" (Vattioni, 1978, no. 149), perhaps the governor of Judea (Judah) mentioned in *2 Kings* 25:22–25. 'ŠR ʿL HMS (Bordreuil, 1992, col. 188ff.) was responsible for forced labor; ŠʿR HMSGR (*ibid.*, col. 189) was the "gatekeeper of the prison"); HʿD (*ibid.*, col. 189) was the "the witness," a ministerial officer; and HRP' (*ibid.*, col. 189) was "the doctor."

Six sealings from seals belonging to L'LYQM NʿR YWKN (NʿR means "page"; Vattioni, 1969, 1978, no. 108) date to the end of the eighth century BCE, as do the LMLK sealings, which are unknown in other periods. Other occupations are PRʿ ("chief"; Vattioni, 1969, no. 126), TRTN ("commander in chief"; Bordreuil, 1992, col. 192), ŠR HʿR ("governor of the city"; *ibid.*, col. 192), and PQD YH⸢D⸣ ("inspector of Ju⸢de⸣a"; *ibid.*, col. 192). The Phoenician fiscal seals of the fourth century BCE bear ʿŠR ("exaction of the tithe"), a place name (Sarepta, etc.), and a regnal year. Royal seals present an "iconographic" version in which a figure bearing an Egyptian crown and scepter with one hand raised: Musuri, king of Moab (MṢRY [?], in Vattioni, 1981, no. 19); Abibaal of Samsimuruna ('BYBʿL [?], *ibid.*, no. 27); and Hanunu of Gaza (ḤNN [?]; Hestrin and Dayagi-Mendels, 1979, no. 123). A Phoenician stamp seal (550 BCE) reads LMLK ṢRPT ("belonging to the king of Sarepta"; Bordreuil, 1992, col. 194ff.). There are seals of priests: ZKRYW KHN D'R ("Zekaryau priest of Dor"; Vattioni, 1978, no. 323) and ḤNN B//N ḤLQYHW // HKHN ("Hanan son of Hilqiyahou the priest"; Bordreuil, 1992, col. 195ff.). On Aramaic seals figures greet a divine representation (Bordreuil, 1986, no. 117) or pray (*ibid.*, no. 123).

Phoenician tesserae (100 BCE) bear the inscriptions LMLQRT BṢR ("belonging to Milqart of Tyre"; Bordreuil, 1992, col. 199) and HYRW'SLS, the latter a transcription of the Greek words *hiera* and *asulos* ("sacred and inviolable"). Others evoked the favor of the goddess Tannit, ḤN(T) TMT. Seals (Vattioni, 1969, no. 31), sometimes made of blue material (lapis lazuli or chalcedony), are decorated with eyes (Bordreuil, 1986, no. 53) intended to ward off the evil eye. Seals with an inscription consisting of the first twelve letters of the alphabet has been explained as magical in nature (Bordreuil, 1992, col. 200). The only seal labeled with the name of Baal (Bordreuil, 1986, no. 37) may have been used to seal documents from a Phoenician sanctuary.

[*See also* Names and Naming; Seals; *and entries on specific languages.*]

BIBLIOGRAPHY

Avigad, Nahman. *Bullae and Seals from a Post-Exilic Judean Archive*. Qedem, vol. 4. Jerusalem, 1976.

Avigad, Nahman. *Hebrew Bullae from the Time of Jeremiah: Remnants of a Burnt Archive*. Jerusalem, 1986.

Bordreuil, Pierre. *Catalogue des sceaux ouest-sémitiques inscrits de la Bibliothèque Nationale, du Musée du Louvre et du Musée Biblique de Bible et Terre Sainte*. Paris, 1986.

Bordreuil, Pierre. "Sceaux inscrits des pays du Levant." In *Dictionnaire de la Bible,* supp. 12, cols. 86–212. Paris, 1992.

Galling, Kurt. "Beschriftete Bildsiegel des ersten Jahrtausends v. Chr. vornehmlich aus Syrien und Palästina." *Zeitschrift des Deutschen Palästina-Vereins* 64 (1941): 121–202.

Herr, Larry G. *The Scripts of Ancient Northwest Semitic Seals*. Harvard Semitic Monograph Series, no. 18. Missoula, 1978.

Hestrin, Ruth, and Michal Dayagi-Mendels. *Inscribed Seals. First Temple Period: Hebrew, Ammonite, Moabite, Phoenician, and Aramaic*. Jerusalem, 1979.

Vattioni, Francesco. "I sigilli ebraici." *Biblica* 50 (1969): 357–388; *Augustinianum* 11 (1971): 433–454.

Vattioni, Francesco. "I sigilli, le monete e gli avori aramaici." *Augustinianum* 11 (1971): 47–87.

Vattioni, Francesco. "I sigilli ebraici, III." *Annali dell'Istituto Orientale di Napoli* 38 (1978): 227–254.

Vattioni, Francesco. "I sigilli fenici." *Annali dell'Istituto Orientale di Napoli* 41 (1981): 177–193.

PIERRE BORDREUIL

Translated from French by Melissa Kaprelian

NOTH, MARTIN (1902–1968), historian and leading figure in the German school of biblical studies. Noth was born in Dresden, Germany, and studied at Erlangen, Rostock, and Leipzig. His central intellectual concern was the history of Israel in the biblical period. As a student of Rudolph Kittel and Albrecht Alt, his early work concentrated on the history of early Israelite religion through a study of personal names (1928). This was followed shortly by *Das System der zwölf Stämme Israels* (1930), a widely influential book proposing the existence of an Israelite twelve-tribe amphictyony in premonarchic Israel. These two works were augmented over the next four decades by studies of the literature of the Hebrew Bible (notably *Genesis–2 Kings, Chronicles, Ezra–Nehemiah*), which Noth believed were the most likely sources of historical information concerning Israel. In his work, archaeology was seen as necessary for understanding the wider context of the written material but limited in the type of information it could provide. Noth's evaluation of the role of archaeology within biblical studies contrasted sharply with that of American scholars of the same period, most notably William Foxwell Albright and G. Ernest Wright. Although he was not directly involved in major excavations, the issues Noth raised in his synthesis in the *History of Israel* (1960), and in the studies that led to the volume, have set the questions for much of the archaeological work since his time.

A major component of Noth's contribution to the field of archaeology is to be found in his numerous studies of topography and written materials (e.g., from Mari, Egypt, and Ugarit). Many of these studies appeared in the journal *Zeitschrift des Deutschen Palästina-Vereins,* which he edited from 1929 to 1964. His approach to archaeological information is illustrated in his 1964 survey of the setting of the biblical material. While acknowledging the independence of archaeology as a discipline, he recognized the difficulty in connecting archaeological material with written evidence (*Die Welt des Alten Testaments,* Berlin 1964). The depth of his involvement with archaeological data is indicated by his participation in *Seminars* at the Deutsches Evangelisches Institute für Altertumswissenschaft des Heiligen Landes in Jerusalem and his directorship of that institution from 1964 until the time of his death. Prior to this he had been professor at the Universities of Königsberg (1930–1944) and Bonn (1945–1967).

Noth's significant contributions within biblical studies include work in the areas of form, redaction, and tradition criticism. Particularly important were his proposals of a Deuteronomistic history stretching from *Deuteronomy* through *2 Kings;* his studies on the development of the Pentateuchal traditions, proposing a common source *(Grundlage)* for the Yahwistic and Elohistic sources; and his work on the Chronicler's history. His wide-ranging interests are exemplified by his editorship of several journals, including *Vetus Testamentum* (1951–1959), *Zeitschrift für Theologie und Kirche* (1950–1962), and *Welt des Orients* (1947–1964).

[*See also the biographies of Albright, Alt, and Wright.*]

BIBLIOGRAPHY

McKenzie, Steven L., and M. Patrick Graham, eds. *The History of Israel's Traditions: The Heritage of Martin Noth.* Journal for the Study of the Old Testament, Supplement Series, 182. Sheffield, 1994.

Noth, Martin. *Die israelitischen Personennamen im Rahmen der gemeinsemitischen Namengebung.* Stuttgart, 1928.

Noth, Martin. *Das System der zwölf Stämme Israels.* Stuttgart, 1930.

Noth, Martin. *A History of Pentateuchal Traditions* (1948). Translated by Bernhard W. Anderson. Englewood Cliffs, N.J., 1972.

Noth, Martin. *The History of Israel* (1950). New York, 1960. Revised translation.

Noth, Martin. *The Deuteronomistic History* (1957). Journal for the Study of the Old Testament, Supplement Series, 15. Sheffield, 1981.

Noth, Martin. *The Old Testament World* (1964). Translated by Victor I. Gruhn. Philadelphia, 1966.

Weippert, Manfred, and Helga Weippert. "German Archaeologists." In *Benchmarks in Time and Culture: An Introduction to Palestinian Archaeology Dedicated to Joseph A. Callaway,* edited by Joel F. Drinkard et al., pp. 87–108. Atlanta, 1988. Survey of the role of German archaeologists in Israel in the twentieth century.

ROBERT D. HAAK

NUBIA, ancient land that extended from Aswan in the north to the region below Khartoum, the capital of the modern Republic of the Sudan. Like Egypt, Nubia was divided into northern and southern regions. The northern part (Lower Nubia), bordered on southern Egypt and the southern part (Upper Nubia) stretched from the Third to the Sixth Cataract of the Nile. Also like Egypt, Nubia was divided by the Nile; however, the river in Nubia was bounded by a very narrow strip of arable land. The Nile remained an important route of transportation between settlements, serving as a conduit to the rest of Africa and enabling the trading of ivory, ebony, gold, and animal skins. Fishing and hunting game in the marshes beside the Nile was an important part of the Nubian diet.

Settlement in Nubia goes back into the Paleolithic period (before c. 25,000 BCE). Evidence of this occupation consists of scatters of stone tools found on the desert margins of the Nile. Later inhabitants left rock drawings and other remains of one of the world's earliest settlements. Traces of this settled Mesolithic culture were found in the area of modern day Khartoum and date to around 6000.

The Lower Nubian Neolithic cultures are closely linked to the Upper Egyptian Predynastic sequence (c. 5000–3100). The first truly distinctive Nubian civilization to be identified by archaeologists is known as the A-Group. It appeared in the area of Lower Nubia in the period immediately preceding the unification of Egypt around 3100. It lasted through the first and second dynasties in Egypt (c. 2985). The A-Group produced very fine ceramics, which were painted to resemble baskets. Along with locally produced wares imported pottery and stone vessels from Egypt are found in A-Group contexts.

Excavations at Qustul by the University of Chicago revealed large, rich graves of local kings (Emery, 1965, Williams, 1986). These tombs date to the period just before the unification of Egypt and represent one of the early states found along the Nile at the end of the Neolithic. The A-Group disappeared suddenly before the end of the Egyptian second dynasty (c. 2650). Neither the written nor the archaeological record provides a satisfactory explanation for the end of the A-Group civilization. Texts indicate that raids were made into Nubia from Egypt by the pharaohs of the Early Dynastic Period and the Old Kingdom.

Egyptian inscriptions dating to the Old Kingdom have been found in the diorite quarries in Lower Nubia and an Old Kingdom town was excavated at Buhen by Walter Emery. Snefru, founder of the fourth dynasty (c. 2575–2465) recorded that he brought from Nubia seven thousand prisoners and two hundred thousand head of cattle. The loss of such an important economic product as that many cattle may account for the "impoverishment" seen in the archaeological record. The prisoners may well belong to the so-called B-Group, the poor successors to the A-Group kingdom.

By the end of the Old Kingdom (late sixth dynasty, c. 2150), the Egyptian record shows peaceful trade relations between Egypt and Nubia, as is recorded in the tomb of Wenis at Saqqara and the tombs of the governors of Aswan, Harkhuf, and Pepinakht. Egypt's power over Nubia decreased during the First Intermediate Period. By the late First Intermediate Period, a new culture known as the C-Group began to appear in Lower Nubia. A reunited Egypt again exerted control over Nubia in the Middle Kingdom. Fortresses were built at Kuban, Aniba, Serra East, Buhen, Kor, Dabenarti, Mirgissa, Askut, Uronarti, Kumma, Semna, and Semna South. These forts were constructed to protect Egypt from the growing power of the first kingdom of Kush. The kingdom was centered in the third cataract area at the site of Kerma, excavated by George A. Reisner for Harvard University and the Museum of Fine Arts, Boston, from 1913 through 1916. [*See the biography of Reisner.*] There were three distinct cultural groups active in Lower Nubia during this time: the Kerma culture; the C-Group peoples, who were nomadic cattle herders; and the Pan-Grave people, desert nomads who served as mercenary soldiers for the Egyptians. The Kerma culture eventually allied itself with the Hyksos (Asiatic) overlords of Egypt in the Second Intermediate Period.

The Kerma kingdom and the Hyksos were eventually destroyed by the Theban pharaohs of the early eighteenth dynasty (c. 1550–1505). The C-Group remained under Egyptian control as evidenced by a fortified settlement of C-Group peoples and Egyptians excavated by the University of Pennsylvania at Areika (Randall-MacIver and Woolley, 1909).

The New Kingdom (eighteenth–twentieth dynasties, c. 1550–1070) marks an important change in the relations between Egypt and Nubia. At the outset of the Egyptian reoccupation the Middle Kingdom fortresses were reoccupied and the temples within them rebuilt. The Egyptians instituted a gradual process of egyptianization. Nubian princes visited the Egyptian court as depicted in the tomb of the governor of Nubia under Tutankhamun, Huy (Davies, 1926).

The temples, rather than the forts served as the main administrative centers by the mid- and later New Kingdom. Rameses II (c. 1290–1224) of the nineteenth dynasty built a great number of temples. One of the more impressive structures was the great temple at Abu Simbel. [*See* Abu Simbel.] However, the most important Egyptian temple complex was that dedicated to Amun at Gebel Barkal; it was established by Thutmosis III (c. 1479–1425) was expanded by nearly every pharaoh of the eighteenth and nineteenth dynasties through Rameses II. It continued to function long after Nubia had again slipped from Egyptian control at the end of the New Kingdom (Davies, 1991; Kemp, 1989; O'Connor, 1983).

Around 800 a local Nubian dynasty began to rise to power in the area of the fourth cataract at Napata. By about 750 it extended its control over all of Nubia, and within another generation it had assumed control of Egypt. The Assyrians invaded Egypt in 663 and the Nubian rule over Egypt came to an end.

The Nubian rulers of the second kingdom of Kush continued to rule for another thousand years. Because Napata remained both the chief cult center of the kingdom and the burial place of its kings, the first half of the second kingdom of Kush is known as the Napatan period. After the third century, the center of political and religious power in the kingdom of Kush shifted south to the city of Meroë. Culturally and politically the ensuing Meroitic period was also very different from the preceding Napatan period. Although the Nubians continued to respect Egyptian traditions, they were also influenced both by Ptolemaic, Roman, and central African ideals. Many of the gods they worshiped were unique; their art and architecture were highly original; and they began to express their own language in an alphabetic script. [*See* Meroë.]

Eventually it appears as though Meroë itself was invaded and destroyed by the armies from Axum in Ethiopia. Nubia was divided into three kingdoms in the Christian period—Nabata in the north, Makouria between the Third and Fourth Cataract, and Alwa at the junction of the Blue and White branches of the Nile. About 350 CE Makouria and Nabata became one kingdom under a single ruler with its capital at Old Dongola.

Nubia became Islamic territory with the treaty of Baqt (640 CE). In that period, Nubia showed a revival in art, literature and architecture, evidencing both Coptic and Byzantine influence. In the sixth century CE missionaries from Egypt and Byzantium converted the various Nubian peoples to Christianity, and two rival Christian kingdoms emerged in the north and south. These survived until the fourteenth century, when they were finally overwhelmed by Arab peoples and superseded by Islamic states.

BIBLIOGRAPHY

Adams, William Y. *Nubia: Corridor to Africa.* Princeton, 1977.

Arkell, Anthony J. *Early Khartoum: An Account of the Excavation of an Early Occupation Site Carried Out by the Sudan Government Antiquities Service in 1944–5.* London, 1949.

Davies, N. deG. *The Theban Tomb Series.* Vol. 4, *The Tomb of Huy.* London, 1926.

Davies, W. V., ed. *Egypt and Africa: Nubia from Prehistory to Islam.* London, 1991.

Emery, W. B. *Egypt in Nubia.* London, 1965.

Gratien, Brigitte. *Les cultures Kerma.* Lille, 1978.

Kadish, Gerald E. "Old Kingdom Egyptian Activity in Nubia: Some Reconsiderations." *Journal of Egyptian Archaeology* 52 (1966): 23–33.

Kemp, Barry. *Ancient Egypt: Anatomy of Civilization.* London and New York, 1989.

O'Connor, David. "Nubia before the New Kingdom." In *Africa in Antiquity: The Arts of Ancient Nubia and the Sudan,* vol. 1, *The Essays,* pp. 46–61. Brooklyn, 1978.

O'Connor, David. "New Kingdom and Third Intermediate Period, 1552–664 B.C." In *Ancient Egypt: A Social History,* edited by Bruce Trigger et al. Cambridge, 1983.

O'Connor, David. *Ancient Nubia: Egypt's Rival in Africa.* Philadelphia, 1993.

Randall-MacIver, D., and C. L. Woolley. *Areika.* Philadelphia, 1909.

Reisner, George. *Excavations at Kerma.* Pts. 1–3 (Harvard African Studies, 5); pts. 4–5 (Harvard African Studies, 6). Cambridge, Mass., 1923.

Säve-Söderbergh, Torgny. *Ägypten und Nubien: Ein Beitrag zur Geschichte altägyptischer Aussenpolitik.* Lund, 1941.

Trigger, Bruce G. *History and Settlement in Lower Nubia.* New Haven, 1965.

Trigger, Bruce G. *Nubia under the Pharaohs.* London, 1976.

Wendorf, Fred, ed. *The Prehistory of Nubia.* 2 vols. Dallas, 1968.

Williams, Bruce. *The University of Chicago Oriental Institute Nubian Expedition.* Vol. 3, pt. 1, *The A-Group Royal Cemetery at Qustal: Cemetery L.* Chicago, 1986.

ZAHI HAWASS

NUZI (genitive of Nuzu, modern Yorgan Tepe), site located in northeastern Iraq, 13 km (8 mi.) southwest of Kirkuk (35°21′47″ N, 44°15′30″ E). Kirkuk (ancient Arrapḫa - *āl-ilāni*) was the source of tablets that had been sold on the antiquities market. Nothing was known about the origin or historical context of these tablets, which were marked by a peculiar dialect of Akkadian and contained Hurrian onomastica that had previously been encountered in letters of the Amarna archive in Egypt and in Kassite-period texts from Nippur. The search for an uninhabited site more suited for excavation led to Nuzi, where a cache of similar tablets had been discovered near the main mound.

Nuzi comprises a main mound and several smaller tells. Oriented northwest–southeast, the mound measures about 200 × 200 m, with an average height of 5 m above the surrounding plain. Only three of the smaller tells were investigated: one prehistoric site (Qudish Ṣaghīr), about 5 km (3 mi.) to the south, and two small mid-second millennium BCE sites, about 300 m to the north. Occupation of the main mound extended from the prehistoric to the Mitannian/Middle Assyrian period, followed by meager remnants of habitation in the Neo-Assyrian, Parthian, and early Sasanian periods (the "late period"). Identified as Gasur by recurrent late third-millennium BCE textual references and as Nuzu/Nuzi in the mid-second millennium BCE, the site is known primarily for the latter occupation. Its stratified Mitannian/Middle Assyrian period archives of more than five thousand sealed tablets span five or six generations of a mainly Hurrian population in the kingdom of Arrapḫa, the easternmost province of Mitanni. Published extensively over the years, the archives sparked intense study of the social, economic, religious, and legal institutions of the Nuzians/Hurrians, whose presumed identity with the biblical Horites *(ḥōrī[m])* prompted several comparisons with the patriarchal customs of the Hebrew Bible. Nuzi replaced Kirkuk as the generic term for analogous tablets and seal impressions from neighboring mounds, including Kirkuk/Arrapḫa and Tell al-Faḫḫar/Kurruḫanni. The associated material culture, notably painted ceramics, glazed wares, and glass and faience objects became diagnostic of the so-called Nuzi period.

Excavations and Division of Finds. At the request of Gertrude Bell, director of antiquities in Iraq, Edward Chiera led the first campaign to Nuzi in 1925–1926, under the joint auspices of the Iraq Museum and the American Schools of Oriental Research. Work began on the small northwestern tell, in the house of Šurki-tilla (two buildings) and the house of Teḫip-tilla. The excavated material was divided between the two supporting institutions.

The subsequent four campaigns, sponsored jointly by the Fogg Art Museum and the Harvard Semitic Museum in Boston and the American Schools of Oriental Research, were directed by Chiera (1927–1928), Robert H. Pfeiffer (1928–1929), and Richard F. S. Starr (1929–1930, 1930–1931). The finds were divided between the Iraq Museum and Harvard University. From the northwestern tell, Chiera moved to the northeastern tell, where he excavated the house of Zike and the house of Šilwa-teššup before turning to the main mound. Pfeiffer introduced a grid system. In addition to completing Chiera's excavation of the palace and adjacent domestic structures to the southwest and northeast, Pfeiffer initiated two test pits in rooms N120 and L4 to establish the sequence of occupation. Starr concentrated on the northwestern ridge and the temple complex. Once the upper levels associated with the widespread Nuzi tablets had been cleared, work focused on an investigation of the lower strata in the temple area (temples A–G), along the northwestern ridge (strata I–IV), and on the southeastern edge in the region of the city wall (strata V–VIII). Pit L4 was extended down to virgin soil, providing a continuous sequence of fifteen occupation levels (pavements I–XII).

Stratigraphy and Chronology. Three stratigraphic schemes were used simultaneously and only tentatively integrated into a single system. Their only contact is during the final Nuzi period between pavement I, stratum II, and temple A, which were also linked by a complicated drainage system and the Nuzi tablets. The date of the tablets hinged until recently on a letter bearing the seal impression of Sauštatar, son of Parsatatar, king of Mitanni, whose reign fluctuates within the fifteenth century BCE. It now appears that the seal was probably an heirloom and that a later date for stratum II conforms with the evidence from other sites where Nuzi-related material is dated by associated texts to the mid-fourteenth and thirteenth centuries BCE. The range of the Nuzi archives is currently posited between 1445/1425 and 1350/1330 BCE, following the low chronology. The variant dating of the latest Nuzi texts and the destruction of the site depends, then, on the Aššur-mutakkil synchronism in the first or second generation at Nuzi and on historical-political factors that best match the socioeconomic turmoil reflected in the latest Nuzi records.

Too little remains of the uppermost stratum I material to extend the duration of the Nuzi period much beyond the stratum II destruction date. The origin of this period is less certain. Although architectural and material remains of the Nuzi period are represented in the lower pavement II, strata III–IV, and temples B–E, Starr's correlation between stratum IV and temple E is contested by Ruth Opificius, who relates stratum IV to temple F, which she considers Old Babylonian by its pottery and figurines (*Das altbabylonische Terrakottarelief*, Untersuchungen zur Assyriologie und vorderasiatischen Archäologie, 2, Berlin, 1961, pp. 18–19). The latter would be compatible with Starr's own comparison between the pottery of strata IV and VII.

Most scholars agree on the synchronism between pavements IIA and IIB, strata V–VII, and temple F. One Old Babylonian tablet and five early Old Assyrian tablets from pavement IIA and one Ur III tablet found in or above pavement IIB–III (a rubbish deposit) provide a tentative chronological range (c. 2100–1650 BCE) for pavements IIA, IIB, and IIB–III, whose contents are considered transitional between those of the upper Nuzi pavements and the lower Gasur pavements. Opinions diverge over the association of the Gasur pavement III, dated by tablets to the Old Akkadian period, with temple G and stratum VIII by virtue of their relative position directly below the transitional phase. Structural as well as ceramic links between temples F and

G and between strata VII and VIII support a later Ur III/Isin-Larsa date instead.

Pavements III to VIII were disturbed by numerous graves, so that any demarcation of the Old Akkadian occupation, linked variously with pavements III–V and III–IX, remains inconclusive. Henry W. Eliot (in Starr, 1939) has tentatively identified pavement VI as Early Dynastic, VII as Late Uruk, and VIII–IX as Uruk. The earliest deposits, pavements XA–XII, belong to the Ubaid period.

Prehistoric period. Represented in pits L4 and G50 and on Qudish Ṣaghir, the lowest levels for the prehistoric period are characterized by packed clay (pisé) walls and incised, knobbed, and painted wares. The painted wares are superseded by unpainted wares in pavement X, which sees the introduction of mud-brick construction and infant burials. A cache of marble stamp seals from G50 is attributed to this period on typological grounds.

Gasur and transitional periods. The Gasur occupation is encountered in pits L4 and G50 and, according to Starr, in the City Wall (stratum VIII) and temples G and F. It is identified and dated by 222 tablets attributed to the early Old Akkadian period on linguistic, orthographic, and paleographic grounds. Most notable among the mainly business documents, in which Semitic names predominate, is an inscribed clay "map" that accompanies a record of land and appears to locate an estate within the district of Gasur. The small finds include a terra-cotta mold for casting animal-shaped amulets and a copper statuette from temple G. The cultural pottery is typified by incised gray-ware vases, zoomorphic vessels, house-shaped stands, and relief decoration in the form of applied snakes, scorpions, and quadrupeds. The glyptic evidence comprises impressions of one cylinder seal and two stamp seals and five cylinder seals (including a shell seal mounted on a copper pin that accompanied a burial).

Nuzi period. The Nuzi period was fully excavated over the entire mound and on both northern tells. The evidence of architecture, texts, glyptic, and luxury products provides the most complete picture of a provincial town on the eastern edge of the Mitannian kingdom toward the end of its hegemony. As such, the Nuzi material complements the evidence from Alalakh levels V and IV, which represents a provincial town on the western edge of the Mitannian kingdom during its formative and mature phase.

Architecture and architectural decoration. Stratum II structures on the main mound include a palace and temple complex surrounded by well-constructed municipal buildings along the northwestern ridge and denser residential sectors on the southeast, southwest, and northeast. Five contemporary buildings, associated by their archives with wealthy landowners and high-ranking officials, were excavated outside the citadel walls on the northern tells.

The tripartite palace plan, incorporating old and new elements, is divided into a formal area consisting of rooms grouped conventionally around courtyards; an agglutinate administrative section south of the outer courtyard; and residential quarters beyond the throne room to the southwest. The main entrance, though not preserved, would have led into the outer courtyard (M94), which was bordered by benches. A connecting room with a hearth (M89) gave indirect access to the inner courtyard (M100), which was flanked by reception rooms and apartments. This separation of the public from the official domain, while reminiscent of the palace plans at Mari and Tell Asmar, becomes a characteristic of Neo-Assyrian palaces. The entrance to the unusually juxtaposed anteroom (L20) and audience hall (L4/11) is marked by two freestanding brick pillars that may have supported a portico or canopy. The supposed chapel directly north of the audience hall was devoid of cult fittings, and Starr's identification of a kitchen in the administrative sector has also been queried on practical grounds. Luxuriously furnished with a sophisticated drainage system, marble paving, and silver-coated copper door studs, the palace is best known for its well-preserved frescoes, also found outside the citadel in the house of Prince Šilwa-teššup, which resembles the palace on a smaller scale. The more elaborate examples show figured designs in panels of solid red and gray framed by geometric patterns arranged in an architectural scheme of bands and metopes. The Hathor head, bucranion, and palmette tree are recurrent motifs that also appear on ceramics, cylinder seals, and plaques. The designs reflect the current taste for foreign, in this case Egyptian and Aegean, imagery.

During the Isin-Larsa/Old Babylonian Period (temple F), the sanctuary was transformed from a single temple (G29) into a double temple (G29, G53) complex with forecourts with subsidiary rooms. Where originally G29 was based on a double-flanked main room (temple G), both temples are Herdhaus types—arranged on the standard Mesopotamian bent-axis scheme, with the hearth or altar and cult podium at the short, southeastern end of a rectangular room that was entered from its northern corner. Apart from structural revetments, neither temple was altered significantly before its destruction in the mid-fourteenth century BCE. The contrasting furnishings of the two cella suggested different patron deities. Temple G29, with its wall decoration of glazed terra-cotta nails, a sheep's head, a boar's head, zoomorphic jars, and glazed terra-cotta lions, was attributed to Ishtar, the Babylonian goddess of love and war, whose association with lions extends back to the Akkadian period. This cella also contained nude female figurines, female amulets, and a unique ivory statuette of a seminude female in Hittite attire, who may represent Ishtar's Hurrian counterpart, Šawuška. Temple G53, marked by its conspicuous lack of contents, was attributed to the Hurrian storm god, Teššup, one of Ishtar-Šawuška's numerous partners, who headed the Mitannian pantheon and whose name is a common onomastic element at Nuzi. Evidence for the cult of Teššup first appears in the early second millennium BCE and supports the later dating of temple F to the Isin-Larsa or early Old Babylonian period.

Tablets and seal impressions. The excavated tablets from Nuzi were stored as public and private archives on the main mound and on both northern tells. Although associated with the upper strata (I–IV), the vast majority come from stratum II. A relative chronological framework is derived from the five-generation scribal family of Apil-sîn and that of the real-estate magnate and crown official Teḫip-tilla. Through ration and personnel lists, contracts, legal records, and letters, the texts, written in a Middle Babylonian dialect of Akkadian mixed with Hurrian idiosyncracies, reflect rapidly declining socioeconomic conditions in the province of Arrapḫa: the grain surplus was decreasing and both debts and litigation were increasing, forcing the majority to cede their property rights to the privileged few. The last years are marked by intensive military activity on both the northern and southern frontiers, but Nuzi's destruction is generally attributed to the Assyrians.

The tablets bore the seals of people from all walks of life in Nuzi and in the surrounding towns. They thus provide a unique source of information on sealing practices and on the relationship between seal design, text type, user, rank, period, and origin. The style is characterized by the extensive, often unmasked use of point and tubular drills; the seals' material is sintered quartz (frit). The iconography is heterogeneous, drawing on a long tradition of assimilation and adaptation. Superimposed on native designs devoted to hunting and animal rituals centered on a tree, are court fashions that shift with the political tide. During the first generations, which coincided with the Mitannian confederacy, contact with the west brought Egyptian and Aegean iconography, such as the Hathor mask, the ankh sign, the sphinx, the griffin, and the winged disk. In time, the tree was replaced by the winged disk and confrontation scenes between human and divine figures, influenced by provincial Kassite-Babylonian traditions from Elam and the Hamrin, gave way to a revival of ancient Mesopotamian contest scenes between mythical beasts—which presumably had survived on the eastern periphery of the region. Among the Akkadian revivals are the storm god on his lion-dragon mount and mythological representations, including scenes from the myth of a Ḫedammu-type dragon and, possibly, the death of Huwawa from the Epic of Gilgamesh. Although associated with the Hurrians in later literary traditions, the origin of these myths is unknown.

Small finds. The material culture associated with the stratum II tablets became diagnostic of the Nuzi period and, by extention, of the Hurrians, who migrated across the Fertile Crescent from the east. Apart from the difficulties of relating any category of archaeological material to an ethnic sector of a composite population, the redating of stratum II to the mid-fourteenth century BCE places the origin of much of the characteristic Nuzi material in the west.

Nuzi ware (formerly called Hurrian ware and Subartu ware) combines elements from a number of earlier ceramic traditions in Mesopotamia with foreign elements of design. Distinguished by a white pattern painted on a dark (red-brown to black) background, this ware is distributed from the Zab valley east of the Tigris River to the ʿAmuq plain and Orontes valley in the west and as far south as Babylonia. At Nuzi, geometric motifs predominate over natural ones. The characteristic shapes include the slender goblet (high cup) with a small foot or button base, and the shoulder cup. Both are thin, fine-grained drinking cups derived from Babylonian prototypes of the Isin-Larsa period. Found predominantly in palaces, temples, and "manor houses," Nuzi ware is considered a luxury product, along with the great quantities of faience, multicolored glass, and glazed wares that are widely distributed during the Mitannian period. At Nuzi, these products include zoomorphic amulets, figurines, beads, vessels, cylinder seals, and plaques. The most common glazed objects are terra-cotta wall nails. They appear to be connected with the cult and may have been dedicated by individuals to decorate the walls following an ancient tradition reaching back to prehistoric times at Qudish Ṣaghīr and to Mesopotamia in general. Cultic paraphernalia cast in copper or bronze include small statuettes and a cylindrical pot stand with excised sides and couchant lions on the upper edge. In a military context, bronze scales were used for the armor of men and horses. Most unusual is a bronze dagger, its hilt decorated with inlaid iron plaques secured by iron rivets. Terrestrial and meteoritic iron was a rare and valued metal used primarily for ornamentation until the late period.

Late period. Structural remains of the late period were concentrated on the northwestern ridge and many low adjacent mounds. Three silver coins of the Parthian king Vologases III and a silver coin of the Sasanian king Shapur I provide a chronological range from the late second to the late third century CE for the settlement and cemetery.

[*See also* Hurrians; Mitanni.]

BIBLIOGRAPHY

Primary Sources

Preliminary reports by the respective excavators published in *Bulletin of the American Schools of Oriental Research,* numbers 18, 20, 29, 30, 32, 34, 38, and 42 (1923–1931) were followed by a final report on the excavations by Starr (1938, 1939) and an ongoing series of text publications. Discrepancies between the preliminary and final reports in the designation of room numbers may account for some of the variation in descriptions of room contents, particularly tablets, which were recorded and published separately. For the excavations, see Richard F. S. Starr, *Nuzi: Report on the Excavation at Yorgen Tepa Near Kirkuk, Iraq,* 2 vols. (Cambridge, Mass., 1939). For a complete listing of primary text publications up to 1992, see Jeanette Fincke, *Die Orts- und Gewässernamen der Nuzi-Texte,* Répertoire Géographique des Textes Cunéiformes, vol. 10 (Wiesbaden, 1993), especially pages xvi–xxx.

Secondary Sources

Cecchini, Serena Maria. *La ceramica di Nuzi.* Studi Semitici, 15. Rome, 1965. Useful assemblage of Nuzi ware and summary of conventional evaluations, though now superseded by new finds and more critical investigations.

Dietrich, Manfried, Oswald Loretz, and Walter Mayer. *Nuzi-Bibliographie.* Alter Orient und Altes Testament, Sonderreihe, vol. 11. Kevelaer and Neukirchen-Vluyn, 1972. Complete listing of primary and secondary publications on Nuzi through 1971.

Eichler, Barry L. "Nuzi and the Bible: A Retrospective." In *DUMU-E₂-DUB-BA-A: Studies in Honor of Åke W. Sjöberg,* edited by Hermann Behrens et al., pp. 117–119. Philadelphia, 1989. Critical review of the impact of Nuzi scholarship on biblical studies from the early comparisons between socio-legal customs at Nuzi and those in the Bible to more recent skepticism regarding the Hurrian background of the customs at Nuzi and their relevance for the dating and interpretation of specific biblical narratives and institutions.

Hrouda, Barthel. *Die bemalte Keramik des zweiten Jahrtausends in Nordmesopotamien und Nordsyrien.* Istanbuler Forschungen, vol. 19. Berlin, 1957. Important, if outdated, examination of Nuzi ware in relation to other painted ceramics, which in one way or another were misconstrued as reflections of Hurrian culture.

Mellink, Machteld J. "A Hittite Figurine from Nuzi." In *Vorderasiatische Archäologie: Studien und Aufsätze Anton Moortgat zum fünfundsechzigsten Geburtstag gewidmet,* edited by Kurt Bittel, pp. 155–164. Berlin, 1964. Unusually convincing description of one Hittite/Hurrian component in Nuzi iconography, citing art historical and archaeological as well as textual and historical arguments.

Porada, Edith. *Seal Impressions from Nuzi.* Annual of the American Schools of Oriental Research, 24. New Haven, 1947. Pioneering art historical study of the Nuzi glyptic based on a representative sample of seal impressions from the five-generation archive of Teḫip-tilla.

Stein, Diana L. "Khabur Ware and Nuzi Ware: Their Origin, Relationship, and Significance." *Assur* 4.1 (1984): 1–65. Redefinition of these two painted wares in terms of their shape, decoration, distribution, and date. Many of the results need to be tested against new evidence from recent excavations in the Khabur triangle.

Stein, Diana L. "Mythologische Inhalte der Nuzi-Glyptik." In *Hurriter und Hurritisch,* edited by Volkert Haas, pp. 173–209. Konstanzer Altorientalische Symposien, vol. 2. Constance, Germany, 1988. Interpretation of mythological imagery in the Nuzi iconography relating, in particular, to Teššup and Ishtar-Šawuška.

Stein, Diana L. "A Reappraisal of the 'Sauštatar Letter' from Nuzi." *Zeitschrift für Assyriologie und Vorderasiatische Archaeologie* 79.1 (1989): 36–60. Casts doubt on the conventional dating of Nuzi and favors a later date based on sealing practice as well as historical and archaeological factors.

Stein, Diana L. *Das Archiv des Šilwa-teššup.* 2 vols. Wiesbaden, 1993. Comprehensive textual and art historical analysis of the sealings and sealing practice in the private archive of Prince Šilwa-teššup; based on a reedition of the texts and line drawings of the seal impressions. The use and designs of seals are investigated in specific legal, administrative, social, and regional contexts within the framework of one community, from about 1440 to 1330 BCE. The results compliment, amend, and extend Porada's study (see above).

DIANA L. STEIN

O

OBODA. *See* Avdat.

ODEUM (Gk., *odeion;* Lat., *odeum*), a small roofed theater, used for musical performances (Gk., *ōdai*), recitations, and lectures. The first monument of this kind was built by Pericles near the theater of Dionysus in Athens and was reconstructed in 52 BCE by two Roman architects. It is recorded only later (Vitruvius, 5.9.1; Plutarch, *Pericles* 13.9) as an odeum. The term is often incorrectly applied to any small theater (especially in cities that have more than one scenical building), to distinguish it from a city's sometimes more ancient (Greek) theater. For all of Greece, however, in the second century CE, Pausanias knew only four odea: those of Agrippa (1.8.6 and 1.14.1) and of Herodes Atticus (7.20.6) in Athens, and those built or rebuilt at Corinth (2.3.6) and Patras (7.20.6) by the same rich rhetor and benefactor; however, Pausanias, in the *Periegeta* was also aware of one at Smyrna (9.35.6). At Caesarea Maritima, in ancient Palestine, Vespasian built an odeum on the site of a destroyed synagogue (Malalas, 10.338, p. 261.13). In Rome, the word is used for, but limited to, the Domitianic construction in the Campus Martius (Suetonius, *Domitianus* 5). This kind of monument therefore seems to be much rarer than might be expected. Epigraphic evidence in the western as well as in the eastern provinces, has, however, added other examples (Carthage in North Africa; Gortyna on Crete; Patara; Qanawat; Thessalonike in Greece; and Vienna), which suggests that the problem of unidentified buildings of this or related types all over the empire needs to be reconsidered.

It was once argued that an odeum was characterized by the absence of *versurae* and of parodoi ("side entrances") leading to the orchestra. However, the identification of the monument in Corinth, which is secured both by a literary source and by an inscription, also has *versurae* and parodoi. It is first of all essential to put aside an important group of monuments that are linked to an agora; they are probable bouleuteria, rather than real odea. Most have but a few, or reduced, scenical installations, others only a podium behind the facade. In some cases, too (e.g., at Gerasa/Jerash, in modern Jordan), the seats are inscribed with the names of the tribes into which the assembly of the people was divided; these point to a completely different use for the monument. Some of these constructions (Alabanda; Anemurium; Arykanda; the island of Cos; Iasos; Pinara; Selinos in Cilicia) have a rectangular plan that facilitated the use of a roof but limited the width of the cavea, or spectators' section; they are relatively small, the largest rivaling the boundary measures adopted, for technical reasons, by the Hellenistic bouleuterion at Miletus (34.84 × 24.28 m). The abandonment of this model in the second century CE, a time of splendor in urban life and architectural renewal in the provinces of the Roman Empire, allowed the development of a plan that is still nearer to—and very often quite the same as—that of the theaters, but roofed. The best examples of this type are at Aphrodisias, Aspendos, Cibyra, Ephesus, Magnesia ad Maeandrum, Sagalassos, and Sillyon in Asia Minor, at Nea-Paphos on Cyprus, and at Amman, Gadara, Gerasa (the North Theater), and Pella in the Near East. The cavea was then wider, with diameters ranging between 30 and 54 m. The building was still placed close to the city's agora or was directly connected to its porticoes. Whether these constructions were used both as bouleuteria and odea has been discussed: Reudiger Meinel (1979) speaks of a mixed type (Ger., *mischtypus,* or *mischgebäude*), on account of the development and magnificence of the rear wall of some of the facades. However, those walls were purely decorative and cannot be considered real *scaenae fronte*—limited as they were to displaying sculptured groups of the house of Augustus and of the municipal elites who took political advantage of acting as benefactors and propagators of the imperial ideology in their own cities. Despite a real influence by the plan of one and the decoration of the other, there are significant distinctions between the two kinds of buildings.

A second group that needs to be excluded is the small *auditoria* (of less than a half-circle) that are usually part of a gymnasium and correspond to what seems to have been called *acroatēria* (Apollonia of Illyria; Arykanda [no. IX on plans of the city]; Cnidus [the so-called bouleuterion], Epidaurus, Syracuse, and perhaps Ariassos and Termessos). Built as they are within the architectural structure of a monument devoted to education, they were clearly intended for lecturing and have no scenical purposes. The so-called odeum of Agrippa in the Athenian agora, dedicated in about 15 BCE, was itself established not far from the gymnasium of Ptolemy—and was probably connected with it.

Cultic assembly halls, either semicircular (as on Delos) or inscribed (as at Dura-Europos in Syria), have also been called odea. Indeed, at Delos, religious processions or epiphanies of the goddess's statue did certainly take place, but the monument has no *scaena* and was evidently not used for real sacred dramas, as has sometimes been thought. On the contrary, the auditorium at Dura, suggested by an imperial dedication and a graffito on one of the seats, was certainly the colony's bouleuterion in the third century CE and has nothing in common with the nearby hall of the Artemis Nanaia temple. Monuments at Gerasa (the festival theater at the Birketein), Saḥr, and El-Hammeh (?) seem to have been dependencies of their respective sanctuaries but do not share architectural characteristics with well-identified odea. They represent a third group of buildings whose purposes and functions were distinct from the odea's.

Real odea are certainly larger than a city's *boulē*, a gymnasium, or auditoria for religious spectacles, as they were intended for larger assemblies. The capacities of the buildings at Corinth, Lyon, and Vienna are calculated to have held some three thousand spectators and that of Herodes Atticus to have approached five thousand. There is, therefore, no comparison with simple *auditoria* and cultal theaters (such as on Delos), which seat only hundreds, and still less with the largest bouleuteria (Aphrodisias, Ephesus), which may have seated fourteen hundred.

With an exterior diameter of about 63–76 m, the odea at Athens, Corinth, Lyon, and Vienna are clearly situated between the largest bouleuteria and medium-sized theaters; the monument at Carthage, with its 95-meter diameter, was still wider, and nearer to real theaters. The smallest (Catania, Nicopolis, Patras) have the same diameter (about 43–48 m) as the largest uninscribed bouleuteria. In plan, many of the real odea "were simply theaters in miniature," as John B. Ward-Perkins put it, which is the sense of the inscription of the *theatroeidēs ōdeion* at Qanawat (W. H. Waddington and P. LeBas, *Voyage archéologiques en Grèce et Asie Mineure: Inscriptions et Applications,* 3 vols., Paris, 1870, 2341) and the expression of the architectural evolution from inscribed rectangular buildings to wider semicircular constructions that clearly resemble theaters. The only significant distinctions seem to have been that odea were covered, in order to facilitate a better acoustic environment for concerts and lectures; their stage was of a simple and more severe design.

Except in the great cities of the empire (Athens, Carthage, Corinth, Lyon, Rome, Smyrna), which were often visited by famous rhetors and in which the spectacles were more diversified than in small cities, odea existed where there were special festivals and games: at Argos, the monument's orchestra is paved with a mosaic that bears an undisputable allusion to the Nemean games; at Nicopolis, it may well be related to the celebration of the *Actiaca;* at Carthage (built in 207 CE) it may be related to the Pythian games; and in Rome itself, the odeum of Domitian was probably intended, just as its stadium was, for the *Certamen Capitolinum,* instituted in 86 CE.

Odea are often directly connected with theaters (Athens, Corinth, Catania, Lyon, and Vienna); both constructions use the same lie of the ground, with its pending particularly adapted for the setting of a cavea. However, at Akrai, Soluntum, and Amman, the bouleuterion also takes the same topographic advantages of this proximity to become, as Statius said for Naples (*Silv.* 3.5.91), this *geminam molem nudi tectique theatri,* an important element in the city's landscape. The joining of the two monuments, interesting as it is for ancient town planning, is thus no absolute criterion by itself for identifying the smaller one as an odeum.

[*See also* Public Buildings; Theaters.]

BIBLIOGRAPHY

Balty, Jean Ch. *Cvria Ordinis: Recherches d'architecture et d'urbanisme antiques sur les curies provinciales du monde romain.* Académie Royale de Belgique, Mémoires de la Classe des Beaux-Arts, Coll. in-4°, 2e sér., XV.2. Brussels, 1991. Devotes an entire chapter to bouleuteria (some of which had been called odea) with an inscribed rectangular and semicircular plan (see pp. 429–600).

Bieber, Margarete. *The History of the Greek and Roman Theater.* 2d ed. Princeton, 1961. Classic study, providing a list of odea throughout the provinces of the Roman Empire (see pp. 174–177, 220–222).

Broneer, Oscar T. *The Odeum.* Corinth, 10. Cambridge, Mass., 1932. Excellent monograph on the building at Corinth.

Crema, Luigi. *L'architettura romana.* Turin, 1959. One of the best guides to Roman architecture, with good coverage of odea (see pp. 92–93, 202–203, 425–428).

Ginouvès, René. *Le théâtron à gradins droits et l'Odéon d'Argos.* Études Péloponnésiennes, 6. Paris, 1972. Exemplary monograph on the odeum at Argos, with extended comparative material on other odea and roofed theaters in the Roman world.

Izenour, George C. *Roofed Theaters of Classical Antiquity.* New Haven, 1992. New and interesting approach to the problem by one of the leading specialists of modern assembly halls, unfortunately confusing odea, bouleuteria, and auditoria.

Meinel, Reudiger. *Das Odeion: Untersuchungen an überdachten antiken Theatergebäuden.* Frankfurt, 1979. Standard work on the subject, drawing special attention to the problem of construction, but uncritically mixing odea, bouleuteria, and auditoria.

Neppi Modona, Aldo. *Gli edifici teatrali greci e romani.* Florence, 1961. Brief, uncritical coverage of odea.

JEAN CH. BALTY

OHNEFALSCH-RICHTER, MAX (1850–1917), German excavator, antique dealer, writer, and one of the pioneers of Cypriot archaeology. After gradation from Halle University, where he studied agriculture, political economy, and natural sciences, Ohnefalsch-Richter traveled extensively in central and southern Europe before going to Cyprus in 1878 to work as a newspaper reporter. He was soon attracted to the archaeology of the island and began a series of excavations, and except for one trip to Germany, stayed there until 1890. Ohnefalsch-Richter returned to his country and wrote his doctoral dissertation on the cult places of Cyprus at Leipzig University. He went back to Cyprus for further research in 1894–1895 and 1910.

Ohnefalsch-Richter excavated throughout the island either for himself or on contract at Athienou, Idalion, Kition, Paphos, Salamis, Tamassos, and at other sites. He located and excavated a large number of very important sites and recovered an enormous quantity of objects. His interests, however, were not always scientific because he also was a dealer in these antiquities. Although he took issue with Luigi Palma di Cesnola and his methods, his own techniques were sometimes considered controversial. Ohnefalsch-Richter did pioneering work, however, and published widely. Being a good draftsman and an accomplished photographer, he left valuable records of his discoveries and of nineteenth-century Cyprus in general. Early in his career he wrote some interesting nonarchaeological articles on Cyprus and later helped his wife, Magda, in photographing objects and people and collecting information pertaining to the folk tradition of the island (Magda Ohnefalsch-Richter, *Griechische Sitten und Gebräuche auf Cypern,* Berlin, 1913). He lectured extensively, illustrating his talks with drawings, watercolors, and photographs, as well as ancient objects from his excavations.

[*See also* Idalion; Kition; Paphos; Salamis; *and the biography of di Cesnola.*]

BIBLIOGRAPHY

Buchholz, Hans-Günter. "Max Ohnefalsch-Richter als Archäologe auf Zypern." *Cahier du Centre d'Études Chypriotes* 11–12 (1989): 3–28.

Fivel, Léon. "Ohnefalsch-Richter, 1850–1917: Essai de bibliographie." *Cahier du Centre d'Études Chypriotes* 11–12 (1989): 35–40.

Krpata, M. "Max Hermann Ohnefalsch-Richter Bibliography and Biographical Remarks." *Report of the Department of Antiquities of Cyprus,* pp. 337–341. Nicosia, 1992.

Malekkos, Andreas. *Studies in Cyprus.* Nicosia, [1994].

Masson, Olivier. "Les visites de Max Ohnefalsch-Richter à Kouklia (Ancienne-Paphos), 1890 et 1910." *Cahier du Centre d'Études Chypriotes* 3 (1985): 19–28.

Masson, Olivier, and Antoine Hermary. "Les fouilles d'Ohnefalsch-Richter à Idalion en 1894." *Cahier du Centre d'Études Chypriotes* 10 (1988): 3–14.

Myres, John L., and Max Ohnefalsch-Richter. *A Catalogue of the Cyprus Museum, with a Chronicle of Excavations Undertaken since the British Occupation and Introductory Notes on Cypriote Archaeology.* Oxford, 1899. Still essential book on the excavations and holdings of the Cyprus Museum in the nineteenth century.

Ohnefalsch-Richter, Max. *Ancient Places of Worship in Kypros.* Berlin, 1891. English version of the German publication of his very important doctoral thesis.

Ohnefalsch-Richter, Max. *Kypros, die Bibel und Homer: Beiträge zur Cultur, Kunst-und Religionsgeschichte des Orients im Alterthume.* Berlin, 1893. Detailed and well-illustrated account of many excavations of the period.

DEMETRIOS MICHAELIDES

OLIVES. The wild olive *(Olea Europaea Var. Oleaster)* is indigenous to the natural forests of the Mediterranean region, whose wet, cool winters and hot, dry summers are ideal for olive cultivation. A mature tree can withstand temperatures as low as −110°C, whereas a young sapling may not survive temperatures below −7°C. On the other hand, to produce maximum fruit yields, the temperature must be below 7°C for a certain number of hours each year.

The wild olive is interfertile with the cultivated varieties, and it is still usual to use wild-olive saplings as root stock: scions are grafted that are taken from the finest tree in the village. Many of the wild trees today are undoubtedly escapees from cultivation.

Origin and Domestication. Olive stones have been found in Natufian and Pre-Pottery Neolithic B (PPNB) contexts and from many Chalcolithic sites in Israel and from Neolithic Ib and II contexts on Cyprus. It was once thought that the stones of wild and cultivated olives could be distinguished. The transitional forms identified between wild and cultivated types on Crete were regarded as evidence for the olive having been domesticated there independently, but today many scholars believe that the wood, stones, and pollen of the wild olive cannot be distinguished from those of cultivated varieties. Proof for the beginning of cultivation is therefore being sought in quantative data and in the archaeological evidence for olive-processing installations. The large number of olive stones found at the Chalcolithic site of Teleilat el-Ghassul was considered proof of cultivation. More recent evidence of large quantities of olive wood and stones at Chalcolithic sites in Jordan and in the Golan region in Israel, and the presence of crushing basins and ceramic oil separators at sites in the Golan, shows clearly that the olive was cultivated in them.

At most sites in Israel, however, olive wood is not found in large quantities until the Early Bronze Age. The evidence suggests that large-scale cultivation coincided with the increase in the size and number of sites now recorded for the period and confirmed by pollen analysis. Colin Renfrew suggested that in the Aegean there was also a connection between the urban revolution of the Early Bronze Age and the beginning of large-scale olive and vine cultivation. This theory has recently been questioned and awaits similar quantitative confirmation.

As the possibility of distinguishing between the stones of the wild and cultivated olive is today considered questionable, the paleobotanical argument for independent domestication of the olive in the Aegean is no longer tenable. It is perhaps relevant, however, that although the vine is not indigenous to the Levant—and was almost certainly introduced from Anatolia—the terms used in Semitic and Indo-European languages for *vine* and *wine* derive from a common source. This is not true for the olive, however. The Greek and Latin terms for the olive and for its oil have no connection to the Semitic roots. This suggests independent domestication in the different regions.

Technology of Olive Oil Production. The quality of olive oil depends on the ripeness and quality of the olive and on the extraction process. Oil made from unripe olives, virgin oil, is more bitter and greener in color than other oil. The first oil to come from a batch of olives is the finest, the quality declining in consecutive pressings.

There are three stages in the production of olive oil: crushing the olives to a pulp, pressing the pulp to express the liquid, and separating the oil (20–30 percent of the liquid expressed) from the resulting black, watery lee, or sediment. The simplest method was to crush the olives with a stone roller. The resultant olive pulp was then put in sacks, or frails (baskets). The oil was then extracted by the weight of stones that were placed on a board on the frails. The oil was allowed to separate, and, when it floated on the lee, was skimmed. An Early Bronze Age oil press from Ugarit in Syria consisted of stone slabs (on which the olives were crushed and pressed) and, at a lower level, a collecting vat (into which the liquid flowed and in which the oil was separated). The installation resembles the wineries/wine presses that are found in the thousands throughout the Levant. In later periods, specific devices evolved for each of the three stages, oil presses and wineries differentiated, and various types of installation developed in different regions.

The first technical change took place in the Late Bronze Age with the introduction of the lever-and-weights press (beam-and-weights press) found on Crete and Cyprus, and in Ugarit. In Israel the earliest examples are from the Iron Age—two distinct types being discernible by Iron II. In the northern part of the country the olives were crushed in round mortars and then pressed on round press beds as found, for example, at Rosh Zayit from which the liquid flowed to lateral collecting vats. The weights were unworked perforated fieldstones. In the south, in Judah, olives were usually crushed with rollers in rectangular crushing basins. The weights were fashioned either with a horizontal bore at the top or with a vertical bore—the doughnut-shaped weight. The characteristic element was the Beth-Mirsham (Beit Mirsim) central vat in which the collecting vat was cut in the center of the press bed and the frails of crushed olive pulp were placed above it (on slats placed criss-cross, to allow the oil to flow down directly into the central vat). William Foxwell Albright mistakenly called the freestanding version of this device a dyeing vat. Similar rock-cut installations are found at sites in the hill country.

The next important technological change was the round

OLIVES. Figure 1. *Phoenician Zabadi weight press.* (Courtesy R. Frankel)

rotary olive crusher. It reached Palestine in the Hellenistic period, but its date and place of origin remain undetermined. The method, however, was used throughout the Mediterranean world until recently. The two main types of presses developed at the same time. At Mareshah/Marisa in the south, a press on either side of the central vat appeared with two plain piers that supported the pile of frails. The weight was also a new type: the bore was in the form of a reversed T; it also is found on Cyprus and in Lebanon. In a press found in the north, in western Galilee at Zabadi (see figure 1), the collection is lateral, and the characteristic element is a monumental slotted pier in which the beam was anchored. The weights in both types of press were raised by a drum attached to the beam. Other types of lever presses developed in other parts of the world. In the Aegean, the Crimea, North Africa, Spain, and southern France the Semana beam weight, which is rectangular and has external dovetailed mortices, is found. In the Semana weight the drum is attached to the weight and not to the beam. It apparently originated in the Aegean or in Anatolia. Both the reversed-T weight and the Semana weight are found on Cyprus, while in North Syria weights were found incorporating the characteristics of both. In Roman Italy, lever and drum presses without weights were used (the drum was attached to the ground). In the second century CE, Cato the Elder described a lever-and-drum press (*De Agricultura* 18; see

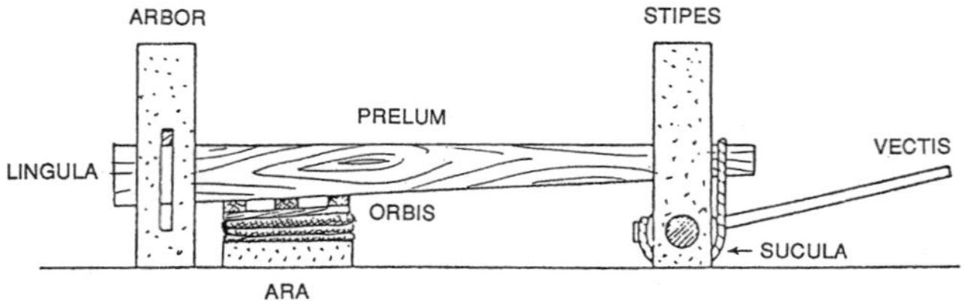

OLIVES. Figure 2. *Cato's lever-and-drum press.* (Courtesy R. Frankel)

OLIVES. Figure 3. *The Judean grooved pier screw press.* (Courtesy R. Frankel)

figure 2) as did Pliny the Elder in the first century (*Historia Naturalis* 18.74.317). Hero of Alexandria (*Mechanica* 3.13–14) described a lever-drum-and-weights press that clearly incorporated the drum of the Roman press and the weight of the Levantine press. There were also regional differences in the manner in which the beam was anchored: large free-standing stone niches were utilized in North Syria, slotted monoliths on Cyprus, and other techniques in the western Mediterranean.

The next technical development was the screw. In Judah, a direct-pressure screw press developed with central collection. A grooved piers press (see figure 3) clearly developed from the plain piers of the press found at Mareshah. In western Galilee, the screw press was a lever-and-screw press—a direct development from the Zabadi Press (see figure 4). Three different types of screw weights developed in the region, the Miʿilya, Beth ha-ʿEmeq, and Dinʿila weights. The Dinʿila weight was the one described by Hero of Alexandria (*Mechanica* 3.15). In Samaria the main press was also a lever-and-screw press, but it used the Samaria screw weight, a type common throughout the Mediterranean; in Lower Galilee and the Golan, direct screw presses were used, but of types different from that in Judah. In North Syria yet another screw weight (the Kafsa weight) was used, a few examples of which have been found in the Jerusalem area. Thus, distinct technical cultures can be discerned that evince strong regional diversity and continuity (figure 5).

The Olive in Written Sources. The Hebrew word for olive is *zyt* (Ugar., *zt*) and for oil, *šmn* (Ugar./Akk., *šamnu*). The Sumerogram (*I*[*A*]) denoting oil and olive oil is *I.GIŠ* (lit., "tree oil," to be read *šamnu*). The olive tree was *[GIŠ] se/irdu,* which, in the peripheral eastern regions, was written *ze/irtu* (Hur., *zirte*), suggesting a connection to the West Semitic *zyt–zt*. In Egyptian, olive oil was *b3Ḳ*, while the olive tree was *dt*, a term introduced only at the time of the New Kingdom, again deriving from *zyt–zt*.

There are many Late Bronze Age administrative tablets from Ugarit that mention the purchase of olive groves and list quantities of oil paid in taxation by individuals (one to four jars) and by whole villages (up to five hundred jars) and allocations of oil from the royal stores to officials, soldiers, and craftsmen, for example (one to ten jars). An estimate of Ugarit's total oil production is 25 tons per village (two hundred villages thus produced 5,000 tons).

Similar documents have been found at Alalakh in Syria and in Hittite archives, both countries where the olive was grown. Hittite texts also describe methods of preparing various foods and perfumed oil, some of the latter used in rituals.

Because oil was either not produced or was produced in negligible quantities in Mesopotamia proper and in Egypt, documents often mention it as an exotic luxury. At Mari, imported oil from Aleppo and the provision of oil for the palace are mentioned but no olive groves. In later Assyrian documents, Assurnasirpal and Sennacherib describe gardens and wildlife reserves they set up based on plants and animals brought from distant regions of their empire that included the olive. Both kings describe sumptuous banquets attended by notables from afar at which olives and olive oil were served. Sennacherib describes how he drenched the heads of his guests with oil mixed with spices.

The Tale of Sinuhe (one of the earliest documents mentioning the land of Israel), from Egypt's Middle Kingdom, describes the land of Yaa (probably in the Galilee or in Syria): "It had more wine than water, abundant was its honey, plentiful its oil." In other documents importing oil from Retenu, Dhaji, and Naharina is referred to. The soldiers of Thutmosis III when in Dhaji "were drunk and anointed with oil as if at feasts in Egypt," and in his lists of

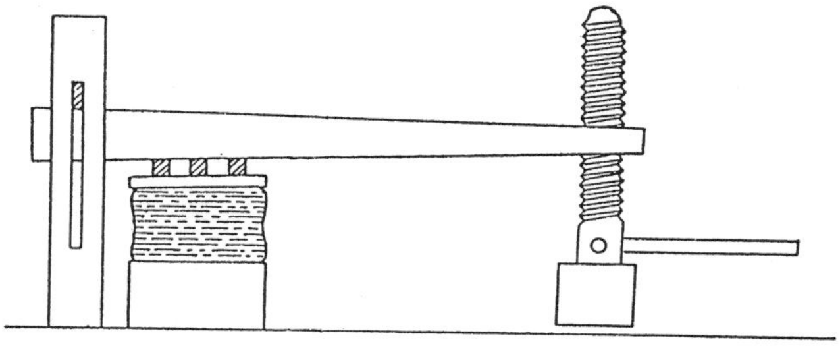

OLIVES. Figure 4. *The lever-and-screw press.* (Courtesy R. Frankel)

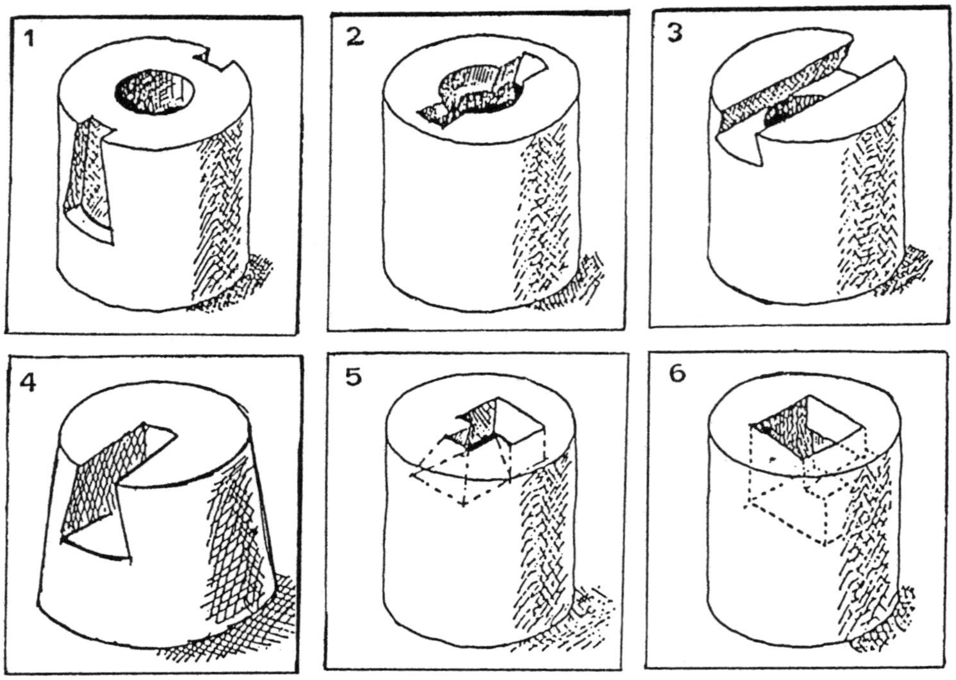

OLIVES. Figure 5. *Six main types of screw weight found in Israel.* (Courtesy R. Frankel)

booty two kinds of oil appear *nḏm* ("sweet") and *w3ḏ* ("fresh/green," probably virgin oil). (See *ANET,* p. 239.)

Hebrew Bible and Hebrew epigraphy. The olive is one of the triad *dgn, tyrwš, yṣhr* ("corn, wine, oil") that appears eighteen times in the Hebrew Bible and is one of the Seven Kinds (*Dt.* 8:8). The two lists have come to symbolize the staple products of Mediterranean dry farming. The olive tree was the first to be asked to be king over the trees in Abimelech's parable (*Jgs.* 9:8–9); similarly, Columella, the Roman agronomist, called the olive "queen of all trees" (*De Re Rustica* 5.8.1).

The names of the officials of King David who were responsible for the olive groves in the Shephelah and for the royal oil stores are specified in *1 Chronicles* (27:28), as are the quantities of oil King Solomon sent to Hiram of Tyre (*1 Kgs.* 5:25; *2 Chr.* 2:29). The export of oil to Egypt is referred to by Hosea (12:2).

No specific term appears in the Bible for an oil press, but, like wine, oil flows into a *yqb* (*Jl.* 4:13; *gt* and *pwrh* usually are translated as "wine press"), a simple treading installation usually cut into rock. Oil production is actually referred to only once (*Mi.* 6:15), and there the oil is expressed by treading.

Four types of spiced oil appear: *šmn rwqḥ* (*Eccl.* 10:1); *šmn hmr,* "myrrh oil" (*Est.* 2:12); *šmn hṭwb* (*2Kgs.* 20:13; *Ps.* 133:2), to be translated "spiced oil," not "good oil"; *šmn twrq* (*Sg.* 1:3), usually translated "poured oil," but should, perhaps, be corrected to *tmrwq,* "cosmetic oil." Of the three other types that appear, *šmn rʿnn,* "fresh oil" (*Ps.* 92:11), may be a technical term for virgin oil; and *šmn ktyt,* literally, "pounded in a mortar" (*Ex.* 27:20, 29:40; *Lv.* 24:2; *Nm.* 28:5; *1 Kgs.* 5:25) and *šmn rḥṣ,* literally, "washed" (Samaria ostraca) designate production techniques—in the first, oil is extracted without pressure after pounding, and in the second, it was extracted with the aid of hot water. [*See* Samaria Ostraca.]

Oil, then, appears in the Samaria ostraca, which are bills of lading found in the palace of the kings of Israel, apparently of taxes assigned to royal officials. Of those ostraca in which the products are known, sixteen mention wine only, eight mention only oil, and two name both products. The Arad inscriptions are on ostraca from the archives of a Judean border fortress. They include fifteen consignment orders to supply soldiers with provisions: wine, oil, and flour—dough or bread, depending on the length of their duty. Oil is mentioned on eight of the fifteen ostraca. It is specifically stated that the oil jar is to be sealed. These documents show that oil was in general use but more scarce and valuable than wine or corn. [*See* Arad Inscriptions.]

Talmudic literature. In Mishnaic Hebrew, unlike biblical Hebrew, there is a clear distinction between a winery, *gt,* and an oil press, *byt bd* (lit., "house of the beam"). The most detailed reference to a press is to a lever-and-weights press (*B.B.* 4:5) that mentions six parts: *btwlwt,* "slotted piers," for anchoring the beam; *mml,* "press bed"; *ym,* "collection vat"; *qwrh,* "beam"; *ʿkyrym/ʿkydym,* "press weights"; and *glgl,* "drum." The term *lwlbyn* for a screw appears in the Tosefta and Talmuds.

An important text is that concerned with the oil to be used in the Temple (*Men.* 8 and related sections in the Talmuds and Tosefta). Lists of types of oil that were forbidden are enumerated, as are the places from which the finest oil came and the factors that affected oil quality. Three grades of olives and of oil are described. Rabbi Yehudah was of the opinion that the oil for the Temple (*šmn ktyt,* "pure oil" or "pounded oil") should be prepared the way it had been for the First Temple: by pounding the olives in mortars and extracting the oil without a beam, using only the weight of stones. Other sages favored more modern methods. The ordinance in the Mishna accepts Rabbi Yehudah's views about the first grade oil but that of the other sages about the second and third.

Uses of Olive Oil. In addition to its use as food and in a ritual context, olive oil was used in cosmetics and perfume and to provide light. These uses are verified in written sources.

1. *Cosmetics.* There is evidence for the use of oil as an unguent or as a base for perfumes in Mesopotamian, Egyptian, and Hittite sources. The Hebrew Bible mentions many perfumed oils: men annoint their beards and hair with oil (*Ps.* 133:2, 141:5; *Eccl.* 9:8), and maidens receive beauty treatments with myrrh oil (*Est.* 2:12). The obvious use for oil was cosmetic (*Mi.* 6:15). In the Greek world, athletes rubbed oil on their body following strenuous activity, and then removed it, the dust, and their sweat with a sicklelike *strigil.* Pliny affirmed that "There are two liquids that are agreeable to the human body, wine inside and oil outside" (*Hist. Nat.* 14.29.150).

2. *Food.* The annual consumption of oil "per capita per annum" in village communities in Greece and Israel in recent times is 17–20 kg (50–55 g per day). It has been suggested that in the Aegean the main use for oil was cosmetic and that its main source, until the end of the Late Bronze Age and beyond, was the wild olive. The written sources from Ugarit in the Late Bronze Age and from Samaria and Arad in the Iron Age show that in the Levant oil was an important element in the diet in these periods, as the biblical triad *dgn, tyrwš, yṣhr* implies.

3. *Light.* Ceramic lamps from the Early Bronze Age used olive oil as their main fuel.

4. *Ritual.* The annointing of kings with olive oil is attested in the Hebrew Bible (*1 Sm.* 16:1–13; *2 Kgs.* 9:1–3) and in Hittite sources. Priests were annointed (*Ex.* 29:7), and the word *messiah* derives from *mšyḥ* (Heb., "annointed"). Stelae were sanctified by annointing them with oil (*Gn.* 28:18, 35:14), as was the tabernacle and all its contents (*Ex.* 30:23–29, 40:9). Oil was used in purification ceremonies (*Lv.* 12–32 and in Hittite sources); was part of meal offerings in the Temple, alone (*Lv.* 2) or with animal sacrifices (*Nm.* 15:1–16); and was used to light the Temple candelabrum (*Ex.* 25:6, 35:15; *Lv.* 24:2; *Men.* 8). Hittite sources refer to annointing the bones of the deceased after cremation.

BIBLIOGRAPHY

Amouretti, Marie-Claire, and Jean-Pierre Brun, eds. *Oil and Wine Production in the Mediterranean Area.* Paris, 1993.

Baruch, Uri. "The Late Holocene Vegetational History of Lake Kinneret (Sea of Galilee), Israel." *Paléorient* 12.2 (1986): 37–48.

Callot, Olivier. *Huileries antiques de Syrie du Nord.* Institut Français d'Archéologie du Proche-Orient, Beyrouth-Damas-Amman, Bibliothèque Archéologique et Historique, vol. 118. Paris, 1984.

Callot, Olivier. "Les huileries et l'huile au Bronze Récent: Quelques exemples syriens et chypriotes." In *Oil and Wine Production in the Mediterranean Area,* edited by Marie-Claire Amouretti and Jean-Pierre Brun, pp. 55–64. Paris, 1993.

Drachmann, A. G. *Ancient Oil Mills and Presses.* Copenhagen, 1932.

Eitam, David. "Olive Presses of the Israelite Period." *Tel Aviv* 6 (1979): 146–155.

Eitam, David. "'Between the [Olives] Rows, Oil Will Be Produced, Presses Will Be Trod . . .' (*Job* 24, 11)" and "Selected Oil and Wine Installations in Ancient Israel." In *Oil and Wine Production in the Mediterranean Area,* edited by Marie-Claire Amouretti and Jean-Pierre Brun, pp. 65–106. Paris, 1993.

Eitam, David, and A. Shomroni. "Research of the Oil-Industry during the Iron Age at Tel Miqne." In *Olive Oil in Antiquity,* edited by Michael Heltzer and David Eitam. Haifa, 1995.

Epstein, C. "Oil Production in the Golan Heights during the Chalcolithic Period." *Tel Aviv* 20 (1993): 133–146.

Frankel, Rafael. "An Oil Press at Tel Ṣafṣafot." *Tel Aviv* 15–16 (1988–1989): 77–91, pls. 5–12.

Frankel, Rafael, et al. "The Olive Press at Ḥorvath Beit Loya." In *Christian Archaeology* in the Holy Land, New Discoveries: Essays in Honour of Virgilio C. Corbo, edited by Giovanni Claudio Bottini et al., pp. 287–300. Studium Biblicum Franciscanum, Collectio Maior, 36. Jerusalem, 1990.

Frankel, Rafael. "Some Oil Presses from Western Galilee." *Bulletin of the American Schools of Oriental Research,* no. 286 (1992): 39–71.

Frankel, Rafael, et al. *Technology of Olive Oil in the Holy Land.* Arlington, Va., and Tel Aviv, 1994.

Frankel, Rafael. "Oil Presses in Western Galilee and the Judea: A Comparison." In *Olive Oil in Antiquity,* edited by Michael Heltzer and David Eitam. Haifa, 1995.

Gal, Zvi, and Rafael Frankel. "An Olive Oil Press Complex at Ḥurbat Rōš Zayit (Rās ez-Zētūn) in Lower Galilee." *Zeitschrift des Deutschen Palästina-Vereins* 109 (1993): 128–140, pls. 16–17.

Güterbock, Hans G. "Oil Plants in Hittite Anatolia." *Journal of the American Oriental Society* 88 (1968): 66–71.

Hadjisavvas, Sophocles. *Olive Oil Processing in Cyprus.* Nicosia, 1992.

Heltzer, Michael. "Olive Oil and Wine Production in Phoenicia and in the Mediterranean Trade." In *Oil and Wine Production in the Mediterranean Area,* edited by Marie-Claire Amouretti and Jean-Pierre Brun, pp. 49–54. Paris, 1993.

Heltzer, Michael, and David Eitam, eds. *Olive Oil in Antiquity.* Haifa, 1995.

Kloner, Amos, and Nahum Sagiv. "The Technology of Oil Production in the Hellenistic Period at Maresha, Israel." In *Oil and Wine Production in the Mediterranean Area,* edited by Marie-Claire Amouretti and Jean-Pierre Brun, pp. 119–136. Paris, 1993.

Liphschitz, Nili, et al. "The Beginning of Olive *(Oleo europaea)* Cultivation in the Old World: A Reassessment." *Journal of Archaeological Science* 18 (1991): 441–453.

Liphschitz, Nili. "Olives in Ancient Israel in View of Dendroarchaeological Investigations." In *Olive Oil in Antiquity,* edited by Michael Heltzer and David Eitam. Haifa, 1995.

Malul, Meir. "Ze/irtu(se/irdu): The Olive Tree and Its Products in Ancient Mesopotamia." In *Olive Oil in Antiquity,* edited by Michael Heltzer and David Eitam. Haifa, 1995.

Melena, J. L. "Olive Oil and Other Sorts of Oil in the Mycenaean Tablets." *Minos* 18 (1983): 110–131.
Neef, Reinder. "Introduction, Development, and Environmental Implications of Olive Culture: The Evidence from Jordan." In *Man's Role in the Shaping of the Eastern Mediterranean Landscape,* edited by Sytze Bottema et al., pp. 295–306. Rotterdam, 1990.
Renfrew, Colin. *The Emergence of Civilisation: The Cyclades and the Aegean in the Third Millennium B.C.* London, 1972.
Runnels, Curtis N., and Julie Hansen. "The Olive in the Prehistoric Aegean: The Evidence for Domestication in the Early Bronze Age." *Oxford Journal of Archaeology* 5 (1986): 299–308.
Singer, Itamar. "Oil in Anatolia according to Hittite Texts." In *Olive Oil in Antiquity,* edited by Michael Heltzer and David Eitam. Haifa, 1995.
Stager, Lawrence E., and Samuel R. Wolff. "Production and Commerce in Temple Courtyards: An Olive Press in the Sacred Precinct at Tel Dan." *Bulletin of the American Schools of Oriental Research,* no. 243 (1981): 95–102.
Stager, Lawrence E. "The Finest Oil in Samaria." *Journal of Semitic Studies* 28 (1983): 241–245.
Stol, Marten. "Remarks on the Cultivation of Sesame and the Extraction of Its Oil." *Bulletin on Sumerian Agriculture* 2 (1985): 119–126.
Waetzoldt, Hartmut. "Ölpflanzen und Pflanzöle in 3. Jahrtausend." *Bulletin on Sumerian Agriculture* 2 (1985): 77–96.
Weinfeld, M. "The Use of Oil in the Cult of Ancient Israel." In *Olive Oil in Antiquity,* edited by Michael Heltzer and David Eitam. Haifa, 1995.
Zohary, Daniel, and F. Spiegel-Roy. "Beginnings of Fruit Growing in the Old World." *Science* 187 (1975): 319–327.

RAFAEL FRANKEL

OMAN. Currently a geopolitical term defining the modern country of the Sultanate of Oman, located on the southeastern portion of the Arabian Peninsula, Oman covers an area of about 192,000 sq km, or 120,000 sq. mi. It is bordered on the north by the United Arab Emirates (UAE) and the Saudi Arabian Rub al-Khali and on the west by Yemen. Its coastline exceeds 1,600 km (1,000 mi.), from the Musandam peninsula to Yemen (Clements, 1980, p. 5). Although a number of geographic subprovinces, or ecological regions, can be observed (Musandam peninsula, Hajar Mountains, Batinah coast, the Nejd, Rub al-Khali, and Dhofar), archaeologically and historically, two basic regions are of paramount importance: the north (the Oman peninsula, broadly) and the south (Dhofar). The summer monsoon that affects the south may be the most important feature in contrasting the two regions. By far the largest amount of archaeological work has taken place in the north. Work in the south by the Transarabian Expedition led by Juris Zarins concluded a four-year field schedule (1992–1995) whose results add to the earlier work of Frank P. Albright (1982), Paolo M. Costa (1979), and Judith Pullar (1974, 1975).

Paleolithic Period. No Paleolithic industries are known in the north, a phenomenon true not only of Oman, but also the UAE, Qatar, Bahrain, and eastern Saudi Arabia (Zarins et al., 1982, pp. 28–29). The dividing line for the Paleolithic appears to run through the Dhofar region. Sites are numerous to the west in Yemen, rare in Dhofar, and nonexistent to the northeast of Dauqa. The largest and earliest Lower Paleolithic site was found in the middle of Wadi Ghadun, on its highest, western terrace. Farther south, along its tributaries, a few scattered artifacts were recovered at Hanun and elsewhere (Biagi, 1994b, p. 84). Oldowan material to the northwest and west, contrasting to the later Early Acheulean handaxe material, suggests a time horizon of about one million years BP for the Wadi Ghadun site and similar sites in western Saudi Arabia and Yemen (Zarins et al., 1981, pp. 13–16; Amirkhanov, 1991, pp. 10–204; 1994, pp. 218–219). Along the southern coast, Paolo Biagi (1994b) suggests that a Late Acheulean industry is to be found at Saiwan. No Middle Paleolithic sites are yet known, but Upper Paleolithic blade industries have been found in the Shisur region of Wadi Ghadun and parallel finds have been found farther west in the Ḥadhraumaut region (Amirkhanov, 1991, pp. 266–312; 1994, p. 220). In light of new evidence concerning Upper Paleolithic industries and the spread of modern hominids, dates may range as far back as 150,000 BP for these sites. [*See* Ḥadhraumaut.]

Holocene "Neolithic" Industries (6000–3400 BCE). Beginning in the early Holocene period (c. 8000 BCE), the Arabian Peninsula (as well as most of North Africa) was affected by a significant increase in precipitation and moisture retention. This is reflected in the quite sudden appearance of blade and bifacial industries found in the north, but more extensively in the south (phase I). The largest percentage of sites are dominated by the blade industry, which produced Pre-Pottery Neolithic (PPN)-type points suggestive of ties with the Levant (Potts, 1993, pp. 170–173). In the north, distinctive coastal adaptations diverge from this pattern (Uerpmann, 1989); however, in the south, numerous sites are known from the Nejd on interior drainages and lakes with Fasad-type (blade) points (Edens, 1988a, p. 115). Sites are either lithic scatters, middens, or contain structures. Known principally from Dhofar, such a culture extended into the Ḥadhramaut province in Yemen and as far north as Jebel Tuwayq in southern Saudi Arabia (cf. McClure, 1994).

Subsequent bifacial projectile-point traditions (phase II) are even more widespread on the peninsula; numerous sites have been found in the south, as well as in adjoining areas of Yemen and in the Saudi Arabian Rub al-Khali (Edens, 1982; 1988b). To the north, such sites are known from eastern Saudi Arabia to the UAE (Potts, 1993, fig. 4). Shell middens in the north continue to follow a divergent stone-tool technology (Biagi, 1994a), that has a common tradition with sites found on the Yemen and Red Sea coastlines. Of particular interest are the Ras al-Hamra sites found near Muscat (Biagi et al., 1984; 1989). While Ubaid period ceramics are now known from the western Oman peninsula inside the Arab-Persian Gulf in the UAE (Haerinck, 1991; Frifelt, 1989), none have been found in the Arabian Sea along the Batinah coast. This suggests that Ubaid seafarers did not leave the Arab-Persian Gulf. [*See* Ubaid; Seafaring.] Other long-distance contacts are known, however, connecting much of the peninsula. Obsidian beads in a Qatari tomb originated in Yemen or southern Saudi Arabia (Zarins, 1990, p. 531); more recently, obsidian from Matafah in Wadi Ghadun was connected to the Dhamar-Reda field in Yemen or to an Eritrean source (Vincenzo Francaviglia, personal communication; Zarins, 1995).

Subsistence activities from the phase I and II groups are most likely attributable to pastoral nomadism and herding. [*See* Pastoral Nomadism.] Rock art in central and southwest Arabia (Anati, 1968; Zarins, 1982) principally depicts cattle and ovicaprids being herded. This evidence is supported by faunal studies (Uerpmann and Uerpmann cited in Potts, 1993, p. 177). Hunting, fishing, and shellfish gathering are also attested. [*See* Hunting; Fishing; Paleozoology.] A unique site in the south (Uruq Ibn Hamuda) produced numerous pestles, mortars, and pounders, confirming that, at most sites, hand-stone grinders were used to process plant remains.

In the south, phase III defines the last stage of the bifacial stone-tool tradition stretching from 3400 to 2500 BCE. There the hallmark is the trihedral rod; peculiar to the south, it is commonly found associated with numerous lithic scatter and structural sites (Ayun, Hailat Araka) and similar sites are reported from the Ḥadhramaut region in Yemen (Amirkhanov, 1994, p. 226, fig. 10). Few examples are known from the Rub al-Khali to the north. The trihedral rods may well be imitations of bronze points that were unavailable locally. In the north, the key stratigraphic site of Hili 8 (3000–1900 BCE) suggests the beginning of complex oasis life involving domesticated animals—sheep, goats, cattle, donkey, dog—and plants—wheat, barley, melons, dates (Cleuziou, 1982; 1989). [*See* Sheep and Goats; Cattle and Oxen; Dogs; Cereals.] Domestic sorghum from Hili 8, dated to the third millennium (Cleuziou and Costantini, 1980), is now superceded by samples from Ras al-Hamra 5 from the late fifth millennium (Nisbet, 1985). The Hamra 5 samples are the earliest known not only from Arabia, but also Sahel Africa and western India. Graves from the north (Hafit type) are single-chambered and double-ring walled. [*See* Burial Techniques.] Pottery types include imported Mesopotamian Jemdet Nasr/Early Dynastic I types. Copper resources are inferred to have been exploited for the first time (Potts, 1993, pp. 178–180). Written evidence from Mesopotamia and Susiana begins in about 3400 BCE, and eastern Arabia is identified as Dilmun. [*See* Dilmun.] Products coming from Dilmun, such as copper and stone, may have originated on the Oman peninsula. Aromatics from Dhofar may have already been imported into Mesopotamia as well (Zarins, 1995).

Protohistoric Cultures (2500–1300 BCE). In phase A (2500–2000 BCE) in the north, Hili 8 (and now Hili 1) define the archaeological sequence for the region. Sites such as Amlah, Bat, Wadi Bahla, Maysar, and the Ras al-Junayz series add to the picture. The tombs and settlement at Umm an-Nar excavated in the 1960s by the Danish archaeological expedition to the Persian Gulf initially defined this mid-third-millennium horizon (Frifelt, 1991; 1995). Now the circular communal tombs are known from Ra's al-Hadd to Khasab. [*See* Ra's al-Hadd.] Subsistence activities at Umm an-Nar pinpointed for the first time the possible domestication of the camel (Hoch, 1979; 1995, pp. 250–252). [*See* Camels.] Both ceramic materials and soft-stone vessels, which first appear in complex, carved designs (*série ancienne*, to use the terminology of Miroschedji, 1973) tie Iran, the Indus Valley, and Mesopotamia to the Arab-Persian Gulf. By 2200 BCE, the soft-stone vessels evolved into a simpler design using dots and circles (*série récente*). Copper sources in Wadi Jizzi and the Maysar complex are known to have been exploited (Weisgerber, 1980; 1981). Historically, the Oman peninsula is mentioned for the first time in the Old Akkadian period as Magan. In the South, Bronze Age sites are defined by megalithic house types, a remnant lithic industry, and the introduction of copper/bronze (Taqa 60, Hagif 241, Khor Rori). Previous Neolithic populations retreated to the fringes of the Dhofar hills.

In phase B (2000–1700 BCE), the north is defined by the Wadi Suq horizon. This subperiod is contemporary to the Isin-Larsa and Old Babylonian periods in Mesopotamia and has ties to the Dilmun culture of eastern Saudi Arabia, Bahrain, and Failaka. [*See* Isin; Larsa; Bahrain; Failaka.] Cist graves contain the distinctive painted Wadi Suq ceramics and the *série tardive* soft-stone vessels. Copper mining continued to play a major role in the region's economy (cf. Oppenheim, 1954), with evidence not only from the Oman peninsula (Wadi Jizzi, Wadi Samad) but from Masirah Island as well. Sites on the Ra's al-Junayz coastline continued to provide evidence of a maritime economy (e.g., RJ1). In the south, Carbon-14 dates from encampments on now fossil lagoons on the Salalah plain define the ongoing Bronze Age tradition. Both shell and copper fishhooks have been recovered, as well as marine and land fauna.

In phase C (1700–1300 BCE), Tell Abraq, Rumeilah, and Hili 2 on the Oman peninsula define the latest phase of the Wadi Suq complex. Ceramic ties connect Elam and Kassite Mesopotamia. Bronze weapons from Nizwa also point to an Iranian connection. In the south, the Bronze Age probably ends by 1300/1100 BCE (Taqa 60, Hagif 241).

Iron Age (1300–300 BCE). In the north, the period between 1300 and 300 BCE is known as Iron A–B, or Lizq. A series of sites is found either as coastal middens (Shimal), agricultural towns (Dibba), piedmont villages at the mouths of wadis (Ghalilah), oases (Rumeilah, Hili 2) or fortifications (Hili 14, Lizq). Graveyards are also known (Qarn Bint Saud, Maysar, Shimal). The largest and most important sites for the period are Rumeilah and Hili 2. Maysar 8 and 42 and Samad 10, among other sites in the area, suggest that the *falaj/qanat* ("channel") system characteristic of irrigation practices in the north probably originated in Iron Age Iran. [*See* Irrigation.] Typical Iron A assemblages include incense burners, Kaftiari ceramic types from Iran, soft-stone vessels, and copper/bronze tools and jewelry (Potts, 1990, p. 376, figs. 41–43). In historical terms, Neo-Assyrian references (640 BCE) to the land of Kade and the city of Iske may refer to modern Izki. The name *Kade* continued to be used into the classical period by Pliny, and Daniel T. Potts has argued that Kade was the Akkadian equivalent of the Persian Maka/Makkaš and its later variants Mykoi/Machiya. Achaemenid control and/or influence over the Oman peninsula was most likely exerted from a coastal center such as Sohar. [*See* Sohar.] In addition, the Azd Omani migrations into Oman may have begun during the Achaemenid period.

In the south, Iron Age sites (1300–300 BCE) have been found principally on high coastal terraces. Some of the structures are superimposed on Bronze Age sites (Taqa, Khor Rori, Hagif), but others represent large Iron Age period homesteads (Wadi Adonhib, Raysut headland). The archaeological assemblages are characterized by red wares and a microlithic flint technique, both having ties to Yemen. The early phases of the formal buildings at Shisur may parallel the Iron Age buildings at Hili 14, the Bahrain fort, or Jumeirah (Potts, 1990, p. 112, figs. 6, 24).

Classical Period (300 BCE–650 CE). Following Hellenistic expansion into the Gulf and across trade routes into central-southern Arabia, Seleucid-period sites on the Omani peninsula such as Mleiha (Potts, 1990, vol. 2, p. 272) parallel northeastern Arabian sites such as Thaj. [*See* Thaj.] From the succeeding Parthian period, more sites, such as ed-Dur, Sohar, and Samad (Maysar 43, Samad ash Shan 1) are known. The majority of these sites continued to be occupied in the following Sasanian period.

First-century historical sources (Pliny, Ptolemy, and the *Periplus of the Erythraean Sea*) refer for the first time to Omana, which is likely Sohar, or perhaps ed-Dur (Groom, 1994). These contemporary sources and later Islamic traditions refer to the Azd Omani as bedouin from the Tanukh confederation (classical Thanuitai). They came from southwest Arabia, perhaps as early as the first century CE, across the south to the north, reaching Basra by 600. The Sasanian name for the Omani was *Mazun,* from the Parthian *mzw(n)* (Potts, 1990, vol. 2, p. 329, n. 309; for the Islamic conversion, see Potts, 1990, pp. 340–348).

In the south, classical sites such as the Shisur fort (probably Marimatha in the territory of the Iobaritae) are datable in part to the Seleucid era, based on the recovery of red appliqué and black-burnished wares. Parthian red wares are paralleled at Sohar (Kervran and Hiebert, 1991). At ʿAin Humran the predominant remains date to the Parthian period, but the baked bricks may be Achaemenid. Other sites along the Salalah plain, such as Taqa and al-Balid have Seleucid- to Parthian-period occupation. The excavations at Khor Rori in the 1950s proved that the site is to be identified as ṢMHRM and belongs to the first century CE as a Ḥadhramaut outpost (Albright, 1982). Survey sites discovered in 1992–1995 on the Salalah plain can be matched with the references in Pliny, the *Periplus,* and Ptolemy.

Islamic Period (650–1500 CE). Until 1150 political control of the north alternated between the local Imamate (Ibadi) and caliphate authorities (Umayyad, ʿAbbasid, and Seljuk). [*See* Umayyad Caliphate; ʿAbbasid Caliphate.] The expansion of Omani influence into India, China, and East Africa took place in the Early Islamic period. Sohar, as the key maritime trade center, peaked in the ninth–tenth centuries and was destroyed by 1225 (Grohmann, 1934; Williamson, 1973; Wilkinson, 1979). By medieval times, the importance of Muscat and Qalhat had grown as a result of increased trade and control through the straits of Hormuz. With the arrival of the Portugese (1507–1625) and their struggles with the Ottomans and Omani in the interior, fortress technology reached new dimensions (Nizwa, Jilani). In the south, Islamic expansion can be documented by ʿAbbasid expansion. Sites such as Jebel Qinqari and Raysut demonstrate the control of harbors and the Indian Ocean coastline. Al-Balid (medieval Mansura), controlled by the Rasulids from Yemen, dominated the Salalah plain (Costa, 1979), and smaller sites such as Taqa were occupied as well.

[*See also* Arabian Peninsula; Qatar; United Arab Emirates; *and* Yemen.]

BIBLIOGRAPHY

Albright, Frank P. *The American Archaeological Expedition in Dhofar, Oman, 1952–1953.* Publications of the American Foundation for the Study of Man, vol. 6. Washington, D.C., 1982.

Amirkhanov, Khizri A. *Paleolit Iuga Aravii* (The Paleolithic in South Arabia). Moscow, 1991.

Amirkhanov, Khizri A. "Research on the Palaeolithic and Neolithic of Ḥadramaut and Mahra." *Arabian Archaeology and Epigraphy* 5 (1994): 217–228.

Anati, Emmanuel. *Rock-Art in Central Arabia,* vol. 1, *The "Oval-Headed" People of Arabia.* Louvain, 1968.

Biagi, Paolo, et al. "Excavation at the RH5 Settlement, Qurm, Winter 1984–1985." *East and West* 34 (1984): 455–465.

Biagi, Paolo, et al. "Excavations at the Aceramic Coastal Settlement of RH5 (Muscat, Sultanate of Oman), 1983–5." In *South Asian Archaeology 1985,* edited by Karen Frifelt and Per Sorensen, pp. 1–8. London, 1989.

Biagi, Paolo. "A Radiocarbon Chronology for the Aceramic Shell Middens of Coastal Oman." *Arabian Archaeology and Epigraphy* 5 (1994a): 17–31.

Biagi, Paolo. "An Early Palaeolithic Site near Saiwan (Sultanate of Oman)." *Arabian Archaeology and Epigraphy* 5 (1994b): 81–88.

Clements, Frank A. *Oman, the Reborn Land.* London, 1980.

Cleuziou, Serge, and Lorenzo Costantini. "Premiers éléments sur l'agriculture protohistorique de l'Arabie orientale." *Paléorient* 6 (1980): 255–261.

Cleuziou, Serge. "Hili and the Beginnings of Oasis Life in Eastern Arabia." *Proceedings of the Seminar for Arabian Studies* 12 (1982): 15–22.

Cleuziou, Serge. "The Chronology of Protohistoric Oman as Seen from Hili 8." In *Oman Studies,* edited by Paolo M. Costa and Maurizio Tosi, pp. 47–78. Serie Orientale Roma, vol. 63. Rome, 1989.

Cleuziou, Serge, and Maurizio Tosi. "The Southeastern Frontier of the Ancient Near East." In *South Asian Archaeology 1985,* edited by

Karen Frifelt and Per Sorensen, pp. 15–48. London, 1989. Includes basic archaeological/historical information for the Oman peninsula before the Islamic period.

Costa, Paolo M. "The Study of the City of Zafar (al-Balid)." *Journal of Oman Studies* 5 (1979): 111–150. Early work at Dhofar.

Edens, Christopher. "Towards a Definition of the Western ar-Rub' al-Khali 'Neolithic.'" *Atlal* 6 (1982): 109–124.

Edens, Christopher. "Archaeology of the Sands and Adjacent Portions of the Sharqiyah." *Journal of Oman Studies Special Report* 3 (1988A): 113–130.

Edens, Christopher. "The Rub al-Khali 'Neolithic' Revisited: The View from Nadqan." In *Araby the Blest: Studies in Arabian Archaeology,* edited by Daniel T. Potts, pp. 15–43. Carsten Niebuhr Institute Publication, 7. Copenhagen, 1988B.

Frifelt, Karen. "'Ubaid in the Gulf Area." In *Upon This Foundation: The 'Ubaid Reconsidered,* edited by Elizabeth F. Henrickson and Ingolf Thuesen, pp. 404–417. Copenhagen, 1989.

Frifelt, Karen. *The Island of Umm an-Nar,* vol. 1, *Third Millennium Graves.* Aarhus, 1991.

Frifelt, Karen, ed. *The Island of Umm an-Nar,* vol. 2, *The Third Millennium Settlement.* Moesgaard, 1995.

Grohmann, Adolf. "Suḥār." In *Encyclopaedia of Islam,* pp. 544–547. Leiden, 1934.

Groom, Nigel. "Oman and the Emirates in Ptolemy's Map." *Arabian Archaeology and Epigraphy* 5 (1994): 198–214.

Haerinck, E. "Heading for the Straits of Hormuz, an Ubaid Site in the Emirate of Ajman (U.A.E.)." *Arabian Archaeology and Epigraphy* 2 (1991): 84–90.

Hoch, Ella. "Reflections on Prehistoric Life at Umm an-Nar (Trucial Oman) Based on Faunal Remains from the Third Millennium B.C." In *South Asian Archaeology 1977,* edited by Maurizio Taddei, pp. 589–638. Naples, 1979.

Hoch, Ella. "Animal Bones from the Umm an-Nar Settlement." In *The Island of Umm an-Nar,* vol. 2, *The Third Millennium Settlement,* edited by Karen Frifelt, pp. 249–256. Moesgaard, 1995.

Kervran, Monik, and Frederik T. Hiebert. "Sohar pré-islamique: Note stratigraphique." *Internationale Archäologie* 6 (1991): 337–348.

McClure, Harold A. "A New Arabian Stone Tool Assemblage and Notes on the Aterian Industry of North Africa." *Arabian Archaeology and Epigraphy* 5 (1994): 1–16.

Miroschedji, Pierre de. "Vases et objets en stéatite susiens des Musée du Louvre." *Cahiers de la Délégation Archéologique Française en Iran* 3 (1973): 9–79.

Nayeem, Muhammad Abdul. *Prehistory and Protohistory of the Arabian Peninsula,* vol. 1, *Saudi Arabia.* Hyderabad, 1990. Oman in the larger context of the Arabian Peninsula.

Nisbet, Renato. "Evidence of Sorghum at Site RH5, Qurm, Muscat." *East and West* 35 (1985): 415–417.

Oppenheim, A. Leo. "Seafaring Merchants of Ur." *Journal of the American Oriental Society* 74 (1954): 6–17.

Potts, Daniel T. *The Arabian Gulf in Antiquity.* 2 vols. Oxford, 1990, passim. Offers basic historical/archaeological information about the Oman peninsula before the Islamic period.

Potts, Daniel T. "The Chronology of the Archaeological Assemblages from the Head of the Arabian Gulf to the Arabian Sea, 8000–1750 B.C." In *Chronologies in Old World Archaeology,* vols. 1–2, edited by Robert W. Ehrich, pp. 63–76, 77–89. 3d ed. Chicago, 1992.

Potts, Daniel T. "The Late Prehistoric, Protohistoric, and Early Historic Periods in Eastern Arabia, ca. 5000–1200 B.C." *Journal of World Prehistory* 7 (1993): 163–212.

Pullar, Judith. "Harvard Archaeological Survey in Oman, 1973, I: Flint Sites in Oman." *Proceedings of the Seminar for Arabian Studies* 4 (1974): 33–48.

Pullar, Judith. "A Selection of Aceramic Sites in the Sultanate of Oman." *Journal of Oman Studies* 1 (1975): 49–88. Includes early work at Dhofar.

Tosi, Maurizio. "The Emerging Picture of Prehistoric Arabia." *Annual Review of Anthropology* 15 (1986): 461–490. Oman in the larger context of the Arabian Peninsula.

Uerpmann, Margarethe. "Some Remarks on Late Stone Age Industries from the Coastal Area of Northern Oman." In *Oman Studies,* edited by Paolo M. Costa and Maurizio Tosi, pp. 169–177. Serie Orientale Roma, vol. 63. Rome, 1989.

Weisgerber, Gerd. ". . . und Kupfer in Oman." *Der Anschnitt* 32 (1980): 62–110.

Weisgerber, Gerd. "Mehr als Kupfer in Oman-Ergebnisse der Expedition 1981." *Der Anschnitt* 33 (1981): 174–263.

Wilkinson, John. "Suḥār in the Early Islamic Period and the Written Evidence." In *South Asian Archaeology 1977,* edited by Maurizio Taddei, pp. 887–907. Naples, 1979.

Williamson, A. *Sohar and Omani Seafaring in the Indian Ocean.* Muscat, 1973.

Zarins, Juris, et al. "The Second Preliminary Report on the Southwestern Province." *Atlal* 5 (1981): 9–42.

Zarins, Juris. "The Early Rock Art of Saudi Arabia." *Archaeology* 35 (1982): 20–27.

Zarins, Juris, et al. "Preliminary Report on the Archaeology Survey of the Riyadh Area." *Atlal* 6 (1982): 25–38.

Zarins, Juris. "Obsidian and the Red Sea Trade: Prehistoric Aspects." In *South Asian Archaeology 1987,* edited by Maurizio Taddei, pp. 507–541. Rome, 1990.

Zarins, Juris. "Dhofar, Frankincense, and Dilmun: Precursors to the Iobaritae and Omani." Paper presented at the Interdisciplinary Archaeology Conference, Harvard University, 15 October 1994 (to be published in 1995).

Zarins, Juris. "Preliminary Results of the Trans-Arabia Expedition to Dhofar, 1992–1995." Paper to be published in the proceedings of the conference "Profumi d'Arabia," Pisa, Italy, 18–22 October 1995.

JURIS ZARINS

ONOMASTICS. *See* Names and Naming.

OSSUARY. A small chest or box, usually made of stone but occasionally of clay or wood, used for reburying human bones after the flesh has decayed, is known as an ossuary. It was used with some frequency in the Early Roman period in Jewish tombs in the vicinity of Jerusalem.

A typical ossuary from that period is hollowed from a single block of limestone and measured about 60 × 35 × 30 cm; there were smaller ossuaries for children. It had a removable lid that might be flat, rounded, or gabled. Most ossuaries were plain, but many were decorated with motifs typical of Jewish art of the period: geometric designs (e.g., the six-petaled rosette) or representations of Jewish architectural and religious themes (e.g., tomb monuments or palm branches). (See figure 1.) Often only one long side of the ossuary was decorated and professionally incised by chip carving. Inscriptions, by contrast, were not professionally done but were scrawled with charcoal or scratched with a sharp object almost anywhere on the ossuary—on its sides, ends, lid, or even along a top edge. Written in Greek, Ara-

OSSUARY. Figure 1. *Stone ossuary.* From Mt. Scopus, first century BCE. (Courtesy ASOR Archives)

maic, or Hebrew, ossuary inscriptions identify the deceased by name, only occasionally adding details about family relations, place of origin, age, or status.

The deceased was initially laid in a niche or on a shelf to decompose in a family burial cave. When decomposition was complete, the bones were gathered in ossuaries for secondary burial and placed in a niche, on a shelf, or in a separate chamber (e.g., in the family tomb located on Reḥov Ruppin in Jerusalem, in the "Goliath" tomb in Jericho, and at Dominus Flevit, a first-century cemetery on the Mount of Olives). The bones of more than one individual could by custom be placed in the same ossuary: according to the third-century rabbinic document *Semaḥot* 13.8, persons who shared a bed in life could share an ossuary in death. Even the "Caiaphas" ossuary contained the bones of more than one person. The Caiaphas ossuary is a large (74 × 29 × 38 cm) richly ornamental ossuary with a vaulted lid inscribed on the side and back with the name "Caiaphas." This name also belonged to the High Priest during the days of Jesus (*Mt.* 26:57). The ossuary was found in 1990 in a tomb located in North Talpiyot, a southern suburb of Jerusalem.

The historical development of Jewish ossuaries is still debated. Eric Meyers sees them as an adaptation of the long-standing ancient Near Eastern custom of secondary burial, with parallels in Chalcolithic bone containers, Cretan larnakes, and Persian astodans. L. Y. Rahmani argues, however, that Jewish secondary burial in ossuaries was unique to Jerusalem in the Early Roman period. Rachel Hachlili and Amos Kloner have in turn questioned Rahmani's view. They note several finds of Jewish ossuaries at locations quite distant from Jerusalem as late as the fourth century CE. Kloner cites the finds at Ḥorvat Tilla, in the southern Shephelah, in particular. Although there presently is no scholarly consensus, ossuaries can reasonably be regarded as the form of secondary burial that was most popular among Jews living near Jerusalem in the Early Roman period.

It is widely agreed (based on literary evidence from the Mishnah and the two Talmuds) that Jewish secondary burial in ossuaries was driven by two theological beliefs: resurrection of the body, and expiation of sin via the decomposition of human flesh. The former motivated the use of an individual burial container and the latter the practice of secondary burial. For Palestinian Jews in the Roman period, bones that had been placed in an ossuary were purified from sin and ready for the resurrection.

[*See also* Burial Techniques; Jerusalem; Sarcophagus.]

BIBLIOGRAPHY

Figueras, Pau. *Decorated Jewish Ossuaries.* Leiden, 1983. Brief introductory study with many useful diagrams and photographs.

Greenhut, Zvi. "The 'Caiaphas' Tomb in North Talpiyot, Jerusalem." *'Atiqot* 21 (1992): 63–71. Exemplary report from a recent excavation of a tomb containing ossuaries, including one marked with the name *Caiaphas.*

Hachlili, Rachel. *Ancient Jewish Art and Archaeology in the Land of Israel.* Leiden, 1988. The most thorough presentation of Hachlili's perspective on Jewish ossuaries, based on her tomb excavations at Jericho.

Meyers, Eric M. *Jewish Ossuaries: Reburial and Rebirth.* Rome, 1971. Early attempt to relate Jewish ossuaries to the wider context of ancient Near Eastern practices of secondary burial. Rahmani's unnecessarily harsh review may be found in *Israel Exploration Journal* 23.2 (1973): 121–126.

Rahmani, L. Y. "Ancient Jerusalem's Funerary Customs and Tombs." *Biblical Archaeologist* 45.1 (1982): 43–53; 45.2 (1982): 109–119. Brief and readable summary of Rahmani's view that ossuaries are "uniquely Jerusalemite."

BYRON R. MCCANE

OSTEN, HANS HENNING ERIMAR VON DER (1899–1960), German archaeologist and Orientalist. In 1923 von der Osten was forced by post-World War I politics to leave his archaeological studies in Berlin. He emigrated to the United States where, from 1924 to 1925, he was an assistant curator at the Metropolitan Museum of Art in New York City. In 1926–1927, he was director of the Hittite Survey for the Oriental Institute of Chicago and from 1927 to 1934 director of its Anatolian Expedition to Alişar Höyük and Kerkenesdağ (1928), Gavurkale (1930), and Terzili Hamam (1932). While chairman of the archaeology department at Ankara University (1936–1939), he worked at Ahlatlıbel (1937), Van (1938), and the Roman baths in Ankara (1938–1939). Imprisoned in 1940 as a result of unsubstantiated accusations of spying, he spent ten years in a Turkish prison. He was rehabilitated in 1950. From 1951 to

1960 he worked at Uppsala University in Sweden, during which time he excavated Tell es-Salihiyeh, Syria (1953); directed the German-Swedish excavation at Takht-i-Suleiman, Iran (1959); and was director of the German Archaeological Institute in Tehran (1960).

Von der Osten's scholarly contribution, some sixty publications and manuscripts, is dominated by his fieldwork, by Anatolian archaeology and historical topography, and ancient Near Eastern glyptics. The main objective of his extensive topographical explorations and surveys in central Anatolia (putting some three hundred sites on the archaeological map) was to find remains of the then newly discovered Hittites. This led to his pioneering, carefully dug, and meticulously published excavation at Alişar Höyük (1927–1932), in collaboration with Erich F. Schmidt (Chicago, 1930–1937). The work produced the first important, albeit controversial, stratigraphy of the Anatolian plateau, with evidence of almost every period except the Hittite. Unfortunately, von der Osten's numerous articles on Anatolian archaeology never culminated in the completion of his long-term study of the historical geography of Anatolia, the unfinished manuscript "Siedlungsgeschichte Kleinasiens."

Osten produced learned volumes on the seal collections of Edward T. Newell (Chicago, 1934), A. Baldwin Brett (Chicago, 1936), and especially Hans S. von Aulock (Uppsala, 1957). A late interest in the archaeology of Iran resulted in the elegant synthesis *Die Welt der Perser* (Stuttgart, 1956) and in his participation on the excavation at the Sasanian site Takht-i Suleiman in Azerbaijan, in 1959.

A forceful, farsighted master of landscape, on an excavation or in a graduate seminar, H. H. von der Osten was caught in the forces of world politics and robbed of his most creative years. Yet, much of his work endures.

BIBLIOGRAPHY

Much material on H. H. von der Osten is available in the archives of the University Library, Uppsala, Sweden. In addition, the reader may consult the following works by von der Osten.

Explorations in Hittite Asia Minor. 3 vols. Oriental Institute Communications, 2, 6, and 8. Chicago, 1927–1930.

Explorations in Central Anatolia, Season of 1926. Oriental Institute Publications, 5. Chicago, 1929.

The Alishar Hüyük (with Erich F. Schmidt). 5 vols. Oriental Institute Publications, 6, 7, 19, 20, 28–30. Chicago, 1930–1937.

Ancient Oriental Seals in the Collection of Mr. Edward T. Newell. Oriental Institute Publications, 22. Chicago, 1934.

Ancient Oriental Seals in the Collection of Mrs. Agnes Baldwin Brett. Oriental Institute Publications, 37. Chicago, 1936.

Die Welt der Perser. Stuttgart, 1956.

Altorientalische Siegelsteine der Sammlung Hans Silvius von Aulock. Studia Ethnographica Upsaliensia, 13. Uppsala, 1957.

CARL NYLANDER

OSTRACON. A loanword from Greek, in which it means "shell" or "sherd," *ostracon* is used in epigraphy to describe generally small inscriptions on shells, irregular pieces of stone, and, most frequently, sherds. Inscriptions were mostly written with ink on these hard materials, although there are a few incised ostraca. In principle, there is a distinction between an ostracon and an inscription on a vessel. In the latter case, there is generally a connection between the inscription and the vessel or its content, such as, perhaps, the name of its owner, its content, place, and date of production. In Egypt and in Palestine occasionally complete jars seem also to have been used for writing exercises. [*See* Kuntillet ʿAjrud.]

The main reason for using sherds was that they were plentiful and cost nothing. However, using such objects presented difficulties: they were relatively heavy and they were difficult to store because they are irregular in shape. In fact, they were mainly used to write provisional notes, administrative lists, short messages, or drafts that could later be copied or registered on leather or papyrus scrolls—though they could be used for official messages when papyrus was unavailable. [*See* Papyrus; Parchment; Writing Materials.] They were also used for school exercises, and, in Egypt at least, for drafts of drawings and sculptures (e.g., at Khirbet el-Medineh).

Because most ostraca were inscribed in ink, they were generally connected with the use of a calamus (rush or reed) to write a linear script. They were therefore unusual and found late in Mesopotamia and Anatolia where cuneiform writing dominated but found frequently in Egypt and in the Levant, especially after the development of alphabetic writing (Canaanite, Hebrew, Phoenician, Aramaic, and, later, Greek and Arabic).

Egypt can be considered the homeland of ostraca, with thousands of Hieratic, Demotic, Greek, and Coptic ostraca, not to mention hundreds of Phoenician and Aramaic ostraca found mainly at Saqqara and Elephantine and dating mostly from the Persian period. [*See* Saqqara; Elephantine.] Those ostraca throw a vivid light on everyday life, with its economical and daily problems. They also contain numerous schoolboys' exercises, including excerpts of literary texts.

In the Levant, scribes chose sherds that were as flat as possible—mainly body sherds from large jars. They sometimes cut or broke them to get a rectangular shape that is easy to hold in the left hand (e.g., in the Elyashib archives at Arad, ostraca are about 5–8 × 7–12 cm). [*See* Arad Inscriptions.] However, there are also very small ostraca of a few centimeters—labels of sorts—and others as large as a modern sheet of paper (e.g., about 21.5 × 28 cm; see Lemaire and Vernus, 1983), or even larger (42 × 60 cm for the Aššur ostracon; see below). [*See* Aššur.] They could be inscribed on both sides, the convex side generally written on first. [*See* Scribes and Scribal Techniques; Writing and Writing Systems.]

Excavations in Israel have produced various kinds or groups of ostraca in addition to a few in Greek and Arabic:

1. *Hieratic.* A few hieratic ostraca have been found in Late Bronze Age strata, mainly at Tell ed-Duweir/Lachish and Tell esh-Shari'a (cf. Goldwasser, 1991). [*See* Lachish.]

2. *"Canaanite" or "Proto-Hebrew."* Ostraca from the Iron Age I, an abecedary and a list of names in Canaanite or Proto-Hebrew, have been found at ʿIzbet Ṣarṭah (Kochavi, 1977) and Beth-Shemesh. [*See* ʿIzbet Ṣarṭah; Beth-Shemesh.]

3. *Philistine.* Several ostraca of Philistine origin have been found at Tell Jemmeh. They contain lists of names and date to the seventh century BCE (cf. Naveh, 1985). [*See* Jemmeh, Tell.]

4. *Paleo-Hebrew.* Many Iron Age II Paleo-Hebrew ostraca, mainly from Samaria, Jerusalem, Lachish, Meṣad Ḥashavyahu, Arad, and Khirbet Ghazza/Ḥorvat ʿUza, are connected with the royal administration of the kingdoms of Israel (for the Samaria ostraca) and Judah (for the others). The latter, dating mainly to about 600 BCE, illuminate the administrative and military organization, as well as the people's state of mind, on the eve of the fall of Judah. [*See* Samaria; Jerusalem; Meṣad Ḥashavyahu.]

5. *Ammonite.* Various ostraca inscribed in Ammonite, generally from the seventh–sixth centuries BCE, have been found in central Transjordan, at Ḥesban/Heshbon, Tell el-Mazar, and Tell el-ʿUmeiri. They are either lists of names or are practically illegible. However, ostracon 3 from Tell el-Mazar is a letter of Palt to his brother. [*See* Ḥesban; Mazar, Tell el-; ʿUmeiri, Tell el-.]

6. *Edomite.* A few small ostraca written in Edomite in about 600 BCE have been found at Umm el-Biyara, Buṣeirah, Tell el-Kheleifeh, and in the Negev; the most interesting is a letter found at Khirbet Ghazza/Ḥorvat ʿUza with a greeting formula mentioning the god Qos. [*See* Umm el-Biyara; Buṣeirah; Kheleifeh, Tell el-; Negev.]

7. *Aramaic.* During the Persian period, Aramaic became the administrative language of Palestine. Aramaic ostraca have been found in Cisjordan and Transjordan, the two main collections being from Arad and Beersheba. Several hundred new Aramaic ostraca have recently appeared on the market. [*See* Aramaic Language and Literature; Beersheba; Idumeans.]

8. *Aramaic and Greek.* A Hellenistic bilingual ostracon, in Aramaic and Greek, was discovered at Khirbet el-Qom (cf. Geraty, 1975, 1981). A dated marriage contract, probably an exercise, was found recently at Mareshah (Kloner and Eshel, 1994). [*See* Qom, Khirbet el-; Mareshah.]

9. *Square Hebrew and Aramaic.* Early Roman ostraca written in Hebrew and Aramaic in a square script have been found at a number of sites: Qumran, Masada, Murabbaʿat, and Herodium. Some were writing exercises—abecedaries or lists of names—while others were simply tags with letter(s) or name(s). [*See* Qumran; Masada; Murabbaʿat; Herodium.]

So far, only a few ostraca have been found in Phoenicia: a small collection of seven ostraca was found in the Temple of Eshmun in Sidon (cf. Vanel, 1967, 1969; Betlyon, 1973) and a single ostracon was found at Tell el-Fukhar/Akko (Dothan, 1985), dating to the Persian period. [*See* Sidon; Akko.]

In Mesopotamia, ostraca are generally rare, late, and connected with the use of Aramaic (cf. Röllig, 1990) and eventually of Greek. However, the large Aššur ostracon (Donner and Röllig 1966–1969, no. 233; Gibson, 1975, no. 20, pp. 98–110) was written by an Assyrian official at the time of the revolt of Shamash-shum-ukin (c. 650 BCE); it shows that Aramaic was already being used between Assyrian officials. In fact, another ostracon, found at Nimrud and containing a list of probably Ammonite names, may be even earlier; it is dated on paleographic grounds to the end of the eighth century BCE. [*See* Nimrud; Ammonite Inscriptions.] The number of these ostraca pales against the some three thousand Parthian ostraca found at Nisa, not far from Ashkhabad (Turkmenistan) and dating to the first century BCE.

BIBLIOGRAPHY

Beit-Arieh, Itzhaq. "A Literary Ostracon from Ḥorvat ʿUza." *Tel Aviv* 20 (1993): 55–65.

Betlyon, John W. "Notes on the Phoenician Ostraca from near Sidon." *Bulletin du Musée de Beyrouth* 26 (1973): 31–34.

Černý, Jaroslav, and Alan H. Gardiner. *Hieratic Ostraca.* Oxford, 1957.

Davies, Graham I., et al. *Ancient Hebrew Inscriptions: Corpus and Concordance.* Cambridge, 1991. See especially pages 1–117.

Devauchelle, Didier. *Ostraca démotiques du Musée du Louvre.* Cairo, 1983.

Diakonoff, Igor M., and Veniamina A. Lifshitz. *Parthian Economic Documents from Nisa.* Corpus Inscriptionum Iranicarum: II. Inscriptions of the Seleucid and Parthian Periods and of Eastern Iran and Central Asia, vol. 2.1. London, 1976.

Donner, Herbert, and Wolfgang Röllig. *Kanaanäische und aramäische Inschriften.* 3 vols. Wiesbaden, 1966–1969.

Dothan, Moshe. "A Phoenician Inscription from ʿAkko." *Israel Exploration Journal* 35 (1985): 81–94.

Fischer-Effert, Hans-Werner. *Literarische Ostraka der Ramessidenzeit in Übersetzung.* Wiesbaden, 1986.

Geraty, Lawrence T. "The Khirbet el-Kom Bilingual Ostracon." *Bulletin of the American Schools of Oriental Research,* no. 220 (1975): 55–61.

Geraty, Lawrence T. "Recent Suggestions on the Bilingual Ostracon from Khirbet el-Kôm." *Andrews University Seminary Studies* 19 (1981): 137–140.

Gibson, John C. L. *Textbook of Syrian Semitic Inscriptions,* vol. 2, *Aramaic Inscriptions.* Oxford, 1975.

Goldwasser, Orly. "An Egyptian Scribe from Lachish and the Hieratic Tradition of the Hebrew Kingdoms." *Tel Aviv* 18 (1991): 248–253.

Gutgesell, Manfred. *Die Datierung der Ostraka und Papyri aus Deir el-Medineh und ihre ökonomische Interpretation,* vol. 1 *Die 20. Dynastie.* Hildesheimer Ägyptologische Beitrage, 18/19. Hildesheim, 1983.

Kaplony-Heckel, Ursula. *Die demotischen Tempeleide.* Ägyptologische Abhandlungen, 6. Wiesbaden, 1963.

Kaplony-Heckel, Ursula. "Niltal und Oasen: Ägyptischer Alltag nach demotischen Ostraka." *Zeitschrift für Ägyptische Sprache und Altertumskunde* 118 (1991): 127–141.

Kasser, Anna Di Bitonto. "Ostraca copti a Deir el Gizāz: Frammenti di lettere." *Aegyptus* 72 (1992): 143–160.
Kloner, Amos, and Ephrat Eshel. "Maresha–1992." *Ḥadashot Archeologiot* 101–102 (1994): 102–104.
Kochavi, Moshe. "An Ostracon of the Period of the Judges from ʿIzbet Ṣarṭah." *Tel Aviv* 4 (1977): 1–13.
Lemaire, André. *Inscriptions hébraïques*, vol. 1, *Les ostraca*. Littératures Anciennes du Proche-Orient, 9. Paris, 1977.
Lemaire, André, and Pascal Vernus. "L'ostracon paléo-hébreu n° 6 de Tell Qudeirat (Qadesh-Barnéa)." In *Fontes atque Pontes: Eine Festgabe für H. Brunner,* edited by Manfred Görg, pp. 302–326. Ägypten und Altes Testament, 5. Wiesbaden, 1983.
Lemaire, André. "Von Ostrakon zur Schriftrolle." In *XXII. Deutscher Orientalistentag vom 21 bis 25 März 1983 in Tübingen,* edited by Wolfgang Röllig, pp. 110–123. Zeitschrift der Deutschen Morgenländischen Gesellschaft, Supplement 6. Stuttgart, 1985.
López, Jesús. *Ostraca ieratici n. 57450–57568, tabelle lignee n. 58001–58007*. Catalogo del Museo Egizio di Torino, Serie Seconda–Collezioni, vol. 3.4. Milan, 1984.
Naveh, Joseph. "The Aramaic Ostraca." In *Beer-Sheba I: Excavations at Tel Beer-Sheba, 1969–1971 Seasons,* edited by Yohanan Aharoni, pp. 79–82. Tel Aviv, 1973.
Naveh, Joseph. "The Aramaic Ostraca from Tel Beer-Sheba (Seasons 1971–1976)." *Tel Aviv* 6 (1979): 182–188.
Naveh, Joseph. "Writing and Scripts in Seventh-Century Philistia: The New Evidence from Tell Jemmeh." *Israel Exploration Journal* 35 (1985): 8–21.
Naveh, Joseph. "Aramaic Ostraca and Jar Inscriptions from Tell Jemmeh." *ʿAtiqot* 21 (1992): 49–53.
Porten, Bezalel, and Ada Yardeni. "Three Unpublished Aramaic Ostraca." *Maarav* 7 (1991): 207–227.
Posener, Georges. *Catalogue des ostraca hiératiques littéraires de Deir el-Médineh.* Documents de Fouilles de l'Institut Français d'Archéologie Orientale, vol. 18. Cairo, 1951.
Renz, Johannes. *Die althebräischen Inschriften, Teil 1. Text und Kommentar.* Darmstadt, 1995.
Röllig, Wolfgang. "Zwei aramäische Inschriften vom Tall Šēḫ Ḥasan/Syrien." *Semitica* 39 (1990): 149–154.
Segal, Judah B. *Aramaic Texts from North Saqqâra.* London, 1983. See pages 139–145.
Vanel, Antoine. "Six 'ostraca' phéniciens trouvés au Temple d'Echmoun, près de Saïda." *Bulletin du Musée de Beyrouth* 20 (1967): 45–95.
Vanel, Antoine. "Le septième ostracon phénicien trouvé au Temple d'Echmoun, près de Saïda." *Mélanges de l'Université Saint-Joseph, Beyrouth* 45 (1969): 345–364.
Wilfong, Terry G. "A Concordance of Published Coptic and Greek Ostraca from the Oriental Institute's Excavations at Medinet Habu." *Enchoria* 17 (1990): 155–160.
Yadin, Yigael, and Joseph Naveh. "The Aramaic and Hebrew Ostraca and Jar Inscriptions." In *Masada I: The Yigael Yadin Excavations, 1963–1965, Final Reports.* Jerusalem, 1989.
Yardeni, Ada. "New Jewish Aramaic Ostraca." *Israel Exploration Journal* 40 (1990): 130–152.

André Lemaire

'OUEILI, TELL EL-, prehistoric site located on the surface of an alluvial plain not far from the present-day Euphrates River, near the ruins of Larsa, a major city and one of the historic capitals of ancient Mesopotamia (31°14′ N, 45°53′ E). The site of Tell el-'Oueili dominates the surrounding plain from a height of about 4 m, with its visible part covering about 4 ha (9 acres, or 200 m in diameter). However, when the modern water table was reached, close to 4.5 m below the level of the plain (following two major soundings), the inhabited layers continued even beyond that level and virgin soil was still not visible. Clearly, the site encompasses much more territory than the area suggested by the visible remains. However, the earliest occupation layers are now under water.

Although the ruins of Larsa were discovered in 1854 and periodically excavated by a French team (led by André Parrot, Musée du Louvre) beginning in 1933, it was not until 1967 that the same team located a small, low tell 3 km (2 mi.) southeast of the historic ruins. That tell, 'Oueili, appeared to consist entirely of prehistoric remains, rendering the site of particular interest, as the prehistoric levels of southern Mesopotamia are generally covered by massive later historical ruins. Prehistoric levels can only be excavated once the area has been carefully investigated, however, as was the case at Ur, Uruk, and Larsa, among other sites. It had long been known that a prehistoric age existed in lower Mesopotamia, but when the sites were not covered over by subsequent cultural layers, they were buried beneath thick layers of alluvial sediment from the Tigris or Euphrates Rivers. The sherds discovered on the surface of 'Oueili pointed to layers dating from Uruk and, in particular, the Ubaid 3 and 4 eras. This presented a unique opportunity to explore 'Oueili's prehistoric levels, in contrast to Larsa where, though present, they remained inaccessible because they were buried underneath more recent deposits 10–15 m deep. The Ubaid period in Lower Mesopotamia was particularly critical because it immediately preceded urbanization. Prior to the discovery of 'Oueili this period was known only from the excavations at Eridu carried out in 1946–1948.

The excavation of 'Oueili was carried out by Jean-Louis Huot and Jean-Daniel Forest (of the Université de Paris I, Panthéon-Sorbonne) beginning in 1976; the work gained momentum between 1981 and 1989. Periods previously believed to exist were uncovered and explored (Ubaid 3–4 and Uruk), as well as earlier, completely unknown phases that had not been detected in the first surface exploration (Ubaid 0–2).

Six periods were identified. They were distinguished from one another by phases of abandonment that were only beginning to become apparent when the excavation was interrupted by the international crisis in the Persian Gulf in 1990. The origins of 'Oueili are unknown. Similarly, the date the village was established is not known. The most ancient levels excavated—albeit not the earliest—were dubbed Ubaid 0 or the 'Oueili phase. They preceded and heralded the Ubaid 1–4 sequence so named in 1960 (on the basis of evidence from Eridu) and still in use, although the phases remain very general. The culture to which Ubaid 0 is linked is unknown (it may be the Pre-Pottery Neolithic B tradition in Syria). Certain architectural similarities suggest a connection between Ubaid 0 and the Hassuna culture of Samarra. [*See* Hassuna.] The two are either contemporaneous or Ubaid 0 is slightly earlier, at least in its final phase. For the time being, Ubaid 0 can only been seen at 'Oueili where its final phase can be dated, on the evidence of two radiocarbon dates (7430 ± 150 and 7320 ± 140 BP), to 5480 and 5370 BCE (uncorrected dates) or 6516–6018 and 6414–5955 BCE (corrected dates).

Three phases can be discerned in Ubaid 0 thanks to mudbrick architectural remains, some bearing finger marks. Small parallel or intersecting walls thought to have functioned as granaries, and three dwellings, each on a tripartite plan, with roofs held up by rows of wooden posts with brick bases were recovered. [*See* Granaries and Silos.] The regular use of posts to support a terracelike roof enabled the rooms, or the surface of the dwelling, to be enlarged and also anchored the building firmly. Two of the houses at 'Oueili measured approximately 140 sq m, while the third one—the oldest—probably measured 240 sq m. Floor-level ovens, a water jar, and other materials found leave no doubt that the buildings were used for housing. Such a discovery considerably alters existing notions with regard to early architecture in Lower Mesopotamia in about the middle of the sixth millennium. With the exception of some burnished sherds (perhaps of Hassuna date) containing vegetal temper, the pottery from this phase is decorated with simple geometric patterns painted dark brown or a very pale pinkish-gray. Among the types found were large bowls, stemmed goblets, large convex-concave earthenware jars (possibly a Hassunian survival or a new technique). The small objects found—lip ornaments of fine clay and dried or baked objects made of bitumen—reveal little variety. A small, painted head of a figurine, probably intact, with oval "coffee-bean" eyes, bears some resemblance to the Samarran figurines at Chogha Mami. Beginning in Ubaid 0, wheat (*Triticum* mono/dicoccum) and especially six-rowed hulled barley were grown, and common domestic animals were bred—goats, sheep, and, in particular, oxen and pigs. [*See* Cereals; Sheep and Goats; Cattle and Oxen; Pigs.]

From the earliest discernible phases, it is obvious that a small, sedentary community cultivated and irrigated cereal crops (the only possible method given the latitude and climate) and bred cattle and pigs as well as sheep and goats in smaller numbers. Fishing and shellfish harvesting were also practiced. Rather remarkable architecture is also visible, though the group appeared to live practically in isolation. Very small amounts of bitumen and some flint were the only raw materials imported. The population was limited in size and was probably highly egalitarian. Unfortunately, the absence of tombs makes it difficult to interpret possible social ranking.

During Ubaid 1 (the available carbon-14 dates are 6710 ± 160, 6680 ± 110, 6460 ± 140 BP—or 4760, 4730, 4550 BCE, uncorrected dates; 5976–5369, 5723–5420, 5608–5236 BCE, corrected dates), the most noticeable development was in the pottery: it is much more elaborately decorated and painted, though still geometric. It closely resembles Eridu ceramics. Architecturally, posts continued to be used, as well

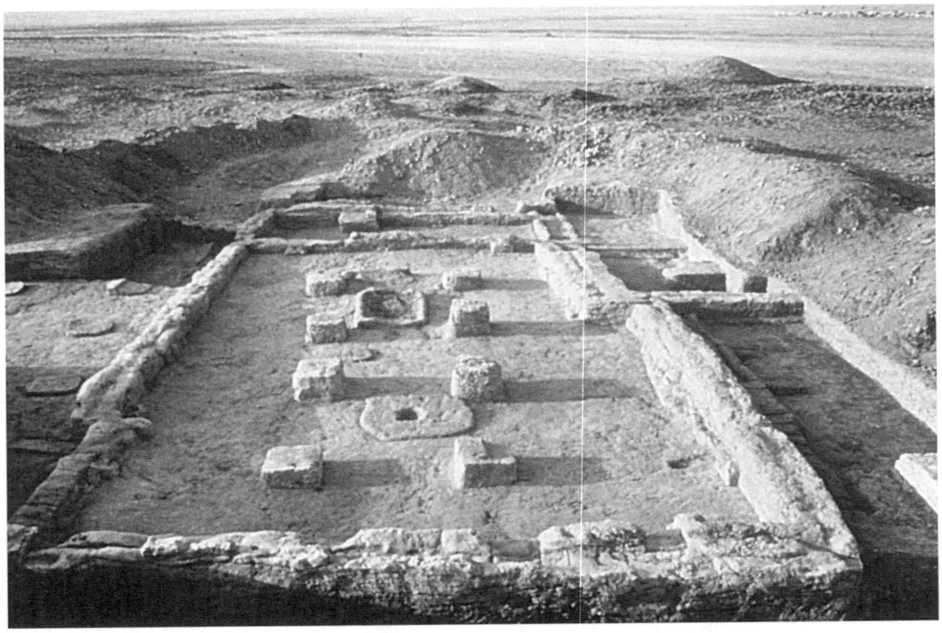

'OUEILI, TELL EL-. *Building* 37, *Ubaid 0, general view.* (Courtesy J.-L. Huot)

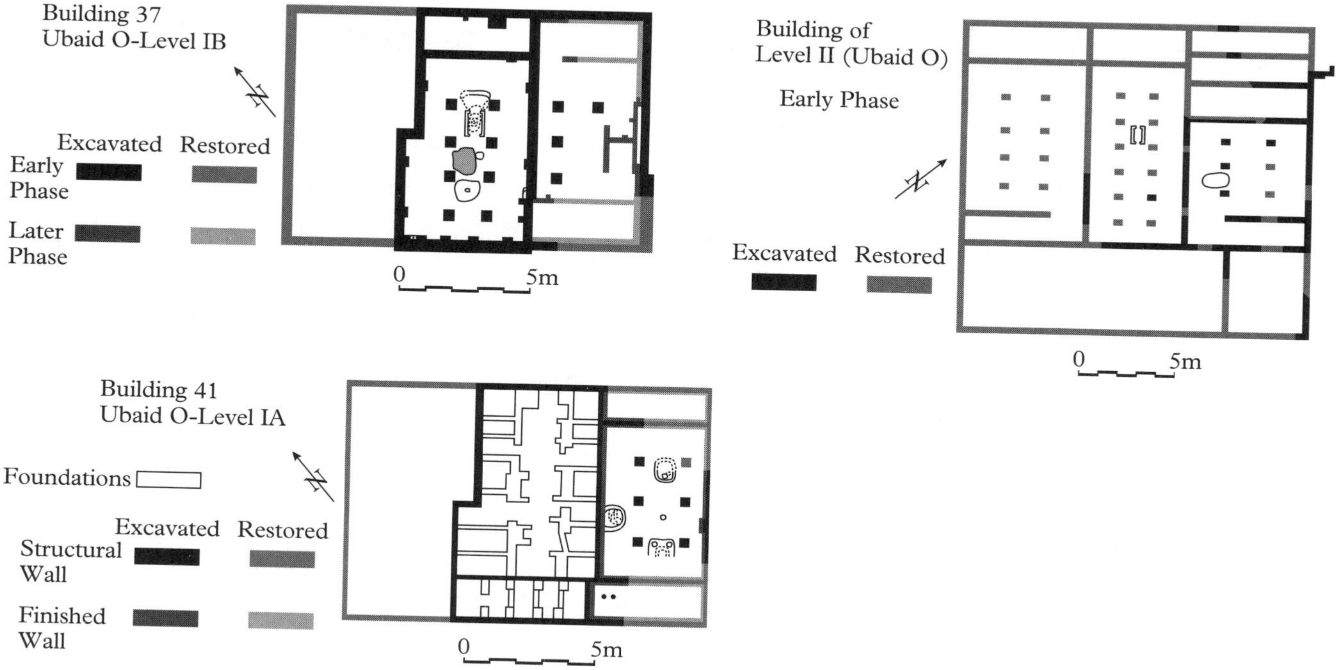

'OUEILI, TELL EL-. *Layout of three three-section buildings, Ubaid 0.* (Courtesy J.-L. Huot)

as mud bricks with markings. Housing is not as easily described as for the preceding period. Two structures consisting of three adjacent rooms were uncovered, undoubtedly sections of houses along the lines of those from Ubaid 0 (despite a period of abandonment between the two phases). Particularly noteworthy are granary infrastructures similar to those from Ubaid 0—that is, a pisé platform with woven reeds supported by small parallel or intersecting walls. In one case, the platform is supported by a tight network of low clay pillars. There is a noticeable difference, however, between the two periods: Ubaid 0 granaries occupied a considerable surface area (approximately 80 sq m), whereas those from Ubaid 1 were much smaller (around 30 sq m). The large collective compounds evident in Ubaid 0 may thus have given way to small, independent family units during Ubaid 1.

The Ubaid 2 phase, clearly evident at Eridu and Hajji Mohammed, is less well-known, albeit present, at 'Oueili. At Ubaid 3, the excavated (but limited) site consists of a vast terrace 40 m long preserved to a height, in some spots, of more than 1.5 m. Unfortunately, neither the extent, the exact layout, nor for that matter the building's function are known. Like all the other construction at 'Oueili, it was made of mud brick. That it resembled the better-known construction at Susa from a later period can only be surmised. [*See* Susa.] The mere existence of such an impressive structure at 'Oueili nonetheless provides some evidence for the settlement's growth and social evolution. Little more can be said, however. Some type of local authority is implied, and, by extension, an increasingly complex society. The pottery from Ubaid 3 resembles that found at all the other sites of the same period in Mesopotamia: fewer painted and decorated examples; standardized motifs on goblets, bowls, and basins; marli dishes; and earthenware jars similar to those discovered at Eridu, Ras al-Amiya, and Tell Abada. From a technical viewpoint, this ceramic pottery heralds the appearance of paint made of "black sand" (containing chromite and iron-titanium minerals) typical of Ubaid 3 and 4 and discovered at Telloh, Ubaid, and Ur as well. This paint was more durable than earlier kinds and gradually replaced them, thus indicating increasingly standardized ceramic techniques.

The Ubaid 4 phase is represented by a tripartite structure that was later reused as a granary, as revealed by the extremely dense network of small intersecting walls. Available carbon-14 dates for Ubaid are 6190 ± 90, 6170 ± 90, 5980 ± 100, 5800 ± 100, 5650 ± 90 BP—or 4240, 4220, 4030, 3850, 3700, BCE, uncorrected dates; 5304–4940, 5293–4926, 5187–4719, 4893–4486, 4725–4357 BCE, corrected dates), a structure divided into three sections was discovered that later functioned as a granary—revealed by the extremely dense network of small, intersecting walls. Ceramics from this period resemble vases from the same period at the large southern sites and on the west coast of the Gulf; at 'Oueili, however, this pottery is less decorated and appears to have been used less frequently. Plain, undecorated vases are far more numerous. Terra-cotta sickles, which began to appear in Ubaid 3, were by this time commonly used, as were small clay knobs (curved nails); clay lip ornaments (practically unchanged since Ubaid 0); animal figures, or ophidians (human figurines with a snake head) polished obsidian "nails"; a few stamp seals (but no seal impressions); and ornaments. [*See* Seals.] Paleobotanical remains attest to the existence of tamarisk, reeds, and the date palm (one of the earliest known examples), as well as wheat (*Triticum* mono/dicoccum) and six-rowed hulled barley, cultivated using stone hoes. Animal breeding continued to revolve around cattle and pigs. Only 5.2 percent of the bones identified belonged to goats and sheep. This rather unusual livestock probably reflects the very marshy terrain during the final Ubaid phase. Fish were numerous and undoubtedly provided most of the protein consumed. Unfortunately, no tombs or prestigious buildings were found. It is known from Eridu's contemporary levels, however, that Ubaid 4 had begun to develop a ranked social order. Furthermore, the large "temples" (according to early interpretations) of Eridu VIII–VI attest to the important position occupied by heads of families or clans within these agricultural settlements because only they could have ordered such construction.

A small worksite at 'Oueili has yielded evidence of a final Ubaid phase (Ubaid 5) characterized by painted pottery found in an area where ceramics were drawn from the kiln, along with obvious wasters. This can be correlated to the discovery of a two-storied pottery kiln, with a preparation area and firing chamber, discovered during the first season of excavation. Pottery remains are the only evidence of this phase. A few Late Uruk remains (bevelled-rim bowls, jugs with a curved spout, incised latticework decoration) represent the final period during which 'Oueili is known to have been inhabited. The site apparently ceased to exist thereafter—abandoned, probably, in favor of Larsa. Following a long period of economic and social growth, society was at the threshold of urbanization.

The excavation at 'Oueili was originally undertaken to pinpoint the transition toward urbanization. The goal was not achieved. On the other hand, discovery of the site led to the identification of the longest sequence known to date in Lower Mesopotamia; despite a few gaps, it encompasses most of the Ubaid phase, from the most ancient levels (previously unidentified) to the late prehistoric era. As a result, what is now known of this transitional phase, which had previously rested entirely on the discovery of Eridu, has been corrected and expanded.

[*See also* Eridu; Larsa; Mesopotamia, *article on* Prehistoric Mesopotamia; Ubaid; Ur; *and* Uruk-Warka.]

BIBLIOGRAPHY

Connan, J. "De la géochimie pétrolière à l'étude des bitumens anciens: L'archéologie moléculaire." *Comptes Rendus de l'Académie des Inscriptions et Belles-Lettres 1993* 4 (1993): 901–921. See pages 910–914 for bitumen from Tell el-'Oueili.

Huot, Jean-Louis, et al. "Larsa . . . et tell el 'Oueili: Première campagne, 1976." *Syria* 55 (1978): 183–223.

Huot, Jean-Louis, et al. *Larsa (8eme et 9eme campagnes, 1978 et 1981) et 'Oueili (2eme et 3eme campagnes, 1978 et 1981): Rapport préliminaire.* Paris, 1983.

Huot, Jean-Louis, et al. *Larsa (10e campagne, 1983) et 'Oueili (4e campagne, 1983): Rapport préliminaire.* Paris, 1987.

Huot, Jean-Louis. "Ubaidian Village of Lower Mesopotamia: Permanence and Evolution from Ubaid 0 to Ubaid 4, as Seen from Tell el-'Oueili." In *Upon This Foundation: The Ubaid Reconsidered,* edited by Elizabeth F. Henrickson and Ingolf Thuesen, pp. 19–42. Copenhagen, 1989.

Huot, Jean-Louis, et al. *'Oueili, travaux de 1985.* Paris, 1991.

Huot, Jean-Louis. "The First Farmers at 'Oueili." *Biblical Archaeologist* 55 (1992): 188–195.

Huot, Jean-Louis, et al. *'Oueili, travaux de 1987–1989.* Paris, in press.

JEAN-LOUIS HUOT

OXEN. *See* Cattle and Oxen.

OXYRHYNCHUS (Ar., Al-Bahnasa), principal town in the nome (province) Oxyrhynchites in Lower Egypt, located approximately 75 km (47 mi.) southwest of modern Bani Suef and 16 km (10 mi.) west of Bani Mazar (28°30′ N, 30°40′ E). Oxyrhynchus flourished chiefly during the Roman era, although it has remains from both the earlier Ptolemaic and later Byzantine and Arab periods. The toponym for both the town and the province derive from the Greek name for a fish of the sturgeon class in whose honor a temple was built at Oxyrhynchus.

Excavations of the ancient rubbish dumps at the site were carried out initially by Bernard P. Grenfell and Arthur S. Hunt, two young papyrologists, in six campaigns from 1897 to 1898 and 1903 to 1907. They were followed by excavators from Italy, led first by Ermenogildo Pistelli and Giulio Farina (1910, 1912, 1913), and later by Evaristo Breccia (1927–1928, 1932, 1934) for the Società per la Ricerca dei Papiri. The principal object of all of these excavators was the acquisition of papyrus texts. The result was the discovery of a stunning number of documents. The number of published volumes in the series The Oxyrhynchus Papyri, for instance, has reached fifty-seven (1990), the edited texts consisting of not only Greek and Latin literary works but chiefly documentary writings, in Greek and Latin as well as other languages. Other Oxyrhynchus texts have been published elsewhere, primarily in the series *Papiri greci e latini* (Pubblicazioni della Società Italiana).

As Grenfell and Hunt described it, the site of the ancient town itself stretched about 2 km (1 mi.) from north to south and .8 km (.5 mi.) from east to west. The rubbish mounds were scattered to the west. From the distribution of papyri in the mounds, Grenfell and Hunt determined that the city had expanded during the Roman period and had then contracted during the Byzantine and Arab periods. The rubbish heaps that lay farthest to the west, running a substantial distance into the uncultivated land, contained a majority of documents from the Roman period, with some Ptolemaic texts, whereas those that lay closer to the modern town preserved a large number of texts from later eras.

According to their initial report, Grenfell and Hunt began excavating in the cemetery but quickly turned to the rubbish mounds lying to the west of the town where the harvest of torn, discarded texts was plentiful. They soon determined that the manuscripts were much better preserved in the portions of the mounds that were above the "damp" line created by underlying groundwater. Their technique was to cut an initial trench directly into a mound until the local laborers, digging chiefly with their hands in order to feel the papyrus fragments, reached the midpoint of the mound. At times, the trenches reached a depth of 7 m (23 ft.) below the upper surfaces of the mounds.

Of the ancient city, almost nothing remained when Grenfell and Hunt arrived. Long before, the stones of the foundations of buildings had been robbed and reused in other structures. Only stone chips and windblown sand could be seen where walls had stood. Now the area is crisscrossed by the trenches of peasants who have dug for fertile soil for their own agricultural purposes. Following the work of Grenfell and Hunt, peasants uncovered the partial remains of two colonmades and a theater that was examined by Flinders Petrie in 1922. Despite the existence of Grenfell's site plan—his work on it was cut short by illness—later scholars have not published it because Grenfell had not completed it.

Although Grenfell and Hunt have been criticized for not employing excavating techniques that would have yielded more archaeological data, it is important to realize that in their day the methods associated with modern archaeology were in their infancy. Furthermore, their efforts, largely carried out with limited funding, led to the discovery of an astonishing number of discarded texts from late antiquity.

[*See also* Oxyrhynchus Papyri.]

BIBLIOGRAPHY

Breccia, Evaristo. "Dove e come si trovano i papiro in Egitto." *Aegyptus* 16 (1936): 296–305.

Brown, S. Kent. "Sayings of Jesus, Oxyrhynchus." In *The Anchor Bible Dictionary,* vol. 5, pp. 999–1001. New York, 1992.

Donadoni, Sergio. "Le prime recerche italiane ad Antinoe." *Aegyptus* 18 (1938): 285–318.

Grenfell, Bernard P. "Oxyrhynchus and Its Papyri." *Egypt Exploration Fund Archaeological Report* 6 (1896–1897): 1–12.

Grenfell, Bernard P., and Arthur S. Hunt. "Graeco-Roman Branch." *Egypt Exploration Fund Archaeological Report* 12 (1902–1903): 1–9; 13 (1904–1905): 13–17; 14 (1905–1906): 8–16; 15 (1906–1907): 8–11.

Kasher, Aryeh. "The Jewish Community of Oxyrhynchus in the Roman Period." *Journal of Jewish Studies* 32 (1981): 151–157.

Turner, Eric G. "Roman Oxyrhynchus." *Journal of Egyptian Archaeology* 38 (1952): 78–93.

Turner, Eric G. "The Graeco-Roman Branch." In *Excavating in Egypt: The Egypt Exploration Society, 1882–1982,* edited by T. G. H. James, pp. 161–178. Chicago, 1982.

S. Kent Brown

OXYRHYNCHUS PAPYRI. British and Italian excavations at Oxyrhynchus in Egypt unearthed several thousand papyri (and parchments), mostly inscribed in Greek, but also including texts in Latin, Coptic, Demotic, and Arabic. The Oxyrhynchus papyri range in date from the Ptolemaic through Early Islamic periods, but the majority come from the Roman period. They are an unusually complete record of the town's culture, society, and economy and form one of the largest and most important groups of texts from Roman Egypt.

The excavation of papyri at Oxyrhynchus began in 1897, under the direction of Bernard P. Grenfell and Arthur S. Hunt for the Egypt Exploration Fund. The great success of this first season, in which thousands of papyri were found, led Grenfell and Hunt to continue digging from 1903 through 1907. Oxyrhynchus was excavated by Italian archaeologists for the Società per la Ricerca dei Papiri intermittently between 1910 and 1934, which resulted in additional papyrus finds. Most of the papyri from the British excavations were found in ancient rubbish dumps and latrines, whereas the papyri from the Italian excavations came from the town itself. The archaeological contexts of the Oxyrhynchus papyri remain largely unpublished, but the papyri themselves have been the object of extensive publication efforts: Greek and Latin texts from the British excavations have regularly appeared in the series *The Oxyrhynchus Papyri* (1898–the present, or sixty-one volumes). Papyri from the Italian excavations were published as *Papiri greci e latini* (1910–1979). In addition, individual Oxyrhynchus papyri have been published in monographs and journal articles.

The contents of the Oxyrhynchus papyri span an enormous range of literary and nonliterary production. The initial goal of the excavation of Oxyrhynchus concentrated on the discovery of Greek literary papyri. In addition to known Greek literature, the Oxyrhynchus papyri have yielded hundreds of fragments of "new" texts by known authors: Sappho, Euripides, Sophocles (including his satyr play *The Trackers*), Menander, Lysias, Hyperides, Callimachus, and Chariton (to name a few), along with anonymous poems, plays, orations, grammars, and scholia. The Oxyrhynchus papyri include fragments of numerous philosophical, rhetorical, and historical works, including the so-called *Hellenica Oxyrhynchia*, published separately (McKechnie and Kern, 1988), which chronicles the events of 396–395 BCE. Scientific, astronomical, astrological, mathematical, medical, and magical works are also represented. In addition to this great assemblage of literary material, the Oxyrhynchus papyri include an extraordinary wealth of documentary, nonliterary papyri: official documents, legal contracts, wills, accounts, lists, private letters—the majority of Roman date and in Greek, with a smaller (but significant) number in Latin. Papyri from the Roman period document the importance of Egyptian cults at Oxyrhynchus and also attest to a significant Jewish presence there. [*See* Cult.] Many important Early Christian texts come from Oxyrhynchus, including fragments of biblical manuscripts and documentary evidence. An important group of Byzantine Greek papyri comes from Oxyrhynchus: the papers of the Apion family, who owned the best attested of the large Byzantine estates in Egypt. Coptic and Arabic papyri from Oxyrhynchus, almost entirely unpublished, include documentary, literary, and magical texts.

[*See also* Arabic; Coptic; Greek; Latin; Oxyrhynchus; Papyrus; *and* Parchment.]

BIBLIOGRAPHY

Grenfell, Bernard P., et al. *The Oxyrhynchus Papyri.* 61 vols. to date. London, 1898–. Ongoing series in which are published Greek and Latin papyri from the Grenfell and Hunt excavations, with text, commentary, and English translations of most papyri.

Hunt, Arthur S., et al. *Select Papyri.* 3 vols. Loeb Classical Library. Cambridge, Mass., 1950–1956. Handy and accessible anthology of Greek and Latin papyri, including many from Oxyrhynchus, with text and English translation of facing pages. Volume 1 contains private documents, volume 2 public documents, and volume 3 literary fragments.

Montserrat, Dominic, et al. "Varia Descripta Oxyrhynchita." *Bulletin of the American Society of Papyrologists* 31 (1994): 11–80. First installment of a larger project to publish the Oxyrhynchus "descripta," papyri that were only briefly described and not fully published in the early volumes of *The Oxyrynchus Papyri.*

Turner, Eric G. *Greek Papyri: An Introduction.* 2d ed. Oxford, 1980. Standard introduction to Greek papyrology, with much useful information on the Oxyrhynchus papyri and their context as well as an extensive bibliography.

Turner, Eric G. "The Graeco-Roman Branch." In *Excavating in Egypt: The Egypt Exploration Society, 1882–1982,* edited by T. G. H. James, pp. 161–178. Chicago, 1982. Concise account of the Grenfell and Hunt excavation of Oxyrhynchus papyri for the Egypt Exploration Fund and their subsequent publication history.

TERRY G. WILFONG

P

PALACE. As the house of the king, his customary residence, the palace contains everything that concerns the activities of daily life in any house, although possibly elaborated in accordance with the wealth of the individual and his family. Because the king exercised a specific function and possessed a unique nature, his house could include specific fixtures (such as a throne room) that would facilitate the exercise of power and of manifesting it materially.

A true palace can exist only in the context of a monarchy, and certainty on this point is possible only when there are texts. Historians date the birth of the first royal dynasties in Mesopotamia, as well as the appearance of the first palaces, to the beginning of the third millennium. The actual situation is, however, less clear. The royal institution was no more born in a day than the palace emerged one fine morning from the head of a genial architect. Throughout the Neolithic period in the Near East, the growing complexity of relationships among agricultural production, the need for exotic raw materials in the river basins, and social organization, all led to the development of a power that often manifested its existence in the creation of specific architecture. By the end of the fifth and in the early fourth millennium, with the first steps toward urbanization, social hierarchy was already marked by clear architectural differentiation. Tepe Gawra, in northern Mesopotamia, demonstrates this situation as early as level XI; the Round House (level XI–A) expresses the real hierarchical social structure because it is the house of the holder of power, sited there, at the summit of the mound. [*See* Tepe Gawra.] In the Uruk period, the great architectural complexes that have been recognized at Uruk itself, such as the E-anna, or at the sites of the Uruk expansion, such as Tell Kannas, also appear as centers of power (without presuming either a theocratic or secular nature). Thus, it is necessary to consider these structures if not palaces in the strict sense, at least as the architectural expression of the exercise of power in a hierarchical society. [*See* Uruk-Warka.]

Early Bronze Age. Mesopotamia has yielded a number of buildings of the Early Dynastic period considered to be palaces, most often because of their scale rather than for precise morphological reasons. It seems, however, that the identification as palaces of the buildings uncovered at Kish (Palace A and the Plano-Convex Building), at Eridu, and at Tell Asmar/Eshnunna (the northern palaces) can be retained (see figure 1). [*See* Kish; Eridu; Eshnunna.] In these cases the palace appears as a complex comprising several autonomous buildings that are connected by long, peripheral corridors that circulated people as well as air and light. Because the palaces expanded to two levels, the definition of functions is a difficult and uncertain exercise. It seems likely, however, that the upper level was devoted to habitation and reception. Perhaps even the throne room, if in fact one existed then, was also located there; the ground floor served mainly for storage (the Akkadian palace at Tell Brak in Khabur) and secondarily as a workplace. The palaces of third-millennium Mari, in the process of excavation since 1964, display the unusual characteristic of being closely associated with a cult place, the Sacred Precinct, but with only this single example, it is difficult to define the existence of any fundamental relationship between palace and temple.

Outside of the Mesopotamian basin, there is still little evidence, for there are hardly any palaces. The discovery of Palace G at Ebla in Syria, and now the large building at Tel Yarmut in Israel, shows, however, that the institution was not confined to Mesopotamia. [*See* Ebla; Yarmut, Tel.] Nevertheless, in these two cases the buildings discovered do not permit a definition of their architectural traits as closely related to those of the region of the Tigris and Euphrates Rivers.

Middle Bronze Age. With the third dynasty of Ur, Mesopotamia saw the birth of a new formula that dominated the river basin completely. Varied solutions were adopted simultaneously in the western (Syria-Palestine) and northern (upper course of the Euphrates) regions. It is at Ur, with the palace of Ur-Nammu and Shulgi, that the formula appears for the first time; it appears again in the palace at Eshnunna/Tell Asmar. Throughout a very long history, the palace formula was transformed many times; however, there is also continuity in the organization of the most significant sectors, such as the complex of official rooms at Mari (the Great Royal Palace and, doubtless, the earlier palaces of the Shakkanakku); at Larsa (the Palace of Nur-Adad, which appears as a veritable architectural drawing); at Aššur (the

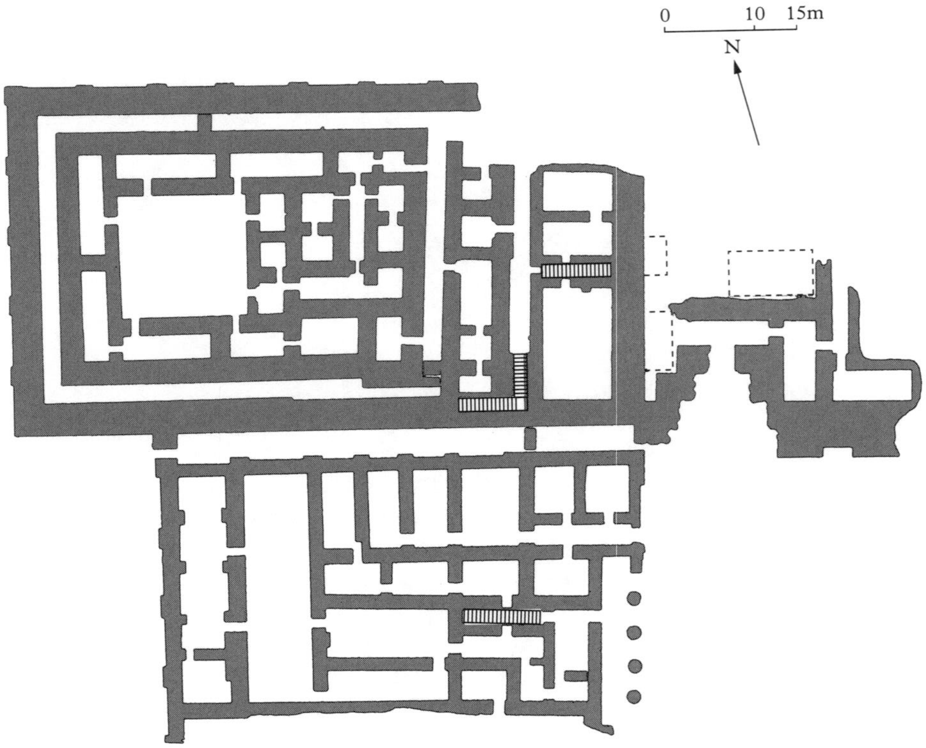

PALACE. Figure 1. *Plan of palace A, Kish.* (Courtesy J.-C. Margueron)

Old Palace); Tell er-Rimah; and, finally, at Uruk (the Palace of Sinkashid). [*See* Mari; Larsa; Aššur; Rimah, Tell er-.]

If Tuttul on the Balikh River has provided an example of a palace close to those at Mari, which belong to the Mesopotamian tradition, Syria and Palestine used formulae whose inspiration was clearly Mediterranean. Occupying a more restricted surface area, these structures developed vertically, occasionally reaching three stories, as was certainly the case in the palace of Yarimlim at Alalakh (eighteenth century BCE), or in the cities of the Upper Euphrates (e.g., Karahöyük). [*See* Alalakh.] There were numerous palaces at Ebla, but they do not seem to represent the morphological traits associated with royal functions that the palaces in Mesopotamia do; they may not be true palaces—places in which the king exercised his authority. The frequent use of the pillar in the columned porch, as well as the court that served as a light well, tended to systematize itself and became a distinctive mark of western architecture.

Late Bronze Age. Mesopotamia does not occupy the foreground in the Late Bronze Age. A single palace, difficult to interpret because it differs totally from the others, and is only partially excavated, is that of ʿAqar Quf (Dur Kurigalzu). The Mitannian period is well represented, however, in the provincial palaces at Nuzi and Tell Brak. [*See* ʿAqar Quf; Mitanni; Nuzi; Brak, Tell.] In Syria-Palestine, the palace is in general small, as in the preceding period; the exception is Ugarit, where a true palatial complex evolved, closer to those of the great capitals of the empire than the Levantine cities. [*See* Ugarit.] Ḫattuša (Boğazköy), capital of the Hittite Empire, is a good example of the complex formed by the association of separate buildings to form a true fortress on an imperial scale. This formula seems to belong to Anatolia. [*See* Boğazköy.]

Iron Age. The evolution toward the formation of the great empires of the Iron Age partly modified the system because if a city possessed a palace, most often a royal governor resided in it. The king inhabited or constructed a palace in the capital city that had to appear in its splendor, dimensions, and wealth like those in other world centers. The Assyrians were particularly prodigious in palatial constructions at Nineveh, Nimrud, and Khorsabad (Dur Sharrukin); however, the approximately ten palaces recovered wholly or in part present great morphological similarities and correspond to a concept well defined by royal function. [*See* Nineveh; Nimrud; Khorsabad.] The Neo-Babylonian kings yielded to the Assyrians in this regard only because of the brief duration of their rule. In this context it is not always easy to know whether, in the Levantine cities, for example, the great residences should be considered royal palaces (which is, however, probable at Megiddo, Ramat Raḥel, and Lachish), or the seats of local governors. [*See* Megiddo; Ramat Raḥel; Lachish.] In the specific form of the *ḫilani*, whose origin goes back to the Late Bronze Age at Emar, the capitals of the small Aramean city-states had a royal building that became very popular, even with the Assyrian kings. [*See* Emar.] The *ḫilani* appears in a very compact form: a columned porch preceded a great elongated room surrounded by smaller rooms, with one or two stories constructed above the whole complex.

Expression of a Civilization. In the course of three millennia in the ancient Near East, the palace has taken diverse forms. Fundamentally, however, the same functions recur, and the final result is always the fruit of a compromise between contradictory demands. Thus, the need to open the building to the city and the realm of which it is the supreme expression, in which the people must see itself, counterbalances the necessity to construct a protected place to assure the security of the king and his belongings and to guard the wealth accumulated there. The palace at Mari from the beginning of the second millennium BCE—because of its exceptional state of preservation and the wealth of the furnishings and archives recovered there, and in spite of its idiosyncrasies—has greatly advanced what is known of what a palace is and how it functioned (see figure 2). Thus, contrary to what is often stated, a Near Eastern palace is neither a city within a city, nor a miniature city. It is an organism that must satisfy specific requirements and whose content varies little.

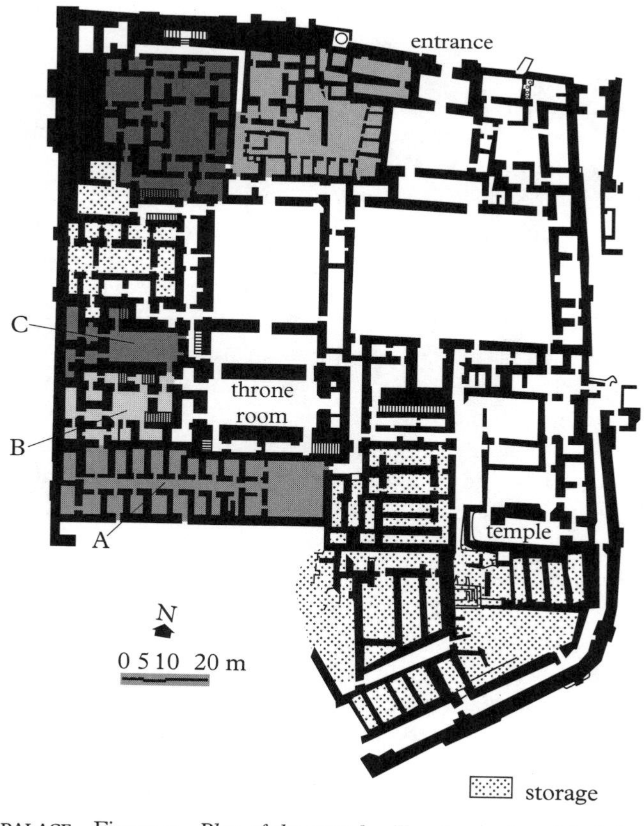

PALACE. Figure 2. *Plan of the second-millennium palace, Mari.* In the northwest corner are the women's quarters. Area C is the administrative center. Area B is the kitchen. In area A are the slaves quarters. (Courtesy J.-C. Margueron)

Royal living quarters. As the quarters of the king and his family, or at least a part of it, the first functions of a palace were consistently to provide comfort, whose nature might vary with the climate, and security. At Mari, the house of the king and the house of the women (the location of the queen, all the wives of the lower ranks, concubines, singers, and dancers) were clearly independent. Each was provided with living quarters for the personnel committed to the service of the king and his queens; this dichotomy is not always so clear at other palaces. The level of comfort was addressed generally by the quality of construction, the size of the rooms, and the character of the sanitary installations. The wealth of decoration that contributed to the splendor of the royal house was not only an aesthetic concern: paintings and reliefs served also to manifest royal power in its basic activities. The themes of the king as hunter, builder, conqueror, protector, and intermediary between the realms of gods and men were repeated endlessly in both the king's apartments and the official quarters.

Official quarters. The palace's official area was often closely connected to the living quarters of the king, who had direct access to it. The situation is not clear in the third millennium, but it becomes more apparent in the Amorite period. The official module at that time was a complex organized around a richly decorated great court, intended to enhance the religious aspect of the royal function (e.g., the Court of the Palm at Mari). This court gave access, by way of an intermediary room marked by a certain cultic character (at Mari the statue of a goddess with a flowing vase [now in the Aleppo Museum] stood there), to the throne room (25 m long × 12 m wide), where the king, seated at one end, held audience. Various ceremonies took place there, certainly including banquets, as the proximity of the kitchens found in room 31 in the palace of Mari suggests. In the Assyrian period, the room that formed an intermediate stage in the progression between the court and the throne room disappeared, but the principle remained the same.

Administrative offices. A meticulous administration characterized the house of the king, but also that of the women. The administrative offices were located in the upper story, connected to the great room where the king presided over administrative operations. Administration was not limited, however, to the service of the king. It also concerned itself with the affairs of the realm, and the principal servants of the king, the viziers and stewards, were responsible for it. The king administered his country from the palace and maintained relations with provincial chieftains and foreign courts; a secretariat functioned to discharge these tasks. The palace steward played an essential role: placed at the doorway of the palace, he controlled entrance and egress and managed some part of the economic activity. In addition, the king was a great employer; he had to compensate his personnel, and for that purpose the palace storerooms contained provisions that were distributed as payment, including cereals, oils, and cloth. These provisions were compensation rather than reserves hoarded to meet future needs. The palace was not a workplace, however, except occasionally for a luxury craftsman. The agricultural estates depended on the palace, and workshops could be located either in the agricultural areas or in the city.

While specific aspects of the palace might vary in importance from one period to another, the arrangement of its various components change, and circumstances lead to the expansion of one characteristic at the expense of others, as a rule, the same functions appear behind the variety of forms. Throughout the history of the ancient Near East, the palace conveyed the very essence of Oriental civilization.

[*See also* Building Materials and Techniques.]

BIBLIOGRAPHY

Aurenche, Olivier, ed. *Dictionnaire illustré multilingue de l'architecture du Proche-Orient ancien.* Lyon, 1977. This reference work, completed by archaeologists and architects specializing in the ancient Near East, aims to clarify mainly technical questions; equivalent terms are given in eight languages.

Garelli, Paul, ed. *Le palais et la royauté: Archéologie et civilisation; compte rendu de la 19e rencontre assyriologique internationale.* Paris, 1974. Contributions are generally philological.

Heinrich, Ernst. *Die Paläste im alten Mesopotamien.* Denkmäler Antiker Architektur, 15. Berlin, 1984.

Kempinski, Aharon, and Ronny Reich, eds. *The Architecture of Ancient Israel: From the Prehistoric to the Persian Periods.* Jerusalem, 1992. The most recent synthesis, which includes the latest archaeological discoveries in ancient Palestine.

Leick, Gwendolyn. *A Dictionary of Ancient Near Eastern Architecture.* London and New York, 1988. Generally concerns the evolution of architectural forms and styles.

Lévy, Edmond, ed. *Le système palatial en Orient, en Grèce, et à Rome: Actes du colloque de Strasbourg, 19–22 juin 1985.* Leiden, 1987. Contributions on the ancient Near East concern the first appearance of the palace, the organization of space in the palace at Mari and the economic role of the palace in the Old Babylonian period based on the texts, the Syrian palaces of the Bronze Age, and Minoan and Mycenaean palaces.

Margueron, Jean-Claude. *Recherches sur les palais mésopotamiens de l'âge du Bronze.* 2 vols. Paris, 1982. By means of a very careful archaeological and architectural analysis, the author arrives at a complete vision of the monuments, which often contradicts accepted ideas, notably about the function and the reconstruction of elevations.

Margueron, Jean-Claude. "Y a-t-il un tracé regulateur dans les palais mésopotamiens du IIe millénaire?" In *Le dessin d'architecte dans les sociétés antiques: Actes du colloque de Strasbourg, 26–28 janvier 1984,* pp. 29–45. Leiden, 1985. Includes five illustrations.

Naumann, Rudolf. *Architektur Kleinasiens.* 2d ed. Tübingen, 1971. Synthetic reference on the architecture of the regions corresponding to modern Turkey from its origins to the eighth century BCE.

Nunn, Astrid. *Die Wandmalerei und der glasierte Wandschmuck im Alten Orient.* Leiden and New York, 1988. Good compilation of mural decoration, from the Neolithic period to the Neo-Babylonian Empire, that treats palace architecture.

Parrot, André. *Mission archéologique de Mari II: Le palais,* vol. 1, *Architecture;* vol. 2, *Peintures murales;* vol. 3, *Documents et monuments.* Paris, 1958–1959. A good number of the interpretations proposed by the excavator of this palace, the best preserved in the ancient Near East, are now out of date. Volume 2 is confined to a catalog.

JEAN-CLAUDE MARGUERON

Translated from French by Nancy W. Leinwand

PALEOBOTANY. To study the interrelationship between humans and plants through time, paleobotany (or paleoethnobotany), recovers and analyzes both macroscopic and microscopic botanical remains. In the Near East, macroscopic plant remains are preserved primarily through carbonization, or charring. Seeds, wood, or other plant parts that have been exposed to heat of sufficient intensity will turn to carbon while essentially retaining their original shape and size. These remains are often found during excavation in ceramic vessels, storage facilities, and hearths or scattered as debris on floor surfaces. Where remains are not dense and have not been collected by hand during excavation, a flotation, or water-sieving, device is used. In flotation, excavated soil is placed in a large container of water and carefully agitated. The carbonized material floats to the surface and can be scooped off, poured off, or directed through an overflow spout into a sieve or other container. When dry, the remains are sorted and identifiable plant remains are removed.

Microscopic plant remains include pollen or phytoliths, which are also important in understanding ancient environments and plant use. Wind disperses pollen from plants over wide areas. Some is deposited in lake beds, bogs, and other permanently wet, still waters, where it sinks to the bottom and is rapidly covered with sediment. There it becomes sealed in an anoxic (oxygen-free) environment, where it can be preserved for thousands of years. Cores of lake-bed sediments (i.e., sample columns of sediment extracted by forcing a tube vertically into the sediment) can yield a record of the pollen deposited, thereby allowing a reconstruction of the vegetation in the region and the changes in this vegetation through time. These changes can be linked to climatic fluctuations or such human action as deforestation, depending on the nature of the change and the types of plants involved. Phytoliths are microscopic silica bodies in plants that take on the shape of certain plant cells when the plant dies. Phytoliths of the particular plant stored or processed are often recovered in storage areas and on stone tools that had been used for plant processing.

The earliest macroscopic remains identified so far from an archaeological site include species of wild plum and hackberry found in the Douara cave in the Palmyra basin in Syria; they date to approximately 100,000 years ago. Palynological data (i.e., data for pollen and spores) from western Syria indicate that these species would not have been growing very near the cave but may have been collected at a higher altitude in the nearby hills. Hunter-gatherer populations throughout the Near East collected a variety of plant food resources, including the wild cereals and legumes that eventually were domesticated. The evidence is that agriculture was developed about ten thousand years ago: palynological studies suggest increased aridity then in parts of the Near East; there was a relatively large, settled population in some areas; and new technology in the form of stone sickles made new harvesting techniques possible for wild cereals, which may have, in part, resulted in the selection of domesticated types. Arboriculture, especially of olives, and viticulture were begun in the Levant at least by 3200 BCE or somewhat earlier. There is written evidence that viticulture was exported to Egypt by 3000 BCE, most likely from the Levant.

Paleobotany is used in conjunction with other biological studies, such as zooarchaeology and paleoanthropology, to address questions of ancient subsistence practices, paleonutrition, and paleodiet. Together with geology and geomorphology paleobotany can provide clues to ancient land use, agricultural practices, and the causes of erosion that may have led to the eventual abandonment of an area. For example, a recent study of the wood-charcoal remains from ʿAin Ghazal in Jordan estimates that deforestation resulted in massive erosion of the arable slopes around the site, thus substantially depleting the potential for agricultural subsistence in the area. The site was abandoned by about 5700 BCE.

[*See also* Agriculture; ʿAin Ghazal; Cereals; Douara; Ethnobotany; Paleoenvironmental Reconstruction; *and* Paleozoology.]

BIBLIOGRAPHY

Moore, A. M. T., and Gordon Hillman. "The Pleistocene to Holocene Transition and Human Economy in Southwest Asia: The Impact of the Younger Dryas." *American Antiquity* 57.3 (1992): 482–494. Discusses the latest palynological data from Lake Huleh in Israel indicating a period of increased aridity between 11,000 and 10,000 BP. Together with the macroscopic plant remains from the Mesolithic levels of Abu Hureyra in Syria, these data suggest an expansion of steppic vegetation at the expense of forest, a change in plant collecting that led to settlement changes over much of the Levant.

Pearsall, Deborah M. *Paleoethnobotany: A Handbook of Procedures*. San Diego, 1989. Complete discussion of all aspects of paleoethnobotany, including their potential to address human-plant interaction through time and attendant significant social and cultural changes.

Rollefson, Gary O., and Ilse Köhler-Rollefson. "The Collapse of Early Neolithic Settlements in the Southern Levant." In *People and Culture in Change*, part 1, edited by Israel Hershkovitz, pp. 73–173. British Archaeological Reports, International Series, no. 508.1. Oxford, 1989. Discusses the results of the authors' analysis of wood charcoal and house construction at Pre-Pottery Neolithic B ʿAin Ghazal, Jordan, concluding that production of lime plaster and the trees used for structural supports for houses led to deforestation and erosion of arable soil. Intensive agriculture and grazing contributed to the settlement's collapse and dispersal of the population.

Zohary, Daniel, and Maria Hopf. *The Domestication of Plants in the Old World*. Oxford, 1988. The most complete compilation of the botanical evidence for domestication of the principal Old World crops, with a discussion of the genetic, geographic, and ecological data and a brief summary of plant remains at the most important Old World prehistoric sites.

JULIE HANSEN

PALEOENVIRONMENTAL RECONSTRUCTION. The foundation for paleoenvironmental studies in archaeology was laid in the early nineteenth century by European geologists such as James Hutton, Ignaz Venetz, A. Bernhardi, Jean de Charpentier, and Louis Agassiz, who convinced the Western world of the evidence for massive glacial movement brought on by striking climatic changes in the past. By the 1860s the concept of a Pleistocene Ice Age was generally accepted, and other types of environmental evidence began to fall into place. Enigmatic fossil remains of cold-loving animals found in temperate climates were suddenly explainable by this new idea. Pollen analysis, first used to identify pollen grains, which could be used as temporal stratigraphic indicators, later became a powerful tool for reconstructing vegetational history in the light of climatic fluctuations, as well as for delineating the climatic changes themselves.

In 1863 T. F. Jamieson, also a geologist, suggested that even semiarid regions had experienced Pleistocene climatic change, and that those areas had once enjoyed climates that were markedly cooler and wetter than existing ones. Paleolimnologists working in the Near East and North Africa began to identify evidence for now extinct pluvial lakes in regions that are today desertic or semiarid. At this time a French archaeologist, Louis Lartet, recognized that the Lisan sediments surrounding the Dead Sea were in fact the remnants of a very much enlarged Pleistocene lake.

The archaeological community of the time soon acquired an awareness of the importance of environmental contexts. Pioneering researchers such as the Danish archaeologist J. J. A. Worsaae maintained in 1840 that environmental information was essential for understanding archaeological finds. In the 1920s and 1930s, these ideas were brought to Near Eastern archaeology and implemented in studies such as those conducted by Dorothy A. E. Garrod and Dorothea M. A. Bate for understanding the prehistory and animal exploitation at the Carmel cave sites in western Palestine, and Gertrude Caton-Thomson and E. Gardiner in studies of the prehistory and environment of the Egyptian Faiyum.

Concepts and Goals. A major goal of paleoenvironmental reconstruction is to understand the social, economic, and spatial relationships between past human groups and the environment. This includes such lines of research as spatial patterns of settlement over a given landscape; ancient subsistence practices; human impact on the landscape; and the influence of climatic change on cultural systems. To achieve this end, techniques have been borrowed from the biological and earth sciences and adapted to address these and other archaeological questions.

In his book *Archaeology as Human Ecology* (1982), Karl W. Butzer outlined five important concepts and methods for approaching paleoenvironmental studies: space, scale, complexity, interaction, and state of equilibrium. The concern with space and spatial distribution applies to landforms and biological communities, as well as to human settlements. The spatial patterning of these three groups is often interrelated and provides insight into the interaction among them.

Paleoenvironmental studies in archaeology are carried out in the framework of three scales of research: macroscale, mesoscale, and microscale. These refer to the physical size of the land area being investigated, the extent of a given biotic zone, the size of a human community, and the magnitude of temporal units. In physical terms, the macroscale refers to major regions with distinctive life zones, or biomes, such as the eastern Mediterranean area or North Africa. Temporally, it can range from about 10,000 to 100,000 years.

The mesoscale is a much smaller unit of space, usually within the vicinity, or catchment, of an archaeological site. It may encompass a variety of different landforms—hills, valleys, dunes, lakes, and streams—each with distinctive groups of biota. Temporal changes at this scale could take place at a magnitude of about 100–10,000 years.

The microscale of investigation includes the site itself, the patterning of residences, and the location of activity areas. Temporally, it is concerned with periods of fewer than one hundred years. Although the three scales of investigation are interrelated, they all impart different information about environmental variability and the interaction between environments and past sociocultural and economic systems. Human perceptions of their natural surroundings also vary with respect to scale, and these perceptions govern the interaction between human groups and their natural milieu.

The concept of interaction refers to the interactive relationships of human communities with each other and their natural environment at varying scales and rates. The relationship between people and their environment is not a deterministic one—with climate, landscape, and biotic communities shaping human responses—or the opposite—with human groups completely manipulating their surroundings. Environmental changes can be viewed as positive or negative stimuli to a human system. The response to this stimuli will differ according to internal factors such as technological level, social organization, and cultural perception of the change.

The complexity factor maintains that environments and human communities are heterogeneous, and that researchers should therefore structure their investigations to account for spatial and temporal variability at different scales of analysis. Finally, the equilibrium state refers to the stability of a given system, either cultural, or environmental, and its vulnerability to changes of differing magnitudes created by stress from outside factors.

Methods of Reconstruction. In reconstructing ancient landscapes and environments, methods have been borrowed from the earth sciences, botany, and zoology. Although the methods resemble those used in the natural sciences, objectives and research questions differ because they are related to archaeological goals and concerns. This has given rise to three basic environmentally oriented subdisciplines in archaeology: geoarchaeology, paleoethnobotany, and archaeozoology. Often, the goals and techniques of these three areas of research overlap.

Geoarchaeology. Some of the major goals of geoarchaeology include reconstructing past climates and interpreting their role in a region's archaeological developments; reconstructing ancient landforms in the vicinity of a site (marshes, springs, floodplains, and streams), including their availability as resources or liabilities and their use in aiding site surveys; assisting in site surveys using methods of geophysical prospecting; identifying the sources of a site's mineral resources; determining the factors that formed an archaeological site; and analyzing areas of diverse activities within a site by chemical tests and microartifact analyses.

One of the cornerstones of paleoenvironmental reconstruction in geoarchaeology is the concept that weathering, transportation, and sediment deposition are controlled by environmental conditions. This life history of sediments is revealed by some of the characteristics of the deposit. Therefore, in describing the color, composition, grain-size distribution, shape, angularity, bedding form, and postdepositional changes of deposits, the geoarchaeologist can find substantial clues for reconstructing ancient land forms and the nature of past environments.

Identifying ancient landforms (abandoned stream or beach terraces, playa lakes, and ancient marshy areas) can aid in locating sites in a site survey, as well as in assessing an area's past agricultural, mineral, and water resource potential. Geophysical prospecting for archaeological sites is conducted by magnetometry, electrical resistivity, and ground-penetrating radar. The appropriate geophysical technique depends on the type of site being investigated, the kind of finds expected (e.g., brick walls, stone walls, or pits), and the nature of the sediment matrix.

Mineral resources at a site include building stone, clay used in ceramic manufacture, metal ores, obsidian and flint for tool production, metals, and precious or semiprecious stones for jewelry and utensils. Locating the sources of this material involves identifying distinctive minerals through heavy mineral, petrographic, and neutron activation analyses and having knowledge of the character of local and regional sources.

On the archaeological site the geoarchaeologist helps to identify the processes of stratigraphic development, factors of site disturbance, and the interface between natural and cultural sediments at the boundary of the archaeological deposits. He or she is concerned with reconstructing the site's formation history and the amount of postdepositional disturbance to artifacts.

The geoarchaeologist may also participate in delineating activity areas. Two procedures used are microartifact and chemical analyses. In microartifact studies, the researcher examines the artifacts, which range in size from about 3 cm down to 0.250 mm. These remains on and in a living surface, too small to be removed or swept away, would have been trampled into the floor or occupation surface. Microartifacts such as sherds, flint chips, charcoal, bone, eggshell, and beads provide a record of activities throughout the life of the living surface. This is one of the only archaeological techniques that allows direct comparisons of percentages of different artifact types.

Chemical analyses of living surfaces include determining pH and phosphate content of the sediments, with a low pH (indicating acid sediment) and high phosphate value indicative of high concentrations of decaying organic matter. These analyses can aid in identifying animal pens and stables. Along the same line of research is soil micromorphology, in which a small unit of sediment from an archaeological site is solidified and thin sections are taken for microscopic examination. This allows the researcher to examine the relationships between site formation and natural soil processes at a microscopic scale.

Paleoethnobotany. The techniques of paleoethnobotany vary with the kinds of research objectives. Some of the aims of paleoethnobotany are paleoenvironmental reconstruction, both at the macroscale of regional vegetation and at the mesoscale of local site environs; investigating ancient plant use for subsistence, fuel, building materials, medicines, and ritual practices; analyzing farming practices; determining the seasonality of site occupation; and understanding the interaction between ancient peoples and their environment. Two techniques commonly applied to the problem of paleoenvironmental reconstruction at the macro- and mesoscales of investigation are palynology and phytolith analysis.

Palynology is the study of pollen grains originating in flowering plants and dispersed primarily through the air. The microscopic (silt sized) pollen is identified according to the size, shape, and surface features of individual grains—which are distinctive to family, often to genus, and sometimes to plant species. At the macroscale of research, pollen samples are usually extracted from water-logged sediments in bog and lake cores and are used to reconstruct regional vegetation and general environmental conditions. This is accomplished by comparing suites of species from the past with modern ones and by identifying "indicator species" that point to a specific ecological situation.

One of the problems facing palynological studies of this kind includes the differential output of pollen by different types of vegetation. This precludes a simple comparison of pollen frequencies without taking into account the amount of pollen produced by each type of plant. Pollen sequences are dated by radiocarbon dates taken from pollen cores. This dating is sometimes problematic because the dated units are often meters apart and changing sedimentation rates can hinder the extrapolation of dates throughout the core. Although a large number of trees and shrubs are identifiable by pollen type, the pollen of grasses is usually indistinguishable.

Identifying grass families and other types of monocotyledons (rushes, sedges, and palms) can be accomplished by another microbotanical technique: phytolith analysis. Phytoliths are microscopic mineralized bodies, usually composed of amorphous silica (opal), that form within the epidermal tissue of living plants. They generally take on the shape of the plant epidermal cells and are seen as microfossils of individual cells or sections of epidermal tissue encompassing from two to hundreds of joined cells. Phytoliths are commonly identifiable to plant family and often to plant genus. Occasional identifications can be made at the species level. As basic research in this field progresses, the range of identifiable plants is rapidly increasing. Phytoliths are initially deposited in the location at which the host plant disintegrated and are generally not dispersed through the air, as is pollen. They are washed into lake sediments by streams in the vicinity.

The combination of pollen and phytolith analyses affords a more exacting method for reconstructing regional vegetation patterns at the macroscale, as well as local plant communities at the mesoscale. The analysis of charred woods from an archaeological site can also offer information about local plant communities, but caution is needed in interpreting this information because humans can transport woods from other ecological zones.

At the microscale of analysis, or site level, the most traditional paleobotanical technique is analyzing macrobotanical remains, usually charred seeds, wood, and sometimes fruit and nuts. The most useful method of retrieving this material is by a system of flotation whereby sediment is mixed with water or a chemical solution. The charred material floats to the top and is removed using a fine-mesh sieve. Macrobotanical remains give information about the types of plants used for subsistence, fuel, building materials, medicines, and ritual pursuits. They are also informative about farming practices, cropping strategies, and the seasonality of site occupation. On a more detailed level of significance, they contribute to what is known about the timing and location of the first cereal domestication.

Phytolith analysis is also an advantageous technique at this level of investigation. Phytoliths are resistant to decay and are commonly preserved where macrobotanical remains are not. Phytoliths have distinctive shapes in different parts of a given plant, which allows differentiation between its stem and its flower. They can therefore aid in identifying activity areas by distinguishing, for example, the remnants of straw, or reed mats, from the remains of cereal glumes. One drawback to this technique is the as yet relatively small corpus of plants with known identifiable forms; however, the list of plant types identifiable by their phytoliths is growing. To date, there are cereals (including maize, wheat, and barley), weed grasses, reeds, sedges, and palms that can be identified at the family and genus level with this technique. Phytoliths are usually extracted from sediment taken from the archaeological site and processed by a researcher specializing in this technique.

Zooarchaeology. Some of the concerns of zooarchaeology, faunal studies of bones from archaeological deposits, include paleoenvironments at the macroscale, as well as the mesoscale, in the vicinity of a site; the season of site occupation; nutritional studies of protein intake from meat; hunting strategies, such as the types and sizes of animals hunted, and the energy expended in the hunt; animal domestication; pastoral strategies of animal species mixtures and patterns of transhumance; the use of secondary products such as milk, wool, and draft power; and how animals were raised for domestic use or market sale.

The most reliable method of bone collection at archaeological sites is the systematic sieving of most archaeological excavation units. This provides the faunal analyst with a large and mostly unbiased sample usable for statistical analyses. Because bones and botanical remains are not independently assignable to a specific period or archaeological level, much care must be taken to record proveniences and note the temporal homogeneity of the archaeological unit. If there are intrusive artifacts, there can also be intrusive bones and botanical remains.

With these considerations in mind, faunal analysts can reconstruct environments in a site's vicinity by the types of wild species present—and sometimes by the size of the species. Seasonality of site occupation is determined by fauna that is only present in the region during specific months in the year (e.g., migratory birds) or by the characteristics of the fauna that change with the seasons (antler growth or juvenile tooth development). Faunal analysts can also approximate the amount of meat consumed by weighing bones because there is a correlation between bone weight and meat. They can also identify butchery practices by the patterns of cut marks on the bones.

Animal husbandry and domestication are recognized by such features as a decrease in species size, signs of draft labor, wear marks from bits, and cultural factors (e.g., the deliberate burial of whole animals and calcium depletion in the bones from milking). The use of secondary products such as milk and wool and the raising of animals for domestic use or market sale are determined by the age profiles of a population of animals at the time of slaughter.

Integration. In reconstructing climates and paleoenvironments at the macroscale of research, each of the three approaches discussed above investigates different and independent data sets that are all environmental responses to climatic factors. In any reconstruction of climatic conditions, it is necessary to compare scenarios from several varied forms of information. Often, these data sets appear to have contradictory facts that, in essence, can be related to inconsistencies in dating the environmental indices. This can sometimes be reconciled by comparing patterns of trends indicating vacillations to wet or dry and cool or warm conditions that are similar to the trends specified by different methodologies.

In applying information about environmental and climatic change to explanations of human responses, it is essential to account for cultural, technological, economic, and settlement variability. All of these factors control the reaction of human groups to their environment, whether stable or changing. This is also true of the impact of the human group on its surroundings. Broadly speaking, hunter-gatherers, pastoralists, subsistence farmers, and cash-crop farmers will respond in different ways to an environmental stimulus such as drought. They will also impact their environments in different manners.

On the meso- and microscale of research, results from landscape reconstructions, combined with analyses of biological and mineral remains from an archaeological site, can assist in delineating site catchment areas or spheres of resource exploitation in the site vicinity. These types of studies are most successful when combined with other factors that influence settlement in a given region: political connections, cultic considerations, and access to resources through long-distance trade. The combination of paleoenvironmental reconstruction with settlement-pattern and catchment analyses provide a powerful body of information that can significantly contribute to our understanding of many aspects of political, social, and economic organizations.

[*See also* Analytical Techniques; Climatology; Environmental Archaeology; Ethnobotany; Ethnozoology; Geology; Paleobotany; *and* Paleozoology.]

BIBLIOGRAPHY

Butzer, Karl W. *Environment and Archaeology: An Ecological Approach to Prehistory*. 2d ed. Chicago, 1971. Essential introduction to environmental archaeology, outlining techniques and their applications to such significant processes as human evolution and the origins of agriculture.

Butzer, Karl W. *Archaeology as Human Ecology: Method and Theory for a Contextual Approach*. Cambridge, 1982. Theoretical framework for integrating environmental studies with archaeological concerns, with a good introduction to geoarchaeology, archaeobotany, and zooarchaeology.

Davis, Simon J. M. *The Archaeology of Animals*. New Haven, 1987. Good introduction to the techniques and concerns of zooarchaeology.

Dincauze, Dena. "Strategies for Paleoenvironmental Reconstruction in Archaeology." *Advances in Archaeological Method and Theory* 11 (1987): 255–336. Integrated approach to environmental studies in archaeology.

Evans, John G. *An Introduction to Environmental Archaeology*. Ithaca, N.Y., 1978. Primarily concerned with technical methods.

Hesse, Brian, and Paula Wapnish. *Animal Bone Archaeology: From Objectives to Analysis*. Washington, D.C., 1985. Good basic source on zooarchaeological techniques and applications to archaeological problems.

Pearsall, Deborah M. *Paleoethnobotany: A Handbook of Procedures*. San Diego, 1989. Thorough survey of field and laboratory techniques, including pollen, phytoliths, and macrobotanical analyses.

Piperno, Dolores R. *Phytolith Analysis: An Archaeological and Geological Perspective*. San Diego, 1988. Introduction to phytolith analysis and its broad applications.

Roberts, Neil. *The Holocene: An Environmental History*. Oxford and New York, 1989. General survey of techniques for environmental reconstruction and an outline of environmental history for the last ten thousand years.

Roper, Donna C. "The Method and Theory of Site Catchment Analysis: A Review." *Advances in Archaeological Method and Theory* 2 (1979): 119–140. Introduction to site-catchment analysis and critical review of previous studies.

Rosen, Arlene Miller. *Cities of Clay: The Geoarchaeology of Tells*. Chicago, 1986. Study of tell formation in a cultural, geomorphological, and environmental context.

Schiffer, Michael B. *Formation Processes of the Archaeological Record*. Albuquerque, 1987. Detailed study of the factors responsible for the placement of artifacts and the formation and erosion of archaeological sites.

Stein, Julie K., and William R. Farrand, eds. *Archaeological Sediments in Context*. Orono, Maine, 1985. Collection of articles on geoarchaeology covering a broad range of site contexts.

ARLENE MILLER ROSEN

PALEOPATHOLOGY. The scientific study of ancient disease, which has historical and medical implications for human, animal, and plant evolution, began in the late nineteenth century. The discipline, known as paleopathology, is today closely allied with archaeology and physical anthropology. Together, those two disciplines provide paleopathologists with the material for their research. Paleopathology's interdisciplinary nature and broad scope place most modern research in universities and medical schools.

According to Calvin Wells, a leader of the field in Europe, one of the main principles of paleopathology is the premise that humans and animals do not exist in isolation from their surroundings: the pattern of disease or injury that affects them is an integral part of that environment. Disease is the manifestation of the stress and strain to which they are exposed. Disease is reflected in their genetic inheritance, the climate in which they lived, the soil that gave them sustenance, and the other animals and plants with which they shared their world. It is influenced by their daily occupations, dietary habits, choice of dwellings, social structure, and even their folklore and mythology (Zias, 1989).

In the Near East, from the mid-nineteenth century until the 1930s, descriptive studies of Egyptian mummies were the prime concern of paleopathologists. Although much of the research appearing in journals is still descriptive, several scholarly attempts (e.g., Cockburn, 1963; Manchester, 1983) to provide a well-formulated theoretical/historical background for the discipline are providing direction for future research. Research today is rapidly moving in the direction of biomolecular studies of ancient disease including the extraction of DNA and polymerase chain reaction (PCR).

The well-established literary tradition in the Near East provides a wealth of information on disease and medical practices spanning five thousand years. While early Assyrian and Egyptian texts deal specifically with the problem of disease and medical practices, perhaps the greatest body of knowledge comes from the Hebrew scriptural writings. Although not intended as medical texts, they are a source of medical practices and folk beliefs.

The scientific value of paleopathology lies in its diachronic approach to illness, which enables researchers to perceive chronic diseases, such as leprosy and tuberculosis, over a long period of time. The paleopathologist can thus determine whether a disease has evolved or changed its pattern. Certain diseases, such as arteriosclerosis, once regarded as the result of diet and modern living conditions, have been found in autopsies performed on Egyptian mummies (Sandison, 1980) calling into question many modern concepts about the etiology of heart disease.

The skeletal remains of all people in all periods are a very valuable scientific-medical resource for tracing the biological history of the human race. This material needs to be studied to understand better our ancestors, our health, and our world.

[*See also* Paleobotany; Paleoenvironmental Reconstruction; Paleozoology; *and* Skeletal Analysis.]

BIBLIOGRAPHY

Cockburn, Aidan. *The Evolution and Eradication of Infectious Diseases*. Baltimore, 1963. Authoritative and comprehensive work presenting diseases in theoretical/historical perspective. The author (d.1981) founded the U.S. Paleopathology Association in 1973, the largest professional association in the field.

Jones, Richard. "Paleopathology." In *The Anchor Bible Dictionary*, vol. 5, pp. 60–69. New York, 1992.

Manchester, Keith. *The Archaeology of Disease*. Bradford, 1983. Excellent survey of the discipline, with a strong emphasis on the Old World, particularly Europe.

Ortner, Donald J., and Walter Putschar. *Identification of Pathological Conditions in Human Skeletal Remains*. 2d ed. Washington, D.C., 1985. The most authoritative and scholarly text on the subject; valuable for its comprehensive coverage of disease worldwide.

Preuss, Julius. *Biblical and Talmudic Medicine* (1911). Translated by Fred Rosner. New York, 1978. Standard reference for diseases mentioned in Jewish scriptural sources. Rosner's English translation corrects certain errors in, but remains faithful to, the original German text.

Rafi, A., et al. "DNA of *Mycobacterium leprae* Detected by PCR in Ancient Bone" *International Journal of Osteoarchaeology* 4 (1994): 287–290. An attempt to utilize modern biomolecular techniques in diagnosing ancient disease on a genetic level.

Sandison, A. T. "Diseases in Ancient Egypt." In *Mummies, Disease, and Ancient Cultures,* edited by Aidan Cockburn and Eve Cockburn, pp. 29–44. Cambridge, 1980.

Wells, Calvin. *Bones, Bodies, and Disease: Evidence of Disease and Abnormality in Early Man.* New York, 1964.

Wood, James, et al. "The Osteological Paradox: Problems of Inferring Prehistoric Health from Skeletal Samples." *Current Anthropology* 33.4 (1992): 343–370. Critical review of the discipline as it relates to prehistoric populations.

Zias, Joseph. "Lust and Leprosy: Confusion or Correlation?" *Bulletin of the American Schools of Oriental Research* 275 (1989): 27–31. This article reflects on how theological and folkloristic concepts are influenced by disease.

Zias, Joseph. "Death and Disease in Ancient Israel." *Biblical Archaeologist* 54.3 (1991): 146–159. The most comprehensive treatment to date on the subject as it pertains to the ancient Holy Land.

JOSEPH ZIAS

PALEOZOOLOGY. The study of animal remains from archaeological sites is known as zooarchaeology, archaeozoology, and faunal analysis as well as paleozoology. As a field it has developed an intellectual territory between and overlapping with several sets of older disciplines. In one dimension it occupies the temporal gap between paleontology, a subject concerned primarily with pre-Holocene phenomena, and neontology, which deals with modern living populations. In another, it overlaps zoology's primary concern with wild animals and veterinary/animal science's preoccupation with domestic species. In a third, archaeological, arena, it has arisen to deal with the collection, identification, and interpretation of the ubiquitous fragments of bone and shell that occur at most sites. Over the century of its existence, paleozoology has developed two overlapping emphases, one primarily concerned with animals and the impact human activity has had on them, the other primarily concerned with human cultures and the way animals affected and were exploited by them.

The zoological side of the discipline emphasizes the development of techniques for identifying remains and describing changes in animal morphology over time. As examples of identification, fragmentary sheep bones are hard to tell from those of goats, and equid remains are notoriously difficult to refer to the various species that inhabited the greater Near East: horses, donkeys, onagers, and their various crosses. However, extensive osteometric analyses in recent years have produced criteria for making some of the separations. Estimating the age at death from teeth and bones has been another achievement. Various methods, including the examination of dental wear and cross-sections of teeth and the study of the schedule of bone maturation, have been developed to assess mortality patterns in many of the more commonly recovered Near Eastern fauna. In the case of domestication, the process of taming and husbanding produces physical changes in animals, some of which are reflected in the skeleton. The horns of goats change from a wild morphology characterized by a quadrilateral cross-section to a domestic morphology of tear-drop shape. Pig and dog skulls are foreshortened and teeth reduced in length by the same process. Many animals also undergo an overall reduction in size and develop greater variability in appearance. An important component of the husbandry of several species is castration. Osteometric analysis of large samples has the potential to demonstrate the use of the technique. Paleozoologists additionally record incidences of disease and pathology. The use of cattle for plowing produces distinctive bony growths on the feet, a feature that appears as early as the Bronze Age in the Near East.

Paleozoology is also charged with contributing to the reconstruction of past environments and the estimation of the seasonality of human occupation. Some species of bird, rodent, and mollusc are diagnostic of past conditions. In the case of snails, the chemical makeup of the shell is also an indicator. In other archaeological problems, it is the relative abundance of different taxa that is the clue.

The development of quantitative measures has been a preoccupation of the field. A number of statistics have been developed (minimum number of individuals, relative frequency, total number of fragments, bone weight), but because each method has significant biases, none has proved a panacea in estimating abundance. Concern with quantification has stimulated concern with taphonomy, the study of processes that affect remains between deposition and recovery. As organic material, bone fragments are subject to attritional processes that tend not to affect lithics and ceramics. Because of these taphonomic biases, the number of bones fragments found and referred to a species is not equivalent to the abundance of that species in the past. Furthermore, because bones in and of themselves are rarely datable directly either by species or morphology (the use of radiocarbon and other physiochemical techniques is prohibitively expensive and is thus restricted to special finds), they must be dated by association with other artifacts, usually pottery. Paleozoologists have found it necessary to distinguish sharply between the stratigraphic date of an archaeological deposit and the date based on its content. Quantitative descriptions of paleozoological data are therefore presented as relative trends through time and space rather than absolute quantities for a given period.

The cultural side of paleozoology targets the reconstruction of past socioeconomic systems. Information about the spatial patterning of bone remains, the relative abundance of different species, and the age of a species at death is evaluated with ethnographic and ethnohistorical data. These models have been applied at regional, site, and household levels. Study of modern pastoralists has shown that their management decisions are shaped by the degree of interaction they have with markets. Application of these principles to archaeological settings reveals how a community's interaction with its network of surrounding communities was constructed. For instance, at Iron Age Tel Dan in the Galilee in Israel, as the village grew to a city, predictable shifts occurred in the abundance of sheep and goats relative to cattle and in the manner of processing carcasses. At Early Iron Age Ai/Raddanah, in the central hill country of Cisjordan, the relative proportions and age at the slaughter of sheep and goats points to a much greater degree of market involvement than has been posited for a small village from this period. Larger forces are also visible. The paleozoological record at Tell Jemmeh in Israel's northern Negev desert and at Tel Miqne (Ekron in ancient Philistia) shows how Assyrian imperial demands for tribute and military provisions severely dislocated local pastoral production systems in the Late Iron Age.

Intrasite spatial variability of animal remains is also informative. Access to different resources is predicated on socioeconomic status and organization of the redistributive system. With respect to animals, this often means that different species and even different parts of the same carcass are distributed to households and sectors of the community based on wealth, prestige, ritual status, or the degree of involvement in pastoral production. Evidence from Tell el-Amarna in Egypt shows that pork was the mainstay of the diet of laborers during the New Kingdom period, while other elements of the society ate cattle, sheep, and a few goats. Faunal remains from Elephantine in the Nile valley, Tell el-Ḥayyat in the Jordan Valley, and al-Hiba in southern Mesopotamia show that although pigs were eaten, remains of the animal are not found in temple complexes at those sites, whereas bones of other domesticates are.

Spatial variability is visible within the household as well. The process of converting animal products to meals is called cuisine. Different stages in food preparation generate distinctive carcass debris. Ethnographically based models of the culinary process have, for example, been used to explain the variability in bone remains found in the various rooms of Byzantine houses at Qaṣrin in the Golan Heights.

[*See also* Animal Husbandry; Camels; Cattle and Oxen; Equids; Ethnoarchaeology; Ethnobotany; Paleobotany; Pigs; *and* Sheep and Goats. *In addition, with the exception of al-Hiba, all of the sites mentioned are the subject of independent entries.*]

BIBLIOGRAPHY

Baker, John, and Don Brothwell. *Animal Diseases in Archaeology*. New York, 1980. Best single source on animal paleopathology.

Chaplin, Raymond E. *The Study of Animal Bones from Archaeological Sites*. New York, 1971. Important early discussion of the modern field.

Cornwall, Ian. *Bones for the Archaeologist*. London, 1964. Classic introduction in English to the field from a zoological perspective.

Davis, Simon J. M. *The Archaeology of Animals*. New Haven, 1987. Global review of paleozoology.

Grayson, Donald K. *Quantitative Zooarchaeology: Topics in the Analysis of Archaeological Faunas*. Orlando, Fla., 1984. Thorough examination of the problems associated with different quantitative methods.

Hesse, Brian, and Paula Wapnish. *Animal Bone Archaeology: From Objectives to Analysis*. Washington, D.C., 1985. Introduction to the methods of paleozoology focused on the archaeology of the late prehistoric and historic periods of the Near East.

Hillson, Simon. *Teeth*. Cambridge, 1986. Guide to the identification of teeth and estimation of age from dental evidence.

Lyman, R. Lee. *Vertebrate Taphonomy*. Cambridge, 1984. Exhaustive review of the effects of burial and exposure processes on animal remains.

Wapnish, Paula, and Brian Hesse. "Faunal Remains from Tel Dan: Perspectives on Animal Production at a Village, Urban, and Rural Center." *ArchaeoZoologia* 4.2 (1991): 9–86. Extensive treatment of the methodology of reconstructing socioeconomic systems from paleozoological data.

BRIAN HESSE and PAULA WAPNISH

PALESTINE. [*This entry provides a broad survey of the history of Palestine as known primarily from archaeological discoveries. It is chronologically divided into six articles:*

Prehistoric Palestine
Palestine in the Bronze Age
Palestine in the Iron Age
Palestine in the Persian through Roman Periods
Palestine in the Byzantine Period
Palestine in the Islamic Period

In addition to the related articles on specific subregions and sites referred to in this entry, see also History of the Field, *article on* Archaeology in Israel.]

Prehistoric Palestine

The earliest occurrences of human artifacts, generally classified as Lower Paleolithic, were found at ʿUbeidiya in the central Jordan Valley. As the archaeological horizons were embedded within a sequence of lacustrine and fluvial deposits, most of the bone and lithic assemblages were recovered from lake shores. The artifacts are characterized by high frequencies of core choppers, from which flakes were removed and used. Polyhedrons, spheroids, and a few handaxes form the rest of the assemblages. Most core choppers and polyhedrons were made of flint pebbles, spheroids were shaped from limestone, and handaxes were predominantly made of basalt but also from flint and limestone. The entire lithic sequence is attributed to the Early Acheulean and is considered to mark the move of *Homo erectus* out of Africa about 1.4–1.0 million years ago. [*See* ʿUbeidiya; Jordan Valley.]

Early hominids at ʿUbeidiya were probably both scavengers and hunters. Their main sources of meat were hippo, horse, and deer. The natural accumulation of more than one hundred different species of fish, reptiles, birds, and mammals indicates that the climate of the Jordan Valley was similar to that of Israel's coastal plain today.

Other Lower Paleolithic sites, all of which are classified as Middle or Upper Acheulean, are found in the Jordan Valley and on the coastal plain. Among these is ʿEvron Quarry, a small site that contained some animal bones and an assemblage of a few large flint bifaces and small flakes, indicating that part of the assemblage was transported there. Gesher Benot Yaʿaqob, on the banks of the Jordan River is known for its assemblages of lava-flake cleavers made in the African technique. Also found were the remains of large mammals, best correlated with Middle Pleistocene fauna that include elephant, rhinoceros, hippopotamus, wild boar, and deer and two fragments of a human femora. The site overlies a lava flow dated by potassium/argon to 0.68 million years ago and is estimated to be around 0.6–0.5 million years old.

Upper Acheulean occurrences, mostly collected from surface scatters, were located throughout the region and at such cave sites as Tabun (Mt. Carmel) and Umm Qaṭafa (Wadi Khareitoun, Judean Desert). [*See* Tabun.] The incorporated animal bones are often those of large-to-medium mammals, probably indicating the scavenging activities of humans.

At several cave sites in the Levant the Upper Acheulean is overlain by the lithic industry known as the Mugharan or Acheulo-Yabrudian tradition. One facies of this entity contains thick scrapers of various shapes, including canted and transverse forms (known as Yabrudian); the second, together with the scrapers, has varying frequencies of often small, oval, or pointed bifaces (called Acheulean); and the third is dominated by blades with a few bifaces and burins (named Amudian). The first two are the most common. The Acheulo-Yabrudian is found in the northern and central Levant. Dating techniques based on the relative amount of uranium in artifacts and teeth known as TL and ESR suggest that this entity lasted from about 500,000/400,000 to 270,000/250,000 years ago. The fragmentary skull recovered in Zuttiyeh cave and a broken femur in Tabun cave are the only human remains. The Zuttiyeh skull is attributed to archaic *Homo sapiens*. The Acheulo-Yabrudian is overlaid by the Mousterian complex. The long sequence of the Tabun cave enabled the general description of three types of lithic industries, mostly made through the use of various core-reduction techniques. Often, other Mousterian assemblages are compared to those of the Tabun sequence:

Tabun D type (earliest Mousterian): contains numerous elongated points and blades not always produced by the Levallois technique. The industry is more common in the Negev desert, southern Jordan, and the Syrian desert.

Tabun C type: often dominated by radial and bidirectional core reduction, this assemblage resulted in large, oval flakes. Convergent flaking to produce Levallois points is quite rare. Similar assemblages are known mainly from the coastal Levant.

Tabun B type: characterized by blanks removed from unidirectional and convergent Levallois cores, this assemblage's short and broad points are common, as are side scrapers. The industry occurs in southern Jordan.

Several human remains were recovered from burials at the Tabun, Skhul, Kebara, Qafzeh, and ʿAmud caves. These fossils were considered to be West Asian Neanderthals (Tabun, Kebara, ʿAmud) and archaic *Homo sapiens* (Qafzeh, Skhul). One school views the entire collection as representing the same population, while others see the Mediterranean Neanderthals as either emerging from local ancestors or as Southeast Europeans who migrated into the Levant with the onset of glacial conditions (115,000 or 75,000 years ago). [*See* Carmel Caves.]

Mousterian people gathered plant foods and hunted gazelles, fallow deer, and other animals. They opportunistically scavenged large animals such as wild oxen, rhinoceros, and hippo. Their tools reflect hide scraping, woodworking, and butchery. Levallois points bear the impact fractures of having been hafted as spear points. The use of red ocher and the collection of marine shells occur rarely. Hearths were rounded or oval; amorphous ashy deposits are common in well-preserved caves (e.g., Kebara).

The transition from the Middle Paleolithic to the Upper Paleolithic is reflected in the lithic industries uncovered at Boqer Taḥtit in the Negev and Ksar 'Akil in Lebanon. [*See* Ksar 'Akil.] The changes demonstrate a transition in the core-reduction methods. Levallois points were removed with blades from bidirectional Upper Paleolithic, mostly prismatic cores. Later, unidirectional cores became the source for blades. The retouched pieces of the transitional industry (also named Emiran) are mainly Upper Paleolithic. Tool types include end scrapers—sometimes made on Levallois blanks—blades, and flakes with a few Emireh points.

The Ahmarian tradition in the lithic industry follows (38,000–20,000/18,000 BP). It is best documented in the Negev, Sinai, and southern Jordan, as well as in a few layers in caves (e.g., Kebara), and is predominantly a blade industry. The Ahmarian sites are interpreted as the residuum of mobile hunter-gatherers who hunted gazelle, fallow deer, roe deer, and ibex in semiarid areas. Several grinding tools indicate a slow change in vegetal food processing to include ground substances in addition to ocher. Bone tools are quite rare, and the use of marine shells began in about 20,000 BP.

The Levantine Aurignacian is only known from the northern and central Levant. It is considered to be the archaeological expression of a social unit foreign to the Near East that arrived in the region and remained for some time between 32,000 and 27,000 BP. The Levantine Aurignacian A and B assemblages include carinated and nosed scrapers. Phase A is rich in blades, and phase B is dominated by flake production. Both contain el-Wad points and are often rich in a bone and antler industry. Two incised slabs from Hayonim cave may represent artistic expressions. The following period (27,000–18,000 BP) incorporates a series of assemblages that are not well dated. Several (previously named Levantine Aurignacian C) are rich in scrapers and burins. In one of the sites, Naḥal ʿEin-Gev I, the flexed burial of a 30–35-year-old woman was uncovered. [*See also* ʿEin-Gev.] Other assemblages, called Late Ahmarian, are dominated by the production of blades and bladelets. Ohalo II, a waterlogged site radiocarbon dated to 19,000 BP, was discovered in Lake Kinneret (Sea of Galilee). Excavations of this site exposed a series of hut bases with numerous lithics, a rich fauna assemblage including fish bones, and a wealth of plant remains.

The Late Ahmarian heralds the onset of what is called the Kebaran cultural complex (c. 19,000/18,000–14,000 BP), in which the main changes in the lithic industries is in the form of the microliths. Nongeometrics such as the obliquely truncated bladelets (Kebara points) give way to the elongated trapeze rectangles that characterize the ensuing cultural complex, the Geometric Kebaran (c. 14,000–13,000/12,800 BP). Kebaran sites are generally small. A shallow base of a brush hut dug into sandy deposits some 5–7 m in diameter was found at ʿEin-Gev I. Repeated occupations resulted in the accumulation of flints and animal bones, including fallow deer and gazelle. A semiflexed burial of a thirty–thirty-five-year-old woman was found under one of the levels in the hut. Mortar and several pestles were used in plant processing. The only art object from this period was found at Urkan er-Rubb II in the lower Jordan Valley: a flat pebble with several incised series of a "ladder" pattern.

The cold and dry climate during the Kebaran, known also as the Late Glacial Maximum, limited occupations to the woodland belt and margins of the steppic belt. Subsequent amelioration brought increased temperatures and precipitation. This enabled the Geometric Kebaran groups to inhabit many of the formerly arid areas and tempted groups from neighboring regions, such as the Mushabian, to penetrate from northeast Africa. During this time period, most people lived in small groups of hunter-gatherers, and the larger sites are considered palimpsests of reoccupations. The consumption of seeds, grain, acorns, and nuts is best recorded in the use of pounding and grinding tools—mortars, pestles, and mullers. Marine shells were brought mainly from the Mediterranean and occasionally from the Red Sea. Two burials with fragmentary skeletons were uncovered at Neveh David (Mt. Carmel), and others are known from the site of Kharraneh, near Azraq (Jordan).

An abrupt climatic shift in about 13,000/12,800 BP, followed by a rapid increase in annual precipitation, has been interpreted as either a "push" or "pull" motivator in the disruption of the previous socioeconomic scenario. Several groups, known as the Natufian culture, resolved the seasonal shortages by becoming sedentary. Large Natufian sites are about 2,000–5,000 sq m in area and contain rounded and oval houses, (ʿAin Mallaha; Hayonim cave, Israel; the Terrace at Wadi Ḥammeh 27), burials, and rich lithic and bone industries. [*See* Hayonim.] The houses are often dug into the ground and have walls of undressed stone slanting toward the interior, although in one large house at ʿAin Mallaha a series of postholes was uncovered. Most superstructures seem to have been made of organic materials.

Natufian burials display various styles. Collective burials are more common in the Early Natufian, when positions are supine, semiflexed, and flexed, and skull removal is rare. The Late Natufian sites contain more single burials in flexed position. Grave goods indicate some possible intergroup social differentiation. Body decorations were made of bone and stone pendants, shell beads, commonly of *Dentalium*. Shell decorations appear on headgear, garments, and belts and were used in necklaces and bracelets. Human burials accompanied by dogs (as at ʿAin Mallaha) indicate canine domestication, as well as a change in religious beliefs. The skeletal remains indicate that the Natufians were generally healthy, with a life expectancy of thirty-two–thirty-five.

Natufian stone tools include geometric microliths, such as lunates shaped by either Helwan or abrupt retouch. Also present are sickle blades, burins, perforators, and some elongated picks. The production of small flakes and short bladelets as blanks for tools distinguishes the Natufian lithic industry from the former cultural complexes. The use of the microburin technique, with which oblique snaps are achieved, may reflect local traditions. Natufian artistic representations include ungulate heads carved on sickle hafts; schematic limestone figurines that represent humans and animals; and zigzag and meander decorations incised or carved on domestic objects. Natufian sites also differ in their use of ornaments, such as bone beads, which are distinctive enough to indicate group identification. The Natufian economy was based on the intensive collection of cereals, which leads some scholars to suggest that the Natufians were the earliest farmers. [*See* Cereals.] However, plant remains are scarce as a result of poor site preservation. Mortars and pestles were used extensively, and the range of hunted game, collected reptiles, and trapped water fowl is wider than for any previous Epipaleolithic entity. Natufian subsistence strategy responded to the increase of basic group size and sedentism.

The Harifian culture (c. 10,700–10,1000 BP) in the Negev and Sinai is interpreted as a cultural adaptation of Late Natufian to the dry and cold conditions of the Younger Dryas. (This brief cold and dry period is now recognized globally and considered the last cold spell of the last glacial cycle.) Their small winter sites were dispersed in the lowlands while the larger summer–fall sites were in the highlands. The latter contain semisubterranean dwellings, mortars, pestles, grinding stones, and slabs with numerous cup holes either inside the huts or around them. No plant remains were recovered. The lithic industry is dominated by lunates and the projectile the Harif point, among other numerous microliths. Gazelle, ibex, and hare were the main game.

The Early Neolithic period (10,300/10,000–8000/7800 BP) saw the emergence of small villages of farmers-hunters and later farmers-herders in a narrow Levantine corridor stretching from the Damascus basin through the Jordan Valley to southern Transjordan. While agriculture as a subsistence strategy expanded, the Lebanese mountains and the arid region remained the territories of hunter-gatherers who continued to interact with farming communities. [*See* Agriculture.]

The few known Pre-Pottery Neolithic A (PPNA; 10,300–9,300/9,200 BP) sites are found in the Jordan Valley. The early levels contain Khiamian assemblages, which include some microliths, perforators, burins, sickle blades, and arrowheads, mostly of the el-Khiam type. The ensuing Sultanian industry includes axes/adzes and polished celts. Cultural change is expressed in the range of site size from 2.5 ha (6 acres) to 100 sq m. Demographic estimates suggest a population of about 450 people for the PPNA site of Jericho. [*See* Demography; Jericho.] In front of Jericho's so-called town wall lies a 3.5-meter-wide shallow ditch dug into the chalky bedrock. Behind the wall, inside the settlement, is the well-known rounded tower (8.5 m high) with a small door and interior staircase. A few large and deep rounded structures built of mud bricks were exposed on the northern side of the tower (Kenyon, 1957). Many have interpreted the wall and tower as a defense system. An alternative is that the wall was built in response to the wetter conditions that prevailed during the PPNA (as compared to the preceding millennium), in order to protect the village from flooding. The tower is seen as having accommodated a mud-brick shrine on top (Bar-Yosef, 1986). The houses were oval, their foundations were dug into the ground, they were lined with stones, and their walls were built of plano-convex mud bricks. The roof was probably flat with wooden beams and woven-reed mats covered with mud. The mud floors also were covered with mats and the hearths were shallow, paved basins.

Burials were found in various places, including open spaces that were later built up. The burials were generally single, with the crania of adults removed. No grave goods were encountered at any of the sites.

The PPNA lithic industry differs from the Natufian by having much lower frequencies of microliths. Among the retouched pieces are small projectiles such as the el-Khiam point and others with small tangs. Perforators and burins are common; sickle blades are often plain and rarely have bifacial retouch. The group of axes/adzes with transverse removal shaping the working edge includes chisels and picks. Polished celts made of basalt and limestone occur, while sickle blades and bifacial tools are missing from the desert sites. The art objects are rare and include small figurines made of limestone or clay that depict seated females, a female with a string skirt, or kneeling females.

The economy of the Sultanian villages was a mixture of cultivation of emmer wheat (on the Damascus plain), barley, and legumes. Fruits and wild seeds were collected, including figs, nuts, and acorns. Gazelle and foxes were the main game sources; fallow deer, bovids, and hare were exploited to a lesser extent; and trapping waterfowl was a seasonal activity. Little is known about the health of the people although their skeletal remains resemble those of the Natufians. In some cases (Jericho) skull deformation was practiced in vivo.

In the following period, the Pre-Pottery Neolithic B (PPNB; 9300/9200–7800/7500 BP) climatic conditions continued to be favorable for farming communities in the Levant, at least until 8000 BP. While most villages remained small, the maximum site size increased to 12 ha or 30 acres (ʿAin Ghazal, Basta), reflecting a population increase evident in both the more lush areas of Palestine and in the desertic regions. [*See* ʿAin Ghazal; Basta.] The excavations at Beidha demonstrate that the building of rectangular houses is a local shift in the villages from round or polygonal buildings, where the roof was supported by wooden posts. [*See* Beidha.] The use of lime plaster on floors, as well as in storage facilities, is recorded from various sites. At ʿAin Ghazal preserved postholes demonstrate the use of timber; in the later phases of the site's history, the diminution of this resource is reflected in smaller enclosed spaces and fewer posts.

PPNB burials are found under floors and in open spaces. Skulls of adults were removed and in a few sites nests of skulls were uncovered. Plastered skulls have been discovered at Jericho, Tel Ramad, ʿAin Ghazal, Beisamoun, and Kefar Hahoresh. At Naḥal Ḥemar skulls modeled in asphalt were found. There is a general consensus that the special treatment of the skulls provides evidence of an ancestor cult. Additional insights into domestic and cultic activities are gained from the numerous clay figurines representing pregnant females, males, and animals. A cache of human figurines, stone masks, modeled skulls, and numerous domestic objects at Naḥal Ḥemar indicates that ritual activities also encompassed special sites, perhaps marking territorial ownership.

The PPNB lithic industry is characterized by blade removal from bipolar cores that, in their more elaborate, elongated form, are known as naviform cores. The punched blades were shaped into arrowheads, perforators, burins, or sickle blades or were used in their original shape. The earliest types of arrowheads are Helwan point (with bilateral notches and a tang) and the Jericho point (with wings or clear-cut shoulders and a tang); later types are the Byblos point (leaf shaped with a tang) and ʿAmuq point (leaf shaped). Sickle blades are either plain blades (which bear the luster resulting from the harvesting of cereals) or elongated, tanged blades, often finely serrated; burins are common at many, but not all, sites.

The group of bifacial tools including axe/adzes and celts also saw some changes through time. While at most early and middle PPNB sites the Tahunian (tranchet) types dominate, there is a shift in the later PPNB to objects with a rounded retouched or polished working edge. These types seem to have been used to cut and work wood and sometimes as hoes. Imported raw materials such as obsidian, which first appeared in the Late Natufian, are more frequent at some PPNB sites—although not necessarily at the large ones. Exotic raw materials include greenstone (serpentine, malachite, rosasite), from which beads and pendants were made. Marine shells were collected on the shores of the Mediterranean and the Red Sea and distributed through the Levant. Cowries (*Cyprea* sp.) and *Glycimerys* sp. were among the most common species.

PPNB village economy was based on the cultivation of domesticated species of cereals and legumes and the continuous collection of wild fruits and seeds. Hunting gazelles, roe deer, fallow deer, wild boar, and hare was supplemented in agricultural villages by the raising of goats and sheep. [*See* Sheep and Goats.] In the late stages of the PPNB new objects for domestic use were introduced. These products, known as white ware, were made of a mixture of ashes and plaster. The forms include bowls, open jars, and bowls on pedestals; most are known from northern Syria and rarely occur in Palestinian contexts.

The collapse of the PPNB in the southern Levant manifested either as a major break or an abrupt change in settlement pattern. At the site of ʿAin Ghazal, where this phase is called PPNC, the lithic industry and mortuary practices changed. The main core-reduction strategy was based on the production of flakes and to a lesser extent of blades. The dominant tool types were the burin, with low frequencies of other formal tool types, including arrowheads. Finally, burials were less organized and lack evidence for skull removal. Speculations on the reasons behind the population shift include group aggression, salinization of fields, mortal epidemic, and the temptation to move to a positive environment.

The Pottery Neolithic (PN) period is poorly known, mainly because of a major change in settlement patterns. This change is archaeologically attested in two ways: at stratified sites, PN remains are found in numerous pits of various sizes that often penetrated and disturbed a wealth of PPNB rectangular buildings (Jericho, Munḥata, Beisamoun); and many new settlements were established either in the Jordan Valley (Shaʿar ha-Golan) or along the coastal plain. [*See* Munḥata; Shaʿar ha-Golan.] The invention of pottery and its introduction for domestic use took place first in the northern Levant and later in Palestine. In Palestine, clay pots outnumber white-ware products; the common forms are simple: jars, cooking pots, and bowls decorated first with chevron patterns and red paint and later with paint alone. The economy of this period was based on the cultivation of cereals and legumes, goat and sheep herding, and raising pigs in the more humid parts of the country and some cattle. [*See* Pigs; Cattle and Oxen.] The activities of pastoral nomads, who partially subsisted on herding goats, are reflected at numerous desertic sites. These groups continued to hunt and may have exchanged meat and other animal products for carbohydrates from the farming communities. [*See* Pastoral Nomadism.]

Evidence of burials is rare but indicates a shift from the earlier pattern. One burial under a small cairn was exposed at Shaʿar ha-Golan, and single flexed and semiflexed burials were found at other sites. Further indications concerning belief systems are reflected in clay and stone figurines. The Yarmukian culture is renown for its seated female clay figurines with tall headgear, masks, and exposed breasts. Temples or shrines are as yet unknown from the more sedentary sites, occurring mainly at such desertic sites as at Biqʿat ʿUvda.

The distribution of the PN sites in Palestine documents a settlement pattern that was based on cultivation and herding with seasonal mobility. The investment in the more permanent sites seems to have been less than in the PPNB period and probably points to a less regular pattern of mobility. This might reflect the unstable climatic conditions that, by the mid-Holocene, were changing from a stable pattern of precipitation to one resembling the modern, less predictable pattern.

BIBLIOGRAPHY

Arensburg, Baruch, and Ofer Bar-Yosef, eds. *Moshé Stekelis Memorial Volume*. Eretz-Israel, vol. 13. Jerusalem, 1977.

Arensburg, Baruch, L. A., Schepartz, A. M. Tillier, Bernard Vandermeersch, and Y. Rak. "A Reappraisal of the Anatomical Basis for Speech in Middle Palaeolithic Hominds." *American Journal of Physical Anthropology* 83 (1990): 137–146.

Bar-Yosef, Ofer. "Prehistory of the Levant." *Annual Review of Anthropology* 9 (1980): 101–133.

Bar-Yosef, Ofer. "The Walls of Jericho: An Alternative Interpretation." *Current Anthropology* 27 (1986): 157–162.

Bar-Yosef, Ofer, and Bernard Vandermeersch, eds. *Investigations in South Levantine Prehistory*. British Archaeological Reports, International Series, no. 497. Oxford, 1989.

Bar-Yosef, Ofer, and François R. Valla, eds. *The Natufian Culture in the Levant*. Ann Arbor, Mich., 1991.

Bar-Yosef, Ofer, and Anna Belfer-Cohen. "From Foraging to Farming in the Mediterranean Levant." In *Transitions to Agriculture in Prehistory*, edited by Anne Birgitte Gebauer and T. Douglas Price, pp. 21–48. Madison, Wis., 1992.

Bar-Yosef, Ofer. "The Role of Western Asia in Modern Human Origins." *Philosophical Transactions of the Royal Society of London, Series B* 337 (1992): 193–200.

Bar-Yosef, Ofer, and Bernard Vandermeersch, eds. *Le Squelette Moustérien de Kébara 2*. Paris, 1992.

Bar-Yosef, Ofer, and Na'ama Goren-Inbar. *The Lithic Assemblages of 'Ubeidiya: A Lower Palaeolithic Site in the Jordan Valley*. Qedem, vol. 34. Jerusalem, 1993.

Garrod, Dorothy A. E., and Dorothea M. A. Bate. *The Stone Age of Mount Carmel: Excavations at the Wady al-Mughara*. Oxford, 1937.

Gopher, Avi. *The Flint Assemblages of Munhata*. Paris, 1989.

Gopher, Avi and Ram Gophna. "Cultures of the Eighth and Seventh Millennium BP in Southern Levant: A Review for the 1990's." *Journal of World Prehistory* (1993): 297–351.

Goren-Inbar, Na'ama. *Quneitra: A Mousterian Site on the Golan Heights*. Qedem, vol. 31. Jerusalem, 1990.

Goren-Inbar, Na'ama. "The Acheulian Site of Gesher Benot Ya'aqov: An African or Asian Entity?" In *The Evolution and Dispersal of Modern Humans in Asia,* edited by T. Akazawa, K. Aoki, and T. Kimura, pp. 67–82. Tokyo, 1992.

Goring-Morris, A. Nigel. *At the Edge: Terminal Pleistocene Hunter-Gatherers in the Negev and Sinai*. 2 vols. British Archaeological Reports, International Series, no. 361. Oxford, 1987.

Goring-Morris, A. N. "The Harifian of the Southern Levant." In *The Natufian Culture in the Levant,* edited by Ofer Bar-Yosef and François R. Valla, pp. 173–216. International Monographs in Prehistory. Ann Arbor, 1991.

Henry, Donald O. "The Prehistory and Paleoenvironments of Jordan: An Overview." *Paléorient* 12.2 (1986): 5–26.

Henry, Donald O. *From Foraging to Agriculture: The Levant at the End of the Ice Age*. Philadelphia, 1989.

Horowitz, Aharon. *The Quaternary of Israel*. New York, 1979.

Howell, F. C. "Upper Pleistocene Stratigraphy and Early Man in the Levant." *Proceedings of the American Philosophical Society* 103 (1959): 1–65.

Kenyon, Kathleen M. *Digging Up Jericho*. London, 1957.

Levy, Thomas. *The Archaeology of Society in the Holy Land*. London, 1994.

Marks, A. E., ed. *Prehistory and Paleoenvironments in the Central Negev, Israel*. 3 vols. Dallas, 1976–1983.

Marks, A. E. "The Early Upper Paleolithic: the View from the Levant." In *Before Lascaux: The Complete Record of the Early Upper Paleolithic,* edited by H. Knecht, A. Pike-Tay, and R. White, pp. 5–22. Boca Raton, 1993.

Neuville, René. *Le Paléolithique et le Mésolithique du désert de Judée*. Archives de l'Institut de Paléontologie Humaine, Mémoire 24. Paris, 1951.

Perrot, Jean. "La préhistoire palestinienne." In *Supplément au Dictionnaire de la Bible,* vol. 8, cols. 286–446. Paris, 1972.

Perrot, Jean, and D. Ladiray. *Les Hommes de Mallaha (Eynan) Israel*. Paris, 1988.

Rak, Y. and Baruch Arensburg. "Kebara 2 Neanderthal Pelvis: First Look at a Complete Inlet." *American Journal of Physical Anthropology* 73 (1987): 227–231.

Ronen, Avraham, ed. *The Transition from Lower to Middle Palaeolithic and the Origin of Modern Man*. British Archaeological Reports, International Series, no. 151. Oxford, 1982.

Ronen, Avraham. *Sefunim Prehistoric Sites, Mount Carmel, Israel*. British International Reports, International Series, no. 230. Oxford, 1984.

Ronen, Avraham. "The Lower Palaeolithic Site Evron-Quarry in Western Galilee, Israel." In *Festschrift Karl Brunnacker,* edited by Wolfgang Boenigk and W. Tillmanns, pp. 187–212. Cologne, 1991.

Tchernov, Eitan, ed. *Les mammifères du pléistocène inférieur de la Vallée du Jourdain à Oubeidiyeh*. Mémoires et Travaux du Centre de Recherche Préhistoriques Français de Jérusalem, no. 5. Paris, 1986.

Tchernov, Eitan. "The Effects of Sedentism on the Exploitation of the Environment in the Southern Levant." In *Exploitation des animaux sauvages à travers le temps,* edited by J. Desse and F. Audoin-Rouzeau, pp. 137–159. Juan-des-Pines, 1993.

Tchernov, Eitan. *An Early Neolithic Village in the Jordan Valley II: The Fauna of Netiv Hagdud*. American School of Prehistoric Research Bulletin, no. 44. Cambridge, 1994.

Tillier, A. M. "The Origins of Modern Humans in Southwest Asia: Ontogenetic Aspects." In *The Evolution and Dispersal of Modern Humans in Asia,* edited by T. Akazawa, K. Aoki, and T. Kimura, pp. 15–28. Tokyo, 1992.

Tillier, A.-M. "Les hommes du Paléolithique moyen et la question de l'ancienneté de l'homme moderne en Afrique." *Archéo-Nil* 2 (1992): 59–69.

Trinkaus, E. "Morphological Contrasts between the Near Eastern Qafzeh-Skhul and Late Archaic Human Samples: Grounds for Behavioral Difference?" In *The Evolution and Dispersal of Modern Humans in Asia,* edited by T. Akazawa, K. Aoki, and T. Kimura, pp. 277–294. Tokyo, 1992.

Valla, François R. *Les industries de silex de Mallaha (Eynan) et du Natoufien dans le Levant*. Mémoires et Travaux du Centre de Recherche Préhistoriques Français de Jérusalem, no. 3. Paris, 1984.

Vandermeersch, Bernard. *Les hommes fossiles de Qafzeh (Israel)*. Paris, 1981.

Vandermeersch, Bernard. "The Near Eastern Hominids and the Origins of Modern Humans in Eurasia." In *The Evolution and Dispersal of Modern Humans in Asia,* edited by T. Akazawa, K. Aoki, and T. Kimura, pp. 29–38. Tokyo, 1992.

Wendorf, Fred, and A. E. Marks, eds. *Problems in Prehistory: North Africa and the Levant*. Dallas, 1975.

OFER BAR-YOSEF

Palestine in the Bronze Age

The period between about 3500 and 1200 BCE in the southern Levant is termed the Bronze Age and is divided into Early, Middle, and Late periods. These in turn are further divided into numbered and lettered subphases. The division of the Bronze Age into three parts was intended to reflect larger contours of sociopolitical, political, and historical development, although transitions continue to be regarded differently. The scholarly literature is replete with periodizations and dating schemes that supplement, contradict, and supersede one another, creating a confusing picture. They are, however, important because they manifest the changing perceptions of internal development during the Bronze Age and the synchronization of the relative chronology of the southern Levant with the more securely fixed chronologies of Egypt and Mesopotamia.

Early Bronze Age. With the end of the Chalcolithic period, in about 3500 BCE, the Early Bronze Age began. The former was a village, agropastoral society with strongly developed craft specialization in copper, ivory, and ceramics and elaborate religious iconography. The reasons for its collapse remain unclear, although climate change may have been involved.

The EB I contains two phases and dates from about 3500 to 3100 BCE. Its early phase is characterized by small settlements with curvilinear architecture, as at Yiftaḥel, ʿEin-Shadud, and Tel Teo. Some sites, such as Tell esh-Shuna in the central Jordan Valley, were occupied in both the Chalcolithic and EB I periods, although it is unclear whether occupation was continuous. Jawa, in Jordan's Black Desert, also straddles the boundary between the Chalcolithic and EB I. The earliest EB I phase is poorly represented in the south, with remains such as pit dwellings at Tell el-Ḥesi and cave dwellings on the Ḥalif terrace. Wadi Gaza site H is an important site, with imported Egyptian ceramics and artifacts. Its copper artifacts originated at the Feinan mines in southern Transjordan. Egyptian material reflects an interest in the resources of the southern coastal plain and the northern Negev desert. The early EB I witnessed settlement in the southern Levant, suggesting individual domestic units with little integration or cooperation, such as village planning or social storage.

Large villages developed late in EB I in both the north and south. Some sites, such as Beth-Yeraḥ, Tell esh-Shuna (North), Tel ʿErani, and Beth-Shean, reached 20 or 25 ha (49 or 62 acres) although their internal layout remains unclear. The overall number of sites increased, especially in the Galilee, Jordan Valley, and Transjordanian highlands. The first unequivocal temples appeared at Megiddo, Jericho, Ai, and Ḥartuv—the last incorporating a previously freestanding row of standing stones into the wall of a structure. In the Negev and Sinai there was an increasing tendency toward sedentarization that peaked in EB II. Egyptian material culture is accompanied by Egyptian architecture, such as the "residency" at the site of ʿEin-Besor and a large building at Tel ʿErani. The Egyptian presence is organized as an official mission, demonstrated by the seal impressions bearing the names of dynasty-"zero" and first-dynasty kings found at ʿEin-Besor. A network of sites provisioned the administrative center at ʿEin-Besor and associated outposts, such as Tel Malḥata and the Ḥalif terrace. Tel ʿErani and Beth-Shemesh are important examples of large sites where Egyptians lived alongside the local population.

Rectilinear architecture predominates at late EB I sites. The new architectural units accommodated larger numbers of residents and were formed into larger blocks, indicating higher levels of cooperation and leadership. Beyond temples, little social architecture is known, save for a few sites like Tell Shalem that may have had fortification walls. There is little evidence of social or political institutions outside extended kinship ties. Temples and fortifications indicate higher levels of organization, however.

The EB II (c. 3100–2700 BCE) was the first "urban" period in the southern Levant. Urban structures—public architecture such as fortifications, gates, and water systems—and urban institutions—"temples" and political institutions—emerge for the first time. A dichotomy between urban and rural segments of society develops, with urban sites controlling the growing international trade. The process of "urbanization" is unclear, given the limited internal chronological resolution available. The transition to urbanism was made on a site or regional basis. Some planned sites, such as Arad, were constructed above small, preexisting EB I communities; others, such as Tel Yarmut, became fortified later in EB II or in EB III.

The EB II settlement landscape shows a decrease in the number of sites and the emergence of size classes, as urban centers dominated rural hinterlands. The increased settlement in the Negev and Sinai is associated by some scholars with the copper trade from southern Sinai controlled by Arad. More likely this was in response to the general social and economic conditions created by urbanism in the Mediterranean core civilizations. Egyptian settlements on the southern coastal plain disappeared at the end of EB I. A trade relationship with Egypt developed instead, the primary evidence being southern Levantine jars and jugs in Egyptian contexts, so-called Abydos wares. The goods involved in this trade remain obscure, but Mediterranean olive crops and grape products in particular may be suspected. Production of Mediterranean crops and containers may have been the basis for elite socioeconomic power during EB II.

Fortifications are the best-known aspect of EB II architecture and were comprised of wall, gate, and tower systems. More than three-dozen fortified sites developed during the course of the period, including Ai, Arad, Tell el-Farʿah (North), Beth-Yeraḥ, and Aphek. Other social architecture includes administrative buildings whose functions are unclear. "Palaces" have been claimed at Arad and Megiddo but lack unequivocal evidence of being elite residences. Religious architecture is better known, with temples found at Ai, Beth-Yeraḥ, Megiddo, and Arad. EB II domestic architecture is based around the broadroom module, the "Arad house," and its variants. Modules are linked with subsidiary structures into compounds, suggesting extended household groups, and also into urban blocks separated by streets. The architectural evidence suggests only weakly developed political institutions during EB II. Economically powerful kin or domestic groups may have been the source of EB II urban planning and civic authority.

The transition from EB II to III is unclear. Ceramic criteria marking this transition were regional, notably the appearance of Khirbet Kerak or Red-Black Burnished Wares in the north and the disappearance of the EB II assemblage known at Arad in the south. The EB III was a period of hypercentralization in the southern Levant. Surveys suggest that the rural component of society was absorbed into urban sites at the beginning of EB III. Many important EB II urban sites did not continue into EB III, including Tell el-Farʿah

(North), Aphek, and Arad. New fortified sites were also founded in Judah and the Shephelah and on the coastal plain, such as Tell Beit Mirsim, Tell Poran, and Tell Nagila. The settlement landscape of the arid zones also changed significantly, with a sharp decline in the number of sites.

Remaining sites become physically larger and were enhanced with fortification systems, with the best examples being Tel Yarmut and Ai. These defenses suggest that society had become more competitive and more violent after about 2700 BCE, and that the ability of urban institutions to mobilize labor was greater than before. Another feature of the urban landscape was the appearance of new urban institutions, notably temples and possibly "palaces." The similarities of temples at Megiddo and Khirbet Zeraqun, comprised of circular altars surrounded by rectangular buildings, suggest a common model. Tel Yarmut provides the best example of a complex or an insula. It is enclosed by a temenos wall and contains large structures and production facilities, interpreted by the excavators as the remains of a palace. The Building with Circles at Beth-Yeraḥ, probably a public granary, also indicates administered redistribution or social storage. During EB III social, political, economic, and religious power were highly centralized at increasingly large urban sites, and rural social institutions and settlements declined correspondingly.

Traditionally ascribed to invading "Amorites," and more recently to climatic fluctuations, the end of EB III has been reinterpreted, particularly as details of the EB IV period become better known. [*See* Amorites.] Some evidence suggests a long-term trend toward desiccation; the EB II and III reliance of urban sites on specialized agricultural production of Mediterranean crops would have made sites vulnerable to climatic change. The abandonment of EB III urban sites is not precisely dated but took place over a long period. Supporting this is the continuation during EB IV of a remnant form of urbanism at lightly fortified sites located on the eastern side of the Dead Sea, such as Khirbet Iskander, Tell Iktanu, and Ader. With village-level occupations in the Mediterranean core, including at formerly urban sites, this may be evidence of less catastrophic collapse than once postulated.

The EB IV period began in about 2300 BCE. Once a "dark age" in the settlement history of the southern Levant—attributed to an influx of Semitic speakers from the north—collapse processes now appear to have been largely internal. The EB IV is also described as a pastoral-nomadic interlude, with cities abandoned and settlement shifting back into arid zones. [*See* Pastoral Nomadism.] There was a tremendous increase in settlement in arid regions, but the village component of society was also becoming better known. Most urban tell sites were abandoned, but at many of them (e.g., Megiddo, Hazor, Beth-Shean, Jericho) damaged remains of EB IV village occupations have been found. The discovery of villages such as Naḥal Rephaim outside of Jerusalem, Naḥal Alexander on the coastal plain, and Shaʿar ha-Golan in the Jordan Valley indicate that sedentary agricultural settlement and production were reconstituted in EB IV. Sites in the arid zones (Be'er Resisim, ʿEin-Ziq) reflect a mobile component of society emphasizing pastoral production—possibly making rounds between the central hill country and perhaps even occupying larger sites in the Negev highlands year-round.

Among the best-known features of the EB IV are the massive cemeteries, often consisting of hundreds or thousands of shaft tombs dug into bedrock, such as Jebel Qaʿaqir near Hebron and ʿAin es-Samiyeh in Samaria. [*See* Tombs.] These cemeteries were used for disarticulated, secondary burials and were reopened when necessary by kin or extended family groups on their seasonal return to the central hills and by agriculturalists residing in nearby villages. Site plans suggest that at arid-zone sites kinship organization was reasserted as the primary form of production and authority, with headmen leading extended domestic groups.

In the Early Bronze Age, the southern Levant was generally a social and cultural backwater. The EB IV period is the height of literate, urban society in Syria, however, with sites like Ebla exerting sociopolitical and economic hegemony over large areas. Akkadian and Ur III interest in Syria had no impact on the southern Levant. Relations with inland Syria and the northern Levant are only attested by the appearance of true tin-bronze and by caliciform ceramic wares, typical at inland Syrian sites such as Hama and Ebla.

Middle Bronze Age. The urban climax of the Bronze Age in the southern Levant took place in the Middle Bronze Age. Renewed urbanism, based on a Syrian model—emulating its material culture, architecture, and perhaps social organization and literacy—is an example of secondary state reformation of sufficient strength and integration to have controlled Lower Egypt for more than a century during the "Hyksos" period. For the first time, sites in the southern Levant were attested in Syrian and Mesopotamian documents, and Egyptian evidence indicates a higher level of development and interaction than the fragmentary and cryptic references from the third millennium. The Middle Bronze Age remains paradoxical because it is difficult to explain the wholesale adoption of Syrian and northern Levantine cultural patterns in the south. Scholars have suggested the influx of one or more waves of migrating or conquering Amorites, but this no longer appears to be an adequate explanation. A series of factors that led to reurbanization on a Syrian model can be enumerated: the migration of both fellow Semitic-speaking and Hurrian groups from north to south, local elites anxious to emulate foreign practices, and generally higher levels of economic interaction with Syria and with a newly reorganized Egypt.

The MB I began after 2000 BCE, and major shifts are evident in the settlement landscape. Village sites occupied during EB IV disappeared on the coastal plain and in the Jordan

Valley and the central hills country. The remnant urbanism on the eastern side of the Dead Sea also disappeared. Finally, settlement disappeared from the arid zones, and there is no evidence of MB occupation or utilization of the Negev and Sinai. A number of urban tell sites on the coastal plain and inland valleys were occupied in MB I (Tell Poleg, Tel Aphek, Tell Burga) and were fortified with characteristic wall and glacis or rampart systems early in the period. Farther inland, however, sites such as Shechem and Tel Dan were not fortified until later. While reurbanization spread quickly, those sites located on trade routes leading from Syria to Egypt were the first to fortify and assume fully urban status. Surveys also indicate many small villages and campsites, especially on the coastal plain.

MB pottery was largely derived from contemporary Syria. Only a few forms may have evolved from EB IV prototypes, such as platter bowls and small burnished juglets. Pottery was made on a fast wheel, with centrifugal force allowing the production of thinner and finer vessels than had been possible with the slow wheel or tournette during the third millennium. Bronze was used exclusively for tools and weapons, and texts indicate the shipment of tin from Mari to Hazor and Dan. Art objects include carved bone and ivory, ceramic and metal figurines, and cylinder seals, all similar to Syrian types. [*See* Seals.] Akkadian cuneiform writing is also found for the first time, indicating that ruling elites were literate, in communication with, and part of the cultural sphere of Syria and Mesopotamia. [*See* Literacy.] Contemporary Egyptian documents, in particular the story of Sinuhe and the Execration texts, reflect the development of sociopolitical organization. Sinuhe was an Egyptian official who fled to the southern Levant shortly after 2000 BCE and who describes a mobile lifestyle. The earlier set of Execration texts lists the names of several leaders in association with each site, indicating that political authority was not centered around individual rulers. Later Execration texts list only one person's name in association with individual sites.

The MB II and III periods represent the peak of urban development in the second millennium BCE. There was widespread settlement in the central hill country during MB II, as third-millennium tells were reoccupied and new locations settled. This settlement wave produced many fortified sites, some of which were cities and others fortresses or redoubts. Settlement geography suggests an increasingly competitive political landscape, perhaps as lowland elites fissioned and established their own sites. Like those of the EB III, fortification systems of the MB II and III were progressively enlarged by the addition of walls and ramparts. This style of fortification is characteristic of contemporary Syrian sites (Qatna, Ebla). Fortifications became so large they created the characteristic bowl shape of many large tells.

The most important MB II and III urban centers include Hazor, Shechem, and Megiddo. During this period Hazor reached its maximum extent of more than 80 ha (198 acres), and is the only site whose size rivals those in Syria. Complex internal organization also appears during this period, suggesting a variety of social institutions. At MB III Megiddo and Shechem there were large, fortified *migdal* temple structures—long rooms with an altar at one end and surrounded by thick walls. Smaller temples are known from such MB rural sites as Tell el-Ḥayyat, Tel Kitan, Nahariya, and Givʿat-Sharett. Curiously, MB II sites such as Megiddo and Shechem do not appear to have temples, suggesting that religious institutions waned temporarily; individualizing forms of worship, especially the veneration of ancestors buried below house floors, took precedence. The palaces at Tel Aphek, Megiddo, and Tel Seraʿ often adjoined temples and were complexes of rooms arrayed around large central courtyards. The examples from Tel Kabri are especially elaborate, with decorated plaster floors and Aegean-style wall paintings. [*See* Wall Paintings.] Urban planning is present during the Middle Bronze Age, as seen by the erection of fortification and gate systems and adjacent plazas and streets. MB domestic architecture at both rural and urban sites consisted of rectilinear courtyard houses, indicating agricultural and pastoral production by domestic units. Larger structures included more elaborate courtyard houses, suggesting class or wealth distinctions, and palaces. The architectural evidence reflects significant stratification and political authority not easily discerned in third-millennium evidence.

During MB II and III, sites with southern Levantine material culture, including Tell ed-Dabʿa, the Hyksos capital of Avaris, Tell el-Yahudiyeh, and Tell el-Maskhuta, flourished in the Nile Delta. *Hyksos,* an Egyptian term meaning "foreign rulers," were southern Levantine elites who had been in Egypt since the end of the third millennium, having come to power during a period of Egyptian weakness. Hyksos sites are known for their rampart fortifications and, at Tell ed-Dabʿa, temples and equid burials, suggesting a military elite. Egyptian sources indicate that the Hyksos fifteenth dynasty ruled Egypt for more than a century and were eventually expelled in about 1540–1525 BCE by Ahmose I of the eighteenth dynasty. The Egyptians destroyed the Hyksos Delta sites and those on the southern coastal plain, in particular Tell el-ʿAjjul (probably the Hyksos capital, Sharuhen) and then exacted revenge on sites farther north. The complex series of destructions makes it difficult to understand the interval between the expulsion of the Hyksos and a renewed series of campaigns by Thutmosis III that marked the beginning of Egyptian imperial domination. [*See* Hyksos.]

Late Bronze Age. Though the height of internationalism, the Late Bronze Age was much diminished by Egyptian vengeance and then domination. The period represents an extreme concentration of wealth and power in the urban elites, at the expense of all other segments of society. It is difficult to determine archaeologically when the Late Bronze

Age began. The final destruction of the Hyksos in about 1525 BCE by Ahmose is a historical turning point. The campaigns of kings of the eighteenth dynasty, beginning with Thutmosis III (c. 1457 BCE), mark the beginning of aggressive efforts to dominate western Asia. The period from about 1450 to 1300 BCE, corresponding in part to the "Amarna age," saw Egyptians periodically moving north through the southern Levant on campaigns into Syria. The Amarna archive reflects conflict and intrigue among petty city-states of the southern Levant and their Egyptian overlords. [*See* Amarna Tablets.] After 1300 BCE, rulers of the nineteenth dynasty moved to control the southern Levant directly, engaging in conflict with the Hittites over boundaries between their respective empires. By 1225 BCE, the Hittites were no longer a threat. The kings of the twentieth dynasty were then forced to engage the "Sea Peoples" in battle, perhaps even in the Nile Delta itself. Egyptian control over the southern Levant declined swiftly after 1225 BCE and ended soon after, bringing the Late Bronze Age to a close.

A few sites escaped the initial Egyptian destructions at the end of MB III, and many others exhibit a gap in occupation until about 1450 BCE. Other decisive changes suggest that LB society never fully recovered. Few, if any, LB sites are fortified, and virtually the entire rural component of society disappeared. The disposition of the rural component is a major outstanding question for scholars. One suggestion is that they became mobile pastoralists who have thus far been invisible to archaeologists. Some recovery of urban society occurred after 1400 BCE, with much-reduced settlements lodged within the areas configured by MB fortifications. MB material culture continued, albeit increasingly impoverished in style and execution. LB pottery styles were derived directly from MB types; only minor decorations and Egyptian-influenced shapes were new. Imported pottery from Cyprus and the Aegean constituted the fine ware of the period. Bronze metallurgy continued, with copper imported from Cyprus and tin probably from southern Anatolia.

Many MB institutional features continued into the Late Bronze Age. Temples are well attested, with multiple examples found at Hazor, Megiddo, Beth-Shean, and Lachish. Some include Egyptian elements, reflecting the deep Egyptian cultural influence, but more generally they reflect Syrian design and practice. Temples were elaborate, often tripartite in design, and decorated with carved orthostats and statues of deities. Palaces were separated from temples (such as the long series at Megiddo) and consisted of rooms around a central courtyard. Numerous imports and luxury goods, such as carved ivories, indicate the wealth of the ruling elites. Cuneiform literacy is attested by the Amarna archives and by a few tablet finds. A number of other elite residential complexes are known (e.g., at Ashdod, Tell el-ʿAjjul, Tell Beit Mirsim), consisting of multiple rooms around courtyards. A final type of elite structure was the square brick Egyptian "governor's residence," found after 1300 BCE at Tell Jemmeh, Tel Seraʿ, Beth-Shean, and possibly Tell es-Saʿidiyeh. The variety of elite structures indicates the growth of institutional power during the Late Bronze Age. Domestic architecture is more poorly known and again consisted of courtyard houses. At urban sites, domestic architecture and planning were placed between palace and temple precincts.

While culturally much diminished from the Middle Bronze Age, the Late Bronze Age did see a number of innovations that set the stage for important later developments. Akkadian cuneiform remained the primary writing form, but the alphabet was also being pioneered. The Proto-Sinaitic or Proto-Canaanite script, parent to the Hebrew and Phoenician alphabets, is found on a small number of inscriptions, mostly votives, and varied in the number of letters and direction. [*See* Proto-Canaanite.] A small number of inscriptions in the simplified cuneiform alphabet used at Ugarit are also found. The plastic arts, such as ivory and seal carving, were influenced by both Egyptian and Syrian styles, reflecting an international exchange of ideas and artisans. International trade reached its zenith, with a range of goods (metals, foodstuffs, wines, oils, art objects) and artisans moving across western Asia and the eastern Mediterranean. The ability of the southern Levant to participate in this trade, despite its diminished state, reflects the concentration of wealth and power.

The breakdown of LB society came swiftly. Tied to both the Egyptian Empire and the international economy, the southern Levant was pulled down along with the rest of western Asia after 1200 BCE. With the collapse of the Egyptian and Hittite Empires for internal reasons and the appearance of the Sea Peoples as a threat to parts of the eastern Mediterranean, including the coast of the southern Levant, the city-state structure of the southern Levant also collapsed. Some sites, such as Megiddo, persisted as independent city-states after 1200 BCE, while others were destroyed in internecine warfare. The subsequent Iron Age, while continuing certain aspects of Bronze Age material culture, such as its ceramic styles, was marked by new technologies and an entirely new sociopolitical and ethnic configuration, notably the rise of national states.

[*See also* Fortifications, *article on* Fortifications of the Bronze and Iron Ages; Palace; *and* Temples, *article on* Syro-Palestinian Temples. *In addition, most of the sites mentioned are the subject of independent entries.*]

BIBLIOGRAPHY

Early Bronze Age

Amiran, Ruth. "The Transition from the Chalcolithic to Early Bronze Age." In *Biblical Archaeology Today: Proceedings of the International Congress on Biblical Archaeology, Jerusalem, April 1984*, edited by Janet Amitai, pp. 108–112. Jerusalem, 1985.

Ben-Tor, Amnon. "The Relations between Egypt and the Land of Ca-

naan during the Third Millennium B.C." *Journal of Jewish Studies* 33 (1982): 3–18.
Ben-Tor, Amnon. "The Trade Relations of Palestine in the Early Bronze Age." *Journal of the Economic and Social History of the Orient* 29 (1986): 1–27.
Ben-Tor, Amnon. "New Light on the Relations between Egypt and Southern Palestine during the Early Bronze Age." *Bulletin of the American Schools of Oriental Research,* no. 281 (1991): 3–10.
Esse, Douglas. "Secondary State Formation and Collapse in Early Bronze Age Palestine." In *L'urbanisation de la Palestine à l'âge du Bronze ancien: Bilan et perspectives des recherches actuelles; Actes du Colloque d'Emmaüs, 20–24 octobre 1986,* edited by Pierre de Miroschedji, pp. 81–96. British Archaeological Reports, International Series, no. 527. Oxford, 1989.
Esse, Douglas. *Subsistence, Trade, and Social Change in Early Bronze Age Palestine.* Studies in Ancient Oriental Civilization, no. 50. Chicago, 1991.
Gophna, Ram. "The Settlement Landscape of Palestine in the Early Bronze Age II–III and Middle Bronze Age II." *Israel Exploration Journal* 34 (1984): 24–31.
Gophna, Ram. "The Contacts between 'En Besor Oasis, Southern Canaan, and Egypt during the Late Predynastic and the Threshold of the First Dynasty: A Further Assessment." In *The Nile Delta in Transition: Fourth–Third Millennium B.C.,* edited by Edwin C. M. van den Brink, pp. 385–394. Tel Aviv, 1992.
Joffe, Alexander H. *Settlement and Society in the Early Bronze I and II, Southern Levant: Complementarity and Contradiction in a Small-Scale Complex Society.* Sheffield, 1993.
Ward, William A. "Early Contacts between Egypt, Canaan, and Sinai: Remarks on the Paper by Amnon Ben-Tor." *Bulletin of the American Schools of Oriental Research,* no. 281 (1991): 11–26.

Middle Bronze Age

Bienkowski, Piotr. "The Division of Middle Bronze IIB-C in Palestine." *Levant* 21 (1989): 169–179.
Broshi, Magen, and Ram Gophna. "Middle Bronze Age II Palestine: Its Settlements and Population." *Bulletin of the American Schools of Oriental Research,* no. 261 (1986): 73–90.
Dever, William G. "The Middle Bronze Age: The Zenith of the Urban Canaanite Era." *Biblical Archaeologist* 50 (1987): 148–177.
Dever, William G. "Hyksos, Egyptian Destructions, and the End of the Palestinian Middle Bronze Age." *Levant* 22 (1990): 75–81.
Dever, William G. "The Chronology of Syria-Palestine in the Second Millennium B.C.E.: A Review of Current Issues." *Bulletin of the American Schools of Oriental Research,* no. 288 (1992): 1–25.
Finkelstein, Israel. "Middle Bronze Age 'Fortifications': A Reflection of Social Organization and Political Formations." *Tel Aviv* 19.2 (1992): 201–220.
Gerstenblith, Patty. *The Levant at the Beginning of the Middle Bronze Age.* American Schools of Oriental Research, Dissertation Series, no. 5. Cambridge, Mass., 1983.
Hoffmeier, J. K. "Reconsidering Egypt's Part in the Termination of the Middle Bronze Age in Palestine." *Levant* 21 (1989): 181–193.
Kochavi, Moshe, et al. "Aphek-Antipatris, Tēl Pōlēg, Tēl Zerōr, and Tēl Burgā: Four Fortified Sites of the Middle Bronze IIA in the Sharon Plain." *Zeitschrift des Deutschen Palästina-Vereins* 95 (1979): 121–165.
Weinstein, James M. "Egyptian Relations with Palestine in the Middle Kingdom." *Bulletin of the American Schools of Oriental Research,* no. 217 (1975): 1–16.
Weinstein, James M. "The Chronology of Palestine in the Early Second Millennium B.C.E." *Bulletin of the American Schools of Oriental Research,* no. 288 (1992): 27–46.

Late Bronze Age

Ahituv, Shmuel. "Economic Factors in the Egyptian Conquest of Canaan." *Israel Exploration Journal* 28 (1978): 93–105.
Dever, William G. "The Late Bronze–Early Iron I Horizon in Syria-Palestine: Egyptians, Canaanites, 'Sea Peoples,' and Proto-Israelites." In *The Crisis Years: The Twelfth Century B.C., from beyond the Danube to the Tigris,* edited by William A. Ward and Martha Sharp Joukowsky, pp. 99–110. Dubuque, 1992.
Finkelstein, Israel. "The Emergence of Israel: A Phase in the Cyclic History of Canaan in the Third and Second Millennia BCE." In *From Nomadism to Monarchy: Archaeological and Historical Aspects of Early Israel,* edited by Israel Finkelstein and Nadav Na'aman, pp. 150–178. Jerusalem and Washington, D.C., 1994.
Gonen, Rivka. "Urban Canaan in the Late Bronze Period." *Bulletin of the American Schools of Oriental Research,* no. 253 (1984): 61–73.
Gonen, Rivka. *Burial Patterns and Cultural Diversity in Late Bronze Age Canaan.* American Schools of Oriental Research, Dissertation Series, no. 7. Winona Lake, Ind., 1992.
Leonard, Albert, Jr. "The Late Bronze Age." *Biblical Archaeologist* 52 (1989): 4–39.
Na'aman, Nadav. "Economic Aspects of the Egyptian Occupation of Canaan." *Israel Exploration Journal* 31 (1981): 172–185.
Ussishkin, David. "Level VII and VI at Tel Lachish and the End of the Bronze Age in Canaan." In *Palestine in the Bronze and Iron Ages: Papers in Honour of Olga Tufnell,* edited by Jonathan N. Tubb, pp. 213–228. University of London, Institute of Archaeology, Occasional Publication, no. 11, London, 1985.
Weinstein, James M. "The Egyptian Empire in Palestine: A Reassessment." *Bulletin of the American Schools of Oriental Research,* no. 241 (1981): 1–28.
Weinstein, James M. "The Collapse of the Egyptian Empire in the Southern Levant." In *The Crisis Years: The Twelfth Century B.C., from beyond the Danube to the Tigris,* edited by William A. Ward and Martha Sharp Joukowsky, pp. 142–150. Dubuque, 1992.

ALEXANDER H. JOFFE

Palestine in the Iron Age

The archaeology of Iron Age Palestine covers most of the period of the Hebrew Bible, from the Israelite settlement until the Babylonian conquest of Jerusalem. To a large extent, the term *biblical archaeology* relates to this period, a field that has inspired extensive research that has, in turn, produced rich and varied data. The mutual relationship between the archaeological data and the biblical texts is one of the crucial methodological problems faced by archaeologists and historians of the period. [*See* Biblical Literature, *article on* Hebrew Scriptures.]

Chronological Framework and Terminology. The Iron Age in Palestine is defined archaeologically as the period that follows the Late Bronze Age (c. 1200 BCE) and terminates with the Babylonian conquests of Philistia and Judah (the latter in 586 BCE). There are, however, alternative proposals concerning the beginning, end, and inner division of this chronological framework, samples of which are provided in figure 1. Some Israeli scholars employ the term *Israelite period* instead of Iron Age. In the following discussion the terminology used is Iron Age I for the twelfth–elev-

PALESTINE: Iron Age. Figure 1. *Comparison of Iron Age Chronologies*

William Foxwell Albright (*The Archaeology of Palestine,* 1949, Harmondsworth, Middlesex, rev. 1960)

Iron Age I	Twelfth–tenth century BCE
Iron Age II	Ninth–beginning of the sixth century BCE
Iron Age III	550-333 BCE

Yohanan Aharoni and Ruth Amiran ("A New Scheme for the Subdivision of the Iron Age in Palestine," *IEJ* 8 [1958]: 016015-016015)

Iron Age I	1200-1000 BCE
Iron Age II	1000-840
Iron Age III	840-586

Philip J. King (*American Archaeology in the Mideast,* Philadelphia, 1983)

Iron Age I	1200-930 BCE
Iron Age IIA	930-721
Iron Age IIB	721-605
Iron Age IIC	605-539

***The Encyclopedia of Archaeological Excavations in the Holy Land* (edited by Michael Avi-Yonah and Ephraim Stern, Jerusalem, 1976)**

Iron Age IA	1200-1150 BCE
Iron Age IB	1150-1000
Iron Age IIA	1000-900
Iron Age IIB	900-800
Iron Age IIC	800-586

***The New Encyclopedia of Archaeological Excavations in the Holy Land* (edited by Ephraim Stern, Jerusalem and New York, 1993)**

Retains the divisions of the earlier encyclopedia, except that the date 800 BCE for the end of Iron IIB was lowered to 700 BCE

Amihai Mazar (*Archaeology of the Land of the Bible,* New York, 1990)

Iron IA	1200-1150 BCE
Iron IB	1150-1000
Iron IIA	1000-925
Iron IIB	925-720
Iron IIC	720-586

Gabriel Barkai (*The Archaeology of Ancient Israel,* edited by Amnon Ben-Tor, New Haven, 1992)

Iron Age IIa	Tenth and ninth centuries BCE
Iron Age IIb	Eighth century
Iron Age IIIa	Seventh century until 586.
Iron Age IIIb	586 until the late sixth century

enth centuries and Iron Age II for the tenth–sixth centuries, disregarding further subdivisions.

Iron Age I (1200–1000 BCE). The first two centuries of the Iron Age are characterized by the disintegration of the Late Bronze Age socioeconomic and political structure and its gradual replacement by a new social organization. The latter was related to the appearance of new ethnic groups bearing individual national and religious identities: the Israelites, the "Sea Peoples" (among them the Philistines), the nations of Transjordan (Ammonites, Moabites, Edomites), the Arameans, and the descendents of the Canaanites, called Phoenicians by both the Greeks and modern scholars. [*See* Philistines; Transjordan, *article on* Transjordan in the Bronze and Iron Ages; Ammon; Moab; Edom; Arameans; *and* Phoenicians.] These ethnic entities did not appear simultaneously, and their impact on the cultural development in Palestine during this period was diverse. Several major trends characterize this era: the decline of international trade; the appearance of new modes in pottery manufacture, architecture, and other aspects of material culture; the emergence of new technologies (particularly the use of iron); and distinct regionalism in the material culture.

Demise of Egyptian hegemony. During the first part of its twentieth dynasty, Egypt retained control over the province of Canaan. Egyptian monuments, inscriptions, pottery, and burials in anthropomorphic coffins are evidence of the continuation of this domination at least until the reign of Rameses VI. Beth-Shean continued to serve as an Egyptian administrative center, as demonstrated by a group of monuments and inscriptions dating to the time of Rameses III, including a full-sized statue of this pharaoh. [*See* Beth-Shean.] Finds at other sites, such as Akko, Megiddo, Lachish, Gezer, Tel Sera', Tell el-Far'ah (South) and the copper mines at Timna', demonstrate the continuity of an Egyptian presence on the coastal and inner plains of the country during the first part of the twelfth century BCE. [*See* Akko; Megiddo; Lachish; Gezer; Sera', Tel; Far'ah, Tell el- (South), Timna' (Negev).] The demise of Egyptian occupation most likely occurred during the reign of Rameses VI, or slightly afterward, when the Egyptian town at Beth-Shean was violently destroyed by fire.

Continuity of Canaanite culture. Although Hazor, the largest Canaanite city, was destroyed in the thirteenth century BCE, other Canaanite cities, such as Lachish (stratum VI) and Megiddo (stratum VIIA), survived well into the twelfth century BCE. [*See* Hazor.] Destructions in the mid-twelfth century BCE, perhaps related to the decline of Egyptian control and the appearance of new ethnic groups (Sea Peoples and Israelites), devastated those cities. While some (e.g., Hazor, Lachish) did not recover for some time, the finds excavated at others reflect a thriving Canaanite culture. The best example is Megiddo (stratum VI) where Canaanite urban life flourished until the late eleventh century BCE. Similarly, a viable Canaanite culture continued on the Plain of

Akko (Akko, Tell Keisan), gradually developing into what can be defined as the Phoenician culture. Canaanites probably persisted as a significant component of the population throughout the country, although their previous mode of urban life was disrupted, and many probably integrated gradually into the new ethnic elements. [*See* Canaanites; Keisan, Tell.]

Sea Peoples. The invasion and settlement of the Sea Peoples is documented by Egyptian and biblical sources, as well as by archaeological evidence. The battles of the Sea Peoples against Rameses III in his eighth regnal year did not appear to have much impact on Palestine, as they probably took place in Lebanon and Egypt. However, the settlement of Sea Peoples, and particularly of the Philistines, is well documented in the archaeological record. The development of the Philistine material culture has been investigated at the principal Philistine cities (Ashdod, Ashkelon, Ekron/Tel Miqne), as well as at peripheral sites (Tell Qasile, Gezer, Timnah/Tel Batash, Tel Sera', Tell el-Far'ah [South]). The Philistines maintained a vital urban culture that combined elements brought from their Aegean homeland with local Canaanite and Egyptian components. Philistia was one of the few regions in the entire Levant where an urban system, including fortifications, temples, and public buildings, thrived in the twelfth–eleventh centuries BCE; cities like Miqne/Ekron reached an area of 20 ha (50 acres). The earliest phase of Philistine pottery was a local variation of the Mycenaean IIIC:1b style. Subsequently, this ware absorbed Canaanite, Egyptian, and Cypriot motifs and forms, developing into an eclectic style (the Philistine Bichrome ware). Philistine clay figurines retained Aegean traditions, and some of the seals are inscribed with a unique, still undeciphered linear script. [*See* Philistines; Ashdod; Ashkelon; Miqne, Tel; Qasile, Tell; Batash, Tel; *and* Ceramics, *article on* Syro-Palestinian Ceramics of the Neolithic, Bronze, and Iron Ages.]

Israelites. The Israelite settlement in the hill country of central Palestine and in the Galilee is archaeologically well attested. Intensive surface surveys have revealed hundreds of small sites founded during Iron I in these regions. A limited number of excavations (at Dan, Hazor, Sasa, Ḥorvat Ḥarashim, the Bull Site, Mt. Ebal, Shiloh, Ai, Khirbet Raddanah, and Giloh) provide data about the nature of the material culture at these sites. The central hill country was the heartland of the settlement process, in territories allocated to the Israelite tribes of Manasseh, Ephraim, and Benjamin. In many cases, the settlements were established on harsh terrain, far from water sources and often in the heart of the hilly woodland. This was a "frontier zone," practically unsettled by the Canaanites of the Late Bronze Age. The new pattern of settlement in these regions reflects the social, economic, environmental, and perhaps ideological factors that distinguished the emerging Israelite society. It appears that this was a sedentary, rural, self-sufficient society that placed an emphasis on familial and tribal relationships. The settlements are usually small and unfortified and display an unsophisticated material culture, although based largely on Canaanite traditions. Somewhat different settlement patterns have been found in the northern Negev desert (Tel Masos) and foothills ('Izbet Ṣarṭah), however. [*See* Dan; Bull Site; Ebal, Mount; Shiloh; Ai; Raddanah; Giloh; Masos, Tel; *and* 'Izbet Ṣarṭah.]

The origin of the settlers in the hill country has been interpreted in various ways. One school of thought pictures this population as local, indigenous peoples, either pastoralists who changed their way of life or farmers who fled to the mountains from the lowlands of Canaan. Another approach claims that the settlers were seminomadic pastoralists who penetrated the country's borders. Still others postulate a complex process in which population groups of the above-suggested origins, as well as immigrants infiltrating from regions north of Palestine, merged to create the new "Israelite" entity. In any event, the archaeological data are source materials for studying the origins of Israel presented in the biblical texts and in the single mention of "Israel" in Merneptah's victory stela (c. 1207 BCE).

Iron Age II (1000–586 BCE). Two key factors determined the material culture of the Iron II period in Palestine: the country's geopolitical history, and the influence of artistic and architectural trends common to the entire Levant. These two opposing trends are discernible in the period's archaeological record.

Israelite kingdoms. Intensive archaeological research has been carried out in the territories of the United Monarchy of David and Solomon, as well as in the realm of the divided monarchies of Judah and Israel. Excavations have been conducted at numerous and diverse sites: the main urban centers (Jerusalem, Samaria, Dan, Hazor, Megiddo, Jezreel, Dor, Gezer, Lachish); smaller towns and villages (Tel Kinnerot, 'Ein-Gev, Yoqne'am, Tel Qiri, Tirzah, Tell en-Naṣbeh, Timnah/Tel Batash, Beth-Shemesh, Tell Beit Mirsim, Tel Ḥalif, 'Ein-Gedi, Tel Sheva/Beersheba, Tel 'Ira, 'Aro'er); royal citadels (Arad, Ḥorvat 'Uza, Qadesh-Barnea); countryside palaces (Ramat Raḥel); desert shrines or cultic centers of worship (Kuntillet 'Ajrud, Qitmit); isolated fortresses and observation towers (Khirbet Abu Tuwein, French Hill [Jerusalem], Giloh); small farmsteads and caravanserais (Vered Jericho, Ḥorvat Shilhah, and various sites in the Judean desert and along the shores of the Dead Sea); and unique phenomena such as the short-lived wave of settlement (probably dating to the tenth century BCE) in the Negev highlands, which includes some fifty main structures ("citadels"), along with hundreds of houses and installations scattered over an extensive area. Surface surveys in many parts of the country round out the excavations by providing data on patterns of settlement in the Israelite territories. [*See* Jerusalem; Samaria; Jezreel; Dor; Lachish; 'Ein-Gev; Yoqne'am; Qiri, Tel; Naṣbeh, Tell en-; Beth Shemesh;

Beit Mirsim, Tell; ʿEin-Gedi; Beersheba; ʿIra, Tel; ʿAroʿer; Arad; Qadesh-Barnea; Ramat Raḥel; Kuntillet ʿAjrud; Qitmit, Ḥorvat; *and* Giloh.]

This extensive research has facilitated detailed studies of many aspects of the material culture, such as settlement patterns, comparative stratigraphy, town planning, architecture, pottery typology, technology, agriculture, industries, trade, religious practices, art, iconography, burial customs, metallurgy, metrology, and paleography. Attempts to reconstruct various aspects of Israelite society, such as demography and family structure, have been made utilizing this vast body of data. Relating these archaeological finds to the political, social, and cultural history of the period, based on the biblical texts as well as on extrabiblical written sources, poses a special challenge, however, often raising serious methodological problems.

Several historically attested military events during this period resulting in severe destructions serve as "datum points" for establishing absolute chronology, the most outstanding of which are David's conquests sometime after 1000 BCE (destruction of Megiddo VIA, Tell Qasile X, Dor); Shishak's conquests during his raid in Israel and the Negev five years after the death of Solomon, in 925 BCE (destruction of Beth-Shean, Tell ʿAmal, Megiddo IVB-VA, Gezer VIII, Tel Qasile VIII, Negev sites); the Assyrian conquest of the northern kingdom of Israel in 735 and 722 BCE (destructions at Dan, Hazor V, Megiddo IVA, Yoqneʿam, Samaria, and other sites); Sennacherib's invasion of Judah in 701 BCE (destruction of Lachish III, Tel Batash III, Tell Beit Mirsim A, Tel Sheva/Beersheba II, Arad VIII, and related sites); and the Babylonian conquest of Judah in 586 BCE (destruction of Jerusalem, ʿEin-Gedi, Ramat Raḥel, Lachish, ʿAroʿer, Arad VI, and other sites).

Material Culture. Only a few selected features of Israelite material culture can be highlighted here, among them the monumental, public architecture of royal Israelite cities. These cities are distinguished by large-scale, meticulous planning, such as evidenced at the royal enclosures at Samaria, Jezreel, Ramat Raḥel, and Lachish, as well as at the sanctuary at Dan. Architectural decoration included the use of ashlar masonry, proto-Aeolic, or "palmette," capitals, and carved windows. These features have been considered typically "Israelite" by some scholars, yet they were probably shared by Israel's neighbors and even invented by Phoenician artists (although this cannot be unequivocably proven). The use of squared-off monolithic pillars became a very common feature in both public structures (storehouses and stables) and private dwellings.

Urban fortifications included both casemate (or double) and solid walls, as well as city gates with two to six chambers, sometimes with an outer gate. These architectural features appear from the reign of Solomon until the end of the monarchy. Although it has been proposed that an inner development and typology exists for these characteristics, there is no consensus on the point. Water-supply projects constitute one of the most enterprising and impressive remains of the period, including shafts and tunnels leading to springs outside the cities or to the underground water table. Aqueducts are rare, the best known being Hezekiah's tunnel in Jerusalem, a unique engineering venture that demonstrates sophisticated hydrological ingenuity. [*See* Water Tunnels.]

Settlement patterns. An important factor in understanding this period is the settlements' spatial distribution and hierarchy. In this respect, the growth of Jerusalem during the eighth–seventh centuries BCE in relation to the rest of Judah is significant; the size of Jerusalem in the eighth–seventh centuries is estimated at 60 ha (150 acres), while most other towns in Judah did not exceed 2–3 ha (5–8 acres). [*See* Judah; Demography.] Thus, the capital became a megalopolis, with a complex, centralized economic, political, and religious system. Jerusalem's agricultural hinterland consisted of many small villages and farmsteads, which enlarged the area of arable land by constructing cultivation terraces on the hillsides.

Religion and cult. What is known of Israelite religious practices comes from two excavated shrines (Arad and Dan), several inscriptions, and numerous clay figurines and other art forms. The central Israelite Temple in Jerusalem is known, only from its description in the Bible (*1 Kgs.* 6–7), which is sufficient to show that its plan was largely akin to earlier and later tripartite temples throughout the Levant. [*See* Temples, *article on* Syro-Palestinian Temples.]

Epigraphy. Epigraphic finds (e.g., ostraca, seals, seal impressions) add important information concerning private names, administrative practices, economic activities, iconography, and even some specific historical events. [*See* Ostracon; Seals.] Some discoveries (such as the Khirbet el-Qom, Kuntillet ʿAjrud, and Ketef Hinnom inscriptions) are of great importance for reconstructing the development of ancient Israelite religion, as well as the history of the transmission of the biblical text. [*See* Qom, Khirbet el-; Ketef Hinnom.]

Other ethnic entities. Archaeological research into the Iron Age elucidates the culture of neighboring regions and other ethnic entities, such as the city-states of Philistia, the nations of Transjordan, and the Phoenicians.

In Philistia, excavations at Ashdod, Ashkelon, and Ekron/Tel Miqne have shed light on the flourishing urban material culture of these city-states in Iron II. They reveal massive fortifications, public buildings, and industries. Their pottery indicates local traditions, which means that a regional material culture was created with its own ethnic and geopolitical affinities (now being called Neo-Philistine). These city-states developed at different rates. Thus, the spurt of growth experienced by Ashdod in the tenth century BCE appears to have allowed it to overtake the role played by the dwindling town of Ekron. The latter, however, expanded to the size of almost 30 ha (75 acres) in the seventh century BCE, when it became a center of olive oil production. Trade relations with Egypt, Greece, Transjordan, and Phoenicia are reflected in the archaeological record, such as the finds from Meṣad Ḥashavyahu on the coast, due west of Tel Miqne/Ekron. [*See* Meṣad Ḥashavyahu.] Severe destructions uncovered at Ekron, Timnah, and Ashkelon mark the Babylonian conquest of Philistia between 605–600 BCE.

The Plain of Akko is by and large the southern extremity of the Phoenician entity, which stretches northward along the Mediterranean coast. At sites such as Achziv, Tel Kabri, Tell Keisan, Tell Abu Hawam, and Dor, the distinctive Phoenician material culture is well represented. [*See* Achziv; Kabri, Tel; Abu Hawam, Tell.] It is particularly well known from the rich cemeteries at Achziv, where different burial customs (rock-cut and ashlar-built chamber tombs and cremations) reflect varying cultural influences. [*See* Burial Techniques.] Phoenician pottery traditions and art are known both from Phoenicia itself and from the objects it exported to Israel, such as the Phoenician ivories found at Samaria, which are a superb example of costly Phoenician art objects. Phoenician influence is also represented in the iconography of many Israelite seals.

The culture of the Moabites, Ammonites, and Edomites in Transjordan is much less known from that of the Israelites, although in recent years important advances have been made in this field. Ammonite tomb groups, watchtowers, seals, and inscriptions, dating mainly to the eight–seventh centuries BCE, have been discovered. The land of Moab has been explored by intensive surface surveys, as well as in excavations at such key sites as Ḥesban (Heshbon) and Dibon; the Moabite stone remains the most important discovery from this region. [*See* Ḥesban; Dibon; Moabite Stone.] Surveys and excavations at several sites in Edom (Buṣeirah, Tawilan, Umm el-Biyara, Tell el-Kheleifeh, and others) provide data concerning settlement history as well as local pottery styles. [*See* Buṣeirah; Tawilan; Umm el-Biyara; Kheleifeh, Tell el-.] However, the majority of these discoveries date to the eight–seventh centuries BCE, so that the earlier part of the Iron Age remains enigmatic. Edomite activity in the ʿArabah and Negev is also known from excavations at Hatzevah and Ḥorvat Qitmit, where an Edomite shrine was uncovered.

Assyrian Domination. Evidence for Assyrian conquests in Palestine after 732 BCE and for Assyrian domination of large parts of the country until about 630 BCE, has been found at various sites. The conquest of Lachish by Sennacherib is illustrated by a unique combination of biblical and Assyrian texts, monumental Assyrian reliefs, and archaeological discoveries at the site, including the only excavated Assyrian siege ramp. Assyrian governmental buildings found at Megiddo (stratum III) and other places, as well as Assyrian objects found at various sites such as Gezer, constitute evidence of local Assyrian administrative centers. A series of sites in the northern Negev (Tell Jemmeh, Tel Seraʿ, Tel Haror, Ruqeish) has produced Assyrian architectural complexes and a variety of objects, indicating a particularly intense Assyrian presence in this region, close to the southern border of Palestine, possibly related to the Assyrian conquest of Egypt. [*See* Jemmeh, Tell; Haror, Tel.]

Conclusion. The archaeology of Iron Age Palestine (including Transjordan) has yielded a vast body of rich and varied information on many aspects of life in the country's various geopolitical zones. The integration of the archaeological data with the biblical and extrabiblical written sources provides a sound basis for reconstructing the material culture, social structure, economy, and technology of the Israelites and their neighbors during most of the period recorded in the Hebrew Bible.

[*See also* Israelites.]

BIBLIOGRAPHY

Only a few selected general books and articles are listed here, out of the many hundreds of publications devoted to this period. The reader will find additional references in the works cited below.

Aharoni, Miriam, and Yohanan Aharoni. "The Stratification of Judahite Sites in the Eighth and Seventh Centuries BCE." *Bulletin of the American Schools of Oriental Research*, no. 224 (1976): 73–90. Proposed relative stratigraphy at Judahite sites.

Aharoni, Yohanan, and Ruth Amiran. "A New Scheme for the Subdivision of the Iron Age in Palestine." *Israel Exploration Journal* 8 (1958): 171–184. Proposed subdivision of the period.

Aharoni, Yohanan. *The Archaeology of the Land of Israel*. Philadelphia, 1982. Discussion of the period based largely on the author's own work (see pp. 153–279).

Bienkowski, Piotr, ed. *Early Edom and Moab: The Beginning of the Iron Age in Southern Jordan*. Sheffield, 1992. Collection of essays on the history and archaeology of Transjordan in the Iron Age.

Biran, Avraham, and Joseph Aviram, eds. *Biblical Archaeology Today, 1990: Proceedings of the Second International Congress on Biblical Archaeology, Jerusalem, June–July 1990*. Jerusalem, 1993. Articles summarizing a session dedicated to the Iron Age II (see pp. 34–115).

Dever, William G. "The Late Bronze–Early Iron I Horizon in Syria-Palestine: Egyptians, Canaanites, 'Sea Peoples,' and Proto-Israelites." In *The Crisis Years: The Twelfth Century B.C., from beyond the Danube to the Tigris*, edited by William A. Ward and Martha Sharp Joukowsky, pp. 99–110. Dubuque, 1992. Cultural features of the transition from the Late Bronze to the Iron Age.

Dothan, Trude. *The Philistines and Their Material Culture*. New Haven, 1982. The most comprehensive work on the subject.

Finkelstein, Israel. *The Archaeology of the Israelite Settlement*. Jerusalem, 1988. Summary and discussion of the archaeological data related to the Israelite settlement.

Gitin, Seymour, and William G. Dever, eds. *Recent Excavations in Israel: Studies in Iron Age Archaeology*. Annual of the American Schools of Oriental Research, 49. Winona Lake, Ind., 1989. Articles on discoveries relating to the Iron Age in Palestine.

Kempinski, Aharon, and Ronny Reich, eds. *The Architecture of Ancient Israel: From the Prehistoric to the Persian Periods*. Jerusalem, 1992. Articles by various authors on town planning and architectural forms of the period (see pp. 183–309).

Kenyon, Kathleen M. *Royal Cities of the Old Testament*. New York, 1971. Review of the main discoveries in the key urban centers of the kingdoms of Israel and Judah.

Mazar, Amihai. *Archaeology of the Land of the Bible, 10,000–586 B.C.E.* New York, 1990. Comprehensive survey in the framework of a general textbook on the archaeology of Palestine (see pp. 295–550).

Mazar, Amihai, and Gabriel Barkay. "The Iron Age." In *The Archaeology of Ancient Israel*, edited by Amnon Ben-Tor, pp. 258–373. New Haven, 1992. Comprehensive survey of the period in the framework of a general textbook on the archaeology of Palestine.

Sauer, James A. "Transjordan in the Bronze and Iron Ages: A Critique of Glueck's Synthesis." *Bulletin of the American Schools of Oriental Research,* no. 263 (1986): 1–26. Summary and discussion of the finds in Transjordan.

Shiloh, Yigal. *The Proto-Aeolic Capital and Israelite Ashlar Masonry.* Qedem, vol. 11. Jerusalem, 1979. Analysis of ashlar masonry and architectural decoration in monumental Israelite masonry.

Stager, Lawrence E. "The Archaeology of the Family in Ancient Israel." *Bulletin of the American Schools of Oriental Research,* no. 260 (November 1985): 1–35. Discussion of archaeological phenomena as a reflection of social structure, particularly the family unit, in ancient Israel.

Stern, Ephraim, ed. *The New Encyclopedia of Archaeological Excavations in the Holy Land.* 4 vols. Jerusalem and New York, 1993. The most authoritative encyclopedia on the archaeology of ancient Palestine, including articles on all excavated sites relating to the period, written in most cases by the excavators; detailed bibliography.

AMIHAI MAZAR

Palestine in the Persian through Roman Periods

After the exile of the Judeans, Palestine fell into obscurity until the return of the exiles under Cyrus the Great in 539 BCE. For the more than a thousand years that followed, the area was administered by imperial powers: the Achaemenid Persian Empire, the Hellenistic Ptolemaic Egyptian and Seleucid Syrian dynasts of Macedonia who succeeded Alexander the Great, and the Roman Empire from Pompey (63 BCE) until the Islamic conquests of the seventh century CE. Until recently, archaeological knowledge of the Persian and Hellenistic periods was veiled in darkness, but exciting discoveries of papyri, coins, seals, and a few inscriptions have begun to provide new insights into the period, which is still basically known best from literary and documentary sources. The century of Jewish independence under the Hasmonean monarchs (167–63 BCE) has also yielded little information from archaeological exploration. In contrast, the archaeological sources for the Roman era are quite substantial and more than amply add to the extensive written sources for the period.

Persian period (539–332 BCE). After the catastrophic conquests by the Mesopotamian empires, Palestine went through a revival under Persian rule. With Cyrus's conquest of Babylon in 539 BCE, the adjacent territories were seized and the Judean exiles permitted to return to Jerusalem and rebuild their temple. [*See* Jerusalem.] The subsequent Egyptian campaign by Cambyses (525 BCE) suggests that political motives and propaganda were involved in the decision. After the uprisings and rebellion in the aftermath of the monarch's death, the rise of Darius to the throne may have instilled hopes in some segments of the population of a Davidic monarch governing the returning exiles in Judah. [*See* Judah.] Under the "governor" Zerubbabel, the grandson of King Jehoiachin, and a scion of the Davidic house, the rebuilding of the temple was completed, with the events recorded by Haggai and Zechariah (516–515 BCE). The next seventy-five years represent somewhat of a literary gap in the Hebrew Bible, casting darkness over the subsequent developments in the region, although the later biblical prophets do offer some vital details. The death of Darius in 486 BCE prompted revolts in Babylon and Egypt, and Judah may not have been unaffected by those events. [*See* Babylon.] A second wave of Judean exiles in the mid-fifth century BCE, under Ezra and Nehemiah, provide the next documented period, and the changes are notable. The previous messianic hopes were gone and the Judeans apparently were settled into life under Persian rule with native hierocratic viceroys supervising their activities. The earlier governors, between Zerubbabel and Nehemiah, remain a matter of speculation (cf. *Neh.* 5:15), as do most of those who subsequently served in this capacity. The recent recovery of a hoard of bullae from Jerusalem makes a partial reconstruction of the governing gap possible today, however (Avigad, 1976; Meyers, 1985).

Because Xerxes' campaign against Greece in 480/79 BCE ended in disaster, it is sometimes assumed that it initiated a period of decline in Persia. However, Persian sources for the period are dismal, forcing the historian to turn to Greek writers for any detailed information about the realm. Nonetheless, little credibility should be ascribed to the picture of a weak and tottering Persian regime contained in Xenophon and the Greek orators. Historical reason, not Greek rhetoric, should be the guide for the events of the fourth century. In spite of periodic revolts, Persian rule was maintained throughout most areas of its extensive domain, including Palestine, for another century and a half, until the Macedonian king Alexander the Great's conquest in 330 BCE. For Palestine, the Hebrew Bible provides a more positive perspective of Persia and the events of the period. These include the prophets Haggai, Zechariah, and Malachi, the Books of *Chronicles, Ezra,* and *Nehemiah,* and the more problematic *Book of Esther.*

It appears that the Persians basically maintained the administrative divisions of Palestine inherited from Neo-Assyrian imperialistic administration, even if subsequent events forced a number of changes in the organization of the region. [*See* Assyrians.] Palestine originally comprised only one part of the substantial territory of the "fifth satrapy," administered by the satrap, or governor *(pḥh),* of the province better known as "Babylon and Beyond the [Euphrates] River" *(Babili u Ebir Nari).* This title is last attested in 486 BCE, sometime after which the territory was divided into two provinces, Babylon and Beyond the River. The latter contained Palestine and the regions of Syria, Phoenicia, and Transjordan. Within Palestine itself, a number of subdistricts existed: Megiddo (or Galilee), Dor (the Carmel coast), and Samaria in the north and Judah, Ashdod (Philistia), and Idumea (Negev) in the south. [*See* Megiddo; Dor; Samaria; Ashdod; Negev.] Only Judah and Samaria are explicitly attested; the other divisions are presumed on the basis of the Neo-Assyrian organization of the region or later evidence. Each of these subdivisions of the satrapy was designated a province (Heb., *medinah*) under the rule of an official called a governor *(phh)*. If Judah is typical, there were also internal districts (Heb., *pelek*) within each of the provinces. Some remains of the administrative centers are known, such as a Persian throne from Samaria and the possible palace of the capital at Beth-Zur. [*See* Beth-Zur.]

Other regions may have been organized differently. Some scholars assume that the coast was comprised of a network of autonomous cities under the political jurisdiction of the Phoenician kings of Tyre and Sidon (excluding Akko and Gaza), but they initially may only have exercised certain economic rights and tax concessions in the area, without any political authority. [*See* Phoenicians; Tyre; Sidon.] By the fourth century BCE, however, there appear to be some changes in the system. The Shamunʿazar sarcophagus from Sidon indicates that the Phoenician king received Dor and Jaffa from the Persian king. [*See* Sarcophagus; Jaffa.] According to Pseudo-Scylax, Ashkelon the former capital of Ashdod, became a Tyrian colony with a royal palace. [*See* Ashkelon.] It is also difficult to ascertain how Samaria was internally organized. Between the time of Nehemiah and Alexander the Great, it was governed by the local native dynasty of Sanballat, but it is not clear how it was administered earlier. The population was of varied ethnic backgrounds as a result of an influx of Babylonians, Iranians, Elamites, and Arabs who settled in the region earlier. [*See* Babylonians; Elamites.] All are represented in the region's onomasticon. Recent excavations on M. Gerazim also reveal that the material culture was influenced by both Persia and Phoenicia, in spite of a strong local component. These early migrants appear to have extensively developed the countryside and established many new sites, including fortified towns, villages, and farms. In addition, the more sparely populated Negev of Palestine and southern Transjordan was under the control of the Qedarite Arab tribal confederation in the fifth century BCE, subsidized by Persia to maintain order in the region. Although centered in northern Arabia at Jauf, these Aramaic-speaking Arabs seem to have controlled the vast territory from Tell el-Maskhuta in the eastern Delta of Egypt across the Negev of Palestine to Transjordan, including the vital trade route between Gaza and ʿAqaba on the Red Sea. [*See* Maskhuta, Tell el-; Delta; ʿAqaba.] By the fourth century BCE, the situation had changed, with the Qedarite Arabs replaced by the Nabateans and a new province named Idumea attested for the Negev (Diodorus Siculus 19.94.7). [*See* Nabateans; Idumeans.] In sum, Judah was surrounded by different ethnic groups: Samaritans to the north, Ammonites to the east, Arabs to the south, and Sidonian and Tyrian merchants to the northwest.

Such ethnic and cultural diversity may help to explain the conservative reforms and transformation of the Jewish community under Ezra and Nehemiah. The latter's struggles with Geshem the Arab, Sanballat of Samaria, and Tyrian merchants resident in the city (*Neh.* 2:19, 6:1–6, 13:16) attest the internal divisions and ethnic tensions within Palestine. Some scholars even assume that Nehemiah freed Judah from prior dependency on Samaria, transforming it into a separate province. Emphasis on purity of language (*Neh.* 13:24), prohibitions against mixed marriages (*Ez.* 10; *Neh.* 10:31, 13:23–28), and the development of strict religious and cultural traditions may have been stimulated by this xenophobia. This ethnic diversity within Palestine is supported by the epigraphic finds in the region. Aramaic, the lingua franca of the Persian realm, was dominant throughout Palestine. [*See* Aramaic Language and Literature.] It is represented by scattered finds of ostraca at Akko, Yoqneʿam in the Galilee, Samaria, throughout Judah, and in the Negev. [*See* Ostracon; Akko; Yoqneʿam.] Phoenician inscriptions appear mainly along the coast, with only random finds inland. [*See* Phoenician-Punic.] From Dor, pottery incised with Greek and Phoenician was recently discovered. Finds of Edomite texts also continue to accumulate in the eastern Negev. In contrast, epigraphic texts in Hebrew are rare for the period.

Judah, however, is rich in other kinds of documentation. Coins of the Philisto-Arabian Attic type and standard were minted in Palestine during the Persian era, but Gaza no longer appears to be the center for the issues. The discovery, since the 1960s, of hundreds of new coins from Judea and Samaria have substantially expanded the existing numismatic corpus of the Persian period. One coin even mentions Yeḥezqiyah, a governor *(phh)* of Judea and a Yohanan the priest *(hkwhn)* of Judah. The legends are mainly in Paleo-Hebrew script and mention the name *yhd* or, less frequently, *yhwd*. Unfortunately, the bulk of the coins lack a precise provenance and none are from a clear, unstratified context. Nevertheless, the reports assign almost all of them to the confines of Judah (Jerusalem, Ramat Raḥel, Beth-Zur, Jericho, and Bethlehem—with a few stray finds outside Judah at Tell Jemmeh near Gaza and also near Jericho). [*See* Ramat Raḥel; Jericho; Bethlehem.] Finds of stamped seal impressions within Judah are even more confined; finds are limited to the 25–40 km (16–25 mi.) around Jerusalem, extending from Bethel/Ai in the north to Hebron and Lachish in the south. [*See* Seals; Ai; Hebron; Lachish.] They bear the imprint of the governor of Judah *(phwh yhd)* and leave the impression that the territory of Judah is far more restricted and compact than what may be assumed from the list of the villages of Judah in the Hebrew Bible (*Neh.* 3:1–32). Stylistic changes in the seals and the possible existence of other governors of Judah have yet to be molded into any chronological scheme.

These finds are rivaled by the discoveries from a cave in Wadi ed-Daliyeh near Jericho that make it clear that the Sanballat dynasty continued to rule over Samaria until Alexander's conquest. [*See* Daliyeh, Wadi ed-.] Coins of the Philisto-Arabian type from the cave were issued by the Samaritan state, matching those known from Judah and Gaza. They date from 375 to 335 BCE. One contains the name of the Samaritan capital (*šmryn*, "Shomron") and another the name of what was probably one of its governors (*yrbʿm*, "Jeroboam"). According to Josephus (*Antiq.* 11.301–309), the last Persian king, Darius III, granted approval for the construction of a temple on Mt. Gerazim, similar to the one in Jerusalem. It was even staffed by some priests from Jerusalem, who were given land and subsidized by Sanballat. The events apparently took place shortly before the conquest of the region by Alexander the Great.

No such contemporary nonbiblical documents survive from Judah, leaving many matters of its history subject to speculation. It is evident that the returning exiles in the 460s stimulated a slow revival in the region for the remainder of the fifth century BCE that reached its zenith in the fourth. There are, however, indications that the native population was restless and that there were periodic revolts. According to Ephraim Stern (1990) some cities in Samaria and Benjamin in the center of Palestine suffered destruction in the 480s, and those of the Shephelah and Negev in the 380s. [*See* Cities, *article on* Cities of the Persian Period.] Revolts in Babylon and Egypt for independence, between 404 and 343 BCE, may account for the latter, producing invasions and counterattacks by Persia that affected southern Palestine. A prior revolt by Egypt in the 450s may have resulted in a chain of fortresses being constructed in Judea, either delineating and protecting its borders or controlling the region's vital roads and trade routes. The second wave of exiles under Ezra and Nehemiah may have served to create a buffer zone against Egypt in Persian interests. A network of forts and royal granaries was constructed along the entire Palestinian coast to control the Mediterannean ports and the rest of the region. [*See* Granaries and Silos.] Akko was an especially important military base for the campaigns against Egypt in 374/73 CE (Diodorus 16.41.3; cf. Strabo 16.2.25 [758]).

A network of roads was also organized as a communication system for the various garrisons of Persian troops or mercenaries in the region. Some of these must have been located at the provincial centers (Samaria, Jerusalem, Dor, Ashkelon, Lachish). Tombs at Gezer and Shechem have been identified with Persian garrisons residing in the area. [*See* Tombs; Gezer; Shechem.] Another string of garrisons appeared in the Negev between Gaza and the Dead Sea. Hebrew ostraca from Arad, Beersheba, Tel ʿIra, Yatta, and Tell Jemmeh and Tell el- Farʿah (south) near Gaza perhaps emanate from these military posts. [*See* Arad; Beersheba; Jemmeh, Tell; Farʿah, Tell el- (South).] The texts from Arad and Beersheba are the most numerous and are basically concerned with the delivery of cereal to various men and animals. There are references to the province *(mdynh),* military units *(degel),* a "treasurer" *(gnzbr),* and perhaps "tax bearers" ([*bnb*]*ryʿ*), but it is not clear if these are rations for local garrisons of soldiers, horsemen, and donkey drivers or tax receipts from the local population or both. There are no architectural remains of a garrison; only store pits from the Persian period attest to an occupation at the sites. Persian occupation of the Negev, farther south, was even more limited; it is represented by only a few ostraca at Ḥorvat Ritma, Qadesh-Barnea, and Tell el-Kheleifeh, near ʿAqaba. [*See* Qadesh-Barnea; Kheleifeh, Tell el-.]

The material culture of the Persian period has been summarized by Stern (1982). Palestine appears to have been culturally divided into two distinct regions. The culture of Judah and Samaria was still influenced by the traditions of Mesopotamia and Egypt. In contrast, the culture of the coastland and Galilee was heavily influenced by foreigners. Throughout Palestine, pottery from Attica, Cyprus, Phoenicia, and of the East Greeks appears at numerous sites. Some of the Greek pottery dates to before 475 BCE, but afterward abundant Attic black-glazed wares signal vigorous trade in the region, following a hiatus of more than a century for any notable evidence of Greek imports. The finds may mainly be a product of Phoenician and Greek mercenaries and traders active in the area, but ceramic imitations of other eastern prototypes are also common. Persian influence itself was minimal; their presence was reflected only in scattered finds of Iranian-type weapons, riding accessories, bronze and silver Persian-type bowls, and Achaemenid-type jewelry. [*See* Weapons; Jewelry.]

Hellenistic Period (332–63 BCE). After the death of Alexander the Great, his Macedonian successors *(Diodochoi)* divided up the conquered territory, with Palestine and Phoenicia becoming the possession of the Ptolemaic dynasty centered in Egypt by 301 BCE. These extraterritorial possession of the Ptolemies were governed by a local provincial official called a strategos, who was empowered with military and civil jurisdiction of the region. [*See* Ptolemies.] For administrative purposes, Syria and Palestine were organized into divisions known as hyparchies or toparchies; minimal literary and archaeological evidence for the period leaves other details unknown. It is known that Ptolemy Philadelphus II (285–246 BCE) created a number of military colonies in the region, including Ptolemais (Akko), Philoteria on Lake Galilee, and perhaps Scythopolis/Beth-Shean in the Jordan Valley. [*See* Beth-Shean.] The major source for the mid-third century in Palestine is the Zenon papyri from the Faiyum in Egypt. [*See* Faiyum.] Zenon was the private agent of Apollonios, the financial minister for Ptolemy II, between 260 and 258 BCE Zenon conducted visits to Gaza, the Idumean cities of Adora and Marisa/Mareshah, and other areas in Palestine, including the cities of Ashkelon, Straton's Tower (Casarea Maritima), Jaffa, Akko/Ptolemais, the royal estates at nearby Beth-ʿAnat and Kedasa, and Jerusalem. [*See* Caesarea.] The focus is obviously the coastal cities and the inland administrative centers. Beginning with Ptolemy II, coins were minted at seven coastal cities (Berytus/Beirut,

Tyre, Sidon, Ptolemais/Akko, Jaffa, Ashkelon, Gaza), but not at any inland city. [*See* Beirut.]

The Macedonian Seleucid dynast Antiochus III defeated Ptolemy V at Panion/Banias in 200 BCE, after which Palestine came under the rule of the Syrian monarchs. [*See* Seleucids; Banias.] At first, the hereditary Zadokite high priests served as the viceroys of Palestine for the Seleucid king. In a similar fashion, Samaria (inclusive perhaps of Galilee) and Idumea were probably also separate spheres governed by native rulers. Macedonian garrisons were located at strategic locations to maintain security in the region, but the focus was still primarily the coastline and Transjordan. Seleucid regional policy is reflected in two recently discovered inscriptions. The Hefzibah inscription found in 1960 near Beth-Shean/Scythopolis provides the correspondence between Antiochus III and the strategos for Syria and Phoenicia in 200–198 BCE regarding the latter's village property in the area and the conduct of his garrison force among the native population. A more recently discovered inscription from the hellenized Sidonian community at Jamnia on the Sea (Yavneh-Yam) indicates that Antiochus V Eupator granted them special status in 163 BCE because of their loyalty to the throne (like the privileges extended by Antiochus IV to the Sidonian community at Shechem in Samaria; (*Antiq.* 12.5.5 [258]). [*See* Yavneh-Yam.] The cities founded by the Macedonian kings were essentially military colonies, not Greek cities with democratic civic organizations disseminating Greek culture to the native population. The language of Jesus and Josephus in the Roman era was still Aramaic, not Greek. The hellenization process was a limited affair sponsored by native monarchs and supported by an urban elite, in contrast to the rural countryside where traditional culture prevailed.

Events in Judea illustrate the phenomenon. The Seleucid appointment of non-Zadokites to the priesthood in Jerusalem and the attempt by a local collaborating elite to transform the city into a hellenized Antiochene community provoked the Maccabean revolt in 167 BCE and eventually led, in 142 BCE, to an independent Jewish state (a native Hasmonean dynasty) under Simon Maccabee. [*See* Hasmoneans.] The real transition to independence was marked later by the hiring of mercenaries by John Hyrcanus I (134–104 BCE) and the territorial expansion of Alexander Jannaeus (104–76 BCE) that resulted in the conquest of the hellenized coastal cities and parts of Transjordan. These efforts produced clashes with the neighboring Nabatean monarchs of Petra over the possession of Gaza and the Golan. [*See* Petra; Golan.] Consolidation of the new territories led to the conversion of the Idumeans by Hyrcanus and of the Itureans of Syria, who had infiltrated Galilee, by Aristobulus. Archaeological evidence for the period is still dominated by the sensational discoveries of the Dead Sea Scrolls from the Qumran Essene community, which remain a center of controversy even after a half century of research. [*See* Dead Sea Scrolls; Qumran.] Their main contribution remains twofold: they provide insights into the transmission of the text of the Hebrew Bible and into the complex and varied Jewish sectarian community they present for the Late Hellenistic and Roman periods, illuminating even further what is known from the Apocrypha and Pseudipigrapha. The scant traces of Hellenistic sites elsewhere remain enigmatic, perhaps concealed by subsequent Roman construction, as indicated by the excavations at Beth-Shean/Scythopolis or still awaiting discovery—such as the Hellenistic tombs recently found at the Maccabee family village of Modiʿin. In spite of this lack of evidence within Judah, a Hellenistic military and commercial presence in the region is evident in peripheral areas: excavations at Tel Anafa in Upper Galilee revealed a prospering Greek community in the second century BCE located on the major trade route between Damascus and Tyre; the Hellenistic necropolis at the Idumean capital of Marisa/Beth-Guvrin reveals Greek and Sidonian influences; and the reconstruction of the Tobiad palace at ʿIraq el-Amir near Amman in Transjordan provides important insights into the art and architecture of the period. [*See* Anafa, Tel; ʿIraq el-Amir.]

Roman Period (63 BCE–324 CE). The Roman commander Pompey's settlement of the East and creation of a province in Syria resulted in the scrambling efforts of neighboring petty kings and tyrants to preserve their rule, including the Hasmonean and Nabatean kings, who were at the mercy of the Roman army. By 63 BCE, Jerusalem was taken by Pompey, the Greek cities of the coast and Transjordan were liberated from Hasmonean rule, and Judea was divided into five administrative districts. The Roman governor of Syria henceforth became the director of affairs in the region, with the Hasmonean Hyrcanus II surviving as a puppet ruler of the Jews supported by his ally Antipater of Idumea. Their later assistance to Caesar in Alexandria won for the former the position of ethnarch of the Jews and for the latter an appointment as procurator of Judea. Antipater's sons, Phasael and Herod, were then given administrative posts in Judea and Galilee, respectively. After Caesar's death, Antony reaffirmed the arrangement and eventually had the Idumean-Nabatean scion Herod declared the "king of the Jews" by the Senate in Rome. Later, Octavian confirmed his rule as a client king of Rome. From 37 to 4 BCE, Herod reigned over Palestine.

At this time, the urbanization of Palestine began in earnest with Herod's massive building program. At the inception of his rule, Palestine was still a world of small villages, but by the time of his death it had been transformed into a network of cities with all of the Greco-Roman features—temples, gymnasia, theaters, amphitheaters, stadia, and hippodromes. [*See* Theaters.] A palace was constructed in Jerusalem, protected by the adjacent Antonia Fortress, and a theater and anphitheater reputedly were constructed in the city. [*See* Palace.] His other foundations include Caesarea

Maritima, with its impressive harbor; Samaria, rebuilt as Sebaste as a tribute to the emperor Augustus; his own tripalatial winter palace at Jericho; and a magnificent marble temple at Panion/Banias in honor of Augustus. In addition, fortress-palaces were constructed at Herodium, Hyrcania, Cypros, Alexandrium, Masada, and Machaerus. [*See* Herodium; Masada; Machaerus.] He also subsidized building projects at major cities outside his realm, including the Lebanese ports of Berytus/Beirut, Tyre, and Sidon; Antioch and Damascus in Syria; and Rhodes, Chios, and Nicopolis in the Greek Aegean. His successors also made their contributions: in Galilee, Sepphoris was rebuilt, Tiberias was founded in 20 CE by Herod Antipas, and Caesarea Philippi (Panion/Banias) was founded by Philip the Tetrarch. [*See* Sepphoris; Tiberias.] To protect his realm, a native garrison force of one cavalry unit and five cohorts of infantry was established; military colonies were created in Batanea of Idumeans and Babylonian Jews; and veterans from his army were settled near Mt. Carmel and in the Golan and in Esbonitis (Ḥesban) in Transjordan. [*See* Ḥesban.] Vestiges of the Herodian cities and fortresses are still visible, unlike the magnificent temple building project that enlarged the sacred Temple Mount in Jerusalem, the elaborate central shrine of Judaism, where only the temenos walls lie exposed.

With Herod's death, the kingdom was assigned by Augustus to Herod's sons. Archelaus received Judea and Samaria, Antipas Galilee and Perea (east of the Dead Sea in Transjordan), and Philip the Tetrarch the territories of the Golan and parts of the Hauran (Iturea and Trachonitis in southern Syria). Archelaus's mismanagement of Judea led to its transformation into a Roman province governed by prefects of equestrian rank appointed and supervised by the governor of Syria. Caesarea Maritima became the seat of the officials who administered Judea from 6 to 41 CE, until the old kingdom of Herod the Great was briefly reinstituted under his grandson Agrippa I (41–44 CE), the friend of the emperor Claudian. With Agrippa's death, Roman procurators were appointed to rule over Judea (44–66 CE), again as a Roman province. His son Agrippa II became ruler of the kingdom of Chalcis in Syria and of Philip's territory while exercising some moral authority in Judea. Nevertheless, Agrippa II could not prevent the Roman procurators' harsh and corrupt policies from precipitating the outbreak of the First Jewish Revolt (66–70 CE). [*See* First Jewish Revolt.] The crushing of the rebellion led to Judea being administered by legates of senatorial rank with legionary troops at their command and directly responsible to the emperor. The effects of a Jewish revolt that broke out in Cyrene and Egypt, before spreading to Cyprus and Mesopotamia in 115 CE, seems to have had repercussions in Judea. [*See* Cyrene; Cyprus.] It is, however, the Bar Kokhba Revolt of 132–135 CE that is better known. This is so partially because of the documentation provided from letters written on papyrus by the rebel leader himself and by the Babatha archive found in caves near the Dead Sea, but mainly because of the disastrous impact it subsequently had on Palestine. [*See* Bar Kokhba Revolt; Judean Desert Caves.]

Prior to the revolt in 66 CE, the Roman army in Judea was composed of the one cavalry unit and five infantry regiments of the former Herodian garrison transformed into regular auxiliary troops serving at Caesarea and in Jerusalem. With the outbreak of the rebellion, the Syrian governor, C. Cestius Gasslus, marched into Palestine with the Twelfth Legion (Fulminata), which suffered a serious defeat by the Jews in an ambush. Consequently, Vespasian sent Titus to Alexandria to withdraw the Fifteenth Legion (Apollinarus), while he brought the Fifth (Macedonia) and Tenth (Fretensis) legions from Syria, accompanied by twenty auxiliary units. Between 68 and 70 the camp of the Fifth Legion was at Emmaus near Jerusalem (*War* 4.8.1 [445]; 5.1.6 [42]). [*See* Emmaus.] After the revolt, the Tenth legion remained in Jerusalem as the permanent Roman garrison in Palestine (*War* 7.1.3 [17]). By 120 it was joined by the Sixth Legion (Ferrata), which was stationed at Caparcotna (Legio) in the Jezreel Valley. This addition signals the transformation of Judea from a single-legion province governed by a legatus of ex-praetor status to a double-legion province under an ex-consul. After the Bar Kokhba Revolt and for the rest of the century (according to military diplomas of 139 and 186), three *alae* (cavalry) and twelve *cohortes* (infantry) units were stationed in Palestine. The ethnic name *Judea* was replaced by *Syria-Palaestinia* for the province, and Jerusalem was transformed into the *colonia* of Aelia Capitolina. By the end of the fourth century, the Tenth Legion was moved to ʿAqaba; a single cavalry unit (Equites Mauri Illyricani) replaced it in Jerusalem.

The development of the Roman road system in Judea is closely associated with Roman military activity in the region. [*See* Roads.] Between 51 and 54, veterans of four Syrian legions were settled in a colony at Ptolemais/Akko that was immediately connected by a coastal road to the Syrian capital at Antioch; it later served as the base of operations against Lower Galilee for Vespasian during the first Jewish Revolt. [*See* Antioch.] During the conflict, a road also was constructed between Caesarea and Scythopolis/Beth-Shean, obviously facilitating the movement of troops for the conflict. A lengthy hiatus followed before there were any signs of such activity again. No milestones of Flavian or Trajanic date are attested in Judea, but under Hadrian a dozen roads were constructed between 120 and 130, just prior to the Bar Kokhba Revolt. The establishment of the Roman colony of Aelia Capitolina (Jerusalem) and the addition of a new legion in Judea seem to have been the motivation, but Hadrian's visit to the region in 129/30 was a spur to construction projects elsewhere and probably in Palestine as well. At Tell Shalem, in the Jordan Valley, a statue of Hadrian was found with a dedication to the emperor by a vexillation of the Sixth Legion, which was probably stationed in the area.

The next documented periods of roadwork are connected with the movement of troops for the Parthian campaigns of the Antonine and Severan dynasties. The final known construction is the Diocletianic road between Aila (ʿAqaba) and Jotapata/Ghadyan, 40 km (25 mi.) north in Wadi ʿArabah. [*See* Jotapata.] Some isolated texts dated to Constantine and other fourth-century emperors are known from the Jordan Valley and Jerusalem. These latest additions to the system probably are to be associated with the administrative and military reorganization of the region.

Jews were excluded from the territory of Jerusalem with its foundation as a Roman *colonia* following the Bar Kokhba Revolt. Even in the rest of Palestine, they were faced with a changed situation as the land underwent an even greater urbanization program under Roman auspices. The Decapolis city of Scythopolis/Beth-Shean was designated one of Coele Syria's Greek cities in the Antonine era and was developed accordingly, as excavations reveal; Sepphoris in Galilee was renamed Diocaesarea under Antoninus Pius; during the Severan dynasty, Lydda/Lod became Diospolis, Beth-Guvrin was renamed Eletheropolis, and Emmaus was called Nicopolis. [*See* Decapolis; Cities, *article on* Cities of the Hellenistic and Roman Periods.] Palestine became a world of Greco-Roman cities in which the Jews were a minority. The center of Judaism consequently shifted to Galilee and the Golan, where the rabbis emerged as the dominant force in villages that were still predominantly Jewish. Throughout the post-135 period, prominent Jews locally and from the Diaspora sought burial in the necropolis of Beth-Sheʿarim on the edge of the Galilee. [*See* Beth-Sheʿarim; Necropolis.] The changed world of Palestine was reflected at Beth-Sheʿarim in the predominance of Greek over Aramaic and Hebrew in funerary inscriptions and in the pagan motifs decorating the tombs. [*See* Greek; Hebrew Language and Literature.] The same emphasis appears in the Graco-Roman mythological and astrological scenes in the synagogue mosaics of the Lower Galilee region. [*See* Synagogues; Mosaics.]

Galilee was apparently extensively developed in the Roman era, with hundreds of towns divided among two distinct regions. Lower Galilee, dominated by the cities of Sepphoris and Tiberias, lay astride the major trade route to the Greek cities of the Palestinian coast and was the center for the majority of the local population in the pre-70 era. Excavations at Yodefat/Jotapata and Gamla provide some insight into the centers of rebellion during the First Revolt. [*See* Gamla.] Upper Galilee appears to have flourished only later, in the second and third centuries, when there may have been a substantial influx of new Jewish migrants. Even there the technical world of Hellenism was absorbed by the population, otherwise known for its religious conservatism. North of the Tiberias-Ptolemais road, there are no Roman roads and there is minimal evidence for any Roman garrisons. The Roman road between Panion/Caesarea Phillipi and Tyre suggests that the contact in Upper Galilee was with the hellenized Phoenician coast, as is reflected in the material culture and coinage of the region produced by excavations of the synagogues at Khirbet Shemaʿ, Meiron, and Gush Ḥalav. [*See* Shemaʿ, Khirbet; Meiron; Gush Ḥalav.] The nature of the population and its relationship to the prerevolt population remains a matter of sharp debate, in spite of the abundant rabbinic literature for the period.

Roman occupation of the rest of Palestine must have been extensive. The royal lands of the Herodian monarchs and much of Judea were confiscated and transformed into imperial property, beginning with the collapse of Archelaus's rule (Josephus, *Antiq.* 17.13.1–2 [340–344]; cf. 18.2.1 [26]), again after the First Revolt (*War* 7.6.6 [216]), and finally in the aftermath of the Bar Kokhba Revolt (Eusebius *H.E.* 4.6.1). Even if much of it was later liquidated, the overwhelming impression is that large tracts of land continued to exist as Roman villae and imperial property. References to Saltus Geraiticus and Saltus Constantinianus, protected by imperial troops to the southeast of Gaza, indicate that vestiges of these imperial lands survived into the Byzantine era. By this time, the tetrarchic reforms had rearranged the provincial borders by adding parts of the province of Arabia (the Negev, Sinai, and southern Transjordan between the southern end of the Dead Sea and ʿAqaba) to Syria-Palestine. [*See* Sinai.] The assumption that the Diocletianic military reforms created a fortified frontier commonly known as the limes Palestinae and limes Arabicus is now a matter of considerable controversy. [*See* Limes Arabicus.] The effects of Diocletian's economic reforms on the region must have been felt by the native population in personal and land taxes, but the extant evidence is limited to parts of Galilee and the Golan. The persecution of the church between 303 and 313 ended with a Christian emperor, Constantine, and a christianized empire that marked the dawn of a new era of prosperity for Palestine.

[*See also* Galilee, *article on* Galilee in the Hellenistic through Byzantine Periods.]

BIBLIOGRAPHY

Avigad, Nahman. *Bullae and Seals from a Post-Exilic Judean Archive.* Qedem, vol. 4. Jerusalem, 1976.

Davies, W. D., and Louis Finkelstein, eds. *The Cambridge History of Judaism,* vol. 1, *Introduction, the Persian Period.* Cambridge, 1984. Uneven collection of studies that still contains valuable information.

Goodman, Martin D. *State and Society in Roman Galilee, A.D. 132–212.* Totowa, N.J., 1982.

Graf, David F. "The Persian Royal Road System in Syria-Palestine." *Transeuphratène* 6 (1993): 149–168.

Graf, David F. "Hellenization and the Decapolis." *Aram* 4 (1994): 1–48. Analysis of Macedonian policies, arguing that Greek civic institutions were a late development in Palestine occurring only under Roman rule.

Hengel, Martin. *Judaism and Hellenism: Studies in Their Encounter in Palestine during the Early Hellenistic Period.* 2 vols. Translated by John Bowden. Philadelphia, 1974. Classic work flawed by its extreme emphasis on the penetration of Hellenistic culture into the Jewish community.

Hoglund, Kenneth G. *Achaemenid Imperial Administration in Syria-Palestine and the Missions of Ezra and Nehemiah.* Society of Biblical Literature, Dissertation Series, no. 125. Atlanta, 1992. Argues, on the basis of a series of forts erected in the mid-fifth century BCE, that Ezra and Nehemiah were imperial collaborators in Persian efforts to consolidate the frontier states as centers of loyalty against rebellious Egypt.

Isaac, Benjamin. "A Seleucid Inscription from Jamnia-on-the-Sea: Antiochus V Eupator and the Sidonians." *Israel Exploration Journal* 41 (1991): 132–144.

Isaac, Benjamin. *The Limits of Empire: The Roman Army in the East.* Rev. ed. Oxford, 1992. Persuasive attempt to demonstrate that the main concerns of the Roman army in Palestine were internal.

Landau, Y. H. "A Greek Inscription Found near Hefzibah." *Israel Exploration Journal* 16 (1966): 54–70.

Lemaire, André. "Les inscriptions palestiniennes d'époque perse: Un bilan provisoire." *Transeuphratène* 1 (1989): 87–105. Exhaustive list of the various finds.

Machinist, Peter. "The First Coins of Judah and Samaria: Numismatics and History in the Achaemenid and Early Hellenistic Periods." In *Achaemenid History VIII: Continuity and Change,* edited by Heleen Sancisi-Weerdenburg et al., pp. 365–380. Leiden, 1994. Provides a recent statement on the coins and seal impressions.

Meyers, Carol L., and Eric M. Meyers. *Haggai, Zechariah 1–8.* Anchor Bible, vol. 25B. Garden City, N.Y., 1987. Extensive commentary with important archaeological data for the sixth and fifth centuries BCE.

Meyers, Carol L., and Eric M. Meyers. *Zechariah 9–14.* Anchor Bible, vol. 25C. New York, 1993. Extensive commentary with important archaeological notes for the fifth century BCE.

Meyers, Eric M. "The Shelomith Seal and Aspects of the Judean Restoration." *Eretz-Israel* 18 (1985): 33–38.

Meyers, Eric M. "Second Temple Studies in the Light of Recent Archaeology. Part I: The Persian and Hellenistic Periods." *Currents in Research: Biblical Studies* 2 (1994): 25–42. Useful synthesis of major developments in the archaeology and historical reconstruction of the period.

Meyers, Eric M. "An Archaeological Response to a New Testament Scholar." *Bulletin of the American Schools of Oriental Research,* no. 297 (1995): 17–26. Commentary on the most recent developments in regionalism and Roman Palestine.

Millar, Fergus. *The Roman Near East, 31 BC–AD 337.* Cambridge, Mass., 1993. Invaluable study of the entire region, with important discussions on Palestine affairs.

Safrai, Zeev. *The Economy of Roman Palestine.* London, 1993. Impressive discussion of the agricultural development and local trading system of the region.

Sherwin-White, Susan, and Amélie Kuhrt. *From Samarkhand to Sardis: A New Approach to the Seleucid Empire.* Berkeley, 1993. Pioneering and provocative analysis of Seleucid policy.

Stern, Ephraim. *Material Culture of the Land of the Bible in the Persian Period, 538–332 B.C.* Warminster, 1982. Fundamental guide for the archaeology of the Persian period.

Stern, Ephraim. "New Evidence on the Administrative Division of Palestine in the Persian Period." In *Achaemenid History IV: Centre and Periphery,* edited by Heleen Sancisi-Weerdenburg and Amélie Kuhrt, pp. 221–226. Leiden, 1990.

Stolper, Matthew W. "The Governor of Babylon and Across-the-River in 486 B.C." *Journal of Near Eastern Studies* 48 (1989): 283–305.

Wenning, Robert. "Griechische importe in Palästina aus der Zeit vor Alexander d. Gr.: Vorbericht über ein Forschungsprojekt." *Boreas* 4 (1981): 29–46.

Wenning, Robert. "Attische Keramik in Palästina: Ein Zwischenbericht." *Transeuphratène* 2 (1990): 157–167. Preliminary report of the Greek pottery finds in Palestine.

David F. Graf

Palestine in the Byzantine Period

The Byzantine period represents one of the most populous, prosperous, and archaeologically rich periods in the entire history of Israel (ancient Palestine). The beginning of the era is usually identified by the date, 324 CE, when the Christian emperor Constantine took control of the East; the end of the period is marked by the Islamic conquest in 640. In archaeological terms, a growing body of stratigraphic evidence from all regions of the country argues against investing too much credibility in these dates. Suffice it to say that the period begins sometime in the fourth century, depending on which site or region of the country is being considered, and continues in some places (like the Galilee and Golan) into the seventh century.

From a political standpoint, the most dramatic change in the country was its enshrinement in the empire as a Holy Land for Christians, as well as Jews, as has been recently documented from literary sources by Robert L. Wilken (1992). Nothing shows this more dramatically than the building programs carried out in Jerusalem by Christian emperors from Constantine onward. The height of this movement to make Palestine a Christian Holy Land is best illustrated by the emperor Justinian's (527–565) building program in Jerusalem, when the *cardo* (the major north–south street) was extended to the south to create a Christian section of the city. A huge basilical church called the Nea was installed near the site of the Church of the Holy Sepulcher in the modern city's Jewish Quarter. [*See* Jerusalem.] Depicted on the sixth century Madaba mosaic map, the *cardo* and a part of the church have now been securely located and excavated by Nahman Avigad (1993, pp. 128–135). [*See* Madaba.]

From an archaeological standpoint, the most dramatic feature of the Byzantine period is the density of site settlement. Byzantine occupation has been found on nearly every known ancient site in what was Palestine. In addition, recent research has focused on the settlement of the area's fragile deserts—in Judaea (Judah) and the Negev and Sinai. After the empire became officially Christian in the late fourth century, the rise of Christian pilgrimage resulted in the settlement of the Judean Desert by Christian monks. They created a new architectural settlement form, the monastery, some fifty-five of which have been studied and systematized into distinct types (Hirschfeld, 1992). [*See* Monasteries.] The presence of the monasteries brought numerous pilgrims and travelers to and through the country's deserts, in addition to the some three thousand permanent inhabitants at the height of the monastic movement. In the northern Negev, superb Byzantine hydrology created a system of runoff agriculture (rainwater diverted to field use by sophisticated dams, terraces, and channels) that was able to sustain the greatest flowering of city culture in the Negev's long history. [*See* Irrigation.] Viticulture was introduced to the Negev, though wine production appears (at least from the Neṣṣana papyri) not to have been carried on. Along with the revitalized city settlements, a flowering of pastoral nomadism occurred. The camping remains of nomads have been mapped (and some excavated) by Steven A. Rosen and Gideon Avni (1993), pp. 189–199). In fact, the very boarders of civilized cultivation were pushed several miles south of Neṣṣana's city territory for the first time, as the boundaries of the "inner desert" receded in the face of the Byzantine presence (Mayerson, 1963, pp. 160–172). Mid-sixth-century Palestine had become an "international" province, with trade links to the wider Mediterranean world, as demonstrated by the Palestinian amphorae found as far west and north as Britain and by the steady flow of imported fine tableware from Asia Minor, Egypt, and North Africa into all regions of the country. Already at the very beginnings of the period in the mid-fourth century, an observant Jewish family in the rural village world of mountainous Upper Galilee had, among its collection of fine-ware bowls, a particularly lovely (and somewhat scarce) red-ware bowl with a flaring rim and a curved body manufactured in far-away Carthage (Groh, 1981, pp. 129–138, pls. 8.29–31). [*See* Galilee, *article on* Galilee in the Hellenistic through Byzantine Periods.]

Yet, curiously, for all the new international flavor of this period, regionalism is most deeply ensconced into both the history and material culture of ancient Palestine precisely in these centuries. Politically, the country was first divided into two halves (north and south) in the late 350s and then, in about 400, into three separate provinces: Palaestina Prima (the northern coastal plain plus Judaea, Idumea, Samaria, Peraea) with its capital at Caesarea Maritima; Palaestina Secunda (Galilee, the Palestinian Decapolis, the Golan region) with its capital at Scythopolis (Beth-Shean); and Palaestina Tertia (formerly Palaestina Salutaris), whose capital has not yet been exactly determined (Gutwein, 1981, p. 8). [*See* Caesarea; Decapolis; Golan; Beth-Shean.] Because almost no Jews lived in the region south of Beersheba (which functioned as the principal city for the region), the development of a virtual southern Christian Holy Land was made possible, organized around the principal northern Negev cities, the bishop's seat for this area being located at Ḥaluṣa. [*See* Ḥaluṣa.]

However, the threefold political division does not do full justice to the vast differences that appear in the material culture of the country's various regions and subregions. It is the recognition of regionalism that best characterizes the professional activity being carried out in surveys, excavations, and the interpretation of material culture from ancient Palestine. Little synthetic work has been done on the country as a whole, however.

Byzantine Aesthetics. The careful attention to architectural balance and proportion, so characteristic of the earlier Roman-period buildings, gave way in the late third century to a heavy reuse of earlier building materials (columns, facings, capitals, inscriptions) employed in ways quite different from their earlier architectonic functions (Groh, 1988, pp. 91–92). For example, in the construction of synagogues and churches in the period, columns with different diameters and bases were used in the same colonnade. [*See* Synagogues; Churches.] Despite attempts to find a rational Byzantine proportionality in planning buildings (see Chen, 1981, 1985), archaeology has recovered buildings that offered overall mass and overall effect (in adaptation to local tastes and topography and availability of materials) as its basic aesthetic. Also, the interiors of public buildings such as synagogues and churches, with their interior forest of basilical columns and their second-story galleries or chapels, were formed by the heightened Byzantine aesthetic commitment to the mysterious interior play of light and shadow on the worshiping faithful. Hanging lamps of metal and glass, found throughout the country in excavations of Jewish or Christian basilical buildings, heightened this play. The glass factories of Asia Minor and Palestine, one of which was found at Jebel Jalme in the Galilee, seem to have been able to keep up with the increased demand (Weinberg, 1988). The tighter and deeper ribbing on the exteriors of fifth–seventh-century crude-ware pottery (especially amphorae) shares in this same aesthetic concern to break up surface appearance into sculptured depth (hence shadow) and light. Most excavators, however, simply consider Byzantine pottery crude and ugly, compared to the more graceful forms and less-severely and more broadly ribbed exterior surfaces of Roman-period pottery. Colored mosaic floors and interior painted plaster walls in both private and public rooms further added to the new aesthetic. [*See* Mosaics; Wall Paintings.]

Common Byzantine Characteristics. Standard Byzantine weights and measures met a shopper in whatever region, and the city dweller walked on a Byzantine street roughly 4.5 m wide. Houses were constructed of stone. The walls were constructed first (floors were added later) and were sometimes mortared, often chinked with rocks and offcuttings. The roofs were made of wood timbers and tile or constructed in the stone-roof slab-and-arch technique of the "Hauranic" style employed in the Golan and the northern Negev. While modern architects point out the utter unsuitability of courtyard houses to a country with (alternately) too much rain and too much sun, residents of Byzantine Palestine were addicted to houses with central courtyards (Shereshevski, 1986)—even apartment-building residences (insulae) had them. Most private housing so far excavated from the period are one or two stories high, with exterior stairways from the courtyard to the upper story or roof. The Galilean split-level house, called the patrician house, excavated at Meiron, the Dionysiac house excavated at Sepphoris, and the numerous houses preserved to the first and second stories in the Golan and Negev, provide excellent examples. [*See* Meiron; Sepphoris.] While private housing can be quite spacious, the huge sprawling urban villas of the rich, so characteristic of these centuries in most other provinces of the empire, are almost completely absent in the three Palestines. The continuous reuse of materials on a site and the wide, contemporaneous variety of plans adapted to local topography, tastes, and pocketbooks, make any attempt to salvage an architectural chronology of synagogue-, housing-, and church-plan types (that is, without careful stratigraphic excavation) relatively hopeless, despite the rigor of its defenders. [*See* Building Materials and Techniques, *article on* Materials and Techniques of the Byzantine and Islamic Periods.]

Regionalism. Eric M. Meyers (1976, 1975) pioneered in identifying an analogous material culture that separated the Galilee from other regions of the country (best represented by the ubiquitous Galilean bowl, seldom found outside the Galilee and Golan) and in separating the Upper Galilee and Upper Golan (following Josephus) into a subregion with its own peculiarities in architectural style, decoration (aniconic and restrained carving), and language preference (primarily Aramaic inscriptions). The material culture of Upper Galilee differed markedly from the Lower Galilee of the Kinneret region (with its highly hellenized artistic tastes and preponderance of the Greek language testified to by the inscriptional evidence). The Jews of the Lower Galilee who lived at sites like Sepphoris or (farther south) Scythopolis/Beth-Shean were wealthy, artistically and linguistically sophisticated people, as their synagogues, inscriptions, and homes attest. Dan Urman (1985) has given even more precision to the Golan and its subregions, suggesting that ethnic preference in settlement took regional archaeology a giant step forward. Identifying the subregions of the northern Negev has furthered helped to see the importance of the way peopled built, lived, adapted, and shopped locally (Gutwein, 1981).

The various regions of the country bought most of their common pottery locally. Although kilns for most regions have not been found, recent discoveries permit the conclusion that certain storage-jar forms and cookers found throughout the Galilee and Golan were manufactured at Kefar Hananyah and Shikhin in Lower Galilee, at least until the Late Roman period (Strange, 1994). It is possible to hypothesize that the characteristically brittle Golan-ware forms were made in that region but did not gain currency in other areas. Judea must have had its own Byzantine pottery factory, located in the Jerusalem area, that produced local fine-ware forms (termed Judean sigillata), as well as other vessels that appear at excavated sites in Jerusalem and its environs. The kilns that produced the Gaza jar, which appears all over the south, have now been found at Ashkelon by the Harvard University Expedition. [*See* Ashkelon.] The distinctive wheel-made southern lamp, which rarely occurs in the north, must be manufactured somewhere in the Negev region, as must the late amphorae so characteristic of the region. The dark-black metallic amphorae, often decorated with paint dribbled down them, must be products of the northern coastal plain because they are found frequently in the north but are rarely seen in the southern regions. [*See* Ceramics, *article on* Ceramics of the Byzantine Period.]

Archaeological Periodization. The vast regional differences in ancient Palestine make a chronological division into subperiods for the Byzantine era impossible at this stage of research. No overall events, either natural or political, cut across all regions of the country to mark a clear and sharp break between one subperiod and another. For example, some recent research and excavations have shown that the so-called Persian destruction layers from the 614 Persian invasion do not appear at carefully excavated sites such as Caesarea Maritima, Capernaum, and Naburiya (Groh, 1989, pp. 62–71). [*See* Capernaum.] Destruction materials that turn up at sites near the Sea of Galilee and in Jerusalem may now be attributable to postinvasion disturbances caused by the populace itself. Similarly, no single event inaugurates the Byzantine period. In Galilee, the revolt of a few of the Jewish cities against Gallus Caesar in 352, which resulted in the military destruction of sites like Sepphoris and Beth-Sheʿarim in the Galilee and Juhada in the Golan Heights, vies with the earthquake of 363, which damaged some sites in Upper Galilee (like Khirbet Shemaʿ), for central importance in precision dating (Nathanson, 1986, pp. 29–36). For all that has been written about the supposed dating and sequencing of synagogues, the precise dating of only a few is known, where there was clean excavating, recording, use of balk sections in conjunction with precise ceramic controls, and clear publication of all finds (see Groh, 1995, pp. 51–69). A similar problem exists in determining church-plan development (Tsafrir, 1993, p. 13).

Appeals to imperial legislation to explain life in Palestine are not helpful either. It is now known that "power decays with distance" (Gill Stein, Northwestern University), and Constantinople was a world away from Palestine. It will fall to the next generation of scholars to trace the exact contours of the subperiodization of material life in Byzantine Palestine.

More Pious Populace. The ethnic/religious groups that inhabited the land (Jews, Christians, Arab tribes, Hellenes, Samaritans, descendents of the Nabateans, and resident foreigners—most of them from Egypt, Asia Minor, Greece, and Syria) are known, but very little is known about their physical appearance, marital patterns, or diets because there has been only limited study of their skeletal remains (Hershkovitz et al., 1988, pp. 193–194). Male skeletons tend to predominate in the evidence, so even less is known about women (even discussions about such basic questions as "gender space" are only at their very inception among archaeologists and historians of this period). The tiny sample suggests that such groups tended to marry within their own intimate ethnic or religious group. The literary evidence for the contact between the two numerically largest groups—Jews and Christians—indicates the same carefully cultivated remoteness. People wanted to keep their distance from outsiders.

This makes the contemporary presence of the beautiful Byzantine synagogue at Capernaum, only a few meters from the Church of the House of St. Peter, all the more intriguing: it signals the ground-level insistence of Jews upon maintaining their own religious and ethnic identity in the face of the encroachment of Christians in the very Jewish heartland, a struggle enacted across the country in previously Jewish areas. Jews in the Holy Land were crowded by the influx of gentiles into their areas; but they were neither repressed nor in internal disarray, as witnessed by the dozens of Byzantine synagogues created all over the country in the fifth–sixth centuries and by the crowning achievement of Talmudic scholarship, the codification of the Palestinian (or Jerusalem) Talmud (c. 400). The patriarchate was eliminated (c. 425), but the communities and their scholars continued in vibrancy.

However, the Jews of the period differed from earlier Jews in one important way: they were more focused in their synagogue life on personal piety and on the study and veneration of Scripture. The synagogue building as a "house of assembly" required a separate *beit midrash* ("house of study") only in this later period. Thus, the great synagogue at Meroth was equipped with both a hall for assembly and a separate hall for study. The growing number of synagogues in the Byzantine era in which rebuildings of the interior bema were carried out to increase its height and majesty underscore this point, as does the new emphasis on prayer in the synagogue (Urman, 1995, pp. 232–255). The veneration of holy sites and burials by the Christians of the era who were residents of the land, and not simply foreign pilgrims, also shows this new dedication to personal piety in their communities. The overwhelming number of synagogue and church donors, as reflected by their dedicatory inscriptions, were neither governmental officials nor official leaders of the communities, but private individuals. In 638, the southern and eastern deserts brought forth a great influx of equally pious people, the faithful of Islam. In their first hundred years of rule, they gradually turned the economy, political links, and orientation of the rulers and peoples of ancient Palestine away from the West and Jerusalem and toward Damascus and Mecca.

BIBLIOGRAPHY

Adan-Bayewitz, David. *Common Pottery in Roman Galilee: A Study of Local Trade.* Ramat Gan, 1993.

Alon, Gedalia. *The Jews in Their Land in the Talmudic Age, 70–640 CE.* Translated and edited by Gershon Levi. 2 vols. Jerusalem, 1980–1984.

Amiran, D. H. K. and E. Arieh. "Earthquakes in Israel and Adjacent Areas: Macroseismic Observations since 100 B.C.E." *Israel Exploration Journal* 44 (1994): 260–305. Most up-to-date listing of earthquakes, including bibliography.

Avigad, Nahman. "The Nea: Justinian's Church of St. Mary, Mother of God, Discovered in the Old City of Jerusalem." In *Ancient Churches Revealed,* edited by Yoram Tsafrir, pp. 128–135. Jerusalem, 1993.

Avi-Yonah, Michael. "The Economics of Byzantine Palestine." *Israel Exploration Journal* 8 (1958): 39–51.

Avi-Yonah, Michael. *The Holy Land from the Persian to the Arab Conquests, 536 B.C.–A.D. 640: A Historical Geography.* Grand Rapids, Mich., 1966.

Avi-Yonah, Michael. *The Jews of Palestine: A Political History from the Bar Kokhba War to the Arab Conquest.* Oxford, 1976.

Broshi, Magen. "The Population of Western Palestine in the Roman-Byzantine Period." *Bulletin of the American Schools of Oriental Research,* no. 236 (Fall 1979): 1–10.

Chen, Doron. "Byzantine Architects at Work in Mampsis and Sobota, Palestina Tertia: A Study in Paleo-Christian Architectural Design." *Studium Biblicum Franciscanum/Liber Annuus* 31 (1981): 235–244.

Chen, Doron. "Byzantine Architects at Work in Oboda, Nessana, and Rehovot, Palestina Tertia: A Study in Paleo-Christian Architectural Design." *Studium Biblicum Franciscanum/Liber Annuus* 35 (1985): 291–296.

Dar, Shimʿon. *Landscape and Pattern: An Archaeological Survey of Samaria, 800 B.C.E.–636 C.E.* 2 vols. British Archaeological Reports, International Series, no. 308. Oxford, 1986.

Figueras, Pau. "Beersheva in the Roman-Byzantine Period." *Boletín de la Asociación Española de Orientalistas* 16 (1980): 135–162.

Figueras, Pau. *Decorated Jewish Ossuaries.* Leiden, 1983. See pages 10–12 for the contention that Christian adoption of the Jewish practice ended its practice by Jews; but for a contrary view, see McCane (below).

Foss, Clive. "The Near Eastern Countryside in Late Antiquity: A Review Article." In *The Roman and Byzantine Near East: Some Recent Archaeological Research,* pp. 213–234. Journal of Roman Archaeology Supplemental Series, 14. Ann Arbor, 1995. Summary article of the most recent studies on Syria/Palestine, including Shereshevski, 1986 (below).

Gafni, I. M. "The World of the Talmud: From the Mishnah to the Arab Conquest." In *Christianity and Rabbinic Judaism: A Parallel History of Their Origins and Early Development,* edited by Hershel Shanks, pp. 225–265. Washington, D.C., 1992.

Groh, Dennis E. "The Fine-Wares of the Patrician and Lintel Houses." In *Excavations at Ancient Meiron, Upper Galilee, Israel, 1971–72, 1974–75, 1977,* edited by Eric M. Meyers et al., pp. 129–138, pls. 8.29–31. Cambridge, Mass., 1981.

Groh, Dennis E. "The *Onomasticon* of Eusebius of Caesarea and the Rise of Christian Palestine." In *Papers of the Ninth International Conference on Patristic Studies, Oxford, 1983,* vol. 1, *Historica, Theologica, Gnostica, Biblica,* edited by Elizabeth A. Livingstone, pp. 23–31. Studia Patristica, 18. Kalamazoo, Mich., 1986.

Groh, Dennis E. "Jews and Christians in Late Roman Palestine: Towards a New Chronology." *Biblical Archaeologist* 51 (1988): 80–96.

Groh, Dennis E. "Judaism in Upper Galilee at the End of Antiquity:

Excavations at Gush Halav and en-Nabratein." In *Papers of the Ninth International Conference on Patristic Studies, Oxford, 1983,* vol. 2, *Critica, classica, ascetica, linguistica,* edited by Elizabeth A. Livingstone, pp. 62–71. Studia Patristica, 19. Louvain, 1989.

Groh, Dennis E. "Recent Indications of Hellenization at Ancient Sepphoris (Lower Galilee), Israel." In *The Ancient Eastern Mediterranean,* edited by Eleanor Guralnik, pp. 39–41, figs. 17–22. Chicago, 1990.

Groh, Dennis E. "The Religion of the Empire: Christianity from Constantine to the Arab Conquest." In *Christianity and Rabbinic Judaism: A Parallel History of Their Origins and Early Development,* edited by Hershel Shanks, pp. 267–303. Washington, D.C., 1992.

Groh, Dennis E. "The Stratigraphic Chronology of the Galilean Synagogue from the Early Roman Period through the Early Byzantine Period, ca. 420 CE." In *Ancient Synagogues: Historical and Archaeological Study,* vol. 1, edited by Dan Urman and Paul V. M. Flesher, pp. 51–69. Studia Post-Biblica, vol. 47.1. Leiden, 1995.

Gutwein, Kenneth C. *Third Palestine: A Regional Study in Byzantine Urbanization.* Washington, D.C., 1981.

Hachlili, Rachel. *Ancient Jewish Art and Archaeology in the Land of Israel.* Leiden, 1988.

Hershkovitz, Israel, et al. "Skeletal Remains from the Northern Church." In *Excavations at Rehovot-in-the-Negev,* vol. 1, edited by Yoram Tsafrir, pp. 193–209. Qedem, vol. 25. Jerusalem, 1988.

Hirschfeld, Yizhar. *The Judean Desert Monasteries in the Byzantine Period.* New Haven, 1992.

Ilan, Zvi. "The Synagogue and *Beth Midrash* of Meroth." In *Ancient Synagogues of Israel, Third–Seventh Century C.E.: Proceedings of the Symposium of the University of Haifa, May 1987,* edited by Rachel Hachlili, pp. 31–36. British Archaeological Reports, International Series, no. 499. Oxford, 1989.

Ilan, Zvi. "The Synagogue and House of Study at Meroth." In *Ancient Synagogues: Historical and Archaeological Study,* vol. 1, edited by Dan Urman and Paul V. M. Flesher, pp. 256–287. Studia Post-Biblica, vol. 47.1 Leiden, 1995.

Magness, Jodi. *Jerusalem Ceramic Chronology, circa 200–800 CE.* Sheffield, 1993. The best overall survey of Byzantine stratigraphic chronology and pottery types for Judah.

Mayerson, Philip. "The Ancient Agricultural Regime of Nessana and the Central Negeb." In *Excavations at Nessana,* vol. 1, edited by Harris D. Colt, pp. 211–269. Princeton, 1962. The most comprehensive study to date of the archaeological remains of Byzantine runoff agricultural technology. Also published as a separate monograph under the same title (Jerusalem, 1960).

Mayerson, Philip. "The Desert of Southern Palestine According to Byzantine Sources." In *Monks, Martyrs, Soldiers and Saracens: Papers on the Near East in Late Antiquity (1962–1993),* pp. 40–52. Jerusalem, 1994.

McCane, Byron R. "Bones of Contention? Ossuaries and Reliquaries in Early Judaism and Christianity." *Second Century* 8 (1991): 235–246. Contrary view to Figueras's position (see above, 1983) that Jews dropped ossuary burial because of Christian practice.

Meyers, Eric M. "Galilean Regionalism as a Factor in Historical Reconstruction." *Bulletin of the American Schools of Oriental Research,* no. 221 (1976): 93–101.

Meyers, Eric M. "Galilean Regionalism: A Reappraisal." In *Approaches to Ancient Judaism,* vol. 5, *Studies in Judaism and Its Greco-Roman Context,* edited by William Scott Green, pp. 115–131. Brown Judaic Studies, 32. Atlanta, 1985.

Nathanson, Barbara G. "Jews, Christians, and the Gallus Revolt in Fourth-Century Palestine." *Biblical Archaeologist* 49 (1986): 26–36.

Negev, Avraham. "House and City Planning in the Ancient Negev and the Provincia Arabia." In *Housing in Arid Lands: Design and Planning,* edited by Gideon Golany, pp. 3–32. London, 1980. Excellent look at stone-roof construction and the central courtyard house plan.

Ovadiah, Asher. *Corpus of the Byzantine Churches in the Holy Land.* Theophaneia, 22. Bonn, 1970. Updated in *Levant* 13 (1981): 200–261 and 16 (1984): 129–165.

Rosen, Steven A., and Gideon Avni. "The Edge of the Empire: The Archaeology of Pastoral Nomads in the Southern Negev Highlands in Late Antiquity." *Biblical Archaeologist* 56 (1993): 189–199.

Russell, Kenneth. "The Earthquake of May 19, A.D. 363." *Bulletin of the American Schools of Oriental Research,* no. 238 (1980): 47–64. Argues for the extensive damage done by this earthquake and, therefore, its importance in archaeological dating.

Russell, Kenneth. "The Earthquake Chronology of Palestine and Northwest Arabia from the Second through the Mid-Eighth Century A.D." *Bulletin of the American Schools of Oriental Research,* no. 260 (1985): 37–59. Standard resource for converting evidence of earthquake damage into a calendar date.

Schäfer, Peter. "Der Aufstand gegen Gallus Caesar." In *Tradition and Re-Interpretation in Jewish and Christian Literature: Essays in Honor of Jürgen C. H. Lebran,* edited by J. W. Van Henten et al., pp. 184–201. Studia Post-Biblica, vol. 36. Leiden, 1986. Questions the trustworthiness of the literary accounts of this revolt.

Schwartz, Joshua. *Jewish Settlement in Judaea after the Bar-Kochba War until the Arab Conquest, 135–640 C.E.* (in Hebrew). Jerusalem, 1986. See the English review by Daniel Sperber and David Adan-Bayewitz in the *Journal for the Study of Judaism* 18 (1987): 248–252.

Shereshevski, Joseph. "Urban Settlements in the Negev in the Byzantine Period." Ph.D. diss., Hebrew University of Jerusalem, 1986. In Hebrew with English summary.

Strange, James F., et al. "Excavations at Sepphoris: The Location and Identification of Shikhin, Part I." *Israel Exploration Journal* 44 (1994): 216–227. The discovery of the Talmudic pottery-making site on an unnamed ridge in Galilee near Sepphoris. Neutron activation of kiln wasters verifies that forms found throughout the Galilee and Golan were made here. The site's Josephan name is *Asochis.*

Tsafrir, Yoram. "The Maps Used by Theodosius: On the Pilgrim Maps of the Holy Land and Jerusalem in the Sixth Century C.E." *Dumbarton Oaks Papers* 40 (1986): 129–145.

Tsafrir, Yoram. "The Development of Ecclesiastical Architecture in Palestine." In *Ancient Churches Revealed,* edited by Yoram Tsafrir, pp. 1–16. Jerusalem, 1993.

Tsafrir, Yoram, et al. *Tabula Imperii Romani, Iudaea Palaestina: Eretz Israel in the Hellenistic, Roman, and Byzantine Periods.* Jerusalem, 1994. Maps and gazetteer.

Urman, Dan. *The Golan: A Profile of a Region during the Roman and Byzantine Periods.* British Archaeological Reports, International Series, no. 269. Oxford, 1985.

Urman, Dan. "The House of Assembly and the House of Study: Are They One and the Same?" In *Ancient Synagogues: Historical and Archaeological Study,* vol. 1, edited by Dan Urman and Paul V. M. Flesher, pp. 232–255. Studia Post-Biblica, vol. 47.1. Leiden, 1995.

Urman, Dan. "Public Structures and Jewish Communities in the Golan Heights." In *Ancient Synagogues: Historical and Archaeological Study,* vol. 2, edited by Dan Urman and Paul V. M. Flesher, pp. 373–605. Studia Post-Biblica, vol. 47.2. Leiden, 1995.

Weinberg, Gladys Davidson, ed. *Excavations at Jalame: Site of a Glass Factory in Late Roman Palestine.* Columbia, Mo., 1988. The discovery of a Late Roman glass factory in Galilee.

Wilken, Robert L. *The Land Called Holy: Palestine in Christian History and Thought.* New Haven, 1992.

Dennis E. Groh

Palestine in the Islamic Period

Just as the Islamic period is the most recent stratum on every archaeological site (if it has an Islamic stratum), so is the study of Islamic archaeology the most recent of archaeological disciplines. In fact, this state of affairs is not confined to ancient Palestine but is shared by many of Israel's neighboring countries. The belated interest in Islamic archaeology has resulted in relatively limited attention to the later levels of excavations, of which the overwhelming majority have concentrated on ancient periods. Few excavations have aimed from the outset at uncovering and studying Islamic remains, which have only recently received the acknowledgement they deserve.

The Islamic history of Palestine (beginning of the seventh century–end of the fifteenth century) can be divided roughly into three main eras—early, middle, and late—each of which is further subdivided. These divisions correspond to the periodization dictated by historical events and, to a considerable extent, reflect the archaeological evidence of their respective material culture. [*See* Periodization.] The weight of the three main periods is far from evenly distributed. Another important factor is that, during the period under discussion, the area of "Palestine" was not a political entity but, from an administrative point of view, comprised two major units: the first, comprising the coastal area, the northern Jordan Valley, and the east bank of the Jordan River was the Jund al-Urdan (the equivalent of the Byzantine Palaestina Secunda); the second included the southern part of the Jordan Valley and Transjordan (echoing Palaestina Prima) and was known as the Jund Filastin. However, historically and politically they shared the same fate and depended, according to shifts in the balance of power, on either Syria or Egypt.

Two factors preceding the advent of Islam had an impact on the character of the country, and both are attested in the archaeological record: a series of infiltrations of nomads, mainly from Arabia via the Red Sea, into the southern part of Palestine; and the Sasanian occupation from 614–628 CE, which was accompanied by the destruction of a large number of churches. [*See* Churches.] Thus, prior to the Islamic occupation there was a phase that did not experience widespread destruction but influenced many of the existing cultural conditions. Evidence for this phase (c. 600–636) is best known from the survey made of the Negev desert, particularly in the area of Sede Boqer. [*See* Negev.] A few pottery sherds that appear to be an extension of Byzantine typologies and an enormous number of rock graffiti in Arabic are finds that should probably be viewed as belonging to an "Arab" stratum (reflecting some degree of Arab infiltration in the pre-Islamic period). However, in the same area there is evidence for the existence of several open-air mosques and several hundreds of rock inscriptions in Arabic dating from the period after 636. [*See* Mosque.] These inscriptions, incidentally, continued into the ninth century, but by then they are Islamic rather than Arabic.

Early Islamic Period. The major turning point in areas of social, political, and cultural developments took place under the Umayyads (661–749). [*See* Umayyad Caliphate.] As early as the reign of ʿAbd al-Malik, Jerusalem benefited from an extraordinary renaissance. The Dome of the Rock was built in AH 72/691–692 CE, a magnificent artistic landmark that expressed the principles of the Islamic art to come—one of them being the use of the Arabic script for decorative purposes. The focal point created by the Dome of the Rock was augmented by a number of buildings, such as the al-Aqṣa mosque and in particular the series of secular buildings discovered during the excavations of Benjamin Mazar to the south and southwest of the Temple Mount. [*See the biography of Mazar.*] These buildings created a new Islamic compound on the Temple Mount, henceforth known as the Ḥaram esh-Sharif. It contributed to transforming Jerusalem into a major administrative center.

In about 712–715, the new city of Ramla was founded by Sulayman, who, as governor of Jund Filastin, chose to establish his capital at this major crossroad. [*See* Ramla.] Excavations at Ramla have permitted the reconstruction of the layout of the city in this early period. The earliest finds were indeed on virgin soil (the *raml* of Ramla). The mosque, a series of mosaic pavements, and particularly a large amount of pottery finds, with some evidence for the existence of a potter's workshop, all combine to offer a new picture of the material culture of Palestine in the eighth century. The phenomenon of the "Umayyad chateau" is exemplified by Khirbat al-Minyeh, on the shore of the Sea of Galilee (beginning of the eighth century) and Khirbat al-Mafjar in the Jericho area (mid-eighth century). [*See* Mafjar, Khirbat al-.] These mansions, linked to agricultural production in the surrounding areas, display a surprising degree of luxury and rich artistic decoration. The excavations of both palaces yielded a varied harvest of sculpture, floor mosaics, carved stone, and carved stucco, each in a most distinctive style. (Only the mosaics resemble their Byzantine counterparts.) During this period the country apparently underwent a considerable reorganization: the roads must have been repaired, for there are several milestones from the reign of ʿAbd al-Malik as testimony. Another significant innovation introduced by ʿAbd al-Malik was in the field of numismatics. The Byzantine coinage, which continued in circulation, eventually received Arabic countermarks. Somewhat later, completely new coins were struck in various centers of the country. A major reform was carried out by ʿAbd al-Malik in which the typical Islamic coin displayed Arabic script on both sides, including a proclamation of the Muslim faith (Ar., *shahādah*), a formula that persisted for centuries.

Islamic pottery deserves particular attention because it changed significantly from that of the preceding Byzantine period. Most of the pottery manufactured during the Early Islamic period was unglazed. However, it was of high artistic quality and great care is exhibited in its manufacture and finish. The shapes, of both vessels and lamps, are indicative of a new era. There was a sophisticated use of molds, enabling a wide variety of decoration—particularly evident in finds at Ramla and in some of the pottery from Khirbat al-Mafjar. The clay is almost always buff, fine, and well levigated. Gradually, glazes made their appearance, and from the ninth century onward, pottery in Palestine was part of the large and varied family of Islamic glazed polychrome ware. [*See also* Ceramics, *article on* Ceramics of the Islamic Period.]

Middle Islamic Period. Under the ʿAbbasids there is little evidence of involvement on the part of the authorities in making improvements in the cities. A rare find is a cistern in Ramla with a dated inscription corresponding to the year 789, during the reign of Harun al-Rashid. [*See* ʿAbbasid Caliphate.] At Abu Ghosh, excavations uncovered the earliest known public hostel (Ar., *khan*), with a rich assemblage of pottery, both unglazed and glazed, dated roughly to the tenth century. The outstanding remains of the Fatimid period that followed are two contemporaneous monumental inscriptions, one in the Dome of the Rock and the other in the al-Aqṣa mosque. Also belonging to the Fatimid period are two spectacular hoards of jewelry, found in the excavations at Caesarea and Ashkelon. [*See* Fatimid Dynasty; Jewelry; Caesarea; Ashkelon.]

Late Medieval Period. The Ayyubid period primarily marks the gradual return to Islamic rule after the interlude of Crusader control. This period, though again a relatively short one (1187–1250), is one of the most fascinating chapters in Islamic history and archaeology in Palestine. The new theological institution of the *madrasa,* or school, became widespread; the new cursive script (Naskhi) was preferred in calligraphy over that of Kufic writing; and the confrontation with the Crusaders led to a most unexpected culmination: the destruction of the coastal cities of the country as far south as Jerusalem. Excavations have produced dramatic evidence of this policy, which was to continue under the Mamluks. Magen Broshi's excavations along the southern wall of Jerusalem revealed a broken inscription commemorating the building of a gate in the wall by the Ayyubid sultan al-Malik al-Muʿazzam ʿIsa. It was known from the written sources that this wall had been destroyed by the same ruler shortly afterward. [*See* Ayyubid-Mamluk Dynasties; Crusader Period.]

The Mamluk period (1250–1517) is represented by monuments all over the country, from Safed in the north to Gaza in the south. It is best exemplified by the concentration of distinctive Mamluk monuments—*madrasas,* markets, and baths–in the Old City of Jerusalem. [*See* Jerusalem.] The modern city's urban plan *inter muros* reflects the Mamluk period to a great extent. Sites excavated in different areas of the country (e.g., Abu Ghosh, Yoqneʿam, Jerusalem) have yielded rather homogeneous pottery, but no local centers of production have yet been located. [See Yoqneʿam.] In the late medieval period, both glazed and unglazed ceramics continued to be manufactured, but they differed in quality, techniques, style, and motifs from their Umayyad and ʿAbbasid predecessors. In the Ayyubid and Mamluk periods, the clay of unglazed pottery is somewhat more green and the shapes are different. A very distinctive family of unglazed pottery made its appearance, consisting of handmade vessels with geometric patterns painted in a dark reddish brown over a pinkish slip. The glazed pottery is characterized by a combination of molded and incised (sgraffito) decoration. Excavations in Jerusalem have uncovered some examples of locally made marvered glass. In the Islamic period, the archaeology of Palestine shares many characteristics of material culture with both Syria and Egypt.

BIBLIOGRAPHY

Avni, Gideon. "Early Mosques in the Negev Highlands: New Archaeological Evidence on Islamic Penetration of Southern Palestine." *Bulletin of the American Schools of Oriental Research,* no. 294 (1994): 83–100.

Broshi, Magen. "Mount Zion (Notes and News)." *Israel Exploration Journal* 24 (1974): 285. Announcement of the discovery in Jerusalem of the Arabic inscription of al-Malik al-Muʿazzam, dated 1212 CE.

King, Geoffrey, C. J. Lenzen, and Gary O. Rollefson. "Survey of Byzantine and Islamic Sites in Jordan: Second Season Report, 1981." *Annual of the Department of Antiquities of Jordan* 27 (1983): 385–435.

Marmardji, A. Sebastianus. *Textes géographiques arabes sur la Palestine.* Paris, 1951.

Northedge, Alastair. *Studies on Roman and Islamic ʿAmman: Excavations of Mrs. C.-M. Bennett and Other Investigations.* Vol. 1, *History, Site, Architecture.* British Academy Monographs in Archaeology, 3. Oxford, 1992. Includes analysis of the Umayyad palace.

Rosen-Ayalon, Myriam. *The Early Islamic Monuments of Ḥaram al-Sharīf: An Iconographic Study.* Qedem 28. Jerusalem, 1989.

Sharon, Moshe. "The Cities of the Holy Land under Islamic Rule." *Cathedra* 40 (1986): 83–120 (Hebrew).

Sourdel, Dominique. "Filasṭīn I: Palestine under Islamic Rule." *Encyclopaedia of Islam,* new ed., B. Lewis, et al. ed. 2: 910–13. Leiden, 1965.

Whitcomb, Donald. "Khirbet al-Mafjar Reconsidered: The Ceramic Evidence." *Bulletin of the American Schools of Oriental Research,* no. 271 (1988): 51–67.

MYRIAM ROSEN-AYALON

PALESTINE EXPLORATION FUND. Founded on 12 May 1865, at a meeting held in the Jerusalem Chamber of Westminster Abbey, the Palestine Exploration Fund was the brainchild of George Grove, then manager of the Crystal Palace. Grove's interest in the fund was sparked by the work he had done on biblical place names for George Adam Smith's *Dictionary of the Bible.* It and the *Ordnance Survey of Jerusalem* appeared in 1864, raising public interest in the subject sufficiently for a society dedicated to studying the land of the Bible to succeed. This interest was heightened by Charles Darwin's *Origin of Species,* published in

1859, and by the text-critical work of the German school of biblical scholars led by Julius Wellhausen in Tübingen: it was felt necessary to buttress the historicity of the Hebrew Bible.

The fund's initial effort was to provide a proper survey and an accurate map of Palestine, as a basis for studying its archaeology (in the broadest sense). In 1865 Charles Wilson of the Royal Engineers carried out a preliminary survey for the fund. The substantial cost and difficulties involved in a full-scale survey were daunting. The fund decided instead to continue the work of exploring Jerusalem, concentrating on the problem of the location of Herod's Temple—a project chosen to raise the profile of the fund and attract the monies necessary for the larger project. Accordingly, from 1867 to 1871 Charles Warren explored "underground Jerusalem" by means of a series of tunnels around the Temple Mount (Ḥaram esh-Sharif). [*See* Jerusalem.] His work revealed for the first time the massive scale of the construction undertaken by Herod and greatly advanced what was known of the location of the Temple. By 1869 the quantity of material resulting from the fund's projects required the regular publication of a journal, the *Palestine Exploration Fund Quarterly Statement (PEFQ)*, the first journal specifically devoted to the study of the region.

By late 1871, the fund had enough money to engage a team of Royal Engineers to survey and map Palestine. The team's initial leader, R. W. Stewart, was sent home within a month of his arrival, a victim of "fever," probably malaria, which was to take the lives of several members of the survey party. He was replaced by Claude R. Conder, who arrived in July 1872 and led the survey until July 1875, when he was injured in an attack at Safed. He had been joined in 1874 by Herbert Horatio Kitchener, who was also injured in the attack. The survey was suspended until 1877, when it was resumed under Kitchener's command. It was completed in September of that year; the map was published in 1880 and the text volumes in 1881–1884. In 1881–1882 the American Palestine Exploration Society attempted to do a similar survey east of the Jordan River, but with the society's demise the work was left incomplete. The fund's attempt was cut short, after more than 800 sq km (500 sq. mi.) of central Jordan had been surveyed, as a result of the opposition of the Ottoman governor of es-Salt. Between 1885 and 1889, Gottlieb Schumacher surveyed the area of Transjordan between Amman and the Syrian border for the fund, while surveying the line of the Hejaz Railway for the Ottoman government. In 1883–1884, an expedition led by Edward Hull, assisted by Kitchener, carried out a geological survey of Wadi ʿArabah. This expedition concluded the first phase of the fund's activities—the mapping and survey of the land.

The next phase began with the first excavation carried out in Palestine by a professional archaeologist, W. M. F. Petrie, who chose Tell el-Ḥesi, believed then to be ancient Lachish. [*See* Ḥesi, Tell el-; Lachish.] Petrie spent six weeks on the site, during which time he laid the foundations for a stratigraphic excavation and established the outlines of the site's ceramic sequence as the basic means of dating the archaeological remains. Although Heinrich Schliemann's work at Troy had already shown that the tells that dotted the Near East were formed by continuous human settlement, this was the first time it was being demonstrated in the Levant. Petrie's use of pottery for dating purposes was at first opposed, notably by Conder, but soon became widely accepted. When Petrie expressed a desire to return to his beloved Egypt, the fund found a replacement in a young American, Frederick Jones Bliss, son of Daniel Bliss, who had founded what was to become the American University of Beirut. Bliss excavated at Ḥesi until the end of 1893.

The fund's international character was reinforced in this period by employing Charles Clermont-Ganneau, a French diplomat and antiquarian who had studied the antiquities of the country in connection with the 1873–1874 survey, and Conrad Schick, a German architect who had originally gone to Jerusalem as a missionary in 1846. Schick maintained a close connection with the fund from its inception until his death in 1901, during which time he carried out extensive research in Jerusalem. From 1894 to 1897, the fund again turned its attention to Jerusalem, and excavations were carried out in a number of areas by Bliss, assisted by the architect A. C. Dickie. Between 1898 and 1900, excavations directed by Bliss, assisted by R. A. S. Macalister, were carried out at four sites in the Shephelah: Tell Zakariya (ʿAzekah), Tell eṣ-Ṣafi (Gath?), Tell el-Judeideh (Moreshet-Gath), and Tell eṣ-Ṣandaḥanna/Mareshah (Marisa). [*See* ʿAzekah; Judeideh, Tell el-; Mareshah.] From 1902 to 1905 and 1907 to 1909, the fund carried out its largest excavation, at Tell el-Jezer (Gezer), under Macalister's direction. [*See* Gezer.] The large-scale and prompt publication of these excavations should have made them the cornerstone of future work in the area; however, Macalister's decision to publish the material by stratum/period, without any indication of findspot, and his crude stratigraphy made his report difficult to use. The fund's final excavation prior to World War I, which brought a halt to archaeology in the field, was in 1911–1912 at ʿAin Shems (Beth-Shemesh), directed by Duncan Mackenzie, assisted by F. G. Newton, an architect. [*See* Beth-Shemesh.] The fund then began to publish a series of annuals, of which only six volumes appeared. In spring 1914, with war looming, Kitchener asked the fund to survey the Negev desert, the last unmapped area in western Palestine. [*See* Negev.] A team of Royal Engineers commanded by S. F. Newcombe, carried out the mapping. The fund had chosen the distinguished Egyptologist T. E. Peet to carry out the archaeological survey, but Peet had a prior commitment. The fund turned to the director of the British Museum, Frederick Kenyon, who, in turn, obtained the services of two young archaeologists then excavating at Carchemish for the museum, C. Leonard Woolley and T. E.

Lawrence. The resulting map was completed in the first year of the war and released for publication in 1921; the archaeological survey results were published in 1915.

The establishment of the British Mandate in Palestine created a new situation. A Mandatory Department of Antiquities was created and in 1918 the British School of Archaeology in Jerusalem was established. A number of other organizations also operating in the field included the American Schools of Oriental Research, the École Biblique et Archéologique Française, and the Jewish Palestine Exploration Society. The fund renewed its own excavations in Jerusalem from 1923 to 1925, directed by Macalister, assisted by J. Garrow Duncan, and from 1925 to 1927, directed by Crowfoot, assisted by G. M. Fitzgerald. In 1934 Alan Rowe carried out a brief excavation at Gezer for the fund, intended to clarify the site's stratigraphy. Unfortunately, the stratigraphy in the area chosen for excavation was so shallow the promised final report never appeared. The fund's last major excavation, at Samaria/Sebaste (1931–1935), was a joint project with Harvard University, the British Academy, the British School of Archaeology in Jerusalem, and the Hebrew University of Jerusalem. [*See* Samaria.] The excavations revealed remains from the tenth century BCE, prior to the foundation of the royal citadel, and from the occupation following the move to the site by Omri in about 880 BCE. An important area of the Hellenistic and Roman city was excavated and the stratified sequence of *terra sigillata* ware became important for the study of the archaeology of the Roman Empire in regions as far away as Scotland.

The period following World War II was a difficult one for the fund. The last of the generation of the founders and their immediate successors was gone, and public interest in biblical matters—and the funds available for them—had greatly diminished. The fund did, however, continue to publish its journal, now known as the *Palestine Exploration Quarterly (PEQ)*, hold lectures, and give some limited financial support to promote research. In 1989 the fund resumed the publication of monographs.

[*See also* American Palestine Exploration Society; British School of Archaeology in Jerusalem; École Biblique et Archéologique Française; Israel Exploration Society; Nationalism and Archaeology; *and the biographies of Bliss, Conder, Clermont-Ganneau, Crowfoot, Kitchener, Lawrence, Macalister, Petrie, Rowe, Schumacher, Schick, Smith, Warren, Wilson, and Woolley*.]

BIBLIOGRAPHY

Bartlett, John R. *Edom and the Edomites*. Journal for the Study of the Old Testament, Supplement 77. Sheffield, 1989.

Condor, Claude R., and Horatio H. Kitchener. *Survey of Western Palestine*. 8 vols. and cased map. London, 1881–1888. Of the many publications (surveys and excavations reports) sponsored by the PEF, this is perhaps the best known.

Hodson, Yolande. "The Palestine Exploration Fund: Recollections of the Past." In *Biblical Archaeology Today 1990*, edited by Avraham Biran et al., pp. 6–8. Jerusalem, 1993.

Lipman, V. D. "The Origins of the Palestine Exploration Fund." *Palestine Exploration Quarterly* 120 (1988): 45–54. Includes extensive notes and bibliography.

Palestine Exploration Fund Annual. London, 1911–1927. Five volumes, issued irregularly.

Palestine Exploration Fund Pamphlets. London, 1878. Covers various subjects; includes proceedings and announcements of early publications.

Palestine Exploration Fund Quarterly Statement (1869–1936); continued from 1937 as *Palestine Exploration Quarterly*.

RUPERT CHAPMAN

PALESTINE ORIENTAL SOCIETY. While in Jerusalem as the first Annual Professor of the American Schools of Oriental Research (ASOR), Albert T. Clay, a professor of Assyriology at Yale University, perceived a need for greater communication and cooperation (from cultural and ecumenical perspectives) among scholars conducting research in Palestine. To that end, on 9 January 1920, he organized a meeting attended by twenty-nine scholars. The society held its first official meeting on 20 March of that year, at which time Père Marie-Joseph Lagrange of the École Biblique et Archéologique Française was elected its first president. Thereafter, the Palestine Oriental Society met quarterly, usually at the ASOR facilities. Other prominent charter members of the society were William F. Albright, Eliezer Ben Yehudah, Herbert Danby, Père Édouard Dhorme, and Père Louis Vincent. The society's last president, serving from 1941 to 1948, was J. H. Iliffe.

The society's stated purposes were to provide scholars from different backgrounds and nationalities with a forum in which to share their findings in all aspects of archaeological and oriental studies; to facilitate greater cooperation and coordination of efforts; to sharpen the focus of research through mutual criticism; to promote publication of findings; and to take advantage of the new openness toward archaeological excavations that characterized British rule in Palestine.

One of the society's major contributions was its publication, the *Journal of the Palestine Oriental Society*. Twenty volumes of the journal were issued from 1920 through 1941; an index was published in 1948, at the end of the British Mandate in Palestine, as its twenty-first and final edition. Virtually every aspect of Near Eastern archaeology is represented in the numerous articles the journal published, including Bible, botany, climatology, folklore, geology, history, inscriptions, epigraphy, linguistics, literature, mosaics, numismatics, pottery, prehistory, religion, and synagogues.

[*See also* American Schools of Oriental Research; École Biblique et Archéologique Française; *and the biographies of Albright, Lagrange, and Vincent*.]

BIBLIOGRAPHY

King, Philip J. *American Archaeology in the Mideast: A History of the American Schools of Oriental Research*. Philadelphia, 1983. In addition to being the standard book on the history of ASOR, this work contains valuable information about significant research organizations related to ASOR.

Glueck, Nelson. *The Journal of the Palestine Oriental Society: Indices to Volumes I–XXI, 1920–1948.* Jerusalem, 1966. Published on the occasion of the reprinting of the complete set of *JPOS* volumes, with a list of all the articles published in the journal by author and subject.

CHARLES E. CARTER

PALESTINIAN ARAMAIC. The language of the corpus of written material from Palestine from roughly 200 BCE to 200 CE are written in Palestinian Aramaic. The corpus principally comprises literary and ephemeral texts from Qumran, Murabbaʿat, and Naḥal Ḥever, but include inscriptions on ossuaries, tombstones, and coins; Aramaic words found in Josephus and the New Testament; and certain very early rabbinic texts, such as *Megillat Taʿanit.* Palestinian Aramaic belongs to the phase of the language that Joseph Fitzmyer (1979) has called Middle Aramaic, distinguishing it from the earlier Official or Imperial Aramaic, on the one hand, and the dialects of Late Aramaic on the other. Contemporary with Palestinian Aramaic are the Aramaic dialects of Nabatea, Edessa, Palmyra, and Hatra.

Morphologically, Palestinian Aramaic differs little from Official Aramaic. The principal differences are the use of third-person plural feminine forms of the pronoun, suffix, and verb; the use of *dn* rather than *dnh* for the demonstrative; and the occasional use of *d* for the earlier relative particle *dy.* Syntactically, Palestinian Aramaic displays a preference for historic Semitic word order (verb-subject-object), whereas Official Aramaic tends to free word order. In comparison with contemporary Aramaic dialects, Palestinian Aramaic tends to make more conservative use of Official Aramaic dialect traits than most. For example, unlike its contemporaries, Palestinian Aramaic retains the use of the jussive.

A major question in research on this dialect is the degree to which it represents the spoken Aramaic of Palestine—that is, how different were the spoken and written forms of the language? In all languages there are some differences, so the question is one of degree. Was there a "Standard Literary Aramaic," as many scholars contend, that was used to write most types of literary text? The existence of such a standard would imply a diglossia, in which different forms of a language serve different functions in complementary distribution. It would also imply, therefore, that various spoken Aramaic dialects existed in Palestine in this period—dialects whose distinctive forms would never appear in written texts except inadvertently. One of the larger issues involved is what sort of Aramaic texts scholars might rightly use in attempting to reconstruct hypothetical Aramaic originals of the sayings of Jesus.

Aramaic texts from Qumran number approximately one hundred, one-sixth of the nonbiblical scrolls; virtually all are literary as opposed to documentary. Broadly speaking, these are theological writings. Their dates correspond to the dates of the Dead Sea Scrolls generally (c. 150 BCE–70 CE). Attempts to date individual texts more precisely have not taken into account the possibility of significantly variant scripts among scribes working in a given period and are therefore unreliable. These Aramaic texts are for the most part written in the Jewish square script that developed from the Aramaic script used in the Persian period. Some are written in cursive or semicursive forms, but those scripts more commonly characterize contracts and other ephemeral writings such as are frequent among the Bar Kokhba materials. Among the best-preserved Aramaic scrolls from the Qumran caves are the *Genesis Apocryphon, 11QTargum Job,* the Enochic literature, and several copies of the *Book of Tobit.* A group of works that are more or less closely related to the biblical *Book of Daniel* are, like several chapters of that book itself, written in Aramaic. These writings include the *Prayer of Nabonidus* (4Q242), the "Son of God" text (4Q246), and the pseudo-*Daniel* apocalypse (4Q243–245).

Numerous Palestinian Aramaic texts from Murabbaʿat and Naḥal Ḥever are associated with the Bar Kokhba-led Second Jewish Revolt (132–135 CE). These texts include marriage contracts and writs of divorce, IOUs, deeds of sale, and subscriptions to contracts. Perhaps most significant is the correspondence from Bar Kokhba to his lieutenants, and from his lieutenants to others. A substantial proportion of the Bar Kokhba letters are in Aramaic, but others are in Hebrew or Greek. Alongside the Aramaic contracts are Nabatean analogs. Thus, these materials illustrate the linguistic complexity that characterized Palestine in this period. How Aramaic functioned socially vis-à-vis the other languages in use in this complex is still uncertain.

Aramaic ossuary and tomb inscriptions come principally from the region of Jerusalem and number nearly one hundred. New ones continue to be discovered almost every year. Excavations at Masada discovered many Aramaic-inscribed ostraca—letters and *tituli picti,* or "labels."

A potentially confusing imprecision in the literature is sometimes encountered in which Palestinian Aramaic is used loosely to connote very different corpora from the one described here. It is important to distinguish the term as defined above from the Aramaic of Palestine: the earliest Aramaic materials found in Palestine date to the ninth century BCE, long before the period under discussion here. The terms Jewish Palestinian Aramaic, denoting materials from the Byzantine period, and Christian Palestinian Aramaic, for materials from the same general period, are also used.

[*See also* Aramaic Language and Literature; Dead Sea Scrolls; Murabbaʿat; *and* Qumran.]

BIBLIOGRAPHY

Fitzmyer, Joseph A. "The Phases of the Aramaic Language." In *A Wandering Aramean: Collected Aramaic Essays,* pp. 57–84. Missoula, 1979. Seminal essay on the division of Aramaic, clearly proposing basic aspects of the view of Palestinian Aramaic adopted in this article.

Fitzmyer, Joseph A., and Daniel J. Harrington. *A Manual of Palestinian Aramaic Texts: Second Century B.C.–Second Century A.D.* Rome, 1978. Handy collection of Palestinian Aramaic texts, including virtually everything then known and a bibliography for each text. Dozens of new texts are available, however, principally from Qumran Cave 4, Masada, and the Babatha archive.

Lewis, Naphtali, et al. *The Documents from the Bar Kokhba Period in the Cave of Letters: Greek Papyri, Aramaic and Nabatean Signatures and Subscriptions.* Jerusalem, 1989. The Greek contracts from the Babatha archive, Papyri 15, 17–19, 20–22, and 27 have Palestinian Aramaic subscriptions that Jonas C. Greenfield treats in a separate section of the book.

Muraoka, Takamitsu, ed. *Studies in Qumran Aramaic.* Abr-Nahrain, Supplement Series, vol. 3. Leiden, 1992. Eight studies on Qumran Aramaic that touch on virtually all the central issues involved in defining Palestinian Aramaic.

Reed, Stephen. *Dead Sea Scroll Inventory Project: List of Documents, Photographs, and Museum Plates.* 14 fascs. Claremont, Calif., 1991–1992. Complete list of all the Dead Sea Scrolls and Bar Kokhba and related materials, including an indication of the language in which the text is inscribed; the place to begin compiling an inclusive text of all Palestinian Aramaic materials. Now revised in Emanuel Tov, et al., eds., *The Dead Sea Scrolls on Microfiche: A Comprehensive Facsimile Edition of the Texts from the Judean Desert* (Leiden, 1993). Note as well Reed's *Dead Sea Scrolls Catalogue: Documents, Photographs, and Museum Inventory Numbers* (Atlanta, 1994).

Tov, Emanuel. "The Unpublished Qumran Texts from Caves 4 and 11." *Journal of Jewish Studies* 43 (1992): 101–136. Provides a quick overview of texts from Qumran caves 4 and 11, indicating those in Palestinian Aramaic.

Yadin, Yigael, and Joseph Naveh. *The Aramaic and Hebrew Ostraca and Jar Inscriptions.* Masada I, the Yigael Yadin Excavations, 1963–1965, Final Reports. Jerusalem, 1989. Includes the Palestinian Aramaic inscriptions, letters, and lists, and *The Coins of Masada* by Ya'acov Meshorer.

MICHAEL O. WISE

PALMER, EDWARD HENRY (1840–1882), British Orientalist. Born in Cambridge, Palmer was a small, slender man with a low and remarkably receding forehead and an inherited tendency to asthma and bronchial disease. Orphaned when he was young, he was raised by an aunt and educated at Perse Grammar School in Oxford, where he studied Latin and Greek. As a boy he spent his pocket money on lessons in Romany from Gypsies passing through the area. He did not excell at school and, instead of going on to the university, went to work as a clerk in a firm of brokers in the City of London. During his time there he learned Italian and French in the same way he had learned Romany. He left the City following a serious attack of bronchial disease, from which he nearly died. He had already begun studying Oriental languages and in 1863 entered St. John's College, Cambridge, from which he received his B.A. degree in 1866; he was elected a fellow of St. John's in 1867.

In 1869 Palmer took part in the Ordnance Survey of Sinai, in which his duties were to collect the traditions, names, and legends of the local people, to copy and decipher any inscriptions encountered, and to observe any dialectical differences that appeared. Following the success of the Sinai expedition, Palmer was engaged by the Palestine Exploration Fund to explore the North Sinai and Negev deserts (December 1869–May 1870). The ten years that followed were taken up with the publication of reports on his explorations and books on the history of the region.

In 1871 Palmer was appointed to fill the vacant post of professor of Arabic at Cambridge, a preferment of a kind then most unusual there because it allowed the holder to keep his position if he married. Palmer married and began a period of intense and productive work. In 1881 the Egyptian army rebelled against the Anglo-French domination of its country, and London feared for the safety of the Suez Canal, the strategic link to India. Britain's military occupation of Egypt made it necessary to secure the loyalty of the bedouin tribes in Sinai, and Palmer was asked to undertake the mission with government backing and a few men. He left Gaza on 15 July 1881 and traveled through the desert, visiting the leaders of the tribes. He reached Suez on 1 August. On 6 August, Palmer and his party again set off into Sinai, but this time one of their guides betrayed them and they were ambushed and murdered in Wadi Sudr.

[*See also* Nationalism and Archaeology; Negev; Palestine Exploration Fund; *and* Sinai.]

BIBLIOGRAPHY

Besant, Walter. *The Life and Achievements of Edward Henry Palmer: Late Lord Almoner's Professor of Arabic in the University of Cambridge and Fellow of Saint John's College.* London and New York, 1883. Appendix 3, pages 427–430 gives a bibliography, "Works of Edward Henry Palmer." A biography by a friend; includes a portrait engraving of Palmer in oriental attire.

Lane-Poole, Stanley. "Palmer, Edward Henry." In *Dictionary of National Biography,* vol. 15, pp. 122–126. London, 1921–1922.

Palmer, Edward Henry. *The Desert of the Exodus: Journeys on Foot in the Wilderness of the Forty Years' Wanderings; undertaken in connection with the ordinance survey of Sinai and the Palestine Exploration Fund.* Cambridge, 1871.

Palmer, Edward Henry. *Arabic and English Name Lists Collected During the Survey.* Survey of Western Palestine. London, 1881.

Palmer, Edward Henry. *The Arabic Manual.* London, 1881.

RUPERT CHAPMAN

PALMYRA (Tadmor), oasis 245 km (152 mi.) east of the Mediterranean Sea and 210 km (30 mi.) west of the Euphrates River, in the center of the Syrian steppe, which is generally known as the Syrian desert (Badiat ash-Sham). Palmyra lies at the northeastern slope of Jebel al-Muntar of the Palmyrene mountain chain at an altitude of about 600 m. Palmyra is 235 km (146 mi.) from Damascus, 155 km (96 mi.) from Homs, and 210 km (130 mi.) from Deiz ez-Zor. It was always a rest stop, and for at least four thousand years a caravan station between Syria and Mesopotamia. The etymology of its ancient, and also actual, name in all Semitic languages, *Tadmor,* is unexplained in all known dialects. It may be derived from the West Semitic *dh-m-r*, which means "protect." It is called Palmyra in Greco-Latin sources, probably because of the extensive palm groves there.

The field of ruins of Palmyra and a part of the oasis are encircled by a rampart of about 6 km (4 mi.) long. A larger enclosure, known as the custom's rampart, rises up toward the mountain; its traces are still visible south of the Afqa Spring.

The city's "Grand Colonnade," a main street more than one km long, has been the city's axis since about the end of the second century CE. (Another axis belonged to the Late Hellenistic city; it was related to the Temple of Bel. The temple was later connected to the new axis through a triangular monumental arch misnamed the Arch of Triumph.)

The Temple of Bel, called the Temple of the Sun in ancient texts, is the largest and the most imposing building at Palmyra: it consists of a large, square courtyard more than 200 × 200 m in area, surrounded by four porticoes, a huge central sanctuary, a propylon, and vestiges of a large banquet hall, a basin, and an altar. The columns of the left portico and four tall columns of a nymphaeum led from the temple to a monumental arch decorated in the Severan-period style (beginning of the third century). Across from the arch, on the left portico, stand the ruins of the Temple of Nabu, which was refounded, with a beautiful propylon, in about the fourth quarter of the first century CE and completed in the second. Its monumental altar was constructed in the third century. On the right portico stands the monumental entrance added to the baths during the reign of Diocletian, at about the end of the third century. Also on the left is an arched path leading to the semicircular colonnaded square around the theater. To the right, near the tetrapylon, is another nymphaeum and two stepped column bases that point the way to a narrow road leading to the Temple of Baʿal Shamin, which was rebuilt in 131. Another street to the left is flanked by a banquet hall and a caesareum. This street leads to the theater, senate, and agora with its annex. Beyond the tetrapylon an Umayyad market was built inside the main street. To the left there is an exedra. At the end of the street, on the hill inside the enclosure of Diocletian's camp, is the Temple of Allat. From it there is a panoramic view of the ruins, the necropolis surrounding the city, and particularly the Valley of the Tombs. The valley was the site of the tower tombs belonging to the city's richest families in the first century CE, with some dating to the first century BCE.

PALMYRA. *The gate of the central building in the Temple of Bel.* (Courtesy Department of Antiquities and Museums, Syria)

Prehistory. In the Upper Paleolithic, the area to the southeast of the site was filled with a large lake whose remains are the present salt flats. It was an excellent place for hunting, which explains the existence of the Levalloiso-Mousterian flint industry from about 75,000 BP in the caves and shelters in the surrounding mountains (Jarf al-ʿAjla, thaniyat al-Baidah, Ad-Dawarah). Neolithic materials are encountered at different mounds in the vicinity of the oasis. Traces of scattered seventh-millennium settlements probably belong to the first sedentarization there, principally encouraged by the abundant sulfuric spring that gave birth to the oasis and subsequently to the city. Recent discoveries at el-Kowm, in the Palmyrene oasis region, confirm that the Uruk culture (end of the fourth millennium) extended to this region.

Bronze and Iron Ages. Excavation on the mound, underneath the courtyard of the Temple of Bel, uncovered primarily Early Bronze Age pottery (c. 2200–2100 BCE) especially that in the calciform Syrian tradition.

The oldest written texts known relating to Palmyra (Tadmor) and the Palmyrenes (Tadmorim) were found at the Assyrian colony of Kaneš (Kültepe) in Cappadocia and date to the nineteenth century BCE. The texts from Mari (Tell Hariri) also mention Palmyra and the Palmyrenes. At Emar (Meskene), texts dealing with Palmyrene citizens have been found. The eleventh-century BCE annals of Tiglath-Pileser refer to Tadmor as being in the country of Amurru. [*See*

PALMYRA. *The main gate of the Temple of Nabu.* (Photograph by Adnan Bounni)

Kültepe Texts; Cappadocia; Mari Texts; Emar Texts; Amorites.]

Seleucid and Roman Periods. Like Emesa/Homs, Petra, and Iturea at that time, Palmyra was independent, keeping its status as an Arab principality. It is known from Polybius (5.79) that at the battle of Raphia (217 BCE), between the Lagid Ptolemy IV and the Seleucid Antiochus III, a certain Zabdibel with ten thousand Arabs supported the Seleucids. These were certainly Palmyrenes because the name of their chieftain is known only in Palmyrene onomastica and means "the gift of (the god) Bel."

While Syria became a Roman province in 63–64 BCE, Palmyra maintained its independence and enjoyed—according to Pliny the Elder (*Nat. Hist.* 5.88)—a privileged position between Rome and Parthia. Both, it seems, were interested in Palmyra. In 41 BCE, Marcus Antonius undertook a futile push toward the city. The Palmyrenes had, as Appian reports (5.9), gained a key trade and political position. They procured exotic goods from India, Arabia, and Persia and then traded them to the Romans. When, precisely, Palmyra was incorporated into the Roman state is a contested issue, but it may have occurred under Tiberius (14–37 CE).

In the second half of the first century CE, Palmyra was occupied by a Roman garrison. Beginning in the reign of Trajan (98–117 CE) the city's own archers, cavalry, and cameleers participated in the defense of the empire's borders on the Danube River, in England, and in Africa. In 106, following the fall of Petra, Palmyra became the most important trading center in the East. Its great prosperity was expressed in the restoration of old monumental buildings and the reconstruction of temples. [*See* Petra.]

Under Hadrian (117–138) Palmyra achieved the status of a free city, as Hadriana Palmyra and, in the name of its senate and people's council, defined its own taxes and proclaimed its own decisions. Under Septimius Severus and the Syrian dynasty (first half of the third century), Palmyra was at its largest (12 km, or 7 mi., in diameter). Emperor Caracalla raised the city to the rank of a Roman colony in 212.

The foundation of the Sasanian Empire in 228 resulted in the loss of Palmyra's control over trade routes. The Palmyrenes then sought new economic opportunities under the leadership of a well-known Arabian family headed by Odainat, who held the title of governor of the Syrian province. In 262 and 267 he led two campaigns against the Sasanian capital. Odainat became dux romanorum, "chief general," of the armies of the East, corrector of the Orient, and king of the kings and imperator. The hope simultaneously of Palmyra and Rome was murdered along with his older son under mysterious circumstances. [*See* Sasanians.]

Because his second son was too young to succeed him, his wife Zenobia took the post of regent. Highly intelligent, knowledgable, and ambitious, Zenobia knew the political situation of the Orient and the weakness of Rome. She did not hesitate to proclaim her independence and took with her son the title of the Augusti. She soon conquered all of Syria, and her armies also occupied Egypt and Anatolia. The emperor Aurelian, forced to react quickly, defeated the Palmyrene army at Antioch and Emesa/Homs. Zenobia retreated to Palmyra, where Aurelian laid siege to her heavy defenses. Zenobia attempted to flee to the Sasanians but was caught and imprisoned in 272. In this critical situation the Palmyrenes rose up and massacred the occupying Roman garrison. Aurelian's retaliation was devastating. The ancient authors offer different versions of Zenobia's end.

In 297, the emperor Diocletian made peace with the Persians in the treaty of Nisibis, which moved the Syrian border to the Khabur River. Palmyra became a center of a network of roads where the principal road was the Strata Diocletiana linking Damascus to the Euphrates River. Inside the city a Roman camp was established and the ramparts were modified to protect the camp.

Byzantine and Islamic Periods. Christianity was well established in Palmyra in the fourth century. During the Byzantine period, the cellas of the temples of Bel and Baʿal Shamin and some other buildings were transformed into churches. At the end of the fifth century and at the beginning of the sixth, Palmyra was one of the residences of the Ghassanid ally of the Byzantines. According to Procopius (*De aedificiis* 2.11), Justinian (527–565) fortified Palmyra's rampart and reestablished its irrigation system.

In 634 Khaled ibn al-Walid, the general of the Muslim armies, occupied Palmyra peacefully. During the Umayyad period Palmyra regained some of its importance but during the ʿAbbasid period was neglected by the caliphs of Baghdad. It became important under the Burids of Damascus (twelfth century), the Ayyubids (twelfth–thirteenth centuries), and the Mamluks (thirteenth–fifteenth centuries). The Temple of Bel was transformed into a fortress, the cella becoming a mosque. The castle overlooking the city is attributed to the emir Ibn Maʿan Fakhr al-Din (1595–1634). The historian and high functionary Ibn Fadl Allah (1301–1349) refers to the splendid homes and gardens of Palmyra and to its prosperous commerce. In 1401 Timur (Tamerlane) sent a detachment against Palmyra that pillaged it. The city's decline accelerated during the Ottoman period (1516–1919). It was soon reduced to a village, at the mercy of nomadic tribes. In the last half of the twentieth century it experienced a renaissance.

Exploration. The story of Palmyra and Zenobia, its beautiful and noble queen, have fascinated the Western world since the Renaissance. They have inspired literary masterpieces by D'Aubignac, Labruyère, and Molière and paintings and tapestries. Many travelers were drawn to Palmyra: the Neapolitan Pietra della Valle (1616–1625); the Frenchman Jean-Baptiste Tavernier (1638); English merchants from Aleppo (1678, 1691), the Frenchmen Girod and Sautet (1705); and the Swede Cornelius Loos (1710). They returned to Europe with copies of inscriptions, drawings of ruins, and sometimes incredible travel stories. The visit of two Englishmen, Robert Wood and H. Dawkins in 1751 had far-reaching effects. Their work, *The Ruins of Palmyra,* which appeared in English and French in 1753, signaled the beginning of systematic exploration at Palmyra. A year later, the Frenchman Jean Jacques Barthelemy and the Englishman John Swinton deciphered the Palmyrene alphabet. An ever-larger number of travelers and researchers then followed: Louis François Cassas (1785), C. F. Volney (c. 1785), Melchior de Vogüé (1853), and J. L. Porter (1851). In 1861 William Henry Waddington copied a number of inscriptions. In 1870 the German A. D. Mordtmann edited several new texts and E. Sachau, who visited the city in 1879, devoted many articles to it.

In 1881 a Russian, S. A. Lazarew, discovered a text of the city's fiscal law, the longest economic text from the ancient world. This important document is now in the Hermitage museum. In 1889 D. Simonsen published the Palmyrene sculptures and texts of the Glyptotheque Ny Carlsberg. The collection is the result principally of the activity of M. J. Loytved, the Danish consul in Beirut.

In 1899 M. Sobernhein discovered a house tomb in the Valley of the Tombs and took the first photographs of Palmyra. Research on the entire city began in 1902 and continued in 1917 under the direction of Theodor Wiegand (1932). In 1908, 1912, and 1915 Alois Musil undertook explorations of the more distant reaches of the city.

In 1914 the French Académie des Inscriptions et Belles-Lettres initiated a project under the direction of Antonin Jaussen and Raphael Savignac to copy all hitherto known texts, which were subsequently published by Jean-Baptiste Chabot (1922).

In 1924 and 1928 Harald Ingolt opened an excavation on Palmyra's western necropolis area, on behalf of the French Académie des Inscriptions et Belles-Lettres and the University of Copenhagen. Again in 1928, with the architect Charles Christensen, he excavated many hypogea in the same area on behalf of the Rask Orsted Foundation. Once again he dug a new hypogeum in 1937 whose excavation was completed by Obeid Taha.

In 1929 A. Gabriel achieved the first precise topographic plan of the city. New epigraphic research was undertaken by Jean Cantineau (1930–1936) that was continued by Jean Starcky in 1949, Javier Teixidor in 1965, and Adnan Bounni and Teixidor in 1975. The large Temple of Bel was cleared in 1929–1930 by Henri Seyrig, who was then director of the Antiquities Service of Syria and Lebanon, with Jaʿfar al-Hasani, director of the National Museum in Damascus (Seyrig, Amy, and Will, 1968–1975). Between 1934 and 1940 Seyrig and al-Hasani were the strongest proponents of carrying out archaeological research at Palmyra. [*See the biographies of Starcky and Seyrig.*]

Robert Amy, Ernest Will, Michel Ecochard, Raymond Duru, and others participated in the excavations or the study of the Temple of Bel, the tomb of Yarhai (now exhibited in the National Museum of Damascus), the agora, the Villa Cassiopeia, and the Valley of the Tombs. Daniel Schlumberger (1951) investigated the environs of Palmyra and Starcky published the first comprehensive summary of Palmyrene research results. [*See the biography of Schlumberger.*]

With independence in 1946, national research at Palmyra expanded considerably. In 1952 Selim Abdul-Hak excavated the Hypogeum of Taʿi in the southeast necropolis. Beginning in 1957 Bounni initiated what is now some twenty years of research at Palmyra. Nassib Saliby, Taha, and Khaled Asʿad have been his principal collaborators. This research has focused on three hypogea in the Valley of the Tombs, the main street, the Temple of Nabu, the annex of the agora, nymphea A and B, and the street of Baʿal Shamin. Asʿad excavated the ramparts, the Temple of Arsu, and the Hypogeum of Amarisha, continued the excavation of the main street, and restored many buildings in collaboration with Ali Taha and Saleh Taha.

Foreign missions have been authorized by the Syrian authorities to participate in the excavations of several monuments: Paul Collart and his Swiss team worked on the temple of Baʿal Shamin in 1954–1956; since 1959 Polish excavations in the area of Diocletian's camp have been led by Kazmierz Michalowski, Anna Sadurska, and Michal Gawlikowski. In 1966–1967 Robert Du Mesnil du Buisson led excavations in the courtyard of the Bel Temple and also excavated the Temple of Belhamon, while Manot worked on the peak of Jebel al Muntar. Joint expeditions—Japanese, Swiss, and Polish—are also working with Syrian teams at Palmyra.

Language and Writing. Palmyrene onomastica, cults, rituals, and several deities represent definitive evidence of the Arab origin of the majority of the inhabitants of the city and its principality. They kept their tribal social organization and were attributed to four main tribes. Palmyrene texts are written mostly in Aramaic, which was the lingua franca in western Asia from the Achaemenid period onward. The Aramaic of Palmyra reflects western and eastern characteristics and has some Arabic expressions.

An essential source on Palmyra is certainly the Palmyrene texts found in different countries, from the Euphrates to northern England. In Palmyra itself about three thousands texts have been recovered. Hundreds of these inscriptions are bilingual (Palmyrene and Greek). Latin texts are very few. The oldest known Palmyrene text is dated to 44 BCE and the latest to 272 CE. In 1754 the Frenchman Barthelemy and the Englishman Swinton deciphered some Palmyrene texts independently. Palmyrenes used the Seleucid era (which began in October 312 BCE) for candendrical dates.

Economy. Palmyra's prosperity made it an important metropolis in the ancient world. An oligarchic class of merchants and caravaneers amassed considerable fortunes from the caravan trade. The luxurious life-style of the Palmyrene aristocracy was displayed in its fondness for temples, colonnaded streets, and monumental tombs. Entertainment was provided by theater, thermal baths, and banquets. Michael Rostovtzeff has correctly identified Palmyra as "the caravan city." The caravans were the hub of Palmyra's economic life. Indeed, Palmyra's social order, religious beliefs,

PALMYRA. *A relief depicting the great Palmyrene goddess and Tyche.* (Courtesy Department of Antiquities and Museums, Syria)

and architecture were all products of its caravan economy. The Palmyrene fiscal law found in 1881 (see above) reflects this clearly and gives an accurate image of daily life.

Religion. Palmyrene cults were characterized by eclecticism and syncretism. The city's pantheon constituted more than sixty deities headed by the Babylonian god Bel/Zeus, often represented with Yarhibol (sun) and ʿAglibol (moon). Nabu/Apollo, son of Bel, also had great popularity in the city, as in the rest of the region. The Canaanite Baʿal Shamin was the chief of another triad. Allat/Athena, the Arab goddess, and Arsu (the Arab Radu) had also their temples in the city. Many Gods were dressed in military costumes and some rode horses and camels.

The main practice in Palmyrene religion was the ritual of procession around the main temple, following the Arab tradition. Attendance at ritual banquets *(thiases)* was widespread. The priesthood was well organized; its highest authority was the symposiarch of the Temple of Bel.

Art and Architecture. All through the three centuries of its history (first–third centuries), Palmyrene art followed the Oriental and Greco-Oriental traditions of Syria and Mesopotamia, with a strong Central Asian influence—particularly Indian and Persian. The Greco-Roman impact on its aesthetics was very strong beginning in the second century.

Palmyrene arts produced mostly sculpture, particularly for religious and funerary purposes. Bas-reliefs predominated, while statuary was rare. In general, Palmyrene art is static, idealized, and stylized, giving little care to dramatic representation and portraiture. Special care was given to details of dress and jewelry, which on many stelae were colored.

Frescoes have been discovered in Palmyrene underground tombs. [*See* Wall Paintings.] They follow the traditional Oriental use of linear technique, frontality, and detailed accessories. In the mosaic pavements, themes are usually related to Greco-Roman mythology. [*See* Mosaics.]

According to Harald Ingholt there were three phases of Palmyrene art, following an Archaic period, from about the first century BCE to the first century CE, that produced more original and naturalistic work whose originality is unanimously recognized (Ingholt, 1928; Ingholt et al., 1955). The Palmyrenes excelled in many aspects of architecture, but their unique achievement was the tomb—and especially tower tomb, such as the Elabel tower tomb built in 103. In the field of religious architecture they built or refounded many temples. From 32 CE through the following two centuries they completed the monumental Temple of Bel, one of the most collossal and beautiful temples in the Orient. The rich decoration on Palmyrene religious architecture developed at about the end of the first century CE from Oriental and Greco-Oriental traditions, while maintaining Syrian traditions, such as vast courtyards adytons, monumental altars, windows in the cella, and merlons. Local limestone was used in the construction of public buildings and streets, but private houses were only partly constructed in stone.

PALMYRA. *Limestone portrait on a funerary monument.* Dated first-second century CE. (Courtesy ASOR Archives)

BIBLIOGRAPHY

Abdul-Hak, Sélim. "L'hypogée de Taʿi à Palmyre." *Annales Archéologiques Arabes Syriennes* 2 (1952): 193–251.

Bounni, Adnan, and Nassib Saliby. "Six nouveaux emplacements fouilles à Palmyre, 1963–1964." *Annales Archéologiques Arabes Syriennes* 15 (1965): 121–138.

Bounni, Adnan, et al. *Le sanctuaire de Nabu à Palmyre.* 1994 (catalog only; printed text due 1997).

Bounni, Adnan, and Javier Teixidor, eds. *Inventaire des inscriptions de Palmyre.* Vol. 12. Damascus, 1975.

Bounni, Adnan, and Khaled al-Asʿad. *Palmyra.* 2d ed. Damascus, 1988.

Cantineau, Jean, ed. *Inventaire des inscriptions de Palmyre.* Vols. 1–9. Beirut, 1930–1936.

Chabot, Jean-Baptiste. *Choix d'inscription de Palmyre.* Paris, 1922.

Collart, Paul, et al. *Sanctuaire de Baalshamîn à Palmyre.* 6 vols. Neuchatel, 1969–1975.

Colledge, Malcolm A. R. *The Art of Palmyra.* Boulder, Colo., 1976.

Dunant, Christiane. *Le sanctuaire de Baalshamin à Palmyre,* vol. 3, *Les inscriptions.* Rome, 1971.

Dunant, Christiane, and R. Fellman. *Le sanctuaire de Baalshamin à Palmyre,* vol. 6, *Kleinfunde/Objets divers.* Rome, 1975.

Fellman, R. *Le sanctuaire de Baalshamin à Palmyre,* vol. 5, *Die Grabanlage.* Rome, 1975.

Février, James-Germain. *Essai sur l'histoire politique et économique de Palmyre.* Paris, 1931.
Février, James-Germain. *La religion des Palmyréniens.* Paris, 1931.
Gawlikowski, Michal. "Die polnischen Ausgrabungen in Palmyra, 1959–1967." *Archäologischer Anzeiger* (1968): 289–307.
Gawlikowski, Michal. *Le temple palmyrénien: Étude d'épigraphie et de topographie historique.* Warsaw, 1973.
Gawlikowski, Michal. *Recueil d'inscriptions palmyréniennes provenant de fouilles syriennes et polonaises récentes à Palmyre.* Mémoires de l'Académie des Inscriptions et Belles-Lettres, vol. 16. Paris, 1974.
Ingholt, Harald. *Studies over palmyresk skulptur.* Copenhagen, 1928.
Ingholt, Harald. "Five Dated Tombs from Palmyra." *Berytus* 2 (1935): 57–120.
Ingholt, Harald, et al. *Recueil des tessères de Palmyre.* Bibliothèque Archéologique et Historique, vol. 58. Paris, 1955.
Michalowski, Kazmierz, et al. *Palmyra, fouilles polonaises, 1959–1964.* 7 vols. Warsaw, 1960–1977.
Milik, J. T. *Dédicaces faites par des dieux.* Paris, 1972.
Rostovtzeff, Michael. *Caravan Cities.* Oxford, 1932.
Schlumberger, Daniel. *La Palmyrène du nord-ouest.* Paris, 1951.
Seyrig, Henri. "Ornamenta palmyrena antiquiora." *Syria* 21 (1940): 277–328.
Seyrig, Henri, Robert Amy, and Ernest Will. *Le temple de Bêl à Palmyre.* 2 vols. Bibliothèque Archéologique et Historique, vol. 83. Paris, 1968–1975.
Starcky, Jean, ed. *Inventaire des inscriptions de Palmyre.* Vol. 10. Beirut, 1949.
Starcky, Jean. *Palmyre.* Paris, 1952.
Starcky, Jean. "Palmyre." In *Supplément du Dictionnaire de la Bible,* vol. 6, cols. 1066–1103. Paris, 1964.
Stark, Jürgen K. *Personal Names in Palmyrene Inscriptions.* Oxford, 1971.
Teixidor, Javier, ed. *Inventaire des inscriptions de Palmyre.* Vol. 11. Beirut, 1965.
Teixidor, Javier. *The Pantheon of Palmyra.* Leiden, 1979.
Wiegand, Theodor. *Palmyra: Ergebnisse der Expeditionen von 1902 und 1917.* Berlin, 1932.
Wood, Robert. *The Ruins of Palmyra, Otherwise Tedmor, in the Desert.* London, 1753.

ADNAN BOUNNI

PALMYRENE INSCRIPTIONS. The Semitic language spoken in the oasis of Palmyra in Syria developed from a dialect of the official ("Imperial") Aramaic used in the Achaemenid Empire. After the settlement of Amorites and Arameans in the oasis, the arrival of the Arabs in the area by the middle of the first millennium BCE made Palmyra the center of major Semitic groups for whom Aramaic, by then an international language, must have served as a common link. Spoken and written all over Western Asia, Aramaic outlasted the end of the empire; distinct dialects appeared once the politically and religiously fragmented region restabilized under the Macedonians and the Romans. It seems, however, that when used by people whose native language was not Aramaic the language developed divergences in syntax and vocabulary that were more conspicuous than in the language of native speakers. This would explain the idiosyncrasies of Palmyrene related in some points to Eastern Aramaic—the plural in *aleph,* the adverbial ending *-âîth,* and the infinitive ending *-û*—but with some features closer to Western Aramaic—the plural in *-yod aleph,* the imperfect with the prefix *y-* instead of *n-* or *l-*, and the relative *dy.* Other noteworthy features are the diacritic point often used, as in Syriac, to distinguish *d* from *r,* ligatures binding some letters to the letter that precedes or follows, and the final form of *n.* Palmyrene is known through some twelve hundred honorary, official, votive, and sepulcral inscriptions dating from the first century BCE to the fourth century CE. No literary text or document on leather has yet been discovered. Palmyrene was the first of the Semitic inscriptional languages to be deciphered (see Daniels, 1988) and new inscriptions appear regularly, both in official excavations and on the antiquities market.

The epigraphic material from Palmyra constitutes a remarkable legacy of an exuberant assemblage of traditions. The substratum of the Aramean tribes who populated the area of Palmyra in the second millennium BCE is perceivable in the names borne by gods and individuals alike. The Babylonian pantheon is present in some liturgical inscriptions discovered in the Temple of Bel. The pervasiveness of Phoenician influence is a less well-known phenomenon, but it cannot be depreciated. The rituals reflect the presence of both Syro-Palestinian traditions and Arabian cults. A statistical survey of the personal names appearing in the inscriptions has revealed that the bulk of the population was of Arab origin—and therefore more than half of the names can be best explained through Arabic; several Arabic words occur, too, in the vocabulary. On the other hand, the technical terms of municipal and administrative life are mostly Greek, and under the Romans the use of Latin words was frequent.

The inscriptions are occasionally given in a Greek version after the Palmyrene. This is particularly the case in the honorary inscriptions written on Corinthian columns that were ranged along the principal streets, or stood in the porticos of the temples and of the agora. On the column there is a bracket for the statue to which the text refers. Two examples of this kind of inscription are "The council and people have made these two statues of Bariki son of Amrisa son of Yarhibola, and of Moqimu his son, lovers of the city and fearers of the gods: to their honor. In the month Nisan, the year 450" (139 CE), and "This statue is that of Taimarṣu son of Taima son of Moqimu Garba, chief of the caravan, which has been made for him by the members of the caravan who came up with him from Charax, because he saved them (their) expenses, three hundred denarii of gold, ancient currency, and was well pleasing to them: to his honor, and to the honor of Yaddai and Abdibol his sons. In the month Nisan, the year 504" (193 CE).

Tombs at Palmyra showed formal variation according to period and resources. The inscriptions outside the hypogea and in the tower tombs are often bilingual, whereas within they are only in Palmyrene. Votive inscriptions are rarely bilingual. The following text is an example of a Palmyrene votive text, commemorating the gift of a column to a deity: "In the month Tebet, the year 363, Amtallat daughter of Bara a son of Attenatan, from the tribe of the Bene Mitha, wife of Taima son of Belhazai son of Zabdibel, from the tribe of the Bene Maazin, dedicated this column to Baal Shamen, the good and bountiful god, for her and the lives of her sons and brothers" (52 CE).

The Palmyrene script is a modified form of the elegant cursive used in the Persian chancelleries, and in many respects it approximates Hebrew square characters. The scribes carved their texts on the local limestone, using either the lapidary or the cursive technique, the former being close to the model of Greek epigraphic letters. No major changes are noticeable in either of the script types during the four centuries they were in use.

[*See also* Palmyra.]

BIBLIOGRAPHY

Bounni, Adnan, and Javier Teixidor, eds. *Inventaire des inscriptions de Palmyre.* Vol. 12. Damascus, 1975.

Cantineau, Jean, ed. *Inventaire des inscriptions de Palmyre.* Vols. 1–9. Beirut, 1930–1936.

Cantineau, Jean. *Grammaire du palmyrénien épigraphique.* Cairo, 1935.

Chabot, Jean-Baptiste. *Corpus inscriptionum semiticarum,* part 2.3, *Inscriptiones Aramaicas continens.* 2 vols. Paris, 1926–1947.

Daniels, Peter T. "'Shewing of Hard Sentences and Dissolving of Doubts': The First Decipherment." *Journal of the American Oriental Society* 108 (1988): 419–436.

Gawlikowski, Michal. *Recueil d'inscriptions palmyréniennes provenant de fouilles syriennes et polonaises récentes à Palmyre.* Mémoires de l'Académie des Inscriptions et Belles-Lettres, vol. 16. Paris, 1974.

Rosenthal, Franz. *Die Sprache der palmyrenischen Inschriften.* Leipzig, 1936.

Starcky, Jean, ed. *Inventaire des inscriptions de Palmyre.* Vol. 10. Beirut, 1949.

Stark, Jürgen K. *Personal Names in Palmyrene Inscriptions.* Oxford, 1971.

Teixidor, Javier, ed. *Inventaire des inscriptions de Palmyre.* Vol. 11. Beirut, 1965.

JAVIER TEIXIDOR

PAPHOS, ancient city on the southwest coast of Cyprus (34°42′ N, 32°35′ E), situated on a low hill above the coastal plain, fewer than 2 km (about 1 mi.) from the shore. The original settlement was also called Paphos, but since the end of the fourth century BCE has been called Old Paphos (Gk., Palaipaphos; Lat., Palaepaphus), to avoid confusion with the recently founded harbor town of New Paphos (Nea Paphos), some 19 km (12 mi.) along the coast to the northwest.

The ancient name of the city was lost during the Middle Ages. In the sixteenth century, the Swiss traveler Ludwig Tschudi (1519) and the Venetian official Francesco Attar (1540) discovered that the ruins outside the village of Kouklia marked the site of the renowned Sanctuary of the Paphian Aphrodite. The first excavations at Palaipaphos-Kouklia were carried out in 1888 by an expedition from the Cyprus Exploration Fund. After an interval of more than seventy years, the British Kouklia Expedition (1950–1955) initiated a systematic archaeological investigation of the city and the sanctuary. Since 1966, regular excavations have been conducted under the auspices of the German Archaeological Institute and the University of Zurich.

Paphos represents the only capital of the ancient kingdoms of Cyprus whose history dates to the early third millennium BCE. The site was inhabited in the Chalcolithic period (c. 2800 BCE). Greek immigrants began to appear in the extensive Late Bronze Age settlement at Paphos (late twelfth or early eleventh century BCE). The city remained the capital of the Kingdom of Paphos from the Iron Age until the conquest of Cyprus by the Ptolemies, in 294 BCE, who abolished the island's local monarchies. The city of Palaipaphos, however, continued to function as a noted place of worship throughout antiquity.

A local fertility cult is attested at Paphos as early as the third millennium. It seems that the Greek immigrants transformed it into the worship of the Paphian Aphrodite, whose cult later also adapted elements of the Syrian Astarte. The shrine at Paphos, situated close to the spot on the coast where the "foam-born" goddess was believed to have risen from the sea, gradually became one of the most famous sanctuaries of Aphrodite in the Greek and Roman world. The sanctuary therefore formed the chief architectural feature of Paphos. The first monumental sanctuary buildings date to about 1200 BCE. Basically, they represent a type of Near Eastern court sanctuary, combining a small, covered hall with a large, open temenos (a sacred precinct), originally filled with altars and votive gifts. The hall probably housed the idol of the goddess in the shape of a conical stone, a symbol of fertility. The aniconic worship of Aphrodite at Paphos throughout the sanctuary's history was a legacy of the original autochthonous cult.

In the large Late Bronze Age city of Paphos, workshops produced refined pottery, jewelery, and ivory objects that exhibit a characteristic fusion of Cypriot, Aegean, and Levantine traditions. Yet, probably the most flourishing phases in the history of the city were the Archaic and Classical periods, as shown by the large number of tombs of the wealthy and by an architectural heritage. In the sanctuary itself, a thorough Roman remodeling destroyed the LB buildings, but the cult's continuity is amply attested by more than four thousand fragments of Geometric, Archaic, and Classical terra-cotta votives. An imposing Late Archaic or Early Classical ashlar building most likely served as a royal residence. It is modeled on Achaemenid prototypes and exhibits a certain monumental elegance. A large Late Classical peristyle mansion, discovered a few years ago, may have served a similar purpose in the fourth century BCE. Another important feature of the Classical period is the vast chamber tomb *Spilaion tis Regainas,* the burial place of two fourth-century kings of Paphos.

The city of Paphos was defended by a circuit of walls built in the Early Archaic period and maintained until about 300 BCE. The northeast gate, which forms a sector of these fortifications, represents an important and, in some respects, unique monument of military architecture. Elaborate siege and countersiege works excavated on the site allow a detailed reconstruction of the siege of Paphos by a Persian army during the Ionian Revolt in 498 BCE. In order to amass the materials to construct a vast siege ramp, the attackers destroyed a sanctuary outside the walls. This debris contained several hundred fragments of sculptures and votive monuments that include some of the finest Archaic Cypriot statues known. These finds testify to a considerable local school of sculptors whose work combines Egyptian trends with Greek and Phoenician influences; they also provide a key date for the art history of ancient Cyprus. The potter's craft also lived on in the Iron Age, as shown by a large number of remarkable vessels decorated in the rather severe Paphian style that relies mainly on austere geometric patterns.

At the beginning of the third century BCE, when a considerable part of the population was transferred to the harbor city of Nea Paphos, the importance of the old city of Paphos declined, but it did retain its fame as an important religious center in the Hellenistic and later the Roman world. The sanctuary was rebuilt in about 100 CE, possibly after a destruction caused by the earthquake of 76/77 CE. This Roman sanctuary, which incorporated part of the LB buildings, was not in the classical Greco-Roman design. The building retained the basic Oriental character of an open-court sanctuary, reminiscent of the cult's Near Eastern antecedents.

The shrine with the longest cult tradition on Cyprus did not survive the final outlawing of all pagan religions by Emperor Theodosius I (391). Yet, several centuries later, at the beginning of the twelfth century, Palaipaphos (then named Couvoucle) regained some of its former importance. The royal manor house was erected adjacent to the sanctuary site, incorporating a thirteenth-century hall that is one of the finest surviving monuments of Gothic secular architecture on Cyprus. The manor served as a center of cane sugar production. On the coastal plain below it, a large and fairly well-preserved cane-sugar refinery was discovered and excavated. Erected in the late thirteenth century, it represents a so-far unique example of a medieval industrial plant; it remained in use until the end of the sixteenth century.

[*See also* Cyprus.]

BIBLIOGRAPHY

Maier, Franz G., ed. *Ausgrabungen in Alt-Paphos*. 4 vols. Konstanz, Germany, 1977–1986.

Maier, Franz G., and Vassos Karageorghis. *Paphos: History and Archaeology*. Nicosia, 1984.

Maier, Franz G. *Alt-Paphos auf Cypern*. Mainz, 1985.

Maier, Franz G., and M.-L. von Wartburg. "Reconstructing History from the Earth, c. 2800 B.C.–1600 A.D.: Excavating at Palaepaphos, 1966–1984." In *Archaeology in Cyprus, 1960–1985*, edited by Vassos Karageorghis, pp. 142–172. Nicosia, 1985.

FRANZ GEORG MAIER

PAPYRUS. The writing material named after the plant from which it is made, papyrus, was manufactured as early as the first Egyptian dynasty (c. 3100 BCE). The emergence of writing and the concomitant use of papyrus seem to be outcomes of the imperial bureaucracy. The Egyptians used papyrus until the ninth–eleventh centuries CE—some four thousand years.

Papyrus was first exported to Syria no later than the twentieth century BCE. It found its way to other societies that had developed writing, such as the Greeks. The majority of extant papyri have been discovered in Egypt, where they survived because of the dry climate, but they have also been found in Asia and Europe. While only a few fragments dating from the Classical period have been found in Greece, dozens of depictions of rolls and papyri appear on vases of the same period. These vase paintings supplement the textual sources with many details of Classical and Hellenistic Greek book culture.

That biblical literature was originally written on papyrus (rather than on parchment) is evident from archaeological finds and textual analysis: a seventh-century BCE papyrus was found in Wadi Murabbaʿat near the Dead Sea and one from the fourth century BCE was found near Jericho. [*See* Murabbaʿat; Jericho.] Imprints of papyrus fibers have been found on the underside of bullae used to seal papyri. These findings support scholarly claims that the "books" mentioned in the Bible (*Jer.* 36:15–16; *Ez.* 2:8, 3:1–3) were actually written on papyrus. Probably only under Hellenistic influence were biblical writings committed to parchment. Jewish sages disqualified biblical scrolls written on papyri for ritual purposes (see Mishnah, *Meg.* 2:2), probably because papyri were considered to be less valuable and less reliable than parchment. This habit of disqualifying papyri is seen also at Qumran: more than eight hundred scrolls have been found there and only some sixty of them (8 percent) are papyrus scrolls. Egyptian Jews, however, continued to use papyrus as was regular in Egypt.

Papyrus was manufactured in Palestine in the Byzantine period (fourth–seventh centuries). According to the Jewish mystical literature of the time, as well as the Testament of Abraham (probably composed in Egypt), in heavenly administration human deeds are written on *pinax* (Gk., wooden tablets with wax) and on papyrus, from which the same practice can be inferred for earthly administration.

Technology. The papyrus-manufacturing process described by Pliny (*Nat. Hist.* 13.74 ff.) did not change over its thousands of years of use. The product was made by tearing off the "skin" of the papyrus reed. The strips thus formed were laid in lengthwise and crosswise layers to achieve strength (sometimes a bit of vegetal glue was added), and the layers were pressed and beaten to meld them. The papyrus was then stretched and smoothed to make it fit for use. To create a roll, the sheets thus produced were glued together with the horizontal fibers on the inside, perpendicular to the join. A text on a scroll was normally arranged in columns, so that the writing followed the horizontal lines of the fibers. Normally, writing was done on only one side of the papyrus, although exceptions are known.

For practical purposes, the papyrus was limited to a standard size: 47 cm long at the most (29–33 cm on the average) and 22 cm wide. The total length of a typical papyrus scroll, consisting of some twenty "pages," was about 4.5 m—although much longer examples are known.

The dependence on a single raw material, a plant that grew mainly in Egypt, determined where papyrus was manufactured and had a significant effect on its cost when it was exported. The Egyptian embargo on exporting papyrus at the end of the seventh century CE opened the way for the use of parchment, and later of paper, its successors. "Ground" paper (the predecessor of modern paper) was invented in China in the second century CE, but reached western Asia only after the Muslim conquest of Turkestan in 751. After the secrets of manufacturing ground paper (from a selection of plants) were disclosed, paper gradually replaced papyrus for economic reasons. In Egypt, the large-scale manufacture of papyrus continued until the end of the eleventh century. It is manufactured today on a small scale, for the tourism industry.

Scribal Technique. The scribe's primary instrument was the pen (Gk., *kalamos*), a reed that was cut to some 15 cm and whose end was chewed to form a brushlike edge. The desired width of the script and the color of the ink determined which of several pens would be used. The ancient Egyptian scribe initially used several colors (with organic and mineral bases) because writing hieroglyphs was so much like drawing. In the course of time, the number of colors was reduced to two: black and red. The scribe's kit included an inkwell, a few pens, two dry inks, and a small container of water to prepare the ink for use. (see, e.g., Pierre Montet, *Everyday Life in Egypt in the Days of Ramesses the Great,* London, 1958, p. 255).

The ancient scribe usually wrote while standing or kneeling, without the aid of a table (as does his modern Yemenite Jewish counterpart). In the second millennium BCE, some Egyptian scribes began to use desks. In Western culture, the desk became an essential accessory only at the beginning of the Middle Ages (or perhaps earlier at Qumran; see Clark, 1963).

A scribe usually worked with other scribes, who were either his equal (official scribes like himself) or of different ranks and subordinate to the chief scribe. Using groups of scribes facilitated writing in more than one language and writing from dictation. Whole families (or a guild) of scribes created an apprenticeship system.

[*See also* Parchment; Scribes and Scribal Techniques; Seals; *and* Writing Materials.]

BIBLIOGRAPHY

Beck, Frederick A. G. *Album of Greek Education.* Sydney, 1975.
Černý, Jaroslav. *Paper and Books in Ancient Egypt* (1952). Chicago, 1977.
Clark, K. W. "The Posture of the Ancient Scribe." *Biblical Archaeologist* 26 (1963): 63–72.
Grohmann, Adolf. *From the World of Arabic Papyri.* Cairo, 1952.
Haran, Menahem. "Book-Scrolls in Israel in Pre-Exilic Times." *Journal of Jewish Studies* 33 (1982): 161–173.
Hunter, Dard. *Papermaking through Eighteen Centuries* (1930). New York, 1971.
Lewis, Naphtali. *Papyrus in Classical Antiquity.* Oxford, 1974.
Metzger, Bruce M. *Historical and Literary Studies.* Leiden, 1968. See pages 123–137.
Porten, Bezalel. "Aramaic Papyri and Parchments: A New Look." *Biblical Archaeologist* 42 (1979): 74–104.
Sirat, Colette. *Les papyrus en caractères hebraïques trouvés en Égypte.* Paris, 1985.
Skeat, T. C. "The Length of the Standard Papyrus Roll and the Cost-Advantage of the Codex." *Zeitschrift für Papyrologie und Epigraphie* 45 (1982): 169–175.

MEIR BAR-ILAN

PARCHMENT. Animal skins have been treated for human use since Paleolithic times, but processing skins for writing (parchment) is a relatively late development, post-dating the invention of papyrus. Early evidence for writing on skins comes from the Egyptian fourth dynasty, before 2750 BCE. The practice was limited to religious and other special writings (such as the Book of the Dead). Although the Assyrians and the Babylonians wrote on clay tablets, there is evidence that they also wrote on parchment, at least from the sixth century BCE onward.

The parchment scroll was unknown in the Hellenistic and Roman world. In the first century CE, Pliny (*Nat. Hist.* 13.70) the statement of Varro (a Roman scholar and politician, 116–27? BCE) that the preparation of skins for writing was invented in Pergamon in Asia Minor at the beginning of the second century BCE (see below). In the Hellenistic world at least, the transition from papyrus to parchment may have been the result of the Egyptian embargo on exporting papyrus. The transition to parchment took place in Palestine as well, and the Jewish sages of the Roman period were of the opinion that any mention of a "book" in the Bible referred to a parchment scroll. It is possible that the use of parchment in Judaism became dominant under the influence of Hellenistic scribal culture: it is attested that the Hebrew and Aramaic languages borrowed more than twenty technical Greek terms pertaining to the manufacture of parchment during that period, among them *diphtera* (Gk., untanned hide for writing), *duchsustos* (the inferior of parchment), *tomos* (scroll), and *tophos* (formula, form).

Unlike papyrus, a strictly Egyptian product, parchment could be produced anywhere and was considerably more durable. In Egypt, low humidity and the ready availability of the papyrus plant kept papyrus the material of choice.

Technology. While the production of papyrus remained virtually unchanged for thousands of years, methods of skin preparation evolved over time. The skin was taken from comestible animals such as sheep, goats, or cows; the hair and fat were removed; and the skin was made smooth.

The traditional method of preparing a hide was to soak it in water, to which calcium ($Ca(OH)_2$) or flour (to cause fermentation) and salt had been added. Subsequently, tannin, made of oak gall, was added, which produced an irreversible chemical reaction that strengthened the product. To remove hair or to improve the product some tanners used dates in the process (or dog dung—although not all the Jewish sages favored it). Different treatment processes applied to the raw skins led to a variety of final products, each with a different name, such as *diphtera* or *gewil* (Gk., the whole, unplaned hide).

A material called *pergamena,* first mentioned in 301 CE, is assumed to have been prepared by the people of Pergamon. The process did not include tanning, so that the skin dried while it was being stretched. The final product was thin and very delicate.

The ancient preparation techniques were passed on into the Middle Ages but were abandoned when the technology for producing paper became available in Europe—in Spain, in the twelfth century. The use of paper increased after the development of printing in the sixteenth-seventeenth centuries. The use of parchment became purely ceremonial or ritualistic; it is, for example, the material of the modern Jewish Torah scroll.

Scribal Technique. Scribes used two types of pens for writing on parchment. One, made of iron or wood, was stiff; the other, the *kalamos* (Gk., "pen"), of reed, was much softer and was used as a brush. The ink used was usually made out of lampblack mixed with the sap of plants. Scribes soon discovered, however, that by adding various minerals to the mixture they could strengthen the dye, making the ink more difficult to erase. Different types of inkwells, from the pharaonic period to the Roman-Byzantine periods, have been found in Egypt, Israel, Jordan, and elsewhere in the Near East (Khairy, 1980).

Scribes writing in Aramaic wrote in ink on clay tablets, using only black ink. Jewish scribes in the Roman period sometimes used ink in other colors, but religious tradition limited writing on the Torah scroll to black only (out of a few examples from Qumran).

[*See also* Leather; Papyrus; Scribes and Scribal Techniques; Tablet; *and* Writing Materials.]

BIBLIOGRAPHY

Carvalho, David N. *Forty Centuries of Ink* (1904). New York, 1971.

Dougherty, Raymond P. "Writing upon Parchment and Papyrus among the Babylonians and the Assyrians." *Journal of the American Oriental Society* 48 (1928): 109–135.

Haran, Menahem. "Book-Scrolls in Israel in Pre-Exilic Times." *Journal of Jewish Studies* 33 (1982): 161–173.

Haran, Menahem. "Book-Scrolls at the Beginning of the Second Temple Period: The Transition from Papyrus to Skins." *Hebrew Union College Annual* 54 (1983): 111–122.

Haran, Menahem. "Bible Scrolls in Eastern and Western Jewish Communities from Qumran to High Middle Ages." *Hebrew Union College Annual* 56 (1985): 21–62.

Haran, Menahem. "Technological Heritage in the Preparation of Skins for Biblical Texts in Medieval Oriental Jewry." In *Pergament: Geschichte, Struktur, Restaurierung, Herstellung,* edited by Peter Rück, pp. 35–43. Sigmaringen, 1991.

Khairy, Nabil I. "Ink-Wells of the Roman Period from Jordan." *Levant* 12 (1980): 155–162.

Olnik, Yael. "Pottery Ink-Wells of the Roman Period from the Land of Israel" (in Hebrew). *Israel: ʿAm waAretz* 1 (1983–1984): 55–66.

Pinner, Harry L. *The World of Books in Classical Antiquity.* Leiden, 1958.

MEIR BAR-ILAN

PARROT, ANDRÉ (1901–1980), French archaeologist noted for his exploration of the site of Mari in Syria. The son of a minister, Parrot studied theology, during which time he first became interested in the ancient Near East when he took some art history courses at the École du Louvre. The year he spent at the École Biblique et Archéologique Française in Jerusalem determined his vocation. He did his first archaeological work in 1926 at Nerab in North Syria and a year later at Baalbek in Lebanon. He participated in the excavation of Sumerian Telloh (1930) and ultimately became director of that project (1931–1933). Parrot also explored at Tell Senkere (ancient Larsa) in 1933, until difficulties with the Iraqi authorities ended his excavation. Although he returned to Larsa for two campaigns in 1967, he concentrated his field research at Mari, where he conducted twenty-one campaigns before 1974.

Throughout his career, Parrot worked at the Louvre museum, first as conservator, then as chief conservator of the Department of Near Eastern Antiquities. He became director of the museum in 1965. After World War II he reorganized the museum's Near Eastern galleries, which remained unchanged until 1992. Especially concerned with the history of art in its traditional form (cf. Parrot, *Sumer* [1960] and *Assur* [1961]), Parrot drew from the exceptionally rich discoveries at Mari, realizing that they would be of interest not only to specialists, but to a broad public. In his studies of the Flood, the Tower of Babel, and the Patriarchs, Parrot sought to show connections between the biblical world and that of other Near Eastern civilizations.

[*See also* Baalbek; Larsa; *and* Mari.]

BIBLIOGRAPHY

Parrot, André. *Tello: Vingt campagnes de fouilles, 1877–1933.* Paris, 1948.
Parrot, André. *Glyptique mésopotamienne, fouilles de Lagash (Tello) et de Larsa (Senkereh), 1931–1933.* Paris, 1954.
Parrot, André. *Mission archéologique de Mari.* 4 vols. Paris, 1956–1968.
Parrot, André. *Sumer.* Paris, 1960.
Parrot, André. *Assur.* Paris, 1961.
Parrot, André. *L'aventure archéologique.* Paris, 1979. Autobiography of the excavator of Larsa, Telloh, and Mari.

JEAN-CLAUDE MARGUERON

Translated from French by Nancy W. Leinwand

PARTHIANS. Parthava, which lies southeast of the Caspian Sea, was part of the Achaemenid Empire. It is recorded in royal inscriptions, including Darius's report of a revolt in 521 BCE. Yet, there is no record of the Parthians in the Hebrew Bible or in Assyrian annals. Those who ruled Parthava in the third century BCE, as Parni, were outsiders related to the Saka (Scythians). They adopted the local Iranian dialect and culture of the Parthian residents, calling themselves Arsacid, after the founder of the dynasty, Arsaces (c. 247 BCE).

In about 171 BCE, Mithridates I expanded the Parthian realm dramatically, at the expense of the Seleucids. By 141 BCE, Babylonia had become the center of the new Parthia. Continuing expansion toward Asia Minor brought the Parthians into conflict with the Romans, who felt their eastern interests threatened. The best-known confrontation, because of the loss of legionary standards, was the Roman proconsul Crassus's defeat at Carrhae, in northern Syria, in 53 BCE. Subsequent rivalries within Parthia weakened the state and eventually allowed the emperor Augustus to engineer the return of the standards, a peace celebrated in his Odes (no. 15) by the poet Horace.

Knowledge of the Parthians comes mostly from these western sources. Parthian sources tend to be rare. Their own successors downplayed Parthian history and deliberately suppressed the Parthian version of Zoroastrianism, so that few texts were consciously preserved. Coins, with individual bust portraits, furnish the outlines of the chronology (247 BCE–226 CE). Commercial documents were often written in ink, as ostraca, or on parchment. As a variant of Aramaic, the script is imprecise, and the heavy use of ideograms makes it difficult to decipher. Used by their successors at first, the Parthian language was abandoned in official inscriptions after seventy-five years of Sasanian rule.

Commentators tend to represent the Parthians as unsophisticated because of their origins as horse-riding tribesmen from the steppes of Central Asia. Fratricide over who should inherit the throne did eradicate most advantages gained through territorial conquest; and the use of Crassus's head as a gruesome stage prop in a performance of the Bacchae is a reasonable example of "eastern barbarity." However, the fact that, as Plutarch tells us *(Life of Crassus),* this Greek play was being watched by the Parthian King Orodes II and Artavazd of Armenia, while drawing up a military alliance through marriage of a son and daughter to counter a Roman invasion, tells a lot about the culture and diplomacy of the first-century BCE Parthians. Greek was one of the formal languages used in Parthian administration. Although the use of the language has been given as an example of Parthian political weakness, it should rather be seen as an astute acknowledgment of the distinct heritage of Parthia's Macedonian settlers and a readiness to use the technical and administrative skills of an immigrant population.

Through his self-claimed title "king of kings," as expressed on all royal coins, the Parthian monarch was a supreme ruler. But there was a variety of governments in the provinces and principalities; some areas occasionally acquired degrees of independence that lasted for a short time, including the right to strike coins, which makes it difficult to define the political boundaries. If describing only those cities ruled directly from the capital, Parthia would appear to have been on the wane as soon as its greatest limit was fixed, in the expansionist years of the second century BCE. A definition by culture allows a broader scope, but it is difficult to know where to stop. Palmyra (Syria) and Taxila (Pakistan) have strong Parthian elements but cannot be claimed to be Parthian, any more than Hatra (Iraq)—because Hatra was the seat of a completely independent Arab principality. Yet, the latter's artwork is always called Parthian. Other excavated sites, such as Nisa (Turkmenistan), Kuh-i-Khwaja (Seistan), and Shahr-i Qumis (Gurgan) were far from the royal capital and eventually lay outside of Parthia proper. Even Qal'eh-i Yazdigird (Media), which lay within easy reach of the capital, was a rebel fortress.

Parthian art is as difficult to define as Parthian government. Rather than be judged as a culture in which Greek standards became debased, Parthian art should be seen as part of an evolution of the distinctive "eastern" modes that became fundamental in later Iranian and Islamic art. In architecture, the vaulted *eyvan/iwan,* or hall, opening onto a courtyard, replaced the older columned style, becoming an Iranian norm. Overall wall coverings of geometric ornament in plaster, based on textile designs, became another distinctive development in Parthian art. In pottery production, the glazed traditions of ancient Assyria were continued, and it is said that the Parthians applied the principle of the battery in the electroplating of metal. The almost five hundred years of Parthian culture formed an important link between the ancient world and the world of Islam.

[*See also* Persia, *article on* Persia from Alexander to the Rise of Islam.]

BIBLIOGRAPHY

The Cambridge History of Iran, vol. 3, parts 1 and 2, *The Seleucid, Parthian, and Sasanian Periods.* Edited by Ehsan Yarshater. Cambridge,

1983. See, in particular, notable contributions by A. D. H. Bivar, "The Political History of Iran under the Arsacids" (pp. 21–100); Mary Boyce, "Parthian Writings and Literature" (1151–1165); and Daniel Schlumberger, "Parthian Art" (1027–1054).

College, Malcolm A. R. *Parthian Art.* Ithaca, N.Y., 1977. Thorough but highly Eurocentric reference work for a wide range of Parthian art.

Debevoise, Neilson C. *A Political History of Parthia.* Chicago, 1938. Slightly out-of-date but extensive overview from the standpoint of Western sources.

Keal [sic], E. J. "The Art of the Parthians." In *The Arts of Persia,* edited by R. W. Ferrier, pp. 49–59. New Haven, 1989. Short essay focusing on Parthian archaeological discoveries but usefully published in a volume in which the wider context of Islamic art in Iran can be appreciated.

Mathiesen, Hans E. *Sculpture in the Parthian Empire.* 2 vols. Aarhus, 1992. Revolutionary look at an old subject, using the well-defined premises of classical art history.

Sellwood, David. *An Introduction to the Coinage of Parthia.* London, 1971. Reasonably up-to-date and complete catalog of the Parthian royal coins that form the basis of the political history.

E. J. KEALL

PASARGADAE, site located in the mountain-ringed Morghab Plain of southwestern Iran at an elevation of 1,900 m above sea level (30°15′ N, 53°14′ E). Pasargadae was founded by Cyrus the Great (559–530 BCE) soon after his conquest of Lydia (c. 547 BCE). According to Strabo (*Geog.* 15.3.8), the site marked the scene of Cyrus's prior victory (c. 550 BCE) over his erstwhile suzerain Astyages of Media. Early Achaemenid art and architecture took shape at Pasargadae and Cyrus, founder of the Persian Empire, was buried

PASARGADAE. Figure 1. *The tomb of Cyrus seen from the west.* The stone elements in the foreground were installed in the thirteenth century CE when the tomb served as the central part of a medieval mosque. (Photograph by O. Kitson, 1961)

there. While the name of the site is rendered as Batrakataš in the Elanite cuneiform of the Persepolis fortification tablets, the name in current usage derives from a Greek transliteration of an Old Persion toponym of still-uncertain meaning.

From the fifteenth century onward, the distinctive, well-preserved Tomb of the Mother of Solomon (the name then ascribed to Cyrus's long-forgotten resting place) was noted by European travelers traversing the main caravan route between Isfahan and Shiraz. Beginning in 1812, a number of such observers raised the possibility that the Morghab monuments might indeed constitute the lost remains of Cyrus's capital, but it took the detailed arguments first of George N. Curzon (1892) and then of Ernst Herzfeld (1908) to affirm the correlation. Herzfeld conducted the first excavations at Pasargadae in 1928. Six years later Aurel Stein examined several of the prehistoric mounds standing on the fringes of the Morghab Plain, and in 1935 E. F. Schmidt took the first aerial photographs of the site. Subsequent excavations were carried out by Ali Sami from 1949 to 1955 under the auspices of the Iranian Antiquities Service and by David Stronach from 1961 to 1963 on behalf of the British Institute of Persian Studies.

The principle remains of Achaemenid Pasargadae are distributed over an area some 3 km (2 mi.) long and 2 km (1 mi.) wide. Individual monuments within this parklike stretch of ground adjacent to the Pulvar River include the tomb of Cyrus, a monumental gatehouse (R), two palaces, a royal garden, an enigmatic stone tower (the Zendan-i Suleiman), two hollow limestone plinths, and an impressive stone platform jutting from the western side of a low hill now known as the Tall-i Takht, or "throne hill."

Tomb of Cyrus. Arguably an intentional synthesis of many separate Near Eastern architectural elements, the tomb of Cyrus stands at the southern limit of the site, approximately one kilometer south of the palace area (see figure 1). With its massive ashlar masonry and plain surfaces balanced by only a minimal number of decorative moldings, the structure creates an indelible impression of dignity, simplicity, and strength. With an estimated original height of 11.10 m, the tomb consists of two parts: a high plinth with six receding tiers and a rectangular cella with a steep-pitched, gabled roof. The stepped plinth measures 13.35 × 12.30 m at the base, and the compact tomb chamber, reached through a low doorway, is 3.17 m long, 2.11 m wide, and 2.11 m high. Until just after the fall of the Achaemenid Empire in 330 BCE, the body of Cyrus is said to have lain here in a golden coffin, on a golden couch beside a table (*Geog.* 15.3.7). Much later, in the thirteenth century CE, a shallow *miḥrab,* or prayer niche, was cut into the southwest wall of the tomb chamber. For an unknown period of time, the tomb served as the focal point of a medieval mosque.

Gate R. Placed on the eastern approach to the palace area, Gate R (also known as the Palace with the Relief) appears to have provided the chief ceremonial means of entrance to the site as a whole. Now greatly denuded, this free-standing rectangular structure originally housed a markedly tall, stone-floored hypostyle hall with two rows of four stone columns and four axial doorways. While the broad, main doorways on the opposed short walls were at one time flanked by paired colossi of Assyrian inspiration, the worn relief of a four-winged apotropaic genius still stands guard over the northeastern side door (see figure 2). Based on yet another kind of Assyrian protective image, the latter figure is distinguished by a short-bearded face with a distinctly Persian physiognomy, a traditional Elamite robe, and an Egyptian *hmhm* crown (an impressive headdress that rested on the long twisted horns of the Abyssinian ram). This last attribute, which was at home in the egyptianizing art of Syria and Phoenicia, may only have been introduced in order to underscore the submission of the eastern Mediterranean seaboard in 539 BCE; equally, however, it may have been intended to advertise what was (at the time) a still-unfulfilled Achaemenid claim to Egypt.

PASARGADAE. Figure 2. *Apotropaic four-winged figure.* The figure is carved in low relief on the one well-preserved door jamb of Gate R. Before the topmost portion of the imposing *hmhm* crown was broken off some 130 years ago, the intact figure measured about 2.85 m in height. (Photograph by O. Kitson, 1961)

Palace S. In reference to this structure's one surviving

13-meter-high stone column, Herzfeld (1908) opted for the label palace S, an abbreviation from *der palast mit der saule* ("the palace with the column"). The architects of palace S succeeded in combining, in one harmonious design, certain longstanding Iranian traditions (e.g., a lofty audience hall with two rows of four columns) with particular imported lonian concepts (such as, most notably, that of placing an open and inviting columned portico on each side of a freestanding building). In terms of innovation, palace S also documents the first known use of one of the more distinctive (and indigenous) emblems of Achaemenid architecture: a stone capital in the form of a double animal protome. At the same time, however, certain of the now severely truncated doorway reliefs of palace S (including one in which the relief shows the legs of a bull man and those of a fish-cloaked genius) show a clear debt to the rich, exotic imagery of Assyria. Seventy years after the fall of Nineveh, Cyrus appears to have realized, in short, that various of the more distinctive elements in the art of Assyria could be borrowed with advantage to proclaim the return of a degree of dominion not seen since the days of Ashurbanipal. [*See* Assyria; Nineveh.]

Palace P. Herzfeld (1908) named palace P (*palast mit der pfleiler,* or "palace with the anta") for its once single visible feature: a protruding stone anta. In contrast to Cyrus's other palatial constructions, this innermost palace appears to have been intended to supply a relatively private, if still representational, setting for royal audiences. This circumstance probably accounts, for example, for the small scale of the thirty columns that once graced the central hall; for the narrow width of even the two main doorways that led into the hall; and for the importance given to the exceptionally long, well-appointed "garden portico" on the southeast side of the building. In many ways, in fact, palace P stands out not so much as a formal palace as a garden pavilion of exceptional size and status. More that this, the building was far from complete when Cyrus died in battle; and, as the latest patterns of research now indicate, neither palace P's Persepolitan-style doorway sculptures (each of which once included a figure of Cyrus followed by an attendant) nor any of the building's three separate inscriptions (including a single example of the standard trilingual building inscription that can be understood to have carried the meaning "I, Cyrus, the king, the Achaemenid [built this]") are to be attributed to Cyrus. Instead, each of these features has to be attributed to Darius: a monarch who apparently found it advisable—not least at the emotive site of Pasargadae—to project his own carefully nuanced image of the memorable ruler whose line he had supplanted.

Palace Garden. Although Cyrus did not live long enough to enjoy the prospect, it is clear that he had an external throne seat placed at the midpoint of the southwest portico of palace P in order to contemplate a well-ordered, luxuriant inner garden. Long, white limestone water channels, studded at intervals by square basins, still define the rectilinear lines of this early Achaemenid garden. It appears to have been divided into four quadrants—a division that may, at the time, have been understood to symbolize the "four quarters" of universal rule. [*See* Gardens, *article on* Gardens in Preclassical Times.]

The possibility that the palace garden was scrupulously maintained for two hundred years (perhaps as one expression of the homage that continued to be paid to Cyrus in his capital and burial place), is not at all improbable. Such a claim not only derives credibility from the long-term, clearly detectable impact of Cyrus's fourfold garden plan (Stronach, 1994, but could also be said to be substantiated by the discovery, within the confines of the garden, of the elegant Pasargadae treasure, a rich hoard of Achaemenid gold and silver objects that, based on the objects themselves, is not likely to have been hidden before 350 BCE.

Zendan-i Suleiman. One of Cyrus's most carefully constructed and enigmatic stone monuments, the Zendan-i Suleiman ("prison of Solomon") originally consisted of an almost square, 14-meter-high tower in which a solitary, raised room was approached by a projecting monumental stone staircase. Copied by Darius at Naqsh-i Rustam, and variously regarded as either a tomb, a fire temple, or a depository, this now-fragmentary construction continues to defy secure interpretation. [*See* Naqsh-i Rustam.]

Stone Plinths. The extreme northern limit of Pasargadae is marked by two isolated limestone plinths, each of which is square in plan and more than 2 m high, and each of which can be ascribed to the reign of Cyrus on the basis of datable stone working techniques. While numerous interpretations of the function of these features have been put forward, it is most likely (on the basis of comparable evidence contained in the funerary relief of Darius) that Cyrus ascended the step-topped southern plinth (by means on an eight-stepped staircase block) in order to worship opposite an elevated altar that stood on the adjacent, northern plinth.

Tall-i Takht. The towering stone platform that protrudes from the west side of this hump-backed hill offers one further proof of the scale and quality of Cyrus's building activities. Left unfinished upon Cyrus's death in 530 BCE, this rigorously constructed palace platform provides a manifest link between the earlier ashlar terraces at Lydian Sardis and the huge, later terrace Darius chose to erect at Persepolis. [*See* Sardis; Persepolis.] In the case of the Tall-i Takht, however, Cyrus's suddenly obsolete platform/terrace came to be incorporated—most probably during Darius's reign—in a sprawling citadel with substantial mud-brick defenses. This fortified complex may in fact represent a notable storehouse, mentioned by Arrian, said to have been surrendered intact to Alexander the Great (*Anabasis* 3.18.10). With reference to the Tall-i Takht's later history, the excavations of the early 1960s served to document a burning of part of the citadel in or near 300 BCE (an event likely to have marked the end of direct Seleucid control in Fars); the subsequent introduction of a more independent local occupation that may have extended down to 180 BCE; and the establishment of a short-lived fortified settlement tentatively dated to the beginning of the Islamic era (seventh and eighth centuries CE).

BIBLIOGRAPHY

Curzon, George N. *Persia and the Persian Question.* 2 vols. London, 1892.

Flandin, Eugène, and Pascal Coste. *Voyage en Perse de MM. E. Flandin, peintre, et P. Coste, architecte, pendant les années 1840 et 1841.* 5 vols. Paris, 1843–1854.

Herzfeld, Ernst. "Pasargadae: Untersuchungen zur persischen Archäologie." *Klio* 8 (1908): 1–68.

Herzfeld, Ernst. "Bericht über die Ausgrabungen von Pasargadae, 1928." *Archäologische Mitteilungen aus Iran* 1 (1929–1930): 4–16.

Herzfeld, Ernst. *Iran in the Ancient East.* London, 1941.

Nagel, Wolfram. "Pasargadae: Ein Lagebericht zum Problem des Beginns achämenidischer Kunst und altpersischer Schrift." *Mitteilungen der Deutschen Orient-Gesellschaft zu Berlin* 111 (1979): 75–88.

Nylander, Carl. "Who Wrote the Inscriptions at Pasargadae?" *Orientalia Suecana* 16 (1967): 135–180.

Nylander, Carl. *Ionians in Pasargadae: Studies in Old Persian Architecture.* Uppsala, 1970.

Sami, Ali. *Pasargadae: The Oldest Imperial Capital of Iran.* Shiraz, 1956.

Stronach, David. *Pasargadae: A Report on the Excavations Conducted by the British Institute of Persian Studies from 1961 to 1963.* Oxford, 1978.

Stronach, David. "Pasargadae." In *The Cambridge History of Iran,* vol. 2, *The Median and Achaemenian Periods,* edited by Ilya Gershevitch, pp. 838–855. Cambridge, 1985.

Stronach, David. "On the Genesis of the Old Persian Cuneiform Script." In *Contributions à l'histoire de l'Iran: Mélanges Jean Perrot,* pp. 195–203. Paris, 1990.

Stronach, David. "Parterres and Stone Watercourses at Pasargadae: Notes on the Achaemenid Contribution to the Evolution of Garden Design." *Journal of Garden History* 14 (1994): 3–12.

Trümpelmann, Leo. "Metrologische Untersuchungen am Kyrosgrab in Pasargadae." In *Memorial Volume of the Sixth International Congress of Iranian Art and Archaeology, Oxford, 11–16 September 1972,* pp. 319–326. Tehran, 1976.

DAVID STRONACH

PASTORAL NOMADISM. A strategy for producing food that emphasizes breeding—the care and use of herd animals, in particular, in the Near East, of camels, cattle, sheep, and goats—is known as pastoral nomadism. Recent research into the history of pastoral nomadism in the Near East has benefited from three independent yet interrelated lines of scholarship. The first is the accumulation of a wealth of ethnographic information on pastoral nomadism in the nineteenth and early part of the twentieth centuries gathered by explorers, missionaries, and colonial administrators. The second is the more recent infusion of ideas and approaches from anthropology into the research agendas of historians and, especially, archaeologists (the so-called New Archaeology revolution). [*See* New Archaeology.] This led not only to renewed interest in ethnography by archaeologists (ethnoarchaeology), but to a virtual explosion of reexaminations by researchers of the documents (reports, artistic renderings, early photographs) of nineteenth-century explorers and missionaries—which has had an impact on biblical scholarship as well (see, e.g., Finkelstein and Na'aman, 1994). The third is the growth of regional archaeological surveys throughout the Near East mandated both by the New Archaeology and by the threat to antiquities sites by the rapid expansion of modern roads, farming, and settlements. Not surprisingly, a very significant proportion of the sites surveyed have produced information relevant to reconstructing the nature and contribution of pastoral nomadism over millennia.

An outcome of this recent escalation of research is an emerging consensus that the lives of nomadic pastoralists in the Near East have always been enmeshed with those of village-based farmers. Thus, the tendency of early scholars to emphasize differences and hostilities between farmers and herders has given way to perspectives emphasizing the varied ways in which raising crops and raising animals presented strategic food-production alternatives. Rural households and whole communities had to chose among them in order to adapt to shifting environmental, economic, and political conditions.

Three factors are especially important for understanding the migratory aspect of food production in the Near East. The first is the availability of water. In much of the region there are two seasons: the rainy season, which usually begins in November and ends in March or April, and summer, when there is little or no rain, only dew. In virtually rainless places, such as Egypt and Iraq (ancient Mesopotamia), the rainy season is nevertheless evident by the annual flooding of the Nile River and the Tigris and Euphrates Rivers, respectively.

Rainwater and floodwater have been counted on not only to irrigate fields, but also to replenish hewn cisterns and reservoirs, as well as natural reservoirs and underground aquifers. In many cases the latter provide fresh water to springs and streams year-round. An important advantage of pastoral nomadism in this regard is that—unlike sedentary agriculture—it is not dependent to the same extent on human labor to maintain irrigation canals, terraced hillsides, cisterns, and reservoirs to provide water for their crops, animals, and households during the dry season. On the contrary, pastoralists rely to a greater degree on their mobility and knowledge of natural pastures and watering places for year-round access to water.

A second factor is the presence of the three great deserts in the region: the Sahara and Sinai in North Africa and the Arabian desert along the frontier of the Fertile Crescent. During the rainy season, these vast deserts produce pastures of sufficient quantity and quality to feed hundreds of thousands of herd animals. By visiting these deserts, herders take advantage of the ability of ruminants to convert cellulose, which humans cannot digest directly, into animal protein, which humans can digest. During the dry season, when the desert becomes too inhospitable for people and animals, most herders bring their herds back to graze them on the stubble that remains following the grain harvest in the well-watered areas surrounding villages and towns.

A third factor affecting an understanding of nomadic pastoralism in the ancient Near East is the shifting of political and economic realities, which at times made sedentary agriculture very risky. This was especially true along the desert frontiers, where settlers sometimes abandoned their villages and farms and moved to safer areas or adopted subsistence pastoralism to provide for their food and security needs. When conditions became more favorable again, they or their descendents often resettled their former homelands.

Such sedentarization and nomadization has been documented by geographers, historians, and archaeologists for the countries along the North African coast, the Levant, and ancient Mesopotamia. Where these processes have been studied intensively—such as in Cyrenaica on the Libyan coast (Johnson, 1973), in the Madaba region of Jordan (LaBianca, 1988), and on the Mesopotamian floodplain (Adams, 1981)—sedentarization has typically been linked with the buildup of permanent settlements such as farmsteads, villages, and towns; with gradual increases in craft specialization; with the production of field crops and tree crops; with the centralization of power and bureaucratization of production; with the stratification of society; and with the delocalization of the food supply. Nomadization, on the other hand, has been linked with the partial or complete abandonment of settled areas; with increased reliance on animals; with dwelling in tents, caves, and abandoned buildings; and with increased reliance on tribal affiliation for access to lands and protection against hostile tribes and states. [*See* Tents.]

There is little scholarly dispute that subsistence pastoralism is a very ancient phenomenon in the Old World. The prevailing view is that nomadic pastoralism emerged as a consequence of the expansion of crop cultivation (Bar-Yosef and Khazarov, 1992). This likely first occurred sometime during Pre-Pottery Neolithic period (c. 6000–5500 BCE), when the first experiments with the migratory herding of animals away from arable areas were made. This early pastoralism likely began with herds of goats, which are a greater hazard to cultivated fields than are sheep. [*See* Sheep and Goats.]

The extent to which pastoralism developed during Pottery Neolithic times (c. 5500–4500 BCE) is uncertain, although it is likely that it was during this period that sheep were added to mobile herding operations. There is some evidence that these animals were raised primarily for their meat until the Chalcolithic period (c. 4500–3500 BCE), when they began to be kept for their milk and wool as well.

The emergence of the first cities during the Early Bronze Age (c. 3500–2300 BCE) provided additional impetus to the specialized production of sheep and goats: expanding urban populations needed to be supplied with meat, milk, fiber, skins, and wool. [*See* Textiles, *article on* Textiles of the Neolithic through Iron Ages.] This "secondary products revolution" coincided with the ass coming into full use as a means of transport, thus facilitating the hauling of the animal products produced in distant pastures to urban centers. [*See* Transportation.]

By the end of the Early Bronze Age, people's experience with the specialized production of animals had developed to the point where pastoral nomadism was fully established as a viable alternative to sedentary agriculture. Throughout most of the Old World, this mobile production of animals typically involved some sort of transhumance, whereby shepherds migrated with their flocks between summer and winter pastures. This ascendancy of nomadic lifestyles—especially toward the end of the Early Bronze Age—signaled the beginning of the cycles of sedentarization and nomadization that thereafter left their marks on the cultural landscape of the ancient Near East.

The secondary products revolution appears to have played a pivotal role in leading to the ascendancy of subsistence pastoralism as an alternative to village agriculture. Three subsequent events had a profound effect on this development in the Near East: the introduction of the camel, the invention of the North Arabian saddle, and the recent introduction of the pickup truck. [*See* Camels.]

Experts seem to agree that the one-humped camel, or dromedary, was domesticated (possibly in Somalia) sometime during the third millennium. Prior to its domestication, herders relied primarily on domestic sheep, goats, cows, and donkeys for their livelihoods. [*See* Cattle and Oxen.] The introduction of the camel allowed them to penetrate deeper into the desert in search of pastures. This increased capacity for mobility in previously uninhabitable desert regions, in turn, led to new opportunities for camel-breeding nomads when it came to long-distance trade.

It is a curious fact that, especially in the Levant, the camel does not appear to have played a very significant role either as a herding animal or as a transport animal until after about 1400 BCE. After that time, however, its importance gradually increased, apparently because of its usefulness to the burgeoning overland trade in incense. The trade was at first controlled by settled merchants; after the invention of the North Arabian saddle in about 500 BCE, however, the usefulness of the dromedary in transport increased so significantly it put the camel-breeding nomads in control. The rise of such desert commercial centers as Petra and Palmyra followed. [*See* Petra; Palmyra.]

The military and economic advantages provided by the camel, the North Arabian saddle, and subsequent technological advances related to riding and raiding by nomads on camel, led to the beginning of what is often referred to as bedouin society (cf. Bulliet, 1975). The auspicious ascent of bedouins as the undisputed masters of the overland trade routes crisscrossing the Arabian desert only lasted a few centuries. Ironically, as Richard W. Bulliet has noted, the very "technological changes that originally made it possible for desert tribes bordering settled empires to gain control of the trade passing through their lands eventually raised the military capacity of all the Arab tribes to such a level that anarchy replaced the control exercised by the first trading states" (1990, p. 104).

No doubt other factors contributed to the waning role of the bedouin when it came to controlling overland trade routes—not the least of which were the deliberate and eventually successful attempts by the Roman overlords of ancient Palestine to take over this control. In the nearly two millennia since then, the fortunes of the bedouin with respect to control of the desert trade routes of Arabia have waxed and waned. Pivotal to the persistence of their way of life in the face of constantly shifting political fortunes has been their skill as breeders of camels, horses, sheep, and goats; their intimate knowledge of the desert; and their resilient tribal organization, which invariably includes complex partnerships not only among their own groups, but also with the villagers and townspeople bordering their desert territories.

The twentieth century brought enormous challenges and changes to the bedouin way of life. In modern Egypt, Israel, Jordan, and Syria their numbers have dwindled as their traditional dry-season pastures in the settled areas have been converted to the intensive cultivation of legumes, vegetables, and fruit trees and their traditional reliance on raiding and collecting protection taxes from villagers and townspeople has been ended by local governments. Furthermore, the introduction of well-guarded national borders has impeded their traditional long-distance migrations.

Despite these changes, bedouin continue to survive. Because of their expertise at utilizing some of the most marginal lands in the world, they have an important contribution to make to the economies of their host countries; their strategies for doing so are likely to change, however, not the least because of modern technology. Thus, the camel as a means of desert transport is rapidly being replaced by trucks, especially small pickup trucks. As new technologies continue to be introduced, the question remains as to whether the bedouin way of life will persist as a type of subsistence pastoralism or, as some predict, it will become a Near Eastern version of commercial ranching.

The infusion of anthropological understanding of pastoral nomadism since the 1960s into historical and archaeological research on the ancient Near East has led to many new insights with broad ramifications for our understanding of the prehistory and history of the Holy Land. For instance, recent scholarship concerned with the cyclic appearance and disappearance of settled villages and towns in ancient Palestine throughout the Chalcolithic, Bronze, and Iron ages has come to rely explicitly on the anthropological concepts of sedentarization and nomadization to understand this phenomenon (cf. Finkelstein and Na'aman, 1994; Levy, 1995). As Israel Finkelstein has argued, the settlement of the Israelites in the highlands of Canaan toward the end of the second millennium BCE was thus not a singular event of some kind, but rather "a phase in the cyclic history of Canaan" (Finkelstein, 1994).

The fluidity that has characterized the social landscape of the Near East over the millennia has in a large measure been possible because of the persistence at the local level of various forms of tribalism. Since prehistoric times, tribal ideology has served as the enabling mechanism whereby small groups of kin have been able shift back and forth between nomadic and sedentary ways in order to adapt to changes in their natural and social environment. Thus, when it comes to understanding the origins, rise, and collapse of such local kingdoms as Israel, Judah, Ammon, Moab, and Edom toward the end of the second and throughout most of the first millennia BCE, insights gained from anthropological research on tribalism—as manifest both among sedentary and nomadic groups—will be crucial to future attempts to understand the nature of the polities of these early kingdoms (cf. LaBianca and Younker, 1995).

[*See also* Agriculture; Egypt, *article on* Prehistoric Egypt; Mesopotamia, *article on* Prehistoric Mesopotamia; North Africa; Palestine, *article on* Prehistoric Palestine; Syria, *article on* Prehistoric Syria; *and* Transjordan, *article on* Prehistoric Transjordan.]

BIBLIOGRAPHY

Adams, Robert McC. *Heartland of Cities*. Chicago, 1981. Documents cycles of sedentarization and nomadization along the Mesopotamian floodplain.

Bar-Yosef, Ofer, and Anatoly Khazanov, eds. *Pastoralism in the Levant: Archaeological Materials in Anthropological Perspectives*. Prehistory Press Monographs in World Archaeology, no. 10. Madison, Wis., 1992. A variety of authors examine the current state of research on pastoralism in the Levant.

Bulliet, Richard W. *The Camel and the Wheel* (1975). Cambridge, 1990. Pivotal study of the history of the camel and its uses in the Old World.

Cribb, Roger. *Nomads in Archaeology*. Cambridge, 1991. Important work on how to investigate nomadic pastoralism using archaeology.

Eph'al, Israel. *The Ancient Arabs: Nomads on the Border of the Fertile Crescent, Ninth–Fifth Century B.C.* Leiden, 1982. Survey of Akkadian and biblical sources dealing with ancient nomads on the border of the Fertile Crescent.

Finkelstein, Israel. "The Emergence of Israel: A Phase in the Cyclic History of Canaan in the Third and Second Millennia BCE." In Finkelstein and Na'aman, eds., 1994 (below), pp. 150–177.

Finkelstein, Israel, and Nadav Na'aman, eds. *From Nomadism to Monarchy: Archaeological and Historical Aspects of Early Israel.* Jerusalem and Washington, D.C., 1994. Examines cycles of sedentarization and nomadization leading to the rise of the monarchy in ancient Israel.

Johnson, Douglas L. *Jabal-al-Akhdar, Cyrenaica: An Historical Geography of Settlement and Livelihood.* University of Chicago, Department of Geography Research Paper, no. 148. Chicago, 1973. Documents cycles of sedentarization and nomadization in Cyrenaica (ancient Libya).

Khazanov, Anatoly. *Nomads and the Outside World.* Cambridge, 1984. Seminal work on the history of nomadism in the Old World.

LaBianca, Øystein S. *Hesban,* vol. 1, *Sedentarization and Nomadization: Food System Cycles at Hesban and Vicinity in Transjordan.* Berrien Springs, Mich., 1990. Documents cycles of sedentarization and nomadization in Central Transjordan.

LaBianca, Øystein, and Randall Younker. "The Kingdoms of Ammon, Moab and Edom: The Archaeology of Society in Late Bronze/Iron Age Transjordan (ca. 1400–500 BCE)." In Levy, ed., 1995 (below), pp. 399–415.

Lancaster, William. *The Rwala Bedouin Today.* Cambridge, 1981. Ethnographic study of the changing lives of bedouin in Jordan and Iraq.

Levy, Thomas E. *The Archaeology of Society in the Holy Land.* London, 1995.

Marx, Emmanuel. *The Bedouin of the Negev.* New York, 1967. Ethnographic study of the changing lives of the bedouin in the Negev desert.

Matthews, Victor H. *Pastoral Nomadism in the Mari Kingdom, ca. 1830–1760 B.C.* American Schools of Oriental Research, Dissertation Series, no. 3. Cambridge, Mass., 1978. Study of pastoral nomadism based on an examination of the Mari texts.

Rowton, M. B. "Enclosed Nomadism." *Journal of the Economic and Social History of the Orient* 17 (1974): 1–30. Study of the role of nomads in Mesopotamia during the third and second millennium BCE.

Shahīd, Irfan. *Rome and the Arabs: A Prolegomenon to the Study of Byzantium and the Arabs.* Washington, D.C., 1984. The role of pastoral nomads on the frontiers of Palestine in the Late Roman and Byzantine periods.

ØYSTEIN S. LABIANCA

PELLA (modern Ṭabaqaṭ Faḥl, Early Islamic Fiḥl), site located in the lower foothills of the eastern Jordan Valley, 28 km (17 mi.) south of the Sea of Galilee and 4 km (2.5 mi.) east of the Jordan River (32°27′ N, 35°37′ E). The site, nestled among rugged hills and deep valleys, overlooks the north Jordan Valley and the plain of Esdraelon. Pella's principal archaeological feature is an oval mound on the north side of Wadi Jirm el-Moz, a small valley that descends from the highlands that lie to the east. On its steep, eroded southern slope the mound rises 30 m (100 ft.) above the valley floor. Beneath its deep occupational remains is a natural hillock, at whose foot a powerful spring has flowed into the valley for thousands of years. On the south side of Wadi Jirm rises a large, dome-shaped natural hill known as Tell el-Ḥusn, which was used both for interment and for occupation at various times in the past. The surrounding region reveals abundant evidence of ancient utilization.

PELLA. *View of excavations from the south.* A portion of the main mound is visible on the left. At center right is the Civic Complex of the Roman-Byzantine period. The Roman odeon (small theater) is visible, as well as the Civic Complex Church, which may have been the city's cathedral. (Photograph courtesy College of Wooster)

Pella was highly desirable as a place of habitation because it commanded the resources of three ecosystems: its own and those in the ascending hills to the east and the Jordan Valley on the west. Although hot in the summer, it had, as it still does, one of the best climates in the region. Even today, after centuries of environmental degradation, it has rich soils and sufficient rainfall to make the vicinity excellent for agriculture. In ancient times it also lay near the junction of two of the major trade and military routes of the ancient Levant, one running along the eastern side of the Jordan Valley and the other descending northwest from the Central Transjordanian highlands, crossing the Jordan River near Beth-Shean and continuing through the Plain of Esdraelon to the coast.

The site has been known to Western travelers and explorers since it was visited, but not identified, by Charles Irby and James Mangles in 1818. It appeared as "Pella" on Heinrich Kiepert's 1842 map, an identification confirmed, on the basis of both research and visitation, by Edward Robinson in his *Later Biblical Researches in Palestine and the Adjacent Regions* (London, 1856). It was recognized by William Foxwell Albright in 1926 as the Piḥil, or Piḥir, in several Egyptian texts, a correlation that opened up a textually documented history going as far back as the Egyptian Middle Kingdom. Several dozen Greek, Latin, and Arabic texts allude briefly to Pella, as does a Talmudic passage (Smith, 1973, pp. 23–82).

Archaeological exploration of the site began with soundings made in 1958 by Robert Funk and Neil Richardson of the American Schools of Oriental Research. The first full-scale excavations were begun in 1967 by the College of Wooster, under the direction of Robert H. Smith, but were curtailed by the June war of that year. Smith returned in 1979 with J. Basil Hennessy and Anthony W. McNicoll as directors of a joint University of Sydney–College of Wooster expedition. The Wooster team had its last season in 1985; Sydney's excavations continued into the 1990s. It is only with this most recent research that the long and rich history of the area has been illuminated.

Surface surveys and excavation have demonstrated occupation in the region of Pella from the Lower Paleolithic (perhaps as many as a million years ago) to the present day. Important Early and Middle Paleolithic sequences predate the formation of the Lisan lake that dominated the region's geography and economy between 100,000 and 14,000 years ago, after which the lake began to retreat and, in its retreat, to create the deep ravines that are so prominent a feature of the existing landscape.

Six sites from the Upper Paleolithic, Kebaran, and Natufian periods have been excavated by the joint expedition; they provide a detailed picture of the environment and human activity in the vicinity of Pella between 30,000 and 12,000 years ago. Excavation of the Early Natufian settlement exposed two large, circular buildings containing deposits of thousands of domestic and agricultural stone tools, as well as carefully worked basalt bowls, pedestal mortars and pestles, small animal sculptures in both basalt and limestone, and large limestone stelae decorated with deeply carved concentric rectangles. Dietary staples included wild barley, lentils, and peas. Human burials and offerings were found beneath some of the domestic structures.

Prepottery Neolithic remains are evidenced so far only in unstratified contexts, but excavation and surface survey indicate a widespread Pottery Neolithic settlement of the Yarmukian horizon in the sixth and fifth millennia, both on the main mound and along the banks of Wadi Jirm el-Moz.

Numerous Chalcolithic settlements are attested throughout the vicinity of Pella. One of these, a large village situated southeast of the central mound on the slope of a large hill known as Jebel Ṣarṭaba, has been excavated. The plan appears to consist of broad courtyard areas between clusters of roughly rectangular stone and mud-brick houses partly cut into the hill's soft bedrock. The ceramic and lithic industries are closely related to those of the upper levels at Teleilat el-Ghassul, the basic levels of the Beersheba Chalcolithic, and some settlements in the Golan in Israel. The village had an agricultural economy based on barley, emmer wheat, lentils, chickpeas, and peas. A radiocarbon sample dates the short-lived settlement to 3480 ± 60 BCE.

Early Bronze Age remains have been found on both the mound and at Tell el-Ḥusn; where many of the areas of deep excavation have reached EB levels. A substantial EB I building has been found on the mound. It is probable that a massive defensive wall exposed in the deep excavations carried out on the southeastern part of the mound had its origin in the Early Bronze Age. An EB IIA large stone platform was discovered at Tell el-Ḥusn. There are few remains of the EB III period. An EB IV cemetery was partly excavated in Wadi Ḥammeh, near the Natufian settlement mentioned above, and there is evidence of a small settlement from the same period in that vicinity.

Piḥil was a city of some significance throughout the Middle and Late Bronze Ages, as might be expected from the Egyptian references. It was defended by a substantial mud-brick wall that continued in use, with occasional patching, into the Iron Age. Rich settlement and tomb remains attest to a continuous and widespread occupation throughout the second millennium BCE, perhaps extending beyond the city wall. Unlike the situation in much of Palestine and Transjordan, there does not appear to have been a reduction in the city's size or any evidence of destruction until the end of LB II, and many MB II buildings continued in use into the Late Bronze Age.

Contact with Egypt is archaeologically attested as early as the MB IIb period by the presence of alabaster and faience vessels, scarabs, and other trade items, and with Cyprus and the Aegean during the Late Bronze Age, when ceramic vessels were imported in some quantity. Fragments of cunei-

PELLA. *Egyptian style box.* Restored ebony box with ivory inlays. Late Bronze Age, fifteenth century BCE. (Photograph courtesy University of Sydney)

form tablets of LB I date suggest a literate society, as do the previously known Amarna letters from Mut-balʿlu of Pella to pharaoh Akhenaten. One substantial building may prove to be the equivalent of the now well-attested governors' residences in contemporary Palestinian cities. There was no marked change in prosperity during LB II, although the town's area may have been more restricted in the thirteenth century BCE. There are very rich burials of LB I and II.

The beginning of the Iron Age saw rebuilding and continuity of local ceramic and other material cultural elements, but the large, MB–LB prosperous city gave way to a somewhat smaller and poorer town. Pella receives no mention in the Hebrew Bible, unless it appears there under some other name. It is possible that during the later biblical period the city was virtually unoccupied, as there is little at the site that is datable to the period from the late seventh through the fourth centuries BCE.

Following the conquests of Alexander the Great in Syria and Palestine in 332–331 BCE and the ensuing reconfigurations in government, economy, and culture, Pella began to revive. Although the late tradition of Stephanos Byzantios (*Ethnica,* pp. 103–104) that the city was refounded by Alexander is probably fictional, it began to rebuild its population and participate in Hellenistic commerce under Ptolemaic suzerainty.

Following the Seleucid conquest of the southern Levant in 200 BCE, Pella experienced a century of expansion and prosperity. New residences and public or military structures were built. Greek became the language of culture and commerce, although the indigenous language of the city was never completely abandoned. The ancient Semitic name of the city was hellenized to *Pella,* calling to mind the city of Alexander's birth. Late Hellenistic artifacts, found in abundance, include not only fine artifacts imported from Syria and elsewhere in the eastern Mediterranean region, but also a new repertoire of local ceramic vessels.

Contemporary with Pella's Late Hellenistic development was the rise of the Maccabean kingdom west of the Jordan River. Having traditionally stood outside the Hebrew cultural sphere, Pella maintained an uneasy relationship with the Jewish state; nevertheless, by keeping a low profile and probably serving as a useful conduit for Seleucid commerce, the city managed to remain relatively free from Hasmonean domination for almost a century. In 83/82 BCE, however, the Hasmonean ruler Alexander Jannaeus, displeased, according to Josephus, that a city so near its border would not accede to Jewish practices, overran and destroyed the city (Josephus, *Antiq.* 13.392–397; *War* 1.103–105). Evidence of extensive burning is present in the Late Hellenistic stratum on the mound.

The advance of the Roman general Pompey through Syria in 63 BCE brought an end to Seleucid and Hasmonean domination alike. Pella was one of ten hellenized cities in southern Syria and northern Transjordan that from this time on were known collectively as the Decapolis—if, indeed, that term had not already come into existence in Late Hellenistic times. Although the cities were placed within the newly created province of Syria, Pompey in fact returned to them much of the independence they had enjoyed under the Seleucid Empire. Archaeological evidence shows that while commerce was important, Pella was no more involved in international trade than many other cities outside that league.

Stratified archaeological deposition from the first three centuries CE has not been found on the mound to the extent that might be expected; nevertheless, it is clear that Pella underwent considerable development during the Roman period. In 82/83 CE the city issued its first modest bronze coinage. Excavations in the Civic Complex near the spring have exposed the remnants of public baths and a small theater constructed about this time, and a forum probably was built in Wadi Jirm. Several of the city's early third-century coins show the facade of a nymphaeum, which was undoubtedly located in the Civic Complex. There was a popular spa at Pella, probably the warm mineral spring that still flows in Wadi Ḥammeh, 3 km (2 mi.) north of the city. The road between Pella and the Decapolis city of Gerasa/Jerash was improved in 160/61 CE, as inscribed milestones found along its route indicate.

Throughout this period the city continued to have its cultural roots in an intermingling of its ancient Syro-Palestinian heritage with Hellenism. The Greco-Roman deities that appear on the coins the city issued between 177 and 222 CE include Athena, an unidentified male deity, and perhaps Heracles, while another coin depicts a large hexastyle temple. Inscriptions found during excavation mention "the elders of Zeus-Ares" and "the Arabian God." Excavations have brought to light scattered evidence of the everyday religious practices of the city's inhabitants, such as the wearing of amulets and the inclusion of hens' eggs in the burial of a newborn child.

Although Pella is not mentioned in the New Testament, the interaction of Judaism and Christianity in the city during this period is of particular interest. Josephus states that Pella was among a number of hellenized cities and villages in Transjordan and Syria that were pillaged by Jews in 66 CE (*War* 2.457–465). Evidently the damage to the city was limited, for some two years later, as Roman troops were on the verge of attacking Jerusalem during the First Jewish Revolt, the Christians who lived in Jerusalem are said to have fled for safety across the Jordan River to the region of Peraea, especially to Pella (Eusebius, *Historia Ecclesiastica* 3.5.3–4; Epiphanius, *Adversus Haereses* 30.2.7–8). The choice of Pella as a city of refuge is further said to have been divinely revealed to a prophet in the Jerusalem church, but it can also be viewed on the pragmatic ground that Pella was the most easily reached of the hellenized cities of Transjordan and would have had no involvement in the insurrection against Rome. In view of the aforesaid distaste that the citizens of Hellenistic Pella had for Jewish customs and nationalism, it is likely that the majority of the Christians who took refuge in Pella came from a hellenized Jewish background. A sarcophagus excavated beneath the floor of the West Church at Pella may originally have contained the remains of a leader of that group who died during the sojourn.

Although these Christians are reported later to have returned to Jerusalem, the fact that the mid-second-century apologist Aristo came from Pella suggests that Christianity continued to exist in the city from that time onward. By the end of the fourth century CE, Pella had become a bishopric and Christianity had displaced most or all of the city's former religions. Three large churches were constructed during the Byzantine period, one of which—probably the city's cathedral—was located in the Civic Complex, another on the west side of the city, and the third on a high slope east of the city. The names of several bishops of the fifth and sixth centuries are known as participants in the church's ecumenical councils.

Pella probably reached its greatest size in the sixth century, when its international trade was extensive and its citizens were enjoying considerable prosperity. The city fell to its Islamic conquerors in 635 CE, after a major battle between the Byzantine and Islamic armies on the nearby plain of Fiḥl. Excavations have demonstrated that the city was taken peacefully into the Early Umayyad Empire, with a gradual transition from its former Byzantine culture and economy.

The city was destroyed in a violent earthquake in 746/47 CE but was not entirely deserted. Excavations to the northeast of the mound have uncovered substantial buildings from the ʿAbbasid period in the ninth and tenth centuries CE. These remains, along with those of the earlier Umayyad occupation, make Pella a type-site for the early Islamic settlement of Jordan. There was some occupation of the site during Mamluk and Early Ottoman times, supported by sugar production. During the Mamluk period a mosque was constructed on top of the mound, but the city itself was never rebuilt.

BIBLIOGRAPHY

Hennessy, J. Basil, et al. "Pella." In *Archaeology of Jordan,* vol. 2, *Field Reports,* edited by Denys Homès-Fredericq and J. Basil Hennessy, pp. 406–441. Louvain, 1989. Lengthy survey of the Pella excavations; the bibliography should also be consulted.

McNicoll, Anthony W., Robert Houston Smith, and J. Basil Hennessy. *Pella in Jordan 1: An Interim Report on the Joint University of Sydney and the College of Wooster Excavations at Pella, 1979–1981.* Canberra, 1982. Contains some material that will not be repeated in the final excavation report series, *Pella of the Decapolis.*

McNicoll, Anthony W., and Robert Houston Smith, et al. *Pella in Jordan 2: The Second Interim Report of the Joint University of Sydney and the College of Wooster Excavations at Pella, 1982–1985.* Sydney, 1992. Detailed report of excavations to the end of 1985, containing some material that will not be repeated in the final excavation report series.

Smith, Robert Houston. *The 1967 Season of the College of Wooster Expedition to Pella.* Pella of the Decapolis, vol. 1. Wooster, Ohio, 1973. First volume in a series of final excavation reports of the Wooster Expedition to Pella and the Sydney-Wooster Joint Expedition.

Smith, Robert Houston. "Excavations at Pella of the Decapolis, 1979–1985." *National Geographic Research* 1 (1985): 470–489. Overview of the results of the first seven seasons of the Sydney-Wooster Joint Expedition to Pella.

Smith, Robert Houston. "Trade in the Life of Pella of the Decapolis." In *Studies in the History and Archaeology of Jordan,* vol. 3, edited by Adnan Hadidi, pp. 53–58. Amman, 1987. Discusses the extent to which international commerce was a factor in Pella's history.

Smith, Robert Houston, and Leslie P. Day. *Final Report on the College of Wooster Excavations in Area IX, the Civic Complex, 1979–1985.* Pella of the Decapolis, vol. 2. Wooster, Ohio, 1989. Second volume in a series of final excavation reports.

Smith, Robert Houston. "The Southern Levant in the Hellenistic Period." *Levant* 22 (1990): 123–130. Discusses the Hellenistic period in Palestine and Transjordan in light of historical and archaeological evidence, with particular reference to Pella.

J. BASIL HENNESSY and ROBERT HOUSTON SMITH

PERGAMON, ancient city situated in the region of Mysia in northwestern Asia Minor. The city occupies the summit and south slope of a dramatic hill that towers over the fertile valley of the Caicus River, about 25 km (15.5 mi.) east of the Aegean coast, opposite the Greek island of Lesbos. The location of Pergamon was never forgotten, and the name survives in that of the modern Turkish town of Bergama. Pergamon was visited and described by numerous early European travelers, starting with Cyriacus of Ancona in the mid-fifteenth century. German excavations sponsored by the Berlin Museum and later by the German Archaeological Institute began in 1878 and have continued intermittently ever since.

In Greek myth, Pergamon was founded by Telephos, the son of Herakles; although prehistoric pottery has been found in places on the Caicus plain, the earliest archaeological evidence for settlement on the hill of Pergamon are scattered Greek Geometric sherds of the seventh century BCE. Until the end of the fourth century BCE, Pergamon was a small fortress settlement, inhabited by a mixed population of Greeks and indigenous peoples. The decisive turning point in the history of the city came in 301 BCE, when the Hellenistic warlord Lysimachos of Thrace secured his war chest in its fortress, entrusting it to a lieutenant named Philetaerus. In 282 BCE, Philetaerus revolted from Lysimachos and founded the so-called Attalid dynasty, which ruled Pergamon for the next century and a half. The Attalids made the city an architectural showpiece and the capital of an increasingly powerful kingdom. This most distinctive epoch in Pergamene history came to an end in 133 BCE, when the last of the Attalid rulers, Attalus III, took the remarkable diplomatic step of leaving his kingdom on his death to the People of Rome. Pergamon continued to grow and prosper under Roman rule, ranking as one of the two or three leading cities in the province of Asia. It became the home, eventually, of one of the seven churches of that province addressed in the *Book of Revelation* (2:12–17). The strategic value of its fortress ensured Pergamon's continued importance in the Byzantine period. Early in the fourteenth century, the city was taken by the Turks and incorporated into the newly founded Ottoman kingdom.

The site of Pergamon falls into three major areas: the fortified hill to which the Hellenistic city was confined; the relatively level area south of the hill, built up in Roman times and now occupied by Bergama; and an extramural sanctuary of Asclepius, southwest of Roman Pergamon. The hill of Pergamon can be divided into two parts: the hilltop, or acropolis, which housed the original fortress; and the south slope, which contained the residential part of town and was entirely enclosed by fortifications in the second century BCE (the total area of Hellenistic city was about 90 ha, or 222 acres).

Although the hilltop was settled as early as the seventh century BCE, the earliest substantial architectural remains belong to the Hellenistic period. The north and east sides—the highest parts—are occupied by the fortress proper: the palaces of the kings (relatively modest peristyle structures) and various military installations. To the west lie the theater, built into the slope of the hill, and a series of grand terraces that run radially around the outside of the theater, stepping down from north to south. The earliest of the building complexes supported by these terraces is the sanctuary of Athena, directly east of the theater. It consists of a Doric temple of the late fourth or third century BCE, which was later enclosed on its north, east, and south sides by stoas and other structures, including a library. An elaborate propylon dates to the reign of Eumenes II (197–159 BCE). South of and below the sanctuary of Athena lies Pergamon's most famous monument, the altar of Zeus, also begun, if not perhaps entirely finished, during the reign of Eumenes (see figure 1). The sculptured frieze that decorated its podium represents the battle between the gods and the giants. It is now the centerpiece of the Pergamon Museum in Berlin. South of the altar lies a monumental marketplace, or agora. By the end of the Hellenistic period, the architectural elaboration of the acropolis of Pergamon was essentially complete. The only major new building from the Roman era is the Trajaneum, a temple on a monumental terrace northeast of the theater, in which colossal statues of both Trajan (98–117 CE) and his successor, Hadrian (117–138 CE), were found. The partial restoration of the Trajaneum was begun in the 1970s and is still underway.

New fortifications which enclosed the whole south slope of the hill of Pergamon were built, like much of the acropolis, during the reigns of Eumenes II (197–159 BCE) and his successor, Attalus II (159–138 BCE). Excavation has concentrated on four areas: the so-called *stadtgrabung*, or "city excavations," a residential area which was a major focus of work from the 1970s into the 1990s; the sanctuary of Demeter, a small Ionic temple enclosed by stoas on a monumental terrace, which was built largely in the third and early second centuries BCE; the gymnasium, a grand complex occupying a series of three terraces, which includes stoas, meeting rooms, public baths, and several small sanctuaries, in addition to a large palaestra, or exercise ground, built in the second century BCE and substantially renovated in the Roman period; and the lower agora, together with a nearby group of houses. The lower agora lies just inside the "Eumenes gate," at the southern edge of the Hellenistic city.

The Roman development of the area south of the hill of Pergamon is largely hidden by Bergama. Monumental buildings include a theater, a stadium, and an amphitheater, as well as the so-called Red Hall, a huge and unusual temple complex from the second century CE which was dedicated to a trio of Egyptian gods. The sanctuary of Asclepius, southwest of the Roman city, was said to have been founded in the fourth century BCE, but the surviving complex belongs largely to the Roman period, especially the second century CE (see figure 2). It consists of a large courtyard flanked by stoas on its north, west, and south sides (with a theater behind the north stoa) and a row of monumental buildings on the east. The most remarkable of those buildings is the Temple of Zeus-Asclepius, a small replica of the Pantheon in Rome.

With the advent of Christianity, many of Pergamon's pagan sanctuaries were converted into churches, including the Asclepium and the Red Hall in the lower city. In Late Antiquity, however, the lower city was abandoned, as the populace retreated to the fortified slopes of the Hellenistic town.

PERGAMON. Figure 1. *Altar of Zeus.* Pergamon Museum, Berlin. (Foto Marburg/Art Resource, NY)

PERGAMON. Figure 2. *General view of the Asklepieon.* (Foto Marburg/Art Resource, NY)

The area between the gymnasium and the acropolis was enclosed by new fortifications (built partly on top of earlier walls). The city enjoyed relative prosperity until as late as the thirteenth century. It fell to the Turks in the early fourteenth century.

BIBLIOGRAPHY

Final reports of the German excavations are published in *Altertümer von Pergamon* (Berlin, 1885–). The supplements (Berlin, 1968–) are devoted especially to the publication of small finds. Preliminary reports on current excavations can be found in *Archäologischer Anzeiger;* see, for example, Wolfgang Radt, "Pergamon: Vorbericht über die Kampagne 1993," *Archäologischer Anzeiger* (1994): 403–432. For further reading, consult the following:

Hansen, Esther V. *The Attalids of Pergamon.* 2d ed. Ithaca, N.Y., 1971. Hellenistic history, with extensive bibliography.

Radt, Wolfgang. *Pergamon: Geschichte und Bauten, Funde und Erforschung einer antiken Metropole.* Cologne, 1988. Excellent introduction to the site, written by the longtime director of excavations.

Smith, R. R. R. *Hellenistic Sculpture.* London, 1991. See chapter 9, "Pergamon and the Great Altar," for the altar of Zeus.

CHRISTOPHER RATTÉ

PERIODICAL LITERATURE. The range of current periodical literature dealing with the archaeology of the ancient Near East and the Mediterranean basin runs the gamut from popular newsletters and magazines to extremely technical, scientific journals. Much of this literature is produced by the major institutes and schools of archaeological research in the United States and Europe; some is regionally specific, while other journals deal with issues that transcend regional boundaries. A growing number of technical journals deal with the scientific aspects of archaeology and related disciplines, including geology, zoology, microbiology, and ethnoarchaeology.

Archaeological and related studies are also found in journals devoted primarily to biblical research, such as the *Journal of Biblical Literature,* the *Catholic Biblical Quarterly, Vetus Testamentum,* and *Zeitschrift für die alttestamentliche Wissenschaft,* which will not be considered here. What follows is an annotated description of the most useful and best-known periodicals dealing with archaeological research and methods, excavation reports, and the artifactual remains (either physical or literary). For a comprehensive list of what is currently available, see the annual *Archäologische Bibliographie* (Deutsches Archäologisches Institut, Werner Hermann and Richard Neudecker et al., eds., Berlin), an index of articles, subjects, and authors on the archaeology of the ancient Near East and the Mediterranean world.

The periodical literature can be organized into two major categories: popular sources and technical sources. Within each category are subcategories of publications. Popular sources include newsletters, abstracts, and popular journals and magazines. Technical sources are comprised of journals of Near Eastern archaeology; Near Eastern history, languages, and culture; classical or Mediterranean archaeology; classical history, languages, and culture; related areas and nonregional archaeological studies; scientific methods that relate to archaeology; and anthropological studies. Within each category and subcategory, the most useful and accessible of these publications are listed here first, in alphabetical order; those that are not as accessible to the general community are listed separately, also in alphabetical order.

Popular Sources

Newsletters. For the general reader or the scholar who wishes to be informed about fellowships, conferences, and preliminary site reports, the newsletter is a helpful publication.

ASOR Newsletters. Quarterly report of news from the archaeological institutes of the American Schools of Oriental Research—the W. F. Albright Institute of Archaeological Research (AIAR), Jerusalem; the American Center of Oriental Research (ACOR), Amman; and the Cyprus American Archaeological Research Institute (CAARI), Nicosia (see below). The newsletter also includes announcements, fellowship opportunities, and general information on ASOR-sponsored activities; illustrated.

Mar Šipri. Biannual newsletter of the Committee on Mesopotamian Civilization; contains short articles, news items, and communications pertaining to research and archaeology in Syria and Iraq; illustrated.

ACOR Newsletter. Biannual published by the American Center of Oriental Research in Amman (see above); contains preliminary excavation reports, news, fellowship information; illustrated.

Art and Archaeology Newsletter. Quarterly in English; occasionally articles contain texts in ancient Egyptian, Greek, and Latin; book reviews; illustrated.

CAARI News. Biannual published by the Cyprus American Archaeological Research Institute in Nicosia; contains research reports, news, fellowship opportunities, and conference information; illustrated.

Diggings. Monthly published in Australia; contains archaeological news on the latest discoveries in the lands of the Bible.

La Tinaja. Quarterly newsletter of archaeological ceramics; contains short reports and announcements.

Newsletter of the American Research Center in Egypt. Quarterly; contains short articles, reports from the field, and announcements; illustrated.

Abstracts. Abstracts provide individuals with the opportunity to review a larger body of information than would otherwise be possible. These short summaries of articles give an overview of current research.

Old Testament Abstracts. Three issues per year; contains sections on "The Ancient Near East: History, Texts, etc." and "Archaeology, Epigraphy, Philology."

Mundus. Quarterly review of German research contributions on Asia, Africa, and Latin America; book notes and abstracts in English.

New Testament Abstracts. Three issues per year; contains a section on the "New Testament World."

Religious and Theological Abstracts. Biannual; contains short abstracts in English, with sections under "Old Testament" on "History and Literature of the Ancient Near East" and on "Archaeology."

Religious Studies Review. Quarterly review of books, including a section on the "Ancient Near East."

Journals and magazines. For the general reader, perhaps the best way to keep up with developments in archaeology is through popular journals and magazines. The following illustrated publications provide semischolarly and popular articles that inform without overwhelming.

Archaeology. Bimonthly publication of the Archaeological Institute of America; contains refereed, lavishly illustrated articles on archaeological excavations throughout the world as well as interpretative research reports, news briefs, and book notes.

Biblical Archaeologist: Perspectives on the Ancient World from Mesopotamia to the Mediterranean. Quarterly ASOR publication; contains refereed, semischolarly, and occasionally thematic issues on current archaeological discoveries in the Near East and Mediterranean area; includes interpretative and historical articles, short book reviews, and news from the field; illustrated.

Biblical Archaeology Review. Six issues per year; contains popular articles, news, short book reviews, and letters from readers. Articles highlight recent excavations, interpretative research, and current developments in the publication and presentation of archaeological information; color illustrations.

Ancient History: Resources for Teachers. Three issues per year, published by the Macquarie Ancient History Association, North Ryder, New South Wales, Australia, for secondary school teachers; contains new developments in ancient history and archaeology.

Antiquaries Journal. Annual publication of the Society of Antiquaries of London; international journal of record within archaeology, reporting the work of specialists to a general readership as well as specific issues of concern for every archaeologist.

Archaeology and Biblical Research. Quarterly (formerly *Bible and Spade*); contains book and film reviews, popular articles on recent discoveries.

Archaeology in the Biblical World. Bimonthly publication of the Near East Archaeological Society, Shafter, California; contains popular articles from a conservative viewpoint, news, letters, and reviews; illustrated.

Biblical Illustrator. Quarterly publication of the Southern Baptist Sunday School Board, devoted to articles to aid teachers and ministers; color illustrations.

Bulletin of the Anglo-Israel Archaeological Society. Annual or biennial dedicated to the subjects of ancient Israel and Jerusalem; contains short articles and book reviews; illustrated.

Buried History. Quarterly journal of the Australian Institute of Archaeology; contains brief articles on aspects of archaeology and social history in the ancient Near East; illustrated.

Expedition. Three issues per year; refereed journal from the University of Pennsylvania; contains short articles on current research in archaeology and anthropology.

Ḥadashot Arkheologiyot. (Hebrew version; English version title is *Excavations and Surveys in Israel*). Published by the Israel Antiquities Authority; contains preliminary excavation reports of sites in Israel; illustrated with color plates and black and white photos.

JACT Review. Biannual publication of the Joint Association of Classical Teachers; contains short articles and book reviews covering all aspects of the classical world.

Technical Journals. Technical journals (all refereed) have a variety of agendas. Some are designed to provide preliminary excavation reports, while others produce final reports or analytical studies of artifactual remains. Still others are concerned with scientific methods or anthropological studies. In every case, however, these publications are written for specialists. The assumption is made that those using them will understand the technical language the authors employ.

Near Eastern archaeology

Bulletin of the American Schools of Oriental Research (BASOR). Quarterly; contains reports from ASOR-sponsored excavations, interpretative research on archaeological data, and a thorough examination of artifactual and philological remains from the ancient Near East; illustrated.

Israel Exploration Journal (IEJ). Quarterly published by the Israel Exploration Society; contains preliminary excavation reports, analysis of newly discovered artifacts, publication of inscriptional materials; illustrated.

Journal of the American Research Center in Egypt. Annual; contains excavation reports as well as philological and historical studies on all periods in Egyptian history.

Levant. Annual jointly published by the British School of Archaeology in Jerusalem and the British Institute at Amman for Archaeology and History; contains studies on the history and archaeology of Near East and eastern Mediterranean world.

Palestine Exploration Quarterly (PEQ). Semiannual published by the Palestine Exploration Fund, London; contains preliminary excavation reports, artifactual analysis, illustrated.

Tel Aviv. Semiannual journal published by Tel Aviv University; contains site reports and interpretative articles on aspects of history and archaeological discoveries in Israel and on the West Bank of the Jordan River; illustrated.

Zeitschrift des Deutschen Palästina-Vereins (ZDPV). Biannual journal; contains articles in English, French, and German on the history, culture, and archaeology of the ancient Near East.

Acta Archaeologica. Quarterly publication, in English, German, French, and Russian, of the Academiae Scientiarum Hungaricae, contains articles on Hittite, Mediterranean, and eastern European archaeology.

Acta Sumerologica. Annual or biennial in English, German, and French published by the Middle Eastern Culture Center in Japan; contains articles about artifacts and inscriptions in Japanese collections.

Anatolica. Annual publication of the Netherlands Historical Archaeological Institute in Istanbul, Turkey; contains historical studies, excavation reports, and archaeological analysis of sites in Turkey—from the prehistoric to the Hittite to the medieval period.

Annual of the Department of Antiquities of Jordan. Annual; contains excavation reports and illustrated articles analyzing newly discovered artifactual and inscriptional materials from sites in Jordan.

ʿAtiqot. Published irregularly, in a Hebrew and an English version, by the Israel Antiquities Authority; contains excavation reports from sites in Israel.

Baghdader Mitteilungen. Annual publication in German of the Deutsches Archäologische Institut; contains analytical articles and excavation reports.

Berytus: Archaeological Studies. Annual of the Faculty of Arts and Sciences of the American University of Beirut; contains historical, philological, and archaeological studies of Syria and Lebanon from prehistoric to Islamic times.

Bulletin of the Society for Near Eastern Studies in Japan. Biannual in Japanese; contains articles discussing the history of the ancient Near East and excavation and survey reports from sites in Syria, Iran, Egypt.

Eretz Israel. Annual published by the Israel Exploration Society, Jerusalem, in English and Hebrew (with English summaries); contains articles on Israeli archaeology, ancient history, and geography.

Journal of Egyptian Archaeology. Annual; contains philological and historical articles dealing with all periods of Egyptian civilization.

Journal of the Israel Prehistoric Society. Annual in English; contains illustrated articles on prehistoric archaeology and methodology.

Judean Desert Studies. Published irregularly in English by the Israel Exploration Society; contains monographs on archaeological discoveries in Israel.

Qadmoniot. Quarterly published in Hebrew by the Israel Exploration Society; contains articles on biblical archaeology, ancient history, the history and archaeology of later periods, and preliminary excavation reports.

Michmanim. Annual publication in Hebrew and English of the University of Haifa; contains articles on archaeological and historical analysis.

Mitteilungen der Deutschen Orient-Gesellschaft zu Berlin. Annual; contains preliminary reports on excavations in the Near East, with an emphasis on philology and archaeology.

Phoenix. Three issues per year in Dutch; contains articles on recent discoveries in the ancient Near East and Egypt.

Qedem. Published irregularly in English by the Institute of Archaeology at the Hebrew University of Jerusalem; contains monographs on current research and excavation reports.

Report of the Department of Antiquities, Cyprus. Annual in English and French; contains preliminary excavation reports for the previous year on Cyprus; illustrated.

Near Eastern history, languages, and culture

Journal of Near Eastern Studies. Quarterly; contains a broad scope of examinations into the ancient and medieval civilizations of the area; the latest theories and research are presented.

Journal of the American Oriental Society. Quarterly; contains articles dealing with the history, culture, and philology of the ancient Near East, Islam in all periods, Asian and African studies, and an extensive book review section and lengthy reviews.

Orientalia. Quarterly in English, French, and German; contains philological and historical studies of ancient Near Eastern civilizations and an extensive book review section.

Revue d'assyriologie et d'archéologie orientale. Biannual in French, German, and English; contains philological and historical examination of the literate cultures of ancient Mesopotamia.

Zeitschrift für Assyriologie und vorderasiatische Archäologie. Biannual in German, French, and English; contains historical, philological, and archaeological studies of the major cultures of ancient Mesopotamia and Anatolia.

Abr-Nahrain. Annual in English, French, and German published by the University of Melbourne; contains studies dealing with the history, languages, and culture of the ancient Near East.

Acta Orientalia. Three issues per year published in English, German, French, and Russian by the Academiae Scientiarum Hungaricae; contains articles on Oriental philology.

Aegyptus: Rivista italiana di egittologia e di papirologia. Semiannual published in English, French, and German; contains scientific articles on the study of ancient Egypt, its culture, people, history, and other related areas.

Akkadica. Five issues per year published in French, English, and German by the Foundation Assyriologique Georges Dossin; contains articles on the history and philology of the ancient Near East, as well as excavation reports; includes the list of papers from the Rencontre Assyriologique Internationale.

Anatolian Studies. Annual journal of the British Institute of Archaeology at Ankara; contains articles on the history, philology, and archaeology of the civilizations of ancient Anatolia.

Annual Review of the Royal Inscriptions of Mesopotamia Project. Annual publication of the RIM Project; contains compilations of cuneiform collections in standard Assyriological format; includes photos.

Archiv für Orientforschung. Annual in German, French, and English; contains articles on the philology and history of the ancient Near East, with an extensive book review section.

Archív orientální. Quarterly publication in English, French, German, and Russian of the Czech Academy of Sciences, Oriental Institute; contains articles on the history, economy, culture, and society of the ancient Near East, Judaica, Asian studies, African studies, and archaeological analysis.

Bibliotheca orientalis. Bimonthly publication in German, French, and English of the Nederlands Instituut voor Het Nabije Oosten; contains lengthy articles and an extensive book review section dealing with the history and philology of the Near East from ancient through Islamic times.

Bulletin for Biblical Research. Annual journal of the Institute for Biblical Research; contains articles primarily on biblical theology and exegesis from a conservative perspective. Some articles deal with issues touching on archaeological research.

Bulletin of the American Society of Papyrologists. Irregularly published journal of philological studies of papyri documents.

Bulletin of the School of Oriental and African Studies (University of London). Three issues per year; contains articles and reviews on ancient Near Eastern history and culture, Islamic studies, Asian and African studies, and anthropology.

Computer Aided Research in Near Eastern Studies. Published irregularly as part of the Cybernetica Mesopotamia series.

Data Sets: Cuneiform Texts. Published irregularly; electronic data processing of Mesopotamian materials, philological and artifactual.

Dilmun. Biannual published in Arabic and English by the Bahrain Historical and Archaeological Society; contains excavation reports and articles on sites on the Arabian Peninsula and in the Persian Gulf area.

Iraq. Annual; articles on the history, archaeology, philology, and culture of ancient Mesopotamian civilizations.

Istanbuler Mitteilungen. Annual; explores the prehistory, archaeology, history and art history of Asia Minor up until the Ottoman period.

Journal of Coptic Studies. Annual; contains articles on all aspects of premodern Coptic society, including its literature, history, archaeology, art, religion, linguistics, and related studies.

Journal of Cuneiform Studies. Semiannual ASOR publication; contains technical articles on the history and languages of ancient Mesopotamian and Anatolian literate cultures.

Journal of Semitic Studies. Biannual; contains articles dealing primarily with the philology of the ancient Near East.

Journal of the Ancient Near Eastern Society of Columbia University. Annual; contains articles on all aspects of the history and culture of the ancient Near East; illustrated.

Journal of the Economic and Social History of the Orient. Quarterly in English, French, and German; contains specialized studies furthering knowledge of the economic and social history of Asia and Africa from the earliest times to the beginning of the nineteenth century.

Oriens antiquus. Quarterly in English, French, and German; contains articles on the history, philology, and archaeology of the ancient Near East.

Orientalia Lovaniensia Periodica. Annual publication of the Catholic University of Leuven; contains studies on the history, languages, and culture of the ancient Near East and Asia.

Orientalia Suecana. Annual published in Sweden; contains philologic studies of Near Eastern languages from Canaanite to Arabic.

Revista degli studi orientali. Quarterly in English, French, German, Italian, and Spanish; covers all fields of Oriental studies from the ancient Near East to modern Japan.

Revue de Qumran. Semiannual published in English, French, German, Italian, Latin, and Spanish; contains studies in linguistics and culture pertaining to the Dead Sea Scrolls.

Sefarad. Quarterly; studies the text of the Hebrew Bible and its ancient versions and cultures, as well as the history and culture of Jews in Spain and the Hebrew and Aramaic languages.

Semitica. Annual; contains articles in French on the history and philology of the classical world and Ugaritic and Islamic studies.

Studi epigrafici e linguistici sul Vicino Oriente antico. Annual in Italian, French, and English; contains articles on philology and ancient Near Eastern studies.

Sumer. Annual in Arabic and English; contains preliminary excavation reports from sites in Iraq and artifactual analysis from all periods.

Syria: Revue d'art oriental et d'archéologie. Quarterly in French and English; a review of art history, philology, and archaeology, primarily from sites in Syria and Iraq.

Ugarit-Forschungen. Annual in English, French, and German; provides linguistic, historical, and cultural studies, with an emphasis on Ugarit and Mesopotamian civilizations.

Wiener Zeitschrift für die Kunde des Morgenlandes. Annual; studies in philology, including Egyptian and Coptic texts, Islamic studies, and an extensive book review section.

Zeitschrift der Deutschen Morgenländischen Gesellschaft. Semiannual in German; studies in the philology of the ancient Near East, Islamic periods, and Asia.

Classical and Mediterranean archaeology

American Journal of Archaeology. Quarterly publication of the American Institute of Archaeology; contains scholarly essays and book reviews on Old World archaeology from prehistoric times to the Middle Ages; illustrated.

Archaeological Reports. Annual publication of the Society for the Promotion of Hellenic Studies and the British School at Athens; contains accounts of recent archaeological work in Greece, with supplementary reports from other parts of the ancient Greek and Byzantine world.

Greece and Rome. Semiannual; contains literary evaluations of the major Greek and Roman authors and articles on ancient history, art, archaeology, the classical tradition, and teaching classics at the tertiary level.

Journal of Mediterranean Archaeology. Biannual; contains articles on local and regional production, development, interaction, and change in the Mediterranean, including Anatolia, with the theoretical implications or methodological assumptions extrapolated from archaeological data.

Journal of Roman Archaeology (JRA). Annual; contains coverage of all aspects of archaeology in every part of the Roman world, from 700 BCE to about 700 CE.

Nestor. Nine issues per year in English, containing original languages; contains bibliographies of material relevant to prehistoric archaeology, Homeric studies, Indo-European linguistics, and related fields in the eastern Mediterranean area and southeast Europe.

Annali dell'Istituto universitario orientale di Napoli. Three issues per year; contains philological and archaeological studies on the ancient Near East, Africa, and Mediterranean cultures.

Mitteilungen des Deutschen Archäologischen Instituts Römische Abteilung. Annual; contains articles, primarily in German, on classical studies and archaeology.

Opuscula atheniensia. Annual published in Stockholm; contains articles on classical archaeology.

Revue archéologique. Semiannual in French; contains recent studies on the Greco-Roman period, Bronze Age, and the start of the Middle Ages.

Classical history, languages, and culture

Classical Antiquity. Biannual; contains interdisciplinary research and discussions of major issues from the entire spectrum of ancient Greek and Roman civilization.

The Classical Journal. Bimonthly; contains philological research and language studies in modern literature and book reviews.

Classical Philology. Quarterly; devoted to research in the language, literature, history, and life of classical antiquity.

The Classical Review. Biannual; contains critical reviews of books dealing with all aspects of classical language, literature, and history from all countries.

Classical World. Bimonthly; contains broad-ranging articles on classical languages and literature and pedagogic aids; includes lists of meeting programs.

Hesperia. Quarterly in English of the American School of Classical Studies in Athens; some articles contain ancient Greek; presents the scholarly research of members and alumni of ASCSA on historical, archaeological, and epigraphic topics on ancient Greece.

Journal of Hellenic Studies. Annual; contains articles covering the Greek language, literature, history, and art in the ancient and Byzantine periods.

Journal of Roman Studies. Annual; contains articles dealing with all aspects of Roman history and culture and linguistics.

Ancient Society. Annual in Dutch, English, French, German, and Italian; articles deal with the cultural history of the Greek, Hellenistic, and Roman world.

Classica et Mediaevalia: Revue danoise de philologie et d'histoire. Annual in English, French, and German; contains studies in classical philology and history through the medieval period.

Das Altertum. Quarterly in German; contains classical studies, including linguistics, history, and culture.

East and West. Annual; includes studies in the language, culture, and philosophy of the classical and eastern Mediterranean world.

Genava. Annual publication of the Musée d'art et d'histoire Genève; contains articles dealing primarily with archaeological remains in Europe; does include studies on ancient Near Eastern archaeology based on items in their museum.

Greek, Roman, and Byzantine Studies. Quarterly; contains research articles on all aspects of the Greek world, from the prehistoric through the Hellenic, Hellenistic, Roman, and Byzantine periods.

Mediterranean Historical Review. Biannual; provides an international forum for a discussion of topics on the ancient, medieval, and modern history of the Mediterranean basin.

Pallas: revue d'études antiques. Annual; contains articles on the literature, linguistics, history, and archaeology of the Greek and Roman periods.

Related areas and nonregional archaeological journals

Antiquity. Quarterly; a periodical review of archaeology with reports on the work of specialists and archaeology and a book review section.

World Archaeology. Three issues per year; presents thematic issues, including interpretative examinations of cultural development, illustrated.

African Archaeological Review. Annual; studies all aspects of the archaeology of Africa and neighboring islands, with an emphasis on new data from the field as well as areas of wider than regional significance.

Journal of the Royal Asiatic Society of Great Britain and Ireland. Three issues per year; contains articles dealing with archaeology, art, anthropology, and the history of Asia, North Africa, and Ethiopia.

Raydan. Published irregularly in Belgium; contains studies dealing with ancient Yemeni antiquities and epigraphy.

Scientific methodology

Journal of Archaeological Science. Six issues per year; articles directed to archaeologists and scientists who have a particular interest in advances in applying scientific techniques and methodologies to all areas of archaeology.

Journal of Field Archaeology. Quarterly publication of Boston University; reports on field excavations and surveys the world over, methodological and technical matters, scientific advances in archaeology, and larger interpretative studies.

Archaeomaterials. Semiannual publication of the University of Pennsylvania Museum; contains articles on the pre- and nonindustrial manipulation of materials, using scientific methods for humanistic ends.

Archaeozoologia. Biannual; devoted to publishing papers presented at the International Congress of Archaeozoology.

Geoarchaeology. Bimonthly; contains original reports on the environmental settings of archaeological sites, materials analysis of artifacts, and process papers describing new techniques and equipment.

International Journal of Nautical Archaeology. Quarterly publication of the Nautical Archaeology Society; contains nonregional studies of marine archaeology.

Radiocarbon. Annual; publishes the radiocarbon dating of archaeological, geological, and other samples and articles on conventional and new techniques and related subjects.

Readings in Glass History. Published irregularly, contains monographs on topics in the history of glass vessels and beads and the glass industry, with a focus on the ancient, medieval, and premodern Near East up to the rise of the Venetian glass industries.

SAS Bulletin. Quarterly published by the Society for Archaeological Sciences; contains articles on cooperative and interdisciplinary research between archaeology and the natural and physical sciences.

Anthropological studies

American Anthropologist. Quarterly; covers cultural, physical, linguistic, and applied anthropology; includes information on archaeology.

Journal of Anthropological Archaeology. Quarterly; nonregional; primarily contains studies in ethnoarchaeological methods and fieldwork.

Man. Quarterly published by the Royal Anthropological Institute of Great Britain and Ireland; covers all areas of anthropology—physical, social, and cultural; includes information on archaeology and linguistics.

Nomadic Peoples. Biannual publication of the Scandinavian Institute of African Studies, ethnographic articles on the peoples of Asia, Africa, and the Middle East.

Tempus. Published irregularly by the University of Queensland; provides a forum for communicating anthropologically oriented studies in archaeology and material culture.

[*See also* Reference Works. *In addition, many of the organizations and institutions mentioned are the subject of independent entries.*]

VICTOR H. MATTHEWS and JAMES C. MOYER

PERIODIZATION. The division of past time into sequential segments based on technological, politico-historical, or religio-ethnic factors is known as periodization. The following discussion is of periodization in ancient Palestine and its application to other parts of the Near East.

Limitations and History. Most periodization charts find their roots in the 1836 publication of Christian Thomsen, who first designated worldwide ancient eras with technological terms (Stone, Bronze, Iron). Although used widely in Europe in the nineteenth century, this "three-age" system was not influential in the Near East until much later. Researchers within some regions of the Near East, especially those with copious written texts, adopted politico-historical terms handed down by ancient authors (e.g., in Egypt, kingdom and dynasty, based on Manetho). In Syria-Palestine in the late nineteenth and early twentieth centuries, most excavators used terms of their own devising. The resulting confusion compelled the British mandatory government of Palestine in 1922 to bring together representatives from the chief foreign schools in Jerusalem to hammer out a common set of terms. The group, which included John Garstang, Louis-Hugues Vincent, and William Foxwell Albright, adopted Thomsen's nomenclature, with subdivisions adapted to Palestine but related to Aegean periodization (Gitin, 1985, p. 101). Primarily because of Albright's forceful scholarship and his prompt publication of the Tell Beit Mirsim excavation in the 1930s, these terms as interpreted by him were accepted as the framework for Syro-Palestinian archaeology. For periods after the Iron Age, the names of various historical empires controlling the area were adopted from classical and medieval authors. [*See* Beit Mirsim, Tell; *and the biographies of Albright, Garstang, and Vincent.*]

Terminology. The term *age* is used for a broad time period, usually for the three technological ages, but could also be used for other macroperiods, such as Classical Age, or Islamic Age. The term *era* is used similarly, but in a less formal sense, especially for post-Iron Age designations (the classical era). *Period* normally refers to a subdivision of an age, such as Late Bronze II period or Roman period, whereas *stage* or *phase* can refer informally to subdivisions of periods. These terms are not used consistently or uniformly.

The different types of names for periodization in Syria-Palestine include technological ones, like those Thomsen introduced; dynastic names for political periods (Persian or Umayyad); religious or ethnic terms for periods in which a dominant group is evident (Islamic, or Arab); and chronological parameters for broad designations (millennium) or specific designations (century).

Technological terms reflect the tools in use during certain periods but, except for the Stone Age, do not necessarily reflect the predominant technologies. While they do accurately present the growth of civilization and can be correlated with broad societal, historical, and technological changes, they span the antiquity of the Near East only until the sixth century BCE, giving the impression that later periods are of less interest.

Dynastic names have the advantage of connecting the archaeological finds with particular political and social events known from written records. Because archaeological change does not necessarily move in concert with or as rapidly as political change, the temptation to ascribe a dynasty's precise range of dates to the archaeological remains can distort the finds, however. For instance, because the Umayyad dynasty ruled from about 640 to 750 CE does not mean that the Umayyad period produced an isolatable archaeological assemblage limited to those precise years. Moreover, although a dynastic term may be appropriate for one period of time in one place, a new dynasty may move in while the original dynasty still holds power elsewhere. For example, the Fatimid period refers to the time when the Fatimid Egyptian dynasty wrested Palestine from the ʿAbbasids of Baghdad; however, farther north and east, where the Fatimids were not in control, it was still the ʿAbbasid period.

Although religious or ethnic terms make sense when they reflect a region's significantly dominant makeup, their deemphasis of minorities can lead to a distorted historical picture: for example, it was once erroneously believed that the arrival of the Islamic or Arab period erased Christianity. Chronological designations are useful approximations, but they do not characterize a period in any way.

No terminology is entirely appropriate or entirely faulty. Moreover, periodization is a dynamic process; it slowly changes its designations as a greater accumulation of data forces a new consensus.

Chronology. None of the above systems relate archaeological assemblages to chronological time with precision. Periodization is relative, emphasizing more the approximate fix of an assemblage in time than precise chronological limits. However, as more data are unearthed, archaeologists tend to become more confident in closer dating schemes.

Using principles he had already outlined in Egypt, William Flinders Petrie was the first to realize that pottery could be a key to date archaeological deposits when he dug Tell el-Ḥesi in 1890. He established a sequential system whereby certain ceramic forms could be ascribed to specific strata. From there, it was an easy step to the principle of comparative stratigraphy, in which deposits from a stratum at one site can be equated with those from another, based on identical or similar finds. The system enabled a comparison of the pottery of Palestine with that of other regions whose chronologies, like Egypt's, were tighter, based on their relationship to written texts. Palestinian pottery found in Egypt (or Egyptian pottery found in Palestine) and Egyptian inscriptions in Palestine thus became the foundation for the absolute dates associated with the periodization of Palestine. [*See* Ḥesi, Tell el-; *and the biography of Petrie.*] Ancient Egyptians sometimes dated their writings by astronomical observations, which modern astronomers can reconstruct. The Sothic cycle is the most significant of these (Rast, 1992, p. 42). For the Iron Age, the Neo-Assyrian eponym lists from Mesopotamia perform a similar function and allow the tie-in of some biblical events (Thiele, 1951, pp. 42–54). For periods before the onset of writing, carbon-14 dates are relied on, corrected by dendroarchaeological computations (tree-ring dating). For Paleolithic dates, other geological time clocks provide only very approximate dates. The following discussion is a summary of periodization for Palestine.

Stone Age. The origins of human material culture until the arrival of bronze is known as the Stone Age.

Lower Paleolithic. The most common artifact of Paleolithic, or Achulean, culture (c. 1,000,000–120,000 BP) is the stone handaxe used by hominids (prehumans); deposits are found in caves or on old lake shores where hunters skinned game. The most important site in Palestine is an old lake bed, now tipped almost vertically by tectonic action, at ʿUbeidiya, south of the Sea of Galilee.

Middle Paleolithic. Found stratigraphically above the Lower Paleolithic at Kebara and other sites, the Middle Paleolithic, or Mousterian, culture (c. 120,000–45,000 BP) is characterized by mostly triangular medium-sized flint tools. Settlements occur in many different ecosystems at sites such as the Mt. Carmel caves, Wadi Zerqa, and the Azraq oasis.

Upper Paleolithic. Mostly contemporary with the Aurignacian culture in Europe, the stone tools typical of Upper Paleolithic (c. 45,000–20,000 BP) include long blades and burins. Sites with these remains are not numerous, but they include Naḥal ʿEin-Gev on the eastern shore of the Sea of Galilee and the Qafzeh cave in Lower Galilee.

Epipaleolithic. Formerly called the Mesolithic period, the Epipaleolithic (c. 18,000–8500 BCE) is equated with the Natufian and Kebaran cultures. Its present name characterizes it accurately as the end of the Paleolithic period. Extremely small flint tools called microliths are ubiquitous at sites like Eynan in the Hulah Valley and the Kebara cave on Mt. Carmel.

Pre-Pottery Neolithic. During the first part of the Pre-Pottery Neolithic (PPNA; c. 8500–7200 BCE), a gradual change in subsistence took place in agricultural communities, with circular huts for dwellings (Jericho was the largest). In its second stage, the PPNB (c. 7200–6000 BCE), the "Neolithic revolution" completed the shift to full-fledged cereal farming and sheep/goat herding. Houses were rectangular in plan and often had thick plaster floors containing finds related to textile production. Mortuary rituals used plastered skulls (portraits?), while at ʿAin Ghazal, the largest settlement of the period, other ceremonial activities are represented by anthropomorphic statues about 90 cm tall. Other important sites were Munḥata, Jericho, and Beidha.

Pottery Neolithic. The earliest of the Pottery Neolithic stages (c. 6000–4500 BCE), called Yarmukian after the location of its discovery (Shaʿar ha-Golan, near the Yarmuk River), includes the first evidence of pottery, similar to that of the Hassuna culture in Mesopotamia. The second stage, called Munḥata after a key site in the Jordan Valley, saw the introduction of dark-faced burnished ware, a ceramic style connecting Palestine, Syria, and Anatolia. The third stage, named after the Wadi Rabbah near the Yarkon River, saw the introduction of weapons of war beyond flint points: slingstones and mace-heads. These weapons also occurred at Halafian sites in Mesopotamia.

Chalcolithic. A diversity of subcultures characterize the Chalcolithic period (c. 4500–3300 BCE). The Ghassulian culture, named after the site in the southern Jordan Valley (Teleilat el-Ghassul), is characterized by colorful paintings on plastered walls, ivory objects, terra-cotta figurines, and basalt bowls. The temple complex at ʿEin-Gedi, and the nearby cache of ceremonial copper objects from a cave in Naḥal Mishmar, may be Ghassulian. The Beersheba culture, comprising fifty-seven sites in the region of the northern Negev desert (Shiqmim is of special importance), displays subterranean dwellings and storerooms and a unique pottery vessel called a churn. In the Golan, villagers built their houses in rows of adjacent broadrooms, in which stylized busts of human heads called pillar figures are found frequently.

Bronze Age. The various phases in the period that marks the beginning of the urbanization process in Palestine, the Bronze Age, are designated Canaanite by some Israeli archaeologists. The practice is now diminishing and a more uniform nomenclature is appearing in the literature.

Early Bronze I. There are four distinct ceramic assemblages related to regions in the Early Bronze I period (c. 3300–3000 BCE): gray-burnished ware in the north; red-burnished ware in the north and south; line-group painted ware (groups of parallel lines) in the central hills and the south; and impressed-slashed ware (relief decoration with pie-crust finger indentations) in the central hills and the south. Until recently, several scholars identified these ware groups as Chalcolithic. Settlements seem to have grown from the valleys and coastal plain into the hills. Connections can be established with Gerzean Egypt and the Proto-Literate period in Mesopotamia via Jawa in the eastern desert. Important sites include Bab edh-Dhraʿ, Arad, Jericho, and Beth-Shean.

Early Bronze II–III. The Early Bronze II–III periods (c. 3000–2250 BCE) represent a unified flow of cultural development. They are a time of reduced regionalism and international trade in which donkey caravans carry wine and oil from Palestine to Egypt (Stager 1992). This provides good synchronisms with Egypt, where nearly two-hundred Palestinian pots have been found in tombs. In Egypt the period includes the Old Kingdom: the first dynasty marks the beginning of EB II, whereas the latest connections in EB III are with Pepi II of the sixth dynasty. In Mesopotamia, it is the Early Dynastic period. The highly burnished EB III pottery known as Khirbet Kerak ware also provides links to Syria and Anatolia. During this long period the largest fortified cities prior to Roman times were built, including Tel Yarmut, Ai, Arad, Tell el-Ḥesi, and Tell el-Farʿah (North). City walls were enormous, sometimes reaching 10 m in width. Houses often were of the broadroom type, as were palaces and temples.

Early Bronze IV. Although not all scholars use the term *Early Bronze IV* (c. 2250–2000 BCE), a rapidly growing consensus favors it. Originally called Middle Bronze I by Albright, others (especially archaeologist William G. Dever; see, e.g., his "The Early Bronze IV Period in Transjordan and Southern Palestine," *BASOR* 210 [1973]: 37–62) noted its closer connections to EB culture and called it Intermediate EB–MB, Intermediate Bronze, or EB IV. The period witnessed a massive change in life-style: gone were the large fortified EB II–III sites (except for moderately sized Khirbet Iskander in Transjordan). Instead, the period is characterized by pastoralists who buried their dead in large cemeteries with shaft tombs, such as at ʿAin es-Samiyeh and Bab edh-Dhraʿ. Sites with small, circular structures (dwellings?) are found in the Negev highlands (Be'er Resisim), and an unfortified hillside village has recently been discovered in the Rephaim Valley near Jerusalem.

Middle Bronze IIA. The renaming of MB I as EB IV created a gap in the nomenclature. Some scholars, therefore, renamed the three phases of MB II: MB IIA became MB I; MB IIB became MB II; and MB IIC became MB III. But this nomenclature has not found consistent support, and most scholars retain the original terms and tolerate the lack of an MB I. MB IIA (c. 2000–1800 BCE) begins the second period of urbanization with settlements refortifying old EB II–III sites or constructing new ones, but in both cases using huge sloping ramparts (glacis) as part of their fortification system. EB pottery had been mostly handmade, but in MBIIA a slow tournette produced some of the most delicate pottery made in Palestine, especially forms with carination (an elegant, sharp bend in the body). The most important site of the period is Aphek, but Tell el-Ḥayyat in the Jordan Valley provides the best continuity from EB IV to MB IIA. This was the Middle Kingdom in Egypt and the Old Assyrian kingdom in Mesopotamia and western Anatolia.

Middle Bronze IIB–C. The cultural direction of MB IIA continued smoothly through MB IIB–C (c. 1800–1550 BCE), and many more sites were fortified with ramparts: Shechem, Gezer, and Hazor (the latter the largest site of any period in Palestine). Pottery forms became more varied, but still maintained the earlier commitment to fine, elegant wares. Burials were often in jars beneath the floors of houses. At this time the Canaanites invented the alphabet, probably in the north. The Old Babylonian kingdom and Mari shared power in Mesopotamia, while the foreign Hyksos ruled Egypt. Indeed, the period comes to an end when the indigenous Egyptians of the seventeenth dynasty chased out the Hyksos and destroyed a number of Palestinian sites in the process. A recent debate about the chronology of this event, spearheaded by the Egyptologist Manfred Bietak, has made some scholars question the date of the end of MB IIB–C.

Late Bronze. At several Palestinian sites there is strong evidence for a three-fold separation of the Late Bronze period into LB I (c. 1550–1400), LB IIA (c. 1400–1300), and LB IIB (c. 1300–1200). Because the culture is a continuous and gradual breakdown of that inherited from the Middle Bronze Age, they will be considered together here. The Late Bronze was an international age, when the Egyptian Empire reached its apogee in Asia (the Amarna period is LB IIA). Large amounts of imported pottery and other objects occur at Palestinian sites, especially Mycenaean pottery from the Aegean and base-ring and white-slipped wares from Cyprus. The most important sites include Megiddo, Hazor, Aphek, Lachish, and Beth-Shean. At the latter, several Egyptian inscriptions connect Palestinian stratigraphy with various New Kingdom pharaohs, while many inscriptions in Egypt speak of pharaonic military campaigns into Palestine. At Aphek a large building may have been an Egyptian governor's residence. In Mesopotamia the Hurrian Empire of Mitanni was influential, while farther west the Hittites were at the height of their power. The period came to an end as part of the larger disruptions in the eastern Mediterranean, most often associated with the Sea Peoples.

Iron Age. Many archaeologists date Iron Age materials by century rather than by period terminology. Among Israeli archaeologists, a few refer to it as the Israelite period.

Iron I. Most Israeli archaeologists date the end of Iron I (c. 1200–925 BCE) to the rise of the United Monarchy in ancient Israel (c. 1000 BCE); other scholars favor the more traditional view that it ended with the invasion of Pharaoh Sheshong (Shishak, dated to about 925 BCE by the Bible and Egyptian texts), which left clear destruction layers at many sites. On the northern coastal plain and in the broad valley regions, the LB Canaanite culture continued (Megiddo) into Early Iron I, while, on the southern coastal plain, a distinctive material culture related to the Aegean and southern Asia Minor undoubtedly represents that of the Philistines (and other Sea Peoples). Sites in the central hills and Transjordan probably represent the coalescence of tribal and some local urban elements toward the national groups known from the Hebrew Bible: Israelites, Ammonites, Moabites, Edomites, and others. The small settlements in the hilly regions, probably of extended families, were farming villages with a limited repertoire of artifacts (Raddanah, Giloh, Shiloh, ʿUmeiri [ʿUmayri]); during the period, however, larger towns and cities gradually developed until, during Israel's United Monarchy, large, fortified cities were built (Jerusalem, Gezer, Megiddo, Hazor). The Iron I period is often subdivided into Iron IA (c. 1200–1125), Iron IB (c. 1125–1000), and Iron IC (c. 1000–925). In Mesopotamia, Assyria was strong only for brief periods and, after the strong leadership of Rameses III at the beginning of the twentieth dynasty, Egyptian influence in Asia was largely absent through the twenty-first dynasty until Sheshonq (twenty-second dynasty).

Iron II. Schemes to subdivide the Iron II period (c. 925–586 BCE) attach a variety of dates to periods labeled Iron IIA, B, C, and sometimes D. It is easiest to subdivide the period into two: Iron IIA from Sheshonq's destruction to the Assyrian invasions at the end of the eighth century BCE, and Iron IIB from those destructions to the Babylonian invasions in the early sixth century BCE. This period witnessed the high points of the region's various national groups (small kingdoms or chiefdoms) and, toward the end of the period, the composition of much of the Hebrew Bible. The various royal courts bred regionalism and an elite social class, both of which are reflected in the archaeological remains. Assemblages of pottery and writing styles are characteristic of definable regions, and finds are richer at royal cities, such as Samaria, Megiddo, Hazor, Jerusalem, Lachish, and Amman than at more provincial sites. In Mesopotamia the dominant power was Assyria, which, in the seventh century BCE, conquered Egypt briefly. The Egyptian twenty-second–twenty-sixth dynasties remained relatively weak until the late seventh century BCE when Neco II (twenty-sixth dynasty) briefly controlled Palestine. In Syria various city-states, such as Damascus and Aleppo, managed to carve out significant kingdoms.

Neo-Babylonian period. Because the culture is still fundamentally Iron II, many attach the Neo-Babylonian period (c. 586–539 BCE) to it as Iron III. However, most begin to use terms that reflect the large empires at this time. Until recently, very few sites were ascribed to these years. There is a new awareness, however, that a significant number of sites existed, especially in Transjordan (ʿUmeiri), in the region north of Jerusalem, and in Phoenician areas along the coast (Dor).

Persian period. The Persian period (539–332 BCE) was also international in scope, with imports into the Levant from Attic Greece reflecting the maritime trade of the Phoenicians and their colonies in the western Mediterranean as well as the presence of Greek travelers and mercenaries. The Persians built small administrative centers and a vast road system to connect them. Important sites in Palestine were Megiddo, Ashdod, Ashkelon, Akko, Dor, Samaria, and Amman. The imperial bureaucratic system, and the common language of Aramaic it used, broke down barriers and allowed the long-range exchange of ideas and material culture. Coins began to be used with frequency.

Classical Age. The term *Classical Age* is not frequent, but it may be used to provide continuity with the preceding "Ages." It includes the Hellenistic, Roman, and Byzantine periods.

Hellenistic period (332–63 BCE). With Alexander the Great's conquest of the Near East in the late fourth century BCE, Greek influence sustained a movement toward Western ideals that lasted into the Islamic Age. The two Greek kingdoms that controlled Palestine, the Ptolemies in Egypt and the Seleucids in Syria, established and supported certain key sites, to which they imported Hellenism: Samaria, Anafa, Jerusalem, and Dor. Indigenously supported settlements tended to be smaller and poorer. Hundreds of amphoras (probably containing wine) were sent from the Aegean to the Levant, many bearing historically important stamped inscriptions in Greek on their handles. The Jewish revolt in the mid-second century BCE against Seleucid inroads of Hellenism into Judaism founded the Hasmonean (Maccabean) dynasty.

Early Roman period (63 BCE –135 CE). Pompey's arrival in Palestine signaled a new era, but the greatest developments took place under the rule of Herod the Great and his followers. Indeed, archaeologists also use *Herodian* to characterize the period until 70 CE. At no time in the past did so much building activity take place in such a short time as under Herod. He built large, opulent Roman-style palaces at Jerusalem, Jericho, Masada, Herodium, and Machaerus. The largest temple complex and harbor in the Roman Empire at the time were at Jerusalem and Caesarea, respectively, with a Roman-style city at the latter site. Other Roman cities, such as the ten cities of the Decapolis (all but one of them in Transjordan), Samaria, and Banias (Caesarea Philippi) were built with huge inflows of capital. Again, indigenous groups lived in more modest surroundings. This was the age of Cleopatra, Julius Caesar, Augustus, the Dead Sea Scrolls, and Jewish sectarianism, out of which rabbinic Judaism and the Talmud, as well as Jesus and the New Testament, grew. Overland trade flourished in the hands of the Nabateans from their capital at Petra and other cities in the Negev. The period came to an end in 135 CE, with the defeat of the Second Jewish Revolt against Rome under Bar Kokhba, although some scholars place it earlier, with the end of the First Revolt, in 70 CE.

Late Roman period (135–c. 325 CE). The Late Roman period is sometimes subdivided into Middle Roman (135–c. 250) and Late Roman (c. 250–325). Emperor Hadrian's restructuring of Palestine gave it Roman temples, palaces, and villas at many sites, including Jerusalem. The Romans took over the Nabatean trade routes and, toward the end of the period, built a line of fortress settlements, known as the limes, fronting the eastern desert. Also toward the end of the period, synagogues and churches began to multiply. Constantine's moving of his capital from Rome to Byzantium, marks the historical end of the period, although some scholars place it at the time of the great earthquake of 363.

Byzantine period (c. 325–640 CE). The period during which churches proliferated in Palestine at almost every non-Jewish settlement larger than a village is known as the Byzantine, or Christian, period. Especially impressive are the roughly fifteen churches in Madaba (a moderately sized town) and another twelve or so churches on Mt. Nebo (a pilgrimage center) in Transjordan. Jewish towns contained synagogues, and both churches and synagogues were built on the basilica plan and paved with beautifully designed mosaic floors, many with historically important Greek and Hebrew inscriptions. [*See also* Churches; Synagogues; Mosaics.] Not until the modern period did the number of settlements and the size of the population of Palestine approach that of the Byzantine period. Many of the Roman cities grew large (Kurnub, Umm el-Jimal, Jerash), and money flowed into the region from pilgrims, who traveled everywhere in the Holy Land. Whereas in the Roman period there had tended to be a wide disparity between the very wealthy and the poor, the booming Byzantine economy allowed a more egalitarian spread of wealth, so that many houses were well built. [*See* Byzantine Empire.]

Islamic Age. With the Islamic conquest of the Near East in the mid-seventh century, a new idealism began to alter the features of the region. A rising consensus among Islamic archaeologists is to abandon the old dynastic names for periodization and instead group them into broad categories. Such categories will facilitate tying Islamic ceramics to chronology. The present divisions belong to this writer.

Early Islamic period (c. 640–1100 CE). The Early Islamic period comprises three foreign dynasties who ruled Palestine: the Umayyads from Damascus (Early Islamic I, c. 640–750 CE); the ʿAbbasids from Baghdad (Early Islamic II, c. 750–969 CE); and the Fatimids from Egypt (Early Islamic III, 969–c.1100). Recent research emphasizes how difficult it is to locate breaks in the stratigraphic record to correspond with these historical and dynastic periods. For instance, much of what used to be limited to Umayyad times is now seen to extend well into the ʿAbbasid period. Thus, Khirbat al-Mafjar in the Jordan Valley, the best known of the Early Islamic palaces, is now known as ʿAbbasid as well as Umayyad.

The coming of Islam did not mean the rejection of Christianity. Many churches continued to function unabated into Umayyad times, and some were even built then, lasting into the ʿAbbasid period. (The mosaic in St. Stephen's Church at Umm er-Rasas, southeast of Madaba, is dated by an inscription to early ʿAbbasid times.) Palestine prospered while the caliphs were in Damascus. They established a provincial capital at Ramla, west of Jerusalem, whose Early Islamic ruins are still preserved. Jerusalem, as a holy city, also saw grandiose building activity, such as the Dome of the Rock, the al-ʿAqṣa mosque, and a major palace. Some of the most pristine structures are the desert castles in the eastern desert. When the caliphate moved to Baghdad, the intensity of settlement abated in Palestine, though cities like ʿAqaba (where a vessel imported from China was found) show that it continued to be productive. [*See* Umayyad Caliphate; ʿAbbasid Caliphate; Fatimid Dynasty.]

Middle Islamic (c. 1100–1516 CE). Comprising foreign rule by the Crusaders (Middle Islamic I, c. 1100–1291 CE), who took over while the ʿAbbasids still ruled in Baghdad; the Ayyubids (1174–1263); and the Mamluks (Middle Islamic II, 1250–1516), the Middle Islamic period illustrates the problem of overlapping dynastic periods. The Crusaders brought European architecture in the form of castles (Nimrud, Kerak, Shobak, Belvoir, ʿAtlit), churches (the Holy Sepulcher and St. Anne's in Jerusalem, the church at Yoqneʿam); institutional structures (monasteries, hospices); and cities/forts (Caesarea, Akko). They also inspired Muslims to follow suit: ʿAjlun Castle was built by the Ayyubid Salah ad-Din. A renaissance of settlements during the Mamluk dynasty made the population the highest in the region since Byzantine times. Many villages and towns dotted the countryside (Heshbon, ʿAqaba, Pella) to complement the major cities (Jerusalem, with its suqs, and Ramla, with the White Mosque). Heightened water control permitted the introduction of sugarcane and its processing sites in the Jordan Valley. Although the period's pottery is mostly handmade, glazed wares were introduced from Egypt, which in turn had been inspired by Chinese ceramics. [*See* Crusader Period; Ayyubid-Mamluk Dynasties.]

Late Islamic period (1516–1918 CE). With the arrival of the Ottoman Turks (after whom the period is also called), consistent administrative neglect gradually produced a chaotic cycle of rebellions by local strongmen (pashas) and crackdowns by Turkish troops. As a result, settlements diminished until Akko, Jaffa, and Jerusalem were virtually all that was left. A concomitant rise in nomadic pastoral lifestyles saw people tenting during the summer and living in caves during the winter. Süleman the Magnificent reconstructed the walls around Jerusalem in the sixteenth century, and much of the Old City of Akko, famous for Napoleon's siege, dates to this period. The most important artifact associated with the period is the clay pipe, which swept the Mediterranean after tobacco was brought from the New World. Toward the end of the period, in the nineteenth century, the European powers became interested in the region and established religious missions and encouraged trade, archaeology, and pilgrimage, bringing an upswing in wealth and settlement.

Modern Period (Since 1918). The period since World War I has been witness to the most rapid rise in settlement intensity in the region's history. Modern construction with bulldozers has destroyed architectural remains from preceding periods, and governments have encouraged sedentarization, so that pastoral and nomadic life-styles have diminished. Rapid technological change has also made traditional artifact types obsolete: the use of pottery is virtually nil, replaced with plastic, glass, and metal, probably the datable artifacts of future excavations, and in a period of international trade objects from all over the world are entering the archaeological record. Copious written records make archaeology more of a historical science than previously. Although it is too early to subdivide the modern period, it may be that, for Palestine, a new subperiod should begin with

1967 when the six-day war caused a massive explosion in the population and settlement of Transjordan and began a process of new settlement in the hill country of Cis-Jordan.

BIBLIOGRAPHY

Bright, John. *A History of Israel.* 3d ed. Philadelphia, 1981.
Fleming, Stuart. *Dating in Archaeology: A Guide to Scientific Techniques.* London, 1976.
Gitin, Seymour. "Stratigraphy and Its Application to Chronology and Terminology." In *Biblical Archaeology Today: Proceedings of the International Congress on Biblical Archaeology, Jerusalem, April 1984,* edited by Janet Amitai, pp. 99–107. Jerusalem, 1985.
Kitchen, K. A. "The Basis of Egyptian Chronology in Relation to the Bronze Age." In *High, Middle, or Low? International Colloquium on Absolute Chronology Held at the University of Gothenburg, 20–22 August 1987,* edited by Paul Åström, pp. 37–55. Gothenburg, 1987.
Porada, Edith. "The Chronology of Mesopotamia, ca. 7000–1600 B.C." In *Chronologies in Old World Archaeology,,* edited by Robert W. Ehrich, vol. 1, pp. 77–121, vol. 2, 90–124. 3d ed. Chicago, 1992.
Rast, Walter E. *Through the Ages in Palestinian Archaeology.* Philadelphia, 1992.
Stager, Lawrence E. "The Periodization of Palestine from the Neolithic through Early Bronze Times." In *Chronologies in Old World Archaeology,* vol. 1, edited by Robert W. Ehrich, pp. 22–41. 3d ed. Chicago, 1992.
Thiele, Edwin R. *The Mysterious Numbers of the Hebrew Kings.* Chicago, 1951.

LARRY G. HERR

PERISTYLE HOUSE. The term *peristyle,* from the Greek words *peri* and *stylos,* refers to the arrangement of columns encircling an architectural feature. In a peristyle temple, for example, the columns surround the outside of the building; in a peristyle house, the columns encircle a central court. The columns in a peristyle house support a roofed porch around the center of the court, which is open to the sky. The rooms of the house surround the four sides of the central court and open onto the porch.

Early examples of peristyle houses dating to the second century BCE are found on the island of Delos. The outside walls of the Delian houses are irregular in shape (i.e., not square or rectangular in layout), but the large central courtyard usually has a perfectly square peristyle. The area within the columns is a sunken impluvium (a shallow depression or sunken area, provided to receive rainwater from the roof), often with a mosaic pavement covering a water cistern. In a variant of the peristyle house known as the Rhodian type, the columns on the south side of the court are taller than the others, enabling the porch to catch the sunlight from that direction.

Peristyle houses enjoyed great popularity throughout the Hellenistic world and beyond. A Hellenistic example from northern Palestine is located at Tel Anafa. [*See* Anafa, Tel.] The northern half of the mound at the site is dominated by a large stucco building that had rooms on four sides of a peristyle courtyard, including a bath complex on the east. Evidence for the adoption of this type by Palestine's Jewish population comes from the Jewish Quarter in Jerusalem, where fragmentary remains of a peristyle house dating to the first century CE were uncovered in Nahman Avigad's excavations. Two of the rooms opening off the peristyle court were paved with opus sectile (colored stone tiles). Peristyle houses found elsewhere in the Near East display adaptations of the type to local building materials and conditions. At Dura-Europos and Nippur, for example, the walls of the houses and sometimes even the columns were constructed of mud brick instead of stone. [*See* Dura-Europos; Nippur.]

A large peristyle building was discovered in the excavations at Ramat Raḥel outside Jerusalem. It appears to have been constructed during the third century CE, when the Tenth Roman Legion occupied the site. During the last phase of the building's use, the floors were deepened, benches were added along some of the walls, and a thin wall was erected in the center of the western colonnade, to the south of which a kitchen was installed. Such subdivisions of peristyle buildings were common throughout the Roman Empire, from the fifth to seventh century CE. While the construction of new peristyle houses declined dramatically then, the few that were constructed were larger than ever. Simon P. Ellis suggests that these developments reflect the increased concentration of wealth in the Late Roman Empire and a more autocratic form of patronage. The construction of peristyle houses appears to have come to an end by the middle of the sixth century CE.

[*See also* Building Materials and Techniques, *article on* Materials and Techniques of the Persian through Roman Periods.]

BIBLIOGRAPHY

Dinsmoor, William Bell. *The Architecture of Ancient Greece.* 3d ed. New York, 1950. Contains a survey of the development of the peristyle house in the classical and Hellenistic worlds.
Ellis, Simon P. "The End of the Roman House." *American Journal of Archaeology* 92 (1988): 565–576. Discussion of the latest examples of peristyle houses in the Roman East and the possible reasons for the disappearance of the type.
Kraeling, Carl H. *The Excavations at Dura-Europos; Final Report VIII, Part I: The Synagogue.* New Haven, 1956. Discussion of the houses at Dura-Europos.

JODI MAGNESS

PERSEPOLIS, site located in the southwest Iranian province of Fars, on the eastern edge of the broad plain called Marv Dasht (29°57′ N, 52°59′ E). The Achaemenid Persian ruler Darius I (522–486 BCE) elected to build a new dynastic seat here to replace the prior capital, Pasargadae, some 40 km (25 mi.) to the north. The site includes a lofty stone terrace close to 450 m long and 300 m wide (see figure 1); the substantial remains of a series of relief-decorated pa-

PERSEPOLIS. Figure 1. *The terrace viewed from the southeast.* Starting clockwise, from the left, this view includes the Palace of Xerxes, the relatively compact Palace of Darius, the apadana (with the building's relief decorated eastern facade hidden beheath a temporary protective covering), the Gate of All Lands, the Hall of One Hundred Columns, and the now severely denuded fabric of the multi-roomed Treasury. (Courtesy D. Stronach)

latial buildings; a fortified hill directly to the east; and a series of lesser representational buildings on the adjacent plain. The settlement in which the common people lived has not been identified. The sheer cliff face at Naqsh-i Rustam, 6 km (3.5 mi.) to the north, is the dramatic setting for the rock-cut tombs of Darius and three others of his line. [*See* Pasargadae; Naqsh-i Rustam.]

Four trilingual cuneiform inscriptions (in Old Persian, Elamite, and Babylonian) on the gate of Persepolis combine with other textual evidence (Hallock, 1969) to affirm that Darius's extensive palace fortress was given the same name, *Parsa,* as the surrounding homeland of the Persians. [*See* Cuneiform; Persians.] Centuries later, when the original name and associations of the terrace had long been forgotten, certain of the carved figures in the doorway reliefs of Darius's palace were taken to represent the mythical Jamshid, the great hunter and paramount ruler of Iran's heroic tradition. Thus, while Biruni, an eleventh-century scientist and geographer at the court of the Ghaznavids, was not without some knowledge of Alexander the Great's fateful actions at the site (see below), most medieval and later Persian visitors appear to have known the terrace and its associated remains as Takht-i Jamshid, or the "throne of Jamshid." At the same time, the site's currently preferred designation, Persepolis, is directly drawn from the name by which it was known to the ancient Greeks (an apparent contraction of Persai polis or "the city in Persis").

The first mention of the ruins appears in the journal of Odoric of Porderone, who passed through Fars in 1318. He refers to the site as Comerun, a corruption of a second popular designation: *chehel sotun* or "forty columns," a term signifying "many columns." In the course of the seventeenth century, however, interest intensified: the first detailed drawings of the well-preserved site and its sculptures began to be published in Europe. Some visitors, such as Don Garcia de Silva y Figueroa, proclaimed their conviction that the ruins had to be those of Persepolis. There matters rested until the early nineteenth century, when G. F. Grotefend of Heidelberg University, working from copies of Old Persian cuneiform texts made earlier at the site, was able to distinguish the names of Darius and several of his successors. This triumph of decipherment cut through all previous speculation and pointed to the undeniable rediscovery of the Persian capital, the Persepolis of classical accounts, that Alexander had sacked and burned in 330 BCE.

Formal excavations were slow to begin. It was only in 1924 that the Iranian government invited Ernst Herzfeld, the foremost Iranologist of the day, to prepare a detailed plan of Persepolis, together with an estimate of what it would cost to clear the site. Then, in the new circumstances that attended the abrogation (c. 1930) of France's hitherto exclusive concession to excavate in Iran, the Oriental Institute of the University of Chicago was invited to sponsor the work and Herzfeld was chosen to head the expedition. Following four campaigns, from 1931 to 1934 (during which the famed reliefs on the east side of the apadana were uncovered), the direction of the work passed to Erich F. Schmidt, who continued to excavate from 1935 to 1939. It was Schmidt, moreover, who published the results of the Oriental Institute's all-important excavations in a comprehensive three-volume final report.

Subsequent excavations, initially conducted by André Godard, M. T. Mostafavi, and Ali Sami on behalf of the Iranian Archaeological Service, did much to reveal the plan of the few remaining unexamined areas of the site. The most productive advances in the last few decades may be said to have come, however, from other directions: in a new interest in the organization and chronology of the work at Persepolis (where the contributions of Carl Nylander, Michael Roaf, Margaret Root, and Ann-Britt Tilia each call for special note) and in a new level of concern for the conservation and restoration of the monuments. [*See* Conservation Archaeology; Restoration and Conservation.]

While work on the massive retaining wall of the partly rubble-filled terrace and on the magnificent stairway in the northwest corner of the site is likely to have begun at least as early as 515 BCE, a string of building inscriptions of Darius himself, his son Xerxes (486–465 BCE), and his grandson Artaxerxes (465–425 BCE) helps to document a subsequent, prolonged sequence of construction on the surface of the terrace from about 500 BCE down to about 440 BCE. Such inscriptions not only reflect the measured pace that was demanded by the uncompromising standards of Achaemenid construction, but they also do much to illustrate the sense of dynastic continuity that apparently inspired the completion of much of an original masterplan. It is also striking that, while there are necessarily many contrasts between the spacious plan of Pasargadae and the more condensed plan of Persepolis, both sites adhere to a distinctive Iranian preference for multiple freestanding units, rather than to the characteristic palace plan of Mesopotamia, which tended to incorporate many disparate elements under one roof (see figure 2). [*See* Palace.]

In a process that was presumably intended to underscore the exalted rank of the Persian king, all visitors to Achaemenid Persepolis were obliged to ascend the 14-meter-high double-return stairway that led to the single formal entrance to the terrace: the freestanding Gate of All Lands. This formidable square structure was marked by a single soaring hall

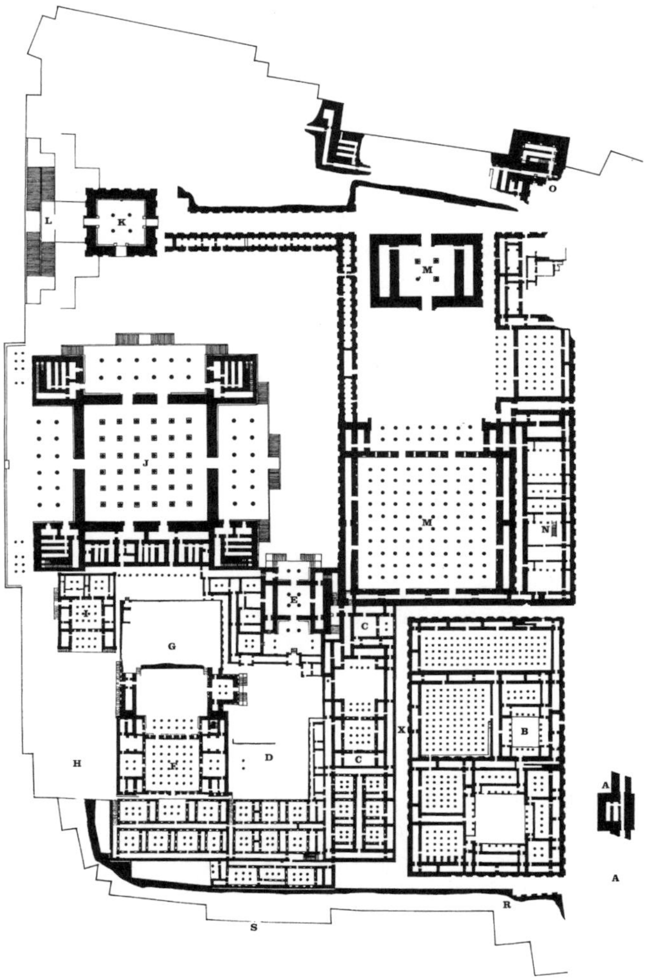

PERSEPOLIS. Figure 2. *Plan of the terrace.* A = Eastern Fortification, garrison; B = Treasury; C/North = Service Quarters of Harem; C/South = Main Wing of Harem; D = Palace D; E = Council Hall; F = Xerxes Palace; G = Palace G; H = Palace H; I = Palace of Darius I; J = Apadana; K = Gate of Xerxes; L = Terrace Stairway; M/North = Unfinished Gate; M/South = Hall of One Hundred Columns; N = Stairway to Drainage Tunnel; O = Northern Fortification; R = Southern Fortification; S = Foundation Inscription of Darius I. The double-return stairway at the northwest corner of the platform provided the only formal access to both the adjacent, supremely spacious public buildings and the more private structures located within the southern half of the terrace. (After Schmidt, 1953)

with four stone columns and three doorways. In keeping with the Assyrian-inspired colossi that once formed part of the fabric of gate R at Pasargadae, two massive stone bulls guarded the outer doorway and two winged human-headed bulls guarded the opposite, inner doorway. Trilingual inscriptions indicate that Xerxes erected, or at least completed, this aptly named structure.

The hub of all else on the terrace was the imposing audience hall, or apadana, a building that was founded by Darius and completed by Xerxes and which stood on a separate podium 2.60 m high. With a plan that can be seen to have followed that of the slightly earlier apadana of Darius at Susa, each side of this square edifice was 110 m long. [*See* Susa.] Six rows of six columns (each with a square base, a fluted shaft, and a composite capital that was crowned by addorsed bull protomes) supported the cedar beams of the main hall, a vast room that stood more than 19 m high and measured 60.50 m on each side. The hall's 5-meter-thick mud-brick walls were flanked by four corner towers and by deep recesses between the towers. To the north, east, and west these recesses took the form of tall porticoes, each marked by two rows of six stone columns set on circular, bell-shaped bases.

While the west portico provided a focal point from which the monarch could review parades on the plain below, the remaining two porticoes were each approached by monumental stairways composed of four symmetrically arranged flights of steps. Effectively carved at eye level, where all who sought an audience could not fail to observe them, the facades of these matching stairways still boast a series of reliefs that rightly remain among the most celebrated expressions of Achaemenid art (see figure 3).

PERSEPOLIS. Figure 3. *Detail from the east facade of the apadana.* Two members of the Cappadocian delegation display gifts of Median-style clothing as they move towards the royal dias. The cape of each figure is fastened by an arched and ribbed fibula. (Courtesy D. Stronach)

When first conceived, each mirror image relief showed a procession of twenty-three tribute-bearing delegations of the empire; a central panel in which the king and the crown prince are giving audience to an official; and a third, complementary tableau that depicts (behind the royal figures) the massed files of royal guards, followed by members of the court entourage. In addition, the left and right edges of the central panel and the extreme limits of the overall composition are each flanked by the sole motif that carried any direct reference to active force: namely, the often-repeated scene of a bull being attacked by a lion (in what appears to be a representation of great power being overcome by yet greater power). Debate will of course persist, but while these and other reliefs from Persepolis were once thought to document the details of an annual new year's festival, it now seems more probable that the above-mentioned scenes were expressly designed to illustrate Darius's personal vision of empire: one of far-reaching, harmonious government at once secure in terms of the power and authority of the monarch and the assured condition of the royal succession.

Like the apadana, Darius's palace stood on its own separate podium near the western edge of the terrace. An archetype for later royal residences, the building was distinguished by a single entrance portico flanked by guardrooms, a hypostyle central hall, and a series of symmetrically planned, adjoining suites. The extant stone elements of this compact structure include highly polished door, window, and niche frames (each capped by fluted, egyptianized cornices), low wall socles, and a series of elegant doorway reliefs. The latter are especially remarkable for those examples in which Darius chose to introduce a novel type of apotropaic relief: the Persian "royal hero" shown in the act of vanquishing one or another real or fabulous beast in defense (in all likelihood) of not only the actual residence of the ruler, but also the realm as a whole.

Darius also founded, but did not himself complete, a three-doored tripylon. This monumental, enigmatic structure appears to have served as the main link between the open courts and public buildings in the northern portion of the site and the more southerly areas of the terrace that largely came to be given over to the private palaces of Darius's successors. He also laid out the first stage of the treasury, an eventually much altered and expanded structure that served as one of the Achaemenid Empire's richest storehouses (as well as one of the more prolific sources of metal objects, administrative tablets, seal impressions, and other notable finds recovered during Schmidt's excavations). After 486 BCE, this latter structure came to be flanked on the west by the so-called Harem of Xerxes and, closer to the southwest corner of the terrace, by Xerxes' palace. In architectural terms, however, the most impressive of all the later buildings at Persepolis consists of the so-called throne hall (or Hall of One Hundred Columns), which was most probably begun by Xerxes and completed by Artaxerxes. Although the square hall of this structure was not given the towering height of the main hall of the apadana, its ground area was substantially larger, with each side measuring 68.50 m.

Subsequent construction at Persepolis was mainly confined to the southeast corner of the terrace and to the creation of a series of private palaces of lesser note. A well-documented exception concerns the addition of a double staircase on the south side of Darius's palace. There an Old Persian inscription proclaims the authorship of Artaxerxes III (359–338 BCE) and an analysis of the associated reliefs shows them to be of the same late date (Roaf, 1983). Elsewhere, both Artaxerxes II (404–359 BCE) and Artaxerxes III chose to locate their sizable rock-cut tombs on the western slope of the fortified hill that overlooks the terrace. With the completion of these last two major monuments, however, a singular record of sustained architectural and artistic accomplishment came to an effective close only a handful of years before the fateful destruction of the site.

[*See also* Persia, *article on* Ancient Persia.]

BIBLIOGRAPHY

Balcer, Jack. "Alexander's Burning of Persepolis." *Iranica Antiqua* 13 (1978): 119–133.

Cahill, Nicholas. "The Treasury at Persepolis." *American Journal of Archaeology* 89 (1985): 373–389.

Calmeyer, Peter. "Textual Sources for the Interpretation of Achaemenian Palace Decoration." *Iran* 18 (1980): 55–63.

Cameron, George G. *Persepolis Treasury Tablets.* Oriental Institute Publications, 45. Chicago, 1948.

Ghirshman, Roman. "Notes iraniennes VII. À propos de Persépolis." *Artibus Asiae* 20 (1957): 265–278.

Hallock, Richard T. *Persepolis Fortification Tablets.* Oriental Institute Publications, 112. Chicago, 1969.

Herzfeld, Ernst. *Iran in the Ancient East.* London, 1941.

Krefter, Friedrich. *Persepolis Rekonstruktionen.* Teheraner Forschungen, 3. Berlin, 1971.

Nylander, Carl. "Mason's Marks in Persepolis: A Progress Report." In *Proceedings of the Second Annual Symposium on Archaeological Research in Iran,* pp. 216–222. Tehran, 1974.

Porada, Edith. "Classic Achaemenian Architecture and Sculpture." In *The Cambridge History of Iran,* vol. 2, *The Median and Achaemenian Periods,* edited by Ilya Gershevitch, pp. 793–827. Cambridge, 1985.

Roaf, Michael. *Sculptures and Sculptors at Persepolis. Iran* 21 (1983).

Root, Margaret Cool. *The King and Kingship in Achaemenid Art: Essays on the Creation of an Iconography of Empire.* Acta Iranica, 19. Leiden, 1979.

Root, Margaret Cool. "Circles of Artistic Programming: Strategies for Studying Creative Process at Persepolis." In *Investigating Artistic Environments in the Ancient Near East,* edited by Ann C. Gunter, pp. 115–139. Washington, D.C., 1990.

Sami, Ali. *Persepolis.* Translated by R. Norman Sharp. 2d ed. Shiraz, 1955.

Schmidt, Erich F. *Persepolis,* vol. 1, *Structures, Reliefs, Inscriptions.* Oriental Institute Publications, 68. Chicago, 1953.

Schmidt, Erich F. *Persepolis,* vol. 2, *Contents of the Treasury and Other Discoveries.* Oriental Institute Publications, 69. Chicago, 1957.

Schmidt, Erich F. *Persepolis,* vol. 3, *The Royal Tombs and Other Monuments.* Oriental Institute Publications, 70. Chicago, 1970.

Shahbazi, A. Shapur. *Persepolis Illustrated.* Tehran, 1976.

Stronach, David. "The Apadana. A Signature of the Line of Darius I." In *De l'Indus aux Balkans. Recueil Jean Deshayes,* pp. 433–445. Paris, 1985.

Tilia, Ann Britt. *Studies and Restorations at Persepolis and Other Sites in Fārs.* Istituto Italiano per il Medio ed Estremo Oriente, *Reports and Memoirs* 16, 18. Rome, 1972, 1978.

Trümpelmann, Leo. *Persepolis: Ein Weltwunder der Antike.* Mainz, 1988.

DAVID STRONACH and KIM CODELLA

PERSIA. [*This entry provides a broad survey of the history of Persia as known primarily from archaeological discoveries. It is chronologically divided into four articles:*

Prehistoric Persia
Ancient Persia
Persia from Alexander to the Rise of Islam
Persia in the Islamic Period

In addition to the related articles on specific subregions and sites referred to in this entry, see also History of the Field, *article on* Archaeology in Persia.]

Prehistoric Persia

Persia is mostly a high, desertic plateau surrounded by forested mountains. As a result of its rugged topography and severe seasonal climates, permanent settlements were always localized around oases or riverine water sources and near the 5–10 percent of the land surface that is arable. About half of the arable land must be farmed with the aid of irrigation.

Persia's prehistory is understood as a result of numerous expeditions to discover sites and then through selective excavations. In the late nineteenth century, French archaeologists pioneered research in Persia, primarily in the central Zagros Mountains and Khuzistan. Following World War II, and until all foreign research ceased with the Iranian Revolution of 1979, archaeologists from the United States, Britain, Canada, and most western European countries, as well as Japan, also carried out projects there. Rather than excavate single sites, many archaeologists during the postwar era explored whole regions. During two decades of intensive research, they surveyed most of western Iran, providing a wealth of information on changes in population from period to period and differences among regions. [*See* Demography.] Nevertheless, this information represents only a preliminary stage in archaeological understanding, for excavations of some critical sites that would provide a solid basis for interpreting the survey results could not be carried out or completed.

Initial Village Period. The first period of human settlement in Persia, following a long and poorly known Paleolithic era, is the Neolithic. Agriculture and the domestication of goats and sheep—a process that may have taken place in the mountains of Persia—were introduced. [*See* Agriculture; Sheep and Goats.] Agriculture appeared in Persia in about 7000 BCE, one thousand years after it began in the southern Levant and probably spread by diffusion from that source. By this time Anatolian obsidian was reaching sites in both the Levant and the Zagros, an indication of very widespread contacts among these early peoples. Beginning with the Neolithic, there was increasing sedentism across Southwest Asia, as farmers began to settle near arable land and build houses out of mud.

A small number of excavated sites, sometimes widely scattered geographically, define the successive archaeological periods. The Aceramic Neolithic, the period when the first permanent agricultural settlements were established, is known from excavations at Ganj Dareh and Tepe Guran; in the mountain plains of Kurdistan; and at Ali Kosh in the lowland Deh Luran plain. [*See* Ali Kosh; Deh Luran.] The inhabitants of each site consumed wild foods, supplemented by cultivated cereals and domestic goats. [*See* Cereals.] Shortly before 6000 BCE, pottery came into common use, and the number of villages began to increase—a trend that was to continue for nearly two thousand years.

Late Village Period. From 5500 to 3800 BCE, cultures arose in Persia that paralleled the Ubaid in Mesopotamia but displayed many regional variants reflecting local, somewhat isolated adaptations to scattered resources. On some of the most favorable agricultural plains, a few sites became much larger than others, but hundreds of villages held fewer than one hundred inhabitants. In addition, a few excavated campsites and cemeteries show that migratory herders, in numbers that are impossible to estimate, utilized the vast stretches of mountain pastures. Patterns of transhumance, similar to those in recent periods, were well established by the mid-fifth millennium. [*See* Pastoral Nomadism.]

After two thousand years of increase, evidence indicates that from 4500 to 4000 BCE there was a general decline in the number of villages and even the abandonment of some regions. The situation may have been related to climatic changes, as well as to regional political and economic ones.

Some of the prominent Late Village period excavated sites are Dalma Tepe, Pisdeli, and Gabrestan in the northern Zagros; Sialk, on the plateau; Giyan, Siabid, and Seh Gabi in the central Zagros; Bakun and Tepe Yahya in the southern Zagros; and Tepe Sabz, Farukhabad, Jaffarabad, Chogha Mish, and Susa in lowland Khuzistan. [*See* Tepe Yahya; Tepe Farukhabad; Susa.]

Susa, on the western edge of the lowland Khuzistan plain, has provided the most information of all these sites. Well known for its historical periods, Susa was founded shortly before 4000 BCE, when the local population had fallen to near its lowest point in two millennia. At Susa, the inhabitants erected a stepped platform of mud bricks on which they placed a number of large buildings, but the ruins give few clues to the buildings' original functions. Nevertheless, by analogy with Eridu and other early temples in Mesopotamia, it is likely that Susa's platform was also the base of at least one religious edifice. [*See* Eridu.] The buildings were destroyed, probably twice, partially by fire, in violent events in about 3800 BCE.

At the base of the platform, the burial remains of a thousand or more individuals, accompanied by elaborately painted ceramics, were crammed into a small cemetery. The conditions that led to this mass interment, often of bones that had been moved from another location, remain a mystery. [*See* Burial Techniques; Grave Goods.]

Known as the Susa I period, this is the final phase of painted pottery in the Ubaid tradition that had begun two thousand years earlier (its demise is later in Persia than in Mesopotamia). The reasons for the disappearance of painted ceramics throughout Southwest Asia at this time are obscure; the type was replaced by undecorated, mass-produced, often wheelmade pots in the Uruk style.

Uruk Period. Without further excavation, it is not possible to resolve debates concerning the nature of the change between Susa I and Uruk in Persia. Some hold that it was a gradual, indigenous transition; others that it signifies an invasion by people from southern Mesopotamia, the region of Warka (Uruk). [*See* Uruk-Warka.] Whatever the case, the pattern of settlement changed. A hierarchy of sites developed, with large ones surrounded by small satellites, implying that some sites may have served regional administrative and economic functions. On the surrounding plain, there was a threefold increase in population. At Susa, a narrow excavation trench has revealed a succession of devices that were precursors of writing: seals, tokens, and bullae (clay envelopes that held tokens and preserved a record of commodity exchange).

At Godin Tepe in the central Zagros, a Late Uruk building is situated in the midst of a local settlement; it may have been an entrepôt, where trade between the lowlands and highlands was effected. [*See* Godin Tepe.] Around Tepe Malyan, on the Marv Dasht plain near Shiraz, there was a severe decline in settlement, and at Tepe Yahya, after a prolonged disruption of settlement in the late fourth millennium, a Proto-Elamite colony was installed. [*See* Malyan.] Both the disruptions of settlement and the incursion of the Proto-Elamites may be related to the emergence of cities in Khuzistan and southern Mesopotamia. By this time, sites in northern Persia were following a trajectory more related to that of Anatolia, the Caucasus, and central Asia than to Mesopotamia. Unfortunately, there have been few excavations of sites pertinent to this dynamic period of social change in

Persia. It resulted, in the third millennium, in an Elamite course of development quite separate from the Sumerian in Mesopotamia.

[*See also* Elamites; Persians; *and* Mesopotamia, *article on* Prehistoric Mesopotamia.]

BIBLIOGRAPHY

Alizadeh, Abbas. *Prehistoric Settlement Patterns and Cultures in Susiana, Southwestern Iran.* Technical Report 24, Museum of Anthropology, University of Michigan. Ann Arbor, 1992. Analysis of prehistoric Khuzistan, based on archaeological survey with many illustrations of ceramics.

Hole, Frank. "Chronologies in the Iranian Neolithic." In *Chronologies in the Near East,* edited by O. Aurenche, J. Évin, and F. Hours, pp. 353–379. British Archaeological Reports, no. 379(i). Oxford, 1987. Along with Voigt (1987), reviews current knowledge of chronology for the prehistoric cultures of Iran.

Hole, Frank, ed. *The Archaeology of Western Iran: Settlement and Society from Prehistory to the Islamic Conquest.* Washington, D.C., 1987. Multiauthored review with an index to sites and a full bibliography.

Hole, Frank. "Cemetery of Mass Grave? Reflections on Susa I." In *Contributions à l'histoire de l'Iran: Mélanges Jean Perrot,* pp. 1–14. Paris, 1990. Interpretive essay.

Lamberg-Karlovsky, C. C., and Thomas Wight Beale. *Excavations at Tepe Yahya, Iran, 1967–1975.* Peabody Museum, Harvard University, American School of Prehistoric Research, Bulletin 38. Cambridge, Mass., 1986. Site report and discussion of the regional implications of developments in southern Persia.

Neely, James A., and Henry T. Wright. *Early Settlement and Irrigation on the Deh Luran Plain: Village and Early State Societies in Southwestern Iran.* Technical Report 26, Museum of Anthropology, University of Michigan. Ann Arbor, 1994. Reports the results of intensive survey of the Deh Luran Plain; includes many figures and maps.

Smith, Philip E. L. *Palaeolithic Archaeology in Iran.* Philadelphia, 1986. Concise summary of current knowledge.

Voigt, Mary. "Relative and Absolute Chronologies for Iran between 6,500 and 3,500 BC." In *Chronologies in the Near East,* edited by O. Aurenche, J. Évin, and F. Hours, pp. 615–646. British Archaeological Reports, no. 379(ii). Oxford, 1987.

FRANK HOLE

Ancient Persia

Persia is an ecological and cultural mosaic characterized by variation rather then uniformity. Variation dominates the geographic and cultural landscape from the Neolithic period (7000 BCE) to the end of the Bronze Age (1200 BCE). Distinctive "culture areas" were characterized by shifting boundaries whose core regions, nevertheless, can be identified. The following list of core areas is in descending order of the extent to which they are known archaeologically: (1) south and southwest Iran—the modern province of Khuzistan; (2) central southern Iran, comprising modern Fars and Luristan; (3) northwest Iran—the provinces of Azerbaijan, Kurdistan, and Kermanshah; (4) southeastern Iran—the provinces of Kerman and Seistan, extending into Baluchistan; and (5) northeastern Iran, comprising the regions southeast of the Caspian Sea and Khorasan, extending to the foothills of the Kopet Dagh Mountains in Turkmenistan.

Neolithic Communities. The earliest Neolithic communities on the Iranian plateau appear in the Zagros Mountains and date to the second half of the eighth millennium (Young et al., 1983). At this time such sites as Ganj Dareh appear, a site approximately one hectare in size (Smith, 1975). It is unlikely that the community represented more than a small number of individual households. The upper levels of this site contain the remains of an early village constructed of mud-brick architecture. Structures took the form of rectilinear two-story structures—the first floor for storage and/or animal pens and the upper story for living accommodations. Ganj Dareh offers the earliest known pottery in the Near East. It is a lightly fired, chaff-tempered coarse ware that takes the form of small pots and large storage vessels. Other clay artifacts included human and animal figurines, as well as small geometric tokens. The stone industry at Ganj Dareh is characterized by numerous blade types, some containing sickle sheen, used to harvest grain. Mortars and pestles for processing cereals occured in abundance. The subsistence economy at Ganj Dareh is incompletely understood, but sheep and goats were certainly domesticated, as was barley. [*See* Sheep and Goats; Cereals.] In one of the rooms, two skulls of wild sheep were discovered embedded in the wall and plastered over with clay. Throughout the Neolithic, either entire structures or parts of buildings were increasingly turned over to ritual functions.

Perhaps the most complete Neolithic sequence in Iran is known from the region of Deh Luran in Khuzistan (Hole et al., 1969). The excavations at Ali Kosh uncovered a Neolithic sequence that ranges from about 7500 to 5500 BCE. Ali Kosh is a roughly circular settlement (135 m in diameter) with an accumulated depth of 7 m of deposit. In the earliest settlement, referred to as the Bus Mordeh phase, the inhabitants relied on a combination of wild and domestic resources. A majority of the seeds recovered were wild annual legumes and grasses native to the environment. The recovery of a limited number of cultivated barley and wheat seeds, of the type not native to the local environment, indicate that the inhabitants were also farming. During this early phase there is also evidence for the primary herding of goats, but less for sheep. It has been suggested that this phase may represent a seasonal settlement—a winter-spring station for the community that moved to higher pastures in the summer months. The Ali Kosh phase (6750–6000 BCE) represents a fully developed Neolithic community. The architecture consisted of large, well-constructed dwellings with a considerably developed material culture. Containers included stone vessels, baskets, and, toward the very end of the phase, pottery. At this time the inhabitants of Ali Kosh participated in far-reaching trade that brought them obsidian from the highland mountains of eastern Anatolia, shells from the Persian Gulf, copper from central Iran, and turquoise from northeastern Iran. Some of the earliest burials on the Iranian plateau belong to the Ali Kosh phase. The dead were buried in a shallow pit beneath the floors of the houses. Frequently, the body was covered with ocher, tightly flexed, wrapped within a reed mat, and buried with items of personal adornment. [*See* Ali Kosh; Tombs; Burial Practices; Grave Goods.]

During the last period of occupation, in about 6000–5600 BCE, (the Muhammad Jaffar phase), the effectiveness of domesticated resources, building techniques, and agricultural tools all continued to increase and pottery is found throughout the Iranian plateau. This earliest pottery is referred to as the Soft Ware horizon, for wherever it is found it is invariably a coarse, low-fired, chaff-tempered ceramic with minimal design motifs. Laboratory studies of this type of pottery from a number of different sites on the Iranian plateau and beyond has shown an identical production technique (Vandiver, 1986). The technique, referred to as consecutive slab construction, endured for more than a millennium, thus typifying the conservative tradition of technological innovation. However, its wide distribution indicates that, by the middle of the sixth millennium, there was considerable diffusion and sharing of technological skills.

Prehistory at Susa and Susiana. Archaeologically, the region of southwestern Iran, Khuzistan, is the best known and most documented in all of Persia. The province of Khuzistan is an extension of the Mesopotamian plain. The lower plains of Khuzistan lie between the Persian Gulf and include the Tigris River marshes. To the west of the Karkheh River, the northern reaches of Khuzistan touch the Zagros Mountains and extend to the eastern edge of the Ram Hormuz plain. In the valleys of Khuzistan, as well as in the lowlands, the yearly rainfall ranges from 250 to 400 mm. This allows for dry farming, which, nevertheless, would be greatly enhanced by irrigation in regions of marginal precipatation.

The archaeology of Khuzistan is responsible for revealing the history and the archaeology of Persia's oldest kingdom, Elam. The most important city within this kingdom was Susa; a site that has been excavated for nearly a century. Beginning in the late nineteenth century, excavations at Susa were directed by a number of French archaeologists: Marcel Dieulafoy, Jacques de Morgan, Roland de Mecquenem, and Roman Ghirshman. The results of these excavations have been published in scores of monographs in *Mémoires de la Délégation en Perse* (Paris). In 1968 Jean Perrot took over the French Archaeological Mission at Susa and provided the first systematic stratigraphic excavation and comprehensive picture of the prehistory of Susa (Perrot, 1976). In addition to the recent excavations at Susa, Geneviève Dollfus (1978), on behalf of the French Mission, excavated several prehistoric settlements in Khuzistan that predate the earliest settlement at Susa and provide an understanding of the region from 6000 to 4000 BCE, when Susa emerged as a regional center. Major excavations at Choga Mish (Kantor, 1976) and Haft Tepe (Negahban, 1991) have also added to what is understood of Elam in the third and second millennia BCE. Archaeological surveys undertaken in Khuzistan by Robert Adams (1962) and Henry Wright and Gregory Johnson (1975) have led to an unparalleled understanding of the local sequences and settlement regimes in this part of Persia. [*See* Susa; Haft Tepe.]

For the Kur River basin of Fars, John R. Alden (1982) and William M. Sumner (1972) have offered an archaeological sequence from both settlement survey and excavation. Research at the site of Malyan in Fars, identified as the Elamite city of Anshan, adds an important understanding of a highland Elamite capital. [*See* Malyan.] In northwestern Iran, survey and excavations in the vicinity of Hasanlu (Dyson, 1965) and Godin Tepe (Young and Levine, 1974) offer a comprehensive picture of settlement and social organization from the Late Neolithic site of Hajji Firuz (Voigt, 1983) to the Median citadel uncovered at Godin Tepe. [*See* Hasanlu; Godin Tepe; Hajji Firuz.] Sites in the Zagros range occasionally exhibit cultural ties to the settlements of Khuzistan. Materials recovered from the excavations at Tepe Sialk (Ghirshman, 1938), Tall-i Iblis (Caldwell, 1967), Tepe Yahya (Lamberg-Karlovsky and Beale, 1986), and Shahdad (Hakemi 1972), at the western edge of the Dasht-i Lut, indicate far-reaching contacts with sites to the west. [*See* Tepe Yahya.] Excavations at Tepe Hissar (Schmidt, 1937; Dyson, 1989) in the Damghan region indicate cultural ties to sites in central Asia as well as with distant Khuzistan. The work of the Italian Mission at Shahr-i Sokhta, in Sistan, has extended what is known of the urban process in this region, as well as this site's role in the production and trade of lapis lazuli (Tosi and Piperno, 1973). Beatrice de Cardi's (1970) excavations in Iranian Baluchistan indicate its cultural relationships with archaeological sites excavated in the Persian Gulf and in the United Arab Emirates. [*See* United Arab Emirates.]

Given what presently is known, there can be little doubt that the emergence of a centralized state is first documented in the region of Khuzistan. The fact that this region was an extension of the Mesopotamian plain readily explains why the prehistoric sequence in Khuzistan is closely related to Mesopotamia's. Throughout the fifth and fourth millennia, Khuzistan was the most densely settled region in Persia. The period in Khuzistan referred to as Susa I, or Susa A, was roughly contemporary with the Ubaid 3–4 culture in southern Mesopotamia (Porada et al., 1992). [*See* Ubaid.] Although there is no doubt that the peoples of Khuzistan were in direct contact with southern Mesopotamia, the developments in the two regions were distinctly different. This may be the result in part to the peoples of southern Mesopotamia being ethnically Sumerian, while those of Khuzistan were Elamite—representatives of entirely distinctive language families. During Susa A, the site of Susa reached 25–30 ha (62–74 acres) in size, and numerous intermediate-sized communities of 10 ha (25 acres) dotted the Khuzistan countryside. These towns, in turn, were surrounded by numerous smaller villages of 2–3 ha (5–7 acres). During this period at Susa, a large terrace or platform (80 × 80 × 10 m) was constructed that is associated with an enigmatic structure called the *massif funéraire* by its excavator, Jacque de Morgan. The structure contained more than two thousand burials and a considerable wealth of grave goods (Hole, 1987). By 4000 BCE, Susa had established itself as the preeminent community in Elam, a position it was to maintain throughout most of the following three thousand years of Elamite history.

Susa I (A) is followed by Susa II. The nature of the transition remains unclear, but there are several phases of abandonment, destruction, and rebuilding of the terrace at the end of Susa I. The nature of the Susa II assemblage is best documented in the recent excavations of Acropole (acropolis) I (levels 22–17) and Acropole II (levels 6–1) (LeBrun, 1978). The material culture of Susa II is of outstanding significance: in private houses pottery, inscribed tablets, sealings, and stone objects were uncovered. The ceramics, tablets, and sealings are identical to those of the Late Uruk period (c. 3400–3200 BCE) in southern Mesopotamia. A comparable assemblage has also been recovered from Godin Tepe (Weiss and Young, 1975). In both instances it appears that the sites were impacted by the "Uruk expansion." [*See* Seals; Uruk-Warka.]

The Uruk expansion represents a massive emigration from southern Mesopotamia to regions as distant as central Anatolia. The reason(s) for the massive exodus remains elusive and is much discussed (Algaze, 1993). There is a predisposition to view the expansion and its colonization of foreign regions as motivated by the desire to control trade routes and exploit resources for shipment to southern Mesopotamia. The southern Mesopotamian artifacts recovered from Susa II represent an inventory of administrative devices dedicated to a technology of social control. The inscribed tablets and bullae (hollow, unbaked clay balls containing geometric tokens believed to represent specific numbers) were devices for monitoring economic production and consumption; the seals and sealings were used to monitor security and access by sealing doors, vessels, and reed bundles. It has been suggested that the beveled-rim bowls were standard units for measuring the rations given in return for labor (Nissen, 1988).

It has been argued that the bullae stratigraphically precede the inscribed numerical tablets, which in turn precede the inscribed tablets containing numbers and text (Schmandt-Besserat, 1992). Should this be further documented it would represent a stratigraphic unfolding from numeracy to literacy, from symbol to writing. The common use of administrative artifacts at Susa, Chogha Mish, and smaller sites in Khuzistan thus suggests an extensive colonization of Khuzistan by the Late Uruk peoples of southern Mesopotamia. The presence of a three-level settlement hierarchy indicates the specialization of settlement function and the emergence of a social organization and political structure dependent upon state-level bureaucracies.

Proto-Elamite Period. Dated to 3400–3200/2600 BCE, the term *Proto-Elamite* refers both to a specific language and to an archaeological assemblage. The beginning of this period, as determined by the excavations at Susa, are in level 16 at the acropolis I and define the nature of Susa III: Proto-Elamite culture (LeBrun and Vallat, 1978). The origins of Proto-Elamite culture are to be sought in Khuzistan following the Late Uruk colonization. Shared features of the Proto-Elamite culture include administrative texts (Damerow and Englund, 1989), heavily influenced by the earlier Uruk IV texts of southern Mesopotamia written in an undeciphered Proto-Elamite script; a distinctive style of cylinder seal known from numerous seals and sealings on tablets; ceramics, particularly the ubiquitous beveled-rim bowl; and miniature zoomorphic stone objects and vessels manufactured from raw resources procured from distant regions on the Iranian plateau.

At the time in which Proto-Elamite culture was emerging in Khuzistan, there was a major decline in population. Gregory Johnson (1973) estimates that by the end of the Late Uruk period there was a 41 percent decline in the occupied area of Khuzistan. Populations were almost entirely concentrated in the urban centers—Susa and Chogha Mish—leaving the village settlements of the hinterland abandoned. Throughout the Proto-Elamite period, the settlement size of Susa ranged between 10 and 20 ha (25 and 50 acres). The appearance of scenes of warfare depicted on cylinder seals suggest that these dramatic shifts in population and settlement occurred within a context of conflict believed to be responsible for the breakdown of the local exchange systems.

In about 3000 BCE, Susiana became independent of the Mesopotamian sphere of influence. The loss of population in Susiana may be related to the unprecedented urban growth that took place in contemporary southern Mesopotamia and the rise of a strong Proto-Elamite state centered around Malyan in Fars. Although Malyan may have been the center of a strong regional polity, it is clear from the archaeological record that a Proto-Elamite influence was felt in virtually every corner of the Iranian plateau. Following the collapse of the Uruk expansion in Khuzistan, the Proto-Elamites replicated the expansionist process and colonized distant sites. Excavated Iranian sites sharing the characteristic Proto-Elamite assemblage include Susa, Chogha Mish, Tall-i Ghazir, Tepe Sialk, Tall-i Malyan, Tall-i Iblis, Tepe Yahya, and Godin Tepe (Lamberg-Karlovsky, 1978). Materials recovered from the surface of Shahdad, a single Proto-Elamite tablet and sealings from Shahr-i Sokhta, and a single tablet from Hissar suggest that these sites and regions were also influenced by the Proto-Elamite expansion. Russian archaeologists, excavating at Altyn Depe (Altin Tepe) in Turkmenistan, have argued that distant reverberations of a Proto-Elamite influence can be detected there in the presence of Proto-Elamite signs on ceramics and figurines (Masson and Sarianidi, 1972).

The sparse settlement in Susiana throughout the Susa III period contrasts with the relatively high populations in western and eastern Khuzistan. In the Deh Luran plain, 60 km (37 mi.) northwest of Susiana, early third-millennium settlement reached a peak unsurpassed until the Achaemenid period. Excavated sites include Tepe Mussian (which may have exceeded contemporary Susa in size), Tepe Farukhabad, Tepe Khazineh, and Tepe Aliabad. [*See* Deh Luran; Tepe Mussian; Tepe Farukhabad.] Many of these sites contained ceramics that can be easily paralleled in the Diyala region of Mesopotamia during the Jemdet Nasr and Early Dynastic I periods. [*See* Diyala; Jemdet Nasr.] At Fars, excavations and extensive surveys in the vicinity of Malyan offer a relatively comprehensive picture of Proto-Elamite culture, referred to as the Banesh phase (c. 3400–2600 BCE, and at Malyan excavators identified five ceramic phases (4500–3400 BCE) preceding it. In the early third millennium, Malyan reached 50 ha (124 acres), almost four times the size of Susa. In the Banesh phase at Malyan three major phases of superimposed architecture were revealed, including public buildings containing extensive wall paintings. From the rooms of private houses, excavators recovered characteristic Proto-Elamite tablets, seals, and sealings. In various areas of excavation, craft production included the working of mother-of-pearl, *Dentalium* shells, bead production, and installations for producing metals and ceramics (Nicholas, 1990).

The results of the settlement surveys undertaken in the vicinity of Malyan (Summer, 1972) are comparable in importance to those in Khuzistan and around Tepe Yahya in Kerman province (Prickett, 1986). The growth of the Banesh phase at Malyan is believed to be the result of the absorption of numerous small surrounding settlements dated to the Susa I and II periods. In about 3000 BCE, Malyan attained the status of an urban center by absorbing the surrounding village populations and by immigration from the lowlands. At this time, toward the end of the Middle Banesh phase, Malyan experienced explosive growth, from 10 to 50 ha (25 to 124 acres) within a couple of centuries, concentrating a regional administration within its authority. The evidence for an immigration to Malyan from Susiana is supported by the increasing similarities between their material culture; the distribution of Proto-Elamite sites east and west of Malyan that link the natural routes connecting the resource-rich areas of the Iranian plateau with resource-poor Mesopotamia; and the marked decline in the population of Susiana, which coincides with the increase at Malyan (Alden, 1982). Other Proto-Elamite communities, represented by such sites as Tepe Yahya, Sialk, and Godin, suggest the presence of a Proto-Elamite colony established within a distinctive local culture. Excavations at each of these distant settlements indicates a local culture that preceded, by at least a millennium, the establishment of the Proto-Elamite colony. The excavators of these sites have independently suggested that the exploitation of local resources and/or commerce was the motivating factor for the establishment of the Proto-Elamite colony.

In the second half of the fourth millennium, a number of widely scattered sites in Khuzistan, Kurdistan, Fars, Kerman, Sistan, and Khorasan participated in a Proto-Elamite ecumene whose primary motivation was economic. It was recognized that differential access to natural resources required economic interdependence between the highlands of the Iranian plateau and the lowlands of Khuzistan and Mesopotamia. It is believed that eventually economic interdependence led to the incorporation of military, political, and even religious alliances. Increased conflict and warfare resulted: late third- and second-millennia BCE texts indicate a nearly constant state of bellicosity between southern Mesopotamia and Elam (Hinz, 1964, 1971). The origins of Proto-Elamite culture in Khuzistan and its dissemination across the Iranian plateau were contemporary with the growing internationalism that characterized the early urban environments in Mesopotamia, the Levant, and Egypt in the Late Uruk period. The foundations for the interaction that united the resource-rich highlands with the resource-poor lowlands, so characteristic of later historical periods, were initially framed within the context of the Uruk and Proto-Elamite expansions.

Third Millennium. Proto-Elamite administrative texts, associated glyptic, and diagnostic ceramics all but disappeared by 2800 BCE. Sites such as Malyan and Yahya were abandoned and only resettled in the last centuries of the third millennium. The precise cause for this decline and abandonment remains elusive. The reabsorption of Susa into the Mesopotamian political community, accomplished by the conquest of Susa by the city-state of Lagash (c. 2450 BCE) and later by the Akkadian and Ur III Empires in the last half of the third millennium, may have been important factors. [*See* Girsu and Lagash; Akkadians; Ur.] Equally significant for the collapse of a centralized Elamite power over the periphery was the rise of powerful independent polities, such as the kingdom of Marhaši, mentioned in numerous Mesopotamian texts of the late third millennium. Marhaši is believed to be centered in eastern Iran in the region that includes Shahdad and Tepe Yahya (Steinkeller, 1982). In the last half of the third millennium, southern Mesopotamian maritime commerce extended to the settlements in the Persian Gulf and reached the Indus Valley (Edens, 1993).

The marked increase in maritime trade appears to have bypassed, if not intentionally replaced, the overland routes that crossed the Iranian plateau. The effort to isolate the plateau may have been the byproduct of the increasing enmity between southern Mesopotamia and Elam.

By the middle of the third millennium, the archaeological picture is embellished by the written texts. The Sumerian king list claims that, as early as 2600 BCE, King En-Mebaragesi of Kish "carried away as spoil the weapons of the land of Elam" (Jacobsen, 1939). The Sumerian king list also attributes 356 years of sovereignty to a "dynasty" of Awan that ruled in about 2500 BCE. Although the existence of these rulers is confirmed in other texts, the kingdom's precise location remains unknown. Early Dynastic inscriptions from the Mesopotamian city-state of Lagash indicate that the king, Eanatum, claimed victory over Elam (c. 2450 BCE) after he conquered Susa. Less then a century later, Enetarzi claims to have defeated a band of Elamites and recovered goods pillaged from Lagash in earlier raiding. Complementing the texts that address the constant conflicts that characterized Elam and the Mesopotamian city-states are tablets that record commercial contacts and literary texts.

One of these literary texts, "Enmerkar and the Lord of Aratta," enjoyed a long popularity in Mesopotamia and involves the relationships of a number of semidivine figures (including Enmerkar, Dumuzi, and Gilgamesh) with the lord of Aratta, who presided over an undiscovered kingdom thought to be on the Iranian plateau (Cohen, 1973). In this epic the Sumerian hero, Enmerkar, sends repeated demands to the ruler of Aratta for craftsmen, metals, and lapis lazuli. En route to the kingdom of Aratta, the messenger passes through Susa and Anshan (Malyan). In failing to obtain the desired materials, another epic relates a siege of Aratta. Yet another fragmentary literary text alludes to an Elamite invasion of Sumer in the time of Dumuzi. Literary traditions also invoke the martial exploits of the great Sumerian hero Gilgamesh in Khuzistan and the mountains beyond. Although these heroic tales are not historical treatises, they can be taken as metaphors of genuine reminiscences that allude to the incessant warfare and administered commerce that characterized southern Mesopotamia and Elamite relations. With the consolidation of the Akkadian Empire by Sargon of Agade (2334–2279 BCE), Mesopotamian texts begin to provide a relatively continuous archive of warfare and commerce with Elam. Mesopotamian boasts of victory can be checked against the contemporary texts of Susa. Sargon's victory over the Elamites is reliably recorded in later Old Babylonian texts. Sargon's successor, Rimush, repeated the war on Elam and Marhaši and is credited with dismantling the fortifications of the Elamite cities. His brother, Manishtushu, succeeded him and in his campaigns against the Elamites is credited with the capture of a king of Anshan. Naram-Sin, one of the greatest of Akkadian conquerors and the first to proclaim himself a divinity, boasts of having attained control "of all Elam, as far as Marhaši and the land of the Subartu" (northern Mesopotamia).

Akkadian influence was well entrenched at Susa throughout the second half of the third millennium. The texts from Susa indicate that the Akkadian language, administrative techniques, and even pedagogical methods were employed in that Elamite city. The texts from both Mesopotamia and Susa indicate that commerce (trading) and warfare (raiding) typified the relations of both the Akkadian and subsequent Ur III empires with Elam. The city of Umma in Mesopotamia appears to have acted as an entrepôt of trade with Khuzistan, while Susa, and its surrounding territory, was integrated into the Akkadian conquest state. Local Elamite rulers continued to hold office, but only as "governors of Susa" under Akkadian patronage.

Although the Akkadians waged war against Anshan, they were less successful in its complete subordination. Beyond Anshan and Elam remained the persistently hostile kingdom of Marhaši. The Akkadian and subsequent Ur III empires managed their relations with these autonomous polities by occasional warfare and diplomatic alliances—one of the daughters of Shulgi (2094–2047 BCE), the greatest of the Ur III kings, married the king of Marhaši, while another married the king of Anshan. Throughout the Ur III period, Mesopotamian relations with Elam were both intensive and extensive. Mesopotamian administrative texts refer to couriers traveling between Susa, Marhaši, Sabum, Adamdun, Huhnuri, the Su-lands, Anshan, Shimashki, and other regions (Carter and Stolper, 1984). The location of most of these regions is elusive, as is the degree of their political subordination to the Ur III Empire. Tantalizing references allude to a "dynasty" of twelve kings that ruled over the "lands of Shimashki" and an equal number of kings that presided over the kingdom of Awan. Such evidence suggests the existence of indigenous political traditions beyond the immediate control of Mesopotamian empires. The locations of Awan and Shimashki are unknown, but the context of these toponyms indicates that the place names refer to regions rather than to specific sites.

Second Millennium (Sukkalmah period, 1900–1500 BCE). Dynastic alliances and diplomatic relations increasingly became the hallmark of Elamite and Mesopotamian political relations. This period was characterized by the rule of the Elamite *sukkalmah,* "grand regent" (see below), whose emergence was contemporary with significant changes in the political life of Mesopotamia. (With the collapse of the Ur III Empire, Mesopotamia reverted to the rule of independent city-states in alliance with powerful leaders of tribal federations.) Excavations at Susa, Chogha Mish, Sharafabad, Chogha Zanbil, and Haft Tepe offer substantial archaeological remains of this period. [*See* Chogha Zanbil.] The site of Malyan, on the other hand, appears to have lost much of its significance after 2000 BCE. Sites on the eastern Iranian plateau—Shahr-i Sokhta, Tepe Yahya, Shahdad, Hissar, and Bampur—all appear to have been abandoned by 1800 BCE. The reason(s) for the large-scale abandonment of these sites remains elusive (Dyson, 1973).

There is evidence at some of the sites (Shahdad, Yahya, Hissar) of a material culture readily paralleled in central Asia in the Murghab and Bactrian oases (Hiebert and Lamberg-Karlovsky, 1992). The discovery of burials in eastern Iran at Shahdad, Khinaman, and Khurab and in Pakistan at Sibri containing artifacts of this central Asian culture suggests a movement of populations. There is an irresistible temptation to associate this migration with the movement of Indo-Iranians onto the Iranian plateau (Parpola, 1988). The role, if any, played by this emigration of central Asian peoples into eastern Iran and the coterminous abandonment of settlements remains an intriguing correlation, but not one necessarily causally related. Thus, on the eastern and central Iranian plateau, the second millennium BCE represents a gap that extends from about 1700 to 1200 BCE (the latter date being when settlements were reestablished).

Archaeological sites in northern and northwestern Iran, largely unrelated to the Elamite polities, appear to sustain their settlement regimes. Excavations at Tureng Tepe (Deshayes, 1975) on the Gurgan plain and at Godin Tepe offer a relatively comprehensive picture of the second millennium BCE in these regions of Iran. The long-term abandonment of numerous sites in the first half of the second millennium; an absence of settlement-pattern studies; and the relatively small number of excavations detailing the period offer only the most limited understanding of the political, economic, and social conditions that characterized the Iranian plateau then. The exceptions are the settlement studies and excavations in Khuzistan and Fars and the excavations at Susa, Haft Tepe, and Chogha Zanbil.

The excavation of and texts from Susa indicate that following the demise of the Ur III dynasty Susiana became independent from Mesopotamia and was ruled by a dynasty of Shimaskian kings. After a few centuries, this dynasty was replaced by the Sukkalmah, a dynasty that may have emanated from Fars and that maintained important diplomatic relations with the Babylonian state of Hammurabi. In Fars, Malyan regained its position as a regional center during the Kaftari phase (2200–1700 BCE) and may have been the point of origin of the Sukkalmah dynasty; later, Malyan, referred to in the Elamite texts as Anshan, was, together with Susa, the cocapital of the Elamite kingdom. Two Elamite rock carvings are believed to be dated to the Late Kaftari phase. One of them, 200 m above the Fahlian plain, depicts a divine couple seated between worshippers. A second relief, at Naqsh-i Rustam, illustrates a number of worshipers and a divine couple seated on a serpent throne. [*See* Naqsh-i Rustam.] The location of these shrines suggests that the Elamites positioned their divinities to indicate symbolically the incorporation of specific territories and to protect the main lines of communication between Susiana and Malyan.

Throughout the first half of the second millennium BCE, the regions surrounding Susa and Malyan experienced an unprecedented prosperity. The extensive use of irrigation near Malyan was not to be replicated until the time of the Achaemenids. Few settlements existed in the valleys and plains separating the two sites, but those known from Luristan (Tepe Guran) suggest that they were culturally distinct from and politically unaligned with the Elamite state. Throughout the first half of the period, the rapid population growth in Khuzistan and Fars was enabled by an increase in agricultural production. It was made possible, at least in part, by the adoption of a Mesopotamian administrative bureaucracy that emphasized agricultural production; alliances with tribal federations and distant autonomous polities; a professional military organization; and a civil bureaucracy dependent upon a tax base for its support.

The textual and archaeological record from the end of the Sukkalmah period (c. 1600 BCE) to the rise of the Middle Elamite kings in the thirteenth century BCE—i.e., Tepti-ahar, 1375 BCE) is poorly known. This gap roughly coincides with the time in which the aforementioned sites on the Iranian plateau were abandoned. In Khuzistan and Fars there is no evidence of continuity from the early (Sukkalmah) to the late (Middle Elamite) second millennium BCE. Nevertheless, archaeological remains from the second half of the period have been recovered from the Ville Royal at Susa, Tepe Sharafabad, and Haft Tepe, 15 km (9 mi.) southeast of Susa, where monumental temple architecture dates to the time of King Tepti-ahar. The royal city of Al Untash-Napirisha (modern Chogha Zanbil), 30 km (19 mi.) southeast of Susa, is the most prominent archaeological monument of the Middle Elamite period (Ghirshman, 1966–1968). The major excavated complex at Chogha Zanbil is a ziggurat surrounded by a double wall. [*See* Ziggurat.] The area enclosed within the city walls is in excess of 100 ha (247 acres). The ziggurat incorporates several different building phases, of which the last resulted in a five-story stepped pyramid crowned by a temple dedicated to the Elamite divine couple Inshushinak and Napirisha. At the foot of the ziggurat archaeologists exposed a number of lesser temples and shrines; several were lavishly decorated with glazed tiles, wooden doors embedded with glass beads, and winged griffins and bulls of glazed frit placed over vaulted stairwells leading to the summit. Large, vaulted structures of baked brick were uncovered at Chogha Zanbil, Haft Tepe, and Susa that served as family tombs. Similarities in the complexity of burial pattern at Haft Tepe and Chogha Zanbil suggest that they were centers of a burial cult.

The last half of the second millennium BCE experienced an "elamization" in southwestern Iran, particularly in Khuzistan and Fars and perhaps in Luristan. The Middle Elamite period was not without its continuing hostility with Mesopotamia: an Elamite stela records the capture of seven hundred towns including Sippar, Opis, Dur Kurigalzu, Eshnunna, and perhaps even Akkad. [*See* Sippar; Eshnunna; Akkade.] War booty was carried off to Susa—the law code of Hammurabi and the victory stela of Naram-Sin—and displayed in the Temple of Inshushinak, tangible evidence that the spoils of war contributed to the wealth of the Middle Elamite kings. Texts recording military campaigns, building projects, and religious commemorations have been recovered from Susa, Haft Tepe, Chogha Zanbil, and Malyan. Archaeological remains recovered from the first three indicate the high level achieved in the production of crafts, especially metalworking.

Many Middle Elamite settlements in Khuzistan were abandoned in about 1000 BCE. The slow decline in the settlements and populations of Susiana indicate that more was involved in the decline of the Middle Elamite period than the defeat of the Elamite king Huteludush-Inshushinak by the Assyrian king Nebuchadrezzar I in 1110 BCE. Once again, it is quite likely that the fortunes of the Elamites were ironically tied to those of their traditional enemy, Mesopotamia. At the turn of the millennium, in Babylonia and Assyria, written texts speak of severe food shortages precipitated by the raiding of nomadic peoples. Susiana may have experienced comparable raids, for one of the tribes responsible, the Arameans, are known to have settled in Khuzistan from the Karkheh River to the Gulf. [*See* Arameans.] In the first half of the first millennium BCE, the general decline in Susiana was complemented by an overall prosperity in Luristan and Kurdistan. In the northeast, the Medes established varying control over independent kingdoms, while the Assyrians exercised dominance over the Mesopotamian borderlands. [*See* Medes.] By 1000 BCE, numerous independent kingdoms are attested in the texts and documented in the archaeological record: Hasanlu, in the northeast, attempted to maintain its independence in the face of a rising ascendancy of Assyrian, Median, and Urartean power.

In 646 BCE, Ashurbanipal plundered Susa with a ferocity unparalleled in the Assyrian annals. The texts detail the razing of all the temples, the destruction of the sacred groves, the desecration of Elamite gods and royal tombs, the deportation of the population and their livestock, and the sowing of salt on the devastated land. Ashurbanipal's lengthy description of the pillaging of Susa was intended to stun the world and deliver the message of Elam's political and cultural eradication. The devastated Elamites were further pressured by the Babylonians to the west, the Medes to the northeast, and the Persians to the southeast. By the mid-sixth century BCE, much of the former Elamite territory was under Achaemenid rule. Inscriptions of Cyrus the Great (559–530 BCE) indicate that his great grandfather, Teispes, claimed to be "king of Anshan." Although it is not documented, it is more than likely that Cyrus took possession of Susa and Khuzistan before he conquered Babylon. The documentation of the decline, fall, and eventual assimilation of Elamite territories by the Achaemenid Empire remains one of the major research questions pertaining to the second half of the first millennium BCE.

[*See also* Elamites; *and* Mesopotamia, *article on* Ancient Mesopotamia.]

BIBLIOGRAPHY

Adams, Robert McC. "Agriculture and Urban Life in Early Southwestern Iran." *Science* 136 (1962): 109–122.

Alden, John R. "Trade and Politics in Proto-Elamite Iran." *Current Anthropology* 23 (1982): 613–640.

Algaze, Guillermo. *The Uruk World System: The Dynamics of Expansion of Early Mesopotamian Civilization.* Chicago, 1993.

Berghe, Louis Vanden. *Bibliographie analytique de l'archéologie de l'Iran ancien.* Leiden, 1979. Comprehensive bibliography of Iranian archaeology. (See also 1981, 1987.)

Berghe, Louis Vanden, and E. Haerinck. *Bibliographie analytique de l'archéologie de l'Iran ancien: Supplément 1, 1978–1980.* Leiden, 1981.

Berghe, Louis Vanden, and E. Haerinck. *Bibliographie analytique de l'archéologie de l'Iran ancien: Supplément 2, 1981–1985.* Leiden, 1987.

Caldwell, Joseph R. *Investigations at Tal-i-Iblis.* Illinois State Museum Preliminary Reports, 9. Springfield, 1967.

Carter, Elizabeth, and Matthew W. Stolper. *Elam: Surveys of Political History and Archaeology.* Berkeley, 1984. Excellent overview of the political history and archaeology of Elam.

Cohen, Sol. "Enmerkar and the Lord of Aratta." Ph.D. diss., University of Pennsylvania, 1973.

Damerow, Peter, and Robert K. Englund. *The Proto-Elamite Texts from Tepe Yahya.* Peabody Museum, Harvard University, American School of Prehistoric Research, Bulletin 39. Cambridge, Mass., 1989. The most recent and thorough discussion of the nature of Proto-Elamite texts.

de Cardi, Beatrice. *Excavations at Bampur: A Third Millennium Settlement in Persian Baluchistan, 1966.* American Museum of Natural History, Anthropological Papers, vol. 51.3. New York, 1970.

Deshayes, Jean. "Les fouilles récentes de Tureng Tépé: La terrasse haute de la fin du IIIe millénaire." *Comptes Rendus de l'Académie des Inscriptions et Belles-Lettres* (1975): 522–530.

Dollfus, Geneviève. "Djaffarabad, Djowi, Bendebal: Contribution à l'étude de la Susiane au Ve millénaire et au début du IVe millénaire." *Paléorient* 4 (1978): 141–167.

Dyson, Robert H., Jr. "Problems of Protohistoric Iran as Seen from Hasanlu." *Journal of Near Eastern Studies* 24.3 (1965): 193–217.

Dyson, Robert H., Jr. "The Archaeological Evidence of the Second Millennium B.C. on the Persian Plateau." In *The Cambridge Ancient History,* vol. 2.1, *History of the Middle East and the Aegean Region c. 1800–1380 B.C.,* edited by I. E. S. Edwards et al., pp. 686–715. 3d ed. Cambridge, 1973.

Dyson, Robert H., Jr., and Susan M. Howard. *Tappeh Hesar: Reports of the Restudy Project, 1976.* Florence, 1989. An important excavation and reanalysis of this site.

Edens, Christopher. "Indus-Arabian Interaction during the Bronze Age: A Review of Evidence." In *Harappan Civilization: A Recent Perspective,* edited by Gregory L. Possehl, pp. 335–364. 2d rev. ed. New Delhi, 1993.

Fisher, William B., ed. "The Land of Iran." In *Cambridge History of Iran,* vol. 1. Cambridge, 1968. Environmental and ecological aspects of Iran.

Ghirshman, Roman. *Fouilles de Sialk près de Kashan 1933, 1934, 1937.* Paris, 1938.

Ghirshman, Roman. *Tchogha Zanbil (Dur Untash),* vol. 1, *La ziggurat;*

vol. 2, *Téménos, temples, palais, tombes*. Mémoires de la Mission Archéologique en Iran, vol. 39. Paris, 1966–1968.
Hakemi, Ali. *Catalogue de l'exposition: Lut, Shahad "Xabis."* Tehran, 1972.
Hiebert, Frederik T., and C. C. Lamberg-Karlovsky. "Central Asia and the Indo-Iranian Borderlands." *Iran* 30 (1992): 1–15.
Hinz, Walther. *Das Reich Elam*. Urban-Bücher, 82. Stuttgart, 1964.
Hinz, Walther. "Persia c. 2400–1800 B.C." In *The Cambridge Ancient History*, vol. 1.2, *Early History of the Middle East*, edited by I. E. S. Edwards et al., pp. 644–680. 3d ed. Cambridge, 1971.
Hole, Frank, et al., eds. *Prehistory and Human Ecology on the Deh Luran Plain: An Early Village Sequence from Khuzistan, Iran*. University of Michigan, Memoirs of the Museum of Anthropology, no. 1. Ann Arbor, 1969.
Hole, Frank, ed. *The Archaeology of Western Iran: Settlement and Society from Prehistory to the Islamic Conquest*. Washington, D.C., 1987.
Jacobsen, Thorkild. *The Sumerian King List*. Oriental Institute, Assyriological Studies, 11. Chicago, 1939.
Johnson, Gregory A. *Local Exchange and Early State Development in Southwestern Iran*. University of Michigan, Museum of Anthropology, Anthropological Papers, no. 51. Ann Arbor, 1973.
Kantor, Helene J. "The Excavations at Čoqa Miš." In *Proceedings of the IVth Annual Symposium of Archaeological Research in Iran*, edited by Firouz Bagherzadeh, pp. 113–142. Tehran, 1976.
Lamberg-Karlovsky, C. C. "The Proto-Elamites on the Iranian Plateau." *Antiquity* 52 (1978): 114–120.
Lamberg-Karlovsky, C. C., and Thomas Wight Beale, eds. *Excavations at Tepe Yahya, Iran, 1967–1975: The Early Periods*. Peabody Museum, Harvard University, American School of Prehistoric Research, Bulletin 38. Cambridge, Mass., 1986.
LeBrun, Alain. "Suse, chantier de 'Acropole 1.'" *Paléorient* 4 (1978): 177–192.
LeBrun, Alain, and François Vallat. "L'origine de l'écriture à Suse." *Cahiers de la Délégation Archéologique Française en Iran* 8 (1978): 11–70.
Masson, Vadim M., and V. I. Sarianidi. *Central Asia: Turkmenia before the Achaemenids*. London, 1972.
Negahban, Ezat O. *Excavations at Haft Tepe, Iran*. Philadelphia, 1991.
Nicholas, Ilene M. *The Proto-Elamite Settlement at TUV*. Malyan Excavation Reports, vol. 1. Philadelphia, 1990.
Nissen, Hans J. *The Early History of the Ancient Near East, 9000–2000 B.C.* Chicago, 1988.
Parpola, Asko. "The Coming of the Aryans to Iran and India and the Cultural and Ethnic Identity of the Dāsas." *Studia Orientalia* (Helsinki) 64 (1988): 195–302.
Perrot, Jean. "Les fouilles de Suse en 1975." In *Proceedings of the IVth Annual Symposium of Archaeological Research in Iran*, edited by Firouz Bagherzadeh, pp. 224–225. Tehran, 1976.
Porada, Edith, et al. "The Chronology of Mesopotamia, ca. 7000–1600 B.C." In *Chronologies in Old World Archaeology*, edited by Robert W. Ehrich, vol. 1 pp. 77–121, vol. 2, pp. 90–124. 3d ed. Chicago, 1992.
Prickett, Martha. *Man, Land and Water: Settlement Distribution and the Development of Irrigation Agriculture in the Rud-i Gushk Drainage, Southeastern Iran*. Ann Arbor, 1986.
Schmandt-Besserat, Denise. *Before Writing*. Austin, 1992.
Schmidt, Erich F. *Excavations at Tepe Hissar, Damghan*. Philadelphia, 1937.
Smith, Philip E. L. "Ganj Dareh Tepe." *Iran* 13 (1975): 178–180.
Steinkeller, Piotr. "The Question of Marḫaši: A Contribution to the Historical Geography of Iran in the Third Millennium B.C." *Zeitschrift für Assyriologie* 72 (1982): 237–265.
Sumner, William M. "Cultural Developments in the Kur River Basin, Iran: An Archaeological Analysis of Settlement Patterns." Ph.D. diss., University of Pennsylvania, 1982.
Tosi, Maurizio, and Marcello Piperno. "Lithic Technology behind the Ancient Lapis Lazuli Trade." *Expedition* 16 (1973): 15–23.
Vandiver, Pamela B. "The Production Technology of Earthenware Ceramics, 4900–2800 B.C." In *Excavations at Tepe Yahya, Iran, 1967–1975: The Early Periods*, edited by C. C. Lamberg-Karlovsky and Thomas Wight Beale, pp. 91–100. Peabody Museum, Harvard University, American School of Prehistoric Research, Bulletin 38. Cambridge, Mass., 1986.
Voigt, Mary M. *Hajji Firuz Tepe, Iran: The Neolithic Settlement*. Hasanlu Excavation Reports, vol. 1. Philadelphia, 1983.
Voigt, Mary M., and Robert H. Dyson, Jr. "The Chronology of Iran, ca. 8000–2000 B.C." In *Chronologies in Old World Archaeology*, edited by Robert W. Ehrich, pp. 122–125. 3d ed. Chicago, 1992. Detailed chronological discussion on the archaeology of Iran, including a synoptic comment on the major sites.
Weiss, Harvey, and T. Cuyler Young, Jr. "The Merchants of Susa: Godin V and Plateau-Lowland Relations in the Late Fourth Millennium B.C." *Iran* 13 (1975): 1–17.
Wright, Henry T., and Gregory A. Johnson. "Population, Exchange, and Early State Formation in Southwestern Iran." *American Anthropologist* 77 (1975): 267–289.
Young, T. Cuyler, Jr., and Louis D. Levine. *Excavations at the Godin Project: Second Progress Report*. Royal Ontario Museum, Occasional Paper, 26. Toronto, 1974.
Young, T. Cuyler, Jr., et al., eds. *The Hilly Flanks and Beyond: Essays on the Prehistory of Southwestern Asia Presented to Robert J. Braidwood*. Studies in Ancient Oriental Civilization, no. 36. Chicago, 1983.

C. C. LAMBERG-KARLOVSKY

Persia from Alexander to the Rise of Islam

With the defeat of the last Achaemenid king, Darius III (336–331 BCE), and the final victory of Alexander the Great at Gaugamela in 331, the vast empire of the Achaemenids came under Hellenistic rule for the next two hundred years. After Alexander's premature death in 323, his empire became the center of a political struggle between his Macedonian generals as well as witnessing opposition by local dynasts. Although the Achaemenid system of satrapies (provinces) was basically maintained under Alexander, it seems that even before his death Macedonian satraps (provincial governors) had replaced the Iranians and that the so-called policy of integration between Greeks and Iranians had been abandoned. Despite the lack of sources reporting on the feelings of the local population, there are some Akkadian texts that indicate hostility toward Alexander and the years of his rule are described as bad (Grayson, 1975, pp. 30–36; Oelsner, 1986, p. 52). At the same time we have an indication of position through Greek rebellions in Bactria where the local population joined the Greeks in a bid for independence.

Seleucus became satrap of Babylonia in 319, and during the years after Alexander's death and the struggle for power, he enjoyed the support of the population of Babylonia, as recorded in the Chronicle of the Diadochoi. After beating off a challenge from Antigonus that had resulted in a period of war ending in 308, Seleucus became sole ruler of Babylonia. He soon turned his attention to Iranian satrapies, such as Media and Susiana, which he successfully incorporated into his kingdom. By 302 his realm included the inner satrapies, that is, Media, Persis, and Susiana as well as outer satrapies—the area of eastern Iran and further east. The empire of Seleucus stretched from Mesopotamia in the west to Central Asia in the east.

With the expansion of the Hellenistic Empire, colonization followed and, particularly during the reign of Seleucus and his son, Antiochus, a number of Greek colonies were established throughout the Seleucid Empire. In Iran these include Seleucia Eulaeus at Susa and Seleucia Hedyphon elsewhere in the southwest, Rhagae (modern Ray) near Tehran and Hecatompylos, probably the site of Shahr-i Qumis near Damghan in northeastern Iran. In the eastern satapies the most famous of the colonies is Antioch-Margiana, Gjar Kala near modern Merv in Turkmenistan, and at Ai Khanum in northern Afghanistan, the first occupation level dates to the early Seleucid period. In the Persian Gulf, the island of Failaka was also occupied during this time. [*See* Failaka.]

Antiochus, who was already acting as joint ruler at the time of his father's murder, came to the throne without any apparent opposition, but there is some suggestion of a local Iranian revolt against Seleucid rule at this time. This is evidenced by the destruction level of the citadel at Pasargadae in southwestern Iran, which on the basis of numismatic evidence dates to the end of Seleucus's reign. [*See* Pasargadae.] In addition, Persian troops in Persis started a mutiny, which resulted in their massacre by Greek infantry and cavalry, and we also hear of a massacre of three thousand Macedonian settlers by local troops in Persis. By the time of his death in 261, Antiochus had consolidated the empire of his father. Both Seleucus and Antiochus attempted to foster an image of tolerance and caring for local beliefs and traditions, but at the same time they were keen to stress their dynastic mythological link with the Greek god Apollo.

The policy of new foundations and refoundations continued under Antiochus and his successors. These included *poleis* or cities as well as military occupations or *strathmoi.* Nihavand-Laodicea, near Hamadan, was an important Greek city, which was placed strategically on the main route from Media to Babylonia. At nearby Kangavar, the monumental architecture and the pottery indicate some Greek Hellenistic influence. Susa in the southwest became a Greek city with Greek law. The various architectural remains such as a gymnasium and a theater with inscriptions in Greek testify to its stature as a city.

During the corulership of Seleucus and Antiochus, the latter had received the eastern part of the empire with its center in Babylonia, and Seleucus had moved his capital from Seleucia on the Tigris to Antiochea on the Orontes in Syria. The reason behind this shift was the ongoing struggle for power in the west between the Ptolemies and the Seleucids, which resulted in the Syrian Wars of 274–271, 260–253, and 246–225. [*See* Seleucia on the Tigris; Antioch on Orontes; Ptolemies; Seleucids; *and* Alexandrian Empire.]

Parthian Period. Danger in the east from the Parthians did not emerge until the middle of the third century during the reign of Seleucus II. The Third Syrian War diverted attention once again to the west and this may have given Andragoras, the Greek satrap of Parthia, the opportunity to declare independence in 245. Already by this time the Parni, a nomadic group of Iranian-speaking tribes, who, according to ancient sources such as Justin and Strabo, were related to the Scythians, had left their homeland in the Atrek Valley (Strabo 11.9.1; Justin 41.4.5–41.5.6). The Parni pose two questions that so far have no answers. Did they conquer the province of Astauene around the middle of the third century? Was their center of power at modern Turkmenistan, that is, the area to the northeast of the Elburz and Kopet Dagh mountains? Archaeological evidence for the early Parthian Period in northeastern Iran is meager because archaeological sites are largely unknown. Further excavation of possible Parthian sites in Iran could radically change the usual reconstruction of early Parthian history.

After the revolt in Bactria under its satrap Diodotos, Arsaces, the eponymous founder of the Parthian Arsacid dynasty, may have conquered Parthia around 238 and shortly afterwards Hyrcania. This triumph of the Parthians over former Seleucid territories resulted in the campaign of Seleucus II against Arsaces sometime between 231 and 227. The result was a victory for Arsaces partly because of Seleucus's enforced retreat to Asia Minor, where revolts had started. Antiochus III (223–187) successfully supressed revolts in Media and Persia in 220 and began a campaign to the east in 209. Peace was eventually made between the Seleucids and the Parthians, however, and the Parthians probably remained vassals of the Seleucids with a certain degree of political freedom. Antiochus returned from his eastern campaign via Arachosia, Drangiana, and Kermania and marched through Persis into Susiana and Seleucia in 205. It was after this campaign that he adopted the title of great king, but he was soon to become the victim of another growing force. In 190 the Seleucid Empire fell to the Romans, and Antiochus himself was brutally murdered while plundering a temple in Elymais.

Thereafter the rise and expansion of the Parthian empire began. Phraates I (c. 176–171) successfully moved the boundaries to the south of the Elburz Mountains and the southern shores of the Caspian Sea, but a significant breakthrough came only with the accession of his brother, Mithridates I, to the throne in 171. Then a new period began in the history of the Arsacid Parthians. After recapturing areas in the east, Mithridates turned his attention to the west where his most important task was to conquer Media for access to Mesopotamia. This process probably took several years, and a Greek inscription on the Herakles relief from Bisitun in western Iran (see Vanden Berghe, 1984, pl. 10) shows that parts of Media were still under Seleucid control between 149 and 148, thus dating the actual transfer of power after 148. [*See* Bisitun.] The conquest of Mesopotamia was likewise not a swift and straightforward matter, as indicated by contemporary cuneiform tablets (Debevoise, 1969, p. 22, n. 99). After a long struggle against the Seleucid king Demetrius II, the Parthians finally gained the upper hand. Mithridates was probably crowned in Seleucia on the Tigris in 141, and in the same year his rule was acknowledged as far south as Uruk in southern Mesopotamia.

After these successes the king soon had to turn his attention to the eastern provinces where he successfully dealt with an invasion by the Saka nomads. While Mithridates I was fighting in the east, part of his army left behind in Mesopotamia entered Elymais and captured Susa, which had become independent under the local Elymaian ruler Kamnaskires I. By the time of his death in 138 or 137 Mithridates' empire had reached its maximum extent; he had transformed the insecure Parthian kingdom into an empire that stretched from eastern Bactria to Mesopotamia. However, his successors were faced with invasions on both eastern and western frontiers, and it was only the accession of a second able ruler, Mithridates II (c. 124–87), that saved the empire.

The new ruler first turned his attention to Babylonia, where an Arab called Hyspaosines had formed the state of Characene at the head of the Persian Gulf. After his victory in southern Mesopotamia, he turned his attention to the north where large areas were annexed in 113. At this time we hear of direct interference of the Parthians in the affairs of Armenia and contact and conflict with Rome (Strabo 11.14.15).

Mithridates II restored the empire of the Arsacids to its maximum extent, and his close control over the empire as well as the overland trade routes gave a great boost to trading activities. Parthia by now seems to have been in control of the so-called Silk Road, which passed through its territories, connecting Rome with China. The Parthians were probably beginning to profit from their position as middlemen in this overland trade and the growing demand of Rome for luxury goods from the East.

Mithridates' increase in power is reflected in his changing title on his coins. As a young king wearing a diadem, he called himself "the great king Arsaces, (god) manifest." As an aged king he wore a tall bejeweled tiara and diadem, and the accompanying legend reads "the great king of kings, Arsaces. . . ." According to cuneiform tablets from Babylonia the new title "king of kings" was introduced around 109.

By the end of his reign, however, there were internal problems, which were to become a recurrent feature in Parthian history. Babylonian tablets of 91 BCE mention a rival king, Gotarzes, who had control over Babylonia, and Mithridates' power probably extended over Iran and northern Mesopotamia. Gotarzes may be the same figure who appears on the so-called Mithridates relief at Bisitun as satrap of satraps. After Mithridates' death in 87, a new ruler, Orodes II, succeeded to the throne. During his reign Roman forces under Crassus came face-to-face with the Parthian army in 53, under Surena at Carrhae in Syria. The result was devastating for the Roman army, which was helpless against the Parthian cavalry and its hail of arrows. By now the Euphrates was definitely recognized as the frontier between the two superpowers. After Mark Antony's unsuccessful march into Media in 36, a period of peace set in between Parthia and Rome. This new peaceful relationship must have provided a boost to the trade of luxury goods across the Euphrates from the east to the west.

Internally Parthian history was overshadowed by rivalry, the emergence of contenders to the throne, and the murder of most of the rulers by their sons or wives. Under Artabanus the superpowers again came into conflict over Armenia, and when the Parthian nobility became discontent with the growing power of Artabanus, they turned to Rome for help. After Tiridates, a grandson of Phraates IV was sent by the Romans to Parthia in 35 CE. Artabanus fled to Hyrcania where he gathered forces. He returned to Mesopotamia, expelled Tiridates, and became sole ruler in 36.

Artabanus's son and successor, Vardanes II, was soon opposed by a certain Gotarzes II, who may have been a brother of the former Gotarzes, but their relationship is unclear. The town of Seleucia began a revolt and forced the two contenders to the throne to come to a temporary agreement in 45. Vardanes was murdered in 47 during a hunting expedition. It was probably at about this time that Elymais in southwestern Iran rebelled against Parthian supremacy and the Elymaians began to issue their own coins by 75. Their control over Susa is evidenced by the find of Elymaian coins at the city. After the death of Vardanes, Gotarzes became the sole ruler but was soon opposed by some of the Parthian nobility, who again turned to Rome for help. Gotarzes captured and killed the Roman puppet king Meherdates. The jousting relief at Bisitun near Kermanshah seems to commemorate his victory (Herrmann, 1977, p. 53). Gotarzes himself died in 51.

Vonones, apparently king of Media, now came to the throne but was soon succeeded by his son Vologases I (c. 51–78). Once again there was conflict with Rome over Armenia but in 63 CE peace was made. [*See* Armenia.] In addition, Vologases was soon faced with a revolt by one of his own sons, Vardanes III but soon reestablished power and gained control over the country. The last years of Vologases' reign were troubled by the advance of the nomadic tribe of the Alani from the Black Sea area. Despite internal and external problems Vologases' rule succeeded in securing Parthia's position and consolidating its share of the growing trade between the west and the Persian Gulf. During Vologases' long reign a few contenders to the throne, namely Pacorus and Osroes, issued coins. Osroes may have been in control over Babylonia and Elymais while Vologases was the "king of kings." Such a division of power was to become a characteristic feature of Parthian politics, indicating the weakness of central authority. In 114 Trajan invaded Armenia, northern Mesopotamia, and also further south but his successor Hadrian made peace with Parthia.

During the long reign of Vologases IV (148–191) relations

with Rome were calm only until the death of Antoninus Pius in 161. For some unknown reason, probably because of economic problems, Vologases declared war on Rome after the accession of Marcus Aurelius. By now trade routes were under the control of Palmyrene merchants who were also keeping them under their protection. Thus, Parthia was no longer in charge of the east–west traffic of luxury goods. Having advanced into Parthian territory in Mesopotamia, the Roman army was forced to retreat in 166 only because of an epidemic of smallpox.

The end of the Parthian era is marked by Roman advances into northern and also southern Mesopotamia under Septimius Severus (193–211). Soon after Vologases came to the Parthian throne, he was challenged by his brother Artabanus IV, who was in control of Media and Susa by 216 CE. The so-called Artabanus relief from Susa dated to 215 shows the enthroned Artabanus handing over the ring of power to the satrap of Susa (Colledge, 1967, pl. 29). Elymais at this time was ruled by its local kings. Rock reliefs from sites such as Tang-i Sarvak, Shimbar, and Hung-i Nauruzi, together with the reliefs and sculpture from Masjid-i Suleiman and Bard-i Nishandeh document a certain degree of independence (Colledge, 1967, pls. 17–20; Vanden Berghe and Schippmann, 1985). [*See* Susa.]

When the request of the Roman emperor Caracalla to marry a daughter of Artabanus was rejected, he went to war against the Parthians in 216, and his forces attacked Media. Artabanus fled to the east but returned when Macrinus, the new Roman emperor, offered him peace. A treaty was finally signed in 218. [*See* Parthians; Roman Empire.]

Sasanian Period. Artabanus had successfully withstood the Roman advance but was soon to become the victim of an internal usurper, who finally put an end to Parthian rule. In 224 Artabanus was killed at Hormizdgan by the forces of Ardashir, the son of Papak, the local ruler of Istakhr in Pars and of the house of the legendary Sasan. This victory of the Sasanians was commemorated on the rock relief of Tang-i Ab at Firuzabad in Fars. Ardashir went on to capture Ctesiphon, in 226. Before 230 he had consolidated his position as the new king of kings of a dynasty that was eager to stress its lineage from the Achaemenids kings. Zoroastrianism became the state religion, and coins of Ardashir show a combination of the fire altar and the royal throne that emphasize the unity of the religion and the state.

In the following years Ardashir concentrated on his western enemy, Rome, and the annexation of territories in northern Mesopotamia, in particular Hatra, which had fallen into Roman hands in the late Parthian period. The advance of the Sasanians into Roman occupied territories resulted in a series of clashes, first in 242 with the emperor Gordian III, with Phillip the Arab who made peace in 244, and finally with Valerian. These historic events and campaigns are documented in the inscriptions and reliefs at Kaaba Zardusht, Naqsh-i Rustam, Bishapur, and Darab. After 239 Ardashir appointed his son Shapur as coregent, and he became sole ruler after the death of his father in 241. Other military and political victories of this time include the conquest of Armenia in the northwest and a final defeat of the Kushan Empire in the east.

New Sasanian cities were built. They include Ardashir Khurrah (Gur Ardashir, Firuzabad), Jundeshapur, and Bishapur, all three situated in the region of Fars, the homeland of the Sasanians. In religious matters Shapur showed a certain degree of tolerance, which is best evidenced in his relationship with Mani, the prophet of the Manichaeans, who spent some years at the royal court and enjoyed religious freedom. After the death of Shapur between 270 and 273 and during the reign of Hormizd I and Bahram I, the policy of tolerance was to change as the power of the Zoroastrian priesthood grew, and finally under Kardir, the high priest of Istakhr, Mani was executed in 276. During the reign of Bahram many Manichaeans, Christians, Jews, and Buddhists were killed. Only after the accession of Bahram III in 293 did tolerance toward minority groups became evident again.

Politically the old conflict with Rome continued, especially over Armenia, which was lost to the Romans during the reign of Narseh (293–302), a son of Shapur I, in 297. By now the Tigris had become the official border between the Roman and Sasanian empires. Not until the reign of Shapur II (c. 309–379), a grandson of Shapur I, did the Sasanian empire once again reach its maximum extent. Shapur's main adversary in the early years of his reign was the emperor Constantine, who had converted to Christianity in 312 and later transferred his capital to Byzantium, later called Constantinople. [*See* Byzantine Empire; Constantinople.] The recognition of Christianity as the official religion of Rome resulted in the persecution of Christians. The latter part of Shapur's long reign of seventy years was overshadowed by continuous clashes with Rome under the emperors Constantine II and Julian and war over Armenia, which finally resulted in an official division of Armenia in 377. The Sasanians now had a new enemy in the East, the Hephthalites, whose first attack on Sasanian territory dates to 427 during the reign of Yazdigird I (c. 399–421), known by Islamic historians as "the Sinner" because of his initially tolerant views toward Christians. This situation was to change at the end of his rule when Christians set fire to a Zoroastrian fire temple in Fars, and mass executions of the Christians followed throughout the empire. After his death, Bahram, one of his three sons who had grown up at the court of the king of Hira, succeeded in gaining support from the nobility and was crowned as Bahram V in 421. He was hailed in Persian literature and art as Bahram Gur ("ass"), the skillful hunter. His successor, Yazdigird II (439–457), continued the persecution of Christians in Armenia that had begun earlier. His vizier, Mihr Narseh, tried to impose Zoroastrianism as the state religion.

After Yazdigird's death in 457 there was a lengthy struggle

between different contenders to the throne, which finally ended in Peroz's victory in 459 with the help of the Hephthalites. When a period of drought paralyzed the country a few years later, however, Peroz turned against his Hephthalite allies in 465. He and his son were imprisoned, and only after a heavy payment to the Hephthalites was he released. Once again Peroz went into battle against the eastern enemy, but the campaign proved abortive, and in 484 Peroz lost his life. The Hephthalites advanced into eastern Iran and forced the Sasanian state to pay an annual tax.

An important event during Peroz' reign was the formation of the Nestorian church named after Nestorius, patriarch of Constantinople. In 484 a meeting of Iranian Christians in Jundeshapur marked the official beginning of this denomination. Throughout their long history, the Nestorians were involved in many struggles with other Christians.

Peace with the Hephthalites was made under Valkash (484–488) but internal struggles overshadowed the reign of this king. Finally, in 488, Kavad, a son of Peroz came to the throne. The most significant feature of his reign was the rise of Mazdakite movement under its leaders, Mazdak and a certain Zardusht. It was initially of a religious nature but then developed into a social uprising, attacking the power of the nobility. This revolutionary movement, which enjoyed Kavad's support at first, was temporarily halted in 496 when the nobility and the Zoroastrian clergy joined forces against the king and imprisoned him in Khuzistan. Kavad managed to escape and sought refuge with the Hephthalites. A few years later he returned with a Hephthalite army and removed his brother Zamasp from the throne. During the latter part of his reign, Kavad ended his support for the Mazdakites, and Mazdak was executed around 528. By this time Kavad had appointed his son Khusrau I Anushirvan "of the immortal soul" (r. 531–579) as his successor. Khusrau introduced a series of reforms, particularly in connection with the army, the nobility, and taxation, which were probably inspired by the Mazdakite movement. A new social level was created, the class of the *dihqan* or land-owning nobility which stood up against the powerful feudal lords or vassals.

In 532 Khusrau made "eternal" peace with Byzantium, but it lasted only for a short while, and war broke out once again. A so-called fifty-year peace began in 556, enabling Khusrau to turn his attention to the Hephthalites in the east. He now had the support of powerful allies, the Turks, and together they defeated the Hephthalites. The result was that the Turks became the eastern neighbors of the Sasanian Empire. Soon a coalition of Byzantium and Turks excluded the Sasanians from the trade of silk, however, and this move led to yet another confrontation between Iran and Byzantium in 572. Before peace could be declared Khusrau died in 579. The Byzantine Empire now proved crucial in the succession to the throne. When Bahram Chubin, a Parthian general of the house of Mihran, who had successfully pushed back an advance of the Turks under Khusrau's father, Hormizd IV (579–590) crowned himself as Bahram VI at Ctesiphon, Khusrau fled to Byzantium where he was given support. With a large Byzantine army Khusrau started his campaign against Bahram Chubin in 591, who fled to the east where he was murdered. During the second part of Khusrau's reign many of the old nobility and generals who had sided with Bahram were removed. His support for the Christian church is shown by his marriage to Mariam, a Byzantine princess, and his legendary love for Shirin, an Armenian princess. This situation created enemies amongst the Zoroastrian clergy. In addition, mistakes in Khusrau's foreign policy and particularly his wars with the Lachmid kingdom and the execution of their king, Numan, proved to be costly in the long run. Also, Khusrau turned against Byzantium in 603 after the murder of his ally, the pro-Sasanian emperor Mauritius. Initially the Sasanians enjoyed victories and recovered important cities in Syria and Mesopotamia. Another part of the Sasanian army reconquered Armenia. The new Byzantine emperor was no longer able to withstand the advance of the Sasanian army, which reached Jerusalem in 614, supposedly taking the Holy Cross with them to Ctesiphon. In 615 the Persian army reached the Bosporus, opposite Constantinople, and in 619 they conquered Egypt, where they went up the Nile to Nubia. The Sasanian empire had reached its maximum extent, only to fall to the forces of Heraclius in 627; in 628 the Byzantine army entered Ctesiphon, the capital of the Sasanian empire. But the final blow came from an Arab army under the banner of Islam in 637 at Qadisiya near Ctesiphon. A further defeat followed at Nihavand in 642 and Yazdigird III (632–651), the last Sasanian king, was forced to flee to Merv, where he was murdered. [*See* Ctesiphon; Sasanians.]

The splendor of the art of the late Sasanian period is best seen in the rock reliefs of Khusrau II at Taq-i Bustan near Kermanshah. Here, the king appears in an investiture scene flanked by Anahita and Ahura Mazda, and another relief shows him as a knight in armor riding a horse. The reliefs on the sides of the iwan depict scenes of the royal hunt with the king standing in a boat and surrounded by boars and elephants (Herrmann, 1977, pp. 132–135; Vanden Berghe, 1984, pls. 37–39).

Among the sites of the late Sasanian period, Takht-i Suleiman in Iranian Azerbaijan, is especially important. Built around a lake, the site was one of the most important religious centers of the time. It is assumed that the Gushnasp fire, the fire of the warriors, burned eternally.

BIBLIOGRAPHY

Christensen, Arthur Emanuel. *L'Iran sous les Sassanides*. 2d. ed. Osnabrück, Germany, 1971.

Colledge, Malcolm A. R. *The Parthians*. London, 1967.

Curtis, John. *Ancient Persia*. London, 1988.

Debevoise, Neilson C. *A Political History of Parthia.* 2d ed. New York, 1969.
Grayson, A. Kirk. *Babylonian Historical-Literary Texts.* Toronto Semitic Texts and Studies, 3. Toronto, 1975.
Herrmann, Georgina. *The Iranian Revival.* Oxford, 1977.
Oelsner, Joachim. *Materialien zur babylonischen Gesellschaft und Kultur in hellenistischer zeit.* Budapest, 1986.
Schippmann, Klaus. *Grundzüge der Parthischen Geschichte.* Darmstadt, 1980.
Schippmann, Klaus. *Grundzüge des Geschichte des Sasaniden Reiches.* Darmstadt, 1990.
Sherwin-White, Susan M., and Amélie Kuhrt. *From Sardis to Samarkand.* London, 1993.
Vanden Berghe, L. *Reliefs rupestres de l'Iran Ancien.* Brussels, 1984.
Vanden Berghe, L., and Klaus Shippmann. *Les reliefs rupestres d'Elymaïde (Irān) de l'époque parthe.* Ghent, 1985.
Yarshater, Ehsan. *Cambridge History of Iran,* vol. 3.1. *The Seleucid, Parthian, and Sasanian Periods.* Cambridge and New York, 1983.

VESTA SARKHOSH CURTIS

Persia in the Islamic Period

The Islamic period in Persia (Iran) was inaugurated politically and historically by the crucial defeat of the Sasanian dynasty in the battle of Nehavend in 642 CE. The transitional period, in which it is difficult to distinguish between the pre-Islamic and Islamic periods, lasted for some time and is unevenly discernible in different parts of Iran, as well as in the various spheres of cultural and artistic activity. Throughout the Middle Ages and even beyond, the Persian-Iranian world comprised vast territories outside the frontiers of modern Iran, such as Afghanistan in the east and Bukhara and Samarkand in the northeast. The heterogeneous nature of the population, then, with its tribal affiliations and local political developments, contributed to the creation of a number of centers of cultural importance. The centers essentially revolved around princely courts that were more or less autonomous and often in competition with one another. This was the case for major capitals—Merv, Bukhara, Nishapur, Rayy/Tehran and Samarkand—each of which became the focus of important intellectual developments while retaining distinct artistic characteristics in pottery, architecture, and literature. [*See* Nishapur.]

In the Late Middle Ages, other centers—Herat, Tabriz (painting), Kashan (ceramics), Kazvin, and Shiraz—rose to fame, culminating, in the seventeenth century, in the extraordinary role played by Isfahan as the cradle and capital of the Safavid dynasty, with its remarkable urbanization project that included a distinctive system of irrigation based on connected underground channels, or *qanats* (Goblot, 1979). [*See* Irrigation; Isfahan.] Throughout this period Iran, despite its adoption of Islam and the Arabic script, retained the Persian language. [*See* Persian.] The country maintained a distinct identity from the Muslim world while remaining part of it.

One of the oldest mosques in Iran has been excavated by Roman Ghirshman (1948, pp. 77–79) at Susa. [*See* Susa.] Its plan appears to reflect the impact of the Mesopotamian mosque type, which can be traced to the Early ʿAbbasid mosque in Isfahan (Galdieri, 1984). The first mosque with a pointed arch occurs, apparently, at Damghan in about 760. By the twelfth century, the plan most typical of Iranian mosques, that of the four iwans, is found at Isfahan. [*See* Mosque.]

Iran's architecture is essentially in brick. Its use entailed a number of distinctive techniques that became integral features of Iranian architecture, particularly in the Islamic period. One of these techniques was the use of stucco decoration. At an early stage, stucco decoration appears in various parts of the Nayin mosque; this form of embellishment continued in use throughout the Middle Ages, as can be seen in the classic example of Gunbad-i Alavian near Hamadan/Ecbatana. [*See* Ecbatana.] Moreover, the medium of brick stimulated the imagination of artists and craftsmen, who created, with much virtuosity, the most extraordinary works of art, such as the incomparable tomb of Ismaʿil the Samanid in Bukhara (c. 907). More than a dozen patterns were created in the tomb's unadorned brick. The tower-tomb at Gunbad-i Qabus in the Gurgan area (c. 1006) displays the opposite concept: apart from a few cartouches with inscriptions, the monument is devoid of decoration. It relies for its effect on its very striking plan and the perfect execution of its severe brickwork. The next step was the integration of glazed tiles into brick structures; eventually, in the Safavid period, the color scheme of the tiles came to dominate the architecture. [*See* Tile.]

Iran has undergone excavations that concentrated primarily on the glory of ancient Iran: at Susa, for example, initiated by the French as early as the nineteenth century, along with those at Persepolis and, more recently, Pasargadae, an exception was the Metropolitan Museum of Art's excavations at Nishapur. It was only after the World War II that Iran's Islamic period began to attract interest. [*See* Persepolis; Pasargadae.] Meanwhile, many clandestine digs have been carried out (e.g., at Gurgan and Rayy, to mention only the most flagrant instances), destroying archaeological contexts and dispersing items on the international antiquities market. [*See* Ethics and Archaeology.] Pottery, metalwork, textiles, and jewelry have found their way into collections, though they lack adequate data as to their provenance.

Islamic archaeology in Iran has concentrated on a relatively limited number of sites. In the northeast, the above-mentioned excavations of Nishapur took place as early as the 1930s. Istakhr, in the center of the country, has yielded important finds of coins, pottery, and other artifacts that are being studied by the Oriental Institute of the University of Chicago. In the south, the port of Siraf was excavated for a number of seasons beginning in 1966 (Whitehouse, 1968, pp. 1–22, and subsequent reports), contributing much to what is understood about the continuity of Sasanian traditions into Islamic Iran and their ultimate integration.

Finally, Susa in the southwest, one of the richest sites in ancient Iran, also yielded a considerable amount of important information for the Islamic period (Boucharlat and Labrousse, 1979, pp. 155–237; Rosen-Ayalon, 1974).

One salient feature clearly emerges: an imaginary diagonal line can be drawn between the very different cultural spheres of the northeast and the southwest. For the ceramics found at Susa, the cultural affiliations are with the area to its west, Mesopotamia, with close connections to Samarra in Iraq; the pottery of Nishapur, however, lacks some of the typical blue-and-white and lusterwares and displays a range of rather different types, such as brown and black-on-white wares. [*See* Samarra, *article on* Islamic Period.]

Unlike the pottery, the spectacular metalwork for which Iran is known has, as yet, no archaeological documentation. Most of the metal artifacts found at Nishapur are rather modest, so that analysis of the stratigraphic contexts of pieces found in the excavations cannot provide answers to the many unsolved questions surrounding metalware.

Some of the most original products of Islamic pottery were devised and manufactured in Iran. The Minai family of ceramics, with its polychrome overglaze painting (thirteenth–fourteenth centuries), is probably the most famous, while the lusterwares in the distinct styles of Rayy and Kashan comprise another category. Iranian potters attempted to compete with Chinese porcelain ware; frit wares were invented under the Seljuks (twelfth–thirteenth centuries), and Chinese wares were imitated under the Safavids (seventeenth century).

[*See also* Ceramics, *article on* Ceramics of the Islamic Period; *and* Sasanians.]

BIBLIOGRAPHY

Boucharlat, Rémy, and Audran Labrousse. "Une sucrerie d'époque islamique sur la rive droite du Chaour à Suse." *Cahiers de la Délégation Archéologique Française en Iran* 10 (1979): 155–237.

Galdieri, Eugenio. *Esfahān: Masgid-i Gumʿa*. 3 vols. Translated from Italian by Ian McGilvray. Rome, 1984.

Ghirshman, Roman. "Une mosquée de Suse du début de l'Hégire." *Bulletin d'Études Orientales* 12 (1947–1948): 77–79.

Goblot, Henri. *Les Qanats, une technique d'acquisition de l'eau*. Paris, 1979.

Rosen-Ayalon, Myriam. *La poterie islamique: Ville royale de Suse IV*. Paris, 1974.

Whitehouse, David. "Excavations at Sīrāf: First Interim Report." *Iran* 6 (1968): 1–22.

MYRIAM ROSEN-AYALON

PERSIAN. The dominant Iranian language, Persian in its oldest documented form was the language of the Achaemenids (559–330 BCE). In its middle form, Persian was the official language of the Sasanian empire (227–651 CE). It emerged in its new form after islamization in the middle of the seventh century CE. The Medes, who preceded the Achaemenids, spoke a language closely related to Old Persian. The Parthians (247 BCE–227 CE), who reasserted Iranian rule after the interregnum of Alexander and the Seleucids, spoke a language closely related to Middle Persian.

These Iranian-speaking empires, centered in Iran, at one time or another extended over two vast areas: (1) much of the Near East and (2) southern Eurasia and the northern Indian subcontinent. As such, they played a major role in the political, cultural, and religious history of two major regions of the world.

Geographically, Parsa and the western Iranian plateau as the bridgehead of the ancient Iranian empires represent the area of the southernmost extension of Iranian speakers, whose historical areas were the vast expanses of southern Eurasia from the western shores of the Black Sea to China.

The English term *Persian* derives from the Greek *Persis* and Old Persian *Parsa*, and originally referred to the southwest region of the Iranian plateau, where the Achaemenids first established their empire. They referred to themselves as "Parsa" or as rulers "in Parsa." The arabicized form of the term is *Fars*, from which derives the Arabo-Persian designation *Farsi* for the language. Although the term *Persian* in its origin referred to a specific region and its local dialect, the term *Iranian* refers to the totality of the members of the large family of related languages called *Iranian*.

The Iranian tongues are a branch of the Indo-Iranian or Aryan family of Indo-European languages together with the Indo-Aryan and Nuristani languages. The latter are found in minute remnants in the mountainous Pakistan-Afghanistan border areas, and recognized as distinct only in this century (Morgenstierne, 1973).

The term *arya*, whose suggested meanings includes "noble," was a self-designation in the Old Persian inscriptions, in the Avesta and Zoroastrian books, as well as in the Old Indic *Vedas* (Schmitt, 1986; 1989, pp. 1–3). It came to refer specifically to the western Aryans, that is, the "Iranians."

Persia and Iran. The name of the country Iran derives from Old Iranian *aryanam khshathram* "realm of the Aryas" (Schmitt, 1989, pp. 1–3), later *eran shahr*, Modern Persian *Iranshahr*, ultimately reduced to *Iran*. The confusion between the terms *Persia* and *Iran* stems from the political decision of the founder of the Pahlavi dynasty early in the twentieth century to identify his country ethnically and all inclusively as Aryan.

It appears that the areas where Indo-Iranian originally began to develop were the middle Volga River and Kazakhstan. From there the ancestors of the later Indo-Aryan branch first moved south into Central Asia, and further south into eastern Iran, Afghanistan, and northwest India in the early second millennium BCE. These were followed by moves of the ancestors of the later Iranian speakers across southern Eurasia to the west, east, and south, probably beginning around the middle of the second millennium. In the eastern regions, there appears to have occurred a long process of symbiosis and interchange with Indo-Aryan, by which the latter became increasingly absorbed and ultimately confined to the southeastern areas of this expanse and the northwestern areas of the Indian subcontinent. In the western regions, between the Caspian and the western shores of the Black Sea, there appear to have occurred similar processes with other Indo-European branches.

This tentative reconstruction is essentially based on the later linguistic evidence. The correlation of linguistic and ethnic dynamics and archaeological evidence is complex by necessity. The most prominent Indo-Iranian archaeological cultures during the second millennium are Andronovo, Namazga, and Tazabagyab in the delta of the Amu Darya River on the southeastern Aral Sea.

Forays to the south as well appear to have happened frequently but without lasting results. Best known are the linguistic Indo-Aryan-type traces in texts of the Mitanni period of the fifteenth century. Similarly, there may have been Indo-European or pre-Indo-Iranian influences on the Kassites in the central Zagros in western Iran. [*See* Kassites.]

The Iranians in Eurasia included such better-known peoples as the Scythians, known in the classical periods as the most numerous barbarians beside the Celts. The Scythians' forays found them in Poland and Siberia; their cousins, the Saka, reigned in eastern Eurasia, Afghanistan, and northern India. Other prominent Eurasian Iranians were the Sarmatians and Alans (from *arya-) in the areas between the Black and Caspian Seas, who at one time entered the Hungarian plains; and the widely urbanized Sogdians who resided between the Aral Sea and Chinese Turkistan, a vital link in east-west commerce. It is possible that the Cimmerians, who were driven by the Scythians from the eastern Pontic areas across the Caucasus in the eighth century BCE had a strong Iranian component.

As to the plateau of Iran proper, the Medes, probably from across the Caucasus were the first Iranians to extend their rule in northwestern Iran. Simultaneously, groups of Persians appear to have made forays from the northeast of the plateau and moved further to the west and finally south. Both were first mentioned as Mada and Parsua in inscriptions of Salmaneser III (858–854). [*See* Medes.]

Overall, it appears that the East, including Sistan, Central Asia, and Afghanistan, remained a major linguistic and cultural Iranian center during the first millennium. In fact, it retained its status throughout the first millennium CE and beyond, until its devastation by the Mongols during the first half of the thirteenth century (Geiger and Kuhn, 1895–1904, vol. 2; Grantovskij, 1970; Burrow, 1973; Ghirshman, 1977; Parpola, 1988; Renfrew, 1987, pp. 178–210; Mallory, 1989, pp. 227–31; Anthony, 1991; Boyce, 1992, with implications for Zoroastrianism).

Dialectology and Periodization. The documented Iranian languages are divided into three diachronic (chronological) stages—Old Iranian, Middle Iranian, and Modern Iranian—roughly following major political changes. The Iranian languages are divided into two major dialects: (1) South Iranian, which comprises the languages of the Iranian plateau and (2) North Iranian, which covers the remainder of the Iranian languages. (The traditional terminological distinction, still often followed, is West vs. East Iranian.) In turn, South Iranian is divided into two subdialects: (1) Southwest Iranian, which comprises Persian and related dialects, and (2) Northwest Iranian, sometimes called *Median*, which includes the remainder of South Iranian. (For general overviews, see Geiger and Kuhn, 1895–1904; Schmitt, 1989, pp. 1–3; and for early history, see Mayrhofer, 1989; Schmitt, 1989, pp. 25–31; Schmitt, 1994).

Old Iranian languages. Only two languages, Old Persian and Avestan, are well documented. Old Persian was the court language of the Achaemenids. It is attested by a rather limited corpus of inscriptions and is probably based on the local dialect of the province Parsa (Kent, 1953; Brandenstein and Mayrhofer, 1964; Schmitt 1989, pp. 56–85).

Avestan (probably a calque on Greek *episteme* "received knowledge"), the sacred language of the Zoroastrian texts, was originally spoken in northeastern Iran and Central Asia. It is documented by a much more extensive corpus, ranging from the Gathas of Zarathushtra (possibly dating from before 1000 BCE) to the so-called Younger Avestan texts, some of which in origin may have predated Zarathushtra, and later compositions. The oldest preserved manuscripts date from the thirteenth century BCE (Jackson, 1892; Reichelt, 1909; Beekes, 1988; Kellens, 1989).

These two languages are also known from references in other languages (Hinz, 1975; Schmitt, 1989, pp. 86–94). A number of other Old Iranian languages are attested only by a small number of words, names, and phrases scattered throughout the writings of additional languages such as Old Scythian in southern Russia, Old Parthian in eastern Iran, and Old Sogdian in Central Asia.

Old Persian and Avestan are southwestern and northern dialects respectively. Within Avestan both diachronic and dialectical differences are apparent. Old Persian has several dialectical features, including "Medisms" and incipient Middle Persian features in later inscriptions.

Middle Iranian languages. The beginning of the Middle Iranian stage can be dated to the third century BCE, based on the evidence found in later Achaemenid inscriptions (Schmitt, 1989, pp. 95–105; Sundermann, 1989, pp. 106–113). Although Middle Persian was replaced by New Persian beginning about the seventh century CE, some other Middle Iranian languages are documented in the thirteenth century. The Middle Iranian languages described in the following paragraphs are documented by texts.

Middle Persian was the official language of the Sasanians. It is best attested in the writings of their state religion, Zoroastrianism, most of which date from the ninth century CE but represent an earlier stage of the language. Middle Persian was also used by Christians, and it was one of the church languages of the Manichaeans in eastern Iran and Central Asia. Mani (d. 277) himself, though an Aramaic speaker, composed a book in Middle Persian for Shapur I. It was used until the eleventh century, as evidenced, e.g., by the signature of witnesses on a copper-plate grant to a Syrian Church in southern India (probably ninth century) and by coins and inscriptions of several local Iranian dynasties (Nyberg, 1964; 1974; Heston, 1976; Brunner, 1977; MacKenzie 1971; Sundermann, 1989, pp. 138–164).

A dialect of the Northwestern subgroup, Parthian was the official language of the Parthians or Arsacids and was spoken in northeastern and partially also northwestern Iran. There are also extensive Manichaean texts in Parthian, which provide evidence for the continuation of this language in Central Asia until the tenth century (Ghilain, 1939; Heston, 1976; Brunner, 1977; Sundermann, 1989, pp. 114–137).

Several languages comprise the northern dialects (Sims-Williams, 1989, pp. 165–172). Sogdian, spoken from Central Asia to the borders of China, is likewise found in many Manichaean texts (Gershevitch, 1954; Sims-Williams, 1989, pp. 173–192). Khwarezmian was spoken in the area south of the Aral Sea and is attested mainly by glosses to Arabic texts (Humbach, 1989). Saka appears in many Buddhist texts found in Chinese Turkestan (Emmerick, 1968, 1989). Bactrian in northern Afghanistan is evidenced by several inscriptions and texts mainly from the first to the third century CE (Humbach and Grahmann, 1966; Humbach, 1989). Scytho-Sarmatian and Alanian were used in the northern Pontic (Bielmeier, 1989; Sims-Williams, 1989, pp. 230–235).

Middle Persian is a successor, albeit with more typical "southwestern" features, of Old Persian. Parthian does not have a known direct ancestor but shows certain northern features attributable to the origin of the dynasty from among the Parni between the Caspian and Aral Seas. No direct successor of Avestan is attested. (On the multiethnic and linguistic variety of Middle Persian with a focus on the Achaemenid Empire, see Rossi, 1981; Delauney, 1985; Schmitt, 1978, 1989, pp. 56–85.)

Modern Iranian languages. Modern Iranian emerged during the eighth century CE. First attested is Modern Persian (three Judeo-Persian inscriptions in Hebraic script, dated 752/3, found in central Afghanistan; and a letter fragment found near Khotan in Xinjiang, China, also dating to the eighth century).

The modern Iranian dialects are spoken in an area that roughly reflects the extent of earlier Iranian rule, stretching from Central Asia and Pakistan through Afghanistan and Iran to Iraq and Turkey, and into the Caucasus. The modern southern Iranian languages include southwestern Persian (in Iran, Afghanistan, and Tajikistan); northwestern Baluchi (in eastern Iran, western Afghanistan, and southwestern Pakistan) and Kurdish (in northwestern Iran, northern Iraq, and eastern Turkey); and numerous remnants of Median and Parthian dialects in central and northwestern Iran, and also in northern Iraq, and eastern Turkey.

The modern northeastern languages include Pashto, which is widely spoken in Afghanistan and Pakistan; Yaghnobi in southern Tajikistan, which is the sole remnant of Sogdian; and a great variety of dialects in northeastern and central Afghanistan and Pakistan. Finally, Ossetic is isolated in the central Caucasus, and the last remnant of the Scytho-Sarmatian dialects that in antiquity were spoken over vast areas of South Russia (see respective chapters in Schmitt, 1989).

Writing Systems. Most Iranian scripts are varieties of and developments from Aramaic, which was the administrative language of the Achaemenid Empire. Subsequently Iranian languages—first Parthian, then Middle Persian—were written in variants of Aramaic. Middle Persian is most familiar from the Zoroastrian books in the script Book-Pahlavi in which the original twenty-two letters had coalesced to some fourteen distinct shapes in cursive and partially connected ligatures. The Avestan script, which was highly differentiated to allow the smallest record of the standard pronunciation of the sacred texts, was developed out of Book-Pahlavi (Morgenstierne, 1942; Windfuhr, 1972).

Scripts not derived from Aramaic are the thirty-six signs of Old Persian cuneiform, which were invented for the inscriptions of Darius I (Diakonoff, 1979; Windfuhr, 1970; LeCoq, 1974); the Greek alphabet of Bactrian; and the central Asian Brahmi variant used for the Saka documents.

[*See also* Parthians; Persia; Persians; *and* Sasanians.]

BIBLIOGRAPHY

Anthony, David W. "The Archaeology of Indo-European Origins." *Journal of Indo-European Studies* 19 (1991): 193–222.

Beekes, R. S. F. *A Grammar of Gatha-Avestan.* Leiden, 1988.

Bielmeier, Roland. "Sarmatisch, Alanisch, Jassisch und Altossetisch." In *Compendium linguarum iranicarum,* edited by Rüdiger Schmitt, pp. 236–245. Wiesbaden, 1989.

Boyce, Mary. *Zoroastrianism: Its Antiquity and Constant Vigour.* Costa Mesa, Calif., 1992.

Brandenstein, Wilhelm, and Manfred Mayrhofer. *Handbuch des Altpersischen.* Wiesbaden, 1964.

Brunner, Christopher J. *A Syntax of Western Middle Iranian.* Delmar, 1977.

Burrow, Christopher B. "The Proto–Indo-Aryans." *Journal of the Royal Asiatic Society of Great Britain and Ireland* (1973): 123–140.

Dandamaev, M. A. *Persien unter den ersten Achämeniden (6. Jahrhundert v. Chr.).* Wiesbaden, 1979.

Delauney, J. A. "L'araméen d'Empire et les débuts de l'écriture en Asie Centrale." *Acta Iranica* 2 (1985): 219–236.

Emmerick, Ronald E. *Saka Grammatical Studies.* London, 1968.

Emmerick, Ronald E. "Khotanese and Tumshuqese." In *Compendium linguarum iranicarum,* edited by Rüdiger Schmitt, pp. 204–229. Wiesbaden, 1989.

Geiger, Wilhelm, and Ernst Kuhn, eds. *Grundriss der iranischen Philologie.* 2 vols. Strassburg, 1895–1904.

Gershevitch, Ilya. *A Grammar of Manichaean Sogdian.* Oxford, 1954.

Ghilain, A. *Essai sur la language parthe. Son système verbal d'après les textes manichéens du Turkestan Oriental.* Louvain, 1939.
Ghirshman, Roman. *L'Iran et la migration des Indo-Aryéns et des Iraniens.* Leiden, 1977.
Grantovskij, E. A. *Rannaja istorija iranskikh plemen Peredneij Azii* (The Early History of the Iranian Peoples of Southwest Asia). Moscow, 1970.
Heston, Wilma. "Selected Problems in Fifth- and Tenth-Century Iranian Syntax." Ph.D. diss., University of Pennsylvania, 1976.
Hinz, Walther. *Altiranisches Sprachgut der Nebenüberlieferungen.* Wiesbaden, 1975.
Humbach, Helmut, and Adolf Grohmann. *Baktrische Sprachdenkmäler.* Vol. 1. Wiesbaden, 1966.
Humbach, Helmut. "Choresmian." In *Compendium linguarum iranicarum,* edited by Rüdiger Schmitt, pp. 193–203. Wiesbaden, 1989.
Jackson, A. V. W. *An Avestan Grammar in Comparison with Sanskrit.* Stuttgart, 1892.
Kellens, Jean. "Avestique." In *Compendium linguarum iranicarum,* edited by Rüdiger Schmitt, pp. 32–55. Wiesbaden, 1989.
Kent, Roland G. *Old Persian: Grammar, Texts, Lexicon.* 2d rev. ed. New Haven, 1953.
LeCoq, Pierre. "La langue des inscriptions achéménides." *Acta Iranica* 2 (1974): 55–62.
MacKenzie, D. N. *A concise Pahlavi dictionary.* London, 1971.
Mallory, J. P. *In Search of the Indo-Europeans: Language, Archaeology, and Myth.* London, 1989.
Mayrhofer, Manfred. "Vorgeschichte der iranischen Sprachen: Uriranisch." In *Compendium linguarum iranicarum,* edited by Rüdiger Schmitt, pp. 4–24. Wiesbaden, 1989.
Mayrhofer, Manfred. "Über die Verschriftung des Altpersischen." *Historische Sprachforschung* 102 (1990): 174–186.
Morgenstierne, Georg. "Orthography and Sound-System of the Avesta." *Norsk Tidsskrift for Sprogvidenskap* 12 (1942): 30–82.
Morgenstierne, Georg. *Irano-Dardica.* Wiesbaden, 1973. See "Die Stellung der Kafirsprachen" (pp. 327–343).
Nyberg, H. S. *A Manual of Pahlavi.* 2 vols. Wiesbaden, 1964–1974.
Parpola, Asko. "The Coming of the Aryans to Iran and India and the Cultural and Ethnic Identity of the Dāsas." *Studia Orientalia* (Helsinki) 64 (1988): 195–302.
Reichelt, Hans. *Awestisches Elementarbuch.* Heidelberg, 1909.
Renfrew, Colin. *Archaeology and Language: The Puzzle of Indo-European Origins.* New York, 1987.
Rossi, Adriano V. "La varietà linguistica nell'Iran achemenide." *Annali del Seminario di Studi del Mondo Classico: Sezione Linguistica* 3 (1981): 141–196.
Schmitt, Rüdiger. "Fragen der Anthroponomastik des achämenidischen Vielvölkerstaates." *Zeitschrift der Deutschen Morgenländischen Gesellschaft* 128 (1978): 116–124.
Schmitt, Rüdiger. "Aryans." In *Encyclopaedia Iranica,* vol. 2, pp. 684–687. London, 1987.
Schmitt, Rüdiger, ed. *Compendium linguarum iranicarum.* Wiesbaden, 1989.
Schmitt, Rüdiger. "Sprachzeugnisse alt- und mitteliranischer Sprachen aus Afghanistan." In *Indogermanica et Caucasica. Festschrift für Karl Horst Schmidt zum 65,* edited by R. Bielmeier and R. Stempel, pp. 168–196. Berlin, 1994.
Sims-Williams, Nicholas. "Eastern Middle Iranian"; "Sogdian"; and "Bactrian." In *Compendium linguarum iranicarum,* edited by Rüdiger Schmitt, pp. 165–192, 230–235. Wiesbaden, 1989.
Sundermann, Werner. "Westmitteliranische Sprachen"; "Parthisch"; and "Mittelpersisch." In *Compendium linguarum iranicarum,* edited by Rüdiger Schmitt, pp. 106–164. Wiesbaden, 1989.
Windfuhr, Gernot L. "Notes on the Old Persian Signs." *Indo-Iranian Journal* 12 (1970): 121–125.
Windfuhr, Gernot L. "Diacritic and Distinctive Features in Avestan." *Journal of the American Oriental Society* 91 (1972): 104–124.
Windfuhr, Gernot L. "Languages of Ancient Iran." In *The Anchor Bible Dictionary,* vol. 4, pp. 217–220. New York, 1992.

GERNOT L. WINDFUHR

PERSIANS. The Persians were one of several Iranian-language groups who migrated onto the Iranian plateau from lands east of the Caspian Sea, perhaps as early as the mid-second millennium BCE. These Old Iranians are divided into three sublanguage groups: Old Northeast Iranian (known from Gathic Avestan); Old Northwest Iranian, or Median (known from Persian personal names and loanwords); and Old Southwest Iranian (known from Old Persian cuneiform inscriptions, the ancestor of modern Persian). [*See* Persian.]

By the mid-ninth century BCE, Mesopotamian records attest the presence of both the Medes and the Persians in the central western Zagros Mountain region. After these sources fall silent (c. 640 BCE), the Persians appear in the southwestern Zagros, in the land of Parsa, modern Fars. The possible relationship between ninth-century BCE Parsua/Parsumash and sixth-century BCE Parsa is a matter of debate. There is no consensus on whether the Persians migrated from north to south; whether two Persias existed at the same time; or which Persia Herodotus described as a Median vassal (1.102). [*See* Medes.] The best explanation may be that there were indeed two groups of Persians, one in the central-western and one in the southwestern Zagros. The former may have been tributary to, and eventually absorbed by, the Medes. The latter, under Cyrus II, may have either rebelled against the Medes, or may, as an independent Iranian group, have attacked them.

Efforts to trace these migrations in the archaeological record have met with little success. One hypothesis, that the radical shift from painted to plain gray-black and buff ceramics at the end of the Bronze Age in central and northwestern Iran represents the arrival of Iranians in about 1450 BCE, is not widely accepted (Young, 1967). Others have suggested that the appearance of the distinctive plain buff pottery of the Iron Age III period in central-western Iran in the ninth century BCE marks the appearance of Iranians in the Zagros. This hypothesis has also gained little support. More widely accepted is the proposition that the rapid spread of Iron III pottery throughout the Zagros in the seventh century BCE may be archaeological evidence of the rise of the unified and powerful Median kingdom that is documented textually (Young, 1988).

In Parsa, the Achaemenid Persian homeland, there is almost no archaeological evidence for the centuries immediately preceding the rise of the Persians to imperial power. This may indicate that these early Persian tribes were tent-dwelling pastoralists.

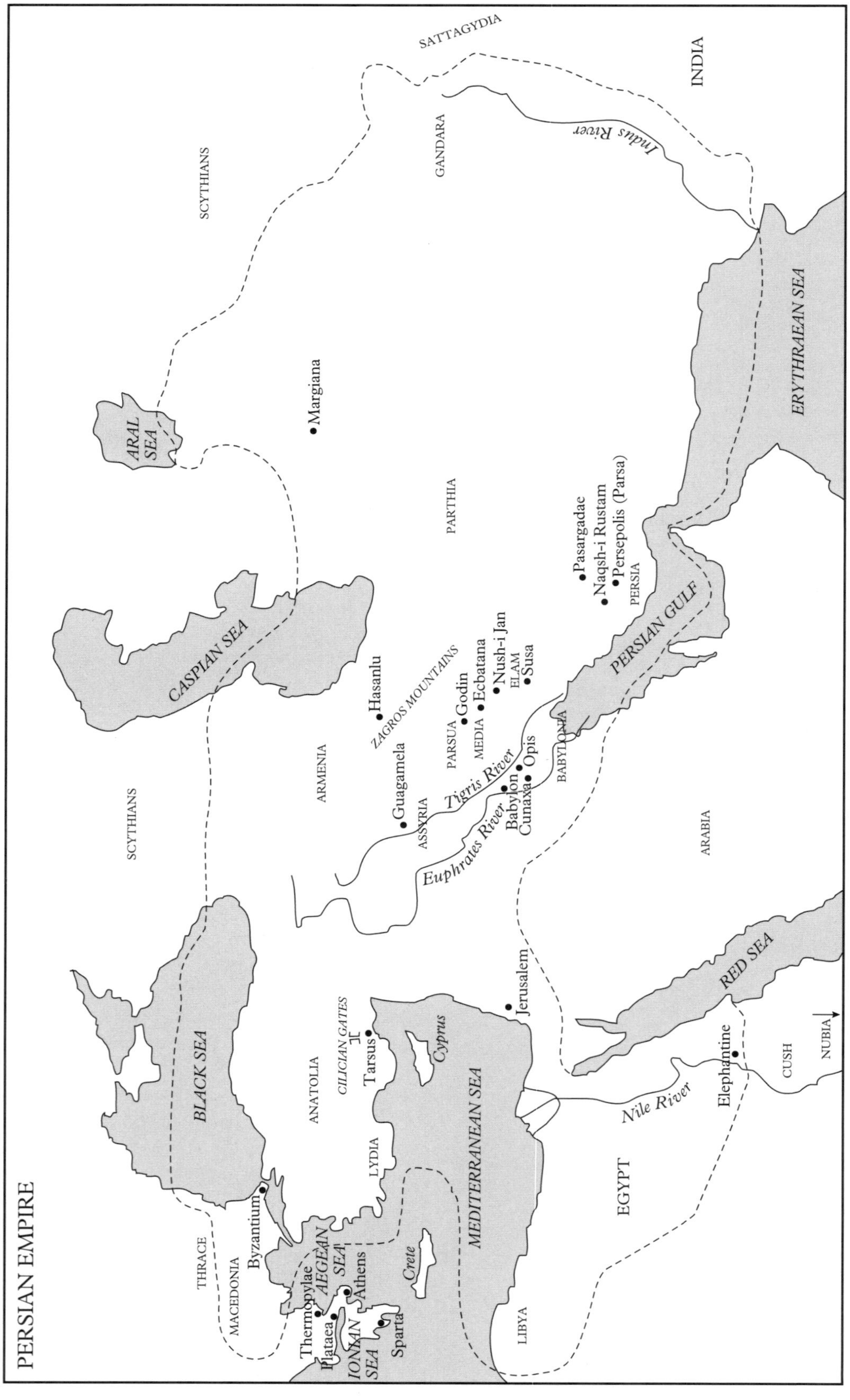
PERSIAN EMPIRE
SATTAGYDIA
INDIA
Indus River
GANDARA
SCYTHIANS
ERYTHRAEAN SEA
Margiana
ARAL SEA
PARTHIA
Pasargadae
Naqsh-i Rustam
Persepolis (Parsa)
PERSIA
PERSIAN GULF
CASPIAN SEA
Hasanlu
ZAGROS MOUNTAINS
Godin
Ecbatana
Nush-i Jan
ELAM
Susa
PARSUA
MEDIA
Opis
Tigris River
BABYLONIA
Babylon
Cunaxa
Guagamela
ASSYRIA
ARMENIA
SCYTHIANS
ARABIA
Euphrates River
Jerusalem
RED SEA
BLACK SEA
CILICIAN GATES
Tarsus
Cyprus
ANATOLIA
MEDITERRANEAN SEA
Nile River
Elephantine
CUSH
NUBIA
EGYPT
LYDIA
Byzantium
THRACE
MACEDONIA
AEGEAN SEA
Athens
Crete
Thermopylae
Plataea
IONIAN SEA
Sparta
LIBYA

Rise to Imperial Power. Cyrus II (559–530 BCE) was the first great king of the Persian royal house, the Achaemenids. His initial task was to unite the Persian tribes. He then successfully attacked the Median king Astyages (550 BCE). Among Iranians this event may have been seen as nothing more than an internal dynastic power struggle, for the Medes became so closely allied with the Persians that the Greeks often had difficulty distinguishing between them.

In 547 BCE Cyrus defended himself against Lydian attack, and after an inconclusive battle, successfully besieged the Lydian capital, Sardis. [*See* Sardis.] Shortly thereafter, all of Asia Minor came under Persian rule (Herodotus, 1.74–84). In October 539 BCE, Cyrus invaded Babylonia, where he fought only one battle, at Opis; the Persians then marched unopposed into Babylon. Cyrus performed the religious rituals required of a Babylonian king and returned confiscated deities to their native Mesopotamian cities. That same year, his decree (*Ez.* 1–4) permitting the Jews to rebuild the Temple in Jerusalem established the Persian custom of ruling with religious and cultural tolerance.

Cyrus died in 530 BCE, fighting the Scythian Massagetae on the northeastern frontier of the empire. His conquests included all of eastern Iran, Afghanistan, much of central Asia, Anatolia, and all of the Babylonian Empire. Of the four kingdoms that held the balance of power in the Near East at the time of Cyrus's succession, only Egypt remained independent.

Cambyses II (530–522 BCE), Cyrus's son, conquered Egypt in 525 BCE in a well-planned campaign. He remained there for three years, extending Persian conquest south into Nubia and west into North Africa. He ruled in Egypt as a legitimate pharaoh, but, probably because of a reorganization of the Egyptian religious establishment, gained a poor historical reputation. While he was in Egypt, rebellion broke out in Persia. He turned homeward in 522 BCE but died en route. It fell to Darius I to suppress the rebellion and to restore the Achaemenid family to power.

Darius I (521–486 BCE) dealt first with the rebellion of Gaumata (Bardiya/Smerdis). The story of the rebellion in Herodotus (3.67–88) and in Darius's Bisitun inscription is that Cambyses killed his brother Bardiya before leaving for Egypt. [*See* Bisitun.] Then Gaumata (Greek Smerdis), a Magian (Median) priest, claiming he was Bardiya, rebelled. Darius and six other nobles were the only Persians willing to challenge the false Bardiya. They killed him and the kingship was given to Darius. He then restored the sanctuaries Gaumata had destroyed, returned confiscated private property, and "reestablished the people on its foundation, both Persia, Media, and the other provinces" (Bisitun inscription, I. 71–72). Clearly, this was more than a palace coup. The empire had been shaken to its foundations by issues involving Mede versus Persian, "haves" versus "have nots," upper versus lower social orders, and different religions.

These confusions provided the climate for widespread rebellion in the first year of Darius's kingship. Elam and Babylon rebelled first but were quickly retaken. In the meantime, Armenia, Persia, Media, Assyria, Parthia, Margiana, Sattagydia, and Scythia rebelled. Subordinate generals were sent to deal with distant trouble spots; the king himself concentrated on the most dangerous core rebellion, in Media and neighboring regions. Once those provinces were under control, troops were available to crush rebellion elsewhere. Darius won because he retained control of the professional army, used his central position to prevent rebel coordination, and was a first-class general.

After an administrative reorganization of the empire, Darius turned to further expansion. Sometime between 520 and 513 BCE, India (the Punjab) was conquered. By 517 BCE Persia controlled the Ionian islands, and in 513 BCE Darius campaigned, with some success, against the Black Sea Scythians and conquered European Thrace and most of the northern Aegean. [*See* Scythians.]

In 499 BCE peace in the west was disturbed by the Ionian Revolt. Fierce fighting restored the power of Persia throughout western Asia Minor and northern Greece by 494 BCE. In response to Athenian support for the Ionians, Darius decided to invade mainland Greece, which the Persians did in 490 BCE, only to lose the battle at Marathon. The Persians retired to Asia. Darius was determined to return, but he died before he could do so, in 486 BCE.

Xerxes (486–465 BCE), Darius's son, assumed the task of conquering Greece. First, however, he had to put down rebellions in both Babylon and Egypt. The invasion of Greece began in 480 BCE, with initial success for the Persians: they outmaneuvered the Spartans at Thermopilae, conquered Attica, and burned the Acropolis in Athens. Their navy, however, was defeated in the confined waters of the Bay of Salamis. Xerxes returned to Persia, leaving general Mardonius in command. In spring 479 BCE, Persians and Greeks fought a close battle at Plataea. Only when Mardonius himself was killed did the Persians collapse and flee both the field and Greece. In the decade that followed, Persian power in western Asia Minor and the Aegean was at its nadir. Xerxes was effectively not heard of again until he was assassinated in 465 BCE.

Late Empire. The Persian Empire survived for 134 years after the death of Xerxes, but its days of expansion were over. Persia continually intervened, to her advantage, with diplomacy and bribery in the internecine wars in Greece. The Peace of Callis was signed with Athens in 448 BCE by Artaxerxes I (464–425 BCE), which left Asia Minor to Persia and the Aegean to the Greeks. The agreement broke down, however, and in 400 BCE Persia and Sparta were at war. Persia supported Sparta's enemies with gold, and eventually Artaxerxes II (405–359 BCE) was invited by the Greeks to mediate their disputes. The result was the so-called King's Peace of 387–386 BCE, with which the Persian Empire firmly reestablished its hold on Asia Minor.

Artaxerxes II had to deal with two major challenges from within. His brother, Cyrus the Younger, rebelled but was defeated at the battle of Cunaxa in 401 BCE. Then, in 373 BCE, the Revolt of the Satraps ("protectors of the Kingdom/Kingship") began. Several satraps, mainly from Asia Minor, combined in rebellion. The rebels, however, fell out among themselves and Artaxerxes triumphed.

Egypt had successfully rebelled in 405 BCE and was not brought back into the empire until 343 BCE under Artaxerxes III (359–338 BCE). The real threat to the Persian Empire by this time, however, was not from rebellion but from the growing power of Macedonia. By the time Darius III (336–331 BCE) was on the throne, Alexander the Great was ready to invade Asia. Alexander won his first battle at the Granicus River in 334 BCE. Victory also went to the invaders at a second battle shortly thereafter, near the Cilician Gates. Alexander spent the next two years consolidating his hold on the Levant and Egypt. The final Persian defeat took place on 1 October 331 BCE, at Gaugamela, near modern Erbil. Alexander captured Persepolis in April 330 BCE, and the fleeing Darius was murdered that summer. [*See* Alexandrian Empire.]

Government and Society. The royal court was the center of imperial government. At its center was the king, so that the capital was wherever the king was. Fixed capitals were Susa, Persepolis, Ecbatana/Hamadan, and sometimes Babylon. [*See* Susa; Persepolis; Ecbatana; Babylon.] King, court, and government were supported by a large scribal bureaucracy concentrated in the treasuries of the empire, for which the best evidence comes from Persepolis. The treasuries were repositories from which stores of imperial wealth in kind were administered. The Persepolis texts tell of provisions issued to work parties, craftsmen, travelers, treasury officials, priests, members of the royal household, and the king himself. These texts make clear that the central government was highly organized and accountable to a hierarchy of officialdom, ending with the king.

Into the reign of Xerxes, the language of the treasury at Persepolis was Elamite. The end of the Elamite record suggests that the language of the treasury became Aramaic, the lingua franca of the empire, which was written not on clay tablets but on perishable materials. [*See* Aramaic.] The language of the royal inscriptions was alphabetic Old Persian, probably invented under Darius I in order to write the Bisitun inscription (see above).

Provincial organization. The empire was organized into provinces (satrapies), each ruled by a satrap. This system existed under Cyrus II but was restructured by Darius I. Satraps were appointed by the king, often from among his relatives. Except for certain royal fortresses, the satrap was both the military and civil commander of his province. Representatives of the king, however—the "king's eyes" or "king's ears"—traveled in the provinces and reported directly to him. Control of the empire was also facilitated by an extensive system of "royal roads," the most famous of which ran from Susa to Sardis.

Military forces. The military was divided into the army and navy. At the core of the standing army were the ten thousand Immortals, a thousand of whom formed the king's elite bodyguard. There were also ten thousand cavalry in the standing army. Troops of the standing army—exclusively Persians, Medes, Elamites, and perhaps Scythians—were often permanently stationed in the satrapies. Provincial forces were supported by native troops and long-term mercenaries, such as the Jewish soldiers stationed at Elephantine on the southern Egyptian frontier. In time of full-scale war, the army was augmented by a levy called up from almost all of the empire's subject peoples. The standing forces in the navy were supplied by Phoenicians, Egyptians, and perhaps Cypriots. Ionian Greeks often participated. All marines were Persians, Medes, or Scythians.

Law and the economy. Little is known of ancient Persian law. Following the model set by Cyrus II, the Achaemenids generally governed with tolerance of, and respect for, the customs, traditions, and laws of its conquered peoples. The best evidence comes from Babylonia, where, in the main, legal affairs were conducted according to long-standing Babylonian law and custom. There is, however, evidence of what might be a "king's" law administered in a "king's" court, though the available texts suggest that even there the Persians were introducing new economic and administrative arrangements rather than rewriting law.

The wealth of the empire was founded on agriculture, but manufacturing and commerce played important roles in the economy. The government taxed with vigor. State and royal properties were rented, funds were collected in lieu of obligations, tribute was paid by peoples outside the provincial structure, customs charges were collected, and selected sales taxes were levied. Most taxes were paid in kind. Some of this wealth, however, went back into the economy. Seed grain and seedlings (probably fruit trees) were issued to private estates by the treasuries. Archaeological evidence demonstrates that state investment in irrigation systems greatly increased productivity in Mesopotamia. [*See* Irrigation.] Manufacturing, at least in cottage industries, was encouraged by payments from the treasuries, and exploratory sea voyages were undertaken at government expense to discover trade routes. Darius dug a canal from the Nile River to the Red Sea, and on land the state-supported road network allowed the peoples of the empire to benefit from what was, for ancient times, a very large common market. [*See* Roads; Transportation.]

Social organization. Persia's tolerance of the customs of her subjects precludes speaking of an imperial social organization. There were two reasons for that tolerance: it was a realistic policy, given the empire's size and cultural diversity; and such a policy fit the Persians' own sense of social structure. Their vertical view of society began at the base, with the family, and progressed upward through the levels of clan, tribe, and country, to culminate in a people or nation. Viewed horizontally, Persian society had four classes: priests, warriors, scribes, and artisans/peasants. At the summit of society was the king, surrounded by the concept *khvarna,* or "kingly glory," that attached itself both to the man and the office. Thus, the king functioned only at the highest level: he was king of countries, peoples, and nations; it was therefore logical that imperial policy not interfere with the affairs of tribes, clans, and families. If the peoples of the empire remained loyal and functioned well, how they did so was not the business of the central government. Tolerance was built into the Persian concept of how the world was organized.

Religion. As wide a variety of religions were practiced in the empire as there were subject peoples. From the Persepolis texts we know that a number of different beliefs and practices were found even in Persia. The critical question, however, remains whether the Achaemenid kings were Zoroastrians, in terms of what Zoroastrianism may have been like in the sixth–fourth centuries BCE. Zoroaster was a great ethical prophet who preached in northeast Iran sometime prior to the rise of the Achaemenids. In due time his message triumphed over the polytheism of the Iranian world, and Zoroastrianism eventually became the state religion of Iran in Sasanian times. [*See* Sasanians.]

There are no data on the religion of Cyrus. Darius I, in several of his inscriptions, uses wording compatible with Zoroaster's teaching, however: truth *(arta)* is in conflict with the lie *(druj)*. Ahuramazda is the supreme and only god mentioned. Darius may have been a Zoroastrian. Xerxes elevated Arta to the role of a deity and seemed particularly concerned about devil worship, as Zoroaster was. The relapse into polytheism must have continued under Artaxerxes I, as the goddess Anahita and the god Mithra appear in royal inscriptions. Yet, with the imperial adoption of the Zoroastrian religious calendar, a clear commitment to Zoroastrianism is made under this king. Thus, beginning with Darius I, the Persian kings seem to move steadily toward a Zoroastrian theology.

Evidence of ritual practice from Persepolis confirms this drift. That fire, whose purity and importance Zoroaster emphasized, was central to Persian royal religious ritual can be seen in the royal tomb reliefs and the great fire altar at Pasargadae. [*See* Pasargadae.] There also appears to have been no animal sacrifice at court—a practice Zoroaster had condemned. The Persepolis texts yield evidence of offerings only of wine, beer, wheat, and flour. Zoroaster had preached against the Haoma cult, a drunken pagan ritual; however, textual and archaeological evidence from Persepolis indicates that the cult was practiced. Nevertheless, on balance, Persian royal religious ritual seems to have come close to Zoroastrian practice at the time.

Art and Architecture. Achaemenid Persian art is a blend of two elements: the experiences Persians had with material culture on the Iranian plateau during the centuries prior to the rise of Cyrus II, and the material culture of the empire's conquered peoples. These elements are most evident in architecture. The artists who decorated the great imperial capitals of Pasargadae, Susa, and Persepolis came from every corner of the empire. Their influence on individual elements is so great as to lead some scholars to argue that Achaemenid art and architecture are only eclectic. A closer look at Pasargadae and Persepolis shows that this is not true.

At Pasargadae, founded by Cyrus II, a clear Egyptian and Mesopotamian influence is evident and a considerable amount of decorative detail; Greek influence is also patent. The layout of the site and the conception of the "whole" is entirely Persian, however. The Pulvar River, which runs through the site, is the key to understanding the plan of the "city": the tomb of Cyrus, the main gate, two major palaces, two pavilions, a bridge, the so-called Zendan, the sacred precinct, and the hilltop fortress, the Tall-i Takht. Most of these structures were oriented to life in the open air. The various water channels feeding off the river and running among the buildings make it clear that the site was in fact a great park, not a city: a physical manifestation of a Persian paradise.

The concept and the details—of the columned halls and pavilions—are fundamentally Persian. Although the columned hall was foreign to the ancient Near East outside of Egypt, it was an architectural tradition that can be traced back in western Iran to Median times at such sites as Tepe Nush-i Jan and Godin II and from there back to the Early Iron Age at Hasanlu V (1450–1150 BCE). It was an architectural concept the Persians brought with them to Parsa. Pasargadae remains a superb expression in stone, wood, and brick of what the city of the king of a new empire (only recently the ruler of tent-dwelling pastoralists) might look like.

That imperial authority was yet more forcefully expressed at Persepolis and Susa—the former grander and better preserved. At Persepolis Darius built a great stone platform jutting westward from the base of the Kuh-i Rahmat ("mountain of mercy"). Xerxes expanded the platform and completed buildings his father had begun and added others. Construction continued under Artaxerxes, and, in a more desultory way, under even later kings. Two large columned audience halls (the Apadana and the Hall of a Hundred Columns), a columned gateway (Gate of All Nations), private columned residence palaces, a treasury, and a harem were the main structures on the platform.

Some of the most remarkable reliefs ever carved in the ancient Near East adorn the walls of these structures. Again, foreign influence is clear, but the basic Persian conception of the totality is equally clear. The carving was done by a team of artisans: a master craftsman working with others, each assigned special elements of each figure. In short, the reliefs were created in an assembly line—the master artist(s) was not the carver of the reliefs (where foreign influences show). Rather, the master was he who conceived, designed, and decided on the final layout of the reliefs. He was a Persian, for the story he told, and the way he told it, was an original contribution of the Achaemenid Persians to the art of the ancient world.

The reliefs are unhistorical. Unlike those of Egypt and Assyria, they tell no story. Instead they are a static picture of accomplishments—they are not scenes of warfare, of the king's conquests, or of enemies defeated, but of contented subject peoples paying homage to their ruler. The king is the central focus, but he is not an individual: he is not Darius or Xerxes or Artaxerxes, but the image of *khvarna,* of the glory of kingship in the abstract. The reliefs are a sculptured statement of the philosophy behind the tolerance of Persian imperial rule, the perfect *pax persica.*

Achaemenid sites have produced few small objects from foreign countries, for the Persians preferred their own products. Relatively plain stone and pottery vessels, with an emphasis on crisp shapes derived from metal prototypes, are common. Bird and animal heads are used as decoration, often on handles—a tradition going back to Median times. Stone-seal cutting was a consummate art, as were metalwork and jewelry. Metal vessels were practical, even when ornate, with an emphasis on intricate, repetitive, and highly geometric decorative elements; animal motifs, long a tradition on the plateau, also were common. Achaemenid jewelry and tableware represent some of the most delicate achievements in ancient metalwork.

Almost nothing is known outside of ceramics of the material culture of the common people for excavation has concentrated on royal sites. At Persepolis the platform was only the acropolis of a large city which may have spread north and west as far as the royal rock-cut tombs at Naqsh-i Rustam. Excavations off the terrace revealed some palaces of the nobility, but no peasant or artisan compound.

The Achaemenids combined the art of others before them with traditions of their own. In doing so they produced an art which, like their empire, marked the end of the ancient world and the beginning of something new.

[*See also* Persia.]

BIBLIOGRAPHY

Balcer, Jack Martin. "The Athenian Episkopos and the Achaemenid 'King's Eye.'" *American Journal of Philology* 98 (1977): 252–263.

Burn, Andrew R. *Persia and the Greeks: The Defense of the West, c. 546–478 B.C.* 2d ed. London, 1984. Authoritative study of Persian-Greek relations from the time of Cyrus to Xerxes.

Cook, J. M. *The Persian Empire.* London, 1983. Expansion of his essay in Gershevitch (below); some excellent insights, but uneven in quality.

Dandamaev, Muhammad A., and Vladimir G. Lukonin. *The Cultural and Social Institutions of Ancient Iran.* Translated by Philip L. Kohl. Cambridge, 1989. Stimulating, somewhat idiosyncratic discussion, very worthy but sometimes marred by factual inaccuracies.

Frye, Richard N. *The History of Ancient Iran.* Handbüch der Altertumswissenschaft, III.7. Munich, 1984. The most recent statement on ancient Iran by a distinguished American scholar.

Gershevitch, Ilya, ed. *The Cambridge History of Iran,* vol. 2, *The Median and Achaemenian Periods.* Cambridge, 1985. Uneven but very useful series of articles, with an excellent bibliography.

Miroschedji, Pierre de. "La fin du royaume d'Anšan et de Suse et la naissance de l'empire perse." *Zeitschrift für Assyriologie* 75 (1985): 265–306. Excellent discussion of the relationship between the Late Elamites and the rise of the first Persian Empire.

Roaf, Michael. "Sculptures and Sculptors at Persepolis." *Iran* 21 (1983). Definitive work on the reliefs at Persepolis.

Schmidt, Erich F. *Persepolis,* vol. 1, *Structures, Reliefs, Inscriptions.* Oriental Institute Publications, 68. Chicago, 1953. The first volume on the University of Chicago excavations at Persepolis. Superseded in some details since, but the starting point for any understanding of the site.

Schmidt, Erich F. *Persepolis,* vol. 2, *Contents of the Treasury and Other Discoveries.* Oriental Institute Publications, 69. Chicago, 1957. Final report on the small finds of the Chicago Persepolis expedition.

Schmidt, Erich F. *Persepolis,* vol. 3, *The Royal Tombs and Other Monuments.* Oriental Institute Publications, 70. Chicago, 1970. The final report on the excavations and investigations of the Achaemenid royal tombs at Naqsh-i Rustam and related structures (some dating to the Sasanian period).

Stronach, David B. *Pasargadae: A Report on the Excavations Conducted by the British Institute of Persian Studies from 1961 to 1963.* Oxford, 1978. Definitive excavation report, incorporating all previous work at the site.

Sumner, William M. "Achaemenid Settlement in the Persepolis Plain." *American Journal of Archaeology* 90 (1986): 3–31. Poses the problem of the lack of archaeological evidence for any settled village life in the Persepolis area immediately prior to the foundation of Persepolis under Darius I.

Vogelsang, W. J. *The Rise and Organisation of the Achaemenid Empire: The Eastern Iranian Evidence.* Leiden, 1992. Stimulating, thoughtful, but not always convincing argument on the organization of the eastern Achaemenid Empire and the role played by the Scythians in the first Persian Empire.

Young, T. Cuyler, Jr. "The Iranian Migration into the Zagros." *Iran* 5 (1967): 11–34. Attempt to demonstrate that both the Medes and the Persians came to western Iran from the northeast, and that their appearance can be traced in the archaeological record; dated but useful.

Young, T. Cuyler, Jr. "The Persian Empire." In *The Cambridge Ancient History,* vol. 4, *Persia, Greece, and the Western Mediterranean,* edited by John Boardman, pp. 1–253. Cambridge, 1988. Narrative report on the early history of the Medes and the Persians to the death of Xerxes, with an excellent bibliography.

T. Cuyler Young, Jr.

PERSONAL HYGIENE.

In the hot, dry climate of the Near East, washing the body and anointing it with oil were hygienic necessities of the first order. The frequency of bathing was influenced not only by the availability of water, but also by social status: wealthy individuals could pay stricter attention to personal hygiene than poor people. Generally, in the ancient Near East people contented themselves with washing only their face, hands, and feet, although the Egyptians appear to have bathed daily and the Babylonians washed their entire body mainly in preparing for religious festivals (Dayagi-Mendels, 1989, pp. 13–34). In the Bible, too, bathing is mentioned most often in connection with ritual purity (*Lv.* 16:24). It was also the rule among the Hebrews to bathe after an illness or a battle, and women were instructed to purify themselves through immersion in the miqveh, or "ritual bath" from their menstrual uncleanness.

Washing the hands was a practice common to all people in the ancient Near East. It was customary to wash the hands upon rising in the morning and before meals (*Mk.* 7:3), and usually after meals, as well. In the Talmud it is said that one must wash one's hands every morning and evening and before prayer (B.T., *Shab.* 109a).

In ancient Greece, banquet guests washed their hands in warm, perfumed water and wiped them on a common towel (Dayagi-Mendels, 1989, p. 14). In the Near East, no special vessels for rinsing the hands are known, with the exception of Egypt, where spouted vessels have been found next to basins. These vessels are frequently depicted on reliefs and in paintings, where they are seen under a table. They are known from the third and second millennia BCE, made mostly of bronze but sometimes of alabaster or pottery.

The custom of washing the feet is mentioned in the Bible as central to the conventions of hospitality (*Gn.* 18:4; 19:2; *2 Sm.* 11:8). It is probably in the context of this custom that the footbaths known from Palestine in the Iron Age should be interpreted. In the bathrooms of first-century CE houses in the Upper City of Jerusalem, stone installations have been found (Nahman Avigad, *Discovering Jerusalem,* Nashville, 1983, pp. 84–86) that probably served as footbaths of the kind mentioned in the Mishnah (*Yad.* 4:1). According to Jewish literary sources it was one of the wife's duties to wash the feet, hands, and face of her husband, even if there were servants in the house (B.T. *Ket.* 61a). This washing was intended to be enjoyable and was done with hot water, in contrast to the hasty washing in the mornings, for which cold water was used.

The tomb of Ruaben, an official of the Egyptian second dynasty, a house containing a bathroom is planned; as in houses of the twelfth dynasty excavated at Kahun, bathrooms were uncovered next to bedrooms; and in houses of the eighteenth dynasty at Tell el-Amarna, the bathrooms were located at the rear. The bathing was actually more like a shower: the bathroom contained a large stone slab raised slightly above the floor, with a drain next to it. The bather stood on the stone while his servant poured water over him through a sieve. Clearly such bathrooms only existed in palaces and in the homes of the wealthy; people of lesser means must have washed in a basin or bathed in the river. The people of Mesopotamia washed their entire body only on festive occasions (see above). The common people bathed in the rivers or in reservoirs in courtyards, while notables and wealthy citizens had special bathing installations in their palaces and mansions. Bathtubs existed also at Mari (see figure 1), where two basins set on a raised platform were uncovered in one of the rooms of the palace (G. E. Men-

PERSONAL HYGIENE. Figure 1. *Bathroom from the palace at Mari.* Two terra-cotta tubs and a toilet area are shown (Courtesy ASOR Archives)

denhall, in *Biblical Archaeologist* 11 [1948]: 8–10). Paved bathrooms equipped with drains and the remains of a bronze bathtub were unearthed at Zincirli in northern Syria. Many bathrooms containing bathtubs have also been found in palaces on Crete and Mycenae from the second millennium BCE (Arthur Evans, *The Palace of Minos,* vol. 3, London, 1930, pp. 384–385). In the Neo-Babylonian period, bathrooms in private houses became commonplace.

Although bathrooms were a rarity in ancient Palestine until the Hellenistic period, several early examples have been discovered (e.g., at Tell el-ʿAjjul, Tell Jemmeh, and Megiddo). Some people also washed in basins or tubs, as demonstrated by the seventh-century BCE figurine of a woman washing herself found in a Phoenician tomb at Achziv. Biblical stories imply that it was also customary to wash in enclosed courtyards (*2 Sm.* 11:2). Presumably, many people also bathed in streams and springs.

Various vegetal or mineral substances were added to the bathwater in antiquity (*Jer.* 2:22), and Pliny says it was the Gauls who invented soap (*Nat. Hist.* 28.191). To prevent the skin from drying and cracking after using harsh minerals, and to protect it in a hot, dry climate, it was customary to anoint the body with oil after bathing (*Ru.* 3:3). Oiling the body was not considered a luxury and in most countries in the ancient Near East, body oils were regarded as an everyday commodity that was in fact used by the majority of the population. It was therefore a sign of mourning to refrain from anointing oneself (*2 Sm.* 14:2). The Egyptians knew more than thirty different oils and ointments for anointing the skin, and in Persia, too, various oils and cosmetics were well differentiated, as is learned in the story of *Esther* (2:12).

In the Greek world, the attitude toward body hygiene was very different, essentially because there the need to take care of the body was connected with sports. As early as the fourth century BCE, the palaestrae and gymnasia in which athletes exercised were equipped with bathing facilities that were continually improved over the centuries. Relatively few remains of bathtubs have been found in private houses in the Greek world. Most of what is known comes from literary sources (e.g., *Odyssey* 4.49–53) and from depictions on vase paintings. The paintings show bathers in a fountain or women washing themselves from a basin. Footbaths were also used, and in banqueting scenes they are depicted underneath the couches. In Greece anointing the body with oil was also part of the daily routine, often even replacing washing or bathing.

In the Hellenistic world, the bathroom became a regular fixture in the homes of the middle class, as seen at Olynthos. At the same time, public baths were established, serving especially those exercizing in the palaestrae and gymnasia, as at Olympia. The Romans took over the concept and construction of bathing installations from the Greeks and perfected them. Under the influence of Hellenistic culture, baths also began to appear in Palestine—and not only in the houses of the nobility (Dayagi-Mendels, 1989, p. 25). The Romans regarded bathing not only as a hygienic necessity, but also as a form of entertainment that went on for many hours. The many public baths they founded were open to all. The patron, after bathing, was massaged with ointments, either by his personal servant or by an individual employed for this task by the baths.

The pampered Roman lady entrusted herself, immediately after her bath, to the hands of her personal staff of maids who massaged her, rubbed her skin with unguents, cared for her hands and feet, and plucked out unwanted hairs. When the lady set out for the baths, she took her creams and unguents with her (Dayagi-Mendels, 1989, p. 25). The unguents used for anointing the skin after bathing were composed of a base of vegetable oils—olive oil, almond oil, or sesame oil—or were made from animal fat taken from geese, sheep, goats, or cattle. To these, various fixatives were added, including milk, honey, and different salts. While the wealthy treated their skin with precious and perfumed unguents, those with lesser means used oils of inferior quality, such as castor oil. The ointment and oil industry led to the development of an entire field devoted to the manufacture of beautiful containers. Stone vessels, especially those made of alabaster, were popular in Egypt, and beautifully painted pottery vessels are known from the classical world.

[*See also* Baths; Cosmetics; Medicine; *and* Ritual Baths. *In addition, many of the sites mentioned are the subject of independent entries.*]

BIBLIOGRAPHY

Dayagi-Mendels, Michal. *Perfumes and Cosmetics in the Ancient World.* Israel Museum Catalogue, 305. Jerusalem, 1989.

Ginouvès, René. *Balaneutiké: Recherches sur le bain dans l'antiquité grecque.* Paris, 1962.

Laser, Siegfried. *Medizin und Körperpflege.* Göttingen, 1983. See pages 138–172.

MICHAL DAYAGI-MENDELS

PETERS, JOHN PUNNETT (1852–1921), professor of Old Testament language and literature at the Episcopal Divinity School, Philadelphia (1884–1891), and professor of Hebrew at the University of Pennsylvania (1886–1893), best known for organizing the first American archaeological excavations in Mesopotamia, at Nippur (1888–1900). Peters was involved in arousing interest in archaeological work in Mesopotamia as early as 1883, soliciting funds from Catherine Lorillard Wolfe, a wealthy New Yorker, to send an exploratory expedition to southern Mesopotamia (1884–1885). Peters then tried to elicit interest in a second expedition to carry out excavations. Nothing came of his efforts until 1887, when he met Edward White Clark, a Philadelphia financier, who, as a young man, had traveled to the Near East and was an avid reader of Austen Henry

Layard's accounts of his travels and excavations. Clark raised the funds for an expedition affiliated with the University of Pennsylvania. In 1888, with pledges of funding in hand, the Babylonian Exploration Fund (with William Pepper, provost of the university, as president) came into existence.

Peters served as director of the first and second excavation campaigns at Nippur (1888–1889, 1889–1900). Despite rivalries and quibbling among the expeditions' crews and limited digging techniques, the first two seasons' excavations were thoroughly recorded and were adequate, held to the standards of the time. Peters' detailed journal, notes, measurements and sketches of walls and buildings, and his catalog of objects from the second campaign, which are in the University Museum's archives at the University of Pennsylvania, constitute a usable source of information on the excavations.

Peters became assistant rector of St. Michael's Church in New York City in 1891 and resigned his position at the Episcopal Divinity School. He became rector when his father died in 1893, at which time he left his position at the University of Pennsylvania.

Although no longer director in the field, Peters nevertheless served as scientific director of the third campaign (1893–1896) to Nippur and maintained an active interest in the excavations throughout his life. From 1905 to 1908 he was embroiled in a bitter dispute with Herman V. Hilprecht, professor of Assyriology at the University of Pennsylvania. The dispute involved not only everyone connected with the Nippur excavations, but also a good number of scholars in the discipline. Peters sparked the so-called Peters-Hilprecht controversy when he alleged that Hilprecht had exaggerated his claims to having found a temple library during the fourth campaign of excavations in 1900, had misrepresented purchased tablets as excavated artifacts, and had falsified the findspots of other excavated artifacts. The trustees of the university appointed a committee to act as a court of inquiry and, in its report dated 26 June 1905, found the charges untrue; its report did not end the controversy, however.

[*See also* Nippur; *and the biography of Hilprecht.*]

BIBLIOGRAPHY

Chamberlain, Joshua Lawrence. *Universities and Their Sons: University of Pennsylvania.* 2 vols. Boston, 1902. See pages 399–400.

Hilprecht, Hermann V. *The So-Called Peters-Hilprecht Controversy.* Philadelphia, 1908. Includes the proceedings of the committee appointed by the University of Pennsylvania's board of trustees to act as a court of inquiry in the Peters-Hilprecht controversy and Hilprecht's response to continued accusations against him.

Peters, John P. "Some Recent Results of the University of Pennsylvania Excavations at Nippur, Especially of the Temple Hill." *American Journal of Archaeology* 10 (1895): 13–46.

Peters, John P. *Nippur.* 2 vols. New York and London, 1897. Peter's account of the background of the Nippur excavations and his public report on the results of the first two campaigns.

Peters, John P. "The Nippur Library." *Journal of the American Oriental Society* 26 (1905): 145–164. Peters's initial charges against Hilprecht.

Peters, John P. *Hilprecht's Answer.* N.p., 1908. Peters's response to Hilprecht's statements in the so-called Peters-Hilprecht controversy, part 2.

Ritterband, Paul, and Harold Wechsler. "A Message to Lushtamar: The Hilprecht Controversy and Semitic Scholarship in America." *History of Higher Education Annual* 1 (1981): 1–41.

RICHARD L. ZETTLER

PETRA.

[*In order to treat the separate phases of excavations at this site, this entry comprises two articles, the first on the history of excavation and the second on more recent finds.*]

History of Excavation

Petra is an ancient city in modern Jordan situated in a broad north-south basin bordered on the east and west by mountain ridges (30°19′ N, 35°26′ E). The traditional entrance to the city is through a cleft in the eastern ridge, El-Kubtha, called the Siq, although access from both the north and the south is possible and was defended by walls during the Nabatean period (from the fourth century onward). The basin is watered by two perennial springs, with a natural water channel running east–west within the city area called Wadi Musa ("valley of Moses"). The Nabateans augmented the water supply with an intricate systems of runnels, cisterns, catchments, and a gravity-fed pipeline extending from another natural spring, ʿAin Musa ("spring of Moses"), about 3 km (2 mi.) from the basin proper.

Occupation of the basin area is documented archaeologically from at least the Neolithic period (6800) and sporadically thereafter, in the biblical Edomite, Hellenistic, Nabatean (to 363 CE), Byzantine, and Crusader periods. With the Islamic conquest in the seventh century CE, the area lost both its place along the major commercial routes and its strategic value. Although known to geographers of the Islamic period, the site became more and more obscure and was not recognized again until its "discovery" by the Swiss explorer Johann Ludwig Burckhardt in 1812. Since that time, most of the "learned travelers" of the late nineteenth and early twentieth centuries have visited the site and left their accounts. They were followed, in 1929 by the first excavations, undertaken by George and Agnes Horsfield working under the Department of Antiquities of Palestine during the mandate period (Horsfield, 1938; 1941). [*See* Nabateans; *and the biography of Horsfield.*]

The major period of modern scientific excavation actually began in the 1950s, with the work of Diana Kirkbride and Peter J. Parr of the British School of Archaeology in Jerusalem (BSAJ), Philip C. Hammond, director of the American Expedition to Petra, Fawzi Zayadine of the Department of Antiquities of Jordan, Manfred Lindner of the Nuremberg Natural History organization, Nabil Khairy of the Jordan University, and Rolf Stucky of the Archaeological Seminar of the University of Basel. Hammond and Parr excavated a Nabatean domestic structure in the city dump area of El-Katute in 1959, the first excavation of built structures on the site. Since that time considerable reconstruction, exploration, and excavations have been conducted, primarily through the activities of the Department of Antiquities of Jordan.

Kirkbride cleared the Paved Street sector of the City Center. Hammond excavated the first major monument on the site at the Main Theater, in cooperation with the Department of Antiquities; and Parr constructed revetment walls along the banks of Wadi Musa and conducted excavations in the temenos area of the temple (Qaṣr Bint Faroun) dedicated to Dhushares, the chief male deity of the Nabateans. The Department of Antiquities excavated a bath complex near the Monumental Gate and partially reconstructed it, rebuilt the frontal area of the Urn Tomb, and carried out other similar projects in the northern suburb of the city at El-Barid.

Parr and G. R. H. Wright investigated the architectural details of the Qaṣr and Zayadine began a durative study of its decorative motifs, as well as more extensive research on Nabatean architecture. Khairy excavated the first "villa" on the southern slope of the City Center. Lindner began extensive surveys of local graves, roads, flora, and geology and investigated the suburb of Sabra, to the south. His investigations also revealed data relating to Nabatean copper mining and discovered a small temple in the southern part of the basin. Stucky began a series of excavations of other residential structures in the Zanṯur sector, paying special attention to the ceramic materials.

Hammond undertook the most extensive work at the site in 1973, beginning with an electronic survey. The long-term excavation of a residential site and a public installation on the north slope of the City Center followed. It uncovered a temple dedicated to Allat, the chief female deity of the Nabateans, with a complex of outbuildings, both residential and industrial. Because of feline-decorated capitals around the altar platform of the building, it acquired the popular name of the Temple of the Winged Lions. The American Center of Oriental Research (ACOR), in Amman, undertook excavations at the site of a suspected Byzantine church to the east of the Temple of the Winged Lions, beginning in 1992.

In addition to the strictly Nabatean interest of the site, other periods were investigated. Crystal-M. Bennett undertook a short excavation project on top of the mountain called Umm el-Biyara, exposing Edomite ruins and recovering considerable materials from that period. Her excavations also called into question the identification of that mountain with biblical Sela, the acropolis of the Edomites during the Iron Age. [*See* Umm el-Biyara; *and the biography of Bennett.*] Hammond and James Jeffers surveyed the small Crusader fort on top of the mountain called El-Habis, during the joint excavation project with the BSAJ in 1959. Kirkbride devoted her attention to materials from earlier periods of occupation in the basin, having discovered and excavated an Early Neolithic settlement at el-Beidha, to the north. [*See* Beidha.]

Because of the relative paucity of Nabatean epigraphic materials from Petra proper, studies on the Nabatean language have concentrated on the hundreds of minor inscriptions in the Sinai and Negev deserts and at Meda'in Saleh in modern Saudi Arabia. [*See* Meda'in Saleh.] Beginning with the work of J. Cantineau in 1930, the basic vocabulary of the Nabateans has been assembled and the language can be read with little difficulty. Excavations on the Paved Street produced a quantity of ostraca, all of which were subsequently lost. Excavations at the Temple of the Winged Lions produced both ostraca and lapidary inscriptions. The former, because of close dating, are of importance for the transition between Nabatean and Arabic script, in keeping with the documentary evidence of a Nabatean teacher of writing during the Early Islamic period, after the destruction of Petra. [*See* Nabatean Inscriptions.]

Horsfield began the study of Nabatean ceramics in 1929 by recognizing fine, thin, red-painted pottery as Nabatean. Since then, a number of studies have been done, including Hammond's on the fine wares, Khairy's on fine and common wares, David Johnson's on unguentaria, and Karl Schmidt-Korte's on decorative patterns and modern replication studies.

Since Burckhardt's rediscovery of the site, a number of maps of the basin have been produced that have benefited from aerial, photogrammetric, plane, and subsurface electronic surveys. However, absolute identification has only been possible by excavation because of the tremendous rock falls that resulted from the earthquakes of 363 and 551 CE in particular. However, the work of Rudolf Ernst Brünnow and Alfred von Domaszewski (1904) at the end of the eighteenth century thoroughly documented the site's more than eight hundred rock-cut monuments and added the modern names of mountains, wadis, and other topographic features. Presently, however, only the Main Theater, the Paved Street, and its related temenos area, the Qaṣr Bint Faroun, the Bath Complex, the excavated residential sites, and the Temple of the Winged Lions represent proper identifications of once-subsurface structures. Judith McKenzie (1990) examined the major architectural structures and has produced a chronology based on typology.

Diodorus of Sicily is the earliest recorder of Nabatean settlement, and he cites an author some three hundred years earlier (*History* 19.94–100). Recent studies have sought to place the original homeland of the Nabateans in what has become modern Saudi Arabia, with the dating of the arrival of the people placed considerably prior to the 312 BCE date of Diodorus's report of Nabatean relations with the Seleucid Greeks. Strabo used an informant in his report of the urbanized city of Petra in the first century CE (*Geog.* 16.4.8; 21). Unfortunately, the informant was blind, and so not all of Strabo's analysis of the culture of the people at that point in history can be trusted as accurate. Nor is the picture of the manner in which the Nabateans urbanized Petra completely understood, in spite of various attempts to analyze the data. It does appear, however, from the archaeological record of building activities, that the main thrust toward urbanization took place under the most energetic of Petra's kings, Aretas IV (9 BCE–40 CE). Although king lists have been reconstructed, the early history of the people remains unclear, and data concerning such societal factors as ranking, actual political organization at lower levels, slavery, and control of sites outside the capital remain to be gathered.

What is known of religious life at Petra is based on its stone-cut monuments and the mention of deities encountered in inscriptional materials within and outside the city (see above). Further information has been made available by the excavations at the Temple of the Winged Lions, including probable cultic practices, the cultic model, and a number of cultic objects recovered, but the story of the cult at Petra, despite lists of deities, two temples known at the site, and many figurines recovered that are presumed to be cultic, is still incomplete.

Recent interest in Nabatean technology, at Petra and elsewhere, has provided a more informed idea of the craftsmanship, products, and even the names of artisan "families" connected with the site and its many tributary areas. Of greatest interest is the profound eclecticism shown by the people in their adoption, adaptation, and innovation of technologies. Thus far, the main areas studied have involved architecture (Parr, Wright, Hammond, Zayadine, Stucky, and Others), metallurgy (Lindner), ceramic production (Hammond, Parr, Khairy, Schmidt-Korte), marble sources (Slaughter), and art.

The Nabatean people have emerged as perhaps the most prominent commercial groups operating in the Near East from the Augustan Age through the Early Byzantine period (first–fourth centuries CE). Their variety of products, reaction to the varying tastes of the western market, and sheer business energy qualify their preeminence in the commercial life of the West. Their assumed earlier seminomadic wandering in the Arabian Peninsula apparently brought knowledge of the trade routes and their skillful choice of products brought profits—especially from oils and balms. The products appear to have been processed from raw materials secured in the area and packaged for sale, with Petra functioning as the main redistribution center. Later sources cite medicinal products from Petra as of the highest quality; along with frankincense, myrrh, bitumen, silk, gems, and spices, they may have been among the luxury items traded to the Western world. Even the Roman occupation of the site (106 CE) does not seem to have reduced the level of the Nabateans' economic activities, as recovered remains from after that date indicate.

BIBLIOGRAPHY

Brock, Sebastian P. "A Letter Attributed to Cyril of Jerusalem on the Rebuilding of the Temple." *Bulletin of the School of Oriental and African Studies* 40.2 (1977): 267–286.

Brünnow, Rudolf-Ernst, and Alfred von Domaszewski. *Die Provincia Arabia.* Vol. 1. Strassburg, 1904.

Hammond, Philip C. *The Excavation of the Main Theater at Petra, 1961–62: Final Report.* London, 1965.

Hammond, Philip C. *The Nabataeans: Their History, Culture, and Archaeology.* Studies in Mediterranean Archaeology, vol. 37. Göteborg, 1973.

Hammond, Philip C. "Survey and Excavation at Petra, 1973–1974." *Annual of the Department of Antiquities of Jordan* 20 (1975): 5–30, 145–154.

Hammond, Philip C. "Excavations at Petra, 1975–1977." *Annual of the Department of Antiquities of Jordan* 22 (1978): 81–101, 229–248.

Hammond, Philip C. "New Evidence for the Fourth-Century A.D. Destruction of Petra." *Bulletin of the American Schools of Oriental Research,* no. 238 (1980): 65–67.

Hammond, Philip C. "Nabataean Settlement Patterns inside Petra." *Ancient History Bulletin* 5.1–2 (1991): 36–46.

Horsfield, George, and Agnes C. Horsfield. "Sela-Petra, the Rock, of Edom and Nabatene." *Quarterly of the Department of Antiquities of Palestine* 7 (1938): 1–42; 8 (1938): 87–115; 9 (1941): 105–204.

Khairy, Nabil. "Nabatäischer Kultplatz und byzantische Kirbe." In *Petra: Neue Ausgrabungen und Entdeckungen,* edited by Manfred Lindner, pp. 58–73. Munich, 1986.

Lindner, Manfred. "Deutsche Ausgrabungen in Petra." *Bonner Jahrbücher* 180 (1980): 253–264.

McKenzie, Judith. *The Architecture of Petra.* British Academy Monographs in Archaeology, 1. London, 1990.

Milik, J. T. "Origines des Nabatéens." In *Studies in the History and Archaeology of Jordan,* vol. 1, edited by Adnan Hadidi, pp. 261–265. Amman, 1982.

Negev, Avraham, ed. "Die Nabatäer." *Antike Welt* 7, Sondernummer (1976). Special issue.

Oldfather, C. H., et al., trans. *Diodorus Siculus.* 12 vols. Loeb Classical Library. Cambridge, Mass., 1933–1957.

Parr, Peter J. "Excavations at Petra, 1958–59." *Palestine Exploration Quarterly* 92 (July–December 1960): 124–135.

Parr, Peter J. "Recent Discoveries in the Sanctuary of the Qasr Bint Farʿun at Petra. I: Account of the Recent Excavations." *Annual of the Department of Antiquities of Jordan* 12–13 (1967–1968): 5–19.

Parr, Peter J. "Découvertes récentes au sanctuaire du Qasr à Pétra. I. Compte rendu des dernières fouilles." *Syria* 45.1 (1968): 1–40.

Russell, Kenneth. "The Earthquake Chronology of Palestine and Northwest Arabia from the Second through the Mid-Eighth Century A.D." *Bulletin of the American Schools of Oriental Research,* no. 260 (1985): 37–59.

Schmidt-Colinet, Andreas. "The Mason's Workshop of Hegra: Its Relations to Petra and the Tomb of Syllaios." In *Studies in the History and Archaeology of Jordan,* vol. 3, edited by Adnan Hadidi, pp. 143–150. Amman, 1987.

Starcky, Jean. "Quelques aspects de la religion des Nabatéens." In *Studies in the History and Archaeology of Jordan,* vol. 1, edited by Adnan Hadidi, pp. 195–196. Amman, 1982.

Strabo. *Geography*. Vol. 12. Translated by Horace L. Jones. Loeb Classical Library. Cambridge, Mass., 1966.

Stucky, Rolf A. "Das Nabatäische Wohnhaus und das urbanistische System der Wohnquartiere in Petra." *Antike Kunst* 35.2 (1992): 129–140.

Wright, G. R. H. "Structure of the Qasr Bint Farʿun: A Preliminary Review." *Palestine Exploration Quarterly* 93 (1961): 8–37.

Wright, G. R. H. "Recent Discoveries in the Sanctuary of the Qasr Bint Farʿun at Petra." *Annual of the Department of Antiquities of Jordan* 12–13 (1967–1968): 20–29.

Zayadine, Fawzi. "Die Götter der Nabatäer." In *Petra und das Königreich der Nabatäer,* edited by Manfred Lindner, pp. 108–117. Munich, 1970.

Zayadine, Fawzi. "Temple, Gräber, Töpferöfen." In *Petra: Neue Ausgrabungen und Entdeckungen,* edited by Manfred Lindner, pp. 214–269. Munich, 1986.

Zayadine, Fawzi. "Decorative Stucco at Petra and Other Hellenistic Sites." In *Studies in the History and Archaeology of Jordan,* vol. 3, edited by Adnan Hadidi, pp. 131–142. Amman, 1987.

PHILIP C. HAMMOND

Recent Finds

Since the initial exploration and excavation of the site, recent finds include a southern temple and a Byzantine church. The temple was first explored by Rudolf-Ernst Brünnow and Alfred von Domaszewski, but it was Walter B. Bachmann, in his 1921 revision of the Petra city plan, who postulated the existence of a "Great Temple." While no structures were revealed before the Brown University 1993 excavations under the direction of Martha Sharp Joukowsky, the precinct, which is constructed on an artificial terrace, was littered with carved architectural fragments toppled by one of the earthquakes that have rocked the site throughout its history. In 1990 Kenneth W. Russell discovered the late fifth-century Byzantine church. Following Russell's death, its excavation was directed by Pierre Bikai of the American Center of Oriental Research (ACOR) with principal archaeologist Zbigniew Fiema assisted by Robert Schick and Khairieh ʿAmr. These excavations, which ended in 1993, were supported by the United States Agency for International Development and Jordan's Ministry of Tourism and Department of Antiquities.

Southern Temple. Located to the south of the colonnaded street and southeast of the temenos gate, the southern temple represents one of the major archaeological and architectural components of central Petra. This precinct (7,000 sq m) is comprised of a propylaeum, a lower temenos, and a monumental grand stairway that in turn leads to

PETRA: Recent Finds. Figure 1. *View of the excavated church.* (Courtesy ACOR)

PETRA: Recent Finds. Figure 2. *Fragments of the Petra scrolls.* (Courtesy ACOR)

the upper temenos—the sacred enclosure for the temple proper. The southern temple was a white-stuccoed building whose impact must have been dramatic set against its rose-red environment. It is tetrastyle in antis with widely spaced (about 7.50 m) central columns at the entrance and two end columns located about 5 m to the east and west, respectively. The porch columns (approximately 15 m high) plus the triangular pediment and the entablature indicate that its height would have been at least 19 m.

The temple measures 28 m east–west and is some 40 m long. The podium rests on a forecourt of hexagonal pavers; a stairway approaches a broad, deep pronaos that leads up and into the naos, or cella. The naos entry is marked by two columns equal in diameter (1.50 m) to those at the temple entrance but larger than either the eight flanking the cella walls or the six at the rear of the temple (whose diameter is 1.20 m). The naos, or cella, is some 29 m north–south by 18 m east–west. In the interior north a massive anta wall rests on a finely carved Attic base. To the south a two-or-three-storied adytum is dominated by a large, central vaulted arch. Twin-stepped, arched passages lead to paved platforms and a series of steps that give access to the temple cella and/or are an exit. Sculpted fragments of faces and fine, deeply carved architectural elements were recovered on an exterior paved walkway in the western part of the temple.

In the lower temenos large white hexagonal pavers were positioned above an extensive system of canals that can be traced to the temple forecourt. In the western exedra there were thousands of architectural fragments, one of them a capital decorated with elephant-headed volutes, and fragments of limestone friezes of faces, in addition to coins, lamps, Roman glass, and ceramics, including figurines, Nabatean bowls, small cups, and juglets. Elaborate floral friezes and acanthus-laden limestone capitals (carved with the ripple technique) suggest that the temple was constructed at the beginning of the first century CE by the Nabateans, who combined their native traditions with the classical spirit.

Byzantine Church. The tripartite basilica (26 m east–west × 15 m north–south) has three entrances on the west, three apses to the east, and walls preserved some 3 m above a mosaic floor (see figure 1). [*See* Basilicas; Mosaics.] In constructing the edifice, the builders recycled Nabatean and Roman architectural elements, including capitals, doorjambs, and reliefs. Although the structure was modified after a fire, its final form included a synthronon in the central apse, with a chancel platform and marble chancel screens. A stone-paved atrium was located to the west.

The side aisles have mosaic pavements dated to the early sixth century. Three parallel rows of roundels depicting native and exotic animals and vessels are found in the pavement in the north aisle; the eastern portion of the pavement in the south aisle is similar. The remaining central panels portray the Seasons, Ocean, Earth, and Wisdom flanked by birds, animals, and fish. The remains of the central nave consist of a fragmented marble opus sectile floor and a marble stylobate that held a row of columns.

Thousands of glass tesserae (some gilded) indicate that the upper walls, arches, and the central apse were decorated with mosaics. Numerous finds include coins, bronze and iron door fittings, glass, ostraca, fragmentary Nabatean and Greek inscriptions, and a large marble vessel decorated with two lioness-shaped handles. The earliest date found is 537

CE and the latest is 559, but earlier or later dates are not precluded. Thereafter, squatters occupied the atrium. The structure was abandoned in the early seventh century.

In a room adjacent to the church, some 152 carbonized papyrus scrolls (30 m wide and some 5–8 cm in diameter) were discovered in 1993 that represent the largest collection of textual material from antiquity yet found in Jordan (see figure 2). They had been crushed under carbonized shelving, on which they originally had been stored, as well as under about 4 m of stone debris. ACOR has assembled an international group of experts to help in the task of conservation and restoration. Ludwig Koenen, professor of papyrology at the University of Michigan, dates the scrolls to the fifth–sixth centuries. Jaakko Frösén, a conservator at the Academy of Finland, has unrolled twelve of the scrolls, which are written by many hands in a cursive Greek "documentary style." The contents are personal records—lectures, sermons, wills, contracts, and agreements with socioeconomic, topographic, and demographic implications for the mid-sixth century in Palestine.

BIBLIOGRAPHY

ACOR Newsletter 6.2 (Winter 1994): 1–3.

MARTHA SHARP JOUKOWSKY

PETRIE, WILLIAM MATTHEW FLINDERS

(1853–1942), British Egyptologist and archaeologist, considered by many scholars to be the founder of modern Near Eastern archaeology. In the course of his long professional career, Petrie excavated more than sixty of the most historically important—and richest—sites in Egypt and Palestine; published well over one hundred excavation reports, general works, and monographs; and wrote almost 450 articles and almost 400 reviews. His lasting importance to the development of Near Eastern archaeology is in his methodological innovations. Petrie was the first excavator in Egypt to recognize the chronological significance of ceramic evidence and, in his 1890 excavations at Tell el-Ḥesi, the first in Palestine to utilize the principles of stratigraphic analysis.

Born in Charlton, Kent, he was a sickly child and was educated at home. From an early age, Petrie showed interest in antiquarian matters: an avid collector of ancient coins, he was also a frequent visitor to the galleries of the British Museum. Under the influence of his chemist father, Petrie was eventually encouraged to take up surveying; his precise, detailed plans of ancient British earthworks and monuments, including Stonehenge, brought him to the attention of the archaeological world. The mystical attraction of Piazzi Smyth's pyramid theories turned Petrie's interest to Egypt. For a survey of the pyramids at Giza, Petrie traveled alone to Egypt in 1881. Ironically, his characteristically meticulous survey, published by the Royal Society, utterly disproved many of Smyth's sweeping mathematical assertions about the design of the Great Pyramid.

Petrie remained in Egypt, where he was employed in 1883 by the newly established Egypt Exploration Fund, and excavated the Delta sites of Tanis and Naukratis, Nebesha, and Daphne. Expressing great dissatisfaction with the financial administration of the fund, however, he set off on his own. Long an admirer of the eugenical theories of Sir Francis Galton, Petrie accepted an assignment to collect accurate measurements and photographs of ancient races as they were depicted in relief on the various temple walls throughout Upper Egypt. The result of this expedition was Petrie's book *Racial Photographs from the Egyptian Monuments* (London, 1887), in which he began to apply Galton's modern ideas about racial mixture and the stability of types to archaeological material.

Petrie's interests and excavation sites were eclectic: in 1887, he discovered a vast cemetery of Roman-period mummies with painted portraits at Hawara in the Faiyum. In 1888, in the Middle Kingdom levels at Lahun and the New Kingdom tombs at nearby Gurob, Petrie perceptively recognized the presence of Bronze Age Aegean pottery. Petrie's initial historical theories in Egypt were based on a collation of finds from widely scattered sites. It was his employment by the Palestine Exploration Fund in 1890 and his subsequent work at Tell el-Ḥesi in southern Judea (Judah), however, that confronted him with the challenge—and opportunity—of utilizing the stratigraphic methods of excavation pioneered by Heinrich Schliemann at Hissarlik in 1870. Although Petrie misidentified the site as ancient Lachish, his excavations there (carried on by Frederick Bliss for several seasons after his departure) inaugurated a new era in Palestinian archaeology. For nearly a century to come, a primary focus of excavation there would be the separation of uniform stratigraphic levels at large tells.

Petrie returned to Egypt in 1891 and explored important sites, including Tell el-Amarna, Coptos, Abydos, Ballas, Hu, Abadiya, and Naqada, at which he introduced his method of pottery seriation to arrange the relative chronology of types. He was appointed professor of Egyptology at the University of London in 1892 and, with his wife Hilda, founded the British School of Archaeology in Egypt in 1906 to support his field research. Race and racial mixture continued to be a main focus of Petrie's historical interpretation; his ideas were fully articulated in his book *The Revolutions of Civilisation* (London, 1911), in which he suggested that "the source of every civilization has lain in race mixture, it may be that Eugenics will, in some future civilization, carefully segregate fine races, until they have a distinct type" (p. 131). This dogma of progress through the triumph of "fine" races was to guide his work for the rest of his life.

With the rise of nationalist agitation in Egypt in the early 1920s, Petrie shifted his work to Palestine, excavating the sites of Tell Jemmeh (1926–1927), Tell el-Far'ah South (1928–1930), and Tell el-'Ajjul (1930–1934, 1937–1938). At these sites he trained a number of young British archaeologists, including James Starkey, Olga Tufnell, and G. Lankester Harding, who would play prominent roles in Palestinian archaeology in the coming years. In recognition for his life's work, Petrie was knighted in 1923. He spent his last years in residence at the American School of Oriental Research in Jerusalem.

[*See also* British School of Archaeology in Egypt; Palestine Exploration Fund; *and the biographies of Bliss, Harding, Starkey, and Tufnell. In addition, many of the sites mentioned are the subject of independent entries.*]

BIBLIOGRAPHY

Callaway, Joseph A. "Sir Flinders Petrie: Father of Palestinian Archaeology." *Biblical Archaeology Review* 6.6 (1980): 44–55.

Drower, Margaret S. *Flinders Petrie: A Life in Archaeology*. London, 1985.

Fargo, Valerie M. "BA Portrait: Sir Flinders Petrie." *Biblical Archaeologist* 47 (1984): 220–223.

Petrie, W. M. Flinders. *Racial Types from Egypt*. London, 1887. Also known as *Racial Photographs from the Egyptian Monuments*.

Petrie, W. M. Flinders. *Methods and Aims in Archaeology*. London, 1904.

Petrie, W. M. Flinders. *The Revolutions of Civilisation*. London, 1911.

Petrie, W. M. Flinders. *Seventy Years in Archaeology*. London, 1931.

Uphill, Eric P. "A Bibliography of Sir William Matthew Flinders Petrie (1853–1942)." *Journal of Near Eastern Studies* 31 (1972): 356–379.

NEIL ASHER SILBERMAN

PETROGRAPHY. The study of rocks and similar materials in thin sections under a microscope, using high magnifications, is known as petrography. The method has been applied to pottery since the end of the nineteenth century—for almost as long as it has been in use in geology to examine rocks. To make a thin section, a 5-millimeter-thick slice of the object to be examined is glued to a glass slide and then ground to a thickness of 30 microns (0.03 mm). At this thickness most minerals become transparent to light. The petrographic microscope includes several components that alter the light passing through the thin section and provide each mineral with a unique set of optical properties that can be identified under the microscope. Thin sections are inexpensive to prepare; the training to analyze them is not complicated; and they can be stored for future reference and reexamination as many times as necessary.

Petrography is applied mainly to pottery, but also to plaster, stone, and metal artifacts. The method has been used to identify the sources of raw materials in pottery production, to locate the provenance of vessels, to assess the techniques used by potters, and to estimate firing temperature.

The fabric (the combination of raw materials and texture as seen under the microscope) consists of matrix and temper. The matrix consists of clay (of clay minerals too fine to be identified under the microscope) and silty components. By identifying microfauna and silty minerals, the source of the clay can be determined. The temper is the sand-size fraction that, in most cases, the potter added to the clay. Rock fragments, minerals, fossils, and plant material are natural tempering materials; grog (crushed pottery) and ash are temper assembled by potters. The composition of the temper reveals which rocks were used; its texture (shape, sorting, size, quantity) reveals how it was prepared before being added to the clay. Firing temperature can be estimated using optical changes that occur in different minerals at different temperatures. Grain counting, a useful petrographic technique, is used to obtain quantitative information on the various temper components.

Thus, from a thin section which ingredients the potter mixed and in what proportion can be determined, as well as how the materials were processed and fired and the source(s) of the raw materials. This kind of technological information is the advantage petrography offers over neutron activation analysis (NAA), a method mainly used in provenance studies. [*See* Neutron Activation Analysis.] Moreover, using petrography to identify the provenance of a sample does not require a large database of vessels from known sources (such as kiln wastes). A thorough knowledge of the regional geology and the raw materials available can tell a petrographer whether a sample is local. Petrography is particularly useful for analyzing coarse, low-fired ware, when abundant information can be obtained; however, it is also applicable to fine ware. It can be used on its own or as a preliminary study preceding other types of analyses to select representative samples for more expensive or less available techniques.

BIBLIOGRAPHY

Amiran, Ruth, et al. "The Interrelationship between Arad and Sites in Southern Sinai in the Early Bronze Age II." *Israel Exploration Journal* 23 (1973): 193–197. Combining typology and petrography to solve an archaeological problem neatly. A classic.

Gilead, Isaac, and Yuval Goren. "Petrographic Analyses of Fourth Millennium B.C. Pottery and Stone Vessels from the Northern Negev, Israel." *Bulletin of the American Schools of Oriental Research,* no. 275 (1989): 5–14. Petrography used for stone artifacts with unexpected results and an application of the grain-counting technique in pottery analysis.

Porat, Naomi. "Petrography of Pottery from Southern Israel and the Negev." In *L'urbanisation de la Palestine à l'âge du Bronze ancien: Bilan et perspectives des recherches actuelles; Actes du Colloque d'Emmaüs, 20–24 octobre 1986,* edited by Pierre de Miroschedji, vol. 1, pp. 169–187. British Archaeological Reports, International Series, no. 527. Oxford, 1989. Demonstrates the wealth of information obtained from petrography and gives an example of the variety of fabrics found in pottery within a limited area and period.

Porat, Naomi, et al. "Correlation between Petrography, NAA, and ICP Analyses: Application to Early Bronze Egyptian Pottery from Canaan." *Geoarchaeology* 6 (1991): 133–149. Petrography used in combination with other analytical techniques, demonstrating its effectiveness.

Rothenberg, Benno, and Jonathan Glass. "The Midianite Pottery." In *Midian, Moab, and Edom: The History and Archaeology of Late Bronze and Iron Age Jordan and North-West Arabia,* edited by John F. A. Sawyer and David J. A. Clines, pp. 65–124. Sheffield, 1983. Methodical study, using petrography to its utmost capacity.

Naomi Porat

PHILISTINES. [*To survey the history of the Philistines as known primarily from the archaeological record, this entry comprises two articles:* Early Philistines *and* Late Philistines.]

Early Philistines

The Philistines were one of the ancient Sea Peoples of unspecified Aegean origin who settled along the coast of Canaan in the Early Iron I period (beginning of the twelfth century BCE), soon after the destruction of the Mycenaean palaces on the Greek mainland. They were a people of cultural and material sophistication who maintained their own sense of cultural identity in their cities and settlements in southern Palestine for about six hundred years.

There are two major sources for the early history of the Philistines after their arrival in the ancient Near East: Egyptian records and the Hebrew Bible. The first specific mention of the Philistines is from the twelfth century BCE (probably 1191 BCE), in the inscriptions and reliefs of the mortuary temple of Rameses III at Medinet Habu in Thebes. The texts refer to a people called the *pršt* or *plšt,* which must be no other than the biblical Philistines. The records describe their defeat, as well as that of other allied peoples, by the Egyptian army led by pharaoh, who repulsed a combined land and sea attack at the mouth of the Nile River. The accompanying battle scenes depict ships with prows decorated with lion or bird heads; the Sea Peoples' warriors wear high feathered headdresses and are armed with straight swords, spears, and round shields. In another scene the women and children are being borne in oxcarts. This information is supplemented by Papyrus Harris I and the Onomasticon of Amenope. Papyrus Harris I also describes Rameses' defeat of the Philistines in which they "are made as ashes." The Onomasticon of Amenope is an encyclopedia of such various subjects as natural history, customs, and foreign peoples. In it the Philistines are reported as dwelling in the coastal cities of Gaza, Ashkelon, and Ashdod. [*See* Ashkelon; Ashdod.]

The Hebrew Bible provides supplemental information on the early history of the Philistines in Palestine and lists the cities of the Philistine Pentapolis as Ashkelon, Gaza, Ashdod, Ekron/Tel Miqne, and Gath/Tel ʿErani (cf. *Jos.* 13:2–3) as well as smaller, semiautonomous centers such as Ziklag (cf. 1 *Sm.* 27:5) and Timnah/Tel Batash (cf. *Jgs.* 14). Other references suggest that their territorial expansion may have reached much farther north and inland, perhaps as far as Beth-Shean. [*See* Miqne, Tel; ʿErani, Tel; Batash, Tel; Beth-Shean.] A number of passages point to the Philistines' technological expertise, suggesting that they possessed a monopoly on smithery (cf. 1 *Sm.* 13:19–23). Their warrior champion, Goliath, is described as having worn a bronze helmet and a coat of chain mail with greaves and having carried a bronze javelin and a spear with an iron tip. Coupled with the description of the battle, whose outcome was decided by a duel between champions, the Goliath narrative is strongly reminiscent of the Homeric epic tales of Greek heroes engaged in single combat.

Modern archaeological investigation of the Philistines began in 1889, when Sir William Flinders Petrie, excavating New Kingdom tombs in the Faiyum discovered evidence of cultural and commercial contacts between Egypt and the Aegean in the fifteenth–twelfth centuries BCE. [*See* Faiyum.] Included among the typically Egyptian tomb goods was Mycenaean pottery that could be dated by the inscribed scarabs found with them. [*See* Grave Goods.] This was followed by the discovery of Mycenaean sherds in Palestine at Tell eṣ-Ṣafi, the presumed site of Philistine Gath. It soon became accepted that a particular repertoire of elaborately decorated red-and-black-painted vessels was the identifying hallmark of Philistine ceramics. Duncan Mackenzie's discovery of similar pottery at Ashkelon in a stratum directly above an earlier thick layer of ash suggested that the Philistines had conquered and razed that flourishing Canaanite city in the twelfth century BCE and subsequently built their own settlement on the ruins.

Recent investigations have expanded upon the Aegean context of Philistine culture with regard to Egyptian, Canaanite, and Israelite cultures, exploring social, economic, and cultic aspects of Philistine life: Ashdod has been extensively excavated and excavations at Ekron/Tel Miqne and Ashkelon are still in progress. Excavations at Tell Qasile near Tel Aviv indicate that Philistine settlement was more widespread than previously thought and its patterns considerably more varied. [*See* Qasile, Tell.]

It is clear from the discovery of underground silos, flint sickle blades, millstones, oil presses, loom weights, and wine jars that the Philistines were not merely the warriors depicted on Egyptian reliefs and in the biblical narratives: they were experienced farmers as well. They were, for the most part, however, urban dwellers, living in well-planned and well-fortified cities with developing industries. The very earliest Philistine levels, exhibited best at Ashdod and at Miqne, show the cities divided into zones: an industrial belt, a central area with monumental public architecture and shrines, and a domestic area. The cities were ringed by thick mudbrick fortification walls. The general plan was more or less adhered to in each successive level as expansion took place.

Philistine cult practices incorporated such Aegean traits as the seated female deity (best exemplified by the numerous examples found at Ashdod), temples with apses (also known from Ashdod), offering benches (Tell Qasile), votive vessels called kernoi, ritual burial pits, hearth rooms (Miqne, Tell Qasile), and connecting cult and industry—exhibited most clearly in the Late Iron II (seventh century BCE) phases by the four-horned alters associated with the olive-oil industry. [*See* Cult; Olives.] Over the course of time, the Philistines gradually assimilated elements of Semitic and Canaanite beliefs into their own religion. The Hebrew Bible, for instance, mentions the Semitic deity Dagon being worshipped in Ashdod (1 *Sm.* 5:2).

So far, no Philistine burials have been uncovered in any of the major cities of the Pentapolis. However, several cemeteries that may be related to Philistine culture on the basis of tomb contents (e.g., Azor), show great diversity in the manner of interment. [*See* Burial Techniques.] Interment practices included simple single inhumations in earthen graves and jars (Azor) and rock-out, communal graves (Tell el-Farʿah [South], Beth-Shean). Two other Philistine burial customs—both ostensibly borrowed from foreign traditions—are the use of anthropoid clay sarcophagi (cf. Deir el-Balaḥ), modeled after Egyptian examples, and rock-cut chamber tombs reminiscent of Mycenaean burial customs. [*See* Deir el-Balaḥ.] There is also some evidence from Azor that cremation may have been employed, a practice unknown in Mycenaean Greece but documented in Asia Minor.

Glimpses of Philistine mourning customs may be gleaned from terra-cotta female mourning figurines with their hands placed on their head or with one hand placed across the breast that have been found at burial sites at Azor and Tell Jemmeh. [*See* Jemmeh, Tell.] Similar examples are known from the Aegean from the cemetery at Perati on the Greek mainland; from Ialysos on Rhodes; the island of Naxos; and eastern Crete. These figurines are often attached to the rims of Philistine kraters and are similar to large Aegean bowls called *kalathoi* that have figurines attached to their rims.

Four different influences can be seen in the decoration of Philistine pottery: first and most dominant is the Mycenaean. A Cypriot, Egyptian, and local Canaanite influence is also evident in form and decoration. The earliest Philistine pottery has a monochrome decoration, but "classical" Philistine pottery is red-and-black bichrome ware on a white slip. Most of the motifs—birds, fish, spirals, concentric semicircles, chevrons—were borrowed from the Mycenaean IIIC:1b decorative repertoire. At a later stage, the white slip gave way to red slip, hand burnished with dark-brown decoration. Common Philistine shapes are the bowl, krater, stirrup jar, pyxis, amphoriskos, three-handled jar, strainer spout, and juglet pinched in at its middle. Types of cult vessels include ring kernoi, kernos bowls, zoomorphic vessels, rhyta, cup-bearing kraters, and seated female terracotta figurines called Ashdoda (named for Ashdod, where they were initially discovered).

Very little is known about the language of the Philistines, except what can be gleaned from the Hebrew Bible. For instance, the title *seren* given to the rulers of the Philistine cities is thought to be Indo-European—perhaps Proto-Greek or Lydian—and related to the Greek word *turanos*, "tyrant." No inscriptions from Iron I Philistine levels have yet been found, although two seals from Ashdod bear as yet undeciphered signs. Some scholars have suggested that clay tablets discovered at Tell Deir ʿAlla may represent Philistine script. [*See* Deir ʿAlla, Tell.] However, both the nature and alphabet of the Philistine language continue to be the subject of controversy.

The Philistines played a significant role in the history of the ancient Near East by furthering the connections between Canaan and the rest of the eastern Mediterranean world. They brought to the region a developed material culture that continued to evolve, even as it was affected by local, indigenous influences. The Philistines were accomplished architects and engineers, artistic potters, textile manufacturers, dyers, metalworkers, silversmiths, farmers, soldiers, and sophisticated urban planners. They played a pivotal role in the political upheavals and population movements that marked the transition from the Bronze to the Iron Age in southern Canaan.

BIBLIOGRAPHY

Aharoni, Yohanan. *The Land of the Bible.* 2d ed. Philadelphia, 1979.

Dothan, Trude. *The Philistines and Their Material Culture.* New Haven, 1982.

Dothan, Trude. "The Arrival of the Sea Peoples: Cultural Diversity in Early Iron Age Canaan." In *Recent Excavations in Israel: Studies in Iron Age Archaeology,* edited by Seymour Gitin and William G. Dever, pp. 1–14. Annual of the American Schools of Oriental Research, 49. Winona Lake, Ind., 1989.

Dothan, Trude. "Ekron of the Philistines, Part I: Where They Came From, How They Settled Down, and the Place They Worshipped In." *Biblical Archaeology Review* 16.1 (1990): 26–36.

Dothan, Trude, and Moshe Dothan. *People of the Sea: The Search for the Philistines.* New York, 1992.

Dothan, Trude. "Tel Miqne Ekron: The Aegean Affinities of the Sea Peoples' (Philistines') Settlement in Canaan in the Iron Age I." In *Recent Excavations in Israel: A View to the West. Reports on Kabri, Nami, Miqne-Ekron, Dor, and Ashkelon,* edited by Seymour Gitin, pp. 41–59. Archaeological Institute of America Colloquia and Conference Papers, no. 1. Dubuque, Iowa, 1995.

Mazar, Amihai. *Excavations at Tell Qasile,* part 1, *The Philistine Sanctuary: Architecture and Cult Objects;* part 2, *The Philistine Sanctuary: Various Finds, the Pottery, Conclusions, Appendixes.* Qedem, vols. 12, 20. Jerusalem, 1980–1985.

TRUDE DOTHAN

Late Philistines

The Late Philistine period (Iron Age II, 1000–600 BCE) represents the second and final chapter in the history of an immigrant society as it adapted to the continuous impact of external forces, while maintaining the features that gave it its own peculiar identity. By the beginning of the tenth century BCE, this dual process was well advanced in Philistia. Most of the material culture traditions of the early immigrant Sea Peoples had disappeared, and new traditions had been adopted from neighboring societies. This process, during which Philistia experienced periods of decline and growth, continued until the end of the Iron Age. The phenomena that demonstrate the long-term regional character of Philistia in Iron II are the continuity of occupation at traditional Philistine sites, the development of Philistine coastal plain material culture traditions, and the dynamics of the behavioral patterns and interactions between Philistia, Judah, and the Neo-Assyrian Empire. [*See* Judah; Assyrians.]

The excavations at Ashdod and Tel Miqne/Ekron, two of the five Philistine capital cities, provide the evidence for the regional character of Philistia throughout Iron II. Thus far, Ashkelon has produced evidence only for the end of the period, and Gaza and Gath (possibly Tel eṣ-Ṣafi), offer little or no secure archaeological data. [*See* Ashdod; Miqne, Tell; Ashkelon.]

Ashdod, following the destruction of its 200-year-old Philistine city at the beginning of the tenth century, was rebuilt in stratum X. This stratum contained pottery characteristic of the end of Iron I, such as bowls with horizontal handles of the "degenerative" Philistine type. It also produced pottery with features that represent new elements of material culture that developed through most of the Iron II period. One such group of pottery forms is Ashdod ware, with its decorative pattern of red-slipped and hand-burnished pottery with black and white bands. Together with the other decorated and coarse ware forms of the Philistine coastal plain ceramic tradition, they belong to a corpus that developed through stratum VI until the end of the seventh century BCE. During these three hundred and fifty years, the acropolis and the large fortified lower city of more than 75 acres were both occupied, although the latter not continuously in all areas.

At Ekron, with the destruction of stratum IV in the first quarter of the tenth century, the large lower Iron I city was abandoned, not to be resettled until the very end of the eighth century. The Northeast Acropolis continued to be occupied, however. Strata III–II (tenth–the eighth centuries) produced new fortifications, monumental architecture, and the continuation of the stratum IV ceramic tradition of red-slipped and burnished decoration. Also, coarse-ware forms, including jars, jugs, and bowls, among others, some of which had developed out of Iron I ceramic traditions, came to constitute part of a new southern coastal tradition. This corpus is fully represented in its final development in stratum I of the seventh century, not only at Ekron, but at Ashdod, Ashkelon, and Timnah/Tel Batash. [*See* Batash, Tel.] It is in stratum I, following the 701 BCE conquest by Sennacherib (see below), that Ekron expanded to more than 75 acres and became an international entrepôt, with the largest industrial center in antiquity known to date for the production of olive oil. [*See* Olives.] The stratum I city also produced five caches of jewelry with two hundred pieces of silver jewelry and silver ingots. [*See* Jewelry.] These were most likely used as currency, vital to the advancement of the multinational Assyrian commercial policies that also involved Phoenician maritime trade. [*See* Phoenicians.] While maintaining its coastal plain traditions in architecture and pottery, Ekron, like Philistia in general, developed into a multicultural society, as indicated by the presence of Israelite, Neo-Assyrian, Phoenician, and Egyptian elements of material culture. At Ekron, these include, among others, the monumental Neo-Assyrian-type palace and cultic objects (e.g., a silver medallion with a Neo-Assyrian motif depicting the goddess Ishtar), Israelite incense-type four-horned stone altars, Phoenicianlike inscriptions (*qdš l'šrt,* "dedicated for the goddess Asherah," and *lmqm,* "for the shrine"), and an Egyptian Hathor sistrum. [*See* Cult; Altars.]

At Ashkelon, to date, only the final (seventh century) Iron Age occupation phase has been exposed on a large scale. This evidence, similar to that at Ashdod and Ekron, but containing a larger sample of imports, has enhanced the scope of material culture features that define the final corpus of Philistine coastal plain material culture. Tell Qasile, Tel Batash/Timnah, and Tell esh-Shariʿa/Tel Seraʿ on the periphery of Philistia provide further evidence of continuity and the impact of other cultures. [*See* Qasile, Tell; Seraʿ, Tel.]

Textual references from as late as the eighth and seventh centuries BCE that reflect Philistia's status as a separate geographic, political, and demographic entity are found in several of the prophetic books of the Bible (*Am.* 1:6–8; *Jer.* 25:20; *Zep.* 2:4; *Zec.* 9:5–8). In them the Philistines are seen as the Israelites' principal "other," or main antagonist. Their separate existence is also documented in Neo-Assyrian texts: in the royal annals, Sargon II cites his 712 BCE conquests of Ashdod, Ekron, Gath; the 701 BCE conquest of Ekron is described in the annals of Sennacherib; in the first half of the seventh century BCE it was recorded in the annals of Esarhaddon that the kings of Ashdod, Ashkelon, Ekron, and Gaza supplied materials for the construction of the palace in Nineveh; in 667 BCE Ashurbanipal, in his royal annals, is quoted as ordering the vassal kings of Ashdod, Ashkelon, Ekron, and Gaza to support his military campaigns against Egypt and Cush; and Nebuchadrezzar's campaign against Ashkelon in 604 BCE and against a Philistine city in 603 BCE (probably Ekron) is described in the Babylonian chronicles. [*See* Nineveh.] The texts use the names *Palaštu* (Philistia), *'Amqar(r)ūna* (Ekron), *Ašdudu* (Ashdod), *Ḫazatu* (Gaza), and *Isqaluna* (Ashkelon) to refer to the region, cities, and people of Philistia.

Philistia's collapse at the end of the seventh century BCE was the result of the cumulative effect of the process of acculturation, accelerated by the new economic patterns established when Philistia became integrated into the Neo-Assyrian Empire in that century and subject to a wide range of cultural influences from Mesopotamia and the Mediterranean basin. The impact was so overwhelming that, by the time of the Neo-Babylonian conquest of 604–601 BCE, Philistia no longer had a sufficiently strong or resilient core culture to survive the destruction of its cities and the deportation of its population.

The ultimate fate of the inhabitants of Philistia is hinted at in the Babylonian ration lists of the first quarter of the sixth century, in which the sons of Aga, the last king of Ashkelon, are mentioned. The final echo of the Philistines can be heard in the second half of the fifth century BCE, in the toponyms from the Murašû archives from Nippur. [*See* Nippur.] They point to ethnic self-identification among the exiles in Babylonia, who are listed by the name of a local region: *Išqalunu,* "Ashkelon," and *Ḫazatu,* "Gaza." With this, the Philistines disappear from the pages of history.

BIBLIOGRAPHY

Gitin, Seymour. "Tel Miqne: A Type-Site for the Inner Coastal Plain in the Iron Age II Period." In *Recent Excavations in Israel: Studies in Iron Age Archaeology,* edited by Seymour Gitin and William G. Dever, pp. 23–58. Annual of the American Schools of Oriental Research, 49 Winona Lake, Ind., 1989.

Gitin, Seymour. "Ekron of the Philistines, Part II: Olive Oil Suppliers to the World." *Biblical Archaeology Review* 16.2 (1990): 32–42, 59.

Gitin, Seymour. "Last Days of the Philistines." *Archaeology* 45.3 (1992): 26–31.

Gitin, Seymour. "Tel Miqne–Ekron in the Seventh Century BCE: The Impact of Economic Innovation and Foreign Cultural Influences on a Neo-Assyrian Vassal City-State." In *Recent Excavations in Israel: A View to the West. Reports on Kabri, Nami, Miqne-Ekron, Dor, and Ashkelon,* edited by Seymour Gitin, pp. 61–79. Archaeological Institute of America Colloquia and Conference Papers, no. 1. Dubuque, Iowa, 1995.

Mazar, Amihai. *Archaeology of the Land of the Bible, 10,000–586 B.C.E.* New York, 1990. See chapter 12, "Philistia."

Porten, Bezalel. "The Identity of King Adon." *Biblical Archaeologist* 44 (1981): 36–52.

Tadmor, Hayim. "Philistia under Assyrian Rule." *Biblical Archaeologist* 29 (1966): 86–102.

SEYMOUR GITIN

PHILLIPS, WENDELL (1921–1975), founder of the American Foundation for the Study of Man (AFSM), a nonprofit research organization, and its first president. Phillips received a bachelor's degree in paleontology with honors from the University of California in 1943. In addition to his work in archaeology, he was an explorer, a successful oilman, and an author.

Archaeology, however, was his first love. Phillips led the University of California African Expedition in 1947 in its successful search for fossil hominid remains. While there, he met the Aga Khan, who told him about the ancient kingdoms of South Arabia. Phillips subsequently assembled some of the leading researchers of his day and in 1950–1952 led an expedition to Yemen. The expedition excavated at several sites, including Timnaʿ, the capital of ancient Qataban, and Marib, the capital of ancient Sheba. Despite the fact that the project had to be terminated prematurely, it generated a wealth of information that was later published in detail by specialists. It also gave Phillips the material for his popular book, *Qataban and Sheba,* cited as one of the fifty best books published in the United States in 1955.

Phillips later began working in Oman. Following a thirty-year hiatus, the AFSM continued its work in Yemen. From 1982 to 1987, it sponsored renewed surveys and some limited excavations in the Wadi al-Jubah. While in Arabia and elsewhere, Phillips was given personal oil concessions and leases, ranking him at one time among the wealthiest men in the United States. He was awarded many honorary degrees and was a member of the Explorers Club.

[*See also* Jubah, Wadi al-; Marib; Oman; Qataban; Sheba; Timnaʿ (Arabia); *and* Yemen.]

BIBLIOGRAPHY

Phillips, Wendell. *Qataban and Sheba: Exploring the Ancient Kingdoms on the Biblical Spice Routes of Arabia.* New York, 1955. Award-winning and fascinating account of the author's 1950–1952 expeditions to southern Arabia (Yemen).

Phillips, Wendell. *Unknown Oman.* London, 1966. Popular account of his 1952–1966 travels, explorations, and excavations.

Phillips, Wendell. *Oman: A History.* London, 1967. Valuable history up to 1966; includes some archaeological background, which should be read in the light of events and work conducted there since publication.

JAMES A. SAUER

PHOENICIA. Coined by the ancient Greeks to designate the narrow strip of land between the Lebanon mountains and the Mediterranean coast from southern Syria to northern Palestine, the term *Phoenicia* now generally refers to this region in the Iron Age (c. 1200–332 BCE), even though the culture had earlier antecedents. The following discussion is restricted to these geographic and chronological limits.

The inhabitants of Phoenicia, because of their seacoast location and the region's limited agricultural land, developed a mercantile economy based on the export of products from the abundant coniferous forests that covered the mountains. This was supplemented by a thriving industrial complex for the manufacture of small objects that became the hallmark of their business interests throughout the Mediterranean world. Iron Age Phoenicia was not a nation, but rather a collection of cities built around natural harbors along the coast. While they shared a common culture, these small states remained independent, competing with each other in the international marketplace. A true history of Phoenicia would thus be that of the individual cities; however, it is a history that cannot be written because there are insufficient textual and archaeological data.

The rare written documents from Iron Age Phoenicia are mostly short funerary inscriptions and brief accounts of temple construction and repair. These texts do not recount history, so that exterior sources, such as contemporary Egyptian and Mesopotamian documents, the Hebrew Bible, and numerous classical writers, must be used. Although there was a native Phoenician literary tradition, this is now known only from quotations in later works, often at third hand. For example, the Roman historian Josephus and the early Christian writer Eusebius preserve portions of histories by earlier classical authors based on still earlier Phoenician originals. Most of the facts and events of internal Phoenician history are gleaned from these and similar works and must therefore be treated with caution.

The archaeological record is inadequate, as many of Phoenicia's principle cities lie beneath modern ones and cannot be examined. Even where excavation is possible, information is disappointing. At Byblos, which has been completely uncovered, for example, most of the Phoenician period is lacking. Sarafand (classical Sarepta) and Tyre have yielded only limited Phoenician remains, and current excavations at Tell Kazel and Tell ʿArqa on the Syro-Lebanese border have discovered small provincial Iron Age towns. Nothing is known of important coastal cities like Arwad, Beirut, and Sidon. Fortunately, there are important cemetery sites of the period near Beirut, Sidon, and elsewhere, and imposing temple complexes at ʿAmrit and Sidon.

History. The end of the Late Bronze Age (twelfth century BCE) was a watershed in ancient history. Throughout the Mediterranean world, socioeconomic systems collapsed, empires disappeared, and a wave of immigrants from the Aegean and western Anatolia moved eastward by land and sea. Dubbed the Sea Peoples by modern scholars, after the Egyptian term for them, they are usually credited with most of the destruction that took place in the eastern Mediterranean. They remain elusive, however, and recent studies suggest they were but one element of a much broader phenomenon. In Phoenicia, there is little trace of these western invaders, and opinion remains divided as to what role, if any, they played there.

The first two centuries of the Iron Age must have been a "golden age" for Phoenicia, in spite of the paucity of data to prove it. Still, the archaeological record and contemporary Egyptian and Assyrian documents show that Tyre, Sidon, Sarafand, Byblos, and Aradus flourished then. As a result of the collapse of the Late Bronze Age palace economies that destroyed all major powers from Greece to the Levant, there was no external interference in the development of the coastal cities. By the beginning of the tenth century BCE, the formation of classical Phoenician civilization was complete, along with a rapidly expanding population indicated by new town sites and cemeteries. The Phoenicians emerged as the chief sea power in eastern Mediterranean waters and, at least as early as the ninth century BCE, began their commercial expansion toward the west. Many reasons have been given for this expansion, but the main stimulus was undoubtedly the search for metals needed for the growing Phoenician manufacturing industry, metals they found in the rich copper mines of Cyprus and in the silver, tin, and copper mines of the Iberian Peninsula.

From the ninth century onward, Phoenicia was subjected to varying degrees of domination by the new empires that succeeded each other in the east. Assyrian kings from Ashurnasirpal II (883–859 BCE) to Ashurbanipal (668–633 BCE) regularly campaigned eastward to the Mediterranean coast. It is clear from the Assyrian annals that while they regularly wreaked punishment and destruction on the Aramean and North Syrian states, they generally did not attack the Phoenician cities but instead exacted tribute. Phoenicia also gave the land-bound Assyrians access to the lucrative Mediterranean commerce from which they extracted additional income.

According to documents from the reign of Tiglath-Pileser III (745–727 BCE) and a treaty between Esarhaddon (680–669 BCE) and the king of Tyre, Assyrian officials were resident at key port cities. They oversaw the shipping there, collecting taxes on the export-import trade and on the felling of cedar trees. As long as the tribute and taxes were forthcoming, Assyrian rule over the Phoenician cities was relatively mild, allowing them a semiautonomous status. While hostile military action may have been undertaken against the Phoenician cities by Tiglath-Pileser III, the first clear indication in the annals is to battles against Sidon and Tyre by Sennacherib (704–681 BCE). The following two rulers describe a second destruction of Sidon and both mainland Tyre and its island stronghold, which, like numerous cities and kingdoms in Assyria's western provinces, had refused to pay tribute. The destruction of Nineveh by the Babylonian king Nabopolassar (626–605 BCE) in 612 BCE ended Assyrian domination in the west. Nebuchadrezzar (605–562 BCE) then led a series of campaigns that brought all of Syria-Palestine under his control. Babylonian rule in Phoenicia was similar to that of Assyria, including annual tribute and taxes and resident officials to assure their payment. A few decades later Nabonidus (556–539 BCE) was defeated by Cyrus of Persia, and the short-lived Babylonian Empire came to a close.

With the creation of an even larger and better-organized Persian Empire under Cyrus (559–530 BCE), Phoenicia, Cyprus, and Egypt formed the Fifth Satrapy (province), whose capital was Sidon. Like the Assyrians and Babylonians, the Persians were interested in the Phoenician commercial ties to the west, but also in the Phoenician fleets and maritime expertise used extensively in Persia's long and ultimately unsuccessful attempt to conquer Greece. The Phoenician cities prospered under the Persians and the whole period (539–

332 BCE) was generally a time of peace. The trade network in which the Phoenicians then played a central role stretched from Gibraltar to Persia, from the Caucasus to Nubia. The introduction of coinage in Phoenicia greatly facilitated this international commerce—at Sidon in about 450 BCE and shortly thereafter at Tyre, Aradus, and Byblos. The material affluence of these cities under the Persians is reflected in the temples at Amrit and Sidon and in the high level of wealth among the populace at large. This prosperous and peaceful life of the Phoenician cities was interrupted several times in the fourth century BCE by local uprisings attempting to get rid of Persian rule. Although such revolts were put down, they were one sign of the unrest and divided loyalties within the Phoenician cities that eventually helped pave the way for the Macedonian conquest in 332 BCE.

It is more difficult to define the role of Egypt in Phoenician affairs during the Iron Age. By the mid-twelfth century BCE, Egypt had ceased to be a power in Southwest Asia. Its foreign policy was reduced to playing one local state against another, to joining Canaanite coalitions against the Assyrians and Babylonians, and to isolated military campaigns of their own. The one attempt to rebuild an empire is credited to Psamtik I (664–610 BCE) and Necho II (610–595 BCE) of the twenty-sixth dynasty. This was brief, however, as Necho II was defeated by the Babylonians at Carchemish in 605 BCE, ending any Egyptian hopes of rebuilding its empire in the region. In the face of the Assyrian and Babylonian empires, Egypt could do little more than safeguard its own frontiers while undertaking a policy of fomenting unrest in Canaan whenever possible. Egypt's northern border was breached in 525 BCE at the battle of Pelusium, when the Persian ruler Cambyses added the Nile kingdom to his expanding empire.

Culture. The Phoenician language is a later form of Canaanite (or West Semitic) used in Phoenicia itself and in North Syria, Cilicia, Cyprus, and elsewhere, preserved in texts dating from the eleventh to the first centuries BCE. Several local dialects can be identified through differing grammatical features. Texts of historical, economic, or religious (other than funerary) content are rare. Phoenician was written from right to left in a consonantal alphabet which, on present evidence, originated in Palestine during the middle centuries of the second millennium BCE. All known texts, however, are inscribed on durable materials such as stone or bronze. Alphabetic writing could well have been used earlier in Phoenicia and elsewhere on a perishable material such as papyrus that has not survived the wet climate of the region. The Phoenicians transmitted this alphabet to Greece, perhaps in about the mid-eighth century BCE, when Greek texts appear in the Phoenician script with a few changes to accommodate the phonemes of the Greek language. Some now argue that this borrowing took place as early as the eleventh century BCE.

The basic characteristic of Phoenician art is its blending of styles borrowed from most artistic traditions of the ancient world. The inventiveness by which the Phoenician artist combined, for example, Aegean, Hittite, and Egyptian artistic forms and motifs formed a distinct style easily recognizable as Phoenician. This style, however, originated in Canaanite antecedents of the Middle and Late Bronze Ages as seen, for example, on North Syrian cylinder seals and the ivories of Ugarit and Megiddo. These illustrate that the Phoenicians of the Iron Age improved upon but did not invent the style that became a hallmark of their civilization.

Phoenician craftsmen excelled in the manufacture of small objects such as gold jewelry, engraved metal dishes, and ivories. They were particularly adept at producing varicolored glass bottles and flasks because the chemical properties of the sand along the Phoenician coast were especially suited to this industry. Among their finest products were scarabs of hard stones based on Egyptian originals but made in a unique Phoenician, or Greco-Phoenician, style. All these objects were easily transported and were an essential element in the Phoenician mercantile economy. Their popularity is evidenced not only by their widespread distribution, but also by local imitations. As Phoenician trade centers were established overseas, immigrant craftsmen set up local workshops, training foreign artists to help meet the demand for Phoenician manufactured items.

The purple dye industry for which the Phoencians are so well known had a similar history. The dye was made from secretions in the Murex marine snail, common around the Mediterranean coastline. Dye installations were already in existence along the Phoenician coast in the Late Bronze Age, but it was in the Iron Age that production reached its height. As they expanded their commercial interests and trade centers, the Phoenicians established dye factories at many sites in the west.

Although they were expert in the production of small objects, Phoenician artists fell short when it came to larger objects in stone, represented mostly by sarcophagi and funerary stelae. While there are some fine pieces, like the marble figures of children dedicated to Eshmun at Sidon and the stone sarcophagi from that site, they are of the Persian and later periods and show the influence of Hellenistic art. Earlier pieces, such as the sarcophagus of Ahiram from Byblos and the newly discovered funerary stelae from Tyre, are clumsy and technically unappealing.

Religion. Most of what is known about Phoenician religious beliefs and practices comes from secondhand sources, primarily classical and early Christian writers and the Hebrew Bible, all of which viewed the Phoenician religion from their own perspective. Philo of Byblos, for example, transmits earlier Phoenician ideas via the euhemeristic approach of his day; statements in the Hebrew Bible, while contemporary to Iron Age Phoenicia, were influenced by the prophetic movement that saw all foreign religious systems as enemies of Yahweh. Even the Late Bronze Age Canaanite religion, as described primarily in the cultic and mythological literature of Ugarit, is not a sure guide to Phoenician thought because it represents a theological system of an earlier time.

Iron Age Phoenicia itself offers only meager textual and archaeological data. While several Phoenician deities are noted in the texts, little is known of their function and character. No national pantheon can be defined as there was no national political identity that required one; deities were, rather, associated with individual cities. The chief god at Byblos is known only from his title Baal, "The Lord," a common appellation of Phoenician gods, often referred to as "Lord" of a place, city, or attribute. Other "Baals" appear in the Byblian texts, namely, Baal Shamêm, "Lord of the sky," and Baal Addîr, "Mighty Lord." Scholars are divided as to whether these should be considered divine epithets or epithets hypostatized into distinct new deities. Is Baal Shamêm, for example, a deity in his own right or is this merely a title of another, perhaps El, head of the older Canaanite pantheon? All these gods were overshadowed by Baalat Gubla, "Mistress of Byblos," a fertility goddess attested from earlier times and portrayed with the attributes of the Egyptian Hathor. She was the protectress of the city and its kings and was later identified with Aphrodite. Texts from Byblos also mention "the assembly of the holy gods of Byblos," recalling similar divine assemblies at Ugarit and elsewhere.

The chief god of Sidon was "the lord of Sidon," though he is mentioned only once and his personal name is unknown. As at Byblos, a fertility goddess, Ashtart (Astarte), held the preeminent position in the Sidonian pantheon. Ashtart played a minor role in the older Canaanite religion but became the protectress of Sidon and its rulers in Phoenician times. Ashtart was similarly an important goddess at Tyre where she was also known as Tannit, probably an attribute of Ashtart later personified as a distinct goddess in the western Punic world. Another prominent god of Sidon was Eshmun, a god of healing worshipped there from the seventh century BCE in his large temple outside the city. As a god of healing, Eshmun was widely honored. It seems likely that he was the god of healing in the temple at ʿAmrit, known there by his epithet Shadrapa, "the protective spirit of healing." Like Tannit, Shadrapa, originally an attribute, became a separate deity (Satrapes) in Hellenistic times.

The chief god of Tyre was Melqart (**Milk-qart*), "King of the City," unknown before the first millennium BCE. It is generally felt that Melqart was the divinized personification of the ideal Phoenician king, perhaps a semidivine ancestor of the Tyrian rulers and founder of the city. Texts from Phoenicia itself mention Melqart only as a human personal name, but the god does appear in the treaty between Tyre and Esarhaddon of Assyria as one of the principle deities of the city (among whom were Ashtart, Baal Shamêm, and Baal Malage, the latter perhaps a maritime deity). Although maritime deities must have been of great importance to Phoenician seafarers, the extant Iron Age documentation produces only one sure example, portrayed but not named on the earliest coinage of Aradus. Classical sources, of course, are replete with Phoenician gods of the sea such as Baal of Beirut, equated with Poseidon.

The religious role of Phoenician kings is little known. By analogy to contemporary societies, priestly functions were part of a ruler's duties. The stela of Yehawmilk of Byblos shows him before the "Lady of Byblos" apparently officiating at some ritual, echoed by the same scene on a small plaque from Byblos of about the same date. A king and queen of Sidon as well as their son carried the title "priest(ess) of Ashtart" but this may have been a local practice and it cannot be assumed that Phoenician kings in general served as high priests of their city goddesses. Kings built and repaired temples, ruled on behalf of the titular deity of their cities, and were referred to as "the father and mother" of their people, perhaps as the earthly representative of that deity.

While the texts indicate that many temples were active, archaeology has produced little more than the temples of Eshmun (Shadrapa) at ʿAmrit and Sidon. A tiny shrine was found in the industrial quarter at Sarepta and a small temple is known from Tell el-Ghassil in the Biqaʿ Valley outside ancient Phoenicia proper.

Nothing is known of the mortuary beliefs of the Phoenicians, but they were probably similar to those in contemporary Canaanite societies. The funerary texts usually include a wish for a long life. One Sidonian king laments: "I was taken away before my time (to die)." Such statements indicate that the Phoenicians shared the common view that the gods meted out reward and punishment in this life, not the next. There is no mention of the underworld, other than in the curse that any who desecrate a burial will have no place among the *rephaim,* the netherworld inhabitants. What deity presided there cannot be determined; the general opinion is that, by analogy to the Canaanite pantheon, it would be Mot.

Tombs of the period were of several types, including vertical shafts leading to a burial chamber, stone-lined pits, and natural caves. Cemeteries throughout Phoenicia show that both inhumation and cremation were practiced side by side, sometimes in the same tomb, for both adults and children. Whether or not the Phoenicians engaged in child sacrifice, as stated by Hebrew and classical writers, has been debated for decades. Both the linguistic and archaeological evidence are inconclusive, and no scholarly consensus has yet been reached. The recent discovery of a possible tophet, or child cemetery, at Tyre has already produced some new information. A final judgment must await the complete excavation of the site.

[*See also* ʿAmrit; Byblos; Glass; Hittites; Nineveh; Phoenician-Punic; Phoenicians; Semitic Languages; Sidon; *and* Tyre.]

BIBLIOGRAPHY

Archaeology 43.2 (1990): 22–56. Special section on Phoenician history and culture.

Baumgarten, Albert I. *The* Phoenician History *of Philo of Byblos*. Leiden, 1981. Detailed study and analysis of a native Phoenician historian of the Roman period.

Bulletin of the American Schools of Oriental Research, no. 279 (1990). Special issue devoted to all aspects of Phoenician history and culture.

Bunnens, Guy. *L'expansion phénicienne en méditerranée: Essai d'interprétation fondé sur une analyse des traditions littéraires*. Brussels, 1979. Balanced approach to the use of classical writers as source material for writing Phoenician history.

Culican, William. *Opera Selecta: From Tyre to Tartessos*. Studies in Mediterranean Archaeology, vol. 40. Göteborg, 1986. Reprint of thirty-one articles on Phoenician art and archaeology by a leading scholar in the field.

Gibson, John C. L. *Textbook of Syrian Semitic Inscriptions,* vol. 3, *Phoenician Inscriptions*. Oxford, 1982. Most of the known Phoenician texts from Phoenicia and elsewhere are translated here, with commentary and philological notes.

Gras, Michel, Pierre Rouillard, and Javier Teixidor. "The Phoenicians and Death." *Berytus Archaeological Studies* 39 (1991): 127–176. Well-balanced discussion of funerary practices throughout the Phoenician and Punic world, including a new look at the alleged practice of child sacrifice.

Harden, Donald B. *The Phoenicians*. 3d ed. Harmondsworth, 1980. Somewhat out of date, but a good survey of history and culture.

Jidejian, Nina. *Byblos through the Ages*. Beirut, 1968. *Tyre through the Ages*. Beirut, 1969. *Sidon through the Ages*. Beirut, 1971. *Beirut through the Ages*. Beirut, 1973. Histories of the major Phoenician cities, especially valuable for the Persian and Hellenistic periods, including extensive photographic documentation and bibliographies of both ancient and modern sources.

Katzenstein, H. Jacob. *The History of Tyre: From the Beginning of the Second Millennium B.C.E. until the Fall of the Neo-Babylonian Empire in 538 B.C.E.* Jerusalem, 1973. Detailed history of the city that perhaps relies too much on classical and biblical sources.

Lipiński, Éduard, et al., eds. *Dictionnaire de la civilisation phénicienne et punique*. Turnhout, 1992. Comprehensive encyclopedia of Phoenician studies written by numerous experts, including bibliographies for each entry.

Moscati, Sabatino, ed. *I Fenici*. Milan, 1988. Translated into English as *The Phoenicians*. New York, 1988. The most authoritative general survey of Phoenician and Punic culture to date, by some thirty leading scholars in the field; lavishly illustrated with an extensive bibliography.

Rivista di studi fenici. Rome, 1973–. Scholarly journal devoted entirely to Phoenician and Punic studies, with an annual bibliography of all works on the subject.

Vance, Donald R. "Literary Sources for the History of Palestine and Syria: The Phoenician Inscriptions." *Biblical Archaeologist* 57.1 (1994): 2–19; 57.2 (1994): 110–120. Well-researched, popular essay on the Phoenician language and the extant texts.

WILLIAM A. WARD

PHOENICIAN-PUNIC. A Northwest Semitic language of the first millennium BCE, Phoenician-Punic belongs to the Canaanite group of languages (Ammonite, Edomite, Moabite, and Hebrew), distinct from Aramaic. [*See* Proto-Canaanite; Ammonite Inscriptions; Hebrew Language and Literature.] In the continuum of Northwest Semitic dialects of the first millennium BCE, Phoenician-Punic stands at one extreme, Aramaic at the other (Garr, 1985, pp. 205–235). Originally spoken on the coastal strip of what are modern Lebanon and southern Syria, it spread, beginning in the ninth century BCE, to those regions reached by Phoenician merchants or mercenaries—Asia Minor, Palestine, Egypt, Greece, and the Aegean Islands. Following its overseas expansion, Phoenician was transplanted to the colonies it founded on Cyprus and westward into North Africa, Malta, Sicily, Sardinia, and southern Spain, including the Balearic Islands. The name *Punic* is used for the phase of language and the type of script developed in Carthage and used throughout its empire, from the beginning of the sixth century BCE onward. As with all the Canaanite languages, with the exception of Hebrew, Phoenician-Punic is attested mainly by inscriptions. The only literary evidence consists of some Punic passages in the Latin comedy *Poenulus,* by Plautus. Phoenician-Punic personal names are attested in Akkadian, Greek, and Latin transcriptions, while some Phoenician-Punic words are cited in classical sources, as late as St. Augustine (fourth century CE). [*See* Akkadian.]

Chronologically, Phoenician-Punic inscriptions range from approximately the eleventh century BCE (Ahiram, *KAI* 1–2) to the second century CE (Bitia in Sardinia, *KAI* 173). [*See* Ahiram Inscription.] A few earlier inscriptions may also plausibly be identified as Phoenician: a small number of brief texts engraved on arrowheads, from different sources, and some on clay objects (cones) from Byblos, dated to the twelfth–eleventh centuries BCE. [*See* Byblos.] On the other hand, a small collection of inscriptions, called Latino-Punic, dated to the fourth–fifth centuries CE and written in Latin characters (with special signs $ and Σ for ṣ and š), express a developed form of the Punic language.

Phases and Dialects. Phoenician-Punic can be divided into broad chronological and geographic phases. Only the inscriptions from Byblos show a clearly distinct dialect, archaic in respect to the rest of Phoenician. That dialect underwent changes over time that can be classified in three phases, the first two of which are usually called Old Byblian: the Ahiram inscription, preceding the tenth century BCE, which is archaic; the royal inscriptions of the tenth–ninth centuries BCE, which are more developed, especially in respect to the form of the pronominal suffix of the third-person masculine singular (Ø/-W, still -H in the preceding phase); and the inscriptions of the Persian and Hellenistic periods that preserved some peculiarities of the ancient dialect (e.g., the suffix Ø/-W) but also adopted some features of the Tyro-Sidonian dialect (e.g., the relative 'Š; Z in the preceding phases).

All other documents from the Phoenician homeland, as well as from the eastern and western colonies (until the sixth century BCE) are written in a homogeneous language. It corresponds to the dialect of Tyre and Sidon and has been named Standard Phoenician. [*See* Tyre; Sidon.] This homogeneity was the result of the supremacy of the Tyro-Sidonian area over all of Phoenicia. The identification of northern Phoenician (ʿAmrit) and Cypriot-Phoenician dialects is problematic. [*See* ʿAmrit.]

In the West, the Punic language, with its own distinctive features (mainly phonological and orthographic), is not attested before the fifth–fourth centuries BCE, although some peculiarities probably existed somewhat earlier. After the fall of Carthage (147 BCE), but again probably after the beginning of the second century BCE, Punic underwent a characteristic phonologic and morphologic development: loss of the laryngeal and pharyngeal consonants, the suffix pronoun -M, and the demonstrative pronoun ST and the relative use of MY and M'. This phase is classified as Late Punic.

Grammar. The grammar of Phoenician-Punic may be discussed in terms of its phonology, morphology, and syntax.

Phonology. The consonants and vowels will be treated separately.

Consonants. Phoenician had twenty-two consonantal phonemes, as is shown by its alphabetic series. As compared with the reconstructed Common Semitic system, the velar fricatives *ḫ* and *ġ* had merged with the pharyngeals *ḥ* and *ʿ*; for example, **ʾaḫ*, "brother"; **ġalmat-* > *ʿalmat*, "girl." The four interdental fricatives—*ṯ*, *ḏ*, *ṯ̣*, and *ḏ̣*—had merged as follows: *ṯ* > *š*, *ḏ* > *z*, and *ṯ̣* and *ḏ̣* > *ṣ*; for example, **ṯalāṯ-* > *šalōš*, "three"; **ḏ-* > *z*, demonstrative-relative element, **ṯ̣or*, "rock" > *ṣōr*, the name of Tyre; and **ʾarḏ̣* > *ʾarṣ*, "land/country." This situation is shared by the other Canaanite dialects. As in Ugaritic, *ś* was not distinct from *š*; compare *nšʾ*, "to lift" (Masoretic Hebrew, *nśʾ*). [*See* Ugaritic; Ugaritic Inscriptions.] Transcriptions indicate that the pronunciation of *š* was probably [ç].

Changing or dropping consonants is attested during the history of Phoenician-Punic, particularly as regards the series of pharyngeals and laryngeals. *Aleph* tends to be dropped in closed or doubly closed syllables: for example, Phoenician RŠ for R'Š, "head/cape" (perhaps in *KAI* 46.1), Punic MLKT, "work" (*CIS* 1.3914.2) for ML'KT (*KAI* 10–11). Punic and Late Punic show a weakening and confusion of pharyngeals and laryngeals, which, in the most recent phase, were dropped in pronunciation and used as vowel-letters (see below). Examples are 'KHN for HKHN, "the priest" (*CIS* 1.246); BʿL HMN for BʿL ḤMN, the name of the deity (*CIS* 1.302); BʿL 'MN (*CIS* 301); ʿMŠ for ḤMŠ, "five" (*KAI* 112.3–4). The assimilation of *nun* to a following consonant is characteristic of all Phoenician-Punic (cf., e.g., YSʿ, **yinsaʿ* > *yissaʿ*, "he pulls down" (*KAI* 26.AIII.15).

Vowels. There are no vowels represented in Phoenician orthography, and *matres lectionis* were used only very rarely—for example, in foreign personal names, such as HRN' for the Greek *erēnē*, (*KAI* 56). A system of marking vowels was used, seldom in Punic but frequently in Late Punic, where, at least in some centers, as in Tripolitania, regular use can be observed of the pharyngeal and laryngeal series and of *yod* and *waw* as vowel-letters (*aleph* is used originally for any vowel, then specifically for *o* and *e*; H is used specifically for *e*, but also for any vowel, and, similarly, but more seldom, Ḥ; ʿ is used frequently for *a*, Y for *i*, and W for *u*). From this late usage and from transcriptions it is possible to reconstruct a system consisting of *a*, *e*, *i*, *o*, *u* and *ā*, *ō*, *ū*.

The following developments of Common Semitic vowels and of diphthongs are characteristic. At Amarna the shift **ā* > *ō*, typical of Canaanite, had already occurred. [*See* Amarna Tablets.] In the development of Phoenician-Punic, this shift remains operative. Indeed, every secondary *ā* changed to *ō*; for example, **maqāmu*, "place" > *maqōm* in Phoenician and in Hebrew; however, the original **naša'tī*, "I carried," with the supposed quiescence of *aleph* in a closed syllable, goes to *našōtī* in Phoenician (cf. *nasot*, "I carried," *Poenulus* v. 937; *nasā'tī* in Hebrew). Later, *ō* changed to *ū*, invariably in open, unstressed syllables, but often also in closed, stressed syllables (Krahmalkov, 1992): for example, **ṯalāṯ-* > *šalōš* > *šalūš*, "three" (cf. *salus*, *Sanctii Aureli Augustini Opera*, section 4, pt. 1, edited by I. Dijvak, Vienna, 1971, pp. 186ff.: *Epistola ad Romanos inchoata Expossitio*, 13). While it has not been proved that every accented *á* changed to *ā* and then to *ō*, there was a tendency for *a* to shift to *o* in stressed syllables. Diphthongs are always reduced: **ay* > *ē* and *a*; for instance, **yadaym-* > *yadēm*, in Latino-Punic *iadem*, "his hands" (dual + suffix; *KAI* 178.1); **aw* > *ō* and *ū*, for instance, **'ittaw-baʿl* (<*'ittahu*), in Greek *ithōbalos* (Josephus, *Against Apion* 1.156, for a personal name), "Baʿl is with him"; and **mawt* > **mōt* > *mūt*. Mouth (Sanchuniaton 34, in *Eusebii Caesariensis Praeparatio Evangelica*, edited by K. Mras, Berlin, 1954, vol. 8), is the name of the deity Mot. Reduction of vowels is attested in pretonic and propretonic syllables: the pretonic *i* is elided in *dobrim*, "saying (pl.)" (*Poenulus* v. 935, < **dābirīm*); the pretonic *a* becomes a vowel of the kind of Hebrew *shewa* in *bynuthi* (*Poenulus* v. 932, *b^{e}nūti < **banāti*).

Morphology

Pronouns. Pronouns take on independent forms in Phoenician-Punic: 1 c. sg. 'NK *'anōki* or *'anīki* ("*anech*" in *Poenulus* v. 995); 2 m. sg. 'T *'atta;* 2 f. sg. 'T *'atti;* 3 m. sg. H' *hu'(a),* Old Byblian H'T, *hu'atu;* 3 f. sg. H' *hi'(a),* Late Punic HY (*KAI* 130.3); 1 c. pl. 'NḤN *'anaḥnū;* and 3 m. pl. HMT *humat(u).* Suffix forms exist for the possessive and object: 1 c. sg., possessive Phoenician, Byblian Ø *-ī*, -Y *-ya;* Phoenician and Punic -Y; object -N *-nī;* 2 m. sg. -K *-kā;* 2f. sg. -K *-kī* (Late Punic -KY); 3 m. sg. Old Byblian -H, -W; Byblian -Ø, *ō*, -W, *w;* Phoenician Ø, *-ō*, -Y, *-yū;* Punic -', *-ō*, -Y, *-yū;* Late Punic, also -M, *-im*/*-em;* 3 f. sg. Byblian

-H; Phoenician Ø, *-ā*, -Y, Punic -', *-ā*, -Y, *-yā;* 1 c. pl. -N, *-nū;* and 3 m. pl. Byblian -HM; Phoenician -M, *-ōm*, -NM, *-nōm;* 3 f. pl. Phoenician probably -M, *-ēm*, -NM, *-nēm.*

In Byblian and in the earliest phase of Phoenician (Old Phoenician) there is a distinction in the form of the first-person object suffix according to the case of the noun. It was *ī*, attached directly to the stem, and unwritten when the case was nominative and accusative, but it was *-ya,* written -Y, when the noun was in the genitive or in the plural: Phoenician, 'B, *'ab-ī,* "my father" (*KAI* 24.3) and 'BY, *'abī/ya,* "of my father" (*KAI* 5); Byblian, HRBT, *ha-rabbot-ī,* "my lady" (*KAI* 10.2), but L-RBT-Y, *la-rabboti-ya,* "to my lady" (*KAI* 3; *-i-* is the genitive ending), BBNY, "among my sons" *bi-banē-ya* (*KAI* 24.13). Early in Phoenician-Punic (but not in Late Byblian), the orthography -Y extended to all cases (ŠMY, "my name" [acc.], *KAI* 26.C4.8).

The possessive suffix at Byblos of the third-person masculine singular was -H (Ahiram inscription: L'ḤRM 'BH, "to Ahiram his father," l.1; SPRH, "his inscription [nom.]," l.2), or Ø, *ō*, -W (tenth–ninth centuries BCE and in the Persian and Hellenistic periods: YMW, "his days"; ŠNTW, "his years" [*KAI* 4.4]; 'DTW, "his mistress" [gen.; *KAI* 6.10]), according to the case and number of the noun, as in Phoenician (see below). The feminine suffix was -H in Late Byblian (MSPNTH, "its ceiling"; *KAI* 10.6). Phoenician and Punic possessive pronouns have complementary forms according to the noun ending. When the singular noun was in the nominative or accusative, the suffix was vocalic (*-ō* for the masculine, *-ā* for the feminine); it was not expressed graphically in Phoenician but was written -' in Punic: for example, R'Š, **rāš-a-hu* > **rō'š-aw* > *rō-šō,* "his head" (nom.; *KAI* 24.15–16); QL and QL', **qōl-a-hu* > **qōl-aw* > *qūlō,* "his voice" (acc.; *KAI* 38.2, 63.3); and *koulō* (*KAI* 175.4). When the singular noun was in the genitive, the original m. **-hū,* f. **-hā,* combining with the genitive ending *-i,* became *-yū* (masc.) or *-yā* (fem.), written -Y in Phoenician-Punic (Late Punic is also -Y')—for example, L-'DNY, **la-'adōn-i-hu* > *la-'adoniyū,* "to his lord" (*KAI* 17.7). An analogous complementarity appears for the suffix of the third-person plural, which is for the masculine *-ōm,* written -M, after the noun in the nominative-accusative, and *-nom,* written -NM, after the noun in the genitive; for example, QLM, "their voice," **qōl-a-humu* > *qōlōm* (*KAI* 39a.3, b.4); L'DNNM, *la-'adoni-nōm,* "to their lord" (*KAI* 40.5). For the feminine it is probably *-ēm/-nēm* (cf. *msprm,* "their [f.] number," *lknnm,* "that they [f.] might belong" [lit., "for their being"]—cf. Krahmalkov, 1993a).

As regards the plural noun, the suffix of the third-person singular is -yū (masc.), -yā (fem.), written -Y, attached to the ending -ē of the bound plural in Phoenician and in Punic (Late Punic is also -Y')—for example, QL DBRY, "the voice of his prayers" (*KAI* 61.6); LBNY', "for his sons" (*IPT* 14.1). The suffix of the third-person plural masculine and feminine is *-nōm,* written -NM—for example, QL DBRNM, "the voice of their prayers" (Gibson, 1982, n. 16, l. 5); ḤBRNM, "their colleagues" (*KAI* 69.14).

In Late Punic, the picture of the possessive suffixes of the third-person singular and plural, masculine and feminine, is slightly different: for the third-person singular masculine the suffixal form -M (pronounced *-im* or *-em* according to the end of the noun) appears. It was probably used with genitive and plural nouns but it soon extended to the nominative-accusative. Its supposed origin is **-i-hū* > **iw* > *-im;* **-ē-hū* > **-ēw* > *-ēm* (Huehnergard, 1991, p. 190). Examples are BNM, "his son" (gen.; *CIS* 1.2805.5); *libinim,* "for his son" (*IRT* 873.4); *baiaem,* "during his life" (*IRT* 828.3); QLM, "his voice" (acc.; *KAI* 77.3). In a similar way, with the complementary use of the variant -', Y of the third-person suffix singular was often lost (cf. SKR DR', "the memorial of his family" [*KAI* 128.2]; QLY, "his voice" [acc.; *KAI* 77.3]).

The object suffix of the third-person (masc. and fem.) singular and plural follows the same rules as the possessive: the complementary distribution of the forms, depending on whether the verbal form ends in a vowel or a consonant. Examples are Byblian YBRK, "may he bless him" (*KAI* 12.4); Punic BRK', "he blessed him" (*CIS* 1 passim); *barakō* (*KAI* 175.4f.); BRKY', "they have blessed him" (*KAI* 105.5); and YBRKYŠ, "may they bless him" (*CIS* 1.5620.4).

For determinative-relative pronouns, Old Byblian has Z *zū* and Standard Phoenician 'Š *'īš*. The use of 'Š, Š, and ŠL is attested to express relationship. For demonstrative pronouns, such as *this,* Old Byblian has ZN and Byblian Z and ZN (fem. Z', only in the Yehawmilk inscription, *KAI* 10 passim). Standard Phoenician and Punic have Z (masc. and fem., differing in vocalization); Z' is attested for masculine in *KAI* 30.2 (ninth century BCE on Cyprus); 'Z, with the prothetic *aleph,* present in the Phoenician homeland and seldom in the western colonies, is frequently used on Cyprus. Late Punic has the innovation ST, used for both genders. 'L (cf. *ily, Poenulus,* v. 938) is the plural for both genders. For *that,* the independent pronouns are used. As adjectives, the demonstratives follow the noun and, with rare exceptions, do not have the article.

As in all Canaanite languages, determination is shown by the preposed article H-. Late Punic orthographies demonstrate the gemination of the following consonant (cf. ʿMMQM, *ammaqōm,* "the [holy] place," *KAI* 173.5). The article does not appear in the Old Byblian Ahiram inscription, although it is already present in that of Yehawmilk, MPLT HBTM 'L, "the ruins of these temples" (*KAI* 4.2.f). Regarding interrogative and indeterminate pronouns, MY and M (M' in Punic) are attested, the first for *who?* and *whoever* and the second for *what?* and *whatever.* Interrogative usage is only attested by Plautus (cf. *Poenulus* v. 1010 [*mi* and *mu*]). Compounds are QNMY, "whoever" (*KAI* 14.20, Eshmunazar); M'Š, for example, in M'Š P'LT, "what

I accomplished" (*KAI* 24.4). [*See* Eshmunazar Inscription.] Late Punic and Latino-Punic use MY and M' *(mu)* as relative pronouns: LMY LPNY = Latin *cui primo,* "to whom, for the first time" (*IPT* 27.7); MNṢBT M' P'L' + BN̊['M], "stela that [his] son[s] made" (*IPT* 77.1 = *mynçysth mu fel* + Bibi [*IRT* 873.1]). For *every* and *each,* Phoenician-Punic uses KL; for *another,* it uses ZR or ŠNY (lit. "the second"; Hebrew uses 'aḥēr) and 'ḤRY, apparently a noun in a construct state (cf. KL 'ḤRY H[MQDŠ]M, "all the other sanctuaries [?]" [*KAI* 19.9f.] and 'ḤRY HŠ'R, "the rest of the flesh" [*KAI* 69.4, 8]).

Nouns and adjectives. When transcriptions are present, it is possible to verify that Phoenician-Punic possessed the main schemes of Common Semitic. The class of the so-called segolate nouns deserves special mention. Unlike Masoretic Hebrew, these nouns only seldom have an anaptyctic vowel. Examples are **'alp,* "ox," in *lasounalph,* a plant name (Pedanii Dioscurides, *De materia medica* 1.128); **milk,* "king" (or the god Milk), in the personal name [I]Mil-ki-a-ša-pa (Asarhaddon 60.59—see R. Borger, *Die Insehriften Asarhaddons Königs von Assyrien,* Graz, 1959); but **zera'* or **zura',* "seed," in *zera* (Dioscurides 2.125); *zura* (Pliny, *Nat. Hist.* 24.71); and **súriš* (?), "root," in *suris* (Dioscurides 2.193).

The inflection of nouns and adjectives is summarized in table 1. The feminine singular retains its original *-t,* as opposed to Hebrew, which has **-at* > *ā* (*â*). As observed, *-at* of the feminine (bound and unbound) was generally pronounced *-ot* (see above). There is no compelling evidence to prove that a long vowel existed between the feminine plural stem and pronominal suffixes, as in Hebrew. *Poenulus* v. 932, *bynuthi,* "my daughters," seems to prove the contrary. The dual is rare, its usage largely limited to parts of the body that occur in pairs, such as hands (cf. Latino-Punic *iadem,* "his two hands" [*KAI* 178.1]).

Declension may have been maintained in the oldest phase of the language. Later, the different forms of the third-person pronominal suffix (and of the first singular in Byblian) indicate preservation of the genitive case ending, at least in the singular bound forms. Only for Late Punic is there evidence of confusion.

Verbal stems. The verbal stems correspond to those attested in Hebrew. There is no evidence before Late Punic of the passive of the D stem (doubled second radical) or of the causative stem. The Ahiram inscription presents two examples of Gt (-t infixed) used as a passive or reflexive: TḤTSP (fem. subject, ḤṬR, the "scepter"), "may it be stripped," and THTPK (fem. subject, KS', "throne"), "may it be overturned" (*KAI* 1.2). The prefix of the causative stem is Y- (H- in Hebrew); consequently, the Dt stem (doubled second radical + t) (Hebrew *hitpael*) must be *yitpael* (perhaps YTLNN, "they used to whimper" [*KAI* 24.10]). As the prefix of the causative normally corresponds to the pronominal suffix of the third-person singular, it is possible that, in its earliest phase, Old Byblian (the Ahiram inscription) still had H-.

Conjugations. The suffix conjugation for Phoenician-Punic has the same consonantal skeleton as Hebrew, with the exception of the third-person feminine singular of the suffixed form, which ends in *-a* (cf. Late Punic NDR' [*CIS* 1.216.3f], and NDR' [*CIS* 1.207.3], "she vowed"); only forms with an object suffix maintain *-t* (cf. Byblian P'LTN [*KAI* 10.2], "she made me"). Vocalization *-tī* of the first-person singular is shown by *Poenulus* v. 930, *ca!ro!thi,* "I implore," and Late Punic KTBTY, "I wrote" (*KAI* 145.6); *-ū* of the third-person plural is shown, for example, by the Late Punic P'L', "they did" (*KAI* 130.5). The prefix conjugation also has the same consonantal structure as Hebrew. Vocalization is not surely attested.

A distinction between indicative and jussive is attested in the third-person plural with the forms ending, respectively, in *-ūn* and *-ū* (cf. YŠ'N, "they shall pay" [*KAI* 60.6], and LKN YD' HSDNYM, "so that the Sidonians might know" [*KAI* 7]). A volitive mood *(energicus)* is attested in 'PQN, "may I find" (*KAI* 50.3). The imperative, participle, and infinitive seem to correspond to Hebrew. However, for the passive participle, Late Punic has the orthography B'RYK, indicating a *qatil* form (CEDAC, Carthage, Bulletin 8, 17ss., 1.3; cf. also personal names, Baric, meaning "blessed," *CIL* 10686).

Particles. Most adverbs and prepositions are Common West Semitic. B- presents the variants 'B-, with the prothetic *aleph,* and BN- expanded with N before suffix pronouns. With the preposition L-, the third-person suffix singular was only vocalic—not written in Phoenician but written -' in Punic. Combinations of prepositions are common: for example, LMN'RY, "from his youth" (*KAI* 24.12), and LMBḤYY, "during my lifetime" (*KAI* 35.2). The prepo-

TABLE 1. *Inflection of Nouns and Adjectives*

	SINGULAR		PLURAL		DUAL	
	Unbound	Bound	Unbound	Bound	Unbound	Bound
Masc.			-M *-īm*	-Ø *-ē*	-M *-ēm*	-Ø *-ē*
Fem.	-T *-(a)t*	-T *-(a)t*	-T *-ōt*	-T *-ōt* (+V?)	-Ø *-ē*	-T *-at-ē*

sition ʿL has the variant ʿLT; for "with," Phoenician uses ʾT (Heb., ʿM). The accusative particle is ʾYT (like ancient Aramaic—later, only ʾT; for a different use, see Krahmalkov, 1992; and Late Punic *4th Poenulus* 939), which governs the genitive: ŠMʿ ʾYT NDRY "(the deity) fulfilled his vow" (suffix -Y and not -ʾ; but later, ŠLM ʾYT NDRʾ, "he fulfilled his vow" [*KAI* 115.1–2]).

To negate, Phoenician-Punic uses ʾY, BL, and ʾBL with the indicative mood (the Hebrew Lʾ does not exist). ʾL is used for prohibitions.

Syntax. Some syntactical rules have already been mentioned. Some remarks concerning the use of tenses need to be made. Phoenician-Punic did not employ, at least extensively, as a narrative past tense, the so-called conversive *waw* + prefixed form. There may be two cases in Hassan Beyli, *KAI* 25. WYBʾ (?), "and he came" (1.4) and WYPʿL, "and he did" (1.5; cf. André Lemaire, 1983, p. 11). Conversely, as early as the second millennium BCE, the *waw* + suffixed form is frequently used in the apodosis of conditional clauses, with a future or jussive sense: (WʾM MLK) WMḤ BʿL ŠMM . . . ʾYT HMLK Hʾ "(and if a king . . .), let Baʿlšamem destroy that king" (*KAI* 26 A3.18f.). In the Ahiram inscription (*KAI* 1.1f.), WʾL MLK . . . ʿLY GBL WYGL ʾRN ZN . . ., "and if a king . . . should come against Byblos and uncover this coffin . . .," has to be explained in a conditional context.

As a narrative past, Phoenician-Punic often uses the independent infinitive followed by the subject, as WŠKB ʾNK, "and I hired" (*KAI* 24.7–8). This "narrative" infinitive can take object pronouns, as in YRDM ʾNK YŠBM ʾNK, "I brought them down; I settled them" (*KAI* 26.A1.20).

The common use of the L- + infinitive construct to express a future action, sometimes with a jussive or an imperative sense, is peculiar: LKTB HʾDMM, "the men shall inscribe (they must inscribe)" (*KAI* 60.4); KL ʾŠ LNGB T ʾBN Z, "every person who shall steal this stone" (*CIS* 1.3784); WʿL KL ZBḤ ʾŠ ʾDM LZBḤ, "for every sacrifice that a man shall offer" (*KAI* 69.14).

Scripts. Phoenician-Punic is written from right to left in an alphabet of twenty-two consonantal signs. It developed from a system already known in Syria-Palestine in about 1600 BCE, from which the Ugaritic cuneiform alphabet had also derived. Phoenician-Punic writing exhibits a clear general chronological development, as well as some local peculiarities. It is possible to identify more formal or more cursive styles, even though a really cursive script is present only in a few papyri and in ostraca. [*See* Papyrus; Ostracon.] Phoenician-Punic script is never completely formal, even in the most accurate stone inscriptions. Chronologically, it is possible to distinguish Phoenician, Punic, and Neo-Punic scripts corresponding roughly to Standard Phoenician, Punic, and Late Punic. Phoenician (including the Byblian inscriptions and those from Cyprus and Greece) undergoes an evolution that is, on the whole, characterized by a progressive lengthening and slanting of the shafts and by specific changes in letter forms. Typical are those that affect the forms of *aleph, he, zayin, kaph, lamed, mem, samekh, shin,* and *taw* (cf. figure 1). Local peculiarities can be distinguished, especially in Byblos (Old, Persian, and Hellenistic), on Cyprus, and in Greece. An uneven concentration of documents prevents wide knowledge of local peculiarities (e.g., the Tyrian script itself is virtually unknown).

Punic script cannot be distinguished from Phoenician script before the fifth–fourth centuries BCE. However, unlike the spoken language, some specificities, like the pointed head of *bet, dalet,* and *resh* and the crossbar of *taw,* which cuts the shaft horizontally (cf. figure 1), are already present in inscriptions of the second half of the sixth century BCE (Motya, Pyrgi). Punic is recognizable at first glance by extremely long shafts that are often shaded. The origin of this script, certainly a cursive one, which was typical of Carthage and the territories under its influence, is not yet clear. Punic script continues to be used in the Late Punic phase of the language, but in the second century BCE, and especially after the fall of Carthage, a new variant, called Neo-Punic, predominates. Once again its origin is unknown. It is likely that Neo-Punic derives from a cursive Phoenician script, already present in a less-developed form in Phoenicia no later than the fifth century BCE (some Neo-Punic forms, for instance, are present on Elephantine ostraca). [*See* Elephantine.] It is probable that this variant became the primary lapidary script with the weakening of a strong scribal tradition, especially in the West and with the fall of the metropolis. Typical of Neo-Punic are the shapes of *aleph, he, waw, ḥet, lamed, mem,* and *shin. Bet, dalet, resh, nun,* and *taw,* being very cursive and schematized, tend to resemble each other and may be confused by the reader. Neo-Punic is attested in North Africa until the end of the first century CE. The latest inscription in Punic letters has been found in Sardinia and is dated to the second century CE (*KAI* 173). It shows a developed form of script that is not, however, Neo-Punic. [*See* Scribes and Scribal Techniques; Writing and Writing Systems.]

Typology of Inscriptions. Phoenician-Punic has a corpus of fewer than ten thousand inscriptions. A small number come from the Phoenician homeland and from the eastern Mediterranean (western Asia, Cyprus, Crete, Rhodes, Cos, the Greek mainland). Most, however, come from the western colonies, especially North Africa. At Carthage, mainly from the tophet, more than six thousand texts have come to light. [*See* Carthage.] The main classes represented are votive, commemorative, and funerary. These classes originally had the same or related typologies in all the Western Semitic areas, and it is likely that they spread along with alphabetic writing. As bureaucratic and literary texts were written on perishable material (especially papyrus), there are only very few administrative texts (cf., e.g., the so-called fiscal seals, the Kition temple tarif, *KAI* 37); the Neo-Punic Cussabat ostracon (*IPT* 86); legal texts (cf., e.g., the "Marseille tariff,"

PHOENICIAN-PUNIC. Figure 1. *Phoenician, Punic, and Late Punic scripts.* (1) Byblos, Ahiram, c. 1000 BCE; (2) Cyprus, ninth century BCE; (3) Zincirli, Kilamuwa, late ninth century BCE; (4) Karatepe, late eighth–early seventh century BCE; (5) Abu Simbel, c. 591 BCE; (6) Byblos, Yehawmilk, fifth century BCE; (7) Byblos, Batnoʿam, late fourth century BCE; (8) Sidon, Tabnit and Eshmunazar, late sixth–fifth century BCE; (9) Cyprus, fourth–third century BCE; (10) Gaulos, third–second century BCE; (11) Sardinia, third–second century BCE; (12) Carthage, third–second century BCE; (13) Leptis Magna, late first century BCE–first century CE. (Courtesy M. Amadasi Guzzo)

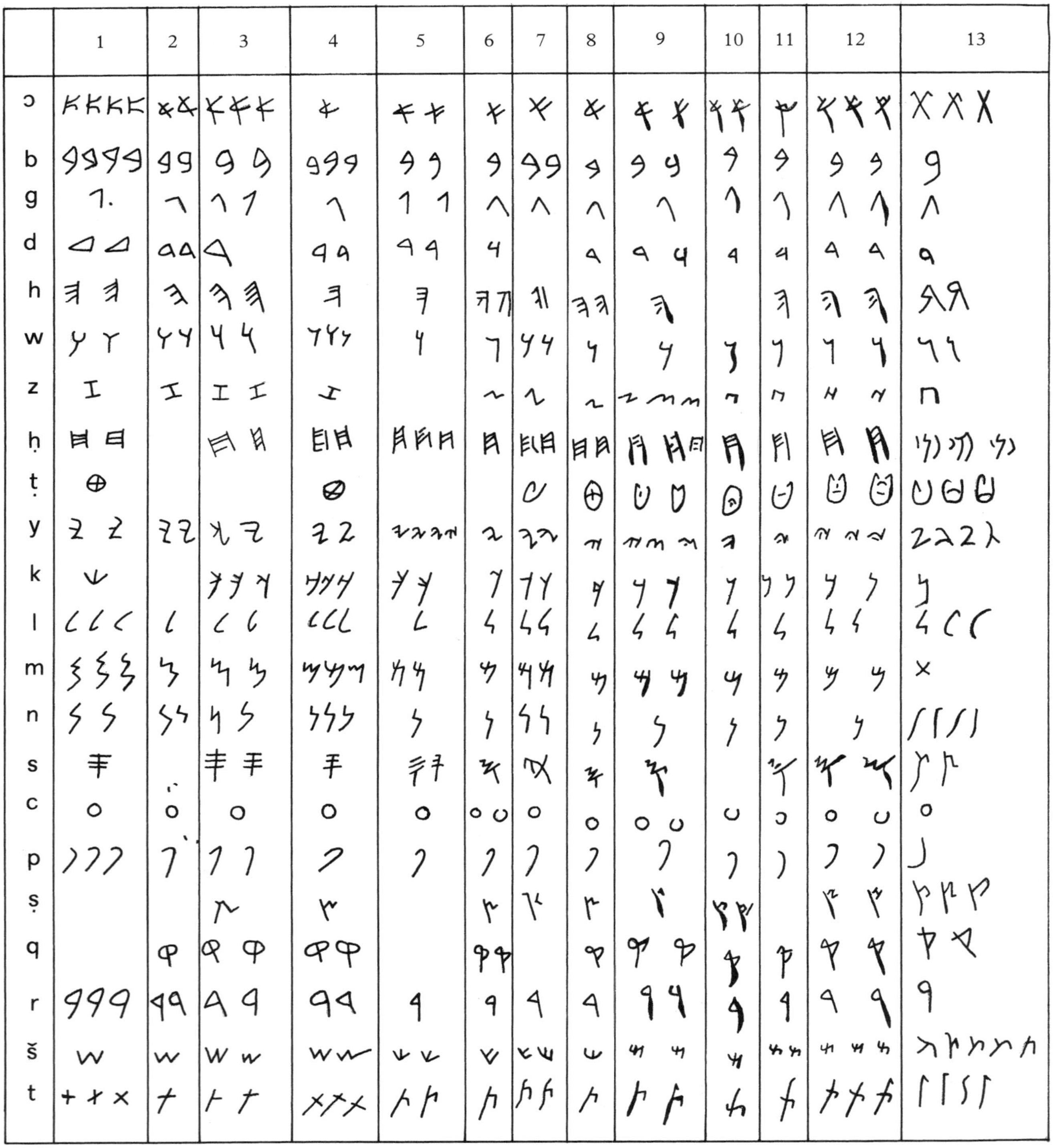
1
2
3
4
5
6
7
8
9
10
11
12
13
ʾ
b
g
d
h
w
z
ḥ
ṭ
y
k
l
m
n
s
ʿ
p
ṣ
q
r
š
t

KAI 69); and letters (cf., e.g., *KAI* 50, the "Saqqara papyrus"). [*See* Marseille Tariff.] The only existing decree (*KAI* 60, from Piraeus) reflects a Greek formulary. A small number of magic texts exist (the Arslan Tash amulets [Degen and Müller, 1972–1974, vol. 2, pp. 17–36], which are still problematic, a pendant [*KAI* 73], a small papyrus from Malta, and metal sheets found at Carthage and in Sardinia). A few objects (especially seals, but also vessels) bear the name of their owner and a few ostraca (especially from Egypt, Sidon, and Kition) contain mainly personal names.

Votive texts dedicate a certain object (a stela, a statuette, a vessel, but also entire buildings) to a deity, in exchange either for a benefit already obtained, or one desired. In the earliest formularies (Byblos [*KAI* 3–7], tenth–ninth centuries BCE), the word designating the object offered, generally followed by a demonstrative and/or a relative pronoun, occupies the first place. The second is occupied by the verb; then comes the name of the dedicator; and then, at the end, the name of the god who receives the gift (preceded by the preposition L-). A concluding formula, which contains the reason for the dedication—a thanksgiving or a request, or both—may follow; a curse against anyone who dares to touch the gift may also be present. This kind of formulary is used through the entire period of Phoenician-Punic. However, it develops and changes, either in general or peculiar to specific places or occasions. The most important variations are in the placement of parts of the dedicatory text and in the choice of vocabulary. From the beginning of the sixth century BCE in the West and later, although rarely in the East, the name of the god takes the first place. It is followed by the other elements in their usual order (i.e., object, relative pronoun and verb, dedicator, final formulas). This change certainly corresponds to the prominence in that period given to the divine sphere, as compared with the offering. The latter can even become purely symbolic: in place of the real objects, models of vessels or of shrines could be dedicated. The god is not only preeminent, it is also probably in a world separated from that of humanity (earlier, the divine sphere appeared to be simply higher in rank). While in the oldest dedications a beautiful object was made (PʿL) for, given (YTN) to, and placed (ŠM) before the god, later, as early as the fifth century BCE, but especially in Hellenistic times, the object is simply a gift (MTNT) or a vow (NDR) that is dedicated (NDR); it gives a merit (ŠM NʿM) to the dedicator, so that he can be remembered (SKR), and probably not only during his lifetime (LʿLM, "for ever"; cf., e.g., *KAI* 19).

Commemorative texts (or propagandistic inscriptions) appear at the same time as votive ones, or only slightly later. They are the longest Phoenician texts preserved and the richest in linguistic data, especially lexical and syntactical. They relate the high deeds of kings (Kilamuwa, *KAI* 24) or governors (Karatepe, *KAI* 26), under the protection of personal or family gods, and are spread across the whole West Semitic area (cf. the Mesha stela, *KAI* 180; the Aramaic Zakkur inscription, *KAI* 202; the Samalian inscriptions, *KAI* 214–215; and the Aramaic Barrakub orthostat *KAI* 216). [*See* Karatepe Phoenician Inscriptions; Moabite Stone; Zakkur Inscription.] Their main characteristic is the narration in the first-person singular, the text beginning with the personal pronoun ʾNK (Aram., ʾNH). They are principally attested in the late ninth through the eighth centuries BCE, corresponding to the period of existence of independent city-states. Being in some cases preserved on dedicatory monuments, commemorative texts can also have the function of votive inscriptions: such is the case of the Karatepe text inscribed on a divine statue. However, the structure of the text is not modified (the Zakkur inscription, on the other hand, begins with dedicatory formulas). Their literary style suggests that they may be copies or abbreviated versions of official documents.

Although it is modified, this form survives in later periods for dedications made by kings, of which the best example is the Yehawmilk inscription from Byblos (*KAI* 10). It combines the usual votive structure, written in the third-person singular, with the commemorative style in the first person. Finally, dedications of kings or persons of high rank, from the middle of the eighth century BCE onward (*KAI* 31, from Limassol), may be written in the third person; as in propagandistic inscriptions, however, the name of the sovereign occupies the first place (cf. also, from Sidon, *KAI* 15–16).

Funerary inscriptions are generally simpler. They first mention the funerary monument itself (QBR, "tomb"; ḤDR, "funerary chamber"; ʾRN, "sarcophagus"; M(N)ṢBT, "[funerary] stela") and then the name of the deceased. Royal funerary inscriptions, however, all of them from Phoenicia (Byblos and Sidon), have more complicated structures, compared to the dedicatory and commemorative ones. The components of Ahiram's inscription have the same order as those of dedicatory texts: name of the object (ʾRN), relative pronoun and verb, donor, name of the deceased preceded by L-, the occasion (thanksgiving or request), and a curse. The later Byblian (Batnoʿam sarcophagus, *KAI* 11) and Sidonian royal inscriptions, on the contrary, show a different structure: the deceased speaks in the first-person singular and the inscription begins with ʾNK, as in the earlier commemorative documents. In the Tabnit funerary inscription (*KAI* 13), the presentation is followed by a long curse against an eventual robber; the Eshmunazar text (see above) is more elaborate and recounts the royal accomplishments (Eshmunazar's mother is associated with the young king) on behalf of the gods (the building of temples) and his "merits" toward the Persian king.

Punic and Late Punic, which, from the earliest times, conform to the typologies discussed above, do not attest the commemorative type (royalty is never attested in the West in antiquity; only indigenous Numidian kings wrote in Punic in the Roman period). The votive and funerary texts may present specific formularies. Peculiar to the western type are the tophet inscriptions (seventh century BCE; *KAI* 61 A–B): votive in structure, they present a technical terminology that has not yet been satisfactorily explained (the "offering" is often designated MLK Bʿ L, MLK 'DM, or MLK 'MR [Lat., *mol/rchomor*], where MLK is probably the name of the sacrifice and the meaning of 'ZRM 'S[T], BŠ[']RM BTM is completely obscure). In Roman times, monumental and funerary texts, sometimes bilingual (in Latin and Punic), may adapt to Punic not only Latin names of specific objects (e.g., QDRYGʿ = *quadriga; KAI* 122.2), buildings (e.g., P'DY = *podium; IPT* 27.10), and names of functions (e.g., ʿYDLYS = *aedilis; KAI* 125), but also entire formularies (cf., e.g., *IPT,* 27).

[*See also* Phoenicians.]

BIBLIOGRAPHY

Amadasi Guzzo, Maria Giulia, and Vassos Karageorghis. *Kition,* vol. 3, *Inscriptions phéniciennes.* Nicosia, 1977.

Amadasi Guzzo, Maria Giulia. *Scavi a Mozia: Le iscrizioni.* Collezione di Studi Fenici, 22. Rome, 1986.

Amadasi Guzzo, Maria Giulia. "Per una classificazione delle iscrizioni fenicie di dono." *Scienze dell'Antichità* 3–4 (1989–1990): 831–843.

Benz, Frank L. *Personal Names in the Phoenician and Punic Inscriptions.* Studia Pohl, 8. Rome, 1972.

Berthier, André, and René Charlier. *Le sanctuaire punique d'El-Hofra à Constantine.* Paris, 1955.

Bertrandy, François, and Maurice Sznycer. *Les stèles puniques de Constantine.* Paris, 1987.

Bordreuil, Pierre. *Catalogue des sceaux ouest-sémitiques inscrits de la Bibliothèque Nationale, du Musée du Louvre et du Musée Biblique de Bible et Terre Sainte.* Paris, 1986.

Bron, François. *Recherches sur les inscriptions phéniciennes de Karatepe.* Hautes Études Orientales, 11. Geneva, 1979.

Chabot, Jean-Baptiste. *Punica.* Paris, 1918.

Corpus inscriptionum semiticarum (CIS), part 1. Paris, 1867–.

Degen, Rainer, and Walter W. Müller. *Neue Ephemeris für semitische Epigraphik.* 3 vols. Wiesbaden 1972–1974.

Donner, Herbert, and Wolfgang Röllig. *Kanaanäische und aramäische Inschriften* (KAI). 3 vols. 2d ed. Wiesbaden, 1966–1969.

Fantar, M'hamed H. *Téboursouk: Stèles anépigraphes et stèles à inscriptions néopuniques.* Paris, 1974.

Février, James-Germain et al. *Inscriptions antiques du Maroc.* Paris, 1966.

Friedrich, Johannes, and Wolfgang Röllig. *Phönizisch-Punische Grammatik.* Analecta Orientalia, 46. 2d ed. Rome, 1970.

Fuentes Estañol, Maria-José. *Vocabulario fenicio.* Barcelona, 1980.

Garr, W. Randall. *Dialect Geography of Syria-Palestine,* 1000–586 *B.C.E.* Philadelphia, 1985.

Gibson, John C. L. *Textbook of Syrian Semitic Inscriptions,* vol. 3, *Phoenician Inscriptions.* Oxford, 1982.

Harris, Zellig S. *A Grammar of the Phoenician Language.* New York, 1936.

Hoftijzer, Jacob, and Karel Jongeling. *Dictionary of the North-West Semitic Inscriptions.* Leiden and New York, 1995.

Huehnergard, John. "The Development of Third Person Suffixes in Phoenician." *Maarav* 7 (1991): 181–194.

Jongeling, Karel. "Names in Neo-Punic Inscriptions." Ph.D. diss., Rijksuniversiteit te Groningen, 1984.

Krahmalkov, Charles R. "The Punic Speech of Hanno." *Orientalia,* n.s. 39 (1970): 52–74.

Krahmalkov, Charles R. "The Punic Monologues of Hanno." *Orientalia,* n.s. 57 (1988): 55–[?].

Krahmalkov, Charles R. "Languages: Phoenician." In *The Anchor Bible Dictionary,* vol. 4, pp. 222–223. New York, 1992.

Krahmalkov, Charles R. "The Third Feminine Plural Possessive Pronoun in Phoenician-Punic." *Journal of Near Eastern Studies* 52 (1993a): 37–41.

Krahmalkov, Charles R. "The Byblian Phoenician Inscription of ʿBD'ŠMN: A Critical Note on Byblian Grammar." *Journal of Semitic Studies* 39 (1993b): 25–32.

Lemaire, André. "L'inscription phénicienne de Hassan Beyli reconsiderée." *Rivistadi Studi Fenici* 11 (1983): 9–19.

Levi Della Vida, Giorgio. "Sulle iscrizioni 'latino-libiche' della Tripolitania." *Oriens Antiquus* 2 (1963): 65–94.

Levi Della Vida, Giorgio, and Maria Giulia Amadasi Guzzo. *Iscrizioni puniche della Tripolitania,* 1927–1967 (IPT). Monografie di Archeologia Libica, 22. Rome, 1987.

Masson, Oliver, and Maurice Sznycer. *Recherches sur les Phéniciens à Chypre.* Hautes Études Orientales, 3. Geneva, 1972.

Peckham, J. Brian. *The Development of the Late Phoenician Scripts.* Harvard Semitic Studies, no. 20. Cambridge, Mass., 1968.

Répertoire d'épigraphie sémitique (RES). Paris, 1900–.

Reynolds, J. M., and J. B. Ward-Perkins. *The Inscriptions of Roman Tripolitania* (IRT). Rome, 1952.

Segert, Stanislav. *A Grammar of Phoenician and Punic.* Munich, 1976.

Sznycer, Maurice. *Les passages puniques en transcription latine dans le Poenulus de Plaute.* Paris, 1967.

Tomback, Richard S. *A Comparative Semitic Lexicon of the Phoenician and Punic Languages.* Society of Biblical Literature, Dissertation Series, 32. Missoula, 1978.

MARIA GIULIA AMADASI GUZZO

PHOENICIANS. In spite of recent advances in historical and archaeological research, the story of the Phoenicians remains an elusive one. The broad geographical spread of their civilization, which extended throughout the Mediterranean basin and beyond, makes any synthesis of the subject difficult. The problem is further complicated by the paucity of written and archaeological evidence for their existence in ancient Phoenicia (modern Lebanon). With the notable exception of Byblos and Sarepta (biblical Zarephath), none of the primary Phoenician coastal sites has been systematically excavated below Roman-period occupation levels. For Byblos itself, the evidence is largely restricted to the preceding Bronze Age (third and second millennia BCE), the period antedating the flourishing of Phoenician culture in the Iron Age.

Even the etymology of the term *Phoenician,* which is adapted from the ancient Greek *Phoinikos,* remains unclear (Muhly, 1970). Among other meanings, it signified the color red-purple or crimson, which may have denated the reddish color of the Phoenicians' hair or skin or perhaps their production of a highly prized purple dye. At any rate, it was clearly a term applied to them by others. As for the designation that the Phoenicians applied collectively to themselves, the evidence is unclear. The term *Canaanite* (used broadly in ancient Near Eastern documents to describe the inhabitants of Syria-Palestine) remains the most likely guess.

The origins and ethnic identity of the Phoenicians are also unclear (Röllig, 1983). Classical antiquity has preserved a tradition associating them with the region of the Red Sea; modern scholars, however, have tended to reject this account as an etiological attempt to explain the color associations of the Greek term *Phoinikos* (Röllig, 1983, p. 80, n. 12). At the heart of this issue is the question of the Phoenicians' ethnic relationship to their Levantine predecessors, the biblical Canaanites. The extent to which the Phoenicians were the direct descendants of these Semitic peoples and the degree to which they were affected racially and politically by the later influx of other Semitic as well as non-Semitic western peoples remains an open question.

In geographical terms, Phoenicia is more easily defined. Its heartland consisted of a narrow strip of Levantine coastal plain between the cities of Aradus (modern Arwad) in the north (some scholars would extend this limit to Tell Sukas) and Akko (modern Acre) in the south. Its inland border is defined by the mountainous region comprising the Lebanon and Anti-Lebanon ranges to the east.

Commerce and Industry. In several important respects, the mountains of Lebanon defined the historical outlook of the Phoenicians—on the one hand, by limiting available agricultural land and on the other, by yielding their most valuable and exportable commodity: timber. Maritime trade thus became the linchpin of Phoenician livelihood and economy. The cedars of Lebanon were coveted in antiquity as building material, especially for ships. An active export trade in timber between Byblos and Egypt is attested as early as the Egyptian fourth dynasty under Pharaoh Snefru, c. 2575–2551). As a result of limited resources, Phoenician industry concentrated largely on the production of finished goods from imported materials. Carved ivory and wood, decorated clothing and textiles of wool and linen, stone sculpture, and engraved metals are just a few of the product categories manufactured for the export trade. The most important native industry, aside from timber, was the production of purple dye, for which the Phoenicians were renowned in antiquity. Derived from the murex shell, which was available in Lebanese coastal waters, "Tyrian purple," as it was known in antiquity, was highly prized as a colorant in garments and textiles. Large piles of crushed murex have been found at numerous coastal sites in Phoenicia and abroad, testifying to the large-scale production of this labor-intensive dye.

As commercial traders, the Phoenicians often acted as middlemen for other peoples' goods as well as their own (Herodotus, 1.1). The objectives of long-range trade were precious natural commodities, such as ivory, ebony, sandalwood, precious stones, and exotic spices and aromatics. Phoenician long-distance trade was, however, driven by another category of natural resource—precious metals (gold, silver, tin, and, to a lesser extent, copper, iron, and lead).

PHOENICIANS. *Depiction of a Phoenician merchant ship.* From a Roman-period sarcophagus relief from Sidon. Musée du Louvre, Paris. (Giraudon/Art Resource, NY)

The Phoenicians' search for precious metals was nothing new. Many of their trade routes and ore sources were already established by the Mycenaeans. The Phoenician contribution lay in expanding the scale and geographic scope of such exploitation.

As the primary medium of ancient Near Eastern commercial exchange, silver attracted Phoenician interest above all. At an early date, perhaps by the eighth century, the Phoenicians had begun to exploit the rich silver mines of southern Spain (in the Rio Tinto region initially and later in upper Andalusia). Archaeological evidence would suggest that they had also targeted the silver resources of southwestern Sardinia and northern Etruria, which, like southern Spain, were rich in silver-bearing lead ores. Phoenician skill and artistry in the working of both gold and silver was highly regarded in antiquity, as Homer records (*Iliad,* 23.741 ff.) and as numerous finds of ornately embellished Phoenician vessels and jewelry attest.

Phoenician History, 1200–64 BCE. Despite a long record of activity in the region extending back to the Early Bronze Age, Phoenician culture today is generally regarded as an Iron Age phenomenon associated with the reemergence of the Levantine city-states at the close of the Late Bronze Age. The arrival of the western Sea Peoples around 1200 and their impact upon Phoenicia is a complex and highly debated issue. In contrast to the northern Levantine coast, where the archaeological evidence speaks unambiguously for destruction and discontinuity at sites such as Ugarit, the archaeological picture for the Phoenician cities reveals evidence of less abrupt change and in some instances outright continuity. This phenomenon, coupled with the strong similarities in material record between the early Phoenician and the Cypriot and Philistine assemblages, has led to the speculation that the Phoenicians were not victims but rather allies of these incoming western sea raiders and benefited from their intervention (Bikai, 1992). The events of the late thirteenth century, at any rate, marked a watershed in the political and economic fortunes of the Phoenician city-states. The documentation for this emergent period, although scanty reveals an era of modest economic prosperity for a number of the Phoenician cities, including Sidon, Byblos, and Aradus. Two historical documents of the period—the Egyptian story of Wenamun (c. 1075) and a foundation text of Tiglath-Pileser I (c. 1100)—indicate that the Phoenicians possessed an active mercantile fleet and were engaged in a prosperous timber trade by the early eleventh century.

Archaeological finds document an active reciprocal trade relationship between Cyprus and the southern Phoenician coast. Moreover, excavations at a number of coastal sites along the Akko Plain attest to a strong Phoenician presence in northern Israel. Under King Hiram I, Tyre entered into commercial alliance with its southern neighbor, under David (*2 Sm.* 5:11) and subsequently under Solomon with whom a joint mercantile expedition in the Red Sea was launched (*1 Kgs.* 9:27).

Phoenicia's growing prosperity attracted the interest of Assyria, beginning in the early ninth century. Ashurnasirpal II's reimposition of tribute on the Phoenician coastal cities in 876 set the stage for a period of more than two hundred years of intermittent Assyrian control and involvement in the economic affairs of Phoenicia. By the second half of the eighth century, Assyrian political control over the region tightened and military activity escalated, resulting initially in the Assyrian capture of Phoenician defensive camps and ultimately, under kings Sennacherib and Esarhaddon, in the siege and reduction of the major Phoenician cities, including Sidon and Tyre. Under Ashurbanipal (668–627), Assyrian control over the Phoenician coast eventually lapsed, ushering in a relatively brief period of Phoenician political independence in the latter half of the seventh century. Following a brief and uncertain interval of Egyptian political supremacy in the region, Phoenicia succumbed in the early sixth century to the Babylonians and Nebuchadrezzar (605–562), under whom the city of Tyre was taken after a thirteen-year siege.

In 539 Phoenicia fell under Achaemenid rule, ushering in a prolonged period of relative peace and prosperity for the Phoenician cities, which were now granted a much greater degree of local autonomy than under previous Near Eastern overlords. Sidon assumed prominence, serving as the administrative seat for the Achaemenid fifth satrapy. With the encouragement of the Persians, Phoenician trade and economy flourished. The impact of Egyptian and Greek culture was now increasingly felt through trade and cultural exchange. The Persians themselves benefited militarily and commercially from their control of the prosperous Phoenician cities, whose fleets (especially those of Sidon) contributed substantially to the Persian war efforts in the fifth century.

With encouragement from Greece and Egypt, a number of the Phoenician cities joined in a series of unsuccessful revolts against Persian authority in the fourth century, ending ultimately in the destruction of Sidon in 347. Shortly thereafter, with the collapse of the Persian Empire, Phoenicia fell under Macedonian Greek control, Tyre alone among the Phoenician cities refusing to submit to the Macedonian authorities. Tyre's resistance was met with a successful siege and sack of the city by Alexander in 332.

Despite blows recently inflicted on its two most prominent cities, the Phoenicians (Tyre and Sidon included) prospered as a whole during the ensuing Hellenistic period. During the third century, the region was contested by the two Greek dynastic houses which had emerged in the Near East following the death of Alexander, the Seleucids and Ptolemies. During this time, most of Phoenicia with the exception of Arwad in the north fell under Ptolemaic rule. At the end of the fifth Syrian war in 198, Phoenicia succumbed to Seleucid control until the final decades of the second century, when the various Phoenician cities regained their autonomy.

Under the Ptolemies and the Seleucids, the process of hellenization in Phoenicia and the Punic (Carthaginian) West accelerated, and numerous Phoenician cities and sanctuaries underwent marked expansion and redevelopment in the Greek style. The period also witnessed the emergence of a number of thriving communities of Phoenician emigrés abroad—on the island of Rhodes and in cities such as Athens and Memphis. Phoenician autonomy ended in 64 with the conquest by Pompey and Phoenicia's incorporation within the Roman Empire. [*See* Ptolemies; Seleucids.]

Phoenician Expansion Abroad and the Punic West. As is attested by numerous ancient accounts of their voyages along the Atlantic coasts of Europe and Africa, the Phoenicians were renowned in antiquity as explorers and navigators. Phoenician exploration laid the groundwork for long-distance trade, which in turn led to the establishment of Phoenician trading posts and relay stations throughout the Mediterranean basin. These were typically situated on offshore islets, promontories, and inlets—wherever safe anchorage was afforded. The majority of these ports-of-call were probably little more than temporary installations (or enclaves within existing harbor towns) and have left little or no archaeological trace.

As for the development of Phoenician trade, a growing number of scattered archaeological finds throughout the Mediterranean attest to a period of incipient or "precolonial" mercantile activity on the part of the Phoenicians, beginning perhaps as early as the twelfth century and persisting through the early first millennium (Negbi, 1992; Niemeyer, 1993). Such incipient entrepreneurial trade may at least partly explain the early foundation dates recorded in the classical sources for the Phoenician cities of Lixus (c. 1180), Cadiz (1110), and Utica (1101). Archaeological proof of Phoenician settlement in the western Mediterranean prior to the second half of the eighth century, however, is presently lacking. Thus, 750 BCE is currently accepted as the starting date for Phoenician territorial expansion abroad.

Unlike the Greek city-states, the Phoenician foundations were not true colonies in the traditional sense, but commercial or industrial facilities of limited scope. A major exception is the city of Carthage, whose urban extent and geographic situation (with extensive agricultural hinterland) clearly identify it as a colonial enterprise. Archaeological work at Carthage has furnished proof of the existence of a large, densely populated urban settlement already in the first half of the eighth century, lending credence to the city's historical foundation date of 814 (Niemeyer in Markoe, 1996).

The subsequent growth of Carthage and other Phoenician settlements within Carthage's cultural and political orbit (in North Africa, Sicily, Sardinia, and Spain) constitute what is known as the Punic horizon. (The emergence of this horizon, while not clearly defined, is usually placed around the mid-sixth century.) The issue of Punic identity, which is based on our often limited understanding of the ethnic and cultural integration between the Phoenicians and the indigenous peoples with whom they settled and traded, is a complex one. As the archaeological evidence shows, various Punic settlements differed widely in character not only from region to region (e.g., Spain and Sicily) but within the same area. This situation is especially true of Tunisia—the Carthaginian heartland—where Punic presence extended inland as well as along the coast. The terminal date of the Punic period is conventionally set in the second century, based on the date of Carthage's destruction (it fell to the Romans in 146 BCE) and the latest attestations of Punic script.

Phoenician Culture: Language, Religion, and Funerary Practices. The language of the Phoenicians represents a later dialect of Canaanite or West Semitic, akin to biblical Hebrew and Aramaic. Its corpus consists of approximately six thousand inscriptions found throughout the Phoenician cultural realm—in the Near East (Anatolia, Syria, Phoenicia, Palestine, and Mesopotamia) and in the Mediterranean basin, including Cyprus, the Aegean, North Africa, Sicily, Sardinia, Italy, Malta, the Balearic Islands, and Spain. Of the once extensive body of Phoenician literature known to have existed, virtually nothing is preserved apart from scattered passages in late classical texts. As for the Phoenician alphabet with its twenty-two consonantal phonemes, the inscriptional evidence presently points to its emergence in the late second millennium (around 1100). Controversy persists over the question of the date and mode of transmission of the Phoenician alphabet to Greece. In spite of recent attempts to place this event in the late second millennium, the current evidence suggests that the process occurred no earlier than the ninth century (McCarter, 1975; Burkert, 1992, pp. 25–33). [*See* Phoenician-Punic.]

The dearth of direct and informative sources on Phoenician civilization in general is even more pronounced for Phoenician religion, a subject that, in spite of recent advances in interpretation, is still poorly understood. Like other polytheistic religions in the Levant, Phoenician worship focused on the processes and phenomena of nature and its cyclical development. Individual deities were local and site specific, often relating to particular places or topographic features considered sacred. A variety of local deities (designated by the generic title of *baʿal* [Phoenician for "lord"]) were associated with mountains: the Amanus, Lebanon, Mt. Zaphon, and Mt. Carmel. Springs and other water sources were often associated with cults of healing and fertility (e.g., the temple of Eshmun at Sidon and its connection with the Yidlal spring). Paired male and female deities, such as Eshmun and Astarte of Sidon, or Baal Hammon and Tanit of Carthage, were frequently associated with individual cities. Many of these, such as Baalat Gubal (the "mistress of Byblos"), were rooted in older indigenous cults which antedated Iron Age Phoenician practice. Others like Tyrian Melqart ("king of the city") were intimately associated with local dynasties, underscoring the central role played by the deity as emblem and protector of the royal house.

Iron Age Phoenician cults owed much to Late Bronze Age Canaanite practice, as attested by the presence of features common to both religions (i.e., a shared focus on natural and cosmic phenomena, the notion of divine assemblies, the adoration of "dying and rising" gods, and the cult of royal ancestors or *rephaim*). Attention has focused on the innovative features and emerging regional character of Phoenician religion in the Iron Age, a phenomenon evident, among other instances, in the elevation of Astarte and the introduction of (previously unattested) deities like Baʿal Hammon, Baʿal Shamêm, Melqart, and Eshmun (S. Ribichini in Moscati, 1988). (The worship of both Astarte and Melqart at Tyre may, in fact, be associated with the religious reforms of King Hiram of Tyre in the tenth century.) Attention may be drawn also to the emergence of various healing cults centered around deities such as Eshmun, Shadrapha, Ḥoron, and Ṣid.

Unfortunately, the varying traditions associated with Phoenician deities are poorly understood; in many instances, we have little more than the etymology of the names themselves to go on. Such uncertainties extend even to prominent deities such as Tyrian Melqart, whose worship was widely exported to the West (e.g., at Carthage and Cadiz). The identity of Melqart has been variously interpreted, as agricultural, maritime, civic, dynastic, and even netherworld deity. Such ambiguities undoubtedly reflect the adaptability and functional flexibility of Phoenician deities.

Like the gods, the rituals and cultic practices of the Phoenicians are poorly understood. Of the Phoenician liturgy itself, nothing is preserved apart from various formulaic benedictions recorded on Phoenician dedicatory reliefs. As documents reveal, the priesthood was a hereditary institution chiefly involving members of royalty and aristocracy. An inscription of the fifth century from Kition on Cyprus offers some idea of the variety of personnel employed in the service of the goddess Astarte. The list includes scribes, choristers, butchers, bakers, barbers, sacrificers, and prostitutes attached to sacred places. Pictorial scenes on Phoenician ivories and metal vessels depict musicians and dancers (principally female) participating in religious votive processions. Sin- and thank offerings (in the form of incense, perfume, milk, oil, wine, honey, fruit, and bread) were proffered to deities in fulfillment of successful prayers. Votive gifts included models of sanctuaries, plaques and stelae, metal bowls and utensils, weapons, and statuettes depicting the deity or offerer. (Such temple offerings were periodically removed and redeposited in special pits or trenches, known as *favissae*). As surviving documents record, blood sacrifices (involving a variety of animals, including birds) were administered by priests and other temple officiants on behalf of the devotee.

Divination, too, played an important role in Phoenician cult. Signs and omens were variously interpeted through the study of dreams, animal livers, natural phenomena, and communication with the spirits of the dead. Prophecy, delivered through ecstatic revelation (often in consultation with a temple oracle), figured prominently as well.

The various Phoenician cults were governed by a calendar of regular feasts and celebrations which revolved around the agricultural cycle. Attention may be drawn in this regard to the Phoenician worship of "dying and rising" vegetation gods (such as Melqart, Eshmun, and Adonis), whose central rite involved the spring "awakening" or resurrection of the deity following his ritual cremation. Sacred prostitution, which was offered at places of worship and involved young women and boys in the service of Astarte, formed another well-known Phoenician custom. This rite is well documented in the Phoenician realm, especially on the island of Cyprus. Although the evidence for its practice on the mainland is primarily late (second–fourth century CE), the prominence of the cults with which it was associated (Aphrodite/Astarte at Byblos, Heliopolis, and Afka) argues strongly for the antiquity of this sacred practice.

As for the private or popular religious practices of the Phoenicians, what little is known may be gleaned from the archaeological record. The importance of magic and a concern with protection against evil spirits is manifest in the numerous occurrence, in tombs, of prophylactic charms, such as painted ostrich eggs, glass head-beads, terra-cotta masks, and a host of Egyptianizing amulets and talismans (including scarabs). Numerous terra-cotta statuettes of the Egyptian god Bes and the ubiquitous "Astarte" figurines (depicting a nude, often pregnant, female with hands held to or clasped beneath the breasts) attest to the popularity of Phoenician domestic cults concerned with procreation and childbirth.

The far-flung commercial interests of the Phoenicians led ultimately to the widespread diffusion of Phoenician cult. This was particularly true in North Africa, where Phoenician and later Punic religious practice exerted a profound and enduring impact upon the indigenous African populations, particularly in the Tunisian heartland. Phoenician cultic influence in Israel is well documented in the Hebrew scriptures, beginning with Solomon (*1 Kgs.* 11:5]) and culminating, in the following century, under Ahab and the Omride Dynasty (*1 Kgs.* 16:31–32; *2 Kgs.* 8:16–24). Recent archaeological investigation at sites in northern Israel supports the veracity of such biblical accounts. Contemporary inscriptional evidence likewise attests to the adoption of Phoenician cult in north Syria (at Zincirli) and Cilicia (at Karatepe). [*See* Cult.]

No traces have yet been found of any of the great mainland Phoenician urban sanctuaries of the Iron Age. (The great temple [I] at Kition on Cyprus remains the only ex-

PHOENICIANS. *Phoenician statuettes.* Musée du Louvre, Paris. (Alinari/Art Resource, NY)

cavated example of a monumental sanctuary complex in the East [Karageorghis, 1976].) The best written source of documentation remains the biblical description of the Temple of Solomon (*1 Kgs.* 6:2–5), whose form must clearly have reflected contemporary Phoenician models and whose construction was, in large part, due to Phoenician artisans (*1 Kgs.* 5:20, 32). Along the Phoenician coast itself, two Iron Age rectangular shrines of modest proportions have been uncovered—at Sarepta (biblical Sarafand) and Tell Sukas. Both provide important evidence for the emplacement of Phoenician cultic furnishings. In addition to a series of low benches along its long walls, the eighth-century structure at Sarepta contained a rear altar or offering table made of ashlar masonry and a stone socket for a dressed standing stone or *betyl* ("house of God").

The most monumental example of a Phoenician open-air precinct or enclosure may be found in the temple of Eshmun at Bostan esh-Sheikh near Sidon (sixth–fifth century BCE), a massive quadrangular podium with central chapel situated upon a series of excavated hillside terraces. At Amrit (ancient Marathus), two rock-cut open-air enclosures are also preserved, the larger of the two (the so-called *maʿabed*) consisting of a raised shrine *(naiskos)* set within a rectangular basin or pool surrounded on three sides by a porticoed enclosure.

Regarding the funerary practices of the Phoenicians, numerous excavated cemetery sites, especially in the Punic west, have provided much information (Gras, 1991). The Phoenicians buried their dead in extramural cemeteries generally located well outside of their settlements. The form of burial varied considerably. Deep rock-cut shaft tombs (often with multiple burial chambers) and built or semibuilt chamber tombs of ashlar masonry were favored by the wealthy, and shallow rectangular pits, often slab-lined and covered with a stone lid, were common with the less affluent. [*See* Shaft Tombs; Pit Graves.] The main Phoenician burial rite was inhumation, but cremation was also widely employed, especially in the Archaic period (eighth–sixth century), when it frequently occurs alongside inhumation in Phoenician burial contexts. (It recurs again in the Punic West during the Hellenistic era.) The practitioners of cremation are assumed to have been foreigners of non-Semitic descent, suggesting that the Iron Age Phoenicians were of mixed ethnic composition. For inhumations, the use of anthropoid stone sarcophagi is widely attested, reflecting Egyptian influence. Phoenician burial ritual is poorly documented; it probably involved some form of ceremonial leave-taking marked by ritual mourning. Surviving evidence suggests that the deceased was wrapped or garbed in linen and anointed with perfumes and other aromatics prior to burial. The wealthy were often elaborately adorned with jewelry (including gold burial masks) and occasionally embalmed, as in the case of King Tabnit I of Sidon. Few surviving texts or inscriptions shed any light on the Phoenician concept of death; a variety of evidence, however, suggests that the Phoenicians believed in an afterlife and in the notion of "rebirth" in the hereafter. The pervasive influence of Egyptian cults on Phoenicia and the widespread belief in a dying and rising god lends support to this assumption. [*See* Burial Techniques.]

The most notorious aspect of Phoenician religion is the practice of child sacrifice. Known as *mulk* in Phoenician, this rite is recorded in various classical texts and in the Hebrew Bible, which refers to the practice of "passing children through fire" (*2 Kgs.* 16:3). Evidence for this phenomenon may be found in the numerous ritual burial precincts or *tophets*, which have been discovered throughout the Phoenician realm: in North Africa, Sicily, and Sardinia. The most extensive *tophet* so far uncovered is at Carthage, where as many as twenty thousand urns with cremated infant and animal remains may have been buried over a six hundred-year period, extending from the late eighth through the second century). Here, as elsewhere, the urns were typically accompanied by stelae bearing dedications to the deities Tanit and Baʿal Hammon. The subject has been recently reexamined by scholars who would argue that the practice was exceptional, undertaken only in circumstances of extreme hardship, and that the *tophet,* far from being a precinct of institutionalized child sacrifice, was actually a cemetery for infants deceased from natural causes (S. Ribicini in Moscati, 1988, pp. 120–122). The extensive archaeological evidence and ancient written documentation, would suggest otherwise, however, and strongly support the existence of this practice and the veracity of the ancient classical accounts (R. J. Clifford in *BASOR* 279 [1990]: 58; see also Lawrence Stager and P. Mosca in Markoe, 1996, for the archaeological and textual evidence for the rite at Carthage).

[*Many of the sites mentioned are the subject of independent entries; see especially* Byblos; Carthage; Sarepta; Sidon; *and* Tyre.]

PHOENICIANS. *Phoenician gold masks from Byblos.* First millennium BCE. Musée du Louvre, Paris. (Giraudon/Art Resource, NY)

BIBLIOGRAPHY

Aubet, María E. *The Phoenicians and the West: Politics, Colonies, and Trade.* New York, 1993. Interesting new study which examines the dynamics of Phoenician trade and colonization in the Mediterranean during the eighth through sixth centuries BCE.

Bikai, Patricia M. "The Phoenicians." In *The Crisis Years: The Twelfth Century B.C.,* edited by William A. Ward and Martha Sharp Joukowsky, pp. 132–141. Dubuque, Iowa, 1992.

Bulletin of the American Schools of Oriental Research, no. 279 (1990). Proceedings of a symposium held at the annual meeting of ASOR in 1988, examining the emergence of Phoenician culture in the Early Iron Age from a wide variety of perspectives; for further readings on the Phoenicians, see especially the article by Patricia M. Bikai, pages 65–66.

Burkert, Walter. *The Orientalizing Revolution: Near Eastern Influence on Greek Culture in the Early Archaic Age.* Cambridge, 1992.

Charles-Picard, Gilbert. *Carthage: A Survey of Punic History and Culture from Its Birth to the Final Tragedy.* London, 1987.

Culican, William. *The First Merchant Venturers: The Ancient Levant in History and Commerce.* London, 1966. Although somewhat outdated, this highly readable work (by one of the great scholars of Phoenician art) outlines the cultural backdrop for the development of Phoenician civilization.

Gras, Michel, et al. *L'univers phénicien.* Paris, 1989.

Gras, Michel, et al. "The Phoenicians and Death." *Berytus* 39 (1991): 127–176.

Gubel, Eric, et al. *Les Phéniciens et le monde méditerranéen.* Brussels, 1986.

Harden, Donald B. *The Phoenicians.* 3d ed. Harmondsworth, 1980. Remains one of the most readable and comprehensive introductory surveys of Phoenician civilization.

Karageorghis, Vassos. *Kition: Mycenaean and Phoenician Discoveries in Cyprus.* London, 1976.

Katzenstein, H. Jacob. *The History of Tyre: From the Beginning of the Second Millennium B.C.E. until the Fall of the Neo-Babylonian Empire in 538 B.C.E.* Jerusalem, 1973.

Lipiński, Éduard, et al., eds. *Dictionnaire de la Civilisation phénicienne et punique.* Turnhout, 1992. Collaborative effort of more than eighty specialists in the field, representing the first comprehensive, encyclopaedic work on Phoenician and Punic civilization.

Markoe, Glenn, ed., *New Perspectives on Phoenician and Punic Carthage.* Cambridge, Mass., 1996.

McCarter, P. Kyle, Jr. *The Antiquity of the Greek Alphabet and the Early Phoenician Scripts.* Cambridge, Mass. 1975.

Moscati, Sabatino. *The World of the Phoenicians.* Translated by Alastair Hamilton. London, 1968.

Moscati, Sabatino, ed. *The Phoenicians.* New York, 1988. Produced in conjunction with an exhibition held at the Palazzo Grassi, Venice, in 1988, this richly illustrated volume explores various aspects of Phoenician civilization in an extended series of essays.

Muhly, James D. "Homer and the Phoenicians." *Berytus* 19 (1970): 19–64.

Negbi, Ora. "Early Phoenician Presence in the Mediterranean Islands: A Reappraisal." *American Journal of Archaeology* 96.4 (1992): 599–615.

Niemeyer, Hans G. "Trade Before the Flag? On the Principles of Phoenician Expansion in the Mediterranean." In *Biblical Archaeology Today,* edited by Avraham Biran and Josef Aviram, pp. 335–344. Jerusalem, 1993.

Niemeyer, Hans G., and Ulrich Gehrig, eds. *Die Phönizier im Zeitalter Homers.* Mainz, 1990.

Pritchard, James B. *Recovering Sarepta, a Phoenician City: Excavations at Sarafand, Lebanon, 1969–1974, by the University of Pennsylvania.* Princeton, 1978.

Röllig, Wolfgang. "On the Origins of the Phoenicians." *Berytus* 31 (1983): 79–93.

Sader, Hélène S. "Phoenician Stelae from Tyre." *Berytus* 39 (1991): 101–124.

Sader, Hélène S. "Phoenician Stelae from Tyre (Continued)." *Studi Epigrafici e Linguistici* 9 (1992): 53–79.

Ward, William A. "Phoenicians." In *Peoples of the Old Testament World,* edited by A. J. Hoerth, Gerald Mattingly, and E. M. Yamauchi, pp. 183–206. Grand Rapids, 1994.

GLENN MARKOE

PHOTOGRAPHY. [*To treat the uses of photography, its features, and its objectives and techniques in archaeological work, this entry comprises two articles:* Photography of Fieldwork and Artifacts *and* Photography of Manuscripts.]

Photography of Fieldwork and Artifacts

Photography has long been a key aspect of the overall recording system in archaeology. Its purpose is to preserve images of excavated areas and of the artifacts discovered, in order to facilitate analysis and dissemination of the data. Because the end product of an archaeological excavation is an empty hole in the ground, thorough and high-quality photographic control over an excavation is essential.

An advantage of photography is that it is detail rich and neither edits nor simplifies arbitrarily. A disadvantage of photography is that it records everything within its view, and does not edit or focus its perspective. As the archaeologist Mortimer Wheeler noted: "The overriding difficulty of the archaeological photographer is to induce his camera to tell the truth" (Wheeler, 1954, p. 174). If the traditional limitations inherent in the medium (the translation of color and tone to monochrome; the reduction of shape, size, depth, and space to two-dimensional prints) are understood, photographs—along with field notes, plans, and drawings—can preserve what is destroyed by the process of excavation. Indeed, the photograph has the capacity to return a viewer to the original site, jog the memory, and help to notice forgotten details. However, as Peter Dorrell of the Institute of Archaeology, University College London, observed, archaeological photography is "rather like the English language, it is easy to learn and even easier to use badly" (Dorrell, 1989, p. ix).

Historically, there have been four practical uses for photographs in archaeology: to locate and evaluate potential archaeological sites; to preserve data as an integrated part of a comprehensive field recording system; to facilitate analysis and interpretation of the discoveries; and to provide illustrations for published reports as well as lectures and other scholarly accountings.

Development. On an oppressively hot evening in August 1839, several hundred people were packed into the auditorium of the French Academy of Sciences to hear the first public report of the work of Louis Jacque Mandé Daguerre, who had succeeded in recording natural images on silver-coated copper plates. It was reported that, for the first time, "the rays of the sun were caught and imprisoned" (New York *Morning Herald,* 30 September 1839).

The technical history of photography has been well documented (e.g., Gernsheim, 1971) and its milestones, from the daguerreotype to Polaroid, are well known. Photographing antiquities began in the nineteenth century. Fox Talbot photographed manuscripts, engravings, and busts in his studio on silver-chloride-impagnated paper. In the early 1850s British Museum officials proposed photographing its collection of cuneiform tablets. In 1853 they considered building a studio and darkroom at the museum for photographing images of their Nineveh artifacts for distribution to scholars. However, the museum ran out of funds for both projects (Dorrell, 1989, p. 1).

During the first years of photography, long before the technology had become either convenient, consistent, or reliable, many field expeditions were quick to employ the powerful new tool to document their discoveries. In 1854 Roger Fenton was sent out with the British Army to the Crimea, ostensibly to photograph monuments and artifacts the troops encountered. No archaeological photographs resulted, but his 350 photographs of the Crimean conflict, a decade before Matthew Brady's photographic record of the American Civil War, were the first to be taken on the battlefield (Dorrell, 1989, p. 2). Baron Gros made daguerreotypes of the monuments of North Africa in 1850, and du Camp took photographs of monuments in Egypt, Nubia, Palestine, and Syria during his travels with Gustav Flaubert from 1849 to 1851 (Dorrell, 1989, p. 3) that he made popular and accessible to scholars and the public. The photographs of Tranchand took in Assyria from 1852 to 1855, in Khorsabad, and later in Armenia and Kurdistan, first by daguerreotype and later by calotype, are of remarkable quality, both technically and artistically (see Dorrell, 1989, p. 3, pl. 1).

When Charles W. Wilson of the British Royal Engineers first excavated Jerusalem's walls in 1864 for the Ordnance Survey, he recorded the finds with pencil and pad, holding a candle in his teeth as he crawled through the tunnels bored along the base of the walls. Because the candle would often be extinguished by rising water in the tunnels, Wilson quickly realized the potential of photography and began systematically making photographic images in 1867 (Wilson, 1871, p. 188). [*See* Jerusalem; *and the biography of Wilson.*]

There was at first no practical printing technology for including these new photographs in publications; editors were forced to have the photos transferred to block cuttings, engravings, or lithographs to be printed. Such images are often described in these early reports as "taken from a photograph." In 1880, the classical archaeologist Alexander Conze was the first to use photographs printed on albumen paper, gold-toned and tipped into the pages, in his excavation report of Samothrace (Conze et al., 1880). The images were made on glass "wet plates" that had to be kept moist throughout preparation, exposure, and development. Dry glass plates replaced them in the late 1870s, making photography much more convenient to do. Although flexible film was popularized by George Eastman as early as 1885, most archaeological photographers continued to use glass plates until World War II and view cameras until the 1960s. As late as 1934, W. F. Badè, excavating at Tell en-Naṣbeh, 10 km (6 mi.) northwest of Jerusalem, had to argue for the use of cut film (Badè, 1934, p. 69). [*See* Naṣbeh, Tell en-; *and the biography of Badè.*]

Tilting-bed view cameras, usually full- (6.5″ × 8.5″), half-plate (4.25″ × 6.5″) or quarter-plate (3.25″ × 4.25″) affairs, with their ground glass and black cloths, were long seen as indispensable to proper composition: for preserving the rectilinear perspective of architecture and for obtaining the image size necessary for quality publication photos. View cameras were recommended in certain circumstances into the late 1980s (V. M. Conlon, *Camera Techniques in Archaeology,* London, 1973, p. 1; Dorrell, 1989, p. 21), but by the mid-1970s, 35-mm cameras were the instruments of choice (Harp, 1975, p. 53), largely because of their low cost and ease of use. A few excavations that could afford the larger "medium format," 2.5 sq. in., found the detail greater while retaining the ease of use of the smaller cameras.

Conditions endured by early photographers were difficult: hot developer, dirty equipment, and oil lamps with leaking safelight filters. One photographer, when his camera jammed in the field, had himself sealed in a Bronze Age tomb until he could safely remove the film from the camera. (Badè, 1934, p. 70). Often, photographers would pitch one camel's hair tent inside another to create a darkroom: the working temperatures of the developer and the sound of sand grinding between the glass photographic plates must have been daunting.

William Flinders Petrie decided to introduce photography to his explorations in 1881 and promptly built his own camera. It was made of japanned tin, about the size, he said, of a biscuit tin. The lens had two apertures, with holes of different sizes drilled in a piece of tin that was slid in front of the lens. It employed a drop shutter, also of tin, and a dark sleeve for changing photographic plates. This simple camera, rebuilt several times during his professional career produced photos of extraordinary detail and clarity (Drower, 1985). [*See the biography of Petrie.*]

The first photographs taken from the air were of Paris in 1858, but the use of aerial photography in archaeology was not attempted until 1891, when a British army officer, Charles Close, used free, unmanned balloons flying glass-plate cameras over the ruins near Agra, India. Although his attempts were unsuccessful, in 1906 P. H. Sharpe, apparently by accident, took aerial photos of Stonehenge in England, producing an impressive vertical image of the entire complex (Deuel, 1969, p. 12; Detweiler, 1948, p. 35). The first underwater archaeological photography was successfully attempted by Antoine Poidebard, a French Jesuit who excavated the harbor installations at Tyre in 1935–1937. Working before the invention of scuba equipment, Poidebard employed helmeted divers and a skin diver holding his breath to map the Phoenician facilities. He photographed the masonry under water, plotted buoys set at critical points, and took aerial photographs; he even took stereophotographs through a glass-bottomed bucket (Bass, 1970, pp. 88–89). [*See* Tyre; *and the biography of Poidebard.*]

During the last decades of the nineteenth century and the first of the twentieth, photography became one of the standard tools in recording excavations and artifacts. Nevertheless, for many decades photography was little more than a way of illustrating monuments, enlivening reports, and providing visual aids for fund-raising efforts. It was not until Wheeler (see above) and his photographer Maurice B. Cookson insisted that site photographs should "reveal every detail of the excavations as they proceeded" (Wheeler, 1954, p. 174ff.) that archaeological photography made the transition from snapshots to scientific recording.

Aerial Photography. As a tool for exploration and recordkeeping, aerial photography can be carried out from a variety of platforms: satellites, aircraft, balloons, kites, and even tall towers. Useful in a rapid initial survey of sites that have excavation potential, air surveys often reveal clear evidence of successive occupations, actual "palimpsests of cultural landscapes," invisible to observers on the ground, that can be readily deciphered. Photogrammetry, the systematic process of aerial survey often used in map production, can provide detailed and accurate mapping for a fraction of the time and cost of a land survey.

Archaeological features appear in aerial photographs in several ways: shadows are visible when photos are taken with low, raking light, allowing the flattened features invisible from the ground to appear; crop marks are the differences in color or density of growth often revealed when plants are growing over underground objects; and soil marks are the visible differences in the color of soil over subsoil installations in a freshly plowed field (Detweiler, 1948, pp. 35–36; Bacon, 1960, p. 303).

At Seleucia on the Tigris, for example, what looked like 8 sq km (5 sq. mi.) of undistinguished sand dunes was revealed from the air to be a grid system of streets interrupted by what proved to be large public buildings (Detweiler, 1948, p. 35). At Gezer, the layout of the site's massive fortifications was first noticed in a balloon photograph, even though the excavators had walked the wall daily for weeks. Periscope cameras were used with great success (and at much less the cost of trial excavations) to inspect Etruscan tombs north of Rome in order to identify those not pillaged in antiquity (Bacon, 1960, p. 304). [*See* Seleucia on the Tigris; Gezer.]

Recording. In recent decades, personnel trained in both archaeological history and photographic technique have been represented on the staff of many excavations. When photography is incorporated into a project's comprehensive recording system, the result is an integrated scheme of documentation that provides a record of progress in the field and of finds, as well as immediate feedback for area supervisors and field directors.

As an excavation progresses, the details of artifacts, structures, strata, and topography contribute to theories of how the site's strata were laid down and what the purpose and function of their tools, buildings, and plans were. Working theories change with the appearance of new data and further reflection. Those emerging reconstructions must be coordinated with the photographic work: photographs should document the evidence as new theories emerge about the sequence of occupation or the purpose of installations, so that when the stratum has been cleared and the level destroyed, the photographic record replaces them.

Because the photographic record must be accurate and comprehensive, considerably more photographs of a site and its objects are taken than will ever be published. However, if details overlooked in the field or considered unimportant take on new significance as the analysis of the finds, plans, and field reports progresses, they often will have been preserved in a well-considered, full-coverage photographic record.

A successful photographic record must be able to fulfill four criteria.

1. *Identification.* Do the photos clearly illustrate the subject? Are the form, outline, and texture of the objects apparent? Are all the features that constitute the character of the subject present in the photograph?
2. *Context.* Do the photos clearly indicate the contextual relationships between the subject and the surrounding area, including vertical relationships (to what has preceded) and horizontal relationships (to other objects and structures in the area)?
3. *Significance.* Have judgments about the identity and importance of the object changed since the photographs were made?
4. *Coverage.* Have enough photographs of the site been taken to assure complete coverage of the subject?

Light and Shadows. The extremes of light and contrast have always posed problems for archaeological photography in the Near East. The light falling on archaeological sites there is about half again as much as on pastoral scenes in Europe and North America. This intense light produces a tonal range between subjects in bright sunlight and those in shadow that is three times as great as is normally encountered. This reality conspires with the limited chromatic range of most archaeological subject matter—tan stones on tan soil—to produce extreme photographic conditions. Thus, photographs at Near Eastern archaeological sites often are taken in the early morning, before the direct light of the sun hits the site (Wheeler, 1954, p. 175; Wright, 1978, p. 185), or late in the afternoon, just before dusk, when the sun's harshness is diminished, and the light of the reflected sky softens the landscape. (The analog is the north studio light preferred by artists.)

Photographic manuals for archaeology emphasize that areas to be photographed must be meticulously clean, for the camera records every intrusive blade of grass, every distracting bit of debris. Anything that might divert from the subject of the photograph should be made as unobtrusive as possible. Surfaces should be evenly brushed to an artificial smoothness so that they do not appear to be significant elements.

Brushing, stippling, wetting, and careful undercutting to provide shadow lines are common techniques used to emphasize a scene's salient features. As Kathleen Kenyon cautioned: "The only justifiable use [of outlining] is to attract the eye to differences which the rest of the visible evidence confirm" (Kenyon, 1953, p. 138). Elements of a scene can be highlighted but should not be falsified. Occasionally, this may mean that the photograph will be ambiguous, for it should not introduce interpretations that were not apparent at the site. It should be no more (or less) certain than the director's original interpretation.

Usually, only one excavation level is shown in a photograph to avoid confusing the presentation of the occupation sequence; however, a photo of where a garbage pit was dug would also show how it cut through earlier layers. Some images are intended to demonstrate the relationships among strata, a point of view for which the photographer must prepare. The goal is to have the photographs, top plans, and balk sections complement each other, so that the dimensions and location of each locus can easily be cross matched to the images.

Technical Control. Photography depends on the several variables inherent in the mechanical and chemical characteristics of the system; changing exposure and shutter speeds and altering development and printing times contribute to the creativity of the craft. However, controlling and standardizing the system's variables can produce precise, uniform photographic prints. Based on Ansel Adams's zone system, the variables are recalibrated at the beginning of an excavation season: film speed, light-meter readings, and film and paper developing time are integrated into a single system of fixed specifications. Beginning with the precise exposure of each scene, not on the object itself, but on a standard photographic 35 percent "gray card," through to fixed-time print processing, eliminating variables will produce uniform photographs throughout the season (see Wright, 1978).

Special Techniques. Underwater photography imposes challenges that do not exist in recording surfaces on land. Even simple tasks, such as laying out a grid and measuring levels, become major feats of planning and dexterity under water. Although nearly any good-quality camera can be used for underwater photography if enclosed in waterproof housing, there are several special cameras that can be used down to more than 1,000 m. The difference in diffraction indices between air and water (e.g., the "bending" of a pencil in a glass of water), causes distortion unless special corrective lenses are added to the camera or its housing.

Because water absorbs light waves at different rates than air does, it absorbs colors sequentially as the depth increases: red fades under just a few feet of water, then orange disappears, and then yellow vanishes. Only blue remains, which gives underwater color photographs a pervasive azure cast, a problem correctable with artificial flood or strobe lights.

Mosaics can be constructed from a series of overlapping photographs to show an area too large to capture in a single image. Because not all of a site is excavated, cleaned, and prepared for photography at the same time, photos are taken in the course of an excavation, as each area is excavated and exposed. Ultimately, photographs may collectively reveal what no one could have seen in a single glance.

Since Poidebard's early efforts at Tyre, many maritime sites have been photographed with increasingly sophisticated equipment. Notable examples are the massive underwater port facilities at Caesarea Maritima in Israel and largely intact ships, such as the Galilee fishing boat, the Maʿagen Mikha'el boat, and the Uluburun and Yassıada wrecks off Turkey. [*See* Caesarea; Galilee Boat; Maʿagen Mikha'el; Uluburun; Yassıada Wrecks.]

Photography using parts of the electromagnetic spectrum beyond visible light has been employed in a variety of attempts to coax information out of archaeological remains. Infrared (IR) and X-ray photography have been useful in illuminating obscured text on damaged parchment and papyrus manuscripts and in revealing palimpsest text where the original text had been scraped or rubbed off. Both have been used to detect degrees of deterioration for the fragments of the Dead Sea Scrolls. IR also has been used to locate painted floors and other decorations invisible to the unaided eye. Infrared and ultraviolet studies have been performed on the Shroud of Turin and Egyptian mummies have been X-rayed with great success to detect whether the wrappings contain a body or to locate jewelry or other decoration. X-rays also aid in paleopathology (the study of disease and medicine) by helping to determine skeletal structure, malformations, and often the cause of death (a broken neck or crushed skull). [*See* Paleopathology.] On a larger scale, X-rays have been used to examine the great pyramids at Giza. [*See* Dead Sea Scrolls; Pyramids; Giza.] Multispectrum "false color" imaging has been used in aerial photography, where the normal spectrum colors of green, blue, and red are shifted so the IR image can be seen as red (Dorrell, 1989, p. 206).

Future Technology. Archaeological photography is changing as new technologies are developed. As desk-top and portable computers and digitizing cameras become more powerful and less expensive, photography may become increasingly digital; it is possible to envision the merging of the photographic recording and computer analysis of excavations and the artifacts they produce into a comprehensive system of recording, manipulation, storage, and publication. When the issues of power, speed, cost, storage, and graphic resolution are resolved, computer graphics may unite still photography, computer and video graphics, motion pictures, color slide photos, and databases into a comprehensive system.

"Field digitalization units" may replace cameras at excavation sites, producing images from a computer printer for field notebooks. The system will provide publication-quality images and, with a computer projection unit, "slides" for public lectures. Powerful personal computers and laser color printers may replace the photo lab and chemicals. The camera obscura, the "dark room," and the fixative hypo, which have been necessary since the beginning of photography, may one day be obsolete.

With CAD (Computer Aided Design) and graphics programs to input the data from photos and site plans, a house or a town may be re-created in "virtual reality," allowing the viewer to "walk" from room to room, down streets, and out city gates. Sequences of levels at a site could be assembled so that each phase of a building or a entire town can be viewed on command. It may be possible to re-create the successive stages of a building's construction, destruction, and reconstruction. These creative sequencings could be recorded on videotape for classroom or public use. As in medical imaging, sequence photos in horizontal "slices" of an excavation area could be reconstructed in a computer program to form coherent occupation levels in three dimensions. The caveat is that with digital imaging, a photo can be altered into something that never existed. Ironically, Wheeler's concern (see above) will have come full-circle: instead of coaxing truth from a photographic image, the new concern may well be to avoid falsifying data by manipulating the digital images.

Secure archival storage is possible with optical CD-ROMs. They provide relatively permanent digital storage that will exceed that of silver photographic images, which deteriorate with handling and storage. Unlike duplicates of photographic negatives and prints, the quality of digital copies is as high as that of the originals.

For photographing small finds, available graphics software for personal computers can scan in a photograph (or start with a profile sketch) of a juglet, for example. It can reconstruct the image in three dimensions, rotate it, apply an appropriate texture pattern, light it with full modeling, slice it into sections, and produce photorealistic renderings. It is now possible to return to early excavation reports and digitize their plans, sections, and photographs, including small objects, and from them produce full-color, photorealistic images. Also on the horizon are holographic imagining techniques that will further enhance the realism of photographic representations.

[*See also* Computer Recording, Analysis, and Interpretation; *and* Recording Techniques.]

BIBLIOGRAPHY

Badè, William Frederic. *A Manual of Excavation in the Near East: Methods of Digging and Recording of the Tell en-Naṣbeth Expedition in Palestine.* Berkeley, 1934.

Bass, George F. *Archaeology under Water.* 2d ed. Harmondsworth, 1970.

Blakely, Jeffrey A., and Lawrence E. Toombs. *The Tell el-Hesi Field Manual.* Edited by Kevin G. O'Connell. Winona Lake, Ind., 1980. One of the best of the manuals describing the new archaeological methods of the mid-twentieth century (see pp. 112–115).

Blaker, Alfred A. *Field Photography.* San Francisco, 1976.

Chéné, Antoine, and Gérard Réveillac. *La photographie en archéologie.* Les Dossiers de l'Archéologie, 13 (November–December 1975).

Conze, Alexander, et al. *Neue Archaeologische Untersuchungen auf Samothrake.* Vienna, 1880.

Cookson, Maurice B. *Photography for Archaeologists.* London, 1954.

Detweiler, A. Henry. *Manual of Archaeological Surveying.* New Haven, 1948. An old classic that has some useful but dated materials on photography.

Deuel, Leo. *Flights into Yesterday: The Story of Aerial Archaeology.* New York, 1969.

Dorrell, Peter G. *Photography in Archaeology and Conservation.* New York and Cambridge, 1989. Probably the best comprehensive survey of archaeological photography.

Drower, Margaret S. *Flinders Petrie: A Life in Archaeology.* London, 1985. Biography of the early pioneer, with some interesting anecdotes on his experiences with photography.

Harp, Elmer, Jr. *Photography in Archaeological Research.* Albuquerque, 1975.

Joukowsky, Martha Sharp. *A Complete Manual of Field Archaeology: Tools and Techniques of Field Work for Archaeologists.* Englewood Cliffs, N.J., 1980.

Kenworthy, Mary Anne, et al. *Preserving Field Records.* Philadelphia, 1985.

Kenyon, Kathleen M. *Beginning in Archaeology.* London, 1953. Classic beginner's book, containing some insights on the use of photography at mid-century.

Malina, Jaroslav, and Vašíč Zdeněk. *Archaeology Yesterday and Today.* Translated by Marek Zvelebil. Cambridge, 1990.

Nassau, W. E. *Practical Photography for the Field Archaeologist.* Ontario, 1976.

Petrie, W. M. Flinders. *Ten Years' Digging in Egypt, 1881–1891.* New York, n.d. Some of Sir Flinders's own comments on his photographs and photography.

Petrie, W. M. Flinders. *Seventy Years in Archaeology.* New York, 1932.

Riley, Derrick N. *Air Photography and Archaeology.* Philadelphia, 1987.

Simmons, Harold C. *Archaeological Photography.* New York, 1969.

Stewart, H. M. "Photogrammetry in Archaeology." In *Archaeological*

Theory and Practice: Essays Presented to W. F. Grimes, edited by Donald E. Strong, pp. 275–282. London, 1973.

Trigger, Bruce G. *A History of Archaeological Thought.* Cambridge, 1989. Contains some conceptual observations on photography.

Warren, Charles, and Charles W. Wilson. *The Recovery of Jerusalem: A Narrative of Exploration and Discovery in the City and the Holy Land.* London, 1871. The classic of Palestinian exploration, including engravings from old photos.

Wheeler, Robert Eric Mortimer. *Archaeology from the Earth.* Oxford, 1954.

White, Minor. *Zone System Manual: Previsualization, Exposure, Development, Printing; the Ansel Adams Zone System as a Basis of Intuitive Photography.* 4th ed. Dobbs Ferry, N.Y., 1972. Technical manual for controlling the photographic system by one of the foremost photographers of the century.

Wilson, Charles N. *1864 Ordnance Survey of Palestine.* New York, 1871.

Wright, Robert B. "Archaeological Photography." In *A Manual of Field Excavation: Handbook for Field Archaeologists,* edited by William G. Dever and H. Darrell Lance, pp. 175–195. Cincinnati, 1978. Practical guide to photographic practices at the Gezer Excavations.

Zayadine, Fawzi, and Ph. Hottier. "Relevé photogrammétrique à Pétra." *Annual of the Department of Antiquities of Jordan* 21 (1976): 93–104.

ROBERT B. WRIGHT

Photography of Manuscripts

When it comes to the study of ancient Near Eastern documents, visual documentation—that is, the record of what a given ancient text actually looks like—is usually an afterthought. Typically, one encounters technically poor images even more poorly reproduced. On the basis of such inferior images, it is usually difficult for a scholar to evaluate whether the readings published for a given text have validity, and rarely is the visual data sufficiently detailed for one to demarcate the kinds of subtle distinctions that often prove crucial to reading a difficult text correctly. Instead, one is usually forced to rely on "eyewitness" testimony as evidenced in a given editor's transcription and commentary or in his or her representation of the text as a line drawing.

However, in recent years there has been an influx of improved techniques, superior technologies, and new, extremely powerful tools that are compelling scholars to rethink how they visually document ancient documents. Indeed, the traditional mode of documentary visualization—the photograph—is gradually being replaced by the digital image conveyed on a computer screen.

Capturing a visual image of an ancient text has always been a daunting and challenging task. For one thing, the vast majority of ancient texts are hardly preserved in mint condition, that is, as beautiful, legible, comprehensive, and highly photogenic manuscripts or inscriptions. Rather, in the vast majority of cases, they come in small bits and pieces; ragged and warped; blackened with age or faded to nearly nothing; full of worm holes, water damaged, and weathered; gouged and dented; even encrusted with bat guano. In order to capture the textual data on these mutilated objects, considerable technical skill—especially photographic and digital imaging skill—is absolutely required. And here the problem has usually been most acute. This is because those having the technical training to photograph and image process the textual data on ancient objects are, from a scholarly standpoint, illiterate. Hence, although they can frequently produce technically "photogenic" pictures, more often than not these pictures are inadequate in conveying crucial evidence for epigraphical and philological analysis simply because the technician cannot distinguish the "signal" from the "noise." On the other hand, those having the scholarly knowledge crucial for producing the most effective and revealing images of ancient texts lack the technical know-how to produce the images themselves.

In order for optimal visual data to be produced, a different sort of archivist is therefore required, a scholar-technician, trained in the study of both ancient Near Eastern documents, their scripts and languages, as well the skills required to reproduce sophisticated visual imagery. As a general rule, the most effective approach has been to train scholars to be technicians rather than the other way around. The reason is that the skills required for scholarly judgment in epigraphy and philology take years to acquire; in contrast, sophisticated training in documentary photography and computer imaging can be done at a far quicker pace.

Basic Photographic Approaches. Photographic documentation involves several techniques adopted from commercial and forensic photography. Foremost is the electronic, or strobe, flash as a light source. Some curators have resisted flash photography in favor of the more traditional tungsten or quartz photo floodlights, in the mistaken belief that the latter are less damaging to ancient manuscript media than the former. In contrast, Marjorie Shelley, conservator of Prints and Drawings for the Metropolitan Museum of Art, New York, forthrightly voices the consensus opinion among most trained conservators that "the safest lighting for photographing vulnerable material is considered to be electronic flash (strobe)" (*The Care and Handling of Art Objects: Practices in the Metropolitan Museum of Art,* (New York, 1987, p. 72). Besides being far less damaging to ancient texts, the use of strobe offers great advantages in terms of both the crispness of the image and the sharpness of the focus.

The second important innovation has been the use of photographic previewing, utilizing special Polaroid films designed for this purpose. Once again, this is a technique long in vogue in commercial photography—especially where strobe flash is employed. Since it is frequently difficult to predict the play of light with strobe flash as well as the exposure, commercial photographers typically make a Polaroid test once they have established what they believe to be the optimal set up. Then after a short wait (30 to 60 seconds, depending on the film type) the set up can be verified by examination of the Polaroid test; moreover, the Polaroid shot becomes a "paper light meter" that verifies the correct exposure. Once a satisfactory preview has been achieved, one can proceed with confidence to do a full documentation in permanent, high resolution films.

This previewing technique has adapted extremely well to the documentation of ancient texts. Besides giving the photographer the ability to know in advance that "what you see is what you get," there is a further, very significant advantage inherent in this ability to preview: It offers an opportunity for the expert scholar to control the documentary process. That is, even when the scholar has no photographic expertise, he or she can still review the previews in order to make sure that the picture misses no subtlety in the data. Moreover, with this methodology photography becomes more than merely a means for documentation; rather, it becomes fully integrated into the investigative process itself. The photographic lens is a powerful tool of visualization which can often see things the eye cannot see. It is typical that a polaroid preview will reveal some aspect of the data of a text that was missed by eye, especially if the text is properly lit. Hence, Polaroid-previewing frequently leads to discovery, especially if an expert is available who can take fullest advantage of the data as it is produced on film.

The third basic technique that leads to better documentation of ancient texts can be summarized in a single phrase: more choice. To be more specific, it is essential to document ancient texts employing a variety of films for each set up as well as a range of exposures for each film type. This is in decided contrast to conventional practices of documentation in which, typically, a single exposure is made in only one film type. This requires a single image to carry all the data, and in fact, no single film or exposure is adequate to this task. Once again, this broadening of choice follows the general practice in commercial photography where the tenet, "when in doubt, shoot more" has long held sway. Films must be used in a complementary fashion, thereby compensating for the inherent weaknesses of one film type with the strengths of another. At minimum at least two films should be employed—a high-resolution black-and-white film and a high quality color-reversal, that is, transparency film. The former allows the epigrapher to study a text in greatest detail while the latter allows him or her to clarify ambiguities of shade and color that black-and-white images can distort or mask. Depending on the circumstance, other films should be used as well—for example, infrared-sensitive films for shooting soft-media documents such as the Dead Sea Scrolls. [*See* Dead Sea Scrolls.] Sometimes color-negative film is also a better choice if the image is to be scanned for digitizing. Moreover, it is essential to do a range of exposures—to bracket the shots—in order to insure that there is sufficient latitude to encompass the wide range from light to dark one frequently finds in the ancient materials upon which textual data have been written. [*See* Papyrus; Parchment; Tablet; Writing Materials.]

The fourth basic concept is closely related to this issue of choice in terms of film and exposure: namely, a range in resolution or scale. In the past the custom has been, once again, to force a single image to cover all the data. A far superior documentation can be achieved, however, working at three levels of resolution/magnification.

1. *Reference shot.* A text should be photographed in the largest reasonable size—for example, a plate of related fragments, a column of text, or the inscribed face of a stela or clay tablet. Even when the very best films are employed, however, this level of documentation will be inadequate to achieve everything needed.

2. *Section shot.* A second level of magnification, the section shot, is also required. That is, the given artifact is shot in sections at a mid-range magnification. This allows for a fairly close survey of the letters or signs as well as the scribal hand or ductus.

3. *High resolution.* A third level of magnification should be used at very high resolution to target specific problems. Virtually all ancient inscriptions have serious problem areas in which a high-resolution photograph at high magnification does wonders to resolve philological ambiguity. This is especially so if an expert on a particular text can target such areas in advance and give the photographer a "shooting script" by which to plan the documentation of problem areas. Even better, if the expert is also available on site, a significant number of problems can often be resolved as he or she reacts and adjusts the documentation based upon what can be seen in successive Polaroid previews.

Resolution problems are dramatically lessened when larger-format films are used. Unfortunately, 35 mm, the most widely available film size and hence the one most often employed for documentation, is inherently poor in resolution regardless of film type employed. Even more significant limitations in resolution are encountered when a microfiche or microfilm is used for primary documentation. A better choice is a mid-format 120 film ($2\frac{1}{4}$ in. wide) and by far the most effective film size for serious, detailed documentation is the standard professional 4 inch by 5 inch film size. For particularly large documents, it is sometimes even necessary to go to an 8 inch by 10 inch format in order to gain a highly detailed reference shot.

There is a further advantage to working with mid- or large-format films. The cameras that can handle these films virtually all allow for the use of interchangeable film magazines. Hence one can line up a shot, verify it with a Polaroid test using a Polaroid magazine, then proceed to do a permanent documentation with several magazines, each containing a different film—all while the camera itself and the photographic set up remain essentially unchanged. Thus, all

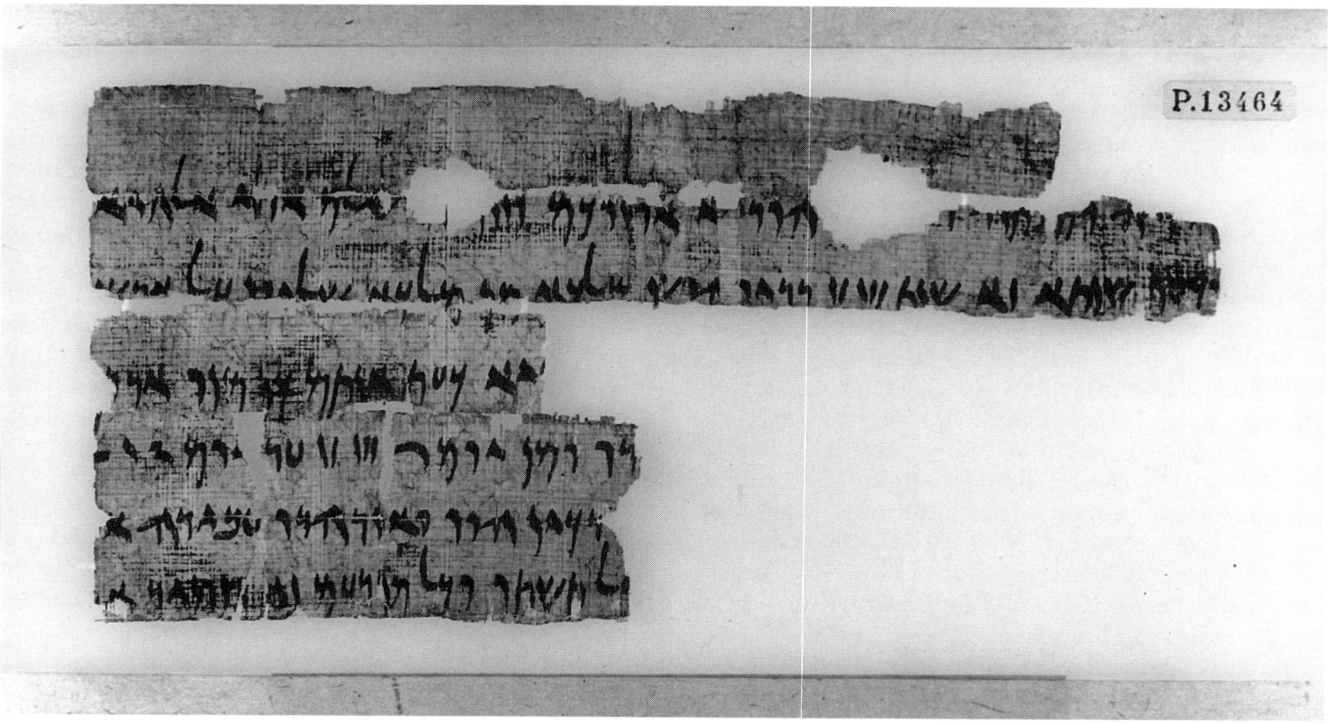

PHOTOGRAPHY: Manuscripts. Figure 1. *Papyrus 13464 (recto), known as the "Passover Papyrus," with both top and backlighting.* (Photography by Bruce and Kenneth Zuckerman, West Semitic Research; courtesy Staatliche Museen, Berlin)

the pictures match precisely in format and scale—an invaluable advantage for purposes of comparison at a later time.

Soft Media. Certain artifacts containing textual data are classified as "soft" media—that is, media that are written on pliable, frequently perishable, organic materials such as animal skin (e.g., Dead Sea Scrolls), parchment or vellum (e.g., early medieval codices), and papyrus (e.g., letters and legal documents like those from Elephantine, Egypt). The media of writing is almost always some form of ink applied to the prepared surface.

Since the ink itself has no significant thickness, soft media documents can essentially be treated as two-dimensional for photographic purposes. Nonetheless, it is still of significant value to employ films of sufficient resolution to be able to distinguish the thicknesses of ink strokes—especially as they cross over one another—on the surface. Such data is invaluable for analysis of the order and direction of strokes in a given scribal hand. Depth-of-field problems are usually minimal as long as extra care is taken to make sure that there is close parallel alignment between the plane of the writing surface, the lens and the film plane. This alignment must be checked and readjusted frequently. On those occasions where the surface has buckled or warped significantly, even greater care in focusing must be taken.

The main concern with regard to lighting is to make sure that the illumination is diffuse (what photographers call a soft light) and even. The use of special diffusers known as soft boxes are ideal for this sort of work and will usually serve to eliminate any shadowing caused by undulations in the writing surface. It is almost impossible to light a surface evenly with a single light source; thus, a typical setup involves two strobe lights set precisely opposite each other on either side of the camera and angled downward at 45°.

If it is practical, soft-media documents should be photographed with backlighting; that is, a highly diffused third strobe placed behind the document. Almost all ancient soft-media documents contain holes and cracks, many of which are extremely small. If the document is only illuminated from above, those imperfections may fall into shadow. Particularly with black-and-white images (but also, to some extent, with color) it can be difficult to distinguish such shadows (sometimes as small as a pinhead) from the ink on the writing surface. Furthermore, if the soft-media text is mounted between glass plates (or some similar material), then, from a photographic standpoint, the document will "float" slightly above the surface on which it is being photographed. When lit only from above, the document will cast a distinct shadow against the backdrop. These shadows not only interfere with reading the ink, but can obscure document edges. Once again, back lighting can be employed to cancel out these shadows so that every edge is sharp and clear, every hole, every hairline crack, no matter how small, distinct from the writing surface. Back lighting offers an added bonus in that it tends to give fine illumination to papyrus and skin grain, thus making the task of matching fragments based on the grain of the writing surface, a far easier endeavor than would otherwise be the case (see figure 1).

A major concern in photographing soft-media texts (typically papyri) mounted between plates is glare. The shiny surface of the mounting plates should be cleaned as well as possible before photographing (even a stray fingerprint can become an occasion for glare), and Polaroid tests must be continually monitored. Glare can be eliminated by using black cardboard and black "gaffer's" tape to mask any reflecting surface.

Considerable success can often be achieved in retrieving information from obscured inks on soft media by photographing and lighting with particular band widths of light, especially ultraviolet and/or infrared illumination. Crucial in this regard is the type of ink employed and the nature of the damage to the writing surface. Where ink has faded, a very effective technique is to photograph the text in black and white with a colored filter over the lens. The filter should match the color of the writing surface—yellow, orange, red, or sepia filters are the most effective. In a black-and-white photograph, the background, correctly filtered, will appear to drop out—either as white or considerably lighter than the surface looks in the visible light spectrum. This, in turn, increases the contrast between the surface and the ink, making the latter more visible. The technique is effective regardless of ink type.

Infrared illumination and photographing in infrared-sensitive film are effective in the opposite scenario: when ink is obscured against a dark or blackened surface—where black is seen against black in visible light. This is typically the case, for example, with obscured ink on the skins of Dead Sea Scrolls. If the inks involved are essentially carbon black in composition, then infrared photographic techniques can deliver surprising, indeed often stunning results for manuscripts that look hopelessly illegible in visible light.

The conventional approach to infrared photography of ancient documents has been to photograph a surface in a relatively broad band of wavelengths. Indeed, the conventional wisdom has been to use a red filter (thereby blocking all illumination beyond red) and to photograph with infra red sensitive films the entire range in which the film is sensitive to infrared illumination. This technique has proven to be generally effective since across the infrared spectrum or-

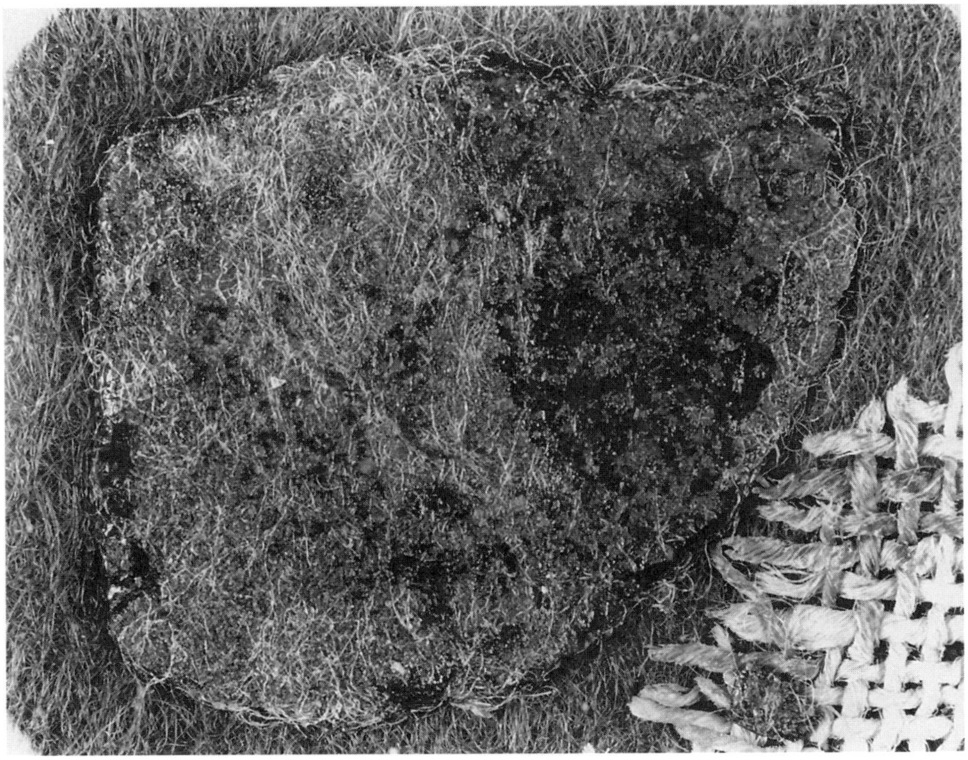

PHOTOGRAPHY: Manuscripts. Figure 2. *Ms* 192614, *fragment C.* A small Dead Sea Scroll fragment as it looks in visible light. (Photograph by Bruce and Kenneth Zuckerman, West Semitic Research; courtesy Schøyen Collection, Oslo)

ganic writing surfaces (animal skin and papyrus) are highly reflective while carbon black ink is not. Thus a surface that appears black in visible light will often drop out as white in a black-and-white infrared image, thus revealing the ink it had previously obscured. On the other hand, when the ink itself has faded against a lighter background, infrared photographic techniques are largely ineffective and generally inferior to the colored-filtration technique discussed above.

Even more dramatic infrared results can be achieved if a target is photographed in discrete narrow bands in the infrared spectrum, where blackened organic materials are not evenly reflective (that is, at given wavelengths they are more reflective). When a surface is photographed in a broad infrared band width, a degree of leveling, or averaging, occurs (i.e., the less reflective are averaged in with the more reflective), thereby lessening the contrast against the ink. A better result is achieved when narrow band-pass filters are used over the camera lens that will only pass illumination where the reflectivity of the surface is optimal. In such instances, startling gains have been achieved that significantly surpass those of infrared photography using the conventional broad band approach (see figures 2 and 3).

After about the fifth century CE, carbon-black inks began to be replaced by what are known as iron-gall inks—inks with a very high iron content as well as tannic acid—extracted from the galls, or irregular growths, that often develop on oak trees. Such inks show up poorly under infrared illumination; indeed, in all areas of the infrared spectrum, they tend to fade away in photographic documentation. On the other hand they respond well to the stimulus of ultraviolet light. That is, under the stimulus of ultraviolet illumination iron gall inks tend to be unusually absorptive.

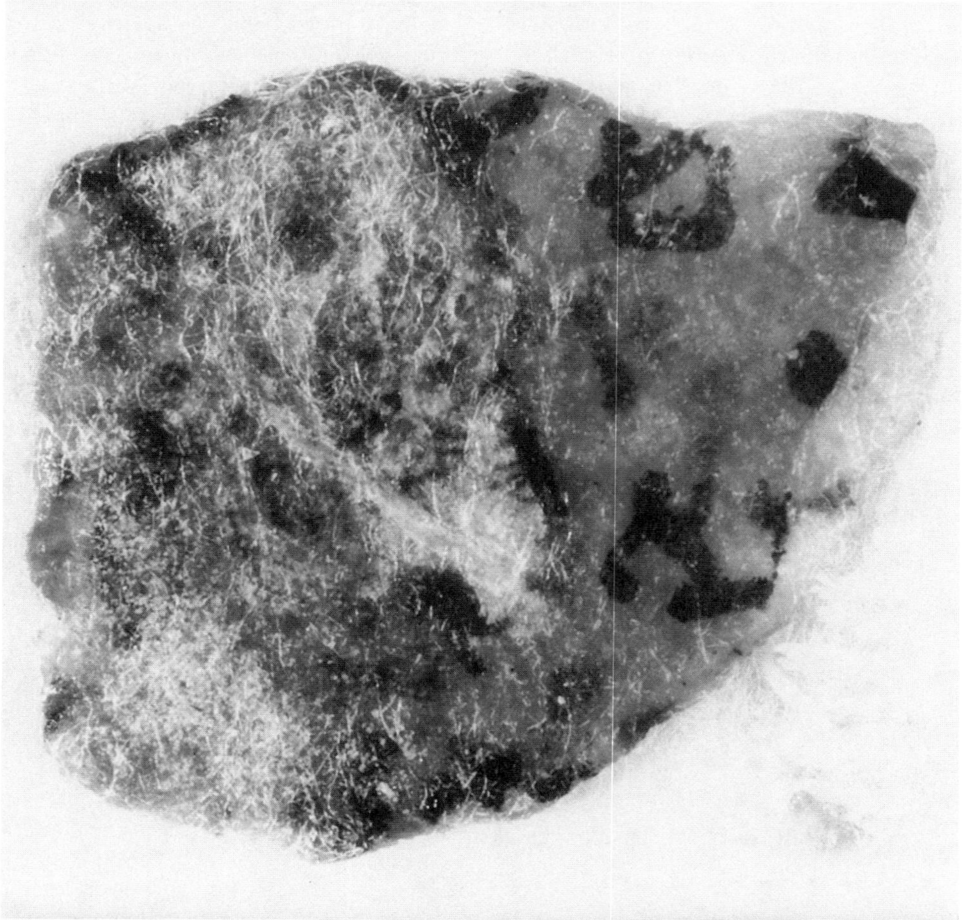

PHOTOGRAPHY: Manuscripts. Figure 3. *Ms* 192614, *fragment C*. The same fragment from figure 2 photographed in a narrow band of infrared illumination. The fragment is revealed to be part of 1QDan[b]. Note that at least two letters (ʿaleph and lamed) are just visible from an underlying layer of skin. (Photograph by Bruce and Kenneth Zuckerman, West Semitic Research; courtesy Schøyen Collection, Oslo)

Thus, in a case where the ink appears in visible light to have faded beyond legibility, under ultraviolet stimulation the ink tracing can often be dramatically retrieved.

While most color and black-and-white films are sensitive well into the ultraviolet spectrum, it is not so much the data in the ultraviolet per se that are the most useful for retrieving information from faded iron-gall inks: it is the fluorescent stimulus that ultraviolet illumination causes in the visible light spectrum that brings out the best data. Thus, the best approach is to use an ultraviolet illuminator (a simple method is to use a filter that only passes ultraviolet light over a strobe flash) and then photograph through a filter that blocks out the ultraviolet. Unfortunately, this technique is not effective for retrieving data from iron-gall inks against a dark background, for example, where the parchment or vellum has darkened due to water staining. In such cases the dark areas of the writing surface become even darker under ultraviolet stimulation and block out the data from the iron-gall ink. Hence it is usually necessary to work with a conventional visible light image in coordination with an image stimulated by ultraviolet light to get the best data from manuscripts written in iron-gall inks.

Occasionally one encounters red-colored inks on soft media, especially scrolls. Such inks usually have a high iron content and seem not to show any especially useful characteristics in either the infrared or ultraviolet range. Colored filtration can be helpful—especially a red filter, which will cause the ink to appear white against the background in a black-and-white print.

Hard Media. Written on durable, usually (but not exclusively) nonorganic materials, hard-media texts are typically pottery, plaster, clay, stone, metal, bone, or gemstones. [*See* Seals; Metals; Bone, Ivory, and Shell.] Ink may be applied to hard writing surfaces (e.g., ostraca, or "pottery sherds"), but more frequently inscriptions are created by carving the surface either through simple incision or impression; occasionally it is done by sculpting or stamping in bas-relief. [*See* Ostracon.]

By far the most common such inscriptions are ostraca, that is, sherds of pottery with ink (usually carbon black) inscribed on either the concave or convex surface, sometimes both. To a large extent, the techniques involved in photographing ostraca are the same as those employed for soft-media manuscripts. The one proviso is that great care must be taken to mount ostraca generally parallel to the film plane, since the curved surface makes depth of field a constant concern. Then focus should be made sharp at the average distance of the curved surface from the film plane. All effort should be made to keep the lens opening as narrow as possible in order to increase the depth of field. If an ostracon is particularly curved, it may be necessary to photograph it in sections in order to compensate for depth-of-field/focus problems.

As with soft-media documents, color filtration increases the contrast between the ink and the writing surface, as described above; it is often extremely effective in increasing the legibility of faded ink on a smooth clay surface. Less effective but still of some value are the infrared techniques noted above. Rarely does such an approach make the ink itself significantly clearer to read; however, an infrared image often is effective in screening out the visual interference that often is the result of the rough or variable texture of the clay. Ultraviolet stimulation has not shown effectiveness in enhancing readings on clay although some gain may be possible when other surfaces are involved, for example, bone. Results similar to those described above for red ink on soft media have been achieved for ostraca as well.

Perhaps the most effective means for making significant gains in readings for ostraca is employing a wetting technique. Considerable caution must be employed when wetting ostraca. Initial testing should be done on a small area of the inked clay to confirm that the ink will not run or otherwise be significantly damaged through the application of water. Only a fine spray of distilled water should be used; the best means of application being short bursts of spray from an airbrush.

When wet, ink traces that are often completely invisible to the eye when the clay surface is dry will suddenly appear. Speed and timing are essential. As an ostracon dries, the ink will begin to fade again. The type of clay and how it was shaped, burnished, slipped, or fired determine the optimal amount of time for photographing—sometimes only seconds. Moreover, when first wet, an ostracon can appear shiny (especially its convex surface) and therefore susceptible to glare reflected from the illumination. Hence, it is sometimes necessary to wait until the surface has dried somewhat to a more matte-like appearance so that this glare problem is minimized.

Other hard-media inscriptions pose different problems because they have a third dimension: height and/or depth. Whereas with soft-media texts and ostraca, an even, diffuse light is preferable, for these other types, readings are clarified by establishing shadows; hence, a low-raking, harsh light is generally preferable. Three-dimensional hard-media inscriptions are divided into two broad subcategories: large and small artifacts.

Large artifacts. In most instances, a "key" and "fill" lighting technique is the best for large artifacts. Dominant shadows are established by a low, raking light positioned to bring out the text readings most clearly. If the text is a cuneiform tablet, conventionally this light is placed so that it sweeps down diagonally from the upper left-hand corner. This establishes continuity with the convention of drawn cuneiform signs. [*See* Cuneiform.] Assyriologists conventionally depict signs graphically as seen with a dominant light from the upper left. In general, this is the convention for other cuneiform drawing (e.g., Ugaritic) as well. The key light should be shifted as irregularities in the surface dictate. With other types of texts, the key is placed where it will best throw the signs into sharp relief—the position being judged by eye and verified by the results of Polaroid testing.

A second light source is typically employed from the precise opposite angle and from the opposite end of the inscribed object, in order to fill and buffer the dominant shadow. This light establishes definition of the opposite end of the signs or letters. This fill light is softer; indeed, it can often be established with a highly reflective white fill card (or sometimes a shinier reflector, such as a mirror) that simply bounces the key light in the opposite direction (see figure 4). Where a stronger fill is needed, a second strobe flash can be used.

In some instances, especially where a surface is curved (as on the incised surface of a jar), dominant, or key, lights are set at both ends of the inscription and are balanced so that they fill for each other. This is also often the best approach

PHOTOGRAPHY: Manuscripts. Figure 4. *The El-Kerak Moabite inscription.* Photographed in typical "key-fill" lighting set-up. The key comes from the upper left and the fill is established with a white card at the lower right. (Photograph by Bruce and Kenneth Zuckerman, West Semitic Research in collaboration with the Princeton Theological Seminary; courtesy Department of Antiquities of Jordan, Amman)

for a long, narrow one- or two-line inscription (e.g., on the base of a statue or votive object). In such cases, "fill-fill" lighting is the only proper approach.

Care must be taken regarding the sort of reflectors used with the lights. In some cases (especially where considerable area needs to be covered) a reflector that throws a fairly broad, diffuse light will work; however, when an inscription is shallow (lightly incised or impressed), where it has been worn away (e.g., weathered), or where the bas-relief is minimal (e.g., on a poorly rolled cylinder seal impression) or partially chipped away, a much narrower light is needed to cast harsher shadows to define the letters or signs. As a general rule, the narrower the conduit of the light, the harsher the shadow created. A "snoot" reflector is the ideal tool for throwing such light. A snoot is essentially an open-ended cylinder about 6 inches long through which the light generated from an electronic strobe is converted into a narrow column. Because the light column is so narrow, it can be sent at an extremely low angle relative to the surface being illuminated; thus, the shadows created often throw even the most subtle indentations into startling relief. The major drawback of working with snoots is that their light covers only a limited amount of area. This makes them especially serviceable for detail work (e.g., a close-up of several letters or signs), but less well-suited for larger surface areas. This problem of coverage can be mitigated by stacking snoots; that is, by positioning two or more snoots diagonally on top of each other so that their lights overlap. Using this technique requires care: the lights must be evenly balanced, so that no unevenness is perceived in the transition from the illumination of one light to the next.

When an even narrower column of light is needed than can be projected through a snoot, black paper (or paper that is black on one side and white on the other) can be rolled into a cone (black on the outside, white on the inside) and taped to the end of a snoot. The end of the cone can then be adjusted to deliver a variable column of light, depending on the size of the area needing coverage. This works especially well for detail shots involving one or two letters or signs. A fiber-optic light source with a small probe can also be used, although it is usually not required for large hard-media objects.

Small artifacts. Essentially, three types of small hard-media objects contain inscriptions: seals, seal impressions, and coins. On occasion, other small artifacts are encountered with minute inscriptions (e.g., the Ketef Hinnom silver scrolls from Jerusalem), but the techniques for photographing them do not differ significantly from those used in the three main categories. [*See* Ketef Hinnom.]

Coins. Probably the easiest and best understood techniques are for photographing coins. Because ancient coins are invariably metal, their reflective surface can be used to advantage in delineating iconography and inscriptions. Usually, all that is required is a fairly diffuse light nearly on top of the target. This can be achieved by employing what is known as a "ring light," that is, an illumination source that literally wraps around the camera lens and projects its illumination down on the target.

Seals. There are two types of seals, stamp and cylinder. The former are typically scaraboid, although other shapes can be encountered. Regardless of a seal's shape, the textual data are found on a stamping surface that is either flat or somewhat rounded. The range of materials for seals is considerable in its variety: from multicolored semiprecious stones (e.g., lapis lazuli, jasper, agate) to single-colored media (e.g., carnelian, shale, limestone, clay, ivory, bone) to nearly clear crystalline stones. Proper lighting is a challenge, since each seal usually involves an individual solution. Still, several basic approaches will yield good results.

If a stamp seal surface is relatively flat and not highly reflective, the key-and-fill technique (see above) is usually effective. A narrow light from a snoot, a coned snoot, or a fiber-optic probe works best as the key; normally, a white card is sufficient as a reflector to bounce back a fill. Care must be taken in establishing the direction of the key light. In cases where the incised strokes of the letters are essentially parallel to the direction of the key light, they will be significantly deemphasized and often will virtually disappear. Hence it is preferable to place the key light in such a position that the beam it projects parallels as few letter strokes as possible. Typically, a diagonal direction works best, although a number of directions should be experimented with. There are instances where no single angle of light is sufficient for gaining the optimal data from a seal of this sort. In such a case, two or several shots should be employed, illuminated from differing light directions in order to give the fullest picture of the letter forms achievable. Obviously, a knowledgeable expert who knows what letters should look like at a given time in a given script is absolutely essential for success in this work.

If a seal's stamping surface tends to be highly rounded rather than flat, a fill-fill approach (see above) needs to be employed—at least two, and sometimes as many as four, light sources should be positioned to cover the surface. For such work, fiber-optic light sources are more serviceable than conventional lights.

If a seal's stamping surface is reflective, it may be almost like a mirror at a particular discrete angle of light. Depending on the polish of the surface and the type of material, this angle can vary from 45° to 70°. Such a reflection is the ideal light in which to illuminate a seal's surface because every aspect of the carving is displayed, down to the finest detail. Indeed, the image often will seem to glow as if lit from within. This reflection cannot be captured in the camera lens if a stamp seal is mounted directly under the camera lens with the stamping surface and the lens plane flat. Rather, the seal should be mounted on a tilt adjusted until the refracted light is bounced into the lens at precisely the optimal angle. Because of this tilt, there is a potential for focusing problems; hence, all effort must be made to achieve the greatest depth of field by closing the lens opening as much as possible (see figure 5). Especially for a seal composed of clear crystal, this is virtually the only way to get a clear picture of the stamping surface.

PHOTOGRAPHY: Manuscripts. Figure 5. *Hebrew seal on a carnelian gemstone belonging to Hananyahu.* The seal was tilted in order to use the reflection of the light off its polished surface to gain optimal detail. (Photograph by Bruce and Kenneth Zuckerman, West Semitic Research; courtesy Harvard Semitic Museum, Cambridge)

Because of the tilt of the seal, the picture can be slightly distorted; however, the image produced will look flat to the viewer. Nonetheless, for greatest precision one should work with a view camera in which both the lens plane and the film plane can be tilted. Then these planes can also be tilted so that the lens and film plane parallel the tilted stamping surface of the seal, thereby minimizing all potential distortion.

In so doing, considerable care must be taken to adjust the planes laterally so that they are in the middle of the lens's imaging circle (the maximum viewing circle covered by the lens); otherwise, a phenomenon known as vignetting may occur and part of the image may be cut off. This can be checked in a Polaroid test.

The conventional practice in photographing a cylinder seal is to photograph its impression rolled out on clay. While the impression gives a general sense of the seal's inscription and design, it inevitably the lacks the precision and detail of the real thing. Conventional photographs of cylinder seals show only a portion of the seal; and, because of the curvature of the surface, proper lighting is always very difficult to achieve. Recently however, an approach has been developed that allows one to make a picture of the actual sealing surface as a 360° time exposure. The technique involves an adaptation of panoramic photographic techniques, which employ specially adapted cameras to photograph a scene in a 360° arc.

In panoramic photography, instead of a standard opening behind the lens and in front of the film plane, a small vertical slit allows light onto the film. As an electric motor rotates the camera at a precise and unvarying speed in a 360° arc, a similar, synchronous motor advances the film in the opposite direction at precisely the same speed. Thus, the scene is "wiped" onto the film during a time exposure. For cylinder seals, this setup is adapted by keeping the camera stationary and rotating the seal in a 360° arc on a small turntable. A motor is used that is synchronized to the one moving the film in the opposite direction in the camera. Illumination is placed so that it highlights the area falling under the slit. Once again, the picture is wiped onto the film in a time exposure.

Previewing with Polaroid film will not work with this arrangement, but Polaroid instant slide film can be used for the same purpose. This is a special 35-millimeter film (available in both color and black and white) loaded and shot in a 35-millimeter camera in the conventional fashion. Once a roll is fully exposed, it can be processed in a small, easy-to-operate portable processor made by Polaroid that produces images for viewing in about five minutes. Thus, a test time exposure employing instant slide film can be reviewed on site. Any necessary adjustments can be made before doing a final documentation with archival-quality color and black-and-white films.

Seal impressions. Seal impressions are typically found on clay jar handles or as bullae. In either case, the inscriptions can be photographed using a standard key-and-fill or a fill-fill setup. Because in antiquity seal designs were often made quickly and with little care, the impressions they leave may only be partially clear and frequently so slight as to be invisible in ambient light. The difficulty of getting the light to fall at precisely the right angle for gaining optimal information becomes particularly acute with impressions. The problem is exacerbated with jar-handle impressions in which the seal creates a tiny bowl-shaped indentation that can be difficult to light.

A fiber-optic light probe is best adapted for illumination, but it is difficult to mount a stationary probe. Instead, a hand-held fiber-optic probe, known as a light brush, often proves to be the easiest and most effective approach. These probes are employed in commercial photography to apply artificial highlights to pictures—for example, to create areas of high reflection on ice cubes. Similarly, this probe can be utilized in a time exposure to "paint" a seal impression with light. In some instances, this is done essentially by holding the probe in one position; frequently, however, the best results are achieved by moving the probe during a time exposure of 5–15 seconds, so that its light illuminates areas of the impression from slightly different angles. Experimenting with combinations of movements and angles with Polaroid tests assesses the results. Again, a trained scholarly observer should examine the tests to ensure the best results. "Light brushing" a seal impression in this manner can achieve dramatic results beyond what is possible with any other lighting (see figure 6).

Digital Imaging. Computers translate an image (digital imaging) into a discrete number of small elements called pixels (short for "picture elements") and assign a color and intensity to each pixel (see below). Subsequently, manipulation of the digital information can change the appearance of the image by adjusting contrast and brightness, sharpening, applying false coloring, and "cutting and pasting," to create composite images and other effects.

Digital images are also convenient for archival storage and electronic transmission. Once an image has been digitized, it can be copied over and over again with no loss of image quality. Even as digital storage media technology changes, the data from older media can be copied onto the new and preserved for the next generation with no loss of information. This is not the case when copying film negatives, transparencies, or photographs, where each subsequent copy produces an image somewhat inferior to its parent. In contrast, electronic transmission of data over any of the available networks including the Internet will give the recipient a perfect clone of the original digital image.

The demands placed on digital-imaging technology when dealing with ancient documents are considerable because of the necessity of preserving minute details. This requires the use of the highest available resolution. This demand can handicap even the most state-of-the-art computer system and frustrate the unsophisticated user.

Input. The first task in digital imaging is to deliver the image so that the computer can read it. This can be achieved in one of two ways: direct-image capture (attaching an electronic camera directly to a computer) or scanning a conventional photographic image (a print, transparency, or negative) with a scanning device driven by a computer.

PHOTOGRAPHY: Manuscripts. Figure 6. *Bulla excavated at Megiddo.* The bulla is illuminated by a light brush. (Photograph by Bruce and Kenneth Zuckerman, West Semitic Research; courtesy Israel Antiquities Authority)

Direct-image capture, sometimes called filmless photography, has the advantage of nearly instant preview of the result (the Polaroid of the electronic world); it also has the ability to work in discrete wavelengths of light, including those beyond the sensitivity of film in the infrared range. Various bands within the spectrum can be selected using an electronic device called a liquid crystal tunable filter (LCTF); the infrared reflective properties of documents can be imaged by cameras designed for that purpose. Within the spectral range of color and infrared films, LCTFs or more conventional narrow band-pass filters can be used with conventional photographic cameras to achieve similar results. The disadvantages of direct-image capture are the need usually to be connected to a fairly powerful (usually cumbersome) computer equipped with a CRT (cathode ray tube) color monitor to control the camera operations, view the results, and save the images. Some stand-alone digital cameras can produce good reference images, but the limitations of the system's resolution preclude enlarging them. In such systems there simply are not enough pixels (typically fewer than 1000 across the longest dimension of the image) to deliver a detailed image. High-end digital cameras that produce dramatically more pixels (5,000–6,000 across the image) are not yet available as stand-alone devices, may require three exposures to capture a color image (a technically more difficult procedure because registration has to be maintained for all three exposures), use slow exposure times that in turn require the use of constant bright light sources (a serious drawback from a conservation standpoint for soft-media documents, as noted above), and are priced substantially beyond the costs of even the finest conventional photographic equipment. As a result, for at least the immediate future, conventional photographic methods will be the preferred image-capture technique for reproducing ancient documents.

The breakdown of an electronic image to the point where it no longer looks photographic but like an assemblage of discrete blocks is called pixelization. The unaided human eye will usually not perceive pixelization if there are at least 300 pixels per inch (ppi) in the image being viewed. As a point of comparison, a conventional photographic image contains the equivalent of at least twice this number of pixels and looks considerably better in a side-by-side comparison with a 300-ppi image. In addition, a digital image can break down if there is an insufficient range of gray levels and colors available for display. In order for computer-imaging output devices to produce a black-and-white image of photographic quality, the device must be based on a scan that contains some 256 levels of gray (sometimes referred to as an 8-bit image). Similarly, a full-color image of photographic quality requires a file with approximately sixteen million colors (called a 24-bit color image: eight bits each of red, green, and blue—if using an additive color system—or eight bits each of cyan, magenta, and yellow—if using a subtractive color system).

As the above statistics suggest, a digital image of any significant resolution involves a tremendous amount of data. For example, to scan a standard 4 by 5 inch original negative without significant pixelization, in order to enlarged it to 11 by 14 inches, the digital image would have to encompass 3,300 × 4,200 pixels for a total of 13.86 million pixels. For a black and white image with 256 levels of gray, this represents 13.86 megabytes (MB) of data; for a full-color image, it represents a considerable 41.58 MB—all for a modest enlargement of less than three times the size of the original. The original 4 by 5 image would need to be scanned into the computer at a pixel density of at least 840 ppi. A 35-millimeter original would need to be captured into the computer at approximately 2,800 ppi.

If the minute details of an image at high magnification are needed, even larger files sizes will be necessary. It is here that the intelligent application of imaging technology becomes important. Just as in conventional photography, only those areas of special concern to the scholar should be digitized at the highest resolutions. (The significance of these numbers will become even more evident in the discussion of film scanners below.) The hybrid use of high-magnification photos digitized with a modestly high-resolution film scanner may be the most efficient use of both technologies.

Scanners. There are three broad categories of scanners: flat-bed scanners, Charged Coupled Device (CCD) film scanners, and drum scanners. Flat-bed scanners look and appear to operate much like a desktop copying machine. A photo (usually a paper print) is placed face down on a glass plate, a cover is lowered over the photo, and a linear light and CCD scanning array pass under the photo to capture the data. Some units are equipped with transparency adapters that allow the device to scan negatives and transparencies. These units are usually limited to 300–600 ppi. Some units make up for this deficiency by adding pixels through software, using a process called interpolation. These extra pixels are not real data, and the images produced should not be confused with images based on true optical data.

Film scanners project a focused image on a CCD that may be linear (in which case the CCD is swept across the image plane) or rectangular (in which there is a rectangular array of sensers that directly captures the image). Color filters may be used to achieve three successive scans to capture a full-color image. The better film scanners have true optical resolution of 1,000–3,000 ppi and can detect more than 256 levels of intensity for each primary color. The ability to record information in more than 256 levels enhances an image's level of detail, especially in its brightest (highlights) and darkest (shadow) areas. Only a few of the high-end film scanners will support large-format (4 × 5 in.) originals. These large-format devices are also slow and require perhaps as much as 10–15 minutes to complete a high-resolution color scan to produce digital files as large as 50 MB.

The best digital scans are obtained with drum scanners. These devices require that the film be mounted on a clear cylindrical drum that is spun at high speed while a very fine point of light is focused on the film. The resulting changes in light intensity and color are measured by a photo multiplier tube (PMT). PMTs are inherently better at detecting light then CCDs. As a result, drum scanners achieve higher resolutions and greater density ranges than any of the other devices discussed above. Drum scanners are also the most expensive and slowest of the choices. However, for the highest quality work, where the application demands file sizes of 100 MB and more, drum scanners are the only choice.

Eastman Kodak has produced a system of film scanners that create files on CD ROMS (compact disks that are "read only" and cannot be edited) called Photo CD. The files on these disks are available in a variety of sizes. The highest resolution is available only on the Pro-Photo CD version, which is capable of scanning a 4-×-5-in. negative or transparency to a file that, when opened with the appropriate software, contains about 70 MB of data. The Kodak system, designed for commercial operations, is very fast; as a result, the cost of the scans is reasonable. A Pro-Photo CD can contain approximately twenty–twenty-five reasonably high-resolution images. Pro-Photo CD is a good place to start for editing images with large file sizes.

Computer enhancement. Once the image of interest is digitized, there are excellent software packages on various computer platforms that can be used to improve and otherwise manipulate images. The manufacturers of imaging-editing programs are constantly improving their products.

When processing large images, work should be limited to selecting areas of interest. Some programs feature a proxy system that enables the user to apply effects to a low-resolution version of the image and subsequently apply identical effects to the high-resolution version while the computer is unattended. Tools that "float" one image or a portion of one image over another are very useful for comparing individual letter shapes in documents or in reconstructing, in a scribe's own hand, a partial letter or words and phrases in lacunae.

Still, such tools cannot be used with impunity. It is necessary to establish protocols for moving and restoring textual data so as not to create a "fake." In any publication or presentation of digital images, both the original and the altered image should be shown; moreover, the manipulations should be documented, explained, and preferably illustrated in detail.

It is also possible to undo effects applied to an image. Image manipulations in some programs only allow the last action to be reversed, whereas others allow unlimited undoing. The power of image processing to correct poorly exposed photographs, sharpen areas in poor focus, build composites, rebuild fragmented texts, cut out individual letters to build script charts, add interpretations by drawing on or electronically tracing over a photograph, and combine photographs made with various filters or at wavelengths beyond the visible are just a few of the tools available to a scholar equipped with a computer and some imaging software.

Many of these approaches to processing and enhancing data have only just begun to be applied by epigraphers and philologists. As this work progresses, the toolbox of techniques easily available to the scholar will undoubtedly grow, thereby dramatically enhancing the ability to see what could not hitherto be seen.

Image processing is one of the most demanding tasks a computer can perform. To work efficiently the computer must be equipped with a fast and powerful processor, have large and fast disk-storage capacity to handle the large files involved, have a high-quality monitor and fast video card with adequate video ram (VRAM), and, most important of all, have very large quantities of internal random access memory (RAM). A further prerequisite is a means of permanent storage beyond the computer's internal hard disk. At the moment, high-capacity tapes, such as digital audiotape (DAT) systems and recordable CD-ROMs, are the storage media of choice. Storage can be increased even more by means of a technology called image compression, which can reduce image sizes for storage. Such compression programs must be used with caution, however, because some programs are designed to discard "unimportant" image data. Such forms of compression may be acceptable for storing images for casual study, but for more rigorous storage, only programs employing "lossless compression" should be used.

`Output` .To produce hard-copy output from digitally enhanced images (i.e., images in tangible form, equivalent to a photographic print), the choices are as varied as on the input side. They range from relatively inexpensive laser and ink-jet printers to much more expensive film recorders that can convert a digital file back into a photographic image. Presently, the best compromise is device called a dye-sublimation (dye-sub) printer. Dye-sub printers produce nearly true photographic quality output at a reasonable price. Sizes are limited typically to 8 by 10 inches, but some models can produce 11 by 14 inch output. For even larger dimensions, high-quality ink-jet devices can produce nearly photo-quality output up to poster size. This is usually achieved by adding extra pixels through interpolation; as mentioned above, however, this method does not add real resolution to the picture.

Image output devices can print directly onto photographic paper or transparency materials at 300 ppi. The output is almost indistinguishable from photographic prints but is now limited to 8 by 10 inches. These are relatively large machines, approximately the size of a freestanding office copier, and are more costly than dye-sub printers, making them practical only in an institutional setting.

If hard-copy output is the primary goal, it is important to balance the resolution of input and output. Sufficient data should be available to produce quality output on the printer or film writer. However, there is little point to processing more data than the output device can handle as this needlessly slows down the processing time without tangible benefit. As already mentioned, in order to have a hard-copy image of photographic quality, it must have in the range of 300 ppi. Higher resolutions are only desirable if images are to be examined under magnification.

Permanence is a problem with dye-sub and ink-jet output: both are subject to fading and physical damage from handling unless special precautions are taken. Some dye-sub printers now apply a protective coating on hard-copy images to protect them from scratching, fingerprints, and rapid ultraviolet fading. Some ink-jet services also offer special fade-resistant dyes and archival paper to create a more permanent image. Ironically, the best means of obtaining hard-copy output, especially for long-term storage, is to record an image back onto a piece of film. The best film recorders can produce output indistinguishable from a camera-made original. Needless to say, achieving an optimal result means beginning with a high-resolution drum scan and image processing the resulting large file.

For purposes of publication, it may not be necessary to produce hard copy or film output at all. Publishers may prefer to receive the digital image file for direct input into their page-makeup system. If the images are to be included in a CD-ROM publication or as part of a multimedia publication, a digital file is ideal. In fact, digital editions of texts are certainly coming in the near future, probably with CD-ROM as the mode of dissemination. Such editions are the ideal tool for scholars, because they offer far superior visual data than could ever be obtained in the photographic reproductions in a conventional book. Moreover, the data invite interaction because they are ready for downloading into computer-imaging and enhancement programs.

Photographic/Digital Recommendations. In the final analysis the large-format camera is still the most suitable tool for the recording of textual data on ancient documents. Digital imaging can then be performed on the high-resolution films. Indeed, today digital scanning, retrieving, and processing of an original film image is now the superior means of getting the most usable data from an ancient inscription and is certainly superior to the chemical processing of a film image in the darkroom. Film should be scanned at high resolution and high bit depth and stored to archival media such as CD-ROM. Processed images should be likewise digitally archived. For hard-copy output dye-sub printers are the most practical at this time; however, prints on dye-sub media should not be considered archival. The best long-term approach for making archival hard copies of digital images is to write the processed images back to film with a high-resolution film recorder.

[*See also* Codex; Libraries and Archives; *and* Scrolls.]

BRUCE ZUCKERMAN and KENNETH ZUCKERMAN

PIGS. The pig, *Sus scrofa,* was domesticated in the Near East from two wild subspecies, *S. s. attila*—a habitant of Turkey, Iran, and Iraq—and *S. s. libycus*—common to the eastern Mediterranean and Egypt. The earliest evidence for domestic pig comes from Hallan Cemi in southeastern Turkey. Based on morphological changes and mortality patterns, domestication is dated by radiocarbon analysis to c. 8500 to 8000 BCE. This preliminary new evidence supersedes the well-known morphological evidence for domestic pig (shortening of the skull and teeth) found at the Neolithic site of Jarmo in northern Iraq, dated to c. 6500 to 6000 BCE. A few sites, particularly in Anatolia, show extensive exploitation of the animal in later phases of the Neolithic. In the Levant, one molar documents pig domestication at Tell Judeideh, a site on the Plain of Antioch, shortly after 6000 BCE. Husbanded pigs spread to the southern Levant by 5000–4000 BCE, at such sites as Tell Turmus in Israel. Pigs were a mainstay of the Levantine diet in the Late Neolithic and Chalcolithic periods, preceding the advent of complex society. Domestic pigs were present in the Nile valley by the Gerzean period (c. 3500–3000 BCE). A number of principles underlie the distribution of pigs. Environmental factors are primary because pigs require habitats receiving more than 300 mm of rain per year or the presence of marshlands. In all periods, increased moisture is predictive of swine exploitation. Pigs also prefer a forested habitat; some of the overall decline in swine husbandry seen over the sweep of Near Eastern history is the result of a steady deforestation of much of the environment.

With the emergence of complex society in the Early Bronze Age, factors beyond environment influenced the use of pigs. Based on the faunal record in the Levant, pigs were a rural subsistence strategy, becoming particularly important in periods and places of decreased political centralization. In general, pigs are substantially less abundant in the whole of the Near East after the onset of the Middle Bronze Age. An exception is the first wave of Philistine settlement, a phenomenon more likely an example of the worldwide pattern in which immigrants in the first phase of settlement turn to pig husbandry than a reflection of ideology. Because the animal reproduces more rapidly than other domestic stock, it provides a quick and abundant source of protein. Certainly, in later phases of Philistine settlement, pig husbandry declines abruptly. Throughout the rest of the Iron Age in the Levant, pork is only a marginal addition to the larder.

Swine were uncommon in other parts of the ancient Near East after the onset of complex society, again with a few exceptions. Pigs were a dietary mainstay at the Early Bronze Age city of Leilan in Syria. Other large and politically important sites in the same region, Lidar Höyük and Korucutepe in modern Turkey, for example, show continued exploitation of the pig into the Late Bronze Age. Hittite texts indicate that the animal was used in ritual contexts, though perhaps not those of the official cult. In southern Mesopotamia—though the faunal record is very sparse—a few large sites, such as Isin, even as late as Neo-Babylonian times, have significant amounts of pig remains. Cuneiform texts indicate that the animal, which lived as a loosely controlled urban scavenger, was held in low esteem. In Egypt, pigs are very infrequently mentioned in texts or depicted in art. Osteological evidence shows that their exploitation was related to the intensity of political control of the economy. Additionally, pig consumption in Egypt was related to social class. The comments of Herodotus about the status of swine herds are reflected in much earlier remains from Amarna, where pork was the food of the working class.

The dietary laws of the Hebrew Bible, a product of the Priestly source (dated variously from the eighth century BCE to the Persian period in the sixth century BCE) were composed when and where swine husbandry was a nearly invisible pursuit, at least on the basis of the archaeological record. The inclusion of the animal in the list of prohibited species would therefore seem to be the incorporation of a region-wide bias into the biblical tradition rather than a theological innovation directed toward pigs.

[*See also* Animal Husbandry.]

BIBLIOGRAPHY

Firmage, Edwin. "The Biblical Dietary Laws and the Concept of Holiness." In *Studies in the Pentateuch,* edited by J. A. Emerton, pp. 177–208. Supplements to Vetus Testamentum, vol. 41. Leiden, 1990. Recent survey of the theological implications of the dietary laws in the Hebrew Bible, with some attention to the archaeological evidence.

Flannery, Kent V. "Early Pig Domestication in the Fertile Crescent: A Retrospective Look." In *The Hilly Flanks and Beyond: Essays on the Prehistory of Southwestern Asia,* edited by T. Cuyler Young, Jr., et al., pp. 163–188. Studies in Ancient Oriental Civilization, no. 36. Chicago, 1983. Thorough review of the Neolithic evidence for domestication of the pig.

Hesse, Brian. "Pig Lovers and Pig Haters: Patterns of Palestinian Pork Production." *Journal of Ethnobiology* 10.2 (1990): 195–225. Survey of pig use from the Neolithic to the Iron Age and the relationship of the archaeological evidence for swine to the anthropological and historical explanation of its use and avoidance.

Redding, R. W. "The Role of the Pig in the Subsistence System of Ancient Egypt: A Parable on the Potential of Faunal Data." In *Animal Use and Culture Change,* edited by Pam J. Crabtree and Kathleen Ryan, pp. 20–30. Philadelphia, 1991. Survey of pig use in Egypt and its relationship to political centralization.

Wilford, John Noble. "First Settlers Domesticated Pigs before Crops." *The New York Times,* 31 May 1994, pp. B6 and B9.

BRIAN HESSE

PIT GRAVES. Simple, or pit, graves consist of a hole cut into sand, rock, or tell debris, to accommodate a body or a collection of bones with mortuary provisions. The cist grave is a more elaborate stone-lined version of a pit grave. Southern Levantine pit graves are either intramural (within settlements), cut into the tell debris (Natufian, Neolithic, Chalcolithic, Middle Bronze Ages), or in extramural cemeteries (Late Bronze, Iron Ages). The deceased were laid either in a flexed position on their side (Natufian–Middle Bronze Ages) or extended on their back (Late Bronze–Iron Ages).

In the Natufian period (10,500–8,500 BCE), intramural graves with one or more individuals were grouped and marked at the surface. At Naḥal Oren, bodies were interred in shallow pits in a designated area around a large stone-built hearth. The single, paired, or multiple bodies, adorned with ornaments, usually lay in a flexed position with the head facing north. Limestone mortars resembling stone pipes placed near several burials have been interpreted as marking the grave location and establishing a conduit between the worlds of the living and the dead (Stern, 1993, vol. 3, p. 1168). At the northern Jordan Valley site of ʿEnan, tomb 9 apparently housed a family (six skulls, plus three adults, one adolescent, and four children). In later burials, many bones were covered with red ocher, and graves were marked with large, flat standing (?) stones, similar to the Naḥal Oren mortars (Stern, 1983, vol. 2, p. 392).

Most Neolithic burials date from the Pre-Pottery Neolithic (PPN) period (8500–6000 BCE). Intramural, primary burial in a contracted position continued from the preceeding period. A PPN innovation was to remove adult skulls, without jaws, to keep in groups in the house, while the bodies were buried under the house floor or in an open space (Jericho, Naḥal Oren). In several cases, skulls were plastered and shells inlaid for eyes, to give a lifelike appearance (ʿAin Ghazal, Jericho). The arid conditions in Jericho have preserved bone needles and points (perhaps used to fasten the clothing of the dead or their wrappings) and traces of matting.

Beginning in the Chalcolithic period (4300–3300 BCE), while the majority of adults were buried in extramural cave and shaft-tomb cemeteries, infants, children, and adults under special circumstances were still being interred beneath house floors. At Beersheba, infants and children lay in the fetal position on their right side; some of the burials were provided with fine pottery vessels.

Pit burial virtually ceased in the region during the Early Bronze Age, but was reintroduced from the north in MB II (2000–1550 BCE). Beginning in MB IIA, intramural pit burial was practiced at sites from Ugarit south to Tell el-ʿAjjul (Dan, Jericho, Lachish, Megiddo, Tell el-Farʿah [South]). One or two mature individuals, positioned on their side with a small selection of pottery vessels and jewelry, were buried in a pit cut into the earth beneath their home or in the courtyard. During this same period, children were interred in jars under the house floor.

The northern-inspired MB intramural pit graves were succeeded by Egyptian-inspired extramural or isolated pit-grave cemeteries in the Late Bronze Age (1550–1200 BCE). Extramural pit-grave cemeteries reached their height of distribution through the Egyptian-administered or influenced lowlands in LB II (1300–1200 BCE; e.g., at Tell Abu Hawam, Tell el-Farʿah [South], Tell es-Saʿidiyeh, Tel Zeror). One person, and rarely two or three, were provisioned with bowls for food, jugs with dipper juglets for liquids, and luxury items such as imported pottery, jewelry, and metal objects.

The pattern of burial practices changed little from the Late Bronze Age through all the social and political upheavals of the Iron Age (1200–586 BCE). Pit and cist graves remained the predominant lowland burial type throughout the Iron Age (Achziv, Tell el-ʿAjjul, Ashdod, Megiddo, Tell el-Farʿah [South]). One or more individuals, of any age or either sex, were laid out on their back, with hands outstretched along their sides or crossed on the chest or pelvis. Continuing the LB practice, bowls and jars were characteristically provided. The lowland distribution of pit graves for individuals diverged markedly from the highland practice of multiple burial in caves. It may be that the lowland cultural group collectively referred to in the Bible as Canaanites practiced pit burial as opposed to the highland Israelites and Amorites.

[*See also* Cave Tombs. *In addition, most of the sites mentioned are the subject of independent entries.*]

BIBLIOGRAPHY

Avi-Yonah, Michael, and Ephraim Stern, eds. *Encyclopedia of Archaeological Excavations in the Holy Land.* 4 vols. Englewood Cliffs, N.J., 1975–1978. Summary of excavations including results of all earlier expeditions to the sites.

Ben-Tor, Amnon, ed. *The Archaeology of Ancient Israel.* Translated by R. Greenberg. New Haven, 1992. Essays with differing emphases on the Neolithic through the Iron II–III.

Bloch-Smith, Elizabeth. *Judahite Burial Practices and Beliefs about the Dead.* Journal for the Study of the Old Testament, Supplement 123. Sheffield, 1992. Summary and comprehensive catalog of the Iron Age burials.

Mazar, Amihai. *Archaeology of the Land of the Bible, 10,000–586 B.C.E.* New York, 1990. Comprehensive, detailed, well-illustrated survey of biblical archaeology, limited only by the traditionalist biblical interpretation.

Stern, Ephraim, ed. *The New Encyclopedia of Archaeological Excavations in the Holy Land.* 4 vols. Jerusalem and New York, 1993. Supplements Avi-Yonah and Stern (above), with results of more recent excavations and revised interpretations.

ELIZABETH BLOCH-SMITH

POIDEBARD, R. P. ANTOINE (1878–1955), officer, explorer, and missionary of the Jesuit order, which he joined in 1897. Born in Lyon, Poidebard was sent to study at Tokat (Turkey), where he learned Turkish and Armenian. He was ordained as a priest in 1910 and sent as a missionary to Armenia from 1911 to 1914. During World War I, he enlisted as a military chaplain with the rank of officer-interpreter in the French military mission in the Caucasus. After having shown his mastery among the Armenians in Erevan, he was sent to Georgia, which was, at that time, independent and at war with Russia. From 1924 onward, he was posted in Beirut.

As a reserve officer, Poidebard was transfered to the air force. During his flights on the edge of the Syrian desert, he noticed that, in a certain light, it was possible to distinguish ruins that though just barely covered, were imperceptible from the ground. Excavations later allowed him to confirm the accuracy of his observations. He involved himself in pioneering research in the border areas between inner Syria and the steppe. The results are available in two majors works as yet unequaled: *La trace de Rome dans le désert de Syrie* and, in collaboration with René Mouterde, *Le limes de Chalcis*.

Poidebard's research methodology was then innovative: observation in flight (at an altitude that might vary but that would be near 300 m for the best light conditions) and above all later verification of the find, either upon landing or through subsequent exploratory expeditions. The result is a work of the first order, with one volume of text and one of plates. Poidebard demonstrated the existence, to the east of Syria, at the edge of the steppe, of a complex network of military routes and small forts representing the successive extensions of the empire from Trajan's time to Justinian's; he described the network's organization, distinguishing above all the presence of an inner and outer boundary line.

In the *Limes of Chalcis,* Mouterde and Poidebard began with Malalas's allusion to *to Limiton Chalkidos*. They then searched the land for vestiges of routes and forts that would permit them to verify the existence of the lines and to understand the organization of this defensive system installed around the ancient village of Chalcis, modern Qinnishrin. [*See* Qinnishrin.] There are many reasons to think that the Limiton Chalkidos was not in reality a "border" in the strategic sense of the term, but that it merely designated the extent of the city. The authors did, however, locate, map, and date a number of very important sites, unknown before their efforts, that proved that in the Byzantine period there was a considerable extension east of the territory occupied by garrisons. While the work does not prove the validity of its initial hypothesis, it reveals the dynamism of the history of the campaigns in northern Syria in the Roman and Byzantine periods. Poidebard was again a pioneer when he applied his method to locate the vanished port of Tyre and study the ancient arrangement of the port of Sidon, the subject of two other works. [*See* Tyre; Sidon.] According to those who knew him, Poidebard was courageous, warm, and cordial. With the perspective of hindsight, he belongs to a small group of men, more imaginative adventurers than researchers in the academic sense of the word. The merit of their enterprise, rather than the possible weakness of their scientific work, should be emphasized. At the time they undertook their research, conditions of instability prevailed. They did things on a vast scale, turning to new methods that have since proven their usefulness. Poidebard died in Beirut, his last years saddened by attacks of amnesia.

BIBLIOGRAPHY

Poidebard, Antoine. *La trace de Rome dans le désert de Syrie*. Paris, 1934.

Poidebard, Antoine, and René Mouterde. *Le limes de Chalcis*. Paris, 1945.

GEORGES TATE

Translated from French by Melissa Kaprelian

POOLS. A pool is an unroofed, built installation, designed to store runoff or spring water, whose length and width are always greater than its depth. A pool requires very thick walls built of large stones (a minimum of 1 m and a maximum of 14 m as the Israin pool in Jerusalem), usually with smaller stones filling in the gaps. An impermeable material was inserted between the stones for reinforcement and to ensure against seepage. A thick layer of plaster applied to the walls after their construction prevented percolation of the water; plaster was also applied to a pool's floor, which often was smooth, bare rock. The corners of the pool were usually curved or formed by two obtuse angles to prevent cracks from developing at weak spots in its perimeter.

Many pools were built in low-lying areas, such as riverbeds, whose topography facilitated construction, as well as the drainage of runoff. A dam was generally first built across the riverbed. The bedrock was then plastered and used as the floor of the pool, longitudinal walls were built along the slopes of the ravine (incorporating the naturally exposed rock), and an upper cross-wall was constructed. This method was used to build the Sultan's Pool and Solomon's Pools in Jerusalem, as well as many others. [*See* Jerusalem.] A pool's large surface area results in a great deal of evaporation—a major drawback because it is virtually impossible to roof such a large area.

Pools were used to store and to regulate the supply of drinking water, as well as water for bathing, swimming, and irrigating gardens and crops. The water entered the pool at its most elevated point, flowed through a filtering basin where heavier materials (detritus, wood, and soil) mixed in the water stream could settle. Pools used for regulating water flow had openings at the bottom, through which the water continued to flow toward its destination. Pools were usually rectangular or trapezoidal; only rarely were they circular.

The most ancient pool so far discovered is at Ai (Khirbet et-Tell) and dated to the Early Bronze Age. [*See* Ai.] It forms part of a system for draining runoff. The capacity of this pool is 1,800 cu m and its maximum dimensions are 29 × 25 m; it is 2.5 deep. Red clay was used for caulking. Other pools from the same period have been found at Arad in Israel's Negev and at Jawa in Jordan's Black Desert. The storage volume for the pool at Arad has been estimated to be 2,000 cu m; at Jawa seven pools were discovered behind dams in the wadi below the city, with a total capacity of about 22,000 cu m of water. These were intended primarily to supply drinking water for the city's inhabitants. [*See* Arad, *article on* Iron Age Period; Jawa.]

The Hebrew Bible mentions several pools: the Old Pool, the Upper Pool, the Lower Pool, the King's Pool, the Artificial Pool, and the Siloam Pool in Jerusalem; as well as pools in Hebron, Gibeon, Samaria, and Ḥesban. Only few of these have been identified. [*See* Hebron; Gibeon; Samaria; Ḥesban.]

The largest pools, Solomon's Pools and one of the pools at Jericho, date to the Second Temple period. Solomon's Pools form part of one of the most impressive and largest water installations in the land of Israel. As part of the water supply system for Jerusalem they served a dual purpose: to regulate the water supply and to store water (reservoirs). The total capacity of the pools is 180,000 cu m; the maximum dimensions of the largest pool are 177 × 83 m; it is 12 m deep. At Jericho, the Musa Pool is the largest reservoir pool (220 × 160 m and 21.5 m deep). It too dates to the Second Temple period. Several swimming pools have been discovered from this period as well, at Jericho (92 × 40 m) and Herodium (70 × 46 m and 3.5 m deep). [*See* Jericho; Herodium.]

During the Second Temple period there were twelve pools in Jerusalem that had originally been quarries and that were subsequently used secondarily for defense purposes.

During the Roman and Byzantine periods in many locations in the Galilee, on Mt. Carmel, and in Samaria, pools were the center of village life. [*See* Samaria.] Their water was used for livestock, laundry, drinking, and bathing. Two large pools at the center of the site of Shivtah in the Negev served as one of the major water sources for that town. A pool on the outskirts of Sepphoris was probably used for swimming. [*See* Sepphoris.] Some of the Byzantine monasteries in Israel also had water installations that included pools, such as Deir Kal'ah in Samaria, whose three pools have crosses engraved on their walls.

From the beginning of the Early Arab period and onward, the development of waterworks in Israel was neglected; only a few pools have been discovered from this period, such as the decorative pools at Hisham's palace and the irrigation pool at ʿEin-ʿEvrona. During the Crusader period a pool was constructed near the Damascus Gate in Jerusalem known as Lac de Leger. No pools are known to have been built in later periods, but Solomon's Pools continued to be used until the middle of the twentieth century.

[*See also* Aqueducts; Hydraulics; Hydrology; Irrigation; Reservoirs.]

BIBLIOGRAPHY

Callaway, Joseph A. "Ai." In *Encyclopedia of Archaeological Excavations in the Holy Land,* vol. 1, pp. 36–52. Englewood Cliffs, N.J., 1976.

Heker, M. "Water . . . in Jerusalem in the Ancient Period" (in Hebrew). In *Sepher Yerushalaim,* edited by Michael Avi-Yonah, pp. 191–218. Jerusalem and Tel Aviv, 1956.

Helms, S. W. *Jawa: Lost City of the Black Desert.* London, 1981.

TSVIKA TSUK

Translated from Hebrew by Ilana Goldberg

POPULATION. *See* Demography.

POTTERY. *See* Ceramics.

PRESERVATION. *See* Restoration and Conservation.

PRIENE, ancient Ionian city (37°38′ N, 27°17′ E) situated on the southern slopes of Mt. Mycale, just north of the Meander River, near the Aegean coast of Turkey, across from the island of Samos. Priene now lies about 15 km (9.3 mi.) inland, but it was originally much closer to the sea; silt carried downstream by the Meander River continues to push the coastline ever westward.

The identification of Priene is secured by numerous inscriptions found on the site. Archaeological investigation began with the expeditions of the British Society of Dilettanti to Ionia in the eighteenth and nineteenth centuries. Extensive excavations were carried out by the Berlin Museum from 1895 to 1899 (Wiegand and Schrader, 1904). A German team resumed investigation of the site in 1977.

The history of Priene may be traced back to at least 700 BCE, but the current site was apparently not settled until the mid-fourth century; the original location of the city remains unknown. The area of new Priene falls into two parts: to the south, a lower city (the main area of occupation), built on gently sloping ground; to the north, an acropolis on a high hill, separated from the lower city by steep cliffs.

Both acropolis and lower city are surrounded by fortifications, enclosing a total area of about 40 ha (99 acres). The lower city was laid out on a grid pattern, oriented north–south and covering an area of about 15 ha (37 acres). The grid is based on a block size of approximately 47.2 m × 35.4 m (160 × 120 Ionic feet). In the center of the city, a nearly square area of three blocks (two full blocks plus two half blocks) was reserved for the agora (marketplace). Northwest of the agora, an area of the same size was set aside for the sanctuary of Athena. The construction of the fortifications, the layout of the city grid, and the basic town-planning all seem to have been parts of the original urban design.

The Ionic temple of Athena rests on a high terrace that dominates the lower city of Priene. The temple was designed by Pytheos, a celebrated architect, and dedicated by Alexander the Great, probably in 334; construction apparently was not finished until the Augustan period (27 BCE–14 CE), however, when the temple received a supplementary dedication to the emperor. The agora and associated structures were also built up over several hundred years; the agora reached its final form, in which it was surrounded on all sides by stoas (portico-like structures), in the second half of the second century. To the east lies a small sanctuary, dedicated either to Zeus or to Asklepios. North of the agora are the *bouleuterion* (council house) and *prytaneion* (administrative headquarters); the former building is unusually well preserved and had an estimated seating capacity of 640 persons.

Other public buildings and lesser sanctuaries are scattered throughout the city. Of these the most important are the theater and the lower gymnasium and accompanying stadium. The theater is built into the hillside on the northern edge of the city grid. The seating area may be as early as the founding of the city in the mid-fourth century; the stage building is somewhat later, but it is still one of the earliest and best-preserved buildings of this type known. The lower gymnasium lies just inside the fortifications on the southern edge of town. It has been dated to the mid-second century, and consists of a colonnaded exercise ground with a row of rooms on the north side, including a large classroom, whose walls are inscribed with the names of hundreds of schoolboys. The stadium lies east of the gymnasium and is the only major building at Priene oriented according to the natural hillslope, rather than the city grid.

Priene is unusual in the preservation and extensive excavation of its residential districts, in which approximately seventy houses have been revealed. These houses, four to a block on average, vary both in size and plan; the state in which they survive is that of the late Hellenistic and Roman periods (second century BCE–fourth century CE), however, and it is possible that they were originally more uniform. Features of these houses often singled out as typical are a square room *(oikos)* on the north side of the house, entered by way of a simple porch *(prostas)*, which opens in turn on an interior court.

There is little new building of the Roman era at Priene, probably because the ever-advancing coastline caused the economic fortunes of the city to decline. Several churches were built in late antiquity, and the city remained the seat of a Christian bishop until the Seljuk conquests of the thirteenth century CE.

BIBLIOGRAPHY

Carter, Joseph C. *The Sculpture of the Sanctuary of Athena Polias at Priene.* London, 1983.

Gerkan, Armin von. *Das Theater von Priene.* Munich, 1921.

Hiller von Gaertringen, Friedrich. *Inschriften von Priene.* Berlin, 1906.

Hoepfner, Wolfram, and Ernst-Ludwig Schwander. *Haus und Stadt im klassischen Griechenland.* 2d ed. Munich, 1994. Controversial study (see pp. 188–225). For criticisms of the first edition's treatment of Priene, see the article by Koenigs below.

Koenigs, Wolf. "Planung und Ausbau der Agora von Priene." *Istanbuler Mitteilungen* 43 (1993): 381–397.

Raeder, Joachim. *Priene: Funde aus einer griechischen Stadt.* Berlin, 1984.

Schede, Martin. *Die Ruinen von Priene.* 2d ed. Berlin, 1964. Very useful short introduction to the site.

Wiegand, Theodor, and Hans Schrader. *Priene.* Berlin, 1904. The basic publication of the German excavations of 1895–1898.

CHRISTOPHER RATTÉ

PROTO-CANAANITE. In the latest thorough treatment of Proto-Canaanite inscriptions (Sass, 1988), twenty-two inscriptions in a quasi-pictographic script from southern Canaan are accepted as representing Proto-Canaanite. They show the evolution, although with many gaps, of the script from the early seventeenth to the twelfth centuries BCE, by which time a script very similar to that of the earliest Phoenician inscriptions had clearly evolved. [*See* Phoenician-Punic.] Depending on the date ascribed to the Proto-Sinaitic inscriptions, written in a similar script, the inscriptions from Canaan either provide the earliest examples of alphabetic writing or come soon after the Sinai inscriptions. (An earlier chronology for the Sinai inscriptions is deemed the more likely. [*See* Proto-Sinaitic.])

The state of preservation of the Proto-Canaanite inscriptions is generally even poorer than that of the Proto-Sinaitic inscriptions. The identification of their script as West Semitic alphabetic rests on its formal similarity with the earlier Proto-Sinaitic script, on the actual decipherment of a minority of the texts, and on the formal evolution toward the script known as Phoenician. Whereas the inscriptions from Sinai are in stone and are relatively long and well preserved, the Proto-Canaanite inscriptions are usually very brief and for the most part are written on pottery, either whole pieces or sherds (ostraca), and have suffered through the millennia. [*See* Ostracon.] For these reasons, there is very little textual material that can be identified with certainty as Proto-Canaanite.

The clearest example of a meaningful Canaanite text is the Lachish Ewer inscription, discovered in the 1933–1934 excavations at Tell ed-Duweir/Lachish and dated to the thirteenth century BCE (Tufnell et al., 1940, frontispiece, pp. 49–54, pls. LI A: 287, LX: 3; Sass, 1988, pp. 60–61, figs. 156–160). [*See* Lachish.] The script is still reasonably close to its pictographic origins and reads {mtn . šy [---]ty 'lt [. . .]}. The first word has been interpreted as a common noun meaning "gift" or as the proper name *Mattan.* Frank M. Cross (1954, pp. 20–21) has plausibly reconstructed the first lacuna as containing the preposition *l,* "for," which may even be partially visible, and the first two letters of the title *rbt,* "lady." The word *'lt* is the standard West Semitic word for "goddess" and could either be a title or function as a divine name. Thus, this text can be interpreted as meaning "a gift of tribute [for the La]dy, the goddess of [. . .]," or perhaps "(From) Mattan: a tribute [a La]dy 'Ilat [. . .]." In any case, the preserved text fits plausibly with the object itself, a large decorated urn found in a temple, inspiring confidence that, had the object been found intact, it would have been possible to decipher the entire inscription.

At the other extreme of comprehensibility are four lines of the five-line inscription on an ostracon from ʿIzbet Ṣarṭah that has been dated to about 1200 BCE (Kochavi, 1977; Demsky, 1977; Cross, 1980, pp. 8–15; Puech, 1983, pp. 563–567; Sass, 1988, pp. 65–69, table 6, figs. 175–177). [*See* ʿIzbet Ṣarṭah.] One line (line 1 or 5, depending on whether the text is read from top to bottom or from bottom to top) is certainly an abecedary, the earliest attested from southern Canaan. [*See* Alphabet.] This abecedary clearly represents the short twenty-two letter alphabet, but the other four lines have so far defied interpretation. It appears likely, therefore, that the West Semitic alphabet was in this instance used to write a text in another language, as yet unidentified. Although it is illegitimate to use this text to call into doubt the West Semitic and alphabetic character of all the Proto-Canaanite inscriptions (Garbini, 1978), this example does show that no given inscription can be considered West Semitic with certainty until it is satisfactorily deciphered (Garbini and Durand, 1994, p. 39).

Forming somewhat of a link between the Proto-Canaanite inscriptions and those in Phoenician is a series of inscriptions on arrowheads, of which the number of known examples is now approaching thirty (Bordreuil, 1992, p. 212, n. 34; Cross, 1992; Cross, 1995), that is dated to about 1100–900 BCE. Some were found in excavations at Bethlehem and in Lebanon, but they have appeared for the most part on the antiquities market. [*See* Bethlehem.] The standard inscription consists of only a personal name, usually preceded by the word *ḥṣ*, "arrow"; sometimes a title is indicated. One, for example, reads {ḥṣ zkrbʿl mlk ʿmr}, "arrow of Zakarbaʿal, king of Amurru" (Starcky, 1982). The function of the inscribed arrowheads is uncertain (Sass, 1988, pp. 72–75; Cross, 1992, p. 25*), and the fact that they have been discovered in two rather widely separated locations constitutes an enigma.

It is plausible to assume that the Proto-Canaanite inscriptions represent the use of the West Semitic alphabet to write the local Canaanite dialects as early as the end of the Middle Bronze period (mid-second millennium BCE). The earliest inscriptions in a similar script presently known are from northern Canaan and Syria—the arrowheads and the very rare and brief "Phoenician" inscriptions dating to before 1000 BCE (primarily from Byblos). [*See* Byblos.] The existence of the Ugaritic alphabetic writing system, which seems to reflect an existing linear alphabetic script, makes it reasonable, however, to posit that a system similar to that used for Proto-Sinaitic and Proto-Canaanite was also in use in the north at the latest by the middle of the second millennium BCE.

[*See also* Writing and Writing Systems.]

BIBLIOGRAPHY

Bordreuil, Pierre. "Flèches phéniciennes inscrites: 1981–1991 I." *Revue Biblique* 99 (1992): 205–213. Overview of recently discovered inscribed arrowheads.

Colles, Brian E. "Recent Discoveries Illuminating the Origin of the Alphabet." *Abr-Nahrain* 26 (1988): 30–67. Rather sanguine attempt at decipherment of the Proto-Canaanite inscriptions.

Cross, Frank Moore. "The Evolution of the Proto-Canaanite Alphabet." *Bulletin of the American Schools of Oriental Research,* no. 134 (1954): 15–24. Proto-Canaanite inscriptions in the context of alphabetic origins.

Cross, Frank Moore. "Newly Found Inscriptions in Old Canaanite and Early Phoenician Scripts." *Bulletin of the American Schools of Oriental Research,* no. 238 (1980): 1–20. Reappraisal of alphabetic origins and developments.

Cross, Frank Moore. "An Inscribed Arrowhead of the Eleventh Century BCE in the Bible Lands Museum in Jerusalem." *Eretz-Israel* 23 (1992): 21–26. Edition of a new arrowhead inscription.

Cross, Frank Moore. "A Note on a Recently Published Arrowhead." *Israel Exploration Journal* 45 (1995): 188–189. Rereading of a recently published arrowhead inscription.

Demsky, Aaron. "A Proto-Canaanite Abecedary Dating from the Period of the Judges and Its Implications for the History of the Alphabet." *Tell Aviv* 4 (1977): 14–27. Attemps to place the ʿIzbet Ṣarṭah ostracon in the history of the alphabet and considers it to be an exercise by an Israelite scribe.

Garbini, Giovanni. "Le iscrizioni 'protocananaiche' del XII e XI secolo a.C." *Annali del Istituto Universitario Orientale di Napoli* 34 (1974): 584–590. Considers the Proto-Canaanite inscriptions to be undeciphered and to have been dated too early by most scholars, arguing that they do not predate the earliest Phoenician inscriptions.

Garbini, Giovanni. "Sull'alfabetario di ʿIzbet Ṣarṭah." *Oriens Antiquus* 17 (1978): 287–295. Uses the ʿIzbet Ṣarṭah ostracon to discredit the West Semitic character of the Proto-Canaanite inscriptions.

Garbini, Giovanni, and Olivier Durand. *Introduzione alle lingue semitiche.* Brescia, 1994. Considers the Proto-Canaanite inscriptions in the context of describing the Semitic languages, emphasizing difficulties of decipherment and linguistic identification.

Kochavi, Moshe. "An Ostracon of the Period of the Judges from ʿIzbet Ṣarṭah." *Tel Aviv* 4 (1977): 1–13. *Editio princeps* of the ʿIzbet Ṣarṭah text, with discussion of the archaeological context.

Naveh, Joseph. *An Early History of the Alphabet: An Introduction to West Semitic Epigraphy and Palaeography.* 2d ed. Jerusalem, 1987. Suggests that some of the Proto-Canaanite texts antedate the Proto-Sinaitic inscriptions.

Puech, Émile. "Quelques remarques sur l'alphabet au deuxième millénaire." In *Atti del I congresso internazionale di studi fenici e punici, Roma, 5–10 novembre 1979,* vol. 2, edited by Piero Bartoloni et al., pp. 564–581. Rome, 1983. Some of the early texts from Canaan seen in the context of the history of the alphabet, with a new hand copy of the ʿIzbet Ṣarṭah inscription.

Puech, Émile. "Origine de l'alphabet: Documents en alphabet linéaire et cunéiforme du IIe millénaire." *Revue Biblique* 93 (1986): 161–213. Early texts from Canaan seen in the context of other second millennium groups of texts.

Sass, Benjamin. *The Genesis of the Alphabet and Its Development in the Second Millenium* [*sic*] *B.C.* Ägypten und Altes Testament, 13. Wiesbaden, 1988. Latest thorough treatment of the Proto-Canaanite inscriptions, which exhibits a very careful epigraphic, philological, and historical method. Highly recommended.

Sass, Benjamin. *Studia Alphabetica: On the Origin and Early History of the Northwest Semitic, South Semitic, and Greek Alphabets.* Orbis Biblicus et Orientalis, 102. Freiburg, 1991. Discusses the place of the Proto-Canaanite inscriptions in the history of the alphabet.

Shea, William H. "The ʿIzbet Ṣarṭah Ostracon." *Andrews University Seminary Studies* 28 (1990): 59–86. Unconvincing attempt to decipher the ʿIzbet Ṣarṭah text.

Starcky, Jean. "La flèche de Zakarbaal roi d'Amurru." In *Archéologie au Levant: Recueil à la mémoire de Roger Saidah*, pp. 179–186. Lyon, 1982. *Editio princeps* of one of the more interesting and important of the arrowhead inscriptions.

Tufnell, Olga, et al. *Lachish II: The Fosse Temple*. London, 1940. Official publication of the Lachish Ewer, with an epigraphic and philological discussion by Theodor H. Gaster.

DENNIS PARDEE

PROTO-SINAITIC. During excavations in 1904–1905 led by W. M. Flinders Petrie at the ancient Egyptian turquoise-mining site in west-central Sinai known as Serabit el-Khadem, ten inscriptions were discovered that were written in a pictographic script that was not Egyptian. [*See* Sinai.] All were engraved in the local sandstone. Petrie (1906, pp. 129–132) reported immediately on these inscriptions, and the texts were published in facsimile in 1917 (Gardiner and Peet, 1917, nos. 345–355; see Gardiner, 1917, pls. III–V). Working from these inscriptions and an eleventh known from a squeeze taken a few years earlier (Weill, 1904, p. 154, no. 44), Alan Gardiner (1916) deciphered the crucial word *bʿlt*, "lady," identified the script as West Semitic alphabetic, and proposed an Egyptian origin for the alphabet. [*See* Alphabet.] Since those first steps, another twenty certain Proto-Sinaitic inscriptions have been discovered and nearly as many dubious proposals have been made (Sass, 1988, pp. 8–50, table I).

As Gardiner (1916, pp. 6–14) observed in his pioneering study, the Proto-Sinaitic letter forms appear to reflect the pictographic form of West Semitic letters according to the so-called acrophonic principle: the sign represents the object corresponding to the name of the letter, while the first letter of the name corresponds to the consonantal phoneme in question. For example, a bovine head represents /ʾ/, and the West Semitic word for *bovine* is *ʾalp-*; a human eye represents /ʿ/, and the word for *eye* is *ʿayn-*; and a human head represents /r/, and the West Semitic word for *head* is *raʾš-*, or *riʾš-*. That the forms of the Proto-Sinaitic signs are to be explained by the acrophonic principle has been accepted by all who identify the script as the precursor of the later West Semitic alphabetic scripts (e.g., Naveh, 1982/1987, pp. 23–27).

Whether this early pictographic form is in fact the earliest known depends on the dating of the inscriptions. No single inscription is dated with certainty and the associated Egyptian finds date from late twelfth dynasty (c. 1800 BCE) to the early New Kingdom (Thutmose III). Joseph Naveh (1982/1987, pp. 26–27), for example, unquestioningly accepts the later date, and thereby places some Proto-Canaanite inscriptions earlier than the Proto-Sinaitic, while Sass (1988, pp. 135–144, pp. 158–159; 1991, p. 4) rejects the dating of some objects on which inscriptions were engraved to the New Kingdom, finding the best parallels in the twelfth dynasty. [*See* Proto-Canaanite.] Accepting Sass's conclusions means that the Proto-Sinaitic inscriptions represent the earliest known attestations of West Semitic alphabetic script. This does not necessarily lead to the conclusion that the alphabet was invented at Serabit el-Khadem, however, for there is insufficient data on the social status of the West Semites who worked there. It is unlikely, in any case, that slaves or uneducated workers would have invented the alphabet. If the Sinai inscriptions do in fact reflect the invention of the alphabetic writing system, they imply the presence there of a West Semite trained in Egyptian who would on the spot have had the idea of reducing the many Egyptian signs to a small number of signs representing the consonantal phonemes of his own language. In fact, the Proto-Sinaitic signs may well represent the borrowing of the pictographic principle from Egyptian hieroglyphs (Sznycer, 1972, p. 1394; 1974, pp. 7–9; Sass, 1988, p. 161)—which in theory could have taken place in any of the centers of Egypto-Canaanite contact since the beginning of writing in Egypt in the late predynastic period. [*See* Hieroglyphs.] According to Benjamin Sass (1991, pp. 24–27), the Egyptian use of certain signs in a quasi-alphabetic fashion for the rendition of foreign names is best attested in the Middle Kingdom, and this usage provides the best contact for the invention of the alphabet by a West Semite. Whatever the relationship may be of the Proto-Sinaitic inscriptions to the invention of the alphabet, the fact that they were carved on stone has meant that this very early group of witnesses to early alphabetic writing has survived to this day in reasonably good condition.

Although claims of virtually complete decipherment have been made (e.g., Albright, 1966; Colless, 1990), and at the other extreme it has been claimed that no decipherment is yet possible (Garbini, 1976, 1980, pp. 89, 103), the most careful treatments (Sznycer, 1972; Sass, 1988, pp. 159–161) accept the decipherment of only a few words. These few words, however, appear sufficient to identify the script as alphabetic and the language as West Semitic: *bʿlt*, "lady"; *mʾhb*, "beloved"; *rb nqbn*, "chief of the mine(rs)." Although they are best identified as West Semitic words, no precise linguistic identification is possible (Garbini and Durand, 1994, p. 34). Until sufficiently well-preserved inscriptions are discovered to permit a full decipherment, such is the hypothesis that commands the highest probability.

BIBLIOGRAPHY

Albright, William Foxwell. *The Proto-Sinaitic Inscriptions and Their Decipherment*. Harvard Theological Studies, 22 Cambridge, Mass., 1966. Attempt at full decipherment of the Proto-Sinaitic inscriptions, which has heuristic value but cannot be accepted as a systematic decipherment.

Colless, Brian E. "The Proto-Alphabetic Inscriptions of Sinai." *Abr-*

Nahrain 28 (1990): 1–52. Another attempt at full decipherment of the Proto-Sinaitic inscriptions that also cannot be accepted.

Garbini, Giovanni. "Gli 'alfabeti' semitici settentrionali." *Parola e Passato* 31 (1976): 66–81. Considers the Proto-Sinaitic inscriptions to be nonalphabetic and undeciphered.

Garbini, Giovanni. *I fenici: Storia e religione.* Naples, 1980. Repeats the stance of the earlier article in the context of the history of writing leading to Phoenician.

Garbini, Giovanni, and Olivier Durand. *Introduzione alle lingue semitiche.* Brescia, 1994. Considers the Proto-Sinaitic inscriptions in the context of describing the Semitic languages, arguing that the language is Semitic and the writing consonantal, that is, alphabetic.

Gardiner, Alan H. "The Egyptian Origin of the Semitic Alphabet." *Journal of Egyptian Archaeology* 3 (1916): 1–16. Pioneering identification of the Proto-Sinaitic inscriptions as alphabetic and West Semitic.

Gardiner, Alan H., and T. Eric Peet. *The Inscriptions of Sinai,* vol. 1, *Introduction and Plates.* Publications of the Egyptian Exploration Fund, 36 London, 1917. Hand copies of the first group of inscriptions discovered during regular excavations.

Naveh, Joseph. *An Early History of the Alphabet: An Introduction to West Semitic Epigraphy and Palaeography.* 2d ed. Jerusalem, 1987. Adopts a low chronology (ca. 1500).

Petrie, W. M. Flinders. *Researches in Sinai.* London, 1906. Discussion of a first group of inscriptions discovered during regular excavations, with photographs of two inscribed objects.

Sass, Benjamin. *The Genesis of the Alphabet and Its Development in the Second Millenium* [*sic*] *B.C.* Ägypten and Altes Testament, 13. Wiesbaden, 1988. Latest thorough treatment of the Proto-Sinaitic inscriptions, which exhibits a very careful epigraphic, philological, and historical method. Highly recommended.

Sass, Benjamin. *Studia Alphabetica: On the Origin and Early History of the Northwest Semitic, South Semitic, and Greek Alphabets.* Orbis Biblicus et Orientalis, 102. Freiburg, 1991. Discusses the place of the Proto-Sinaitic inscriptions in the history of the alphabet.

Sznycer, Maurice. "Protosinaïtiques (Inscriptions)." In *Supplément au Dictionnaire de la Bible,* vol. 8, cols. 1384–1395. Paris, 1972. Thorough overview of discovery, publication, and decipherment, with a balanced assessment of the contribution of these texts to knowledge of alphabetic origins.

Sznycer, Maurice. "Quelques remarques à propos de la formation de l'alphabet phénicien." *Semitica* 24 (1974): 5–12. Broader and briefer treatment of alphabetic origins, including the contribution of the Proto-Sinaitic inscriptions.

Weill, Raymond. *Recueil des inscriptions égyptiennes du Sinai.* Paris, 1904. Earliest publication of a Proto-Sinaitic inscription, from a squeeze taken near Serabit el-Khadem, in the Wadi Magharah.

DENNIS PARDEE

PTOLEMAIS, provincial capital of the Libyan Pentapolis from the time of Diocletian (284–305 CE) until the beginning of the fifth century CE (32°40′ N, 20°55′ E). Ptolemais occupied a coastal position 88 km (55 mi.) west of Cyrene and 105 km (65 mi.) northeast of Benghazi (ancient Euesperides/Berenice). Random pottery finds suggest that it may have already served as a harbor facility by the late seventh century BCE. Nonetheless, the name of the settlement during the Archaic or Classical periods has not survived. Eventually Ptolemy III (262–221 BCE) refounded it as Ptolemais, and it is as a Hellenistic, Roman, and Byzantine center that the town is best known. It came into Roman possession in 96 BCE and flourished until various poorly understood factors (perhaps tribal incursions and the silting up of its harbor) forced the city to cede its role as the head of the provincial government to nearby Apollonia-Sosuza. Although the invasions under Amr ibn al-ʿAṣ in the seventh century CE brought an end to the Greek settlement, recent excavations provide clear evidence for a continued occupation well into the Islamic period.

Excavations that had been undertaken by Italian archaeologists between the two world wars were later extended by the Libyan Department of Antiquities and were directed by Richard Goodchild and others. Carl Kraeling undertook a major clearance in the later 1950s for the University of Chicago, and more recently, various British archaeologists have conducted tests of both the harbor and land portions of the site for the Society for Libyan Studies.

The main harbor basin was sheltered by a small promontory to its west on which stands an ancient pharos (lighthouse). The urban plan occupies a rectangle about 1,650 × 1,400 m (5,413 × 4,593 ft.) with two major cardines (north–south streets) and five *decumani* (east–west streets) creating standard blocks of 180 × 36 m (590 × 118 ft.). The east–west Road of the Monuments was lined with *cippi* or stone bases carrying honorific statues, as well as decorated with a triple-arcaded triumphal arch of the time of Constantine. Although little remains of the Hellenistic defensive walls apart from elements of projecting rectangular towers set out at regular intervals, the Tocra gate to the west is still imposing. Traces exist of an amphitheater (see plan, item 1) in the northwest corner, a hippodrome (27) to the south and three theaters (7, 9, 28). Urban water needs were partially met by the Court of the Cisterns (10), whose seventeen underground vaulted cisterns had a combined capacity of more than 8.5 million gallons, and a nearby open public reservoir (12) supplied an additional 26 million gallons. Private cisterns and an aqueduct from Wadi Habbun 24 km (15 mi.) to the east supplied the remainder of the city's water. Although the nearby extramural quarries are honeycombed with chamber tombs, the most impressive expression of funerary architecture is unquestionably the Qaṣr Faraoun, modeled after the pharos at Alexandria, that lies a short distance west of the city. The more important later civic monuments include the city's Byzantine baths (15), its ducal headquarters (23), and the important fortified church (2).

The private town houses of the wealthy, providing some of the best examples of their type thus far uncovered in the Pentapolis region ("land of the five cities"—Cyrene, Apollonia, Ptolemais, Tauchira, and Berenice) have been the target of considerable recent investigation. The substantial "Palazzo delle Colonne" (13), which was built around two peristyles, occupies the entire width of a city block and half its length. Known since the 1930s, it remains the most familiar monument of Ptolemais, as well as a model for urban villa construction throughout the eastern Mediterranean region.

Ptolemais has yielded a number of important inscriptions, including a copy of the price edict of Diocletian and a decree of Anastasius. The local museum contains important sculptures and other locally discovered artifacts. Despite what has been accomplished, much remains to be excavated inside the walls, and useful survey should be undertaken some day in the neighboring environs.

BIBLIOGRAPHY

Kennet, D. "Some Notes on Islamic Tolmeita." *Libyan Studies* 22 (1991): 83–89. Summarizes recent work on the post-Greek phase of urban occupation.

Kraeling, Carl H. *Ptolemais, City of the Libyan Pentapolis*. Chicago, 1962. The principal site monograph, which includes an extensive discussion of Ptolemais's history.

Lloyd, J. "Urban Archaeology in Cyrenaica, 1969–1989: The Hellenistic, Roman, and Byzantine Periods." *Libyan Studies* 20 (1989): 77–90. Contains a useful summary of fieldwork carried out at Ptolemais since the conclusion of the Chicago Expedition led by Kraeling.

Pesce, Gennaro. *Il "Palazzo delle Colonne" in Tolemaide di Cirenaica*. Monografie di Archeologia Libica, 2. Rome, 1950. The definitive description of the city's most important architectural monument.

Ward-Perkins, J. B., et al. "Town Houses at Ptolemais." *Libyan Studies* 17 (1986): 109–153. Analysis of work on various urban villas carried out for the Society of Libyan Studies during the previous decade.

DONALD WHITE

PTOLEMIES. Ptolemy, a general of Alexander the Great and the author of a history of Alexander (now lost), received Egypt as his domain as a result of the partitioning of the empire following Alexander's death. Ptolemy was crowned king of Egypt in 304 BCE. This date marks the beginning of the Ptolemaic dynasty that ruled Egypt until 30 BCE, when the Romans conquered the country.

From the outset the Ptolemies were crowned at Memphis, Egypt's traditional capital (although firm evidence exists only for the crowning ceremony of Ptolemy V). The first four Ptolemies were extremely active in foreign policy and ruled over many regions outside Egypt, including Cyrene, Cyprus, southern Asia Minor, some of the Aegean islands, and Palestine. Most of these regions were lost between the end of the third and the second centuries BCE.

The Ptolemies were well aware from the start of their rule how to conduct themselves as kings both for the Greek colonizers of Egypt and its native population. For the latter, they were Pharaohs who had been Horus and upon their death had become Osiris. In Egyptian temples they were considered Egyptian deities. The temples they erected for the indigenous population followed traditional Egyptian temple architecture but with some Hellenistic additions, such as at Philae and Edfu. The literature composed by native Egyptians such as Manetho (third century BCE) seems to be full of legitimations of the dualism their reign reflected, of their pharaonic and Hellenistic traits. As the Greek rulers of Egypt, however, they stressed their Greek aspects, recruiting Greek *philoi* ("friends of the king"—namely, his advisory board), speaking Greek in the royal court, appearing on their coins as Greek deities, and founding Greek temples. They also supported the many Greek scholars who gathered in Alexandria around the Mousseion (Museum, a kind of academy), and some of the Ptolemies were ardent collectors of Greek manuscripts. Thus, the Ptolemies posed, to varying degrees, as dualistic kings.

During the Hellenistic era (323–30 BCE) the Ptolemies faced several crucial challenges. Foremost was dealing with Egypt's internal dynastic power politics, which became more troublesome in the second and, in particular, the first centuries BCE. They also had to contend with a strong local priesthood, which played a leading role among native Egyptians. Two documents from the Hellenistic period reflect those tensions: the Canopus document (238 BCE) and the Rosetta Stone (196 BCE). Finally, the Ptolemies had to confront harsh international power politics, especially in their relationships with the Seleucids and Macedonians (until the downfall of Macedonia in 168 BCE). Throughout the third century BCE, Egypt fought the Seleucids at least five times, in the so-called Syrian Wars—about most of which we have little information. Egypt had the upper hand in Palestine in the third century BCE. Some useful information concerning economic activities during Ptolemaic rule in Palestine is preserved in the Zenon papyri.

At the turn of the century (204 BCE), following the death of Ptolemy IV, Philip V of Macedonia and the Seleucid king Antiochus III made a pact to divide Egypt's overseas possessions between them. This brought about the Second Macedonian War (Rome and her Greek allies against Macedonia, in 200–197 BCE). The Seleucid Empire, under Antiochus III, annexed Palestine after the battle of Panion, in which he crushed the Ptolemaic army. The Ptolemies also lost many of their other possessions outside Egypt. Rome defeated the Seleucids in the so-called Roman-Syrian War (192–189/88 BCE), and then crushed Macedonia (in the Third Macedonian War in 172–168 BCE), the beginning of their more intensive intervention in the affairs of the ancient Near East. During the second century BCE, Rome often supported Egypt against the Seleucids. Antiochus IV's well-attested second invasion of Egypt in 169/68 BCE illustrates Rome's position vis-à-vis Ptolemaic Egypt at the time. The Roman envoy issued an ultimatum and Antiochus obeyed: he left Egypt, which he had wished to treat as his own domain. Later, it was Ptolemaic Egypt, along with Pergamon and Rome, that supported the Seleucid pretender Alexander Balas against Demetrius. Rome was interested in a weak Egypt but supported it against other powers in the region. From the end of the second century BCE onward, the Ptolemaic dynasty declined sharply, with Egypt embroiled in the continuous strife among the Ptolemaic princes.

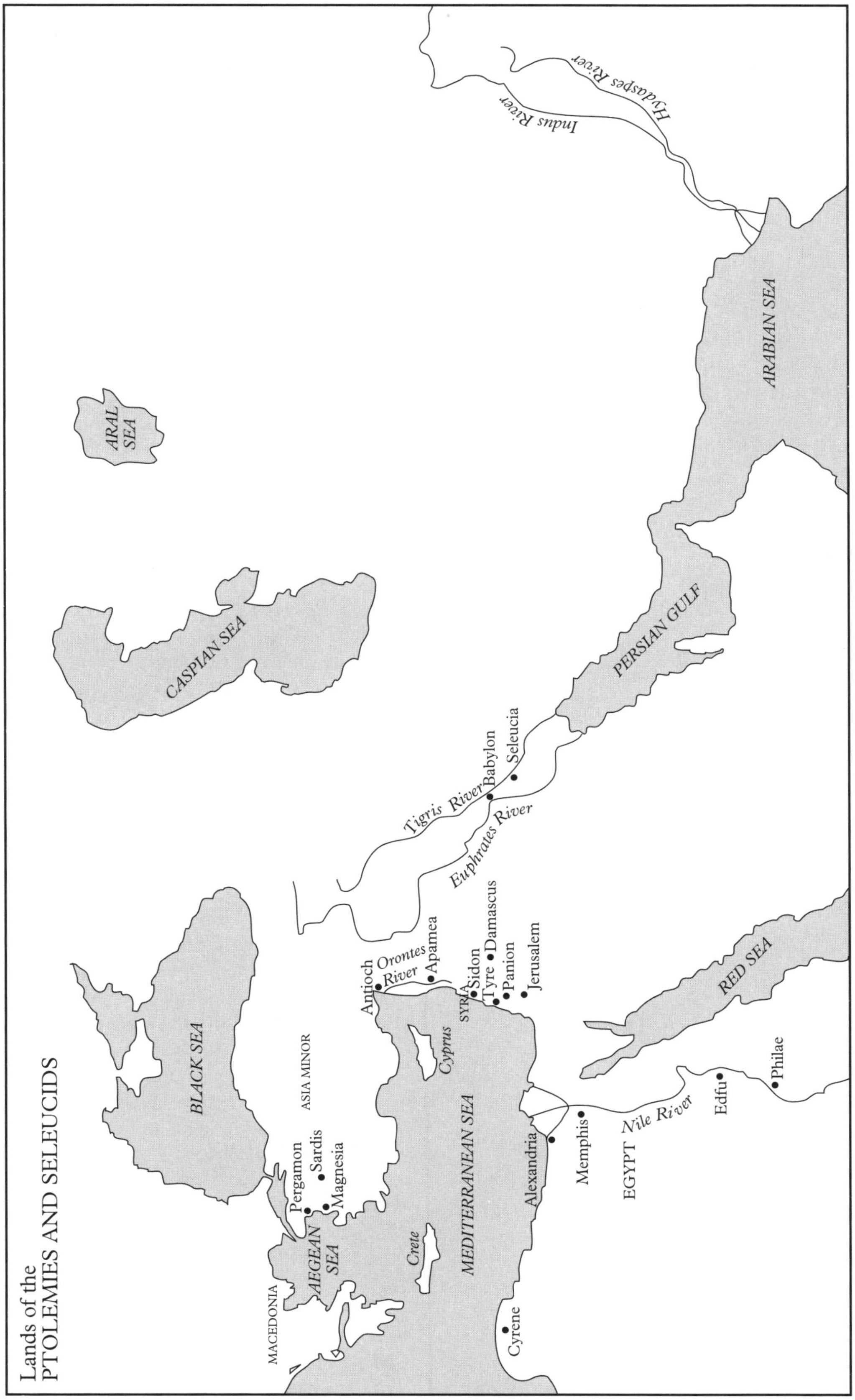
Lands of the
PTOLEMIES AND SELEUCIDS
MACEDONIA
AEGEAN SEA
Crete
MEDITERRANEAN SEA
Cyrene
Pergamon
Sardis
Magnesia
ASIA MINOR
BLACK SEA
Alexandria
Memphis
EGYPT
Nile River
Edfu
Philae
Cyprus
SYRIA
Antioch
Orontes River
Apamea
Sidon
Tyre
Damascus
Panion
Jerusalem
RED SEA
Euphrates River
Tigris River
Babylon
Seleucia
CASPIAN SEA
PERSIAN GULF
ARAL SEA
ARABIAN SEA
Indus River
Hydaspes River

Ptolemaic Egypt was organized into forty districts called nomes. Every *nomos* was subdivided into *topoi.* The *nomos* was managed by the *nomarches,* apparently until the third century BCE, when their functions were gradually taken over by the *stratēgos,* who had until then been in charge of the army in the district. The *stratēgos* was assisted by an *oikonomos,* who was in charge of finances, and by a *basilikos grammateus,* who administered the district's land register. All of these magistrates received their orders from the *dioikētēs,* the chief administrator of Egypt, stationed at Alexandria, the new capital. High officials in Ptolemaic Egypt in the time of the first Ptolemies were recruited mainly from among the Greek colonizing stratum of the society; later, people indigenous to Egypt were also recruited, provided they were Hellenized. The same pattern held for the higher ranks in the Ptolemaic army.

Like other Hellenistic armies, the Ptolemaic army was composed of mercenaries (from Crete, Greece, and Asia Minor) and soldiers who received allotments *(klērouchiai)* and were recruited when needed. Even indigenous Egyptians were recruited, such as the twenty thousand Egyptians who participated in the battle of Raphia (217 BCE). This recruitment of Egyptians led to unrest, however, when they demanded more freedom from Ptolemaic rule.

The economy of Ptolemaic Egypt was based on tightly centralized management. There was intense commercial activity in the Greek cities (of which there were only three), and particularly in Alexandria. The cities were the main consumers of imported goods, as well as of goods from the *chōra* (the land around the cities). The lands of Egypt were divided into the *gē basilikē,* "the king's land"—and therefore under his direct control—cultivated by Egyptian farmers who received part of the crops; *gē en ephesei,* land the king alloted to soldiers *(gē klērouchikē)* and senior magistrates in the Ptolemaic bureaucracy *(gē en dōrea);* and land owned by the temples *(gē hiera),* perhaps a third of all Egyptian lands.

The Egyptian legal system also was dualistic in character. The Greek population adhered to Greek law while the native population followed the local law. Ptolemaic Alexandria was famous for its rich cultural life, which included being an important center of Jewish life in the Greco-Roman period.

[*See also* Egypt, *article on* Postdynastic Egypt; *and* Seleucids.]

BIBLIOGRAPHY

Bevan, Edwyn Robert. *A History of Egypt under the Ptolemaic Dynasty.* London, 1927.

Bowman, Alan K. *Egypt after the Pharaohs, 332 BC–AD 642.* London, 1986.

Fraser, P. M. *Ptolemaic Alexandria.* 3 vols. Oxford, 1972.

Mendels, Doron. "The Polemical Character of Manetho's *Aegyptiaca.*" In *Purposes of History,* edited by H. Verdin et al., pp. 92–110. Louvain, 1990.

DORON MENDELS

PUBLIC BUILDINGS.

Although frequently used, the term *public buildings* is somewhat misleading when applied to palaces, temples, storehouses and other administrative units, which were not intended to serve the "public": they were built exclusively to meet the needs of the ruling class and should, thus, be labeled elite structures. [*See* Palace.] Along with fortification systems, elite structures signify the architectural manifestation of the institutions controlled by the ruling class—political, military, administrative, religious, and economic. In many cases elite structures were built on a monumental scale, with a unique plan that expressed the high status of their users. The architecture of elite structures thus became an ideological tool used by rulers to sustain social order and their high standing within it.

Temples. Ceremonial, cultic structures usually are referred to as temples. [*See* Cult.] The earliest example of this type is the colossal round tower assigned to the Pre-Pottery Neolithic A period at Jericho. [*See* Jericho.] The tower apparently served as a podium for a brick-made ceremonial structure that was not preserved (Bar-Yosef, 1986). Entry into this shrine was through an inner staircase incorporated within the solid building.

From the Chalcolithic period throughout the Iron Age, monumental temples in Israel were constructed either as a broad-room house type or in the long-room style (Ottosson, 1980). A group of temples common in the Middle Bronze Age IIB throughout the Late Bronze Age is identified as monumental symmetrical temples or Syrian temples (Mazar, 1992). Temples with a long-room or with a broad-room hall are included in this category, despite the basic difference between the two architectural types. In Mesopotamia, a third type of temple was common, the bent-axis temple. All other cultic structures should be considered composite in type.

Unlike modern churches, synagogues, and mosques, which serve the community for cultic ceremony, ancient temples were considered to be the dwelling place of the gods. [*See* Churches; Synagogues; Mosque.] The presence of the deity was exhibited by a statue or a stela, usually erected on a podium. The participants in the ceremonies gathered in the courtyard outside the temple. The basic shape of the sanctuary dictated the level of intimacy the builders of the temple allowed the worshippers with their deity. In a broad-room temple, the platform for the deity was usually placed next to the rear wall, in line with the central entrance, providing a close and direct view from outside. In a long-room temple, the podium was set in the back and could not be seen by most of the audience. The bent-axis temples common in Mesopotamia totally prevented a view of the deity.

Broad-room temple. Like broad-room houses, broad-room temples were the prevalent form of rectangular buildings in ancient Israel (Herzog, 1980). Compounds consisting of a broad-room temple encompassed by a fence had been commonly used as ceremonial-cultic centers since the Chalcolithic period. Typical examples are the compounds at ʿEin-Gedi and Teleilat el-Ghassul. [*See* ʿEin-Gedi; Teleilat el-Ghassul.] The continuity of this plan into the Early Bronze I period is evident in the plans of Megiddo stratum XIX and the Ḥartuv compounds. [*See* Megiddo; Ḥartuv.] The EB II broad-room temples at Ai and Megiddo XVIII apparently were also incorporated into such compounds. [*See* Ai.] The broad-room temple is the dominant type in EB III, as attested in the plan of the White Building at Tel Yarmut, at Beth-Yeraḥ (where the structure was surrounded by circular silos), and in the temples at Bab edh-Dhraʿ and Khirbet ez-Zeraqun in Jordan. [*See* Yarmut, Tel; Beth-Yeraḥ; Bab edh-Dhraʿ; Zeraqun, Khirbet ez-; Granaries and Silos.] The EB III temples of Megiddo strata XVII–XV present an architectural combination of a broad-room plan with a portico of the megaron (long-room) house type.

The later history of the broad-room temple type is notable in MB IIA temples at Nahariya and Kefar Shemaryahu and in the MB IIB temples at Hazor (stratum 3 in area H). [*See* Hazor.] The latter temple was built with heavy walls, and two towerlike rooms were added to the front of the broad room. This temple is usually listed among the Syrian-type temples, although most temples in this category were long-room sanctuaries. Excavations at Tell el-Ḥayyat in Jordan uncovered a sequence of four temple phases, at the same location, covering the entire Middle Bronze Age (Magness-Gardiner and Falconer, 1994). [*See* Ḥayyat, Tell el-.] Other temples in the Jordan Valley are known from Kfar Ruppin and Tel Kitan. [*See* Jordan Valley; Kitan, Tel.] An almost square temple dating to LB II was exposed at ʿAin Daraʿ in northern Syria, but the broad-room form was reintroduced into the religious architecture of the Iron Age, as evidenced by the temple at Arad. [*See* ʿAin Daraʿ; Arad, *article on* Iron Age Period.] The form was further utilized in the Hellenistic temple at Lachish. [*See* Lachish.]

Long-room temples. The long-room form was popular in the northern part of the ancient Near East (Heinrich, 1973). Typical long-room temples have been uncovered at MB IIB Megiddo and Shechem. [*See* Shechem.] At both sites the structures had been rebuilt and reused during the Late Bronze Age. A smaller long-room temple was erected on the high tell at Hazor in LB I. Long-room temples were common in Syria: since the late third millennium BCE at Tell Chuera, the first half of the second millennium BCE at Tell Mardikh (Ebla), and in the second half of the second millennium BCE at Tell Munbaqa (Mumbaqat) and Tell Meskene (Emar). [*See* Chuera, Tell; Ebla; Emar.] Solomon's Temple in Jerusalem was also constructed on the long-room principle.

Palaces. The political elite operated and resided in the same building, namely the palace. The presence of palaces indicates a considerable accumulation of wealth and power in the hands of the ruling family. In the Early Bronze Age, well-defined palaces appeared later than temples and fortifications. At Arad the excavator identified a palace in the largest residential unit in stratum 2, dating to EB II (Amiran and Ilan, 1992). However, other scholars doubt this attribution and assume that the palace at Arad stood on one of the site's summits. Nevertheless, the structure lacks any monumental qualities. If it was a palace, it reflects a very low level of social stratification. It is only for the EB III period that buildings are found that clearly justify the term *palace*. One such structure was exposed in strata XVII–XVI at Megiddo and another in the lower city at Tel Yarmut. The latter building consists of a rectangular wall with internal buttresses covering an area of 84 × 72 m. The northwestern wing of the building was filled with a series of rectangular rooms that served as dwelling and storage units. The rest of the space was utilized as an open courtyard. The large palace at Tel Yarmut indicates a crystallization of the political role of the urban elite.

During the Middle Bronze Age, the palace became the dominant building in cities. Large palaces, commonly arranged around internal courtyards, have been uncovered throughout Syria and Palestine. Large structures are known in Syria at Mari, Ebla, and Alalakh and in Israel at Hazor, Tel Kabri, Megiddo, Shechem, Aphek, Tell el-ʿAjjul, and Tel Seraʿ. [*See* Mari; Alalakh; Kabri, Tel; Aphek; ʿAjjul, Tell el-; Seraʿ, Tel.] During the Late Bronze Age, builders erected palaces next to the gate area and not on the city's acropolis. Examples of the shift are observable at Ugarit and Alalakh in Syria and perhaps also at Megiddo. [*See* Ugarit.] Locating the palace near the city gate provided rulers with a protected royal compound, while the rest of the city was enclosed only by the rear walls of an outer belt of houses.

During the thirteenth century BCE, isolated palaces were erected over the ruins of several Canaanite cities. [*See* Canaanites.] These were relatively small and compact structures (about 25 × 25 m) with a central hall surrounded by rows of rectangular rooms on all four sides. The roofing over the central hall was supported by wooden pillars, as indicated by the stone bases found. Such buildings may have been used as a residency for the Egyptian governor at the administrative sites of Beth-Shean, Tell el-Farʿah (South), Tel Seraʿ, and Deir el-Balaḥ (Oren, 1992). [*See* Beth-Shean; Farʿah, Tell el- (South); Deir el-Balaḥ.] At other sites, such as Aphek and Tel Gerisa, the palaces were inhabited by the local rulers. [*See* Gerisa, Tel.] Some of the LB palaces were also used in the Iron Age IA, during the first half of the twelfth century BCE.

Few examples of palaces are known from the eleventh century BCE: building 2072 in stratum VIA at Megiddo is the clearest one. From the tenth century BCE onward, a new type of palace appeared, called the *bit-ḫilani.* It consisted of a broad-room main hall and a broad-room porch with a pillared facade wall. Palaces attributed to this type (foundations only) were uncovered in stratum VA at Megiddo (buildings 1723 and 6000). These palaces were constructed of ashlar masonry with drafted margins. Proto-Aeolic capitals may have adorned the buildings, but they, as most of the wall stones, were removed and reused by builders in later periods. Characteristic examples of *bit-ḫilani* palaces were exposed in North Syrian cities dated to the ninth-eighth centuries BCE—Zincirli, Carchemish, and Tell Taʿyinat. [*See* Carchemish.] Monumentally built palaces, but of no distinct type, have been exposed at Lachish (strata V–III), Samaria, Hazor, Ramat Raḥel, and Beersheba (Fritz, 1983). [*See* Ramat Raḥel; Beersheba.]

Following the Assyrian conquest, palaces with characteristics of royal Assyrian architecture were constructed in northern Syria, northern Israel, and Transjordan. [*See* Assyrians.] These were rectangular buildings, often built over a raised podium, with a central courtyard surrounded by rooms. On one side a reception wing contained a large audience hall, usually entered through a doorway whose threshold was ornamented with horseshoe-shaped stones. Additional Assyrian elements include a shallow niche in the reception room and a bathroom with a drainage system. Examples have been found in stratum III at Megiddo (buildings 1369 and 1052), below Tel Hazor (Kibbutz Ayyelet ha-Shaḥar), and at Buṣeirah in Edom. [*See* Buṣeirah.] Later development of this type in the Babylonian and Persian periods can be observed in the Lachish "residency" and in stratum III at Hazor (Reich, 1992).

Silos, Storehouses (or Stables), Treasuries, and Scribes' Chambers. The agricultural basis of ancient economies and the fact that taxes in kind were paid by farmers necessitated the erection of storage facilities by the ruling administration. [*See* Agriculture.] Foodstuffs were redistributed as supplies for military forces, cult functionaries, merchant caravans, and other dependents of royal courts.

The simplest form of storage was achieved by silos for grain. An elaborate example is seen in the large granary complex at Beth-Yeraḥ, which contained nine circular silos (arranged around a broadroom temple; see above). The round structure behind temple 4040 in stratum XVI at Megiddo also seems to be a stone base for a granary made of bricks, rather than an altar. [*See* Altars.] In MB and LB city-states, rooms within the royal palace were used for storage.

Structures built specifically for administrative purposes are observed from the late eleventh century BCE onward, throughout Iron II. The best-known type is the tripartite pillared building found all over ancient Israel: at Tel Hadar, ʿEin-Gev, Hazor, Tell Abu Hawam, Megiddo, Tell Qasile, Beth-Shemesh, Tell el-Ḥesi, Beersheba, Tel Malḥata and Tel Masos. [*See* Hadar, Tel; ʿEin-Gev; Abu Hawam, Tell; Qasile, Tell; Ḥesi, Tell el-; Masos, Tel.] Wide scholarly debate exists regarding the functional interpretation of these buildings, whether stables (Holladay, 1986), storehouses (Herzog, 1973), army barracks (Fritz, 1977), or markets (Herr, 1988). [*See* Stables.] They should be identified with the biblical term *miskenot* (2 Chr. 32:28). The assemblage of objects found in the three tripartite pillared buildings at Beersheba suggests that these houses contained not only the foodstuffs for redistribution but also pottery vessels and other household tools, assumingly delivered to the state functionaries acting in the region.

Elongated rooms without pillars have been found at several sites: at Hazor (next to the tripartite pillared building), at Lachish, Megiddo, and Samaria. [*See* Samaria.] These long halls (up to 30 m long at Lachish) may be interpreted as treasuries for weapons and other precious objects. [*See* Weapons and Warfare.] Such materials did not require the light and ventilation offered by the pillared buildings. These structures may be identified with the biblical *osarot* in *2 Chronicles* 32:27 (Herzog, 1992).

A third type of building contained a series of adjacent units, each of which included a long corridor flanked by two or three square rooms. These structures served the city administrators as recording and documentation centers and have been found in several Iron Age cities. This type of house may be the scribe's chamber of Jeremiah 36:12 (Avi-Yonah and Yeivin, 1955, pp. 118). This attribution is based primarily on the scores of administrative documents found at Samaria in one such house, known as the Ostraca House. Similar houses have also been found at Megiddo (building 1482 in strata VA and IVB) and Hazor (stratum VB in area B).

Water-Supply Systems. A supply of water was essential to every settlement (Miller, 1980). However, it was military considerations that dictated the need to provide city dwellers with direct access to a water source from within the city walls. With this type of water system, a city under attack could sustain a durable siege. Every fortified city can be expected to have found some kind of solution for this necessity. Indeed, from the first urban phase of EB II, a large cistern was exposed at Ai and some kind of a reservoir existed at Arad. [*See* Cisterns; Reservoirs.] A circular water system hewn in the rock at Tel Gerisa is attributed to MB IIA. The straight, sloping tunnel at Gezer is dated to MB IIB, and a deep well is attributed to Iron I at Tel Beersheba.

In Iron II, the systems became considerably more elaborate (Shiloh, 1992). In the northern part of Israel a natural water source (spring or water table) was reached through a deep shaft and sloping tunnel. Such systems are found at Hazor, Megiddo, Gibeon, and Ibleʿam and in Warren's Shaft in Jerusalem. [*See* Gibeon; Jerusalem.] In the southern regions, water was directed into reservoirs from a source outside the city. A well-preserved system at Beersheba consists of a staired shaft, five plastered reservoirs, and a feeding tunnel. The system could be filled by floodwaters from the nearby wadi. The same principle, but with a spring as the source, was used in Hezekiah's Tunnel in Jerusalem, at Qadesh-Barnea, and possibly also at Beth-Shemesh. [*See* Qadesh-Barnea; Beth-Shemesh.] At Arad, underground cisterns were fed by a rock-hewn channel, to which water was brought in containers from the well at the foot of the hill. At Tell es-Saʿidiyeh, an ascent of constructed stairs led from the top of the mound to the spring at the base of the hill.

[*See also* Building Materials and Techniques; Fortifications; *and* Temples.]

BIBLIOGRAPHY

Amiran, Ruth, and Ornit Ilan. *Arad: Eine 5000 Jahre alte Stadt in der wuste Negev, Israel.* Neumuenster, 1992.

Avi-Yonah, Michael, and Shmuel Yeivin. *The Antiquities of Our Land* (in Hebrew). Tel Aviv, 1955.

Bar-Yosef, Ofer. "The Walls of Jericho: An Alternative Interpretation." *Current Anthropology* 27 (1986): 157–162.

Fritz, Volkmar. "Bestimmung und Herkunft des Pfeilerhauses in Israel." *Zeitschrift des Deutschen Palästina-Vereins* 93 (1977): 30–45.

Fritz, Volkmar. "Paläste während der Bronze und Eisenzeit in Palästina." *Zeitschrift des Deutschen Palästina-Vereins* 99 (1983): 1–42.

Henrich, Ernst. "Haus. B: Archäologisch." In *Reallexikon der Assyriologie,* vol. 4, pp. 173–220. Berlin, 1928–.

Herr, Larry G. "Tripartite Pillared Buildings and the Market Place in Iron Age Palestine." *Bulletin of the American Schools of Oriental Research,* no. 272 (1988): 46–67.

Herzog, Ze'ev. "The Storehouses." In *Beer-Sheba I,* edited by Yohanan Aharoni, pp. 23–30. Tel Aviv, 1973.

Herzog, Ze'ev. "A Functional Interpretation of the Broadroom and Longroom House Types." *Tel Aviv* 7 (1980): 82–89.

Herzog, Ze'ev. "Administrative Structures in the Iron Age." In *The Architecture of Ancient Israel,* edited by Aharon Kempinski and Ronnie Reich, pp. 223–230. Jerusalem, 1992.

Holladay, John S. "The Stables of Ancient Israel." In *The Archaeology of Jordan and Other Studies: Presented to S. H. Horn,* edited by Lawrence T. Geraty and Larry G. Herr, pp. 103–165. Berrien Springs, Mich., 1986.

Magness-Gardiner, Bonnie, and Steven Falconer. "Community, Polity and Temple in a Middle Bronze Age Levantine Village." *Journal of Mediterranean Archaeology* 7 (1994): 127–164.

Mazar, Amihai. "Temples of the Middle and Late Bronze Ages and the Iron Age." In *The Architecture of Ancient Israel,* edited by Aharon Kempinski and Ronnie Reich, pp. 161–187. Jerusalem, 1992.

Miller, R. "Water Use in Syria and Palestine from the Neolothic to the Bronze Age." *World Archaeology* 11 (1980): 331–341.

Oren, Eliezer D. "Palaces and Patrician Houses in the Middle and Late Bronze Ages." In *The Architecture of Ancient Israel,* edited by Aharon Kempinski and Ronnie Reich, pp. 105–120. Jerusalem, 1992.

Ottosson, Magnus. *Temples and Cult Places in Palestine.* Uppsala, 1980.

Reich, Ronnie. "Palaces and Residences in the Iron Age." In *The Architecture of Ancient Israel,* edited by Aharon Kempinski and Ronnie Reich, pp. 202–222. Jerusalem, 1992.

Shiloh, Yigal. "Underground Water Systems in the Land of Israel in the Iron Age." In *The Architecture of Ancient Israel,* edited by Aharon Kempinski and Ronnie Reich, pp. 275–293. Jerusalem, 1992.

ZE'EV HERZOG

PUBLIC HYGIENE. *See* Medicine.

PYRAMIDS. For more than a millennium—from the twenty-seventh century BCE to the early sixteenth century BCE—pyramids served as monumental funerary structures (tombs) for the kings of Egypt and sometimes also their principal queens. Pyramids have a square base and four sloping, triangular sides (most have an angle of incline of between 50 and 54 degrees) that meet at the top and are oriented toward the cardinal points. There were two major periods of pyramid construction: the Old Kingdom (third–sixth dynasties, c. 2700–2190 BCE) and the Middle Kingdom–early Second Intermediate period (mid-eleventh–thirteenth dynasties, c. 2033–1633 BCE). From the fourth dynasty onward, each pyramid had its own name.

The Egyptian word for pyramid, *mr,* is of uncertain origin. The hieroglyphic determinative (meaning sign) in the word shows a *pyramid* with one side of an enclosure wall around the base. The English word *pyramid* comes not from the Egyptian term, but from a Greek word, *pyramis,* meaning "wheaten cake."

Most Old Kingdom pyramids were built in the Memphite necropolis, which stretches about 80 km (50 mi.) north–south from Abu Roash to Meidum, along the edge of the desert plateau west of the Nile River. Pyramid complexes were built close enough to the river to facilitate the hauling of heavy stone blocks on sledges from river barges to the construction site, where they were dragged up ramps and set into position with the aid of levers. The core of an Old Kingdom pyramid generally was of local limestone, with the smoothed casing blocks made of fine limestone from the quarries at Tura on the east bank of the Nile, south of Cairo; the lower levels of some pyramids were faced with granite blocks.

From the fourth dynasty onward, the standard pyramid complex contained several basic elements: a valley temple where the king's body underwent purification and mummification, a mortuary temple for the daily cult of the deceased king, and a long connecting causeway, all on the east side of the pyramid; one or two enclosure walls around the pyramid itself; and a small pyramid south or southeast of the main pyramid, perhaps for the spirit (Egyp., *ka*) of the dead ruler. The passage leading to the burial chamber normally began on the north side of the pyramid in the Old Kingdom, but was switched to one of the other sides in the twelfth dynasty. A pyramid-shaped stone *(pyramidion)* served as the capstone for the pyramid. Finally, there might be one or more subsidiary pyramids or shaft tombs for important queens.

The history of Egyptian pyramids begins in the early dynastic period (first–second dynasties, c. 3100–2700 BCE). At that time, both royalty and important officials were interred in funerary structures now known as mastabas (Ar., "benches"). These tombs, which first appeared just prior to the first dynasty, were so named because they looked like the benches outside the homes of modern Egyptians. Early mastabas had a rectangular mud-brick superstructure with internal cells and a flat top, and a subterranean burial pit (often divided by walls into a series of chambers). Some first-dynasty mastabas at Saqqara had a brick-enclosed mound of rubble and sand immediately above the burial pit. The outer support for these internal mounds developed into a series of brick-encased "steps," or terraces (as in the case of tomb 3038 at Saqqara, attributed to King Anedjib or his reign). Already in the early first dynasty, a long pit was sometimes dug outside the mastaba's enclosure wall to contain a boat, perhaps intended for use by the deceased in the afterworld. (Boats occur in conjunction with both royal and private mastabas during the early dynastic period; in the Old Kingdom these ships have been found only with royal burials.) In addition, small models of buildings of uncertain function were occasionally constructed outside the tomb (e.g., at tomb 3357 at Saqqara, attributed to King Aha or his reign). An innovation of the second dynasty was the conversion of the mastaba superstructure into a mass of rubble enclosed in brick, with an increase in the number of rooms in the substructure. Another change was the use (at Helwan, on the east bank of the Nile) of stone for some architectural elements in private tombs.

The "step pyramids" of the third dynasty mark the transition from mastaba to pyramid. The most famous of these structures is the Step Pyramid of Netjerikhet (later known as Djoser) at Saqqara. The architect of this extraordinary complex was Imhotep. The Step Pyramid began as a square mastaba built entirely of limestone blocks (the oldest preserved building in Egypt made entirely of stone). Subsequently, the mastaba was enlarged on all four sides to form a rectangular structure, and a series of progressively smaller "mastabas" was placed on top of it. The resulting tomb had six levels and was about 62 m (204 ft.) high. A deep shaft beneath the original mastaba led to the burial chamber and a network of rooms and corridors.

A conglomeration of buildings set within a rectangular limestone enclosure wall nearly 10 m (33 ft.) high surrounded the Step Pyramid. A courtyard southeast of the pyramid was flanked on its east and west by a series of small dummy structures; this complex was designed to allow Netjerikhet to perform his periodic jubilee ceremony (Egyp., *heb-sed*) in the afterworld. A mastaba with subterranean chambers at the southern end of the Step Pyramid complex may have served as the king's cenotaph. The engaged columns in the Step Pyramid complex are the oldest known columns in Egypt; the builder's failure to let the pillars stand alone may reflect his lack of confidence in the structural integrity of stone columns.

The fourth dynasty saw the construction of the earliest as well as the largest of the true pyramids. The first king of the dynasty, Snefru, built two pyramids at Dahshur. The southern pyramid is often called the Bent Pyramid because it has a change in angle about halfway up the sides. The later, northern pyramid was designed from the start as a true pyramid. Snefru also completed as a true pyramid a step pyramid possibly started by his third-dynasty predecessor, Huni, at Meidum. Because of a structural failure, the outer casing of that pyramid later collapsed, leaving the structure looking like a pyramid having three steps.

The pyramids erected at Giza by several pharaohs of the fourth dynasty—Khufu (Gk., Cheops), Khafre (Gk., Chephren), and Menkaure (Gk., Mycerinus)—are the best-known monuments of ancient Egypt. The largest of the three great pyramids, that of Khufu, originally contained an estimated 2,300,00 blocks weighing an average of 2.5 tons, stood about 145 m (481 ft.) high, and was 229 m (756 ft.) long at the base of each side. The structure has three burial chambers: an unfinished one below ground level, a second chamber (popularly known as the Queen's Chamber) just above the base of the pyramid, and the magnificent King's Chamber near the center of the structure. The King's Chamber was lined and roofed with huge granite blocks and was reached through a 46-meter-long (153 ft.) ascending corridor known as the Grand Gallery. Herodotus reports that one hundred thousand men labored twenty years to build Khufu's pyramid, and another ten years to construct its causeway. Regardless of whether these figures have a factual basis, large numbers of workmen would have been available during the annual flood season, when work in the fields came to a halt.

On the eastern and southern sides of Khufu's pyramid was a series of pits for the royal funerary barges. One of these boats was uncovered in 1954 in a pit immediately south of the pyramid. When reconstructed, the ship, built mostly of Lebanese cedar, was found to be approximately 43 m (143 ft.) long.

Close to the Giza pyramids is a series of small pyramids for some of the queens, while nearby there are extensive fields of mastaba tombs for major officials, important mortuary priests, and members of the royal family. On the north side of the valley temple of Khafre's pyramid is the Sphinx, an enormous rock sculpture (about 72 m [240 ft.] long and 20 m [66 ft.] high) in the form of a recumbent lion with a head that is a representation of the king himself.

The last ruler of the fourth dynasty, Shepseskaf, constructed a tomb at Saqqara known as the Mastabat Faraʿun. Built in the form of a huge stone sarcophagus with a vaulted roof, this structure lies outside the evolutionary path of the Old Kingdom pyramid.

Change and innovation highlight pyramid construction in the fifth–sixth dynasties. A gradual weakening in the authority of the central administration resulted in a decline in the size of the mastaba fields, many officials choosing to be buried in provincial cemeteries rather than near their king. The pyramids themselves were smaller than their fourth-dynasty predecessors and often had cores of small limestone blocks. The pyramids of the fifth dynasty were built at Saqqara (for Userkaf, Djedkare Isesi, and Wenis) and Abu Sir (for Sahure, Neferirkare, Neuserre, and an unidentified king), while the pyramids known from the sixth dynasty were all built at Saqqara (for Teti, Pepi I, Merenre, and Pepi II).

Fifth-dynasty pyramid complexes are notable for their use of columns with plant-shaped capitals; the expanded use of reliefs in the temples and causeway; and, starting in the pyramid of Wenis at the end of the dynasty, the writing of inscriptions collectively known as the Pyramid Texts on the walls of the burial chamber and corridors. These magical texts, which include spells designed to protect and assist the king in the afterworld, as well as hymns and prayers to the gods, regularly occur in pyramids through the eighth dynasty.

The pyramid complexes of the sixth dynasty are remarkably similar because the funerary complex of the first king of the dynasty, Teti, was used as a model for those erected later by Pepi I, Merenre, and Pepi II. The pyramids of these four kings have the same height (about 52 m) and the same base length on each side (about 79m); are all made of small stones held together with mud and an outer casing of Tura limestone; and are part of mortuary complexes having the same overall layout. The complex of Pepi II is the best preserved and most interesting. Outside the enclosure wall are miniature versions of the king's complex for three of his queens; each of these complexes had its own subsidiary pyramid as well as Pyramid texts.

The First Intermediate period (seventh–mid-eleventh dynasties, c. 2190–2033 BCE) witnessed a sharp decline in pyramid building. The country's internal disarray left it without the highly centralized authority required to construct, decorate, and staff such large mortuary complexes. In such circumstances, only a few pyramids were built: the best known is that of an eighth-dynasty ruler, Ibi, in the southern sector of Saqqara. His pyramid, which lacks a valley temple and causeway, is made of mud brick (a forerunner of the pyramids of the Middle Kingdom). At the end of the First Intermediate period, the Theban kings of the early eleventh dynasty were buried in long *saff* (Ar., "row") tombs cut back into the rock; at least some of these tombs were surmounted by small brick pyramids.

The reunification of Egypt in the mid-eleventh dynasty and the transfer of the capital at the beginning of the twelfth dynasty to Itjtawy near Lisht in the Faiyum region inaugurated the Middle Kingdom. Although the mortuary temple of the eleventh-dynasty ruler Nebhepetre Mentuhotep at Deir el-Baḥri is now thought to have been surmounted by a flat roof rather than a pyramid, about a dozen true pyramids are attested for the twelfth–thirteenth dynasties. These were built at Dahshur, Mazghuneh (situated just south of Dahshur), and in the Faiyum region (at Lisht, Lahun, and Hawara).

Twelfth-dynasty pyramids were larger than those built during the fifth and sixth dynasties. One king, Amenemhet III, built two pyramids—one at Dahshur (which was abandoned after a partial structural collapse) and another (his actual burial place) at Hawara. Classical writers later described his enormous mortuary temple at Hawara as the Labyrinth.

Middle Kingdom pyramids differ considerably from earlier ones. Although the first twelfth-dynasty pyramid—that of Amenemhet I at Lisht—was made entirely of stone (including many removed from Old Kingdom pyramid complexes), those of his three immediate successors (Senwosret I, Amenemhet II, and Senwosret II) had interior stone walls with rubble and/or sand fill. Later Middle Kingdom pyramids were constructed of brick with a casing of limestone blocks.

The other principal development in pyramid construction during the Middle Kingdom was the emphasis placed on the security of the royal burial. The entrance to the passage leading to the burial chamber was shifted from the north face to one of the other sides. Some other devices used in (unsuccessful) efforts to protect the dead king included blind corridors and false shafts, ingeniously set portcullis blocks, large granite plugs, trap doors, and sarcophagi cut from huge monolithic blocks of stones.

Information on the people who built pyramid complexes comes mainly from the excavation of a town occupied by the workmen for Senwosret II's pyramid at Lahun. (Excavations have recently begun on an Old Kingdom workmen's village at Giza.) This planned town, surrounded by a nearly square enclosure wall and divided by a long wall into two main sections, contained a number of mansions for senior officials as well as many parallel rows of small houses for ordinary workmen and artisans.

Three unfinished mud-brick pyramids are known from the thirteenth dynasty—two at Saqqara (one belonging to Khendjer, the other being anonymous) and one at Dahshur (for Amenyqemau). No pyramids have survived from the late Second Intermediate period (the fifteenth–seventeenth dynasties, c. 1648–1540 BCE), but there are references in a late New Kingdom document known as the Abbott Tomb Robbery Papyrus to pyramids associated with the royal tombs of the seventeenth dynasty at Thebes. Observations made by nineteenth-century observers indicate that these small mud-brick pyramids had one or more interior chambers, were topped by a stone *pyramidion,* and sat on the hillside above the rock-cut tombs.

The first king of the New Kingdom, Ahmose, constructed a small pyramid at Abydos to serve as a cenotaph for his grandmother, Tetisheri; this solid structure was made of rubble and small stones and was held together by a stone facing. Through most of the New Kingdom, Egyptian royalty was buried in less obtrusive, rock-cut tombs in western Thebes (in the Valley of the Kings and the Valley of the Queens), while the mortuary temples were erected out on the plain, well away from the tombs.

The pyramid continued in use in New Kingdom (c. 1550–

1069 BCE) Egypt and Nubia in conjunction with private tombs. Such tombs are especially well known at Deir el-Medineh and Dra'Abu 'n-Naga in the Theban necropolis. Typically they had a small steep-sided mud-brick pyramid topped by a stone *pyramidion* set above a columned portico or chapel.

No pyramids were built in Egypt after the New Kingdom. Later on, however, the pyramidal tradition was revived for kings as well as some queens and princesses in the northern Sudanese kingdoms of Napata (c. 900–300 BCE) and Meroë (c. 300 BCE–300 CE). Small pyramids (all fewer than 30 m high) were built in the Napatan royal cemeteries at el-Kurru and Nuri, and subsequently in the Meroitic royal cemeteries at Gebel Barkal and Meroë. These steep-sided pyramids had a chapel on the east side and the burial chamber cut into the rock below the pyramid. Initially they were built of stone, but later pyramids at Meroë were constructed of stone over a rubble core and, finally, of brick.

[*See also* Abydos; Egypt, *article on* Dynastic Egypt; Giza; Meroë; *and* Saqqara.]

BIBLIOGRAPHY

Arnold, Dieter. *Der Pyramidenbezirk des Königs Amenemhet III. in Dahschur,* vol. 1, *Die Pyramide.* Mainz am Rhein, 1987. Deutsches Archäologisches Institut, Abteilung Kairo, Archäologische Veröffentlichungen, vol. 53. Best modern report on the excavation of a Middle Kingdom pyramid.

Arnold, Dieter. *Building in Egypt: Pharaonic Stone Masonry.* New York, 1991. Fundamental reference work on ancient Egyptian stone construction, essential for understanding how the pyramids were built.

Badawy, Alexander. *A History of Egyptian Architecture.* 3 vols. Berkeley, 1954–1968. Survey of Egyptian architecture through the New Kingdom, including basic descriptions, plans, and drawings of many pyramids.

David, A. Rosalie. *The Pyramid Builders of Ancient Egypt.* London, 1986. Study of the Middle Kingdom town in which the officials and workers associated with Senusert II's pyramid at Lahun lived.

Dunham, Dows. *The Royal Cemeteries of Kush.* 5 vols. Cambridge, Mass., 1950–1963. Final publication of the Harvard University–Museum of Fine Arts, Boston, excavations at the royal cemeteries of the Napatan and Meroitic kingdoms in northern Sudan.

Edwards, I. E. S. *The Pyramids of Egypt.* Rev. ed. London, 1991. The most readable and authoritative introduction to the pyramids in the English language.

Emery, Walter B. *Archaic Egypt.* Baltimore, 1961. Good introduction, though now somewhat outdated, to the archaeology of Egypt during the early dynastic period, focused principally on the tombs at Abydos and Saqqara.

Fakhry, Ahmed. *The Pyramids.* 2d ed. Chicago, 1969. General introduction to the pyramids, now somewhat out of date and not as comprehensive as Edwards (1991).

Faulkner, Raymond O. *The Ancient Egyptian Pyramid Texts.* 2 vols. Oxford, 1969. Provides excellent translations of the texts as well as a limited amount of background information.

Jéquier, Gustave. *Deux pyramides du Moyen Empire.* Cairo, 1933. Excavation report on the two thirteenth-dynasty pyramids at Saqqara.

Jéquier, Gustave. *La pyramide d'Aba.* Cairo, 1935. Excavation report on the eighth-dynasty pyramid of Iby at Saqqara.

Lauer, Jean-Philippe. *La pyramide à degrés.* 5 vols. Cairo, 1936–1965. Volumes 1–3 of this excavation report cover the architecture of the Step Pyramid complex; volumes 4–5 (coauthored by Pierre Lacau) are devoted to the vase inscriptions.

Lauer, Jean-Philippe. *Histoire monumentale des pyramides d'Égypte,* vol. 1, *Les pyramides à degrés (IIIe dynastie).* Institut Français d'Archéologie Orientale, Bibliothèque d'Études, vol. 39. Cairo, 1962. Comprehensive study of the step pyramids of the third dynasty.

Lauer, Jean-Philippe. *Saqqara, the Royal Cemetery of Memphis: Excavations and Discoveries since 1850.* London, 1976. Authoritative and well-illustrated history of research on the Old Kingdom pyramid complexes at Saqqara.

Lauer, Jean-Philippe. *Les pyramides de Sakkarah.* 6th ed., rev. and exp. Cairo, 1991. Basic guidebook, in French and English, for the pyramids at Saqqara.

Málek, Jaromir. *In the Shadow of the Pyramids: Egypt during the Old Kingdom.* Norman, Okla., 1986. Good popular survey, with excellent color photographs, of Egypt in the age of the pyramid.

Nour, Moḥammad Zaki, et al. *The Cheops Boats.* Cairo, 1960. Preliminary report on the Khufu funerary boat discovered in 1954.

Spencer, A. Jeffrey. *Brick Architecture in Ancient Egypt.* Warminster, 1979. Detailed study of brick architecture and construction, with a discussion of the brick pyramids of the second millennium BCE.

JAMES M. WEINSTEIN

Q

QADESH-BARNEA, site identified with Tell el-Qudeirat in northern Sinai (30°38′ N, 34°27′ E; map reference 0949 × 0064), a central camp for nomadic and seminomadic tribes in the Negev-Sinai deserts. Encompassing about three-quarters of an acre, the site, which overlooks the Wadi el-Qudeirat ravine, is situated just to the west of ʿEin-Mishpat, the Sinai's most bountiful spring (the biblical "waters of Meribah" of, for example, *Nm.* 20:13).

In the biblical tradition, Qadesh-Barnea played an important role in the Israelite wilderness wanderings. It was the site from which Moses, at God's command, sent a group of twelve men, one from each tribe, to investigate the Promised Land (*Nm.* 13:26). Later it was where the king of Edom, meeting with another delegation, denied the Israelites permission to pass through his realm on their way to Canaan (*Nm.* 20:14). Kadesh is also where Miriam, the sister of Moses and Aaron (*Nm.* 20:1) died and was buried. However, the lack of any material at Qadesh-Barnea earlier than the tenth century BCE, especially datable pottery, calls the biblical traditions into question. The Exodus stories, in their present form, may have originated instead in the period of the monarchy, when pilgrimages to the site may have begun. The traditions would then be best understood as etiologies.

In 1914 C. L. Woolley and T. E. Lawrence found the first remains at Qadesh-Barnea, fortress with eight towers (see below). [*See the biographies of Woolley and Lawrence.*] In 1956 a team led by Moshe Dothan for the Israel Department of Antiquities partially excavated the fortress, further exposing its ground plan and dating it. Rudolph Cohen excavated for ten seasons between 1976 and 1982, during which he completed the exposure of the upper fortress and uncovered two additional fortresses, each built on the remains of the other following a succession of destructions and indicating occupation at the site from the tenth through the sixth centuries BCE, probably with periods of abandonment. Cohen also discovered, built on the remains of the last fortress, an unfortified settlement dating to the fifth–fourth centuries BCE.

Lower Fortress. The earliest—and apparently the smallest (27 m in diameter)—of the three fortresses dates to the tenth century BCE. Its remains indicate that this lower fortress was made up of casement rooms arranged in an elongated circle around a central courtyard. Thick layers of ash above the floors in the rooms contained the wheel-made vessels typically found at tenth-century BCE sites in Israel as well as handmade Negebite ware.

An adjacent settlement, made up of several buildings and silos, was uncovered 5 m below the surface just west of the fortress. It too dates to the tenth century BCE. At the northwestern edge of the site, a room (about 4 × 6 m) lined with stone benches was found in one of the buildings.

Middle Fortress. In the eighth century BCE following what appears to have been a long period of abandonment after the lower fortress was destroyed, a second fortress was erected over its remains. The design of this second, or middle, fortress differed from that of the first: it was rectangular (about 40 × 60 m) and had eight towers protruding from an outer wall (4 m wide, preserved to a height of 1.8 m). The fortress itself was surrounded by an earthen rampart supported by a revetment wall (2.5 m tall) and by a 4-meter-wide fosse that was 2.5 m deep on all but the south side, where the fortress was protected by the steep wall of the wadi.

Two silos, one rectangular (3.8 × 5.5 m) and the other round (2 m in diameter), were found inside the fortress. Just outside the north wall of the fortress, flanked by two of the eight towers, were four stone-built granaries, the largest measuring 1.8 m in diameter. West of the granaries, a clay oven *(tabun)* was found in a room (3 × 4 m) abutting the wall of the fortress.

Among the material remains were wheel-made vessels characteristic of the eighth and seventh centuries BCE and many examples of Negebite ware. Two ostraca were found, one the base of an oil lamp and the other the rim of a Negebite bowl; each carries a fragmentary Hebrew inscription that is probably part of a name.

The internal structures indicated three settlement phases, which demonstrates that the middle fortress was inhabited for a long period of time. The principal phase was distinguished by the division of buildings inside the fortress into northern and southern blocks separated by a street (3.5 m wide). The remains of five mud-brick structures (each about 10 m long) were uncovered in the northern block. These structures also were separated from each other by narrow streets (1.5 m wide). In the northwestern block, adjacent units (each 7 × 10 m) contained five elongated rooms (about 2.5 × 4 m) and mud-brick installations showed evidence of fire damage. South of the adjacent units a plastered channel and cistern were uncovered. The cistern (about 10 m in diameter), which was twenty-five steps deep, could hold about 180 cu m of water and was fed via the channel by a spring outside the fortress. [*See* Cisterns.]

Upper Fortress. Not very long after the middle fortress was destroyed—possibly in the mid-seventh century BCE—another fortress was built on its remains. This third, or upper, fortress also was rectangular; it made use of features of the second fortress, but its outer wall was ringed by about twenty casement rooms. As a result, although the fosse was still useful, the earthern rampart had to be brought into alignment with the casements' outer wall.

The internal plan of the upper fortress differed importantly from that of the second in that its inside structures were not divided into distinct blocks. In the northwest corner of the upper fortress was a rectangular building (10 × 25 m) with three elongated rooms whose floors were covered with a thick layer of ash and to which access was through an open courtyard (10 × 15 m). At the western end of the stone-paved courtyard a round mud-brick structure (1.9 m in diameter) was preserved to a height of 1.2 m. As was the case with the two earlier fortresses, an abundance of pottery was found on the floors of structures inside the upper fortress, both sherds and complete specimens, including wheel-made vessels characteristic of the seventh and sixth centuries BCE and of Negebite ware. Because the level of the fortress had been raised, the number of steps to enter the cistern was increased.

Many ostraca were found throughout the upper fortress. East of the cistern and alongside the casement rooms on the south, a large ostracon was found in a building with many rooms. Of these inscribed sherds, one (22 × 23 cm) consists of six columns of numbers and measurements in a hieratic script. The numbers are arranged in columns of one to ten, ten to one hundred (in units of ten), one hundred to one thousand (in units of one hundred), and one thousand to ten thousand (in units of one thousand), and may have been used to practice arithmetic. Another ostracon (10 × 15 cm) has three columns of script, mostly numbers. The last column is the clearest: it contains a series of hieratic numerals that reaches 800; next to each number is inscribed *grh*, the Hebrew word for the smallest unit of weight then known (about half a gram). A third ostracon (45 × 45 cm), consisting of the Hebrew letters *zḥṭ*, probably is a fragment of an abecedary.

The upper fortress was most likely destroyed by fire in a violent attack. The destruction likely took place concurrently with the conquest of Judah and the destruction in Jerusalem of the First Temple in 586 BCE.

Postexilic Period: An Unfortified Settlement. In the northern and southern parts of the upper fortress, two small rooms dating to the postexilic period (fifth–fourth centuries BCE)—the period following the return of the Exiles from Babylon—were found that had been used by an unfortified settlement. The casements of the Early Iron Age fortresses also provided temporary housing for the new settlers. Most

QADESH-BARNEA. *General overview of excavations.* (Courtesy R. Cohen)

of the finds from this period, including imported Greek ware, however, were recovered from pits. Among them was a *yhd* seal impression, found elsewhere as well in postexilic Judah, and an ostracon containing the Hebrew words *'skr ṭb* ("offering" or "merchandise").

BIBLIOGRAPHY

Cohen, Rudolph. "Did I Excavate Kadesh-Barnea?" *Biblical Archaeology Review* 7.3 (1981): 21–33.

Cohen, Rudolph. "Excavations at Kadesh-Barnea, 1976–1978." *Biblical Archaeologist* 44 (1981): 93–107.

Cohen, Rudolph. *Kadesh-Barnea: A Fortress from the Time of the Judaean Kingdom.* Israel Museum Catalogue, no. 233. Jerusalem, 1983.

Cohen, Rudolph. "Qadesh-Barnea." *Le Monde de la Bible* 39 (1985): 9–27.

Dothan, Moshe. "The Fortress at Kadesh-Barnea." *Israel Exploration Journal* 15 (1965): 134–151.

Hogarth, David G. "The Wilderness of Zin." *Palestine Exploration Fund* 23 (1914–1915): 61–63.

Raumer, Karl Georg von. *Palästina.* 2d ed. Leipzig, 1838. See pages 480–486.

Robinson, Edward. *Biblical Researches in Palestine and in the Adjacent Regions: A Journal of Travels in the Year 1838.* 2d ed. Boston, 1860. See pages 175ff.

Schmidt, Nathaniel. "Kadesh Barnea." *Journal of Biblical Literature* 29 (1910): 61–76.

Vaux, Roland de. "Nouvelles recherches dans la région de Cades I–IV." *Revue Biblique* 47 (1938): 89–97.

RUDOLPH COHEN

QALʿAT AL-BAHRAIN, site in the Arabian Gulf, located on the north coast of the island of Bahrain, with an areal extent of about 18 ha (46 acres), and its largest settlement (26°13′28″ N, 50°28′45″ E). Excavations began at the site in 1954, when Peter Vilhelm Glob and a Danish team from the University of Aarhus's Prehistoric Museum Moesgård, initiated work that was to continue uninterrupted until 1965. A follow-up season was carried out by T. Geoffrey Bibby in 1970, and in 1977 a new program of excavations, concentrating principally on a Parthian/Early Islamic fortress to the north of the main mound, was begun by the French archaeologist Monique Kervran. During the 1980s, the Bahrain Department of Antiquities carried out extensive restoration of the sixteenth-century Portuguese fort that crowns the site. In 1988 the French excavations were resumed under the direction of Pierre Lombard, who began work near the site of an Iron Age building originally exposed by the Danes, in a project which is still in progress.

The occupation of Qalʿat al-Bahrain dates to about 2400 BCE. Late Early Dynastic and/or Early Akkadian-related pottery, as well as sherds of painted Umm an-Nar pottery from the Oman peninsula occur in the settlement's basal city I levels alongside a local "chain-ridged" ware typical of Bahrain and the adjacent parts of the northeast Arabian mainland during that period. Soft-stone weights (imported from Oman) and cubical chert weights of Harappan type also appear in late city I contexts. At the beginning of the period known as city II (c. 2100 BCE), a distinctive stamp-seal form appears. The earliest so-called Persian Gulf seals are round, with a high, grooved boss and display animals and other nonhuman motifs. Nearly a dozen of the earliest seals also bear short Harappan inscriptions together with a humped bull (zebu) shown in profile. The iconography suggests that an Indian element in the population, or trade with India, played an important role at the site in the late third millennium.

In about 2000 BCE, a 3.5-meter-thick stone wall with a rubble core was built around the settlement. A system of lanes and streets, with well-planned houses, was exposed in the Danish excavation of levels dating to this period. A more developed seal type (Dilmun seals) with incised lines and four dotted double circles on the boss was in use from about 2000 to 1700 BCE. Seals of this type show a complex iconography that includes a wide variety of human, animal, and architectural features. Certain iconographic and stylistic details suggest that Dilmun glyptic may have influenced Anatolian glyptic of the Old Assyrian caravan period (e.g., at sites like Acemhöyük). Links to Isin-Larsa and Old Babylonian Ur are also clear, both from cuneiform and glyptic evidence. An Amorite element, perhaps originating on the mainland opposite Bahrain, appears to have been present at Qalʿat al-Bahrain as well, for at least one cuneiform text found there contains several Amorite personal names.

City III shows strong ties to the Kassite state, and a sizable proportion of Kassite pottery types appears in Qalʿat al-Bahrain's ceramic assemblage of the mid-second millennium BCE [*See* Kassites.] A large building from that period, which contained thousands of burnt date stones, has been identified as a storehouse. Above this level, in city IV levels, is a building complex that is, in some ways, reminiscent of Neo-Assyrian and Neo-Babylonian palace architecture. Ceramic bathtub coffins, with close analogues in Neo-Babylonian Mesopotamia, were buried in the ruins of the building after its abandonment. City V represents the Hellenistic and Parthian occupation of the site, probably extending into the Early Sasanian period; city VI was the designation used for the later Islamic remains. A square fortress with round corner towers, originally excavated by the Danish expedition and later reinvestigated in 1977–1983 by Monique Kervran for the Centre Nationale de la Recherche Scientifique, was probably founded in the second or third century CE under Parthian or Characene influence and then rebuilt and reused in the thirteenth century. Imported Chinese ceramics and coins bear witness to the existence of far-flung trade with East Asia at this time. The largest monument on the site, however, is a fortress originally built by a local Arab dynasty and taken over and remodeled by the Portuguese in the six-

QALʿAT AL-BAHRAIN. *View of Qalʿat al-Bahrain.* The Portuguese fort lies in the background, the Neo-Assyrian building complex in the foreground. (Courtesy D. Potts)

teenth century. The fortress, which is shown clearly on Portuguese drawings of the period, was surrounded by a dry moat. As the main ancient settlement on the north coast of Bahrain island, Qalʿat al-Bahrain was ancestral to the later population centers of Bilad al-Qadim and Manama.

[*See also* Bahrain; Dilmun.]

BIBLIOGRAPHY

Bibby, Geoffrey. *Looking for Dilmun.* New York, 1969. Popular account of the Danish Gulf expedition, with primary reference to the work carried out on Bahrain and the search for Dilmun.

Khalifa, Shaikha Haya A. al, and Michael Rice, eds. *Bahrain through the Ages: The Archaeology.* London, 1986. Proceedings of a conference held in 1983; touches on most aspects of Bahraini archaeology.

Kervran, Monik, et al. *Fouilles à Qalʿat al-Bahrein/Excavation of Qalʿat al-Bahrain, 1ère partie/1st part, 1977–1979.* Bahrain, 1982. Preliminary report on the first three seasons of excavation at Qalʿat al-Bahrain by the French mission.

Lombard, Pierre, and Monik Kervran, eds. *Bahrain National Museum Archaeological Collections,* vol. 1, *A Selection of Pre-Islamic Antiquities from Excavations, 1954–1975.* Bahrain, 1989. Catalog of objects in the Bahrain National Museum, many of which come from the Danish excavations at Qalʿat al-Bahrain.

Potts, Daniel T. *The Arabian Gulf in Antiquity.* 2 vols. Oxford, 1990. General survey of the archaeology of the Gulf region, with reference to the occupation of Qalʿat al-Bahrain in all periods.

D. T. POTTS

QALʿAT SIMʿAN (Ar., "sanctuary of St. Simeon"), site situated on a promontory overlooking the ʿAfrin Valley, at the heart of the Syrian *tetrapolis* in Antiochea, 60 km (37 mi.) from Aleppo; 80 km (50 mi.) from Antioch, 140 km (87 mi.) from Apamea, and 180 km (112 mi.) from Latakia.

Although some of the earliest visitors to the site published descriptions and drawings (A. Drummond, 1754), it is since the middle of the nineteenth century that this monumental group of buildings has been the subject of exploration and detailed publications. Melchior de Vogüé completed the first important study of the site, and those by M. van Berchem and E. Fatio, Howard C. Butler, J. Mattern, D. Krencker, and Georges Tchalenko followed. Since 1980, Jean-Pierre Sodini and Jean-Luc Biscop have made regular expeditions for purposes of excavation and survey, under the aegis of the French Institute of Archaeology of the Near East (IFAPO) in Damascus. [*See the biographies of Vogüé* and *Butler.*]

The promontory the sanctuary occupies is the site of the column where St. Simeon practiced his asceticism from 412 to 459. According to Tchalenko, the sanctuary is on an artificial platform formed by the leveling of the north–south ridge and by the embankment of the east and west flanks. The monuments cover a surface of approximately 1,200 sq m. The buildings are divided into two groups: to the north, a cross-shaped martyrion, a monastery, and a conventual tomb; and to the south, a baptistery bordered by a church and propylaeum. In between are many inns on the east, west, and south. A sacred way from the village of Telanissos (Deir Simʿan), situated below, leads to the sanctuary from the south; this sacred way, with shops on both sides, passes through an arch and then climbs the slope to the propylaeum.

Verifying the date of the construction of Qalʿat Simʿan remains elusive. What is known is that in 472/73, the date the life of St. Simeon was written in Syriac, there was as yet no edifice around the column. By 517, however, monks from Apamea were making pilgrimages to the sanctuary. Its construction should be placed in the context of the politics of Zeno: St. Daniel had learned from him that he had had the relics of St. Simeon transported from Antioch to Constantinople, and so between 471 and 474 a martyrion was constructed to shelter them. It was perhaps on the urging of St. Daniel, and finally to appease the religious discord dividing the patriarchate of Antioch, which was well within the line of the Henoticon (482), that Zeno had the martyrion built around the column on which the first of the Stylites had lived. The work must have been finished before 491/92, for by that time the church at Basufan, a partial copy of the sanctuary of Qalʿat Simʿan, had been built. For an enterprise of this magnitude, it took a relatively short amount of time to build. Tchalenko calls attention to the results of that haste: faulty connections in the different decorative elements of the martyrion, demonstrating that the gantry had been open in many places at once. [*See* Martyrion.]

The martyrion is made up of four three-naved basilicas positioned in the form of the Greek cross. [*See* Basilicas.] The basilicas meet again in the shape of an octagon formed by eight large arches. The column of the saint (18–20 m high), stands in the center of this arrangement. Only the rocky base and a block of stone of the column remain, perhaps because it was cut up to be sold as relics. The column was square-cut and had three superimposed shafts. The saint lived on a platform enclosed by a railing. Of the eight arches, four open onto the basilicas and the other four onto small apses which made the links. The largest of the basilicas is on the east. It is the true sanctuary in which the liturgy unfolds. It ends in three projecting apses. The west basilica, which opens to the outside, has the function of a rostrum. The cult of the saint was therefore disassociated from the divine cult, which had its center around the octagon. The south basilica is preceded by a narthex to which access was through a great central arch of two arches of weaker bearing.

The monastery, which is adjacent to the martyrion to the southeast, includes a two-story building with porticoes on three sides (there is none on the east), placed at right angles. The porticoes form, with the martyrion's south and east basilicas, a rectangular court that opens to the outside onto a small church. Outbuildings were joined to the principal building.

To the north of the martyrion, the collective tomb is an example of a one-nave basilica. [*See* Tombs.]

The southern group of buildings includes, most importantly, the propylaeum, which is situated 80 m south of the baptistery: it opens with two series of three arches onto a vast space bordered to the south and west by inns and to the east by the baptistery. [*See* Baptisteries.] The inns are one-story buildings that open on one side, like the houses, and are preceded by pillared porticoes. The baptistery is an octagon inscribed in a square. The principal room is square in plan. It is topped by an octagonal drum covered by an eight-sided pyramidal roof and flanked by three long rooms replaced on the east by an apse that contains the baptismal tank. Entrance and egress are by means of stairs located in side rooms, not in the central room.

Qalʿat Simʿan poses three archaeological problems: how the octagon of the martyrion was covered; its place in the evolution of the architecture and ornamentation of churches in Syria's limestone massif; and the duration of its occupation.

By observing and identifying fallen blocks, Krencker was the first to show that the octagon was not originally open but covered. He proposed a wooden dome, an untenable hypothesis because wood would have been too heavy for the stone construction on which it must have rested. Taking its span into account, an exterior diameter of 29 m, with a height of 18 m, the drum, with a height of 10 m, on which the roof would have exerted its force, would have inevitably been dislocated. (It is made of courses not exceeding 90 cm in width and its blocks are laid on top of each other without mortar or another bonding substance. Tchalenko has proposed an eight-sided pyramidal roof, like that of the baptistery. To reduce the load and the lateral thrust, he suggested that there were intermediate supports between the column and the pillars bearing the arches of the octagon. In the tenth century, at the time of the Byzantine reconquest, the floor of the octagon was recovered with tiles. Sodini and Biscop removed that floor, under which a beaten-earth floor revealed no trace of the base of an intermediary pillar. They hypothesize that the roof was in fact an eight-sided pyramid, as Tchalenko thought, but that it covered the entire surface of the octagon.

The second problem, the place of Qalʿat Simʿan in the religious architecture of the limestone massif of northern Syria, has been studied by Butler, Tchalenko, Charles Strube, F. W. Deichmann, Sodini, and A. Naccache. For Butler, Qalʿat Simʿan marks a break in the architectural and ornamental evolution of the churches of the massif, in which methods and ornamentation appear that were to experience wide diffusion in the churches of the sixth century, and notably in the basilica of Qalbloze, which he dates later than St. Simeon. Tchalenko, however, followed by Strube and Deichmann, placed the construction of Qalbloze in about 450, before that of Qalʿat Simʿan. He established also that the church of Bettir, close to Qalbloze in the Jebel el-Aʿla, and dated by inscription to 471, was a pared-down copy of its neighbor—each using pillars, rather than columns, to support the great arches of the nave, in a pure local tradition.

This long-accepted view is now challenged by Sodini and Biscop, who show that Bettir combines two stages (perhaps three according to Naccache) and that the inscription dating the church refers only to the first stage; they show further that the inscription describes a one-nave basilica, which owes nothing to Qalbloze. The terminus ante quem of 471 for Qalbloze thus disappears. In one study (Biscop and Sodini, 1984), the two authors show that the apse of Qalʿat Simʿan combined two superimposed rows of columns. This feature gave the basilica a plan constituting a truly ornamental overlaid order. The other churches of northern Syria with columned apses show the same device, but incompletely: they were imperfect copies and Qalbloze does not belong to the category.

Naccache, in his work on the churches of Antiochea, drew up a complete inventory of ornamental innovations at Qalʿat Simʿan that had also been found in later churches. If Qalbloze is dated to about 450, these innovations would have had to have existed without imitation for nearly forty years before being reprised at Qalʿat Simʿan. It is thus preferable to reestablish the evolution of the decoration of churches by saying that the great edifice of Qalʿat Simʿan, constructed by the state, owes its form to a foreign master worker and that its innovations were imported.

On the third problem, the duration of occupation at the site, the excavations have been less helpful. It is known, from Michael the Syrian, that the sanctuary was burned in about 546 and that it was then that the octagon became open—a description confirmed by Evagrius after his visit in about 561. According to him, the neighboring peasants used to go into the sanctuary with their beasts of burden and dance around the column. The monastery was in use until nearly the second third of the tenth century. The emperors of Byzantium, Nikephoros II Phokas (963–969) and John I Tzimiskes, reconquered the occidental part of northern Syria. The soldiers who occupied Qalʿat Simʿan evicted its monks and turned the sanctuary into a fortress to guard the border that henceforth separated the empire from the emirate of Aleppo. It was they who built the surrounding wall and the towers that still stand and who placed a tiled floor in the octagon (see above). The Byzantine garrison remained in place until the end of the eleventh century and the conquest by the Ottoman Turks. Sodini's excavation in the area west of the baptistery attests to an occupation uninterrupted until the Mamluk period.

BIBLIOGRAPHY

Biscop, Jean-Luc, and Jean-Pierre Sodini. "Qalʿat Semʿan et les chevets à colonnes de Syrie du Nord." *Syria* 61 (1984): 267–330.

Biscop, Jean-Luc, and Jean-Pierre Sodini. "Travaux à Qalʿat Semʿan." In *Acts of the Eleventh International Congress of Christian Archaeology,* vol. 2, pp. 1675–1695. Rome, 1989.

Biscop, Jean-Luc, et al. "Qalʿat Semʿan: Quelques données nouvelles." In *Acts of the Twelfth International Congress of Christian Archaeology.* Rome, 1996.

Deichmann, F. W. *Qalb Löze und Qalʿat Semʿan.* Munich, 1982.

Shaath, Shawqi. *Qalʿat Simʿan* (in Arabic). 2d ed. Halab, Syria, 1991.

Sodini, Jean-Pierre. "Qalʿat Semʿan: Ein Wallfahrtszentrum." In *Syrien: Von den Aposteln zu den Kalifen,* edited by Erwin M. Ruprechtsberger, pp. 128–143. Linzer Archäologische Forschungen, 21. Linz, Austria, 1993.

Tchalenko, Georges. *Villages antiques de la Syrie du Nord: Le massif du Bélus à l'époque romaine.* 3 vols. Paris, 1953–1958. See volume 1, pages 205–276; volume 3, page 124.

GEORGES TATE

QARQUR, TELL, site located less than 2 km (1 mi.) east of the Orontes River and about 7 km (4 mi.) south of Djisr Choghour, the major crossing point on the Orontes for the road from Aleppo to Latakia, Syria (35°44′ N, 36°20′ E). The fertile Orontes Valley at this point is about 10 km (6 mi.) wide. Tell Qarqur is situated at the northern end of the portion of the valley known as the Ghab. The Ghab was once a marshy area that extended south for about 42 km (26 mi.) to Asharneh. According to inscriptions on temple walls at Luxor, in antiquity Egyptian New Kingdom pharaohs hunted elephants in the marshy area. Much later, the Carthaginian Hannibal trained soldiers there in the art of using the elephant in warfare.

Tell Qarqur has been equated with Karkara/Qarqar mentioned in the records of Shalmaneser III (958–824 BCE) and Sargon II (721–705 BCE) of Assyria. The texts mention that the site was destroyed several times. In Shalmaneser III's monolith inscription it is called the royal residence of King Irhuleni of Hamath. In the annals of the second year of Sargon II it is mentioned as the favorite city of Iaubi'di, king of Hama. Both Assyrian rulers fought battles in the vicinity of Karkara/Qarqar and confronted the king of Hama and a coalition of armies from states in Syria and Palestine. The coalition of twelve kings against Shalmaneser included Ahab of Israel, Ba'asa of Ammon, and a contingent of Arab camel riders.

The equation of Tell Qarqur with Karkara/Qarqar is still not confirmed. Excavations were undertaken by the American Schools of Oriental Research in 1983 and 1984 under the direction of John Lundquist and resumed in 1993 under the direction of Rudolph H. Dornemann. They indicate quite clearly that Tell Qarqur was a major site during the ninth and eighth centuries BCE, the period that includes the two Assyrian rulers mentioned above. The total 55 acres covered by the site may have been occupied then. Iron Age II material was found close to the surface on the highest part of the mound, in area B, in area C (on the western side of the tell), in area A (in a gateway area), and in area D (on the lower portion of the mound).

The tell consists of two portions, a high, 20-acre southern tell and a lower, 35-acre northern tell. Excavation has been limited to the four areas mentioned. Pottery from the Ayyubid, Umayyad, Byzantine, Roman, Hellenistic, and Persian periods has been found scattered over the entire surface of the mound; however, only limited architectural remains of any of these periods have been encountered so far. The most extensive excavations have concentrated on the gateway area (area A), where several Iron IIA phases have been encountered as well as other substantial wall foundations. Inside the gateway a 2-meter-wide stone-paved street has been traced to 15 m beyond the gateway; the street is covered in places by 3 m of later erosional deposits washed into the area. The ceramic inventory parallels very closely the ʿAmuq phase O materials of the ninth and eighth centuries BCE. Red-burnished platters and characteristic jar and cook-pot rims are well represented, as are typical painted wares and imported Cypriot pottery.

Bronze Age walls were found downslope in area A, but the most extensive evidence for earlier occupation on the site comes from pottery found in fills associated with the gateway complex. MB II pottery is present in addition to a very complete third-millennium sequence. This raises the possibility that the name of the site may have continued for many millennia and that the reference to a Qarqar in Egyptian execration texts may prove to be associated with Qarqur as well.

A few sherds indicate still earlier material on the site. Dark-faced burnished and impressed sherds of the Neolithic period are contemporary with phases A–B on the ʿAmuq plain to the north; painted sherds demonstrate the Ubaid tradition of ʿAmuq phases E–F; and beveled-rim bowl rims and triangular lug handles indicate the ʿAmuq phases F–G range of the Uruk through Early Bronze I periods.

EB remains include ceramic materials well known from the ʿAmuq area, from the early reserved-slip wares, cross-combed metallic ware sherds, and diminutive ring bases that go with cyma-recta profiled cups, to later plain simple and scrabbled wares with distinctive washes and painted and incised bands. Also well represented are sherds of red and black burnished or "Khirbet Kerak" ware with its typical range of colors and shapes and incised and molded decoration.

BIBLIOGRAPHY

Dornemann, Rudolph H. "The 1993 Excavations at Tell Qarqur." *Annales Archéologique Arabes Syriennes* (1994), in press.

Dornemann, Rudolph H. "Excavations at Tell Qarqur, 1994." *Annales Archéologique Arabes Syriennes* (1995), in press.

Dornemann, Rudolph H. "Comparisons in the Bronze and Iron Age Inventories between Orontes Valley Sites, Ugarit and Ebla, from the Point of View of Tell Qarqur." In Proceedings of the International Colloquium, Aleppo and the Silk Road, Aleppo, Syria, September, 1994. *Annales Archéologique Arabes Syriennes* (1995), in press.

Lundquist, John. "Tell Qarqur—The 1983 Season." *Annales Archéologique Arabes Syriennes* 33.2 (1983): 273–288.

RUDOLPH H. DORNEMANN

QARYAT AL-FAU, site located in southwestern Saudi Arabia at the escarpment of Wadi al-Dawasir and the Tuwaiq Mountains on the ancient transpeninsular trade routes linking the South Arabian states not only with Arabian trade centers but with neighboring countries. The site is located at the mouth of a dry channel, al-Fau ("the gap"), from which the village acquired its name. Sabaean inscriptions refer to it as Qaryat or Qaryat Dhat Kahl, a deity whose life-sized figure is found on the mountain adjoining al-Fau.

The site was discovered accidentally by officials of the Saudi Arabian Oil Company in the 1940s. In 1952 H. St. John Philby, Jacques Ryckmans, and P. Lippens visited the site and wrote about its archaeological importance. Albert Jamme, with the collaboration of Saudi Arabia's Department of Archaeology and Museums, in 1969 made a study of the Sabaean rock inscriptions on the Tuwaiq Mountains

QARYAT AL-FAU. Figure 1. *Architectural remains of the suq at al-Fau.* (Courtesy A. T. al-Ansary)

flanking al-Fau. In 1971 Abd al-Rahman al-Ansary surveyed the site and undertook excavations the following year.

Twenty seasons of excavations were conducted from 1972 to 1994 that unearthed a full-fledged settlement with unique features and an enormous number of artifacts. The work revealed an advanced stage of civilization that had flourished between about 300 BCE and 300 CE. Stratigraphy revealed two phases at the site: the Minaean period and the Kindite period. The former lasted from the third century BCE to the beginning of the first century CE, and the latter from the first half of the first century BCE to the end of third century. For a certain amount of time, the two overlapped and coexisted.

The site's geographic location was the main factor contributing to the rise and flourishing of civilization at al-Fau. This is manifested in the large variety of small finds and architectural remains, recovered through excavation: coins; pottery and stone vessels; glass; jewelry; metal objects, including figurines; textiles; ivory and bone objects; inscriptions; and frescoes. The architectural remains include a double-storied market, or *suq* (30.25 × 25.20 m), which is so far unique in Arabia, with well-planned shops, a courtyard, corridors leading to the shops, staircases, wells, and lavatories (see figure 1). Built of stone and mud brick, its wide doors are capped with semicircular lintels.

Al-Fau's five temples are also unique: they are the only ones discovered to date within Saudi Arabia. They are devoted to the gods Shams, Sin, Wud, Abat, and al-Hawar, and seem to belong to different periods. The figurines found inside and outside the temples resemble those from Syria, Egypt, and the Mediterranean basin, suggesting foreign links and influences in religion and civilization at al-Fau (see figure 2). The lower portion of an alabaster statuette was recovered from the Wud temple along with an incense burner for burning aromatics for the god. [*See* Incense.] From a room adjoining the Wud temple were recovered bronze figurines of Herakles and Hippocrates. The blending of different architectural elements is evident in the general plan of the temples, which are rectangular and similar to those found in contemporary South Arabian states as well as at the Awratian temple at Altin Tepe in Anatolia. All the inscriptions, are in South Arabian. [*See* South Arabian.]

The site's social organization is demonstrated by the variety of burial tombs. Three groups of tombs for three categories of people were distinguished: kings, nobility, and the general population. The tombs are underground, permanent stone structures with arches over the doorways and stairs. Rectangular sections, or chambers, to accommodate several peole, suggest that these were family tombs. The tombs are like underground houses. A Sabaean inscription on one tombstone reads "The tomb of Muʿawiyah ibn Rabia al / al-Qahtani king of Qahtan and Mudhhyg built by. . . . / His servant Haf'am ibn Beran of al-tl. . . ." Gold jewelry was

QARYAT AL-FAU. Figure 2. *Statuette of Harpocrates found during excavation of al-Fau.* (Courtesy A. T. al-Ansary)

recovered from one of the tombs. [*See* Tombs; Grave Goods.]

Its municipal planners assigned particular areas for the different town functions—the king's palace, the market, religious shrines, public buildings, tombs, and so forth. A residential area with well-planned houses, streets, lanes, hotels, rest-houses, water channels, a water-storage tank, overns, hearths, and lavatories gives a vivid picture of the life and society in the town in pre-Islamic Arabia. By all standards, apparent from the artifacts, its society was learned and advanced.

A variety of pottery (coarse, fine, and glazed) for different domestic purposes has been used in dating the town. Some sherds, inscribed in South Arabian, bear the name of the god Kahl or the name of the Ḥimyarite king. [*See* Ḥimyar.] Nabatean sherds found at al-Fau suggest commercial relations with the Nabateans who ruled in north-western Arabia. [*See* Nabateans.] Soft-stone vessels with geometric designs similar to those found in the Arabian Gulf states were recovered from the houses at al-Fau. They probably were locally made, for the raw material was available nearby, in Saudi Arabia, at ad-Dawadmi, aṭ-Ṭa'if, and Hajlah-Abha, among other sites.

The Kinda kingdom minted its own silver and bronze coins in various denominations for domestic consumption and for commercial transactions with traders passing through it. The coins depict their god Kahl and bear the monogram of Kahl in South Arabian. Their nature and mode of manufacture suggest the profound influence of the South Arabian states.

Wall paintings found in the settlement depict daily life, socioeconomic conditions, manners, customs, costumes, and leisure activities. Among the scenes depicted are a hunt, chasing game, royalty on horseback, and a man holding on to a camel. Animals, fruits, and naked people are also depicted. The paintings also carry rather short inscriptions in South Arabian.

BIBLIOGRAPHY

Ansary, Abdul Rahman T. al-. "Inscriptions from Qaryat al-Fau" (in Arabic). *Bulletin of the Faculty of Arts, University of Riyadh* 3 (1973–1974).

Ansary, Abdul Rahman T. al-. "New Light on the State of Kinda from the Antiquities and Inscriptions of Qaryat al-Fau" (in Arabic). In *Sources for the History of Arabia: Proceedings of the First International Symposium on Studies in the History of Arabia, 23rd–28th April 1977*, edited by Abdul Rahman T. al-Ansary et al., pp. 3–11. Studies in the History of Arabia, vol. 1. Riyadh, 1979.

Ansary, Abdul Rahman T. al-. *Qaryat al-Fau: A Portrait of Pre-Islamic Civilization in Saudi Arabia*. New York, 1982.

Jamme, Albert. "Sabaean Rock Inscriptions from Qaryat al-Fau." *Miscellanées d'Ancient Arabe* 4 (1973): 2–96.

Lippens, Philippe. *Expedition en Arabia Centrale*. Paris, 1956.

Philby, H. St. John. "Two Notes from Central Arabia." *Geographical Journal* 113 (1949): 86–93.

ABDUL RAHMAN T. AL-ANSARY

QASILE, TELL, small mound (14 acres) located on a sandstone ridge on the northern bank of the Yarkon River, about 1.5 km (1 mi.) from the Mediterranean coast (today in the center of a northern suburb of Tel Aviv). The ancient name of the site is unknown, but it may be one of the towns of the tribe of Dan in the region of the Yarkon, such as Harakon (*Jos.* 19:46). The site's proximity to the river and the coast made it a convenient harbor for trading ships. In the Iron Age I, its location made Tell Qasile a commercial center, a role formerly played by the Canaanite town at Tel Gerisa, on the opposite bank of the river. While maritime trade was probably a major feature in the town's economy, agriculture was as well. A relatively large number of hippopotamus bones found at the site suggests that the animal was part of the local diet.

The site came to the attention of scholars in the late 1940s, when two Paleo-Hebrew inscriptions incised on potsherds were found on its surface. One reads "Gold of Ophir (belonging) to Beth-Ḥoron, thirty shekels." The second reads "(Belonging) to the king, one thousand and one hundred [units] of oil . . . Hiyahu.")

Excavations at the site were conducted by Benjamin Mazar from 1949 to 1951 and in 1959, and by Amihai Mazar from 1971–1974 and from 1982–1992, on behalf of the Institute of Archaeology of the Hebrew University of Jerusalem and the Ha-aretz Museum in Tel Aviv.

Iron Age I: Urban Development. The major period of occupation at Tell Qasile was in Iron Age I (twelfth–eleventh centuries BCE). The town was probably founded by the Philistines in connection with their expansion from the nucleus of their settlement in the heart of Philistia. Philistine bichrome ware was introduced during this period (c. 1150 BCE), replacing the earlier Philistine monochrome pottery, a local product made in the Mycenaean IIIC style. The latter pottery was not found at Tell Qasile, but bichrome ware was abundant in the earliest occupation level on the mound (stratum XII). It continued to appear in large quantities in the following level (stratum XI) and to some extent also in the third level (stratum X). In stratum X, however, a local decorative style appeared, characterized by black paint on red slip, a degeneration of the original Philistine pottery.

Strata XII–X represent the town's gradual development, with transitions unmarked by violent destruction. However, stratum X, the level in which the town reached the peak of its urban development and economic prosperity, came to a violent end, probably as a result of King David's annexation of the coast north of Jaffa to his kingdom in the early tenth century BCE.

Evidence of the town's urban development in Iron I was uncovered over a large area: more than 2,500 sq. m were excavated. In its earliest phase (stratum XII), the town was only partially built up. Thick deposits of gray ashy earth in the remaining large open areas constitute evidence of a comparatively long occupation. Mud-brick structures without stone foundations were built on bedrock in this stratum. A public building south of the temple (see below) had a large hall with benches along the walls and a hearth at its center. The latter element is foreign to Canaanite architecture and may reflect Aegean or Cypriot traditions brought by the Philistines from their homeland.

In the following phase (stratum XI), more substantial buildings were erected with stone foundations and a mud-brick superstructure. Many of the stratum X buildings had probably been founded in stratum XI, yet their exact plans in stratum XI are not entirely clear. In the third phase (stratum X), the town was fully developed. As a result of the fire that destroyed the town, its mud-brick walls were found fired and, thus, well preserved. The excavations revealed a careful planning, with an orthogonal grid of streets that created clearly defined blocks of buildings. In a residential quarter in the southern part of the mound, seven houses, almost identical in plan, were excavated. Most of them are rectangular (about 100 sq m), of the pillared house, or four-room house type. [*See* Four-room House.] Such houses are one of the cultural features that characterize various ethnic groups coexisting during the Iron Age I in ancient Palestine. The structures contained a central space (open courtyard?) with a roofed side space paved with flagstones that was probably used as an animal shelter. This side space was separated from the courtyard by a row of four or five pillars made of wooden beams standing on end on stone bases. On one or both sides of the courtyard were additional rooms. In the courtyard itself were various installations: baking ovens, grinding stones, wine presses, looms (piles of up to forty clay loom weights were found in almost every house, evidence for home industry). In one house a bronze workshop was found that contained a circular kiln and two smelting crucibles. Each of the houses contained dozens of pottery vessels; some houses had storerooms, each containing more than fifty storejars of about 20 liters in volume. The storejars were probably used as portable containers in the trade of liquid commodities such as wine and oil. They would have been transported by the ships anchored in the Yarkon.

Two public buildings were also constructed in this quarter: a storehouse composed of a rectangular hall divided by two rows of pillars (one of the earliest examples of the storehouses that became common in the Iron II period). Another building probably served an administrative function: it contained three rectangular storerooms, in addition to a number of other rooms, and a large hall. No fortifications could be detected because of severe erosion along the edge of the mound. However, on the western slope of the mound, a short segment of a thick mud-brick wall was recovered that may be a remnant of a city wall.

Iron Age I: Sacred Area. The Iron Age sacred area at Tell Qasile is the only one in ancient Philistia that has been completely excavated. It exhibits extensive architectural

QASILE, TELL. Figure 1. *View of the Philistine temple (stratum X), looking east.* (Courtesy A. Mazar)

changes over a comparatively short time. The architecture and many of the cult objects from its sanctuary are unique. Although rooted mainly in local Canaanite traditions, some Aegean and Cypriot components are recognizable.

In stratum XII, a modest shrine was constructed on bedrock: a one-room structure (outer dimensions 6.4 × 6.6 m) with benches along its walls and a raised platform in front of the entrance, which was at the center of the east facade. A large courtyard with an auxiliary room was found east of the shrine. In stratum XI, the older shrine went out of use and was replaced by a larger temple with stone walls (outer dimensions 7.75 × 8.50 m). The entrance was at the end of the east facade; inside the building benches lined the walls and an inner room served as a treasury. The holy of holies was probably in a niche opposite the entrance. Attached to the temple on the west was a small mud-brick shrine with a bent-axis approach, benches lining its walls, and a raised platform in its southwestern corner. In the large courtyard in front of the temple were two attached auxiliary rooms. A *bothros* (Gk., a pit where sacred objects were buried) found in the courtyard contained layers of animal bones, discarded cult vessels, and many pottery vessels. The plans of both the temple and the shrine are unknown in Canaanite architecture. This unique combination of a main temple and a side shrine with a bent-axis approach recalls the somewhat earlier sacred complex at Philakopi, on the island of Melos.

The stratum X temple represents a rebuilding and enlargement of the previous structure (see figure 1). An antechamber was added on the east, enlarging the building to 8 × 14.5 m. The antechamber created a bent-axis approach to the main hall. Stepped plastered benches were constructed along the walls of the antechamber and the main hall. The roof of the latter was supported by two cedar-wood columns that stood on cylindrical stone bases running along the hall's long axis. A raised platform was located opposite the entrance to the main hall; behind the platform a narrow cell was used perhaps as a treasury. A courtyard north and east of the temple was enclosed by stone walls. In the courtyard in front of the temple the square foundation of a sacrificial altar was found. The small shrine of the previous stratum continued in use, but with its own fenced courtyard and an auxiliary room used as a kitchen.

A considerable number of ceramic cult objects was found in the sanctuary. Some are based on local Canaanite or Egyptian traditions, while others are original shapes with almost no precedents. Among them is a plaque showing the facade of a shrine and two figures of what may be goddesses that were intentionally destroyed in antiquity; an anthropomorphic vessel with breasts serving as spouts (see figure 2); a lion-shaped cup made in a tradition known from Ugarit and paralleled at other Iron I sites settled by Sea Peoples; a large jar with five openings that may have been used to hold sacred plants in the temple; various cylindrical stands decorated with animal and human figures; and offering bowls decorated with bird figurines. Among the metal objects were an iron knife with bronze rivets and an ivory handle that ends in a ring-shaped pommel and a bronze ax/adze, both known in the Aegean and Cyprus but foreign to local Canaanite traditions.

QASILE, TELL. Figure 2. *Anthropomorphic libation vessel found in the Philistine sanctuary.* (Courtesy A. Mazar)

The Iron I culture at Tell Qasile as revealed in the dwellings and sanctuary retains many Canaanite characteristics; it can therefore be assumed that indigenous Canaanites were an important component of the local population. However, the abundance of Philistine pottery and the appearance of Philistine motifs on several cult objects, as well as cultural elements that retain Aegean traditions, lead to the conclusion that Philistines founded the site and were the leading element in its social structure.

Following the violent destruction and burning of stratum X, the town was rebuilt, in the tenth century BCE. The two strata that can be dated to this period (strata IX–VIII) give evidence of the town's partial rebuilding. The new town was a pale reflection of its predecessor—smaller in area and much less densely built. Some of the older buildings were reconstructed with modifications, but other houses went out of use and paved open spaces replaced them. Stone-lined silos were found in several places. The ruined stratum X temple was reconstructed to some extent, but it is doubtful whether it was a roofed structure in this phase. Around it was a large open space that was occasionally repaved with a new lime floor. The pottery in this period is characterized by red slip and hand burnishing, typical of the tenth century BCE; Philistine painted pottery disappeared altogether.

It seems that during this period Tell Qasile served as a port town for the united kingdom under David and Solomon. The town was probably destroyed by Pharaoh Sheshonq on his return to Egypt from Megiddo. Yet, it is difficult to say whether he destroyed stratum IX or VIII. If the former is the case, than stratum VIII denotes a partial rebuilding of the town after this destruction, in the ninth century BCE.

End of the Iron Age. After a long gap in occupation, a small settlement was founded at Tell Qasile in the late seventh century BCE. Agricultural installations found around the tell are evidence of a small farm. However, the Hebrew inscriptions mentioned above hint that the site had been an administrative and trading center in the eighth–seventh centuries BCE.

Persian Period. A single building with a frontal fenced courtyard probably served as an agricultural or administrative center in the fifth–fourth centuries BCE. Refuse pits from this period were dug around the building, and a square well was found at the foot of the mound. Imported Greek pottery is evidence of maritime trade connections. The site may have been destroyed during the conquest of Alexander the Great.

Late Periods. Evidence of some limited activity during the Hellenistic and Roman periods was found on the summit of the mound. A large building with rows of pillars may have been a marketplace. In the Byzantine period a small village was scattered over and around the mound. A synagogue with a Samaritan inscription was found at the foot of the mound, and a bathhouse was uncovered on its summit.

In the Early Islamic period a caravanserai was located at the summit of the mound. In the Middle Ages a small sugar factory was constructed there, probably to process the sugar cane being grown in the vicinity.

BIBLIOGRAPHY

Maisler [Mazar], Benjamin. "The Excavations at Tell Qasîle: Preliminary Report." *Israel Exploration Journal* 1.2 (1950–1951): 61–76, 125–140. The first seasons of excavations.

Mazar, Amihai. *Excavations at Tell Qasile,* part 1, *The Philistine Sanctuary: Architecture and Cult Objects.* Qedem, vol. 12. Jerusalem, 1980.

Mazar, Amihai. *Excavations at Tell Qasile,* part 2, *The Philistine Sanctuary: Various Finds, the Pottery, Conclusions, Appendixes.* Qedem, vol. 20. Jerusalem, 1985. Final report (with Mazar [1980]) of the 1972–1974 excavation seasons, covering mainly the Iron Age sanctuary.

Mazar, Amihai. "Excavations at Tell Qasile, 1982–1984: Preliminary Report." *Israel Exploration Journal* 36 (1986): 1–15.

Mazar, Amihai. "Qasile, Tell." In *The New Encyclopedia of Archaeological Excavations in the Holy Land,* edited by Ephraim Stern, vol. 4, pp. 1204–1212. Jerusalem and New York, 1993.

AMIHAI MAZAR

QAṢR AL-ḤALLABAT, site located in Jordan (32°06′ N, 36°20′ E), 25 km (15.5 mi.) northeast of Zerqa, 55 km (34 mi.) northwest of Azraq, and about 18 km (11 mi.) from the nearest point (to the northwest) of the Via Nova Trajana. It comprises a conglomerate of separate and widely spaced units that include a *qaṣr* ("castle"; see figure 1), a mosque, a huge reservoir, and eight cisterns dug into the western slope and into the plain alongside the reservoir. The site also includes an irregularly shaped agricultural enclosure with an elaborate system of sluices and a cluster of poorly built houses that extends to the northwest of the reservoir. To these units should be added the bath complex at Ḥammam aṣ-Ṣaraḥ, 2 km east of the castle.

The Princeton Archaeological Expedition to Syria, under the direction of Howard C. Butler (1907–1921), visited the site twice in 1905 and 1909. They drew plans of the castle and mosque, published numerous inscribed stones, and mentioned the reservoir, at the bottom of which they had pitched their camp. The remains are also mentioned by, among others, Rudolf-Ernst Brünnow and Alfred von Domaszewski, Henry Field, G. Lankester Harding, Nelson Glueck, Aurel Stein, Jean Sauvaget, and L. W. B. Rees. Rees published a vertical aerial view that reveals many of the ancient remains associated with the castle. [*See the biographies of Harding, Glueck, and Sauvaget.*] More recently, Ḥallabat was the subject of detailed investigation by David Kennedy (1982), who published a new plan for the castle and additional inscribed stones, and by Fawwāz Touqan, who emphasized the Early Islamic aspect of the site. Between 1979 and 1985, five seasons of excavation were carried out jointly by the Department of Antiquities of Jordan and La Maison de L'Orient Méditerranéen de Lyon. In the course of these excavations, the plan of the mosque was confirmed and the agricultural enclosure investigated. In addition, all the rooms along the north, south, and east walls of the castle were cleared to floor levels, and eleven probes, placed inside the rooms and outside the castle, penetrated the floors down to bedrock. The pottery sherds the probes in the castle produced cannot be assigned earlier than the Umayyad period (661–750 CE). This would indicate that, in the last phase of construction, the earlier occupational debris and whatever floors existed within the castle were thoroughly removed. That there was a pre-Umayyad building, however, is beyond doubt, confirmed by the ceramic evidence from outside the castle as well as by the fact that the enclosure and partition

QAṢR AL-ḤALLABAT. Figure 1. *General view of the ruins.* (Courtesy G. Bisheh)

walls were set on the outer edges of earlier walls. This may explain the anomalous plan of Qaṣr al-Ḥallabat compared to other Umayyad buildings.

The plan of the castle (see figure 2) is square (44 m to the side), with square towers and a single entrance in the eastern wall. A central courtyard paved with flagstones is surrounded on three sides by a series of oblong and nearly square rooms. The northwestern quadrant is occupied by a structure that also consists of a central courtyard surrounded on all but the south side by a number of rooms. This quadrant, which is set apart from the rest of the castle, may have been a low-status area reserved for servants. There is a cistern in each of the two courtyards.

Two inscriptions are thought to have some bearing on the architectural phases of the castle: one in Latin, dated to 212 CE that refers to the construction of a *novum castellum;* and the other in Greek, dated to 529 CE. Excavations and clearance work inside the castle uncovered a total of 146 Greek inscriptions—as well as two in Nabatean, one in Safaitic, and a fourth in modern Armenian—engraved on regularly cut basalt stones. [*See* Safaitic-Thamudic Inscriptions; Nabatean Inscriptions.] The vast majority of these inscribed stones belong to an edict issued by the Byzantine emperor Anastasius (491–518) for the administrative and economic reorganization of the Provincia Arabia. It is quite likely that all of the inscribed stones were brought from a nearby settlement, possibly Umm el-Jimal, and reused as building material during the Umayyad reconstruction of the castle. [*See* Umm el-Jimal.] In the course of this reconstruction, the castle was elaborately decorated with carved stucco, frescoes,

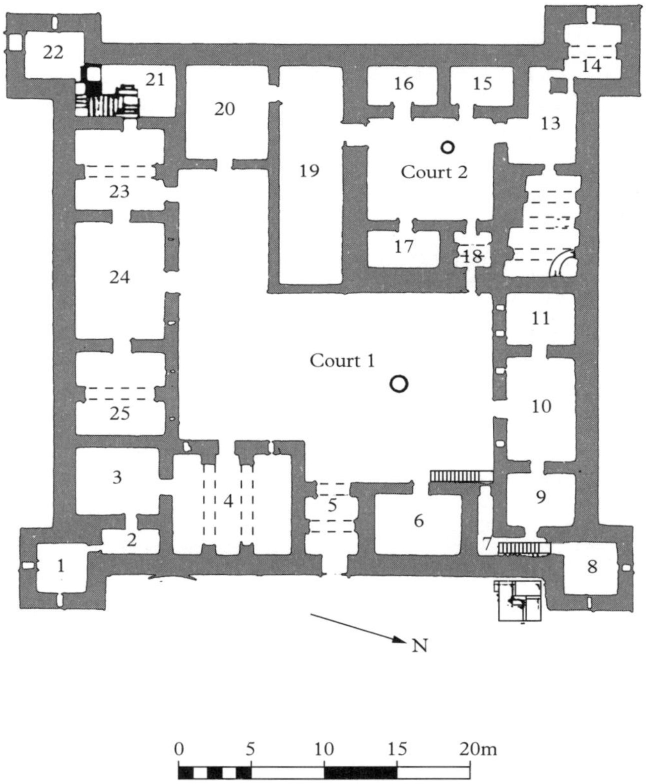

QAṢR AL-ḤALLABAT. Figure 2. *Plan of the castle.* (Courtesy G. Bisheh)

and colored mosaics, thus transformed from a fortified building into a palatial residence. The transformation was accompanied by a remarkable development of the site, apparent in its extramural mosque, agricultural enclosure with its elaborate irrigation systems, and the bath complex at Ḥammam aṣ-Ṣaraḥ.

BIBLIOGRAPHY

Bisheh, Ghazi. "Excavations at Qasr al-Hallabat, 1979." *Annual of the Department of Antiquities of Jordan* 24 (1980): 69–77.

Bisheh, Ghazi. "The Second Season of Excavations at Hallabat, 1980." *Annual of the Department of Antiquities of Jordan* 26 (1982): 133–143.

Bisheh, Ghazi. "Qaṣr al-Ḥallābāt: A Summary of the 1984 and 1985 Excavations." *Archiv für Orientforschung* 33 (1986): 158–162.

Butler, Howard Crosby, et al. *Publications of the Princeton University Archaeological Expeditions to Syria in 1904–1905 and 1909.* 4 vols. in 9. Leiden, 1907–1921. See Division II, Section A, pp. 70–77 (architecture); Division III, Section A, pp. 21–42 (Greek and Latin inscriptions); and Division IV, Section A, pp. 1ff. (Nabatean inscriptions).

Kennedy, David L. *Archaeological Explorations on the Roman Frontier in North-East Jordan.* British Archaeological Reports, International Series, no. 134. Oxford, 1982. See pages 17–65.

Marcillet-Jaubert, Jean. "Recherches au Qasr el-Hallabat." *Annual of the Department of Antiquities of Jordan* 24 (1980): 121–124.

Marcillet-Jaubert, Jean. "Les inscriptions grecques de Hallabat, II." *Annual of the Department of Antiquities of Jordan* 26 (1982): 145–158.

GHAZI BISHEH

QAṢR AL-ḤAYR AL-GHARBI, one of the two desert estates of the Umayyad caliph Hisham (r. AH 105–125/724–793 CE) that is part of a group of ten structures extending for 20 km (12 mi.) and connected by a sophisticated system of water channels starting at the Kharbaqa dam on the northern fringes of the Jabal Rawaq. The caliph resided mostly at Rusafa in Syria, the former Sergiopolis, between Palmyra and ar-Raqqa. He first commissioned the Palace of the Western Game Park, about 180 km (112 mi.) southwest of Rusafa, built in about AH 109/727 CE; shortly thereafter he commissioned the Palace of the Eastern Game Park (Qaṣr al-Ḥayr ash-Sharqi), dated to AH 110/728–729 CE, about 70 km (43 mi.) southeast of Rusafa. [*See* Rusafa; Raqqa, ar-; Qaṣr al-Ḥayr ash-Sharqi.] Antoine Poidebard (1930) carried out an aerial and topographical survey and Daniel Schlumberger excavated the site in 1936–1938. [*See the biographies of Poidebard and Schlumberger.*]

The Kharbaqa dam is a mighty construction 345 m long and more than 20 m high that originally created a storage lake of more than one square kilometer. From it the water is channeled north in a surface canal. About 4 km (2.5 mi.) away is an almost square building (63 × 58 m), supposedly a Roman post on the Strata Diocletiana. About 11 km (7 mi.) farther north the channel's first bifurcation conducts the water west, to the palace proper, and to an isolated bath in the immediate vicinity. About 2 km later the main channel leads to a square pool (60 m on each side). Close by, a second western bifurcation leads to another square structure (55 × 55 m), probably a caravanserai, with a reused Roman doorframe inscribed with an Arabic text commemorating its construction in AH 109/727 CE, now exhibited in the Damascus Museum; two wings project from the facade: one contains a small oratory *(masjid)* and the other a water trough. About 500 m along the main canal, a side channel operates a water mill (about 5 × 7 m), a clear indication of local grain production. The neighboring courtyard structures to the east of the mill have not yet been excavated. To the west another barrage (i.e., a dam) with a 560-meter-long wall, in the shape of a horseshoe, from which the collected rainwater was conducted to the garden at the northwestern end of the complex. The large, walled, rectangular garden compound (1,050 × 440 m) is subdivided into square compartments (80 m on each side). It is watered by the main canal, which originates at the Kharbaqa dam, more than 18 km (11 mi.) away, and occasionally by the surplus rainwater from the horseshoe barrage. This pleasure ground, accessible through two portals accentuated by flanking columns, may have been a game park, as the traditional name of the site suggests. [*See* Irrigation.]

The focal point of this artificial oasis is the square building (about 72 m on each side) initially distinguished by double stories and exceptionally rich architectural decoration, which obviously served as the part-time residence of Caliph Hisham. Of its original splendor almost nothing remains. Only half of the tower of a monastery founded in 559 by the Christian Ghassanid ruler al-Harith ibn Jabala, to which the palace was attached, dramatically surmounts the surrounding field of ruins. In a new wing of the Damascus Museum, the building's original entrance has been reconstructed by the architect Michel Ecochard from the excavated fragments, including the facade's stucco decoration and the upper story's stately reception rooms, in which plaster sculptures, fresco floors, ornamented window grills, and wood lintels are exhibited. The sumptuous decoration program was evidently executed by artists from various parts of the Umayyad Empire. They created an architectural masterpiece that borrows from classical Syrian as well as Sasanian (Persian) features. [*See* Umayyad Caliphate.]

Although an Umayyad origin, based on the inscription in the caravanserai (see above), is generally accepted for the palace and most of the other structures, the excavators assumed that the artificial oasis was first designed in the Roman period. They thus dated the Kharbaqa dam to the second or third century, assuming the existence of a pre-Islamic military post on the ancient road crossing the Syrian desert. An extensive Umayyad estate that included agricultural land, gardens, and a game preserve seems a reasonable benefactor for the construction of a sophisticated irrigation project that depended on a water supply from the sizable reservoir the monumental dam created. The dam, therefore, probably also originated in the Umayyad period.

Eventually, the history of the site may reach back into the Roman period, but the first attested building activity so far is for the Ghassanid monastery tower incorporated into the palace by Caliph Hisham shortly before AH 109/727 CE (see above), when the new oasis in the desert, at the crossroad of major nomadic routes, was installed as a visual symbol of imperial might. The tower probably fell into disuse soon after Hisham's death in AH 125/743 CE. Its partial reactivation in medieval times is attested by a restoration inscription of AH 583/1187 CE on the massive Ghassanid tower, and by later construction in the palace area identified by Jean Sauvaget (*La poste aux chevaux dans l'Empire des Mamelouks,* Paris, 1941) as a way station of the Syrian postal route, established by the Mamluk sultan al-Ẓahir Baybars (r. AH 658–676/1260–1277 CE). [*See* Ayyubid–Mamluk Dynasties.]

BIBLIOGRAPHY

Creswell, K. A. C. *Early Muslim Architecture,* vol. 1, *Umayyads, A.D. 622–750* (1940). 2d ed. Oxford, 1969. See pages 506–518 for a summary of Schlumberger's excavation report (1939), with a complete bibliography.

Creswell, K. A. C. *A Short Account of Early Muslim Architecture.* Rev. ed. Aldershot, 1989. The most accessible standard reference; see pages 135–146.

Grabar, Oleg. "Umayyad Palaces Reconsidered." *Ars Orientalis* 23 (1993): 93–108. Analysis of Early Islamic imperial architecture, including Qaṣr al-Ḥayr al-Gharbi.

Poidebard, Antoine. *La trace de Rome dans le désert de Syrie: Le limes de Trajan à la conquête arabe; recherches aériennes, 1925–1932.* Paris, 1934. The first modern study of the site using aerial photography; see pages 187–190.

Schlumberger, Daniel. "Les fouilles de Qasr el-Heir el-Gharbi, 1936–1938: Rapport préliminaire." *Syria* 20 (1939): 195–238, 324–373. Extensive excavation report.

Schlumberger, Daniel. "Deux fresques omeyyades." *Syria* 25 (1946–1948): 86–102. The floor frescoes of the palace, now in the Damascus Museum.

Schlumberger, Daniel. *Qasr el-Heir el Gharbi.* Edited by Odile Échard and Agnes Schlumberger. Bibliothèque Archéologique et Historique, vol. 120. Paris, 1986. Mainly a reprint of Schlumberger's (1939) preliminary report, but with extended documentation and thus the best available publication on the subject; includes contributions by Michel Écochard and Nassib Saliby.

MICHAEL MEINECKE

QAṢR AL-ḤAYR ASH-SHARQI, site located about 110 km (68 mi.) north–northeast of Palmyra, Syria, at the northern end of a flat steppic area, at the foot of a low mountain chain, the Jebel Bishri. This is more or less the area in which the rains from higher altitudes gather toward the plain and occasionally flood it. It is also located at the approximate place where the Baghdad to Aleppo and Damascus to ar-Raqqa routes cross. Long assumed to be a Roman defensive establishment against nomads, Qaṣr al-Ḥayr has now been shown to have been one of the many early Islamic foundations that cover the entire area from the Euphrates River to the Gulf of ʿAqaba.

Because of its spectacular ruins, which are visible from afar, the site has been recorded by travelers since the first decade of the nineteenth century. It was partially mapped and surveyed by the more thorough explorers, such as the Czech Alois Musil, of the decades before World War I. During the French Mandate, the site was surveyed by André Gabriel and entered into the various reconstructions of Late Antique and Early Medieval Syria by René Dussaud. It was the subject of an extensive archaeological investigation directed by Oleg Grabar under the auspices of the University of Michigan and Harvard University between 1964 and 1972. The results of those excavations were published in 1978 (see Grabar, 1978). The material remains are in the archaeological museum in Palmyra.

The site (7 sq km, or roughly 2.75 sq. mi.) is enclosed by a wall 15 km (9 mi.) long. The wall has been provided with sluices and retaining walls at strategic points where sudden flooding could become harmful. The technology of these waterworks seems to have been imported from southern Arabia and Yemen rather than to be indigenous to Syria. At the northern end of this enclosure three buildings were erected. The largest, a square of about 167 m to the side, was provided with four gates leading up to a large central open area surrounded by a portico. Around the central area, twelve approximately equal squares were mapped out with a single course of stones. They included four backyards in the corners, one mosque, one oil press, and seven dwellings, each of which had a central porticoed court and rooms of varying sizes around the portico. The living unit nearest to the mosque had elaborate stucco decoration of vegetal and geometric motifs and may well have been an official building. An inscription, now gone, identifies this enclosure as a *madinah,* "a city"—although the word should probably be understood in its earlier meaning, "estate." In spite of the enclosure having been laid out at one time, the various units were not completed together or with the same construction techniques. The inscription dates the foundation of the enclosure to 728–729 CE and the rule of the caliph Hisham. However, the wall decoration and some of the material remains indicate that much of the "city" was not really in full activity before the early ninth century.

The second building is a well-preserved and massive square (70 m to the side) monument with a single entrance, walls preserved to a height of more than 11 m, and corner towers that offer views of the terrain for miles. Around a porticoed courtyard, the interior consisted of large numbers of high and dark halls vaulted in a brick technique hitherto unknown in Syria. These halls appear to have existed without any amenities or apparent differentiations in function. The second floor has not been preserved, but such evidence as exists suggests the repetition of the same plan. The excavators have interpreted the building as a work of commercial architecture, as a caravanserai for the repose of travelers and the safeguarding of goods; the huge area surrounding it would have served for animals.

The third major building was a bath, typical in all respects of the Early Islamic baths that came out of the architectural traditions of Late Antiquity. In addition, cisterns and complex systems of canals distributed water to the walled enclosures. Ceramic finds also point to the existence of rather simple and short-lived residential quarters to the north of the main buildings. [*See* Baths.]

Excavation made it possible to establish the history of the site. It was planned in Umayyad times as an estate for agriculture and trade (perhaps the Zaytunah of medieval Arabic texts). Using remains from earlier Roman and Palmyrene monuments, the site was completed and flourished throughout the Early ʿAbbasid period (until about 900). It was then almost completely abandoned. It was revived as a small and miserable twelfth–fourteenth-century city, and then finally abandoned in about 1350. The material culture of all but the first of these periods can be reconstructed from excavated fragments and from analysis of the architectural remains.

[*See also* Qaṣr al-Ḥayr al-Gharbi; *and the biography of* Dussaud.]

BIBLIOGRAPHY

Creswell, K. A. C. *A Short Account of Early Muslim Architecture.* Rev. ed. Aldershot, 1989. See pages 149–163 for Qaṣr al-Ḥayr esh-Sharqi.

Grabar, Oleg, et al. *City in the Desert: Qasr al-Hayr East.* Cambridge, Mass., 1978.

Hillenbrand, Robert. *Islamic Architecture.* Edinburgh, 1994.

OLEG GRABAR

QAṢR AL-MESHATTA (Ar., "palace of wintering"), site located on the edge of the Jordanian desert (31°49′ N, 36°28′ E). At approximately 200 m above sea level, al-Meshatta commands a strategically broad view in all directions and is the largest and most ambitious of the Islamic palaces in Jordan. The site was discovered by H. B. Tristram in 1865 (*The Land of Moab,* London, 1873). Its date and origin were once disputed, but it is now generally accepted as an Umayyad structure and is identified as the work of Caliph al-Walid II (r. 743–744 CE).

The *qaṣr,* or palace, is a square, walled enclosure constructed of burnt clay brick (144 m to a side) and is flanked by polygonal towers at its corners. Two octagonal salient angles, to the right and left of the entrance, formed a splendid limestone facade (60 m long, 5 m high) covered with highly formalized ornaments and sculpture carved in delicate relief. Only a few lower courses are preserved.

The carvings on the facade of the palace are of floral, animal, and geometric motifs: bold rosettes; large, rhythmic triangles; looped and grape-laden vine stalks; birds; lions; acanthus leaves; and great octagons. The motifs in the decorations varied from bastion to bastion, and the work of several distinct hands can be discerned. Some of the motifs are essentially Hellenistic, while others show a Sasanian (Persian) influence, especially in the frontal poses of animals, with candelabra forms or double wings. The other sides were undecorated. Almost the entire palace facade was given as a gift to the German Kaiser Wilhelm II by the Ottoman sultan Abdülhamid, just before World War I. It was removed and dispatched to Berlin, where it was set up in the Kaiser Friedrich-Museum (Pergamon Museum).

The palace itself is considerable in size but had only one entrance, which led to the living quarters (see above). Those quarters were arranged in three sections, separated from one another by large rectangular courts. The courtyards apparently were used to stable camels and horses and to store goods. The palace mosque was sited in the traditional position, inside and to the right of the main entrance. [*See* Mosque.]

The palace interior, including a three-apsed hall, remained in various stages of completion. Some walls and vaults were built with light-brown fired bricks. There is symmetry throughout, created by its plan, on an axis, with a tendency to compartmentalization, often into three sections. The vaulting systems are essentially Mesopotamian in style, but the masonry is Hellenistic. The style of the carved decoration is both Sasanian and Hellenistic, a fusion of the two traditions in Umayyad architecture.

[*See* Palace.]

BIBLIOGRAPHY

Berchem, Max van. *Opera Minora I.* Geneva, 1978. Comprehensive and well-documented presentation of the scholarly dispute over the date and origin of this Islamic monument.

Creswell, K. A. C. *Early Muslim Architecture.* 2 vols. Rev. ed. Oxford, 1969. Basic and essential study for students of Islamic architecture in general and Qaṣr al-Meshatta in particular.

Grabar, Oleg. "Al-Mushatta, Baghdād, and Wāsiṭ." In *The World of Islam: Studies in Honour of Philip K. Hitti,* edited by James Kritzeck and R. Bayly Winder, pp. 99–108. London, 1959. Accurate, up-to-date, and concise description of Qaṣr al-Meshatta and its plan.

Schulz, Bruno, and Josef Strzygowski. *Mschatta.* Berlin, 1904. Publication prepared on the occasion of the opening ceremony of the Kaiser Friedrich–Museum, Berlin, in October 1904, which consists of a detailed description of the Qaṣr al-Meshatta by Schulz and an analytical study of its character, origin, and importance.

Trümpelmann, Leo. *Mschatta.* Tübingen, 1962. Highly scholarly contribution to the study of Qaṣr al-Meshatta, with an emphasis on the problem of the date, character, and origin of its facade's stone decorations. Essential reference for an understanding of this monument and its artistic aspects.

ADNAN HADIDI

QAṢR BURQUʿ, structural complex in northeastern Jordan comprising a tower and rooms that surround a small courtyard (32°40′ N, 37°50′ E). The buildings were constructed next to a large seasonal pool whose water-storage capacity was at some time augmented by a stone dam. The site lies on the eastern edge of the basalt *harra,* some 150 km (93 mi.) beyond the *limes Arabicus,* in a zone that receives between 50–100 mm of rain per year. The main inner "desert" route from North Arabia (Jauf/Dumatha) to Damascus and Palmya passes near the site; many east-west routes lead through the *hammada/wudiyan* to the Euphrates River in the east.

Several building phases have been identified. The first consisted of a massive rectangular tower of at least four stories, probably more than 12 meters high. The tower had only one small door and a few narrow ventilation slits in the upper levels. Larger openings may once have existed near the roof line. At ground level there are three chambers, one of which has a low rounded transverse arch. The upper floors were stone corbeled. Excavations into the foundations did not reveal conclusive dating evidence, although it is clear that the tower must predate at least 700 CE. Its original function is, similarly, uncertain. It could have been built as a watchtower to control the site's water resources or as a hermit's tower (Syr., *burga*). The project may have been financed by the Ghassanids in the sixth century, the period in which the dam must have been built. It was repaired and rebuilt often.

At some time between the towers' construction and 700 CE, a series of rooms was built in a rough square surrounding the tower. These buildings consist of a round structure that may have been a windmill, several small storage rooms, five or six long rooms, and a small, two-storied tower at one corner. The "windmill" has a small cross carved on the lintel of its entrance; one of the rooms leads to a small apse under a possibly pointed arch. These features suggest a monastic function for the buildings. Several gravestones were found inside these structures, among them two with (undated) Greek inscriptions, mostly lists of names. Excavations at several points along the walls have produced both Umayyad and pre-Umayyad pottery. The new buildings at Burquʿ may have served as a monastery between the sixth and the early eighth centuries. An Arabic inscription in Kufic script was cut into the lintel of the doorway into one of the long rooms. The lintel may have been reused. The inscription is dated to 700 CE. It tells of rooms (Ar., *buyut*) being built on behalf of the Amir Walid, son of Abd al-Malik (Umayyad caliph, 685–705). Walid's gift may be viewed in the light of Abd al-Malik's diplomacy with the bedouin, notably the Kalbi in the Badiyat ash-Sham, in order to assure the succession of his son. The room with the apse has also been identified as a humble version of an audience chamber, rather than a chapel. It may, like the rest of the buildings, have served both of these functions at various times, as well as others—which can be subsumed under the notion of a *badiya,* a formal venue for tribe-state relations. Qaṣr Burquʿ may still have functioned as a Monophysite monastery in Kalbi territory well into the eighth century. How long after the eighth century the place was used, and for what purpose(s), is not known. The next epigraphic evidence comes from an Arabic inscription, dated to the early fifteenth century, mentioning the "discovery" of the Kufic inscription of al-Walid.

BIBLIOGRAPHY

Field, Henry. *North Arabian Desert Archaeological Survey, 1925–50.* Papers of the Peabody Museum of Archaeology and Ethnology, vol. 45.2. Cambridge, Mass., 1960. Contains a brief mention of an early examination of Qaṣr Burquʿ, including the first plan of the site.

Gaube, Heinz. "An Examination of the Ruins at Qaṣr Burquʿ." *Annual of the Department of Antiquities of Jordan* 19 (1974): 93–100. Short technical survey report.

Helms, S. W. *Early Islamic Architecture of the Desert: A Bedouin Station in Eastern Jordan.* Edinburgh, 1990. Historical and archaeological study of an early Islamic site in eastern Jordan; includes a discussion of the area's history and the nature of nomad/state relations, as well as a short section on the most recent work at Burquʿ.

Helms, S. W. "A New Architectural Survey of Qaṣr Burquʿ, Eastern Jordan." *Antiquaries Journal* 71 (1991): 191–215. Detailed technical report on the most recent architectural survey of the Qaṣr and the ancient dam.

S. W. HELMS

QAṢRIN, site located in the central Golan Heights, approximately 13 km (8 mi.) northeast of the Sea of Galilee and 1 km southeast of the modern city of Qaṣrin (32°59′15″ N, 35°42′15″ E; map reference 2161 × 2661). The site's ancient name is unknown. It was first recorded and identified by Gottlieb Schumacher during his surveys of the region in 1884; he revisited it in 1913 and described "Kiṣrin" as a "small Bedouin winter village with a group of beautiful oak trees and old ruins" (Schumacher, 1888, p. 194). The name *Kiṣrin,* perhaps derived from the Arabic word *qaṣr,* meaning "fort" or "palace," may refer to the monumental ancient remains visible to the inhabitants of this nineteenth- and twentieth-century village (see figure 1).

During archaeological surveys of the region in 1967, Shmaryahu Gutman identified the remains of an ancient synagogue inside the modern Syrian village of Kiṣrin. Subsequent surveys by Dan Urman from 1969 to 1971 revealed numerous architectural elements originally belonging to the synagogue and several ancient Hebrew and Aramaic inscriptions. In 1971–1972, Urman initiated excavations in the synagogue, which continued under the direction of Muni Ben-Ari (1975–1976) and Zvi Maʿoz (1978). From 1982 to 1984, Rachel Hachlili, Ann Killebrew, and Zvi Maʿoz conducted a new series of excavations in the synagogue; from 1983 to 1990, Killebrew directed excavations in the adjacent

QAṢRIN. Figure 1. *General view of the site, looking west toward the synagogue.* The village houses, before reconstruction, are in the foreground with house B to the left. Complex C is to the right and house A is next to the southeast corner of the synagogue. (Courtesy Israel Antiquities Authority)

village. Approximately 1,500 sq m, or nearly 10 percent of the site, has been uncovered.

The excavators identified nine strata at Qaṣrin. Ceramic finds and fragmentary architectural remains indicate that the site was inhabited during the Middle Bronze II (stratum IX), Iron II (stratum VIII), Hellenistic (stratum VII), and Late Roman (stratum VI) periods. The main periods of occupation were the Late Roman through Early Islamic periods (synagogues A and B, strata V–IV); the Mamluk period (mosque, stratum II); and the late nineteenth century–1967 CE (stratum I).

Late Roman–Early Byzantine Periods (Stratum VA–B). The construction and use of synagogue A span stratum VA–B) (fourth–fifth centuries CE). The earlier phase of the village, VA, dates to late third–mid-fourth centuries CE, based on pottery assemblages found in the structures and coin hoards, including a deposit of nine thousand coins hidden under a stratum VA courtyard floor. Stratum VB (late fourth–fifth centuries CE) follows the earthquake of 363 and is characterized by the continued use of synagogue A and the repair of the village houses.

The earliest monument, synagogue A, was nearly square (15.2 × 15.3 m), with two rows of three columns each. Its main entrance was located in the northern facade wall, with a side entrance in the western wall. The hall was lined with benches on three sides, and a stone platform was constructed against the southern wall, facing Jerusalem, to hold the Ark of the Law. Artifacts sealed below the white plaster floor of synagogue A included Late Roman period pottery sherds and a coin minted in 218–219, indicating a late third- or early fourth-century date for the building's construction.

Most of the village houses built at the same time as synagogue A continued in use until the mid-eighth century, but were remodeled numerous times. The plan of a typical domestic unit at Qaṣrin consisted of a large, rectangular multipurpose room *(traclin;* Lat., *traclinium),* a smaller rectangular storage room, a sleeping loft above the storage room, and an unroofed courtyard. Additions to this typical domestic unit included small storage spaces or indoor kitchens. Generally, several of these household units were connected to form a large complex, or insula, inhabited by several generations of an extended family.

Byzantine–Early Islamic Periods (Stratum IVA–B). Synagogue B, constructed on top of synagogue A, marks the beginning of stratum IVA (sixth century). Although the general plan of the two synagogues is similar, in synagogue B the northern facade wall was extended northward for 2–2.5 m, increasing the size of the synagogue, necessitating two rows of four columns each. The building's exterior measurements became 15.4 m along the north wall; 14.95 m along the south wall; 17.95 m along the east wall and 17.4 m along the west wall. Two surfaces are related to synagogue B's use: an earlier mosaic floor (stratum IVA), dated to the sixth century by coins found inside the benches along the rebuilt northern wall of synagogue B; and a later plaster floor (stratum IVB) laid over the dismantled mosaic floor, dated to the seventh century, based on a coin hoard found sealed below the plaster floor.

During stratum IVA–B, a street and drain were added to the area outside and adjacent to the northeastern half of the synagogue, converting it for use as a public space. Most of the original domestic structures remained in use during the period, and the village reached its maximum size (approximately 5 acres).

Analysis of the faunal evidence from the strata V–IV village reveals that sheep and goat were the largest category of species, followed by cattle and then chicken. The relative percentages of different domesticated livestock indicate that animal production, consumption, and processing occurred at the household level. In addition to the rearing of sheep, goats, and cattle, the economic base of the Byzantine village was diverse, depending mainly on household production of cereals, wine, and a surplus market production of oil.

The synagogue remained in use through the mid-eighth century. Based on the uniform direction of the superstructure's collapse, the destruction of this synagogue is attributed to the earthquake of 749. In the village, several rooms showed signs of reuse by squatters (stratum III) on top of the collapsed rubble.

Mamluk Period (Stratum II). Following a settlement gap of nearly five hundred years, the site was reoccupied during the Mamluk period (thirteenth–fifteenth centuries). The inhabitants constructed a mosque (8.1 × 15.5 m) in the northern third of the ruined synagogue, reusing several of the earlier walls and architectural elements. The southern wall and its niche *(miḥrab)* were added then. The poorly preserved Mamluk village covered the entire 5-acre Byzantine site.

Faunal analysis for the Mamluk period indicates that cattle were far more numerous than previously at Qaṣrin. The more specialized approach taken by the stratum II inhabitants and the relatively higher proportion of cattle suggest participation in a larger market economy.

In the nineteenth century, bedouin resettled the site, repairing ancient structures or constructing new houses reusing the ancient basalt building stones. The stratum I site was in use until 1967.

[*See also* Golan; Mosque; Synagogues; *and the biography of Schumacher.*]

BIBLIOGRAPHY

Grantham, Billy. "Modern Bugata and Ancient Qasrin: The Ethnoarchaeology of Cuisine in the Golan Heights." Master's thesis, University of Alabama, 1992.

Killebrew, Ann, and Steven Fine. "Qatzrin: Reconstructing Village Life in Talmudic Times." *Biblical Archaeology Review* 17 (1991): 44–56.

Maʿoz, Zvi, and Ann Killebrew. "Ancient Qasrin: Synagogue and Village." *Biblical Archaeologist* 51 (1988): 5–19.

Schumacher, Gottlieb. *The Jaulân.* London, 1888.

Ann Killebrew

QATABAN, pre-Islamic state in southern Arabia, located in modern Yemen. Adjoining Sheba on the northwest and west, Ausan on the south, and Ḥadhramaut on the east, Qataban, at its zenith, included a territory of mountains and valleys extending from Bab al-Mandeb to the sands of the Ramlat as-Sabʿatayn on the north, and to the western border of the Ḥadhramaut on the east.

Qataban is not mentioned in the Table of Nations (*Gn.* 10), or elsewhere in the Hebrew Bible, probably because it was not an independent kingdom at the time of writing. Qataban was known to Strabo (*Geography* 16.4.2–4, 19, 22–25) as Cattabania and to Pliny the Elder (*Natural History* 6.26.104; 32.153–55, 160–62; 12.30–35, 41) as Gebbanitae (i.e., Qatabanians), in conjunction with international trade in frankincense and myrrh. Both mention Timnaʿ, the Qatabanian capital—spelled "Tamna" by Strabo, and "Thomna" by Pliny the Elder—as an important city on the incense route. Pliny reports that Timnaʿ was 1487.5 (Roman) miles from Gaza.

Exploration and Excavation. Early visitors to Qataban include G. Wyman Bury (1898–1899), who recorded inscriptions at Timnaʿ, its capital; Stewart Perowne (1938), who described Timnaʿ and collected artifacts; and Nigel Groom (1948), a British political officer. Timnaʿ, its cemetery, and Hajar Bin Ḥumeid, a town under the aegis of Timnaʿ, were excavated in 1950 and 1951 by an expedition of the American Foundation for the Study of Man, organized and led by Wendell Phillips, with William Foxwell Albright as archaeological director. During the 1980s, investigations in Qataban were resumed under the direction of J. F. Breton for the French Archaeological Mission in Sanʿa. [*See* Hajar Bin Ḥumeid; Timnaʿ.]

History. Although settlement in Qataban can be traced from the eleventh to tenth centuries BCE, human occupation probably goes back a millennium or so earlier, to at least a Neolithic stage of cultural development. Linguistic evidence seems to indicate that southern Arabia was populated by various waves of migration from the Levant and Mesopotamia. Qataban, Maʿin, and Ḥadhramaut share common language characteristics: the use of the *sh* prefix for the causative verb form and third-person pronouns, corresponding to structure and usage in East Semitic, such as Akkadian. Saba' (Sheba) differs in employing the *h* prefix for causative verbs and third-person pronouns, as is common in Northwest Semitic, such as Canaanite and Hebrew. Early pottery recovered in archaeological excavations appear to support a similar diversity of sources. Immigrants brought many cultural features to southern Arabia from their homelands. With the passage of time and the selective acceptance of indigeneous and foreign ideas and designs, a distinctive South Arabian culture emerged and soon prevailed throughout the region.

As in Sheba, centralized authority prevailed in Qataban. The first royal inscriptions of Hawfiʿamm Yuhanʿim, son of Sumhuʿalay Watar, appear in the late seventh–early sixth centuries BCE, when rulers were known as *mkrb (mukarrib),* a title perhaps meaning "priest-king." Inscriptions of this period are written either left to right, or boustrophedon (the direction of successive lines is right–left and then left–right). At about the end of the fifth century BCE, Qataban freed itself from Saba' (Sheba) and became a dominant power along with Ḥadhramaut and Maʿin. Rulers adopted the title "king," which was used thereafter. Qataban conquered Maʿin in the second century BCE, but later lost the southwestern part of its kingdom to Dhu-Raydan, which had joined with Saba'. Thus, the zenith of Qatabanian power extended from the fifth to the first centuries BCE. In the first century CE Qataban was conquered and Timnaʿ was burned in a great conflagration; soon after, it was incorporated into the kingdom of Ḥadhramaut.

The economy was based on subsistence agriculture, trade in frankincense and myrrh, and transshipping South Asian products. Farmers developed flash-flood irrigation systems that were more ingenious than the constant-flow systems of the ancient Near East. Well irrigation was utilized year round for crops.

Religion seems to have been highly organized, with temples ranging from simple to elaborate. The principal deity of the Qatabanian pantheon was the moon god 'Anbay. This is to be expected among a people heavily involved in the caravan trade, in which the advantages of traveling at night included the precise navigational aid of the night sky. The supremacy of the moon over the sun is represented in a pair of Hellenistic sculptures, each featuring a bronze lion (the sun) and small boy rider (the moon). The boy controls the lion by holding its chain, attached to its collar, in one hand and a small dart in the other, which were found inside the South Gate of Timnaʿ by the American Foundation excavators in 1950.

[*See also* Ḥadhramaut; Marib; *and* Sheba.]

BIBLIOGRAPHY

Albright, William Foxwell. "The Chronology of Ancient South Arabia in the Light of the First Campaign of Excavation in Qataban." *Bulletin of the American Schools of Oriental Research,* no. 119 (1950): 5–15. Succinct, conservative chronological listing of the kings of Qataban, Maʿin, and Ḥadhramaut and their relationships.

Cleveland, Ray L. *An Ancient South Arabian Necropolis: Objects from the Second Campaign (1951) in the Timnaʿ Cemetery.* Publications of the American Foundation for the Study of Man, vol. 4. Baltimore, 1965. Excellent resource for Qatabanian material culture.

Phillips, Wendell. *Qataban and Sheba: Exploring the Ancient Kingdoms on the Biblical Spice Routes of Arabia.* New York, 1955. Semipopular, highly readable account of the American Foundation for the Study of Man archaeological expeditions to Qataban (1950–1951) and to Sheba and Dhofar (1952–1953).

Van Beek, Gus W. "Prolegomenon" to reprinted edition of James A. Montgomery, *Arabia and the Bible.* New York, 1969. Updates developments in what is known of the relationship between Arabia and the Bible as described by Montgomery in the Haskell Lectures at Oberlin College in 1930.

GUS W. VAN BEEK

QATAR. The State of Qatar occupies a small peninsula roughly 160 km, (99 mi.) long and, at most, 80 km (50 mi.) wide (about 10,437 sq km, or 6,471 sq. mi.), on the east coast of the Arabian Peninsula. It borders the Eastern Province of the Kingdom of Saudi Arabia and the Western Region of the United Arab Emirates (UAE). A generally flat, semidesertic area with a maximum elevation of 120 m above sea level, Qatar's topography ranges from a limestone plateau (Dukhan Heights) opposite Salwa Bay on the southwestern side of the peninsula, through sandy desert throughout most of the interior, to low-lying *sabkha,* or salt flats, along much of the east coast.

The archaeological exploration of Qatar dates back to 1956, when a Danish expedition from the University of Aarhus, under the direction of Peter Vilhelm Glob, discovered several lithic sites and burial mounds there during a brief visit. This was followed by Danish fieldwork, concentrating mainly on lithic sites, between 1957 and 1964, and ultimately by the publication of the first major work on Qatar's prehistory by Holger Kapel (1967). In 1973 a British team, led by Beatrice de Cardi, conducted a season of survey and excavation (di Cardi, 1978). An important French mission under the direction of Jacques Tixier worked in Qatar from 1976 to 1982 (Inizan, 1980; Hardy-Guilbert, 1984), and in 1988 a Japanese team under the direction of Masatoshi A. Konishi, Takeshi Gotoh, and Yoshihako Akashi returned to the site of Umm al-Ma', the scene of some preliminary investigations by the Danish expedition thirty years earlier, to excavate two burial cairns (Konishi, 1989).

Kapel grouped the lithic material discovered by the Danish expedition into four categories: Qatar A, a Middle Paleolithic industry in the Levalloiso-Mousterian tradition; Qatar B, a Mesolithic blade-arrowhead industry; Qatar C, a Late Mesolithic scraper culture; and Qatar D, a Neolithic industry characterized by tanged and barbed arrowheads and fine, pressure-flaked bifaces. The work of the French mission showed conclusively, however, that all of the material assigned to groups A, C, and D is late prehistoric, dating principally to the late fifth and fourth millennia. This is borne out by the presence, on some sites belonging to this group (such as Khor F.P.P., an abbreviation used to designate this particular site at Khor, of which there are many), of imported pottery from Mesopotamia of the Ubaid 3–4 type.

The earliest material found by any of the teams working in Qatar is Kapel's Qatar B (e.g., at Shagra), excavated by the French at site 36 near Acila in western Qatar. This complex includes blade arrowheads that compare closely with material found on Pre-Pottery Neolithic B sites in Syria and Israel; it probably represents the remains of the hunting camps of a mobile population that originated in the Syro-Palestinian desert region and colonized eastern Arabia sometime around 5000 BCE. Pollen analysis suggests that site 36 may have been situated alongside a lake ringed by halophytic plants, reeds, and trees, no doubt a watering hole that attracted game.

The later prehistoric sites, on the other hand, provide evidence for the intensive exploitation of fish (particularly Sparidae) and shellfish (*Turbo*, Veneridae, and oyster). The local population at this time was in contact with Ubaid-period Mesopotamia. This was demonstrated, inter alia, by the presence of small numbers of Ubaid 3–4 sherds in the simple pit burials the French team excavated at Khor F.P.P. At least two other exotic materials, carnelian and obsidian, also reached Qatar at this time as beads.

Qatar's later pre-Islamic past is poorly represented in the archaeological record. An early to mid-second millennium BCE site at Khor excavated by the French mission yielded small numbers of Barbar city II red-ridged sherds, probably originating on Bahrain, as well as a small amount of so-called Wadi Suq pottery with close parallels at Tell Abraq in the UAE. These were found in connection with the stone foundations of several small huts or tents. The British team similarly found red-ridged pottery at the site of Bir Abaruk 3. The presence of large quantities of the shellfish (gastropod) *Drupa concactenata* at Khor led to the suggestion that purple dye may have been produced at the site, but some malacologists dispute this.

Some slight indication of Qatar's occupation during the Hellenistic and/or Parthian period was provided in 1961–1962 by a single sherd found outside of a cairn burial excavated by the Danish team. It belongs to a type of pottery well represented at the major Hellenistic metropolis of Thaj, in northeastern Saudi Arabia. In 1962–1963 the Danish mission carried out excavations at a settlement on Ras Uwainat Ali, just north of Dukhan on the west coast of the peninsula, where more Thaj-type pottery was recovered. The presence of the toponym *Kadara polis* (cf. Qatar) on Claudius Ptolemy's map of Arabia and of the tribal name *Catharrei* in Pliny's *Natural History* (6.32.149) also gives a hint of occupation in Qatar in the Hellenistic/Parthian period. Contemporary, or just slightly later, remains of Parthian or Sasanian date were also discovered at Mezruah, south of Khor, where the Danish expedition uncovered two camel burials, one of which contained a glass vessel. Comparable camel burials are now known in Oman, the UAE, eastern Saudi Arabia, and Yemen.

The Islamic archaeology of Qatar was investigated by Claire Hardy-Guildbert for the Centre Nationale de la Recherche Scientifique between 1977 and 1986, when an inventory of more than two hundred monuments was made. Excavations were also conducted by the French team in 1979 and 1982–1983 at the site of Murwab, a large rural site covering about 125 ha (309 acres) in northeastern Qatar. Material dating to about 800–850 CE was recovered during the course of excavating a small fort, private houses, two mosques, and a cemetery. The most important later Islamic site in Qatar is surely al-Huwaila, which appears on Carsten Niebuhr's map of the Arabian Gulf as Huäle. (Niebuhr was the surveyor on the Danish expedition of 1761–1767 charged with exploring Arabia.) Al-Huwaila was the principal town on Qatar until the nineteenth century. Finally, at various points along the east coast of Qatar, cup marks, small holes, gaming boards, and representations of ships have been carved into the surface of rock outcrops. Although the dating of these features is difficult, it has been suggested that they are the work of pearl divers working off the coast of Qatar in the last several centuries who whiled away their free time playing board games and carving pictures of local seacraft.

BIBLIOGRAPHY

de Cardi, Beatrice. *Qatar Archaeological Report: Excavations, 1973*. Oxford, 1978. Final report of the 1973 British expedition.

Facey, William. "The Boat Carvings at Jabal al-Jussasiyah, Northeast Qatar." *Proceedings of the Seminar for Arabian Studies* 17 (1987): 199–222.

Hardy-Guilbert, C. "Fouilles archéologiques à Murwab, Qatar." In *Arabie orientale: Mésopotamie et Iran méridional, de l'âge du fer au début de la période islamique,* edited by Rémy Boucharlat and Jean-François Salles, pp. 169–188. Paris, 1984.

Inizan, Marie-Louise. *Préhistoire à Qatar*. Mission Archéologique Française à Qatar, vol. 2. Paris, 1980. Final publication of the work of the French mission under Jacques Tixier on the Qatar peninsula. Supersedes all earlier publications on the prehistory of Qatar by the Danish, British, and French missions.

Kapel, Holger. *Atlas of the Stone-Age Cultures of Qatar*. Aarhus, 1967.

Konishi, M. A., et al. *Excavations in Bahrain and Qatar, 1987/8*. Tokyo, 1989.

Potts, Daniel T. *The Arabian Gulf in Antiquity*. 2 vols. Oxford, 1990. General survey of the archaeology of the Gulf region, with references to the occupation of Qatar in all periods.

D. T. Potts

QINNISHRIN (Ar., "eagle's nest"; Chalcis ad Belum), settlement located in North Syria about 28 km (17 mi.) south-southwest of Aleppo (39°46′ N, 41°10′ E). The local name for the place was already attested in the Talmud and has always remained alive among the Arab population; it certainly derives from the widely visible, striking limestone mountain on whose south slope the settlement lies. It was one of many new Syrian cities founded by Seleucus Nicator (Appianus, *Syria* 57; Kai Brodersen, *Appians Abriss der Seleukidengeschichte,* Munich, 1989, p. 156).

The identification of the city is supported by the *Itinerarium Antonini* (Antonine Itinerary), according to which it lies 29 km (18 mi.) south of Beroea (Aleppo) on the way to Emesa (Homs), and by the *Tabula Peutingeriana* (Peutinger map), which on the way from Antioch to Beroea incorrectly gives a distance of 47 km (29 mi.). It is at least clear that Chalcis lay on a geographical crossroads and formed one of the centers in North Syria. Claudius Ptolemaeus (*Geog.* 5.18) mentions it as the chief city of the district of Chalcidike, a region he places between the Chalybonitis and the Apamene, proceeding from east to west. To differentiate it from Chalcis ad Libanum, Pliny (*Nat. Hist.* 5.19) calls the place in question Chalcis ad Belum. According to a new and convincing interpretation, Belus refers to the Qoueiq River and not to the easternmost foothills of the Syrian limestone mountain range opposite the flat, arable land stretching toward the Euphrates River (Balty, 1982). Strabo (16.2.11) mentions only the district of Chalcidike, which he says is inhabited primarily by the Skaenites (tent dwellers), a nomadic population expressly differentiated from the Arabs that displayed only a low standard of civilization. This remark, recorded during the Augustan period, is pertinent because it contrasts with numerous pieces of archaeological evidence from the imperial and early Christian periods. That evidence bears witness to dense settlement of the area and suggests a change from a nomadic mode to a larger and more fixed one, which in turn should have had an effect on the makeup of the population of Chalcis.

The first concrete historical events after the founding of the city are recorded for the year 145 BCE, when Diodotos Tryphon from Apamea, at the beginning of a revolt against Demetrius II, captured Chalcis with the help of the native leader Malchos, or Iamblichos, and then became the first non-Seleucid to ascend the Seleucid throne (Grainger, 1990). [*See* Seleucids.] In 92 CE the coins show the beginning of a new era, providing a basis for the plausible supposition that at this time the city was "freed" by a native dynast (who could have been a successor of Iamblichos or Malchos). Like many other places ruled by local dynasts, it was made completely subject to Roman administration (Grainger, 1990, pp. 132, 162). In 256 CE, Sapor I overran the "limes of Chalcis" (Malalas 295.17), whereupon he completely captured Syria and Antioch. This historical notice provided modern researchers with a name for the section of the limes between the Euphrates and the mountains of Palmyra (Poidebard and Mouterde, 1945). After that, however, Chalcis must have again been considered a secure place because, in 363 CE, the population of the Euphrates fortress Anatha was resettled there (Ammianus Marcellinus 24.1.9). In 529 CE it was again devastated by the Ghassamid leader al-Mundhir (cf. D. Feissel, "Remarques de toponymie syrienne," *Syria* 59 [1982]: 326).

During Justinian's Persian wars, his general, Belisarius, moved south via Chalcis (Procopius, *De Bellis Persicis* 1.18.8; 90.21; 181.3). After being captured by Chosroes, the city had to ransom itself with 200 pounds of gold (Procopius, *De Bellis Persicis* 1.205.5). Furthermore, Procopius reports in two places that after the withdrawal of the Persians, the fortifications of Chalcis were renewed under Justinian in 550 and were also supplemented with an outwork. If there is no oversight on the part of the author here, perhaps both Chalcis ad Libanum and Chalcis ad Belum are meant (Procopius, *De Aedificiis* 2.11.1.8). An inscription from Qinnishrin preserved in situ as a door lintel (Jalabert and Mouterde, 1939, no. 348) further specifies that the city wall was built by Isidorus of Miletus, a nephew of Justinian's chief architect of the same name (cf. Procopius, *De Aedificiis* 1.1.24). After the Battle of the Yarmuk in 636, the city was finally conquered by Abu Ubayda in the course of his conquest of North Syria. Furthermore, in the Umayyad period the city possessed a military garrison and remained the chief city of the djund Qinnishrin. After being destroyed a number of times, in the eleventh century it finally lost its significance to Aleppo (Elisséeff, 1986).

The ancient settlement, like the modern one, lay on a plain between two mountains. The Nebi Is, a foothill of the northern limestone mountain range, lies to the northwest; to the south there is a fortified tell. To the north, the Qoueiq River forms a natural boundary. The remains of the settlement that are visible on the surface have been mapped and described (Monceaux and Brossé, 1925; Jean Lauffray in Poidebard and Mouterde, 1945, p. 7, plan 1). No excavations have been carried out. Accordingly, it can only be reasonably assumed that the pre-Greek settlement lay on the eastern tell. This still shows an approximately trapezoidal fortification wall along the flanks of the hill and can be designated as the upper city. Its wall is certainly older than the walling off of the lower city that can be ascribed to Isidorus of Miletus; however, it would be difficult to provide a more precise date. Only a number of unconnected traces of foundations and ruins have been preserved of the city's architecture. The massiveness of the foundations and the use of columns of Egyptian granite show that presentation architecture was a element here. The large quarries on the south slope of the Nebi Is that extend up to the settlement provided abundant construction material for the building activity in Chalcis. Numerous hypogea, with arcosolia arranged in a cross-shaped pattern, were situated here. Some of the burial chambers are decorated with reliefs.

BIBLIOGRAPHY

Balty, Jean Ch. "Le belus de Chalcis et les fleures de Baʿal de Syrie-Palestine." In *Archéologie au Levant: Recueil à la mémoire de Roger Saidah,* pp. 287–298. Lyon, 1982.

Brodersen, Kai. *Appians Abriss der Seleukidengeschichte.* Munich, 1989.

Elisséeff, Nikita. "Ḳinnasrīn." In *Encyclopaedia of Islam,* new ed., vol. 5, pp. 124–125. Leiden, 1960–.

Grainger, John D. *The Cities of Seleukid Syria.* Oxford, 1990.

Jalabert, Louis, and René Mouterde. *Inscriptions grecques et latines de la Syrie.* Vol. 2. Paris, 1939.

Monceaux, Paul, and Léonce Brossé. "Chalcis ad Belum." *Syria* 6 (1925): 339–350.

Poidebard, Antoine, and René Mouterde. *Le limes de Chalcis.* Paris, 1945.

Rüdiger Gogräfe

Translated from German by Susan I. Schiedel

QIRI, TEL, (Heb., Hazorea) village site situated on the eastern end of a spur of the Carmel ridge that slopes steeply into Naḥal Shofet, near the site's main water supply (map reference 1611 × 2278). Tel Qiri is approximately 2 km (1.2 mi.) southeast of Tel Yoqneʿam, the major site in the vicinity, of which it was undoubtedly a satellite. The pottery, coins, tombs, and other remains noted in various surveys here range in date from the Neolithic to the Early Arab period, but no historical identification has ever been suggested. A considerable part of the site has been damaged by modern building activity. When rescue excavations were begun in 1975, less than half of its original area (estimated at approximately 2.5 acres) was intact. Today, the entire site is covered by modern houses. Tel Qiri was excavated between 1975 and 1978 as part of the Yoqneʿam Regional Project, under the direction of Amnon Ben-Tor, on behalf of the Institute of Archaeology of the Hebrew University of Jerusalem.

The main period of occupation at the site was in the Iron Age, of which an accumulation of about 4 m was noted. Remains of earlier as well as later periods were also encountered, some represented only by isolated small finds such as coins and sherds. Stratum numbers were assigned only to periods for which there are architectural remains. The uppermost remains of the later periods (strata I–IV) were severely damaged across the site by recent building activity, so that the Ottoman, Crusader, and Umayyad periods are represented only by stray finds. A few isolated walls of what were apparently private houses date to the Byzantine–Early Roman periods. Remnants of an impressive public building,

QIRI, TEL. *Israelite houses and agricultural installations.* Ninth–eighth century BCE. (Courtesy A. Ben-Tor)

with a large paved courtyard, date to the Hellenistic period. A few walls, which are not part of a coherent plan, and some twenty rock-cut tombs in the higher, western part of the site, are dated to the Persian period. An anthropological study of the bones indicates that the interred population was not local but is related to types common in Iran. Some of the tombs were reused in the Roman period.

Five strata of the Iron Age (strata V–IX), divided into twelve phases, were identified that form a continuous sequence. Most of the buildings remain in use during several phases. A significant change in the plan of buildings is noticeable only once in the sequence: in the transition from stratum VIII to VII—that is, from Iron I to Early Iron II. This change may reflect the arrival of the Israelites: neighboring Yoqneʿam was thoroughly destroyed at that time, whereas at Tel Qiri the transition seems to have occurred peacefully. The ceramic repertoire indicates an occupation beginning in the twelfth century BCE (stratum IX), including Philistine ware and collar-rim storejars, down to the eighth century (stratum V), characterized by an Iron IIB assemblage. The agricultural nature of the site is clearly indicated by the large number of silos scattered throughout and by a large oil press. Agricultural remains include mainly wheat, peas, vetch, and olive pits, while sheep and goats constitute about 80 percent of the faunal remains. Of particular interest is a building of regular plan in stratum VIII, in which a fine assemblage of clay vessels, cultic in nature, and a few dozen right foreleg bones of goats and sheep, undoubtedly remains of the right thigh offerings (*Lv.* 7:32–33), were found.

Two strata (X–XI) are associated with earlier periods. Walls of residential structures, found in a deep section cut into the eastern slope of the site, belong to the Middle Bronze Age. Sherds from the Early Bronze Age, including gray-burnished and band-slip wares, as well as Chalcolithic churn and cornet fragments, indicate occupation during those periods. A few narrow stone walls, a stone-lined silo, and a large assemblage of stone tools and sherds, including dark-faced burnished ware, probably represent the first settlement at Tel Qiri and are attributed to the Late Neolithic period (second half of the fifth millennium BCE).

QIRI, TEL. *Cultic vessel assemblage.* From stratum VIII, eleventh century BCE. (Courtesy A. Ben-Tor)

BIBLIOGRAPHY

Ben-Tor, Amnon. "Tell Qiri (Hazorea)." *Israel Exploration Journal* 25 (1975): 168–169; 26 (1976): 200–201.

Ben-Tor, Amnon. "Tell Qiri (Hazorea)." *Revue Biblique* 83 (1976): 272–274.

Ben-Tor, Amnon. "Tell Qiri: A Look at Village Life." *Biblical Archaeologist* 42 (1979): 105–113.

Ben-Tor, Amnon. "The Regional Study: A New Approach to Archaeological Investigation." *Biblical Archaeology Review* 6.2 (1980): 30–44.

Ben-Tor, Amnon, et al. *Tell Qiri, a Village in the Jezreel Valley: Report of the Archaeological Excavations, 1975–1978*. Qedem, vol. 24. Jerusalem, 1987.

Brandl, Baruch, and Aviva Schwarzfeld. "Tell Qiri (Hazorea), 1977." *Israel Exploration Journal* 28 (1978): 124–125.

Hunt, Melvin L. "The Iron Age Pottery of the Yoqneʿam Regional Project." Ph.D. diss., University of California, Berkeley, 1985.

AMNON BEN-TOR

QITAR, EL- (Til-Abnu in Hittite hieroglyphs), Late Bronze Age mountain fortress, located on the right bank of the Euphrates River in Syria, about 60 km (37 mi.) south of Carchemish, at a narrows from which traffic along the river could be controlled and where the Tishreen dam is under construction. Excavations were conducted at el-Qitar in 1976 by the Milwaukee Public Museum under the direction of Rudolph Dornemann; from 1982 to 1985 by Thomas L. McClellan for the University of Melbourne; and in 1986–1987 by McClellan for the University of Chicago. Prior to excavation, large portions of the settlement's layout were visible on top of the mountain and on a lower eastern spur; their plans were recorded, utilizing kite photography and photogrammetry.

Ceramics and radiocarbon dates indicate that the main period of occupation was in the fifteenth century BCE, possibly under the loose suzerainty of the Mitanni. Reoccupation during the fourteenth–thirteenth centuries BCE of this military position was probably under Hittite direction. Earlier occupation from the Middle Bronze Age was largely masked by subsequent construction, but portions were excavated of what may have been an official residence, the Orthostat Building (its rooms were lined with limestone orthostats). Traces of Early Bronze IV material (third millennium) were also recovered within the lower settlement. During the Hellenistic period, four tumuli were constructed on the northern part of the mountaintop and graves were located nearby. A stone circle grave, probably from the Roman period, was found near the water's edge, in the lower settlement.

In the Late Bronze Age (and possibly earlier) the upper and lower settlements were connected by a rock-cut stairway. A fortification wall could be traced along the western and southern sides of the upper settlement that connected to a North Tower, the Lower West Gate, and a South Tower. Streets divide the settlement into several residential blocks.

Triangular in layout, the lower settlement was on a spur that jutted into the river. The mountain's steep slope protected the base of the triangle; the two other sides were defended by fortification walls, the northeastern portion utilizing the natural cliff line along the river. The settlement was divided into blocks of houses; some buildings were constructed against the fortification walls and opened onto streets that ran parallel to the walls and led to the River Gate.

The LB fortifications consisted of curtain walls, made of large, irregularly cut limestone blocks, as were towers and two city gates. Both the River Gate and the Lower West Gate were designed with two sets of shallow piers of limestone orthostats. The absence of public buildings is notable, although one structure (building 10) had two rooms that contained benches and platforms. Although originally identified as a temple or shrine, this interpretation is called into question by the many domestic houses nearby at Munbaqa with similar installations.

Objects from the Late Bronze Age included a Middle Assyrian cuneiform tablet with a Syro-Hittite sealing on it whose hieroglyphs may identify the site as Til-Abnu. It is an adoption contract in which more than twenty personal names are Hurrian. A silver cache weighing 2.5 kg contained bent and broken pins, medallions, and blanks.

Although neither the domestic architecture nor the artifacts hint at the site's military function, its mountain setting identifies it as a fortress. Among the faunal remains many species were present: seven domesticated species (including numbers of Equidae—the horse *Equus caballus*, donkey, mule, and wild half-donkey), nine wild mammals (including beaver, fox, wild boar, brown bear, and Indian elephant), and sixteen bird species. This large number of hunted animals, compared to other sites on the Middle Euphrates, may indicate the inhabitants' privileged or military status.

[*See also* Euphrates Dams, Survey of.]

BIBLIOGRAPHY

Archi, Alfonso. "A Seal Impression from el-Qiṭār/Til-Abnu (Syria)." *Anatolian Studies* 43 (1993): 203–206.

Culican, William, and Thomas L. McClellan. "El-Qitar, 1982–83: A Preliminary Report." *Annales Archéologiques Arabes Syriennes* 23.2 (1983): 289–297.

Culican, William, and Thomas L. McClellan. "El-Qitar: First Season of Excavations, 1982–83." *Abr-Nahrain* 22 (1983–1984): 29–63.

McClellan, Thomas L. "The Second Season of the Australian Excavations at el-Qitar, 1983–84." *Annales Archéologiques Arabes Syriennes* 23.2 (1983): 315–324.

McClellan, Thomas L. "El-Qitar: Second Season of Excavations, 1983–84." *Abr-Nahrain* 23 (1984–1985): 39–72.

McClellan, Thomas L. "A Syrian Fortress of the Bronze Age: El-Qitar." *National Geographic Research* 2 (1986): 418–440.

McClellan, Thomas L. "El-Qitar: Third Season of Excavations, 1984–85." *Abr-Nahrain* 24 (1986): 83–106.

THOMAS L. MCCLELLAN

QITMIT, ḤORVAT, site located along the eastern margin of a broad valley some 10 km (6 mi.) south of Tel Arad (31°11′00″ N, 35°03′10″ E; map reference 1564 × 0660) in Israel. The site is on a long, flat, stone-covered hilltop whose slopes are stepped flint cliffs. Naḥal Qitmit (Wadi Qatamat), cuts the hilltop off from the surrounding range of hills.

Ḥorvat Qitmit lies within a radius of approximately 5–10 km (3–6 mi.) of other contemporary sites—Tel ʿAroʿer, Tel Masos, Tel ʿIra, Tel Malḥata, Tel Arad, Ḥorvat Ṭov, Ḥorvat ʿUza, and Ḥorvat Radum. It is located between two major ancient roads: one that leads to the "Land of Edom" to the east and one to the Negev highlands to the southwest, within sight of Tel ʿIra, Tel Malḥata, and Tel Arad. No permanent water sources are known to be within its immediate vicinity, but wells near Tel Malḥata probably served as a water supply for Qitmit in antiquity. Ḥorvat Qitmit is a one-period site from the end of the seventh century BCE, erected directly on the limestone bedrock. The site covers an area of about 650 sq m. It consists of two complexes on its west side: A and B; each comprises a number of rooms, a courtyard with various installations, and two enclosures (nos. 114 and 60). Complex A consists of one structure with three rooms, a *bāmâ* ("platform"), bounded on three sides by a stone wall (hereafter referred to as the *bāmâ* enclosure); and a stone basin and an altar, also apparently enclosed by a stone wall (hereafter referred to as the altar enclosure).

The structure is rectangular and measures 10.5 × 5 m, with each room opening to the south for its entire width. Podiumlike wall segments, whose upper courses consist of large, flat stones, were erected perpendicular to the entrances in all three rooms. It is fairly clear, however, that these podiumlike elements served no structural function. Rather, they should be seen as elements of the room's furniture. They may have served as a table on which rituals were performed in the room's entrance spaces.

The platform, or *bāmâ,* measures 1.25 × 1 m. It was built of medium-sized fieldstones directly on the bedrock and is preserved to a height of about 30 cm. It was enclosed on three sides—south, east, and west—by straight walls; its northern side, which faces the rooms, was left open. Crevices and hollows in the rock were filled with pebbles and the entire surface completely covered with a heavy coat of plaster, creating a table with a smooth surface for placing cult vessels around the *bāmâ.* The altar enclosure (locus 24) is located south of the rooms, near the eastern wall of the *bāmâ* enclosure, on a smooth rock surface that slopes to the southeast. It comprises a stone altar, a basin, and a pit enclosed by an elliptical or circular wall.

Complex B was erected on level ground about 15 m north of complex A. Enclosed by a massive wall (1.20 m thick), it contains a number of rooms and an open courtyard. Near the southeast corner of room 108, a rectangular flintstone was found in situ, probably a *maṣṣēbâ* (a ritual standing stone, 0.8 × 0.6 × 0.3 m). An area (1.3 × 1.1 m) in front of the courtyard was paved with small flintstones slabs framed by rectangular stones.

Most of the finds are from complex A. They were scattered over the enclosure area, concentrated either in groups on the rock surface or in the shallow earth layer. The largest quantity is from the *bāmâ* enclosure. The finds include various clay figurines, different types of ceramic cult stands, pottery vessels, bronze and stone artifacts, and seashells.

The pottery from the site can be divided into three groups: domestic vessels, Edomite-type vessels, and vessels widely found at sites in Judah and Transjordan. Five potsherds bear fragmentary incised inscriptions (four from complex B and one from complex A). One consists of only a single line, too fragmentary to be interpreted, with the exception of the letters *qws* in the middle, the name of the principal Edomite god, Qos. The same name is found in another inscription on a rim fragments of a krater and in a bronze stamp from complex A.

The largest accumulation of iconographic finds was ex-

QITMIT, ḤORVAT. Figure 1. *Three-horned goddess.* Height, 13 cm. (Photograph by Avraham Hay; courtesy I. Beit-Arieh)

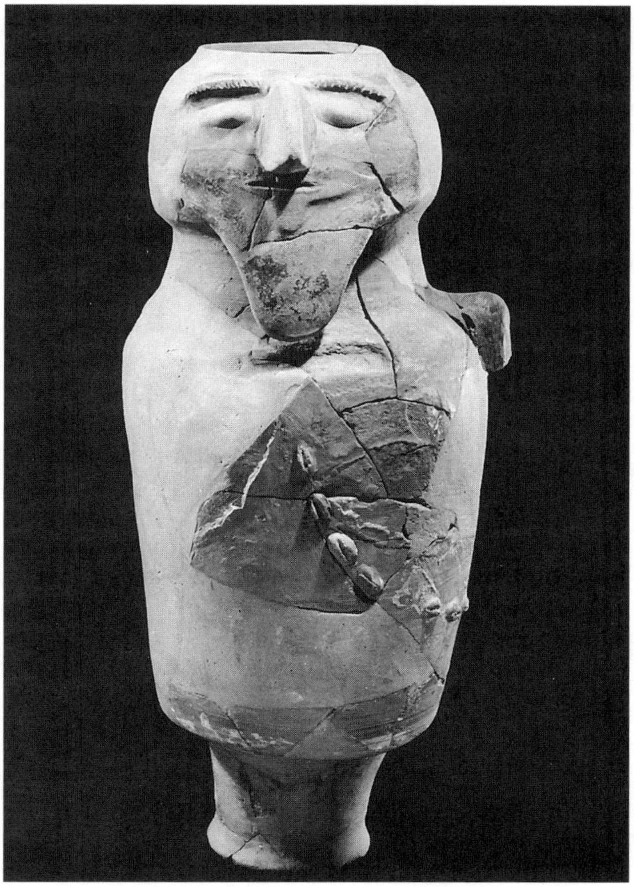

QITMIT, ḤORVAT. Figure 2. *Anthropomorphic stand.* Height, 60 cm. (Photograph by Avraham Hay; courtesy I. Beit-Arieh)

posed in the *bāmâ* enclosure. In addition to everyday pottery vessels, more than one hundred ceramic figurines, statues, reliefs, stands, and cultic vessels were discovered in this area. The figurines depict humans and animals (sheep, cattle, and birds). All the large animal figurines are hollow; some were punctured with small holes both on their sides and underneath their tail. Of special interest are the head of a three-horned goddess (see figure 1), a sphinx with a bearded human head, the body of an animal (perhaps a lion) that has wings spread loftily upward, and assorted anthropomorphic stands (see figure 2).

Cultic vessels include chalices covered with pendant pomegranates as surface decoration; fragments of a square, windowed stand; and perforated incense bowls. The pottery figurines and cultic stands are tentatively interpreted as closely related to the eastern Mediterranean traditions embodied in Phoenician culture.

The shrine at Qitmit in the Judean Desert is indicative of relations between Edom and Judah at the end of the period of the Judean kingdom. It may be construed as evidence of Edomite domination of several regions in Judah at the end of the First Temple period or a few years later. The biblical prophets' wrathful denunciations of Edom, along with expressed sentiments for revenge, reflect a historical reality of dire conflict between the two kingdoms that may have had many causes (*Jos.* 34; 63:1–6; *Jer.* 49:7–22; *Ez.* 25:12–14, 35:1–6; *Jl.* 4:19; *Am.* 1:11–12). The most plausible explanation of this enmity may be Edom's attempt to exploit the weakness of the Judean kingdom at the very time that the latter was engaged in a life-and-death struggle against the Babylonian army.

BIBLIOGRAPHY

Aharoni, Yohanan. *Arad Inscriptions.* Translated by Judith Ben-Or. Jerusalem, 1981.

Bartlett, J. R. *Edom and the Edomites.* Sheffield, 1989.

Beit-Arieh, Itzhaq. "New Data on the Relationship between Judah and Edom toward the End of the Iron Age." *Annual of the American Schools of Oriental Research* 49 (1989): 125–131.

Beit-Arieh, Itzhaq. "The Edomite Shrine at Ḥorvat Qitmit in the Judean Negev: Preliminary Excavation Report." *Tel Aviv* 18.1 (1991): 93–116.

ITZHAQ BEIT-ARIEH

QOM, KHIRBET EL-, small hilltop site 20 km (12 mi.) west of Hebron at the border of the Shephelah and the Judean foothills (map reference 1465 × 1045). It is probably to be identified with the Makkedah of *Joshua* 10.

Khirbet el-Qom was discovered after the 1967 war by the Archaeological Survey of Israel and then excavated by William G. Dever in salvage campaigns in 1967–1968, sponsored by the Hebrew Union College in Jerusalem. The principal find was a recently robbed Iron Age cemetery on the slopes below the modern Arab village. In addition to dozens of pieces of pottery dated to the ninth–seventh century BCE, there were recovered Hebrew shekel-weights; an inscribed decanter reading "(Belonging to) Yaḥmol"; and a bowl reading "El" (or "God"). Several of the eighth-century BCE tombs recleared and planned were typical Iron Age bench-tombs. Tomb I had an inscription to the left of the doorway into one chamber reading "Belonging to ʿOphai Ben-Nethanyahu; this is his tomb-chamber." Over the doorway the lintel read "Belonging to ʿUzza Bat-Nethanyahu." A longer inscription from tomb III read:

> Uriyahu the Governor (or singer) wrote it.
> May Uriyahu be blessed by Yahweh,
> For from his enemies he has been saved by his a/Asherah.

The reference to "his (i.e., Yahweh's) a/Asherah" is problematic, but it is now paralleled almost exactly by eighth-century BCE inscriptions from the Judean fort-sanctuary at Kuntillet ʿAjrud in the eastern Sinai. [*See* Kuntillet ʿAjrud.] Some scholars prefer to see in "asherah" merely a symbol of the old Canaanite Mother Goddess, such as the treelike effigies condemned in many passages in the Hebrew Bible.

Others see evidence here for the continuation of the cult of the Asherah, "Asherah" being either a hypostatization of some aspect of Yahweh, or perhaps his consort.

In 1971 John S. Holladay, James F. Strange, and Lawrence T. Geraty conducted soundings in the modern village. These were scattered Early Bronze Age remains, but the principal settlement was that of the tenth–early sixth century BCE. Part of the cyclopean Iron Age wall is still visible, and remains of a two-entryway gate were brought to light.

The Babylonian destruction evidently ended the Iron Age site, but several domestic houses of the fourth–third century BCE were found, reusing earlier dwellings. In some of the rooms were ostraca, six in Aramaic, one in Greek, and one bilingual text of nine lines. The latter records a transaction between a certain "Qos-yada" and a Greek named "Nikeratos," noting the payment of 32 drachmas. The date given is the 12th of Tammuz, year 6, no doubt of Ptolemy II Philadelphus, or 277 BCE.

BIBLIOGRAPHY

Dever, William G. "Iron Age Epigraphic Material from the Area of Kh. el-Kôm, West of Hebron." *Hebrew Union College Annual* 40–41 (1969–1970): 139–204.

Geraty, Lawrence T. "The Khirbet el-Kôm Bilingual Ostracon." *Bulletin of the American Schools of Oriental Research,* no. 220 (1975): 55–61.

Hadley, Judith M. "The Khirbet el-Qôm Inscription." *Vetus Testamentum* 37 (1987): 50–62.

Holladay, John S. "Khirbet el-Qôm." *Israel Exploration Journal* 21 (1971): 175–177.

Lemaire, André. "Les inscriptions des Khirbet El-Qôm et l'Ashérah de YHWH." *Revue Biblique* 84 (1977): 597–608.

Mittmann, Siegfried. "Die Grabinschrift des Sängers Uriahu." *Zeitschrift des Deutschen Palästina-Vereins* 97 (1981): 139–152.

Zevit, Ziony. "The Khirbet el Qom Inscription Mentioning a Goddess." *Bulletin of the American Schools of Oriental Research,* no. 255 (1984): 39–47.

WILLIAM G. DEVER

QUADRANT PLAN. The standard method for laying out a large site is the grid plan, according to which the site is configured like a checkerboard in 5-meter squares and each square is given an identifying control number. Although a large site can be effectively controlled in this way, the grid plan is overly complex for digging a small area, which does not require numerous squares.

At small sites, especially round ones, therefore, the quadrant plan is utilized. It involves dividing the site into four areas, or sections, by drawing 90 degree intersecting lines through its center, which produces a quadrant, each quarter of which is then numbered. When opposite quadrants are dug, the balks of their axes reveal the full stratigraphy of the area. Thus, it is not necessary to dig all four quadrants: four balks have been exposed, providing the stratigraphical history of the entire area.

An area is divided into quadrants following a full site survey. The survey will determine where the most productive excavation areas are likely to be found and where the first trenches should be dug. The use of subsurface interface radar, magnetometers, and aerial infrared photography enhances the surface survey by locating stone structures beneath the surface. In countries whose entire landscape has been plotted onto a national grid and for which elevation benchmarks exist, site surveys correlate with the grid and utilize quadrant plans within its framework.

[*See also* Excavation Strategy; Grid Plan; *and* Site Survey.]

BIBLIOGRAPHY

McRay, John. *Archaeology and the New Testament.* Grand Rapids, Mich., 1991. See pages 17–34.

Sharer, Robert J., and Wendy Ashmore. *Fundamentals of Archaeology.* Menlo Park, Calif., 1979. See pages 177–210.

JOHN MCRAY

QUMRAN, site located near the northwestern shore of the Dead Sea, 12 km (7 mi.) south of Jericho, some 32 km (20 mi.) north of ʿEin-Gedi, and 21 km (13 mi.) east of Jerusalem (31°44′18″ N, 35°27′30″ E; map reference 193 × 127). The ruins of Qumran stand on a marl terrace, 338 m below sea level, at the foot of cliffs edging the Judean Desert, whose caves yielded part of the remarkable manuscripts known as the Dead Sea Scrolls.

The site was visited in the nineteenth century by Félicien de Saulcy, Baron Rey, Claude R. Conder and Horatio Herbert Kitchener, and Charles Clermont-Ganneau, when it was known as Khirbet Yahud (Ar., "ruins of the Jew") or Khirbet Qumran ("the grayish spot," according to E. H. Palmer, *The Survey of Western Palestine: Arabic and English Name Lists,* London, 1881, folio 18, p. 345). Wadi Qumran, which is the lower course of the Kidron Valley runs along its southern edge. John M. Allegro (*The Copper Scroll from Qumran,* Transactions Glasgow University Oriental Society, 1959–1960, p. 64) proposed a synonymy between *Qimrôn,* which is not attested textually, and the Kippah torrent mentioned in the Copper Scroll from nearby Cave 3, along which there is a place called Sekaka. Other proposals for the ancient name of the khirbeh ("ruins") are de Saulcy's Gomorrha, Martin Noth's Ir ha-Melah (Heb., "salt city," from *Jos.* 15:62, for which Pessah Bar Adon proposes ʿEin Ghuweir: "Another Settlement of the Judean Desert Sect, *BASOR* 227 [1977]: 22–23); Allegro's other synonym, Meṣilla (*Zec.* 1:1, 8), which may be Josephus's Bemeselis (*War,* 1.4.6); and, for its last period of occupation, Meṣad Ḥasidin (Heb., "Fortress of the Hasidim/the Pious"), known from document 45 from the nearby Wadi Murabbaʿat caves as having played a role during the Second Jewish War (134–135 CE; J. T. Milik, *Discoveries in the Judaean Desert,* vol. 2, 1961, p. 163).

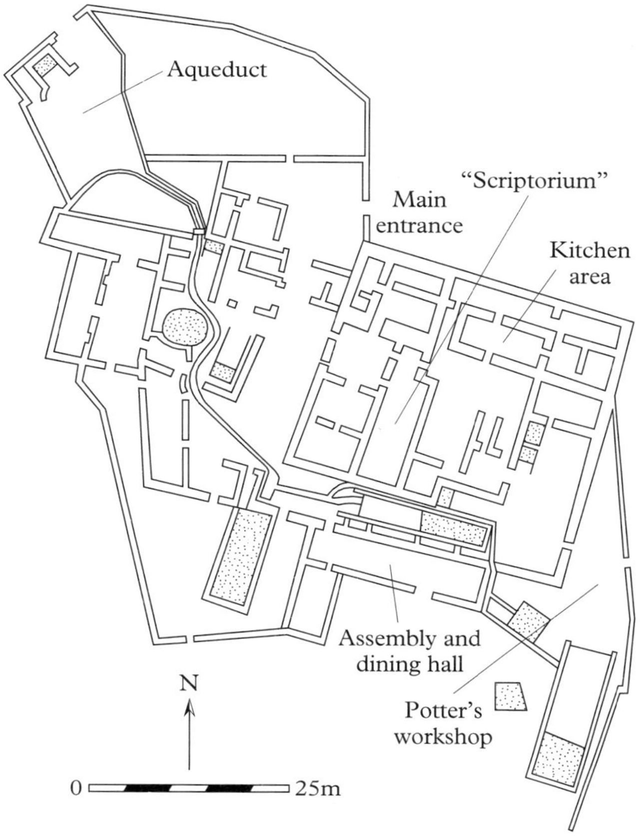

QUMRAN. *Plan of the site.* (Courtesy R. Donceel)

Except for the tomb cleared in 1873 by Clermont-Ganneau, the Qumran ruins were first excavated in November-December 1951 by a small team led by Fr. Roland Guérin de Vaux, director of the École Biblique et Archéologique Française (EBAF) in Jerusalem, and G. Lankester Harding, for the Department of Antiquities of Jordan, with technical assistance (restoration and photography) from the Palestine Archaeological Museum of Jerusalem (now the Rockefeller Museum). Five campaigns followed regularly between 1953 and 1958 under de Vaux's direction. (Work was suspended in 1957 because of the Suez conflict.) The neighboring site of ʿAin Feshkha was also uncovered, evidencing the same historical periods, but with an additional occupation in the Byzantine period. The caves were further explored between and during the seasons in the field.

Between December 1959 and April 1960, a year after the Franco-Jordanian excavations, Allegro undertook deep soundings at a series of Qumran loci (at twenty-nine, mostly peripheral, locations), causing damage under certain walls. Extensive restoration was subsequently carried out by Jordan and then Israel, during which other discoveries were made ("Chronique archéologique," *Revue Biblique* 73 [1966]: 147). Solomon H. Steckoll excavated ten tombs in the main cemetery, which the de Vaux team had only partially explored (principally Joseph T. Milik and Henri de Contenson). There are traces of unofficial digging there in recent years.

A comparison of the photographs taken in the 1950s and 1980s shows the extent of the damage caused by excavation, erosion, and tourism—many installations and some loci having entirely disappeared. De Vaux proposed the following chronology of the site's occupational phases:

1. *Period Ia.* The Iron Age fortress was reoccupied at the end of the second century BCE, in the reign of Alexander Jannaeus or even of his predecessor, John Hyrcanus (134–104 BCE).

2. *Period Ib.* The site's greatest expansion and wealth took place prior to the earthquake in spring 31 BCE that caused its abandonment for most of the reign of Herod the Great (37–4 BCE).

3. *Period II.* Reoccupation took place between 4 and 1 BCE (see de Vaux, 1973, p. 36), a date de Vaux determined from a hoard of 561 silver coins discovered in locus 120. All are from the mint of Tyre, mostly tetradrachmae but also didrachmae. The earliest may date back to the Seleucid kings, but the majority comes from the autonomous mint of Tyre; the latest date is 118 of the Tyrene era, that is, 9/8 BCE. The hoard, in three different pots, must have been hidden between then and 1 BCE/1 CE. De Vaux suggested that this was during the site's period of temporary abandonment, after which life continued along the same lines it had prior to the earthquake.

4. *Period III.* The locality was taken by a Roman detachment during the First Jewish War either at the end of June 68 CE, or immediately afterward. Some of the ruins were restored by a small garrison that may have been stationed there for about ten years, until the entire region had been completely pacified (by the time of the fall of Masada, in 73 CE). The site was then abandoned for about half a century. Traces of a wall and some coins signify that what was left of the buildings knew a brief reoccupation, related to the Second Jewish War.

De Vaux's outline has been contested on some significant points. Milik, one of his field collaborators, questions whether the site had been completely abandoned during Herod's reign, as well as the chronology of the successive Ib and II periods of locus 84/89 (the "crockery" room found near to what de Vaux interpreted as a refectory, great quantities of which are intact; cf. Milik, 1959, p. 55, and de Vaux's response, 1973, pp. 11–12). Ernest M. Laperrousaz (1976) disputes the use de Vaux made of the coins, especially of the silver ones, to date the Hellenistic occupation (cf., e.g., Philip R. Davies, "How Not to Do Archaeology—The Story of Qumran," *Biblical Archaeologist* 51.4 [1988]: 204; Davies also favors lower dates). Laperrousaz sees the site first abandoned at about the time of Pompey's conquest of Palestine, in relation to the 67–63 BCE Jewish internecine war; consequently, the earthquake, for which de Vaux's evidence has frequently been disputed, would have taken place while the site was abandoned. De Vaux's distinction between phases Ia and Ib, which he admits is not clear ("Fouilles de Khirbet Qumrân," *Revue Biblique* 63 [1956]: 551), is rejected by many archaeologists.

The building techniques used at Qumran are strikingly basic. Walls are of local rough-hewn stone and dry joints, but mortar and stucco were used generously for their faces. Most of the internal fittings—seats, benches, cupboards, raised platforms—and a few walls are of unbaked mud brick, carefully plastered over. Most door and window frames, of local soft coral limestone, were finished with care, while column bases and drums carry traces of a stucco revetment. De Vaux retraced the evolution of the architecture at Qumran from an Iron Age rectangle to a wider and more complex settlement; the tower, which still dominates the center of its north flank, was built in period Ib and restored after the earthquake according to him. The hypothesis that it was there from the start was made by a team member, R. F. M. du Buit (*Le Monde de la Bible* 4 [1978]: 22).

The site's most striking feature is its important water system. The volume of water that can be collected per year has been estimated at some 100,000 liters (Laperrousaz, 1976, p. 107). This water is caught in natural basins in the Wadi Qumran torrent situated upstream and is brought to the site by an aqueduct that is in all ways comparable to those of neighboring Hasmonean fortresses and residences. Passing through decantation basins, it is then distributed among the different cisterns. Except for one round cistern (locus 110), that appears to have been built in the Iron Age, all are rectangular, though of different sizes. There are two small, neatly finished reservoirs that the excavators maintain are baths—ritual or not (locus 138, northwest, near one of the entrances, and locus 68, southeast; cf. de Vaux, 1973, p. 132). The annual local rainfall is less than 100 mm in ten to twenty days, and Qumran has no springs. About 3 km south, and on even lower ground, ʿAin Feshkha enjoys the water of several somewhat briny springs.

The buildings, at ground level, mainly consist of what the excavators describe as collective facilities (e.g., a refectory, places to wash, workshops, ovens, mills, stables, and lavatories). De Vaux interpreted the plastered furniture from the upper floor of locus 30 as proving the existence of a scrip-

QUMRAN. *The so-called "Scriptorium."* (Courtesy ASOR Archives)

torium, an installation in which texts were copied. The cemetery is notable for its tombs' orderly distribution although their north-south, rather than east-west, disposition is not traditional for a Jewish population.

The precise chronological framework de Vaux proposed and the abundant archaeological material from the site have become a chronological point of reference for archaeologists working on this period of Near Eastern history (cf. Paul W. Lapp, *Palestinian Ceramic Chronology, 200 B.C.–A.D. 70,* New Haven, 1961; p. 12). De Vaux's finds included numerous very fragmentary items not selected for the inventory and the publication but that were kept and marked with their date and place of discovery. Except for the few dozen artifacts used to illustrate his preliminary reports and his only, relatively short, synthesis (see *Archaeology and the Dead Sea Scrolls,* 1973), the finds were left unpublished, much as those of the more recent excavations at the site. The EBAF launched the final publication of all the finds on the occasion of its centenary (Donceel and Donceel-Voûte, 1994).

At the time of the excavations, the pottery, including the lamps, together with the material from the caves, appeared to be unique when compared with same-period sites (cf. de Vaux, 1973, pp. 17–18, in which he is slightly more reserved on this point than in the French edition, pp. 13–14). However, Lapp (1961) had already shown that certain Qumran I and II pottery shapes were akin to other Hellenistic and Eastern Terra Sigillata wares. The initial publications say little about other categories of objects that might be significant for the history and chronology of Qumran, such as the stone- and glassware, and the metal objects, mainly tools, which offer insights into everyday activities. More than twelve hundred coins were recovered from all over the site, including several hoards. Organic material—wood, reeds, and palm leaves—was found, but no scrolls were discovered in or among the buildings.

Endeavoring to explain the topographical relationship between the site and the nearby scroll caves, and struck by characteristics that, according to him, only communal life could explain, de Vaux proposed an occupation of the buildings in periods I and II by a monastic community of Essene inspiration ("Fouilles de Khirbet Qumrân," *Revue Biblique* 60 [1953]: 104). He was encouraged by the contents of certain Qumran cave scrolls and the indication of a dwelling place of the "Essene" sect, localized as having ʿEin-Gedi "underneath them," by Pliny the Elder (*Nat. Hist.,* 5.17.4). De Vaux and other supporters of a Qumrano-Essenic theory have been accused of forcing the archaeological evidence from Qumran, and from other nearby sites, into the frame of this theory (see Norman Golb, "Who Hid the Dead Sea Scrolls?" *Biblical Archaeologist* 48.2 [1985]: 68–82).

With the increase in comparative archaeological material for the region of ancient Syria-Palestine, other hypotheses have been formulated. Scholars such as Golb, for example, have underlined the military character of the site's defensive features; as early as 1914 Gustaf Dalman had suggested that Qumran had been a Roman fort (*Palästina Jahrbuch* 10 [1914]: 9). Even though the tower is sturdy, especially in its last phase, the circumference of the site would not be easily defended; the long east wall, to which de Vaux also attributed a ritual function (separating the worlds of the living and the dead in the cemetery on the east), encloses the large southern terrace that is characteristic of the site; it may have been a cultivated area because it received water from the central system and its outlets, as from cistern 71, at the southern end of the buildings. This may have served to irrigate a vineyard—as Robert Donceel was able, in 1988, to identify a wine-press in the isolated southern locus 75—and/or other plantations, in relation with regional products, such as palm dates, or balsam, well known from classical authors. Indeed, Qumran pottery counts a good number of a type of narrow-necked, round-bellied juglets, one of which was found intact in a nearby cave still containing a vegetable extract, which is akin to the famous essences retrieved from such shrubs as the Balsamodendron Opobalsamon that were among the area's main economic assets in antiquity (J. Patrich and B. Arubas, "A Juglet Containing Balsam Oil(?) from a Cave near Qumran," *Israel Exploration Journal* 39 [1989]: 43–59).

The finds at the site include quantities of soft limestone objects: chip-cut mugs, small jugs, deep dishes and bowls, as well as lathe-turned vessels such as flat-based semi-globular goblets and large pedestalled urns, often finely ornamented with a fluted band. Lamps show a diversity of clays, production methods, and shapes. The few "cornucopia" lamps, the series of current, small, "Herodian" anvil nozzled types, and an unusual, large and long-nozzled model are wheel turned. Molded lamps can be delphiniformic, or carry simple radiating designs or richer vegetable motifs. The blown glassware is quite abundant and presents some rare colors and mold-blown pieces, the shapes being mostly of small bowls, balsamaria, and bottles. The pottery includes some fine wares, such as "painted Jerusalem" plates, Hellenistic black ware, Western and Eastern A Terra Sigillata, beside vast quantities of common wares for the table, cooking, and storage, among the more remarkable of which are the cream ware with combed and punched decoration, the large lopsided flasks, and the delicate shapes of cups, bowls, and rimmed plates.

The archaeological remains at Qumran included at least three stone staircases to upper floors and comprised both a complex of industrial installations—workshops, various shallow basins, tall plastered earthen vats, different kilns and heating installations—and a residential core that includes the multistoried tower and an upstairs dining room (de Vaux's scriptorium; see P. Donceel-Voûte, "'Coenaculum'—la salle à manger à l'étage du locus 30 à Khirbet Qumrân sur la Mer Morte," *Res Orientales* 4 [1992]: 61–84). These workshops, the few defensive structures, and the number of coins found at the site suggest economic activities whose yield was great. Roads and far-reaching defensive systems had been built in the area well before the common era, as part of the exploitation of salt and bitumen from the Dead Sea, while all of the Jericho region, which may have included Qumran and ʿAin Feshkha, traditionally produced and traded precious vegetable essences and the various yields of its extensive palm groves.

The date of the necropolis is still considered uncertain. Part of the excavated tombs were found in one of the fill levels, maybe the same as those, in the northern part of the site, which the excavators described as having an inverted stratigraphy (sounding A). In 1956 grave 26 was found dug into earth that contained a Herodian lamp, of the type common in de Vaux's period II of the site (ending in 68 BCE). For other graves, stone blocks had been reused to build the tomb's side chamber. However, Carbon-14 datings confirmed the antiquity of the necropolis. It included more than eleven hundred burials, remarkably poor and deep, and regularly laid out, which suggests a strong organization for quite an important human group (a religious community, according to de Vaux, or possibly an abundant labor force, eventually "forced," with distinct funerary practices).

Certain rooms offer evidence for occupational periods more numerous than those described in print by the excavators (e.g., the case of locus 4 "council hall") or for a denser later occupation (probably second century CE) of the settlement (e.g., loci 32 and 36).

[*See also* Essenes; Dead Sea Scrolls; *and the biographies of Harding and Vaux.*]

BIBLIOGRAPHY

Bibliography for the archaeological remains is less abundant than for the texts; only publications by excavators and archaeologists in direct contact with the material appear here.

Cross, Frank Moore. *The Ancient Library of Qumrân and Modern Biblical Studies.* Rev. ed. Garden City, N.Y., 1961. Traditional presentation of the site as the center of an Essene community by one of the driving forces behind the early activities in the field for the American Schools of Oriental Research. The German edition (1967) has a more up-to-date bibliography.

Donceel, Robert, and Pauline Donceel-Voûte. "The Archaeology of Khirbet Qumran." In *Methods of Investigation of the Dead Sea Scrolls and the Khirbet Qumran Site,* edited by Michael O. Wise et al., pp. 1–38. Annals of the New York Academy of Sciences, vol. 722. New York, 1994. The available evidence and final publication plan by the École Biblique and the Catholic University of Louvain team.

Goranson, Stephen. "Further Qumran Archaeology Publications in Progress." *Biblical Archaeologist* 54.2 (1991): 110–111. Inkwells from the site.

Harding, G. Lankester. *The Antiquities of Jordan.* London, 1959. Good presentation of the site by one of the two archaeologists responsible for the first excavation (see pp. 195–200).

Laperrousaz, Ernest M. *Qoumrân, l'établissement essénien des bords de la Mer Morte: Histoire et archéologie du site.* Paris, 1976. Collection and classification of all the published evidence, by a member of the team during the last campaigns. Includes this excavator's complete diary, bibliography (on the modern and ancient place names), and discussion of certain points of de Vaux's interpretations. For a shorter, updated version, see "Qumran et découvertes au désert de Juda" in *Dictionnaire de la Bible, Supplément,* vol. 9, cols. 783–789 (Paris, 1978).

Milik, J. T. *Ten Years of Discovery in the Wilderness of Judaea.* Studies in Biblical Theology, vol. 26. London, 1959. Translation, with minor additions, of the French edition of 1957. Evidence of the excavation presented by a member of the team, with his original views on certain aspects of uncovering Qumran and ʿAin Feshkha.

Milik, J. T. "Qumrân." In *Encyclopaedia Universalis,* vol. 19, pp. 417–419. Paris, 1990.

North, R. "The Qumran Reservoirs." In *The Bible in Current Catholic Thought,* edited by John L. McKenzie, pp. 100–132. New York, 1962.

Sharabani, Marcia. "Monnaies de Qumrân au Musée Rockefeller de Jérusalem." *Revue Biblique* 87 (1980): 274–284, pls. 3–4. Study of the silver coin hoard.

Steckoll, Solomon H. "Preliminary Excavation Report in the Qumran Cemetery." *Revue de Qumran* 6.3 (February 1968): 323–336. Excavations in the necropolis.

Vaux, Roland de. "Une hachette essénienne?" *Vetus Testamentum* 9 (1959): 399–407. Study of a small hatchet found at the site, presented as a ritual object.

Vaux, Roland de. *Archaeology and the Dead Sea Scrolls.* London, 1973. The excavator's only synthesis (although only half of the book covers the site), with basic information on the site and finds; slightly amplified and posthumous version of the first French edition (1961), with references to de Vaux's preliminary reports in the *Revue Biblique* (1951–1958).

Zeuner, F. E. "Notes on Qumrân." *Palestine Exploration Quarterly* 92 (1960): 27–36. Results of laboratory analyses of animal bones, C14 in wood, and the sediment and clay deposits in cisterns from a ceramological perspective.

ROBERT DONCEEL

QURAYYAH, site located in northwest Arabia (28°47′ N, 36°00′ E), about 63 km (39 mi.) northwest of Tabuk. It lies near the main pilgrim and trade route through the peninsula connecting Yemen with the Levant. Qurayyah is situated in a region of broken sandstone hills and gravel plains which, though barren throughout most of the year, receives flash floods in the spring from the higher granite mountains to the west. It was mentioned by nineteenth-century European travelers such as Augustus Wallin, Richard Burton, and Charles M. Doughty but not visited and described until 1906, by Bernard Moritz. The next European visitor seems to have been St. John Philby in 1951, who left a reasonably accurate account of the visible remains. The first real archaeological exploration was not undertaken until 1968, however, when a team from the University of London made a rapid survey of the site and its surroundings, described by Peter J. Parr et al. ("Preliminary Survey in N. W. Arabia, 1968," *Bulletin of the Institute of Archaeology, University of London* 8–9 [1970]: 219–241, pls. 21–42). Archaeologists from the Saudi Arabian Antiquities Department have made a few minor soundings at the site, but it remains poorly explored and recorded. Any account of its historical and cultural significance is, thus, necessarily tentative and speculative.

Qurayyah's ruins comprise three main elements. The first is an isolated hill, the citadel (about 1,000 × 350 m), whose nearly vertical sides rise some 50 m above the surrounding terrain to a flattish summit. The summit is divided into three parts by two walls built of thin slabs of the local shale (approximately 1.40 m thick at their base and 3 m high). Several towers attached to them and a possible gateway are visible. The remains of other buildings on the summit are of the same masonry style and may be watchtowers or aboveground tombs. The second element appears about 200 m away, at the foot of the citadel: the remains of a small settlement (about 400 × 300 m) are surrounded by a stone wall now largely buried by wind-blown sand. Finally, over many square kilometers to the east the third element, the outlines of small fields can be traced, delineated by single lines of stones and crossed by stone irrigation channels. Extensive areas of these fields are enclosed by substantial stone walls, mostly covered by sand but similar where visible to the walls on top of the hill. Only three other structures are visible whose style of ashlar masonry is very different, and they clearly are later than the other remains. They exhibit architectural features characteristic of the Nabatean/Roman period.

Despite the lack of detailed examination and excavation, it seems evident that these remains (with the exception of the three late buildings) form part of a single contemporary occupational complex. An idea of their date can, at present, only be gained from the surface pottery. This includes quantities of a distinctive ware decorated with naturalistic and geometric motifs derived from the Aegean and Egypt and reminiscent of Late Bronze and Early Iron Age decorated pottery found elsewhere in the Levant. However, that the ware was locally made is indicated by the number of sherds lying near a ruined kiln and has been confirmed by petrographic analysis. This Qurayyah painted ware has also been discovered at other sites, notably at Timnaʿ in the Wadi ʿArabah in Israel, by Benno Rothenberg, where it is associated with Egyptian copper mining and smelting installations dated by inscriptions to the nineteenth dynasty (c. 1300–1150 BCE). [*See* Timnaʿ (Negev).] The main occupation at Qurayyah is thus tentatively attributed to this period.

This part of Arabia is usually identified with ancient Midian. According to the Hebrew Bible, Moses took refuge there after he murdered an Egyptian overseer and married the daughter of its ruler, Jethro; these events are usually also dated to the time of the nineteenth dynasty. In the Bible the Midianites are portrayed as pastoralists and camel raiders, but if Qurayyah is, as the evidence suggests, a Midianite settlement, this picture needs revision. [*See* Midian.] The inhabitants of Qurayyah built fortification walls and practiced irrigation agriculture; they almost certainly were participating with the Egyptians in the metallurgical industry at Timnaʿ. Judging from the location of the site, they may well have already been active in the incense trade. Although this interpretation of the evidence is controversial, so is the part played by Egypt in this "urban" development (Parr, 1988, 1993; Bawden, 1992).

BIBLIOGRAPHY

The following articles represent a discussion between the authors over the dating and implications of the material from Qurayyah and elsewhere in northwest Arabia.

Bawden, Garth. "Continuity and Disruption in the Ancient Hejaz: An Assessment of Current Archaeological Strategies." *Arabian Archaeology and Epigraphy* 3 (1992): 1–22.

Parr, Peter J. "Pottery of the Late Second Millennium B.C. from North West Arabia and Its Historical Implications." In *Araby the Blest: Studies in Arabian Archaeology*, edited by Daniel T. Potts, pp. 73–89. Copenhagen, 1988.

Parr, Peter J. "The Early History of the Hejaz: A Response to G. Bawden." *Arabian Archaeology and Epigraphy* 4 (1993): 48–58.

PETER J. PARR

QUṢAYR ʿAMRA, site located 85 km (53 mi.) east of Amman, Jordan, and 32 km (20 mi.) southwest of the oasis of Azraq (31°48′ N, 36°33′ E). This bathhouse complex was built in the first half of the eighth-century CE on the Jordanian steppe, unconnected to any visible earlier settlement. The Austrian Orientalist-explorer Alois Musil discovered the monument in 1898. Soon afterward, he made two additional trips to the site, the third in the company of a painter, A. L. Meilich, who copied the frescoes that cover virtually all the interior surfaces, which the Academy of Vienna published in 1907. Following Musil's rediscovery, the paintings became smoke blackened by bedouin campfires. Visitors and passersby caused additional damage by scratching their names on the frescoes. Perceiving the precarious condition of the paintings, the Department of Antiquities of Jordan commissioned a Spanish team from the National Museum of Madrid to clean them. This task was accomplished in three seasons of work (1971–1973).

The complex is built of roughly shaped, hard limestone blocks, except the doorjambs and the monolithic lintel above the main doorway, which are of basalt. The plan consists of three main elements: a rectangular audience hall, a bath complex, and hydraulic structures.

The audience hall is divided into three bays by two slightly pointed transverse arches that spring from low pilasters. The bays are roofed by three tunnel vaults; on the axis of the entrance doorway a tunnel-vaulted alcove is flanked by two small, poorly lit rooms paved with colored mosaics. The northeastern corner of the audience hall is occupied by a shallow fountain pool. To the east of the audience hall is a bath complex consisting of three small rooms corresponding to the apodyterium, tepidarium, and caldarium. The floors of the second and third rooms rested on basalt supports; the space between the supports allowed for the circulation of hot air (hypocaust). On the east side of the caldarium is a tunnel-vaulted passage; at the far end, below this passage, are the strokehole and furnaces. The passage opens onto an unroofed enclosure that served as the stroking area and for fuel storage. At a distance of 5 m to the north is an elevated water tank, along-side which is a deep masonry-lined well. Immediately to the west of the well two piers of masonry stand opposite each other alongside a low circle; originally there must have been a third pier in the middle. These piers formed part of the apparatus for drawing water from the well into the water tank. From the elevated tank two feeder pipes set in slab-covered channels led to the fountain pool in the audience hall and to a plastered tank set above the furnace.

The first impression to strike the visitor to Quṣayr ʿAmra is the sharp contrast between the rough appearance of the exterior walls and the extensive paintings, in the interior (see figure 1). These paintings include bathing and hunting scenes, dancing, athletes practicing, wrestlers, gift bearers, various activities connected with the builder's trade, as well as a cluster of isolated scenes of pastoral life. The dome of the caldarium is decorated with the constellations of the Northern Hemisphere and the signs of the zodiac.

It has long been recognized that the roots of these paintings lay in the Greco-Syrian artistic tradition, apparent in the themes adopted from the classical repertoire: flying angels; putti; the personifications of history, philosophy, and poetry identified by accompanying Greek inscriptions; and the flamboyant represention of bathing scenes. However, a closer look at the figural representations shows that more than one style existed concurrently in the paintings—from elegantly formed shapes whose poses differ to formalized Byzantine figural representations and compositions of clumsy proportions and woodenlike, frozen shapes drawn schematically with heavily charged brushstrokes. These styles sum up the possibility of assimilation of the various local artistic traditions enriched by Eastern ideas. Another striking feature of these paintings is their rich and varied iconographic repertoire. The themes are very diverse with no apparent unity or relationship to each other. The scenes of dancing females, hunting figures, and figures listening to music were considered by Oleg Grabar to be reflections of royal pleasures and pastimes, *majlis al-lahwa* ("a place used for ceremonial entertainment"), in which the life of the prince was expressed through his association with hunting, banqueting, and dancing—amusements common in the Sasanian court. It is also likely that such themes were stock motifs and subjects in the decorations of high-quality baths.

Quṣayr ʿAmra was not a residential building. It may have served as a stopping place for caravans of high government officials and civil servants traveling from the Belqa to Iraq and the Hijaz via Wadi es-Sirḥan.

BIBLIOGRAPHY

Almagro Basch, Martin, et al. *Qusayr' Amra: Residencia y Baños Omeyas en el Desierto de Jordania.* Madrid, 1975. General discussion (with

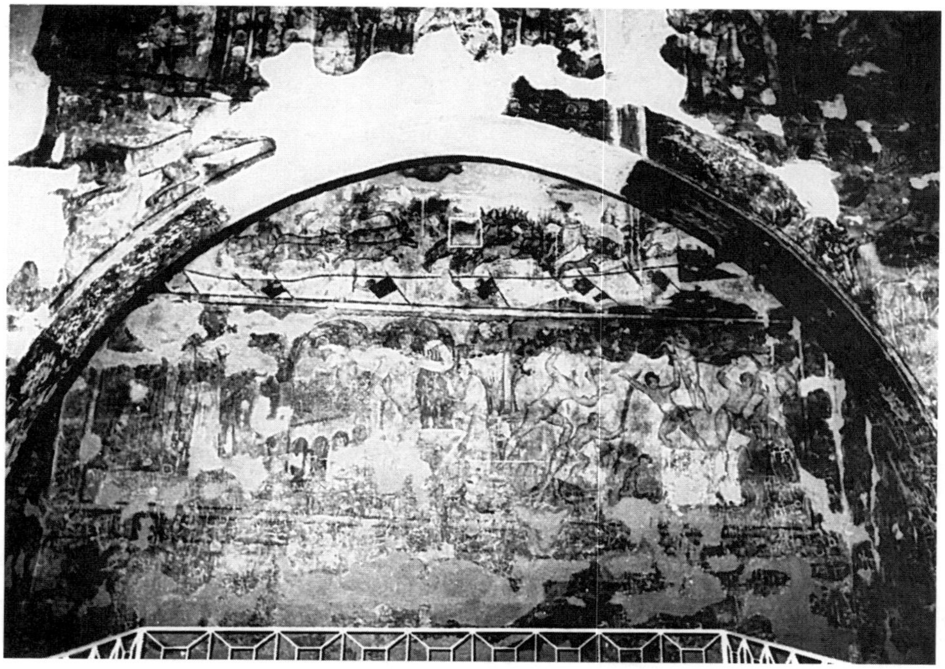

QUṢAYR ʿAMRA. Figure 1. *Interior paintings of the audience hall, looking west.* (Courtesy G. Bisheh)

summaries in English, Arabic, and French), useful for its accompanying plans and photographs.

Bisheh, Ghazi. "Qusayr Amra: Les fresques d'un Palais Omeyyade." *Dossiers Histoire et Archéologie,* no. 118 (1987): 70–73. Attempt to interpret the paintings in an Umayyad context.

Blazquez, J. M. "La pintura helenística de Qusayr 'Amra (Jordania) y sus fuentes." *Archivo Español de Arqueología,* no. 54 (1981): 157–202; no. 56 (1983): 169–212.

Creswell, K. A. C. *Early Muslim Architecture,* vol. 1, *Umayyads, A.D. 622–750* (1940). 2d ed. Oxford, 1969. See pages 390–449 for a detailed description of the monument, with a full bibliography arranged chronologically.

Grabar, Oleg. *The Formation of Islamic Art.* New Haven and London, 1973. See pages 139–187 for a sustained analysis of secular art and architecture in the Umayyad period.

Grabar, Oleg. "La place de Qusayr Amrah dans l'art profane du haut moyen âge." *Cahiers Archéologiques* 36 (1988): 75–83.

GHAZI BISHEH

R

RABUD, KHIRBET, site located south of Hebron, surrounded by the namesake river Wadi en-Nar, a region that experiences meager precipitation (31°25′ N, 35°01′ E; map reference 151 × 093). For water sources, residents of Khirbet Rabud depended on cisterns and two wells, about 3 km (2 mi.) north of the site.

Based on topographic clues in the Hebrew Bible, Kurt Galling identified the site with biblical Debir ("Zur Lokalisierung von Debir," *Zeitschrift des Deutschen Pälastina-Vereins* 70 [1954]: 135–141), an identification challenged by William Foxwell Albright ("Debir," in *Archaeology and Old Testament Study,* edited by David Winston Thomas, Oxford, 1967, pp. 207–220), who believed Debir to be his own site, Tell Beit Mirsim. [*See* Beit Mirsim, Tell.] However, recent surveys in the Judean hill country and the excavation of Khirbet Rabud support Galling's proposal: Khirbet Rabud and biblical Debir are located in the same southern Judean district as ʿAnab, Socoh, and Eshtemoa (*Jos.* 15:49); Khirbet Rabud is the only Late Bronze Age city located south of Jerusalem (the Bible depicts Debir as the major Canaanite city in the area [*Jos.* 11:21, 15:15–17; *Jg.* 1:11–15]); and the town is located in a dry region that depended on cisterns and an upper and lower water source (the Wells of ʿAlaqa), like the ones described in the story of Achsa, daughter of Caleb, in *Joshua* 15:19 and *Judges* 1:15. [*See* Judah.]

In 1968–1969, Moshe Kochavi directed excavations at the site on behalf of Tel Aviv University's Institute of Archaeology. Rescue excavations were also carried out at several robbed burial caves, part of the large burial ground, ʿUsh eṣ-Ṣaqra, across the wadi. Because, like many hill country sites, most of Khirbet Rabud is eroded to bedrock, remains of ancient occupation were discerned only in a narrow strip adjacent to the city wall, in two trenches, A and B, on the mound's western slope.

Early Bronze Age I and IV sherds were found in the cemetery and in the excavated areas. A stone wall running along the mound's lowest terrace on the northwest was encountered in trench A and dated to the Late Bronze Age. Four strata of the fourteenth–thirteenth centuries BCE were associated with this wall. LB I sherds found on the mound and in its cemetery may indicate an earlier date for the construction of the LB city wall. The LB II pottery from trench A and from the cemetery included a high percentage of imported Mycenaean and Cypriot wares. An Iron I stratum and a tenth-century BCE cistern were also exposed at the lower part of trench A.

A massive stone wall, 4 m wide and about 1 km long, had been noted prior to the excavation. It encircles about 5 ha (12 acres) of this 6-ha (15 acres) mound and was encountered in both trenches and dated to the ninth century BCE. The wall was built in straight sections, in uneven lengths, with half-meter projections at their joints. The topography of the site suggests the existence of a gateway on the southeastern slope, where the modern hamlet of Khirbet Rabud now stands.

A major destruction level, with large amounts of pottery and other finds lying in the ashes, was detected in both trenches and attributed to Senacherib's campaign against Judah in 701 BCE. Two stamp seals inscribed in Hebrew, ŠLM BN ʾḤʾ ("Shalom son of Aha") and a four-winged *lamelekh* seal, found in this stratum fit the suggested chronological horizon. In the seventh century BCE the city wall was doubled in width and a small, unwalled suburb, Khirbet Rabda, was built at the foot of the mound. Some buildings from the Persian period and a Roman lookout tower represent the end of the site's occupational history.

BIBLIOGRAPHY

Albright, William Foxwell. "The Excavations at Tell Beit Mirsim." *Bulletin of the American Schools of Oriental Research,* no. 23 (1926): 2–14. Albright's identification of Debir with his excavation at Tell Beit Mirsim.

Donner, Herbert. "Das Deutsche evangelische Institut für Altertumswissenschaft des Heiligen Landes, Lehrkursus 1963, 2. Die Exkursionen in Palästina." *Zeitschrift des Deutschen Palästina-Vereins* 81 (1965): 3–53. The first report on LB sherds found at Khirbet Rabud.

Kochavi, Moshe. "Khirbet Rabûd = Debir." *Tel Aviv* 1 (1974): 2–33. Report on the excavation and discussion of the identification.

Moshe Kochavi

RADANNAH, site located on the northern perimeter of Ramallah, 16 km (10 mi.) north of Jerusalem on a ridge surrounded on three sides by deep valleys with perennial springs (map reference 70835 × 553305). It was, therefore, strategically located with regard to security. Radannah is not mentioned in the Bible and remains essentially anonymous. Yohanan Aharoni (1971) proposed identifying the site with biblical 'Ataroth (*Jos.* 16:5, 18:13), a border town between Benjamin and Ephraim.

Four seasons of excavation were conducted at the site (about 32–40 acres) between 1969 and 1974 by Joseph Callaway and Robert Cooley on behalf of the Israel Department of Antiquities. Its occupational history includes four phases. The earliest evidence is represented by a few Early Bronze I sherds and no definable structures. The second and third phases appear to be an Iron Age I settlement comprised of five–six structures that give evidence of their original construction and subsequent remodeling. Settlers of unknown origins seem to have arrived at the site toward the end of the thirteenth century or early twelfth century BCE, lived through two phases of village life, and then disappeared in the middle of the eleventh century BCE. Ashes and disturbed architecture indicate that this phase was terminated by a violent destruction. After a long period of abandonment there is evidence of a fourth occupational phase, during the Byzantine period. The site was excavated in three major areas (R, S, T), moving east–west.

The first and fourth phases suggest minimal human activity, whereas the second and third phases point to a well-preserved single-period site with a relatively well-developed material culture. A common feature of the Iron I settlement is the pillared house. [*See* Four-Room House.] A large room was divided by hewn pillars or stacked stone piers to support the roof beams, and there was a chamber at the back. Multiple chisel marks were preserved on the top and sides of the hewn pillars. Benches were built against the outer wall of the largest room, and in one case they were cut into bedrock on two sides. A hearth was located in the center of the room. Bell-shaped cisterns for water storage and silos for grain storage were regular features in the houses. These pillared houses were clustered around the top of the ridge, leaving a common open space in the middle area of the settlement that probably served as an animal enclosure and storage space for grain. Below the settlement the hillsides were shaped by agricultural terraces.

An abundance of cereal food-processing tools was found throughout the site, including large, well-worn saddles and querns, stone mortars and pestles, rubbing stones, and flint sickle blades. There is considerable evidence for primitive metalworking. Fragments of crucibles, some with slag adhering to the inside, were discovered, along with pieces of tuyeres, or bellow tips. Numerous bronze objects were identified along with three iron implements.

Other significant finds include an inscribed jar handle with three letters in Proto-Canaanite script and a large multihandled krater. A channel built into the Krater's upper wall terminated in spouts on the inside of the bowl, each of which is in the shape of a bull's head. A cultic function may be inferred. Large collar-rim storage jars were recovered throughout the site.

BIBLIOGRAPHY

Aharoni, Yohanan. "Khirbet Raddana and Its Inscription." *Israel Exploration Journal* 21 (1971): 130–135. A useful discussion of the date for the inscribed jar handle and the identification of the site with biblical 'Ataroth.

Callaway, Joseph A., and Robert E. Cooley. "A Salvage Excavation at Raddana, in Bireh." *Bulletin of the American Schools of Oriental Research,* no. 201 (1971): 9–19. The first synthesis of archaeological work at this site, which must be supplemented by later reports.

Cooley, Robert E. "Four Seasons of Excavation at Khirbet Raddana." *Near Eastern Archaeological Society Bulletin,* no. 5 (1975): 5–20. Features a reconstruction of the cultural pattern at the Radannah settlement.

Cross, Frank Moore, and David Noel Freedman. "An Inscribed Jar Handle from Raddana." *Bulletin of the American Schools of Oriental Research,* no. 201 (1971): 19–22. A brief description of the jar handle and its chronological significance.

Finkelstein, Israel. *The Archaeology of the Israelite Settlement.* Jerusalem, 1988. Provides a cultural context for Radannah as a flourishing farming village in the Israelite settlement pattern.

ROBERT E. COOLEY

RAMAT RAḤEL, site located on a hill midway between Jerusalem and Bethlehem (31°40′ N, 35°15′ E; map reference 1708 × 1275). Yohanan Aharoni excavated the site for four seasons between 1954 and 1962 under the auspices of the Hebrew University of Jerusalem, the Israel Department of Antiquities, the Israel Exploration Society (IES), and the University of Rome. In 1984 Gabriel Barkay excavated there for Tel Aviv University and the IES. In 1931 Benjamin Mazar and Moshe Stekelis excavated a burial cave south of the site for the Palestine Exploration Society. Five main strata were identified dating from the Iron Age IIC through the Early Arab period. The ancient name of the site is unknown, although Aharoni suggests that it may be Beth-ha-Kerem; Barkay rejects this identification.

Stratum VB was founded on bedrock. Though little remains of its architecture, there is some evidence of a casemate wall and a stone quarry. Two seal impressions similar to impressions known from Tel Nagila and Lachish mention "to Shebna [son of] Shahar." [*See* Lachish.] One hundred and seventy *lmlk* stamped handles, of both the two-winged and four-winged varieties, were found in constructional fills used in stratum VA. Private seal impressions were also recovered, some of whose names correspond to seals from Tell en-Naṣbeh, Beth-Shemesh, and Lachish. [*See* Naṣbeh, Tell en-; Beth-Shemesh.] The *lmlk* handles found in fills below stratum VA surfaces help date stratum VB to the reign of Hezekiah. The destruction of the site can be attributed presumably to Sennacherib's campaign of 701 BCE.

A new citadel, dated to the late seventh–early sixth centuries BCE, was constructed in stratum VA. A double wall system, enclosing 2.5 acres, partially surrounded the citadel. The area between the walls and the citadel was intentionally leveled with extensive fills. Only fragments of the outer wall were excavated and it appears to surround the citadel only partially. The citadel itself is rectangular (56 × 72 m). It consists of the fragments of two buildings along the western and northern sides of its inner casemate wall. The casemates functioned as storerooms. In the center of the eastern wall a paved opening served as a gate and led to a well-plastered courtyard. A second, smaller gate was found to the south of the main gate. A hewn tunnel outside the citadel may originally have been linked to a narrow postern along the north wall. Architectural elements from the citadel include fine ashlar masonry, header-stretcher construction, the remains of ten proto-Aeolic capitals (see figure 1), carved stone crenelation fragments, and carved stone window balustrades. These types of balustrades are identical to those portrayed in Phoenician ivory plaques depicting the "woman in the window" motif. A small quantity of Assyrian Palace ware was found, along with a sherd depicting a seated individual. Originally, this painted sherd was thought to imitate an Assyrian pictoral style. However, Shulamit Geva (1981) has suggested that this sherd better reflects Aegean traditions. Rosette stamp impressions, which may have been used as royal sealings after the seventh century BCE, were also found. A seal impression "to Eliakim, steward of Yochin" is identical to seal impressions from Tell Beit Mirsim and Beth-Shemesh. [*See* Beit Mirsim, Tell.] The high quality of the ashlar masonry, the types of architectural adornments, and the overall site plan are reminiscent of Samaria and suggest a Phoenician influence [*See* Samaria; Phoenicians.] The use of these distinctive architectural elements, along with the small finds, supports the contention that Ramat Raḥel was indeed a royal citadel, perhaps during the reign of Jehoiachin.

The Late Persian/Early Hellenistic ceramic assemblage dates stratum IVB to the fourth century BCE. This stratum is poorly preserved, but two hundred and seventy seal impressions were recovered. The wide variety of inscribed seal impressions includes the use of name *Jerusalem,* Yehud stamps, and private names. The anepigraphous seal assemblage is also rich and diverse. Most of these seals belong to Stern's type A, which depicts lions in various positions (Stern, 1982).

The Herodian remains of stratum IVA are limited to scattered architectural fragments and burial caves on the slopes. Stratum III is dated to the late third century CE, when the site was utilized by the Roman Tenth Legion. The Church of Kathisma and a monastery from stratum II date to the Byzantine period (fifth–late seventh centuries). The last use of the site (stratum I) was in the Early Arab period.

BIBLIOGRAPHY

Aharoni, Yohanan. "Excavations at Ramat Raḥel, 1954: Preliminary Report." *Israel Exploration Journal* 6 (1956): 102–111, 137–157. Report of the first season, complimentary to and in part superseded by the excavation volumes (below).

Aharoni, Yohanan. *Excavations at Ramat Raḥel.* 2 vols. Rome, 1962–1964. Preliminary reports with architectural plans, photographs, and

RAMAT RAḤEL. Figure 1. *Proto-Aeolic capital.* (Courtesy ASOR Archives)

pottery plates. Although not a final report, includes all the archaeological work done by Aharoni.

Geva, Shulamit. "The Painted Sherd of Ramat Raḥel." *Israel Exploration Journal* 31 (1981): 186–189.

Reich, Ronny. "Palaces and Residencies in the Iron Age." In *The Architecture of Ancient Israel: From the Prehistoric to the Persian Periods,* edited by Aharon Kempinski and Ronny Reich, pp. 202–222. Jerusalem, 1992. Excellent synthetic article on Iron Age architectural traditions.

Shiloh, Yigal. *The Proto-Aeolic Capital and Israelite Ashlar Masonry.* Qedem, vol. 11. Jerusalem, 1979. Comprehensive analysis of proto-Aeolic capitals found in Palestine, with important discussions of ashlar masonry and Phoenician influences on Israelite architectural traditions. Though a few new capitals have been found at sites such as Dan, this volume remains the definitive study.

Stern, Ephraim. *Material Culture of the Land of the Bible in the Persian Period, 538–332 B.C.* Warminster, 1982.

Stern, Ephraim. "The Phoenician Architectural Elements in Palestine during the Late Iron Age and Persian Period." In *The Architecture of Ancient Israel: From the Prehistoric to the Persian Periods,* edited by Aharon Kempinski and Ronny Reich, pp. 302–309. Jerusalem, 1992. Excellent synopsis of Phoenician influences on Israel from the Late Iron Age through the Hellenistic period.

Yadin, Yigael. "The 'House of Baʿal' of Ahab and Jezebel in Samaria, and That of Athalia in Judah." In *Archaeology in the Levant: Essays for Kathleen Kenyon,* edited by P. R. S. Moorey and Peter J. Parr, pp. 127–135. Warminster, 1978. Important, though dated, critique of Aharoni's work at Ramat Raḥel, questioning his methodology, chronological conclusions, and historical reconstructions.

J. P. DESSEL

RAMLA, site located at the crossroads leading from Israel's western seacoast (Jaffa) to Jerusalem on the east, and from Syria in the north to Egypt in the south, about 4 km (2.5 mi.) south of Lod (map reference 138 × 148). The name *ar-Ramla* is believed to derive from the Arabic word *raml,* meaning "sand," referring to the sand dunes of the region. Ramla was the only new city founded in Palestine during the Islamic period; its founder was Sulayman, son of ʿAbd al-Malik, who, as governor of the Jund Filastin, established his capital there. This must have taken place sometime between 712 and 715, when Sulayman became caliph after his brother Walid I.

The first excavation at the site was conducted by Jacob Kaplan in 1949, on behalf of the Ministry of Religious Affairs and the Department of Antiquities of Israel. The excavation focused on the White Mosque, which was at the core of the first buildings constructed at the site in the eighth century. Excavation established that the mosque was built in the form of a quadrangle (93 × 84 m), with its walls oriented to the cardinal points. The right half of the mosque deviates some 6° to the north of the traditional east–west orientation. The major remains are the foundations of the east and west porticoes, the *qiblah* wall (the wall oriented toward Mecca) on the south with its *miḥrab* (niche) in the middle, and two rows of massive pillars running parallel to the *qiblah* wall. These remains appear to be from a later restoration under the Ayyubids, after the Crusader period, as there are clear remnants of cross vaulting for the roof. The mosque's most prominent feature is its square minaret, which was rebuilt in the Mamluk period and still preserves an inscription giving the name of Sultan Muhammad ibn Qala'un and the date AH 714/1318 CE. Another building was discovered in the center whose function is as yet unidentified (it may be an ablution basin). Three subterranean cisterns were revealed in the courtyard.

In 1965 Myriam Rosen-Ayalon and Avraham Eitan, on behalf of the Israel Department of Antiquities and Museums, conducted an excavation that concentrated on the southwestern part of the town; they also made several smaller-scale trial soundings that contributed to understanding the city's topography and urban development in antiquity.

A large number of finds—mainly pottery, but also glass, stone, and metal—were recovered immediately beneath the surface. The material was homogeneous in character and could be ascribed to the eighth or beginning of the ninth century CE. Although this suggests a relatively brief period of occupation, four settlement levels were distinguished, the lowest resting directly on virgin soil. The nature of the finds, together with evidence of elements of installations, points to what might have been a potter's workshop.

In 1973, in the southeastern part of the town, (the Old Quarter), in the courtyard of a private house, Magen Broshi excavated a mosaic pavement comprised of three "carpets." Two are geometric compositions reminiscent of pre-Islamic patterns; the third bears an inscription of a Qur'anic verse in an early Kufic script set within an arch supported by two columns. The ceramic material found with the mosaic also lay on virgin soil, confirming the eighth-century date.

BIBLIOGRAPHY

Conder, Claude R., and H. H. Kitchener. *The Survey of Western Palestine: Memoirs of the Topography, Orography, Hydrography, and Archaeology,* vol. 2, *Samaria.* London, 1882. See pages 264ff.

Kaplan, Jacob. "Excavations at the White Mosque in Ramla." *ʿAtiqot* 2 (1959): 106–115.

Le Strange, Guy, trans. *Palestine under the Moslems: A Description of Syria and the Holy Land from A.D. 650 to 1500.* London, 1890. See pages 15–16, 20, 28, 39, 41, 56, and 303–308.

Rosen-Ayalon, Myriam, and Avraham Eitan. *Ramla Excavations: Finds from the VIIIth Century C.E.* Jerusalem, 1969.

Rosen-Ayalon, Myriam. "The First Mosaic Discovered in Ramla." *Israel Exploration Journal* 26 (1976): 104–119.

Wüstenfeld, Ferdinand, ed. *Jacut's Geographisches Wörterbuch,* vol. 11, p. 817. Leipzig, 1866–.

MYRIAM ROSEN-AYALON

RAQQA, AR-, site located on the eastern (left) or Mesopotamian (Syrian Jezireh) bank of the Upper Euphrates River, where the river meets its tributary, the Balikh River. Facing Deir az-Zor, Mari is to the east and Hama to the west; facing Harran, to the north, Palmyra is to the south-southwest.

Today, ar-Raqqa is the capital of the governorate of ar-Raqqa, one of fourteen that constitute the Syrian Arab Republic. The name is as old as the Islamic domination of Syria: the area was peacefully conquered by ʿIyad ibn Ganm in AH 18/638–639 CE.

Medieval Muslim historians such as al-Baladhuri and geographers such as Yaqut used its post-Islamic name, whose Arabic meaning corresponds to its topography: according to Yaqut, it means "flat land, marshland, or soft land." In fact, the city is situated on the flat, soft, partial marshland of the Euphrates Valley. Ar-Raqqa is identified with a pre-Islamic city known by three different names—Nicephorion, Callinicos, and Leontopolis—and most probably founded during the Seleucid era (third century CE). Cuneiform texts from Mari (second millennium BCE) had situated the city of Tutul at the same site. It is commonly believed that Tutul must be identified with Tell Biʿa, 800 m north of ar-Raqqa (see below). Recent discoveries at the tell itself in 1990 confirmed this identification.

Between AH 18/638 CE and AH 155/772 CE, the only major architectural changes at the site were the building of a Friday mosque, markets, and probably some extramural extensions. In AH 155/772 CE, the ʿAbbasid caliph Abu Jaʿfar al-Manṣur, after having built the round city of Baghdad as a new capital of the caliphate, ordered a similar city built west of old ar-Raqqa/Nicephorion. He named it ar-Rafiqa ("the companion"). His grandson, Harun al-Rashid, made ar-Rafiqa/ar-Raqqa his permanent residence for thirteen years (AH 180–192/796–809 CE). During this period, the sister cities witnessed an urban explosion. The area north of them became residential, full of spacious palaces and mansions for the caliph Harun ar-Rashid and members of his family and court. A large canal, 16 km (10 mi.) long, which terminates in marshes near the Balikh River, was dug to carry water from the Euphrates to the area.

After some periods of instability, the city was revived under the Zangid Atabeg Nur ad-Din and the Ayyubids in the twelfth–thirteenth centuries CE. The fourteenth-century geographer Abu al-Fida' reported that in 1258 the Mongols devastated ar-Raqqa.

European travelers began visiting ar-Raqqa in the sixteenth century. The first archaeological exploration there was conducted in 1907 by the German scholars Frederich Sarre and Ernst Herzfeld, who photographed and sketched its ruins. The French Geographical Institute took the first aerial photographs in 1924, introducing scholars to the palaces of Harun ar-Rashid and the course of the canal. The first archaeological excavation carried out in ar-Raqqa was by Maurice Dunand and Raymond Duru (1944–1945). They unveiled the northeastern part of a representative building labeled palace A, which lay about 400 m north of the city wall (see below). Between 1966 and 1970, Kassem Toueir of the Department of Antiquities and Museums of Syria resumed the excavation of palace A. This rectangular building (140 × 110 m) is oriented east–west and has annexes on the south. It is constructed of mud brick and whitish limestone plaster. On the west are corner towers, buttresses, and a gate. The coins found refer to Harun al-Rashid and his successor, al-Ma'mun (early ninth century CE). Thin-walled subdivisions of rooms and halls indicate a rehabitation in the twelfth–thirteenth centuries.

Between 1950 and 1954, Nassib Saliby, also for the Department of Antiquities, excavated three palaces (B–D) some 1,200 m northeast of the city wall that resemble palace A. A painted inscription in palace B is attributed to the son of Harun al-Rashid, al-Muʿtaṣim.

Beginning in 1982, Michael Meinecke of the German Archaeological Institute, Damascus, excavated three palaces some 800 m north of the city wall that are similar to palaces A–D and also show evidence of rehabitation in the twelfth–thirteenth centuries. Between 1977 and 1990 Kassem Toueir excavated and restored the Qaṣr al-Banat, a palace of the period of Harun al-Rashid in the southeastern part of ar-Rafiqa. The building, whose perimeter has not yet been revealed, is constructed entirely of baked bricks and consists of a central courtyard with fountains in the middle that are shaped like eight-pointed stars. Four iwans open to the four sides of the courtyard. The building was erected on virgin soil, which dates it to the foundation of the city in 772 CE or shortly afterward. It was reused in the twelfth–thirteenth centuries as a storehouse and workshop for producing glazed Raqqa ware.

The Great Mosque (108 × 92 m), in the northern part of the city, within the city wall, was also erected when the city was founded. Built of mud brick with a baked-brick coating on the outer faces of its walls, it is the second-largest mosque in Syria (after the Umayyad mosque in Damascus). Its square courtyard and the round towers buttressing its corners and sides follow the Iraqi model, but its three-aisled division and its prayer hall's gabled roofing follow the Syrian type (Damascus mosque).

The Department of Antiquities is also clearing and restoring the unique horseshoe-shaped city wall (1,500 × 1,500 m) with its double enceinte and intervallum. The wall, the only surviving one of the Early ʿAbbasid period, is massive, buttressed with round towers at regular distances, and built of mud brick with baked-brick coating. The outer wall was thinner than the inner one. The only surviving gate on the outer wall, known as the Gate of Baghdad, is in the southeastern corner. It is constructed entirely of baked brick and is richly decorated in the Hazarbaff technique (arranging bricks in the face of a wall in a way that creates an ornamental design). The outer wall has disappeared since 1980, but its original height, if it followed the Baghdad example, would have been about 20 m.

In 1983, Kay Kohlmeyer, on behalf of the Department of

RAQQA, AR-. *Qaṣr el-Banat after excavation and restoration.* (Courtesy K. Toueir)

RAQQA, AR-. *Corner room of Qaṣr el-Banat.* (Courtesy K. Toueir)

Antiquities and the German Institute made soundings in the area of old ar-Raqqa/Nicephorion, currently the suburb al-Mašlab, in order to observe its pre-Islamic rectangular city wall (1,200 × 650 m). The wall is 2.5 m thick and built of baked brick. It dates to the time of Justinian (first half of the sixth century).

Since 1980, Eva Strommenger (1981) has been excavating at Tell Biʿa, some 800 m north of ar-Raqqa/Nicephorion. In addition to unveiling third- and second-millennium BCE material in the 1990 season (including part of a royal palace similar in plan to the palace at Mari and cuneiform tablets confirming identification of Tell Biʿa with Tutul), she uncovered two mosaic pavements with Syriac inscriptions referring to the building of a Christian monastery (sixth century), which is, perhaps, to be identified with the much-celebrated Early ʿAbbasid church/convent of Dayr Zakkai (Krebernik, 1991, 1993).

[*See also* ʿAbbasid Caliphate.]

BIBLIOGRAPHY

For the history of Islamic Ar-Raqqa, the reader may consult *Jacut's Geographisches Wörterbuch,* edited by Ferdinand Wüstenfeld (Leipzig, 1866–); Aḥmad ibn Yaḥyā Balādurī, *The Origins of the Islamic State,* translated by Philip K. Hitti (New York, 1916); and Muḥammad al-Ṭabarī, *Kitāb ahbār ar-rusūl wa-al-mulūk,* vol. 2 (1879). The reconstruction of Ar-Raqqa is covered in Friedrich P. T. Sarre and Ernst Herzfeld, *Archäologische Reise im Euphrat- und Tigris-begiet,* 4 vols. (Berlin, 1911–1920), and K. A. C. Creswell, *Early Muslim Architecture,* vol. 2 (Oxford, 1940). For excavation reports, see Nassib Saliby, "Rapport préliminaire sur la deuxième campagne (automne 1952) de fouilles à Raqqa," *Annales Archéologiques Arabes Syriennes* 4–5 (1954–1955): 205–212; and the following articles from *Damaszener Mitteilungen* 2 (1985): Jan-Christoph Heusch and Michael Meinecke, "Grabungen im ʿabbāsidischen Palastareal von ar-Raqqa/ar-Rāfiqa, 1982–1983" (pp. 85–105); Murhaf al-Khalaf and Kay Kohlmeyer, "Untersuchungen zur ar-Raqqa–Nikephorion/callinicum" (pp. 133–162); Kassem Toueir, "Der Qaṣr al-Banāt in ar-Raqqa: Ausgrabung, Rekonstruktion und Wiederaufbau, 1977–1982" (pp. 297–319); and Murhaf al-Khalaf, "Die ʿabbāsidische Stadtmauer von ar-Raqqa/ar-Rāfiqa mit einem Beitrag von Norbert Hagen" (pp. 123–131). Tell Biʿa is discussed in Eva Strommenger, "Die archäologischen Forshungen in Tall Biʿa, 1980," *Mitteilungen der Deutschen Orient-Gesellschaft (MDOG)* 113 (1981): 23–34, and "Ausgrabungen in Tall Biʿa 1990," *MDOG* 123 (1991): 7–34; in addition, the mosaic and Syriac inscriptions and cuneiform tablets of Tell Biʿa were published by Manfred Krebernik, "Schriftfunde aus Tall Biʿa," *MDOG* 123 (1991): 41–70, 125 (1993): 51–60. Kay Kohlmeyer discusses the statements of pre-Islamic historians and European travelers in the survey, "Untersuchungen zu ar-Raqqa/Nikephorion/Calinicum," *Damaszener Mitteilungen* 2 (1985): 146–161.

KASSEM TOUEIR

RAS, TELL ER- (32°12′30″ N, 35°17′30″ E), site located on top of one of the northernmost peaks of Mt. Gerizim (Jebel et-Tur), 831 m above sea level, overlooking the short, narrow east–west pass between Mt. Gerizim (881 m above sea level) and the higher Mt. Ebal (940 m above sea level) to the north. On the western watershed of the pass 350 m below the tell, lies Nablus (ancient Neapolis), the largest city in Samaria. Jacob's well (Bir Yaqob) and Tell Balaṭah (ancient Shechem), once the chief city of the Samaritans, lie at the entrance to the pass on the eastern watershed. On the highest peak of Mt. Gerizim, 750 m south of Tell er-Ras, an expanse of limestone bedrock, devoid of structure, marks for the Samaritan community the location of their temple. Nearby are the octagonal remains of the Theotokos church built in about 484 CE by the emperor Zeno and the remains of fortifications built around the church by the emperor Justinian in about 532 CE. Farther south lie the Hellenistic remains of the walled Samaritan town of Lozeh.

Charles W. Wilson of the Survey of Western Palestine examined Tell er-Ras in 1866 and noted it was a partly artificial mound containing building remains. A century later, Robert J. Bull of Drew University discovered frusta of red Aswan granite columns at the foot of Mt. Gerizim and, in a search for the structure from which the columns came, led a team, formed initially from the Drew-McCormick Expedition to Tell Balaṭah, to excavate Tell er-Ras 1964, 1966, and 1968. The tell, 120 m long by 80 m wide, covered with limestone chips and marble architectural fragments, was isolated from the rest of Mt. Gerizim by an east–west fosse approximately 100 m long, 30 m wide, and 8 m deep cut into the limestone bedrock. Stratigraphic excavation uncovered the remains of building A (21.48 m long north–south × 14.14 m wide), with a three-stepped stylobate, a 8.24 m × 3.05 m pronaos and a 8.24 m × 10.13 m naos, a marble floor, and Corinthian captial fragments. The .85-meter-diameter Aswan granite column frusta discovered at the foot of Mt. Gerizim matched the diameter of the column bases excavated at the tell. Building A was identified as a tetrastyle, prostyle, pseudoperiptal temple centered on a platform 64.91 m long north–south × 44.21 m wide. The platform, made up of earth, rubble and cement, was encompassed by a rectangle of stone walls 9 m high and 2 m thick. At the northern end of the platform, a 7.74-meter-wide staircase descended to a broad esplanade of green marble squares and areas of patterned mosaic. The esplanade served as the upper terminus of a very long and very steep stairway that led from the city of Neapolis up the side of Mt. Gerizim to Tell er-Ras. In 1968, Bull excavated eighty of the 7.50-meter-wide stairway steps, some cut into bedrock, some arranged in flights of five steps or more between landings, some with evidence of marble facing, and all on a line from a point beside the mosque, Rijal el-ʿAmud, at the foot of Mt. Gerizim, to the temple at Tell er-Ras.

In the second and third centuries CE, the reverse of coins struck at the Neapolis mint exhibited the likeness of a tetrastyle, peripteral temple at the top of a mountain peak. A stairway ran from a colonnade at the mountain's base up the mountain side to the temple on top (Hill, 1914, pp. 48–50, pls. 5–7). The earliest and most detailed coins were issued under Antoninus Pius (138–161 CE) and the last and least detailed, under Volusianus (251–253 CE). Marinus of Neapolis (fl. 440 CE) indicated that the emperor Hadrian had built a temple to Zeus Hypsistos on Mt. Gerizim (Photius, *Bibliotheca* 242.348B. 18–20). A stairway of three hundred steps *(gradii)* on the side of Mt. Gerizim was reported by the Bordeaux Pilgrim (fl. 333 CE; *Itineraarium Burdigalense* 587.3), but Epiphanius (315–403 CE; *Libri de XII Gemmis* 258) stated that the stairway contained more than fifteen hundred steps, a number confirmed by Procopius of Gaza (d. 440 CE; *Commentarii in Deuteronomium* 440). The discrepancy in the number of steps reported in the stairway was due to the fact that broad steps or platforms were discovered at intervals of five steps or more in the line of steps up the side of the mountain. The Bordeaux Pilgrim counted the platforms *(gradii)* while Epiphanius and Procopius knew or counted the individual steps.

The temple was modified in the third century when six vaulted cisterns were built in front of and against the north platform wall necessitating a new approach to the temple. In the fourth century, earthquakes collapsed the vaulted cisterns, filling the cisterns with voussoir and architectural elements from the temple. The latest coins recovered from the sealed silt layers of the cisterns were those of Julian II (360–363 CE).

In 1966, beneath the foundations of the Zeus temple, Bull excavated a second major structure, building B, 20.94 m long north–south × 20.04 m wide and 8.50 m high. Stratigraphic excavation disclosed that building B was founded on the leveled bedrock of Tell er-Ras at 819 m above sea level and constructed of at least eighteen courses of unhewn limestone slab taken from the local geological bedding planes and laid in without mortar. No construction was found internal to building B. Its geometric form was roughly that of a half cube with approximately 4,000 cubic m of limestone slab laid in courses with obvious care and precision. It was first assumed that building B was a foundation built by the Roman builders of the Zeus temple, but after further excavation, it was discovered that building B stood in the center of a rectangular courtyard of stone walls 60 m long × 40 m wide and 1.50 m thick made of unhewn stone and without mortar. The 7-meter-high courtyard of walls rested on leveled bedrock and a gateway 7.50 m wide was found at the center of the north courtyard wall. The 2-meter-wide walls of the Zeus temple platform, built of ashlar and mortar, were constructed against the standing 1.50-meter-wide unhewn stone walls that formed the building B courtyard. After building B at the center of the double-walled courtyard was stabilized with revetments of rubble and cement, the courtyard was filled earth and stone to form the massive platform on which the Zeus temple stood. Thick layers of sterile white *huwwar* were found in trenches dug against the sides of building B. The tip lines of the *huwwar* visible in the balks of the trenches beside building B have an angle of repose for the dumped *huwwar* that indicates it was dumpted from a height two or more meters higher than the discovered hight of building B. Prior to building A, building B and at least part of its courtyard had been covered by layers of sterile earth that contained no dating material. Below the *huwwar,* earth, rubble, and cement makeup of the temple platform and at the bottom of the walls in the northeast corner of the building B courtyard, pottery dating from the third and second centuries BCE was found. Also in the lowest silt layers of a rock-hewn cistern found beside the steps of the temple platform, water vessels of the third century BCE were recovered.

From 1983 to 1988 Yitzhak Magen of the Israel Department of Antiquities uncovered additional stairways and extensive Hellenistic remains on Mt. Gerizim, including Lozeh.

The identification of building A with the Zeus temple at Tell er-Ras seems assured. The identification of building B is less clearly understood. The fact that a massive, carefully fashioned structure of unhewn stones was constructed on the leveled bedrock of Mt. Gerizim and surrounded by a courtyard of walls built of unhewn stone indicates that a major building complex predated the Zeus temple at Tell er-Ras. Limited ceramic evidence indicates that the building B complex was standing in the third century BCE. The massive size of the building B complex, its location directly above the ancient Samaritan capital city of Shechem, and its third-century BCE date suggest it was part of the Samaritan temple that Josephus (*Antiq.* 11.302ff., 13.255ff.; *War* 1.62ff.) notes was built on Mt. Gerizim and modeled after the Jerusalem temple.

BIBLIOGRAPHY

The Site

Adler, Elkan N., and M. Seligsohn. "Une nouvelle chronique Samaratine." *Revue des Études Juives* 30 (1902): 188–222.

Anderson, Robert T. "Mount Gerizim: Naval of the World." *Biblical Archaeologist* 43 (1980): 217–221.

Bull, Robert J., and G. Ernest Wright. "Newly Discovered Temples on Mt. Gerizim in Jordan." *Harvard Theological Review* 58 (1965): 234–237.

Bull, Robert J. "A Preliminary Excavation of an Hadrianic Temple at Tell er Ras on Mount Gerizim." *American Journal of Archaeology* 71 (1967): 387–393.

Bull, Robert J. "The Excavation of Tell er-Ras on Mt. Gerizim." *Biblical Archaeologist* 31 (1968): 58–72.

Bull, Robert J., and Edward F. Campbell. "The Sixth Campaign at Balatah (Shechem)." *Bulletin of the American Schools of Oriental Research,* no. 190 (1968): 2–41.

Bull, Robert J. "Towards a 'Corpus Inscriptionum Latinarum Britannicarum in Palentina.'" *Palestine Exploration Quarterly* 102 (1970): 108–110.

Bull, Robert J. "An Archaeological Context for Understanding John 4:20." *Biblical Archaeologist* 38 (1975): 54–59.

Bull, Robert J. "A Tripartite Sundial from Tell Er Ras on Mt. Gerizim." *Bulletin of the American Schools of Oriental Research,* no. 219 (1975): 29–37.

Bull, Robert J. "Tel er-Ras (Mount Gerizim)." In *Encyclopedia of Archaeological Excavations in the Holy Land,* vol. 4, pp. 1015–1022. Englewood Cliffs, N.J., 1978.

Conder, Claude R., and H. H. Kitchener. *The Survey of Western Pal-*

estine: Memoirs of the Topography, Orography, Hydrography, and Archaeology, vol. 2, *Samaria.* London, 1882.

Hill, George F. *Catalogue of the Greek Coins in Palestine.* London, 1914. See pages 25–34, plates 5–7, 39.

Kee, Howard C. "Tell-er-Ras and the Samaritan Temple." *New Testament Studies* 13 (1967): 401–402.

Magen, Yitzhak. "Mount Gerizim, a Temple City" (in Hebrew). *Qadmoniot* 23 (1990): 70–96.

Magen, Yitzhak. "Gerizim, Mount." In *The New Encyclopedia of Archaeological Excavations in the Holy Land,* vol. 2, pp. 484–492. Jerusalem and New York, 1993.

Schneider, A. M. "Römische und byzantinische Bauten auf dem Garizim." *Zeitschrift des Deutschen Palästina-Vereins* 68 (1951): 211–234.

Wilson, Charles W. "Ebal and Gerizim." *Palestine Exploration Fund* 2 (1873): 66–71.

The Samaritans

Dexinger, Ferdinand, and Reinhard Pummer, eds. *Die Samaritaner.* Darmstadt, 1992.

Montgomery, James A. *The Samaritans: The Earliest Jewish Sect.* Philadelphia, 1907.

Pummer, Reinhard. *The Samaritans.* Iconography of Religions 23, 5. Leiden, 1987.

Purvis, James D. *The Samaritan Pentateuch and the Origin of the Samaritan Sect.* Harvard Semitic Monographs, 2. Cambridge, Mass., 1968.

Rowley, Harold Henry. *Men of God: Studies in Old Testament History and Prophecy.* London, 1963.

ROBERT J. BULL

RA'S AL-HADD, site located in the Sultanate of Oman (22°31′ N, 50°47′ E), at the point where the Arabian coast turns from running southeastward to running southwestward and the Gulf of Oman joins the Arabian Sea. The Arabic name, meaning "headland of the limit," corresponding roughly to "Land's End," describes its situation and has been used since before AD 1500 when the Portuguese recorded the toponym.

A small modern town stands on the neck of a sandy promontory which encloses a shallow lagoon, with low hills behind. Though strategically placed, the region has little fresh water, but marine resources are abundant. Archaeological remains, scattered at different sites (designated HD 1–HD 27) across some 1,000 ha (2,470 acres) and representing most periods from modern times back to 4000–3000 BC or earlier, document substantial continuity in lifestyle coupled with long-distance trading relations overseas. Remains of fish, shellfish, and turtles dominate the organic finds from excavation; there is also evidence for dates, today grown in inland oases with which there are close traditional links. Donald Whitcomb (1975) first drew attention to the Islamic remains. Bronze Age material was identified in 1986 by Julian Reade, who directed excavations during 1988, 1989, and 1992. The site complements nearby Ra's al-Junayz.

The earliest site identified, HD 2, is a midden producing small flints and molluscs, to be dated before 3000; terebralia shells suggest the presence of a mangrove swamp in the lagoon. At HD 6, dating to about 3000–2500, there is evidence for the use of copper and of distinctive large flint tools, and for the manufacture of stone and shell ornaments; contemporary tombs at HD 10 are circular stone structures with corbelled roofs.

HD 1 (c. 2500–2000), has stone ovens (for fish preparation) and much cooper, including fishhooks and a bun ingot; there are a few bronze pieces. Pottery was introduced during the occupation of HD 1 and mainly comprises Mature Harappan types, including one inscribed with two Indus signs. Buildings of this phase have not been located. The mangroves were declining. An aceramic village at HD 18, beside the lagoon, with subrectangular stone house-footings, is tentatively dated about 2000–1500.

Early "Iron Age" tombs abound on the hills. Those excavated at HD 9, perhaps dated about 1000, are stone, roughly oblong in shape, often abutting on one another. Copper or bronze arrowheads and some pottery vessels recall Wadi Suq types. There are many beads, stone vessels, and scraps of copper or bronze bowls. No contemporary settlement has been identified, but a Late Iron Age village was established at HD 21 (perhaps c. 500 BC), significantly located on the hills out of sight of the sea and exploiting animal rather than mainly marine resources. The village comprises agglomerations of rounded rooms and yards, with stone footings to the walls. The pottery is mainly a very coarse gritty ware similar to that found at Samad (in central northern Oman).

Hellenistic-Sasanian settlement has not been securely identified, but traces of a well-built stone structure with rectangular walls suggest a strongpoint near the lagoon. Islamic occupation is widely attested, and the HD 2 area on the promontory is rich in sherds dating from before AD 1000 to recent times. Plain and glazed wares probably derive from Oman, the Gulf, Iran, India, and Pakistan; Chinese and African wares are common. Excavations at HD 4 exposed a building of coral blocks. There is much glass, and evidence exists for the manufacture of lapis lazuli and carnelian beads. An oyster midden extends beside the sea.

The modern town has developed around a castle, which may have been built within a century of AD 1700, because no older traces were observed during restoration work about 1990.

BIBLIOGRAPHY

Reade, Julian E. "Excavations at Ra's al-Hadd, 1988: Preliminary Report." In *The Joint Hadd Project,* edited by Serge Cleuziou et al., pp. 33–43. Rome, 1990.

Whitcomb, Donald S. "The Archaeology of Oman: A Preliminary Discussion of the Islamic Periods." *Journal of Oman Studies* 1 (1975): 123–157.

JULIAN E. READE

RAS EN-NAQB, a commanding promontory, located near a village of the same name, in the mountainous region of southern Jordan (29°55′ N, 35°30′ E). A long-term, ongoing research program, directed by Donald O. Henry and sponsored by the University of Tulsa, the American Center of Oriental Research, and the Jordanian Department of Antiquities was initiated in the vicinity of Ras en-Naqb in 1977. By 1994, exploration of approximately 32 square kilometers had resulted in the discovery of more than 130 prehistoric sites with occupations spanning the late Lower Paleolithic through the Chalcolithic periods. The research focused on understanding the prehistoric human ecology and the evolution of human adaptation in the area.

Excavation exposed Middle Paleolithic, Upper Paleolithic, Epipaleolithic, Neolithic, and Chalcolithic occupations at twenty-nine sites. Paleoenvironmental studies of pollen, geological, and faunal evidence recovered by excavation generated paleoclimatic reconstructions covering much of the last sixty-five thousand years.

Strategy of Transhumance. Perhaps the most significant result of the research was establishing the length of time (on the order of sixty-five thousand years) the inhabitants of the region had followed a transhumance strategy. To utilize transhumance, the area's prehistoric groups followed an annual settlement schedule that involved seasonal shifts to different elevational belts, ranging from 800 to 1,700 m above mean sea level. Such a settlement schedule enabled them to exploit area-specific resources seasonally. This meant occupying an elevation when it offered optimum creature comforts.

Transhumance is typically associated with pastoral nomads, such as the modern bedouin. Few research efforts have yielded the quantity and diversity of evidence confirming the strategy for such a temporal sweep during the Paleolithic era, however. Comparing sites by elevation revealed a time-transgressive pattern. This pattern showed an asymmetry within several data sets (e.g., site area, thickness of cultural deposit, artifact density, artifact inventory) that was linked to the different elevational belts. Pleistocene settlement remains (Middle, Upper, and Early Epipaleolithic periods) in the high-elevation belts reflected short-term, warm-season camps. Pleistocene on the low-elevation belts revealed apparent settlement remains from long-term winter camps. In contrast, sites occupied at the end of the Pleistocene and Holocene (Natufian and Chalcolithic) reversed the pattern: sites indicating long-term winter camps were found in the high-elevation belts, whereas small, ephemeral camps were found in the lowlands.

Lower Paleolithic. Wadi Qalkha, identified as a Late Acheulean site, exhibited an artifact-bearing horizon near the top of a 30-meter-thick section of alluvial silts and sands. A geomorphic study placed the alluvial fill in the last interglacial period. The lithic assemblage is composed mainly of finely fashioned ovate handaxes.

Middle Paleolithic. Tor Faraj and Tor Sabiha are rockshelters with extensive Levantine Mousterian deposits. The differences in natural setting and artifacts between the two sites suggest that they represent winter (Tor Faraj) and summer (Tor Sabiha) segments of an annual cycle of transhumance. The artifact assemblages are dominated by Levallois points. Microscopic analysis suggests that most of the points were hafted and used for various tasks, ranging from cutting to scraping and to use as projectiles. Amino acid racemization and uranium series dates indicate that the occupations were contemporaneous, archaeologically, dating to about 62,000 BP. Examination of the pollen, sediments, and animal remains from the deposits points to very dry climatic conditions during the time of occupation.

Upper Paleolithic. The rockshelter sites of Tor Hamar, Tor Aeid, and Jebel Ḥumeima contain the most important of several Upper Paleolithic occupations. Based on artifact analysis, these occupations include both Ahmarian and Levantine Aurignacian industries. The Ahmarian horizons at Tor Hamar and Tor Aeid most likely date from about 38,000 to 29,000 BP, whereas Jebel Ḥumeima's Levantine Aurignacian occupation may be somewhat younger. The Upper Paleolithic deposits, formed of pinkish silt, yielded pollen that traced a succession from slightly humid conditions (represented by trees and grasses) to drier conditions (defined by desert shrubs).

Epipaleolithic. About 40 percent of the sites encompassed by this research belong to the Epipaleolithic, an interval of considerable cultural-historic complexity. Five cultural-historic complexes (Qalkhan, Kebaran, Geometric Kebaran, Mushabian, and Natufian) were identified, with the Qalkhan being newly defined and unique to southern Jordan. At a more specific taxonomic level, new industries were identified within the Kebaran (Early Hamran), Geometric Kebaran (Middle, Late, and Final Hamaran), and the Mushabian (Madamaghan).

1. *Qalkhan occupations.* Characterized by a large triangular point type, Qalkhan occupations have been recovered from several sites, including Tor Hamar. The industry has been fixed stratigraphically between Upper Paleolithic and Kebaran horizons at the site of Wadi Aoud, in area B (although without radiometric dates).

2. *Kebaran complex occupations.* Represented by Early Hamran assemblages, Kebaran occupations were identified in the stratified deposits of several rockshelter sites, of which the most important are Jebel Hamra and Jebel Misraq. Dated to between 18,000 and 15,000 BP, these occupations were linked to quite moist conditions, as indicated by high frequencies of tree (especially oak) and grass pollen.

3. *Geometric Kebaran complex occupations.* Represented by Middle, Late, and Final Hamran assemblages, Geometric Kebaran occupations occur within several stratified rockshelter deposits adjacent to Pleistocene lake beds in the lowlands, as well as in open-air sites in the uplands. The most important of these include Jebel Hamra, Qa Salab, and el-Quweira. The cultural-stratigraphic sequences tracing the Late and Final Hamran at Qa Salab and el-Quweira are of special significance: they show a progressive change in di-

agnostic microlithic artifacts—lunates replace trapeze-rectangles—that suggests an age immediately preceding the Natufian (i.e., 14,000–13,000 BP). Pollen evidence indicates that dry conditions during the Middle Hamran (c. 15,000–14,000 BP) were followed by warm, moist conditions during the Late Hamran—which, in turn, were replaced by dry, cold conditions during the Final Hamran.

4. *Natufian Complex.* Represented by early (Wadi Judaiyid) and late (Wadi Aoud, area A) phases of occupations, the Natufian deposit at Wadi Judaiyid yielded rich flint and bone assemblages radiometrically dated to about 12,500 BP. It is one of the earliest Natufian sites yet recorded. The presence of wild sheep remains in the deposit is also noteworthy, for this significantly extends the species's known biogeographic range. Paleoenvironmental data point to an initial extension of the dry, cold conditions of the Final Hamran followed by climatic amelioration and a return to drier conditions during the Late Natufian (after c. 11,000 BP).

Neolithic and Chalcolithic. The Neolithic is poorly represented in the research area, but Chalcolithic sites dating to about 6,000 BP are common. These sites reflect an economy based on pastoral nomadism following a transhumant settlement strategy. Material culture inventories include a wide range of ground stone, worked bone, pottery, and a microlithic flint industry. Stone-lined pit houses and stone corrals occur at several sites, the most important of which include Jebel el-Jill and Jebel Queisa.

BIBLIOGRAPHY

Henry, Donald O. "The Prehistory of Southern Jordan and Relationships with the Levant." *Journal of Field Archaeology* 9 (1982): 417–444. Summary of the initial stages of research and a description of the finds for each of the major Paleolithic periods, with comparisons to those in the rest of the Levant.

Henry, Donald O., and Priscilla F. Turnbull. "Archaeological and Faunal Evidence from Natufian and Timnian Sites in Southern Jordan." *Bulletin of the American Schools of Oriental Research,* no. 257 (1985): 45–64. Site reports for Jebel el-Jill, Jebel Queisa (Chalcolithic-Timnian), and Wadi Judaiyid (Natufian).

Henry, Donald O. "Topographic Influences on Epipaleolithic Land-Use Patterns in Southern Jordan." In *Studies in the History and Archaeology of Jordan,* vol. 3, edited by Adnan Hadidi, pp. 21–27. Amman, 1987. A pattern of transhumance reconstructed for the Epipaleolithic by comparing cultural and natural data linked to numerous sites.

Henry, Donald O. "Summary of Prehistoric and Paleoenvironmental Research in the Northern Hisma." In *The Prehistory of Jordan,* edited by Andrew N. Garrard and Hans G. Gebel, pp. 7–37. British Archaeological Reports, International Series, no. 396.1. Oxford, 1988. Detailed description of the cultural-historical units, diagnostic artifacts, chronology, and paleoenvironmental reconstructions.

Henry, Donald O., and Andrew N. Garrard. "Tor Hamar: An Epipaleolithic Rockshelter in Southern Jordan." *Palestine Exploration Quarterly* 120 (1988): 1–25. Detailed description of the newly found Mushabian presence in southern Jordan; includes a discussion of its relationship to occupations in the Negev and Sinai deserts and early evidence for the use of the bow and arrow.

Henry, Donald O. "The Epipaleolithic Sequence within the Ras En Naqb-El Quweira Area, Southern Jordan." *Paléorient* 14.2 (1988): 245–256. Paris, 1990. In-depth discussion of the complex and richly diverse Epipaleolithic period, along with an organizational framework for the various archaeological units.

Henry, Donald O. "Transhumance during the Late Levantine Mousterian." In *The Middle Paleolithic: Adaptation, Behavior, and Variability,* edited by Harold L. Dibble and Paul Mellars, pp. 143–162. Philadelphia, 1992. Compares the Middle Paleolithic sites of Tor Faraj and Tor Sabiha, emphasizing reconstructing settlement-procurement strategies and hominid cognitive development.

Henry, Donald O. "Prehistoric Cultural Ecology in Southern Jordan." *Science* 265 (1994): 336–341. Stresses the importance of seasonal shifts in surface water and temperature in defining prehistoric settlement patterns.

Henry, Donald O. *Prehistoric Cultural Ecology and Evolution: Insights from Southern Jordan.* New York, 1995. Detailed overview of the research in the area conducted between 1979 and 1988.

DONALD O. HENRY

RAS IBN HANI (Ar., "cape of Ibn Hani"), site extending 2.5 km (1.5 mi.) into the Mediterranean Sea, 8 km (5 mi.) north of old Latakia (35°35′ N, 35°44′ E). Ras Shamra (ancient Ugarit) is 4.5 km (3 mi.) northeast, about 1.6 km (1 mi.) inland, and Cyprus is 100 km (62 mi.) across the sea. The cape is 0.4–1 km wide; its rocky western part, originally an island, was eventually connected with the coast by sand deposits. Two bays offer good harbors for small ships.

Hellenistic and Roman remains were noted as early as the eighteenth century. They include (Hellenistic?) moles in both bays and a large, built Late Hellenistic tomb with loculi. An archaeological mound was reported by Gabriel Saadé (1964). A Late Bronze Age tomb was accidentally discovered and subsequently excavated by the Directorate General of Antiquities of Syria in 1973. A joint Syrian and French expedition, headed by Adnan Bounni and Jacques Lagarce, with Elisabeth Lagarce and Nassib Saliby, began work in 1975, holding its twentieth season in 1995.

Excavation began on the southern slope and summit of the tell (9.40 m above sea level). The examination of walls in areas where modern buildings were under construction led to the discovery of a Hellenistic city wall (third century BCE). In 1977, work was initiated near the Bronze Age tomb, close to the northern coast of the cape; excavation has gradually been concentrated on that area.

In the thirteenth century BCE, the last century of the Late Bronze Age, a complex of palaces and residencies was built by a king of Ugarit. [*See* Ugarit.] The site offered excellent possibilities for controlling seaborne traffic. Two main areas have been excavated. The Southern Palace covers more than 5,000 sq m. [*See* Palace.] Its construction was an enormous undertaking: sand was dumped 4 m high on the natural rock, between the 1.80-meter-thick walls, to raise the levels of the floors. Despite the scarcity of finds, such a building could only be interpreted as a royal palace. On its northeastern limit, it is maintained and protected by an embankment faced with an ashlar wall.

The Northern Palace covers about 2,000 sq m. Its unusual

plan allows only one obligatory way to circulate through the entire building (i.e., having entered a group of rooms, one must return to the main passage in order to reach any other group). Staircases lead to the upper story(ies). Each group of rooms around the main, paved courtyard seems to have a specific function: an office and archive on the east; a possible throne room with a two-columned porch on the north; and two areas devoted to metallurgical activities on the west. The eastern part of the palace also produced an administrative archive. To the east, another building, considered a satellite of the administrative building, held a bread-making workshop with two large ovens *(tannurs)* and a toilet provided with a seat.

The finds were few, but significant, and include two groups of tablets. The first group, mostly in Ugaritic, sometimes in Akkadian, illustrates nearly all types of texts attested in Ugarit, except contracts: letters to and from the king, the queen mother and officials; ritual, magical, and lexical texts; and administrative documents. [*See* Ugaritic; Akkadian.] They shed considerable light on Ugaritic culture and show that the Northern Palace belonged to a queen of Ugarit, perhaps to King ʿAmmishtamru II's (c. 1260–1230 BCE) mother. According to one of the letters, the city could have been called Biruti. The second group of texts is exclusively administrative: receipts and memoranda, "banking" practices apparently used a silver standard. A clay sealing bears ʿAmmishtamru II's name.

The ashlar-built chamber tomb matches the aristocratic sepulchers of Ugarit. A stepped dromos leads to a rectangular corbeled chamber. [*See* Tombs.] At the farther end is a closet, connected with the chamber only through a narrow hole. The purpose of this annex is not clear. Looted in antiquity, the tomb still contained local, Cypriot, and Aegean material of the fourteenth–thirteenth centuries BCE.

Workshops were numerous in this palace. One was devoted to cutting and polishing hard stone with emery. In the metal workshops, the main find was a mold for "oxhide" copper ingots—a large and thick slab of beach sandstone with the shape of the ingot hollowed in its upper surface. Based on analysis, the copper came from Cyprus. Oxhide ingots (rectangular with concave sides and elongated corners) have been recovered by the hundreds in the Mediterranean area. Copper was one of the staple commodities of LB trade, and considerable quantities were imported by Egypt from Alashiya (Cyprus?), Syria, and the Aegean. The Ras Ibn Hani mold, the only one ever found, is a document of utmost significance for the technology of ingots and the implication of Ugarit in the metal trade.

West of the Northern Palace another, similar building held two large kilns, one built into a platform (2 × 2 m) accessible via four steps. The palace had been nearly deserted before it was destroyed by heavy fire, early in the twelfth century BCE apparently by "Sea Peoples" whose precise nature is a debated question. On a part of the ruins that was leveled, small dwellings were built bordered by perpendicular streets. The painted pottery recovered, of types common on Cyprus and in Palestine in the twelfth century, are considered to be the last development of Mycenaean pottery, suggesting that this settlement was founded by the very sackers of the Ugaritic city.

Destructions and rebuilding phases alternate during the twelfth–tenth centuries BCE. New types of pottery show connections with Cyprus, but also with Hama on the Orontes River. With al-Mina, Ras el-Bassit, and Tell Sukas, Ras Ibn Hani is one of very few sites in the area containing information about this period, the Early Iron Age. [*See* Hama; Bassit; Sukas, Tell.] No architectural remains were recovered for the remainder of the Iron Age, but settlement was uninterrupted until the early fifth century BCE at least.

In the Hellenistic period, a fortified city, nearly 1 km long, was built on the cape. A list of mercenaries and Ptolemaic coins point to the Lagid king of Egypt, Ptolemy III (246–221 BCE), as its founder. In 246, he conquered Seleucia and Antioch. [*See* Seleucia; Antioch on Orontes.] The city at Ras Ibn Hani was probably meant to secure these new possessions against an attack from Seleucid Laodicea (Latakia). It demonstrates that the king's domination reached much farther south than had been thought. The city wall is rare testimony of the Hellenistic art of fortification in this region. Mainly the wall's eastern part has been studied by Pierre Leriche, a member of the Ras Ibn Hani expedition. It comprised an inner wall of large blocks, with massive foundations supporting coffered masonry, an outer wall of boulders, and a fosse. Alternately square and U-shaped towers protected the curtain and a gate opened into a circular area surrounded by columns.

Ras Ibn Hani probably returned to Seleucid hegemony under Antiochus III, in about 200 BCE. Life went on eagerly during the second and part of the first centuries BCE, as demonstrated by stamped amphora handles, bronze coins, clay figurines, and rich pottery finds. At some time in the first century BCE, a stronghold was built, reusing part of the ancient city wall. It was destroyed violently, perhaps the first decades of the Roman conquest of Syria, around 30 BCE. The site experienced a final revival from the time of Constantine (fourth century CE) to Justinianus or to the early seventh century CE. Remains of large houses, fishing and agricultural tools, small bronze coins, and a necropolis illustrate the life of a medium-sized city. The diversity of the pottery, with many imports, is nevertheless typical of the prosperity and overseas connections of this coastal area.

BIBLIOGRAPHY

Preliminary reports on the results of the excavations and on the texts have been published by members of the excavation team in French in the journal *Syria:* 53 (1976): 233–279; 55 (1978): 233–325; 56 (1979): 217–234; 57 (1980): 343–373; 58 (1981): 215–299; and 61 (1984): 1–23, 153–179; and in *Comptes rendus de l'Académie des inscriptions et belles-*

lettres (1978): 45–65; (1979): 277–294; (1980): 10–34; (1983): 249–290; (1984): 398–438; and (1987): 274–301; and in Arabic in *Annales archéologiques arabes syriennes* (1976): 27–64; (1977–1978): 23–84; and (1983): 31–59. Additional publications include the following:

Dussaud, René. *Topographie historique de la Syrie antique et médiévale.* Paris, 1927. The first mention of Ras Ibn Hani in archaeological literature appears on pages 416–417.

Lagarce, Jacques, and Elisabeth Lagarce. *Ras Ibn Hani. Archéologie et histoire.* Damascus, 1987. Brief and synthetic presentation of the site, primarily intended for visitors. With a similar version in Arabic by Adnan Bounni and Nassib Saliby.

Lagarce, Jacques, and Elisabeth Lagarce. "Ras Ibn Hani au Bronze récent. Recherches et réflexions en cours." In *Acts of the Colloquium "Le pays d'Ougarit autour de 1200 av. J.-C."* Paris, 1995.

Saadé, Gabriel. *Histoire de Lattaquié.* Vol. 1, *Ramitha, problèmes des origines.* Damascus, 1964. First mention and cursory description of the archaeological mound; see page 94, fig. 11, and pages 98–99.

ADNAN BOUNNI and JACQUES LAGARCE

RAS SHAMRA. *See* Ugarit.

RAWLINSON, HENRY CRESWICKE (1810–1895), known as the "father of cuneiform." Rawlinson was born in Oxfordshire, England. While an officer cadet in the East India Company in 1827, he demonstrated a remarkable ability for languages, mastering five Oriental languages in a very short time. In 1833, he was one of a party of British officers sent to reorganize the shah of Persia's army. Posted to Kurdistan, he decided to attempt a decipherment of King Darius's trilingual inscription on the Great Rock of Bisitun, commemorating that monarch's victory over five rebel chiefs. Over the next decade, Rawlinson copied and deciphered the Old Persian, Elamite, and Babylonian texts, establishing that Babylonian was a Semitic, polyphonic language.

Rawlinson shares credit for the decipherment of cuneiform with the Irish cleric Edward Hincks and the Frenchman Jules Oppert, who worked on vowels, syllables, and word values. He was appointed British consul in Baghdad in 1843. This gave him ample time to work on the cuneiform tablets Austen Henry Layard found at Nimrud and Nineveh, which he identified as Assyrian cities. In 1850–1851, Layard unearthed the royal archives of the Assyrian monarch Ashurbanipal at Nineveh. It was Rawlinson who realized the crucial importance of this unique library with its grammars and rich archives and arranged for their study in the British Museum. Rawlinson excavated on his own account only once, at the ziggurat of Borsippa, near Babylon, in southern Mesopotamia, in 1853, where he unearthed the commemorative cylinders that recorded how Nebuchadnezzar, king of Babylon had rebuilt and repaired the temple. He resigned from the East India Company in the same year. In later life, Rawlinson continued in cuneiform research. He fostered long-term research on the Ashurbanipal collection, which yielded the celebrated Deluge tablets, deciphered by one of his protégés, George Adam Smith, in 1872.

[*See also* Bisitun; Cuneiform; Nimrud; Nineveh; *and the biographies of Layard and Smith.*]

BIBLIOGRAPHY

Lloyd, Seton. *Foundations in the Dust: The Story of Mesopotamian Exploration.* Rev. and enl. ed. London, 1980. General history of Mesopotamian archaeology that offers an assessment of Rawlinson's work.

Rawlinson, George. *Memoir of Major-General Sir Henry Creswicke Rawlinson.* London, 1898. Hagiographic biography of Rawlinson by his brother; useful as a narrative summary of his life.

Rawlinson, Henry Creswicke. *The Persian Cuneiform Inscription at Behistun Decyphered and Translated.* London, 1846. Rawlinson's description of his decipherment of Behistun (Bisitun).

Rawlinson, Henry Creswicke. *A Commentary on the Cuneiform Inscriptions of Babylonia and Assyria.* London, 1850. The first description of the Assyrians from cuneiform sources.

BRIAN FAGAN

RECONNAISSANCE, ARCHAEOLOGICAL. *See* Survey, Archaeological.

RECORDING TECHNIQUES. Archaeologists document the process of removing debris and successive occupational remains in a controlled excavation by means of recording techniques. By its nature, archaeological excavation is a nonrepeatable experiment, destroying its evidence as it produces data. Any information not recorded accurately and fully when a site is being excavated is knowledge lost forever. The goal of archaeological recording is to document fully how and where each element encountered in a site's systematic excavation was found and recovered. The degree of detail provided in such an effort is determined by an excavation project's research design.

Excavations differ in how they are organized, but generally a series of 5-×-5-meter squares in the same portion of a site are grouped into a "field" or "area." Each square is established by a project surveyor or an architect, who maintains a large-scale plan of the site grid and the specific location of each excavation area in relation to the grid. [*See* Grid Plan.] A staff member is assigned to supervise each area and is responsible for ensuring that all excavation activities at the location are comprehensively documented. This documentation is in both descriptive and graphic form and is entered in a notebook that contains the excavation season's records for the area.

Daily activity in each square is recorded in a running commentary that creates a daily log of excavation. Details such as the changing of loci, brief descriptive assessments of characteristics of new loci, notable finds, or questions regarding occupational activities are recorded, as are lists of recovered materials sent to laboratories for further analysis. For each day, a precisely scaled top plan of the excavation unit is prepared, showing not only new architectural elements encountered in excavation but also, by shading or coloration, indicating where various soil loci or artifact concentrations were located. The end-of-day elevations of each locus, which chart the daily progress of revealing successive cultural deposits, are also a normal part of field recording. As the excavation of an area progresses, informal photographs of significant features often are taken to allow for the clear identification of loci and related features. [*See* Photography, *article on* Photography of Fieldwork and Artifacts.] Many excavations use instant photographs for this purpose, with the resulting prints being glued into the area supervisor's notebook.

Because working in the field presents many possibilities for overlooking essential information, most excavations use a variety of supplementary recording forms in an attempt to ensure complete documentation. The registration and description of each soil locus and each architectural unit (e.g., walls, doorways, cisterns) and special features such as burials are recorded on special forms usually maintained by the area supervisor.

As artifacts are uncovered in the field, the use of field tags becomes an integral part of the recording system. Most tagging systems utilize some form of reference to the specific excavation location, the soil locus from which the artifact came, and some designation of the class of the artifact (metal, glass, ceramic) that will guide the registrar in further processing the item and the project expert in evaluating it.

Once an occupational level is fully excavated, the results are recorded by some combination of architect's drawing, formal photography, and section drawing. [*See* Architectural Drafting and Drawing.] The excavation architect prepares a precisely scaled drawing of the full excavation area, showing all relevant features. The excavation photographer takes several carefully planned photographs of the area, seeking to show as completely as possible the relationships of the various features to each other. The area supervisor prepares a section drawing showing at least one face of the balk in the excavation area in which all soil layers will have been distinguished and labeled. [*See* Balk.] These primary recording elements are frequently among the more important of the published forms of excavation documentation.

Once the excavation of an area has been completed, the supervisor is responsible for writing up a final report, summarizing the main periods, or phases, of occupation and connecting the area's various features to them. While much of the excavation's recordkeeping up to this point has been descriptive, the area report is interpretive, correlating soil loci and architectural elements into a coherent picture of human activity. This final area report becomes part of the area notebook and of the permanent record of the excavation in an area. Other records are usually inserted in the notebook as well: field reports of ceramic dating and identification, preliminary coin reports, and flora and fauna reports.

While every excavator strives to maintain a comprehensive documentation of an excavation, there are always conditions that call for a balance between recording the detail of every facet of excavation and the practical limitations of fieldwork. Each excavator is confronted with the need to determine which information is of such central importance that time and money should be allocated for its retrieval and recording. These decisions are made on the basis of the project's research design, which not only should address the general goals of the excavation but also should include some consideration of the analytical processes and recording techniques to be used to meet those goals. Collecting and recording vast amounts of information about issues that are of limited analytical value may only complicate the excavation process and the eventual publication of its research results.

The development of increasingly computerized fieldwork has meant significant time saving for archaeological recording. Laser transits generate digitalized data that can be readily converted into a variety of renderings, making it possible to produce top plans of excavation areas with greater accuracy and speed. The use of digitalizing imaging equipment, still in its infancy in archaeological fieldwork, may enable archaeologists to produce images of an excavation's progress that can be further enhanced to show greater or fewer details, in ways that are impossible with conventional instant photography. Establishing local computer networks on a site now allows field excavators instant access to the results of specialized analyses of materials from across the site; as a consequence, excavation techniques or sampling strategies can be adjusted to the data flow. As more powerful portable computer equipment becomes available to excavation projects, field recording will be the beneficiary.

[*See also* Computer Recording, Analysis, and Interpretation; Excavation Tools; *and* Excavation Strategy.]

BIBLIOGRAPHY

Blakely, Jeffrey A., and Lawrence E. Toombs. *The Tell el-Hesi Field Manual.* Joint Archaeological Expedition to Tell el-Hesi, vol. 1. Winona Lake, Ind., 1980. Very complete assessment of the goals and processes of field recording, including many forms and plans used in the excavation of Tell el-Hesi (see pp. 28–59).

Dever, William G., and H. Darrell Lance, eds. *A Manual of Field Excavation: Handbook for Field Archaeologists.* Cincinnati, 1978. Comprehensive description with examples of the actual system used for field recording during the ASOR excavations at Gezer in the 1970s (see pp. 74–97). Most contemporary excavations in the Near East use some variation of this same system.

Dibble, Harold L., and Shannon P. McPherron. "On the Computerization of Archaeological Projects." *Journal of Field Archaeology* 15 (1988): 431–440. Report on the successful computerization of field recording for the excavation of a European prehistoric site. While written before the ready accessibility of powerful portable equipment, the authors' insights on the need to incorporate computer recording at the inception of a project's development are still valuable.

McMillon, Bill. *The Archaeology Handbook: A Field Manual and Resource Guide.* New York, 1991. Very readable work for a general North American audience, with a brief chapter devoted to the recording process (see pp. 102–110).

Meyers, Carol L., and Eric M. Meyers. "Recording and Reporting: New Challenges in Archaeological Research." *Eretz-Israel* 23 (1992): 80–86. Readable essay on the use of quantification in archaeology, its applicability to studies in the world of the Bible, and the potential that computerization may hold for enabling such studies to appear in published form with greater rapidity.

Raab, L. Mark. "Laboratory Automation: Computer-Linked Measurement Devices and Videomicroscopy." *Journal of Field Archaeology* 20 (1993): 219–224. Brief overview of the problems and one working solution to automating the measuration and registration of artifacts in the archaeological field lab.

Schiffer, Michael B., et al. "The Design of Archaeological Surveys." *World Archaeology* 10 (1978): 1–28. Excellent overview of the interrelated problems of research design, methodology, and recording of archaeological fieldwork.

KENNETH G. HOGLUND

REFERENCE WORKS. There are numerous reference works available to those studying archaeology and the ancient Near East. What follows is a corpus of the most significant recent volumes, with emphasis on English-language works. The first section covers the ancient Near Eastern world; the second section offers a selective survey of the New Testament (Greco-Roman) world, but does not repeat those works in the first part that cover both the Hebrew Bible and the New Testament. The annotations attempt to give the scope of each work along with its strengths and weaknesses.

Ancient Near Eastern World

Primary sources in translation

Charlesworth, James H., ed. *Old Testament Pseudepigrapha.* 2 vols. Garden City, N.Y., 1983–1985. Over fifty scholars introduce, translate, and annotate more than sixty ancient texts. Despite its unevenness, inconsistent inclusion criteria, and the need for a revision, this remains the definitive work.

Coogan, Michael David. *Stories from Ancient Canaan.* Philadelphia, 1978. Readable translations of four important myths from ancient Ugarit.

Lichtheim, Miriam, comp. *Ancient Egyptian Literature: A Book of Readings.* 3 vols. Berkeley, 1973–1980. [Annotation]

Matthews, Victor H., and D. C. Benjamin. *Old Testament Parallels: Laws and Stories from the Ancient Near East.* New York, 1991. Readable translations of ancient Near Eastern texts designed for students.

Pritchard, James B. *Ancient Near Eastern Texts.* 2d ed. Princeton, 1955. Abridged in *The Ancient Near East.* 2 vols. Princeton, 1958–1975. Literal and traditional translations of the more important texts of the ancient Near East, none too readable and somewhat dated.

Smelik, K. A. D. *Writings from Ancient Israel: A Handbook of Historical and Religious Documents.* Translated by Graham I. Davies. Louisville, 1991. Translations are limited to inscriptions from Israel and Jordan, dated to 1000–500 BCE, and selected for their historical and religious value.

Commentaries. There are many commentary series and numerous commentaries on individual books of both the Hebrew Bible and the New Testament. Most are devoted to biblical books rather than ancient Near Eastern literature, and the use of archaeological data varies widely. Two recent texts, both by Philip J. King, which set a superb standard for deploying archaeological information to illuminate the text are *Amos, Hosea, Micah: An Archaeological Commentary* (Philadelphia, 1988), and *Jeremiah: An Archaeological Companion* (Louisville, 1993).

Anchor Bible. Garden City, N.Y., 1964–. Multivolume series. Individual commentaries vary immensely in the use of archaeological information. Originally intended for the educated general reader, the series (nearly complete) has evolved into lengthy technical works for scholars.

Brown, Raymond E., Joseph A. Fitzmyer, and Roland E. Murphy, eds. *The New Jerome Biblical Commentary.* Englewood Cliffs, N.J., 1990. Revision of the 1968 edition, with significant additional material. The most comprehensive coverage of any one-volume Bible commentary available. Extensive topical articles do full justice to the archaeological data, with an extremely useful subject index for locating such information. However, the scholarly style and verse-by-verse format is tedious and difficult.

Bruce, Frederick F., ed. *The International Bible Commentary.* Grand Rapids, Mich., 1986. The best of the one-volume conservative commentaries, including topical articles on archaeology and the Bible. Makes good use of archaeological information, but needs a subject index.

Hermeneia. Philadelphia and Minneapolis, 1971–. Multivolume series. Lengthy technical commentaries on individual books, with varying use of archaeological information.

International Critical Commentary on the Holy Scriptures. Edinburgh, 1895–. Multivolume series. Standard technical coverage, but the archaeological information is too old to have value. The series is being extended and renewed, with new commentaries in preparation.

Mays, James Luther, ed. *Harper's Bible Commentary.* San Francisco, 1988. Mainline, up-to-date, readable scholarship with an emphasis on literary analysis and very limited use of archaeological information. Includes good maps and a map index, but no subject index.

Word Biblical Commentary. Waco, Texas, 1982–. Multivolume series, nearly complete. Fairly technical evangelical critical commentaries, with varying use of archaeological information.

Bible atlases. Bible atlases can be divided into reference and student works. Reference atlases generally feature extensive color photos and maps with textual commentary. Student atlases, less expensively produced are also more reasonably priced and often available in paperback editions.

Bahat, Dan, with Chaim T. Rubenstein. *The Illustrated Atlas of Jerusalem*. New York, 1990. Excellent maps and line drawings by Carta. Bahat is the official archaeologist for the city of Jerusalem. The text serves the general reader well, but specialists will find some issues addressed too briefly.

Baines, John, and Jaromir Málek. *Atlas of Ancient Egypt*. New York, 1980. Includes color photos and maps. The nontechnical text deals with individual sites, the cultural setting, and Egyptian society.

Beek, Martinus A. *Atlas of Mesopotamia*. Translated by D. R. Welsh. Edited by H. H. Rowley. London, 1962. Though somewhat dated, includes good maps and black-and-white photos.

Beitzel, Barry J. *The Moody Atlas of Bible Lands*. Chicago, 1985. Reference Bible atlas. Balanced, conservative treatment with excellent color maps designed to aid the colorblind. The geographical commentary is exhaustive and often too detailed for the general reader. Archaeological data is minimal but current. A gazetteer would be helpful.

Bimson, John J., and John P. Kane. *New Bible Atlas*. Wheaton, Ill., 1985. Student Bible atlas. Balanced conservative approach, organized according to archaeological periods, with extensive discussion of important sites and archaeological methods and limitations. The color maps and illustrations are well coordinated with the text. This is the best of the student atlases, along with *The Harper Concise Atlas of the Bible* (Pritchard 1991).

Freeman-Grenville, G. S. P. *Historical Atlas of the Middle East*. New York, 1993. Designed for the general reader, with an emphasis on the medieval and modern Middle East. Includes excellent maps by Carta; the brief commentary is accompanied by many smaller maps.

Gardner, Joseph, ed., with Harry Thomas Frank. *Reader's Digest Atlas of the Bible*. Pleasantville, N.Y., 1981. Reference Bible atlas. Mainstream approach, lavishly illustrated with excellent color maps. The accessible text, now somewhat dated, is augmented with an informative gazetteer. The volume would be more useful geographically if the maps were gridded and clear topographical distinctions shown.

Pritchard, James B., ed. *The Harper Atlas of the Bible*. San Francisco, 1987. Reference Bible atlas. Mainstream scholarship, visually beautiful, with excellent maps and illustrations. The large size and high production cost of the horizontal maps restrict use. A scripture column should be added in the site index and more focus placed on geographical features.

Pritchard, James B., gen. ed. *The Harper Concise Atlas of the Bible*. New York, 1991. Student Bible atlas. Mainstream approach. An abridged version of the *Harper Atlas of the Bible* (Bimson and Kane 1985), with some improvements and most of the maps retained. Selected commentary has been rewritten and improved.

Rainey, Anson F., et al., eds. *Macmillan Bible Atlas*. 3d ed. New York, 1993. Reference Bible atlas. Standard work, revised and improved.

Rasmussen, Carl G. *Zondervan NIV Atlas of the Bible*. Grand Rapids, Mich., 1989. Reference Bible atlas, notable for its visual quality, with excellent color maps (especially the block maps depicting physical features) and numerous illustrations. The conservative commentary is written for the general reader, with an extensive gazetteer. Occasionally the coordination between text and maps is not apparent.

Rogerson, Joseph W. *Atlas of the Bible*. New York, 1985. Reference Bible atlas. Mainstream commentary, with lavish use of color illustrations and maps. The regional approach to historical geography is helpful, but the maps should be more colorful and less cluttered. The gazetteer should be expanded.

Archaeological dictionaries. Dictionaries that cover archaeology broadly, for instance, *The Facts on File Dictionary of Archaeology* (New York, 1983) or *The Cambridge Encyclopedia of Archaeology* (New York, 1983), provide limited coverage of the ancient Near East. The reader would find much more information in the following works.

Ben-Tor, Amnon, ed. *The Archaeology of Ancient Israel*. New Haven, 1992. Eight Israeli scholars have collaborated to provide the full sequence of archaeological periods for sites in ancient Canaan from the Neolithic to Iron III. The volume is effectively illustrated with color and black-and-white photos, maps, and line drawings. Technological advances and cultural transitions are discussed with a minimum of technical language. Information on sites and artifacts provide both specific topical data as well as an excellent overview.

Blaiklock, Edward M., and R. K. Harrison, eds. *The New International Dictionary of Biblical Archaeology*. Grand Rapids, Mich., 1983. Twenty scholars cover a wide range of topics and provide brief bibliographies, although the articles are uneven in quality and becoming dated. Includes black-and-white photos and sixteen pages of color photos in the center of the volume.

Mazar, Amihai. *Archaeology of the Land of the Bible, 10,000–586 B.C.E.* New York, 1990. Advanced survey from an Israeli perspective.

Negev, Avraham, ed. *The Archaeological Encyclopedia of the Holy Land.* 3d ed. Englewood Cliffs, N.J., 1990. More than twenty American and Israeli archaeologists contribute about six hundred entries covering approximately ten millennia, from the earliest societies down to the Arab conquest. Includes a glossary of archaeological terms and about three hundred black-and-white photos, charts, and maps. Generally reliable and up to date, but coverage is more limited than Stern.

Pfeiffer, Charles F., ed. *The Biblical World: A Dictionary of Biblical Archaeology.* Grand Rapids, Mich., 1966. Pioneering effort when it appeared, but the archaeological information is badly dated now. Includes articles on texts (e.g., Sinuhe, Enuma Elish), people (e.g., Moab, Moabites), and sites (e.g., Masada).

Rast, Walter E. *Through the Ages in Palestinian Archaeology: An Introductory Handbook.* Philadelphia, 1992. A more popular survey than Mazar by an American archaeologist.

Sasson, Jack M., et al., eds. *Civilizations of the Ancient Near East.* 4 vols. New York, 1995. A welcome addition to the secondary literature, this work is a very useful and ambitious collection of essays on many aspects of the ancient Near East. It is particularly strong in areas of the history and literatures of the region but touches less systematically on the physical and cultural aspects of ancient society.

Stern, Ephraim, et al., eds. *The New Encyclopedia of Archaeological Excavations in the Holy Land.* 4 vols. Jerusalem and New York, 1993. Definitive work (revised and updated from the 1975–1977 edition), covering excavations in Israel and parts of Jordan, Syria, and the Sinai Peninsula. Features some four hundred articles by international scholars (primarily Israeli) on 420 sites as well as regions and topics (i.e., "Churches, Monasteries, and Synagogues"), with excellent bibliographies. Each site is discussed in detail, often by the original excavator.

Bible dictionaries

Achtemeier, Paul J., ed. *Harper's Bible Dictionary.* San Francisco, 1985. Balanced mainstream approach. Excellent presentation of up-to-date archaeological information written by many of the leading scholars in their fields. Bibliographic data is limited, even in the longest articles. Includes excellent color maps, numerous illustrations, and an index. Overall this is the best one-volume Bible dictionary, but it is becoming dated.

Bromiley, Geoffrey W., ed. *The International Standard Bible Encyclopedia.* 4 vols. Grand Rapids, Mich., 1979–1988. The definitive conservative work, almost completely revised from the 1915 and 1929 editions. Delays in publication have produced some unevenness. Generally balanced approach; many articles interact with the full range of critical scholarship.

Butler, Trent C., ed. *Holman Bible Dictionary.* Nashville, 1991. About 5,000 popularly written articles (without bibliographies), authored by 250 teachers and ministers, with lavish use of color illustrations and maps and fairly balanced use of archaeological information. Conservative approach. A good Bible dictionary for the general reader.

Buttrick, George A., ed. *The Interpreter's Dictionary of the Bible.* 4 vols. Nashville, 1962. Remained the definitive work until the publication of *The Anchor Bible Dictionary* (Freedman 1992), although because of the latter's uneven quality, this volume is still very useful, especially in philological studies. A supplementary volume was published in 1976.

Douglas, James D., ed. *The New Bible Dictionary.* 2d ed. Wheaton, Ill., 1982. Excellent presentation of archaeological information with good bibliographies for the longer articles. Includes a comprehensive index useful for locating archaeological information, but no map section or color photos. Balanced conservative approach, but slightly dated, making this a close second to *Eerdmans* (Myers 1987) as the best conservative Bible dictionary.

Freedman, David Noel, ed. *The Anchor Bible Dictionary.* 6 vols. New York, 1992. The definitive work in English, with over six thousand entries authored by nearly a thousand contributors. The articles and bibliographies are extensive, up to date, and often written by the leading international scholars. Archaeological information is comprehensive and includes articles on the newest approaches. However, the selection of sites and coverage given to those included is uneven, for instance, there is no article on Carchemish, and the article on Hazor is less than one page. Though the arrangement is alphabetical, the forthcoming index volume will help the reader to make full use of the massive amount of information.

Mills, Watson E., ed. *Mercer Dictionary of the Bible.* Macon, Ga., 1990. The best coverage of extra-biblical literature, with signed contributions by more than 225 scholar/teachers and bibliographies. Features up-to-date archaeological information but fewer (1,450) entries than other Bible dictionaries; limited but visually attractive illustrations; and color maps (but no map index). Succeeds well as a volume designed for students and classroom use.

Myers, Allen C., ed. *The Eerdmans Bible Dictionary.* Grand Rapids, Mich., 1987. The best conservative Bible dictionary, a revision and translation of *Bijbelse Encyclopedia* (1975), with substantial additions of up-to-date archaeological information. Articles are balanced (though unsigned) and frequently accompanied by bibliographies. Includes excellent color maps by Hammond, but no map index. No other color illustrations and a limited number of black-and-white photos make this dictionary less visually appealing.

Flora and Fauna

Cansdale, George S. *All the Animals of the Bible Lands.* Grand Rapids, Mich., 1970. Comprehensive discussion of animals, birds, and fish, with drawings and pictures (some in color), plus good indices.

Zohary, Michael. *Plants of the Bible.* New York, 1982. Handbook to all the plants of the Bible, with bibliography, index, and about two hundred color illustrations.

Dissertations. Often technical and difficult to read, dissertations nevertheless represent a source for the most current research available. The *Dissertation Abstracts International* (Ann Arbor, Mich., 1938–) provides abstracts of the latest archaeological dissertations from all over the world (although coverage of European dissertations is limited). Section A of *DAI* covers the humanities and social sciences, with several relevant categories for the archaeological researcher (anthropology, archaeology, history: ancient, religion, biblical studies, language: ancient, etc.), as well as a keyword title index and an author index. *Religious Studies Review* (Atlanta, 1975–) notes completed dissertations as well as research in progress. The *Zeitschrift für die Alttestamentliche Wissenschaft* (Berlin, 1881–) lists dissertations in progress.

Indices and bibliographies

Annual Egyptological Bibliography. Leiden, 1947–. The most comprehensive annual bibliography of ancient Egypt, with numbered abstracts classified in ten sections, and author and title indices.

Art Index. New York, 1929–. Indexes several journals devoted to art and archaeology, with a separate section for book reviews. Well indexed.

Elenchus Bibliographicus Biblicus. Rome, 1920–. The most comprehensive annual biblical bibliography, indexing virtually every relevant journal, as well as newsletters and occasional publications. Archaeology and the ancient Near East are very well covered. Extensive indices are very helpful. Unfortunately, there is a delay of a few years before publication.

Heizer, Robert F. *Archaeology: A Bibliographical Guide to the Basic Literature.* New York, 1980. Almost five thousand unannotated items, with a very thorough review of the literature.

Hospers, J. H., ed. *A Basic Bibliography for the Study of the Semitic Languages.* 2 vols. Leiden, 1973–1974. Volume 1 has chapters devoted to several languages, written by specialists, and a section on comparative Semitics. Volume 2 covers all aspects of Arabic. Includes almost ten thousand entries, but no annotations or index.

Humanities Index. New York, 1974–. Separated from the *Social Science and Humanities Index* in 1974, with significantly improved humanities coverage. Indexes several journals dealing with archaeology, with a separate section for book reviews.

Hupper, William G. *An Index to English Periodical Literature on the Old Testament and Ancient Near Eastern Studies.* Metuchen, N.J., 1987–. Five volumes of this projected ten-volume series have appeared to date. Indexes English-language works in over six hundred journals of archaeology, history, language, science, and theology from 1793 to 1970. The special value of this index is the extensive coverage of nineteenth- and twentieth-century articles, including many on archaeology which are compiled in no other source. Includes articles not found in Part I of Vogel's bibliography. Not yet indexed.

Index of Articles on Jewish Studies. Jerusalem, 1969–. Valuable for Hebrew-language publications, but not especially useful for archaeology. Includes festschrifts and several journals not indexed elsewhere. Well indexed.

Keilschriftbibliographie. Rome, 1940–. Published as part of the periodical *Orientalia.* Biannual index for the ancient Near East arranged alphabetically in a continuously numbered list, with subject and name indices. This index does for the ancient Near East what *Elenchus* does for the Bible.

Langevin, Paul-Émile. *Biblical Bibliography.* 3 vols. Quebec, 1972–1985. Covers journals and some books from 1930 to 1983. Well indexed with many subcategories dealing with archaeology. Organization of biblical sections by verse references make the biblical sections very useful. Includes an introduction in five languages.

Purvis, James D. *Jerusalem, the Holy City: A Bibliography.* 2 vols. Metuchen, N.J., 1988–1991. The definitive bibliography on all aspects of Jerusalem.

Religion Index One. Chicago, 1949–. Originally titled *Index to Religious Periodical Literature.* Indexes journals relating to a much broader spectrum of topics than *Elenchus,* including biblical archaeology, but ancient Near Eastern coverage is limited. Features subject, author, editor, and scripture indices.

Religion Index Two. Chicago, 1960–. Companion to *Religion Index One,* with additional indexing of multi-authored books, series, and festschrifts.

Vogel, Eleanor K., et al. "Bibliography of Holy Land Sites." *Hebrew Union College Annual* 42 (1971): 1–96; 52 (1981): 1–92; 58 (1987): 1–63. The definitive bibliography of individual sites in Israel and parts of Jordan and Syria. Each articles brings the bibliography up to date to the time of publication. Also available in offprint.

New Testament (Greco-Roman) World. Archaeology has not been utilized as much to illuminate the New Testament as it has for the Hebrew Bible. The following list is very selective. In addition, many items above deal with both the Hebrew Bible and the New Testament, and will not be relisted in this section.

Primary sources in translation

Hennecke, Edgar, Wilhelm Schneemelcher, and Robert McL. Wilson, eds. *New Testament Apocrypha.* 2 vols. Rev. ed. Philadelphia, 1991–1992. The revision brings the translation fully up to date.

The Loeb Classical Library. Cambridge, Mass. The most extensive collection of Greek and Latin texts with English translations.

Robinson, James M., ed. *The Nag Hammadi Library in English.* 3d ed. San Francisco, 1988. Thorough revision of the Gnostic texts, and the definitive translation of the world's leading Gnostic scholars.

Atlases

Cornell, Tim, and John Matthews. *Atlas of the Roman World.* New York, 1982. Excellent color maps and pictures and a popularly written text. Includes a gazetteer, index, and bibliography.

Levi, Peter. *Atlas of the Greek World.* New York, 1980. Excellent color maps and pictures and a popularly written text. Includes a gazetteer, glossary, index, and bibliography.

Meer, Frederik van der, and Christine Mohrmann. *Atlas of the Early Christian World.* Translated and edited by Mary F. Hedlund and H. H. Rowley. London, 1966. Older and still valuable standard work which should be supplemented by the Levi and Cornell/Matthews volumes.

Archaeological dictionaries and textbooks

Finegan, Jack. *The Archaeology of the New Testament: The Mediterranean World of the Early Christian Apostles.* Boulder, Colo., 1981. *The Archaeology of the New Testament: The Life of Jesus and the Beginning of the Early Church.* Rev. ed. Princeton, 1992. Companion volumes, the latter extensively revised from the 1969 edition. Fairly detailed archaeological review, lavishly illustrated, with an alphabetical list of ancient sources, an index of biblical references, and a general index.

McRay, John. *Archaeology and the New Testament.* Grand Rapids, Mich., 1991. The most comprehensive and up-to-date undergraduate textbook available in this field.

Pauly, August, and Georg Wissowa, et al., eds. *Real-Encyclopädie der classichen Altertumswissenschaft.* Stuttgart, 1839–. The definitive reference work covering all aspects of classical antiquity. A supplement, *Der Kleine Pauly,* 5 vols., edited by Konrat Ziegler and Walther Sontheimer (Stuttgart, 1964–1975), is more accessible than the original publication.

Rousseau, John J., and Rami Arav. *Jesus and His World: An Archaeological and Cultural Dictionary.* Minneapolis, 1994. A work that includes entries on sites, customs, and artifacts relating to the New Testament; to be used critically.

Stillwell, Richard, et al., eds. *The Princeton Encyclopedia of Classical Sites.* Princeton, 1976. Covers sites that show remains from the Classical period, mid-eighth century BCE to the beginning of the sixth century CE, with the exception of Early Christian sites of the fourth and fifth centuries. Includes maps, map indices, and a glossary, but no illustrations or drawings. Helpful bibliographies accompany each article.

Dictionaries

Ferguson, Everett, ed. *The Encyclopedia of Early Christianity.* New York, 1990. Helpful overall, but often inadequate on excavations.

Hammond, N. G. L., and H. H. Scullard. *The Oxford Classical Dictionary.* 2d ed. Oxford, 1970. The best single-volume reference work, though somewhat dated. Articles are signed and include bibliographies.

Bibliographies

L'année philologique: Bibliographie critique et analytique de l'antiquité gréco-latine. Paris, 1928–. The definitive annual bibliography of Greek and Latin philology. Includes helpful indices of collections, ancient authors, modern authors, humanists, and geography.

Charlesworth, James H. *The New Testament Apocrypha and Pseudepigrapha: A Guide to Publications with Excursuses on Apocalypses.* Metuchen, N.J., 1987. Introduction to and extensive bibliography on Christian extracanonical writings dating from 125 to 425.

Oster, Richard E. *A Bibliography of Ancient Ephesus.* Metuchen, N.J., 1987. Extensive bibliography of ancient Ephesus, including archaeological aspects.

Scholer, David M. *Nag Hammadi Bibliography.* Leiden, 1971. The definitive bibliography of Nag Hammadi, updated annually as "Bibliographia gnostica" in *Novum Testamentum.*

Other

Ferguson, Everett. *Backgrounds of Early Christianity.* 2d ed. Grand Rapids, Mich., 1993. Encyclopedic work covering Hellenistic-Roman and Jewish backgrounds to early canonical Christianity. Includes archaeological remains.

Meshorer, Yaʿacov. *Ancient Jewish Coinage.* 2 vols. Dix Hills, N.Y., 1982. Definitive work on Jewish coins.

White, L. Michael. *Building God's House in the Roman World: Architectural Adaptation among Pagans, Jews, and Christians.* Baltimore, 1990. Traces the architectural development of the meeting places of Christians from the earliest evidence until after Constantine.

VICTOR H. MATTHEWS and JAMES C. MOYER

REḤOVOT (Ar., Ruḥeibe), site located 32 km (18 mi.) southwest of Beersheba, 11 km (7 mi.) southwest of Elusa (Ḥaluṣa), and 22 km (13 mi.) northeast of Neṣṣana, on the northeast side of Wadi Ruḥeiba. Positioned on the biblical Way of Shur (*Gn.* 16:7; 20:1), this second-largest Negev city (after Elusa) functioned as an important caravan stop and, in the Byzantine period, as a rest stop for pilgrims traveling between the Sinai desert and Jerusalem, as the Byzantine khan and stable excavated in area C and the city's four churches indicate.

The Hebrew name of the site (Reḥovot) derives in modern times from the similarity of its Arabic name (Ruḥeibe) to the biblical Reḥovot, where a patriarchal well was located (*Gn.* 26:2). The huge, ancient well (largest in the Negev), located outside the town near a now-destroyed Byzantine bathhouse, was mistaken for the well mentioned in *Genesis.* The ancient name of the site is not known, although it is probably one of the towns mentioned inNeṣṣana papyrus 79, as Yoram Tsafrir argues (Tsafrir, 1993, p. 295).

Excavations carried out by Tsafrir from 1975 to 1979 and in 1986 indicate that the site was founded in the first century BCE/CE and terminated in about 700. The presence of post-abandonment Arab squatters in the site's north church and the absence of Arab glazed pottery indicate the probability of such a date. Estimates of the site's size vary in the literature, but the most recent estimate by Tsafrir of about 30 acres, with a population of about 4,800 at the city's height in the Byzantine period, is probably best.

Very little of the site has been excavated: some domestic housing (areas A and B), the khan and stable (area C), and only two (one partially) of the city's four churches (Tsafrir, 1988). Partial excavation of the central church (area D) revealed a well-preserved synthronon in a single-apsed building. Extensive excavation of the northern church revealed one of the largest triapsidal church buildings in the Negev, erected in several stages, with a chapel to the north and a large atrium that may have functioned as a monastery at the southern end of the nave. The dedicatory inscription dates its construction to the mid-sixth century. The most remarkable feature of this church is its crypt, equipped with a stairway for pilgrims to visit and venerate the unknown saint buried there.

The 1986 excavations carried out at the site under the auspices of the Institute of Archaeology of the Hebrew University of Jerusalem and the University of Maryland gave welcome stratigraphic precision to particular areas (Tsafrir and Holum, 1987–1988 and 1988). On ceramic grounds, the southern edge of the town (area B) cannot have been built before the fifth or sixth centuries CE; and the floor of the stable house (area C) overlay pottery of the first centuries BCE/CE. In addition to excavations carried out in the Byzantine cemetary, work in the atrium of the North Church (area E) yielded a Kufic officer's inscription with the earliest epigraphic mention of ʿAmr ibn al-ʿAṣ, the conqueror of Byzantine Palestine.

Studies of the names of the city's inhabitants (as revealed by dedicatory and cemetery inscriptions) indicate a preponderance of Greek personal names of Nabatean and Arab origin in the early sixth century. They are replaced by a preponderance of Semitic personal names by the end of the century (Gutwein, 1981). This pattern seems to be reinforced by the small skeletal sample recovered and published, which indicates a nomadic, rather than either Jewish or Greek, ethnic type. Among the skeletal samples are those of three females, which are significant because so little is known about female skeletons in general.

[*See also* Churches; Ḥaluṣa; *and* Nabateans.]

BIBLIOGRAPHY

Gutwein, Kenneth C. *Third Palestine: A Regional Study in Byzantine Urbanization.* Washington, D.C., 1981.

Shereshevski, Joseph. "Urban Settlements in the Negev in the Byzantine Period." Ph.D. diss., Hebrew University of Jerusalem, 1986. In Hebrew with English summary.

Tsafrir, Yoram, and Kenneth G. Holum. "Rehovot—1986." *Excavations and Surveys in Israel, 1987/88* (1987–1988): 89–91.

Tsafrir, Yoram, and Kenneth G. Holum. "Rehovot-in-the-Negev: Preliminary Report, 1986." *Israel Exploration Journal* 38 (1988): 117–127.

Tsafrir, Yoram, et al. *Excavations at Rehovot-in-the-Negev,* vol. 1, *The Northern Church.* Qedem, vol. 25. Jerusalem, 1988.

Tsafrir, Yoram. "On the Pre-Planning of Ancient Churches and Synagogues: A Test Case—The Northern Church at Rehovot in the Negev." In *Christian Archaeology in the Holy Land, New Discoveries: Essays in Honour of Virgilio C. Corbo,* edited by Giovanni Claudio Bottini et al., pp. 535–544. Studium Biblicum Franciscanum, Collectio Maior, 36. Jerusalem, 1990.

Tsafrir, Yoram. "The Early Byzantine Town of Reḥovot-in-the-Negev and Its Churches." In *Ancient Churches Revealed,* edited by Yoram Tsafrir, pp. 294–302. Jerusalem, 1993.

Tsafrir, Yoram, and Kenneth G. Holum. "Rehovot-in-the-Negev." In *The New Encyclopedia of Archaeological Excavations in the Holy Land,* edited by Ephraim Stern, vol. 4, pp. 1274–1277. Jerusalem and New York, 1993.

DENNIS E. GROH

REISNER, GEORGE ANDREW, (1867–1942), American Egyptologist. Born of German-American parents in Indianapolis, Reisner obtained a Ph.D. from Harvard University in Semitic history and languages in 1892 and received a traveling fellowship to continue his studies in Germany, where he became fascinated by ancient Egypt. In 1899 he entered into an agreement with Phoebe Apperson Hearst to direct excavations at several sites in Egypt on behalf of the University of California. From 1905 until his death he worked almost continuously for the Harvard University–Museum of Fine Arts (Boston) Egyptian Expedition. Reisner died at his house behind the Great Pyramid of Giza, where he had spent most of his adult life.

Although he held academic appointments, primarily at Harvard University, and was curator of the Egyptian Department at the Museum of Fine Arts, Boston, (1910–1942), Reisner spent most of his time in the field. He worked longest at Giza, but many other areas also drew his attention including Deir el-Ballas and Nag ed-Deir (Upper Egypt), Samaria (Israel), and Lower Nubia (Sudan). Reisner set the highest standards in field methods, insisting on meticulous recordkeeping in all aspects of excavation. He was among the first to use complete photographic recording as a standard field technique. Although he spent only three seasons at Samaria (1908–1910), his work there greatly influenced Byro-Palestinian archaeology.

Reisner's contributions on a scholarly level were no less important. The publications of his fieldwork were unusually complete, both as catalogs of remains recovered and as detailed historical and cultural syntheses. His *History of the Giza Necropolis,* volume 1 (1942) and *The Development of the Egyptian Tomb Down to the Accession of Cheops* (1936) remain two of the most important works published on these subjects. He made another lasting contribution by training a succeeding generation of Egyptologists and archaeologists in his meticulous scholarly and field methods.

[*See also* Giza; Samaria.]

BIBLIOGRAPHY

Dawson, Warren R., and Eric P. Uphill. *Who Was Who in Egyptology.* 2d rev. ed. London, 1972. Contains biographic entries on most Western and Egyptian scholars of ancient Egypt of the past two to three centuries.

Reisner, George A. *Israelite Ostraca from Samaria.* Cambridge, Mass., [191?].

Reisner, George A. *The Archaeological Survey of Nubia: Report for 1907–1908.* vol. 1, *Archaeological Report;* vol. 2, *Plates and Plans.* Cairo, 1910.

Reisner, George A., Clarence S. Fisher, and David G. Lyon. *Harvard Excavations at Samaria, 1908–1910,* vol. 1, *The Text;* vol. 2, *Plans and Plates.* Cambridge, Mass., 1924.

Reisner, George A. *Mycerinus: The Temples of the Third Pyramid at Giza.* Cambridge, Mass., 1931.

Reisner, George A. *The Development of the Egyptian Tomb Down to the Accession of Cheops.* Cambridge, Mass., 1936.

Reisner, George A. *History of the Giza Necropolis.* 2 vols. Cambridge, Mass., 1942–1955.

PATRICIA V. PODZORSKI

RENAN, JOSEPH ERNEST (1823–1892), French philosopher, Semitist, historian of religions, archaeologist, and prolific writer. Ernest Renan was born at Tréguier in Brittany, the third and last child of Philibert Renan, a marine merchant, and his wife Magdeleine Féger, a grocer. Destined to the priesthood, he studied rhetoric, theology, Latin, and Hebrew at the Grand Séminaire de Saint-Sulpice in Paris but left the seminary to do graduate work at the Sorbonne. He completed his doctoral degree in 1852 with a dissertation on Ibn Rushd (d. 1198) "Averroes et l'Averroïsme, essai historique."

In 1856 Renan married and joined the Académie des Inscriptions et Belles-Lettres. He published his translation of the *Book of Job* in 1859 and a year later, of the *Song of Songs.* In 1860 Renan was given the opportunity to lead an archaeological expedition to Phoenicia, where his research focused on four areas: Ruad/Aradus, Tortose/Antarados, and Amrit/Marathus; Jbail/Byblos; Saïda/Sidon; and Sour/Tyre. He began by excavating at Byblos; two months later he went to Sidon and the region of Tyre, where he opened several more digs. Until his departure for France in late 1861, Renan traveled widely in Phoenicia and Palestine. He began publishing his monumental *Mission de Phénicie* in Paris in 1864. Completed in 1874, the survey details his exploration and excavations in Phoenicia. The work is topographical, historical, ethnological, descriptive, and archaeological.

Upon his return from the Near East, Renan was elected professor of Hebrew, Chaldean, and Syrian at the Collège de France. His opening lecture upset the college's clerical faction and his lectures were suspended within the week. However, the government allowed him to lecture at home and did not deprive him of his title or salary. Within imperial circles Renan enjoyed the protection of Prince Jérome Bonaparte and Princess Mathilde.

In 1863 he published his *Life of Jesus* (vol. 1 of *Les Origines du christianisme*). The work questions scientifically the supernatural in the Gospels and was reprinted ten times before the end of the year. It generated such fierce attacks that Renan was forced to spend the summer of 1863 in Jersey and Brittany. The book was translated and published outside France in 1864. A revised thirteenth edition was published, he was dismissed from the Collège de France by the Ministry of Culture, and he was appointed assistant director of the Department of Manuscripts at the Bibliothèque Imperiale, all in that same year. His professorship was reinstated in 1870, after the Franco-Prussian War and the fall of Napoleon III.

Meanwhile, in 1866, he published *Les Apôtres* (as vol. 2 of

Les Origines du christianisme) and in 1867 initiated the *Corpus Inscriptionum Semiticarum.* Elected to the Académie Française in 1878, he received the Legion of Honor *(grand officier)* in 1888. Renan died in Paris after a long illness.

[*See also* Byblos; Phoenicia; Sidon; *and* Tyre.]

BIBLIOGRAPHY

For a comprehensive bibliography of Renan's works, see Henri Girard and Henri Moncel, *Bibliographie des oeuvres d'Ernest Renan* (Paris, 1923). Biographical entries on Renan may be found in the *Chambers Biographical Dictionary* (Cambridge, 1990); *Dictionnaire des biographies* (Paris, 1958); *Encyclopaedia Universalis* (Paris, 1992); *Encyclopaedia Britannica,* 14th ed. (London, 1929); *La grande encyclopédie* (Paris, 1976); *The Jewish Encyclopedia* (New York, 1905); *The Macmillan Dictionary of Biography,* new ed. (London, 1986); and *Webster's New Biographical Dictionary* (Springfield, Mass., 1988).

Works by Renan

Histoire générale et système comparé des langues sémitiques. Paris, 1855.

Mission de Phénicie. Paris, 1864.

L'Antéchrist. Paris, 1873.

Marc-Aurèle et la fin du monde antique. Paris, 1882.

Histoire du peuple d'Israël. 5 vols. Paris, 1887.

L'avenir de la science. Paris, 1890.

Oeuvres complètes. 10 vols. Edited by Henriette Psichari. Paris, 1947–1961. Not comprehensive.

Works about Renan

Chadbourne, Richard M. *Ernest Renan.* New York, 1968.

Dussaud, René. *L'oeuvre scientifique d'Ernest Renan.* Paris, 1951. The best reference on Renan's *Mission de Phénicie.*

Espinasse, Francis. *Life of Ernest Renan.* London, 1895. See chapter 5, pages 87–91.

Exposition Ernest Renan: Souvenirs d'enfance et de jeunesse, 20 avril–13 juin 1959. Paris, 1959.

Inauguration du Musée Renan le 20 juillet 1947 à Tréquier (discours sténographiés). Paris, 1948.

Mercury, Francis. *Renan.* Paris, 1990. See pages 317–332 for a discussion of *Mission de Phénicie.*

Robinson, Agnes Mary F. *The Life of Ernest Renan.* Boston, 1898.

Wardman, Harold W. *Ernest Renan: A Critical Biography.* London, 1964. See pages 72–77 for the *Mission de Phénicie.*

Hafez K. Chehab

RESERVOIRS.

RESERVOIRS. A large natural or an artificial underground space enhanced to store large quantities of water, primarily for drinking, is known as a reservoir. Water storage is essential to life in regions where there is no rainfall during part of the year and the total amount of precipitation is low enough to require conservation of water from one period to the next: winter to summer, night to day, and a rainy year to a drought year. Syria-Palestine abounds with reservoirs created for this purpose.

Reservoirs were either hewn from natural rock or built of stone; sometimes both engineering methods were combined. In several cases, large supporting pillars were constructed to hold up the installation's ceiling. The walls were thickly plastered, usually with a layer 5–10 cm thick, to prevent loss of water from percolation.

The earliest reservoirs discovered in the region are small and should properly be designated cisterns. The earliest reservoir in the land of Israel was discovered at Hazor and dates to the Middle or Late Bronze Age. [*See* Hazor.] This reservoir, located beneath a Canaanite palace, is shaped like a cross or a clover leaf and is coated with white plaster. The water entered the reservoir by means of a monumental drain made of basalt. Its volume is 150 cu m.

Two reservoirs for the collection of runoff are known from the Iron Age II period: at Beth-Shemesh, at Eitam, and at Beersheba. [*See* Beth-Shemesh; Beersheba.] The reservoir at Eitam is a system of natural caves whose volume is 240 cu m. The Beth-Shemesh reservoir is hewn out of soft, chalky rock; it is square and has four extensions and a capacity of 500 cu m. Both reservoirs display a double layer of plaster, one gray and the other yellow. The one at Beersheba has a volume of about 600 cu m and the plaster is similar to the one at Beth-Shemesh.

During the Second Temple period (Hellenistic and Early Roman periods) several reservoirs were cut out of the rock to serve the desert fortresses at Sartaba (nine reservoirs with a total capacity of 5,000 cu m), Duk (Dagon/Mt. Quarantale; nine reservoirs with a capacity of about 2,000 cu m), Cypros (four reservoirs, one with a volume of 500 cu m), Hyrkania (twenty-four reservoirs with a capacity of 20,000 cu m), Herodium (four reservoirs), and Masada (twelve reservoirs with a volume of 40,000 cu m). [See Herodium; Masada.] The water reached the reservoirs by means of conduits or aqueducts that either diverted water from flash floods, collected runoff, or conveyed water from natural springs, such as at Cypros (phase II).

Also from the Second Temple period are the thirty-four reservoirs beneath the Temple Mount in Jerusalem, whose total capacity is 36,000 cu m. The largest of these, with a volume of 12,000 cu m, located not far from the al-Aqṣa mosque, is called the Small Sea; it is the largest ancient reservoir in the region. [*See* Jerusalem.]

In the Roman and Byzantine periods, many more reservoirs were hewn or constructed. At Sepphoris, a sausage-shaped reservoir was hewn from the rock with a volume of 4,300 cu m (see figure 1). [*See* Sepphoris.] A reservoir at Beit Ras (Capitolias) in Jordan has a similar shape and size to the one found in Sepphoris. [*See* Beit Ras.] In Jerusalem, the domed reservoir of the Nea Church, built of two longitudinal galleries and two cross galleries, has a total volume of 3,500 cu m (its wall has an inscription dating it to the reign of Justinian). The built reservoir at Tiberias has a volume of 2,000 cu m; and the partly hewn and partly constructed reservoir at Hippos/Susita has a volume of 1,500 cu

RESERVOIRS. Figure 1. *Entrance to the reservoir at Sepphoris.* (Courtesy E. M. Meyers)

m. [*See* Tiberias.] These large reservoirs were fed by aqueducts, with the exception of the ones in Jerusalem. In the Byzantine period, large reservoirs were built for the monasteries in the Judean Desert. The Martyrius monastery has a reservoir of 2,000 cu m; the Haritun monastery has a reservoir of 1,000 cu m and walls decorated with crosses.

In the Early Arab period, four underground reservoirs were built in the city of Ramla (the Pool of Arches and three located next to the White Mosque). [*See* Ramla.] These were fed by an aqueduct that originated at Tel Gezer; their total volume is 10,000 cu m. Numerous pillars support these reservoirs' ceilings. In the Crusader period, reservoirs were built inside fortresses to collect runoff; especially well known are those at Qalʿat Nimrod and Belvoir (Kokhav ha-Yarden). In the Ottoman period a large reservoir was built at Acre/Akko underneath the courtyard of the Jazzar mosque, which had been a Crusader church. This reservoir was the terminal point for the Kabri aqueduct. [*See* Akko; Kabri, Tel.]

[*See also* Aqueducts; Cisterns; Hydraulics; *and* Hydrology.]

BIBLIOGRAPHY

ʿAmit, David, et al., eds. *The Aqueducts of Ancient Palestine* (in Hebrew). Jerusalem, 1989.

Brinker, Werner. "Antike Zisternen: Stationen ihrer Entwicklungsgeschichte." *Mitteilungen: Leichtweiss-Institut für Wasserbau der Technischen Universität Braunschweig* 103 (1989): 247–279.

Heker, M. "Water . . . in Jerusalem in the Ancient Period" (in Hebrew). In *Sepher Yerushalaim,* edited by Michael Avi-Yonah, pp. 191–218. Jerusalem and Tel Aviv, 1956.

Tsuk, Tsvika. "The Aqueducts to Sepphoris." Master's thesis, Tel Aviv University, 1985. In Hebrew with an English summary.

TSVIKA TSUK

Translated from Hebrew by Ilana Goldberg

RESISTIVITY. Subsurface electrical resistivity surveying exploits the fact that soil masses and rocks are able to conduct electricity because water in their interstices contains dissolved mineral salts and/or humic acids of biological origin. Measurement equipment includes a set of four or more electrodes, an electrical source, and a metering device. Survey technique involves placing the electrodes in the ground at regular intervals in a linear array and then connecting them sequentially in pairs to respective positive and negative voltage sources. Electrical resistance is measured as voltage is passed through the ground between the electrodes. The resistivity is the ratio of the applied voltage to the magnitude of the current. Ditches and pits with loose silts and soils generally show low resistivity readings, while structures and deposits with clay, brick, and stone will be relatively high. Testing is most successful when the linear transverse runs perpendicular to subsurface features—across ditches or stone or brick walls.

Soil resistivity measurement has been used by geologists and civil engineers since World War I. However, the first major application to archaeological work was only made in 1946, by R. J. C. Atkinson (1953), on a group of Neolithic monuments at Dorchester, England. One advantage of resistivity testing is that deep-current penetration can be obtained with only short probe insertion because the depth of electrical penetration is governed by, and is roughly equal to, the spacing between the electrodes. Another advantage is that the equipment setup is simple and of reasonable cost—although the development of more modern and sophisticated electronic instruments and of complicated probe array systems may now belie that claim. The advent of magnetic detection in the late 1950s provided archaeologists with an alternative tool to supplement the linear-array limitation of resistivity survey by providing a means for sweeping coverage of a survey area. [*See* Magnetic Archaeometry.]

Like other systems that test subsurface conditions, the resistivity surveyor must contend with a multitude of variables within the test environment. Stone-filled soils make inserting probes difficult and produce erratic resistivity results; dry, sandy soils are often incapable of conducting current; and subsurface features parallel and adjacent to the array transverse may skew resistivity readings. Accordingly, while analysis of resistivity readings can help the archaeologist to develop a plot of assumed subsurface features, "ground truth" can be finally determined only by excavation.

[*See also* Survey, Archaeological.]

BIBLIOGRAPHY

Aitken, Martin J. *Physics and Archaeology*. 2d ed. Oxford, 1974.

Atkinson, R. J. C. *Field Archaeology*. London, 1953.

Clark, Anthony. "Resistivity Surveying." In *Science in Archaeology*, edited by Don Brothwell et al., pp. 694–707. London, 1971.

JOE D. SEGER

RESTORATION AND CONSERVATION. To discuss restoration of monuments is to speak of a very vexed and controversial matter—and to avoid the controversy is to avoid the substance. The social factors standing behind restoration are complex (and mutually antagonistic), the interests to be served in the monument itself are conflicting, and in some essential respects the technical means available are limited to nonexistent. Thus, popular expectations may be quite out of proportion to possibilities. It is possible to exhibit ancient monuments for the short term in a manner agreeable to contemporary taste, but very frequently this does little to preserve them across the ages. On the other hand it is possible to preserve them well (e.g., by building a shelter over them or, in extremis, by burying them), but this is often at the expense of exhibiting them in an agreeable manner. There is no magic in the words *conservation* and *restoration* to ensure perfect preservation and exhibition concurrently. All that is material is subject to decay, stones and men alike. Sometimes results can be achieved which will last for more or less limited time. Results can not always be achieved. And no results can be guaranteed for ever. In the final instance perhaps the restorer must serve his generation.

Origin and Theory of Restoration. The theory of restoration of monuments is very well developed. It originated in specific circumstances in western Europe during the nineteenth century but is now reckoned to be of international application. Nonetheless, since the theory is based on European concepts of aesthetics and history, there is no reason why this should be so, and it would always be quite reasonable for another region to reject this theory in favor of one based on different cultural values—for example, on those of Confucianism or Islam. However, as yet this attitude has not been manifested in practice.

The concept of restoration emerged out of the historicism of the Romantic movement *sub specie* the Gothic Revival and the basic principle was established in the polemics surrounding its enunciation. The first person to deal systematically with the term and the activity (both novelties) was Viollet-le-Duc (1814–1879). Both in word and deed he proclaimed a concept of restoration which was immediately refuted (in theory) by his English contemporaries Ruskin and Morris. For Viollet the subject of restoration was the "form" of the building, its style—the Zeitgeist which the builders had realized (or sought to realize) in their structure. Thus, the restorer must be a master of building history together with all the techniques of construction necessary to reproduce perfectly the exact style in question. Metaphysically considered, Viollet's approach was Platonic (and he was much concerned with the ideal castle or church). In their often unsuccessful efforts to prevent its practice in England, Ruskin and Morris denigrated this theory, which they called the worst form of destruction.

Metaphysically considered their understanding was Aristotelian. The monumental form was a quality of the material—it was embodied in the material and existed nowhere outside of it: destroy the surviving material and you destroy the monumentality. The problem of restoration was thus how to preserve the surviving material in such a manner as to exhibit its monumentality to maximum effect. This has remained ever since the basic principle of restoring monuments and thus the controversy between three men of great genius (expressed equally in literature, art, and society) on the correct manner of caring for Gothic churches in nineteenth-century England and France has been extended automatically to monuments of all types, periods, and places (e.g., by influence to the newly independent countries of Greece and Italy and by colonialism to the ancient Near East).

This basic concept was systematized and elaborated a century later in the aftermath of World War II. In the first instance the enormous destruction by high explosives in Europe made restoration an issue of the moment. Supervening on this was the anticolonialism and prointernationalism which expressed itself emphatically on the cultural plane (cf. the idea of UNESCO). As a result, Rome became the international center for restoration of monuments, with a special provision for disseminating its teaching to underdeveloped countries. Men of great practical experience and/or acute analytical disposition refined experience into principles during the mid-twentieth century, and it is those principles which have since been applied in restoration work in the Near East. As a condition precedent to any discussion of this work, it is therefore necessary to outline the principles on which it is based. (Even if this is restricted to a cursory naming, it will show the severe conflicts inherent in the activity).

Restoration distinguishes itself from simple repairs, renovation, and rebuilding by having as its subject monumentality. An architectural monument reminds the viewer of some significant human experience; it calls to mind history and does so through art. That is, it can be viewed in an aesthetic instance and in a historic instance. Monumentality is incorporated in a twofold manner: as material and image, structure and aspect (this latter be it noted only partly of human design being partly of natural development over time). Both structure and aspect are equally constituted in the building material and are equally proper vehicles for intervention by the restorer. All interventions are per se undesirable and are to be limited to the minimum necessary (in restoration very definitely "least is most"). They operate via two modes: by removal and by addition. Restoration by removal is directed to the aspect and can be astonishingly rewarding. The attendant problem is that of periods: it may be difficult to decide between the aesthetic significance of one period and the historic significance of another. Addition of new material can be to the aspect or to the structure. Addition to the aspect must be kept to the minimum and never be practiced for its own sake. It must proceed by way of representation not reproduction: that is, it must always be clearly seen to be not original (otherwise it is falsification), but this distinction in appearance should not detract from the surviving monumental aspect. In short, restoration does not consist in reproducing the appearance of the monument as originally constructed, far less as it would or should have appeared in some ideal circumstances as Viollet le Duc taught. With additions to the structure, the limiting consideration is possible adverse reaction between old and new material. Thus, the safest practice is to consolidate the structure with the same material as the original.

The first step in restoring damage to monumentality is the investigation of the causes of damage. These may be human or natural, catastrophic or continuous. And it is based on the understanding of these causes that interventions are decided on to provide either for better preservation and/or better exhibition of the monument, but regrettably these two claims are often irreconcilable.

The prerequisite analysis of any restoration project into its constituent problems according to the above-mentioned categories is straightforward. However, difficulty arises in the endemic conflicts between the various categories: between the historic instance and the aesthetic instance; between monumental demands and functional demands; and the bitter conflict between exhibition and preservation. The analytical categories bring these conflicts into consciousness, so that an intervention is only made in some interest and with an awareness of its damage to another.

The nature and incidence of these conflicts vary according to the class of monuments, and in this connection, monuments can be classified as follows.

1. *Archaeological ruins.* When only vestiges of the original building survive (often retrieved by clearance or excavation) and the original integrity of the monument cannot be recognized. The ruin is thus the subject of the intervention and not the original building.

2. *Ruined monuments.* These are structures which are no longer functional as monuments but where the original form is or can be made recognizable; here the original building is the subject of the intervention.

3. *Living monuments.* Where the monument is still in use for its designed purpose (church, mosque) but the art by which it was built no longer survives, great problems arise between monumental and functional interests and it is by no means assured that any restoration qua monument will prove acceptable to the current functional interest.

4. *Modern monuments.* The monument is built entirely within the artistic and social framework of contemporary society. These are exceptional to the theory and can be treated in the same way as other contemporary buildings (maintained, repaired). The new work will be matched up with the old and a normal building inscription will satisfy the demands of history.

Practice in the Near East. As the place of origin of civilization, the Near East contains monuments of all types and ages, from the earliest Neolithic to recent Islamic times. Furthermore, because of its archaeological interest, new monumental remains are continually being unearthed. Almost the entire region was under Ottoman (or quasi-Ottoman) rule until the present century. The Ottoman authorities made provision for archaeological excavation and in special instances they permitted the excision of monumental remains for transport to European museums. However they did not receive the practice of restoration of monuments. This was introduced only with colonial (mandatory) administrations, in the twentieth century, namely French activity in the Maghrib, Syria, and Egypt, and Italian activity in Cyrenaica and Tripolitania. The British antiquities services in Iraq, Palestine, and Transjordan did not carry out routine restoration work but provided for some exceptional projects only. The striking majority of these activities dealt with Greco-Roman building but some work on Pharoanic remains was carried out in Egypt and there was also work on Early Christian and Mediaeval remains (Crusader or Arab castles, etc.). All the work was done more or less in the light of the above theory and certainly no local or regional style of restoration was evolved. This colonial activity, however, was only a curtain raiser to the large-scale restoration programs instituted in the region from the 1960s onward (often provided with international funds and/or international "experts").

Archaeological ruins. Very successful work has been carried out with archaeological ruins all over the Near East (e.g., in Tripolitania, Cyrenaica, Jordan, Syria, etc). It is much appreciated by the public and arouses little if any controversy. With appropriate landscaping it is equally at home in frequented antiquities sites and in remote deserted regions. The ruined aspect which is the subject of the work is maximized by setting up any coherent fragments and arranging *disjecta membra* in a systematic fashion, without any additions in the interest of the original form. Column drums, which often form the principal surviving material on classical and Early Christian sites, are its stock-in-trade and thus the colonnaded streets of the hellenized Orient are excellent vehicles. Familiar scenes from, for example, Palmyra, Jerash, Petra, and elsewhere illustrate this "anastylosis." One complicated factor here may be the presence of mosaics. Their exhibition in situ greatly adds to the picturesqueness of the ruins but in this event their preservation will inevitably demand measures which compromise the overall aspect.

The situation is very different with less durable remains which nonetheless may be of considerable monumental value in the historic instance. It may be possible to exhibit, and also preserve to some degree, vestigial rubble walls by regular seasonal consolidation, but this site maintenance is a heavy burden on departmental budgets. The critical problem of mud-brick remains will be referred to in this conclusion.

Ruined monuments. These form the core of restoration projects in the Middle East—temples, tombs, theatres, triumphal arches, towers, and so forth, sometimes more or less standing, sometimes more or less fallen to the ground and more or less buried. Architectural scholarship finds relatively little difficulty in correctly placing the surviving remains and engineering resources permit their effective reintegration. The difficulty here is the question of the aspect of the "new work." And, even within the rule of "representation without reproduction," taste in this matter changes as drastically as that in restoration of sculpture.

Some types of monuments are especially rewarding to restore. Underground (or rock cut) monuments of interior architectural development provide for their own preservation after their internal aspect has been restored (cf. e.g., the Greco-Roman cemeteries in Alexandria and the pharaonic Tombs of the Kings at Thebes). However even this advantage is not proof against tourist invasion. Other types of favored monuments are those of vertical development, for example, the monumental gate, triumphal arches, tetrapylons, and so forth. Here the plan generally involves the repetition of a standard element (e.g., a pier) and the new work can be safely concentrated on the lowest preserved element leaving the surviving remains of the others to maintain the original monumental aspect.

Ruined monuments are the class which has been subject to rescue operations occasioned by the epidemic of dam building in the later twentieth century. The dismantling, transfer and re-erection of ashlar masonry is a straightforward operation (but regrettable unless absolutely necessary). The excellence of the result is largely dependent on sympathetic new siting (cf. the transfer of the Nubian Temples consequent on the building of the High Dam).

Living monuments. Although recently medieval mosques and the like have been restored in Cairo, Iraq, and Iran, the restoration of living monuments has not been as prominent in the Near East as much as in Europe. The conflict of monumental and functional interest here can be insuperable and it is to be noted that the established Church of England from the beginning has refused to allow the fabric of its cathedrals to pass into the care of the Ancient Monuments Commission. Similarly when structural instability occasioned by earthquake necessitated restoration of the Church of the Holy Sepulcher in Jerusalem, the work was controlled and carried out by church authorities. Here a half-dozen sects had to reconcile their claims, and with these was involved a very acute problem of conflicting periods (i.e., Byzantine = Eastern Churches, Crusader = Western Churches). On the other hand an example of good cooperation between the monumental authority (Antiquities Department) and the functional authority (Orthodox church) exists in Cyprus, where functioning mid-Byzantine churches have been restored by the antiquities service with the good offices of the church.

However of recent years a related problem has emerged in the Near East—what might be called conversion restoration, or transferred function. Arab castles make good antiquities offices, Ottoman city gates good cultural centers, and so on. Above all is the question of site museums which everyone agrees are a good thing, and if some salient ruin can be restored and converted to this end there is a double gain. Yet, such restoration can be completely beyond or contrary to the general dictates of theory. In this event instead of killing a reasonably preserved monument with a mass of new work, the better solution may be to take a suitable plan (e.g., a basilica) where only vestiges survive and rebuild its form, with complete freedom to detail according to functional requirements.

Somewhat similar considerations apply to ancient theaters. On occasions the superb siting of a rock-cut Greek theater (e.g., Kourion, Cyprus) recommends very strongly that it be put into commission for staging theatrical performances (particularly in conjunction with festivals). Quite frequently so far as the cavea is concerned there is virtually not a block in place, although it may be perfectly possible to work out the scheme of the seating quite accurately. In such case, it is reasonable to rebuild the cavea out of new stone and leave the scaena untouched, allowing the performances to provide their own sets. In this way a restricted passage of fine masonry will not be "killed" and an excellent venue will be provided for performances. On the other hand to reproduce the elaborate architectural ornament of a *scaena frons* in new work is a monumental error.

Another allied category of restoration work has become of great importance in the Near East—"ethnological restoration." Palaces and palatial houses fallen into decay during the previous century or so have been renovated and rebuilt according to the original model to serve as ethnological museums or otherwise to illustrate the traditional life of the region (Emir Shihab's palace at Beit ed-Din in the Lebanon; the Azm palace at Damascus together with numbers of instances in Isfahan and Shiraz).

Modern monuments. This class of monuments, which normally only comes into consideration with catastrophic destruction by war or natural disasters, has acquired great importance in the Near East because of drastic social changes in the last generation. The almost instant disappearance of traditional domestic architecture has evoked concern for preserving and exhibiting what relics can be salvaged, with the consequent designation of "Old Towns," "Traditional Quarters," and so forth. All this stands within the theory of modern monuments since artisans and craftsmen still survive who can carry out this work and their continued survival can be promoted if this becomes an established activity. The challenge here is to establish the social framework so that the restored buildings remain alive.

The principles reviewed here have a fragile foundation and may seem somewhat recondite. However, surprisingly they are generally apprehended by the public, and public condemnation quickly attaches to illogical solutions founded on no principle at all.

Difficulties in restoration are not in consolidating the structure of ancient monuments. With the resources of modern engineering this can be done without impairing the aspect of the monument. The abiding difficulty is in preserving the aspect from deterioration by weathering or action of time without impairing the exhibition. A small mudbrick building was constructed in antiquity with the expectation that its fabric might survive for a generation or so. Yet, when the ruins of these structures are dug up out of the ground, the mere fact that they are ancient ruins raises the expectation in common belief that they can/should be made to survive indefinitely with their agreeable aspect agreeably exhibited. It is commonly thought that some (liquid) preparation is available which can be sprayed on to delicate surfaces (decaying stone or mud brick) which will consolidate and preserve them without damaging their aspect. Many such preparations have been publicized but hitherto none has been found to give satisfactory results for any extended period of time—and many have done great damage. This is the "elixir of life" which is lacking in restoration of monuments—or the lack could equally well be described as that of the simplest and most basic technical device.

Finally a great difficulty in restoration is not technical but social. This is the difficulty of carrying out restoration of monuments according to the accepted theory free from social interests which operate directly to the destruction of monumentality. Proposals to make circus grounds or popular entertainment centers out of an ancient monument's site can have no place in the discussion of the theory of restoration.

[*See also* Conservation Archaeology; Field Conservation.]

BIBLIOGRAPHY

Brandi, Cesare. *Teoria del restauro.* Rome, 1963. Collected papers which give excellent coverage strongly developed on the conceptual basis of restoration.

Crema, Luigi. *Monumenti e restauro.* Milan, 1959. Fully illustrated manual of practice and procedure.

Monuments and Sites of History and Art and Archaeological Excavations: Problems of Today. Paris, 1950. Global survey which provides a manifesto of the new concern for restoration arising out of the destructiveness of World War II and supplied to the Middle East. A UNESCO publication.

Morris, William. *Manifesto of the Society for the Protection of Ancient Buildings.* London, 1877. Embodies Ruskin's attitude and has remained the policy of the SPAB, which is still influential.

Ruskin, John. *The Seven Lamps of Architecture (VI The Lamp of Memory).* London, 1849. Clear presentation of the essential premise of restoration theory, set against a system of aesthetic and social philosophy.

Thompson, Michael W. *Ruins: Their Preservation and Display.* London, 1981. Very clear exposition of general principles as derived from long practice.

Viollet-le-Duc, Eugène. "Restauration." In *Dictionnaire raisonné de l'architecture française.* Paris, 1858–. A resumé which needs to be supplemented by further reading from and about this giant of his age who is both the patriarch and heresiarch of restoration.

Ward, Pamela, ed. *Conservation and Development in Historic Towns and Cities.* Newcastle-on-Tyne, 1968. Provides useful background information on restoration of modern monuments with indication of legal, economic, and administrative considerations.

Wright, G. R. H. *Kalabsha: The Preserving of the Temple.* Berlin, 1972. Details how accepted principles of restoration were applied in practice to a major project of dismantling and reerecting an Egyptian temple.

Wright, G. R. H. *The Ptolemaic Sanctuary of Kalabsha: Its Reconstruction.* Mainz, 1987. Detailed account of a highly unusual project and its attempted justification in terms of accepted theory.

G. R. H. Wright

RIFAʿAT, TELL, site located 35 km (22 mi.) north of Aleppo, Syria, in the middle of a village of the same name (36°5′ N, 37°1′ E). The village is 5 km (3 mi.) east of the Aleppo-Iʿazaz road and about 14 km (9 mi.) southeast of the modern city Iʿazaz. Tell Rifaʿat is strategically positioned on the plain between the Qouiq River in the east and Jebel

Sama'an in the west. It is the largest tell in the area and is about 360 m above sea level.

The tell itself is composed of two parts: the citadel and the lower city. The citadel (30 m high and 142 × 142 m at the top and 250 × 233 m at its base) stands approximately in the middle of the lower city. The citadel is freestanding, with extremely steep slopes; the lower city is partially occupied with modern houses.

The inhabitants of the village Tell Rifa'at reported that the old name of the site was Arpad, an identification that can be made on etymological and geographical grounds as well. In antiquity, Arpad was the capital city of the Aramean state of Bit-Agusi. The Aramean kingdom emerged in the tenth century BCE and appears in Assyrian texts as the land of Arpad or as the land of Bit-Agusi. Like all Aramean kingdoms in Syria and Mesopotamia, Arpad paid tribute to the Assyrian kings approximately every year. Arpad finally lost its independence in 740 BCE, when it was made a province and given an Assyrian governor.

The equation of Tell Rifa'at with Arpad remains a hypothesis, however, for none of the excavations at the site succeeded in recovering sufficient evidence for the identification. Limited excavations on the tell have been conducted. From fall 1924 to spring 1925, the Czech philologist Bedrich Hrozny excavated Tell Rifa'at and identified it as biblical Arpad. Hrozny abandoned his investigation after three months without publishing a report. Only a very brief report appeared in a Prague newspaper, *The Central European Observer* (16 July 1929, p. 512). In 1956, 1960, and 1964, an expedition from the Institute of Archaeology, University of London, directed by M. V. Seton-Williams undertook excavations at Tell Rifa'at, during which the team made soundings and distinguished five levels, from the Chalcolithic period (fifth–fourth millennia) through the Roman period (first–fourth centuries CE).

According to Seton-William's preliminary reports (1961, 1967), the old city of Arpad had been surrounded by a very strong brick fortification wall. In the northwestern part of the tell his team unearthed a monumental limestone staircase that led through the fortifications and was later in date, probably Greco-Roman. On the western side of the tell he discovered a large palace (923 m wide and 30 m long) with a large porch with two columns and a great paved courtyard. The palace was flanked by two rooms, in front of which there had been a large hall. The palace belongs to the first millennium BCE.

Seton-Williams also discovered the east gate in the Bronze Age city wall. The gate's first phase belongs to the sixteenth–fifteenth centuries BCE. In its last phase, it was 3.90 m wide, was lined with limestone orthostats, and had a drain 60 cm wide running down the center of the passageway. The entrance area was paved with limestone and basalt slabs and broken glazed bricks.

Among the small finds recovered by Seton-Williams are stamp seals—seventh-century BCE Assyrian and sixth-century BCE Neo-Babylonian and Achaemenid—and elaborate and common style Mitannian cylinder seals; Late Bronze and Iron Age terra-cotta figurines, among them numerous examples of the so-called Scythian horseman and an Astarte plaque; a limestone Aramean grave stela (0.57 m high and 0.37 m wide) depicting a banquet; and eight fragments of Assyrian cuneiform tablets and a fragment of an inscription in Phoenician.

BIBLIOGRAPHY

Matthers, John. *The River Qoueiq, Northern Syria, and Its Catchment: Studies Arising from the Tell Rifa'at Survey, 1977–79.* 2 vols. British Archaeological Reports, International Series, no. 98. Oxford, 1981.

Sader, Hélène. *Les états araméens de Syrie depuis leur fondation jusqu'à leur transformation en provinces assyriennes.* Beirut, 1987. See pages 99–152.

Seton-Williams, M. V. "Preliminary Report on the Excavations at Tell Rifa'at." *Iraq* 23 (1961): 68–87.

Seton-Williams, M. V. "The Excavations at Tell Rifa'at, 1964: Second Preliminary Report." *Iraq* 29 (1967): 16–33.

Ali Abou Assaf

RIMAH, TELL ER-, also known as Tell Ermah, site located in northern Iraq (36°15′ N, 42°37′ E), 13 km (8 mi.) due south of modern Telafar and 65 km (40 mi.) west of Mosul. Austen Layard, under the auspices of the British School of Archaeology in Iraq, visited and described the site in 1850, and Seton Lloyd, under the auspices of the University Museum of the University of Pennsylvania, surveyed it. The walled city of the second millennium BCE enclosed an area about 600 m in diameter. British and American excavation teams, led respectively by David Oates and Theresa Howard-Carter, worked jointly from 1964 to 1966; the British worked alone there from 1967 to 1971.

Occupation of the site goes back to prehistoric times, although excavation did not reach the lowest levels. A building with pitched brick vaults was dated to about 2000 BCE and several cylinder seals, perhaps heirlooms, were found that are earlier than the Old Babylonian period (c. 1900–1600 BCE).

Early second millennium texts show that Tell er-Rimah benefited from the caravan trade passing between Aššur and central Anatolia. The temple was the central and highest feature of the city, which was walled. The temple may have been built by Shamshi-Adad I of Assyria. It sits on two massive terraces that are approached via a monumental staircase from a courtyard. The temple faced roughly eastward and was backed on its west side by a solid tower, or ziggurat. The shrine inside the temple could be reached directly from the main door by passing through a central courtyard. An internal stairway in the northeast corner of the building led to the roof, and perhaps also to a shrine on top of the tower. The exterior facades were decorated with semiengaged mud-brick columns imitating the trunks of two kinds of palm trees. Similar architectural decoration is known from Larsa, on the temple of the sun god; at Tell Leilan in the Upper Khabur; and on the so-called bastion of Warad-Sin at Ur. Clay tablets consisting of administrative letters and records were found in the temple of this phase and beside the main stairway. The temple may have been dedicated to the storm god Adad or to the goddess Geshtin-anna. In it were found two sculptured heads of Humbada and a stone relief of a goddess between palm trees.

A palace, perhaps contemporary with the temple, was built on virgin soil to the northeast of the temple. Most of one wing was excavated, which included a throne room with a dais. A small number of early Old Babylonian personnel lists was found in the wing. That palace was demolished almost to ground level and replaced by a new building that followed a slightly different alignment, perhaps soon after the death of Shamshi-Adad I. In it were found letters, records, and seal impressions indicating association with four rulers: Hatnu-rapi, a contemporary of Zimrilim of Mari, now identified from Mari texts as a king of Qaṭṭara; Ashkur-Addu, also contemporary with Zimrilim, identified from Mari texts as a king of Karana; Zimrilim, king of Mari, whose official seal was found impressed on two envelope fragments; and Aqba-Ḫammu, brother-in-law of Ashkur-Addu, whose wife Iltani was at the center of the main archive of letters and administrative records and who appears to have ruled the city as a vassal of Hammurabi of Babylon after the latter brought the reign of Zimrilim at Mari to an end.

The kingdom to which Tell er-Rimah belonged is now thought to have contained two major cities, Karana and Qaṭṭara, that were alternatively named according to the residency of the current ruler. Therefore, it is still uncertain from the Old Babylonian evidence whether the site is Karana or Qaṭṭara. A foundation inscription of a king of Razama, found out of stratigraphic context, may be loot from a siege of that neighboring city.

During the Nuzi period, in the third quarter of the second millennium, the site was still extensively occupied, with a large administrative building and domestic houses built over the old palace area. Much fine glass and frit work was found, especially in connection with a small domestic shrine, and many cylinder seals, but no inscribed material. Texts of the period found at Nuzi mention a Karana, but that may refer to another town with the same name on the Lower Zab, depending on the interpretation of the texts. The temple continued in use.

During the Middle Assyrian period, in the last quarter of the second millennium, the temple and domestic structures continued to flourish under the aegis of Assyrian kings. Business records found in the temple, mainly concerned with tin and barley, date to the reigns of Shalmaneser I and Tukulti-Ninurta I. The place name *Qaṭṭara* is frequently attested in them; Karana does not occur. In texts of this time from Aššur, both Karana and Qaṭṭara are found, but without indications for locating them.

The site was completely abandoned after the Middle Assyrian period. It was partly resettled in the Neo-Assyrian period, but the old temple was not restored. Under the Assyrian king Adad-Nirari III, it belonged to the province of Rasappa and was renamed Zamahe. There, the semi-independent governor Nergal- (or Palil-) Eresh set up a stela beside the altar in a small, new temple dedicated to Adad, built into the north side of the old temple mound. The new temple had a different alignment, and its entrance on the northeast gave direct access to the cella through a long hall. The entrance to the cella was decorated with stone pillar bases in the shape of lion heads with huge, protruding dagger-blade tongues; it featured a gigantic lion-headed bird made from a bitumen core. The stela recorded the titles and deeds of Adad-Nirari III, including his taking tribute from Syrian rulers and from Jehoash of Israel, as well as new settlements built in the vicinity by Nergal-Eresh; the latter part of the inscription was erased in antiquity. A tablet recording a real estate transaction by Nergal-Eresh also was found.

BIBLIOGRAPHY

Charpin, Dominique, and Jean-Marie Durand. "Le nom antique de Tell Rimāh." *Revue d'Assyriologie et d'Archéologie Orientale* 81.2 (1987): 125–146.

Dalley, Stephanie. "Karanā." In *Reallexikon der Assyriologie und Vorderasiatischen Archäologie*, vol. 5, pp. 405–407. Berlin and New York, 1980.

Dalley, Stephanie, C. B. F. Walker and J. D. Hawkins. *The Old Babylonian Tablets from Tell al Rimah.* London, 1976.

Fadhil, Abdulillah. *Studien zur Topographie und Prosopographie der Provinzstädte des Königreichs Arraphe.* Mainz am Rhein, 1983. See pages 92–101.

Howard-Carter, Theresa. "Excavations at Tell al-Rimah, 1964." *Bulletin of the American Schools of Oriental Research,* no. 178 (April 1965): 40–69.

Howard-Carter, Theresa. "An Interpretation of the Sculptural Decoration of the Second Millennium Temple at Tell al-Rimah." *Iraq* 45 (1983): 64–72.

Layard, Austen H. *Discoveries in the Ruins of Nineveh and Babylon.* London, 1853. See page 243.

Lloyd, Seton. "Some Ancient Sites in the Sinjar District." *Iraq* 5 (1938): 123–142.

Oates, David. "The Excavations at Tell al Rimah." *Iraq* 27 (1965): 62–80; 28 (1966): 122–139; 29 (1967): 70–96; 30 (1968): 115–138; 32 (1970): 1–26; 34 (1972): 77–86.

Oates, Joan. "Late Assyrian Temple Furniture from Tell al Rimah." *Iraq* 36 (1974): 179–184.

Page, Stephanie M. "A Stela of Adad-Nirari III and Nergal Ereš from Tell al Rimah." *Iraq* 30 (1968): 139–153. See Tadmor (below) for corrections.

Parker, Barbara. "Cylinder Seals from Tell al Rimah." *Iraq* 37 (1975): 21–38.

Postgate, J. N. "A Neo-Assyrian Tablet from Tell al Rimah." *Iraq* 32 (1970): 31–50.

Saggs, H. W. F. "The Tell al Rimah Tablets, 1965." *Iraq* 30 (1968): 154–174.

Tadmor, Hayim. "The Historical Inscriptions of Adad-Nirari III." *Iraq* 35 (1973): 141–150.
Wiseman, D. J. "The Tell al Rimah Tablets, 1966." *Iraq* 30 (1968): 175–205.

STEPHANIE DALLEY

RITUAL BATHS (Heb., *miqvaʿot;* sg., *miqveh;* lit. "a gathering of water"). A *miqveh* is a built water installation whose construction complies with tenets of Jewish law *(halakhah),* and in which the observant Jew, disrobed, purifies him- or herself through total immersion. In the late Second Temple period, the Jews developed an elaborate system of regulations concerning matters of ritual purity, based on biblical law but emended and influenced by the dominant contemporary religious interpreters of the time (e.g., Pharisees and Saduccees). In the early stages of the practice, a state of purity was achieved through immersion in a natural body of water—a spring, river, or lake. Eventually, however, the demand for pools of natural water to service the community was met via the introduction of the *miqveh.*

To draw a distinction between a ritual immersion and ordinary washing, the sages decreed that the *miqveh*'s waters should be "in the hands of heaven," distinct from waters that are "in the hands of man." They decreed that *miqveh* waters meeting the following requirements have intrinsic powers of purification. The *miqveh* was to be cut into bedrock or built directly into the ground—it could not be a precast container. It was not to be filled with drawn (i.e., "in the hands of man" and therefore impure) water. Only rainwater that collected by itself into the *miqveh* (i.e., by gravity) was acceptable. Spring water led by aqueduct was also permissible. The *miqveh* must hold a minimum volume of 40 *seʿah* of water (somewhat less than a cubic meter). The water in the *miqveh* must maintain the natural appearance of water (meaning, for example, that oil finding its way into a *miqveh* defiled it, even though all other requirements were met). The rabbis did not set regulations for the shape or the number of steps leading into the *miqveh,* which is attested in the archaeological record, as installations are found in various shapes and with differing numbers of steps.

The main rabbinic sources for the tradition are the tractates *Miqvaʿot* in the Mishnah and Tosefta. These are compilations of *halakhot* ("religious regulations") prescribing the minimal requirements for a *miqveh* and of discussions of problems already solved by the sages regarding the use of this installation (they are not manuals of instruction for how to build a *miqveh*).

Archaeologist Yigael Yadin first drew attention to the installation in the excavations on Masada (1963–1964). However, it was not until the findings from Nahman Avigad's excavations in the Jewish Quarter and those of Benjamin Mazar near the Temple Mount, both in Jerusalem, that *miqvaʿot* began to be studied formally. Such installations have been found in large numbers in archaeological contexts in Israel, mainly in bathrooms in the basements of every one of the large private houses dated to the first century BCE and the first century CE until the year 70, where they appear in addition to cisterns, bathtubs, and footbaths. A recent comprehensive study by Ronny Reich (1990), based on the above-mentioned excavations and others, has proven the identification of these installations with the *miqveh* known from the written sources and has defined their characteristics and significance.

The lower part of the *miqveh* typically was cut into bedrock, while its upper part was built and roofed with a barrel-shaped vault or, alternatively, also hewn completely out of bedrock. Its average size was 2 × 4 m. The steps in the *miqveh* usually occupy its entire width and have risers about 25–30 cm high; the lowest step usually has the highest rise (60–70 cm) and one or two small auxiliary steps are cut at the bottom expressly to overcome this height. The tread of the steps also varies in depth. In many cases a step with a deep (50–70 cm) tread alternates with two–four 30-cm steps enabling the use of the *miqveh* in different water levels. Variations of *miqvaʿot* occur: there are installations with a narrow staircase attached to one or two sides of the basin (typical to Hasmonean Jericho), and *miqvaʿot* equipped with two adjacent openings (instead of one) and/or a low built partition (10–30 cm high) that divides the staircase into two lanes (to separate the descending impure person from contact with the ascending purified individual), a type typical mainly to Jerusalem.

Miqvaʿot are filled with rainwater during the first rainstorm of each year. The chief operational/maintenance problem with *miqvaʿot* in ancient Israel was guaranteeing a constant supply of pure water throughout the year in a land with a long rainless season (April–November). The sages decreed that a minimum volume of 40 *seʿah* can also purify drawn water; thus, a solution for maintaining the purity of the water was simply occasionally to add drawn water to the *miqveh* as long as the amount of the original pure water in the pool was more than 40 *seʿah*—instantaneously purifying the drawn water (which was probably the common means to purify additional amounts of water). In addition, an operational device is in evidence based on the principle given in the Mishnah that any body of water linked to the water in a valid *miqveh* becomes equally pure: at a few sites (Masada, Herodium, and Jericho, and in a few examples in Jerusalem) a pair of *miqvaʿot* were excavated that are linked at their rims by a pipe or channel. Both *miqvaʿot* were initially filled with pure rainwater, but only one was used for ritual immersion (in later periods the unused one is referred to as an *oṣar,* "treasury"). When the water in the *miqveh* in frequent use became dirty, it was replaced with clean drawn water (still unqualified for purification). When the stopper was pulled from the connecting pipe, and momentary contact occurred between the two bodies of water, the water

RITUAL BATHS. *A plaster bath with steps, from excavations at Sepphoris.* (Courtesy E. M. Meyers)

from the "treasury" purified the freshly drawn water. This procedure could be repeated as often as required. The method was used only rarely in the Second Temple period, probably reflecting the habits of certain religious/social segments of Jewish society at that time, but is obligatory today.

In addition to domestic *miqvaʿot* and those excavated near the gates of the Temple Mount in Jerusalem are examples excavated in the palaces and mansions of the Hasmonean and Herodian dynasties in Jericho (which were supplied by spring water conducted by aqueducts) and at Masada, Herodium, and Cypros. Others have been found at Qumran, Gezer, Gamla, and elsewhere, in rural areas near oil and wine presses. The latter examples enabled commodities to be produced in a state of ritual purity.

Frequently used in the Second Temple period in Judea (Judah) and the Galilee, *miqvaʿot* were absent from the Late Hellenistic and Early Roman world. Like Jewish inscriptions and symbols, the *miqveh* is a clue (an architectural one) for identifying a Jewish presence at sites. After the Romans destroyed Jerusalem and the Temple in 70 CE, the need for ritual purity was considerably minimized, resulting in a sharp decline in the number of the *miqvaʿot* in use, which is attested in the archaeological record. From an average frequency of two–three installations per private house (in Jerusalem), the number declined to one–two *miqvaʿot* per village or neighborhood at most sites. (Although the site of Sepphoris in Galilee seems to present a much higher rate of frequency in the period after 70 CE.) In medieval Europe the installation rate was also one or two per Jewish neighborhood.

[*See also* Personal Hygiene; Public Baths. *In addition, most of the sites mentioned are the subject of independent entries.*]

BIBLIOGRAPHY

Netzer, Ehud. "Ancient Ritual Baths *(Miqvaot)* in Jericho." In *The Jerusalem Cathedra,* vol. 2, edited by Lee I. Levine, pp. 106–119. Detroit, 1982.

Reich, Ronny. "The Hot Bath-House *(balneum),* the *Miqweh,* and the Jewish Community in the Second Temple Period." *Journal of Jewish Studies* 39.1 (1988): 102–107.

Reich, Ronny. "Miqwa'ot (Jewish Ritual Immersion Baths) in Eretz-Israel in the Second Temple and Mishnah and Talmud Periods." Ph.D. diss., Hebrew University, 1990. In Hebrew with English abstract.

RONNY REICH

ROADS. A region's geopolitical history cannot be understood without a basic knowledge of its roads. The roads and highways in the ancient Near East determined its demographic patterns to a large degree because population centers generally developed along them. Moreover, the locations of roads dictated, or at least prescribed, the movements of armies, merchants, and ordinary citizens. Consequently, they exerted a profound influence on a region's development and history.

Road Dimensions. In order to bear the traffic of wheeled vehicles such as chariots, carts, and wagons, roads in the ancient world were generally two or more lanes wide. In Mesopotamia, for example, city streets were often several meters wide. Aiburšabum Street in Babylon was as much as 20 m wide in its excavated sections. Other excavated streets in Babylon varied in width from 2 to 10 m, most having been about 3–6 m wide. In Neo-Babylonian warranty deeds from Babylon and Erech, "broad streets" (Akk., *sūqu rapšu*) and "narrow streets" *(sūqu qatnu)* are frequently mentioned. Sennacherib boasts that he broadened Nineveh's market streets for the passage of the "royal road" and made this road 62 large cubits (about 30 m) wide. Open roads were also wide, probably averaging 3–6 m. The Assyrians rarely encountered roads too narrow for their wagons and chariots. According to their records, they drove freely throughout the land and considered it a matter worthy of note when they met with narrow roads outside Assyria.

In Egypt an Old Kingdom road was discovered leading to the alabaster quarries east of el-Amarna; it was 5 m wide, with two branches, one 9 m and one 3 m wide. A road system discovered in the environs of el-Amarna comprised roads approximately 5 m wide, with rows of stones marking the edges. Another network of roads from the Old Kingdom has been traced in the region of the Second Cataract of the Nile. These also were about 5 m wide, with one widening to 8 m as it approached the fortress of Mirgissa. Evidence indicates that most open roads in ancient Egypt were relatively wide. Rameses II boasted that he marched northward to Qadesh with his infantry and chariotry, with his army "traveling on the narrow paths as if on the roads of Egypt."

The same picture holds for Syria-Palestine. From the excavated remains it appears that streets in this region were generally 2–3 m wide (as found, for example, in the Iron Age strata at Megiddo, Tell Deir ʿAlla, Tell Qasile, Tell en-Naṣbeh, Beth-Shemesh, Ashdod, and Tell Beersheba), with streets 4.5 m wide being fairly common (for example, in Iron Age levels at Megiddo, Tell Qasile, Gezer, and Beth-Shemesh). Evidence suggests that open roads in ancient Israel were typically two lanes wide (3–4 m), although roads of three or more lanes also undoubtedly existed (wider than 5 m).

During the Roman period, roads in the ancient Near East were generally two to four lanes wide. Roman roads discovered in the Judean Wilderness measured from 3 to 12 m in width. One of the Roman roads through the Beth-Shean valley measured 9–10 m in width—at least the width of a modern five-lane highway.

In the Byzantine period, the standard width of streets in Palestinian cities seems to have been 5.4 m. More than a dozen streets this wide have been excavated in Jerusalem alone, and additional examples have been found elsewhere in the Near East, including Gerasa in Jordan and Dura-Europos in Syria. On the other hand, the main streets of cities were much wider: those in Jerusalem, Samaria, and Gerasa/Jerash, for example, were 22 m wide, four times the width of the average street.

Until the Roman period, roads in the open countryside were generally unpaved, and city streets were only occasionally paved. (Josephus's assertion that Solomon paved the roads leading to Jerusalem with black stones [*Antiquities* 8.7.4] is anachronistic.) No paved road from the pre-Roman period has been found in Palestine, and unpaved thoroughfares are assumed in the biblical literature—briers, thorny bushes, and other plants may be found growing in a road (cf. *Hos.* 2:6 [Hebrew, verse 8]; *Prv.* 15:19, 22:5). The same was generally true throughout the Fertile Crescent. According to a third-millennium inscription from Sumer, when Agade fell and the Gutians took over the land, these barbarians "made the weeds grow tall on the highways of the land." Even stretches of the Persian Royal Road often became impassable mud holes, in which, on one occasion, the retreating Greeks repeatedly became stuck. In the Letter of the Satirical Scribe, the road through the Megiddo pass is described as filled with boulders and pebbles and overgrown with reeds, brambles, briers, and "wolf's paw."

Road Construction. Certainly the technology of paving existed in the pre-Roman period (Walter Andrae, *Alte Feststrassen im Nahen Osten,* Leipzig, 1941). Aiburšabum Street in Babylon, like similar streets in ancient Mesopotamia, was constructed with a technique almost matching that of the Romans: a foundation layer of bricks was set in asphalt, a surface of heavy limestone slabs was laid over it, and the joints were sealed with more asphalt. Other examples of such paving include the processional streets discovered in Aššur, the approach road at Khorsabad, and the paved streets Sennacherib constructed in Nineveh. In Egypt, approach roads to temples were often paved.

In Israel, paving is attested as early as the Early Bronze Age, witnessed, for example, by the paved street at Beth-Yeraḥ near the Sea of Galilee. Examples of other paved streets from pre-Israelite periods include a cobbled street at Shechem, from the Middle Bronze II period, and a paved street from the Late Bronze period discovered at Jaffa. Paving is also well attested in the Iron Age. The Iron Age streets at Tell Deir ʿAlla were paved, and the paving was regularly refurbished. The main street of the Israelite city of Dan was paved with stone. Cobbled streets from the Iron Age include the 3.5-m-wide street discovered at Ashdod and the tenth–ninth-century BCE street found at Gezer. At Megiddo the approach road to the city gate (eleventh century BCE) was paved with a hard, cementlike plaster on a crushed-stone base. The parapet and retaining wall on the outside and inside of the roadway were also of rubble and plastered like the roadway.

It was the Romans, however, who brought to the ancient Near East the practice of paving open highways; and during the Roman era many of the thoroughfares of the region were paved. The technology of Roman roads, featured superb foundations, adequate drainage, and one or more layers of cement or stone paving designed to last for centuries (see Forbes, 1934, 1965; and Casson, 1974, pp. 163–175). The remains of many of these paved Roman highways can be seen throughout the Near East.

Preparation of road surfaces during the pre-Roman period is occasionally referred to in contemporary records. The Assyrian king Tukulti-Ninurta I recounts that during his campaign against the mountainous Nairi-lands, he cut through the mountain ranges with copper pickaxes and widened their closed paths. Tiglath-Pileser I describes how, in his campaign against the land of Kutmuhi, he attacked the rugged highlands and their difficult paths with copper pickaxes, improving the roads so that his chariots and army might advance. When Sargon II encountered a road too difficult for his chariots, he summoned his engineering corps to hew out a better one. When the road was completed, he marched ahead, followed by his chariotry, cavalry, army, and baggage train. Nebuchadrezzar recounts how he opened passes to make a road for transporting cedars. The tool most often referred to as employed in road preparation is the *akkulu,* a pickaxe often used otherwise for hewing building blocks and tunneling through mountainsides.

In Egypt, road construction is also occasionally mentioned in the records. During the twelfth dynasty, Thuthotep describes how he employed miners, quarrymen, and others to help hew a rocky trail, whose rugged surface was hard stone, to create a smooth road along which he was attempting to haul a 60-ton block of stone. From the remains of Egyptian roads from the pre-Roman period, it appears that road preparation in Egypt consisted of leveling out a track by scraping smooth the surface and lining the sides with the scrapings and gravel.

In the Hebrew Scriptures, the process of road building is apparently alluded to in *Isaiah* 40:3, 57:14, and 62:10 and in *Malachi* 3:1. There, too, the procedure appears to have involved simply "clearing" *(pinnâ)* the roadway and "smoothing" *(yiššēr)* and "leveling" *(sālal)* the surface.

Generally, the government was responsible for both constructing and maintaining roads. Road maintenance and repair were regularly carried out during the spring, following the damage done by the winter rains (Mishnah, *Sheq* 1:1 and *Moʿed Q.* 1:2; B.T.; *San.* 11a).

Road Markings. Roads were generally named according to their destinations. The "Uruk Road" was, thus, the name of a Mesopotamian road that led to Uruk. This custom was common throughout the ancient Near East. In the Hebrew Scriptures, for example, the "Beth-Shemesh Road" mentioned in *1 Samuel* 6:12 was the road that led to the town of Beth-Shemesh; the "Bashan Road" (*Nm.* 14:25; *Dt.* 3:1) was the highway leading to Bashan; and the Beth-Gan Road (*2 Kgs.* 9:27) was the road leading to Beth-Gan. The major exception to this practice would appear to be the designation "the king's highway." However, this designation, which occurs in Sumerian *(kaskal lugal),* Akkadian *(ḫarrān šarri),* Aramaic *(ʾōraḥ mālkāʾ),* and Hebrew *derek ha-melek),* was not the name of a road but a descriptive designation of a particular kind of road, to be translated "the main road" or "the public road."

Roads do not generally appear to have been marked by signs in the pre-Roman period. In Egypt a road dating from the Old Kingdom that led to the alabaster quarries east of el-Amarna was marked by a series of cairns constructed of black stones, limestone, and flints. Similar markers were used in the road network in the el-Amarna region during the Late Kingdom. Although in Mesopotamia Sennacherib set up stelae along his great processional road in Nineveh, they are not to be equated with road markers in the open countryside, for which there is little evidence in Mesopotamia. In the Hebrew Bible, road markers similar to those used occasionally in Egypt may be alluded to in *Jeremiah* 31:21 *(ṣiyyunîm).* The Romans, on the other hand, marked their highways with inscribed mile markers, many of which can still be seen along Roman roads in the Near East.

Because few clearly identifiable physical traces of roads in the ancient Near East prior to the Roman era have been discovered, reconstructing their courses is inferential, involving at least four lines of evidence. First, there are the historical sources: for example, the highway that went from Bethel to Shechem, passing west of Shiloh, is mentioned in *Judges* 21:19. Second, lines of ancient settlements, revealed by archaeological excavations and surveys, can be testimony to the existence of an ancient thoroughfare. Cities, towns, villages, way stations, and forts, for example, tended to grow up along roads. Long after a road had fallen into disuse and disappeared, settlement ruins attested to its erstwhile existence. Third, the courses of later routes—Roman, medieval, and nineteenth-century—may preserve the courses of earlier, unpaved roads they simply followed. Finally, an area's geographic and topographic conditions determined to a large degree the courses roads took: mountain passes, river fords, harbors, easily traversed valleys, ascents, and springs attracted roads; whereas deep canyons, high mountains, swamps, deserts, and unfordable rivers were natural barriers to be avoided.

[*See also* Carts; Chariots; Transportation.]

BIBLIOGRAPHY

Aharoni, Yohanan. *The Land of the Bible: A Historical Geography.* Rev. ed. Translated and edited by Anson F. Rainey. Philadelphia, 1979. Good overview of the nature of roads in ancient Israel, with a reconstruction of the country's main routes.

Andrae, Walter. *Alte Feststrassen im Nahen Osten.* Leipzig, 1941.

Avi-Yonah, Michael. "Map of Roman Palestine." *Quarterly of the Department of Antiquities in Palestine* 5 (1936): 139–193. Extensive study of the Roman road system in Palestine, brought current by the continuing work of Israel Rol and others.

Broshi, Magen. "Standards of Street Widths in the Roman-Byzantine Period." *Israel Exploration Journal* 27.4 (1977): 232–235. Suggests that the average width of city streets during this period was 5.4 m, perhaps a standard at the time.

Casson, Lionel. *Travel in the Ancient World.* London, 1974.
Dorsey, David A. "Schechem and the Road Network of Central Samaria." *Bulletin of the American Schools of Oriental Research,* no. 268 (November 1987): 57–70. Reconstructs the course of about two dozen routes comprising the road network in the central highlands of Iron Age Samaria.
Dorsey, David A. *The Roads and Highways of Ancient Israel.* Baltimore, 1991. The only comprehensive treatment of the subject in the ancient Near East, particularly in Israel. Deals with the nature and physical characteristics of roads, road terminology in the ancient Near East and in the Hebrew Bible, and methodology in reconstructing ancient Israel's road network. Reconstructs the course of some 245 routes that comprised Israel's road network in the Iron Age.
Forbes, Robert J. *Notes on the History of Ancient Roads and their Construction.* Amsterdam, 1934.
Forbes, Robert J. "Land Transport and Road Building" in *A History of Technology,* edited by C. Singer, et al., vol. 2, pp. 493–516. Leiden, 1965.
Goodchild, R. G. "Evolution of the Roman Roads." In *A History of Technology,* edited by Charles Singer et al., vol. 2, pp. 500–509. London, 1956. Helpful survey.
Karmon, Yehuda. "Geographical Influences on the Historical Routes in the Sharon Plain." *Palestine Exploration Quarterly* 93 (1961): 43–60. Illustrates how topographic and geographic factors determined the course of roads in ancient times, particularly in the Sharon plain.
Roll, Israel. *Roman Road System.* Historical Geography of the Bible Lands, Wide Screen Project, Map 12. Tel Aviv, 1979. Convenient, up-to-date wall map of the Roman road network in Palestine, based on Rol's extensive research.
Wilkinson, John. "The Way from Jerusalem to Jericho." *Biblical Archaeologist* 38.1 (1975): 10–24. An example of good methodology in reconstructing the course of an ancient road.

DAVID A. DORSEY

ROBINSON, EDWARD (1794–1863), American biblical scholar, philologist, and explorer. Although Robinson belongs to an era before the inception of modern archaeological excavation in Palestine, his influence on the later development of the discipline was enormous. In his utilization of historical sources, linguistic evidence, and physical explorations throughout Palestine and the Sinai Desert, Robinson was among the first to attempt to reconstruct a historical geography of the Holy Land based on scholarly research rather than ecclesiastical tradition.

Born in Southington, Connecticut, Robinson, the son of a Congregationalist minister, was educated at Hamilton College. After briefly studying law, he returned to Hamilton as an instructor in Greek and mathematics. He published a detailed commentary on the *Iliad* in 1822. After ordination as a Congregationalist minister, he devoted himself to biblical studies under the guidance of Moses Stuart at the Andover Theological Seminary. Robinson subsequently spent several years in Germany, becoming familiar with the latest techniques of historical research and textual criticism. A theological conservative, he returned to America intent on utilizing these methods in defense of the historical reliability of the biblical text.

In 1831, Robinson accepted a professorship in biblical literature at Andover and founded the *American Biblical Repository,* a journal devoted to biblical research. After publishing lexicons of the Hebrew and New Testaments, Robinson accepted a position on the faculty of the Union Theological Seminary in New York City. Before assuming his teaching responsibilities, however, Robinson set off in 1838 on an extended exploration of Sinai and Palestine, in which he hoped to establish the historical geography of the Holy Land as a serious and systematic discipline.

Robinson was well aware that the initial attempts at sound geographical identifications for localities mentioned in the Bible were for the most part desultory and unsystematic, based on the often haphazard guesses of Western travelers. He was therefore determined to prepare his own exploration carefully. His most important achievement in this respect was gaining the services of Eli Smith, an American missionary, fluent in Arabic and a long-time resident in Lebanon. During the course of his ambitious three-month journey in 1838 from Suez to Beirut, Robinson and Smith succeeded in identifying dozens of previously overlooked biblical localities, speculated on the ancient landscape of the country, and formulated a system of linguistic rules to account for the transformation of ancient Hebrew geographical terminology into modern Arabic.

Robinson and Smith's analysis of the transformation of geographical terminology was deeply influenced by contemporary German comparative philology, with its theoretical emphasis on linguistic "degenerationism." That theory, which Robinson had studied under the philologists Wilhelm Gesenius and Emil Rödiger and the geographer Karl Ritter, posited the existence of several original, primitive languages (suggestively named for the migrating sons of Noah: Hamitic, Semitic, and Japhetic), each of which had undergone distortion and grammatical deterioration over the centuries. The modern geographical terminology of Palestine, Robinson believed, was the result of "a truly national and native tradition," which was "deeply seated in the genius of the Semitic languages," through which the transformations from Hebrew to Aramaic to Arabic could be traced (Robinson, 1841, vol. 1, p. 255).

The goal, then, in Robinson's study of the historical geography of Palestine was "a first attempt to lay open the treasures of biblical geography and history still remaining in the Holy Land; treasures which have lain for ages unexplored, and had become so covered with the dust and rubbish of many centuries, that their very existence was forgotten" (*ibid.,* p. xi). The distinct intellectual strains of conservative American Protestantism and German scientific linguistics were merged in the service of Robinson's brand of biblical geography. The impact of this scholarly undertaking was far-reaching: a new, modern territorial entity was effectively defined through the replacement of an existing landscape of Arabic place-names with a "biblical" geography.

Robinson's three-volume report on his expedition, *Biblical Researches in Palestine, Mount Sinai, and Arabia Petraea* (Boston, 1841) quickly became a standard work. An additional volume, *Later Biblical Researches in Palestine and the Adjacent Regions* (Boston, 1856), was based on an expedition to Palestine Robinson undertook in 1852, again in the company of Eli Smith. The continuing influence of Robinson's work can be seen in its use by the British-sponsored Survey of Western Palestine (1871–1882), which followed Robinson and Smith's linguistic lead by compiling an encyclopedic list of Arabic place-names and their relationship to biblical localities.

Plagued by poor health and failing eyesight in later years, Robinson was gradually forced to restrict his teaching and research responsibilities; yet, by the time of his death, he was already regarded as the father of a uniquely American brand of biblical geography.

[*See also* Biblical Archaeology; Historical Geography.]

BIBLIOGRAPHY

Ben-Arieh, Yehoshua. *The Rediscovery of the Holy Land in the Nineteenth Century*. Jerusalem, 1979.

Bliss, Frederick Jones. *The Development of Palestine Exploration*. New York, 1906.

Hitchcock, Roswell D., and Henry B. Smith. *The Life, Writings, and Character of Edward Robinson*. New York, 1863.

King, Philip J. *American Archaeology in the Mideast: A History of the American Schools of Oriental Research*. Winona Lake, Ind., 1983.

Robinson, Edward. *Biblical Researches in Palestine, Mount Sinai, and Arabia Petraea*. 3 vols. Boston, 1841.

Robinson, Edward. *Later Biblical Researches in Palestine and the Adjacent Regions*. Boston, 1856.

Silberman, Neil Asher. *Digging for God and Country: Exploration, Archaeology, and the Secret Struggle for the Holy Land, 1799–1917*. New York, 1982.

Silberman, Neil Asher. "Desolation and Restoration: The Impact of a Biblical Concept on Near Eastern Archaeology." *Biblical Archaeologist* 54 (1991): 76–87.

NEIL ASHER SILBERMAN

ROMAN EMPIRE. The lands around the Mediterranean have been politically and administratively united only during the Roman period. For four centuries (first to fourth century CE) Rome presided over an empire that at its height around 200 CE covered some 5 million sq km extending from central Scotland to northwestern Saudi Arabia. Complete control was achieved only in the first century BCE. Even in the fifth century CE when barbarian kingdoms emerged in the western half, the Byzantine Empire lived on in the east for an additional one thousand years.

Beginning with the province of Asia (western Anatolia) in 133 BCE Rome embarked on a series of conquests that culminated in 30 BCE with the overthrow of Cleopatra's Egypt. For the Near East in the narrower sense, there were provinces of Syria (63 BCE); Judaea (70 CE), later called Syria Palaestina; Arabia (106 CE), and Mesopotamia (198 CE). Direct administration in the first century BCE was restricted mainly to the northwest where the major cities of Hellenistic Syria were located. Later acquisitions extended direct control to the Gulf of ʿAqaba and to the Tigris at Mosul. Military expeditions saw Roman armies campaigning as far as the Caspian Sea, Persian Gulf, and Yemen.

Government was in the hands of a *legatus* (called *praefectus* in Mesopotamia) drawn from the imperial aristocracy. Equipped with a slim and largely unprofessional bureaucracy, these officials controlled their extensive provinces through a combination of delegation to internally self-governing cities and the threat of intervention by an efficient and ruthless army. In addition to the cities and often extensive territories that were administered by local aristocracies, there were various principalities and petty kingdoms. The emperor Augustus (30 BCE–14 CE) swept away many of these in Syria, but some well-known allied states remained. Best known is Herod the Great's Judaea, but longer lasting was the Nabatean kingdom, which was only annexed in 106 CE.

The quality of government improved after the civil wars (49–30 BCE). The monarchy of Augustus replaced the Roman republic. Governors resided in palaces in their provincial capitals but were often absent on tours of assize (legal and juridicial) centers or on campaigns. Their primary responsibilities were security, the administration of justice, and the collection of tax. Despite the great Jewish rebellions (66–70, 116–118, and 132–135 CE) the eastern empire enjoyed a long period of largely peaceful, stable administration for nearly three centuries. [*See* Bar Kokhba Revolt; First Jewish Revolt.]

Eastern Cities. Greco-Roman civilization was essentially urban, and the East had many cities. Antioch and Alexandria reached populations of about 200,000 to 250,000. There were many other great cities, such as the provincial capitals at Ephesus (Asia), Ancyra (Galatia), Nisibis (Mesopotamia), and Caesarea (Palaestina) with scores of others, mostly of already great antiquity. The pattern of cities—overwhelmingly pre-Roman in origin—was largely determined by geography: fertile soils, trade routes and ports, and strategic requirements. Most of the cities in greater Syria were on or within fifty miles of the coast.

The Roman impact was superficially modest. A few new cities, *coloniae,* were founded in southwestern Anatolia, with fewer still in Syria, although Berytus (now Beirut) grew into one of the great cities of the East. But this overlooks the contribution of the allied rulers who founded Greco-Roman cities, some of which—Herod's Caesarea Maritima in Palestine is the outstanding example—flourished and helped transform the character of the region. The real impact of

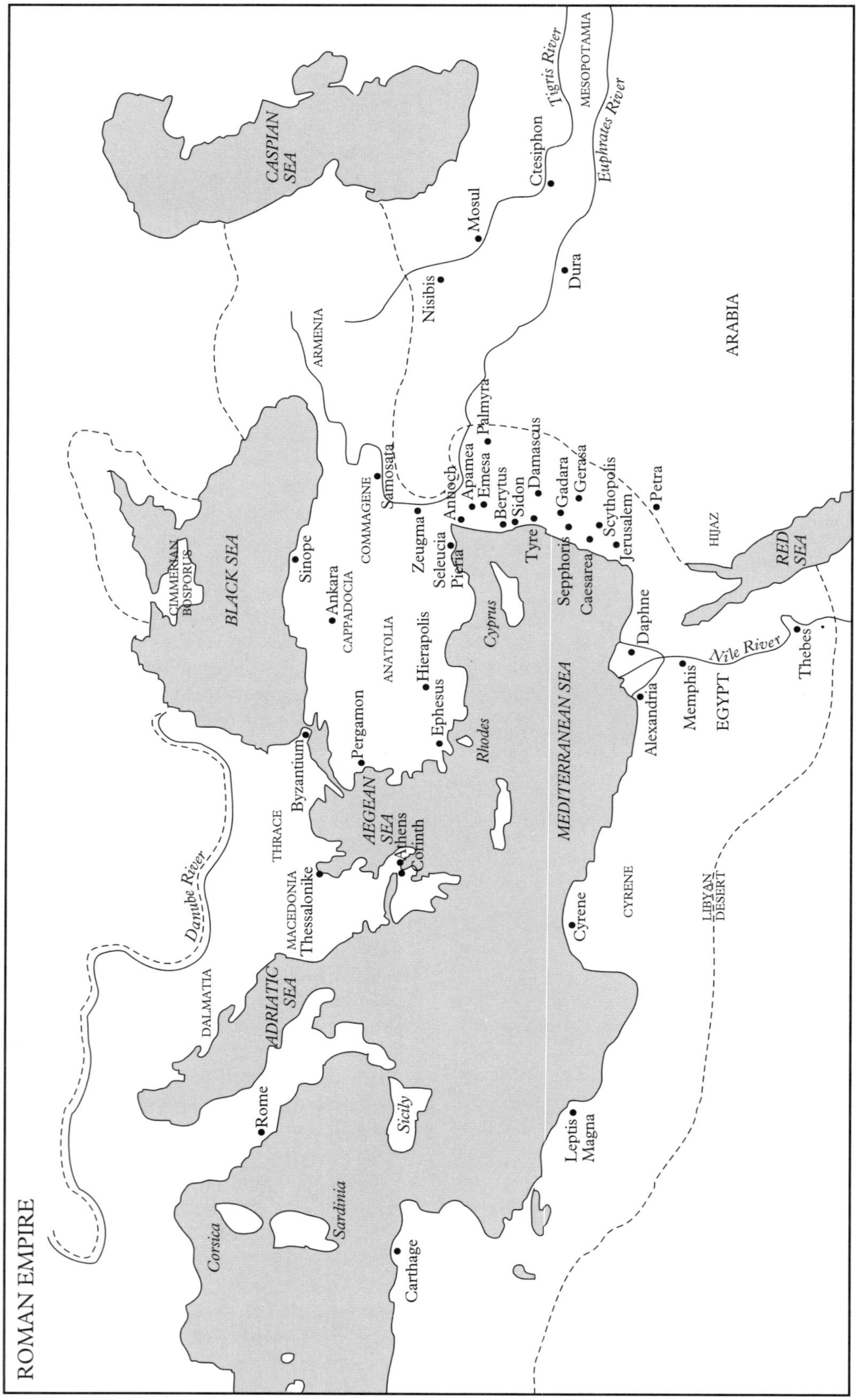
ROMAN EMPIRE
CASPIAN SEA
BLACK SEA
CIMMERIAN BOSPORUS
ARMENIA
MESOPOTAMIA
Tigris River
Euphrates River
Ctesiphon
Mosul
Nisibis
Dura
ARABIA
Sinope
Ankara
CAPPADOCIA
COMMAGENE
Samosata
Zeugma
ANATOLIA
Hierapolis
Ephesus
Pergamon
Byzantium
THRACE
Danube River
AEGEAN SEA
Athens
Corinth
MACEDONIA
Thessalonike
DALMATIA
ADRIATIC SEA
Rome
Sicily
Sardinia
Corsica
Carthage
Rhodes
Cyprus
Seleucia Pieria
Antioch
Apamea
Emesa
Palmyra
Berytus
Sidon
Damascus
Tyre
Gadara
Gerasa
Scythopolis
Sepphoris
Caesarea
Jerusalem
Petra
HIJAZ
RED SEA
MEDITERRANEAN SEA
Daphne
Alexandria
Memphis
EGYPT
Nile River
Thebes
Cyrene
CYRENE
LIBYAN DESERT
Leptis Magna

Rome on the urban landscape was more subtle but important. Peace and stability provided the ideal conditions which permitted growth, prosperity and development. It was only in the Roman period that most cities achieved their fullest flowering.

Under Roman prosperity civic architecture flourished. Theaters, stoas, and gymnasia became regular features of Greek cities in the Roman Empire. The Roman contribution, however, was uneven. The basilica is rarely found in the East. The amphitheater occurs in such "Roman" cities as Berytus and Caesarea Maritima but is otherwise rare. In contrast, the hippodrome and that quintessentially Roman structure, the monumental arch, were popular features. Probably the best-preserved hippodrome in the empire is at Tyre, and there are fine combinations of city gate, hippodrome-stadium, and monumental arch at Gadara (Umm Qeis) and nearby Gerasa (Jerash) in Palestine in what may be an example of civic rivalry. Public amenities were most developed in the Roman period, whether the great public baths or aqueducts, such as those to be seen still at Caesarea (drawing water from 14.5 km distant), Apamea (75 km long), and around the cities of eastern Cilicia.

Overall, however, the greatest Roman contribution was grandeur. It is most striking in the treatment of the main streets. Broadened, lengthened, flanked by shady colonnades and shops, they became monuments in their own right. The street at Antioch in Syria two miles long, is known only from excavation. Their character can be seen readily at Apamea also in Syria, Gerasa, and elsewhere. [*See* Cities, *article on* Cities of the Hellenistic and Roman Periods.]

Art and Architecture. Despite numerous Greco-Roman features, the eastern cities lay in an alien environment. At Palmyra in Syria, for example, the column brackets that were intended for statues are a native embellishment. In most cities the pre-Roman tradition of post-and-lintel architecture remained dominant in the face of Roman preference for brick-faced concrete, and there was a continued confident Hellenistic artistic tradition.

At Samosata the native rulers used *opus reticulatum,* diamond-shaped facing stones on a concrete core, even on their city walls, a construction style rarely found outside Italy. At Caesarea Maritima, Herod the Great evidently employed not just Roman engineers and craftsmen but Roman techniques and material for his great artificial harbor. In Herod's palace at Masada, however, the wall paintings were of Alexandrian (Hellenistic) style. Most representational art of the period is known to us only through the many fine mosaics to survive—more than three hundred at Antioch and Daphne alone and many more superb examples from Apamea, Zeugma, Palmyra, and Scythopolis in Syria-Palestine, reflecting a vigorous Hellenistic style of three dimensionality and illusionism. Where wall painting does survive extensively, it is in peripheral areas, providing the evidence for a continuing oriental tradition. At Dura-Europos, for example, a city with a strong army presence, the figured scenes in the synagogue are in the unrealistic, frontal poses of the Near East. Even the third-century painting in the temple of Bel at the same site depicting the Roman tribune Julius Terentius sacrificing with his soldiers, is in the same style. [*See* Wall Paintings.]

Sculpture was common. Full-size bronzes such as that of Hadrian from Tirat Zevi near Scythopolis are rare anywhere, but there is much fine heavily classical stone statuary and relief sculpture from the towns. Once again, native tastes remained vibrant. Best known are the relief sculpture and depictions on tombstones from northern Syria, especially Palmyra, where it is the staring frontal pose which strikes the observer rather than the Greek of the inscription. Syrian style was exported to imperial art where it appears in the relief portraits of Septimius Severus (193–211 CE) and his family on the Porta Argentariorum in the Roman forum. The porphyry sculpture of the four tetrarchs now at St. Mark's Cathedral in Venice is perhaps the most obvious example of Palmyrene tradition in the art of the Roman East (Rice, 1968, pp. 52, 390).

Popular art and architecture remained little changed: mud-brick and pisé (clay) for houses in many areas, stone orthostats (supports) and arches in the villages of the largely treeless limestone massif of northern Syria and the lava lands of the Hauran. Amongst the sedentary population, artwork tended to be cruder versions of traditional oriental forms. The thousands of so-called Safaitic graffiti of the desert and semidesert often reveal the tastes of the nomads for scenes of everyday life, especially hunting and herding. [*See* Building Materials and Techniques, *article on* Materials and Techniques of the Persian through Roman Periods.]

Religion and Funerary Practices. The deified Roman emperors and the "classical" deities were certainly worshiped in the eastern empire; nonetheless, the Greco-Roman pantheon figured only superficially in local cults. The god of Doliche in northern Syria may have been called *Jupiter,* but he was an oriental syncretism, Jupiter Dolichenus, clad in Hellenistic military costume and standing on the back of a bull. The important excavations at Dura-Europos illustrate the complexity and diversity of religious belief. Worshipers had access to Palmyrene deities such as Bel and Atargatis, Greco-Roman personifications of Nemesis and the Fortune of Dura, and to a synagogue. Alongside these mixed practices, the army was engaged in the official commemoration of defied emperors and the gods of Rome, as we know from a unique military religious calendar (see Welles et al., 1959). In the south the important Nabatean sanctuary at Si in the Hauran and numerous smaller Nabatean temples and "high places" continued to flourish under Roman rule, giving way to Christianity only in the third century. In the northwest, too, oriental religions dominated. The oriental priest of the cult of Atargatis at Hierapolis is depicted in traditional long robe and conical hat. At Emesa,

Diadumenianus, priest of the sun god Elagabalus, became emperor in 218.

The most famous temples of Roman Syria were those at the great sanctuary of Heliopolis at Baalbek. Nominally dedicated to a Roman triad of Jupiter, Venus, and Mercury, they rapidly became powerful, elevated, oriental deities, the temples themselves incorporating features alien to Roman tradition. Monumentality on the scale of Baalbek was not a Roman innovation, but it was surely Roman wealth and determination that finally completed the vast sanctuary. At a much lower level at Dura, we find small, irregular mud-brick temples to Semitic deities that are quite unlike even the semi-classical monumental stone versions at Palmyra.

Funerary practices, too, were less touched by Roman rule, much of the impact being superficial. Notable native traditions which continue are the great tower tombs of Palmyra and Dura and the royal examples at Emesa, and the superb rock-cut tomb facades of Petra in Jordan and Meda'in Saleh in Saudi Arabia. Even when cremation was the common practice in much of the Roman Empire through the first to third centuries CE, inhumation remained the norm in the East. The well-to-do were interred in stone sarcophagi or in niches in rock-cut tombs such as those which are found in the cemeteries of Roman Zeugma. Also found at Zeugma and elsewhere in northern Syria, are a handful of tumulus graves, a fashion most strikingly found in use among the rulers of Samosata farther north. A novel feature, which does reflect a characteristically Roman fashion, is the great increase in the erection of inscribed stelae. Most carry little more than a brief text—usually in Greek—but many bear relief portraits of the deceased. Throughout much of the Near East, however, symbols of the Sun are common on tombstones, especially the eagle, which also implies apotheosis.

ROMAN EMPIRE. *Roman tomb in Syria.* Dated to the second century CE. (Courtesy D. L. Kennedy)

Material Culture. Throughout the East the material culture of the pre-Roman societies continued. The novelty was less one of new characteristically Roman artifacts than a broadening of the range and quantity. Finds are generally much more abundant and the drier conditions of much of Syria and Egypt have preserved even organic materials from human hair through textiles to wood and foodstuffs. Especially useful are the huge numbers of papyri recovered in Egypt and, now, from similar conditions around the Dead Sea at Dura-Europos and in Mesopotamia.

Coinage became more abundant with the proliferation of both local and imperial mints. Many towns such as Zeugma, Damascus, Pella, Philadelphia (Amman), and even little Areopolis (modern Rabba, Jordan) occasionally struck their own coins, but the principal imperial mints in the Near East were at Antioch and Alexandria. Glass is much more common too, best preserved when recovered among grave goods. Pottery is well made and includes the major fine wares of the Roman world, the red-gloss wares known as Eastern sigillata and African red slip. Metalwork, especially in bronze, is common too for jewelry, tools, and household cult images. [*See* Coins; Glass; *and* Ceramics, *article on* Ceramics of the Hellenistic and Roman Periods.]

Rural Areas. Agriculture was already well-developed and widespread in the Near East and Roman rule brought no great technological breakthroughs. What Rome did contribute, however, was the long period of sustained peace which permitted the easier spread of ideas and what may have been the fullest expansion of agriculture until modern times. For the former, it was the spread of technical inventions, largely those developed at Alexandria in the Hellenistic and early Roman periods. For example, the geographer Strabo describes a water screw used for raising water from the Nile to the Roman fortress at Babylon in Egypt in the early first century CE; half a century later an example is attested epigraphically on the Euphrates near Samosata. No certain trace has yet been found anywhere in the Near East of the characteristic Roman practice, so common in Europe and parts of North Africa, of centuriation—dividing the landscape up for colonists into great regular squares of, typically, 776 yards. Farmsteads dated to the Roman period are emerging in large numbers from the landscape surveys now so common in Jordan and Israel in particular. In the marginal regions of the Hauran in southern Syria into which agriculture spread very fully in the Roman period, old air photographs preserve traces of fossilized field systems probably belonging to the Roman and Byzantine settlements in their midst. Not the Roman centurial squares but fairly regular long, narrow strip fields, marked by stone boundary walls. The pattern emerging from field surveys is uneven, but the impression is of a densely settled landscape in which even in marginal regions with inadequate rainfall, pre-Roman methods of water harvesting, permitted farming to be sustained for generations. [*See* Agriculture.]

In supply, communications, and transport there was a major impact. The change was brought about not so much by Roman engineering skill as by the opportunity for development of native traditions in the construction of dams, reservoirs, and cisterns which now abound in the region. The Romans, however, were great bridge builders and many of the finest surviving examples are to be seen in the Near East, especially those on the tributaries of the Euphrates around Samosata. Many ancient roads became Roman highways, and scores of new roads were constructed, creating a network that in scale and quality was unsurpassed till the nineteenth and twentieth centuries. Superb examples can be viewed all over the region from the frontier roads of the upper Euphrates, through the desert roads of Syria and Arabia, to the great highways which bound together the region as a whole. The ancient coast road of the Levant, the Via Maris to Egypt, was paved and marked by milestones under Roman rule, other roads were built to join Palmyra to the Euphrates and southwards to Damascus, and numerous new surfaced roads connected the towns of the Near East to one another. Especially notable is the Via Nova Traiana in Jordan where not just the road but even the regular towers and groups of inscribed milestones at each Roman mile is often visible. Terrain was no impediment, as the zigzags which carry the Via Nova across the great slash of Jordan's Wadi el-Mujib attest. [*See* Transportation; Roads.]

Trade and Industry. The remarkable sea captain's handbook, *The Periplus of the Erythraean Sea* (c. 40–70 CE), provides details of trade between Egypt and India, which is confirmed by finds of Roman artifacts, including terra sigillata (at Arikamedu in Tamil Nadu) and coins (in southern India and Sri Lanka). Trade provided a wider range of items from distant points within the empire and beyond. Thus amphorae attest to wine imports from the Aegean, fine red-gloss terra sigillata to trade with Gaul and the province of Africa, and numerous marbles can be traced to their origins in Asia Minor and North Africa, the Aegean, and Italy. Exotic commodities from outside the empire include Chinese silk from a Palmyrene tomb, lapis lazuli from the Hindu Kush in Afghanistan, ivory from Sub-Saharan Africa, amber from the Baltic. To facilitate trade, not only Caesarea Maritima but also Seleucia Pieria were given sophisticated artificial harbors to supplement the many others along the coast from Cilica to Egypt. At Antioch, the river Orontes was tamed by canals, which allowed goods to be brought upriver, possibly as part of a military supply route linking the Mediterranean to the Euphrates.

Industries included the dyeworks of the Levant, fulling at Antioch, silk weaving at Damascus, and the production of fine linen, jewelry and glass. Natural resources were exploited: copper from the Wadi ʿArabah, the cedar forests of Lebanon, and bitumen from the Dead Sea.

ROMAN EMPIRE. *Via Nova Trajana, looking south.* (Courtesy D. L. Kennedy)

The nature and role of Roman influence on provincial economies is keenly debated. Although most scholars accept that there was little direct intervention, the needs of the frontier armies, the effects of taxation, and the impact of transforming large areas into imperial estates, will certainly have brought about changes in scale, character and direction. More passively, peace and political unification permitted the gradual filtering of ideas around the region as a whole. In agriculture, the ubiquitous olive presses still to be seen on the limestone massif illustrate one area of development, and recent surveys and examination of air photos have revealed how farming penetrated even the more marginal areas.

Roman Army. The work of the military is much harder to trace. We know that upward of one hundred thousand soldiers were based in the eastern provinces, over half in greater Syria but, unlike the West, few of their bases have been located or investigated. Most are known only from literary references or artifacts, such as military tombstones and stamped tiles. There is a legion fortress at Satala in northeastern Anatolia, and the outline of that at Bostra in Arabia is visible from the air, but the location of a first-century fort has been excavated at Tell el-Hajj on the Euphrates, revealing typical round corners, which contrast with the possibly second-century fort at Ḥumeima in Jordan where the circuit has small projecting towers. The best evidence comes from the third century CE, when the Diocletianic *castella* or fortresses appear along the desert fringes of Syria and Arabia. Part of the explanation for the spotty attestation for military structures seems to be that troops were largely based in earlier periods in the towns where the evidence is lost or hidden. The classic case is at Dura-Europos, where excavation has revealed how an entire quarter within the town walls had been taken over—indeed, walled off—by the military. The garrison built new, characteristically Roman military structures, such as barrack blocks, and also made use of what was there, as in the case of the temple of Azzanathkona, which became the regimental archive. Finally, the East has superb examples of Roman siege works; not just the well-known first-century CE example at Masada, but another at Machaerus, in Jordan. There are also second-century examples at Battir and Naḥal Ḥever in Israel and a possibly third century example at Hatra in Iraq. [*See* Fortifications; *article on* Fortifications of the Hellenistic and Roman Periods.]

Population. Ethnic Italians were rare outside the administration and army; even Greeks were few and scattered in the newer urban centres. Many urban natives throughout the eastern provinces, however, became Hellenized in language and, to some extent, culture. In greater Syria the native population was largely Semitic. Latin is rare in inscriptions; Greek is much more common. Indigenous languages such as Palmyrene and Nabatean are preserved on numerous inscriptions; even more startling is the survival of tens of thousands of so-called Safaitic graffiti scratched on the rocks of the harra (the boulder-strewn southern part of the Syrian desert) and hammada (the gravel- and pebble-strewn parts) farther south, attesting to a degree of literacy and self-awareness amongst the nomads. [*See* Greek; Latin; Palmyrene Inscriptions; Nabatean Inscriptions; Safaitic-Thamudic Inscriptions.]

Soldiers from distant provinces settled and intermarried in the East. Traders and refugees from the Parthian (Persian) Empire came as well. In crude terms we can measure the size of the military impact. Initially most of the approximately 100,000 soldiers were foreigners, but there continued to be recruitment from throughout the East as well as beyond—Italians in the legions and Thracians, Gauls, Moors, and Goths in the auxiliary regiments.

An inscription (*ILS* 2683) records the tally of 117,000 *homines* (probably those citizens of tax-paying age) at Apamea in Syria one of the larger cities, under Augustus. Antioch may have reached 250,000 in habitants. Archaeology can assist. Scholars will dispute likely and possible population densities, and must make subjective allowances for the amounts of open space. Nevertheless, broad population parameters may be calculated for individual towns from the extent of area walled; at Samosata, for example, the walls run for 5 km (3 mi.). Then there is the impressionistic value of the numbers and supposed sizes of towns. There is also the evidence of field survey for the size and number of sites of all kinds in the Roman period. Finally, there is the mounting evidence for the extent and intensity of agriculture, implying a large population. At its peak, a population of thirty to fifty million persons may have lived between Bosphorus and Cyrenaica in the second century CE and about ten million in greater Syria.

Future of Research. Roman sites abound in the Near East. Cities have always been attractive to archaeologists, but excavation has extended now to military sites—especially in Jordan—and field survey has produced rich harvests of "Roman" sites of all kinds. The pressing need today for the understanding of the Roman period, as for other historical eras, is for salvage of the many sites threatened not only by population growth and land development but also by hydroelectric projects and other irrigation schemes.

[*See also* Byzantine Empire. *In addition, most of the sites mentioned are the subject of independent entries.*]

BIBLIOGRAPHY

Bowersock, Glen W. *Roman Arabia.* Cambridge, Mass., 1983. Standard study of an area undergoing increasingly intensive research.

Bowman, Alan K. *Egypt after the Pharaohs, 332 BC–AD 642.* London, 1986. Beautifully illustrated and evocative study of a key and highly distinctive province.

The Cambridge Ancient History. 3d ed. London, 1970–. This revised edition of volumes 9– incorporates solid accounts by international scholars of all the major themes of the Roman period, including chapters devoted to specific eastern provinces (e.g., David L. Kennedy, "Syria," vol. 10).

Cornell, Tim, and John Matthews. *Atlas of the Roman World.* New York, 1982. Superb maps and color photographs illustrate and evoke the Roman Empire.

Dentzer, Jean-Marie, and Winfried Orthmann, eds. *Archéologie et histoire de la Syrie,* vol. 2 *La Syrie de l'époque achéménide à l'avènement de l'Islam.* Saarbrücken, 1989. A most valuable collection of essays by leading scholars on numerous aspects of Classical Syria not often surveyed outside specialist publications.

Isaac, Benjamin. *The Limits of Empire: The Roman Army in the East.* Rev. ed. Oxford, 1992. Broad-ranging and provocative study.

Jones, Arnold H. M. *The Cities of the Eastern Roman Provinces.* 2d ed. Oxford, 1971. Classic study of the many cities of the region, here revised by several regional experts.

Kennedy, David L. "The Archaeology of the Umm el-Jimal Area: Maps, Air Photographs, and Surface Survey." In *Umm el-Jimal, a Nabataean, Roman, Byzantine and Early Islamic Rural Community in Northern Jordan, I,* edited by Bert De Vries. Journal of Roman Archaeology Supplementary Series. In press (due October 1995). Based mainly on air photographs, this study illustrated the extent to which even marginal areas were settled intensely.

Kennedy, David L. "Syria," In *Cambridge Ancient History.* 3d ed. Vol. 10, pp. 703–736. Cambridge, in press (due 1996).

Kennedy, David L., and Derrick N. Riley. *Rome's Desert Frontier from the Air.* Austin, 1990. Air views illustrate the range, character, and context of Rome's military installations.

Levi, Doro. *Antioch Mosaic Pavements.* Princeton, 1947. The principal collection of Roman mosaics from, in this case, the provincial capital.

MacDonald, Burton. *The Wadi el-Hasa Archaeological Survey, 1979–1983, West-Central Jordan.* Waterloo, Ontario, 1988. One of the first and most fully published field surveys which has helped to quantify the Roman presence in the Near Eastern landscape and place it in a broader chronological context.

Macready, Sarah, and Frederick H. Thompson, eds. *Roman Architecture in the Greek World.* London, 1987. Superb collection of essays on an increasingly popular theme; note in particular references to other works by Dodge.

Millar, Fergus. *The Roman Near East, 31 BC–AD 337.* Cambridge, Mass., 1993. The first major study of the region to appear for many years, by a leading historian of Rome.

Mitchell, Stephen. *Anatolia: Land, Men, and Gods in Asia Minor.* 2 vols. New York, 1993. Substantial and thoughtful study of Roman Anatolia.

Perkins, Ann. *The Art of Dura-Europos.* Oxford, 1973. A short but lively survey of the art and architecture, including the wall paintings.

Rice, David Talbot. *Byzantine Art.* Rev. ed. Harmondsworth, 1968. General, well-illustrated discussion of art from the Roman East.

Schürer, Emil. *The History of the Jewish People in the Age of Jesus Christ, 175 B.C.–A.D. 135.* 4 vols. Revised and edited by Géza Vermès et al. Edinburgh, 1973–1987. Superbly documented study of Judaea and neighboring regions.

Ward-Perkins, J. B. *Roman Imperial Architecture.* 2d ed. Harmondsworth, 1989. Classic treatment whose major chapters on the Near East provide both analysis and context.

Welles, C. Bradford, Robert O. Fink, and J. Frank Gillian. *The Excavations at Dura-Europos: The Parchments and Papyri. Final Report, Vol. 1.* New Haven, 1959. Superb collection of military papyri from Syria and including the military calendar.

Wells, Colin. *The Roman Empire.* Stanford, Calif., 1984. Short but stimulating study of the Roman Empire as a whole, combining documentary and archaeological sources in an enterprising manner.

DAVID L. KENNEDY

ROWE, ALAN (1891–1968), British archaeologist and Egyptologist. Born in Horshonds, Essex, England, Rowe spent his early years in Australia. Between 1922 and 1928 he worked at Beth-Shean on the Palestine Expedition of the University of Pennsylvania Museum. He was director from 1925 to 1928. Rowe uncovered a series of Canaanite temples, which he partially published in 1940. Full publication and reanalysis of the Beth Shean excavations has lowered the dates and produced a new evaluation of much of the material (Kenyon, 1970, p. 219; James, 1966). The site is being reexcavated by Amihai Mazar for the Hebrew University of Jerusalem.

From 1923 to 1925 Rowe worked as assistant to George A. Reisner at Giza, Egypt, where in 1925 he discovered the fourth-dynasty tomb of Hetepheres J, wife of Pharaoh Snefru and mother of Khufu (Smith, 1956, pp. 144–145). From 1929 through 1931 Rowe directed the University Museum's excavations at Meidum, Egypt, for which he provided detailed documentation of the earliest classic "residence-cemetery" of the Old Kingdom, including the funerary temple and causeway to the pyramid, which dates to the end of the third and the beginning of the fourth dynasty (Rowe, 1931). In 1934 he undertook minor explorations at the site of Gezer for the Palestine Exploration Fund. In 1936 Rowe published his important *A Catalogue of Egyptian Scarabs, Scaraboids, Seals, and Amulets in the Palestine Archaeological Museum.* From 1942 to 1943 Rowe reported twice to the British War Office in Cairo on the state of monuments in Cyrenaica, formerly an ancient Greek kingdom in Libya. This activity led to Rowe's excavations (1952, 1955–1957) around the ancient capital Cyrene for the University of Manchester (Rowe, 1956, 1959). While curator at the Greco-Roman Museum in Alexandria (1940–1949), he explored the remains of ancient Athribis (also Kom el-Atrib or Tell Atrib) near Benha in the central Delta. From 1945 to 1946 he excavated the temple and enclosure of the god Serapis (discovered in 1943) at Alexandria (Rowe, 1946, 1957). In 1950 he joined the faculty at the University of Manchester, where he remained until his death in 1968. During this time, when not in the field, Rowe wrote about the archaeology of Egypt, its western desert, and other areas of the Near East (Rowe 1953–1957, 1961).

[*See also* Beth-Shean; Cyrene; Gezer; Giza; *and the biography of Reisner.*]

BIBLIOGRAPHY

Anonymous. "Excavations in Palestine, 1932–4: Gezer." *Quarterly of the Department of Antiquities of Palestine* 4 (1935): 198–201.

James, Francis W. *The Iron Age at Beth Shan: A Study of Levels VI–IV.* Philadelphia, 1966.

Kenyon, Kathleen M. *Archaeology in the Holy Land.* 3d ed. New York, 1970.

Rowe, Alan. *The Four Canaanite Temples of Beth-Shan.* 2 vols. Philadelphia, 1930–1940.

Rowe, Alan. *The Topography and History of Beth-Shan.* Philadelphia, 1930.

Rowe, Alan. "Excavations of the Eckley B. Coxe, Jr. Expedition at Meydûm, Egypt, 1929–30." *Museum Journal* (University of Pennsylvania) 22 (1931): 5–36.

Rowe, Alan. "The 1934 Excavations at Gezer." *Palestine Exploration Quarterly* 4.4 (1935): 19–33.

Rowe, Alan. *A Catalogue of Egyptian Scarabs, Scaraboids, Seals, and Amulets in the Palestine Archaeological Museum.* Cairo, 1936.

Rowe, Alan. *Discovery of the Famous Temple and Enclosure of Serapis at Alexandria.* Annales du Service des Antiquités de l'Égypte, Cahier no. 2. Cairo, 1946.

Rowe, Alan. "A Contribution to the Archaeology of the Western Desert." *Bulletin of the John Rylands Library* 36.1 (1953–1954): 128–145; 36.2 (1953–1954): 484–500; 38.1 (1955): 139–165; 39.2 (1957): 485–520.

Rowe, Alan. *Cyrenaican Expedition of the University of Manchester, 1952.* Manchester, 1956.

Rowe, Alan. *Cyrenaican Expeditions of the University of Manchester, 1955, 1956, 1957.* Manchester, 1959.

Rowe, Alan. "Studies in the Archaeology of the Near East." *Bulletin of the John Rylands Library* 43.2 (1960–1961): 480–491; 44.1 (1961–1962): 100–118.

Smith, Joseph L. *Tombs, Temples, and Ancient Art.* Norman, Okla., 1956.

Winegrad, Dilys P. *Through Time, Across Continents: A Hundred Years of Archaeology and Anthropology at the University Museum.* Philadelphia, 1993.

ROBERT H. DYSON, JR.

RUJM EL-HIRI (Ar., "stone heap of the wild cat"), a large Bronze Age megalithic complex also known as Rogem Hiri and Gilgal Rephaim, situated in the central Golan, about 16 km (10 mi.) east of the northern shore of the Sea of Galilee (map reference 2254 × 2573), about 515 m above sea level. With major occupational remains from the Early and the Late Bronze Ages, the site consists of a massive, carefully constructed central cairn roughly 20 m in diameter and 4.5 m high, encircled by several concentric stone circles. The outermost circle is about 156 m in diameter and 500 m in circumference. The 2.5-meter-high and 3.5-meter-wide stone rings are sporadically connected by a series of short radial walls. There are two monumental entryways to the complex, one facing the northeast and the other the southeast. The cairn, circles, and hundreds of dolmens—the straight, shallow stone walls that surround the monument—constitute a large megalithic complex that is one of the most impressive archaeological stone monuments in the southern Levant. Petroglyphs have been reported both from the monument and from areas neighboring it.

Rujm el-Hiri was discovered during the 1967–1968 archaeological survey of the Golan Heights. Initial explanations for the function and the date of the complex described it as a ceremonial center, a defense enclosure, a central storage facility, a large burial complex, a center for astronomical observations, and a calendrical device. Rujm el-Hiri yielded almost no surface artifacts, limiting the possibilities for dating it. Tentative dates offered for the site were usually within the temporal framework of the third millennium BCE, although both slightly earlier and later dates were also suggested. The ongoing debates over the date and the function of Rujm el-Hiri triggered the Rujm el-Hiri Project (1988–1991), directed by Yonathan Mizrachi of Harvard University, as part of the Land of Geshur Project of Tel Aviv University, in cooperation with the Israeli Antiquities Authority. The research program at Rujm el-Hiri was designed from the outset as a long-term, problem-oriented multidisciplinary effort, including a large excavation project, a geophysical survey program, a lichenometric study, and a comprehensive study of the geometry and astronomy of the complex. A preliminary geophysical survey provided data on subsurface elements and valuable information on the central cairn: data from a magnetometer survey suggested that the cairn was built on a naturally elevated basalt formation. Based on the radar data, several targets were identified within the central cairn, one of which was excavated and turned out to be a carefully constructed burial chamber. Seismic data helped in isolating areas with deep stratification for future excavations. Four main excavation areas were opened in the circular complex: NE-I and NE-II in the northeast quadrant, SW-I in the southwest quadrant, and cairn I in the central cairn. Excavation exposed substantial examples of architecture in the northeast gate and the central cairn and a dromos-based burial chamber measuring 2 × 2 m within the central cairn. The looted chamber contained the remains of a dozen carnelian beads, arrowheads, and three gold earrings.

Excavation and survey data, lichenometric studies, and studies of the geometry and astronomy of the complex indicate that the concentric stone circles and the two gates were already in place by the later part of the third millennium BCE. By contrast, evidence excavated from the central cairn and analysis of the geometry of the complex all point to the surprising possibility that the cairn in its present format was extensively used, and probably built, sometime during the late second millennium BCE. Although alternative reconstructions are possible, it appears that Rujm el-Hiri is a LB megalithic cairn built within a preexisting EB monumental complex, rather than a single contemporary EB monumental complex built around a megalithic cairn (for the latter view, that the LB material represents a secondary usage of the cairn, see Kochavi, 1989).

During the mid-third millennium BCE, a large ceremonial center was erected at Rujm el-Hiri. The complex reflects such care in engineering and design that there can be little doubt that the alignments of the architecture were intentional and meant to manifest notions of religion and cosmology and permanently record culturally significant alignments (e.g., alignments associated with the agricultural calender) by using the entryways and the radial walls as alignments fixing devices for both celestial and noncelestial elements or phenomena. This EB monument served as a socioeconomic and a political central place for the local third-millennium urban populations—the inhabitants of the Golan enclosure sites. Concurrently, the site served as a spiritual focal point for these populations, a node at which religious ceremonies associated with ritual observations were performed. The fact that the Rujm el-Hiri complex falls within the temporal horizon in which complex society and subsequent urbanization emerged in this region is of special significance. Thus, Mizrachi interprets the hyper-monumentality of the complex as a means of symbolizing power through the conspicuous consumption of energy, control of which is the fundamental measure of power in complex, urban societies.

By the late second millennium BCE, the central cairn was built in its present format. This reconstruction is plausible in light of the accumulated evidence for construction and reuse of dolmens in the late second millennium that has been reported from other sites in neighboring areas and from the northern Golan. It is known from the astronomical and geometric analyses that during this time the complex could not have functioned as a celestial-bodies alignments-fixing device. This observation, as well as the nature and the association of the late second-millennium material recovered, leads to the suggestion that the primary function of the complex during the Late Bronze Age was associated with burial. Something during the post-LB era, Rujm el-Hiri ceased being a focus of ceremonial or burial activity, and its primary function shifted toward something more earthly. It seems that by this time the large stone complex had been used as a source of construction material, a cattle pen, a storage place, and perhaps even as a defense post.

[*See also* Dolmen; *and* Golan.]

BIBLIOGRAPHY

Aveni, Anthony, and Yonathan Mizrachi. "A Study of the Geometry and Astronomy of Rogem Hiri, a Megalithic Monument from the Southern Levant." Forthcoming. Detailed study of the astronomical and geometric aspects of the complex. Essential reading.

Kochavi, Moshe. "The Land of Geshur Project: Regional Archaeology of the Southern Golan, 1987–1988 Seasons." *Israel Exploration Journal* 39.1–2 (1989): 1–17. Survey of some recent Bronze and Iron Age work in the Golan.

Mizrachi, Yonathan. "Mystery Circles on the Golan." *Biblical Archaeology Review* 18.4 (1992): 46–57. The story of five years of research at Rujm el-Hiri, including a description of each of the major research programs, color photos, drawings, and reconstructions.

Mizrachi, Yonathan. "Rujm el-Hiri: Toward an Understanding of a Bronze Age Megalithic Monument in the Levant." Ph.D. diss., Harvard University, 1993. The most detailed and comprehensive study available on Rujm el-Hiri, including site plans, drawings, and color plates.

Mizrachi, Yonathan, Mattanyah Zohar, Moshe Kochari, Pirhiya Beck, Vincent Murphy, Anthony Aveni, and Simcha Lev-Yadun. "Report of the 1988–1991 Exploration Efforts at Rogem Hiri, Golan Heights." *Israel Exploration Journal* (forthcoming). Detailed technical report of the Rujm el-Hiri excavations.

Zohar, Mattanyah. "Rogem Hiri: A Megalithic Monument in the Golan." *Israel Exploration Journal* 39.1–2 (1989): 18–31. Summary of the available information about Rujm el-Hiri prior to the Rujm el-Hiri Project, with detailed description of the complex's architecture.

Zohar, Mattanyah. "Megalithic Cemeteries in the Levant." In *Pastoralism in the Levant: Archaeological Materials in Anthropological Perspectives,* edited by Ofer Bar-Yosef and Anatoly Khazanov, pp. 43–63. Prehistory Press Monographs in World Archaeology, no. 10. Madison, Wis., 1992. Comprehensive survey of megalithic remains in the Levant.

YONATHAN MIZRACHI

RULE OF THE COMMUNITY. The abbreviated title of the *Rule of the Community* is 1QS; the *1Q* indicates that it comes from the first cave at Qumran to yield manuscripts. The original find was made in 1947, and the text, photographs of its eleven columns, and a transcription into Hebrew characters were published by their editors, Millar M. Burrows, John C. Trever, and William H. Brownlee, in 1951. The *S* in the abbreviated title represents the Hebrew word *serek* ("rule"), which occurs several times in the scroll. The closest analogy to the scroll's contents is to be found in the rules of monastic orders, with their mixture of disciplinary directives and idealistic exhortation. The *Rule* reveals the internal organization of the Qumran community, whose institutions, many believe, identify its members as Essenes. Surveys of research into the scroll have been published by Hans Bardtke and Mathias Delcor (851–857).

Ten badly damaged manuscripts of the *Rule* were found among the thousands of fragments scattered in Cave 4 at Qumran. One other extremely fragmentary copy (5Q11) was found in Cave 5 (Milik, 1962). Fragments detached from the scroll when it was removed from the cave were published by Dominique Barthélemy and J. T. Milik (1955, pp. 107–130). They are the *Rule of the Congregation* (1QSa) and the *Book of Blessings* (1QSb). All these texts are now available in volume 1 of the Princeton Theological Seminary Dead Sea Scrolls Project edited by J. H. Charlesworth.

On paleographic grounds, Nahman Avigad (1958, p. 71) and Frank M. Cross (1961, p. 258, n. 116) assign 1QS to the first quarter of the first century BCE. Neither it nor any of the extant copies of the *Rule* is the original. Hence, the composition of the *Rule* in its present form must be dated sometime in the second century BCE (Cross, 1967, p. 120).

The earliest commentators noted, but did not analyze, the scroll's composite character (Dupont-Sommer, 1953, p. 90; Wernberg-Møller, 1957, p. 56, n. 49). Although acute in their observations, the attempts of Jürgen Becker (1963, pp. 39–42) and Alfred R. C. Leaney (1966) to define the scroll's component elements ultimately proved unsatisfactory because they failed to explain how and why the elements were assembled. Jerome Murphy-O'Connor (1969) was the first to suggest a general hypothesis of composition; his conclusions were accepted with minor modifications by Jean Pouilly (1976). Their hypothesis integrates the partial hypotheses of their predecessors (Denis, 40–44; Duhaime, 1977; and von der Osten-Sacken, 1969, pp. 17–27) and has raised no decisive objections (Schürer, 1986, vol. 1, p. 383; Davies, 1987, p. 60). It postulates that 1QS developed in four stages in order to meet the community's changing needs.

The first stage of development (1QS 8:1–10a, 12b–16a, 9:3–10:8) represents the manifesto in which the Teacher of Righteousness proposed the establishment of a community in the desert to the Essenes (Murphy-O'Connor, 1974, p. 237; Knibb, 1987, p. 127). The community would be a spiritual temple (1QS 8:5) in which spiritual sacrifices (1QS 9:4–5) are offered to expiate the sins of the land (1QS 8:6, 10). Its core would be composed of priests (1QS 9:7).

The second stage, consisting of two interpolations (1QS 8:10–12a, 8:16b–9:2), was inserted into the manifesto not long after the community was established (Knibb, 1987, p. 136). The manifesto continued to define the community, but legislation to deal with failures of obedience had become necessary.

The third stage reflects a completely different social situation. The community's need to redefine itself as a democracy (1QS 5:1–13), to enact legislation for the conduct of a general assembly (1QS 6:8–13), and to admit new recruits (1QS 6:13–23) suggests that the original idealism had been institutionalized. The casuistry of the penal code (1QS 6:24–7:25) confirms the inference that we have here the problems typical of a late stage of development in a large community (Weinfeld, 1986).

The fourth stage is designed to counteract the community's descent into formalism by revitalizing its spiritual life. It bracketed stages 1–3 with material taken from the liturgy of the renewal of the covenant (1QS 1:1–3:12, 10:9–11:22), during which members recommitted themselves. The addition of 1QS 4:23b–26, which stresses the crucial importance of individual decision, adapted the originally independent *Instruction on the Two Spirits* (1QS 3:13–4:23a) to the same end (Duhaime, 1977). Such indirect appeals were strengthened by new legislation regarding the quality of entrants and the continuous study of the Law (1QS 5:13b–6:8).

[*See also* Dead Sea Scrolls; Qumran.]

BIBLIOGRAPHY

Avigad, Nahman. "The Palaeography of the Dead Sea Scrolls and Related Documents." In *Aspects of the Dead Sea Scrolls,* edited by Chaim Rabin and Yigael Yadin, pp. 56–87. Scripta Hierosolymitana, vol. 4. Jerusalem, 1958.

Baillet, Maurice, J. T. Milik, and Roland de Vaux. *Les "petites grottes" de Qumrân.* Discoveries in the Judaean Desert of Jordan, vol. 3. Oxford, 1962.

Bardtke, H. "Literaturbericht über Qumran VII: Die Sektenrolle 1QS." *Theologische Rundschau* 38 (1973): 257–291.

Barthélemy, Dominique, and J. T. Milik. *Qumran Cave I.* Discoveries in the Judaean Desert, vol. 1. Oxford, 1955.

Becker, Jürgen. *Das Heil Gottes: Heils- und Sündenbegriffe in den Qumrantexten und im Neuen Testament.* Studien zur Umwelt des Neuen Testaments, 3. Göttingen, 1963.

Burrows, Millar, ed., with John C. Trevor and William H. Brownlee. *The Dead Sea Scrolls of St. Mark's Monastery,* vol. 2, fasc. 2, *Plates and Transcription of the Manual of Discipline.* New Haven, 1951.

Charlesworth, J. H., ed., with Frank Moore Cross, J. Milgrom, Elisha Qimron, Lawrence H. Schiffman, L. T. Stuckenbruck, and R. E. Whitaker. *The Dead Sea Scrolls: Hebrew, Aramaic, and Greek Texts with English Translations.* vol. 1, *Rule of the community and Related Documents.* Tübingen, 1994.

Cross, Frank Moore. "The Development of the Jewish Scripts." In *The Bible and the Ancient Near East: Essays in Honor of William Foxwell Albright,* edited by G. Ernest Wright, pp. 133–202. Garden City, N.Y., 1961.

Cross, Frank Moore. *The Ancient Library of Qumran and Modern Biblical Studies.* Rev. ed. Garden City, N.Y., 1976.

Davies, Philip R. *Behind the Essenes: History and Ideology in the Dead Sea Scrolls.* Brown Judaic Studies, no. 94. Atlanta, 1987.

Delcor, Mathias. "Littératur essénienne." In *Dictionnaire de la Bible, Supplément,* vol. 9, cols. 828–960. Paris, 1978.

Duhaime, Jean. "L'instruction sur les deux esprits et les interpolations dualistes à Qumrân." *Revue Biblique* 84 (1977): 566–594.

Dupont-Sommer, André. *Nouveau aperçus sur les manuscrits de la Mer Morte.* Paris, 1953.

Knibb, Michael A. *The Qumran Community.* Cambridge, 1987.

Leaney, Alfred R. C. *The Rule of Qumran and Its Meaning.* London, 1966.

Milik, J. T. "Review of P. Wernberg-Møller, *The Manual of Discipline.*" *Revue Biblique* 67 (1960): 410–416.

Murphy-O'Connor, Jerome. "La genèse littéraire de la Règle de la Communauté." *Revue Biblique* 76 (1969): 528–549.

Murphy-O'Connor, Jerome. "The Essenes and Their History." *Revue Biblique* 81 (1974): 215–244.

Osten-Sacken, Peter von der. *Gott und Belial: Traditionsgeschichtliche Untersuchungen zum Dualismus in den Texten aus Qumran.* Studien zur Umwelt des Neuen Testaments, 6. Göttingen, 1969.

Pouilly, Jean. *La Règle de la Communauté de Qumrân: Son évolution littéraire.* Cahiers de la Revue Biblique, 17. Paris, 1976.

Schürer, Emil. *The History of the Jewish People in the Age of Jesus Christ, 175 B.C.–A.D. 135.* Vol. 3, part 1. New English version revised and edited by Géza Vermès et al. Edinburgh, 1986.

Weinfeld, M. *The Organisational Pattern and the Penal Code of the Qumran Sect: A Comparison with Guilds and Religious Associations of the Hellenistic-Roman Period.* Novum Testamentum et Orbis Antiquus, vol. 2. Fribourg and Göttingen, 1986.

Wernberg-Møller, Preben C. H. *The Manual of Discipline Translated and Annotated.* Studies on the Texts of the Desert of Judah, vol. 1. Leiden, 1957.

JEROME MURPHY-O'CONNOR, O.P.

RUMEITH, TELL ER-, site located near the northern border of Jordan and the town of Ramtha (map reference 247 × 212). The site's excavator, Paul W. Lapp, identified it with Ramat-Gilead based on the apparent linguistic similarity, its location, and the occupational evidence. The site's small size could disqualify the identification, but it is the only excavated site in the area whose occupational history corresponds to the biblical record. Tell el-Ḥusn, for example, the largest site in the area with any archaeological remains, has not been excavated.

In a sounding at Rumeith in 1962, sponsored by the American Schools of Oriental Research (ASOR), Lapp investigated the occupation on the mound, and he uncovered Hellenistic and later material to the east, which, without substantial architecture, seemed to indicate only transient occupation. He returned for a six-week excavation in 1967 with the additional sponsorship of the Pittsburgh Theological Seminary, limiting the second campaign to the fort on the mound, which had been occupied for about two centuries during the Iron Age. Lapp investigated the four Iron Age strata (VIII–V) by clearing the northeast quadrant of the fortress down to bedrock and clearing a portion of the southeast quadrant along the east wall. The plans of the four strata were recovered and ceramic groups whose typology is Syrian were collected.

The contours of the mound suggest that the stratum VIII fort, believed to be Solomonic, was symmetrical (approximately 37 × 32 m). Its mud-brick walls were about 1.5 m thick and the north wall had a recessed gate. Excavation to bedrock revealed a leveling operation prior to construction. The destruction debris above the stratum VIII floors was as much as a half-meter thick. The stone grinding implements, craters and bowls, ovens, and bins recovered indicate that the occupants had produced and processed grain. In stratum VII (probably when the site was under the control of the Arameans), which followed soon after the stratum VIII destruction, a stone defense line more than 1.5 m wide was built of very large and roughly dressed boulders around the mud-brick fort. Thin walls divided the space between the stone and mud-brick walls into casemates and the earlier gateways were reused. The Arameans may have converted the site into a border fort. About 2 m of destruction debris preserved the stratum VII plan and assemblages of pottery and stone implements that show a distinct Syrian influence of the mid-ninth century BCE. The destructions could date to the reigns of Jehoshaphat and Ahab or to Ahaziah and Jehoram.

The stratum VI occupation could be attributed to the Arameans and Hazael's extending Syria's borders to the south. The entire area within the walls of the stratum VI fort had been leveled in order to construct a platform out of thick gray clay. The houses in the southeast quadrant consisted of two rooms with a cobbled floor and evidence of a stairway to the roof. The lower half-meter of the 50-cm-thick walls was constructed of small rough stones topped by mud brick. Ceramic assemblages, found on the floor in the thick destruction layer, dated the destruction to about 800 BCE, possibly relating it to Joash's defeat of the Arameans at Aphek.

The strata VI and V occupations extended beyond the fortress walls, but there was no sign of their defenses. Inside the lines of the fort, the stratum V walls were preserved to a height of 1.5 m. Rooms were filled with destruction debris that may belong to Tiglath-Pileser III's 733 BCE campaign in Palestine.

BIBLIOGRAPHY

Lapp, Nancy L. "Rumeith." In *Archaeology of Jordan,* vol. 2, *Field Reports,* edited by Denys Homès-Fredericq and J. Basil Hennessy, pp. 494–497. Louvain, 1989.

Lapp, Paul W. "Tell er-Rumeith." *Revue Biblique* 70 (1963): 406–411; 75 (1968): 98–105. Preliminary reports after the excavations.

Lapp, Paul W. "Excavations at Tell er-Rumeith." In *The Tale of the Tell: Archaeological Studies,* edited by Nancy L. Lapp, pp. 111–119. Pittsburgh Theological Monograph Series, 5. Pittsburgh, 1975. Popular report of the excavations reprinted from an ASOR newsletter.

NANCY L. LAPP

RUSAFA (Old Syriac, Rasappa; in Ptolemy, Rēsapha; Lat., Rosapha, Risapha; since the sixth century CE also Sergiopolis; Ar., Ruṣāfat Hishām), site located 180 km (112 mi.) east of Aleppo, Syria, and 35 km (22 mi.) south of the Euphrates River. Excavations were conducted by the German Archaeological Institute from 1952 to 1965 under the direction of Johannes Kollwitz and since 1975 of Tilo Ulbert.

To date, no traces of a pre-Roman settlement have been found. The most recent excavations have recovered evidence for the presence of the Roman army beginning in the first century CE (see below). In about 300 CE the Christian officer Sergius suffered a martyr's death in the Diocletianic limes fort of Rusafa (Vita Ss. Sergii et Bacchi, Acta Martyrum, Analecta Boll. 14, 1895, 373ff.). The fort later grew into a city that prospered as a result of the number of pilgrims visiting the grave of St. Sergius. It became in the fifth century the seat of a bishop and later of a metropolitan. In the Byzantine period (sixth century), the city was fortified (Procopius, *de Aedificiis* 2.9.3–8). From 724 to 745 it was the residence of the Umayyad caliph Hisham and was a Christian/Islamic city until the Mongol invasion of Syria in 1259–1260. The site has been uninhabited since.

In the sixth century the fortification walls were expanded to enclose a rectangular city area of 21 ha (62 acres). Their four monumental main gates and fifty towers have been largely preserved. Vaulted cisterns in the southwest area of the city also belong to this period. In 1986, in the course of investigating the ancient city's water supply system, it was possible to determine that there had been a dam outside the walls that collected the water from winter and spring rains and directed it into the city. Through a complicated canal system, the water flowed into four giant cisterns, whose annual levels would have sufficed for about six thousand inhabitants for one year, based on an assumed use of 10 l per person. In addition, each residential unit possessed its own cistern for collecting rainwater. Deep shafts, from which the saline groundwater could be drawn for watering livestock and gardens, were also distributed throughout the city.

The investigation of a residential quarter in the vicinity of the cisterns showed a continuity of settlement in the same stone houses from the sixth to the thirteenth century CE. The most recent excavations also permit a better understanding of the system of streets and open squares in the city. The sixth-century public buildings, such as the forum, baths, and pilgrim lodgings, have not yet been excavated. It is the ruins of the city's large churches that have determined Rusafa's appearance and that were the object of past investigations. [*See* Churches.] The oldest preserved church (Basilica B) was erected in the early sixth century on the site of an earlier structure. [*See* Basilicas.] The most recent excavations have produced finds from the first century CE from under its floor (the evidence of the first phase of Roman occupation on the Syrian limes). The so-called Central Building also dates to the sixth century; this is a church that manifests both a basilican and a centralizing architectural schema. Basilica A, the bishop's church probably originally dedicated to the Holy Cross, also housed the relics of the city's patron, St. Sergius, from the Early Byzantine period until the city's demise in the thirteenth century. In antiquity, this basilica, with its wide arcade (54.40 m long, 28.60 m wide, and preserved to a height of 18 m), suffered repeated earthquake damage; however, in contrast to the two other large Christian buildings at the site, it was always repaired. Both a baptistery and a residential building for the metropolitan were annexed to the basilica. [*See* Baptisteries.] A spacious peristyle courtyard in the northern part of the church was probably reserved for pilgrims. The grave itself was housed in the especially artfully outfitted subsidiary room in the north, next to the basilica's apse.

The large three-nave mosque of Hisham built in the pilgrim courtyard in the early eighth century is evidence of the probably peaceful coexistence of the Christian and Islamic communities at Rusafa at the start of the Umayyad period. [*See* Mosque.] During this period, a *suq* ("market") was established to the west of the mosque and the church. To judge from the finds, it was still functioning into the thirteenth century. The few rooms excavated so far have given valuable indications about the types of crafts produced (metal handicrafts, dye-works). In 1982 a hoard of five gilded silver vessels decorated in niello was discovered concealed in a pottery vessel in the pilgrim courtyard. This unique treasure was restored in the Rheinisches Landesmuseum in Bonn, Germany, and is now on display in the National Museum in Damascus. It consists of votive offerings to the grave of Sergius that were hidden shortly before the Mongolian invasion. All of the pieces date to the twelfth–thirteenth centuries; some were made in Syria, partially following western models. At least two of the other vessels came from western workshops and has reached the Near East in conjunction with the Crusades. Especially interesting is the drinking vessel that belonged to Raoul I of Couzy, a French noble, who took part in the Third Crusade and fell in the Battle of Akko in 1193. His own coat of arms and that of his family are engraved on the cup.

Inside the city, the fourth of the large basilicas (the so-called Basilica C, a columned basilica from the fifth–sixth centuries with a surrounding step podium) has also been investigated, as has a khan (a caravanserai within the walls). Research into the extensive construction outside the city walls has begun. This includes a fortified Late Antique suburban villa, occupied until the Umayyad period, and the so-called al-Mundir building, probably a reception hall of the sixth-century Ghassanid ruler of the same name. In an area south of Rusafa, the remains of large buildings constructed from mud bricks can still be recognized. One was excavated by Katarina Otto-Dorn during the first Rusafa campaign in 1952 and published as the Palace of Hisham. The most recent excavations have revealed a garden pavilion, richly decorated with stucco, that is also dated to the Umayyad period. It belonged to another very extensive palace area.

BIBLIOGRAPHY

Brinker, Werner. "Zur Wasserversorgung von Resafa-Sergiupolis." *Damaszener Mitteilungen* 5 (1991): 119–146.

Gatier, Pierre-Louis, and Thilo Ulbert. "Eine Türsturzinschrift aus Resafa-Sergiupolis." *Damaszener Mitteilungen* 5 (1991): 169–182.

Karnapp, Walter. *Die Stadtmauer von Resafa in Syrien.* Berlin, 1976.

Kollwitz, Johannes, et al. "Vorberichte über die Grabungen." *Archäologischer Anzeiger* (1954): 119–159; (1957): 64–109; (1963): 328–360; (1968): 307–343. Preliminary reports of the excavations.

Kollwitz, Johannes. "Die Grabungen in Resafa." In *Neue deutsche Ausgrabungen im Mittelmeergebiet und im Vorderen Orient,* edited by Erich Boehringer, pp. 45–70. Berlin, 1959.

Konrad, Michaela. "Flavische und spätantike Bebauung unter der Basilika B von Resafa-Sergiupolis." *Damaszener Mitteilungen* 6 (1992): 313–402.

Logar, Nuša. "Katalog der Keramikfunde aus dem Wasserverteiler." *Damaszener Mitteilungen* 5 (1991): 147–168.

Logar, Nuša. "Die Kleinfunde aus dem Westhofbereich der Groβen Basilika von Resafa." *Damaszener Mitteilungen* 6 (1992): 417–478.

Mackensen, Michael. *Resafa I: Eine Befestigte spätantike Anlage vor den Stadtmauern von Resafa.* Mainz am Rhein, 1984.

Sack-Gauβ, D.. *Resafa IV: Die Groβe Moschee von Resafa-Ruṣafāt Hišām.* Mainz am Rhein, 1995.

Sarre, Friedrich P. T., and Ernst Herzfeld. *Archäologische Reise im Euphrat- und Tigris-Gebiet.* Berlin, 1920. See volume 2, pages 1–45.

Spanner, Harry, and Samuel Guyer. *Rusafa: Die Wallfahrtsstadt des Heiligen Sergios.* Berlin, 1926.

Ulbert, Thilo (Tilo). "Eine neuentdeckte Inschrift aus Resafa." *Archäologischer Anzeiger* (1977): 563–569.

Ulbert, Thilo. *Resafa II: Die Basilika des Heiligen Kreuzes in Resafa-Sergiupolis.* Mainz am Rhein, 1986.

Ulbert, Thilo. *Resafa III: Der kreuzfahrerzeitliche Silberschatz aus Resafa-Sergiupolis.* Mainz am Rhein, 1990.

Ulbert, Thilo. "Beobachtungen im Westhofbereich der Groβen Basilika von Resafa." *Damaszener Mitteilungen* 6 (1992): 403–416.

Ulbert, Thilo. "Ein umaiyadischer Pavillon in Resafa-Ruṣafāt Hišām." *Damaszener Mitteilungen* 7 (1994): 213–231.

TILO ULBERT

Translated from German by Susan I. Schiedel

S

SAFAITIC-THAMUDIC INSCRIPTIONS.

Old Arabian script was used from perhaps as early as the eighth century BCE to as late as the fourth century CE, undergoing alterations as it spread across the vast Arabian Peninsula. Of the regional varieties, it is those conventionally termed Thamudic and Safaitic that appear in North Arabia. Occasionally, finds have been made of Old Arabian texts in the Levant of the Hijaz variety called Dedanite and Lihyanite, but the vast majority are concentrated at al-ʿUla (Dedan) in the Hijaz. The terms *Thamudic* and *Safaitic* are commonly used as conventional labels for these North Arabian inscriptions. They are in a South Semitic script and appear mainly on the desert fringe of the Levant. It is commonly assumed that the script evolved from South Arabian through the influence of Dedanite and Lihyanite, with the various script types of Thamudic developing from those earlier writing systems and ending with the Safaitic texts. The language of the Thamudic and Safaitic texts represents the linguistic family of what has been called Early North Arabian. The most distinguishing linguistic feature of these dialects is the use of the definite article *h*-.

Thamudic texts are found throughout the Arabian Peninsula and represent the oldest of the North Arabian texts. The concentration of such texts in the northern Hijaz led initially to their ascription to the tribe of Thamud, known from the Assyrian annals and the Qur'an. Attempts have also been made by some scholars to associate the users of the script with the descendents of the Midianites. Neither theory has gained acceptance. The earliest forms of the script seemed to have emanated from the North Arabian oases of Tayma' and Dedan in the Hijaz, from which they spread elsewhere. [*See* Tayma'; Dedan.] In 1937, Fred V. Winnett proposed classifying the texts into five types labeled A–E, suggesting a sequential chronological and geographic development for the script. The problem with this classification is that the categories are not ironclad: some texts exhibit the characteristics of more than one group. Primitive forms also appear with more evolved forms of the script, defying any simple chronological arrangement of the texts. In 1970, Winnett revised the categories into geographic designations, with Najdi (B), Hijazi (C, D), and Tabuki (E) replacing the older categories. Both systems are still utilized for convenience, in full recognition that further modification is needed. [*See the biography of Winnett.*] The now more than fifteen thousand recorded Thamudic texts are mainly graffiti, containing the name and patronymic of an individual, sometimes with a petition to a deity or an individual and accompanying phrase. Their laconic nature makes dating precarious.

Safaitic inscriptions primarily appear in southern Syria, northern Jordan, and northern Saudi Arabia, but a few isolated finds have been made in western Iraq, on Lebanon's coasts and Biqaʿ Valley, and as far afield as Pompeii, Italy. The name *Safaitic* is derived from the *ṣafa,* the basalt desert southeast of Damascus, Syria; the term is, however, a misnomer resulting from the initial discovery of the texts in the region in 1857. Most of the fourteen thousand published texts are concentrated in the basalt desert, or *ḥarra,* of northeast Jordan and neighboring southern Syria. Literally thousands more exist in this region and need to be recorded. The main contributors to the decipherment of the texts were Joseph Halévy in 1877, F. Praetorius in 1883, and E. Littmann in 1901. The latter was the first to recognize that the alphabet consisted of twenty-eight letters comparable to the Arabic alphabet. Some of the Thamudic E, or Tabuki, texts have a more marked similarity with the orthography of Safaitic than the common varieties of Thamudic and have been designated South Safaitic by some. The texts frequently contain extensive geneaologies that trace the lineage back to an eponymous ancestor; they sometimes include an individual's social group or tribe *('l),* along with various formulae and religious petitions, with occasional allusions to some historical event. The date is normally of an unidentifiable or ambiguous nature.

Few of the Safaitic texts can be dated with any precision, but they seem generally to begin as early as the first century BCE and cease probably by the fourth century CE because they reflect no evidence of any Christian or Islamic influence. The overwhelming impression is that they mainly stem from the first century CE, based on references to the Herodian dynasts, Nabatean kings, and Roman authorities, as well as the "Jews" *(yhd),* Itureans *(yẓr),* and Persians *(mḏḫy).* Because most of the Thamudic and Safaitic inscriptions are found in the remote desert regions of North Arabia, some distance from settled regions and villages, they have traditionally been perceived as the product of a nomadic population. Many of the texts speak of seasonal migrations with flocks and herds and many are accompanied by rock-art drawings of camels and horses, suggesting that pastoralists are the authors. Others, however, speak of attachments to villages and express intimate knowledge of political developments and imperial authorities, implying a population that was not just on the fringe of the sedentary population. The deities mentioned in the texts also include the Syrian Baʿal Shamin and Nabatean Dushara—cults associated with the shrines and temples of the settled population. Additional texts are being found scattered along the villages and settlements of the Transjordanian plateau and southern Syria.

BIBLIOGRAPHY

Graf, David F. "Rome and the Saracens: Reassessing the Nomadic Menace." In *L'Arabie préislamique et son environnement historique et culturel: Actes du Colloque de Strasbourg,* edited by Toufic Fahd, pp. 341–400. Leiden, 1989. Adventuresome reappraisal of the traditional "nomadic" interpretation that needs to be refined in light of newly published texts.

Harding, G. Lankester. *An Index and Concordance of Pre-Islamic Arabian Names and Inscriptions.* Toronto, 1971. Complete listing of the publications and onomasticon of the texts.

Macdonald, M. C. A. "Nomads and the Ḥawrān in the Late Hellenistic and Roman Periods: A Reassessment of the Epigraphic Evidence." *Syria* 70 (1993): 303–413. Defense of the traditional "nomadic" view (formulated by the pioneer interpreters of the texts) that ignores the implications of many of the texts.

Winnett, Fred V., and G. Lankester Harding. *Inscriptions from Fifty Safaitic Cairns.* Toronto, 1978. Valuable collection and discussion of many of the texts.

David F. Graf

SAFAR, FUAD (1913–1978), Iraqi archaeologist. Born in Mosul, Safar studied at Safed College in Palestine (1931–1932) and then graduated from the American University in Beirut (1933) with a degree in history and archaeology. He continued his studies (1934–1938) on a scholarship at the Oriental Institute of the University of Chicago, where he earned a master's degree. Upon returning to Baghdad, he joined the antiquities department, where he began his career as Iraq's most outstanding excavator and archaeologist.

In 1940–1941, Safar and Seton Lloyd excavated Tell ʿUqair in Lower Mesopotamia, whose material belongs to the Uruk and Jemdet Nasr periods. The remarkable painted murals in a temple from the Late Uruk period (c. 2800 BCE) remain the only known examples from predynastic levels in southern Mesopotamia. In 1942 Safar directed the excavations at the Islamic city of Wassit, near the modern town of Kut, built by al-Hajaj, the Umayyad governor of Iraq. He subsequently published the results of the excavations in 1952. This publication is the only source of information about one of the most important Islamic ruins in Iraq. Safar joined Seton Lloyd again in 1943–1944 at Hassuna, a small mound south of Mosul, where they identified a new Chalcolithic culture with distinctive pottery. In 1948 Safar and Lloyd began excavations on the ancient mound of Eridu, which proved to be of great importance in understanding the origin of the Sumerians and the development of the religious beliefs of ancient Mesopotamians. A sequence of eighteen occupation levels was established. A small temple belonging to the late Ubaid period was found at the top of the mound and primitive chapel founded on clean sand was uncovered on the lowest level.

Safar's excavations undertaken at the Parthian-Arab site of Hatra in 1950 are still underway. He directed only the first few seasons himself, but greatly influenced the subsequent fieldwork. He published numerous articles about the site, particularly its Aramaic inscriptions. [*See* Hatra Inscriptions.] In 1951–1952, Safar was one of the founders of the Faculty of Archaeology at the University of Baghdad, in which he lectured in addition to his work at the Department of Antiquities. In 1956, Safar was appointed inspector general of excavations, a post he held until his death, with the exception of a brief period when he was director general of antiquities.

Fuad Safar died in an automobile accident while on his way to inspect the international rescue excavations in the Hamrin basin. His work covered nearly all of Iraq's major historical periods, and his interpretation of his discoveries was influential. His students are today distinguished archaeologists in Iraq.

[*See also* Eridu; Hassuna; Hatra; *and the biography of Lloyd.*]

BIBLIOGRAPHY

Lloyd, Seton, and Fuad Safar. "Tell ʿUqair: Excavations by the Iraq Government Directorate of Antiquities in 1940–41." *Journal of Near Eastern Studies* 2 (1943).

Lloyd, Seton, and Fuad Safar. "Tell Hassuna: Excavations by the Iraq Government Directorate of Antiquities in 1943 and 1944." *Journal of Near Eastern Studies* 4 (1945): 255–289.

Safar, Fuad. *Wasit, the Sixth Season's Excavations* (in Arabic). Cairo, 1945.

Safar, Fuad, and Muhammad A. Mustafa. *Hatra, the City of the Sun God* (in Arabic). Baghdad, 1974.

Safar, Fuad, et al. *Eridu.* Baghdad, 1981.

Lamia al-Gailani Werr

ṢAFUṬ, TELL, site located geologically on the central Transjordan plateau at 927 m above sea level, overlooking the amply watered Baqʿah Valley, whose agricultural activities it administered on behalf of ancient Ammon (32°5′10″ N, 35°40′20″ E; map reference 228 × 168). Today, the tell stands within the northwest boundary of Greater Amman, just north of Suweileh and east of the modern village after which it is named. It is on the main Amman–Jerash road. In antiquity, Tell Ṣafuṭ also functioned as gatekeeper on a main access route to the capital of Transjordan, Rabbat Ammon, approximately 12 km (7 mi.) to the southeast.

Selah Merrill visited Tell Ṣafuṭ in 1868 and named it as one of four major sites surrounding Amman. Subsequent published accounts of tours of biblical lands included Tell Ṣafuṭ on the Transjordanian leg of the journey. An archaeological survey by Alexis Mallon in 1934 noted the existence of rampart fortifications built of large stones. Mallon suggested that the ancient name of the place was Nobah (near Jogbehah, cf. *Jgs.* 8:11) Roland de Vaux (1978, p. 590), has, however, shown that Nobah of *Numbers* 32:42 has to be located elsewhere. Surveys by Nelson Glueck (1939) and de Vaux (1938) noted the importance of Tell Ṣafuṭ relative to controlling the Baqʿah Valley. Except for some foundation stones of a (possibly square) tower, practically no architecture remained on the surface. In the mid-1950s, however, the rerouted Amman–Jerash road carved its way past the tell, cutting off a portion of the southern sector. Farah Maʿayeh (1960) and de Vaux (1960) believed that the bulldozing revealed a Middle Bronze Age glacis.

Further widening of the highway occasioned initial excavations in 1982 that are, under the direction of Donald Wimmer, jointly sponsored by Seton Hall University (New Jersey) and the Department of Antiquities of the Hashemite Kingdom of Jordan. The new cut revealed flat, geologically laid stratigraphy that the bulldozer had cut at an angle, giving the false (but frequently cited) impression of a glacis. Five seasons of excavation followed (1983, 1985, 1987, 1989, 1995). Material cultural remains clearly correlate with other Ammonite sites: the Amman citadel, Tell el-ʿUmeiri, Tell Jawa, and Umm ad-Dananir. [*See* Amman; ʿUmeiri, Tell el-.]

At Tell Ṣafuṭ excavation activity has been divided into areas A–J, omitting I. Squares are generally 5 × 5 m but no larger. Area A contains five squares at the eastern end of the southern slope, where the largest highway cut was made; to the north and adjacent to area A, area B contains nine squares, and, continuing in counterclockwise fashion, area C rises to the summit through three 5 × 10 m squares directly west of area B, with four more squares directly north of these three. South of area C, separated from and lower by 10–15 m because of the highway cut, was the now almost totally eroded area D, two squares to bedrock shaved to a 45 degree angle by bulldozers in the 1950s. Area E has a single shallow square that is off the tell and across the wadi to the east; area F has one square, on the northern perimeter defense wall, directly across from areas A and B; area G has a single Iron Age tomb (fragment) and is where two probes were made, along the wadi at the northern base of the tell, that were occasioned by construction activity; area H has two squares on the hill across the wadi to the east; and area J has twelve squares on the southeast slope of the tell, where the surface has been excavated only to expose architecture in order to forestall modern development.

Major architectural remains on the tell itself date to the Late Bronze Age and the Late Iron Age into the Persian period. Some reuse of architectural materials on the summit in the Byzantine period is clear, but the material culture remains from the Middle Bronze Age and Hellenistic period are scant. Late Roman ware seems to be continuous with the Byzantine ware off the tell in area E and across the wadi in area H, where the overview of the valley seems to have moved permanently by Islamic times. Two seasons of diachronic excavation penetrating vertically reached LB architecture built directly on bedrock (areas B, D) or virgin soil (area A). In subsequent seasons understanding the Late Iron phases was sought by synchronic excavation, which exposes as much material from a single period as possible.

Settlement at the site was fully underway in the Late Bronze Age, when a major perimeter defense wall was constructed running through area B into area J. It enclosed a stone structure (square B.5) into which a mud-brick superstructure had collapsed, crushing a once-gilded bronze LB deity and associated sacred vessels. In all likelihood, despite destruction layers elsewhere on the tell, this enclosed sacred area, possibly a temple or shrine, and the perimeter wall continued in use through the Iron Age. In the adjacent square (B.4), Iron I pottery characterized a few intervening layers under an extensively expanded Late Iron occupation that had overflowed earlier walls, including a lower Late Iron perimeter defense wall that, by itself, had already more than doubled the area of concentrated architecture.

To date, no inscriptions have been recovered, but several seals and seal impressions, mostly on jar handles, have been. Tell Ṣafuṭ boasts of an excellent repertoire of Ammonite painted pottery reconstructed from sealed destruction layers. [*See* Ammon.] Terra-cotta pillar figurines complemented the seated bronze deity of this Ammonite agricultural administrative center, where fertility religious beliefs undoubtedly prevailed. The high point of life at the tell seems to have occurred under Assyrian and then Babylonian hegemony. [*See* Assyrians; Babylonians.] The discovery of a four-winged Assyrian-type scarab stamp seal was accompanied by probably locally made Assyrian-type bottles and bowls. A Late Babylonian seal impression that was once affixed to a document was also found (Wimmer, 1987a, p. 281).

After a modest Byzantine-period presence, settlement activity moved to the east. Tell Ṣafuṭ was then used only for burials (on the summit) and farming (along the terraces).

[*See also* Transjordan; *and the biographies of Glueck and Vaux.*]

BIBLIOGRAPHY

Dornemann, Rudolph. *The Archaeology of the Transjordan in the Bronze and Iron Ages.* Milwaukee, 1983. Incorporates discussion about surface pottery taken from Tell Ṣafuṭ prior to stratigraphy excavation.

Glueck, Nelson. "Exploration in the Land of Amman." *Bulletin of the American Schools of Oriental Research,* no. 68 (1937): 13–21.

Glueck, Nelson. "Exploration in Eastern Palestine, III." *Annual of the American Schools of Oriental Research,* nos. 18–19. New Haven, 1939. Glueck's exploration summaries amply illustrate the vast multiplicity of sites now lost to modern development. For example, in his day, Ṣafuṭ is the only village in the valley. Today, there are at least three municipalities in addition to a very large Palestinian refugee camp.

Maʿayeh, Farah S. "Recent Archaeological Discoveries in Jordan: Tel Safut (Sweileh)." *Annual of the Department of Antiquities of Jordan* 4–5 (1960): 115. A single paragraph on the site providing the first attribution of a glacis to Tell Ṣafuṭ, based only on visual observation after bulldozing and before excavation. This assumed attributation, picked up by Dornemann, Sauer, and others, becomes a commonplace in the literature.

Mallon, Alexis. "Les Tells riverains du Jabbok inférieur (Sukkoth, Phanuel, Nobé)." In *Miscellanea Biblica Edita a Pontificio Instituto Biblico ad celebrandum annum XXV ex quo conditum est institutum,* pp. 57–68. Rome, 1934. Describes the site as a classical example of an ancient town whose pottery spans from 1200 to 600, and is suitably identified with Nobah of Gideon's travels as narrated in the *Book of Judges.*

Vaux, Roland de. "Chronique: Exploration de la région de Salt." *Revue Biblique* 47 (1938): 398–425. Includes Tell Ṣafuṭ and associated tombs in megaliths nearly.

Vaux, Roland de. *The Early History of Israel,* translated by David Smith. Philadelphia, 1978. Discusses Nobah of the *Book of Numbers* 32:34 relating it to research about a town called Kenath. The historian cannot use this information in connection with the Nobah of the *Book of Judges* 8:11, which, with Jogbehah = modern Jubeihat, is on the road from es-Salt to Amman.

Wimmer, Donald H. "The Third Archaeological Expedition to Tell Ṣâfûṭ," *Liber Annuus,* 35 (1985): 408–410.

Wimmer, Donald H. "The Excavations at Tell Ṣāfûṭ." In *Studies in the History and Archaeology of Jordan,* vol. 3, edited by Adnan Hadidi, pp. 279–282. Amman, 1987a. Highlights include a gilded bronze deity, Late Babylonian seal impression, and Late Iron Age casemate wall reinforced in its most vulnerable segment by a battered wall.

Wimmer, Donald H. "Tell Ṣāfûṭ Excavations, 1982–1985: A Preliminary Report." *Annual of the Department of Antiquities of Jordan.* 31 (1987b): 159–174. Discusses findings from areas A–E, including especially area D and segments of area A subsequently removed as part of the highway construction project.

Wimmer, Donald H. "Tell Ṣāfûṭ." In *Archaeology of Jordan.* In *Akkadica. Supplementum VII,* edited by Denyse Homes-Fredericq and J. Basil Hennessy, vol. 2, pp. 512–515. 1989.

Wimmer, Donald H. "Tell Ṣāfûṭ." In Bert De Vries, "Archaeology of Jordan," *American Journal of Archaeology,* 95 (1991): 268. A thumbnail sketch of five architectural phases divided into three strata: I, Byzantine; II, Iron IIC/Persian; III, possibly Iron I/Late Bronze Age, depending upon unresolved questions about ceramic typology related to historical periods.

Wimmer, Donald H. "Tell Ṣāfûṭ." In *The Anchor Bible Dictionary,* edited by David Noel Freedman et al, vol. 5, pp. 896–897. New York, 1992. Summarizes location and history of occupation from the Middle Bronze Age to the Late Iron Age and Late Byzantine period in light of the history of exploration and excavation.

Wimmer, Donald H. "Tell Ṣāfûṭ: The Northern Perimeter Wall." In Glen L. Peterman, "Archaeology in Jordan." *American Journal of Archaeology* 98 (1994): 540–541. The northern counterpart (area F) of the perimeter defense wall in area A.

Zayadine, Fawzi. *The Archaeological Heritage of Jordan.* Amman, 1973. Of all surveys, this accurately attests to the broadest range of historical periods reflected in the ceramic corpus.

DONALD WIMMER

SAḤAB, site located about 12 km (7 mi.) southeast of Amman, Jordan, in a transitional zone between the highlands and the desert. It has a long history of occupation, extending from the Late Neolithic/Chalcolithic period (fifth and fourth millennia) to the Late Iron Age. After the sixth century BCE, the site was probably abandoned until the Medieval Arabic period (eleventh–thirteenth centuries CE) as evidenced by the Ayyubid–Mamluk handmade sherds found there.

Neolithic/Chalcolithic Periods. Saḥab was largest in area during its earliest period of habitation, when it supported itself with extensive agriculture and evidently produced an abundance of food. This agricultural abundance is demonstrated by the large number of storage facilities both inside houses and outside in courtyards. A unit was excavated in area E that consists of several rooms (built of mostly unhewn stone) surrounding a courtyard in which large storage pits were cut into virgin soil and lined with small stones. These settlers coexisted with cave dwellers: caves were found in areas A, B, Cave C, and D. Some show a series of floors, the uppermost of which date to the Early Bronze Age. It is quite possible that the inhabitants continued to live in caves even after the main Neolithic/Chalcolithic settlement was deserted or destroyed.

Transitional Period. There appears to have been a transitional period just prior to the beginning of the Early Bronze Age, in which there was no permanent settlement at the site. In area E, above the Neolithic/Chalcolithic levels, several fragmentary walls were uncovered. These wall remains do not conform to any definite architectural plan. The present evidence suggests that the site was a seasonal settlement toward the end of the fourth millennium, probably at the very beginning of the Early Bronze Age (Kathleen Kenyon's Proto-Urban period). Related to this transitional period were two burial jars with human skeletons and a reused pit with seven–nine animal burials excavated in area E.

Bronze Age. The Early Bronze Age proper is represented at Saḥab by a number of sherds found in a sounding in area B; they were not associated with any structure. During the first and second seasons of the 1972–1973 excavations, two caves reused as burials in the Middle Bronze Age were excavated in areas A and B north of the site. Each of the graves has a deep shaft dug into earlier deposits. The shaft leads to a pavement on which the skeletons and objects were placed. In the last excavation campaign of 1980, close to the center of the site, part of an MB fort connected to a typical glacis rampart was excavated. The area was too limited to recover more definite information about the extent of the MB settlement. In another area (area H III), a massive MB wall was excavated. Unfortunately, no direct connection between it and the rampart in area GII can yet be established because the area between them is covered with modern houses. Saḥab is probably the closest of the MB II forts to the desert area, and its location must have been significant in defending the highland from attacks from the desert.

The Late Bronze Age is well represented but because of the location of the modern settlement, investigations were mainly restricted to the LB town wall. Most of the portion excavated (nearly 75 m) is in the western part of the LB settlement (areas G II, G III, B IV). Soundings made in other areas of the tell to the south and southeast (areas H III, H IV), to the east (area H II), and to the north (areas H II, B019) allow the reconstruction of the town wall; the inner part of the LB settlement remains largely unexcavated. What is left from the LB wall are, in effect, its foundations, sunk in earlier deposits in the form of a deep trench lined on both sides with large- and medium-sized stones, which most probably served as a secret corridor. The complete enclosure appears to have been symmetrical—oval with rounded angles—and oriented north–south along its long axis.

The LB town may have had a long occupation, from the fifteenth into the late thirteenth centuries BCE. The earlier date is based on a seal impression on a typical LB storage jar handle found in association with the foundation trench of the town wall. The scene as a whole is typical of the period at about the time of Thutmosis III of the eighteenth dynasty. It combines the three signs of seated sphinx, uraeus (snake), and god beard. In front of the sphinx (at the left of the scene) is an ankh.

The pottery associated with the town wall shows a range of types, including imports and imitations of Mycenaean pieces, as well as examples of local ware. Although the final pottery analysis is not yet complete, it appears that the types represented cover most of the Late Bronze Age up to the late thirteenth century BCE. Information about the inner structure of the LB town comes primarily from an important public building partially uncovered in area E, south of the main mound. It consists mainly of a long, massive wall (more than 17 m long) with a projecting towerlike room. The building's inner parts appear to be under a deep accumulation of Iron Age deposits and modern structures that have made excavation difficult. Apart from a rich LB–Iron Age tomb excavated by Rafik Dajani in 1968 (Dajani, 1970), no other LB tombs were found in the course of the 1972–1980 excavations.

Iron Age. The Early Iron Age settlement is well represented and—at least on the west and north—seems to extend beyond the LB town. Domestic architecture from this period appeared in most of the areas (A, B, D, E, E/W, H, G). The evidence, though, is fragmentary and does not give a clear picture of Iron I. Two houses have almost complete ground plans. In general, the houses (especially in area B) follow a pattern of rectangular rooms that were, in most cases, plastered with stones. In one of them, in area A, a large number of storage jars (pithoi) were excavated. Since their excavation at Tell Beit Mirsim, these jars have been designated collared-rim jars. William Foxwell Albright and others considered them evidence for the presence of early Israelite settlers in Canaan. However, more recent research (Ibrahim, 1978) concludes that the makers of this type of jar cannot be ethnically identified. The jar was, however, produced on a large scale in central workshops and played an important role in storing products and in the trade of various parts of Bilad ash-Sham, ("Greater Syria") in the Early Iron Age. [*See* Beit Mirsim, Tell; *and the biography of Albright.*]

Some of these twelfth-century storage jars bear seal impressions or fingerprints (Ibrahim 1978; 1983, pp. 48–50). One seal impression, identified on the rims of two jars, shows an animal with long horns followed by a human being raising his hands. Another impression of a roughly circular seal, repeated three times on a single jar, depicts two seated animals: an ibex on top and a lioness below.

It is not obvious to what extent LB structures were reused in the Iron I period, but in area GII (squares 15–17) it was evident that part of the LB town wall was reused in the Iron I for domestic housing. This continuity can also be observed in the continuous reuse of the tomb excavated by Dajani in 1968 (see above) that was in use in the LB I(?)–II until the Iron I–II periods. Certain LB bronze weapons and pottery types, including bowls, small craters, jugs, dipper juglets, and flasks, were also found in the Iron I tomb in area C excavated in 1972 (Ibrahim, 1972).

The Iron II period was attested mainly in area B019, where an extensive architectural complex and a piece of the town wall have been uncovered. It could also be found in area GII and in two soundings in the center of the site and in the deep bulldozer cut at the north edge of the excavated area in E. During the Iron II period, the walled town became smaller but better planned than it had been in Iron I. Its eastern border is defined by the town wall on that side of the site. A small area in the center, to the south, probably of the same wall, was visible on line with the area excavated in B019. This wall cannot extend much farther north because there was no Iron II material in area A or B fewer than 10 m from this wall. In area GII, in the west, the Iron II settlement goes beyond the LB town wall. The excavated evidence shows that the walled settlement was planned.

The main architectural complex in area B019 consists of rectangular rooms oriented north–south. The largest is a spacious, rectangular, pillared room in the center of the excavated area. Four pillars of large stones were built in a row along the central length of the room. There are at least two other rooms on the west that join with this one to form a house or unit separated by a corridor from another unit in the west. Another pillared room was excavated in area GII. It resembles the one mentioned above but is smaller. It is clear that these columns supported the roof of large rooms and probably had a special function within the architectural unit. On the basis of the finds from area B019, the pillared house at Saḥab most probably served as an industrial and perhaps a commercial and guest facility. The finds include a large number of loom weights of two main types (conical and round), weights in at least three units, and various tools and pots made of stone and basalt, used mainly for grinding and polishing. The pottery included storage jars and red- and black-burnished pottery with bowls and platters often slip painted in bands inside and outside. Some of the bowls and small jars were painted with dark, thin bands.

BIBLIOGRAPHY

Albright, William Foxwell. "An Anthropoid Coffin from Saḥâb in Transjordan." *American Journal of Archaeology* 36 (1932): 295–306.

Dajani, R. "A Late Bronze–Iron Age Tomb Excavated at Sahab, 1968." *Annual of the Department of Antiquities of Jordan* 15 (1970): 29–34.

Ibrahim, Moawiyah. "Archaeological Excavations at Sahab, 1972." *Annual of the Department of Antiquities of Jordan* 17 (1972): 23–36.

Ibrahim, Moawiyah. "Second Season of Excavations at Sahab, 1973." *Annual of the Department of Antiquities of Jordan* 19 (1974): 55–61.

Ibrahim, Moawiyah. "Third Season of Excavations at Sahab, 1975." *Annual of the Department of Antiquities of Jordan* 20 (1975): 69–82.

Ibrahim, Moawiyah. "The Collared-Rim Jar of the Early Iron Age." In *Archaeology in the Levant: Essays for Kathleen Kenyon,* edited by P. R. S. Moorey and Peter J. Parr, pp. 116–126. Warminster, 1978.

Ibrahim, Moawiyah. "Siegel und Seigelabdrücke aus Saḥāb." *Zeitschrift des Deutschen Palästina-Vereins* 99 (1983): 43–53.

Ibrahim, Moawiyah. "Saḥāb and Its Foreign Relations." In *Studies in the History and Archaeology of Jordan,* vol. 3, edited by Adnan Hadidi, pp. 73–81. Amman, 1987.

MOAWIYAH IBRAHIM

SAʿIDIYEH, TELL ES-, large double mound tentatively identified as the biblical Zarethan, situated in the central Jordan Valley, approximately 1.8 km (1.1 mi.) east of the Jordan River, on the south side of Wadi Kafranja (32°16′15″ N, 35°35′00″ E; map reference 2046 × 1861). The higher of the two mounds lies to the east, rising to about 40 m above the present plain level. Approximately 20 m below the summit, the Lower Tell extends from the western side as a benchlike projection. Altogether, the site occupies an area of about 10 hectares (25 acres).

The first detailed archaeological survey of the site was undertaken by Nelson Glueck during his Survey of Eastern Palestine between 1939 and 1947. His collections of surface pottery indicated a long history of occupation from the Chalcolithic period to the Byzantine era. In 1953, small-scale soundings were made by Henri de Contenson at yet a third element of the site, Tell es-Saʿidiyeh et-Taḥta, a small, almost imperceptible mound lying about 400 m west of the Lower Tell. A thin occupation layer was found, with flints and pottery, dating to the Middle Chalcolithic period (fourth millennium).

It was not until 1964, however, that large-scale systematic excavations were begun at the main double mound. Between 1964 and 1967, four seasons were undertaken by a University of Pennsylvania expedition directed by James B. Pritchard. In 1985, a new campaign of excavations was initiated by Jonathan N. Tubb on behalf of the British Museum; to date (1993), seven seasons have taken place.

Combining the results of the two expeditions, the earliest remains so far excavated belong to the Early Bronze II period. At this time, occupation was extensive, covering not only the Lower Tell, but also, in all probability, the base area of the Upper Tell.

On the Lower Tell, three main areas have yielded significant and sophisticated architectural remains. In the best-preserved exposure, part of a large domestic complex shows a suite of carefully planned and well-constructed rooms built of mud brick on stone foundations (see figure 1). This complex, together with most of the buildings revealed in the other excavation areas, is assigned to stratum L2, which was destroyed by fire toward the end of the first quarter of the third millennium.

Following the destruction of L2, there seems to have been some short-lived occupation within the burnt ruins. This somewhat ephemeral phase of campsite occupation (stratum L1) is characterized by the patching and modification of surviving L2 structures, with only minor and poorly constructed additions.

Stratum L1 has all the appearances of a temporary squatter occupation. It is not yet known whether occupation continued uninterrupted on the eastern. Upper Tell; however, as far as the Lower Tell is concerned, it appears to have been completely abandoned until the very end of the Late Bronze Age, when it became the site of an extensive and intensively used cemetery.

Between 1985 and 1992, some 480 graves were excavated in an area toward the center of the mound; fifty had been excavated on the north side by the Pennsylvania expedition. Of the total, about 5 percent can be attributed to the Late Iron–Persian periods; the remainder, possessing datable finds, can all be assigned to LB III (end of the thirteenth, beginning of the twelfth centuries BCE). The graves show considerable variety with regard to construction method, disposition of the deceased, grave goods, and burial customs—indicative indeed of a mixed population.

Many of the graves consist of simple pits without further elaboration. In some instances, use was made of structural elements (foundation stones, mud bricks) from the underlying EB occupation to create kerbs or markers. Toward the center of the area, a group of more elaborate graves was found. These should more correctly be considered tombs and were clearly intended to be partially visible above ground level: they are constructed of purpose-made mud bricks and roofed with slabs of the same material.

The grave goods and burial practices pertaining to the Saʿidiyeh cemetery make it quite clear that the site was under Egyptian control during this period. The richness and variety of the finds indicate society's affluence. Large numbers of bronzes have been found—vessels, weapons, and orna-

SAʿIDIYEH, TELL ES-. Figure 1. *Early Bronze Age house.* This residence was destroyed by fire around 2700 BCE. The photograph shows the nature of the destruction debris and a fine collection of pottery vessels on the floor. (Courtesy J. N. Tubb)

ments—many of them Egyptian in style. It is, however, the seals, amulets, stone vases, items of jewelry and ivory objects which most clearly display Egyptian craftsmanship. More significantly, perhaps, the burial practices also appear to be Egyptian in origin: the use of linen for wrapping the burial gifts and for the tight binding of the deceased.

One of the most interesting and important burial types found in the cemetery is the so-called double pithos, in which the deceased was enclosed in a "coffin" composed of two large storejars joined shoulder to shoulder. This type of burial, represented at Saʿidiyeh by twenty-seven examples, while extremely rare elsewhere in ancient Palestine, is quite commonly found in LB cemeteries in southern and southwestern Anatolia. Its occurrence in some number at Saʿidiyeh may well indicate the presence within the population of an alien, perhaps Sea Peoples, element—not altogether unexpected for a city under Egyptian control. The results of the cemetery are supplemented by those from the Upper Tell, where excavation revealed remains of the contemporary settlement. [*See* Jar Burials.]

Stratum XII, the lowest phase of occupation so far reached on the Upper Tell, has been examined in three excavation areas. Toward the center of the mound, parts of a large and impressive public building were found whose plan and construction methods conform to the so-called Egyptian Governors' Residency. This type of building, known from a number of Egyptian-controlled sites west of the Jordan River (e.g. Beth-Shean, Tell el-Farʿah [South]), is characterized by a peculiarly Egyptian method of construction which, for example, utilizes deep brick foundations instead of the more usual stone.

On the west side of the tell, behind a substantial casemate

city wall, a second administrative complex has been partly excavated (see figure 2). Termed loosely the Western Palace, this complex consists of a series of rooms, courtyards, and chambers laid out on either side of a narrow passageway which leads through the city wall to the exterior by means of a small opening (possibly a postern). The complex's most interesting features are a pair of interconnecting vaulted cisterns and a semicircular pool with an elaborate system of inlet and outflow channels. That the pool was concerned with commercial activities rather than purely domestic functions is clear from the large number of storejars of Egyptian design found at its base. It is possible that this pool served as a cooling tank, perhaps for storing wine.

The third main structure which can be assigned to stratum XII is the water-system staircase, beautifully constructed out of stone and cut into the tell's north slope. Having descended the mound in a series of broad, shallow steps, the staircase turns 90 degrees at the base and continues down through a flight of much steeper steps to a depth of some 8 m below plain level. At this point, the two sidewalls curve in to enclose a small semicircular pool; the water is supplied to the system by an underground spring and fed into the pool by a skillfully manufactured conduit.

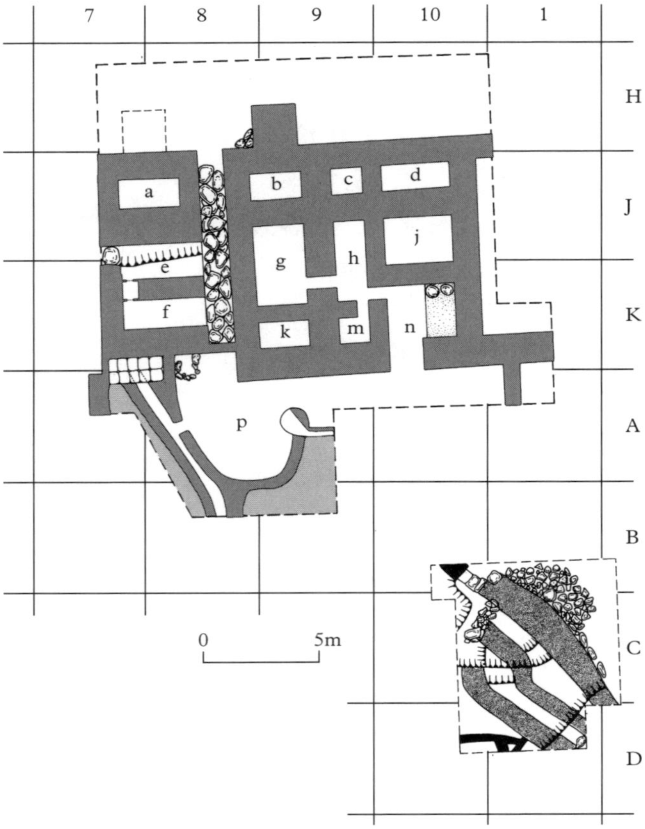

SAʿIDIYEH, TELL ES-. Figure 2. *Plan of the Western Palace complex.* Twelfth century BCE. (Courtesy J. N. Tubb)

The stratum XII architecture and the contemporary cemetery provide clear evidence for an Egyptian presence at Saʿidiyeh during the twelfth century BCE. It seems likely that the city was a major taxation center or entrepôt, serving the needs of the Egyptian Empire during its final phase under the pharaohs of the twentieth dynasty.

Stratum XII was destroyed by fire toward the middle of the twelve century BCE, when use of the Lower Tell cemetery also came to an end. The site appears to have been abandoned for some time following, perhaps for as long as one hundred years. Toward the end of the eleventh century BCE, a rather ephemeral phase of campsite occupation (stratum XIB) was established within the now silted-up stratum XII ruins. Consisting of little more than beaten-earth surfaces, fireplaces, and postholes—presumably for shelters—this phase seems to have been preconstruction rather than post-destruction. In any event, stratum XIA, which follows it, represents a very restricted occupation. It remains, which can be dated to the early tenth century BCE, have only been found near the center of the tell. A single, rather poorly constructed building was excavated which, for reasons of its proportions and ground plan, is thought to be a type of temple. It is bipartite, with the smaller room to the rear. This rear room, or sanctuary, had a plastered bench against the back wall, incorporating an inset niche; a burnt area with an incense stand and a pile of gazelle bones was found in front of the niche.

Little can be said of the next three phases (strata X–VIII). Again, they appear to represent restricted and poor settlements which, in the area examined, consisted of roughly paved, cobbled courtyards with traces of flimsily built mud-brick walls.

The next important period in the site's history appears with stratum VII (late ninth–early eighth centuries BCE). Perhaps as a consequence of the renewed occupation of Transjordan by the Israelite king Jeroboam II, Saʿidiyeh underwent a major expansion at this time. Stratum VII, extensively excavated by both the Pennsylvania and the British Museum expeditions, shows a densely packed settlement consisting of houses, stores, workshops, and industrial installations arranged on a well-planned grid of intersecting streets and alleyways. For the first time since stratum XII, a city wall encircled the settlement. Weaving and textile preparation seem to have been the main industrial activities: many hundreds of clay loom weights were found in what must have been workshops, often in distinctive alignments indicating the configuration of the looms.

Almost all of the stratum VII housing units had bathrooms containing both basins and toilets, suggesting that cleanliness and sanitation were major concerns of the inhabitants. The best-preserved example consisted of a raised room approached by three steps. Inside was a large plastered basin and a sitting-height mud-brick pedestal with a comfortably rounded seat made of fine mud plaster. Both units could be flushed through with water, being provided in each case with inlet and outflow channels, the latter leading to a combined soak-away drain (a drainage basin that does not have a constructed conduit) in the courtyard below.

By the end of the first decade of the eighth century BCE, the prosperity of the city had declined; stratum VI, which succeeded VII without any evidence of a catastrophe of any sort, shows Saʿidiyeh, once again, as a small settlement confined to an inner zone on the tell's surface. Fortunes must have revived, by the middle of the eighth century BCE, however, for stratum V is extensive. It has a new city wall and is similar in most respects to stratum VII, with the same pattern of workshops and industrial units arranged on a grid. In stratum V, however, the plan is even more strictly formalized, with insulae of workshop complexes, all with very similar internal room arrangements. Again, like stratum VII, the emphasis of the industry was on textile manufacture. Stratum V was relatively short-lived. It was destroyed by fire around 720 BCE, perhaps by the Assyrians. Although the inhabitants probably had time to escape, some of their unfortunate animals were abandoned: several burnt-out stalls have been excavated, each containing the charred bones of equids (donkeys).

The destruction of 720 BCE was one from which the city never really recovered. Stratum V was succeeded by an enigmatic phase (stratum IV) represented solely by large numbers of deep, unlined storage pits which had contained animal fodder. During the Persian period (fifth century BCE), an administrative building, or perhaps a fort, was established on the highest point on the Upper Tell (the so-called acropolis), but remains of any contemporary settlement (stratum III) have proved to be elusive. It may well be that occupation moved to the as-yet completely unexplored eastern side of the mound. Certainly some occupation is indicated by the presence in the Lower Tell cemetery of a number of graves of this period.

The Persian period building on the acropolis was replaced by a similar, but larger fortress in the Hellenistic period (stratum II); by then, however, the presence at the site may have been little more than token or strategic: no finds from this period have been found anywhere else on the site. The Roman period (stratum I) is represented by a solitary watchtower guarding the northwest corner of the Upper Tell. The very last traces of occupation consist of a single-roomed farmhouse on the Upper Tell and what may be a type of khan, or caravanserai, on the north side of the Lower Tell, both dating to the seventh–eighth centuries CE.

BIBLIOGRAPHY

Contenson, Henri de. "Three Soundings in the Jordan Valley." *Annual of the Department of Antiquities of Jordan* 4–5 (1960): 12–98, 36 figs. Account of the soundings undertaken at Tell es-Saʿidiyeh et-Taḥta.

Glueck, Nelson. *Explorations in Eastern Palestine*. Vol. 4. Annual of the American Schools of Oriental Research, 25/28. New Haven, 1951. The first detailed survey of the site, including an extended discussion of the identification.

Pritchard, James B. "Two Tombs and a Tunnel in the Jordan Valley: Discoveries at the Biblical Zarethan." *Expedition* 6.4 (1964): 2–9.

Pritchard, James B. "A Cosmopolitan Culture of the Late Bronze Age." *Expedition* 7.4 (1965): 26–33. Popular account of the work of the Pennsylvania expedition; see also Pritchard (1964).

Pritchard, James B. *The Cemetery at Tell es-Saʿidiyeh, Jordan*. University Museum, Monograph 41. Philadelphia, 1980. Definitive report on Pritchard's excavation in the cemetery.

Pritchard, James B. *Tell es-Saʿidiyeh: Excavations on the Tell, 1964–1966*. University Museum, Monograph 60. Philadelphia, 1985. Final report of the Pennsylvania expedition's work on the Upper Tell.

Tubb, Jonathan N. "Tell es-Saʿidiyeh: Preliminary Report on the First Three Seasons of Renewed Excavations." *Levant* 20 (1988): 23–88.

Tubb, Jonathan N. "Preliminary Report on the Fourth Season of Excavations at Tell es-Saʿidiyeh in the Jordan Valley." *Levant* 22 (1990a): 21–42.

Tubb, Jonathan N., and Rupert L. Chapman. *Archaeology and the Bible*. London, 1990b. Chapter 4 offers a popular account of the British Museum excavations.

Tubb, Jonathan N., and Peter G. Dorrell. "Tell es-Saʿidiyeh: Interim Report on the Fifth (1990) Season of Excavations." *Levant* 23 (1991): 67–86.

Tubb, Jonathan N. "Tell es-Saʿidiyeh: Interim Report on the Sixth Season of Excavations." *Palestine Exploration Quarterly* 125 (1993): 50–74.

JONATHAN N. TUBB

SAID NAYA (Sardenay, Saydeneia), predominantly Christian settlement located about 20 km (12 mi.) northeast of Damascus on one of the high plateaus of the Qalamun Mountains, which comprises a section of the Anti-Lebanon range (37°43′ N, 40°40′ E). Following the orientation of the mountain chains, the high valley stretches out in a north–south direction. The chief routes from Damascus to Emesa/Homs and farther on to North Syria described in ancient itineraries seem, however, not to have touched this region. They led north either through the Biqaʿ plain via Heliopolis/Baalbek in the west or via a route that lay farther east. Consequently, the identification with the Danaba mentioned in the Peutinger map, which was championed in the older literature (J. L. Porter, *Five Years in Damascus,* London, 1855), cannot be maintained. Monuments from the Roman imperial period demonstrate that the place had a certain significance then.

There are two explanations of the place name. In the first it derives from the Old Syriac *sayda* ("lady") and *naya* ("our"). According to this explanation, the name of the cloister on the cliff that dominates the entire area was transferred to the city. The second and more popular explanation is closely connected with one of the legends of the founding of the cloister (see below); according to this variant, the name means "hunting place" (Old Syriac *seid,* "to hunt"; *dnaya,* "place"). Old Syriac was still spoken in Said Naya in the nineteenth century CE. It is possible that a Christian legend attached itself to a local place name, but more exact details are unknown.

Three rock tombs are located below the cloister and are dated to 198 CE (W. H. Waddington, *Inscriptiones grecques et latines de la Syrie,* 25620, vol. 3 of Philippe Le Bas, *Voyage archéologique en Grèce et en Asie Mineure,* Paris, 1870). The tombs are decorated with reliefs of deceased couples. In the older literature these were often misinterpreted as pictures of saints.

A mausoleum in an area to the east, below the cloister, is today Peter and Paul's Church, a windowless rectangular building on three steps. A small entrance door is located in the east side; a partially worked outline of a base and a ledge are the only architectonic decoration on this otherwise undated building (second–fourth centuries CE?). The interior is in the form of a cross with three large arcosolia formed from massive blocks. In one of the building's resulting massive corner pilasters, a stairway leads to the roof. (Jean Lassus, "Deux églises cruciformes du Hauran, *Bulletin d'Études Orientales* 1 [1931]: 45–48).

St. Mary's Cloister, which is Greek Orthodox, is today occupied only by nuns (in the Middle Ages it was occupied by nuns and monks). There are various versions of the founding of the cloister in numerous legends; however, there are no certain historical or archaeological data. Since the Middle Ages it has been repeatedly visited, even by European travelers (the first known visitor was Magister Thietmar in 1217), because of the Mary icon, which was already widely known. According to the earliest travelers, the cloister was founded either by a pious lady from Damascus or by a monk from Jerusalem. Ernst H. Maundrell (*Voyage d'Alep à Jèrusalem à Paques en l'année 1697,* Paris, 1706) mentions the legend that is today most popular and disseminated by the Orthodox patriarchy. In it the cloister was founded in 547 by Justinian, before whose eyes, during the course of a hunt, a gazelle transformed itself into an image of the Virgin Mary on the spot of the current cloister. There are other widely different legends concerning the icon's age and origin. Later variants report that Eudoxia, the wife of the emperor Theodosius, brought this picture painted by St. Luke the Evangelist to Said Naya and built a cloister for the icon there. In the foundation of the current, drastically renovated and enlarged structure, some masonry may be ancient; however, clearer indications of a date are absent.

Deir Mar Tuma, to the west, above the settlement, is a church integrated into a Roman building that was in the form of a small porticoed temple with a north–south orientation. There is no inscription to provide information about the building's original purpose. It stands in an ancient rectangular precinct that was hewn into the cliff and constructed from massive blocks. In the immediate vicinity are other rock tombs and rooms hewn into the cliff, one of which was designated a meeting room by Richard Pococke, (*A Description of the East,* London, 1743–1745).

The Cherubim Cloister is located on a 2,011-meter-high mountain peak northwest of the settlement. Numerous ruins show that a very holy shrine has stood there since at least the early imperial period. A series of rock-cut rooms is associated with later use as a hermitage.

BIBLIOGRAPHY

Peeters, Paul. *La légende de Saidnaya.* Analecta Bollandiana, 25. Brussels, 1985. See pages 137–157. More easily obtained but less complete in its inclusion of older literature than Zeiad (below).

Zeiad, H. *Geschichte von Said Naya* (in Arabic). Damascus, 1932. Contains citations from all of the older literature, but not readily serviceable as a modern historical reappraisal.

RÜDIGER GOGRÄFE

Translated from German by Susan I. Schiedel

SALAMIS, fortified city on Cyprus, settled in the eleventh century BCE. Located on the eastern coast of Cyprus on the northern side of the Pediaios River where it enters Famagusta Bay approximately 7.5 km (4.6 mi) north of Famagusta. Salamis was one of the leading cities on the island from the earlier Iron Age through the Late Roman period. A portion of the city was occupied until at least the early eighth century CE and probably as late as the twelveth century CE. Although the architectural and sculptural remains of Salamis always have been visible, it was not until the 1860s and 1870s that the epigraphical finding of the first European visitors identified the church and monastery of Apostolos Varnavas immediately to the west of the site as part of the ruins of Salamis.

According to the legend of the eighth to fifth century BCE, the Homeric hero Teukros, son of Telamon, who was the king of the island of Salamis in the Saronic Gulf in Greece, founded the city in 1184 after the Trojan War. Actually the settlement was established in the mid- to late eleventh century BCE, probably as a consequence of the destruction by earthquake(?) and abandonment of the nearby Late Cypriot city of Enkomi, about 2 km (1.25 mi.) inland to the southwest. [*See* Enkomi.] The estuary of the Pediaios River may have silted up around this time, making Enkomi inaccessible directly to the Mediterranean. The southern portion of the city was occupied continuously from the eleventh through second centuries BCE. This region then appears to have been uninhabited until the late fourth century CE. The city was the metropolis of the island under the Ptolemies from the end of the fourth through the second century BCE when this role shifted to Nea-Paphos. At its height Salamis covered about 150–275 ha. Major earthquakes shook the city in 16/17, 76/77, 342, and 394 CE. A revolt by the Jewish population in 116/117 CE caused extensive damage within the city. Under the aegis of the emperor Constantius II (344–361 CE) the city was rebuilt after the earthquake of 342. In his honor the new city was called Constantia and resumed its earlier position as the metropolis of the island. The Arab raids, beginning in 647/48 CE, resulted in more destruction. Although there is evidence for limited reoccupation in the late seventh through early eighth centuries CE, including a defensive fortification built around the basilica of Ayios Epiphanios, most of the urban area was abandoned. The remnants of the large residence called L'huilerie ("the olive press") provide evidence of continued use in this section after the seventh century.

Exploration and Excavation. Small sections of the ancient city were inhabited through the twelveth century CE. Marble and granite architectural fragments and an inscribed statue base from the gymnasium were used in some late medieval and Venetian buildings in Famagusta demonstrating that the ruins of the city were accessible in the thirteenth through sixteenth centuries. The first published description of Salamis was in 1862 by Melchior de Vogüé, William Waddington, and Edmond Duthoit. Luigi Palma di Cesnola and later his brother, Alexander, were the first non-Cypriots to "excavate" at Salamis (1866–1878). In 1888 D. G. Hogarth published his observations of his visit. Formal excavations of the western and northern cemeteries and a Roman house with floor mosaics were carried out by Max Ohnefalsch-Richter in 1880–1882 for the British Museum under the direction of Charles Newton. H. H. Kitchener and G. Hake excavated more tombs in the western cemetery in 1882 for the South Kensington Museum (now the Victoria and Albert Museum). The Cyprus Exploration Fund organized by the British Museum, the Ashmolean Museum (Oxford), and the FitzWilliam Museum (Cambridge) and led by J. A. R. Munro and H. A. Tubbs in 1890 and 1891 opened up many trenches within the city itself. Another British team consisting of A. S. Murray, A. H. Smith, and P. Christian excavated more tombs in 1896 in the western cemetery for the British Museum.

In 1913 J. L. Myres and G. E. Jeffrey worked at the "prison/tomb of St. Catherine/Haghia Haikaterini" in the western cemetery. Jeffrey in 1923–1925 and Joan duPlat Taylor in 1933 carried out small-scale excavations of primarily Late Roman structures. In 1952 the Department of Antiquities began regular large-scale excavations within the city which continued until 1974. The systematic excavation of the western cemeteries by the Cypriot Department of Antiquities began in 1957 first under the direction of Porphyrios Dikaios and then from 1962 to 1967 by Vassos Karageorghis. A French expedition from the Institut F. Courby, Université de Lyon, dug in the southern section of the city from 1964 to 1974, focusing on the Temple of Zeus and the Late Roman Christian basilica called Campanopetra. In 1973 N. C. Flemming undertook a preliminary underwater survey of the harbor facilities of Salamis.

Major Remains. The earliest remains of the city date to the late eleventh century BCE: French tomb no. 1, a cult place (through the sixth century BCE), and the southern rampart. Iron age elite burials were located in various extramural cemeteries: "Royal tombs" (c. 800–500 BCE), Cellarka (c. 700–400 BCE), and Koufoumeron (c. 550–500 BCE). There were extramural sanctuaries dating to the sixth century BCE to the west around Apostolos Varnavas (site A; Great Goddess/Aphrodite) and to the south at Toumba (site G). Tumulus/tomb 77 represents the funerary pyre and cenotaph of King Nikokreon(?), the last king of Salamis, and his family, about 311 BCE. The Temple of Zeus Olympios (Zeus Salaminios?) was first constructed in late second century BCE and a ramp was added at the end of first century CE. It was destroyed by earthquakes in 332 and/or 342 CE. To the north of the temple there was an elongated porticoed forum or "Agora" (site C), probably constructed before 22 BCE and then reconstructed in the first or second century CE.

At the north end of the forum a large rectangular cistern or loutron with a vaulted roof was built during reign of Septimius Serverus (fl. 193–211). It was fed by an aqueduct from the spring at Kythrea. An elevated arched section is preserved southeast of Ayios Sergios. The gymnasium (site B) probably existed in the second and first centuries BCE. There were major building phases and repairs to it at the beginning of the first century CE and again during the reigns of Trajan (fl. 97–117) and Hadrian (fl. 117–138). After damage by the fourth-century earthquakes, it was restored as public baths by Justinian (fl. 527–565) then abandoned. Adjacent to the gymnasium there was a xystos or stadium with eight rows of seats on the north. A propylaeum entrance or vestibule (c. 100–150 CE?) on the western end opened on a north–south colonnaded street leading from the gymnasium to the theater. The theater was built at end of first century BCE. It was reconstructed after earthquake of 76/77 CE with additional repairs and reconstruction under Hadrian. Further modifications followed in the third century CE. Following its destruction by the fourth-century earthquakes the stage was rebuilt in a crude fashion about 375–425. Abandonment occurred in the sixth century CE. The amphitheater built in the late first century CE completed the city's entertainment complex.

Ayios Epiphanios (site H) was the earliest and largest Christian basilica on the island. It was built in 375–400 and later partially reconstructed. This "cathedral" of Epiphanios, the first archbishop of Salamis (fl. 368–403), was enclosed within a limited defensive circuit around the core of the city. The wall was built in the early seventh century in response to Arab raids. After the basilica was destroyed in 447/48 by the Arabs, a church was built immediately to the southeast to replace it in around 698. This church was rebuilt in the ninth century and continued in use through at least 1344.

Three important edifices were built around 470–500. The "Campanopetra" Christian basilica and monastery (? site E) is one of the largest and most refined known on the island. After 647 the baptistery was turned into a chapel. Immediately to the west across a street was an official residency. Nearby was a large elite residence, "L'huilerie" (see above). Following its destruction during Arab raids squatters inhabited it in the mid- to late seventh century. Afterward the complex was divided into at least three independent structures, one of which was an olive oil pressing establishment. They were occupied through the twelfth century.

[*See also the biographies of Di Cesnola, Dikaios, Hogarth, Kitchener, Myres, Newton, Ohnefalsch-Richter, and Vogüé.*]

BIBLIOGRAPHY

Karageorghis, Vassos. *Salamis: Recent Discoveries in Cyprus.* New York, 1969. General introduction to the history of the site and the Department of Antiquities excavations in the "Royal Tombs" and Cellarka cemeteries, as well as the gymnasium and theater.

Rupp, David W. "The 'Royal Tombs' at Salamis (Cyprus): Ideological Messages of Power and Authority." *Journal of Mediterranean Archaeology* 1.1 (1988): 111–139. Analysis of the eighth to sixth century BCE "Royal Tombs" in the context of a study of the reemergence of sociopolitical complexity in Iron Age Cyprus under the stimulus of Phoenician trade and colonization.

Wallace, Paul W., and Andreas G. Orphanides, eds. *Sources for the History of Cyprus,* vol. 1, *Greek and Latin Texts to the Third Century A.D.* Albany, N.Y., and Nicosia, 1990. Translation of Greek and Latin Texts which refer to Cyprus, including an index with references to Salamis.

Yon, Marguerite, ed. *Salamine de Chypre: Histoire et archéologie, état des recherches.* Éditions du Centre National de la Recherche Scientifique, no. 578. Paris, 1980. Proceedings of an international colloquium held in Lyon in 1978 on the various excavations and research relating to Salamis.

Yon, Marguerite, ed. *Kinyras. L'Archéologie française à Chypre/French Archaeology in Cyprus.* Travaux de la Maison de l'Orient, no. 22. Paris, 1993. An up-to-date summary in French and English of the results of the French excavations at Salamis; with extensive bibliography. See Yon's article "La ville de Salamine/The Town of Salamis," pp. 139–158; and Georges Roux, "Basiliques et residences byzantines/Byzantine Basilicas and Residences," pp. 195–204.

Excavation Reports: French Expedition

Argoud, Gilbert, et al. *Une résidence byzantine "l'Huilerie."* Salamine de Chypre, 11. Paris, 1980.

Calvet, Yves. *Les timbres amphoriques, 1965–1970.* Salamine de Chypre, 3. Paris, 1972.

Chavane, Marie-José. *Les petits objets.* Salamine de Chypre, 6. Paris, 1975.

Chavane, Marie-José, and Marguerite Yon. *Testimonia Salaminia 1.* Salamine de Chypre, 10.1. Paris, 1978.

Diederichs, Catherine. *Céramiques hellénistiques, romaines et byzantines.* Salamine de Chypre, 9. Paris, 1980.

Institute Fernand Courby. *Anthologie salaminienne.* Salamine de Chypre, 4. Paris, 1973.

Jehasse, Laurence. *La céramique à vernis noir du rempart méridional.* Salamine de Chypre, 8. Paris, 1978.

Monloup, Thérèse. *Les figurines de terre cuite de tradition archaïque.* Salamine de Chypre, 12. Paris, 1984.

Oziol, Thérèse, and Jean Pouilloux. *Les lampes (octobre 1964–mai 1967).* Salamine de Chypre, 1. Paris, 1969.

Oziol, Thérèse. *Les lampes du Musée de Chypre.* Salamine de Chypre, 7. Paris, 1977.

Pouilloux, Jean, et al. *Testimonia Salaminia 2.* Salamine de Chypre, 13. Paris, 1987.

Yon, Marguerite. *La Tomba T 1 du XIe s. av. J.-C.* Salamine de Chypre, 2. Paris, 1971.

Yon, Marguerite. *Un dépôt de sculptures archaïques: Ayios Varnavas, Site A.* Salamine de Chypre, 5. Paris, 1974.

Excavation Reports: Department of Antiquities Expedition

Karageorghis, Vassos, and Cornelius C. Vermeule. *Sculptures from Salamis.* 2 vols. Salamis, 1.1–2. Nicosia, 1964–1966.

Karageorghis, Vassos. *Excavations in the Necropolis of Salamis.* 4 vols. Salamis, 1.3–5/7. Nicosia, 1967–1978.

Mitford, Terence B., and Ino K. Nicolaou. *The Greek and Latin Inscriptions from Salamis.* Salamis, 1.6. Nicosia, 1974.

DAVID W. RUPP

SALLER, SYLVESTER JOHN (1895–1976),

American Franciscan archaeologist based in Jerusalem. S. J. Saller was born in Petosky, Michigan. He entered the Franciscans in 1913 and was ordained a priest in 1922. He taught at the Franciscan house of studies in Teutopolis, Illinois, until he was invited to study Scripture at the Antonianum in Rome in 1928. After two years in Rome he moved to the school's Jerusalem campus, where, two years later, he graduated as a lector generalis in Scripture. From 1932 until his death, he remained, with rare exceptions, in Jerusalem, as a professor at the Studium Biblicaum Franciscanum (SBF). There he taught biblical archaeology and Greek and directed excavations on Mt. Nebo (Siyagha, Jordan), at 'Ein-Kerem, and at Bethany. His two-volume work on Nebo inaugurated the SBF's publication series. He also helped launch and edit the SBF's periodical *Liber Annuus* (1950–). Saller initiated the SBF's Collectio Minor (Minor Series) with his study of Bethphage. He followed this with the important "Catalogue of the Ancient Synagogues of the Holy Land" (*Liber Annuus* 4[1954]: 219–246), updated and separately printed in the Collectio Minor (Jerusalem, 1969, 1972).

Saller was elected a member of the Palestine Archaeological Council during the British Mandate and was religious superior in the SBF community (in the Flagellation Convent, on the Via Dolorosa); he generally avoided the limelight, living the life of an exemplary friar. His principal articles are to be found in *Liber Annuus.*

[*See also* Franciscan Custody of the Holy Land; Nebo, Mount.]

BIBLIOGRAPHY

Bagatti, Bellarmino. "P. Sylvester Saller, 1895–1976." *Studii Biblici Franciscani/Liber Annuus* 26 (1976): 334–339. Includes a bibliography of Saller's work.

Saller, Sylvester J. *The Memorial of Moses on Mount Nebo.* 2 vols. Studium Biblicum Franciscanum (SBF), Collectio Maior, 1. Jerusalem, 1941. Comprehensive report of the 1933, 1935, and 1937 seasons on the hill of Siyagha. Part 1 was completely reedited in 1965.

Saller, Sylvester J. *Discoveries at St. John's 'Ein Kerem, 1941–42.* SBF, Collectio Maior, 3. Jerusalem, 1946.

Saller, Sylvester J., and Bellarmino Bagatti. *The Town of Nebo (Khirbet el-Mekhayyat) with a Brief Survey of Other Ancient Christian Monuments in Transjordan.* SBF, Collectio Maior, 7. Jerusalem, 1949. Treats the Greek inscriptions and lists the Christian towns, with bibliography.

Saller, Sylvester J. *Excavations at Bethany, 1949–1953.* SBF, Collectio Maior, 12. Jerusalem, 1957. Covers digs near the Tomb of Lazarus and the early history of the village.

Saller, Sylvester J. *The Jebusite Burial Place.* SBF, Collectio Maior, 13. Jerusalem, 1964. Excavation report of the Bronze Age burial cave at the Dominus Flevit on the Mount of Olives.

BENEDICT T. VIVIANO

SALT. Although salt is an essential mineral in the human diet, it is generally believed that hunter-gatherer and fishing groups do not require it as a diet supplement, whereas agriculturists do. In addition to its dietary role, salt has many industrial uses. It is employed, for example, to treat hides, preserve fish, and separate silver from gold (the cupellation process). Salt occurs naturally in various forms, and its method of extraction varies accordingly. In Western Asia, rock salt has been mined (e.g., in northern Arabia, Anatolia, Assyria, Yemen); sea salt has been evaporated (e.g., on the west coast of Turkey); and certain salt-rich plants may occasionally have been used to produce salt, as in parts of Africa (Potts, 1984). Salines, however, present another, easily accessible source of salt. The intense heat in the Near East evaporates the saline solution leaving the crystalized salt behind. Extraction can then take place by digging the salt out of the ground, often in the form of "bricks" of salt that can be transported by pack animals.

The ubiquity of salines throughout the Near East has meant that it was always the most important source of salt in antiquity—particularly Mesopotamia, Syria, and Anatolia. Cuneiform texts contain a number of pertinent references. The profession of salt gatherer *(mun-ur4)* is attested at Fara in the early dynastic period, and designations for leather bags for salt (Sum., *kuš-dùg-gan-mun;* Akk. *tukkan ṭâbti*) are found in lexical lists. A list of salines (Ugar., *ṣṣ* or *ṣiṣūma*) and their harvesters (?) is contained in a pair of Ugaritic texts (*Palais Royale d'Ugarit,* vol. 5, 96 and 97). The division of a saline (Akk., *eqil ṭâbti*) between the kings of Ugarit and Siyannu is mentioned in a letter from Mursilis II. Prices for salt are specified in Ur III economic texts, as well as in the laws of Eshnunna (sec. 1: A i 14). Ur III sources also mention bricks of salt (*sig4-mun;* e.g., *Ur Excavation Texts,* III 1021), while a text (*Ur Excavation Texts* III 1498) which lists 20 *sìla* of salt in the inventory of a goldsmith's workshop during the reign of Ibbi-Sin points to the practice of the salt method of cupellation in Mesopotamia by the late third millennium.

In addition to its utilitarian uses, salt played a role in ancient Near Eastern cultic practices. This is best exemplified in the *Maqlû* series: "O salt, created in a clean place, for food of gods did Enlil destine thee, without thee no meal is set out in Ekur, without thee god, king, lord and prince do not smell incense" (tablet VI: 111–119, trans. T. Jacobsen). Salt was burned in a number of different Assyrian and Hittite magical spells, ceremonies, and incantations. It was included in ritual meals prepared for Ishtar and other deities, and was strewn on the ground at the conclusion of certain rituals performed at Aššur. Finally, salt was a component in a number of ancient Mesopotamian medicinal recipes. The Akkadian idiom "to eat the salt of a person" *(ṭâbat PN leḫemum)* signified the making of a covenant or arriving at a reconciliation.

BIBLIOGRAPHY

Buccellati, Giorgio. "Salt at the Dawn of History." In *Resurrecting the Past: A Joint Tribute to Adnan Bounni,* edited by Paolo Matthiae, et al., pp. 17–40. Istanbul, 1990. Attempt to link salt use and the bevel-rim bowl, with particular reference to Syria.

Butz, Kilian. "On Salt Again . . . Lexikalische Randbemerkungen." *Journal of the Economic and Social History of the Orient* 27 (1984): 272–316. Philological discussion of the technical vocabulary of salt in Sumerian and Akkadian, with particular reference to the lexical sources.

Levey, Martin. "Gypsum, Salt, and Soda in Ancient Mesopotamian Chemical Technology." *Isis* 49 (1958): 336–341. Early attempt to elucidate the industrial uses of salt in ancient Mesopotamia.

Potts, Daniel T. "Salt of the Earth: The Role of a Non-Pastoral Resource in a Pastoral Economy." *Oriens Antiquus* 22 (1983): 205–215. Study of salt exploitation by pastoral nomads in greater Mesopotamia, drawing on anthropological, ethnohistoric, and cuneiform evidence.

Potts, Daniel T. "On Salt and Salt Gathering in Ancient Mesopotamia." *Journal of the Economic and Social History of the Orient* 27 (1984): 225–271. Wide-ranging look at salt extraction and use in ancient Mesopotamia, combining philological and archaeological evidence.

DANIEL T. POTTS

SALVAGE EXCAVATION. [*To treat the archaeological process known as salvage excavation, this entry comprises an overview of the method's procedures, objectives, potentials, and limitations, and a study of specific salvage excavation operations in Israel.*]

An Overview

Stepped-up destruction of the world's archaeological heritage has been a by-product of the intensified economic and industrial development of the later twentieth century. Confronted with this challenge, archaeologists have scrambled to rescue what evidence they can. In the Near East, salvage archaeology began in earnest in the 1960s, when the first large-scale dam construction projects were announced, initiated to harness hydroelectric power and to facilitate large-scale agricultural development. Faced with the imminent flooding of sites in the threatened river valleys, national antiquities organizations, often in concert with UNESCO, organized salvage programs and encouraged archaeologists to excavate doomed sites. Salvage excavation has become an increasingly important concern in Near Eastern archaeology. In Syria, for example, new excavation permits granted in recent years have almost exclusively been limited to salvage projects, and such trends may well persist if not intensify.

The major dam projects in southwest Asia have largely been in the valleys of the Euphrates and Tigris Rivers and their tributaries. [*See* Euphrates; Tigris.] Sponsoring countries include Syria (the Tabqa and Tishrin dams on the Euphrates, and the Khabur dams), Turkey (the Keban, Karakaya, Atatürk, Birecik, and Karkam dams on the Euphrates and a set of dams on the Tigris), and Iraq (the Hamrin dam on the Diyala, Saddam/Eski Mosul dam on the Tigris, and Haditha/Qadisiyah dam on the Euphrates). [*See* Khabur; Hamrin Dam Salvage Project; Diyala; Eski Mosul Dam Salvage Project.] The archaeological heritage is also threatened by the trend toward large-scale agricultural intensification: regions formerly cultivated with traditional technologies and methods are now subjected to mechanized agriculture with tractors and deep plowing. Such activity results in the destruction of archaeological sites as well as such off-site features as ancient roads, canals, and sherd scatters. The North Jezireh project in northern Iraq is an example of a salvage operation organized specifically to collect archaeological evidence from an area of some 800 sq km (496 sq. mi.) targeted for agricultural development.

Other types of economic development also encroach. The important Neolithic site of ʿAin Ghazal near Amman, Jordan, was discovered when highway construction damaged it; more recently the site was endangered by real estate development. [*See* ʿAin Ghazal.] In Beirut, plans for massive urban renewal in the downtown area precipitated salvage excavations of the ancient city below. The developers are said to be planning the integration of excavated remains into the modern constructions with an eye to the cultural and touristic value of those remains—an increasingly common practice. [*See* Beirut; Tourism and Archaeology; Restoration and Conservation.]

There has been relatively little discussion of methodologies for mounting salvage projects in the Near East. Generally, national antiquities organizations sponsor surveys of threatened regions that locate sites for excavation (Whallon, 1979). After survey, excavation projects are speedily organized to sample as much as possible before sites are destroyed. Unfortunately, haste only compounds the problem of the site's destruction: the archaeologist cannot return to check the results after the site has vanished.

Although the destruction of archaeological sites can only be viewed as a calamity, there are some positive aspects to salvage archaeology. One is the concentration of intensive archaeological efforts in specific geographic areas, facilitating an unusually comprehensive and coherent understanding of regions and their changes through time. In the case of the Euphrates valley, continual dam construction resulted in an almost unbroken zone of archaeological research from the Keban dam area in eastern Turkey to the Tabqa dam in Syria. Because of the association with dam projects, large-scale salvage operations are typically focused on (and biased toward) riverine communities.

Coordination of salvage excavations, both foreign and locally sponsored, is usually undertaken by the national antiquities organizations, which often organize international symposia of scholars involved in salvage work (for published proceedings on symposia held in Iraq, for example, see *Sumer* 35 [1979], 40 [1982], 42 [1983]). Such cooperation allows archaeologists to compare results and work toward an integrated perspective of societal changes in the relevant regions. Antiquities organizations have also offered inducements for foreign participation in salvage work, by providing labor, equipment, housing, and even financial support (in the case of Iraq), and permission to retain and exhibit a portion of the excavated museum-quality objects (Syria).

A second "blessing in disguise" provided by salvage projects is their tendency to compel archaeologists to concentrate their efforts on "peripheral" or "marginal" regions that would otherwise be neglected in favor of the urban heartlands (e.g., Uruk, Babylon, Aššur, Mari). The investigation of marginal areas has produced surprising results that the core areas could never have yielded. For example, excavations at Mureybet and Abu Hureyra in the Tabqa dam region supplied crucial data on the transition from mobile hunting-gathering to Neolithic agricultural lifestyles, providing evidence that sedentary village life preceded agriculture by several millennia. [*See* Mureybet.] Excavations in the Euphrates valley in Syria and Turkey have provided testimony of a southern Mesopotamian "expansion" and colonization of the region coincident with the appearance of the first urban societies in southern Mesopotamia (Uruk period, c. 3600–3100 BCE). A rich body of material has been obtained from a range of relevant sites, including the full-fledged colonies of Habuba Kabira and Jebel ʿAruda (Syria), smaller outposts like Hassek Höyük (Turkey), and southern Mesopotamian "enclaves" in local towns, as at Hacinebi (Turkey). [*See* Habuba Kabira.]

The Hamrin salvage region in Iraq and the Middle Khabur project in Syria have both revealed networks of specialized small third-millennium communities apparently associated with (and established by?) emerging urban centers. The results indicate that the development of urban civilization had a significant effect even on marginal rural areas, where local resources were mobilized or exploited within newly established regional economic systems. Unexpected results have also been supplied by excavations in more recent historical periods. The excavations at Khirbet-ed Diniye (ancient Haradum) in the Haditha dam region exposed a centrally planned small city of the Old Babylonian period

(c. 1800 BCE); the thirteenth-century BCE cuneiform archives from the city of Emar in the Tabqa dam area have provided an invaluable textual source for a prosperous Late Bronze Syrian city, supplying an alternative model from that of Ugarit. [*See* Emar; Ugarit.]

BIBLIOGRAPHY

Algaze, Guillermo, ed. *Town and Country in South-Eastern Anatolia,* vol. 2, *The Stratigraphic Sequence at Kurban Höyük.* Chicago, 1990. Final report from a Turkish salvage project. See Wilkinson (1990).

Algaze, Guillermo, et al. "The Tigris-Euphrates Archaeological Reconnaissance Project: A Preliminary Report of the 1989–1990 Seasons." *Anatolica* 17 (1991): 175–240. Report on surveys conducted in the Euphrates and Tigris salvage regions of southeastern Turkey, with general comments on the nature of the rescue programs.

Ball, Warwick, et al. "The Tell al-Hawa Project: Archaeological Investigations in the North Jazira, 1986–87." *Iraq* 51 (1989): 1–66. Excavation and survey in the northern Jezireh salvage area of Iraq.

Huot, Jean-Louis, ed. *Préhistoire de la Mésopotamie: La Mésopotamie préhistoire et l'exploration récente du djebel Hamrin, Paris 17–19 décembre 1984.* Paris, 1987. Reports from an international colloquium on the Hamrin excavations, illustrating the cooperative character of salvage work.

Margueron, Jean-Claude, ed. *Le Moyen Euphrate, zone de contacts et d'échanges: Acts du colloque de Strasbourg, 10–12 mars 1977.* Leiden, 1980. Proceedings of a symposium on the results of excavations in the Tabqa salvage area.

Whallon, Robert. *An Archaeological Survey of the Keban Reservoir Area of East-Central Turkey.* Memoirs of the Museum of Anthropology University of Michigan, no. 11. Ann Arbor, 1979. Report of an unusually systematic and detailed survey conducted prior to salvage excavation.

Wilkinson, T. J. *Town and Country in South-Eastern Anatolia,* vol. 1, *Settlement and Land Use at Kurban Höyük and Other Sites in the Lower Karababa Basin.* Chicago, 1990. Final report from a Turkish salvage project. See Algaze (1990).

Glenn M. Schwartz

Salvage Excavation in Israel

Also known as rescue excavation, the term *salvage excavation* does not appear in Israel's Antiquities Law of 1978; it is, rather, a technical term used, since the early 1960s, by officials of the Israel Antiquities Authority (IAA, previously the Israel Department of Antiquities) to describe small archaeological excavations IAA archaeologists conduct at sites discovered and damaged in the process of building and highway construction and other development work. In the last thirty years, nearly two thousand licenses have been issued for such excavations.

A salvage excavation is not planned and prepared for in the way that a large-scale archaeological excavation is, with the specific goals of providing a key to a historical or an archaeological problem, within a time frame of several seasons stretching over many years. Instead, it is organized in a matter of days, conducted under time pressure, and in a general environment and under physical conditions inimical to its goals and objectives: to learn as much as possible in a short time about a site and to register, describe, and photograph a maximum of its archaeological data. The archaeologist assigned to a salvage excavation has had no time to study the site to prepare for the dig. He or she learns about it, appreciating its importance and special contributions to the archaeology and history of the land, only as the excavation proceeds. The small size and scope of such an excavation does not, however, diminish its importance.

One of the principal limitations of a salvage excavation is that it is conducted in the part of the site threatened with destruction, which is not always the most important area in terms of its history and material culture.

The initial archaeological information recovered from a salvage excavation is published in the IAA's *Ḥadashot Arkheologiyot* (Hebrew) and its English version, *Excavations and Surveys in Israel.* Final reports are published in *ʿAtiqot* (English and Hebrew), the IAA's official journal.

In recent years, salvage excavations have been carried out in several of Israel's larger cities (Jerusalem, Beersheba, Ashkelon, Qiryat Ata), where intensive development work has been underway to provide housing for new immigrants.

Tens of salvage excavations in Jerusalem alone have provided archaeological data of cardinal importance. For example, the "Third Wall," segments of which had already been revealed through excavation, was excavated in 1990 by Vassilios Tzaferis, Alexander Onn, and Nurit Feig when new road construction uncovered additional sections, as well as the remains of an American monastery and a number of Armenian inscriptions.

Discoveries at other salvage excavations necessitated by roadwork in Jerusalem in 1990 include the Tomb of Caiaphas, the high priest in whose time Jesus was tried and sentenced, found during Zvi Greenhut's excavations in East Talpiyot (Yaʿar ha-Shalom). Salvage excavations directed by Ronny Reich in the Mamilla Street area, where a major development project is underway, led to the discovery of several Iron Age and Byzantine period tombs: a huge Byzantine burial cave containing hundreds of human remains was found adjoined by a small chapel whose walls are decorated with frescoes. One such fresco represents an angel facing to the right and extending its arms. In adjacent excavations, Aren Maeir exposed an aqueduct built in the third or fourth century CE that was in use through the Middle Ages. Parts of this aqueduct had previously been exposed north and west of this area.

The 1990 construction and expansion of Jerusalem's suburbs have resulted in a large number of salvage excavations in the area. At Pisgat Zeʿev, Rina Avner uncovered a Byzantine monastery, part of a complex that included an oil press, flour mill, and wine presses. In a later phase, prior to its destruction in a fierce conflagration, this complex served as an inn. Other parts of the same suburb revealed a site dating from the Early Bronze IV–Early Arab period, whose Roman-Byzantine remains include a complex system of buildings and installations: three *miqva'ot* (ritual baths), a lever-and-screw oil press, and a wine press (excavated by Jon Seligmann, 1990); a large Persian period fortress (60 × 70 m) with an outer casemate wall (uncovered by Yonatan Nadelman, 1990); and a Second Temple period farmstead with an adjacent hidden cave, *miqveh,* wine press, and underground oil press (excavated by Eli Shukron, 1991). [*See* Jerusalem; Ritual Baths.]

In Beersheba, building construction in the Ḥorvat Maṭar area in 1990–1991 exposed an Early Arab farmhouse excavated by Itzhaq Gilead and Steven Rosen. The farmhouse was built on top of a monumental Byzantine building that in turn was erected over scanty Chalcolithic remains. The walls of the Byzantine structure were plastered and were faced either with mosaics or red paint; its floors were paved with plastered stone slabs. Nearby, several farmhouses from the Iron Age and Byzantine periods were uncovered. At the construction site of a shopping mall northwest of the Beersheba central bus station, Yehudah Govrin unearthed twenty-five Byzantine graves in 1988–1989. At Naḥal Kovshim, in northern Beersheba, where building construction is planned, buildings dating to the Byzantine period were uncovered during excavations directed by Pirhiya Nahshoni, Yulia Ustinova, and Hayim Bar-Ziv. Remains included several structures, a complex of rooms arranged around a courtyard, a bell-shaped cistern, and a cistern and plastered sediment pool connected by clay pipes. Remains of a Chalcolithic settlement were also evident at the site and included twelve cisterns containing pottery. Of note is a violin-shaped limestone figurine. [*See* Beersheba.]

In the Afridar neighborhood in Ashkelon, salvage excavations directed by Baruch Brandl and Ram Gophna uncovered a site dating to the Early Bronze Age I. Massive wall remains from a large public building were located throughout the site. Seven rooms have been identified. A locally manufactured Egyptian-type bowl was found top of a staircase in one of the rooms. One of the earliest Canaanite copper daggers found in Israel was unearthed in these excavations, along with a considerable amount of Egyptian pottery, providing invaluable information regarding the Egyptian presence in the country's southern coastal region in the EB I.

Application for a building permit in Qiryat Ata, an eastern suburb of Haifa, led to salvage excavations in 1990 by Eliot Braun and Amir Golani at a site covering more than 240 acres. Several well-preserved EB I oval structures were uncovered, oriented east–west. One of the structures was destroyed by fire. At a second site in Qiryat Ata, salvage excavations were conducted in a previously robbed burial cave damaged during foundation work on a building. The cave contained several clay saroophagi.

Salvage excavations were conducted in northern Israel during construction of the new Tefen-Karmiel road. Three Middle Bronze I burial caves, containing skeletal remains, pottery, and a bronze dagger, were discovered and excavated by Mordechai Aviʿam in 1990. Each cave comprised at least two burial chambers.

Preparations for laying a water pipe at Bab el-Hawa, near Quneitra, revealed a 400-acre ancient site. Moshe Hartal's excavation of 1988–1990 unearthed, among other remains, an elongated Byzantine structure built over an Iron II building. The walls and doorjambs are of smoothed basalt blocks and still stand more than 2 m high. Of the eight rooms uncovered, two had round pottery installations (*tabuns* or silos). The building was used from the fourth–seventh centuries CE, with various changes made to its floors, doorways, and walls. Ceramic remains included imported ware and eight hundred decorated lamps. Also found were nine hundred coins; bronze, bone, metal, and glass jewelry; cosmetic utensils; and a stone seal carved with a seated figure milking a goat. The settlement was probably involved in animal husbandry (as evidenced by the hundreds of animal bones found), weaving, and milling and was most likely Christian (a large number of cruciform pendants were unearthed, and many of the lamps were decorated with crosses). A stone-built tomb was also discovered at the site containing pottery, human skeletal remains, animal bones, and turtle shells that may have been associated with funerary rites.

A group of interconnected rock-out caves was uncovered during construction work at Gush Ḥalav. The caves date to the first–second centuries CE and were probably used for storage. Their concentration indicates the location of ancient Gush Ḥalav. One cave, excavated in 1989 by Emanuel Damati and Hana Abu ʿUqsa, revealed four chambers and a corridor. Round and triangular hollows dug into the walls were used as shelves. Pottery and forty-one lines of graffiti were also found.

Ṭirat ha-Carmel was the cemetery of a large settlement in existence from the Roman–Byzantine to the Early Arab period. Twenty-two of its sixty caves were excavated in 1990 by Shalom Yankelevitch; those belonging to the Roman and Byzantine periods were irregular in plan and contained clay saroophagi. The Early Arab period caves were arcosolia caves containing burial troughs. All the caves had been looted, so that the finds were out of context: bronze coins; shell, bronze, and glass jewelry; pottery; glass vessels; and cosmetic objects. Of note is a fragment of a blue duck-shaped glass vessel. The site is first mentioned in Crusader sources as having been named after the Christian saint Jean of Tyre.

In the Tel Aviv area, during a sounding conducted in 1989 by Yossi Levy along the projected "Netiv Ayalon North" Project, a (Samaritan?) burial complex consisting of a courtyard and two chambers was uncovered. Finds included skeletal remains, pottery, lamps, jewelry, coins, and glass dating to the second–third centuries CE.

At Gelilot, during road-widening work on one of the area's main arteries in 1990, Levy uncovered rock-out wine presses characteristic of the Late Roman and Byzantine periods, including a treading surface, pools, and collection vats; an underground storehouse; a bathhouse, whose hypocaust and tepidarium are now partially excavated; a subterranean *miqveh* complex (with steps and a step bench, an entrance, and a threshold) covered with several layers of plaster (evidence of its extended use); a bell-shaped cistern used secondarily as a refuse pit; and a burial cave consisting of an entrance and small burial chamber that had been pillaged and thus produced few finds. All were probably used by a Late Roman period Samaritan agricultural settlement. [*See* Samaritans.]

In the south, in Israel's Negev desert, Chalcolithic remains were discovered during preparations for roadwork on the Kissufim-Katif road at Naḥal Kissufim. Excavations directed by Yuval Goren and Peter Fabian revealed limestone ossuaries containing human bones, pottery, and a bird figurine engraved in ivory. A large pit contained remains of a least ten burials. West of this area, which was damaged in the construction, was an underground rectangular burial chamber. Several shallow pits contained clay ossuaries. Small rectangular niches, one of which held an ossuary, were carved into two of the chamber's walls. Offering vessels were also found, some containing organic material. People of esteemed social status were probably buried there. Individual and group burials were also found around the periphery of the chamber, accompanied by very simple pottery forms. A secondary burial of three individuals was found nearby. The pottery at this site suggests a strong connection with the sites along Israel's coastal plain.

Several tumulus burials, including nine that are well-preserved, were uncovered when construction began in a new residential suburb on the outskirts of Eilat. Excavation in 1988–1989 by Uzi Avner and Israel Hershkovitz revealed that most were secondary burials and include the skeletal remains of at least one child. Finds included Neolithic arrowheads, grinding stones, flint scrapers, a sandstone bowl and fragments, pottery, and beads. An MB IIB cooking pot and a complete, primary male burial were found nearby, the first remains of this period found south of Tel Masos and Tel Malḥata.

An Iron II burial cave containing the fragmentary skeletal remains of ten people and dozens of pottery vessels was uncovered during road building operations at Ḥorvat ʿAnim. Yeshayahu Lender's 1989 excavations revealed a single burial chamber with arcosolia hewn into three of its walls.

[*See also* Israel Antiquities Authority; Survey of Israel.]

BIBLIOGRAPHY

Excavations and Surveys in Israel. Vols. 1–12. Jerusalem, 1982–1993. English edition of *Ḥadashot Arkheologiyot,* the IAA's archaeological newsletter.

RUDOLPH COHEN

SAMARIA, site located 56 km (35 mi.) north of Jerusalem (map reference 168 × 187) and west of the Ephraimite watershed, rising to a summit height of 430 m above sea level at 32°17′ N, 35°12′ E, near the center of the Northern Kingdom of Israel. Samaria overlooked the main road (Via Maris) connecting Egypt and the Southern Kingdom of Judah with the strategic Jezreel Valley and northern routes to Phoenicia and Damascus. Its biblical names *Šāmîr* (*Jgs.* 10:1–2) and, somewhat later, *Šōmĕrôn* (*1 Kgs.* 16:24 *et passim*), mean "watch" or "Watchman." Both designations stem from an original **qātil* participle and reflect successive changes in the pronunciation of that verb form (**šāmir-v* → **šōmir* → *šōmēr*). The name of the site's earliest recorded private owner, *Šemer,* represents a secondary nominal formation from this verbal antecedent.

Archaeology. Excavation at Samaria began in 1908 with the Harvard expedition directed by Gottlieb Schumacher. George Andrew Reisner and architect Clarence Fisher succeeded him in the second phase of the project, which ran from 1909 to 1910. Their combined efforts concentrated on the western half of the summit and exposed a substantial portion of the Israelite royal palace and, immediately to its west, a sizable storeroom complex. Reisner called the latter feature the Ostraca House because of the discovery inside of more than one hundred laconic shipping dockets recording the transfer of various commodities (primarily wine and oil) to the capital during the early eighth century BCE, in the time of Jehoash/Jeroboam II (see figure 1). [*See* Samaria Ostraca.]

Between 1932 and 1935, five institutions (mostly from England and Israel) sent a Joint Expedition to Samaria under the leadership of John W. Crowfoot. As primary field supervisor in the royal quarter, Kathleen M. Kenyon introduced new techniques of debris-layer analysis to the project. She exposed a north–south section across the entire summit east of Schumacher's and Reisner's earlier excavations. In the final reports, Kenyon held that Samaria's pottery provided crucial guidelines for evaluating the stratigraphic history and ceramic traditions at other Iron II sites in Palestine. Her publications quickly became the standard references for studying Samaria and the early Iron Age II generally; moreover, Aegean archaeologists began mooring their chronologies to Kenyon's proposed framework at Samaria.

Though Kenyon found some Early Bronze Age I pottery on the rock surface, most remains came from the Iron Age. Here she distinguished eight major building phases (periods I–VIII) and concluded that periods I–VI spanned the earliest Iron Age II occupation under Omri to the Assyrian destruction of Samaria in 722/21 BCE. Kenyon also believed that each new building phase corresponded directly to a shift in ceramic tradition. Appealing to *1 Kgs.* 16:24 to buttress her archaeological interpretations, she argued decidedly against any Iron Age occupation of Samaria earlier than Omri's reign.

Prior to Kenyon's official publication of the pottery (1957), however, Roland de Vaux (1955) suggested that her two earliest ceramic phases actually predated all Omride building activities and indicated an Iron I occupation of the site. Whereas this view merely questioned the direct correlation of architectural and ceramic periods, George Ernest Wright (1959) later proposed a formal distinction between them. Other contemporaneous studies by William Foxwell Albright (1958) and Yohanan Aharoni and Ruth Amiran (1958) agreed that the earliest Iron Age pottery predated the first royal architecture at Samaria. The resulting controversy stemmed mainly from differences in archaeological method and interpretation.

Kenyon's assertion that *1 Kgs.* 16:24 precluded any occupation on the hill prior to Omri compelled her to correlate the earliest ceramic remains with the earliest royal architecture and to assign both to Omri. Although the earliest Omride courtyard lay several depositional layers above bedrock, Kenyon's system demanded that she associated all Iron Age pottery lying directly on the bedrock (and often mixed with scrappy Early Bronze Age remains) with that higher floor level. Having started this way, she dated each successive floor level by the material found beneath it. Wright and others, however, proposed dating these surfaces by the material lying directly on them. In fact, both systems had merit; they simply addressed different aspects of the same methodological issue. Kenyon's approach yielded a floor's *terminus post quem* (construction date), whereas Wright's provided its *terminus ante quem* (occupational dates).

The early studies that challenged Kenyon's principles of dating had only her published pottery to evaluate. More recent ceramic (Stager, 1990) and stratigraphic (Tappy, 1992) investigations have examined unpublished material to determine the original findspots of the pottery and thereby settle the unanswered questions. The results have confirmed a pre-Omride occupation of Samaria and have associated the Iron I pottery there with various nonmonumental architectural features resting immediately on or set into the rock surface (remains of a possible beam press, numerous rock cuttings, storage pits, separator vats, and cisterns). A narrow reading of *1 Kgs.* 16:24, therefore, can no longer support Kenyon's proposed chronological framework for Israelite Samaria.

Kenyon's initial pottery analysis raised hopes that the strict stratigraphic controls that presumably attended her excavation method might strengthen typologies for the ninth–eighth centuries BCE. However, Tappy's recent stratigraphic study has shown that much of the published pottery came from secondary or disturbed contexts, while those pieces from primary contexts often came from deposits several layers above or below the floors and architecture they purportedly dated. When analyzed typologically against ceramic groups from traditional and more recently excavated sites, the pottery recovered from these deposits supports the new stratigraphic analysis. The collective attributes of vessels such as bar-handle bowls, cup-and-saucer forms, lentoid flasks, collar-rim store jars, and Early Iron Age krater, chalice, and cooking pot rims point to a significant Iron I

SAMARIA. Figure 1. *Ostraca house.* (Courtesy Reisner-Samaria Archive/Semitic Museum, Harvard University)

occupation for many of the levels exposed in Kenyon's large section across the summit and labeled "periods I–II."

In short, while Kenyon correctly associated the first monumental building activities with the early ninth-century Omride dynasty, recent studies have demonstrated the need to adjust her proposed ceramic chronology. Pottery Periods 1–2 belong to as early as the eleventh (possibly late twelfth) century BCE. It does not follow, however, that we should automatically shift the pottery from Pottery Period 3 upward to fill the resultant gap in the Omride era. In fact, only some of the Pottery Period 3 wares can relate to the Omrides. Other vessels in that assemblage must remain in Jehu's time period, while a significant number extend into the early eighth century. Clearly, we have many fewer stratigraphically secure archaeological data pertaining to ninth-century Samaria than the excavation report implies. Therefore, we must exercise caution when relying on the published materials from Samaria to establish or adjust chronologies at sites elsewhere in the Levantine and Aegean worlds.

History. When Omri rose to power over Israel in the early ninth century BCE, he soon moved the capital from Tirzah to Samaria (*1 Kgs.* 16:21–24). Together with Ahab, his son and successor, Omri subsequently transformed this one-time family estate of Shemer into a cosmopolitan royal city complete with impressive fortification walls, a palace, large courtyards with rectangular pools, public buildings, and storerooms. Ahab's politically motivated marriage to the Sidonian princess Jezebel opened the way to Phoenician wealth and religious influence. Later biblical references (*1 Kgs.* 22:39; *Am.* 3:15, 6:4; *Ps.* 45:9 [MT]) to ivory-appointed houses preserve a memory of the site's grandeur, confirmed by the discovery of numerous ivory furnishings spanning the period from Ahab to Jeroboam II. At the same time, Ahab's syncretistic tendencies won him the scorn of the religious establishment, epitomized in the figure of Elijah (*1 Kgs.* 17–19), whose victory against the prophets of Baal on Mount Carmel enhanced the credibility of the monotheistic Yahweh Alone Party. With backing from this faction, comprised mainly of prophets, ultra-conservative social groups such as the Rechabites, and undoubtedly some segments of the military, Jehu seized control of the throne in Samaria sometime around 842 BCE (*2 Kgs.* 9–10). Nevertheless, long after this event the Assyrians continued to refer to Samaria as the House of Omri.

Over a span of roughly 150 years (c. 870–722 BCE), fourteen Israelite kings ruled from Samaria as the city became Israel's political and cultural center, the undisputed "head of Ephraim" (*Is.* 7:9). Yet its newly acquired centrality also made Samaria the clearest and most dangerous symbol of opposition to the Southern Kingdom of Judah and its cult in Jerusalem. This deeply rooted north–south schism and the Judahite perspective taken in the final Deuteronomistic History produced a critical treatment of the rulers and activities at Samaria in the Hebrew Bible, while extrabiblical sources (Mesha Stele; Assyrian annals) often pointed to the capital's regional and international prominence. The complexities attending both textual and archaeological investigations into the Israelite period have led historians to concentrate their research on this phase of the city's existence.

In 722/21 BCE, Assyrian armies led by Shalmaneser V and Sargon II besieged and occupied Samaria, deporting large numbers of Israelites and resettling the site primarily with South Arabians (*2 Kgs.* 17; the Display, Bull, Khorsabad Pavement, and Cylinder inscriptions of Sargon). Though excavators recovered few building remains from this occupation, an Assyrian stele fragment (attributable to Sargon II), pieces of various cuneiform tablets (some apparently representing a letter to Avi-aḫi, the local governor), and significant quantities of Assyrian palace ware attest to Samaria's use then as an administrative center. Following Assyrian rule, the city passed into the hands of each successive world power. Although archaeology has revealed little from the subsequent Babylonian period, *Jeremiah* 41 alludes to the site's occupation during that time.

From the late sixth to the late fifth centuries BCE, Persia retained Samaria as an administrative center. Concurrent efforts to restore and strengthen Jerusalem rekindled old antagonisms between the two cities (*Ez.* 4; *Neh.* 2, 4, 6; 1 *Esd.* 2). Though few architectural remains survive from these years, excavators did recover a .25 m-thick deposit of fertile brown soil spread over a 45 × 50 m area of the summit. This area surrounded the district governor's palace and seems to have served as a large garden similar to those found elsewhere in the Babylonian-Persian empires. Small finds from this period include seal impressions in both Neo-Babylonian and Achaemenid styles; fragments of an Achaemenid throne; a fifth-century Athenian coin; three Sidonian coins (from the reign of Abdastart I, 370–358 BCE); painted and incised limestone incense altars; an alabaster alabastron; fourteen Aramaic ostraca (bearing dates from the late sixth to early fourth centuries); plus significant quantities of black- and red-figure, white-ground, and black-burnish wares imported from the Aegean world during the late sixth to late fourth centuries BCE.

The conquests of Alexander the Great initiated the turbulent Hellenistic period throughout the Levant. Following Alexander's death, the Ptolomies and Seleucids competed bitterly for control over Palestine. At Samaria, a series of beautifully constructed round towers and a subsequent massive defense wall (4 m thick) with square towers attest to the political vicissitudes of the time (see figure 2). The round towers, originally misdated to the Israelite period, stand 8.5 m high, with diameters ranging from 13 to 14.7 m. They represent some of the most impressive Hellenistic architecture unearthed anywhere in the country. Significant quantities of Megarian bowls and fragments from thousands of

SAMARIA. Figure 2. *Hellenistic round tower.* (Courtesy Reisner-Samaria Archive/Semitic Museum, Harvard University)

SAMARIA. Figure 3. *S-2 foundation of Herodian stair.* (Courtesy Reisner-Samaria Archive/Semitic Museum, Harvard University)

Rhodian stamped jars reflect Samaria's international commercial contacts during this era. Late in the period (c. 108/07 BCE), the Hasmonean high priest John Hyrcanus (135/34–104 BCE) led an assault against the city, destroying much of the so-called Fortress Wall and bringing Samaria temporarily under Judean control (Josephus, *Antiquities* 13.275–281; *War* 1.64–65).

Following Pompey's conquest of Palestine in 63 BCE, Samaria underwent its period of greatest physical change. The provincial governor, Gabinius (57–55 BCE), rebuilt its walls and residential areas and established a forum with an adjoining basilica northeast of the summit. But the most dramatic program of construction came under Herod the Great (Josephus, *Antiquities* 15.292; *War* 1.403), who renamed the city Sebaste (a Greek name honoring Emperor Augustus) and commissioned the Augusteum, a summit temple (35 × 24 m) with portico and cella, all situated on a platform whose retaining walls stood 15 m high. A 21-m-wide staircase led from the forecourt up 4.4 m to the temple proper (see figure 3). Other impressive features, including another temple and altar dedicated to the goddess Kore and a large stadium (230 × 60 m), lay on the city's north and northeast slopes, then enclosed by an outer city wall more than 3 kilometers (almost 2 mi.) in circumference (encompassing roughly 160 acres). A main entrance gate, flanked by two massive round towers, stood west of the city, and shops of all kinds lined the columned street (12.5 m wide) that angled around the south side of the hill and eventually approached the summit from the east.

Under Constantinian rule, in the Byzantine period, Samaria-Sebaste sent bishops to councils at Nicea, Constantinople, and Chalcedon and to the Synod of Jerusalem. Few remains from this period have survived. Between this time and the Middle Ages, tradition identified Samaria as the burial site of John the Baptist, and two separate shrines marked the proposed resting places of his body and head.

BIBLIOGRAPHY

Albright, William Foxwell. "Recent Progress in Palestinian Archaeology: Samaria-Sebaste III and Hazor I." *Bulletin of the American Schools of Oriental Research* 150 (1958): 21–25. An early and quite positive review of Kenyon's 1957 publication of the Samaria pottery, though it questioned her dating of some early Iron Age vessels.

Avigad, Nahman. "Samaria." In *The New Encyclopedia of Archaeological Excavations in the Holy Land,* vol. 4, pp. 1300–1310. New York, 1993. Well-balanced article written by a participant in the Joint Expedition to Samaria.

Crowfoot, J. W., and G. M. Crowfoot. *Early Ivories from Samaria.* Samaria Sebaste: Report of the Work of the Joint Expedition in 1931–1933 and of the Work of the British Expedition in 1935, no. 2. London, 1938.

Crowfoot, J. W., G. M. Crowfoot, and Kathleen M. Kenyon. *The Objects from Samaria.* Samaria-Sebaste: Report of the Work of the Joint Expedition in 1931–1933 and of the Work of the British Expedition in 1935, no. 3. London, 1957. This volume and the two published earlier by Crowfoot et al. comprise the official excavation report of the Joint Expedition (1931–1935). Although the report received praise as a hallmark in the study of Palestinian archaeology, it failed to present the stratigraphic data necessary to evaluate critically the authors' opinions.

Crowfoot, J. W., Kathleen M. Kenyon, and E. L. Sukenik. *The Buildings at Samaria.* Samaria-Sebaste: Report of the Work of the Joint Expedition in 1931–1933 and of the Work of the British Expedition in 1935, no. 1. London, 1942.

Kaufman, Ivan T. "The Samaria Ostraca: An Early Witness to Hebrew Writing." *Biblical Archaeologist* 45.4 (1982): 229–239. Synopsis of the author's 1966 dissertation, "The Samaria Ostraca: A Study in Ancient Hebrew Palaeography," summarizing the evidence available from archaeology and from the study of early scripts and hieratic numerals.

Rainey, Anson F. "Toward a Precise Date for the Samaria Ostraca." *Bulletin of the American Schools of Oriental Research,* no. 272 (November 1988): 69–74. Presents a viable new proposal to clarify the dating of the Samaria ostraca, explaining how they can be assigned to Jehoash and his coregent, Jeroboam II.

Reisner, George A. *Israelite Ostraca from Samaria.* Cambridge, Mass., [191?].

Reisner, George A., Clarence S. Fisher, and David G. Lyon. *Harvard Excavations at Samaria, 1908–1910,* vol. 1, *The Text;* vol. 2, *Plans and Plates.* Cambridge, Mass., 1924. The official excavation report from the initial exploration of Samaria by Harvard University from 1908 to 1910, including Lyon's brief summary of Schumacher's work in 1908; it is often difficult to relocate specific findspots on the basis of these reports.

Stager, Lawrence E. "Shemer's Estate." *Bulletin of the American Schools of Oriental Research,* no. 277–278 (February–May 1990): 93–107. Salient study of Early Iron Age bedrock installations that represent facilities for processing wine and oil.

Tappy, Ron E. *The Archaeology of Israelite Samaria,* vol. 1, *Early Iron Age through the Ninth Century BCE.* Harvard Semitic Studies, no. 44. Atlanta, 1992. Thorough evaluation of Kenyon's proposed chronological framework for the occupation of Early Iron Age Samaria, based on a critical assessment of data contained in both published reports and unpublished field notebooks. The discussion is technical and intended for the specialist.

Tappy, Ron E. *The Archaeology of Israelite Samaria,* vol. 2, *The Eighth Century BCE.* Forthcoming.

Vaux, Roland de. "Les fouilles de Tell el-Farʿah, près Naplouse, Cinquième Campagne." *Revue Biblique* 62 (1955): 541–589. An essay that predated Kenyon's official publication of the pottery from Samaria and that proposed tentative correlations between the Samaria pottery and that which de Vaux had recovered at Tell el-Farʿah (North); the correlations disagreed with Kenyon's conclusions regarding the earliest Iron Age materials from Samaria.

Wright, G. Ernest. "Israelite Samaria and Iron Age Chronology." *Bulletin of the American Schools of Oriental Research,* no. 155 (October 1959): 13–29. Praises Kenyon's work at Samaria as "one of the most remarkable achievements in the history of Palestinian excavation" (p. 17), but disagrees strongly with both her methodology and conclusions.

Wright, G. Ernest. "Samaria." *Biblical Archaeologist* 22.1 (1959): 67–78.

Wright, G. Ernest. "Archaeological Fills and Strata." *Biblical Archaeologist* 25.2 (1962): 34–40. Although here the author analyzes selected vessels from among Kenyon's published assemblage, his articles in *Biblical Archaeologist* function more as brief methodological treatises than comprehensive ceramic studies.

RON TAPPY

SAMARIA OSTRACA. Inscribed broken pieces of pottery (ostraca) recording the delivery of wine and oil to Samaria, the capital of Northern Israel, in the late first/early second quarter of the eighth century BCE were excavated at Samaria in 1910 by George A. Reisner of Harvard University. They are now in the Archaeological Museum in Istanbul. There are sixty-three ostraca as published by Reisner and forty others that he considered too illegible to publish. Nevertheless these latter ostraca are useful for study of the shapes of individual letters of the alphabet. These ostraca comprise the earliest corpus of Hebrew writing and were inscribed by a number of distinguishable hands. Their fine cursive script is pen drawn, with ink, in the early Hebrew forms derived from Phoenician. F. Briquel argues, however, that the language of the ostraca is a dialect of Hebrew (*Journal Asiatique* 274 [1986]: 478–479). In constructing a relative typology of early Hebrew scripts, the ostraca provide priceless evidence for how the forms of the alphabet developed, including how letters were made. They flow in a style that resembles Egyptian hieratic writing.

The ostraca could be dated with reasonable accuracy to a period considerably earlier than the destruction of samaria in 722/21 BCE. As if discarded, they were found widely scattered in the fill beneath the floor of a large building complex that, after it was built, underwent reconstruction of rooms and doorways before the fall of the city. Some of the ostraca bear the Egyptian hieratic numerals for 5 and 10, indicating the fifteenth year of the king, which dates them as far back as Jeroboam II (786–746), as has been clear since 1966, when Yohanon Aharoni wrote that the numerals on the Samaria Ostraca are to be read with the Egyptian values (Aharoni, 1966). Finally, a typologically later form of writing than that on the Samaria Ostraca is known on a type of pottery that is datable to the last period before the fall of the city, according to Kathleen M. Kenyon (Crowfoot, 1957).

The ostraca functioned as an accounting system when aged wine and refined oil were delivered from towns to the royal city. There is, however, a division of opinion over the precise function of the inscriptions. The issue centers on the identity of the person whose name on the ostraca is preceded by the preposition *lamed*. Frank M. Cross and Ivan Kaufman, following Yigael Yadin, have held the view that this person, now commonly referred to as the *l*-man, was a property owner who sent the wine or oil to the city of Samaria as tax paid in kind, and that the ostraca are records and perhaps receipts for goods received and credited to the *l*-man. There are eleven named *l*-men in the Samaria Ostraca. The other main point of view, held by Anson Rainey, is that the *l*-man was an official who resided in Samaria, was favored by the king, and received the commodity from land given to him by the king. He was, in effect, providing for himself from the produce of his land. The ostraca in this case were directives that the commodities be sent to the official for his use. Rainey's argument is detailed, and it fits some Ugaritic inscriptions in which the preposition *lamed* means "to" with reference to a person named (Rainey, 1988). Whether it holds for the Samaria ostraca is not entirely clear.

The ostraca show that the towns related to the *l*-men are clustered around the city of Samaria, within a radius of 6–13 km (4–8 mi.), with only two exceptions, and that all are within the tribal area of southern Manasseh. None are in Ephraim, which would rule out identifying the operation with the administration of the first Solomonic district. The configuration suggests local sources for wine and oil, rather than a broad system of taxation. The reading of some town names has been clarified, as is *spr* (Sefer) earlier read as *sq*. The *qoph,* which Reisner identified as an "S-headed" type is now understood to be a joined *pe* and *resh*. Sefer, if identified with modern Saffarin, locates the clan of Shemeida, as Cross has pointed out (1961).

A number of new readings of personal names have come to light in the ostraca as has a significant sociological datum: while the ratio of Baal names to Yahwistic or non-Baal names is 7:11. (Albright, 1956), all but one of the Baal names belong to men secondarily listed who appear to work for an "*l*-man."

The Samaria Ostraca are important to the study of the early Hebrew language and writing practices. Their precise function is elusive and will probably only become clearer with future discoveries and research.

[*See also* Samaria.]

BIBLIOGRAPHY

Aharoni, Yohanan "The Use of Hieratic Numerals in Hebrew Ostraca and the Sheckel Weights." *Bulletin of the American Schools of Oriental Research* 184 (1966): 13–19.

Albright, William T. *Archaeology and the Religion of Israel.* Baltimore, 1956.

Cross, Frank Moore "Epigraphic Notes on Hebrew Documents of the Eighth-Sixth Centuries B.C.: A New Reading of a Place Name in the Samaria Ostraca." *Bulletin of the American Schools of Oriental Research* 163 (1961): 12–14.

Cross, Frank Moore "Ammonite Ostraca from Heshbon." *Andrews University Seminary Studies* 13 (1975): 1–20. The author's fullest argument for interpreting the Samaria ostraca as tax receipts. Includes bibliographical notes and a discussion of Rainey's position.

Crowfoot, J. W. *The Objects from Samaria.* London, 1957.

Kaufman, Ivan T. "The Samaria Ostraca: A Study in Ancient Hebrew Palaeography." Th.D. diss., Harvard University, 1966. Extensive paleographic study based on infrared photographs of the ostraca.

Kaufman, Ivan T. "The Samaria Ostraca: An Early Witness to Hebrew Writing." *Biblical Archaeologist* 45 (1982): 229–239. Summarizes the conclusions of his dissertation (above), with samples of the text, photographs of the ostraca, charts, hand-drawn examples of the alphabet, and a bibliography.

Kaufman, Ivan T. "Samaria Ostraca." In *The Anchor Bible Dictionary,* vol. 5, pp. 921–926. New York, 1992. Alternative to the article in *Biblical Archaeologist* (see above).

Lemaire, André. "Writing and Writing Materials." In *The Anchor Bible Dictionary,* edited by David Noel Freedman, vol. 6, pp. 999–1008.

New York, 1992. Treats the early history of the alphabet, broad aspects of ancient writing, and has an extensive bibliography.

Rainey, Anson F. "Toward a Precise Date for the Samaria Ostraca." *Bulletin of the American Schools of Oriental Research,* no. 272 (November 1988): 69–74. Significant article with bibliography. The author supports Kaufman's dating of the ostraca to Jeroboam II on the basis of the paleographic and archaeological evidence, but dates Jeroboam's first year to 793 as coregent with Jehoash, with the resulting date of 784–783 for nineth-, tenth-, and fifteenth-year ostraca. Rainey further defines his position that the ostraca functioned as directives for delivery to residents in Samaria from their estates.

Reisner, George A., Clarence S. Fisher, and David G. Lyon. *Harvard Excavations at Samaria, 1908–1910,* vol. 1, *The Text;* vol. 2, *Plans and Plates.* Cambridge, Mass., 1924. Reisner's major publication on Samaria.

IVAN T. KAUFMAN

SAMARITANS. The origin of Samaritanism and the Samaritans is in the second–first centuries BCE, as an ancient off-shoot of Judaism. This date is now generally accepted by scholars of Samaritanism. The Samaritans themselves still hold the view that a schism occurred in the time of Eli, the priest at Shiloh (*1 Sm.* 1:9, 2:11). According to Samaritan tradition Eli, "the insidious one" (Samaritan *Book of Joshua,* ch. 43), left Mt. Gerizim and settled in Shiloh, where "he gathered the children of Israel into a schismatical sect" (Samaritan *Book of Joshua,* ch. 43; cf. also Abu 'l-Fatḥ, *Kitāb al-Tarīkh,* ch. 10). Jewish tradition, on the other hand, holds that Samaritanism arose after the fall of the northern kingdom when, according to *2 Kings* 17, Israelites were deported and pagans were settled in their stead. The same view was current in early scholarship. Gradually, it was realized that it was untenable and that the split between Jews and Samaritans must have occurred much later. On the basis of *Ezra* 4:1–5, many thought that the separation had taken place after the Exile, in the time of Ezra. It is now clear, however, that in the early post-Exilic period there was no real break, only the beginning of tensions between northern and southern Israelites. Thus, the prehistory of the Samaritans, as it were, begins then. The history of the Samaritans proper (as opposed to the Samarians, or inhabitants of Samaria, and "proto-Samaritans"—i.e., northern Israelites in the time leading up to the break) begins in the Maccabean period, with the hostilities they endured from the southern Israelites, which culminated in the destruction of their temple by John Hyrcanus in approximately 110 BCE. [*See* Samaria.] Jerusalem and its Temple ceased to be of importance to the northern Israelites, whose main defining criterion became their exclusive orientation toward Mt. Gerizim. Although the two communities went their separate ways, they did have contacts with each other throughout the centuries.

During Byzantine and Muslim rule, the number of Samaritans dwindled rapidly, until there were fewer than two hundred individuals left. It was only in the twentieth century that their numbers increased from approximately 139 in 1909 to 560 in 1994. Today the Samaritans live in two centers, Nablus and Ḥolon, the latter a southern suburb of Tel Aviv. However, from the Hellenistic period to the eighteenth century CE a far-flung diaspora existed whose traces are to be found in literary, epigraphic, and archaeological sources. Samaritans have lived in Egypt, Greece, Syria, Italy, and North Africa.

As a branch of Judaism, Samaritan religion shares its foundations. The Samaritan Bible, however, comprises only the Pentateuch but excludes the Prophets and Writings. The Samaritans do not of course recognize rabbinic writings; they developed their own traditions, albeit in a less structured and canonical form than those of the Jews. They also have their own Aramaic Targum, their specific liturgy and liturgical compositions, and their chronicles.

The center of Samaritanism is and has always been Mt. Gerizim (map reference 175 × 178) south of Nablus, ancient Shechem. [*See* Shechem.] According to Josephus, the Samaritans built a temple on the mountain in the time of Alexander the Great (*Antiq.* 11:302–347) that was destroyed two hundred years later by John Hyrcanus (*Antiq.* 13:255–256; *War* 1:63). Before Yitzhak Magen's recent excavations on the main peak (map reference 175 × 178), which began in 1984, archaeological finds had suggested that the temple mentioned by Josephus stood on Tell er-Ras (map reference 1761 × 1793), a lower peak of Mt. Gerizim, north of the main peak. [*See* Ras, Tell er-.] Beneath the Roman temple to Zeus, built in the time of Antoninus Pius (138–161 CE) and probably renewed by Caracalla (211–217 CE), a large

SAMARITANS. *Roman coin of the city of Neapolis.* Depicts Roman temple to Zeus at Tell er-Ras. Second/third century CE. (Photograph by R. Pummer)

structure was discovered that was thought to have been somehow connected with a Hellenistic Samaritan sanctuary, a hypothesis subsequently questioned. Magen's extensive excavations on the main peak (1995 was the twelfth season) have, however, brought to light remains of a large settlement from the Hellenistic period.

The fortified city on Mt. Gerizim was approximately 40.5 hectares (100 acres) in size; it was built in about 200 BCE, in the time of Antiochus III (223–187 BCE), and destroyed by John Hyrcanus (134–104 BCE) between 114 and 111 BCE. The finds include sections of the city wall, towers, large dwellings and service buildings, oil presses, storage jars, lamps, numerous coins, and inscriptions in Hebrew, Aramaic, and Greek. Magen identifies an area of more than 2 hectares (5 acres) on the summit as a sacred precinct, enclosed by a wall and accessed via a 10-meter-wide staircase ascending from the west. The excavations in 1995 have brought to light remains of a gate and enclosure walls from the Persian period. Ashes and bones found at the site have been dated by the C-14 method to the fifth century BCE. The implications of the new finds have yet to be assessed. The Hellenistic pottery and coins found under the temple to Zeus and dating from the second century BCE come, in Magen's opinion, from the Hellenistic city on the main peak (see his article in *New Encyclopedia of Archaeological Excavations in the Holy Land,* Jerusalem and New York, 1993, vol. 2, p. 489).

Outside Samaria, Samaritan settlements are known from literary and epigraphic sources, the most important of which are Damascus, Egypt, Athens, Delos, Corinth, Rome, and Syracuse. From a seventh-century CE literary source, Samaritans are known to have lived also in Carthage (*Vat. gr.* 1502, fol. 175). No archaeological remains, apart from inscriptions, that can be identified as Samaritan have been uncovered in the diaspora. It should be kept in mind for the literary sources, that the occurrence of such terms as *Samareus, Samaritēs,* and *Samaritis* are not unequivocal references to Samaritans in the religious sense; they may well be, and probably often are, an ethnic designation characterizing colonists from Samaria. Only terms such as *Samaritai tēn thrēscheian (Corpus Papyrorum Judaicarum,* sixth century CE) or *Israeleitai hoi aparchomenoi eis hieron Argarizein* (two inscriptions found on Delos and tentatively dated to the third/second and second/first centuries BCE respectively); clearly designate Samaritans by religion. Inscriptions engraved in Samaritan script or in Greek and Samaritan letters are of course also clear indications.

In antiquity, the Samaritans used a modified form of Hebrew script, known as Samaritan script, although for inscriptions they also utilized Greek; Samaritan script remains distinctive of the group. Its immediate ancestor is the Hebrew script of the end of the Second Temple period. The languages used by the Samaritans in antiquity were Hebrew, Aramaic, and Greek. They began to use Arabic in the Middle Ages. Eventually, a hybrid Samaritan Hebrew language developed.

Samaritan material culture in Greco-Roman times and in the Byzantine era was practically indistinguishable from its

SAMARITANS. *Hellenistic remains.* Section of the Hellenistic city recently unearthed on the main peak of Mt. Gerizim and, in the background, Tell er-Ras. (Photograph by R. Pummer)

Jewish counterpart. In the last analysis, only the presence of Samaritan script allows the attribution of remains to the Samaritan sphere. In Samaria, the fact that the area was inhabited primarily or exclusively by Samaritans is another means by which the provenance of material remains can be determined.

On the basis of the latter criterion, oil presses, *miqva'ot* ("ritual baths") jars, oil lamps, and tools excavated at Qedumim (map reference 165 × 179), located 10 km (6 mi.) west of Nablus, have been identified as Samaritan. Similarly, a considerable number of oil lamps found in the region of Samaria are considered to be of Samaritan origin, even though only a very small number are inscribed in Samaritan script. The symbols on the lamps are the same as on Jewish lamps—the *menorot* ("candelabra") and other cultic implements used in the Temple in Jerusalem. The Samaritan lamps exclusively are decorated with daggers or knives and ladder or steplike designs as well. The former may be connected to the Offering of Isaac, the latter to the staircase leading from Neapolis (Nablus) up to the temple on Tell er-Ras, although the latter was a Roman temple. A number of sarcophagi were found that were called Samaritan, even though the same type was also found outside the area of Samaria; they clearly show Roman and Jewish influences.

The city of Samaria probably began minting coins in about 375 BCE and continued to do so until 333/32 BCE. The coins bear the inscription *šmryn,* either in full or in various abbreviations; it is not clear whether this refers to the city or the region. Much discussed are those coins bearing the name *yrbʿm.* However, the evidence of these coins is too vague to shed light on the development of Samaritanism, or proto-Samaritanism.

Roman coins from the cities of Samaria depict emperors and symbols from Greco-Roman mythology. Of particular interest are the city coins of Neapolis minted between the reigns of Antoninus Pius and Volusian (251–253 CE), with a gap in the reign of Septimius Severus (193–211 CE). They depict Mt. Gerizim with a colonnade at its foot, a staircase leading up to a temple, and a second, smaller structure on the second peak. Whereas the identity of the latter building is unknown, the temple must represent the Roman temple to Zeus built in the second century CE on Tell er-Ras. The many gods and goddesses, together with their temples or cult places, depicted on the coins from Neapolis after Domitian (81–96 CE), are testimony to the predominantly pagan character of the city. Under Domitian the city coins of Neapolis do not depict any pagan symbols. Some scholars therefore believe that this was out of regard for the Samaritan population. In contrast, contemporary coins of the city of Samaria, a Roman settlement at the time, do bear symbols proper to the worship of Kore/Persephone.

Although it was known from literary sources and inscriptions that the Samaritans had a number of synagogues during the Roman-Byzantine period, archaeological remains of some of them were only recently uncovered. They are identified as Samaritan either by mosaic inscriptions in Samaritan script or by their location within the core area of the Samaritan settlement. To the former category belong synagogues in Shaalbim (map reference 148 × 141), Beth-Shean (197 × 213), and Ramat Aviv (131 × 167); and to the latter, Ḥusn Yaʿqub in Nablus, Mt. Gerizim, Khirbet Samara (1609 × 1872), El-Khirbe (1671 × 1846), Ṣur Natan (Khirbet Majdal) (1508 × 1832), and Kefar Faḥma (167 × 199). Epigraphic evidence shows that Samaritan synagogues also existed outside of Palestine: in Thessalonike, or Delos, and in Syracuse. Literary evidence alone is available for the existence of a Samaritan synagogue in Rome in the sixth century CE. The synagogues in Palestine were built in the fourth/fifth–sixth/seventh centuries CE. They were probably destroyed during the Samaritan revolts in the sixth century; some were rebuilt in the late Byzantine period. The synagogue on Delos has been tentatively dated to the third/second century BCE, the one in Thessalonike to between the fourth and sixth centuries CE, and the one in Sicily to the third/fourth centuries; the existence of a Samaritan synagogue in Rome is inferred for the fifth century CE.

The architecture and mosaic art of Samaritan synagogues are virtually identical to those of Jewish synagogues. Differences exist in the orientations of the buildings—toward Mt. Gerizim rather than Jerusalem—and possibly also in the complete avoidance of the depiction of living beings on mosaics, which no Samaritan synagogue has but some Jewish synagogues do. Because a large part of the region of Samaria still awaits thorough archaeological exploration, the picture that has begun to emerge can only be considered preliminary.

BIBLIOGRAPHY

Coggins, Richard J. *Samaritans and Jews: The Origins of Samaritanism Reconsidered.* Atlanta, 1975. Thorough assessment of biblical and postbiblical Jewish texts, archaeological evidence, and Samaritan literature concerning the early history of Samaritanism.

Crane, Oliver T. *The Samaritan Chronicle, or, The Book of Joshua the Son of Nun.* New York, 1890. An old translation, but the only one in print.

Crown, Alan D., ed. *The Samaritans.* Tübingen, 1989. The most comprehensive modern treatment of all major questions related to the Samaritan tradition by specialists.

Crown, Alan D. *A Bibliography of the Samaritans.* 2d ed. Metuchen, N.J., 1993. Complete bibliography on all aspects of Samaritanism.

Crown, Alan D., Reinhard Pummer, and Abraham Tal, eds. *A Companion to Samaritan Studies.* Tübingen, 1993. Encyclopaedic dictionary that complements and expands the anthology by Crown (1989).

Dexinger, Ferdinand, and Reinhard Pummer, eds. *Die Samaritaner.* Darmstadt, 1992. Besides tracing the development of Samaritan studies in German and English contributions, the book contains an article assessing the present state of research and a comprehensive discussion of the origins of Samaritanism.

Magen, Yitzhak. "Mount Gerizim and the Samaritans"; "The 'Samaritan' Sarcophagi"; "Qedumim: A Samaritan Site of the Roman-Byzantine Period"; "The Ritual Baths *(Miqva'ot)* at Qedumim and the

Observance of Ritual Purity among the Samaritans"; and "Samaritan Synagogues." In *Early Christianity in Context: Monuments and Documents,* edited by Frédéric Manns and Eugenio Alliata, pp. 91–230. Studium Biblicum Franciscanum, Collectio Maior, 38. Jerusalem, 1993. The most complete and up-to-date accounts in English of the excavator's recent findings.

Meshorer, Ya'acov. *City-Coins of Eretz-Israel and the Decapolis in the Roman Period.* Jerusalem, 1985.

Pummer, Reinhard. *The Samaritans.* Leiden, 1987. Concise introduction with forty-eight plates illustrating historical and contemporary aspects of Samaritanism.

Purvis, James D. *The Samaritan Pentateuch and the Origin of the Samaritan Sect.* Harvard Semitic Monographs, 2. Cambridge, Mass., 1968. Seminal work with a detailed discussion of the Samaritan script.

Reeg, Gottfried. *Die antiken Synagogen in Israel,* vol. 2, *Die samaritanischen Synagogen.* Beihefte zum Tübinger Atlas des Vorderen Orients, Reihe B, no. 12.2. Wiesbaden, 1977. Discusses all those places for which literary or epigraphic evidence exists. However, it is now believed that not all stone inscriptions necessarily come from synagogues. The new excavations of synagogues were not yet known (see Magen above).

Stenhouse, Paul. *The Kitāb al-Tarīkh of Abū 'l-Fatḥ.* Sydney, 1985. English translation with notes of the most important Samaritan chronicle, based on the author's unpublished critical edition of the Arabic text.

Sussman, Varda. "Samaritan Lamps of the Third–Fourth Centuries A.D." *Israel Exploration Journal* 28 (1978): 238–250.

Tal, Abraham. *The Samaritan Targum of the Pentateuch: A Critical Edition.* 3 vols. Tel Aviv, 1980–1983. New, critical edition with an extensive introduction (in English and Hebrew).

REINHARD PUMMER

SAMARRA. [*This entry comprises two articles treating the remains of the Chalcolithic and Islamic periods, respectively.*]

Chalcolithic Period

Located on the Tigris River some 96 km (60 mi.) north of Baghdad (34°13′ N, 43°52′ E), Samarra was a capital of the ʿAbbasid caliphs in the ninth century CE. It was built for the most part by al-Muʿtasim (833–842) and his son al-Mutawakkil (847–861), and it remained the seat of government for fifty-six years before the capital was moved back to Baghdad. Next to the Great Mosque at Samarra still stands the minaret known as Malwiyah. It has an external spiral staircase and has been thought by many to be a descendant of the ancient Mesopotamian ziggurat or temple tower.

There is a long history of exploration and excavation of the Islamic city of Samarra, but of special interest to the archaeology of early Mesopotamia was the find of Chalcolithic period remains by Ernst Herzfeld in 1904–1905 and published by him in 1930. Beneath some private houses of the ninth century CE was a layer of earth approximately 1.5 m (5 ft.) thick, a stratum resting apparently on virgin soil. Badly preserved unstratified simple inhumations accompanied by a very distinctive handmade painted pottery were recovered from this layer. The stratum was so disturbed that it was impossible to determine proper grave groups. As this was the first time such pottery was excavated, it came to be known as Samarra ware, and the duration of time in which it was produced is known as the Samarra period or phase.

Usually of a medium thickness, Samarra ware is relatively well made. In many small vessels, however, the ware is very thin. Because a wide range of firing temperatures were used, the ware varied in color. In many cases the pottery was overfired and even vitrified. The matte-finish painted decoration also varied in color ranging from reddish earth tones to a deep black. Much of the paint was also what is now a gray green. The painted designs included geometric patterns as well as abstract animal and human motifs. The painters often exhibited an extraordinary sensitivity to design problems and produced "tour de force" pieces like jar necks made into the faces of women with "coffee-bean" shaped appliques for eyes.

The Samarra pottery is distributed over a wide geographical area ranging from north of Baghdad and the foothills to the east of Baghdad throughout the central part of northern Mesopotamia. Some of the major sites in which the ware has been found include the following: Chogha Mami to the east of Baghdad in the Mandali region, Tell Songor, and Tell Rihan in the Hamrin region of the upper Diyala, Tell as-Sawwan next to Samarra north of Baghdad, Mattarah near Kirkuk, Shemshara in the Rania plain in the northeast hills, Hassuna south of Mosul, Yarim Tepe in the Sinjar, and Baghouz in the west on the upper Euphrates. The archaeological remains associated with this pottery are part of a distinct culture of village farmers that dates to the first half of the sixth millennium and may begin as early as the late seventh millennium. At some sites the Samarra culture stands alone while at others the pottery coexists with traditional pottery of the Hassuna culture. At Hassuna itself the Samarra pottery first appears in Hassuna III–IV and continues to be found in the later levels of that site. It seems clear that the Samarra ware is an import into Hassuna. The fact that so much of the pottery was repaired in antiquity would suggest that it was a valued commodity. The stratification of Hassuna also indicates that chronologically the Samarra phase overlaps with the Hassuna period which begins somewhat earlier. The more recent excavations at Yarim Tepe I would support the conclusions derived from the Hassuna excavations. The archaic phase of the Hassuna culture is represented at Yarim Tepe I by levels 8 through 12, and the "standard" Hassuna pottery characterizes levels 1 through 7. Painted Samarra ware first appears in level 6. Generally, the Hassuna sites are situated further north than the majority of Samarra sites; however, the stratigraphic situation at Tell as-Sawwan, where the Samarra pottery first appeared in Level III along with Hassuna wares, indicates that the Hassuna potteries extended further south in Mesopotamia than is sometimes assumed.

Evidence would suggest that the Samarra culture overlapped with the following Halaf period, an archaeological phase characterized by a new painted pottery first found at Tell Ḥalaf in the Khabur region of northern Syria. Some Ḥalaf pottery dating to the early Halaf period was found at Samarra itself, although the sherds from Samarra do not include any of the famed polychrome painted pottery of the later part of the Halaf period. [*See* Ḥalaf, Tell.]

Besides Yarim Tepe in the Sinjar, comparatively extensive exposures of Samarra period remains have been excavated further south at such sites as Tell as-Sawwan and Chogha Mami where there is evidence that farming was dependent on irrigation. At Tell as-Sawwan the third level of the settlement had a defensive wall and a protective ditch at least three meters wide. Impressive large mud-brick buildings with T-shaped plans were found, and beneath the first and earliest level there were very rich graves with stone idols and stone vessels of superior workmanship. No pottery accompanied these burials that must predate the actual appearance of Samarra pottery at Tell as-Sawwan and belong to an early Hassuna or even Proto-Hassuna period of the second half of the seventh millennium. At Chogha Mami the excavators distinguished a late phase of Samarra pottery which was termed "Transitional Ware." This pottery is related to pottery in Iran and to pottery of the early Ubaid period in the south of Mesopotamia. It forms an important chronological link between north and south. It is now clear from the excavations at Tell el-'Oueili that there is a phase in the south earlier than the period represented by the Chogha Mami "Transitional Ware" probably contemporary in part with the earlier Hassuna.

[*See also* Hassuna; 'Oueili, Tell el-.]

BIBLIOGRAPHY

Herzfeld, Ernst. *Die Vorgeschichtlichen Töpfereien von Samarra.* Forschungen zur Islamischen Kunst, 2, Die Ausgrabungen von Samarra, vol. 5. Berlin, 1930. Original publication of the pottery from Samarra.

Porada, Edith. "The Chronology of Mesopotamia, ca. 7000–1600 B.C." In *Chronologies in Old World Archaeology,* edited by Robert W. Ehrich, vol. 1, pp. 77–121, vol. 2, pp. 90–124. 3d ed. Chicago, 1992. Provides good bibliography for the Samarra sites and discussions of the period.

Yoffee, Norman, and Jeffery Clark, eds. *Early Stages in the Evolution of Mesopotamian Civilization: Soviet Excavations in Northern Iraq.* Tucson, 1993.

DONALD P. HANSEN

Islamic Period

Samarra, capital of the ʿAbbasid caliphate from 836 to 892 CE, located on the left bank of the Tigris River, 96 km (60 mi.) north of Baghdad, Iraq (34°13′ N, 43°52′ E). It may be the largest archaeological settlement site in the world.

History. Before the advent of Islam, Samarra was known only as the site of a fort near which the Roman emperor Julian the Apostate was killed in battle in 364 CE. In the sixth century CE the Sasanian king Khusrau Anushirvan dug the Qatul al-Kisrawi, a northern extension to the Nahrawan canal, which watered the left bank of the Tigris below Baghdad. There were two inlets north and south of Samarra: the modern Nahr al-Rasasi and the Nahr al-Qa'im. A palace was built at the entrance to the first, and a monumental tower, the Burj al-Qa'im, at the entrance to the second. The ʿAbbasid caliph Harun al-Rashid (786–809) added the Qatul Abi al-Jund, whose inlet lay south of Samarra (now largely eroded), and built a palace city there called al-Mubarak.

The caliph al-Muʿtasim (833–842) sought a new site for a city after disturbances between the population of Baghdad, and the Turkish army corps. In 836 he settled in Samarra, formally called *Surra man ra'a* ("He who sees it is delighted"). Although considered a city, Samarra was mainly a court residence and cantonment of the ʿAbbasid army.

Al-Muʿtasim's second successor, Jaʿfar al-Mutawakkil (847–861), the greatest of the builders of Samarra, doubled the size of the city and is credited with nineteen palaces. Mutawakkil was murdered in 861, and during the following decade the leaders of the Turkish corps made and unmade four caliphs. In 892 al-Muʿtaḍid (caliph, 892–908) returned to Baghdad. During the 880s the city declined rapidly, contracting into the market areas of the ʿAbbasid city. Today it is a small town whose economy is supported by the pilgrimage to the tombs of the Shiʿi Imams al-'Askari and al-Hadi.

Archaeology. The site was first worked on by the French architect Henri Viollet, who dug soundings in the palace in 1910. The first major excavation was the German Samarra Expedition (1911, 1913), directed by Ernst Herzfeld. The expedition conducted rapid large-scale excavations of nineteen sites in twenty months. The series *Ausgrabungen von Samarra* (Herzfeld, 1923–1948) published most of the finds and a history of the city, but not the excavations themselves. The major architectural findings were summarized by K. A. C. Creswell (1940). The Iraq Directorate-General of Antiquities initiated excavations 1936 that are still underway. In the 1980s Alastair Northedge, in an archaeological survey, recorded surface remains on behalf of the British School of Archaeology in Iraq and excavated soundings at Qadisiyya.

The site extends for 50 km (31 mi.) along the bank of the Tigris and consists of 57 sq km (35 sq. mi.) of mounds whose arrangement reveals the lines of avenues and plans of buildings in aerial photographs. Samarra is, thus, an excellent subject for the application of the principle of horizontal stratigraphy and comparison of archaeological evidence with historical texts. ʿAbbasid building construction at Samarra used fired brick, mud brick, and pisé. About 5,700 ʿAbbasid buildings have been identified. While only

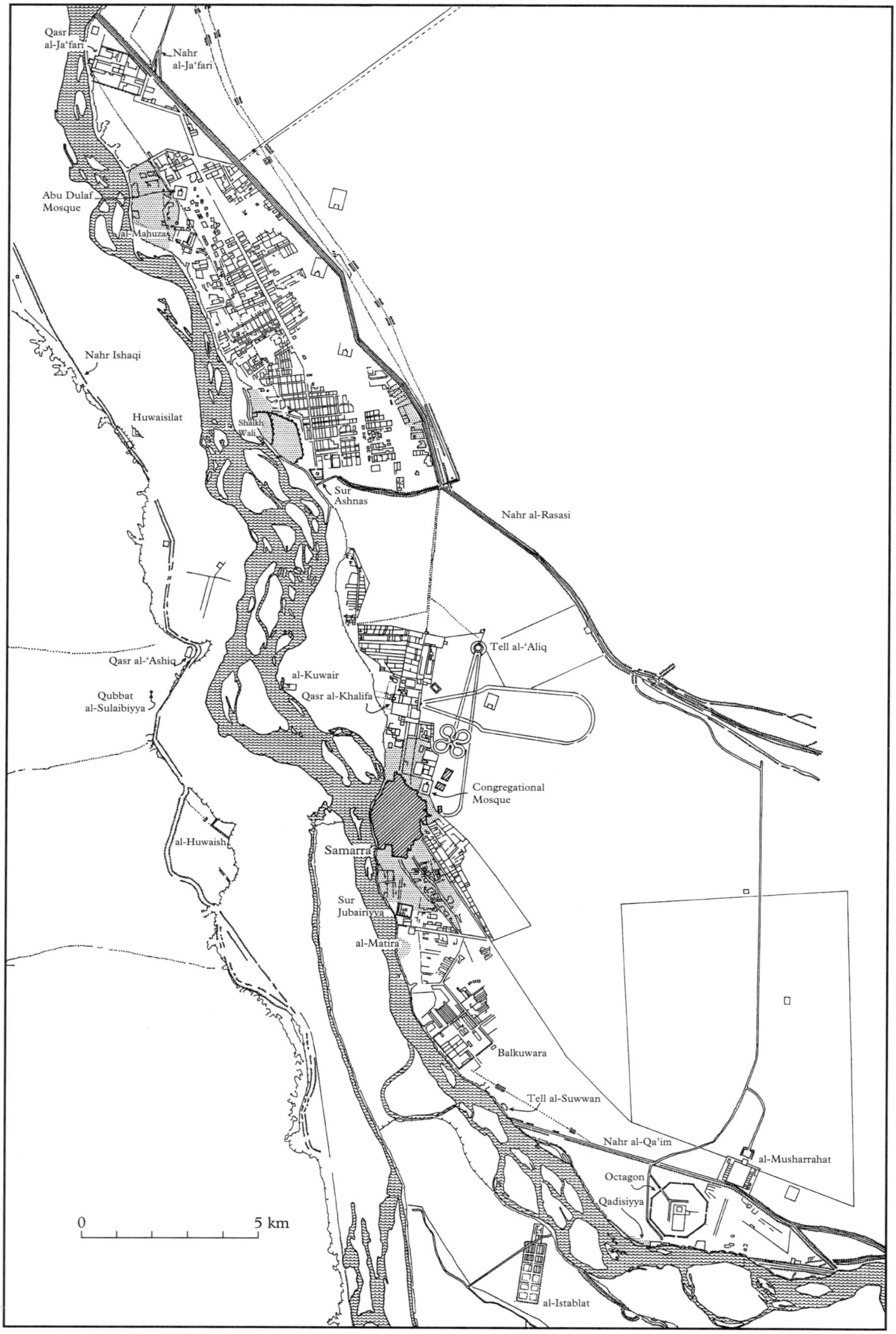

SAMARRA: Islamic Period. *Plan of the site.* (Courtesy A. Northedge)

one or two major phases of construction can be seen over much of the site, four sites, representing pre-Islamic towns on the bank of the Tigris, have a complex stratigraphy extending from the Sasanian period to the thirteenth century CE.

Octagon of Ḥusn al-Qadisiyya. Ḥusn al-Qadisiyya, a regular octagon 1,500 m in diameter, is an unfinished complex; only its mud-brick outer walls were built, but the lines were laid out for a mosque, a palace, a central square, and three avenues. Historical sources suggest an identification with the palace of Harun al-Rashid, al-Mubarak, whose construction was abandoned in 796.

Dar al-Khilafa (Jawsaq al-Khaqani). The main palace of al-Muʿtasim, a vast complex of 125 ha (309 acres), included a block of reception halls, excavated by Herzfeld in 1913. The halls were fronted by a triple *iwan* known as the Bab al-ʿAmma. Behind them was a large rectangular courtyard, two *birka*s ("sunken pools"), a polo ground, and a residential palace to the north. The *birka*s, excavated in the 1980s, were cut into the conglomerate, one square and one circular, each surrounded by a four-*iwan* plan of rooms for occupation in the summer. Herzfeld identified the complex as the Jawsaq al-Khaqani, but the palace is more likely to have included both the official palace of Muʿtasim (the Dar al-ʿAmmi) and the residence (al-Jawsaq).

Military cantonments. The military cantonments (Ar., *qatiʿa*) all follow a similar plan that includes a major palace, a number of lesser residences, a ceremonial avenue, and a grid of streets. Istablat and Balkuwara are walled; others are not. The troops were quartered in houses rather than barracks; al-Muʿtasim arranged for the purchase of Turkish slave girls for marriage partners, in order to avoid the mixing of Turks with the indigenous population.

In the north, and separated from the main city, the cantonment of the Turkish general Ashnas was built outside the walls of the former Sasanian town of Karkh Fairuz. The palace, now called Sur Ashnas, is quadrilateral, with a mosque in the center. Adjacent to the Dar al-Khilafa, the cantonment of Khaqan Urtuj has a palace facing onto the steppe. South of Samarra, and at first separated from it, the cantonment of the Central Asian Iranian prince Afshin was built at Matira, with a square palace on the river, now called Sur Jubairiyya.

In the 850s a new cantonment for Mutawakkil's son al-Muʿtazz was built in the south, at Balkuwara, with a rectangular palace facing the river, set in an 1,171 meter square enclosure. The reception halls, excavated by Herzfeld in 1911, form a square block with a central dome chamber and four *iwans* in a cruciform pattern.

Al-Istablat is a cantonment on the west bank of the Tigris, with a rectangular palace and a second walled rectangle. The rectangle contains a partly finished cantonment, 2.5 km (2 mi.) long and 500 m wide. It is apparently the short-lived palace of al-ʿArus, constructed in the 850s by al-Mutawakkil and demolished a decade later.

Congregational mosque of al-Mutawakkil. Between 848/49 and 852, al-Mutawakkil built a new congregational mosque (239 × 156 m) that was, for a long time, the largest mosque in the Islamic world. Its exterior is marked by semicircular buttresses and a minaret 52 m high, with an external

SAMARRA: Islamic Period. *Congregational mosque of al-Mutawakkil.* (Courtesy A. Northedge)

spiral ramp. This unusual style of minaret is apparently derived from the Assyrian ziggurat (cf. Khorsabad) and provided the inspiration for European depictions of the Tower of Babel.

Al-Mutawakkiliyya (al-Jaʿfariyya). In 859 al-Mutawakkil began a new caliphal city to the north, called al-Mutawakkiliyya. The new main palace, al-Jaʿfari, has its reception halls at the junction of the Tigris and the Qatul al-Kisrawi, while residential blocks spread for 1.7 km to the east. A major avenue, 98 m wide, leads south to Sur Ashnas, with palaces and houses on either side. In 861 Mutawakkil was murdered and al-Mutawakkiliyya abandoned. The mosque of Abu Dulaf, bordering on the preexisting town of al-Mahuza, was the congregational mosque for al-Mutawakkiliyya and a smaller replica of Mutawakkil's congregational mosque at Samarra, with a spiral minaret and fired brick arcades supported on piers.

Racecourses. To the east of the city, in the steppe, are three racecourses for horse racing. Two are out-and-back courses, each 10.42 km (6.5 mi.) long, and 80 m wide. One has a rest house for the caliph and a viewing mound, Tell al-ʿAliq, on which Herzfeld found a small pavilion. The third is a closed cloverleaf, 5.31 km (3.3 mi.) long, also with a central viewing pavilion. A fourth, linear course, 9.78 km (6.1 mi.) long, and 104 m wide, lies adjacent to the Turkish cantonments at al-Karkh.

Hunting parks. A quadrilateral enclosure (9 × 6 km, or 5 × 4 mi.) to the southeast appears to be a *hayr,* or "hunting park"; a palace on the south, at al-Musharrahat, faces a basin. A second park, to the north of the al-Jaʿfari, has a double enclosure wall with four gates and a viewing mound at Tell al-Banat.

[*See also* ʿAbbasid Caliphate.]

BIBLIOGRAPHY

Adams, Robert McC. *Land behind Baghdad: A History of Settlement on the Diyala Plains.* Chicago, 1965. The major reference on regional history and environment.

Creswell, K. A. C. *Early Muslim Architecture.* Vol. 2. Oxford, 1940.

Directorate General of Antiquities. *Excavations at Samarra, 1936–1939.* 2 vols. Baghdad, 1940. The palace of al-Huwaisilat and large houses.

Herzfeld, Ernst. *Ausgrabungen von Samarra,* vol. 1, *Der Wandschmuck der Bauten von Samarra und seine Ornamentik;* vol. 3, *Die Malereien von Samarra;* vol. 6, *Geschichte der Stadt Samarra.* Berlin and Hamburg, 1923–1948.

Northedge, Alastair. "Karkh Fairūz at Sāmarrā'." *Mesopotamia* 22 (1987): 251–263.

Northedge, Alastair, and Robin Falkner. "The 1986 Survey Season at Sāmarrā'." *Iraq* 49 (1987): 143–173. Treats the Octagon of Ḥusn al-Qadisiyya and surrounding sites.

Northedge, Alastair. "The Racecourses at Sāmarrā'." *Bulletin of the School of Oriental and African Studies* 53.1 (1990): 31–56.

Northedge, Alastair. "The Palace at Istabulat, Samarra'." *Archéologie Islamique* 3 (1992): 61–86.

Northedge, Alastair. "An Interpretation of the Palace of the Caliph at Samarra (Dar al-Khilafa or Jawsaq al-Khaqani)." *Ars Orientalis* 23 (1993): 143–170.

Rogers, J. M. "Sāmarrā: A Study in Medieval Town-Planning." In *The Islamic City,* edited by Albert Hourani and S. M. Stern, pp. 119–155. Oxford, 1970.

Susā, Ahmad. *Rayy Samarra' fi ʿAhd al-Khilafa al-ʿAbbasiyya* ("The Irrigation of Samarra' under the ʿAbbasid Caliphate"). 2 vols. Baghdad, 1948–1949. The major Iraqi work, in principle on the canal system, but actually treats everything, including questions not dealt with in Western works.

Alastair Northedge

SAMOSATA (Tk., modern Samsat; Ar., Sumaisat; Syr., Semisat), ancient capital of Commagene, located on the right bank of the Euphrates River, 64 km (40 mi.) downstream from the river's rapids and 116 km (72 mi.) upstream from Zeugma (Pliny, *Nat. Hist.* 5.85), 21 km (13 mi.) from Tarsus in Cilicia, and 19 km (12 mi.) from Edessa in Osrhoene. It occupies a site of confluence with the Marsyas River.

W. F. Ainsworth visited its ruins in 1836 and V. Moltke in 1838; it was the late publications of Carl Humann and Otto Puchstein (1890), however, that provided a plan and illustrations. Finally, in 1896, David G. Hogarth and Vincent Yorke published four of the site's inscriptions. No excavation is known to have been undertaken or published. The site has been in danger of disappearing since the great dams on the Euphrates were constructed.

The site lent itself admirably to the development of a large city: it is on a plain 1,200 m wide lying between the Euphrates on the west and a mountainous area on the east—a position that destined it to be an important crossroads on a north–south axis. It supplied the Euphrates valley and the valley between Osrhoene and Cilicia with access through the passes in the Anti-Taurus Mountains. [*See* Cilicia.]

The oldest evidence of the existence of Samosata is a Hittite stela that reveals that the city already had its name. During the Assyrian period it was the capital of Kummuh. It survived the attacks of the Assyrian kings until Sargon II reduced it to an Assyrian province. It became the capital of the kingdom of Commagene, which Pompey entrusted in 62 or 61 BCE to King Antiochus I, son of Mithridates Kallinikos. His reign is known for the building projects he undertook at Arsameia, which his ancestor Arsames founded and where his father Mithridates had his tomb, as well as for the monumental tomb he had made for himself at the summit of Nemrud Dağı. Its enormous seated statues of gods and of kings reflect a Greco-Oriental art in which Persian influences, notably in dress, combine with the purest Greek style. These composite traits testify to the mixed civilization that characterized Commagene.

From 17 to 38 CE, the kingdom was merely a Roman province. Caligula reestablished the dynasty in the person of Antiochus IV, but Antiochus was accused of collusion with the Parthians under Vespasian, who then authorized the governor of Syria, L. Caesennius Paetus, to annex Commagene

(72 CE). Vespasian sent the sixteenth Flavian Legion to occupy Samosata. The legion sprang into action and was cited in Trajan's war against the Parthians in 114. Samosata's fame in the third century is owed to Lucien and the bishop Paul, who was deprived of his office for his heretical ideas. According to the Peutinger map, Samosata is at the convergence of five routes that lead to Melitene, Comana, Heracome, Tarsus, and Zeugma. In the fourth century, Libanios described it as a large, heavily populated city. It may have suffered misfortune in 531, under Justinian, when the area was ravaged by Arab tribes allied with the Persians (Procopius 1.17.22f.). Under Heraclius it was conquered by the Arabs and became Muslim, but it was briefly reconquered many times by the Byzantines, in 700, 836, 858, 872, 927, and 958. Moltke (see above) identified a fragment belonging to a decorated marble entrance that was no doubt Byzantine.

The city was fortified during the Roman period and, according to Strabo and Lucien, it had a basilica of which no trace remains. Its murals, on the other hand, have survived, with many alterations, but without their layout being greatly modified. The city's perimeter is nearly 8 km long, and its border on the east, for 2 km, is the Euphrates. The acropolis (45 m high) lies to the south of the city, rather than at its center. Remains of walls belonging to a house from the Roman period were seen at the foot of the acropolis, on the south side. At the beginning of the twentieth century the south side of the city was the best preserved, but there were no more than one hundred houses in the village. Today, the village is a medium-sized town.

BIBLIOGRAPHY

Ainsworth, William F. *A Personal Narrative of the Euphrates Expedition.* 2 vols. London, 1988.

Honigmann, Ernst. *Die Ostgrenze des byzantinischen reiches von 363 bis 1071 nach griechischen, arabischen, syrischen und armenischen Quellen.* Brussels, 1935. See especially pages 134–137.

Humann, Carl, and Otto Puchstein. *Reisen in Kleinasien und Nordsyrien.* 2 vols. Berlin, 1890.

Yorke, Vincent W. "A Journey in the Valley of the Upper Euphrates." *Geographical Journal* 8 (1896): 317–335, 453–474. David G. Hogarth led the expedition on which Yorke reports.

GEORGES TATE

Translated from French by Melissa Kaprelian

SANʿA, since 1990 the capital of the unified Republic of Yemen, located 2,200 m above sea level, in the middle of a plain between tall mountains, through which the Yislaḥ pass (altitude 2,700 m) enables communication with the south and another, the bin Ghaylan pass (altitude 2,300 m), with Marib in the east; there are no obstructions to the north (15°21′ N, 44°13′ E). The walled city is cut by Wadi al-Sa'ilah, and encompasses about 100 ha (247 acres) with about six thousand tower houses (multi-story brick, stone, and wood houses) built in it.

Sanʿa has its roots in prehistory. Pre-Islamic Sanʿa is known primarily from late sources that recount its history. Very few inscriptions have been found in Sanʿa, and sources from elsewhere mentioning it are rare. A Swiss Mission directed by J. Schneider began excavations in Sanʿa, as yet unpublished, in the Bayt al-Ambassi.

The only available stratigraphy of the Old City of Sanʿa was salvaged from a pit sunk in the courtyard of the Imam ʿAli mosque, at the site of the house where ʿAli ibn Abi Ṭalib, the first Shiʿi Imam, reportedly stayed during the lifetime of the Prophet, on the edge of the contemporary suq. Daily life in Sanʿa takes place in the upper stories of the tower houses, so that leveling operations, which leave little more than wall stumps on the ground floor (where animals and grain were kept), limit the value of the archaeological material, as human living floors are not preserved.

The observed stratigraphy is no earlier than the seventh century CE, but pottery suggests that settlement at the site of the mosque may date to the late prehistoric period (c. second millennium BCE) in Yemen. The sherds and wall stumps found there, along with reused bits of monumental architecture encountered elsewhere in the city, confirm textual sources indicating that Sanʿa was a town of at least 7 ha (17 acres) in the first centuries CE, with commercial, residential, public, and religious areas. It continued to grow during the centuries of upheaval as the Sabaean rulers gave way to the Ḥimyarites, who were overthrown by the Ethiopians and Sasanians before adhering to Islam. [*See* Sheba; Ḥimyar; Ethiopia; Sasanians.] Under the ʿAbbasids, Sanʿa was increasingly subjected to local pressures: the native Yu'firid dynasty competed with both the Fatimids and the ʿAbbasids, as well as the emerging Zaydis. [*See* ʿAbbasid Caliphate; Fatimid Dynasty.] Serious damage may have been done to the city in about 905 CE and again in 911 CE, when it changed hands, but this may not have taken place, being merely slanderous accusations against the Fatimid general Ibn al-Faḍl. Sanʿa probably grew to about 50 ha (124 acres) before the period of Ayyubid hegemony. [*See* Ayyubid–Mamluk Dynasties.]

A Sabaean inscription records the presence of an Awa sanctuary at Sanʿa that has been interpreted as indicating that Sanʿa was a supratribal Sabaean national center. Sanʿa was also a Sabaean *maḥram*, a "protected place." The name *Sanʿa* is interpreted as meaning "well fortified"; it was the base of Sabaean military operations against the southern and western areas. Texts occasionally refer to Sanʿa as Azal, perhaps related to Uzal (*Gn.* 10:27).

A Sabaean king named Ilisharaḥ is cited in later Muslim sources as having constructed the Ghumdan palace in about the middle of the third century CE, when the city was very prosperous. It was a very large building with windows of thinly cut, transluscent alabaster and bronze lions at the corners that "roared" when the wind blew. The ruins of the Ghumdan palace form a large mound facing the eastern doors of the Grand Mosque, reputedly built in about 630 CE (during the Prophet's lifetime) in the Sasanian governor's garden.

The citadel is situated on a rock outcrop on the eastern edge of the city. Within its walls are both a fortified acropolis and a lower town. The oldest structures yet identified appear to date to the ninth century CE, but there may be earlier material. Urban Sanʿa grew from the citadel to the west, rather than from the area of the Ghumdan east, as the etymological connotation of *Sanʿa* can only be applied to the citadel. To the west of the citadel is the site of an enormous church built by the Axumite general and ruler Abrahah at the time of the Ethiopian occupation, in about 540 CE.

[*See also* Yemen.]

BIBLIOGRAPHY

Lewcock, Ronald. *The Old Walled City of Ṣanʿā.* Paris, 1986.

Serjeant, R. B., and Ronald Lewcock, eds. *Ṣanʿā: An Arabian Islamic City.* London, 1983. Contains articles by some of the foremost authorities on ancient and medieval Sanʿa. Some minor details will necessarily be corrected, such as the date of the Imām ʿAlī mosque.

Warburton, David A. "A Stratigraphic Section in the Old City of Ṣanʿā." *Proceedings of the Seminar for Arabian Studies* (forthcoming). Account of the stratigraphy of Sanʿa based on a last-minute rescue operation making levels from the seventh-eighth centuries to the twentieth century CE accessible.

DAVID A. WARBURTON

SANIDHA, small village lying in the Troodos Mountain foothills, adjacent to the southern coast of Cyprus, 20 km (12.5 mi.) northeast of Limassol (34°49′ N, 33°12′ E). The Late Bronze Age ceramic manufacturing site, however, is situated 1 km (.6 mi.) northeast of the village at the locality Moutti tou Ayiou Serkou at an elevation of 520 m (1,706 ft.). No other sites are known in the area, but a detailed field survey has not been undertaken. The discovery of the Late Bronze Age site in 1988 was accidental, and it highlights the potential archaeological wealth of the mountain zone. Following an extensive collection of surface material, an initial season of rescue excavation, under taken by Ian A. Todd for the Vasilikos Valley Project, was necessary in 1990 because the site was destined for significant agricultural disturbance. The second and third excavation seasons were undertaken in the autumn and spring of 1991–1992.

Attention was drawn to Sanidha because of the dense scatter of Late Bronze Age White-Slip II sherds on the surface. The concentration is greater than that on any other known Cypriot site. Some wasters (sherds deformed in firing) were identified, and the surface survey suggested that the site must have served a specialized function. The surface ceramics comprised White-Slip and Monochrome types, but almost none of the other types such as Base Ring, which commonly occur on the surface of settlement sites. In addition to ceramics, quantities of "brick" fragments were also found. These "bricks" are formed of mud and vegetable matter with parallel sides, rounded ends, flat bottoms, and curved tops. No complete "bricks" were found, and all fragments showed evidence of firing or burning. According to the surface survey the site measures about 675 × 325 m (2,215 × 1,066 ft.) and was certainly large, even if not used for a long duration.

Three seasons of excavation have failed to reveal any pottery kilns in situ, but abundant evidence has been retrieved which derives from different stages in pottery manufacture. Several activity areas were located consisting of extensive scatters of sherds and other artifacts in one place in association with shallow pits. Two larger pits were filled with rubbish, probably derived from nearby manufacturing activities. Around the edges of one pit were found approximately five hundred well-preserved "brick" fragments in association with small amounts of sherds. In the other, large quantities of sherds were found, but only few and poorly preserved "brick" fragments. Such variety within a small area is characteristic of Sanidha.

Few scientific analyses of White-Slip ware have been conducted, but it seems that all the required raw materials for the manufacture of pottery were available locally, including timber for fuel, water, clay, and the minerals necessary for the temper. "Bricks" of somewhat similar shape to those at Sanidha were used in a Roman kiln at Tell Qasile in Israel and in modern kilns in Crete. All available evidence, therefore, suggests ceramic production as the purpose of the Sanidha site. Further excavations are planned, and a program of ceramic analysis will be undertaken to establish the sites in Cyprus and abroad to which the ceramics were traded.

BIBLIOGRAPHY

Todd, Ian A. "Sanidha-Moutti tou Ayiou Serkou: A Late Bronze Age Site in the Troodos Foothills." *Archaeologia Cypria* 2 (1990): 53–62. Report on the initial discovery and surface collection of the site.

Todd, Ian A., and Maria Hadjicosti. "Excavations at Sanidha, 1990." *Report of the Department of Antiquities, Cyprus* (1991): 37–74. Preliminary report on the first season of excavation, containing references to technical analyses of Cypriot ceramics.

Todd, Ian A., et al. "Excavations at Sanida 1991." *Report of the Department of Antiquities, Cyprus* (1992): 75–112. Preliminary report on the second season of excavation.

Todd, Ian A., and Despo Pilides. "Excavations at Sanida 1992." *Report of the Department of Antiquities, Cyprus* (1993): 97–146. Preliminary report on the third season of excavation.

IAN A. TODD

SAQQARA, largest and most important necropolis in Egypt (29°50–53′ N, 31°13′ E), stretched out along the desert plateau west of the capital city of Memphis for 6 km (3.7 mi.). At Abu Sir and Giza just to the north and at Dahshur to the south there are pyramid cemeteries. Altogether these desert sites comprise one vast cemetery that served the

Memphite region for more than three thousand years, from the first dynasty until the rise of Christianity in Egypt (c. 2920 BCE–late second century CE). The name is derived from Sokar, Memphite god of the dead, and carries over to Arabic as the name of the nearby village, Saqqara.

Located along the edge of the north escarpment, the earliest monumental tombs at Saqqara are those of the first dynasty. The site was excavated by James E. Quibell in 1912 and by Cecil M. Firth in 1932. The most extensive excavations were those of Walter Emery from 1936 until 1952. Influenced by the impressions on mud sealings of pottery in the tomb chambers, Emery initially understood the great mud-brick mastabas with elaborate "palace facade" niches as tombs of high officials. He later changed his mind and assigned several of the fourteen mastabas to first-dynasty kings beginning with Hor-Aha, whom most Egyptologists equate with Menes, first king of the dynasty. According to literary tradition, Menes established Memphis as the new capital. There followed an Egyptological dispute that pitted the tombs of Abydos against the Saqqara mastabas as the actual, as opposed to symbolic, burial place of these earliest kings. Although the argument is unresolved, most Egyptologists accept that the Saqqara mastabas do belong to high officials of the first dynasty (Kaiser, 1969, 1981; Kaiser and Dreyer, 1982; Kemp, 1967; Stadelmann, 1985; Trigger, 1983).

Saqqara has about thirty pyramids, fifteen of which are king's tombs, the rest being for queens or royal children. Egypt's first pyramid, and first major monument in stone, is the third-dynasty Step Pyramid, which rises in six courses to 140 m (460 ft.) and still dominates the Saqqara plateau (see figure 1). It was built for King Djoser (c. 2630–2611), whose Horus name, Netjerikhet, found in the chambers of the complex, is the only one of Djoser's five official names inscribed in the pyramid. The structure is surrounded by a great rectangular enclosure with "dummy" models in stone of courtyards and reed and wood shrines that were actually used in Memphis for ceremonies, rituals, and administration. The stone simulation magically function for the king and his court into the afterlife.

The Djoser pyramid had no real precedent, except for the great enclosure at Abydos of Khasekhemwy (died c. 2650), last king of the second dynasty although it is a mud-brick rather than a stone monument Sekhemkhet, who ruled just after Djoser, attempted another step pyramid in a rectangular complex just to the southeast of the latter, but it was left unfinished. The only fourth-dynasty monument at Saqqara is the huge mastaba-shaped tomb, the "Mastabat Faraoun" in the southern part of the site. It was built for King Shepseskaf, who ruled after Menkaure, builder of the third and smallest pyramid at Giza. All the other fourth-dynasty pyramids, which were built on a gigantic scale, were erected at Meidum, Dahshur, and Giza. With the collapse of the fourth dynasty, however, the first fifth-dynasty king, Userkaf (2465–2458) returned to Saqqara to build his pyramid just off the northeast corner of the Djoser enclosure.

During the reigns of the next three kings (Sahure, Neferirkare, and Neuserre), pyramid building, now on a smaller scale with a standard design, moved to Abu Sir, until Djedkare Isesi built the first of the pyramids, known as Ḥaram

SAQQARA. Figure 1. *Step pyramid of Djoser.* In the foreground are subsidiary shrines. (Photograph by J. S. Jorgensen)

es-Shawaf, at South Saqqara. Unas (c. 2356–2323), last king of the fifth dynasty, built his pyramid just off the southwest corner of the Djoser enclosure. Because it is so far out in the desert, this pyramid had an extraordinarily long causeway to a valley temple and a harbor, the ruins of which are just beside the modern entrance to Saqqara. Unas was the first king to inscribe within his burial the *Pyramid Texts,* which were Egypt's oldest funerary literature and the precursor of the later *Coffin Texts* and the *Book of the Dead.*

Teti, first king of the sixth dynasty, located his pyramid to the northeast of Userkaf's. The other pyramids of the sixth dynasty, belonging to Pepi I, Merenre, and Pepi II, are all in south Saqqara. The name of the pyramid of Pepi I, Men Nefer, is the origin of the name of the capital city, Memphis. Jean Leclant and Jean-Philippe Lauer are excavating the sixth-dynasty pyramids, carrying out conservation work, and studying the *Pyramid Texts* in the inner chambers of these pyramids. In the Pepi I complex, south of the king's pyramid, they found four subsidiary queens' pyramids, names of two of the queens, and four obelisks.

Zahi Hawass excavated around the pyramid-temple of Queen Iput, one of the wives of Pepi I. A stela that must belong to the Djoser complex was found; it contains the name Netjerikhet within a palace-facade emblem known as a *serekh,* which is surmounted by a falcon wearing the double crown of Egypt with repeating registers below alternating with enclosed jackals and lions (Hawass, 1994).

The king's family and court officials were buried near their ruler's pyramid in tombs that became larger and more elaborately decorated as the period progressed. The scenes of everyday life sculptured on the walls insured a magical supply of commodities for the deceased in the Afterlife. Some of the finest of these Old Kingdom tombs are in the Saqqara necropolis. The most famous is the tomb of Ti (Wild, 1953–1966), a high official of the fifth dynasty who served kings Neferirkare and Neuserre. Ti's tomb, found by Auguste Mariette, is north of the Serapeum. [*See the biography of Mariette.*] Other fine tombs include the fifth-dynasty burials of Ptahhotep and Akhethotep south of the Djoser pyramid, the "Two brothers tomb" of Niankhkhnum and Khnumhotep in the line of the Unas causeway, and the sixth-dynasty tomb of Mereruka in front of the Teti pyramid.

King Ibi of the eighth dynasty built a small brick pyramid to the east of that of Pepi II. Its small size indicates the dramatic disintegration of the Old Kingdom at the end of Pepi II's long reign. East of the pyramid of Teti are the remains of another small pyramid that may date to the ninth or tenth dynasties of the First Intermediate Period (c. 2150–2040). At the southernmost end of Saqqara are two thirteenth-dynasty pyramids, one of which belongs to a king named Khendjer.

During the New Kingdom (beginning c. 1550 BCE), Memphis became the second capital of Egypt after Thebes. The sons of kings used the site as a base for their military training. Amenhotep II left an inscription inside his temple located northeast of the sphinx indicating his military training. Although the administration was established in Thebes and that city became the place of burial for the officials of Upper Egypt, those who controlled Lower Egypt lived in Memphis and were buried in Saqqara.

Most of the tombs are dated to the eighteenth-dynasty reigns of Amenhotep III, Amenhotep IV (known as Akhenaten) and Tutankhamun. Geoffrey Martin reexavated the tomb that Horemheb built for himself before he became pharaoh, while he was still the overseer of the army. Martin also found the tomb of Maya, the treasurer of King Tutankhamun. Alain Zivie found the tomb of the vizier Aper-El, whose name was shortened to Aperia. He served as the prime minister of Lower Egypt in the fourteenth century BCE under King Amenhotep III and under his son Akhenaten. The tomb was discovered in 1987. In addition the funerary room, full of funerary equipment and other furnishings, was discovered hidden behind the stair. Zivie found other tombs, such as the tomb of the royal scribe and chief of the granaries Mery-Sekhmet, who lived in the nineteenth dynasty. Sayed Tawfik has excavated the New Kingdom cemetery south of the causeway of Unas for Cairo University. He found the tombs of the officials in charge of Lower Egypt during the Ramesside period.

The Serapeum lies southwest of the Djoser pyramid. When Mariette discovered it in 1852, there was an avenue lined with sphinxes leading from the escarpment of the Saqqara plateau to the opening in the desert floor. This avenue gives access to vast underground galleries with individual caverns for burial of the successive sacred Apis bulls, each one considered an incarnation of Osiris. The burials began in the reign of Amenhotep III and continued into the Ptolemaic and Roman periods. One of the latest ruins of antiquity at Saqqara is the monastery of St. Jeremias, located southeast of the Unas Pyramid and dated to 43 CE. The architecture and painting from this site are among the finest of Coptic remains.

[*See also* Pyramids.]

BIBLIOGRAPHY

Edwards, I. E. S. *The Pyramids of Egypt.* Rev. ed. London, 1991.

Emery, Walter B. *Archaic Egypt.* Baltimore, 1961.

Ghunaim, Muhammad Zakariya. *The Buried Pyramid.* London, 1956.

Hawass, Zahi. *The Pyramids of Ancient Egypt.* Pittsburgh, 1990.

Hawass, Zahi. "A Fragmentary Monument of Djoser from Saqqara." *Journal of Egyptian Archaeology* 80 (1994): 45–56.

Jéquier, Gustave. *Fouilles à Saqqarah: Le monument funéraire de Pepi II.* 3 vols. Paris, 1936–1940.

Kaiser, Werner. "Zu dem königichen Talbezirken der 1. und 2. Dynastie in Abydos und zur Baugeschichte des Djoser-Grabmals." *Mittelungen des Deutschen Archäologischen Instituts, Kairo* 25 (1969): 1–21.

Kaiser, Werner. "Zu den Königsgräbern der 1. Dynastie in Umm el-

Qaab." *Mittelungen des Deutschen Archäologischen Instituts, Kairo* 37 (1981): 247–254.
Kaiser, Werner, and Günter Dreyer. "Umm el-Qaab: Nachuntersuchungen im frühzeitlichen Königsfriedhof. 2. Vorbericht." *Mitteilungen des Deutschen Archäologischen Instituts, Kairo* 38 (1982): 262–269.
Kemp, Barry J. "The Egyptian 1st Dynasty Royal Cemetery." *Antiquity* 41 (1967): 22–32.
Lauer, Jean-Philippe. *Saqqara, the Royal Cemetery of Memphis: Excavations and Discoveries since 1850*. London, 1976.
Martin, Geoffrey T. *The Hidden Tombs of Memphis: New Discoveries from the Time of Tutankhamun and Ramesses the Great*. London, 1991.
Stadelmann, Rainer. *Die ägyptischen Pyramiden vom Ziegelbau zum Weltwunder*. Mainz, 1985.
Trigger, Bruce. "The Rise of Egyptian Civilization." In *Ancient Egypt: A Social History*, edited by Bruce Trigger et al., pp. 1–70. Cambridge, 1983.
Wild, Henri. *Le tombeau de Ti*. 2 vols. Cairo, 1953–1966.

ZAHI HAWASS

SARCOPHAGUS. From the Greek *sarx* ("flesh") and *phagein* ("to eat"), a sarcophagus (pl., sarcophagi) is a container for the primary burial of a human corpse. Sarcophagi were widely used throughout the ancient Near East.

Made of wood, clay, or stone, sarcophagi range in size from small specimens like the Jebel el-Mukabbir sarcophagus (2.02 × 0.65 × 0.56 m) to the very large examples found in catacomb 20 at Beth-Sheʿarim (approaching 2 × 1.5 × 0.75 m) in Israel. [*See* Beth-Sheʿarim.] Stone sarcophagi were typically hollowed out from large blocks of basalt, limestone, or marble, with limestone being the most common material used. The rims of stone sarcophagi are typically at least 10–12 cm thick, although R. H. Smith has reported on several samples with rims as thin as 4.5 cm (Smith, 1973). The interiors of many sarcophagi feature a rounded headrest at one end, indicating the expected orientation of the corpse. Most specimens bear ornamentation on the sides and/or lid, including decorative friezes, gabled lids, acroteria on the corners of lids, and carrying handles on the short sides. Decorations frequently appear only on those sides of a sarcophagus that remained visible after placement in the burial site. Sarcophagi stand on two brackets running beneath the short sides, on feet located under each corner, or on a flat bottom.

Anthropoid clay sarcophagi appear as early as the fourteenth century BCE, in Bronze Age graves at Deir el-Balaḥ, southwest of modern Gaza. [*See* Deir el-Balaḥ.] Such burial containers, in the form of a human body (including representations of facial features, hands, feet, and calves) were first introduced into Canaan from Egypt during the Late Bronze Age. Similar anthropoid sarcophagi are also known from Iron Age sites in Jordan, including Saḥab, Jebel el-Quṣur and Dibon, and in Lebanon during the Persian period in and around Sidon. In each case Egyptian influence is present, as anthropoid sarcophagi had been employed in Egypt since about 1900 BCE. [*See* Saḥab; Dibon.]

One of the earliest examples of an ornamented sarcophagus is the Ahiram sarcophagus from the Early Iron Age (early tenth century BCE) at Byblos. Decorative friezes on its sides and lid include depictions of King Ahiram, votive ceremonies, and recumbent lions that typify Phoenician art during this period, particularly in their increasingly Syrian (rather than Egyptian) themes and motifs.

Greek influence becomes evident during the Persian period (late fifth century BCE) in, for example, the so-called Satrap Sarcophagus from Sidon. It bears decorative friezes depicting scenes of a banquet, a procession, and the Persian court. Interpretation of these scenes is vexed by the question of whether they represent episodes from real life or visions of the afterlife: is the deceased being remembered as he was, or is he being depicted as heroized among the divinities? The possible presence of mythological elements, including perhaps Dionysus and Pluto, renders such questions problematic, and the likelihood of polyvalent symbolism cannot be discounted.

Mythological symbolism is certainly present—indeed, is prevalent—in decorated sarcophagi from the Roman period, especially from the second and third centuries CE, when primary burial in sarcophagi was very widely practiced by pagans. Three specimens from Caesarea Maritima in Israel, for example, are extensively ornamented with Dionysiac scenes of satyrs, maenads, erotes, and even Leda and the

SARCOPHAGUS. *Lid of a sarcophagus.* From Beth-Shean, dated to the Iron I period. (Courtesy ASOR Archives)

swan; several sarcophagus reliefs from Tyre from the second century CE also feature elaborate mythological scenes of Achilles and Dionysus. A basalt sarcophagus from Umm Qeis (Gadara) in Jordan from the third century CE bears a depiction of Dea Syria at each end. Such decorations seem to express hopes for immortality in the afterlife through mythic union with the gods. [*See* Umm Qeis.]

Jewish sarcophagi from the Roman period, by contrast, are noteworthy for their geometric and floral rather than mythological decorative themes. Specimens from Benyamina; Dominus Flevit, Mt. Scopus, and Sanhedria in Jerusalem; Nablus; and Rosh ha-ʿAyin all feature carved friezes of geometric design on their anterior faces or lids, without iconic representations. As such, these sarcophagi cohere with patterns of decoration on Jewish ossuaries from the Roman period typically ornamented with compass-drawn rosettes. Later, by the third century CE, Jewish sarcophagi at Beth-Sheʿarim display images of lions, eagles, shells, and masks; even there, however, mythological depictions are generally lacking, except in the Leda sarcophagus discussed by Michael Avi-Yonah (1967).

Early Christian sarcophagi appear outside of Palestine by the third century CE, exploiting and transforming typical pagan mythical motifs. Decorative depictions of Jonah in particular symbolize Christian hopes for resurrection.

[*See also* Burial Techniques.]

BIBLIOGRAPHY

Avigad, Nahman. *Beth Sheʿarim: Report on the Excavations during 1953–1958*, vol. 3, *Catacombs 12–23*. Jerusalem, 1971. Report and discussion, including plates and drawings, of the Jewish sarcophagi of the Roman period from catacomb 20.

Avi-Yonah, Michael. "The Leda Coffin from Beth Sheʿarim" (in Hebrew). *Eretz-Israel* 8 (1967): 143–148. Brief but very useful discussion of this specimen and its mythological symbols.

Bivar, A. D. H. "Document and Symbol in the Art of the Achaemenids." In *Monumentum H. S. Nyberg*, vol. 1, pp. 49–67. Leiden, 1975. Photographs and discussion of the Satrap Sarcophagus.

Dothan, Trude. *Excavations at the Cemetery of Deir el-Balah*. Jerusalem, 1979. Report and discussion of Bronze Age anthropoid clay sarcophagi, including instructive typological distinctions.

Koch, Guntran, and Hellmut Sichtermann. *Römische Sarkophage*. Munich, 1982. Standard reference work for Roman sarcophagi in the Mediterranean world.

Smith, R. H. "An Early Roman Sarcophagus of Palestine and Its School." *Palestine Exploration Quarterly* 103 (1973): 71–82.

BYRON R. MCCANE

SARDINIA. The largest island in the western Mediterranean, Sardinia is within easy sailing distance of Italy, North Africa, and southern France. Its coasts tend to be rugged and lacking in maritime approaches, but the west and south have some safe harbors, where Phoenician, Punic, and Roman cities arose. Although there are very few high mountains, Sardinia is a mountainous region. About 20 percent of the island is comprised of low-lying plains with adjacent terraces to about 200 m; about two-thirds of the island's surface lies between these zones and the 500-m line.

Disregarding the still enigmatic Paleolithic period, the beginning of Sardinia's prehistory can be dated to the arrival of cardial impressed ware early in the sixth millennium. From the earliest period, Sardinia was in contact with Corsica, Liguria, Lombardy, and Provence, as is attested by the presence of Sardinian obsidian in those regions. This earliest Neolithic culture evolved into the Middle Neolithic culture known as Bonu Ighinu (c. 4500–4000 BCE). The obsidian trade produced in Sardinia ceramic parallels with a wide range of cultures in the 5500–4000 BCE horizons from northern Italy and Provence. The size of the known early sites suggests that society was based on small bands, perhaps no more than individual extended families, whose economy was based largely on herding, foraging, and the small-scale cultivation of barley, wheat, and legumes. Settlement in the Bonu Ighinu period was more widespread and more developed. Local groups began to exercise control over the obsidian sources and trade was probably mediated through the coastal villages. These factors suggest the development of social and economic hierarchies, which find their material manifestations in jewelry and fine pottery in mortuary contexts. During this period the first indications of cultural interactions occur, either direct or indirect, with the Balkans and the eastern Mediterranean.

By about the end of the fifth millennium, Bonu Ighinu had evolved into the Late Neolithic San Michele or Ozieri culture (c. 4000–3400 BCE). This was a period of profound, often rapid, changes and marked increases in prosperity that began in the eastern Mediterranean (notably in Gerzean Egypt) and southeastern Europe and rippled westward. Except for a few habitations in caves, Ozieri was a culture of unwalled open-air villages with marked social and economic hierarchies. During the latter phases of this period, large stone architecture makes its first appearance at the sacred site of Monte d'Accoddi-Sassari, an artificial "high place" with a ramp and village. The presence of copper and silver allows us now to consider the Late Neolithic as transitional to the Chalcolithic, or Copper, Age, which on Sardinia is almost coterminous with the third millenium BCE and is transitional to the Bronze Age culture known as Nuragic. Large stone architecture now developed into the first defensive structures, suggesting a further evolution of society and economy. Extrainsular contacts include the late fourth-/early third-millennium Copper Age cultures of southern France, Iberia, Italy, and Sicily, the latter being the probable mediator of more widespread parallels with material from the eastern Mediterranean.

During the Copper Age, megalithic architecture produced fortifications known collectively as protonuraghi, essentially rectangular, ovoid, or circular raised platforms on top of which one or more huts were constructed. These eventually evolved into corbeled tholoi, or true nuraghi, the characteristic feature of the Bronze Age. Most nuraghi were simple, single-towered structures, but some were made more elaborate by the addition of a walled courtyard, sometimes with a second tower in it. A few walled courtyards, apparently through a series of additions over time, became even more developed, until, by about 1200 BCE, a small number of them had been transformed into veritable fortresses with multiple-towered, interconnected external bastions.

Most, if not all, nuraghi had associated villages, but there are many nuragic villages without nuragic towers. With few exceptions, the huts in these villages are circular stone constructions that would have supported thatched roofs; their interior diameters range from about 5 to about 8 m. In some cases, several huts are interconnected, appearing to form part of a single domicile; in an apparently later development, groups of interconnected huts appear around a courtyard, each group remaining isolated from its counterparts, perhaps the dwellings of the village's elites. Evidence for the social and economic activities of nuragic villages is exiguous. Faunal remains attest to the continued importance of hunting alongside stock raising and cultivation, and many villages have yielded evidence for the production of wool and cheese. Copper and bronze were worked in some villages, but it is excessive to suggest that these were widespread cottage industries. An extensive obisidian industry continued.

Probably the most important and certainly the most visible of nuragic cults is that of water. In its most fully developed form, the water cult focuses on sacred wells, most of which are associated with nuragic villages. Many of these sacred sites have yielded remarkable amounts of bronze objects, jewelry, and imports. Some of the sites were surely the religious centers of tribes or confederations whose names are known from later texts and inscriptions, but any attempt to make direct correlations seems futile. It was at such centers that the Romans would find attacking the natives most efficient.

There is virtually no evidence in Sardinia of external contacts in the late third and early second millennia, apart from late bell beakers and the remarkably close parallels, perhaps fortuitous, between indigenous pottery and that of the northern Italian Polada culture. By about 1400 BCE, however, if not earlier, Sardinia was an integral part of a commercial network that extended from the Near East to northwestern Europe. The principal eastern component of this network was Cyprus, and it seems that the peak period of the Sardinia-Cyprus nexus was the twelfth century BCE; it is evident that the connection continued to the end of the second millennium, or even beyond, when it can be considered part of the Phoenician trade. During the high-water period of Cypriot trade, Sardinia was also in direct and/or indirect contact with the Mycenaean world. It is arguable that indigenous Sardinians, known in the east as Sherden, were carriers of some of the eastern material found on the island.

An inscription that may date to the eleventh century BCE and some bronze figurines found at nuragic sites and dated to around 1000 BCE provide the first clear evidence for Phoenician contacts, probably at this time no more than the sporadic or periodic visits of merchants making ports of call on their way to or from the Iberian Peninsula. Contact with Iberia put Sardinia from the tenth to the eighth century indirectly in contact with the broader world of the west, and it may be that Phoenician Sardinia was the mediator between the Atlantic world and the Italian mainland. Three Sardinian bronze figurines found in the Cavalupo tomb at Vulci have been interpreted as evidence for (surely not unique) marriage relationship between Sardinian and Villanovan aristocrats.

In the eighth and seventh centuries, BCE the Phoenicians began to develop permanent settlements. Shortly after the middle of the sixth century, Carthage directly intervened in Sardinia by sending an expeditionary force that was at first defeated; over the course of the next century, however, the Carthaginians vigorously and successfully pursued a policy of active imperialism which resulted, in around 450 BCE, in the establishment of an interior frontier system. By the fifth century, the Phoenician coastal settlements and some more recently established Punic ones had arrived at a mature level of urbanization; they would continue to evolve and play important social and economic roles throughout the Roman period and into the Middle Ages. After the establishment of the Punic internal frontier, Carthaginian influences on the native populations—both within their sphere of control and beyond—intensified, imported goods at native sites increased dramatically, and some rural colonies were founded.

As far as we can tell from surviving accounts, Sardinia played a minor role in the First Punic War between Rome and Carthage, although in the earliest phases of the conflict it would have seemed destined to be a major battleground. In 238 or 237 BCE, in response to Carthage's Mercenary War, the Romans, in a complete transformation of policy, sent a naval expedition to the island. When Carthage expressed indignation at Rome's action and informed the Romans that they were preparing to recover the island, the Romans declared war, causing the Carthaginians to abandon their claim to Sardinia and to pay an additional indemnity of 1,200 talents. The consul of 238, Tiberius Sempronius Gracchus, with a fleet and troops, took possession (probably in 237) of Sardinia without a struggle—that is, he established control over the Punic cities of the littoral. From this began a long series of wars in the interior and the gradual transformation of the island into a Roman province, one of the chief suppliers of grain to the imperial capital. Roman culture, including the Latin language, supplanted the indigenous culture, elements of which, nonetheless, survived for centuries, as is best evidenced by the fact that some natives were still worshiping wooden and stone idols in the late sixth century CE, undoubtedly a continuation of customs that had evolved from the Neolithic. Pre-Roman words (including the Punic *mitza* for "spring" or "fountain") persist in the modern Sardinian language, the closest to Latin of all Romance languages. As excavation and archaeological surveys have demonstrated, a very large number of indigenous sites continued to be occupied, or were reoccupied, during the Roman period, especially during the high empire. Some of these indigenes have left us epigraphic records of their names, such as, Tarammon, Urseccur Tertelli (filius), Miaricora Turi (filius), and Asadiso Osurbali (filius).

Punic culture also survived. We know from Cicero's speech in defence of Scaurus, who had governed the island in 55, that the ruling class of the city of Nora still had Punic names (Aris, Bostar), a phenomenon repeated elsewhere. The magistrates *(sufetes)* in the city of Cagliari, perhaps in about 40 BCE, were named Aristo and Muthumbal, and the name of the modern city of Oristano evidently derives from the landholdings of someone name Aris (i.e., *ager Aristanus*). In Cagliari, the atrium of a Roman house had a mosaic floor with the symbol of the goddess Tanit. At Bithia, coins associated with the votive deposits made to the Egyptian god Bes continued into the time of the early empire; and the temple to that deity was restructured by the people—*sufetes* and other citizens—an activity recorded on a neo-Punic inscription from the late second or early third century CE.

Very little is known of the formerly Punic cities during the Republican and early imperial periods. Even where extensive excavations have been conducted, scholarly interest has focused on the imperial and the Punic periods. Tharros and other cities (Othoca, Neapolis, Sulcis/Sant' Antioco, Bithia, Nora, Cagliari, Olbia, Cornus) became relatively more prosperous and well appointed during the high empire, but they were probably not excessively depressed in the interval. The extensive agricultural settlements in the hinterland, which archaeological survey has recently elucidated, required a port to export their products and to import, if nothing else, the black-glazed wares and Dressel-1 amphoras that are often the only witnesses to the villages' existence.

In the fifth century CE, the Romans were replaced by the Vandals, who were soon ousted by the Byzantines. Traditionally, in Sardinia the Dark Ages begin earlier than elsewhere. However, archaeological evidence is beginning to provide a clearer picture of Late Roman and early medieval Sardinia than was available only a few years ago, when the evidence consisted largely of literary and legal texts along with a few inscriptions; although the gaps in our knowledge are so great that many years of research will be required to provide adequate documentation, the trend is manifest. For example, the importation of African Red-Slip Ware, which continued long after the Vandal conquest of the island c. 450 CE, reveals that trade and economic life continued. It invites a vastly different understanding of life in Sardinia between about 450 and 600 CE than was possible when the only evidence was the pages of Procopius: if nothing else, we now know that the countryside was much more populated than it had seemed to be. Our knowledge of early Christianity is constantly increasing, almost annually revising an outdated conclusion (that Sardinia was largely pagan) based on a single literary text. Most importantly, recent years have witnessed a revolution in our understanding of the impact on Sardinia of the Byzantine world, which began with Justinian's reconquest in 533/34. Future research should allow us eventually to fashion a more comprehensive analysis of the processes by which Sardinia was transformed between the fifth and eleventh centuries CE.

[*See also* Carthage; Cyprus; *and* Phoenicians.]

BIBLIOGRAPHY

Atzeni, Enrico. et al. *Ichnussa: La Sardegna dalle origini all' età classica.* 2d ed. Milan, 1985. Lavishly illustrated overview, particularly of prehistory.

Balmuth, Miriam S., and Robert J. Rowland, Jr., eds. *Studies in Sardinian Archaeology.* Ann Arbor, 1984. A collection of up-to-date essays by an international group of specialists.

Balmuth, Miriam S., ed. *Studies in Sardinian Archaeology,* vol. 2. Ann Arbor, 1986. Similar to the above, with a focus on pan-Mediterranean contacts.

Barreca, Ferruccio. *La civiltà fenicio-punica in Sardegna.* Sassari, 1986. Comprehensive and well-illustrated overview by the late archaeological superintendant of the provinces of Cagliari and Oristano.

Bondí, S. F., et al. *Storia dei Sardi e dell Sardegna,* vol. 1, *Dalle origini alla fine dell' età bizantina.* Milan, 1987. A comprehensive survey written by a team of specialists.

Boscolo, Alberto. *La Sardegna bizantina e alto-giudicale.* Sassari, 1978. The standard survey.

Dyson, Stephen L., and Robert J. Rowland, Jr. "Survey and Settlement Reconstruction in West-Central Sardinia." *American Journal of Archaeology* 96 (1992): 203–224. Presents a summary of the results of a large-scale, multi-phased survey archaeology project.

Lilliu, Giovanni. *La civiltà dei Sardi dal paleolitico all' età dei nuraghi.* 3d ed. Turin, 1988. The standard survey.

Meloni, Piero. *La Sardegna romana.* 2d ed. Sassari, 1990. The standard survey.

Paulis, G. *Lingua e cultura nella Sardegna bizantina.* Sassari, 1983. The best starting point for Sardinia in the Byzantine period.

ROBERT J. ROWLAND, JR.

SARDIS, site located in western Anatolia about 100 km (62 mi.) due east of Smyrna (Izmir), where the valley of the Hermus River (Gediz çayı) meets the foothills of Mt. Tmolus (Boz dağı). Sardis has always been identifiable because the toponym (Sart today) has survived, occurring in many ancient in situ stone inscriptions. The factors that account for the growth and prosperity of the city are the natural corridor of the river valley, which connects the Aegean coast with the interior of Anatolia; the fertility of the valley and of mountain highlands; the perennial water source of a mountain stream, the Pactolus River (Sart çayı), which empties into the Hermus; and the security of a high spur of Mt. Tmolus, which provided a defensible place of refuge (a citadel or acropolis) and mineral resources, notably gold (for which the Pactolus with its placer deposits was the most famous source in antiquity).

History. The oldest stratified occupation dates to the Late Bronze Age (c. 1500–1400 BCE), but Early Bronze Age and Neolithic artifacts have been recovered out of context. In the first millennium, Sardis was the chief city of the Lydians, an Anatolian people who occupied the central western river valleys, especially those of the Hermus and Kayster (Küçük Menderes çayı), and who spoke an Indo-European language (belonging to the Palaic-Anatolian subgroup). The Lydian language is known from a relatively small number of texts (somewhat more than 110), mostly from Sardis and mostly dedicatory and funerary inscriptions on stone and pottery. Before the seventh century their history (under a five-hundred-year-old Heracleid dynasty that traced its descent from Herakles) is shadowy. From about 780 to 546, under their aggressive Mermnad dynasty (and successive kings Gyges, Ardys, Sadyattes, Alyattes, and Croesus), the Lydians were masters of an empire in western Anatolia that extended as far east as the Halys River (Kızılırmak çayı). Around 546 the Lydian Empire was conquered by the Persians, under Cyrus the Great, who besieged and captured Sardis and made it the capital of an important *satrapy* or viceroyalty, named Sparda, like the city. Sardis was the chief western terminus of a major administrative route, the Persian "royal road," which originated at Susa in Iran.

During more than two centuries as a western outpost of the Persian Empire, Sardis played a role in Persian relations with the Greeks. Capture and burning of the lower city by Athenians and Eretrians around 498 during the Ionian revolt led to the Persian Wars of 490 and 480–479; and Sardis was a stopping place for King Xerxes and his forces before their invasion of Greece in 480. The Athenian Alcibiades was a guest and councilor of the satrap Tissaphernes at Sardis in 412–411, where King Lysander of Sparta visited the satrap Cyrus the Younger, younger son of King Darius II, in 405. Sardis was the mustering place for Cyrus the Younger's ill-fated expedition with ten thousand Greek mercenaries against his brother, King Artaxerxes II, in 401. The Spartan king Aegesilaus won a victory over troops of satrap Tissaphernes in 395, which resulted in the latter's disgrace and execution. The Athenian admiral Konon was briefly imprisoned at Sardis by the satrap Tiribazus, in 392. The terms of the Peace of Antalcidas or the King's Peace, favorable to Persia and Sparta, were announced at Sardis in 387.

Persian rule ended in 334 when Sardis surrendered to Alexander the Great, who restored "to Sardians and other Lydians the ancient *nomoi* (customs or laws) of the Lydians" (Arrian, *Anabasis Alexandri,* 1.17.3–8). In the Hellenistic Period, Sardis was controlled first by Antigonus and Lysimachus, around 323–281. During part of this time, it was the residence of Alexander's only full sister, Cleopatra. Then Sardis was ruled by the Seleucid kings from 281 to 190 BCE and next by Pergamon from 190 to 133. During Seleucid rule, the city was for a time headquarters of the rebel Seleucid prince Achaeus, uncle of the legitimate king, Antiochus III, who besieged the city and captured and executed Achaeus in 214. Antiochus's reparations to Sardis thereafter were recorded in an inscription on the Metroon at Sardis. After the bequest of Attalus III of Pergamon in 133, Sardis became part of the Roman province of Asia.

In Roman times, Sardis was the principal city of a *assize* or judicial district *(dioecesis, conventus),* which included twenty-seven or more other settlements of Lydia and Phrygia. In 17 CE extensive destruction by an earthquake, which also damaged eleven other cities of western Anatolia, was the occasion for a five-year tax remission and a grant-in-aid of ten million sesterces from Emperor Tiberius. Sardis was visited by the emperors Hadrian and Marcus Aurelius with Commodus and perhaps also by Lucius Verus and Caracalla.

With Diocletian's provincial reorganization in the late third and early fourth centuries CE, Sardis became capital of the province of Lydia within the larger diocese of Asiana. Under Diocletian or Constantine I it was the site of a weapons factory. Beginning in the first century CE, Sardis was an important center of Christianity, as one of the "seven churches which are in Asia" (*Rev.* 1:11; 3:1–6) and the seat of a high-ranking bishop until 1369. It also had a privileged Jewish community. (Josephus, *Antiq.,* 12.147–153; 14.235, 260). The city barely escaped capture by the Goths in 399, may have been raided and partly sacked by the Sassanian Persians in 616, was taken by the Arabs in 716, and was in Turkish hands intermittently from the eleventh century, permanently from the beginning of the fifteenth century.

Topography, Monuments, Culture. Sardis grew up around the high acropolis, mainly at the edge of the Hermus plain on the north side, also in the Pactolus Valley on the west side. Some settlement regularly existed on the acropolis summit. Cemeteries were located at the periphery of settlement, mainly in hilly terrain of the Pactolus Valley and also 8 km (5 mi.) away to the north on a low limestone ridge (Bin Tepe) located between the Hermus plain and the Gygaean Lake or the Lake of Koloe (Marmara Gölü). Of satellite communities—villages, hamlets, farms, military outposts—in the surrounding plain and mountains, some are named in ancient texts (e.g., Kombdilipia and Tbalmoura in a Hellenistic inscription on the temple of Artemis; and Metallon, in Nonnus, *Dionysiaca* 13.464–478), and some are known from sites and their archaeological remains (e.g., Dedemezari and Karadut).

Little is known about the nature and extent of settlement in the Late Bronze Age and early centuries of the first millennium BCE. The Lydian city of the sixth century probably covered at least 115 hectares (285 acres), over which excavated occupation remains are distributed). As topography and later settlement patterns suggest, the city may have spread over twice as much land. (Herodotus, 3.4.2, judged Kadytis [Gaza] in Palestine comparable to Sardis in size.) The lower city was partly surrounded by a fortification wall, and the acropolis had its own triple-walled fortifications (Arrian, *Anabasis Alexandri,* 1.17.5; Lucian, *Charon,* 9). A few segments of them survive. Residences (some associated with small glass industry), perhaps a market, a quarter near the Pactolus stream where gold and silver were separated from placer (waterborne or glacial deposits) electrum, and a modest altar (probably associated with the goddess Cybele), are known from excavation. Also attested by archaeological work is a chthonic cult attested by ritual offerings in the form of dinners. Immature dogs are the main course. Each offering included a pitcher, cup, dish, iron knife, and cooking pot with dog skeleton buried near houses. A temple of Cybele and palace or palaces of the Lydian kings are cited in literature (for the temple, see Herodotus, 5.102; Plutarch, *Themistocles,* 31; for the palace[s], see Xanthus of Lydia cited by Nicolaus of Damascus; see Felix Jacoby, *Die Fragmente der griechischen Historiker* [Berlin and Leiden, 1923–1958], 90.44[7]; Vitruvius, 2.8.9–10; Arrian, *Anabasis Alexandri,* 1.17.6).

Ordinary houses were built with walls of mud-brick on fieldstone socles and roofs of reed construction. Grander buildings had terra-cotta roof and revetment tiles with molded and painted decoration (figural, floral, and pattern motifs in red, black, and white), and precisely cut ashlar (dressed) masonry in white limestone and marble. The physical size and conceptual grandeur of several monuments testify to the wealth and power of the Lydian capital: the massive 20 m (65.5 ft.)-thick fortification wall of the lower city; the terracing in white, crisp, ashlar masonry that regularized and redefined natural slopes of the acropolis; the huge tumuli (two with diameters exceeding 350 m [1148 ft.]) and dramatic landscape created by them in the cemetery at Bin Tepe.

Lydian culture of Sardis attested in the archaeological record combines Anatolian and Greek traditions. Anatolian are the tumulus and rock-cut chamber tombs, some pottery shapes (notably the *lydion* unguent container) and decorative conventions (distinctive varieties of Anatolian bichrome and black-on-red wares, and the highly distinctive "marbling"). Greek are the architectural ornament, including the terra-cotta roof and revetment tiles and their motifs, as well as the Ionic repertory (column design, moldings, pattern, individual motifs) in stone; sculptural motifs, design, and style (e.g., *kouroi, kourai,* lions), many vessel forms, mainly attested in pottery (column crater, skyphos); and the alphabetic writing system (adapted with certain changes). Conceivably Greek cultural components may have been more prominent at Sardis than at other settlements of Lydia (the Lydian archaeological record of which is still little known) because of greater foreign contacts at the capital. If so, however, it was well entrenched, as is shown by the use of Greek design for plain and ordinary pottery of the seventh and sixth centuries, and by close similarities to Greek forms in the shapes and decoration of earlier Sardis pottery, about 1300–700. Anatolian and Greek motifs can be originally combined, as in the highly decorative painted pottery called Ephesian ware, probably made at Sardis and elsewhere in western Anatolia in the seventh and early sixth centuries. Some design features are at home in both western Anatolia and Greece and probably reflect a shared cultural heritage.

There is little evidence for cultural interchange with Mesopotamia or Iran (although Lydian contact with Assyrians, Babylonians, and Medes is reported by the Assyrian records of Ashurbanipal and by Herodotus (1.16, 73–74, 77). The "nomadic" animal style of some objects probably reflects the presence at Sardis of Cimmerians or Scythians.

Persian conquest initially had little effect on the material culture of Sardis, except in lavish art forms (plate, jewelry, glyptic). Cults of Sardis during the Persian era include those of Artemis of Sardis, attested by Lydian grave epitaphs and by a monumental altar in the Pactolus Valley (perhaps the one cited by Xenophon, *Anabasis,* 1.6.7); Artemis of Koloe, whose sanctuary by the Gygaean Lake is reported by Strabo, 13.4.5/626, and is attested by Lydian grave epitaphs; and Zeus Baradates (perhaps Ahuramazda of the Zoroastrian religion), known from a Greek inscription of Roman imperial times that refers to his statue and *adyton* in the time of King Artaxerxes. Gardens and hunting parks *(paradeisoi)* of the satraps Tissaphernes and Cyrus the Younger are reported in literature (Xenophon, *Oeconomicus,* 4.20–24; Diodorus, 14.80.2).

Early in Hellenistic times the altar of Artemis of Sardis in the Pactolus Valley was greatly enlarged and a huge temple built to the east of it. The temple faced west, like the temple of Artemis at Ephesus, which may have been the model. A metroon of more modest size (perhaps a successor of the Temple of Cybele reported by Herodotus, 5.102, and the same or the successor of one cited by Plutarch, *Themistocles,* 31) is attested by marble blocks inscribed with correspondence between the Seleucid King Antiochus III; his queen, Laodike; and the Sardians. A gymnasium is cited in one of the same inscriptions; and a theater, city walls and gates, hippodrome, and temple of Zeus Olympius (vowed by Alexander the Great) are cited in the literature (Polybius, 7.15–18; Arrian, *Anabasis Alexandri,* 1.17.3–6).

City institutions, cults, and monuments of Roman times are documented in greater number than for any other era. Most major Roman archaeological features postdate the earthquake of 17 CE. A series of vast terraces on the lower slopes and skirt of the acropolis supported many buildings. Two or three gymnasium-bath complexes (one of them possibly a basilica), a theater, stadium, and large pseudodipteral temple are known from archaeological remains, as are additions to the temple of Artemis of Sardis (pseudodipteral peristyle, cella-partition wall, perhaps designed to create separate halls for cults of Artemis and Zeus Polieus). A mud-brick building reportedly once the palace of Croesus served for the *gerousia,* council of elders (Vitruvius, 2.8.9–10). An agora, nearly twenty fountains, an *odeion,* and many cults with sanctuaries and temples, including those of Hera, Demeter, Mēn, and Augustus and Gaius, are attested in inscriptions. A goddess called Kore, represented in Roman sculpture and on coins of Sardis as a semi-aniconic image (analagous to the Ephesian Artemis type) may belong to a pre-Roman cult.

In late Roman times (fourth–seventh centuries CE), the urban traditions of a great metropolis were maintained but with increasing strain. Major buildings, colonnaded thoroughfares (one with a tetrapylon or four-sided arch), and commodious, multiroom private residences were repaired, rebuilt, or freshly created, often substantially constructed and decorated with lavish expanses of mosaic paving. The tomb of an arms-factory director (Chrysanthius) is one of many painted tombs of barrel-vaulted, subterranean type *(hypogaeum)* in the city cemeteries. Increasing reuse of building materials, however, suggests significant abandonment or ruin in the city as well as economic recession; one colonnaded street and its sidewalks were never paved. Sardis was refortified: the lower city in the late fourth century, with a circuit wall that enclosed a space of about 150 hectares (350 acres); the acropolis in the seventh–ninth centuries, with massive, well-designed fortifications at strategic places. Three churches, two of them substantial in size, and an unusually large synagogue about 80 m (262 ft.) long were built and flourished in the fifth and sixth centuries.

From the seventh century onward, Sardis steadily diminished in size. Over foundations of one of the larger churches a modest-size, ornately decorated church of multidome type (like the church of the Holy Apostles in Salonica) was built in the thirteenth century. The city was apparently a community of villages, one on the acropolis and several in the lower city and Artemis of Sardis sanctuary, in the fourteenth and fifteenth centuries.

Research and Excavation. Antiquarian research began in the fifteenth century with Cyriacus of Ancona, who visited Sardis in 1446, explored the site, and recorded inscriptions on stone. From the seventeenth to the early nineteenth century, many British and European travelers recorded topography and architecture, notably Thomas Smith in 1670, Edmund Chishull in 1699, Robert Wood and Charles de Peysonnel in 1750, Richard Chandler in 1765, Charles Cockerell in 1812, and Anton von Prokesch (Anton Prokesch von Osten) in 1825. Their records are valuable for references to then-existing conditions and for monuments that disappeared after their visits. Tumuli at Bin Tepe were explored and excavated (without discovery of intact burial chambers) by Ludwig Spiegelthal (who excavated the tumulus of Alyattes) in 1853, George Dennis beginning in 1868 and again in 1882, and Auguste Choisy in 1875. Excavations at the temple of Artemis in the Pactolus Valley were also conducted by Dennis in 1882 and by Gustave Mendel on behalf of the Imperial Ottoman Museum in Constantinople in 1904. Systematic long-term excavations were undertaken by the American Society for the Excavation of Sardis, founded and directed by Howard Crosby Butler, in 1910–1914 and 1922. The temple of Artemis and graves in the Pactolus Valley were the focus of Butler's excavations, but exploration and test excavation in other parts of the city site and at Bin Tepe also were undertaken. [*See the biography of Butler.*] Since 1959, excavation and other archaeological research in many parts of the city site and at Bin Tepe have been conducted by the Archaeological Exploration of Sardis, a project begun by George M. A. Hanfmann and jointly sponsored by the Harvard University Art Museums, Cornell University, the American Schools of Oriental Research, and the Corning Museum of Glass.

BIBLIOGRAPHY

Buckler, William H, and David M. Robinson. *Greek and Latin Inscriptions.* Publications of the American Society for the Excavation of Sardis, vol. 7.1. Leiden, 1932. Texts, translations, and commentary on Greek and Latin inscriptions studied up to 1922.

Butler, Howard Crosby. *Sardis: The Excavations, 1910–1914.* Publications of the American Society for the Excavation of Sardis, vol. 1.1. Leiden, 1922. Summary of excavations between 1910 and 1914, primarily concerned with the Temple of Artemis of Sardis and graves and including a general introduction to topography, city history, and the history of scholarly research at Sardis.

Foss, Clive. *Byzantine and Turkish Sardis.* Sardis Monograph, 4. Cambridge, Mass., 1976. Political, military, and cultural history, with archaeological interpretation and key sources.

Gauthier, Philippe. *Nouvelles inscriptions de Sardes.* Vol. 2. Centre de Recherche d'Histoire et de Philologie de la IVe Section de l'École Pratique des Hautes Études, 3; Hautes Études du Monde Gréco-Romain, 15. Geneva, 1989. Hellenistic inscriptions from the Metroon, recording correspondence between King Antiochus II, Queen Laodike, and the Sardians.

Greenewalt, Crawford H., Jr. "When a Mighty Empire Was Destroyed: The Common Man at the Fall of Sardis, ca. 546 B.C." *Proceedings of the American Philosophical Society* 136 (1992): 247–272. Covers Lydian defenses of the lower city and evidence for the siege and capture by Cyrus the Great.

Hanfmann, George M. A. *From Croesus to Constantine: The Cities of Western Asia Minor and Their Arts in Greek and Roman Times.* Ann Arbor, 1975. Urban history of Sardis in Anatolian context.

Hanfmann, George M. A., and N. H. Ramage. *Sculpture from Sardis: The Finds through 1975.* Sardis Report, 2. Cambridge, Mass., 1978. Primarily concerned with Lydian, Hellenistic, and Roman sculpture.

Hanfmann, George M. A. *Sardis from Prehistoric to Roman Times.* Cambridge, Mass., 1983. Comprehensive account of Sardis.

Pedley, John G. *Ancient Literary Sources on Sardis.* Sardis Monograph, 2. Cambridge, Mass., 1972. Texts with translations and commentary, organized chonrologically and thematically.

Yegül, Fikret K. *The Bath-Gymnasium Complex at Sardis.* Sardis Report, 3. Cambridge, Mass., 1986. Comprehensive report on one of the Roman bath-gymnasium complexes.

CRAWFORD H. GREENEWALT, JR.

SAREPTA (modern Sarafand), a low mound on the shore of the Mediterranean Sea in south Lebanon, 50 km (31 mi.) south of Beirut (33°27′ N, 35°18′ E). The name *Sarepta* stems from a Semitic root, *saraph* or *sarapu,* meaning "to refine" or "to color red," a connection enhanced after numerous pottery kilns were recovered at Sarepta (see below).

Sarepta's long and varied history can be traced through more than fifty references in ancient sources, namely the fourteenth-century BCE Ugaritic texts, thirteenth-century BCE Egyptian papyri, and eighth-century BCE Assyrian sources. The Bible mentions the visit of the prophet Elijah to Sarepta (Zarephath) in *1 Kings* 17:8–28, in about the ninth century BCE, where he performed two of his miracles. This story was given prominence in Christian writings (*Lk.* 4:24–26) and is kept alive as a legend in Islamic tradition, where a shrine for the Wely el-Khudr still stands today beside the modern motor road between Sidon and Tyre, about 2 km southwest of the site where Elijah's story took place.

The Greek sources Pseudo-Scylax in the fourth century BCE and Lycophron, a third-century poet, mention Sarepta. The Latin poet Sidonius Apollinaris was quoted about the area's famous wines. The "holy god of Sarepta" appears in three Greek inscriptions (Pritchard, 1978). Arab geographers and historians of the twelfth and thirteenth centuries knew Sarafand: al-Idrisi and Yaqut speak of a beautiful town surrounded by gardens.

Exploration and Excavation. When the explorer and historian George Sandys visited Sarepta in 1611, he noted its mosque, the new town on the hills, and Roman period tombs. The pilgrim and traveler Chevalier Laurent d'Arvieux in 1659 and pilgrim and explorer Richard Pococke in 1738 noted the modern town, the sepulchers, and various ruins. In 1838 the American biblical geographer Edward Robinson saw the Wely el-Khudr and mentioned "Zarephath" (see above).

The first archaeologist to visit was Ernest Renan, in 1861. He wrote a scientific account of Sarepta, describing the necropolis and two rooms cut into the rock at the seashore. In 1929 Sarafand villagers found a burial cave, from which the Museum of the American University of Beirut purchased sixty-seven pots. In 1932 Harold Inghold and Ejnar Fugmann studied the collection (mostly Late Bronze Age pottery, including Mycenaean imports), which was published by Dimitri Baramki in 1959. [*See the biographies of Renan and Baramki.*] In 1968 Roger Saidah explored forty rock-cut tombs to the east of the coastal road north of Sarafand. Three were intact and date to about the sixth and fifth centuries BCE (Saidah, 1969).

Between 1969 and 1974, with a study season in 1978, James B. Pritchard, then assistant director at the University Museum of the University of Pennsylvania, directed excavations at Sarepta whose main goal was to obtain a record of the successive periods of Phoenician cultural history there. While the early and late periods had been fairly well documented, information about the Iron Age was limited, often coming from Phoenician colonies in the western Mediterranean.

In the first season of excavations, a Roman port was uncovered and designated area I. Subsequent excavations took place on top of the tell, designated area II, and two soundings were made: sounding X, in an area of 875 sq m, and sounding Y, in an area of 100 sq m.

The excavations produced the Roman-Byzantine port. A rectangular quay (14.50 × 12.60 m) had been constructed on a natural promontory in order to make the city accessible from the sea on three of its sides. A mooring ring was discovered, in addition to four rock-cut basins to hold fresh water brought from the hills by a conduit. An L-shaped natural reef, 1 m below the surface, acted as a natural mole to provide shelter from the open sea and to keep the harbor from silting up. To judge from the frequency of datable coins, the harbor was opened in the first century CE. Two major periods of expansion could be attested in the fourth and the sixth centuries: a bath and the foundation of a church were uncovered from the Byzantine period. After that, the datable coins become scarce. It seems that, by the seventh century, the harbor was almost deserted (see Pritchard, 1975).

Phoenician Settlement. The search for Phoenician remains was conducted on the tell, in area II, in soundings X and Y. Based on the stratigraphic sequence, the soundings exhibited essential differences in the uses to which each area had been put: sounding X revealed an industrial sector (Khalifeh, 1988) and sounding Y had been mainly residential and thus was less disturbed (Anderson, 1988). Table 1 correlates the different periods in both soundings with a sounding dug at the neighboring city of Tyre. [*See* Tyre.]

These correlations are based on the development of ar-

TABLE 1. *Comparison of Soundings at Sarepta and Tyre*

Sounding X Periods	Sounding Y Strata	Tyre Strata	Approximate Date
I	K	XVI	1550–1450 BCE
I–II	J–H	XVI–XV	1450–1350
III–IV	G	XV–XIV	1350–1275
V	F	XIV	1275–1150
VI	E	XIV–XIII	1150–1025
VII	D	XIII–VIII	1025–800
VIIIa–VIIIb	C–B	VII–I	800–350
VIIIb–IX?	B–A2	—	350–100?
X?	A1	—	100(?)BCE–(?)CE

chitectural plans and on the fluctuations of statistically studied frequencies for pottery-type series and related modes of surface finish and decoration. The results show that LB Sarepta was a peaceful settlement. The LB transition to the Iron Age was smooth, with no evidence of destruction. Iron Age Sarepta continued to be the center of a pottery industry, with an increase in the frequency of storage jars as an indictor of an increase in trade. The major change was the introduction of new ceramic forms—red-slipped burnished bowls and jugs—and a new building technique called pier and rubble construction.

Pottery production center. Twenty-two kilns with related facilities were uncovered in sounding X. The kilns were constructed according to a plan that remained standard for centuries, with only slight changes in shape and dimension. They are oval chambers divided into two kidney-shaped lobes by a wall that projects from the side opposite the doorway (see figure 1). Kiln G, recovered in sounding X, is well preserved, with a complete firing chamber, a roof with flues, and a doorway leading to a stoking room, from which it had been fired. Next to kiln G is room 74, which served as a work area. Kiln G can be dated within the thirteenth century BCE.

Purple dye industry. In the Roman port, a square tank cut into the rock, with four openings in the walls to allow the circulation of water, is thought to have been used to grow Murex shells, the source of purple dye. Similar tanks were attested on the north coast of Crete for the same purpose (Pritchard, 1975, 1978). Additional evidence came from a deposit of crushed Murex shells near the kiln G complex.

Three sherds were unearthed whose interior was covered with a purple accumulation of the purple dye. Spectroscopic and chemical investigations proved it to be the original purple dye. This is the earliest chemical confirmation of the ancient "royal purple" dye. It was produced locally and the industry can be dated to the end of the Late Bronze Age/Early Iron Age. (The production of the purple dye, for which the Phoenicians were famous, played a major role in the dyeing industry and in promoting the textile industry in general.)

Metallurgy. Amorphous pieces of metal and bits of slag were found, along with a rim sherd from a crucible whose inside surface was coated with slag. A mold for jewelry evidenced both the method employed in casting and the forms of the pieces produced. The various objects cast included an elongated bead, a pendant or an earring, and a finger ring.

Oil press. A complete oil press was found in the southeastern corner of sounding X that had been in use during the Hellenistic and Roman period. The main elements uncovered were a crushing basin, a large circular stone with a

SAREPTA. Figure 1. *Aerial view of the industrial quarter from a tethered balloon.* Note the circular kilns. (Courtesy J. B. Pritchard)

low rim (for collecting the olive pulp produced in the crushing process), an oil vat hewn from a solid stone column drum, and a large column drum. [*See* Olives.]

Inscriptions. Twenty-one inscriptions in Phoenician script were found in sounding X that vary in length from a single letter to a complete text of thirty-two Phoenician letters dedicated to the goddess Tannit (see below). [*See* Phoenician-Punic.] They are mostly notations incised or painted on jars and bowls. (Greek and Latin scripts appeared in the later periods, also in sounding X.) Most of the Phoenician inscriptions denote ownership by a god or a person, for example, "belonging to Eshmunyaton," or "client of Melqart."

Among the small finds is a greenish-brown stone inscribed with the name *Sarepta* that was used as a seal stamp. [*See* Seals.] An ivory plaque (3.3 × 5 cm) incised with a complete thirty-two-letter Phoenician inscription is a dedication to Tannit and Ashtart (see figure 2), both of whom were served at the same time—probably in the seventh century BCE (see below). The sign of Tannit also appears on a molded glass disk a centimeter in diameter that may have fit the bezel of a ring (see figure 3). The large ribbed handle of an amphora is incised with an inscription in Ugaritic script. [*See* Ugaritic.] Its text, dated approximately to the thirteenth century BCE, reads:

> (This) ewer, the work of my hands,
> ʿObal made for (the festival ? of) the new moon.

Shrines. In the eighth century BCE, evidenced by an ivory carving of a woman's head, a shrine was built at the edge of the mound, north of sounding X, whose walls were constructed with well-cut sandstone blocks set in the header-and-stretcher technique. The ivory plaque dedicates the shrine to Tannit-Ashtart. An adjacent room uncovered north of the shrine included votive objects of the same type as those found within the shrine. The shrine is characterized by three distinctive features: benches located along each of the room's four walls; a table built against the west wall, probably used as an alter on which worshipers placed gifts for the deity (two hundred votive objects were found nearby); and a socket for a pillar firmly set in the cement floor immediately in front of the offering table. Among the votive objects were figurines, pieces of carved ivory, amulets in human and animal form and the Egyptian "Eye of Horus," cosmetic equipment, beads, a cult mask, gaming pieces, and lamps. An Egyptian influence is obvious.

SAREPTA. Figure 2. *Incised ivory plaque.* (Courtesy J. B. Pritchard)

SAREPTA. Figure 3. *Sign of Tannit.* (Courtesy J. B. Pritchard)

A later shrine with a different plan was built over the earlier one, also dedicated to Tannit-Ashtart. Stones from the north wall of the earlier shrine were robbed to built it. Most of the figurines came from the debris that filled the later shrine. Terra-cotta figurines from the earlier shrine vary from a woman holding a stylized bird in her arms to a seated woman playing a hand drum or tambourine, while figurines of the later shrine are mostly of the type known as the seated pregnant woman figurine (see Pritchard, 1978). The presence of the figurines suggests a date for the later shrine between the fifth and the fourth centuries BCE, a span of use for the shrines of some four centuries.

[*See also* Phoenicia; Phoenicians.]

BIBLIOGRAPHY

Anderson, William P. *Sarepta,* vol. 1, *The Late Bronze and Iron Age Strata of Area II, Y. The University Museum of the University of Pennsylvania Excavations at Sarafand, Lebanon.* Beirut, 1988. The best

source on the development of the site's pottery-type series and residential area.
Baramki, Dimitri C. "A Late Bronze Age Tomb at Sarafend, Ancient Sarepta." *Berytus* 12 (1956–1958): 129–142. Early explorations at Sarepta.
Khalifeh, Issam Ali. *Sarepta,* vol. 2, *The Late Bronze and Iron Age Periods of Area II, X. The University Museum of the University of Pennsylvania Excavations at Sarafand, Lebanon.* Beirut, 1988. The industrial quarter and the correlations between soundings X and Y and Tyre.
Koehl, Robert. *Sarepta,* vol. 3, *The Imported Bronze and Iron Age Wares from Area II, X. The University Museum of the University of Pennsylvania Excavations at Sarafand, Lebanon.* Beirut, 1985. Traces imports and trade in the Phoenician period.
Pritchard, James B. *Sarepta: A Preliminary Report on the Iron Age. Excavations of the University Museum of the University of Pennsylvania, 1970–1972.* Philadelphia, 1975. The pottery industry, shrines, and votive objects.
Pritchard, James B. *Recovering Sarepta, a Phoenician City: Excavations at Sarafand, Lebanon, 1969–1974, by the University Museum of the University of Pennsylvania.* Princeton, 1978. Good source for Phoenician civilization.
Pritchard, James B. *Sarepta,* vol. 4, *The Objects from Area II, X. The University Museum of the University of Pennsylvania Excavations at Sarafand, Lebanon.* Beirut, 1988. The only source to identify all the objects and to provide a full record of the Phoenician material culture.
Saidah, Roger. "Archaeology in the Lebanon, 1968–1969." *Berytus* 18 (1969): 119–142. Useful information on early archaeological activities at Sarafand.

ISSAM ALI KHALIFEH

SARRE, FRIEDRICH (1865–1945), German art historian specializing in Islamic and pre-Islamic Iranian art. After earning his doctorate in art history in 1890, Sarre made several extended trips to Asia Minor, Iran, Turkestan, and Mesopotamia (1895–1908). In 1910 he published the photographs he had taken on those trips in two large volumes: *Monuments of Persian Architecture,* in which he gave special attention to the wall decoration in Islamic buildings, and (with Ernst Herzfeld) *Iranian Rock Reliefs,* in which he focused on Sasanian rock reliefs and Achaemenid monuments. *An Archaeological Journey in the Area of the Tigris and Euphrates, 1911–1920,* also published with Herzfeld, was of value to future archaeological research. As a direct result of his travels, Sarre organized the excavations in Samarra, which Herzfeld carried out from 1911 to 1913. In 1910, in Munich, in conjunction with colleagues, Sarre also organized the most comprehensive "Exhibition of Masterpieces of Muslim Art" that had ever been displayed; the most important aspects of the exhibition were published in 1912 in a work edited by Sarre and F. R. Martin.

In conjunction with the Islamic Division of the Kaiser-Friedrich Museum in Berlin, which was founded in 1904 and which he directed from 1921 to 1931, Sarre published numerous monographs and essays on all areas of Islamic art. His examinations of miniature painting, metalworking, ceramics, and carpets were a fundamental contribution. In 1921 he presented the museum with a large part of his private collection of Islamic arts and crafts.

In the German-speaking world, Sarre is considered one of the founders of Islamic art history. His study of Islamic art followed the style-critical method, always viewing the various genres of arts and crafts in conjunction with overall developments in Islamic art. His interests in art extended beyond his subject matter, which allowed him to recognize its East Asian and Western influences.

BIBLIOGRAPHY

Herzfeld, Ernst. "Friedrich Sarre." *Ars Islamica* 11–12 (1946): 210–212.
Kühnel, Ernst. "Friedrich Sarre." *Der Islam* 29 (1950): 291–295.
Schmidt, J. Heinrich. *Friedrich Sarre Schriften: Zum 22. Juni 1935.* Forschungen zur Islamischen Kunst, vol. 6. Berlin, 1935.
Völks, Margarete. "Bibliographie Friedrich Sarre nach 1935." *Kunst des Orients* 6 (1969): 184.

VOLKMAR ENDERLEIN

Translated from German by Susan I. Schiedel

SASANIANS. Traced to a legendary ruler named Sasan, the Sasanian regime (226–651 CE) began with a revolt against Parthia. Coins, primarily silver dirhems, portray individual kings. The main chronology comes from Western accounts; Sasanian texts were written in the hard-to-decipher Middle Persian (Pahlavi) script, and few are preserved. The archaeological record is very poor.

The Dynasty. In 228 CE, Ardashir, the first monarch, was imperially titled *shahanshah* ("king of kings"), and a new capital was founded at Ctesiphon that started a pattern that became the state's trademark whereby victories were commemorated with the foundation of new cities. The capture of Hatra extended Sasanian control into the region of the Euphrates River, where struggles with the West were to remain a constant theme. Like Ardashir, Shapur I (241–272) was aggressive along the Sasanians' frontiers. He adopted the title "King of Kings of Iran and non-Iran," referring to conquests beyond Iranian-speaking territory. In 244, Shapur's northeastern campaign tempted Philip the Arab to invade from the West. Shapur's reaction was immediate; Philip withdrew, paying a ransom of 500,000 gold dinars for safe passage, and ceded suzerainty over Armenia.

The assassination of the Armenian king in 252 became a pretext for aggression against Roman Syria. The Sasanians sacked Antioch and commemorated the event by founding a new city, Gundeshapur. The emperor Valerian's counter-invasion was a disaster, and Shapur's victory inscription at Naqsh-i Rustam celebrates the capture of seventy thousand Romans and thirty-six Roman cities plundered. [*See* Naqsh-i Rustam.] Yet, the Sasanians neglected the region, interested more in plunder than settlement.

Internal power struggles are reflected in Narseh's (293–302) anachronistic insertion of his name on his predecessor's

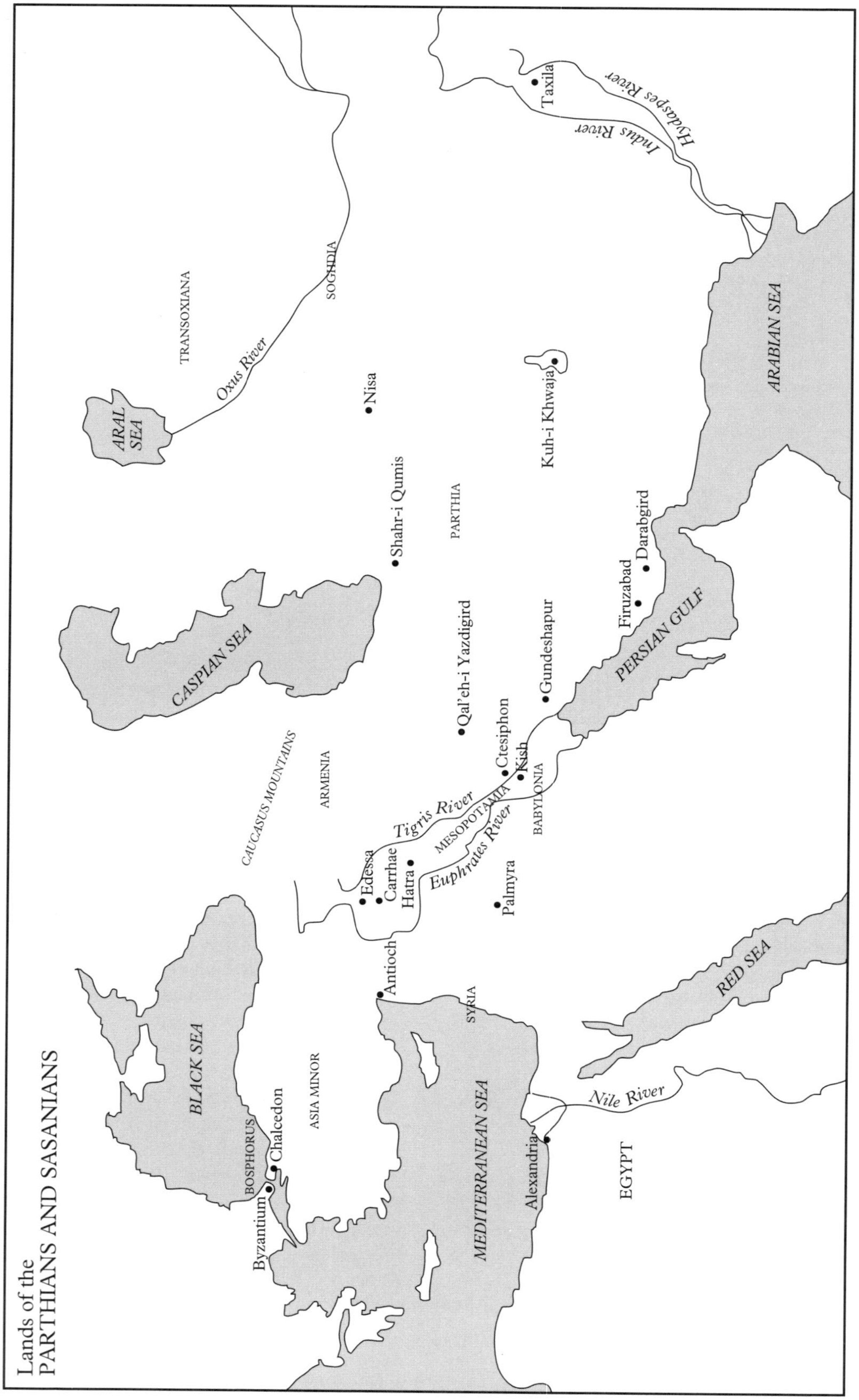

Lands of the PARTHIANS AND SASANIANS

victory relief. Narseh's own Paikuli victory monument lists his backers, from which the rulers of central Iran and the Parthian feudal families were notably absent. Narseh largely had fringe support.

With Rome officially Christian, as was Byzantium, Iran subjected believers to harsh taxes and often to persecution. Yet, Christian fortunes fluctuated wildly, for at the end of the fourth century, Yazdigird I earned the reputation amongst Zoroastrians of being "sinful," for his Christian tolerance. Christian issues were interwoven with the long-standing Armenian problem. Under Yazdigird II (438–457), his minister, Mihr Narseh, tried to convert Armenia to Zoroastrianism with bloody violence. Only disasters against the Huns in the East, including King Peroz (457–484) losing his life fighting them, forced Sasanian concessions for religious freedom in Armenia.

Internal disruptions followed Kavad II's sympathizing with the revolutionary movement of Mazdakism, which touted social equality and women's rights. Khusrau I (531–579) restored the power of the state. The revolutionary Mazdak and his followers were murdered treacherously while banqueting. Later, Khusrau was called Anushirvan ("of immortal soul") for fostering orthodox Zoroastrianism. His administrative reforms improved systems of taxation and created a professional army, rather than rely on levies from the nobles. Khusrau's most effective campaign started in 540, with the sack of Antioch. Prisoners and spoil were taken, as usual, to a new city near the capital. Like Shapur I, however, Khusrau failed to master the Arab, and now Christian, reaches of the upper Euphrates. Like others, he had to face the East. Arranging a truce with Emperor Justinian, and allying with the new Turkish groups in Transoxiana, Khusrau won dramatically over the Huns. The truce with Justinian was supposed to last fifty years. Sasanian aggression, however, was transferred to the Red Sea, where Byzantine rivalry for trade with India persuaded them to interfere in southern Arabia. In about 575, the Sasanians took Yemen as a province.

Military professionalism impacted upon state security, however. A jealous Hormizd IV (579–590) forced General Bahram Chubin to become a revolutionary who exiled the king, as well as Hormizd's successor, Khusrau II (591–628). Emperor Maurice received the fugitive Khusrau's overtures, and Bahram Chubin was overwhelmed by two Byzantine forces sent against him. As Khusrau II, the new king upheld his promise and ceded territorial rights in the Caucasus.

Khusrau earned his title, *parvez* ("victorious"), through subsequent victories. His spoils included the previously impregnable Edessa, taken in 609. After taking Antioch, in 611, the Sasanians went on to Palestine and Lower Egypt: in 614, the Holy Cross was taken as part of the Jerusalem loot, and in 619 Alexandria fell. A Sasanian army reached the Bosphorus and threatened Byzantium itself.

Only Heraclius, whose brilliant reforms involved rebuilding the army and realigning troop loyalties, rescued Byzantium. In 622, with a superior navy, Heraclius moved quickly into Armenia, twice defeating the Sasanians. Attempts to divide Byzantium in the Caucasus failed, and Heraclius's offensive penetrated deep into Iranian territory, moving to within reach of Ctesiphon, where only winter forced his withdrawal.

In 628 Khusrau was executed by his own generals, and his son, Kavad II, expediently evacuated the newly conquered territories. Assassinations brought a series of rulers to the throne, including a female, about whom little is known. A grandson of Khusrau II became Yazdigird III (633–651). He faced the challenge of Islam, whose armies conquered Syria in 636, Mesopotamia in 639, and Egypt and Iran in 640 and 641. For all its professionalism, the Sasanian army failed to stem this novel tide of invaders, and the people of Iran had no spirit to resist.

Religious Thought and State Religion. During his reign Ardashir established Zoroastrianism as a state religion, and idolatry was abolished. Fire worship, introduced by the priesthood in Achaemenid times, became mainstream in the new orthodoxy. Coronation fires were consecrated in the king's name, and coins bore images of fire altars. Excavations have exposed walls of simple domed pavilions recognized as fire temples, whose altars are positioned centrally on the floor beneath the dome of the sanctuary. Discreet ceremonies would have been held inside the building, where the sacred fire was held pure. Altars located on hillsides served the need for public display.

Ardashir proposed reforms to simplify the calendar. Their failure underlies the complexity of Iranian society, whose faiths were a millennium old. Zoroastrianism remained an oral tradition, its main texts archaic and obscure. People honored the new calendar but celebrated traditional festivals as well. Ironically, the now traditional March equinox new year (Naw Ruz) was introduced much later.

The nature of god was intensely debated. One school maintained that Zurvan ("time") begot the twins Ohrmazd (Ahura Mazda), who created the world, and Ahriman (Anru Mainyu) its evil. Some members of the royal family favored Zurvanism. Equalizing good with evil, the Zurvanites lessened Ohrmazd's stature, despite his responsibility for all subsequent creation. Orthodox Mazda worshipers believed in only one creator. Zurvanism was treated as a heresy in the sixth century, when Khusrau I initiated his program of state purges. Mysticism and the Eastern sects of Christianity made inroads, and the Eastern-rite Nestorians became freer in Iran after the 525 Council of Chalcedon (they were seen as separate from Byzantium). In the third century the prophet Mani, influenced by a number of faiths and aware of the teachings of Buddha, preached worldly withdrawal. Zoroastrians considered him a dangerous heretic. Mani's fame is the result of the discovery of Manichaean texts unearthed from old monasteries in Chinese Turkistan, where

Manichaeans fled from persecution after their prophet's death in 276.

Architectural Remains. There have been virtually no modern surveys or settlement studies in the region and no scientific excavations. What is known mostly comes from texts. Of these, the majority are from Islamic times. Typical of what is known is how the colorful figure of Bahram V (420–438) became part of Persian literature through his skills as a hunter. He earned the epithet Gur ("wild ass"), being frequently portrayed in Islamic art performing virtuoso acts with his bow. His real exploits, particularly campaigns in the East, are much less well known because written Sasanian sources are lacking.

In Mesopotamia, canal networks supporting large-scale irrigation have been recorded through survey. Intended to increase revenues, as much as feed people, these networks remained viable after the dynasty's fall. Systems of communication survived, but the newly founded cities were less enduring, lacking base support after the reign of the monarch.

Some sites have striking patterns visible from the air. At Gundeshapur, the rectangular city grid is seen as Roman work. However, it is uncertain whether this interpretation is sound. Darabgird, a round city, is also seen as a prototype for the first Sasanian capital, at Firuzabad. Others claim that Darabgird is post-Sasanian, underlining the primitive state of Sasanian archaeological studies. What is known comes from architectural, and mostly freestanding, remains.

Architectural innovations begun under the Parthians became entrenched. Barrel-vaulted chambers surrounded by corridors serving as buttresses continued to appear. On the Iranian plateau, round domes in solid masonry over square chambers were erected, but these are rare in Mesopotamia. Their interpretation as fire sanctuaries is based mostly on the observation that they are standing structures and by drawing analogies from the religious ceremonies in the fire temples of the Zoroastrian Parsees of nineteenth-century Iran and India.

In palaces, the use of piers allowed for the opening up of internal spaces, giving halls a Roman basilica look. Western decorative devices were popular, but indigenous building techniques continued, particularly the use of blind facades. At Kish, excavated structures, including palace courts with ornamental pools and throne halls reflect the nobility's growing pretensions. The stucco ornament at Kish, characterized by the use of heraldic figures and human busts, is similar to that at the capital, Ctesiphon.

Trade. Long-distance trade impacted on the quality of portable goods. Cosmas Indoplasticus, a sixth-century Indian navigator, reports Arab and Persian merchants trading as far as Ceylon. Controlling the maritime routes toward the Arabian and Red Seas, the Sasanians held a monopoly over eastern routes, exporting raw silk to Byzantium, Egypt, and Syria. When Justinian received live silkworms from China in the sixteenth century, the West's own sericulture broke the Persian monopoly.

In Central Asia, Soghdia's Iranian speaking rulers, whose merchants visited China, encouraged trade. Monasteries in Soghdia provided havens for merchants and served as exchange points for goods and ideas. Nestorian missionary activity brought Westerners into contact with China, where an Iranian presence is also described in texts and inscriptions such as the Xian monument dated 781. When the last Sasanian king fled before the advancing Arab armies of Islam in 641, his descendants sought refuge in the Tang court.

Remarkably, China imported from Iran fabrics made from Chinese silk, "Persian brocades" characterized by animal and bird motifs carried within pearl-bordered medallions. Although quite different from designs found in Chinese art, they are comparable to Central Asian wall paintings and silver vessels from the Sasanian period.

Sasanian silver and gold vessels are found in China, traded there from as early as the fourth century. Some may have been made by Iranians in China. Sasanian cut glass was popular. Many Sasanian artifacts were buried after the fall of the Chinese Tang dynasty, reflecting an influx of royal refugees. Thousands of coins, extending in date for more than three centuries, have also been unearthed, the earliest from the time of Shapur II. The largest group dates from Khusrau II, which is also true in Iran itself as a result of fiscal reforms. Mint marks reveal that the coins found in Tang China were struck in both central and eastern Iran. Some bear a counterstrike mark of the Huns, for whom there is otherwise little tangible evidence.

[*See also* Byzantine Empire; Ctesiphon; Kish; *and* Persia, *article on* Persia from Alexander to the Rise of Islam.]

BIBLIOGRAPHY

Adams, Robert McC., and Hans J. Nissen. *The Uruk Countryside: The Natural Setting of Urban Societies*. Chicago, 1972. Historical interpretation of changes to canal systems in Mesopotamia.

Frye, Richard N. *The Heritage of Persia*. Cleveland, 1963. Iranian history by a specialist in Iranian languages.

Ghirshman, Roman. *Iran: Parthians and Sassanians*. London, 1962. Colorful picture book with a personal viewpoint.

Göbl, Robert. *Sasanian Numismatics*. Braunschweig, 1971. Basic catalog of the dynasty's coins, with details of all the variations.

Harper, Prudence Oliver. *The Royal Hunter: Art of the Sasanian Empire*. New York, 1978. Extensive commentary on a wide range of objects shown at an Asia House (New York City) exhibition.

Hayashi, Ryōichi. *The Silk Road and the Shoso-in*. New York, 1975. Treasury of Persian art found and housed in the Far East.

Herrmann, Georgina. *The Iranian Revival*. Oxford, 1977. Picture essays with insightful commentary.

Lukonin, Vladimir G. *Persia II*. New York, 1967. Rich inventory of artifacts from Soviet collections.

Millar, Fergus. *The Roman Near East, 31 BC–AD 337*. Cambridge, Mass., 1993. Historical background and the reign of Shapur.

Trümpelmann, Leo. *Zwischen Persepolis und Firuzabad*. Mainz, 1992. Survey of ancient Iranian monuments and reliefs including aerial photographs.

Yarshater, Ehsan, ed. *The Cambridge History of Iran,* vol. 3, *The Seleucid, Parthian, and Sasanian Periods.* 2 vols. Cambridge, 1983. Numerous contributions on political, numismatic, and social issues by specialists.

E. J. KEALL

SAUDI ARABIA. *See* Arabian Peninsula.

SAULCY, FÉLICIEN DE, more fully, Louis Félicien Joseph Caignart de Saulcy (1807–1880), French numismatist and archaeologist. De Saulcy studied at the École Polytechnique in Paris and chose a career in the military. Caught up in the romanticism of the 1820s in France, which involved looking at the nation's past, including its artistic heritage, de Saulcy became interested in some of the archaeology carried out in French territory of that period. He published some numismatic discoveries and was among the first participants in the newly created *Revue de numismatique.*

He might have continued this amateur work had not the death of his wife in 1850 led him to seek consolation through religion and travel by visiting the Holy Land. De Saulcy was also drawn to the Holy Land through his study of Crusader coins. His two trips—from 1849 to 1851 and later in 1863–1864—and the results of his investigations greatly influenced emerging French Orientalism. De Saulcy studied the principal monuments in Jerusalem, analyzing the masonry of the wall surrounding the Haram esh-Sharif. He excavated the Tombs of the Kings, where he discovered the sarcophagus of Sadan, a queen of Adiabene who converted to Judaism with her family and is better known by her Greek name, Helen. De Saulcy thought that these monuments dated to the time of the Israelite monarchy and therefore preceded classical Greek architecture. We now know that they belong to the first century CE.

De Saulcy was among the pioneers of Palestinian archaeology. He explored the Dead Sea area and produced excellent maps, which his military training had prepared him to draw, in what was the first scientific exploration of the region. He also was the first to use photography as a tool in archaeological research. To bolster his theories on the dating of Jerusalem's monuments, de Saulcy hired a painter, Auguste Salzmann, to photograph them. Salzmann's plates, made in 1854, were published in an album in Paris in 1856. They constitute the first collection of photographic images of Jerusalem.

[*See also* Jerusalem.]

BIBLIOGRAPHY

Bassan, Fernande. *F. L. Caignart de Saulcy: Carnets de voyage en Orient, 1845–1869.* Paris, 1955.

Félix de Saulcy et la Terre Sainte. Notes et Documents des Musées de France, 5. Paris, 1982.

Salzmann, Auguste. *Jérusalem: Étude et reproduction photographique des monuments de la Ville Sainte depuis l'époque judaïque jusqu'à nos jours.* Paris, 1856.

Saulcy, Félicien de. *Numismatique des Croisades.* Paris, 1847.

Saulcy, Félicien de. *Voyage autour de la Mer Morte et dans les terres bibliques exécuté de décembre 1850 à avril 1851.* 3 vols. Paris, 1853. Translated as *Narrative of a Journey around the Dead Sea and in the Bible Lands in 1850 and 1851.* 2 vols. Edited by Edward de Warren. London, 1853.

ANNIE CAUBET

Translated from French by Melissa Kaprelian

SAUVAGET, JEAN (1901–1950), French historian of the Islamic Near East. After completing classical studies in Arabic and history, Sauvaget went to Syria as secretary of the French Institute in Damascus (1924–1937). He then taught in Paris at the École des Hautes Études and the Collège de France. He was a brilliant teacher who influenced, by the force of his personality and of his ideas, nearly two generations of scholars.

Sauvaget never participated in field archaeology, but he developed, for the study of the medieval Near East, another type of archaeology: through it, a land or a space is illuminated by the simultaneous consideration of literary texts, inscriptions, standing monuments, surface and other surveys, and the analytic techniques of geography, ethnography, urban and rurals studies, and sociology. He was aiming toward what was later called total history, a history from which no source would be omitted. Sauvaget was often critical of the lack of rigor in the works of historians of art, and he liked to show, sometimes playfully, the absurdity of many accepted conclusions. As a result of his concern about the physical character of the land on which people build and work, he was able to demonstrate the economic bases of early Islamic settlements; to propose novel and exciting interpretations for the growth of Syrian cities (especially Aleppo, Damascus, and Latakia); and to outline, based on texts, cultural history, and logic, the history of the early mosque in a book about the mosque in Medina in Arabia. A careful and critical observer of the world around him, Sauvaget transformed his experience of the present into an appraisal of the past. While his studies on ceramics are less useful for archaeological purposes than for understanding the functions of pottery and some of his conclusions and hypotheses have not stood the test of time, his rigorous method and constant questioning of all bits of evidence remain models for all scholarly enterprise.

BIBLIOGRAPHY

For a good introduction to Sauvaget's life and work the reader may consult *Memorial Jean Sauvaget,* published by the Institut Français de Damas (Damascus, 1954), which contains a full bibliography, an excellent survey of Sauvaget's work by Louis Robert, and several notable articles. Sauvaget's contributions to the field are well illustrated in two important articles, published posthumously in the *Revue des Études Islamiques:* "Introduction à l'étude de la ceramique musulmane," *REI* 33

(1965): 1–67; and "Châteaux Umayyades de Syrie," *REI* 35 (1967): 1–49.

OLEG GRABAR

SCHAEFFER, CLAUDE F.-A. (1898–1982), primary excavator of Ras Shamra (Ugarit). Arguably the most renowned French archaeologist of his generation, Claude Frédéric-Armand Schaeffer was a man of great energy who for many years simultaneously directed two major field projects while holding a university chair and important administrative positions in the government. Also a scholar with wide-ranging interests, he was responsible for novel and often controversial interpretations of archaeological material.

A native of Alsace, which had been annexed by Germany in 1871, Schaeffer was drafted into the Kriegsmarine as a cryptographer in World War I and learned skills that would serve him well both in his archaeological career and in the French navy during World War II. In the early 1920s he studied European prehistory at the University of Strasbourg, excavated in Alsace, and was soon offered a museum position in Strasbourg. He married Odile Forrer, eldest daughter of the prominent archaeologist Robert Forrer. Odile became the able camp manager of all his expeditions.

Schaeffer's methodological approach to large assemblages of artifacts, such as those excavated in burial mounds, resulted in several much acclaimed syntheses. Schaeffer's role in exposing the fraudulant nature of inscriptions vaguely Phoenician in character that were supposedly discovered at the Neolithic site of Glozel in the Allier region caught the eye of the prominent French scholar René Dussaud, who later sent him to investigate the peninsula of Minet-el-Beida, north of Latakia in Syria, where a rich Mycenaean tomb had been discovered in 1928. This work began an exceptionally successful field career spanning four decades in Syria and Cyprus. The very first campaigns at the ancient harbor of Minet el-Beida and nearby Ras Shamra—soon to be identified as the capital of the kingdom of Ugarit—established the importance of these sites in the history of the ancient Near East.

Always a restless, questioning spirit, Schaeffer was so intrigued by the evidence for Levantine trade with the West—notably with Cyprus—that he visited the island in 1932 to search for meaningful parallels. His excavations at the rich Early–Middle Bronze Age cemetery of Bellapais *Vounous* in 1933 yielded quantities of remarkable Red Polished pottery, though few eastern parallels were recognized. His subsequent discovery of a major Late Bronze Age urban center at Enkomi *Ayios Iakovos*—a site hitherto viewed as a mere cemetery—convinced him that further investigation would supply useful comparative material for his work on the mainland.

Schaeffer spent much of the Second World War in England, serving as head of Charles de Gaulle's Free French Historical Service. Research in London and Oxford led to a major volume (Schaeffer, 1948), which heralded a new, sweeping vision of interdependent cultures stretching from the Mediterranean to the Caucasus and a fresh approach to archaeological enquiry.

In 1946 Schaeffer directed the first of four field seasons at Arslantepe on the Euphrates and also began excavating at Enkomi *Ayios Iakovos,* where he discovered many tombs as well as fine domestic and public buildings of ashlar masonry (dressed, square-cut stone), all rich in finds.

Schaeffer was appointed general secretary and then vice president of the Committee on Excavations of the Ministry of Foreign Affairs (1946–1949) and member of the French Academy 1953. In the following year a chair in Near Eastern archaeology was created for him at the Collège de France. His inaugural address closed with the enjoinder "to continue with courage, objectivity, and tenacity the pursuit of research," and so Schaeffer himself did, until the very end of his long life.

[*See also* Arslantepe; Enkomi; Ugarit; Vounos; *and the biography of Dussaud.*]

BIBLIOGRAPHY

Amiet, Pierre. "Hommage à Claude Schaeffer." *Archeologia,* no. 175 (February 1983): 14–16.

Bergerhof, Kurt, Manfried Dietrich, and Oswald Loretz, eds. *Festschrift für Slaude F. A. Schaeffer.* Ugarit-Forschungen, vol. 11. Kevelaer, 1979. This 900-page volume has contributions by eighty-eight scholars covering the full range of Ugaritic studies. The publication includes a perceptive review (pp. vii–ix) of Schaeffer's life and achievements by his contemporary and colleague of equal renown, Kurt Bittel.

Schaeffer, Claude F.-A. *Les tertres funéraires préhistoriques de la fôret de Haguenau* (1926–1930). 2d ed. Brussels, 1979. The first two-volume edition earned Schaeffer the reputation as one of the best and most productive French prehistorians of his generation.

Schaeffer, Claude F.-A. *Missions en Chypre, 1932 à 1935.* Paris, 1936. Accounts of short visits to explore Cyprus and to undertake preliminary excavations at several sites.

Schaeffer, Claude F.-A. *Ugaritica.* 7 vols. Paris and Leiden, 1939–1978. Field reports and studies of material relating to the excavations of Ras Shamra-Ugarit. These volumes are part of the general *Mission de Ras Shamra* series.

Schaeffer, Claude F.-A. *Stratigraphie comparée et chronologie de l'Asie occidentale (IIIe et IIe millénaires).* London, 1948. Although outdated, this was a major contribution to ancient Near Eastern studies at the time of its publication.

Schaeffer, Claude F.-A. *Enkomi-Alasia: Nouvelles missions en Chypre, 1946–1950.* Paris, 1952. Contains six chapters dealing with different aspects of the site, some of the richer tombs, finer objects, and a major building. This is not, however, a comprehensive excavation report, as none was ever published by Schaeffer. For such reports, see Porphyrios Dikaios, *Enkomi: Excavations, 1948–1958,* 3 vols. (Mainz, 1969).

Schaeffer, Claude F.-A., et al. *Alasia I.* Mission Archéologique d'Alasia, vol. 4. Paris, 1971. Contains eighteen field reports and studies of material from Enkomi *Ayios Iakovos* by an international group of scholars in honor of the twentieth season of excavations.

Vercoutter, Jean. "Notice sur la vie et les travaux de Claude Schaeffer-Forrer, membre de l'Académie." *Compte-rendus de l'Académie des Inscriptions et Belles-Lettres, Paris* (1989): 178–188.

STUART SWINY

SCHICK, CONRAD (1822–1901), missionary and architect. Schick was born in the village of Bitz, Wupperthal, Germany, and educated in Kornthal, Germany, and at the Pilgrim-Missions College of St. Chrischona, Switzerland. In 1845, at the age of twenty four, he was one of four missionaries sent to Jerusalem to teach mechanical trades to young men. When the program failed, Schick became an agent of the London Jews Society, entrusted with teaching carpentry and other trades to young Jews under the society's auspices at the School of Industry. Schick became the leading architect in Jerusalem in his day. Many of his buildings still stand, including his own home, on the Street of the Prophets. He married in 1853.

Early in his residency in Jerusalem, Schick became interested in the city's antiquities. When Charles Wilson of the British Royal Engineers arrived in Jerusalem in 1864 to carry out the Ordnance Survey of Jerusalem for the Palestine Exploration Fund, he found a willing and able assistant in Schick, who frequently accompanied him on his explorations of ancient cisterns and tunnels. When Wilson returned to Jerusalem in 1866, he made Schick responsible for observing all evidence of construction in Wilson's excavations and for drawing plans of all remains exposed as well as the level of any exposed bedrock. With this series of observations, Schick began his long association with the PEF, and subsequently with the Deutscher Palästina-Verein. During the next thirty-one years, Schick produced a constant stream of articles for the PEF. Because not all of them were published, some of his discoveries are known only from his papers in the fund's archives.

Schick assisted many of the scholars and explorers who worked in Jerusalem and in Palestine generally, including Canon Tristram, Charles Warren, and Claude R. Conder. On his fiftieth year of residence in Jerusalem, Schick received congratulations from the members of all of the ethnic and religious communities then living in the city, an expression of the universal regard and friendship in which he was held. Perhaps the greatest event of Schick's life was the visit of Kaiser Wilhelm II of Germany to Jerusalem in 1898.

Schick remained active to the end of his long life. Much of the work of his contemporaries and their successors owes a great debt to his work. His contributions are only now beginning to be properly appreciated. Although not an archaeologist, but rather an antiquary in the great tradition, he was a careful and meticulous observer known for his honesty, warm personality and his eagerness to share his knowledge of Jerusalem.

[*See also* Deutscher Palästina-Verein; Jerusalem; Palestine Exploration Fund; *and the biographies of* Conder, Warren, *and* Wilson.]

BIBLIOGRAPHY

Schick, Conrad. "Die Wasserversorgung der Stadt Jerusalem in geschichtlichler und topographischer Darstellung mit Originalkarten und Plännen." *Zeitschrift des Deutschen Palästina-Vereins* 1 (1878): 132–176.

Schick, Conrad. *Beit el Makdas: Oder der alte Templeplatz zu Jerusalem: wie er jetzt ist.* Jerusalem, 1887.

Schick, Conrad. *Die Stiftshütte, der Tempel in Jerusalem und der Tempelplatz der jetztzeit.* Berlin, 1896.

Wilson, C. W. "Obituary of Dr. Conrad Schick." *Palestine Exploration Fund Quarterly Statement* (1902): 139–142. Includes a photograph portrait of the author of dozens of articles in this journal.

RUPERT CHAPMAN

SCHLIEMANN, HEINRICH (1822–1890), German businessman and archaeologist. A disrupted education gave Johann Ludwig Heinrich Julius Schliemann a sense of unfulfilled potential, which propelled him to extraordinary achievement. A clerk's position in Amsterdam (1844) and an aptitude for languages led to an agency in St. Petersburg (1846) where he made his fortune as a commodities dealer. His wealth enabled him to travel widely. Looking for a more genteel activity, Schliemann settled on archaeology, which he pursued by moving just to Paris (1866). In 1869 he fraudulently obtained both American citizenship and an American divorce from his Russian wife, Katharina Lyschina. He rapidly remarried a Greek girl, Sophia Kastromenos, and moved to Athens. Despite Schliemann's claims, Sophia seems to have taken very little part in his subsequent archaeological career. In a derivative archaeological travel book, *Ithaka, der Peloponnes und Troja* (1869), he accepted the identification of the site of Hisarlik, in northwestern Turkey, with Homer's Troy. Excavations followed in 1870–1873, 1878–1879, 1882, and 1890 revealed an impressive little citadel, which had been destroyed by fire and is dated to around 2500 BCE. Much of the metalwork from this citadel disappeared from the Berlin Museum in 1945 and is now in Moscow and St. Petersburg. Schliemann's excavations at Mycenae (1876), Orchomenos (1880) and Tiryns (1884–1885) unearthed Mycenaean-period remains (c.1600–1100 BCE). His final season at Troy produced Mycenaean pottery from overlying strata previously missed, and allowed a correct correlation with the other sites.

Schliemann put archaeology in the public eye. Study of the Aegean in the Bronze Age has grown up around the materials he excavated. He resurrected belief in a historical kernel to the Homeric poems. It is now accepted that his Greek sites document the Heroic Age, but it is not agreed that the Troy excavations prove the historicity of the Trojan War. A rough excavator, Schliemann was nevertheless keenly observant of strata and objects; and the complexity he discerned at Troy alerted other archaeologists to the need to attempt stratigraphic excavation. Wilhelm Dörpfeld, his assistant from 1882, introduced meticulous architectural recording and analysis into his work. His encouragement of photography and ancillary scientific studies was ahead of its time. Schliemann's business ethics were questionable and his thinking was not always disciplined. Attempts to prove fraudulence in his archaeology, however, have largely failed.

BIBLIOGRAPHY

Calder, William M., and Justus Cobet, eds. *Heinrich Schliemann nach hundert Jahren.* Frankfurt am Main, 1990. Articles on many aspects of Schliemann's background, character, and writings.

Easton, D. F. "Was Schliemann a Liar?" In *Heinrich Schliemann: Grundlagen und Ergebnisse moderner Archäologie 100 Jahre nach Schliemanns Tod,* edited by Joachim Herrmann, pp. 191–198. Berlin, 1992.

Easton, D. F. "The Troy Treasures in Russia." *Antiquity* 69. Forthcoming.

Hawkes, Jacquetta, ed. *The World of the Past,* vol. 2. New York, 1963. Contains lively accounts by Schliemann about his life and excavations—including no doubt some of his lies and inconsistencies.

Ludwig, Emil. *Schliemann: The Story of a Gold-Seeker.* Boston, 1931. Classic biography.

Schliemann, Heinrich. *Ithaka, der Peloponnes und Troja.* Leipzig, 1869.

Schliemann, Heinrich. *Troy and Its Remains.* London, 1875.

Schliemann, Heinrich. *Mycenae.* London, 1878.

Schliemann, Heinrich. *Ilios.* London, 1881.

Schliemann, Heinrich. *Orchomenos.* Leipzig, 1881.

Schliemann, Heinrich. *Troja.* London, 1884.

Schliemann, Heinrich. *Tiryns.* New York, 1885.

Traill, David A. *Excavating Schliemann: Collected Papers on Schliemann.* Illinois Classical Studies, Supplement 4. Atlanta, 1993. Collection of republished articles containing useful biographical material and bibliography, but marred by a determination to prove Schliemann a liar at every turn.

Wood, Michael. *In Search of the Trojan War.* London, 1985. Lively reexamination of the archaeological and historical ground first covered by Schliemann, based on a successful television series.

D. F. EASTON

SCHLUMBERGER, DANIEL (1904–1972), archaeologist and educator, born at Mulhouse, Alsace. Schlumberger studied history and archaeology at Strasbourg and Paris Universities. From 1929 to 1939 he was an inspector in the Department of Antiquities of Syria and Lebanon, then under the French Mandate. His research in Syria centered on the area of Palmyra. From 1936 to 1939, he excavated Qaṣr al-Ḥayr al-Gharbi, uncovering the remains of an Umayyad palace complex (his excavation house is the stage of Agatha Christie's novel *Murder in Mesopotamia*). His preliminary reports—"Les fouilles de Qaṣr el-Heir el-Gharbi" (1939) and "Les origines antiques de l'art islamique à la lumière des fouilles de Qasr el-Heir" (1940) and his subsequent "Deux fresques omayyades" (1946–1948)—shed new light on the origins of Islamic art. He published "Le temple de Mercure à Baalbek-Héliopolis" in 1939.

After World War II, Schlumberger headed the French archaeological delegation to Afghanistan, publishing (1946–1970) a series of articles on his excavations at Lashkari Bazar (1947–1952) and Surkh Kotal (1952–1963) and on his research in Bactria, which culminated with his discovery, in 1964, of a large Hellenistic city, Ai Khanum (Schlumberger, 1965). His publications on Bactria, the Kushan dynasty, Ghandaran art, and the Hellenistic East were summed up in *L'Orient hellénisé* (1970).

A dedicated professor at Strasbourg University beginning in 1955, Schlumberger became a member of the Académie des Inscriptions et Belles-Lettres in 1958. He succeeded Henri Seyrig in 1967 as director of the French Institute of Archaeology in Beirut, where he published additional articles on Palmyra and other sites in Syro-Phoenicia. He died after a partial stroke while at the Institute for Advanced Studies in Princeton, New Jersey. His wife Agnès made possible the posthumous publication of his manuscript for *Qasr el-Heir el Gharbi* (1986).

[*See also* Institut Français d'Archéologie du Proche Orient; Palmyra; Qaṣr al-Ḥayr al-Gharbi; *and the biography of* Seyrig.]

BIBLIOGRAPHY

Chéhab, Maurice. *Bulletin du Musée de Beyrouth* 24 (1971): 1–2.

Frézouls, Édmond. "Allocution d'ouverture." In *Palmyre, bilan et perspective: Colloque de Strasbourg (18–20 octobre 1973) organisé par le C.R.P.O.G.A. à la mémoire de Daniel Schlumberger et de Henri Seyrig,* pp. 5–9. Strasbourg, 1976.

Schlumberger, Daniel. "Les fouilles de Qaṣr al-Heir al-Gharbi." *Syria* 20 (1939): 195–238, 324–373.

Schlumberger, Daniel. "Le temple de Mercure à Baalbek-Héliopolis." *Bulletin du Musée de Beyrouth* 3 (1939): 25–36.

Schlumberger, Daniel. "Les origines antiques de l'art islamique à la lumière des fouilles de Qasr el-Heir." In *Bericht über den VI. Internationalen Kongress für Archäologie,* pp. 241–249. Berlin, 1940.

Schlumberger, Daniel. "Deux fresques omayyades." *Syria* 25 (1946–1948): 86–102.

Schlumberger, Daniel. "Aï H̱anom, ville hellénistique d'Afghanistan." *Comptes Rendus de l'Académie des Inscriptions et Belles-Lettres* (1965): 36–46.

Schlumberger, Daniel. "Aï Khanoum." *Bulletin de Correspondance Hellénique* 89 (1965): 590–603.

Schlumberger, Daniel. *L'Orient hellénisé.* Paris, 1970.

Schlumberger, Daniel. *Qasr el-Heir el Gharbi.* Paris, 1986.

Will, Ernest. "Daniel Schlumberger." *Syria* 50 (1973): 267–276.

HAFEZ K. CHEHAB

SCHRÖDER, PAUL G. A. (1844–1915), diplomat and linguist whose major contribution to the study of ancient oriental civilization is his grammar of the Phoenician language (1869), which was in use until 1936. Schröder was born in Elsterwerda, Germany, and died in Jena. After studying oriental languages at the universities of Halle and Berlin, he received a Ph.D. from Halle in 1867. Schröder entered the diplomatic service and in 1869 was appointed a dragoman (translator) at the German consulate, later the

German embassy, in Constantinople. From 1888 to 1909 he served as a consul general for Germany in Beirut. Schröder's grammar, an expanded version of his Ph.D. thesis, to a great extent used the traditions about Phoenician and Punic from classical sources, including the Punic passages in Plautus's comedy *Poenulus*. He also utilized newly discovered epigraphic material from Phoenicia and North Africa. He tried to establish a reliable text although he did not have access to the original inscriptions. The grammar thus also contains an appendix of the most important Phoenician and Punic inscriptions in facsimile available at the time. During the forty years of his diplomatic service in Constantinople and Beirut, Schröder published a series of articles about newly found Semitic inscriptions written in Phoenician, Palmyrene, and Nabatean and on topics pertaining to the history and geography of the Ottoman Empire. He also supported by his political influence the geographical survey of Gottlieb Schumacher in Transjordan.

[*See also* Phoenician-Punic.]

BIBLIOGRAPHY

Schröder, Paul. *Die phönizische Sprache: Entwurf einer Grammatik nebst Sprach- und Schriftproben.* Halle, 1869.

WOLFGANG RÖLLIG

SCHUMACHER, GOTTLIEB (1857–1925), architect, engineer, and surveyor. Born in Zanesville, Ohio, Schumacher received his early education in Buffalo, New York. His father, Jakob, had emigrated from Tübingen, Germany, to the United States, together with other members of a religious sect called the Tempelgesellschaft. The family moved to Palestine in 1869 and settled in Haifa, where Jakob Schumacher worked as an architect and engineer. He designed most of Haifa's German Colony, as well as many buildings for the Christian communities in the Galilee. Gottlieb Schumacher finished high school in Haifa and studied engineering in Stuttgart from 1876 to 1881. He then returned to Haifa, where he soon became the leading figure in house and road construction. The Ottoman government promoted him to chief engineer of the province of Akko. Among the many buildings he designed are the Scottish hostels in Safed and Tiberias, the bridge over the Kishon River, the Russian hostel in Nazareth, and the wine cellars in Rishon Lezion.

Schumacher also carried out a survey of the Golan in order to determine the line for the railway to be built from Damascus to Haifa, and he constructed the extension of the mole in the port of Haifa. His surveys of the Golan, Hauran, and Ajlun stirred his interest in archaeological remains. He subsequently not only drew the map of Transjordan, published in ten sheets, but also recorded its ancient monuments and sites. Beginning in 1886 he published numerous articles about his discoveries, mainly in the *Zeitschrift des Deutschen Palästina-Vereins*. Between 1903 and 1905 Schumacher directed excavations at Megiddo, the first investigation of this important tell, on behalf of the Deutscher Verein zur Erforschung Palästinas. Even though field methods were in their infancy, he managed to establish eight levels of occupation. He published the results in 1908; a second volume, by Carl Watzinger, followed in 1929.

An outstanding architect and scholar, Schumacher was given an honorary Ph.D. by the University of Halle in 1893 and the title Königlicher Baurat by the king of Württemberg in 1904. After World War I he did not return to Haifa until 1924, where he died in his house on the Carmel.

[*See also* Ajlun; Golan; Megiddo; *and the biography of Watzinger.*]

BIBLIOGRAPHY

Writings on Schumacher

Carmel, Alex. "Christen und Juden in Israel." *Die Neue Ordnung* 5 (1988): 375–387.

Guthe, Hermann. "Zum Gedächtnis an Gottlieb Schumacher." *Zeitschrift des Deutschen Palästina-Vereins* 49 (1926): 218–221.

Writings by Schumacher

Across the Jordan: Being an Exploration and Survey of Part of Hauran and Jaulan. New York, 1886.

The Jaulân. London, 1888.

Pella. London, 1888.

"Der Dscholan." *Zeitschrift des Deutschen Palästina-Vereins* 9 (1886): 165–368.

Abila of the Decapolis. London, 1889.

"Der arabische Pflug." *Zeitschrift des Deutschen Palästina-Vereins* 12 (1889): 157–166.

"Grabkammern bei Ḥaifā." *Zeitschrift des Deutschen Palästina-Vereins* 13 (1890): 175–180.

"Das jetzige Nazareth." *Zeitschrift des Deutschen Palästina-Vereins* 13 (1890): 235–245.

Northern 'Ajlûn, "within the Decapolis." London, 1890.

"Von Tiberias zum Ḥūle-See." *Zeitschrift des Deutschen Palästina-Vereins* 13 (1890): 65–75.

"Der Hiobstein, Sachrat Eijub, im Hauran." *Zeitschrift des Deutschen Palästina-Vereins* 14 (1891): 142–147.

"Ergebnisse meiner Reise durch Ḥaurān, 'Adschlün und Belḳā." *Zeitschrift des Deutschen Palästina-Vereins* 16 (1893): 153–170.

"Es-Salt." *Zeitschrift des Deutchen Palästina-Vereins* 18 (1895): 65–72.

"Madaba." *Zeitschrift des Deutschen Palästina-Vereins* 18 (1895): 126–140.

"Das südliche Basan." *Zeitschrift des Deutschen Palästina-Vereins* 20 (1897): 65–227.

"Ergäzungen zu meiner Karte des Dschōlān und westlichen Ḥaurān." *Zeitschrift des Deutschen Palästina-Vereins* 22 (1899): 178–184.

"Dscherasch." *Zeitschrift des Deutschen Palästina-Vereins* 25 (1902): 109–177.

Tell el-Mutesellim: Bericht über die 1903–1905. 2 vols. Leipzig, 1908–1929. (vol. 2 by Carl Watzinger).

"El-Maḳārin und der Tell ed-Dschamīd." *Zeitschrift des Deutschen Palästina-Vereins* 36 (1913): 114–123.

"Unsere Arbeiten im Ostjordanland." *Zeitschrift des Deutschen Palästina-Vereins* 36 (1913): 123–129; 37 (1914): 123–134, 260–266; 38 (1915): 136–148.

"Zur Verkehrsgeographie Palästinas." *Zeitschrift des Deutschen Palästina-Vereins* 37 (1914): 55–58.

VOLKMAR FRITZ

SCRIBES AND SCRIBAL TECHNIQUES.

Widespread literacy is a phenomenon strictly of the modern world. In ancient times and long after, the chore of creating, maintaining, and interpreting written records fell to a small cadre of professionally trained scribes. What is known of their training and activities is perforce limited by accidents of preservation of written materials from antiquity and so is virtually restricted to those from Mesopotamia and Egypt. (See the extensive summaries on this subject by Jeremy A. Black and W. J. Tait, Edward Wente, and Laurie E. Pearce in Sasson, 1995, pp. 2197–2209, 2211–2221, and 2265–2278, respectively). James L. Crenshaw (1985) insists that far less can be asserted about biblical education than has been believed, and Paul S. Ash argues (necessarily from silence, primarily) that tenth-century BCE Palestine "held a society which knew of writing but had little or no use for it" (Ash, 1995, p. 72).

Craft. Mesopotamian scribes wrote with light touches of the corner of a reed stylus of triangular cross section, impressing wedges into the smoothed surfaces of a shaped mass of clay, usually of a size to be comfortably held in the palm of a hand. There are on average more wedges in a cuneiform sign than there are strokes in a letter of an alphabet, but since a sign represents a whole syllable or a whole word, the speed and efficiency of writing are probably comparable in the two systems. Cuneiform is more economical in the use of materials: in mundane documents, virtually no space is left between signs or between lines of signs; scribes were good at using the right amount of clay to accommodate approximately the length of the text to be written. When monumental inscriptions were incised on walls, the stonecarvers were not necessarily themselves literate, but imitated a text prepared on a clay tablet. [*See* Cuneiform.]

Egyptian scribes wrote with a reed pen on papyrus; the hieroglyph for *scribe* represents the tool-kit, including pen, water-jar, and palette with cakes of dried ink. A scribe would usually work in a cross-legged seated position, with the papyrus sheet or the exposed portion of the papyrus roll resting on the lap. Hieroglyphic inscriptions on walls would be roughed out initially by a literate scribe, and subsequently painted with color and decorative detail.

West Semitic writing was primarily with pen and ink on receptive surfaces—papyrus, skins, or potsherds. The nature of the writing instrument and the physical process of writing can be determined by careful examination of some original documents (Daniels, 1984). Scribes writing in Akkadian and in Aramaic are depicted in Assyrian reliefs standing side by side (Driver, 1976, fig. 4 and pls. 23–24), with the latter rather awkwardly, it seems, holding a sheet of flexible papyrus or leather draped over his outstretched left hand. Kurt Galling (1971, p. 212) states that when the free end of the material hangs free, it is papyrus, and when it is rolled, it is leather. At Ugarit, one of doubtless many places where Egyptian and Mesopotamian culture mingled, the pen-written West Semitic script was successfully adapted to the clay medium by imitating the letterforms with impressed wedges, rather than trying to incise the shapes with a pointed tool (as most West Semitic monumental inscriptions were done) or by writing with pen and ink on the surface of pliable clay as a supplement to a cuneiform text (as was done later on in the so-called "Aramaic dockets" of Neo-Babylonian and Achaemenid times).

Duties. Mesopotamian scribes could work either in private enterprise (even some merchants were literate) or for the temple or palace. [*See* Palace.] Scribes in the first group drew up commercial and legal documents, saw to the payment of rents and wages, and overall kept the economy going. They could also do free-lance work (e.g., writing letters for ordinary people), and their offices were often at the city's gates. Temple scribes (distinct from the priesthood) were responsible for administering the considerable assets and operations of the temple complex. Palace scribes prepared diplomatic documents—letters and treaties—and maintained annals; it was also in connection with the palace that cuneiform scholars maintained their belletristic and scientific traditions—both the poetry echoed in biblical and modern literature and the specialities of divination, astronomy, and astrology. Colophons at the close of literary and scientific tablets attest to the care with which valued texts were preserved. (Elaborate colophons also characterize manuscripts from the Islamic world virtually to the present day.)

Owing to the fragility of papyrus, fewer ordinary documents have survived from Egypt than from Mesopotamia, where clay tablets were used. [*See* Papyrus; Tablet.] As a result, what is understood of the place of writing in everyday life in Egypt is limited to what was believed worthy of preservation in temples or in tombs, rather than the ephemera of commerce such as make up the great majority of extant cuneiform tablets. [*See* Tombs.] In Egypt, all scribes seem to have been government workers, engaged in surveying land and assessing the harvest, for the purpose of levying taxes; they also supervised construction and kept the accounts involved in maintaining workers and armies. Ordinary persons in need of a legal document would go to a government clerk to have it drawn up. Scribes also produced and maintained Egypt's literary heritage, although there seems to have been little antiquarian sense: wisdom was valued for itself, not for its lineage.

From the Levant, climate prohibits all but the scarcest survival of documents from antiquity; the clay tablets from Ugarit suggest that scribes there engaged in essentially the same activities as their Mesopotamian counterparts. [*See* Ugarit.] The neatness of script on most surviving ostraca indicates that care was taken in the education of scribes during the first millennium BCE, but little can be said about their everyday business. [*See* Ostracon.] Most surviving inscriptions are royal assertions of dominion, probably not typical of written output.

Archives. From Mesopotamia, three main kinds of collections of tablets have survived: accidental conglomerations, private archives, and palace archives. (Temples do not seem to have been in the business of collecting documents, and tablets found there pertain to their own mundane administrative activities.) Much the most common sort of grouping is the first, and tablets recovered from chance accumulations represent the discards of the scribal trade: tablets would not usually be saved for more than a few decades. Private archives could represent the records of a business covering a couple of generations; also counting as a private archive are the libraries of individual scholar-scribes, who might own a fine collection of literary and scientific works. Palaces would need to preserve records of diplomacy and of the glorious deeds of rulers—and could bear on their walls monumental illustrated accounts of the same. Several kings, notably Ashurbanipal, are renowned for their activities in preserving the Mesopotamian literary heritage.

Egyptians distinguished "libraries" from "archives." Mundane documents had no particular value, and the papyrus on which they were written could be routinely reused. The fourteenth-century BCE Amarna tablets represent an archive that survived presumably because it was simply abandoned along with the city of Akhetaten. [*See* Amarna Tablets; Amarna, Tell el-.] Libraries, however, are mentioned as early as the Old Kingdom, and in Egypt temples did serve as repositories for valued literary works: Ptolemaic temples include rooms whose inscriptions include catalogs of the books to be kept there. Private libraries could be interred in chests in their owners' tombs. Some of the earliest texts of Egyptian literature, the Pyramid texts, continued to be copied down to the Roman period.

Biblical attestation of the storage of documents is found in the naming of works including the *Book of the Wars of the Lord* (some five such titles are found in the Hebrew Bible)—no trace of which has survived—and in the incorporation of supposed verbatim texts of letters and decrees in the historical books. Some theories of the composition of the prophetic books would seem to require that records were kept of prophets' utterances, which were subsequently arranged and transcribed. Most forms of the Documentary Hypothesis would require extensive compositions (J, P, E, etc.) to have been written down, collated, copied, and subsequently lost or destroyed. Again, no physical evidence of such texts survives. [*See* Libraries and Archives; Biblical Literature.]

Education. From earliest times, there is evidence that scribes in Sumer were trained in schools. Mesopotamian children intended for the scribal life (some of their copybooks survive) had to learn to shape tablets and to make the various wedges that comprise cuneiform characters, to write the signs, and to read Sumerian (their native language being Akkadian or Amorite). [*See* Sumerian; Akkadian.] They learned Sumerian by copying out, and thus incidentally preserving, literary compositions. The standard formulary of letters and contracts was also mastered. Besides language and literature, the students learned mathematics and music.

Education in Old Kingdom Egypt seems to have been on an individual apprenticeship basis, with officials training their successors. Schools appear in the First Intermediate period, with decentralization of the government. Children began their studies at about the age of ten. Writing lessons involved well-known literary works in hieratic script; the language remained that of the Middle Kingdom, during which the works were composed, although the spoken language eventually diverged greatly. After some years, the young scribes chose whether to enter administration, the priesthood, or the military. Only late in the educational process would a student learn hieroglyphs. [*See* Hieroglyphs.]

Textbooks. Among the very earliest documents known (from Uruk IV, c. 3200 BCE) are prototypes of the lexical lists that dominated Mesopotamian scholarship for thousands of years, serving as both textbooks and reference works. [*See* Uruk-Warka.] Philological lists include sign lists, vocabularies, syllabaries, and grammatical lists; eventually, lists were maintained of everything under the sun and served both advanced students and mature scholars.

Egyptian study materials began with the Satire on the Trades, which mocks professions other than that of the scribe; portions of other literary works found on cheap ostraca (rather than carefully prepared papyrus), replete with errors, show that these too were studied in school. There were also, as in Mesopotamia, lists of signs and of vocabulary organized by topic.

It is often suggested that the wisdom literature of the Hebrew Bible comprises instructional texts, but nothing in the nature of school materials has survived beyond a handful of sloppily written abecedaries.

Multilingualism. Mesopotamian scribes, who spoke Akkadian or Amorite and in the first millennium BCE probably Aramaic, studied Sumerian long after it had passed out of use. Scribes in outlying lands, such as Urartu or the Aramean kingdoms, presumably had to learn a form of Akkadian, since bilingual monuments exist with native and Assyrian versions of their inscriptions. In Hittite-speaking Anatolia, Hattic and primarily Hurrian served a purpose analogous to that of Sumerian in Semitic-speaking Mesopotamia. [*See* Hittite; Hurrian.] From Ugarit, along with ordinary Sumerian–Akkadian vocabularies, a few quadrilingual ones include Ugaritic and Hurrian translations. In the Mesopotamian heartland, however, there seems to have been little interest in the languages of the "barbarians" of other countries.

A select handful of New Kingdom Egyptian scribes

learned Akkadian, Canaanite, Hittite, and one or another Aegean language for use in international relations.

Scattered anecdotes in the Bible (e.g., *2 Kgs.* 18:26), as well as the presence of extended passages in Aramaic within the Hebrew context, show that, from at least the early first millennium BCE, scribes (though not the common people) could converse in the lingua franca, Aramaic. The scholars of Rabbinic Judaism (beginning in the early first millennium CE) were fully at home in both Hebrew and Aramaic, but by some point toward the middle of the first millennium, at the latest, Hebrew was no longer spoken. The scriptures were translated into Greek (the Septuagint) for the Jewish community in Alexandria, Egypt, by the second century BCE, and into Aramaic (the Targums) beginning at about the same time (Aramaic versions of several books are found among the Dead Sea Scrolls). [*See* Hebrew Language and Literature; Greek; Dead Sea Scrolls.]

[*See also* Literacy; Writing and Writing Systems; *and* Writing Materials.]

BIBLIOGRAPHY

Ash, Paul S. "Solomon's? District? List." *Journal for the Study of the Old Testament* 67 (1995): 67–86.

Atiyeh, George N., ed. *The Book in the Islamic World: The Written Word and Communication in the Middle East.* Albany, N.Y., 1995.

Crenshaw, James L. "Education in Ancient Israel." *Journal of Biblical Literature* 104 (1985): 601–615.

Daniels, Peter T. "A Calligraphic Approach to Aramaic Paleography." *Journal of Near Eastern Studies* 43 (1984): 55–68.

Driver, G. R. *Semitic Writing: From Pictograph to Alphabet.* Newly revised edition edited by S. A. Hopkins. London, 1976.

Galling, Kurt. "Tafel, Buch und Blatt." In *Near Eastern Studies in Honor of William Foxwell Albright,* edited by Hans Goedicke, pp. 207–223. Baltimore, 1971.

Lemaire, André. *Les écoles et la formation de la Bible dans l'ancien Israël.* Fribourg, 1981. The standard treatment, though criticized for excessive speculation.

Pedersen, Johannes. *The Arabic Book* (orig. Danish ed., 1946.). Translated by Geoffrey French. Princeton, 1984.

Sasson, Jack M., ed. *Civilizations of the Ancient Near East.* 4 vols. New York, 1995. See J. A. Black and W. J. Tait, "Archives and Libraries in the Ancient Near East"; Edward F. Wente, "The Scribes of Ancient Egypt"; and Laurie E. Pearce, "The Scribes and Scholars of Ancient Mesopotamia."

Williams, Ronald J. "Scribal Training in Ancient Egypt." *Journal of the American Oriental Society* 92 (1972): 214–221.

PETER T. DANIELS

SCROLL. In antiquity the exercise of writing employed lengths of pliable material, generally papyrus or parchment, stored by rolling from end to end and known as a scroll. The advantages of the scroll for recording and storing lengthy texts in a relatively compact form made it a widely used and enduring device in the ancient Near East from earliest times until the medieval period. Although the literary contents of ancient scrolls remain the interest of all students of antiquity, archaeologists are also concerned with the technical and material aspects of this pervasive and influential bibliographic form.

Given the factors of a climate favorable to both the cultivation and the preservation of papyrus, and the particular funerary practices (i.e., entombment) of the ancient Egyptians, it is no surprise that the oldest and most numerous discoveries of ancient scrolls are from Egypt. The oldest extant writing on papyrus dates from the fifth dynasty (c. 2750–2625 BCE). Although papyrus was by far the most commonly used scroll material, Egyptian documents of equal antiquity written on parchment are also attested. Owing to its capacity to contain lengthy texts, the scroll was the primary vehicle of Egyptian literature, the most commonly preserved example being the collection of funerary texts referred to as the Book of the Dead. The Aramaic papyri from Elephantine in southern Egypt also illustrate the suitability of the scroll for transmitting literary texts. Most of the texts from the archives of the Jewish military colony at Elephantine were letters or legal documents consisting of single sheets of papyrus folded from bottom to top and then sealed. Two of the texts, however, The Sayings of Aḥiqar and a copy of the Persian emperor Darius's Behistun inscription, were written in multiple columns on lengths of papyrus rolled from left to right into scrolls (Bezalel Porten, "Aramaic Papyri and Parchments: A New Look," *Biblical Archaeologist* 42 [1979]: 74–104). Numerous Greco-Roman papyri have been recovered from excavations of rubbish dumps in ancient Egyptian towns, further demonstrating the historical persistence of this writing device. [*See* Elephantine.]

The features of compactness and portability that afforded convenience and economy of use for ancient writers also made the scroll the most vulnerable to decay. The use of the scroll outside of Egypt is therefore attested primarily from literary sources rather than archaeological remains. The earliest references to the use of scrolls in Mesopotamia date to the Neo-Assyrian period (mid-eighth–mid-seventh centuries BCE). The archaeological evidence is limited primarily to depictions in Assyrian reliefs of two scribes, one writing in cuneiform script on a tablet and the other writing in Aramaic on rolled material (James B. Pritchard, ed., *The Ancient Near East in Pictures Relating to the Old Testament,* 2d ed. Princeton, 1969, nos. 235, 236). Although the earliest references to written documents in biblical literature are to tablets or stones, the historical influence of Egypt over the southern Levant suggests the use of the scroll there by at least the mid-second millennium BCE. Archaeological evidence of the use of papyrus scrolls in ancient Israel includes impressions of papyrus fibers on the reverse side of clay seals and bullae, such as the one bearing the name of Baruch, son of Neriah, the seventh-century BCE scribe described in *Jeremiah* 36:4 as writing a scroll of the prophet's utterances (Nahman Avigad, *Hebrew Bullae From the Time of Jeremiah,* Jerusalem, 1986).

The Dead Sea Scrolls provide the best example of ancient scrolls from an identifiable, though secondary, archaeological context. Beyond the wealth of information contained within the texts themselves, they reveal many technical details regarding the manufacture, use, storage, and repair of parchment scrolls in antiquity. Common scribal techniques such as ruled lines and margins and a columnar arrangement of the text are readily observable from these scrolls. Other technical aspects of manuscript preparation are observable as well, such as the fastening of parchment sheets by sewing or gluing, the mixing of the carbon-based ink, and the storage of the scrolls in linen wrappers and clay jars.

Studying the material and technical aspects of ancient scrolls yields a greater understanding of the material and economic prerequisites for writing in antiquity, such as the manufacture or acquisition of papyrus, parchment, ink, and implements; it also reveals the technical skills, daily functions, and the social, political, and religious roles of scribes in the cultural systems of the ancient Near East.

[*See also* Codex; Papyrus; Parchment; Scribes and Scribal Techniques; Writing Materials.]

BIBLIOGRAPHY

Černý, Jaroslav. *Paper and Books in Ancient Egypt.* London, 1952.

Davies, Philip R. *Qumran.* Grand Rapids, Mich., 1982. Summary of the discovery, archaeology, and contents of the Dead Sea Scrolls, with judicious criticisms of previous conclusions.

Haran, Menahem. "Book Scrolls in Israel in Pre-Exilic Times." *Journal of Jewish Studies* 33 (1982): 161–173. Surveys the available archaeological evidence in conjunction with literary analyses of biblical and extrabiblical sources.

Haran, Menahem. "Book-Scrolls at the Beginning of the Second Temple Period: The Transition from Papyrus to Skins." *Hebrew Union College Annual* 54 (1983): 111–122. Includes a discussion of the (limited) evidence for the use of scrolls in Mesopotamia and the influence of Babylonian and Persian bibliographic traditions on the transmission of biblical literature.

Reed, Ronald. *Ancient Skins, Parchments, and Leathers.* London, 1972. Introduction to ancient technologies of the preparation of skins, written by a materials scientist for students of archaeology and the humanities.

Roberts, C. H., and T. C. Skeat. *The Birth of the Codex.* London, 1983. Lucid treatment of the transition from scroll to codex in Western letters that demonstrates the persistence of the use of the scroll in late antiquity.

Turner, Eric G. *Greek Papyri: An Introduction.* Rev. ed. Oxford, 1980. Includes a summary of the history and manufacture of papyrus scrolls and also a treatment of the archaeology of the Greco-Roman papyri discovered in Egypt in the twentieth century.

Vaux, Roland de. *Archaeology and the Dead Sea Scrolls.* London, 1973. Summation of de Vaux's definitive reports on the excavations at Khirbet Qumran and ʿAin Feshkha and their illumination of the Qumran manuscript discoveries.

BARRY A. JONES

SCYTHIANS. The earliest mention of the Scythians is in Assyrian records dating to the reign of Sargon II (prior to 713 BCE). They were called Ashkuzi by the Assyrians; a similar name is known from the Hebrew Bible in the pedigree of Noah's descendency (*Gn.* 10:1–3): Askeneze was the son of Gomer (i.e., Cimmerians). According to Herodotus (4.11) the Scythians came from the steppes east of the Araxes River (modern Syr Darya) and were pushed westward by the drying up of the steppe and by their wilder eastern neighbors, the Massagetes (cf. also Diodorus Sicarus 2.43–37). The language of the Scythians belongs to the Iranian group. Herodotus (1.5–10) gives two legends of their origin. The first describes Skythes as the youngest son of the first man, Targitaos (son of Zeus and the daughter of the Borystenes River, now the Don). He had two elder brothers, but only Skythes was able to touch the four gold objects that had fallen from the sky: plow, yoke, axe, and bowl. In the second version, the mother of the three sons is a goddess whose upper body is human and whose lower body is in the shape of a snake; their father is Herakles. Because Skythes was the only one who could successfully handle their father's bow, he became the ancestor of the Royal Scythians. A gold vessel from the Kul'-Oba kurgan displays this myth: two men hurt themselves while trying to handle the bow, and only the third is successful. Though the first mythological story speaks in favor of an agricultural ancestry, the Scythians were true nomads, with mounted archers as their main military force.

The earliest Scythian finds from the Kelermes kurgans (discovered in 1903–1904 and dated to the mid-seventh century BCE) suggest that their earliest material culture strongly resembles that of the late Cimmerians (known from the Novocherkassk hoard), but their own artistic expression initially combined the traditional Animal Style of northern Eurasia with the arts of Media and neighboring areas in the Near East, where the Scythians carried out their military activities. [*See* Cimmerians.] According to Herodotus (4.1) Scythian military supremacy there lasted twenty-eight years, but their actual presence in the Near East extended for more than a century. Their center north of the Caucasus Mountains remained in the Kuban area (there are only a few early rich Scythian tumuli in the Ukraine); in the Near East, their kingdom had its core in the area of Lake Urmia. In the 670s BCE, the Scythians became dangerous neighbors for Urartu and also for the Assyrians. [*See* Urartu; Assyrians.] In 673 BCE Esarhaddon gave his daughter in marriage to the Scythian king Parthatua (Protothyes in Greek sources), apparently seeking an alliance against Urartu and the Medes. [*See* Medes.] Protothyes' son Madyas later helped the Assyrians when the Medes attacked Nineveh (Herodotus 1.103). [*See* Nineveh.]

Scythian power apparently grew after the middle of the century, but the peak of their military raids in the Near East falls between 630 and 625 BCE. Using the opportunity created by the Assyrian loss of power, Scythian cavalry plundered Syria and Palestine. They were only stopped at the

Egyptian frontier by Psammetichus, who had to pay the Scythians richly to spare his country. The impact of the military success of the Scythian cavalry and its savagery and cruelty made a strong impression: the Hebrew prophets (Isaiah, Jeremiah) used these campaigns in their imagery to describe their terrifying visions. At the end of the seventh century BCE, the time of the final collapse of the Assyrian Empire (609–605 BCE) and then of Urartu in the sixth century (between 590 and 585 BCE), the Scythians experienced problems with the rising power of the Medes. Herodotus (1.106) describes the killing of Scythian leaders during a feast given by the Median king Cyaxares. In the early sixth century BCE, the core of the Scythian Empire returned, slowly, from the Kuban region to the northern Pontic steppes.

Characteristic Scythian art appeared in the late seventh century BCE, during the period of their military campaigns. It joined Iranian traditions with the Eurasian Animal Style to create a new style that owes much to the artistic mastery of the Ionians. The best works of early Scythian art found in Asia Minor (at Sardis and Ephesus), in the Kuban region, the northern Pontic area, and in Hungary may well have been executed by Ionian artists, who also served the Persians (see R. Stucky, "Kleinplastiken, Anatolisches Zaumzeug aus Ost und West," *Archäologie Mittelungen aus Iran* 18 [1985]: 119–124; 20 [1987]: 161–165). [*See* Sardis; Ephesus.] One of the earliest complexes of Scythian art is found in the treasure associated with the site of Ziweye, in Iranian Kurdistan, and in several of the Kelermes kurgans (see Schiltz, 1994).

The Royal Scythians inhabited the Pontic steppes. They were nomads in the full sense of the word, moving with their herds across that vast pastureland. Their families lived in wagons, and horses served not only for riding and transport but as a food source. Herodotus (4.110–117) reports Scythian farmers, plowmen and other inhabitants of the Pontic area between the Danube and Don Rivers (east of the latter was the territory of the Sauromatae). Archaeological investigations have uncovered cultures with settled population and forts in the forest-steppe zone north of the Royal Scythians, to whom their neighbors paid some kind of tribute. The Scythians, also in the sixth century BCE, attacked their western neighbors, and their military raids reached as far west as present-day Austria and the Polish western frontier. In the latter area, a hoard was found at Witaszkowo (Vettersfelde) with Scythian parade armor: pieces of Ionian manufacture dated to about 540 BCE (see Schiltz, 1994). Scythian military supremacy reached its peak there, and the peoples affected by their raids learned their technique of horsemanship. Herodotus (4.118–143) describes the Scythian campaign of Darius in 512 BCE, from which the great king of Persia had to retreat, when his army became exhausted from chasing the Scythians across the steppe.

As with other nomadic cultures without characteristic traces of dwellings, the main archaeological source for Scythian culture is their monumental tombs under barrows of extraordinary dimensions. The one at Tolstaja mogila (see Mozolevs'kij, 1979) was 8.5 m high and consisted of 1,500 cu m of earth: the preserved lateral chamber (the central burial was partially destroyed by tomb robbers) was 7 m under the present ground level—more than 15 m under the top of the tumulus. Horses and even servants were sacrificed to the noble dead, and the body of a woman, deposited later in the undisturbed chamber, was buried with a small boy and several servants. Her body and funeral bed were lavishly equipped with precious objects: gold jewelry, toilet equipment, glass vessels, and fine Greek pottery. Hidden in a special pit, near the main chamber, was a sword in a gold sheath and a gold pectoral weighing 1,150 gr. There are more than twenty truly royal barrows; the more numerous graves of middle-class Scythians are less well equipped and lack gold objects.

The bow and arrow were the main weapons used by the Scythians. The *gorytus* was a sheath protecting them, while a short sword called an *akinakes* was protected by a sheath. In the burials of the wealthy, both were covered by sheet gold decorated in relief. Most of the known examples are Greek works depicting animal fights or scenes from Greek mythology. Horse harnesses included many decorated ornamental parts for covering the animal's forehead, nose, and chest. Scythian noblewomen wore a high tiara; the dress in which they were buried was covered with sheet gold ornaments decorated in relief. Poles topped with bells and other objects were paraphernalia used in shamanistic rituals; the Animal Style was the art of shamanistic religion.

The Scythians rejected the Greek way of life, but their aristocracy frequently used jewelry and toreutics made by the Greeks especially for them and adapted to their taste. The best works of Scythian art were made by Greek craftsmen, first by the Ionians and then, in the late fifth century BCE, by those from the Athenian confederacy (e.g., the Solokha comb). The golden age of Scythian art in the fourth century BCE was created by masters who stemmed from both Athenian and Macedonian schools.

Representations of Scythians beginning in the latter part of the fifth century BCE show them in distinctive clothing, including trousers; fourth-century iconography shows a turn from warlike scenes to amicable negotiations and myths propagating the legitimacy of the dynastic rule. The simpler objects in the Animal Style, mainly showing predators attacking herbivores, were made by local craftsmen in a style reminiscent of woodcarvings. Early Animal Style Scythian art in the represents organic forms, while the later works dissolve the bodies into individual parts.

In the fifth century BCE, the Scythians were a fairly strong military power respected by both the Greek Pontic cities (Olbia was a Scythian protectorate) and their more barbarian neighbors—the Getae and other Thracians living in the eastern Balkans and the Sauromatae (later called Sarmatians) east of Don—though the last mentioned slowly moved westward. A second peak of Scythian power and the golden age of their art were reached toward the middle of the fourth century BCE under King Ateas. Ateas subdued Dobrodgea (since called Scythia Minor), south of the Danube River, and fought battles against the Triballoi in the central Balkans and against Philip II of Macedon. To Ateas's reign date the best-known Scythian tumuli, with royal jewelry and toreutics (as at Tolstaya mogila, Kul'-Oba, and Great Bliznitsa), and the introduction of Scythian coinage. In his last battle against Philip, in 339 BCE, Ateas (then ninety years old) was killed and his army defeated. Philip II took twenty thousand women and children as part of the booty, in addition to an equal number of horses. In 331 BCE, Olbia, with the help of the Scythians, resisted an attack of the Macedonian general Zopyrion, sent by Alexander the Great; during the third century BCE, however, the Scythians lost most of the Pontic steppe to the Sarmatians, and their kingdom became confined to the inner Crimea and to a coastal strip between Crimea and Olbia.

The Scythian kingdom in the Crimea, with its capital at Scythian Neapolis, fought, with more or less success, its Greek neighbors and the mountainous Taurae in the southern Crimea. In 110 BCE, the Scythians were severely defeated by Diofantes, a general of Mithridates VI of Pontus, but they maintained some of their positions until the third century CE, when they finally disappeared from history.

[*See also* Anatolia, *article on* Ancient Anatolia.]

BIBLIOGRAPHY

Artamonov, Mikhail I., and Werner Forman. *The Splendor of Scythian Art.* London, 1969.

From the Land of the Scythians. New York, 1980. Exhibition catalog, Metropolitan Museum of Art.

Mozolevs'kij, B. M. *Tvosta Mogila.* Kiev, 1979.

Piotrovsky, Boris B., and Nonna Grach. *Scythian Art: The Legacy of the Scythian World, Mid-Seventh to Third Century B.C.* Leningrad, 1986.

Piotrovsky, Boris B., and Klaus Vierneisel. *L'or des Scythes.* Brussels, 1991. Exhibition catalogue, Musée Royaux d'Art et d'Histoire.

Polosmak, N. V., and Francis van Noten. "Les Scythes de l'Altaï." *La Recherche* 26 (1995): 524–530.

Rolle, Renate, et al., eds. *Gold der Steppe: Archäologie der Ukraine.* Schlesswig, 1991.

Schiltz, Véronique. *Les Scythes et les nomades des steppes, 8e siècle av. J.-C.–1er siècle après J.-C.* Paris, 1994.

JAN BOUZEK

SCYTHOPOLIS. *See* Beth-Shean.

SEAFARING.

By learning to build vessels that could travel over open water and by attaining the knowledge necessary to operate and guide them, sailors in antiquity transformed watery frontiers from insurmountable barriers to superhighways. Over those routes, cultures were able to communicate in the widest sense of the term, facilitating the process of human development. The earliest evidence for Mediterranean seafaring are flakes of obsidian found on the Greek mainland in Franchthi cave in Upper Paleolithic and Neolithic strata (c. eleventh–fourth millennia) that originated on the Aegean island of Melos. This material could only have reached the mainland by means of water transport, as Melos was never connected to the mainland. It is not known how Paleolithic seafarers learned of the existence of obsidian on Melos, but it seems likely that Melos was only one of many islands visited by them without their leaving any evidence of their visits.

There are no known depictions of the vessels employed by these early seafarers. Perhaps they voyaged on primitive reed rafts, similar in construction to the *papirella* built until recently on Corfu. In an archaeological experiment, a modern 6-meter-long *papirella* was paddled successfully from Lavrion on the southwest coast of Attica to Melos, indicating that such voyages were at least theoretically possible. Skin craft are another, although less likely, possibility. Later, Neolithic tools would have permitted the construction of dugouts (monoxylons).

In antiquity, hulls were built in a method quite different from that used today. After raising the keel and posts, a modern shipwright attaches the frames to the keel and then builds up the hull's shell around the framing system, known as frame-first, or frame-based, construction. The shipwright's ancient counterpart, however, after preparing the vessel's keel and posts, built the shell of the hull's planking before inserting the frames into it. This method is known as shell-first, or shell-based, construction.

The hulls of all seagoing ships built before the end of the Roman period that have been excavated in eastern Mediterranean waters were edge-joined with closely spaced mortise-and-tenon joints. The joints were locked in place with wooden pegs, usually driven from inside the hull. No caulking was required, as the wooden planks swelled upon contact with water, effectively sealing the planking seams.

Other forms of hull construction existed simultaneously. Pharaonic Egyptians went to sea in hulls that apparently were held together primarily with longitudinal lashings. Unpegged mortise-and-tenon joints served to seat the planking. This construction method was used on the (nonseagoing) Cheops ship found at Giza. [*See* Giza.] Lashed hulls were particularly useful for ships on the Red Sea run to Punt. For those ventures, ships were built on the Nile River and then dismantled to permit them to be carried overland to the Red Sea coast, where they were reassembled for the voyage.

Until fairly recently, blue-water sailors had only three options for propelling their vessels: paddling, rowing and sailing. Paddlers sit facing the vessel's bow, usually in a kneeling position. Energy is transferred through the bodies of the paddlers to the vessel because the paddles are used as levers.

SEAFARING. *Painted vase showing a ship and animals.* Egypt, Predynastic period (c. 3400-3000 BCE). Inv. EO 304. (Erich Lessing/Art Resource, NY)

The earliest-known depictions of Aegean ships (third millennium) illustrate what appears to be a type of vessel that is long and narrow with rows of lines on either side. The lines probably represent paddles rather than oars. Paddling requires significantly less inboard space than rowing, as paddlers must sit next to the sides of a vessel; therefore, narrow boats would have been paddled rather than rowed. Aegean ships were still being paddled in waterborne cultic races/processions as late as the seventeenth century BCE, even though this mode of propulsion was no longer suited to the contemporary craft used in the celebrations. Paddling thus appears to have had a long tradition in the Aegean.

In rowing, the oar is held in an oarlock or rope grommet attached to the vessel's caprails, which transfers energy directly to the vessel. Normally, the oarsman sits facing the vessel's stern and pulled the oar toward his chest while leaning backward. As rowing requires the use of lower-body muscles during the stroke, it is a far more energy-efficient manner of propulsion than paddling.

The Neolithic colonization of Crete, during the latter part of the eighth millennium or the early seventh, appears to have been a result of an organized migration. In order to establish themselves on Crete, those early colonists must have transported at least 15 tons of breeding-stock grain and personal items in a single sailing season. Moving such masses of material would have been virtually impossible if the vessels were paddled. This consideration suggests that rowing, and/or the sail, was known by the Neolithic period in the Aegean.

A ship painted on a Gerzean-period jar carries the earliest known depiction of a sail; it is roughly square in shape and spread on a mast stepped in the ship's bow. Throughout the Bronze Age, the boom-footed sail, in a variety of shapes and variations, remained the only sail in use. In this sail system, the boom was lashed to the mast and the sail was set and lowered by raising the yard to the masthead by means of halyards. Such a rig did not permit reducing the sail. To take the sail in, the crew had to lower and remove it and then replace it with another, smaller sail.

The boom prevented the use of shrouds—the lines running from the masthead to the sides of a ship that normally supply lateral support. In place of shrouds, at least on Bronze Age Egyptian, Syro-Canaanite, and Cypriot ships, seagoing ships employed lateral cables attached to the bottom of the mast, about the height of the boom.

Toward the end of the Late Bronze Age, a new and innovative form of sail came into use. This rig, termed the brailed sail, did away with the boom. Instead, a system of lines (brails) attached to the foot of the sail was carried through vertical rows of rings sewn to the sail and carried over the yard back toward the stern. The brails acted like modern Venetian blinds. The sail could be more easily controlled by hauling on—or releasing—the brails. This apparently permitted greater ability in sailing to windward. Indeed, the enhanced seafaring abilities that mark the beginning of the Iron Age are probably to be attributed primarily to the appearance of the brailed sail.

The origins of the brailed sail are unclear. Some New

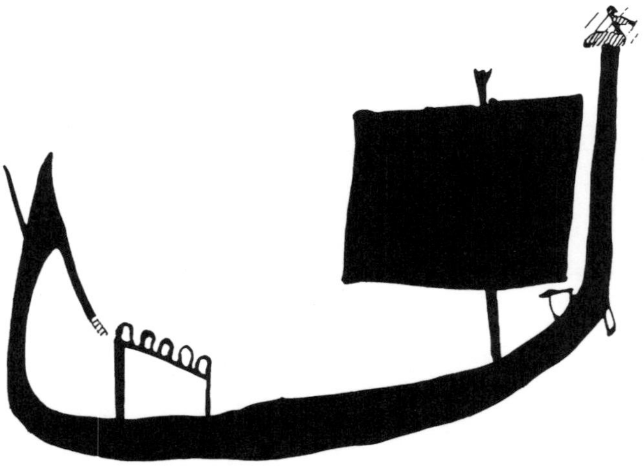

SEAFARING. *Earliest known depiction of a sail, painted on a Gerzean jar.* (After Frankfort, 1924, pl. XIII)

Kingdom depictions show ships carrying a prototype sail that was raised to the yard, yet still carries a boom. It is unlikely, however, that the brailed sail was an Egyptian invention. The brailed rig seems to have come into general use in the eastern Mediterranean in about 1200 BCE. It appears prominently on both the ships of the attacking Sea Peoples as well as those of the defending Egyptians in the scene of Rameses III's naval battle at Medinet Habu (see below). All depictions of Aegean ships, down to the end of the thirteenth century BCE (Late Helladic IIIB), in which the type of rig can be identified, show them carrying boom-footed rigs; those dating to the twelfth century BCE (and later) are all depicted carrying brailed rigs.

Sails were woven primarily of linen. No remains of sails have been found on any ancient Mediterranean shipwrecks; however, part of a sail, with a wooden fairlead still attached, was found among the wrappings of a second-century BCE mummy.

The square sail was intended primarily for sailing before the wind. Crews either took to their oars or bided their time when winds were contrary. The ability of a ship mounting a square sail to sail into the wind depends on a variety of considerations, including the specific type of rig and the design of the hull and its ability to prevent drift to leeward. The *Kyrenia* II, a replica of a fourth-century BCE merchantman, employing a brailed sail, was able to sail 50–60 degrees (4–5 points) off windward. A boom-footed sail would have severely hampered these abilities.

The lack of shrouds, and the curious consideration that seagoing ships were built with their keel (or keel planks) rising upward, inside the hull, instead of protruding below it (where it would have served to prevent leeward drift), both suggest that the Bronze Age seafarers who employed the boom-footed square sail were not unduly concerned with utilizing winds from far off the stern.

From the lines used to control ships' sails to the hawsers, which allowed ships to anchor, ropes were an integral part of ships' equipment, used for a variety of purposes. In antiquity, a variety of fibers were used in rope making.

Models of Middle and New Kingdom ships that have been preserved with their rigging have a number of recognizable knots, primarily hitches and lashings. While the use on models of such knots does not necessarily prove their use at sea, it does indicate that such knots were known.

The ability to navigate to a destination after crossing an expanse of water, often out of sight of land and seemingly lacking in directional signs, is a prerequisite of seafaring. In antiquity the sailing season was relegated primarily, although not exclusively, to the summer months. During those months the predominant wind in the eastern Mediterranean is northwesterly. This had a profound influence on sea routes. With a square sail it was relatively easy to reach Africa from Europe. Returning was, however, another matter. A return trip required a counterclockwise voyage around the entire Levantine coastline. Although there is little archaeological evidence for it, ancient Mediterranean seafarers must have had access to a broad body of knowledge relating to navigational techniques and meteorology. At the same time, a lack of navigational tools need not reflect a lack of navigational knowledge. It is possible to have a remarkably developed navigational system that would leave no trace in the archaeological record, beyond evidence that voyages were indeed being made.

Ancient navigation was an art, rather than a science, and was based on an broad knowledge of position-locating factors committed entirely to memory, as studies of Polynesian navigational techniques have demonstrated. In Oceania, no position-determining instruments were ever carried on board ships, despite remarkable feats of navigational skill. Theoretically at least, a similar situation may have existed in the Mediterranean during the Bronze and Iron Ages.

There are two methods for determining the direction of land lying beyond the horizon with birds. In one, land birds that were unable to land on water—ravens, crows, doves, and swallows—were carried on board ship and released when needed. Upon gaining height, if the bird saw land it would invariably make a beeline toward it, and freedom, indicating the direction of the nearest landfall. If, however, it did not sight land, the bird had no choice but to return to the ship. This land-finding technique is of high antiquity; Noah (*Gn.* 8:6–12), as well as his Mesopotamian counterpart Utnapishtim, are reported to have used this land-finding method. Seabirds have also been utilized as a navigational aid. By acquiring an intimate knowledge of the habits of seabirds that nest on rookeries on shore yet feed far out to sea, it is possible to determine landfall by taking careful note of the direction in which flocks of seabirds fly in the morning or during the late afternoon.

As has been shown by Oceanic navigators, winds can be significant indicators of direction. Before the introduction of the magnetic compass there was the wind rose. By noting the "signature" characteristics of each wind, it was possible to determine the direction from which it blew. The Phoenicians are credited with introducing the wind rose into the Mediterranean. [*See* Phoenicians.] Homer knew of four winds. Later Greeks developed this wind rose into the eight-wind system portrayed on the first-century BCE Athenian Tower of the Winds (horologium or water clock).

Winds, however, are directional indicators of a secondary nature that must be compared with more reliable directional phenomena. When in sight of land, landmarks were valuable navigational aids. In classical times, seafarers could avail themselves of *periploi,* "handbooks" containing information on anchorages, landmarks, and other details valuable to seafarers. The sun could also be used as a navigational aid, although its points of rising and setting vary throughout the year. However, only stellar navigation—a sidereal compass—can supply fixed points in open water. As demonstrated by Oceanic navigators, stellar navigation is based on an intimate knowledge of the rising and setting points on the horizon of numerous stars.

Ships are at the mercy of the weather, and therefore seafarers, no doubt from earliest times, developed an intimate knowledge of weather lore. The biblical writers considered the east wind particularly dangerous and repeatedly describe it as destroying the large seagoing merchantmen called Tarshish ships (*Ps.* 48:7; *Ez.* 27:26). Josephus describes the "black norther" that destroyed the Jewish rebel fleet at Jaffa in 67 CE, as well as the destructive tendencies of the southwest wind (*War* 1.409; 3.421–426; *Antiq.* 15.333). The best-known weather lore from antiquity appears in the New Testament (*Mt.* 16:2–3; *Lk.* 12:54).

International and local trade were carried out by ships that were able to move heavy and bulky cargoes for great distances at appreciably lower rates than land-based transport. Shipwrecks, like those uncovered at Uluburun and Cape Gelidonya in Turkey and off Kyrenia on Cyprus, have provided intimate, and often surprising, information about the types of cargoes carried. [*See* Uluburun.] Ships, as well as timber for their construction, were in themselves also an important trade item.

Ugaritic texts and the Tale of Wenamun indicate that by the end of the Late Bronze Age a code of maritime laws existed along Levantine shores. This was a prerequisite for maintaining seaborne commerce and diplomacy.

Ship-based warfare played a predominant role in seafaring. By the sixth dynasty, and probably earlier, Egyptian oared ships were employed as rapid military transports for attacks along the Syro-Canaanite coast and for transporting the resultant spoils back to Egypt. Unas (Wenis), an officer who served under Pepi I, describes in his cenotaph at Abydos how he used ships to transport forces, landing them behind a prominent landmark he calls the Antelope's Nose, perhaps an early name for the Carmel Mountains in the region of Haifa, Israel. Throughout the Bronze Age, the purpose of ships in military ventures was the rapid transport of forces to their destination. In sea battles, ships were used as floating platforms on which soldiers fought. Šuppiluliuma II, the last king of the Hittite Empire, refers to three sea battles in which he fought against "the ships of Alashiya," perhaps an allusion to contingents of ship-based Sea Peoples who used Cyprus as their base of operations. Rameses II mentions doing battle against ships of the Shardanu, one of the groups of Sea Peoples, on a stela from Tanis. [*See* Hittites.]

The earliest-known depiction of a naval battle is carved in relief on the outer wall of Rameses III's mortuary temple at Medinet Habu. The scene graphically describes a successful surprise attack by Rameses' forces against an invading fleet of Sea Peoples. The engagement apparently took

SEAFARING. *Naval battle depicted at Medinet Habu.* (After Nelson et al., 1930, pl. 37)

place in the Nile Delta region. In the first phase of the engagement, Egyptian archers, located on ships and on shore, used composite bows to pick off the invading warriors at long range. Against this, the Sea Peoples, armed only with medium-range throwing javelins and swords, were defenseless. Once the enemy was neutralized, the invading ships were capsized by tossing four-armed grapnels into their rigging. The grapnel is the only strictly nautical weapon depicted in the relief.

The naval weapon par excellence of antiquity was the waterline ram, which is believed to have evolved first in Greece during the Geometric period. A badly damaged Assyrian wall painting dating to about 700 BCE is the earliest pictorial representation of one war galley ramming another ship. The first battle known to have taken place after the introduction of the ram transpired off Alalia on the eastern coast of Corsica in 535 BCE. From then until the Battle of Actium (31 BCE), some sixty naval battles of varying size and intensity are recorded.

The ram went through four distinct evolutionary phases. Between about 900–600 BCE, it was a metal-sheathed point, apparently a development of the protruding bow structures that appear on Mycenaean galleys. In the sixth century BCE, a blunt ram in the form of a boar's snout replaced the point. The boar's head ram was popular for the next two centuries. Then, toward the end of the fifth century BCE, a three-finned ram came into widespread use. It was this device, typified by the ʿAtlit ram, that destroyed Anthony's fleet at Actium—and it may have been used earlier, in the waning years of the Peloponnesian wars. [*See* ʿAtlit Ram.] The fins apparently were intended to prevent the ram from piercing the enemy's hull, which would have endangered the attacking ship by locking her into a deadly embrace while other ships could ram her. The three-finned ram was employed to open the planking seams by breaking the mortise-and-tenon joints holding them together, thus permitting seawater to enter the hull and render it inoperable. To use the ram effectively, galleys had to be heavy: the weight contributed the momentum necessary to damage the enemy's hull. The ship itself was the weapon; the ram was only the "warhead" by means of which the attacking ship's momentum was imparted to its victim. In about 100 CE, the three-finned ram fell out of use. The last phase of the ram was during the Byzantine period.

[*See also* Anchors; Fishing; *and* Ships and Boats.]

BIBLIOGRAPHY

Basch, Lucien. *Le musée imaginaire de la marine antique*. Athens, 1987. A comprehensive collection of ancient Mediterranean ship depictions.

Broodbank, Cyprian, and Thomas F. Strasser. "Migrant Farmers and the Neolithic Colonization of Crete." *Antiquity* 65 (1991): 233–245. Discussion of Crete's earliest settlement.

Casson, Lionel. *Ships and Seamanship in the Ancient World*. 2d ed. Princeton, 1986. Textbook for ancient Mediterranean seafaring, with a focus on the classical period.

Casson, Lionel, and J. Richard Steffy, eds. *The ʿAthlit Ram*. College Station, Tex., 1990. Report on the only waterline ram known from antiquity.

Frankfort, Henri. *Mesopatamia, Syria, and Egypt and Their Earliest Interrelations*. Studies in Early Pottery in the Near East, 1. London, 1924.

Haldane, Cheryl Ward. "Ancient Egyptian Hull Construction." Ph.D. diss., Texas A&M University, 1993. Monograph on ancient Egyptian shipbuilding.

Hornell, James. "The Role of Birds in Early Navigation." *Antiquity* 20 (1946): 142–149.

Lewis, David. *We, the Navigators: The Ancient Art of Landfinding in the Pacific*. Honolulu, 1975. Study of Polynesian navigational techniques.

Steffy, J. Richard. *Wooden Ship Building and the Interpretation of Shipwrecks*. College Station, Tex., 1994. Textbook on ancient hull construction.

Wachsmann, Shelley. "The Ships of the Sea Peoples." *International Journal of Nautical Archaeology and Underwater Exploration* 10 (1981): 187–220.

Wachsmann, Shelley. *Seagoing Ships and Seamanship in the Bronze Age Levant*. College Station, Tex., 1996. Textbook on Bronze Age eastern Mediterranean seafaring.

SHELLEY WACHSMANN

SEALS. Small stones (5–10 cm) whose flat or cylindrical surfaces are carved in intaglio with a design or inscription have been used as seals since the Late Neolithic period (7600–6000 BCE) in Syria (Wickede, 1990). The engraved surface was designed to be read in the impression left on receptive materials (clay, wax, soft metal). Through the impression a seal could convey a message of ownership, authorization, or responsibility (Gibson and Biggs, 1977). An inscription most commonly contains the owner's name, patronymic, and office, although prayers and religious dedications are not uncommon. As Dominique Collon demonstrates in *First Impressions* (1988), the inscription and the design offer information on onomastics, political hierarchy, myth, ritual, and activities of daily life. Not all engraved stones were used as seals: some were amulets and others were used as personal ornaments. Seal impressions themselves also may have had an apotropaic, magical, or purely decorative function. Seal stones often were pierced to be worn as rings, pendents, or bracelets. Fired clay, wood, bone, ivory, and metal are used for seals as well, but these more fragile materials have not survived in the quantities stone seals have. Flat-surfaced stamp seals appear before cylinder seals in the Near East and were the preferred form of seal in Anatolia, Egypt, and the Levant. Stamp seals are divided into typological classes according to the presence or absence of a handle and according to shape. Cylinder seals were the preferred form of seal in Mesopotamia, Iran, and Syria-Palestine, areas that used cuneiform script during the Bronze Age. Cylinder seals are characterized by place of manufacture, historical phase, and design.

The earliest recorded seals and seal impressions, from the Late Aceramic Neolithic period in Syria, are impressions made on the plaster vessels (white ware) that preceded true ceramics (Wickede, 1990). In the Pottery Neolithic and Early Chalcolithic periods, seals continued to be used on vessels in Iraq and coastal Syria and Cilicia. Pyramidal and conoid stamps were common. Their designs, simple cross-hatching, zigzags, and other linear motifs, probably had decorative or apotropaic value. During the Halaf period (5500–5000 BCE), seal impressions occur for the first time on fired ceramic vessels and on soft clay nodules (bullae) used to seal containers. More elaborate in shape and in their engraved design, the Halaf-period seals continue the tradition of primarily geometric, linear, or hatched designs, crosses, and dots but add animal motifs to the repertoire. The Ubaid period (5000–4000 BCE) sees a widening use of seals to control access to objects and rooms, as well as an expansion of motifs to include complex designs and human figures. Tepe Gawra strata XII and XI have some of the best examples of complex seal impressions; they illustrate an early use of sealings to control access to rooms and other containers, probably in an administrative context (Rothman and Blackman, 1990). [*See* Tepe Gawra.] The use of seals to control access, as well as the particular style associated with them, spread to Anatolia and can be found in examples from Degirmentepe.

Although stamp seals were used throughout the Uruk period (4000–3300 BCE) in southern Mesopotamia, cylinder seals gradually took over their function. The development of the cylinder seal accompanied the increasing sophistication of the recordkeeping and writing system that began with small tokens contained in clay balls. The earliest use of a cylinder seal was to impress the surface of the clay ball, thereby verifying or securing its contents. These have been found at Susa in Iran, but also occur at Uruk in Mesopotamia, in contemporary contexts. [*See* Susa; Uruk-Warka.]

SEALS. *Clay bulla from Habuba Kabira South.* This bulla is dated to about 3500-3000 BCE. (Courtesy ASOR Archives)

Uruk cylinder seals are large and made of soft limestone and often have a knob at one end. The incised motifs were adapted to the cylindrical surface and designed to repeat indefinitely on rolling. The number and quality of designs expanded considerably to include scenes of hunting, boating, grain storage, and fighting. Mark A. Brandes (1979) suggests that these were used in state/temple administration. A male figure is possibly the "priest-king," often depicted as taking part in rituals and in scenes with prisoners. Seals from Jemdet Nasr are contemporary with Uruk-style seals but probably were used by individuals rather than administrators. Small, harder, and more common, the Jemdet Nasr seals either show women at work spinning, weaving, and making pottery (Asher-Greve, 1985) or files of animals and geometric patterns. [*See* Jemdet Nasr.] Cylinder seals of this period are found throughout the Near East, from Susa to Egypt. Collon (1987, pp. 20–24) divides the cylinders seals from the Early Dynastic Period (3200–2600 BCE) into two broad chronological groups: Early Dynastic A and Early Dynastic B. The Early Dynastic A group was produced at the end of the fourth millennium and consists of material from the sites along the trade route between Susa, northern Mesopotamia, and Syria. The tall thin steatite seals have very elaborate, almost brocade, designs that use hatched lines, lozenges, circles, and chevrons. The Early Dynastic B group dates to the middle of the third millennium and is more closely associated with southern Mesopotamian types. Geometric designs based on herringbone patterns and arches in registers are common. More figural designs occur on the cylinder seals created in southern Mesopotamia: animals in human posture, the bull-man, and human-headed bulls may relate to the myths of Mesopotamia. The two major themes, however, are the contest scene between lion and bull or bull-man and the banquet scene at which two seated figures drink through straws from the same vessel or share a meal at the table placed between them.

Although cylinder seals and impressions are found as early as Early Bronze I (3500–3100 BCE) in Byblos on the coast of Syria, the majority of seals and impressions in Palestine date to the EB II–EB III period contemporary with the Early Dynastic B group in Mesopotamia. Unlike Mesopotamia—where seals were rolled on tablets and the unfired clay was used to close doors, bags, boxes, and other containers—in Palestine seals were rolled only on fired-clay vessels as decoration. The material of the seals used for making impressions was probably wood or bone. Designs include the herringbone pattern, concentric circles, lozenges, spirals, and ladders, as well as animals, structures, and a few very schematic human figures (Ben-Tor, 1978).

Beginning in about 2350 BCE, Sargon and his successors in the Akkadian Empire sponsored craftsmen who developed a new, more naturalistic style of seal carving and who added new themes and motifs to the repertoire derived from the Early Dynastic period. One new scene was the presentation scene, in which a supplicant is introduced to an enthroned god or goddess by a minor deity. Deities in general are more prevalent on Akkadian seals than on Early Dynastic seals, and for the first time appear in postures or with attributes that allow their identification with members of the Mesopotamian pantheon (Frankfort, 1939). While contemporary with the Akkadian period, the impressions found at Ebla in Syria are related more to developed Early Dynastic styles, even though they also show some knowledge of Akkadian iconography (Collon, 1988, p. 39). Ur III seals continue to use and to standardize the themes from earlier periods: the banquet, contest, and presentation scenes. An innovation in the latter is the use of the deified king receiving a supplicant in place of the seated god or goddess (Winter, 1986). [*See* Akkadians; Ebla; Ebla Texts.]

Assyrian seals of the Colony period in Anatolia (1950–1750 BCE) are known from the business letters and houses of the merchants stationed at Karum Kaneš in eastern Anatolia. [*See* Kültepe Texts.] The Assyrian seals contain presentation scenes, deities, lines of animals, or figures that were present in the Ur III period but are more crudely executed in two basic styles: one with flat, linear figures and the other with more stylized, elongated, but deeply cut figures (Collon, 1988, p. 41). The local Anatolian group of seals is very finely cut and takes some inspiration from Assyrian seals. In design, however, the spaces on local seals are filled with a jumble of objects, animals, and human figures, all extremely detailed and finely hatched and rehatched. The iconography of the local seals is a good source of information on local Anatolian deities and ritual.

The Old Babylonian Period (1800–1600 BCE) was, like the Akkadian period, a high point in the development of cylinder seals. Returning to the Early Dynastic and Akkadian prototypes, Old Babylonian seal cutters produced very carefully cut hematite seals using a few standardized versions of old themes. The presentation scene, for example, was reduced to two standing figures, the king and the goddess. Old Babylonian seals appear almost mass produced, except for the inscription of the owner's name. Peripheral sites such as Mari in Syria were heavily influenced by the new style, particularly for royal seals. Syrian seals are, however, much more elaborate and naturalistic, with an iconography that includes elements of Egyptian, Hittite, and Minoan design. In Iran, Elamite seals are often indistinguishable from Old Babylonian examples, except for certain isolated elements of coiffure or gesture (ibid., p. 55). New cutting techniques were introduced shortly after Hammurabi's death in 1750 BCE. The use of the drill and the unmasked use of the cutting wheel resulted in a much more schematic treatment of the human and animal elements in the design.

The Late Bronze Age saw many regional developments in seal materials, use, and design. Mitanni craftsman in northern Mesopotamia developed sintered quartz (known also as faience, paste, or frit) to manufacture seals. Easy to cut or drill and fire, masses of Common Style Mitanni seals were produced all over the Near East, primarily as jewelry and amulets. Designs were often split into a major and minor scene, and abstract geometric forms were used for animals and figures (Porada, 1985, p. 99). Elaborate Style cylinder seals were made of hard stone, were more carefully cut, were inscribed, and are more often found impressed on government and legal documents. [*See* Mitanni.]

SEALS. *Hebrew seal depicting a sailing ship.* The inscription reads "Belonging to Amiyahu, son of Marab." Dated to the eighth-seventh century BCE. (Courtesy ASOR Archives)

In the Levant and coastal Syria, only scarab seals rival Mitannian seals in popularity. These stamp seals, shaped like scarab beetles, appear first in Egypt at the end of the Old Kingdom and are found in the Levant throughout the Middle and Late Bronze Ages. As Egyptian political power spread to the southern Levant, so did the popularity of scarab seals. Usually found in burials, scarabs are only occasionally used to impress objects, and then only under the influence of the Egyptian administrative system (Buchanan and Moorey, 1988, p. xii). During the Late Bronze Age, the Hittite Empire expanded from the Anatolian plateau to include much of Syria. In their homeland, the Hittites stopped using cylinder seals after the Colony period and returned to the use of button-shaped stamp seals for personal and official use. Many seals are inscribed with its owner's name and title in Hittite hieroglyphic, and others have a simple heraldic design. Only in the Syrian vassal states did the Hittite officials use cylinder seals to impress official documents (Güterbock, 1980).

After the beginning of the first millennium BCE, only the Assyrians continued to use the cylinder seal because only in

Mesopotamia did cuneiform continue to be the preferred form for inscribing records. The increase in literacy and the shift to new writing materials, languages, and scripts in Syria and the Levant are reflected in the replacement of the stamp seal with the cylinder seal there. Pyramidal, conical, or scaraboid, the stamp seal had little room for elaborate design, but it was more suited to impressing the small nodules of clay affixed to string around papyrus and leather documents. Iron Age stamp seals usually have a single figure or more often a simple inscription of the owner's name and patronymic, or title. In use, however, stamp seals parallel cylinder seals as means of validating legal documents or preventing access to documents or containers (Hestrin and Dayagi-Mendels, 1979).

[*See also* Northwest Semitic Seal Inscriptions.]

BIBLIOGRAPHY

Asher-Greve, Julia M. *Frauen in altsumerischer Zeit.* Malibu, 1985.

Ben-Tor, Amnon. *Cylinder Seals of Third-Millennium Palestine.* Bulletin of the American Schools of Oriental Research, Supplement, no. 22. Cambridge, 1978.

Brandes, Mark A. *Siegelabrollungen aus den archaischen Bauschichten in Uruk-Warka.* Wiesbaden, 1979.

Buchanan, Briggs, and P. R. S. Moorey. *Catalogue of Ancient Near Eastern Seals in the Ashmolean Museum,* vol. 3, *The Iron Age Stamp Seals.* Oxford, 1988.

Collon, Dominique. *First Impressions: Cylinder Seals in the Ancient Near East.* Chicago, 1988. Good introduction to periods and styles of seals, with a comprehensive bibliography.

Frankfort, Henri. *Cylinder Seals: A Documentary Essay on the Art and Religion of the Ancient Near East.* London, 1939. Basic reference on the style and iconography of Mesopotamian cylinder seals, somewhat out of date but still useful.

Gibson, McGuire, and Robert D. Biggs, eds. *Seals and Sealing in the Ancient Near East.* Malibu, 1977. Covers the function of cylinder seals in a series of contributions.

Güterbock, Hans. "Seals and Sealing in Hittite Lands." In *From Athens to Gordion,* edited by Keith DeVries, pp. 51–57. Philadelphia, 1980.

Hestrin, Ruth, and Michal Dayagi-Mendels. *Inscribed Seals.* Jerusalem, 1979. Good introduction to and catalog of the Iron Age seals of ancient Palestine.

Matthews, Donald M. *Principles of Composition in Near Eastern Glyptic of the Later Second Millennium B.C.* Freiburg, 1990. Art historical study of Mitannian seals. Excellent discussion and bibliography.

Porada, Edith. "Syrian Seals from the Late Fourth to the Late Second Millennium." In *Ebla to Damascus,* edited by Harvey Weiss, pp. 90–104. Washington, D.C., 1985.

Rothman, M., and M. James Blackman. "Monitoring Administrative Spheres of Action in Late Prehistoric Northern Mesopotamia with the Aid of Chemical Characterization (INAA) of Sealing Clays." In *Economy and Settlement in the Near East,* edited by Naomi F. Miller, pp. 19–46. Philadelphia, 1990.

Wickede, Alwo von. *Prähistorische Stempelglyptik in Vorderasien.* Munich, 1990. The most recent comprehensive treatment of the shape, design, and function of early stamp seals.

Winter, Irene J. "The King and the Cup: Iconography of the Royal Presentation Scene on Ur III Seals." In *Insight through Images: Studies in Honor of Edith Porada,* edited by Marilyn Kelly-Buccellati, pp. 253–268. Malibu, 1986.

BONNIE MAGNESS-GARDINER

SEA PEOPLES. *See* Philistines.

SECTION. *See* Balk.

SEFIRE ARAMAIC INSCRIPTIONS. The three Aramaic inscriptions on basalt stelae from Sefire, in Syria, constitute one of the most important sources for our knowledge of Aramaic in the first half of the first millennium BCE. The stelae were discovered at Sefire, 25 km (16 mi.) southeast of Aleppo, in the late 1920s. Stelae I and II were acquired by the Damascus Museum in 1948, and stela III by the Beirut Museum in 1956.

Stela I was first called the Sujin stela because Sébastien Ronzevalle, a French Jesuit and professor at Université St. Joseph, Beirut, had been misled about its findspot by the natives who claimed to have discovered it at Sujin. The stela is inscribed on three sides of a rectangular basalt stone. Because the stone was cut after it was engraved, not only was the text on the left side of face A lost, but also the beginnings of the upper lines on face A and the ends of the upper lines on face B. The stone had also been broken in the center, so that at least three lines are missing from the middle of the text extant on three sides. As reconstructed, stela I stands 131 cm high. Face A originally had forty-two lines; face B, forty-five lines; and face C, twenty-five lines. Stela II, reconstructed from a dozen fragments, must have resembled stela I. Its face A today has only fourteen fragmentary lines; face B, twenty-one lines; and face C, seventeen lines. Stela III was pieced together from nine fragments, forming a broad slab 102 cm wide and 72 cm high; it is inscribed only on the reverse, with twenty-nine fragmentary lines. Stela III also is of basalt and has the same kind of writing, absence of word dividers, and the same mention of "kings of Arpad." Hence, it is certainly related to stelae I and II, and all three probably form the text of one and the same treaty, although this is presently debated.

The stelae are inscribed in Aramaic script dated to the middle of the eighth century BCE. They preserve the text of a treaty/treaties made by the north-Syrian ruler, Matiʿel, son of ʿAttarsamak, vassal-king of Arpad, with his overlord, Bar-Ga'yah, king of KTK. The *terminus ante quem* for the stelae is 740 BCE, when Tiglath-Pileser III conquered Arpad, making it part of the Assyrian Empire. The inscriptions presuppose the political autonomy of Arpad. As king of Arpad, Matiʿel had concluded a pact with Ashurnirari V in 754 BCE. He was also an ally of Sardur III of Urartu, prior to the resurgence of Neo-Assyrian might. These stelae, then, were important factors in the history of Syria in the time of Jeroboam II (786–747 BCE) of Israel and of Uzziah (783–742 BCE) of Judah.

The stelae record a suzerainty treaty, a pact concluded between a vassal and his overload. Their text identifies the contracting parties, sets forth the stipulations of the pact, mentions the curses invoked against Matiʿel if he is not faithful to them, and lists the gods, Canaanite and Babylonian, who are witnesses to the treaty. The main problem in the interpretation is the identification of the overlord Bar-Ga'yah, possibly Shamshi-Ilu, and of the country, KTK, over which he ruled, possibly the Kittakka of some Assyrian texts.

[*See also* Aramaic Language and Literature.]

BIBLIOGRAPHY

Dupont-Sommer, André. "Une inscription araméenne inédite de Sfiré." *Bulletin du Musée de Beyrouth* 13 (1956): 23–41, pls. 1–6. *Editio princeps* of stela III.

Dupont-Sommer, André. "Les inscriptions araméennes de Sfiré (stèles I et II)." *Mémoires présentées par divers savants à l'Académie des Inscriptions et Belles-Lettres* 15 (1960) 195–351, pls. 1–29. New edition of stela I and *editio princeps* of stela II.

Fitzmyer, Joseph A. *The Aramaic Inscriptions of Sefire.* Biblica et Orientalia, 19. Rome, 1967. Extensive commentary on the Aramaic text of the stelae, with a study of its grammar and a glossary.

Lemaire, André, and Jean-Marie Durand. *Les inscriptions araméennes de Sfiré et l'Assyrie de Shamshi-Ilu.* École Pratique des Hautes Études, 2. Hautes Études Orientales, 20. Geneva and Paris, 1984. Good *status quaestionis* and up-to-date bibliography.

Ronzevalle, Sébastien. "Fragments d'inscriptions araméennes des environs d'Alep." *Mélanges de l'Université Saint-Joseph* 15 (1930–1931): 237–260. *Editio princeps* of stela I.

Rooy, H. F. van. "The Structure of the Aramaic Treaties of Sefire." *Journal of Semitics* 1 (1989): 133–139.

JOSEPH A. FITZMYER, S.J.

SELEUCIA ON THE TIGRIS, site located approximately 60 km (37 mi.) northwest of Babylon and 35 km (22 mi.) south of Baghdad. Seleucia was founded in the late fourth century BCE by Seleukos Nikator (Lat., Seleucus Nicator), one of the generals of Alexander the Great. According to Greek and Latin writers, the Greek colony was placed near the earlier site of Opis. Pliny (Nat. Hist. 6.30.121ff.) records that Seleucia was founded for the purpose of drawing away the population of Babylon. The Parthians captured the city in 141 BCE. Its inhabitants rebelled between 35 and 42 CE, after which the Parthians may have transferred the seat of government across the river to Ctesiphon. Seleucia's continued importance during the period of Parthian rule is shown, inter alia, by the recent find, unfortunately not in an archaeological context, of a bronze statue of Heracles. According to an inscription in Greek and Pahlavi, the statue was brought from Messene in 150/51 CE by the Parthian king Vologeses IV after a victory over his challenger, Mithridates, and erected at Seleucia in the Temple of Apollo. The Romans took the city three times: under Trajan, in 116 CE; by Avidius Cassius in 165/66; and by Septimius Severus in 198/99. Abundant traces of fire mark the Trajanic destruction, and its capture by Septimius Severus is represented on that emperor's arch in the Roman Forum. The city fell to the Sasanians in the middle of the third century CE, and they moved the capital to the neighboring site of Coche.

Excavations at Seleucia were conducted by the University of Michigan from 1927 through 1937 and by the University of Torino from 1964 through 1976 and from 1986 through 1989. The catalyst for the University of Michigan excavations was a topographical study by Leroy Waterman that attempted to locate the Babylonian city of Opis. Arguing that the area of approximately 100 sq km (62 mi.) covered by the mounds surrounding the prominent artificial mound called Tell ʿUmar was too large for a Babylonian city, he identified the site as Seleucia, whose population Pliny gave as 600,000. The Michigan excavations were the first deliberately to target a Greek city in Mesopotamia.

The excavators established the general outline of the city plan by a contour survey and air photography, showing that the city was laid out on a grid plan of Hippodamean type. The blocks are the largest used in the Hellenistic world (144.70 × 72.35 m). A canal running through the center of the city seems to have divided a largely public northern sector from a primarily residential southern area. One large square in the northern sector is bounded on the west by a long, narrow mud-brick building housing official Seleucid archives and on the north by Tell ʿUmar. A second square enclosed the two structures the American expedition identified as temples. The Hellenistic remains, heavily overlaid by those of the Parthian city, are extremely fragmentary. It is nonetheless striking that essentially no typically Greek structures have been identified. The locations of an agora and theater remain uncertain. It seems unlikely that Seleucia, founded as the capital of a Greek kingdom, should have lacked a theater, as one was built in nearby Babylon. The Michigan excavator Clark Hopkins's identification of remains in the southern part of the city as those of a theater have not been confirmed, and the suggestion made by the Italian excavator Antonio Invernizzi that Tell ʿUmar was originally the theater of the Greek city, though probable, remains hypothetical. The early history of Tell ʿUmar has been obscured by Parthian rebuilding and the Sasanian construction of a defensive tower surrounded by a wall. The two structures tentatively identified as temples are square enclosures that are formally related to temples in both Iran and Syria and may date to the Parthian period.

The American excavations were concentrated in three areas: On Tell ʿUmar, in a nearby block that held a building of uncertain function, and in a residential block in the southern part of the city. The Italians have worked primarily in the Archives building, with some soundings in the southern part of the city.

The plan of only the latest phase of the building excavated by Michigan near Tell ʿUmar can be established with any degree of certainty; it shows a series of rooms around an open court, with elaborate provisions for drainage in one section. The architect considered it a Parthian villa. An inscription of an uncertain Seleucid ruler reused in the later phase of the structure seems to show the existence of a Seleucid *heroon* (i.e., a shrine to a heroized founder of the city); Hopkins argued that the building should be identified as that *heroon*. It differs, however, from known Hellenistic *heroa*.

During the Seleucid period, the building excavated by Michigan in the southern part of the city housed private and official archives. The block contained one or more large residences with shops on the street facades and a number of small rooms arranged around larger rooms and courts. Columns are still used in level III, built during the period of Parthian rule (142 BCE–43 CE), but disappear thereafter. The next phase is characterized by the presence of *iwan*s (large rooms open to one side), an architectural form probably developed in Mesopotamia in the first century BCE that figures prominently in Parthian and Sasanian architecture. Architectural decoration in stucco, such as figured capitals and coverings for walls and vaults with abstract patterns, is related to that known at Uruk and Aššur.

That the inhabitants of this block were not entirely Greek, or at least did not adhere to Greek customs, is shown by the presence of burials in walls and under the floors of the residential area, a continuation of a Babylonian practice. The method of burial varies. Some bodies were simply interred in walls and under floors, but most were placed in jars or coffins of pottery or baked brick. Vaulted family tombs occur thorough level II (approximately 43–118 CE) but disappear entirely in the latest phase. At least initially, the Greek settlers must have been buried outside the city. In any case, the number of burials found in block G6 does not seem large enough for its presumed population, suggesting that people of Greek extraction continued to be interred outside the city.

Both archives end in 154–152 BCE. The documents, presumably written on papyrus, are lost, but the clay bullae that sealed them survive, burnt in the fire that destroyed the buildings, a fire probably associated with the Parthian invasion. The bullae provide valuable evidence about Seleucid administration and the economic life of the city: they give the titles of administrators and show, for example, the importance of a tax on salt. During the Parthian period the archive building near Tell ʿUmar was converted into a commercial quarter that was used largely for the production and sale of terra-cotta figurines.

Little monumental art has been found at Seleucia, but large numbers of terra-cotta figurines and the images on the bullae give some indication of its creative vitality in the Hellenistic period. It is of interest that figurines that are Greek in style and subject appear alongside Near Eastern types throughout the Parthian period. Seleucia was a major force in establishing Hellenism in Mesopotamia, and it remained a creative center in the Parthian period.

[*See also* Ctesiphon; Parthians; Ptolemies; *and* Seleucids.]

BIBLIOGRAPHY

Downey, Susan B. *Mesopotamian Religious Architecture: Alexander through the Parthians.* Princeton, 1988. Survey and analysis of Near Eastern religious architecture dating after the Greek conquest and utilizing Mesopotamian forms; includes a chapter on Seleucia.

Invernizzi, Antonio, et al. In *La terra tra i due fiumi,* pp. 87–141. Turin, 1985. Well-illustrated exhibition catalog providing recent information about Italian excavations at Seleucia and other cities in Iraq; includes a bibliography.

McDowell, Robert Harbold. *Stamped and Inscribed Objects from Seleucia on the Tigris.* University of Michigan Studies, Humanistic Series, vol. 36. Ann Arbor, 1935. Includes the seals and bullae found in the Michigan excavations, and provides useful information on the history and economy of the city.

McDowell, Robert Harbold. *Coins from Seleucia on the Tigris.* University of Michigan Studies, Humanistic Series, vol. 37. Ann Arbor, 1935.

Mesopotamia. Turin, 1966–. Journal containing reports of the Italian excavations at Seleucia on the Tigris, as well as specialized articles on the finds (most in English).

Van Ingen, Wilhelmina. *Figurines from Seleucia on the Tigris.* University of Michigan Studies, Humanistic Series, vol. 45. Ann Arbor, 1939.

Waterman, Leroy. *Preliminary Report upon the Excavations at Tel Umar, Iraq.* Ann Arbor, 1931.

Waterman, Leroy. *Second Preliminary Report upon the Excavations at Tel Umar, Iraq.* Ann Arbor, 1931.

SUSAN B. DOWNEY

SELEUCIDS. The Seleucid kingdom was founded by Seleucus Nicator (Gk., Seleukos Nikator), a general of Alexander the Great. Seleucus was allotted part of the territories that had been under Alexander's control and then partitioned. In 305 BCE, Seleucus I was crowned king of the Seleucid Empire. He founded a dynasty that was to become very powerful in the eastern Mediterranean, ruling over the largest kingdom in the ancient Near East for most of the Hellenistic period.

Whereas the Seleucid Empire was heterogeneous in its ethnic makeup, its Greek cities were populated mainly by their Greek colonizers, who preserved their Greek way of life. The Greek stratum coexisted with the various *ethnē* ("indigenous peoples"), who continued to worship their local gods, kept their traditional languages, and maintained other specifically ethnic traits. Local coinage, for instance, was minted under the auspices of the Seleucid kings, but it expressed a great deal of the native heritage, as may be seen in local coins from Tyre and Sidon. Between Greeks and natives, a stratum of hellenists emerged. These people were syncretistic in all aspects of life.

During most of the Hellenistic era, the Seleucids competed with the Ptolemies of Egypt, especially over Coele-Syria. The two powers fought five wars between the end of the fourth and the third centuries BCE for the domination of Palestine, the so-called Syrian Wars. Toward the end of the third century, the Seleucids, as well as other powers in the

Near East, became more and more preoccupied with Rome, which had begun to intervene in the region's affairs.

In 204/203 BCE, Antiochus III, one of the great Seleucid kings, made a pact with Philip V of Macedon to divide Egyptian possessions overseas between them. This evinced a Roman reaction that resulted in the Second Macedonian War, which ended in a Macedonian defeat in 197 BCE. Rome subsequently defeated the Seleucids. Antiochus III invaded Greece but was defeated at Magnesia in 189 BCE. The treaty of Apamea, which marked the end of that war, and that ceded most of Asia Minor west of the Taurus mountains to Rome, signified a deeper involvement by the Romans in the affairs of the East. The defeat also signified the beginning of the decline of the Seleucid Empire.

In 200 BCE, the Seleucids, under Antiochus III, managed to take Palestine from the Ptolemies in the battle at Panion. As a result, many concessions were granted to the Jews in Jerusalem, which led essentially to comprehensive religious autonomy. During the reign of Seleucus IV (c. 187–175 BCE), relations between the Seleucids and the Jews in Jerusalem worsened. This occurred primarily because the Hellenistic high priests of Jerusalem convinced the Seleucids that the Jews should be hellenized. Severe restrictions on the religious autonomy of the Jews followed, initiated by Antiochus IV Epiphanes in 167 BCE. The result was a revolt by the indigenous Jewish population against the Seleucids. By 170–169 BCE, Antiochus IV aspired to conquer Egypt, but during his second invasion he was forced by a Roman ultimatum to return to Syria. Antiochus IV died in 164 BCE, and his young son, Antiochus V, was subsequently murdered, in 162, in the midst of terrible intrigues at the Seleucid court.

In 162 BCE, Demetrius, the son of Seleucus IV, escaped from Rome, where he had been kept as a hostage, and crowned himself Demetrius I, king of the Seleucid Empire. Many struggles ensued, and he was finally killed in 150 BCE by another claimant to the Seleucid throne, Alexander Balas, who claimed to be the son of Antiochus IV. These struggles further weakened the Seleucid kingdom. Rome threw its support to Egypt and Alexander Balas in their struggle against Demetrius I's son, Demetrius II. The Jews in Palestine profited from these developments and, with the support of Rome, the Ptolemies, and Pergamon, succeeded in 143/42 BCE in declaring their independence from the Seleucids.

The last impressive figure in the Seleucid court was Antiochus VII Sidetes, son of Demetrius I. In one attempt to renew the grandeur of the Seleucid Empire, he invaded Palestine, in 134 BCE. After laying siege to Jerusalem, he left, however, in 130, to fight the more important Parthians in the East.

Like most Hellenistic monarchs and princes, the Seleucids were tolerant of the indigenous cultures in lands they conquered and usually did not interfere in native cultures and religions. When they did, the result was disastrous (e.g., the Maccabean revolt). During the Seleucid period, there is evidence for the continuity of local religions and of writing in Neo-Babylonian as well as in Aramaic and Hebrew and other Eastern languages. The Seleucids also supported their Greek population and encouraged the foundation of Greek cities throughout their realm. One such example was the founding of their new capital, Seleucia, on the Tigris River, which they erected just 37 km (60 mi.) from the old traditional capital, Babylon. For the Greek population, the Seleucids posed as Greek deities, while for the natives they were local gods. The Seleucids supported literary activities that praised and legitimized their own deeds through a reinterpretation of the past. Authors like Megasthenes and Berossus flourished in the cultural centers of the Seleucid kingdom. Berossus's *Babyloniaca,* apparently written at the beginning of the third century BCE, is a typical Seleucid interpretation of Babylonian history.

Seleucid administration was based on the old Persian division into satrapies. The chief administrator of the satrapy was a *stratēgos* (at first called a satrap). The *stratēgoi* were at times also "high priests" (cf. the Hefzibah inscription from 199/98 BCE). This gave them authority over the temples and priesthoods in their domains. There are cases of a local leader being placed at the head of the satrapy. The *stratēgos* was assisted by an *oikonomos,* who was responsible for the satrapy's financial activities and for the king's property.

The Seleucid king was the head of state and was assisted by a council of *philoi* ("friends"). The highest offical was the *epi tōn pragmatōn,* who was assisted by the *dioiketes,* a financial administrator. The latter function could be found in both the central and local governments. An *oikonomos* at the court was responsible for the king's treasury. Instead of the *oikonomos,* we later find a magistrate called *epi tōn prosodōn* (the one responsible for the income of the king). The Seleucids usually chose their *philoi* and other administrators from among the Greek (i.e., Macedonian) stratum of society. Because the Seleucid Empire was so vast, the Seleucids had, in addition to their new capital in Seleucia on the Tigris, other centers, such as Antioch on Orontes and Sardis.

The end of the Seleucid kingdom came with Rome's conquest of the East in the 60s BCE.

[*See also* Antioch on Orontes; Ptolomies; Sardis; *and* Seleucia on the Tigris.]

BIBLIOGRAPHY

Astin, A. E., et al., eds. *The Cambridge Ancient History,* vol. 7.1, *The Hellenistic World;* vol. 7.2, *The Rise of Rome to 220 B.C.;* vol. 8, *Rome and the Mediterranean to 133 B.C.* 2d ed. Cambridge, 1989.

Bilde, Per, et al., eds. *Religion and Religious Practice in the Seleucid Kingdom.* Aarhus, 1990.

Kuhrt, Amélie, and Susan Sherwin-White, eds. *Hellenism in the East.* Berkeley, 1987.

Sherwin-White, Susan, and Amélie Kuhrt. *From Samarkhand to Sardis.* London, 1993.

DORON MENDELS

SELLIN, ERNST (1867–1946), German scholar of Old Testament studies and biblical archaeologist. Born in Altschwerin, Mecklenburg, Sellin studied Protestant theology and then worked as a high school teacher in Parchim, a city close to his birthplace, from 1892 until 1894. After qualifying as a lecturer in 1894, he taught Old Testament in Erlangen. He was appointed an associate professor of Old Testament in Vienna in 1897 and became a full professor there in 1899. Between 1908 and 1921, he held chairs in Rostock, Kiel, and finally in Berlin, his last post until he retired in 1935. He died in Epichnellen near Eisenach.

Sellin published numerous works on topics relating to the religion of ancient Israel (1896–1897), on *Job* (1919) and on "Second Isaiah" (1908). He also wrote monographs on Zerubbabel (1898), Gilgal (1917), Shechem (1922), and Moses (1922), a commentary on the minor prophets (1922), and a two-volume history of Israel (1924 and 1932). His most famous work is an introduction to Old Testament literature *(Einleitung in das Alte Testament),* which saw many editions after its first appearance in 1910. This handbook was later republished by L. Rost (1959) and G. Fohrer (1965).

The only scholar of Old Testament studies of his generation to do fieldwork in biblical archaeology, Sellin directed the German excavations at Taʿanach (1901–1904) and at Jericho (1907–1909). In 1913–1914 he worked at Shechem, to which he returned in 1926–1927 and 1934. His work there was interrupted not only by World War I but also by an intrigue against him and was eventually halted because of the political situation in Germany. While his first excavations were well published for the standards of the time, the results of the Shechem project were never properly presented: the manuscript of the final publication was burned in an allied air raid over Berlin in fall 1943. Sellin's preliminary reports on Shechem in the *Zeitschrift des Deutschen Palästina-Vereins* between 1926 and 1941 are, however, of great value. His fieldwork and his publications made Sellin the leading German scholar in the field of biblical archaeology in the first half of the twentieth century.

[*See also* Jericho; Shechem; *and* Taʿanach.]

BIBLIOGRAPHY

Writings by Sellin

Beiträge zur israelitischen und jüdischen Religionsgeschichte. Leipzig, 1896–1897.

Serubbabel: Ein Beitrag zur Geschichte der messianischen Erwartung und der Entstehung des Judentums. Leipzig, 1898.

Tell Taʿannek. Vienna, 1904.

Das Rätsel des Deuterojesajanischen Buches. Leipzig, 1908.

Einleitung in das Alte Testament. Leipzig, 1910.

Jericho: Die Ergebnisse der Ausgrabungen (with Carl Watzinger). Leipzig, 1913.

Gilgal: Ein Beitrag zur Geschichte der Einwanderung Israels in Palästina. Leipzig, 1917.

Das Problem des Hiobbuches. Leipzig, 1919.

Mose und seine Bedeutung für die israelitisch-jüdische Religionsgeschichte. Leipzig, 1922.

Wie wurde Sichem eine israelitische Stadt. Leipzig, 1922.

Das Zwölfprophetenbuch. Leipzig, 1922.

Geschichte des israelitisch-jüdischen Volkes. 2 vols. Leipzig, 1924–1932.

"Die Ausgrabung von Sichem." *Zeitschrift des Deutschen Palästina-Vereins* 49 (1926): 229–236, 304–320; 50 (1927): 205–211, 265–274.

"Die Masseben des El-Berit in Sichem." *Zeitschrift des Deutschen Palästina-Vereins* 51 (1928): 119–123.

"Drei um strittene Stellen des Amosbuches." *Zeitschrift des Deutschen Palästina-Vereins* 52 (1929): 141–148.

"Zur Lage von Ezion-Geber." *Zeitschrift des Deutschen Palästina-Vereins* 59 (1936): 123–128.

"Kurzer vorläufiger Bericht über die Ausgrabungen in *balāṭa* (Sichem) im Herbst 1934." *Zeitschrift des Deutschen Palästina-Vereins* 64 (1941): 1–20.

"Die palästinischen Krughenkel mit den Königsstempeln." *Zeitschrift des Deutschen Palästina-Vereins* 66 (1943): 216–232.

"Zu dem Goldschmuckfund von Sichem." *Zeitschrift des Deutschen Palästina-Vereins* 66 (1943): 20–24.

Volkmar Fritz

SEMITIC LANGUAGES. Since at least the fourth millennium BCE, the Semitic languages, which constitute a relatively close-knit linguistic family, have occupied core areas of western Asia (Mesopotamia, Syria, Palestine, and the Arabian Peninsula). They extended their presence at some point into coastal and highland Ethiopia and, more recently, into substantial parts of northern Africa. As is becoming increasingly evident, the Semitic language family in turn is related to a much more widespread, highly differentiated Afro-Asiatic superfamily whose members, beside Semitic, are Egyptian (the Nile valley, from the Delta to the first cataract); Berber (North Africa, from Libya to Morocco, and, at least since the domestication of the camel, south into the deep Sahara); Cushitic (more than fifty languages from the Red Sea hills and the Horn of Africa, down the Rift Valley into Tanzania); Omotic (several dozen languages in southwest Ethiopia, perhaps to be counted as Western Cushitic); and Chadic (Hausa in northern Nigeria and more than two hundred other languages roughly in the Lake Chad watershed).

The close resemblance of the Semitic languages is obvious on casual inspection of cognate lexical, phonological, and grammatical data. For lexical resemblance note, for example, the word for *dog* in Akkadian *kalbum,* Hebrew *keleb,* Aramaic *kalbā,* Arabic *kalbun,* and Geʿez (Ethiopic) *kalb*—to give just a sample. (For more detailed phonological and grammatical resemblances, see below.) It had long been speculated (since the Jewish grammarians of the Middle Ages at least) that the special resemblances such as exist among the Semitic languages could only be explained as the result of a long process of historical development, whereby an ancestral speech community gradually broke up into communities with similar, but increasingly distinct languages. Lexical evidence for the relatedness of Afro-Asiatic is much sparser, but over the last century there has been a slow accumulation of cognates, such as the word for "die": Akkadian *mūt-*, Egyptian *m(w)t,* Berber *əmmət,* Hausa *mutu.* Even more striking have been a number of grammatical correspondences. Compare, for example, with the Akkadian pronouns given in table 6 below, the following pronominal forms of Cushitic Oromo: *ani* "I," *ati* "you" (sg.), *isa* "him," *isee* "her," *nu* "we," *isin* "you" (pl.), *isaani* "they."

Semitic languages already hold a unique position in their own right within the study of language evolution because their early development, differentiation, and often palimpsestlike diffusion pattern (one Semitic language frequently replaced an earlier member of the same family) coincided in period and area with the elaboration of the earliest writing systems. As a result, the Semitic languages offer a unique record of textual attestation of the process of language diversification. Beyond this—on the level of Afro-Asiatic—Egyptian, although it remains relatively uniform at any given period, has a history of written attestation that goes back at least as far as that of Semitic. The other Afro-Asiatic languages are attested only in modern times, but their differentiation and spread guarantee a time depth that places Semitic into a perspective of recorded and reconstructable history stretching far back into the Near Eastern and East African Neolithic.

This survey will offer first a broad overview of the temporal and geographic distribution of the historically attested Semitic languages. It will then characterize in outline form some of the major phonological and grammatical features of Semitic. Finally, one possible scenario, or model, will be sketched for the family's origin, initial differentiation, and spread.

The Evidence. A mass of material widely distributed geographically and chronologically over the ancient and modern Near East provides the evidence for the evolution and diversification of the Semitic language family. The main clusters follow.

Akkadian. Texts in Akkadian are abundantly attested in Mesopotamia and peripheral regions from the mid-third millennium onward. They are written on thousands of clay tablets in the cuneiform logographic-syllabic system the speakers of Old Akkadian adapted from the Sumerians. Even before the first real Akkadian texts, Akkadian proper names and Akkadian loanwords in early Sumerian texts show that Akkadians were present in Mesopotamia almost from the beginnings of Sumerian writing early in the third millennium. Akkadian in its Northern and Southern dialect forms, Assyrian and Babylonian, continued as a living, evolving language (through stages conventionally schematized as Old, Middle, and Neo-) down into the first millennium BCE. In the second millennium BCE, Akkadian was widely used throughout western Asia as an international language of scholarship and correspondence. In the course of the first millennium BCE, Akkadian was gradually replaced by Aramaic as a spoken language, but some texts continued to be written in Akkadian into the first century CE. [*See* Akkadian.]

Eblaite. A couple of centuries after the first Old Akkadian texts in Mesopotamia, for a period of about two centuries, another Semitic language used a related, but distinct adaptation of the cuneiform writing system in the northern Syrian city of Ebla. Although most of the many tablets recently discovered at this site are in Sumerian, a variety of text genres are written in the local language, which is Semitic and certainly not identical with any known variety of Akkadian. A better understanding of the language will be necessary to determine exactly its genetic relationship to Akkadian. [*See* Ebla Texts.]

Amorite. No texts are preserved in Amorite, a variety of Semitic. Its existence is inferred from a large, recognizably distinct corpus of proper names in texts (about six thousand) that are otherwise Akkadian or Sumerian, from the late third through the first half of the second millennium. Appearing first as foreigners, bearers of these names come to represent a widespread, stable segment of the population in Akkadian-using Mesopotamia and Syria. Indeed, several ruling dynasties in the Mesopotamian heartland in the early second millennium BCE, including that of Hammurabi, bear names of this kind. Because the bearers of these names, when they are ethnically identified, are sometimes referred to as Sumerian *mar-tu* (Akk., *amurru,* "westerners"), the language (or group of languages) represented by these names is called generically Amorite (from the related biblical term). [*See* Amorites.]

Old Canaanite. The label Old Canaanite is used here as a cover term for a heterogeneous set of materials yielding evidence for the linguistic situation in Palestine, for the most part in the second and third quarters of the second millennium BCE. Linguistically, some of this material may overlap with what is referred to above as Amorite. Most of the material is scattered through Akkadian and, to a lesser extent, Egyptian texts originating in or referring to the Syro-Palestinian area. It takes the form of personal names, place names, glosses, loanwords, morphological forms, and syntactic calques. The most important corpus of Akkadian texts, preserved at el-Amarna in Egypt, is the archive of mid-second millennium diplomatic correspondence with the Egyptian court from local rulers in Syria-Palestine. To be assigned provisionally to this group also are the earliest alphabetic inscriptions, approximately contemporary with the Akkadian and Egyptian texts just mentioned and only partially interpretable, found in Palestine and in the Sinai Desert. [*See* Amarna Tablets; Canaanites; Proto-Canaanite; *and* Proto-Sinaitic.]

Ugaritic. The North Syrian site of Ras-Shamra has yielded a corpus of more than a thousand texts, dating from just after the middle of the second millennium BCE and written in a locally developed writing system that is cuneiform in shape but genuinely alphabetic in design and function. Given the uncertainties surrounding Eblaite, and the very sketchy nature of the Amorite and Old Canaanite material, Ugaritic gives the first clear view of a Western Semitic language. The relationship of Ugaritic to Canaanite proper has been intensively discussed but cannot be considered settled. [*See* Ugaritic; Ugarit Inscriptions.]

Hebrew. The main evidence for Hebrew here is of course the text of the Hebrew Bible, to which can be added a small corpus of epigraphic materials in Hebrew and some limited inscriptional materials in the closely related Moabite, Ammonite, and Edomite languages. Together with Phoenician, these languages are the linguistic continuation of Old Canaanite. Even after the homogenization of the text by later editors, the Hebrew Bible shows a succession of stages of development of Palestinian Semitic from the very end of the second millennium up to the last centuries of the first millennium. By the time of the latest biblical Hebrew texts, Hebrew had already been, for a century or more, in the process of being replaced as a spoken language in Palestine by Aramaic—a process that had surely gone to completion by the beginning of the second century CE. A standardized form of a final stage of Hebrew remained as a liturgical and scholastic language through Late Antiquity, the Middle Ages, and on into modern times. Finally, in a unique development in language history, Hebrew, revived for general use in the nineteenth century, has once more entered the list of spoken languages—with all the unforeseeable linguistic results that that entails. [*See* Hebrew Language and Literature.]

Phoenician. Because of the abundance and widespread distribution of its inscriptions and the influence of its writing system, special notice must be taken of a close northern relative of Hebrew. Phoenician began to be attested in what is now coastal Lebanon late in the second millennium BCE and continued there and in various Mediterranean sites until Roman times. Punic is a variety of Phoenician attested in inscriptions from the North African colony of Carthage from its founding in the fifth century BCE to its destruction by Rome in the second century BCE. Punic continued to be written in various locations in North Africa up until the fifth century CE. [*See* Phoenician-Punic.]

Old/Official Aramaic. A very large number of closely related languages is grouped under the heading of Aramaic. The group's literary and epigraphic output constitutes, after Arabic, the largest corpus of writing in Semitic. Old Aramaic inscriptions are first attested in North Syria and Mesopotamia in the ninth century BCE, and the beginning of a gradual aramaicization of Mesopotamia, Syria, and Palestine can be dated from this period. A standardized form of Aramaic became an official language of the Persian Empire and was used for written communication all over the Near East—including parts of some late additions to the Hebrew Bible *(Ezra).*

Middle Aramaic. During the Seleucid and Roman periods, Aramaic continued to be used for inscriptional purposes in a number of localities, including some where the language and ethnic affiliation of the local population was probably Northern Arabic (Nabatean, Palmyrene). A corpus of religious literature in Aramaic continued to be developed in Palestine: Bible translations (targums) and the Aramaic texts from Qumran. [*See* Nabatean Inscriptions; Palmyrene Inscriptions; Qumran.]

Late Aramaic. Apart from the evidence of the continued use of Aramaic in Mesopotamia ("magic bowls," texts of the Gnostic baptist sect of the Mandaeans [*see* Mandaic]), the period from the third to the seventh centuries CE saw a massive development of religious writing in Western and Eastern varieties of Aramaic, first in a Jewish milieu (the Palestinian and Babylonian Talmuds and related writings), and then in a Christian one (Christian Palestinian and, especially, Syriac literature). Although Aramaic remained a spoken language in some of these communities after the seventh century, a standard form of Late Aramaic continued a more general existence in its own right in Christian and Jewish contexts as a language of liturgy and religious scholarship, much as was the case for Hebrew.

Neo-Aramaic. Although Aramaic was gradually replaced by Arabic throughout much of its former territory, in those areas where the dominant Islamic groups were Kurdish speaking (in what is now northwestern Iran, northern Iraq, and southeastern Turkey), Aramaic was often retained as the primary spoken language by urban and village Jewish and Christian communities. In addition, a couple of mountain villages not far from Damascus, Syria, also retained a unique Western form of Neo-Aramaic. From the point of view of morphology and syntax, the Neo-Aramaic dialects have to be counted as the most thoroughly transformed Semitic languages ever attested—more so, for example, than any modern Ethiopian Semitic language. It can be shown, however, that many, if not most, of the deviations from the Semitic "norm" are continuations of tendencies observable in some of the earliest forms of Aramaic. [*See* Aramaic Language and Literature.]

Old Northern Arabic. Thousands of short graffiti written in a Southern variant of the general ancestral West Semitic alphabet have been found scattered over the Syrian and, especially, northern Arabian desert, generally dated between the sixth century BCE and the fourth century CE. Frequently little more than apersonal name or pronoun and a nominal or verbal predicate, they are sufficient to show that these are the earliest attestation of what was to become Classical Arabic. The most general type of the script is called Thamudic and was probably used to write a variety of dialects. Special local varieties, Dedanite and Lihyanite, arose in the Hijaz oasis of al-ʿUla. A subtype of Old Northern Arabic inscription known as Safaitic is especially abundant in the southern Syrian desert in the latter half of this period. [*See* Safaitic-Thamudic Inscriptions; Dedan.]

Classical Arabic. A few inscriptions from the fourth century BCE in a modified Nabatean Aramaic script, plus a body of oral poetry that had its origins in the same period are the precursors of Classical Arabic, which received its definitive form in the seventh century CE in the Qur'an. A written standard, purged of some of the more marked dialect forms of the Qur'an, was quickly elaborated, codified by grammarians and lexicographers, and spread as the official medium of communication of the new Arabic-Islamic administrative structures. This written standard, which has produced a voluminous literature over the centuries, remains the official language of literacy, public life, literate oral communication, and mass media in the Arabic-speaking world up to the present day.

Modern Arabic. Spoken Arabic continued developing alongside the standard languages, in a well-studied relationship called diglossia. Certain phonological, morphological, and syntactic simplifications and/or innovations are common to many varieties of Modern Arabic, but there has been enough differentiation that mutual intelligibility between spoken varieties at the geographic extremes can be quite limited. There are glimpses of these changes in process in some medieval texts (sometimes referred to as Middle Arabic), especially those coming from Christian and Jewish Arabic-speaking milieus less constrained by the norms of the Classical standard. [*See* Arabic.]

Old South Arabian. A large body of monumental texts from what is now Yemen reveals a subfamily of Semitic completely distinct from anything considered up to now. Written in an elegant monumental development of the South Semitic alphabet that also appears in Old North Arabic, the oldest inscriptions may be as early as the first third of the first millennium BCE. They testify to the political power and cultural achievements of the city-states along the spice route from south to north between the Yemeni highlands and the Arabian desert. There are marked differences between the languages (or dialects—it is difficult to tell) of the principal city-states: Maʿin, Saba', Qataban, Ḥadhramaut. The inscriptions continue into the sixth century CE, by which time Yemen had been politically unified, the center of power had moved to the highlands, and the Sabaean variety of Old South Arabian (perhaps no longer a spoken language) had replaced other varieties. [*See* South Arabian; Qataban; Ḥadhramaut.]

Modern South Arabian. After a thirteen-hundred-year hiatus barely touched upon by scattered notices in Arab geographers, historians, and lexicographers, nineteenth-century travelers and scholars discovered in the southern extremity of the Arabian Peninsula (eastern Yemen, western Oman, and some offshore islands) a half-dozen languages and dialects of the South Arabian type. The most important languages are Mehri (with the dialect Harsusi), Jibbali, and Soqotri—together they have fewer than one hundred thousand speakers. Although they are clearly closely related to Old South Arabian (as well as to Ethiopian Semitic), it is not certain that the Modern South Arabian languages are linear descendants of any member of the older group. Reliable lexical and grammatical information about these languages is only now becoming available, and much work needs to be done before the historical development behind them becomes clear.

Classical Ethiopic (Geʿez). Old South Arabian inscriptions of the Sabaean type found in Ethiopia and dating from the fifth-century BCE trading colony show that there was a long-standing cultural and economic relationship between southern Arabia and Ethiopia. Accordingly, it is not surprising to find in the Ethiopian highlands fourth-century CE inscriptions in a new variety of Semitic—written in a South Semitic script that seems in some respects closer to that of the Thamudic graffiti than the Old South Arabian monumental inscriptions. Like Modern South Arabian, Ethiopic (native designation, *gəʕəz,* "Geʿez") is related to, but not derivable from, any known variety of Old South Arabian. Shortly after the first unvocalized inscriptions, a unique system of vocalization was introduced, and at the same time the Ethiopian court was converted to Christianity. A standard literary language was elaborated in the next couple of centuries (e.g., with a Bible translation, liturgical texts, and patristic excerpts); this language remains the official church and court language and was the only written language well up into the nineteenth century.

Modern Ethiopic Semitic. The members of the group of Modern Semitic language—about a dozen, of them—differ at least as much from one another as do the members of the Romance family of languages. Two of these languages constitute a Northern group (Tigre and Tigrinya, one of the official languages of Eritrea); the rest form a fairly coherent Southern group (Amharic, until recently the only official language of Ethiopia, Harari, Gaffat, Argobba; and a cluster of languages and dialects referred to as Gurage). Of all these languages, only Tigrinya can be plausibly derived from Geʿez, which thus cannot be identified with Proto-Ethiopic Semitic. [*See* Ethiopic.]

The very approximate time chart in figure 1 gives a rough summary of the distribution in time of attestation of the major languages or groups of languages of the Semitic family. Figure 1 of course does not try to fix the point in time at which different varieties of Semitic come into existence, but only the period over which actual texts attest to the existence of a language or group of languages. In addition, the chart tries to delimit for some languages two additional types, or stages, of attestation. In a preliminary type of attestation (light stipple in figure 1) even though there is not a usable

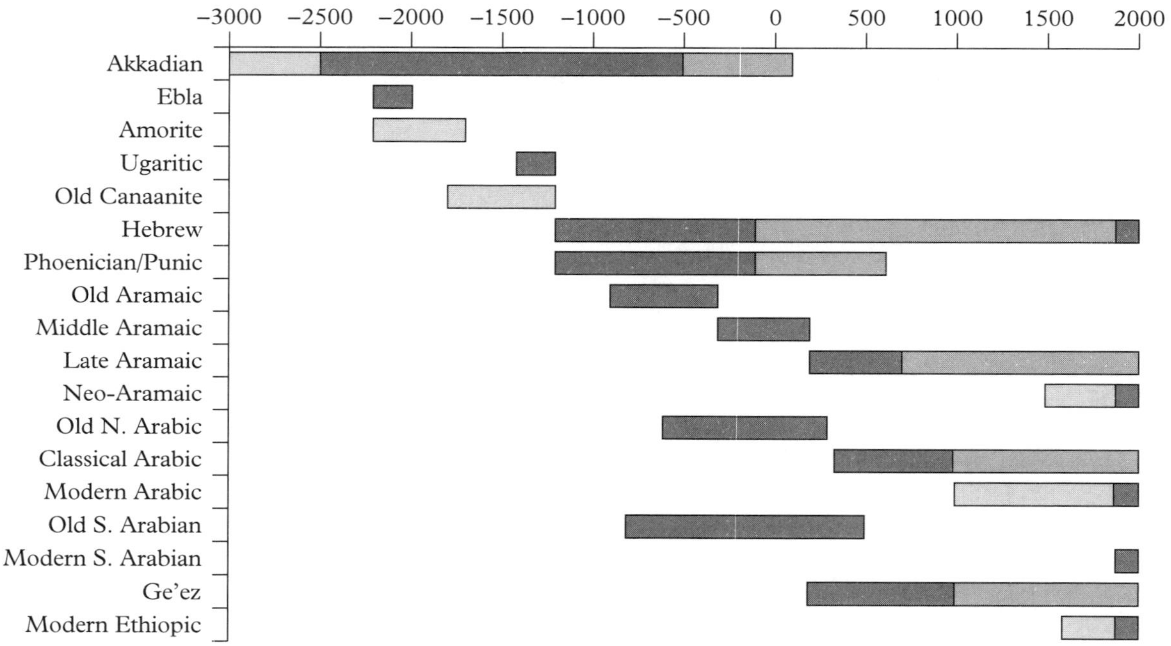

SEMITIC LANGUAGES. Figure 1. *Chronological distribution of the Semitic languages.*

corpus of texts, there may still be evidence for the existence of the speech community in the form of personal names, references to the language or the ethnic group that speaks it in texts in other languages, and even sporadic and isolated attempts to write the language.

In addition, as a kind of postexistence, it can be useful to distinguish a period when the language in question was superceded as a living, spoken language by other languages but continued to be understood in a community, and perhaps used as a (or even the only) medium of written communication to generate new texts (dark stipple in figure 1). It is of course difficult or impossible to determine at what point a community's spoken language no longer corresponds to the written language: by definition there is no written attestation of the former—thus, the location of the point of transition in figure 1 is somewhat arbitrary. Given the nature of written language, it is probable that a certain gap between written and spoken varieties of a language develops early on in most speech communities. In any case, there is clear evidence that in the absence of a relatively sudden replacement or notable transformation of the vernacular, the gap can become very wide indeed before speakers are willing or able to perceive a traditional vehicle of written communication as "not the same language as" the spoken one (cf. Latin in European Romania, Greek in Byzantium, or Arabic in the Near East).

Phonological and Grammatical Features. Comparative Semitic linguistics has been engaged for more than a century in the twin tasks of gathering data about the range of phonological, lexical, and grammatical phenomena in the attested Semitic languages and inferring from this evidence the corresponding features of Proto-Semitic, the language of the parent Semitic speech community.

Phonological features. In the realm of phonology, the relevant primary data are cognate sets—that is, sets of lexical items whose resemblance in meaning and form is of such a kind that it is highly unlikely that it could have arisen either by chance or by borrowing; the sets are much more likely to represent material inherited from an ancestral speech community. (Historical linguistics can only deal with probabilistic judgments, although this probability can sometimes be very high.) Finding such cognate sets in Semitic is a much simpler process than in many other domains of historical linguistics, given the relatively close relationships of the member languages. One such particularly obvious set is the one already alluded to: Akkadian *kalbum* "dog," Hebrew *keleb* "dog," Aramaic *kalbā* "dog," Arabic *kalbun* "dog," and Geʿez *kalb* "dog." From the pattern of occurrence of phonemes in this and interlocking cognate sets like the Arabic *kullun* = Hebrew *kōl* "all," or the Akkadian *libbum* and Geʿez *ləbb* "heart," general correspondence sets can be inferred: Akkadian /k/ = Hebrew /k/ = Aramaic /k/ = Arabic /k/ = Geʿez /k/, Akkadian /l/ = Hebrew /l/ = Aramaic /l/ = Arabic /l/ = Geʿez /l/, Akkadian /b/ = Hebrew /b/ = Aramaic /b/ = Arabic /b/ = Geʿez /b/, Akkadian /a/ = Hebrew /e/ = Aramaic /a/ = Arabic /a/ = Geʿez /a/. The cognate sets and correspondence sets together then permit a number of conclusions: that Proto-Semitic had the four phonemes /*k/, /*l/, /*b/ /*a/; that Proto-Semitic had the stems **kalb-*, "dog"; **kull-* "all," **libb-* "heart," and so forth. (The asterisk

TABLE 1. *Stop Consonants of Semitic*

	Akk.	Ugr.	Heb.	Syr.	Ar.	OSA	Jib.	Gez.	PSem.
Labial	p	p	p	p	f	f	f	f	*p
	b	b	b	b	b	b	b	b	*b
Alveolar	t	t	t	t	t	t	t	t	*t
	d	d	d	d	d	d	d	d	*d
	ṭ	ṭ	ṭ	ṭ	ṭ	ṭ	ṭ	ṭ	*ṭ
Velar	k	k	k	k	k	k	k	k	*k
	g	g	g	g	g	g	g	g	*g
	q	q	q	q	q	q	q	q	*q

means that the form is not directly attested but is reconstructed.)

Of course not all correspondence sets are identity sets like the consonantal ones just used. Without going through the cognate sets that justify them, tables 1–4 give the major correspondence sets defining the Proto-Semitic (PSem) consonant system, using the languages Akkadian (Akk.), Ugaritic (Ugr.), Hebrew (Heb.), Syriac (Syr.), Arabic (Ar.), Old South Arabian (OSA), Jibbali (Jib., Modern South Arabian), and Geʿez (Gez.).

The stop consonants are given in table 1, in the order voiceless, voiced, and emphatic. The latter feature is realized as pharyngealized in Arabic (i.e., produced with a simultaneous constriction of the throat in the velar-pharynx region), but glottalized in Modern South Arabian and Ethiopian Semitic (i.e., produced with a coarticulated glottal stop)—for the other pronunciation traditions the situation is not certain. Scholars are increasingly of the opinion that pharyngealization is a special development in Arabic, and that the general Semitic pronunciation of emphatics was with glottalization. With the exception of the voiceless labial, the correspondence sets are of the identity kind, and the reconstruction in Proto-Semitic poses no problems. It is noteworthy that a "southern tier" of languages has /f/ in place of the more northern /p/. The sonorants (see table 2) give an equally homogeneous and unproblematic picture. Here note that Ugaritic, Hebrew and other Canaanite languages, and Aramaic (and also Amorite) have /y/ in the initial position where the other languages have /w/—a feature sometimes adduced as a Northwest Semitic isogloss (a shared feature among a group of languages).

TABLE 2. *Sonorants of Semitic*

	Akk.	Ugr.	Heb.	Syr.	Arb.	OSA	Jib.	Gez.	PSem.
Nasal	m	m	m	m	m	m	m	m	*m
	n	n	n	n	n	n	n	n	*n
Liquid	l	l	l	l	l	l	l	l	*l
	r	r	r	r	r	r	r	r	*r
Glide	w	y, w	y, w	y, w	w	w	w	w	*w
	y	y	y	y	y	y	y	y	*y

On the other hand, the situation becomes much more complex with the spirants—a part of the phonology where the Semitic languages show a larger number of distinctions than is common in the world's languages. As can be seen from table 3, there is also evidence of a great deal of divergent and independent phonological change. Parenthesized symbols in quotes in table 3 indicate that a language's orthography has a distinct symbol for a segment (and, hence, presumably had a distinct phoneme at one point) whose pronunciation has since merged with that of another segment; "s^1", "s^2", and "s^3" are the conventional transcription symbols for the "s-like" phonemes of Old South Arabian (the superscripts correspond roughly to order of frequency); "θ" and "δ" are like "th" in the English "thin" and "then," respectively; "ɬ" is a voiceless [l]. Note that because of the interlocking correspondence sets, even without the Southern Arabian material the reconstruction of nine Proto-Semitic spirants would be obligatory, even though no one language makes more than eight distinctions (Ugaritic, Syriac, and Arabic—versus five for Geʿez and Hebrew and four for Akkadian). However, all nine distinctions are present in the most conservative branch of Semitic, Southern Arabian—graphically in Old South Arabian and pronounced in Middle South Arabian. With some reservations the pronunciation of one variety of Middle South Arabian is assigned to Proto-Semitic. It is beginning to look increasingly possible, however, that the pronunciation of the segment noted /*š/, far and away the most common of the "s" sounds, might in fact have been [s] (as in Arabic), and the series noted /*s *z *ṣ/ might be the affricates [ts dz tsʕ].

Semitic languages tend also to have an unusually large inventory of consonantal distinctions in the postvelar or laryngeal region. The most plausible reconstruction assigns to Proto-Semitic the same set of laryngeals as in Ugaritic, Arabic, Old South Arabian, and Middle South Arabian (see table 4). Noteworthy here is the almost complete disappearance of these characteristically "Semitic" consonants in Akkadian—presumably the result of language contact with laryngeal-poor Sumerian (the same phenomenon can be ob-

TABLE 3. *Spirants of Semitic*

	Akk.	Ugr.	Heb.	Syr.	Ar.	OSA	Jib.	Gez.	PSem.
Dental	š	θ	š	t	θ	θ	θ	s	*θ
	z	δ	z	d	δ	δ	δ	z	*δ
	ṣ	θ̣	ṣ	ṭ	ẓ	θ̣	θ̣	ṣ	*θ̣
Alveolar	s	s	s	s	s	s^3	s	s	*$s^?$
	z	z	z	z	z	z	z	z	*$z^?$
	ṣ	ṣ	ṣ	ṣ	ṣ	ṣ	ṣ	ṣ	*ṣ$^?$
Palatal$^?$	š	š	š	š	s	s^1	š	s	*š$^?$
Lateral	š	š	s("ś")	s	š	s^2	ɬ	s("š")	*ɬ
	ṣ	ṣ	ṣ	ʕ	ḍ	ḍ	ɬ̣	ṣ("ḍ")	*ɬ̣

TABLE 4. *Laryngeals of Semitic*

	Akk.	Ugr.	Heb.	Syr.	Ar.	OSA	Jib.	Gez.	PSem.
velar/	ḫ	ḫ	ḥ	ḥ	ḫ	ḫ	ḫ	ḥ("ḫ")	*ḫ
uvular	∅	γ	ʕ	ʕ	γ	γ	γ	ʕ	*γ
pharyngeal	∅	ḥ	ḥ	ḥ	ḥ	ḥ	ḥ	ḥ	*ḥ
	∅	ʕ	ʕ	ʕ	ʕ	ʕ	ʕ	ʕ	*ʕ
glottal	∅	h	h	h	h	h	h	h	*h
	∅	ʔ	ʔ	ʔ	ʔ	ʔ	ʔ	ʔ	*ʔ

served in other Semitic languages in situations of language contact, such as Amharic within Ethiopic).

Of the writing systems used to represent Semitic languages, only those used for Akkadian and Ethiopic have a built-in system of vowel representation. For the others, vowel representation is either virtually nonexistent (Old South Arabian, Phoenician), relatively limited (Ugaritic), optional (the other Western Semitic writing systems), or relatively recent (almost a thousand years lapse between the demise of Hebrew as a spoken language and the fixing of the standard Masoretic vowel notation). Although there is much that is not known about the history of the vowel systems in some individual branches, the Proto-Semitic vowel system from which the attested systems derive seems to have been the following rather simple one:

i u ī ū

a ā

with three long and three short vowels, plus diphthongs /ay, aw/. This vowel system is preserved virtually intact in Classical Arabic, and with only slight modification in Akkadian. Where it interacts with stress and syllabic structure, as in Hebrew, Aramaic, and Modern South Arabian, the result can be a relatively complex vowel system and set of vocalic alternations.

No detailed history of the phonological development of the Semitic languages is possible without taking into account a good deal of additional evidence. However, an important general conclusion can already be pointed out on the basis of the data in tables 1–4. Although there is a large number of parallel developments (/θ/ ends up as /š/ in both Akkadian and Hebrew; /ḥ ḫ/ end up merging in Canaanite, Aramaic, and Ethiopic; and /ɬ š/ merge in Akkadian, Arabic, and Ugaritic), the more evidence there is, the more it seems likely that each of the major branches of Semitic began its existence as a separate speech community with the Proto-Semitic phoneme inventory virtually intact. It seems that they developed toward their historically attested forms as distinct (but perhaps mutually interacting) entities. On the level of phonology, thus, very little content can be given to such traditional labels such as Northwest Semitic (for Canaanite and Aramaic) and South Semitic (for Arabic, South Arabian, and Ethiopic) as designations for hypothetical intermediate unified speech communities—however useful these terms may be for zones of greater mutual influence and interaction.

Grammatical features. In principle, grammatical features should cover both morphological and syntactic features. Comparative Semitic syntax, however, is an area of study that barely exists. Indeed, basic data collections can be hard to find even for the syntax of major stages of well-attested individual languages. Apart from an occasional discussion of so-called polarity switches in agreement patterns (e.g., the tendency for numerals agreeing with masculine nouns to have typically feminine morphology, and vice versa), the one topic regularly touched on in the literature is word order. The frequently repeated observation is that "verb, subject, object" seems to be the preferred sentence-level word order in the earliest stages of Semitic. The two major exceptions seem to confirm the rule: the "subject, object, verb" order of Akkadian and Modern Ethiopic Semitic can be attributed to substratum influences—Sumerian and Cushitic, respectively. Even in Akkadian, the oldest onomastic evidence suggests an earlier "verb, subject, object" stage. The Semitic languages are, however, characterized by a rich inflectional and derivational morphology, and a framework for comparative Semitic morphology has been steadily built up over the last century.

Noun. The inflectional categories of the noun are illustrated in table 5, which gives the nominal paradigms for the two languages with the best-preserved systems, Akkadian (*šarrum*/*šarratum* "king/queen") and Arabic (*ʕālim(at)un* "wise man/woman"). As for the other languages, the data on nominal inflection are obscured by the writing system, partially in Ugaritic and almost totally in Old South Arabian, whereas the system has undergone considerable simplification in Canaanite, Aramaic, Middle South Arabian, and Geʿez. As can be seen from the table, Semitic has two grammatical genders, with the feminine frequently marked by a suffix *-(a)t* (in addition to a number of less common ones). The core of the case system for Proto-Semitic seems clear: nominative **-u*; genitive **-i*; and accusative **-a* in the singular, and nominative **-u*, and oblique **-i/y* in the dual and plural. The Proto-Semitic status of some other cases marginally attested in some of the individual languages is less certain. In its fullest form Semitic distinguishes three number categories, although the dual, marked basically by *-ā*, either becomes reduced in scope (with fewer case distinctions and limited to a small number of nouns) or disappears altogether in the course of the history of each of the branches.

The basic mark of the plural in Semitic, when it is formed by suffixation, is a lengthening of the first suffix vowel (the

TABLE 5. *Akkadian and Arabic Noun Inflection*

	Akkadian			Arabic		
	Sg.	Du.	Pl.	Sg.	Du.	Pl.
Masc.						
Nom.	*šarrum*	*šarrān*	*šarrū*	*ʕālimun*	*ʕālimāni*	*ʕālimūna*
Gen.	*šarrim*	*šarrīn*	*šarrī*	*ʕalimin*	*ʕālimayni*	*ʕālimīna*
Acc.	*šarram*			*ʕāliman*		
Fem.						
Nom.	*šarratum*	*šarratān*	*šarrātum*	*ʕālimatun*	*ʕālimatāni*	*ʕālimātun*
Gen.	*šarratim*	*šarratīn*	*šarrātim*	*ʕālimatin*	*ʕālimatayni*	*ʕālimātin*
Acc.	*šarratam*			*ʕālimatan*		

case vowel *u* or *i* for masculines; the vowel of the feminine suffix *-at* for feminines). In Arabic (and probably Proto-Semitic) there is an added suffix, *-nV,* in the nonsingular, where V is high (/ni/) after a low vowel (/ā/) and low (/na/) after a high vowel (/ūī/). This suffix shows up as *-n* in the Akkadian dual, as *-n* in Aramaic and as *-m(V)* in Canaanite and Ugaritic. In addition to suffix plurals, Semitic could also form plurals by changing the vowel pattern of a noun (with or without additional affixes). This is an inflectional process abundantly attested in the Southern Semitic languages (Arabic *kilāb* and Geʿez *ʕakləbt* "dogs"), but also marginally in Hebrew, where it cooccurs with the usual plural suffix *-īm (klābīm).*

Lastly, the singular nouns of table 5 show also one final suffix that has the shape *-m* in Akkadian (also in Old South Arabian) and *-n* in Arabic. This suffix eventually disappears in all the branches—it is no longer present in Modern Arabic, Modern Southern Arabian, or the most recent dialects of Akkadian. Its function is not certain. It is not present, however, in Classical Arabic when the noun occurs with the definite article prefix *al-*, and it is not present in any language when a noun is followed by a "possessor" noun (i.e., a noun in the genitive, if the language has preserved case): Arabic *baytu* "house," and *malikun* "king," but *baytu al-maliku* "house of the king." Note that nouns in this position are said to be in the construct state. This construction exists in all branches of Semitic and is characterized by a grammatically (e.g., fewer case distinctions) and sometimes phonologically reduced version of the "possessed," or "governed," noun, which often forms some sort of accentual unit with the "governing" noun: Akkadian *bītum* "house," *šarrum* "king," but *bīt šarrim* "house of the king"; and Hebrew *bayit* "house," *melek* "king," but *bêt melek* "(a) king's house."

Pronoun. Table 6 gives the principal pronomina paradigms for two representative Semitic languages, Akkadian and Arabic. The independent pronouns are used in emphatic subject and predicate nominal function. The suffix pronouns are interpreted as possessives when attached to nouns and as objects when attached to verbs. In every branch of Semitic only the first-person singular has a different form in these two functions (*-ī* when possessive and *-ni* when object). The one major distinction between the two languages in table 6 is in the pronominal base for the third-person forms, masculine and feminine, singular and plural: *š-* versus *h-* (which sometimes becomes *ʾ-*). This turns out to be a major isogloss in Semitic generally. All Old South Arabian languages except Sabean agree with Akkadian in having *š-*; Sabean and the rest of the Semitic languages follow Arabic—except for Middle South Arabian, which has a mixture of both (sometimes *h-* in masculine and *š-* in feminine forms). It is difficult to determine whether this alternation is fundamentally morphological or phonological: that is, whether two different pronominal bases coexisted in Proto-Semitic, of which different branches generalized one or the other, or whether a mysteriously conditioned sound change *š* > *h* occurred. The latter possibility has certainly come to be the case in the branch that leads to Middle South Arabian, in which various languages show sporadic *h* < *š* correspondences in nonpronominal general vocabulary (cf. Soqotri *hémaʕ* "hear" versus the common Semitic **šamaʕ-*). Finally, the Semitic languages tend to use the same conso-

TABLE 6. *Akkadian and Arabic Pronouns*

	Akkadian		Arabic	
	Sg.	Pl.	Sg.	Pl.
Independent				
1	*anāku*	*nīnu*	*ʔana*	*naḥnu*
2 masc.	*atta*	*attunu*	*ʔanta*	*ʔantum*
2 fem.	*atti*	*attina*	*ʔanti*	*ʔantunna*
3 masc.	*šū*	*šunu*	*huwa*	*hum*
3 fem.	*šī*	*šina*	*hiya*	*hunna*
Suffix				
1	*-ī, -nī*	*-nī*	*-ī, -nī*	*-nā*
2 masc.	*-ka*	*-kunu*	*-ka*	*-kum*
2 fem.	*-ki*	*-kina*	*-ki*	*-kunna*
3 masc.	*-šu*	*-šunu*	*-hū*	*-hum*
3 fem.	*-ši*	*-šina*	*-hā*	*-hunna*

nant both as third-person pronominal base and as prefix for the causative form of the verb: Akkadian *šu* "he" *-šalbas* "cause to dress," Arabic *huwa, ʕalbas* (cf. Old North Arabic *hlbs*). Ugaritic, with *hw* "he" *šlbš* "cause to dress," seems to show a transitional stage (but in which direction?).

Verb. Although each Semitic language has its own system of verbal inflection, there is a common core of categories and formal processes visible in the different systems. It permits a fairly accurate approximation of the essential features of the protosystem. In all Semitic languages, finite verb paradigms can be analyzed into two subparadigms: one subparadigm marks the subject affixes; the other subparadigm accounts for the stem form and marks the combination of root, derived stem, and tense mode.

The subject subparadigms divide the verb forms into two inflectional classes: those marking the verbal subject with prefixes (plus supplemental suffixes for distinctions of gender and number), and those marking the verbal subject with suffixes only. Table 7 gives these subject-marking subparadigms for three languages that among them cover most of the range of forms resconstructable for Proto-Semitic subject marking: Ugaritic, Canaanite, and Aramaic in general follow the Arabic pattern; Middle South Arabian follows the Geʿez—Old South Arabian, with its huge corpus of inscriptions formulated solely in the third person (singular, dual, and plural), cannot be classified. In Akkadian, the prefixing subparadigm is used with different stems for the past tense (*ta-lbaš* "she wore"), the present tense (*ta-labbaš* "she wears"), and the jussive (*ta-lbaš* "may she wear"). The suffixing subparadigm is used only with a form generally termed stative (*labš-at* "she is dressed"). In Arabic and Geʿez the prefixing form is also used with the present tense and the jussive (Ar. *ta-lbas-u, ta-lbas;* Gez. *tə-labbəs-i, tə-lbas-i* "she wears," "may she wear"), but the suffixing form is used with an innovated past tense, homologous with the Akkadian stative (Ar. *labis-at*, Gez. *lab(ə)s-at* "she wore").

As can be seen from table 7, the prefixing subparadigms differ very little from one another, and presumably all continue fairly directly an ancestral Proto-Semitic system. The suffixing subparadigms, however, seem to be subject to a certain amount of transformation. In the first place, the first- and second-person suffix forms, especially in the Akkadian, look very much like reduced enclitic forms of the independent pronouns given in table 6, with the *-ā-* perhaps as some linking element. The third-person forms, on the other hand, look like elements from the nominal inflection—as a matter of fact, the Akkadian stative can be formed on the basis of any noun or adjective (e.g., *damq-at* "she is good," *šarr-āku* "I am king"). The major difference in the Arabiclike languages (Canaanite, Aramaic) is that the *-k-* ~ *-t-* alternations in the paradigm have been leveled out in favor of *-t-*, whereas in Geʿez and Middle South Arabian they have been leveled out in favor of *-k-*. As was pointed out by Robert Hetzron (1976), this is important evidence in favor of the temporal priority of an Akkadianlike system over the other two. It is now widely supposed therefore that the Proto-Semitic system resembled the Akkadian one, and that the Western Semitic past tense evolved out of something like a verbal adjective with enclitic reduced pronouns.

The second set of subparadigms governs the shape of the stem to which the subject affixes are attached. The essential features of this system are shown in table 8, where Akkadian and Geʿez illustrate eastern and southern varieties of Semitic, and where Arabic illustrates the state of affairs in a central group including Canaanite and Aramaic. In table 8 it can be seen that all branches have a jussive at some point (this becomes marginal in Canaanite and disappears in Aramaic). The verbal form of the jussive is, as far as is known, homophonous with the past tense in Akkadian. Each of the branches also has a specialized past tense, however (called Past_2 in table 8), which has the form of the jussive. In Arabic the jussive with *lam,* "not," is the ordinary negative past tense: *talbas,* "may she wear"; *lam talbas,* "she did not wear." In Hebrew this is the so-called waw-consecutive

TABLE 7. *Akkadian, Arabic, and Geʿez Verb Subject*

	Akkadian		Arabic		Geʿez	
	Sg.	Pl.	Sg.	Pl.	Sg.	Pl.
Prefixing/Suffixing						
1	*a-*	*ni-*	*a-*	*na-*	*ʔə-*	*nə-*
2 masc.	*ta-*	*ta- . . . -ā*	*ta-*	*ta- . . . -ū*	*tə-*	*tə- . . . -u*
2 fem.	*ta- . . . -ī*	*ta- . . . -ā*	*ta- . . . -ī*	*ta- . . . -na*	*tə- . . . -i*	*tə- . . . -ā*
3 masc.	*i-*	*i- . . . -ū*	*ya-*	*ya- . . . -ū*	*yə-*	*yə- . . . -u*
3 fem.	*ta-*	*i- . . . -ā*	*ta-*	*ta- . . . -na*	*tə-*	*yə- . . . -ā*
Suffixing						
1	*-āku*	*-ānu*	*-tu*	*-nā*	*-ka*	*-na*
2 masc.	*-āta*	*-ātunu*	*-ta*	*-tum*	*-ka*	*-kəmmu*
2 fem.	*-āti*	*-ātina*	*-ti*	*-tunna*	*-ki*	*-kən*
3 masc.	*-∅*	*-ū*	*-a*	*-ū*	*-a*	*-u*
3 fem.	*-at*	*-ā*	*-at*	*-na*	*-at*	*-ā*

TABLE 8. *Strong Base-Form Tense Stems in Akkadian, Arabic, and Geʿez.* All forms are feminine third-person singular.

	Akkadian		Arabic		Geʿez	
	Function	Form	Function	Form	Function	Form
1	Present	*ta-labbaš*			Present	*tə-labbəs*
2	(Cf. Subjunctive *ta-lbaš-u*)		Present	*ta-lbas-u*		
3	Jussive	*(lu) ta-lbaš*	Jussive	*ta-lbas*	Jussive	*tə-lbas*
4	Past	*ta-lbaš*	Past_2	*ta-lbas*	(Past_2)	*(tə-bel-)*
5	Stative	*lab(i)š-at*	Past	*labis-at*	Past	*lab(ə)s-at*

form: *tilbaš* "may she wear," "she wears," *wattilbaš* "and she wore." In Geʿez this form exists with only one lexical item, the verb *bhl* "say," whose ordinary past tense is formed with subject prefixes: *təbe* "she said," *yəbelā* "they [fem] said," (vs *təbəl* "she says"—note the form of the jussive *təbal* "may she say"). The normal past tense in all of the Western languages, however, is a suffixing form, homologous with the Akkadian stative. Finally, the present-tense form, which in the Southern languages is the same as in Akkadian, has a new base in the central languages, which is akin to the Akkadian past/jussive, and may, with its *-u* suffix, be related to a subjunctive form in Akkadian.

Two characteristic aspects of Semitic verbal inflection are not touched upon in table 8: the derived (as opposed to the base) stem form, and the so-called weak (as opposed to the strong) verbal root. The stem system illustrated involves only the basic (nonderived) form of the stem. The essential features of the stem system hold also for each language's inventory of so-called derived stems. Some of the principal common derived stems can be illustrated in Akkadian, Hebrew, and Arabic using, for the sake of illustration, the root **lbš* (which does not actually occur in each derived stem form in each language). The derived stem form will be given in the stative for Akkadian and in the past tense for Hebrew and Arabic: causative, with the prefix *š/h/ʕ* (Akk. *šulbuš-*, Heb. *hilbīš-*, Ar. *ʕalbas-*); passive, with the prefix *n* (Akk. *nalbuš-*, Heb. *nilbaš-*, Ar. *inlabas-*); reflexive, with the prefix or infix *t* (Akk. *litbuš-*, Heb. *hitlabbeš-*, Ar. *iltabas-*); factative, with the geminated middle root consonant (Akk. *lubbuš-*, Heb. *libbeš-*, Ar. *labbas-*).

The distinction between strong versus weak root involves the fact that Semitic inflection and derivation typically involve a triconsonantal strong root, such as *lbs*, "wear," for Arabic, into which are inserted different vowel patterns (combined with different prefixes, suffixes, and infixes): *labisa*, "he wore"; *lubs*, "wearing"; *labs*, "tangle"; *libs*, "clothing"; *lubūs*, "articles of clothing"; *libsa*, "style of dressing"; *libās*, "clothes"; *albisa*, "clothes [pl]"; *labīs*, "worn"; *talbīs*, "dressing". A number of words, however, do not have three true consonants, and the place of the "missing" consonant is occupied by a glide /w/ or /y/ (sometimes also /n/ and /ʕ/), yielding weak roots of the form *wCC, yCC, CwC, CyC, CCw, CCy*, and so on. Because some of the oldest and most widespread Semitic vocabulary items (*wld* "bear," *qwm* "stand," *bky* "cry") are of this form, it has been suggested that the unique phonological organization involved in triconsonantal strong roots is a tendency (already incipient in Afro-Asiatic) that only gradually overtook large portions of Semitic morphology and lexicon. In it the weak roots are an attempt to fit older, nontriconsonantal lexical items onto the innovative triconsonantal patterns. Semitic languages differ in the extent to which weak verbs are assimilated to the strong patterns—in general Akkadian tends to be the most conservative (i.e., the least assimilating), whereas Geʿez is the most assimilating; Arabic is somewhere in the middle; and Hebrew is somewhat more conservative than Arabic. Table 9 gives an idea of how this works out for selected tense-person forms of the very archaic weak root **mwt*, "die."

Scenario for Semitic Prehistory. The picture of the "dawn of Semitic" that emerges from a consideration of the Semitic and parallel Afro-Asiatic evidence is that of a group

TABLE 9. *Weak Verb Forms in Akkadian, Arabic, and Geʿez*

	Akkadian		Arabic		Geʿez	
	Present	Past	Present	Past	Present	Past
3 Sg. masc.	*i-mūat*	*i-mūt*	*ya-mūt-u*	*māt-a*	*yə-maww t*	*mot-a*
2 Sg. masc.	*ta-mūat*	*ta-mūt*	*ta-mūtu*	*mut-ta*	*tə-maww t*	*mot-ka*
3 Pl. masc.	*i-mutt-ū*	*i-mūt-ū*	*ya-mūt-ū-na*	*māt-ū*	*yə-maww t-u*	*mot-u*

of languages distributed over what may have been a relatively restricted range in Northeast Africa, with one subgroup occupying the African-Asian (hence, "Afro-Asiatic") bridge and gateway into western Asia that is Palestine (with adjacent parts of Syria and northern and western Arabia). It is impossible to fix a definite time of origin for this distribution, but a *terminus ante quem* is clearly provided by the fact that an Afro-Asiatic-speaking group, the Egyptians, is present at, and apparently responsible for, the construction of irrigation-based urban civilization in the Nile valley at the end of the fourth millennium. Slightly later, representatives of the Western Asian Afro-Asiatic branch arrive on the scene in the early stages (but not as originators) of the parallel development in Mesopotamia. Given the language distributions, the center of dispersion of this group would seem more likely to be Northeast Africa than Western Asia—but a lot of linguistic and archeological work will have to be done before this can be taken as certain. Apart from the group that settled in the Nile valley, a common cultural profile of important segments of the other Afro-Asiatic groups—Semitic, Cushitic, and Berber—would, in any case, seem to be that of a mobile, if not nomadic, society with a special adaptation to food production and animal raising in arid environments.

Research into the nature of the language of this group is barely at a beginning stage. However, evidence from Berber and Cushitic may indicate that the language possessed a prefixing present and past tense distinguished by a variety of vowel patterns and syllabic structures: Berber *i-krəz, t-krəz,* "he/she plowed," versus *i-kərrəz, t-kərrəz,* "he/she is plowing"; Bedja (Cushitic) *ʕa-dbil, ʕi-dbíl,* "I/he collected," versus *ʕa-danbíil, danbíil,* "I/he collect(s)." On the other hand, Egyptian shows that a verbal form with encliticlike pronominal suffixes could also have been part of the inflectional repertoire. Compare the Akkadian stative suffixes in table 7 with Egyptian: *sḏm.kwỉ, sḏm.tỉ, sḏm.wyn, sḏm.tỉwny,* "I/you[sg], we/you[pl] heard." In other words, in these and other respects, a picture emerges of a Proto-Afro-Asiatic as it begins to differentiate, whose essential features are not all that different from what might be conjectured of an older stage of Akkadian.

Assuming an area in and around Palestine as the region of most intense contact between the Proto-Semitic speech communities, where innovations are most likely to be spread and shared, one scenario for the differentiation of the major branches of Semitic might run as follows: an eastern part of the Proto-Semitic speech community, including, or consisting exclusively of, a forerunner of Akkadian, moving toward North Syria and the Euphrates River, might have become isolated from the other dialects at some point before a tendency spread in the rest of the speech community to replace the (homophonous?; cf. Table 8) past-tense form with a new past tense based on the perfective stative (a development with many parallels in language history—including, e.g., that of the modern Romance languages). There was evidently a simultaneous tendency to level out the shape of the suffixed pronouns, now part of the core verbal inflexional system. In the southern extremity of the contact area, dialects tended to replaced the *t* forms with a *k*. In the north, the leveling took place in the opposite direction. Subsequently, the southern dialects in turn lost contact with the rest of the community (perhaps they crossed the highland barrier that roughly corresponds to the southwestern border between Saudi Arabia and Yemen) before they were reached by a new reinterpretation of the verbal system coming out of the central dialects. The reinterpretation would have ended up replacing the bisyllabic present-tense form preserved in Akkadian and Geʿez with a monosyllabic form (and in Middle South Arabian; the nature of the written evidence does not permit including Old South Arabian with any certainty). The present state of knowledge only allows speculation on the nature of this reinterpretation. One possibility is that Proto-Semitic already possessed both forms, and that one of them tended to drop out at the periphery and take over in the center. Another possibility is that an older main-clause form was replaced by a (clefted?, more emphatic?) version,

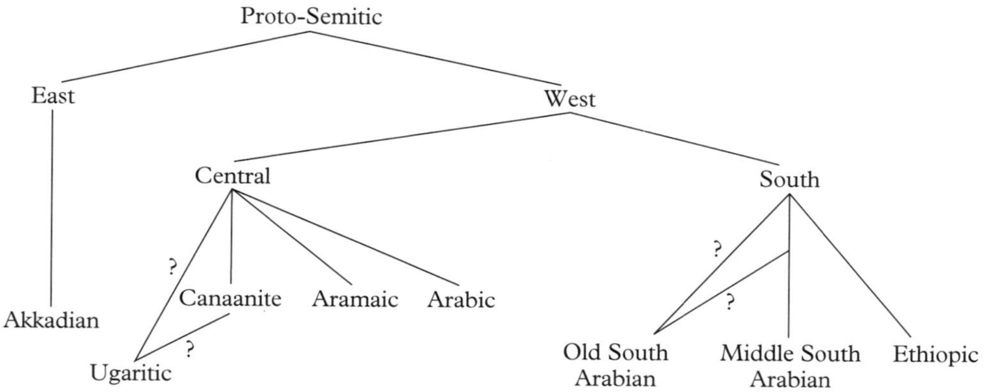

SEMITIC LANGUAGES. Figure 2. *Relations and subgrouping of Early Semitic speech communities.*

in which "she wears" is replaced with a quasi-subordinate form ("it is that she wore," or the like).

Whether or not this scenario turns out to be tenable, it is generally admitted today that the the data summarized in tables 7–9 dictate a primary major differentiation of Semitic into an Eastern, Central, and Southern group, in which Arabic belongs to the Central, and not the Southern group. This picture still leaves open the possibility for the spread of phonological (/f/ instead of /p/) and grammatical (internal plural patterns) preferences among dialects in the southern range of Semitic. It also leaves open the question of whether or to what extent Aramaic and Canaanite may have constituted an independent regional speech community, or a communicating group of dialects—thus justifying the old term *Northwest Semitic*. In any case, the essential features of this view are captured in figure 2, where the status of Ugaritic as a Canaanite language, and the relationship between Old and Middle South Arabian are left open.

BIBLIOGRAPHY

Bergsträsser, Gotthelf. *Introduction to the Semitic Languages.* Translated with notes, bibliography, and an appendix on the scripts by Peter Daniels. Winona Lake, Ind., 1983. Translation, with updated notes, of a classic work from 1928.

Brockelmann, Carl. *Grundriss der vergleichenden Grammatik der semitischen Sprachen.* 2 vols. Berlin, 1908–1913. Terribly out of date in many respects, but at the same time the only attempt ever made to survey the entire field in detail.

Brockelmann, Carl. *Kurzgefasste vergleichende Grammatik der semitischen Sprachen.* Berlin, 1908. Based on the same data as his two-volume work (see above), but much more concise and easier to consult.

Cantineau, Jean. "Le consonantisme du sémitique." *Semitica* 4 (1952): 78–94. The still classic statement of the Proto-Semitic consonant inventory.

Cohen, Marcel. *Le système verbal sémitique et l'expression du temps.* Paris, 1924. Surveys basic morphosyntactic data.

Diakonoff, Igor M. *Afrasian Languages.* Moscow, 1988. The most complete summary available of general Afro-Asiatic morphological data.

Diakonoff, Igor M. *Proto-Afrasian and Old Akkadian: A Study in Historical Phonetics.* Journal of Afroasiatic Languages, vol. 4.1–2. Princeton, 1992. Radical, reconstruction-based proposals à propos of some long-held assumptions.

Faber, Alice. "Akkadian Evidence for Proto-Semitic Affricates." *Journal of Cuneiform Studies* 37 (1985): 101–107. Reinterpretation of part of a commonly reconstructed sibilant series.

Fleisch, Henri. *Les verbes à allongement vocalique interne en sémitique.* Paris, 1944. Study of one of the classes of the derived stem in Semitic.

Garr, W. Randall. *Dialect Geography of Syria-Palestine, 1000–586 B.C.E.* Philadelphia, 1985. Organization of the available data on Canaanite.

Greenberg, Joseph H. "The Patterning of Root Morphemes in Semitic." *Word* 6 (1950): 162–181. Basic and very influential study on Semitic root structure.

Greenberg, Joseph H. *The Languages of Africa.* Bloomington, 1963. Revised edition of a work that launched the term *Afro-Asiatic* and set its scope, proposing cognate sets for family.

Hetzron, Robert. *Ethiopian Semitic: Studies in Classification.* Manchester, 1972. Classification of Ethiopic within the context of Semitic.

Hetzron, Robert. "Two Principles of Genetic Reconstruction." *Lingua* 38 (1976): 89–108. Proposes principles that have been influential in all recent attempts to draw a Semitic family tree.

Hetzron, Robert. "Afroasiatic Languages" and "Semitic Languages." In *The World's Major Languages,* edited by Bernard Comrie, pp. 647–653, 654–663. New York, 1990. Very concise but useful surveys of the principal features of families.

Huehnergard, John. "Remarks on the Classification of the Northwest Semitic Languages." In *The Balaam Text from Deir ʿAlla Reevaluated,* edited by Jacob Hoftijzer and Gerrit van der Kooij, pp. 282–293. Leiden, 1991. Reviews the state of the question about the relationship of Central to Northwest Semitic.

Kuryłowicz, Jerzy. *Studies in Semitic Grammar and Metrics.* Warsaw, 1973. Adventurous reconstructions of Semitic by an eminent linguist and Indo-Europeanist.

Moscati, Sabatino, et al. *Introduction to the Comparative Grammar of the Semitic Languages.* Wiesbaden, 1964. Cautious, committee-based approach to the basic features of common Semitic.

Nöldeke, Theodor. "Semitic Languages." In *Encyclopaedia Britannica,* 11th ed., vol. 24, pp. 617–630. London, 1911. Still classic statement of the basic facts about Semitic.

Solá-Solé, José M. *L'infinitif sémitique.* Paris, 1961. Form and function of verbal nouns in the various Semitic languages.

Steiner, Richard. *The Case for Fricative-Laterals in Proto-Semitic.* American Oriental Series, vol. 59. New Haven, 1977. Synthesis of data on lateral series in Semitic.

Steiner, Richard. *Affricated Sade in the Semitic Languages.* New York, 1982. Explores evidence for affricates in Semitic.

Voigt, Rainer M. *Die infirmen Verbaltypen des Arabischen und das Biradikalismus-Problem.* Wiesbaden, 1988. Relationship between weak verbs and Semitic triconsonantal root structure.

Gene B. Gragg

SEPPHORIS (Heb., Zippori), site located in the heart of Lower Galilee in northern Israel (map reference 176 × 239), along the ancient east–west trans-Galilean roadway that linked the Mediterranean Sea, some 29 km (18 mi.) to the west, with the city of Tiberias on the Sea of Galilee, some 29 km to the east. The site is approximately 6 km (4 mi.) northwest of Nazareth and sits on a hill that rises about 300 m above the surrounding valleys: to the north lies the Beth-Neṭofa Valley and to the south, the Nazareth basin. The ancient site of Sepphoris was occupied from early modern times until 1948 by inhabitants of the Arab village of Ṣafuriyye and subsequently by Jewish settlers at Moshav Ẓippori, located just south of the ancient city. Sepphoris consisted of an upper city (summit, or acropolis) and a large lower city surrounding the summit (see figure 1a–b). The medieval citadel, which crowns the summit, was the focal point of the early modern settlement, for which it served as a school until 1948; it was renovated in the mid-eighteenth century by Ẓahir al-ʿUmar al-Zaydani, the bedouin governor of Galilee, and again in about 1889 by the Turkish sultan Abdülhamid II (1876–1909), when a second story was added.

Archaeological Excavations. The first excavations at Sepphoris were carried out in the early 1900s by Prosper Viaud in the ruins of the Church of St. Anne, a Crusader structure just north of the summit (see figure 2). Acquired

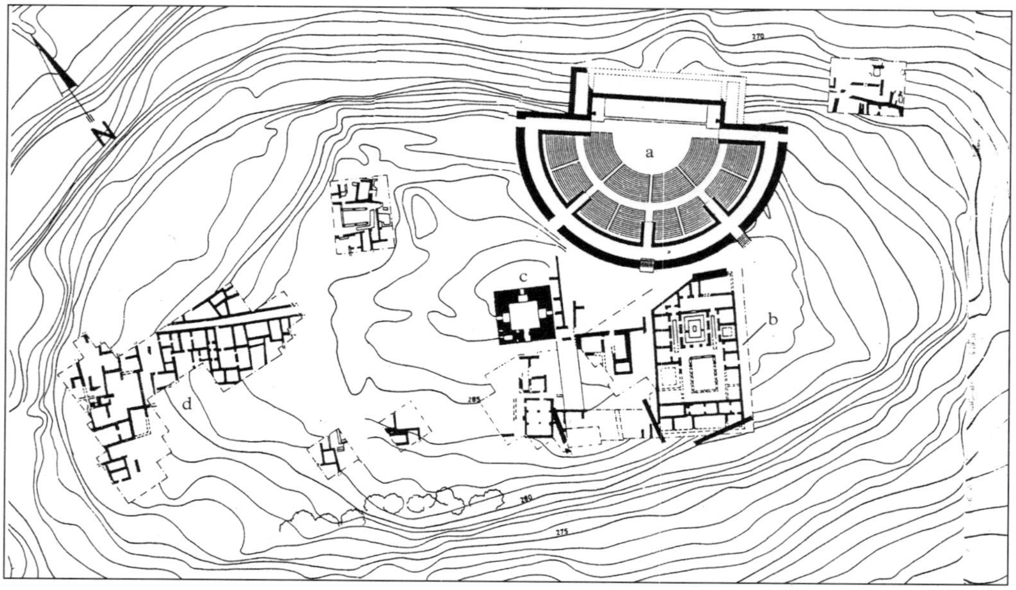

SEPPHORIS. Figure 1a. *Plan of the upper city.* (a) Theater; (b) Roman villa of Dionysus; (c) citadel; (d) western summit. (Courtesy Joint Sepphoris Project)

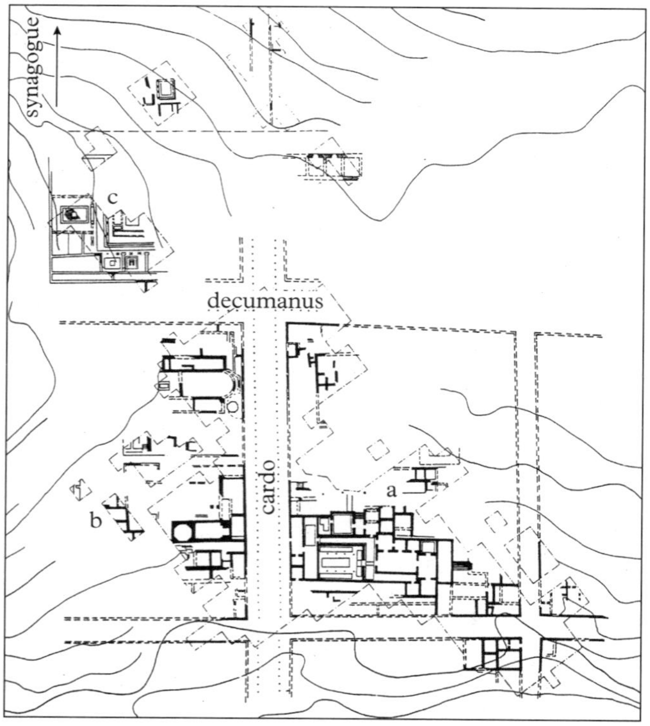

SEPPHORIS. Figure 1b. *Plan of the lower city.* (a) Festival building; (b) Byzantine church; (c) Roman-period public building. (Based on the excavation map of Z. Weiss and E. Netzer, Hebrew University of Jerusalem)

by the Franciscans in 1870, the church still belongs to the Custody of the Holy Land, although it is now administered through the orphanage of the Sisters of St. Anne, founded in 1924. The limited work in the church produced no evidence of a pre-Crusader building. However, mosaic fragments were found just north of the church. One large fragment, probably dating to the Late Roman period, has an Aramaic text: "Be remembered for good, Rabbi Yudan son of Tanḥum, son of . . . who gave one [dinar]. . . ." Another Late Roman or perhaps Byzantine inscription on a stone lintel uncovered in this general area by W. Ewing (1895) is in Greek and refers to several apparently well-known leaders, including the *archisynagogus* ("head of the synagogue") of Sidon and also of Tyre. This inscription ends with a chi-rho symbol, which has caused some scholars to identify it as a Jewish-Christian synagogue inscription.

The first major archaeological excavations at Sepphoris were carried out in 1931 under the direction of Leroy Waterman of the University of Michigan. This expedition discovered the theater on the northeastern summit and excavated a large building, identified as a Christian basilica, on the northwestern summit (Waterman, 1937). Michael Avi-Yonah (1978) argued that the so-called church was in fact in a large house with a peristyle courtyard. In 1976 Eric M. Meyers and James F. Strange conducted a preliminary site survey under the rubric of the Meiron Excavation Project; in 1982 and 1984, Strange (1982) conducted a systematic survey of the site—its buildings, cisterns, and burial caves—under the sponsorship of the University of South Florida. In 1983 and 1984, the South Florida team, under Strange's direction, began excavations on the western summit, along-

SEPPHORIS. Figure 2. *Aerial view of the medieval church of St. Anne.* (Courtesy Joint Sepphoris Project)

side the citadel, and on the western side of the theater; in 1986, the team reopened the areas around Waterman's "church." In later seasons the South Florida expedition focused its energies on a large public building in the eastern lower city.

In 1985 the Joint Sepphoris Project was launched, bringing together Duke University and the Hebrew University of Jerusalem for five seasons under the direction of Meyers, Ehud Netzer, and Carol L. Meyers. This project concentrated on the domestic areas on the western summit, the theater, and a large Roman villa with a Dionysus mosaic on the eastern summit. The Hebrew University team continued under Netzer and Zeev Weiss until 1995, when Weiss took over the directorship. Their work on the summit since 1990 continued work on the theater and also uncovered a storage building east of the citadel. In addition, they opened extensive areas of the eastern lower city and excavated a Byzantine synagogue in the northeast. The Duke University team reorganized in 1993, adding Kenneth G. Hoglund to the directorship and renaming its project the Sepphoris Regional Project. Work at Sepphoris in 1993 and 1994 concentrated exclusively on domestic areas of the western summit; the team also began excavation of a small tell nearby, Tel ʿEin-Zippori. [*See* ʿEin-Zippori, Tel.] Between 1975 and 1985, Tsvika Tsuk carried out systematic surveys of the water systems in the site's environs. From 1992 to 1995, under the sponsorship of the National Parks Authority and Tel Aviv University, he directed the excavation and preservation of the aqueducts, reservoir, and associated structures.

In October 1992, Zippori National Park was opened to the public; in 1993, a permanent structure to house the Roman villa and mosaic was constructed; and in 1995, the citadel was converted into a museum and information center. Restoration of selected buildings in the residential area of the western summit and in the public areas of the lower city is underway.

History. Reconstructing the history of Sepphoris from the abundance of literary sources and archaeological materials is a complicated task. The Joint Sepphoris Project and the Sepphoris Regional Project identified a large amount of pottery from the Iron Age (Iron I and especially Iron II), mostly on bedrock and in fills on the summit, but without accompanying structural or stratified remains. The Mishnah's apparent awareness of an "old" settlement going back to the time of Joshua (*ʿArakh.* 9.6) should not be dismissed. After several seasons of excavations at nearby Tel ʿEin-Zippori, however, it now appears that the Late Bronze–Iron Age settlement in the area was located more to the southeast. It is still too soon to determine whether there was a gap between the eighth century BCE and the Persian period in the sixth. The presence of black Attic ware sherds and the chance discovery of a beautiful Attic animal-shaped rhyton from the fifth century BCE indicate that the site was occupied by that time. Whether it was a military garrison serving the Persian authorities or another sort of settlement cannot be established. Similarly, the presence of large amounts of late Persian and Early Hellenistic pottery on the western summit suggests that there was a settlement of some kind (its nature also remains unclear) during the early Second Temple period.

The name *Sepphoris* does not appear in the Bible. The first literary reference to it is in Josephus in connection with the Hasmonean king, Alexander Jannaeus, who successfully repelled the attack of Ptolemy Lathyrus of Egypt at the beginning of his reign (*Antiq.* 13.338). Although few stratified remains of the Hellenistic period have been found on the western summit, many coins of Jannaeus have been recovered. The settlement of this period was substantial enough to warrant an attack by Ptolemy, in which he lost many soldiers (*Antiq.* 3.337). In the Hasmonean era, Sepphoris was probably the administrative capital of Galilee because by about 57 BCE Gabinius, Pompey's legate to Syria, assigned a *synedria,* or "council," to Sepphoris (*Antiq.* 14.91; *War*

1.170), making it officially the capital of the Galilee. The city was captured by Herod the Great in a snowstorm, in about 37 BCE, which prevented it from going over to Mattathias Antigonus and the Parthians (*Antiq.* 17.271). [*See* Parthians.] The city presumably remained Herod's northern command post for the rest of his reign. Upon his death in 4 BCE, a rebellion broke out at the site—the so-called War of Varus—that sought to remove Sepphoris from Herodian rule. The rebellion was crushed, and the city was supposedly burned and many of its inhabitants taken as slaves (*War* 2.68; *Antiq.* 17.289). Archaeological evidence of only scattered burning suggests that Josephus's report of destruction may be somewhat exaggerated.

Sepphoris was inherited by Herod's son Antipas as part of the tetrarchy of Galilee and Peraea (Transjordan). Antipas no doubt did much to contribute to the site's recovery: he "fortified Sepphoris to be the ornament of all Galilee, and called it Autocratoris" (*Antiq.* 18.27). Josephus's use of the term *ornament (proschema)* is to be understood in the sense of an impregnable nature and fortification, and "Autocratoris" refers to the fact that it enjoyed autonomous rule and also honored Augustus. The precise nature of the renovations and rebuilding Antipas undertook before he moved the capital of Galilee to Tiberias is not known. The theater, parts of which have been excavated by four expeditions, seems to date to a period later than Antipas, though there is no unanimity of opinion about the date, and no known public buildings of any great size have been recovered from the period of his rule. [*See* Theaters.] However, other kinds of first-century remains, including partially preserved sections of a large villa and several ritual baths, have been recovered on the summit, giving support to the considerable literature that mentions the presence of priests at Sepphoris during this period. [*See* Ritual Baths.] The fragmentary nature of the Early Roman deposits on the site certainly is a result of extensive building and rebuilding in later periods.

The role of Sepphoris during the First Jewish Revolt against Rome was clearly pro-Roman, the residents having "displayed pacific sentiments" (*War* 2.30–31); coins minted in 66–67 CE commemorate the surrender of the city to Vespasian by naming it Eirenopolis, "City of Peace" (Meshorer, 1985, p. 36). [*See* First Jewish Revolt.] Josephus, however, is inconsistent about the city's pro-Roman stance during the war. Coins minted during the reign of Nero read: "Sepphoris Neronias, the city of peace named after the Caesar Nero."

After the fall of Jerusalem in 70 CE, many Jews fled north; some, including the priestly clan of Jedaiah, apparently settled in Sepphoris. This demographic shift influenced the city's character: it became the foremost Jewish city in Galilee. The city coins minted in Trajan's reign (98–117 CE) all bear Jewish symbols on the reverse: wreath, palm tree, caduceus, and ears of grain. A Capitoline temple, however, was apparently erected during or shortly after the reign of Hadrian (117–138 CE), who appointed a gentile administration in the city. It was at the end of his reign, or at the beginning of the reign of Antoninus Pius (138–161 CE), that the city became known as Diocaesarea, in honor of Caesar and Zeus. It was at this time, too, that Roman soldiers of the Sixth Legion were stationed at nearby Leggio (modern Lejjun), testifying to a dramatic change in the population at Sepphoris and in the region as a whole. The impact of the Second Revolt against Rome (132–135 CE) on Sepphoris and nearby areas is unclear in both the archaeological record and the literary sources. [*See* Second Jewish Revolt.]

During the reign of Caracalla (198–217 CE), for some seventeen years, Sepphoris was the seat of the Sanhedrin under the leadership of Rabbi Judah the Patriarch (ha-Nasi). The municipal government apparently reverted to Jewish control, judging from a coin of the early third century CE that commemorates an accord between the *boule* ("council") of Sepphoris and the Roman senate: "Covenant of friendship and mutual aid between the holy council and the senate of the Roman people" (Meshorer, 1985, p. 37). This coin provides a unique glimpse into the city of Rabbi Judah, well known as the redactor of the Mishnah and presumed to be a friend of the emperor Caracalla, who was well disposed toward the Jews, perhaps as part of his policy of developing the eastern empire.

Sepphoris remained a major Jewish center of learning even after the publication of the Mishnah and the removal of the Sanhedrin to Tiberias during the time of Judah's grandson, Rabbi Judah Nesiah. The so-called Gallus Revolt, against Gallus Caesar, is reported to have broken out in Sepphoris in 351 CE led by Patricius; the extent of the damage done when the revolt was quelled by the Roman commander Ursicinus is unclear. In any case the city was badly damaged by the earthquake of 363, one of the strongest of antiquity and is specifically mentioned in a letter to Cyril, bishop of Jerusalem. The archaeological evidence indicates that Sepphoris was extensively rebuilt fairly soon after the earthquake. By the sixth century there was a Christian community headed by a bishop; the bishops of Sepphoris at this time participated in synods in Jerusalem. By late Byzantine times there is some indication that Sepphoris had a connection to the Umayyad dynasty: Umayya, a great grandfather of three caliphs and a businessman in Mecca, is reported to have been given a Jewish slavegirl from Sepphoris when he lived in Palestine. During this period, Sepphoris is referred to as Ṣaffuriyya, not Diocaesarea.

Sepphoris may have been conquered by a general named Shuraḥbil during the caliphate of ʿUmar ibn al-Khaṭṭab (after 634) and is included on a short list of cities that also mentions Akko and Tyre—indicating that Sepphoris was a city of considerable size and power. Islamic coinage was introduced at Ṣaffuriyya in 697 for a short time. At present, only limited archaeological remains of this period have been recovered. During the Crusades, Sepphoris was captured by the Franks, who called it Le Saphorie and (re)fortified its citadel. Benjamin of Tudela visited the city in about 1160 and noted only that it was in Crusader hands, mentioning no Jewish families. In 1187, Crusaders gathered at the site for war with Salah edh-Din (Saladin), who retook the city. Saladin himself visited the site en route to Akko on the fifteenth of Rajab, the seventh month of the Muslim year.

Upper City. The earliest occupation of the site was apparently on the highest part, or acropolis, of the Sepphoris hill. The major expeditions to Sepphoris all began their projects on this upper city.

Western residential area. Although no clear stratigraphic remains have yet been discovered, numerous Black Attic ware sherds and quantities of Late Hellenistic pottery, small finds, and coins indicate that occupation began on the summit in the Hasmonean era, if not earlier (in the Late

SEPPHORIS. Figure 3. *Small street in western residential area, looking east.* Note the citadel in the background (Courtesy Joint Sepphoris Project)

SEPPHORIS. Figure 4. *Metal figurine of Prometheus.* Found in a Roman-period house on the western summit (Courtesy Joint Sepphoris Project)

Persian period). At the extreme west of the summit, rock-cut quarries testify to building activities during the Hellenistic and the Early Roman periods. The best-preserved Late Hellenistic remains are close to the citadel.

In the Roman period, a 2.20-meter-wide east–west street connected the summit with areas to the west; because of the rising slope, the street is not preserved at its eastern end (see figure 3). Two large residential buildings of this period have been identified along the southern side of the street in units II and IV; another one probably stood in unit III, though Byzantine remains dominate in this area. Unit VIII appears to be mainly agricultural, although several well-preserved *miqvaʿot* (ritual baths) there suggest domestic use or, possibly, public space. Four ritual baths appear in unit II and at least four in unit IV; numerous others were also uncovered in the western residence area.

The residential area on the western summit is characterized by a large number of underground chambers cut from bedrock. Some are cisterns; many others, including ones converted from cisterns, are silos, storage rooms, and olive presses, judging from their configuration and from the number of storage vessels found in them. [*See* Cisterns; Granaries and Silos.] Some of the cavities were ultimately used as garbage pits, primarily for broken pottery vessels. An unusually large variety of vessels, including a unique assemblage of ceramic incense shovels and decorated discus lamps, have been recovered from such cavities.

The abundance of *miqvaʿot* and the presence of two lamps decorated with menorahs and one with a Torah shrine suggest the presence of a Jewish population on the western summit during the Roman period. At the same time, the recovery of two exceptionally fine bronze statuettes, one of Pan and the other of Prometheus (see figure 4), from an underground cavity points to a Hellenistic or cosmopolitan aesthetic for the population.

Like the rest of the site, the western summit was almost totally destroyed by the 363 earthquake at the end of the Late Roman period. A major reconfiguration of the area, which may be the result of a demographic change, occurred in the subsequent Byzantine period. New structures, which included some workshops, notably one for glass, were built. [*See* Glass.] The late fourth- and fifth-century remains, best preserved in units III and V, are replete with pig bones, and units II and IV have pig bones in post-363 fills; such was not the case in the Roman period. [*See* Pigs.] The faunal remains, along with several ostraca with Christian names and prayers and several late red-ware stamped crosses, suggest that the Byzantine inhabitants of the western summit were Christian.

Citadel and storehouse. Crowning the upper city is a massive, fortresslike structure known as the citadel (see figure 5). As already indicated, its present form, reaching 10.5 m above ground level, is the result of eighteenth- and nineteenth-century renovations. The rounded corners below the uppermost story of this square building (14.95 m to a side) suggest that it may have been built as a watchtower in the Crusader period. Like many Crusader buildings in Palestine, the ashlar stones used to construct its walls were apparently taken from earlier structures; the cornerstones, for example, are rubble-filled Roman sarcophagi. Excavations of its foundations indicate that the citadel was first erected early in the Byzantine period, near the end of the fourth or early in the fifth century.

Just south of the citadel the remains of a large building feature a central rectangular room (9.4 × 6.2 m). Two columns and two rectangular pilasters set into each of its long walls supported the ceiling, and a white mosaic floor covers it. Because of the many large storage jars discovered in the central room, as well as in two adjacent ones, the building has been tentatively identified as a storehouse. The jars, typical Byzantine wares, were found on the floor, crushed by the building's ashy collapse in the seventh century, the result of either the Persian (614) or Arab (640) conquest. One of the jars was decorated with menorahs, providing some evi-

SEPPHORIS. Figure 5. *The citadel, looking north.* Though originally built in Byzantine times, it was rebuilt by the Crusaders and again in the eighteenth century. (Courtesy E. M. Meyers)

dence of a continued Jewish presence in the eastern part of the summit in the Byzantine period—in contrast to the apparent shift then to a Christian population on the western summit.

Theater. Set into the steep northern scarp of the summit and offering a panoramic view of the Beth Neṭofa Valley, the theater at Sepphoris occupies a prominent position in the upper city. It nearly abuts the Roman villa to its south—only a narrow path separates the two monumental structures. With a diameter of about 74 m, the theater probably could seat some forty-five hundred people. Like contemporary theaters in Roman Palestine, the plan of this building places the semicircular cavea (auditorium) opposite the stage. The natural slope of the summit together with a series of vaults provided the necessary gradient for the cavea's tiered seating. Three of these 2.2-meter-wide vaults served as exists and and entrances, or vomitoria. In addition, two side entrances *(paradoi),* 3.2 m wide, lead to the semicircular area, or orchestra, in front of the cavea and to the stage. Built of stone and probably featuring a wooden floor, the stage 31 × 6 m stretched across the northern edge of the building. No trace of the *scaenae frons,* or backdrop, survives.

Although it was first assumed that the theater was constructed early in the first century by Herod Antipas, extensive soundings under its foundations indicate a later date, perhaps as late as the early to mid-second century, when the city underwent extensive rebuilding after the First Jewish Revolt. The theater probably remained in use until the end of the Late Roman period. Whether it still functioned early in the Byzantine period is questionable. Clearly, it was abandoned by the Late Byzantine period, when its ruins were used as a limestone quarry and most of its architectural members were destroyed.

Roman villa. Just south of the theater, at the eastern end of the acropolis, is a palatial residential building (about 40 m long and 23 m wide). Some of its 6-meter-wide walls, built mainly of large, plaster-covered ashlars, are preserved to a height of 2 m. Fragments of colored floral and geometric frescoes indicate that the plastered ceilings or walls, or both, were decorated. [*See* Wall Paintings.] This two-storied structure consists of a peristyle courtyard and a series of living and service rooms, many of whose floors are covered with geometric mosaics or plain buff-colored or white tesserae. [*See* Mosaics.] In one of these rooms, a small trapezoidal chamber, the Greek word *hygei* ("health") is set in black tiles into the tesselated floor; along with the room's water channels; the inscription is compatible with the room's use as a restroom.

Built early in the third century, as attested by the latest material under its floors as well as by stylistic elements of its architecture and decoration, this building collapsed in the earthquake of 363. Its Roman period of usage, of about 120–150 years, was extended into the Byzantine period in its southern portion, where domestic remains, including two ritual baths and a stable, were found that had been built into the remnants of the Roman villa.

The villa's most noteworthy feature is its splendid triclinium, or reception and banquet hall, located just to the north of the courtyard. The room (7 × 5.5 m) is covered with a mosaic carpet. One part of the floor, consisting of white tesserae, forms a U shape around the rest, which features an elaborate T-shaped colored mosaic utilizing twenty-eight colors; the mosaic is composed of three major elements, each adorned with elaborate geometric and figural borders.

The central part of the colored portion is a large rectangle composed of fifteen panels that depict aspects of the life story of Dionysus and the rituals that celebrated him. The largest (1.35 × .78 m) of these panels, in the center, depicts the Symposium, or Drinking Contest of Dionysus and Herakles. Several of the other fourteen panels, only three of which are damaged beyond recognition, reflect similar aspects of Dionysus's role as a god of feasting, fertility, drunkenness, ecstasy, and revelry. Greek inscriptions on each of the panels, all of which have a white background, assist in interpreting them; the word ΜΕΘΗ ("drunkenness"), for example, accompanies a scene in which the bearded hero Herakles, apparently in a drunken stupor, is attended by two devotees.

Surrounding the fifteen Dionysos panels is a frame consisting of twenty-two circular acanthus-leaf medallions against a background of black tesserae. The leafy wreaths contain hunting scenes featuring various wild animals as well as naked erotes, or *putti* ("cupids"), holding weapons such as the bow and arrow. In the central medallion of the northern and southern sides of the frame are female portraits. The one on the north is damaged, but the southern portrait depicts the bust of a strikingly beautiful woman (see figure 6). So exquisite is this portrait of an unknown woman that this masterpiece of ancient art has been nicknamed "Mona Lisa of the Galilee."

The third component of the colored carpet is a set of three border panels—one across the southern end of the floor and the other two extending partway along each of the eastern and western sides, giving the decorated mosaic the T-shape typical of triclinium mosaics. The eastern and western panels depict processions of people carrying items (flowers, fruit, ducks, roosters) that were probably offerings. These panels were apparently once part of one long procession scene surrounding the southern end of the carpet; damage to the scene along the south side led to its replacement with a Nilotic scene, lively and charming in its own right, but quite different from the Dionysiac character of the other elements of the triclinium floor.

The themes from Roman art, centering on mythological figures, may indicate that a Roman official with his family and servitors lived in this villa. Yet, the cosmopolitan nature of Sepphoris and the fact that even ancient synagogues were adorned with mosaics using non-Jewish motifs allows for the

SEPPHORIS. Figure 6. *"Mona Lisa" of the Galilee from the House of Dionysos.* Third century CE. (Courtesy Joint Sepphoris Project)

possibility that the villa and its superb mosaic floor reflect the Hellenistic aesthetics of Jewish occupants. [*See* Villas.]

Lower City. Excavations at Sepphoris, especially since 1990, have uncovered extensive areas of a relatively flat area or plateau extending along the eastern and southeastern sides of the summit.

Eastern insulae. As early as the second century CE, the original settlement on the summit had spread to the east, on the adjacent plateau. Two broad streets—an east–west *decumanus* and a north–south *cardo*—and several smaller streets parallel and perpendicular to these main thoroughfares created spacious orthogonal grid with blocks, or insulae, of buildings. The *cardo* (13.7 m wide) is paved with hard white limestone blocks set in diagonal rows. The original Roman pavers, with deep wheel ruts testifying to centuries of wagon traffic, lasted well into the Byzantine period.

Both the *cardo* and *decumanus* are flanked by colonnaded sidewalks, or stoas. These roofed walkways were initially paved with mosaics. Unlike the streets, they were repaved with mosaics at least once—near the intersection of the two major streets, geometric mosaics covered earlier ones. Three inscriptions set into the later mosaics give tribute to a Bishop Eutropius, whose exact dates are not known but who apparently held office near the end of the Byzantine period. These inscriptions, one of which reads "Under our most saintly father Eutropius the episcopus, the whole city in the time of the fourteenth interdiction," are part of the evidence for a flourishing Christian community at Sepphoris in the Byzantine period. At the same time, a menorah carved into one of the paving stones of the *cardo* is one of several indications of a continued Jewish presence in the fourth–seventh centuries.

Along the streets of the lower city a series of small shops, in use for centuries, contribute to the sense that this part of Sepphoris was the commercial center of the city during the Roman and Byzantine periods. A rabbinic tradition about the "lower marketplace" of Zippori may well refer to this area. Similarly, a lead market weight discovered in the upper city depicts a colonnaded street, perhaps the market of the lower city. A large building in the insula northeast of the intersection of the *decumanus* and *cardo* was built as early as the Early or Middle Roman period and then rebuilt in Byzantine times. It was paved with colorful mosaics and a Greek inscription reading "Good Fortune" and may have been the site's central marketplace, or agora.

The public character of the eastern insulae is further supported by the presence of a Roman-style bathhouse in the western insula—the one west of the *cardo* and south of the *decumanus.* Although not yet fully excavated, its two *caladaria* (hot rooms), one of them octagonally shaped, have been revealed. With renovation, the bathhouse continued to be used in the Byzantine period. Fragmentary remains of a building with a triclinium, probably dating to the Middle Roman period, were also found in this area beneath Byzantine construction.

Byzantine church. Also in the insula west of the *cardo* are the remains of a church, probably constructed under the direction of Bishop Eutropius along with one Marianus, a physician and leading citizen of the community, also mentioned in one of the mosaic inscriptions described above. Thus far, only the width (18 m) of this long building has been established. The basilical plan—a nave and two aisles—of its main room is clear, as is its orientation to the east. [*See* Basilicas.] Additional rooms that may have served as chapels are found on its northern and southern sides; a narthex and atrium may be located at its western end.

Nile festival building. In the central insula, opposite the bathhouse, is another building with Roman foundations that was extensively expanded and renovated in the Byzantine period. An eight-line inscription in the mosaic sidewalk of the *cardo* in front of its main entrance mentions two artists, Patricius and his father-in-law Procopius, presumably the artisans responsible for the stunning mosaics discovered in the building. The building itself (roughly 35 × 50 m) consists of eastern and western sections connected by corridors. A courtyard surrounded by variously sized rooms comprises the eastern section.

The western section consists of two large rooms and several subsidiary ones, with mosaic flooring in nearly every room. The largest of the rooms is a basilical hall (about 13.5 × 10.5 m). The existence of this hall, in addition to the building's size and central location, suggests that this structure was a public building. Its basilica is not a religious hall but, rather, a large room of the sort referred to in Byzantine texts: a place for public meetings, discussions, and even lectures. An inscription discovered at Sepphoris in the late 1950s refers to the renovation of a "basilica." At the time it was thought that the restoration of a church was at issue, but it now seems that it was work on a civic building.

Among the many mosaics in this building, the tesselated floor of the second largest room (7.6 × 6.2 m) in the western section is a nearly intact figural mosaic with scenes celebrating the Nile River—hence the name given to the entire building. Surrounded by elaborate geometric bands and featuring a row of birds across the top with a Greek inscription reading "Have Success," the floor contains various features of a Nile River festival and associated Nilotic hunting scenes.

The Nile River runs across the center of the floor. Rising above its banks a "nilometer" is depicted: a slender tower, marked with numbers (in cubits) used to measure the height of the Nile during its flood stage; the higher the water, the more fertile the surrounding land—and, thus, the higher the taxes. On either side of the nilometer are reclining figures: on the left the female personification of Egypt (labeled AIGY[PTOS]) holds a cornucopia; on the right is the god of the Nile. Below the river several hunting scenes are composed of a wide array of animals and plants, as well as a representation of the gate, flanked by two round towers, to the city of Alexandria. A flame shooting up from one of the towers probably depicts that city's famous lighthouse, known as the Pharos and said to be one of the seven wonders of the ancient world.

Other mosaic floors found in this building were once equally spectacular but survive in less complete form. The corridors of the building include figural panels within overall geometric designs. One of those panels depicts a rearing centaur; his uplifted arms hold a Greek inscription, "God is [our] Helper." Near the entrance to the basilical hall a panel features two armed Amazons on horseback; in another panel in the eastern wing, three bare-breasted Amazons are shown dancing. The several Amazon scenes, like the Nile River floor, seem to represent festivities; the water installations and special drainage channels in the building suggest that a harvest water festival, known as the Maiuma, may have been celebrated in this building in the Byzantine period. Despite the mythological figures in the mosaics, the building could have been used by either the Byzantine city's Jewish or Christian groups, or both—although no motifs or symbols associated with either group have been found.

Synagogue. Rabbinic sources indicate that a large number of synagogues—eighteen or more—functioned in Sepphoris in the Roman period, during the time of Rabbi Judah's sojourn in the city. Excavations and chance discoveries, however, had recovered only the fragments of the synagogue inscriptions mentioned above. Evidence of synagogue building finally emerged in 1993 when land was being cleared for a parking area north of the summit. A large rectangular structure, probably built in the sixth century, the synagogue is situated near a north–south street running west of an parallel to the *cardo*. Although it has several subsidiary rooms, the main hall is outstanding because of its narrowness (16 × 6.5 m) and unusual floor plan. Unlike most ancient synagogues, the hall has only one row of columns: the internal space thus consists of the nave and only a single aisle, on the north. Yet it shares with the synagogues north of Jerusalem the placement of its entry on the southern, Jerusalem-oriented wall.

The hall is also significant for its mosaic carpet: the floor is covered with a rich variety of biblical and ritual scenes and symbols, as well as geometric forms. Its repertoire of designs includes a magnificent zodiac, at whose four corners the four seasons of the year are represented by attractive females dressed in seasonally appropriate garb. Its centerpiece is the chariot of the sun god Helios, accompanied by the moon and a star; unlike similar zodiacs at Beth Alpha and Hammath Tiberias, the god himself is not depicted. [*See* Beth Alpha; Hammath Tiberias.]

The biblical scenes, not all of which have survived, apparently present several aspects of the Abraham story. Depictions of various temple furnishings, such as the table for the bread of the Presence (*Ex.* 25:23–30), and renderings of musical instruments and of sacrifices preserve aspects of temple ritual. The high priest was also pictured, although only the inscription "Aaron" remains intact. In addition to such captions, longer dedicatory inscriptions, in Greek and in Aramaic, appear in profusion: in the geometric panels that fill the single aisle, adjacent to many of the scenes of the figural mosaics, and even surrounding the central area of the zodiac. [*See* Synagogues.]

Water system. The elaborate and complex water system of Sepphoris, especially the aqueducts and reservoirs to the east of the site, has been thoroughly investigated (see above). [*See* Aqueducts; Reservoirs.] A freshwater spring, located just to the west of Tel 'Ein-Zippori in the Nazareth basin and some 2 km south of Sepphoris, still supplies water to the region and was no doubt a perennial source of water in antiquity. Because the spring is lower in elevation than the city, water had to be transported to the site by pack animals. This water supply was probably supplemented by stored rainwater collected in cisterns in many of the domestic units.

By about 100 CE, when the city's population began to expand, the nearby spring proved inadequate. The residents of Sepphoris began to exploit the springs to the east, at Raineh and Mashad, by constructing a series of gravity-drawn aqueducts that led westward to the site. Large quantities of water were stored in an enormous underground reservoir some 1.5 km east of the city. Nearly 200 m long, the reservoir could hold more than 10,000 cu m of water. When water was needed for drinking, bathing, agriculture, or other purposes, it was released through a lead pipe fitted with a valve for regulating water flow; pressure then apparently forced the water through a series of channels and aqueducts to the site for distribution. This system of water storage and transfer has a close parallel at the site of Capitolias (Irbid) of the Decapolis in Transjordan. [*See* Irbid; Decapolis.]

Tombs. The cemetery at ancient Sepphoris was situated on the hills surrounding the site on the southwest, southeast, and east. Although only a few tombs have been explored or excavated, it seems certain that the cemetery was as extensive as the one at Beth-Sheʿarim. [*See* Tombs; Beth-Sheʿarim.] The first tomb excavations were conducted by the Hebrew University in 1930, when Eleazar L. Sukenik (1932) identified a large complex of rooms with loculi and several inscriptions, one referring to a Rabbi Yudan. [*See the biography of Sukenik.*] Another group of rock-cut caves, which contained several bilingual (Greek and Hebrew) inscriptions, was excavated by Adam Druks for the Israel Department of Antiquities in 1980. Both groups date to the Roman period (second–third centuries). Northwest of the site lies a tomb traditionally identified as the burial place of Rabbi Judah Nesiah, the grandson of Rabbi Judah the Patriarch. A mausoleum known as the Tomb of Jacob's Daughters was excavated by Nahman Avigad. Its interior walls are constructed of unmortared ashlars, and the ceiling is barrel vaulted. The mausoleum is a loculus tomb and may date to the Roman period. Several small Byzantine-period burial caves on the western spur of Sepphoris may be part of a Christian cemetery, for a cross was found carved on the wall of one of them.

BIBLIOGRAPHY

Avi-Yonah, Michael. "A Sixth-Century Inscription from Sepphoris." *Israel Exploration Journal* 11 (1961): 184–187.

Avi-Yonah, Michael. "Sepphoris." In *Encyclopedia of Archaeological Excavations in the Holy Land,* vol. 4, pp. 1051–1055. Englewood Cliffs, N.J., 1975–.

Folda, Jaroslav. "The Church of Saint Anne." *Biblical Archaeologist* 54 (1991): 88–96.

Frey, Jean-Baptiste. *Corpus inscriptionum iudaicarum,* vol. 2, *Asie-Afrique.* Rome, 1952. See inscriptions 989–992.

Meshorer, Yaʿacov. *City-Coins of Eretz-Israel and the Decapolis in the Roman Period.* Jerusalem, 1985.

Meyers, Eric M., Ehud Netzer, and Carol L. Meyers. "Sepphoris, 'Ornament of All Galilee.'" *Biblical Archaeologist* 49 (1986): 4–19.

Meyers, Eric M., Ehud Netzer, and Carol L. Meyers. "Artistry in Stone: The Mosaics of Ancient Sepphoris." *Biblical Archaeologist* 50 (1987): 223–231.

Meyers, Eric M., Ehud Netzer, and Carol L. Meyers. "A Mansion in the Sepphoris Acropolis and Its Splendid Mosaic" (in Hebrew). *Qadmoniot* 21 (1988): 87–92.

Meyers, Eric M., Carol L. Meyers, and Ehud Netzer. *Sepphoris.* Winona Lake, Ind., 1992. Short account, lavishly illustrated, of the work of the Joint Sepphoris Project from 1985–1989.

Meyers, Eric M. "Aspects of Roman Sepphoris in the Light of Recent Archaeology." In *Early Christianity in Context,* edited by Frédéric Manns and Eugenio Alliata, pp. 29–36. Jerusalem, 1993.

Meyers, Eric M., Carol L. Meyers, and Kenneth G. Hoglund. "Sepphoris (Ṣippori)." *Israel Exploration Journal* 44 (1994): 247–250; 45 (1995): 68–71.

Miller, Stuart S. *Studies in the History and Traditions of Sepphoris.* Studies in Judaism and Late Antiquity, vol. 37. Leiden, 1984. Major study of the literary traditions regarding Sepphoris, primarily in rabbinic literature.

Ne'eman, Yehuda. *Sepphoris in the Period of the Second Temple, the Mishna, and the Talmud* (in Hebrew). Jerusalem, 1993. Comprehensive but not always reliable treatment of archaeological and literary sources.

Netzer, Ehud, and Zeev Weiss. "New Mosaic Art from Sepphoris." *Biblical Archaeology Review* 18.6 (1992): 36–43.

Netzer, Ehud, and Zeev Weiss. *Zippori.* Jerusalem, 1994. Popular summary of the work of the Joint Sepphoris Project plus the additional work of the Hebrew University in the lower city on the east (including the Nile Festival building) and the synagogue with the zodiac in the north.

Netzer, Ehud, and Zeev Weiss. "New Evidence for Late-Roman and Byzantine Sepphoris." In *The Roman and Byzantine Near East: Some Recent Archaeological Research,* edited by John H. Humphrey, pp. 164–176. Journal of Roman Archaeology, Supplementary Series, no. 14. New York, 1995.

Strange, James F., et al. "Sepphoris (Ṣippori)." *Israel Exploration Journal* 34 (1984): 269–270; 35 (1985): 297–299; 37 (1987): 278–280; 38 (1988): 188–190; 39 (1989): 104–106.

Strange, James F. "Sepphoris." In *The Anchor Bible Dictionary,* vol. 5, pp. 1090–1093. New York, 1992.

Sukenik, Eleazar L. "Some Remains of Sepphoris" (in Hebrew). *Tarbiz* 3 (1932): 107–109.

Tsuk, Tsvika. "Ṣippori: The Aqueducts." *Excavations and Surveys in Israel* 1 (1982): 105–107; 9 (1989–1990): 20.

Tsuk, Tsvika. "The Aqueducts of Sepphoris" (in Hebrew). In *The Aqueducts of Ancient Palestine,* edited by David ʿAmit et al., pp. 101–108. Jerusalem, 1989.

Ward, Seth. "Sepphoris in the Arab Period." In *Sepphoris in the Galilee: Crosscurrents of Culture,* edited by Rebecca M. Nagy, Eric M. Meyers, Carol L. Meyers, and Zeev Weiss. Raleigh, N.C., 1996.

Waterman, Leroy, et al. *Preliminary Report of the University of Michigan Excavations at Sepphoris, Palestine in 1931.* Ann Arbor, Mich., 1937. The only publication of the Michigan excavations.

Weiss, Zeev. "Sepphoris." In *The New Encyclopedia of Archaeological Excavations in the Holy Land,* vol. 4, pp. 1324–1328. Jerusalem and New York, 1993.

Carol L. Meyers and Eric M. Meyers

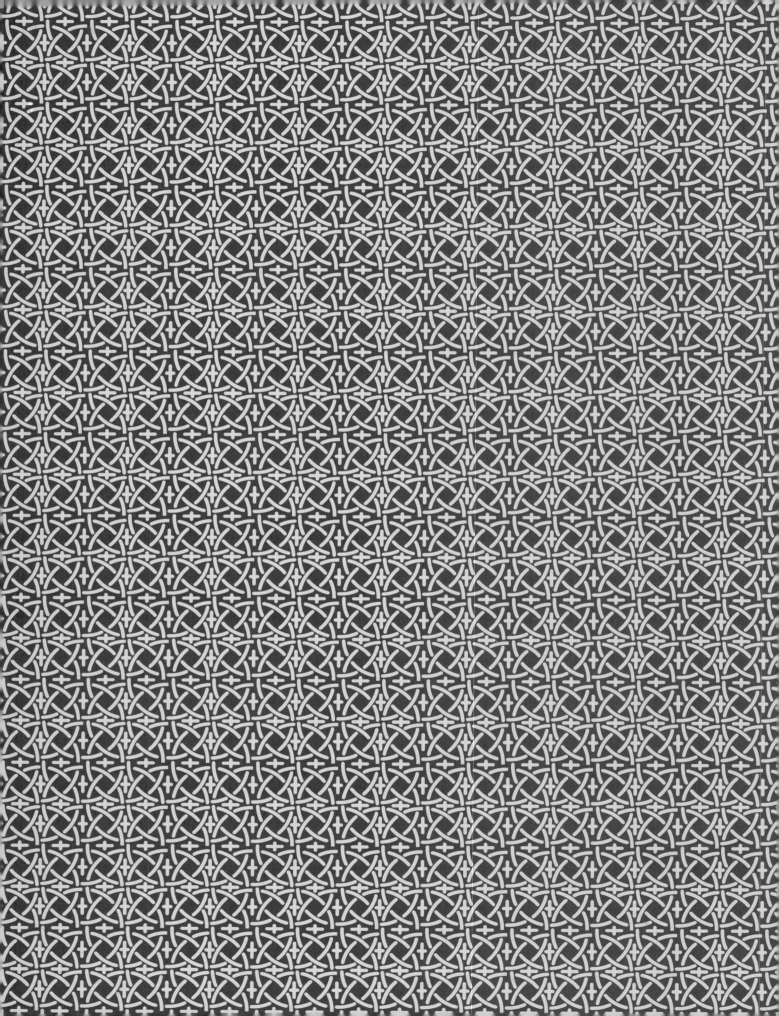